GALE

FIVE LANGUAGE
FINANCE

DICTIONARY

**ENGLISH   FRENCH   GERMAN
ITALIAN   SPANISH**

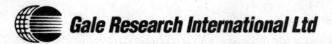 **Gale Research International Ltd**

LONDON • DETROIT • WASHINGTON D.C.

© 1993 Compact Verlag München

Published in the United Kingdom by
  Gale Research International Limited
  PO Box 699
  Cheriton House
  North Way
  Andover
  Hants SP10 5YE *

ISBN 1-873477-01-5

A CIP catalogue record for this book is available from the British Library.

Printed in Germany

Foreword

In the context of a new, united Europe, the command of multiple languages assumes an ever-growing importance in college and workplace. With networking and international collaboration on the increase, notably in the world of finance, this multilingual dictionary will be found essential as an authoritative and reliable reference book.

Approximately 20,000 headwords, with 80,000 translations, supply the most common technical terms concerning all aspects of the financial world, given in the five major Europoean languages: German, English, French, Italian and Spanish. Whichever of the five languages a particular headword is looked up in, the arrangement of all entries in alphabetical order allows rapid access to that headword and its translations.

This comprehensive international vocabulary of finance is thus an indispensable aid in all areas of modern professional activity.

Abbreviations

D = German
E = English
F = French
I = Italian
Es = Spanish
f = feminine
m = masculine
n = neuter
pl = plural

	D	E	F	I	Es
Abandon (D)	—	abandonment	abandon *m*	abbandono *m*	abandono *m*
abandon (F)	Abandon *m*	abandonment	—	abbandono *m*	abandono *m*
abandonment (E)	Abandon *m*	—	abandon *m*	abbandono *m*	abandono *m*
abandono (Es)	Abandon *m*	abandonment	abandon *m*	abbandono *m*	—
abbandono (I)	Abandon *m*	abandonment	abandon *m*	—	abandono *m*
abbassamento del tasso d'interesse (I)	Zinssenkung *f*	reduction of the interest rate	réduction des intérêts *f*	—	reducción del tipo de interés *f*
Abbuchungs- verfahren (D)	—	direct debit procedure	système de prélève- ment automatique *m*	procedimento di addebito *m*	procedimiento de adeudo en cuenta *m*
Abendbörse (D)	—	evening stock exchange	bourse nocturne *f*	borsa pomeridiana *f*	bolsa nocturna *f*
Aberdepot (D)	—	fungible security deposit	dépôt de choses fongibles *m*	deposito irregolare di titoli *m*	depósito de títulos fungibles *m*
Abfindung (D)	—	compensation	indemnité *f*	indennizzo *m*	compensación *f*
Abfindungs- angebot (D)	—	compensation offer	offre d'indemnité *f*	offerta di riscatto *f*	oferta de compensación *f*
Abgabenordnung (D)	—	fiscal code	code des impôts *m*	legislazione tributaria *f*	ordenanza tributaria *f*
Ablösungsanleihe (D)	—	redemption loan	emprunt de revalorisation *m*	prestito di ammortamento *m*	empréstito de amortización *m*
Abrechnungsstelle (D)	—	clearing house	bureau de liquidation *m*	stanza di compensazione *f*	oficina de compensación *f*
Abrechnungs verkehr (D)	—	clearing system	opérations de compensation *f/pl*	clearing *m*	operaciones de compensación *f/pl*
Abschlags- dividende (D)	—	dividend on account	acompte sur dividende *m*	acconto dividendo *m*	dividendo a cuenta *m*
Abschlagszahlung (D)	—	down payment	acompte *m*	acconto *m*	pago a cuenta *m*
Abschluß (D)	—	conclusion	conclusion *f*	chiusura *f*	conclusión *f*
Abschlußauftrag (D)	—	final order	ordre final *f*	operazione di chiusura *f*	orden final *f*
Abschreibung (D)	—	writing off	amortissement *m*	ammortamento *m*	amortización *f*
Abschreibungs- gesellschaft (D)	—	project write-off company	société d'amortissement *f*	società d'ammortamento *f*	sociedad de amortización *f*
absorptive capacity of the market (E)	Aufnahmefähigkeit des Marktes *f*	—	capacité d'absorption du marché *f*	assorbimento di mercato *m*	capacidad de absor- ción del mercado *f*
Abstempelung (D)	—	stamping	estampillage *m*	bollatura *f*	estampillado *m*
Abtretungsverbot (D)	—	prohibition of assignment	défense de cession *f*	divieto di cessione *m*	prohibición de cesión *f*
abus de confiance (F)	Untreue *f*	disloyalty	—	infedeltà *f*	infidelidad *f*
Abwertung (D)	—	devaluation	dévaluation *f*	svalutazione *f*	desvalorización *f*
Abwertungs- wettlauf (D)	—	devaluation race	course de dévaluation *f*	corsa alla svalutazione *f*	carrera de desvalorización *f*
Abwicklung (D)	—	settlement	exécution *f*	esecuzione *f*	ejecución *f*
Abzahlungs- geschäft (D)	—	instalment sale transaction	vente a tempérament *f*	operazione con pagamento rateale *f*	operación a plazos *f*
Abzahlungs- hypothek (D)	—	instalment mortgage	hypothèque réductible *f*	ipoteca di pagamento a rate *f*	hipoteca a plazos *f*
Abzinsung (D)	—	discounting	déduction des inté- rêts non courus *f*	deduzione di interessi *f*	deducción de intereses no acumulados *f*
academia de banqueros (Es)	Bankakademie *f*	banking academy	académie de banquiers *f*	accademia bancaria *f*	—
académie de banquiers (F)	Bankakademie *f*	banking academy	—	accademia bancaria *f*	academia de banqueros *f*
accademia bancaria (I)	Bankakademie *f*	banking academy	académie de banquiers *f*	—	academia de banqueros *f*
accantonamenti (I)	Rücklagen *f/pl*	reserves	réserves *f/pl*	—	reservas *f/pl*
accaparement spéculatif (F)	Aufkaufspekulation *f*	take-over speculation	—	speculazione in accaparramenti *f*	especulación de acaparamiento *f*
accélération de l'inflation (F)	Inflations- beschleunigung *f*	acceleration of inflation	—	accelerazione dell'inflazione *f*	aceleración de la inflación *f*
acceleration of inflation (E)	Inflations- beschleunigung *f*	—	accélération de l'inflation *f*	accelerazione dell'inflazione *f*	aceleración de la inflación *f*

	D	E	F	I	Es
accelerazione dell'inflazione (I)	Inflationsbeschleunigung f	acceleration of inflation	accélération de l'inflation f	—	aceleración de la inflación f
accensione di credito (I)	Kreditaufnahme f	raising of credits	recours à l'emprunt m	—	apelación al crédito f
accept (E)	Übernahme f	—	acceptation f	accettazione f	aceptación f
acceptability as collateral (E)	Lombardfähigkeit f	—	capacité d'être déposé à titre de gage f	idoneitá di titoli all'anticipazione f	capacidad de ser pignorable f
acceptance (F)	Akzept n	acceptance	—	accettazione f	aceptación f
acceptance (E)	Akzept n	—	acceptance f	accettazione f	aceptación f
acceptance banks (E)	Akzepthäuser n/pl	—	banques d'acceptation f/pl	acceptance banks f/pl	bancos de aceptación m/pl
acceptance banks (I)	Akzepthäuser n/pl	acceptance banks	banques d'acceptation f/pl	—	bancos de aceptación m/pl
acceptance bill (E)	Dokumententratte f	—	traite documentaire f	tratta documentaria f	letra documentaria f
acceptance credit (E)	Trassierungskredit m	—	crédit bancaire sur documents m	credito di traenza m	crédito de reembolso m
acceptance credit (E)	Akzeptkredit m	—	crédit par traite acceptée m	credito d'accettazione m	crédito de aceptación m
acceptance for collection (E)	Inkassoakzept n	—	acceptation pour encaissement f	accettazione in attesa d'incasso f	aceptación de cobranza f
acceptance in blank (E)	Blanko-Akzept n	—	acceptation en blanc f	accettazione in bianco f	aceptación en blanco f
acceptance liability (E)	Akzeptverbindlichkeit f	—	engagement par acceptation m	effetto passivo m	obligación de aceptación f
acceptance of a bill (E)	Wechselakzept n	—	acceptation d'un effet f	accettazione cambiaria f	aceptación cambiaria f
acceptation (F)	Übernahme f	accept	—	accettazione f	aceptación f
acceptation de banque (F)	Bankakzept n	bank acceptance	—	accettazione bancaria f	aceptación bancaria f
acceptation de complaisance (F)	Gefälligkeitsakzept n	accommodation acceptance	—	accettazione di favore f	aceptación de favor f
acceptation d'un effet (F)	Wechselakzept n	acceptance of a bill	—	accettazione cambiaria f	aceptación cambiaria f
acceptation en blanc (F)	Blanko-Akzept n	acceptance in blank	—	accettazione in bianco f	aceptación en blanco f
acceptation partielle (F)	Teilakzept n	partial acceptance	—	accettazione parziale f	aceptación parcial f
acceptation pour encaissement (F)	Inkassoakzept n	acceptance for collection	—	accettazione in attesa d'incasso f	aceptación de cobranza f
accepted finance bill (E)	Finanzakzept n	—	traite financière acceptée f	accettazione bancaria f	letra de cambio bancaria f
accesso libero al mercato (I)	freier Marktzutritt m	free access to the market	liberté d'accès au marché f	—	libertad de acceso a un mercado f
accettazione (I)	Akzept n	acceptance	acceptance f	—	aceptación f
accettazione (I)	Übernahme f	accept	acceptation f	—	aceptación f
accettazione bancaria (I)	Kreditakzept n	financial acceptance	traite tirée en garantie d'un crédit f	—	aceptación de crédito f
accettazione bancaria (I)	Bankakzept n	bank acceptance	acceptation de banque f	—	aceptación bancaria f
accettazione bancaria (I)	Finanzakzept n	accepted finance bill	traite financière acceptée f	—	letra de cambio bancaria f
accettazione cambiaria (I)	Wechselakzept n	acceptance of a bill	acceptation d'un effet f	—	aceptación cambiaria f
accettazione di favore (I)	Gefälligkeitsakzept n	accommodation acceptance	acceptation de complaisance f	—	aceptación de favor f
accettazione estera (I)	Auslandsakzept n	bill in foreign currency	traite tirée sur l'étranger f	—	letra sobre el extranjero f
accettazione in attesa d'incasso (I)	Inkassoakzept n	acceptance for collection	acceptation pour encaissement f	—	aceptación de cobranza f
accettazione in bianco (I)	Blanko-Akzept n	acceptance in blank	acceptation en blanc f	—	aceptación en blanco f
accettazione in valuta estera (I)	Valuta-Akzept n	foreign currency accept	traite libellée en monnaie étrangère f	—	aceptación en moneda extranjera f
accettazione parziale (I)	Teilakzept n	partial acceptance	acceptation partielle f	—	aceptación parcial f

	D	E	F	I	Es
acción (Es)	Aktie f	share	action f	azione f	—
acción al descubierto (Es)	Leeraktie f	shares not fully paid up	action non entièrement libérée f	azione non interamente versata f	—
acción al portador (Es)	Inhaberaktie f	bearer share	action au porteur f	azione al portatore f	—
acción al público (Es)	Publikumsaktie f	popular share	action populaire f	azione preferita dai risparmiatori f	—
acción con derecho a voto (Es)	Stimmrechtsaktie f	voting share	action à droit de vote simple f	azione con diritto di voto f	—
acción con posibilidad de incremento (Es)	Wuchsaktie f	growth share	action avec possibilité d'acroissement f	azione con possibilità di sviluppo f	—
acción de compañías de seguros (Es)	Versicherungsaktie f	insurance company share	action d'une société d'assurance f	azione assicurativa f	—
acción de cuota (Es)	Quotenaktie f	share of no par value	action de quotité f	parte di capitale f	—
acción de depósito (Es)	Depotaktie f	deposited share	action déposée en compte courant f	azione in deposito f	—
acción de oro (Es)	Goldaktie f	gold share	action-or f	azione di miniere d'oro f	—
acción de personal (Es)	Belegschaftsaktie f	staff shares	action de travail f	azione per dipendenti f	—
acción de provisión (Es)	Vorratsaktie f	disposable share	action en réserve f	azione di riserva f	—
acción de reajuste (Es)	Berichtigungsaktie f	bonus share	action gratuite f	azione gratuita f	—
acción de suma (Es)	Nennwertaktie f	par value share	action nominale f	azione a valore nominale f	—
acción de sustitución (Es)	Ersatzaktie f	replacement share certificate	action supplétive en remplacement d'un titre adiré f	azione sostitutiva f	—
acción deteriorada (Es)	beschädigte Aktie f	damaged share certificates	certificat d'action endommagé m	azione danneggiata f	—
acción de trabajo (Es)	Arbeitnehmeraktie f	employees' shares	action de travail f	azione di lavoro f	—
acción de valor determinado (Es)	Summenaktie f	share at a fixed amount	action d'un montant fixe f	azione a valore nominale determinato f	—
acción de voto plural (Es)	Mehrstimmrechtsaktie f	multiple voting share	action à droit de vote plural f	azione a voto plurimo f	—
acciones de preferencia (Es)	Prioritätsaktien f/pl	preference shares	actions de priorité f/pl	azioni privilegiate f/pl	—
acciones de tesorería (Es)	Verwaltungsaktien f/pl	treasury stock	actions de Trésor f/pl	azioni amministrate f/pl	—
acciones nuevas (Es)	junge Aktien f/pl	new shares	actions nouvelles f/pl	nuove azioni f/pl	—
acciones propias (Es)	eigene Aktien f/pl	company-owned shares	actions propres f/pl	azioni sociali f/pl	—
acción global (Es)	Sammelaktie f	global share	titre représentant globalement un paquet d'actions m	azione globale f	—
acción gratuita (Es)	Gratisaktie f	bonus share	action gratuite f	azione gratuita f	—
acción industrial (Es)	Industrieaktie f	industrial shares	action industrielle f	azione industriale f	—
accionista (Es)	Aktionär m	shareholder	actionnaire m	azionista m	—
accionista comanditario (Es)	Kommanditaktionär m	limited liability shareholder	actionnaire d'une société en commandite par actions m	socio di una società in accomandita per azioni m	—
accionista importante (Es)	Großaktionär m	major shareholder	gros actionnaire m	grande azionista m	—
accionista intermedio (Es)	Zwischenaktionär m	interim shareholder	actionnaire intermédiaire m	azionista non permanente m	—
accionista pequeño (Es)	Kleinaktionär m	small shareholder	petit actionnaire m	piccolo azionista m	—
accionista permanente (Es)	Daueraktionär m	permanent shareholder	actionnaire permanent m	azionista permanente m	—
acción minera (Es)	Kux m	mining share	part de mines f	azione mineraria f	—
acción no cotizada (Es)	nichtnotierte Aktie f	unquoted share	action non cotée f	azione non quotata ufficialmente f	—
acción nominal (Es)	Namensaktie f	registered share	action nominative f	azione nominativa f	—
acción ordinaria (Es)	Stammaktie f	ordinary share	action ordinaire f	azione ordinaria f	—

	D	E	F	I	Es
acción pequeña (Es)	Kleinaktie f	share with low par value	action minimale f	piccola azione f	—
acción popular (Es)	Volksaktie f	low-denomination share for small savers	action populaire f	azione popolare f	—
acción preferente (Es)	Vorzugsaktie f	preference share	action privilégiée f	azione privilegiata f	—
acción preferente sin derecho a voto (Es)	stimmrechtslose Vorzugsaktie f	non-voting share	action privilégiée sans droit de vote f	azione privilegiata senza diritto di voto f	—
acción sin valor nominal (Es)	nennwertlose Aktie f	no par value share	action sans valeur nominale f	azione senza valore nominale f	—
acción suplementaria (Es)	Zusatzaktie f	bonus share	action supplémentaire f	azione gratuita f	—
acción vinculada (Es)	vinkulierte Aktie f	restricted share	action négociable sous réserve f	azione vincolata f	—
accomandante (I)	Kommanditist m	limited partner	commanditaire m	—	comanditario m
accomandatario (I)	Komplementär m	general partner	commandité m	—	socio colectivo m
accommodation acceptance (E)	Gefälligkeitsakzept n	—	acceptation de complaisance f	accettazione di favore f	aceptación de favor f
accommodation endorsement (E)	Gefälligkeitsgiro m	—	endossement de complaisance m	girata di favore f	endoso de favor m
accomplissement (F)	Erfüllung f	performance	—	adempimento m	cumplimiento m
acconto (I)	Abschlagszahlung f	down payment	acompte m	—	pago a cuenta m
acconto (I)	Anzahlung f	deposit	acompte m	—	pago a cuenta m
acconto dividendo (I)	Abschlagsdividende f	dividend on account	acompte sur dividende m	—	dividendo a cuenta m
accord (F)	Zustimmung f	consent	—	approvazione f	consentimiento m
accord de contrôle (F)	Beherrschungs-vertrag m	control agreement	—	contratto di controllo m	contrato de dominación m
accord de réciprocité (F)	gegenseitiger Vertrag m	reciprocal contract	—	contratto bilaterale m	contrato recíproco m
accord de transfert des résultats (F)	Ergebnisabführungs-vertrag m	profit and loss transfer agreement	—	contratto di trasferi-mento profitto m	acuerdo de pago del resultado m
accord d'un plafond d'intérêt (F)	Zinskappenverein-bahrung f	cap rate of interest agreement	—	accordo sul tetto interessi m	acuerdo de un plafón de interés m
accord général de crédits (F)	allgemeine Kreditvereinbarung f	General Arrange-ments to Borrow	—	accordo generale di credito m	acuerdo general de empréstito m
accord monétaire européen (F)	Europäisches Wäh-rungsabkommen n	European Monetary Agreement	·	Accordo Monetario Europeo m	Acuerdo Monetario Europeo m
accord sur la protec-tion de capital (F)	Kapitalschutz-vertrag m	capital protection agreement	—	accordo di tutela degli investimenti m	contrato de protec-ción del capital m
accord sur l'encourage-ment de la for-mation de capital (F)	Kapitalförderungs-vertrag m	capital encourage-ment treaty	—	accordo sulla forma-zione di capitale m	contrato de fomento de capital m
accordo di tutela degli investimenti (I)	Kapitalschutz-vertrag m	capital protection agreement	accord sur la pro-tection de capital m	—	contrato de protección del capital m
accordo generale di credito (I)	allgemeine Kreditvereinbarung f	General Arrange-ments to Borrow	accord général de crédits m	—	acuerdo general de empréstito m
Accordo Monetario Europeo (I)	Europäisches Wäh-rungsabkommen n	European Monetary Agreement	accord monétaire européen m	—	Acuerdo Monetario Europeo m
accordo sulla forma-zione di capitale (I)	Kapitalförderungs-vertrag m	capital encourage-ment treaty	accord sur l'encou-ragement de la for-mation de capital m	—	contrato de fomento de capital m
accordo sul tetto interessi (I)	Zinskappen-vereinbahrung f	cap rate of interest agreement	accord d'un plafond d'intérêt m	—	acuerdo de un plafón de interés m
accord swap (F)	Swapabkommen n	swap agreement	—	contratto swap m	acuerdo de swap m
account (E)	Konto n	—	compte m	conto m	cuenta f
account costing (E)	Kontenkalkulation f	—	calcul des comptes m	calcolo dei conti m	calculación por cuentas f
account for reimburse-ments of expenses (E)	Aufwandsausgleich-konto n	—	compte de frais à reporter m	conto compensazione spese m	cuenta de compensa-ción de gastos m
account in foreign currency (E)	Fremdwährungs-konto n	—	compte en monnaie étrangère m	conto in valuta estera m	cuenta de moneda extranjera f
accounting (E)	Rechnungslegung f	—	reddition des comptes f	chiusura dei conti f	rendición de cuentas f

	D	E	F	I	Es
accounting (E)	Buchführung f	—	comptabilité f	contabilità f	contabilidad f
Accounting and Reporting Law (E)	Bilanzrichtlinien-gesetz n	—	loi sur les directives de l'établissement du bilan f	legge sulla formazione del bilancio f	ley sobre directivas en materia de balances f
accounting exchange on the liabilities side (E)	Passivtausch m	—	écritures entre postes de passif f/pl	rettifica del passivo f	cambio de asientos en el pasivo m
accounting regulations (E)	Bilanzierungs-vorschriften f/pl	—	prescriptions concernant l'établissement du bilan f/pl	norme per la redazione del bilancio f/pl	normas sobre balances f/pl
accounting transparency (E)	Bilanzklarheit f	—	clarté du bilan f	chiarezza del bilancio f	transparencia del balance f
accounting value (E)	Buchwert m	—	valeur comptable f	valore di libro m	valor contable m
accounting voucher (E)	Buchungsbeleg m	—	pièce comptable f	documento contabile m	comprobante de asiento m
account number (E)	Kontonummer f	—	numéro de compte m	numero di conto m	número de la cuenta m
account numbering (E)	Konten-nummerierung f	—	numérotage des comptes m	classificazione dei conti f	numeración de cuentas f
account receivable (E)	Buchforderung f	—	créance en compte f	credito contabile m	crédito en cuenta m
accounts collection method (E)	Rechnungseinzugs-verfahren n	—	système d'encaissement automatique de factures m	procedimento d'incasso di fatture m	procedimiento de cobranza de pagos pendientes m
accounts payable (E)	Lieferkonto n	—	compte de fournisseurs m	conto fornitori m	cuenta de suministradores f
accreditare (I)	akkreditieren	to open a credit	accréditer	—	acreditar
accréditer (F)	akkreditieren	to open a credit	—	accreditare	acreditar
accréditif (F)	Akkreditiv n	letter of credit	—	lettera di credito f	crédito documentario m
accréditif payable en espèce (F)	Bar-Akkreditiv m	clean credit	—	apertura di credito per cassa f	crédito simple m
accréditif rotatif (F)	revolvierendes Akkreditiv n	revolving letter of credit	—	credito rinnovabile m	crédito rotativo m
accumulation de capital (F)	Kapital-akkumulation f	accumulation of capital	—	accumulazione di capitale f	acumulación de capital f
accumulation of capital (E)	Kapital-akkumulation f	—	accumulation de capital f	accumulazione di capitale f	acumulación de capital f
accumulation of capital (E)	Thesaurierung f	—	thésauration f	tesaurizzazione f	atesoramiento m
accumulative investment fund (E)	Thesaurierungs-fonds m	—	fonds de thésauration m	fondo di accumulazione m	fondo de atesoramiento m
accumulazione di capitale (I)	Kapital-akkumulation f	accumulation of capital	accumulation de capital f	—	acumulación de capital f
aceleración de la inflación (Es)	Inflations-beschleunigung f	acceleration of inflation	accélération de l'inflation f	accelerazione dell'inflazione f	—
aceptación (Es)	Übernahme f	accept	acceptation f	accettazione f	—
aceptación (Es)	Akzept n	acceptance	acceptance f	accettazione f	—
aceptación bancaria (Es)	Bankakzept n	bank acceptance	acceptation de banque f	accettazione bancaria f	—
aceptación cambiaria (Es)	Wechselakzept n	acceptance of a bill	acceptation d'un effet f	accettazione cambiaria f	—
aceptación de cobranza (Es)	Inkassoakzept n	acceptance for collection	acceptation pour encaissement f	accettazione in attesa d'incasso f	—
aceptación de crédito (Es)	Kreditakzept n	financial acceptance	traite tirée en garantie d'un crédit f	accettazione bancaria f	—
aceptación de deuda (Es)	Schuldübernahme f	assumption of an obligation	reprise de dette f	espromissione f	—
aceptación de favor (Es)	Gefälligkeitsakzept n	accommodation acceptance	acceptation de complaisance f	accettazione di favore f	—
aceptación en blanco (Es)	Blanko-Akzept n	acceptance in blank	acceptation en blanc f	accettazione in bianco f	—
aceptación en moneda extranjera (Es)	Valuta-Akzept n	foreign currency accept	traite libellée en monnaie étrangère f	accettazione in valuta estera f	—
aceptación parcial (Es)	Teilakzept n	partial acceptance	acceptation partielle f	accettazione parziale f	—
achat (F)	Kauf m	purchase	—	acquisto m	compra f

	D	E	F	I	Es
achat à crédit (F)	Kreditkauf *m*	credit purchase	—	acquisto di credito *m*	compra de crédito *f*
achat au comptant (F)	Barkauf *m*	cash purchase	—	acquisto in contanti *m*	compra en efectivo *f*
achat de soutien (F)	Stützungskauf *m*	support buying	—	acquisto di sostegno *m*	compra para sostener precios *f*
achat de titres (F)	Effektenkauf *m*	purchase of securities	—	acquisto di titoli *m*	compra de valores *f*
achats majoritaires (F)	Majoritätskäufe *m/pl*	buying of shares to secure the controlling interest in a company	—	acquisti di maggioranza *m/pl*	compras mayoritarias *f/pl*
achats off shore (F)	Offshore-Käufe *m/pl*	offshore purchases	—	acquisti off-shore *m/pl*	compras offshore *f/pl*
acknowledgement of a debt (E)	Schuldanerkenntnis *f*	—	reconnaissance de dette *f*	ricognizione di debito *f*	reconocimiento de la deuda *m*
acompte (F)	Anzahlung *f*	deposit	—	acconto *m*	pago a cuenta *m*
acompte (F)	Abschlagszahlung *f*	down payment	—	acconto *m*	pago a cuenta *m*
acompte sur dividende (F)	Abschlagsdividende *f*	dividend on account	—	acconto dividendo *m*	dividendo a cuenta *m*
acquirer model (E)	Erwerbermodell *n*	—	modèle d'acquéreur *m*	acquisto di immobili affittati *m*	modelo de adquirente *m*
acquisitions complémentaires de la société (F)	Nachgründung *f*	post-formation acquisition	—	costituzione successiva *f*	adquisición de instalaciones por una sociedad después de su fundación *f*
acquisition value (E)	Anschaffungswert *m*	—	valeur d'acquisition *f*	valore d'acquisto *m*	valor de adquisición *m*
acquisizione di crediti (I)	Forderungskauf *m*	purchase of accounts receivable	vente d'une créance *f*	—	compra de créditos *f*
acquisti di maggioranza (I)	Majoritätskäufe *m/pl*	buying of shares to secure the controlling interest in a company	achats majoritaires *m/pl*	—	compras mayoritarias *f/pl*
acquisti off-shore (I)	Offshore-Käufe *m/pl*	offshore purchases	achats off shore *m/pl*	—	compras offshore *f/pl*
acquisto (I)	Kauf *m*	purchase	achat *m*	—	compra *f*
acquisto di beni e servizi da terzi (I)	Fremdbezug *m*	external procurement	matériel acheté au-dehors *m*	—	suministro externo *m*
acquisto di credito (I)	Kreditkauf *m*	credit purchase	achat à crédit *m*	—	compra de crédito *f*
acquisto di immobili affittati (I)	Erwerbermodell *n*	acquirer model	modèle d'acquéreur *m*	—	modelo de adquirente *m*
acquisto di sostegno (I)	Stützungskauf *m*	support buying	achat de soutien *m*	—	compra para sostener precios *f*
acquisto di titoli (I)	Effektenkauf *m*	purchase of securities	achat de titres *m*	—	compra de valores *f*
acquisto in contanti (I)	Barkauf *m*	cash purchase	achat au comptant *m*	—	compra en efectivo *f*
acreditante (Es)	Akkreditivsteller *m*	person opening a credit in favour of somebody	émetteur d'un accréditif *m*	ordinante il credito *m*	—
acreditar (Es)	akkreditieren	to open a credit	accréditer	accreditare	—
acreedor (Es)	Gläubiger *m*	creditor	créancier *m*	creditore *m*	—
acreedor de la quiebra (Es)	Konkursgläubiger *m*	bankrupt's creditor	créancier de la faillite *m*	creditore della massa fallimentare *m*	—
acreedores (Es)	Kreditoren *m/pl*	creditors	créanciers *m/pl*	creditori *m/pl*	—
acreedores varios (Es)	sonstige Verbindlichkeiten *f/pl*	other liabilities	autres obligations *f/pl*	debiti diversi *m/pl*	—
acreedor sin garantía (Es)	Massegläubiger *m*	preferential creditor	créancier de la masse *m*	creditore della massa *m*	—
acte de protêt pour non-restitution d'effet (F)	Ausfolgungsprotest *m*	protest for non-delivery	—	protesto mancata consegna cambiale *m*	protesta de incumplimiento *f*
acte passé avec soi-même (F)	Insichgeschäft *n*	self-dealing	—	operazione fine a se stessa *f*	negocio consigo mismo *m*
action (F)	Aktie *f*	share	—	azione *f*	acción *f*
action à droit de vote plural (F)	Mehrstimmrechtsaktie *f*	multiple voting share	—	azione a voto plurimo *f*	acción de voto plural *f*
action à droit de vote simple (F)	Stimmrechtsaktie *f*	voting share	—	azione con diritto di voto *f*	acción con derecho a voto *f*
action au porteur (F)	Inhaberaktie *f*	bearer share	—	azione al portatore *f*	acción al portador *f*

	D	E	F	I	Es
action avec possibilité d'acroissement (F)	Wuchsaktie *f*	growth share	—	azione con possibilità di sviluppo *f*	acción con posibilidad de incremento *f*
action déposée en compte courant (F)	Depotaktie *f*	deposited share	—	azione in deposito *f*	acción de depósito *f*
action de quotité (F)	Quotenaktie *f*	share of no par value	—	parte di capitale *f*	acción de cuota *f*
action de travail (F)	Belegschaftsaktie *f*	staff shares	—	azione per dipendenti *f*	acción de personal *f*
action de travail (F)	Arbeitnehmeraktie *f*	employees' shares	—	azione di lavoro *f*	acción de trabajo *f*
action d'une société d'assurance (F)	Versicherungsaktie *f*	insurance company share	—	azione assicurativa *f*	acción de compañías de seguros *f*
action d'un montant fixe (F)	Summenaktie *f*	share at a fixed amount	—	azione a valore nominale determinato *f*	acción de valor determinado *f*
action en réserve (F)	Vorratsaktie *f*	disposable share	—	azione di riserva *f*	acción de provisión *f*
action gratuite (F)	Gratisaktie *f*	bonus share	—	azione gratuita *f*	acción gratuita *f*
action gratuite (F)	Berichtigungsaktie *f*	bonus share	—	azione gratuita *f*	acción de reajuste *f*
action industrielle (F)	Industrieaktie *f*	industrial shares	—	azione industriale *f*	acción industrial *f*
action minimale (F)	Kleinaktie *f*	share with low par value	—	piccola azione *f*	acción pequeña *f*
actionnaire (F)	Aktionär *m*	shareholder		azionista *m*	accionista *m*
actionnaire d'une société en commandite par actions (F)	Kommanditaktionär *m*	limited liability shareholder	—	socio di una società in accomandita per azioni *m*	accionista comanditario *m*
actionnaire étranger (F)	ausländischer Anteilseigner *m*	foreign shareholder	—	azionista estero *m*	titular de acciones extranjero *m*
actionnaire intermédiaire (F)	Zwischenaktionär *m*	interim shareholder	—	azionista non permanente *m*	accionista intermedio *m*
actionnaire permanent (F)	Daueraktionär *m*	permanent shareholder	—	azionista permanente *m*	accionista permanente *m*
action négociable sous réserve (F)	vinkulierte Aktie *f*	restricted share	—	azione vincolata *f*	acción vinculada *f*
action nominale (F)	Nennwertaktie *f*	par value share	—	azione a valore nominale *f*	acción de suma *f*
action nominative (F)	Namensaktie *f*	registered share	—	azione nominativa *f*	acción nominal *f*
action non cotée (F)	nichtnotierte Aktie *f*	unquoted share	—	azione non quotata ufficialmente *f*	acción no cotizada *f*
action non entière-ment libérée (F)	Leeraktie *f*	shares not fully paid up	—	azione non intera-mente versata *f*	acción al descubierto *f*
action-or (F)	Goldaktie *f*	gold share	—	azione di miniere d'oro *f*	acción de oro *f*
action ordinaire (F)	Stammaktie *f*	ordinary share	—	azione ordinaria *f*	acción ordinaria *f*
action populaire (F)	Publikumsaktie *f*	popular share	—	azione preferita dai risparmiatori *f*	acción al público *f*
action populaire (F)	Volksaktie *f*	low-denomination share for small savers	—	azione popolare *f*	acción popular *f*
action privilégiée (F)	Vorzugsaktie *f*	preference share	—	azione privilegiata *f*	acción preferente *f*
action privilégiée sans droit de vote (F)	stimmrechtslose Vorzugsaktie *f*	non-voting share	—	azione privilegiata senza diritto di voto *f*	acción preferente sin derecho a voto *f*
action qui fait l'objet d'un achat par un groupe intéressé (F)	Interessenwert *m*	vested interest stock	—	titolo primario *m*	valor de interés *m*
action sans valeur nominale (F)	nennwertlose Aktie *f*	no par value share	—	azione senza valore nominale *f*	acción sin valor nominal *f*
actions de priorité (F)	Prioritätsaktien *f/pl*	preference shares	—	azioni privilegiate *f/pl*	acciónes de preferencia *f/pl*
actions de Trésor (F)	Verwaltungsaktien *f/pl*	treasury stock	—	azioni amministrate *f/pl*	acciones de tesorería *f/pl*
actions nouvelles (F)	junge Aktien *f/pl*	new shares	—	nuove azioni *f/pl*	acciones nuevas *f/pl*
actions propres (F)	eigene Aktien *f/pl*	company-owned shares	—	azioni sociali *f/pl*	acciones propias *f/pl*
action supplémentaire (F)	Zusatzaktie *f*	bonus share	—	azione gratuita *f*	acción suplementaria *f*
action supplétive en remplacement d'un titre adiré (F)	Ersatzaktie *f*	replacement share certificate	—	azione sostitutiva *f*	acción de sustitución *f*

	D	E	F	I	Es
actividades bancarias cooperativas (Es)	genossenschaftlicher Bankensektor *m*	cooperative banking sector	activités bancaires coopératives *f/pl*	settore bancario cooperativo *m*	—
activités bancaires coopératives (F)	genossenschaftlicher Bankensektor *m*	cooperative banking sector	—	settore bancario cooperativo *m*	actividades bancarias cooperativas *f/pl*
activo (Es)	Guthaben *n*	credit balance	avoir *m*	avere *m*	—
activo (Es)	Aktiva *n/pl*	assets	masse active *f*	attività di bilancio *f/pl*	—
activo casi líquido (Es)	Quasigeld *n*	quasi money	quasi-argent *m*	quasi moneta *f*	—
activo efectivo (Es)	Barvermögen *n*	cash assets	valeurs réalisables à court terme ou disponibles *f/pl*	capitale liquido *m*	—
activo en fondos públicos (Es)	Fondsvermögen *n*	fund assets	capital constituant le fonds *m*	patrimonio del fondo *m*	—
activo fijo (Es)	Anlagevermögen *n*	fixed assets	valeurs immobilisées *f/pl*	attivo fisso *m*	—
activo fijo neto (Es)	Netto-Anlagevermögen *n*	net fixed assets	capital fixe net *m*	capitale immobilizzato netto *m*	—
activo inmobiliario (Es)	Realvermögen *n*	real wealth	patrimoine réel *m*	patrimonio reale *m*	—
activo social (Es)	Gesellschafts-vermögen *n*	partnership assets	patrimoine social *m*	attivo sociale *m*	—
Act on Foreign Trade and Payments (E)	Außenwirtschafts-gesetz *n*	—	loi sur le commerce extérieur *f*	legge sul commercio estero *f*	ley de transacciones exteriores *f*
actual amount (E)	ausmachender Betrag *m*	—	montant calculé *m*	controvalore della contrattazione *m*	importe calculado *m*
actual currency clause (E)	Effektivvermerk *m*	—	clause de payement en monnaie étrangère *f*	clausola di pagamento effettivo in moneta estera *f*	cláusula de efectividad *f*
actual profit (E)	bereinigter Gewinn *m*	—	produit net d'exploitation *m*	utile rettificato *m*	beneficio real *m*
actual reserve (E)	Ist-Reserve *f*	—	réserve effective *f*	riserva effettiva *f*	reserva efectiva *f*
actual transaction (E)	Effektivgeschäft *n*	—	marché en disponible *m*	operazione in effettivo *f*	operación al contado *f*
acuerdo de pago del resultado (Es)	Ergebnisabführungs-vertrag *m*	profit and loss transfer agreement	accord de transfer des résultats *m*	contratto di trasferi-mento profitto *m*	—
acuerdo de swap (Es)	Swapabkommen *n*	swap agreement	accord swap *m*	contratto swap *m*	—
acuerdo de un plafón de interés (Es)	Zinskappen-vereinbährung *f*	cap rate of interest agreement	accord d'un plafond d'intérêt *m*	accordo sul tetto interessi *m*	—
acuerdo general de empréstito (Es)	allgemeine Kreditvereinbarung *f*	General Arrange-ments to Borrow	accord général de crédits *m*	accordo generale di credito *m*	—
Acuerdo Monetario Europeo (Es)	Europäisches Wäh-rungsabkommen *n*	European Monetary Agreement	accord monétaire européen *m*	Accordo Monetario Europeo *m*	—
acumulación de capital (Es)	Kapitalakkumulation *f*	accumulation of capital	accumulation de capital *f*	accumulazione di capitale *f*	—
acuñación (Es)	Prägung *f*	minting	frappe *f*	coniatura *f*	—
acuñación (Es)	Ausprägung *f*	markedness	monnayage *m*	coniazione *f*	—
adaptation du marché (F)	Marktanpassung *f*	market adjustment	—	adattamento del mercato *m*	ajuste de mercado *m*
adaptation d'une monnaie (F)	Währungs-umstellung *f*	currency conversion	—	riforma monetaria *f*	reforma monetaria *f*
adaptive inflation (E)	Anpassungsinflation *f*	—	inflation adaptive *f*	inflazione di adattamento *f*	inflación adaptiva *f*
adattamento delle parità flessibile (I)	gleitende Paritätsanpassung *f*	crawling exchange rate adjustment	ajustement continu de parités *m*	—	ajuste continuado de paridades *m*
adattamento del mercato (I)	Marktanpassung *f*	market adjustment	adaptation du marché *f*	—	ajuste de mercado *m*
addebitamento (I)	Lastschrift *f*	debit entry	note de débit *f*	—	cargo en cuenta *m*
addebiti (I)	Lastschriftverkehr *m*	direct debiting transactions	prélèvements automatiques *m/pl*	—	sistema de cargo en cuenta *m*
addebito (I)	Debet *n*	debit	débit *m*	—	debe *m*
additional capital (E)	Zusatzkapital *n*	—	capital supplémentaire *m*	capitale addizionale *m*	capital suplementario *m*
additional contribution (E)	Zuzahlung *f*	—	payement supplémentaire *m*	pagamento supplementare *m*	pago suplementario *m*
additional risk premium (E)	Risikozuschlag *m*	—	surprime de risque *f*	soprappremio di rischio *m*	recargo de riesgo *m*

	D	E	F	I	Es
addition des intérêts accumulés (F)	Aufzinsung *f*	addition of accrued interest	—	capitalizzazione *f*	adición de los intereses acumulados *f*
addition of accrued interest (E)	Aufzinsung *f*	—	addition des intérêts accumulés *f*	capitalizzazione *f*	adición de los intereses acumulados *f*
adeguamento di struttura (I)	Strukturwandel *m*	structural change	changement dans les structures *m*	—	cambio de estructura *m*
adelanto sobre valores (Es)	Effektenlombard *m*	advances against securities	prêt sur tites *m*	anticipazione su titoli *f*	—
adempimento (I)	Erfüllung *f*	performance	accomplissement *m*	—	cumplimiento *m*
adesione (I)	Beitritt *m*	joining	adhésion *f*	—	adhesión *f*
adhesión (Es)	Beitritt *m*	joining	adhésion *f*	adesione *f*	—
adhésion (F)	Beitritt *m*	joining	—	adesione *f*	adhesión *f*
adición de los intereses acumulados (Es)	Aufzinsung *f*	addition of accrued interest	addition des intérêts accumulés *f*	capitalizzazione *f*	—
adjudicated bankrupt (E)	Gemeinschuldner *m*	—	débiteur en failli *m*	debitore fallito *m*	deudor común *m*
Adjustable Peg (D)	—	adjustable peg	cours adaptable *m*	adjustable peg *m*	cotización ajustable *f*
adjustable peg (E)	Adjustable Peg *m*	—	cours adaptable *m*	adjustable peg *m*	cotización ajustable *f*
adjustable peg (I)	Adjustable Peg *m*	adjustable peg	cours adaptable *m*	—	cotización ajustable *f*
adjustment project (E)	Anpassungs-investition *f*	—	investissement d'ajustement *m*	investimento di aggiornamento *m*	inversión de ajuste *f*
administración (Es)	Verwaltung *f*	administration	administration *f*	amministrazione *f*	—
administración de depósito (Es)	Depotverwaltung *f*	portfolio management	administration des titres déposés *f*	amministrazione di un deposito *f*	—
administración de valores (Es)	Effektenverwaltung *f*	portfolio management	administration de titres *f*	amministrazione di titoli *f*	—
administración fiduciaria (Es)	Treuhand *f*	trust	substitution fidéicommissaire *f*	amministrazione fiduciaria *f*	—
administración fiscal (Es)	Finanzverwaltung *f*	administration of the finances	administration des finances *f*	amministrazione delle finanze *f*	—
administration (E)	Verwaltung *f*	—	administration *f*	amministrazione *f*	administración *f*
administration (F)	Verwaltung *f*	administration	—	amministrazione *f*	administración *f*
administration des finances (F)	Finanzverwaltung *f*	administration of the finances	—	amministrazione delle finanze *f*	administración fiscal *f*
administration des titres déposés (F)	Depotverwaltung *f*	portfolio management	—	amministrazione di un deposito *f*	administración de depósito *f*
administration de titres (F)	Effektenverwaltung *f*	portfolio management	—	amministrazione di titoli *f*	administración de valores *f*
administration fédérale pour la réglementation des cartels (F)	Bundeskartellamt *n*	Federal Cartel Authority	—	ufficio federale dei cartelli *m*	Oficina Federal de Cártel *f*
administration of the finances (E)	Finanzverwaltung *f*	—	administration des finances *f*	amministrazione delle finanze *f*	administración fiscal *f*
administrator in bankruptcy proceedings (E)	Konkursverwalter *m*	—	liquidateur de la faillite *m*	curatore del fallimento *m*	síndico de quiebra *m*
admisión (Es)	Zulassung *f*	admission	admission *f*	ammissione *f*	—
admisión en la bolsa (Es)	Börsenzulassung *f*	admission to the stock exchange	admission en bourse *f*	ammissione alla quotazione di borsa *f*	—
admission (E)	Zulassung *f*	—	admission *f*	ammissione *f*	admisión *f*
admission (F)	Zulassung *f*	admission	—	ammissione *f*	admisión *f*
admission board (E)	Zulassungsstelle *f*	—	commission pour l'admission des valeurs à la cote *f*	ufficio d'ammissione *m*	oficina de matrícula *f*
admission en bourse (F)	Börsenzulassung *f*	admission to the stock exchange	—	ammissione alla quotazione di borsa *f*	admisión en la bolsa *f*
admission of shares to official quotation (E)	Kotierung *f*	—	cotation *f*	ammissione alla quotazione *f*	cotización *f*
admission to the stock exchange (E)	Börsenzulassung *f*	—	admission en bourse *f*	ammissione alla quotazione di borsa *f*	admisión en la bolsa *f*
adquisición de instalaciones por una sociedad después de su fundación (Es)	Nachgründung *f*	post-formation acquisition	acquisitions complémentaires de la société *f/pl*	costituzione successiva *f*	—

	D	E	F	I	Es
adquisición original (Es)	Ersterwerb *m*	first acquisition	première acquisition *f*	primo acquisto *m*	—
aduana (Es)	Zoll *m*	customs duty	droit de douane *m*	dazio *m*	—
advance (E)	Vorschuß *m*	—	avance *f*	anticipo *m*	anticipo *m*
advance performance (E)	Vorleistung *f*	—	prestation exécutée avant l'échéance *f*	prestazione anticipata *f*	anticipo *m*
advances against securities (E)	Effektenlombard *m*	—	prêt sur tites *m*	anticipazione su titoli *f*	adelanto sobre valores *m*
advice (E)	Rat *m*	—	conseil *m*	consiglio *m*	consejo *m*
affaire de compensation (F)	Kompensationsgeschäft *n*	offset transaction	—	operazione di compensazione *f*	operación de compensación *f*
affaire de médiation (F)	Vermittlungsgeschäft *n*	brokerage business	—	operazione di intermediazione *f*	transacción de mediación *f*
affaire en commission (F)	Kommissionsgeschäft *n*	commission business	—	contratto di commissione *f*	operación de comisión *f*
affaire en contrepartie (F)	Gegengeschäft *n*	countertrade	—	operazione di compensazione *f*	transacción en contra *f*
affaire privée (F)	Privatgeschäft *n*	private transaction	—	transazione tra privati *f*	operación privada *f*
affaires commerciales (F)	Handelsgeschäfte *n/pl*	commercial transactions	—	affari commerciali *m/pl*	negocio *m*
affaires en suspens (F)	schwebende Geschäfte *n/pl*	pending transactions	—	affari pendenti *m/pl*	negocios en curso *m/pl*
affare all'estero (I)	Auslandsgeschäft *n*	business in foreign countries	opération avec l'étranger *f*	—	negocio de exportación *m*
affare in contanti (I)	Bargeschäft *n*	cash transactions	marché au comptant *m*	—	operación al contado *f*
affare in proprio (I)	Eigengeschäft *n*	transactions on own account	opération en nom personnel et à propre compte *f*	—	operación por cuenta propia *f*
affari commerciali (I)	Handelsgeschäfte *n/pl*	commercial transactions	affaires commerciales *f/pl*	—	negocio *m*
affari pendenti (I)	schwebende Geschäfte *n/pl*	pending transactions	affaires en suspens *f/pl*	—	negocios en curso *m/pl*
affectation à des règles (F)	Regelbindung *f*	rule-bound policy	—	attività vincolata *f*	vinculación a reglas *f*
affiche de bourse (F)	Börsenaushang *m*	stock market notice board	—	affissione in borsa *f*	anuncio bursátil *m*
Affidavit (D)	—	affidavit	affidavit *m*	affidavit *m*	afidávit *m*
affidavit (E)	Affidavit *m*	—	affidavit *m*	affidavit *m*	afidávit *m*
affidavit (F)	Affidavit *m*	affidavit	—	affidavit *m*	afidávit *m*
affidavit (I)	Affidavit *m*	affidavit	affidavit *m*	—	afidávit *m*
affiliata (I)	Affiliation *f*	affiliation	affiliation *f*	—	afiliación *f*
Affiliation (D)	—	affiliation	affiliation *f*	affiliata *f*	afiliación *f*
affiliation (E)	Affiliation *f*	—	affiliation *f*	affiliata *f*	afiliación *f*
affiliation (F)	Affiliation *f*	affiliation	—	affiliata *f*	afiliación *f*
affissione in borsa (I)	Börsenaushang *m*	stock market notice board	affiche de bourse *f*	—	anuncio bursátil *m*
affisso (I)	Aushang *m*	notice board	tableau de signalisation *m*	—	tablilla *f*
afflusso di ordini (I)	Auftragseingang *m*	incoming order	entrée de commandes *f*	—	entrada de pedidos *f*
afidávit (Es)	Affidavit *m*	affidavit	affidavit *m*	affidavit *m*	—
afiliación (Es)	Affiliation *f*	affiliation	affiliation *f*	affiliata *f*	—
a fin de mes (Es)	per Ultimo	for the monthly settlement	à fin de mois	quotazione a fine corrente *f*	—
à fin de mois (F)	per Ultimo	for the monthly settlement	—	quotazione a fine corrente *f*	a fin de mes
a forfait (I)	pauschal	global	forfaitaire	—	global
after-date bill (E)	Datowechsel *m*	—	effet payable à un certain délai de date *m*	cambiale a certo tempo data *f*	letra a tantos días fecha *f*

	D	E	F	I	Es
after-hours dealing (E)	Nachbörse *f*	—	marché après-bourse *m*	dopolistino *m*	operaciones después del cierre de la bolsa *f/pl*
after-sight bill (E)	Nachsichtwechsel *m*	—	traite à un certain délai de vue *f*	cambiale a certo tempo vista *f*	letra a tantos días vista *f*
agence (F)	Zweigstelle *f*	branch	—	filiale *f*	sucursal *f*
agence de renseignements (F)	Auskunftei *f*	commercial agency	—	agenzia d'informazioni *f*	agencia de información *f*
agence d'opérations de financement par participation (F)	Beteiligungsvermittlung *f*	agency of equity financing transactions		mediazione di partecipazioni *f*	mediación en las operaciones de financiación de participación *f*
agencia de información (Es)	Auskunftei *f*	commercial agency	agence de renseignements *f*	agenzia d'informazioni *f*	—
agency agreement (E)	Geschäftsbesorgungsvertrag *m*	—	contrat de gestion d'affaires *m*	contratto d'agenzia *m*	contrato de mandato *m*
agency of equity financing transactions (E)	Beteiligungsvermittlung *f*	—	agence d'opérations de financement par participation *f*	mediazione di partecipazioni *f*	mediación en las operaciones de financiación de participación *f*
agent commercial (F)	Handelsmakler *m*	commercial broker	—	mediatore di commercio *m*	corredor de comercio *m*
agent de change (F)	Parkettmakler *m*	official market broker	—	agente di cambio *m*	corredor de parqué *m*
agente comercial (Es)	Handelsbevollmächtigter *m*	general agent	personne ayant le pouvoir commercial *f*	rappresentante commerciale *m*	—
agente de bolsa (Es)	Börsenmakler *m*	stockbroker	courtier en bourse *m*	agente di borsa *m*	—
agente de cambio y bolsa (Es)	Kursmakler *m*	stockbroker	courtier en bourse *m*	agente di borsa *m*	—
agente di borsa (I)	Börsenmakler *m*	stockbroker	courtier en bourse *m*	—	agente de bolsa *m*
agente di borsa (I)	Kursmakler *m*	stockbroker	courtier en bourse *m*	—	agente de cambio y bolsa *m*
agente di cambio (I)	Effektenmakler *m*	stockbroker	courtier en valeurs mobilières *m*	—	corredor de bolsa *m*
agente di cambio (I)	Parkettmakler *m*	official market broker	agent de change *m*	—	corredor de parqué *m*
agente di cambio (I)	Devisenkursmakler *m*	exchange broker	courtier en devises *m*	—	corredor de cambios *m*
agente di commercio (I)	Handelsvertreter *m*	commercial agent	représentant de commerce *m*	—	representante comercial *m*
agente in valori (I)	Effektenhändler *m*	dealer in securities	courtier en valeurs mobilières *m*	—	corredor de bolsa *m*
agente profesional (Es)	Berufshändler *m*	professional trader	agent professionnel *m*	operatore professionale *m*	—
agent financier (F)	Kreditvermittler *f*	money broker	—	intermediario finanziario *m*	operador de negociación de créditos *m*
agent professionnel (F)	Berufshändler *m*	professional trader	—	operatore professionale *m*	agente profesional *m*
agenzia d'informazioni (I)	Auskunftei *f*	commercial agency	agence de renseignements *f*	—	agencia de información *f*
agevolazione all'esportazione (I)	Exportförderung *f*	export promotion	encouragement à l'exportation *m*	—	fomento de la exportación *m*
aggio (I)	Agio *n*	agio	agio *m*	—	agio *m*
aggio d'emissione (I)	Aufgeld *n*	agio	agio *m*	—	agio *m*
aggio di rimborso (I)	Rückzahlungsagio *n*	premium payable on redemption	prime de remboursement *f*	—	agio de reembolso *m*
aggiotaggio (I)	Agiotage *f*	agiotage	agiotage *m*	—	agiotaje *m*
aggiunta (I)	Zuschuß *m*	allowance	allocation *f*	—	suplemento *m*
aggregate property (E)	Gesamtvermögen *n*	—	avoir total *m*	patrimonio complessivo *m*	totalidad del patrimonio *f*
Agio (D)	—	agio	agio *m*	aggio *m*	agio *m*
agio (E)	Aufgeld *n*	—	agio *m*	aggio *m*	agio *m*
agio (E)	Agio *n*	—	agio *m*	aggio *m*	agio *m*
agio (Es)	Agio *n*	agio	agio *m*	aggio *m*	—
agio (Es)	Aufgeld *n*	agio	agio *m*	aggio d'emissione *m*	—
agio (F)	Aufgeld *n*	agio	—	aggio d'emissione *m*	agio *m*

	D	E	F	I	Es
agio (F)	Agio *n*	agio	—	aggio *m*	agio *m*
agio de reembolso (Es)	Rückzahlungsagio *n*	premium payable on redemption	prime de remboursement *f*	aggio di rimborso *m*	—
Agiopapiere (D)	—	securities redeemable at a premium	obligations remboursables avec prime *f/pl*	titoli a premio *m/pl*	valores de renta fija reembolsados con una prima *m/pl*
Agiotage (D)	—	agiotage	agiotage *m*	aggiotaggio *m*	agiotaje *m*
agiotage (E)	Agiotage *f*	—	agiotage *m*	aggiotaggio *m*	agiotaje *m*
agiotage (F)	Agiotage *f*	agiotage	—	aggiotaggio *m*	agiotaje *m*
agiotaje (Es)	Agiotage *f*	agiotage	agiotage *m*	aggiotaggio *m*	—
agreement of purchase and sale (E)	Kaufvertrag *m*	—	contrat de vente *m*	contratto di compravendita *m*	contrato de compraventa *m*
agricultural loan (E)	Landwirtschaftskredit *m*	—	crédit agricole *m*	credito all'agricoltura *m*	crédito agrario *m*
agricultural mortgage bond (E)	Landwirtschaftsbrief *m*	—	cédule hypothéquaire agricole *f*	obbligazione di una banca agricola *f*	cédula hipotecaria agrícola *f*
ahorrador (Es)	Sparer *m*	saver	épargnant *m*	risparmiatore *m*	—
ahorradores de menor importancia (Es)	Kleinsparer *m*	small saver	petit épargnant *m*	piccolo risparmiatore *m*	—
ahorrar (Es)	sparen	saving	économiser	risparmiare	—
ahorrar para la construcción (Es)	bausparen	saving through building societies	épargner pour la construction	risparmiare per l'edilizia	—
ahorro colectivo (Es)	Kollektivsparen *n*	collective saving	épargne collective *f*	risparmio collettivo *m*	—
ahorro común (Es)	Gemeinschaftssparen *n*	joint saving	épargne collective *f*	risparmio collettivo *m*	—
ahorro con primas (Es)	Prämiensparen *n*	bonus-aided saving	épargne à primes *f*	risparmio a premi *m*	—
ahorro con un fin determinado (Es)	Zwecksparen *n*	target saving	épargne à un but déterminée *f*	risparmio ad investimento vincolato *m*	—
ahorro de beneficios (Es)	Gewinnsparen *n*	lottery premium saving	épargne à lots *f*	risparmio a premi *m*	—
ahorro de excedentes (Es)	Plus-Sparen *n*	surplus saving	épargne d'excédents *f*	risparmio restanti del conto corrente *m*	—
ahorro de los importes excesivos (Es)	Überschuß-Sparen *n*	surplus saving	épargne d'excédents *f*	risparmio con ordine permanente *m*	—
ahorro favorecido por ventajas fiscales (Es)	steuerbegünstigtes Sparen *n*	tax-privileged saving	épargne jouissant d'avantages fiscaux *f*	risparmio con privilegi fiscali *m*	—
ahorro fórzoso (Es)	Zwangssparen *n*	compulsory saving	épargne forcée *f*	risparmio forzato *m*	—
ahorro individual (Es)	individuelles Sparen *n*	saving by private households	épargne individuelle *f*	risparmio individuale *m*	—
ahorro negativo (Es)	Entsparen *n*	dissaving	épargne négative *f*	diminuzione dei risparmi accumulati *f*	—
ahorros (Es)	Ersparnis *f*	savings	épargne *f*	risparmio *m*	—
aide financière (F)	Kapitalhilfe *f*	capital aid	—	aiuto finanziario *m*	ayuda financiera *f*
aide financière (F)	finanzieller Beistand *m*	financial assistance	—	assistenza finanziaria *f*	ayuda financiera *f*
aide financière à l'éxportation (F)	Außenhandelsfinanzierung *f*	foreign trade financing	—	finanziamento commercio estero *m*	financiación del comercio exterior *f*
aiuti agli investimenti (I)	Investitionshilfe *f*	investment assistance	subvention en faveur des investissements *f*	—	ayuda de inversión *f*
aiuto finanziario (I)	Kapitalhilfe *f*	capital aid	aide financière *f*	—	ayuda financiera *f*
ajuste continuado de paridades (Es)	gleitende Paritätsanpassung *f*	crawling exchange rate adjustment	ajustement continu de parités *m*	adattamento delle parità flessibile *m*	—
ajuste de mercado (Es)	Marktanpassung *f*	market adjustment	adaptation du marché *f*	adattamento del mercato *m*	—
ajuste financiero (Es)	Finanzausgleich *m*	financial equalization	compensation financière *f*	conguaglio finanziario *m*	—
ajustement continu de parités (F)	gleitende Paritätsanpassung *f*	crawling exchange rate adjustment	—	adattamento delle parità flessibile *m*	ajuste continuado de paridades *m*
ajustes por periodificación (Es)	Rechnungsabgrenzung *f*	apportionment between accounting periods	délimitation des comptes non encore soldés en fin d'exercice *f*	ratei e risconti *m/pl*	—

	D	E	F	I	Es
AKA-Kredite (D)	—	export credits	crédits en faveur de l'exportation *m/pl*	crediti speciali all'esportazione *m/pl*	créditos a la exportación *m/pl*
akkreditieren (D)	—	to open a credit	accréditer	accreditare	acreditar
Akkreditiv (D)	—	letter of credit	accréditif *m*	credito documentario *m*	crédito documentario *m*
Akkreditivsteller (D)	—	person opening a credit in favour of somebody	émetteur d'un accréditif *m*	ordinante il credito *m*	acreditante *m*
Aktie (D)	—	share	action *f*	azione *f*	acción *f*
Aktienanalyse (D)	—	analysis of shares	analyse d'actions *f*	analisi di azioni *f*	análisis de acciones *m*
Aktienausgabe (D)	—	issuing of shares	émission d'actions *f*	emissione di azioni *f*	emisión de acciones *f*
Aktienaustausch (D)	—	exchange of shares	échange d'actions *f*	scambio di azioni *m*	canje de acciones *m*
Aktienbanken (D)	—	joint stock banks	banques par actions *f/pl*	banche per azioni *f/pl*	bancos por acciones *m/pl*
Aktienbuch (D)	—	share register	registre des actions *m*	registro delle azioni *m*	libro de acciones *m*
Aktieneinziehung (D)	—	withdrawal of shares	retrait d'actions *m*	ritiro di azioni *m*	redención de acciones *f*
Aktienfonds (D)	—	share fund	fonds d'actions *m*	fondo azionario *m*	fondo de acciones *m*
Aktiengesellschaft (D)	—	joint stock company	société anonyme *f*	società per azioni *f*	sociedad anónima *f*
Aktiengesetz (D)	—	Company Law	loi sur des sociétés par actions *f*	legge sulle società per azioni *f*	ley sobre régimen jurídico de las socie-dades anónimas *f*
Aktienindex (D)	—	share index	indice du cours des actions *m*	indice azionario *m*	índice de cotización *m*
Aktienkapital (D)	—	share capital	fonds social *m*	capitale azionario *m*	capital en acciones *m*
Aktienkurs (D)	—	share price	cours des actions *f*	quotazione azionaria *f*	cotización de las acciones *f*
Aktienmarkt (D)	—	share market	marché d'actions *m*	mercato azionario *m*	mercado de acciones *m*
Aktienoption (D)	—	share stock option	option d'échanger des titres con-vertibles en actions *f*	diritto di prelazione *m*	opción de cambiar títulos convertibles en acciones *f*
Aktienpaket (D)	—	block of shares	paquet d'actions *m*	pacchetto azionario *m*	paquete de acciones *m*
Aktienquorum (D)	—	share quorum	quorum d'actions *m*	quorum azioni *m*	quórum de acciones *m*
Aktienrecht (D)	—	company law	loi sur les sociétés anonymes *f*	diritto delle società per azioni *m*	derecho de socieda-des anónimas *m*
Aktienregister (D)	—	share register	registre d'actions *f*	registro delle azioni *m*	registro de acciones *m*
Aktienrendite (D)	—	yield on shares	produit de l' action *m*	reddito effettivo di azioni *m*	rédito de las acciones *m*
Aktienumtausch (D)	—	exchange of share certificates for new ones	échange d'actions *m*	cambio di azioni *m*	cambio de acciones *m*
Aktienzeichnung (D)	—	subscription for shares	souscription d'actions *f*	sottoscrizione di azioni *f*	suscripción de acciones *f*
Aktienzertifikat (D)	—	share certificate	certificat d'actions *m*	certificato azionario *m*	certificado de acciones *m*
Aktienzusammen-legung (D)	—	consolidation of shares	regroupement d'actions *m*	raggruppamento di azioni *m*	fusión de acciones *f*
Aktionär (D)	—	shareholder	actionnaire *m*	azionista *m*	accionista *m*
Aktionärsbrief (D)	—	circular letter from board to shareholders	circulaire d'actionnaires *f*	lettera degli azionisti *f*	circular de accionistas *f*
Aktionärs-vereinigungen (D)	—	associations of shareholders	assemblée des actionnaires *f*	associazioni di azionisti *f/pl*	juntas de accionistas *f/pl*
Aktiva (D)	—	assets	actif *f*	attivo *m*	activo *m*
Aktivgeschäft (D)	—	credit transaction	opération de prêt *f*	operazione attiva *f*	operación activa *f*
Aktivposten (D)	—	credit item	poste de l'actif *m*	attività *f*	asiento activo *m*
Aktivzins (D)	—	interest receivable	intérêt demandé par la banque *m*	interessi attivi *m/pl*	intereses deudores *m/pl*
Akzept (D)	—	acceptance	acceptance *f*	accettazione *f*	aceptación *f*
Akzeptaustausch (D)	—	exchange of acceptances	échange d'acceptations *m*	scambio di accettazioni *m*	intercambio de acceptaciones *m*

	D	E	F	I	Es
Akzepthäuser (D)	—	acceptance banks	banques d'acceptation f/pl	acceptance banks f/pl	bancos de aceptación m/pl
Akzeptkredit (D)	—	acceptance credit	crédit par traite acceptée m	credito d'accettazione m	crédito de aceptación m
Akzeptlinie (D)	—	line of acceptance	plafond des crédits sur effets acceptés m	linea di credito d'accettazione f	línea de aceptación f
Akzeptprovision (D)	—	commission for acceptance	commission bancaire sur crédit d'acceptation f	commissione d'accettazione f	comisión de aceptación f
Akzept-verbindlichkeit (D)	—	acceptance liability	engagement par acceptation m	effetto passivo m	obligación de aceptación f
a la par (Es)	pari	par	pair	pari	—
a largo plazo (Es)	lange Sicht f	long run	échéance longue f	a lunga scadenza	—
al cambio más barato (Es)	billigst	at lowest	au meilleur prix	al meglio	—
alcancía (Es)	Sparbüchse f	piggy bank	tirelire f	salvadanaio m	—
alcista (Es)	Haussier m	bull	haussier m	rialzista m	—
alcista (Es)	Bullish n	bullish	haussier m	bullish m	—
al contado (Es)	bar	cash	comptant	in contanti	—
alias (Es)	genannt	indicated	indiqué	stimato	—
alignement des monnaies (F)	Währungs-ausgleich m	currency conversion compensation	—	conguaglio dei cambi m	compensación de cambios f
aliquota (I)	Anteil m	share	part f	—	parte alícuota f
aliquota di risparmio (I)	Sparquote f	savings ratio	quote-part de revenu réservé à des fins d'épargne f	—	cuota de ahorro f
Alleinvertrieb (D)	—	sole distribution	distribution exclusive f	esclusiva f	distribución exclusiva f
allgemeine Kredit-vereinbarung (D)	—	General Arrangements to Borrow	accord général de crédits m	accordo generale di credito m	acuerdo general de empréstito m
allocation (E)	Allokation f	—	allocation f	allocazione f	asignación f
allocation (F)	Zuschuß m	allowance	—	aggiunta f	suplemento m
allocation (F)	Allokation f	allocation	—	allocazione f	asignación f
allocation de capital (F)	Kapitalallokation f	allocation of capital	—	allocazione di capitale f	alocación de capital f
allocation of capital (E)	Kapitalallokation f	—	allocation de capital f	allocazione di capitale f	alocación de capital f
allocazione (I)	Allokation f	allocation	allocation f	—	asignación f
allocazione di capitale (I)	Kapitalallokation f	allocation of capital	allocation de capital f	—	alocación de capital f
Allokation (D)	—	allocation	allocation f	allocazione f	asignación f
allotment right (E)	Zuteilungsrechte n/pl	—	droits de répartition m/pl	diritti d'assegnazione m/pl	derechos de acceso m/pl
allowance (E)	Zuschuß m	—	allocation f	aggiunta f	suplemento m
allowance (E)	Bewilligung f	—	consentement m	autorizzazione f	concesión f
all-round bank (E)	Universalbank f	—	banque universelle f	banca universale f	banco mixto m
all-share certificate (E)	Global-Anleihe f	—	titre représentant globalement un pa-quet d'emprunts m	credito globale m	empréstito global m
allungamento del bilancio (I)	Bilanzverlängerung f	increase in total assets and liabilities	extension du bilan f	—	extensión del balance f
al meglio (I)	billigst	at lowest	au meilleur prix	—	al cambio más barato
al meglio (I)	bestens	at best	au mieux	—	al mejor cambio
al mejor cambio (Es)	bestens	at best	au mieux	al meglio	—
alocación de capital (Es)	Kapitalallokation f	allocation of capital	allocation de capital f	allocazione di capitale f	—
alta congiuntura (I)	Hochkonjunktur f	boom	haute conjoncture f	—	alta coyuntura f
alta coyuntura (Es)	Hochkonjunktur f	boom	haute conjoncture f	alta congiuntura f	—
alteración del balance (Es)	Bilanzänderung f	alteration of a balance sheet	modification apportée au bilan f	modifica del bilancio f	—

	D	E	F	I	Es
alteration of a balance sheet (E)	Bilanzänderung f	—	modification apportée au bilan f	modifica del bilancio f	alteración del balance f
a lunga scadenza (I)	lange Sicht f	long run	échéance longue f	—	a largo plazo
alza (Es)	Hausse f	bull market	hausse f	contegno rialzistico m	—
alza considerable de las cotizaciones (Es)	Kurssprung m	jump in prices	hausse sensible des cours f	balzo delle quotazioni m	—
amalgamation (E)	Fusion f	—	fusion f	fusione f	fusión f
amalgamation tax (E)	Fusionssteuer f	—	impôt sur la fusion de sociétés m	tassa di fusione f	impuesto sobre la fusión de sociedades m
ambiente de crisis (Es)	Krisenstimmung f	crisis feeling	climat de crise m	atmosfera di crisi f	—
amenaza del crédito (Es)	Kreditgefährdung f	endangering the credit of a person or a firm	atteinte au crédit f	pregiudizio della capacità creditizia m	—
American accounting system (E)	amerikanisches Rechnungswesen n	—	comptabilité dite américaine f	contabilità americana f	contabilidad americana f
American Bankers Association (D)	—	American Bankers Association	Association des Banquiers Américains f	American Bankers Association f	Asociación de Banqueros Estadounidenses f
American Bankers Association (E)	American Bankers Association f	—	Association des Banquiers Américains f	American Bankers Association f	Asociación de Banqueros Estadounidenses f
American Bankers Association (I)	American Bankers Association f	American Bankers Association	Association des Banquiers Américains f	—	Asociación de Banqueros Estadounidenses f
amerikanisches Rechnungswesen (D)	—	American accounting system	comptabilité dite américaine f	contabilità americana f	contabilidad americana f
amministrazione (I)	Verwaltung f	administration	administration f	—	administración f
amministrazione delle finanze (I)	Finanzverwaltung f	administration of the finances	administration des finances f	—	administración fiscal f
amministrazione di titoli (I)	Effektenverwaltung f	portfolio management	administration de titres f	—	administración de valores f
amministrazione di un deposito (I)	Depotverwaltung f	portfolio management	administration des titres déposés f	—	administración de depósito f
amministrazione fiduciaria (I)	Treuhand f	trust	substitution fidéicommissaire f	—	administración fiduciaria f
amministrazione fiduciaria prestiti (I)	Anleihetreuhänder-schaft f	loan custodianship	fidéicommis d'emprunts m	—	fideicomiso de empréstitos m
ammissione (I)	Zulassung f	admission	admission f	—	admisión f
ammissione alla quotazione (I)	Kotierung f	admission of shares to official quotation	cotation f	—	cotización f
ammissione alla quo-tazione di borsa (I)	Börsenzulassung f	admission to the stock exchange	admission en bourse f	—	admisión en la bolsa f
ammortamento (I)	Amortisation f	amortization	amortissement m	—	amortización f
ammortamento (I)	Abschreibung f	writing off	amortissement m	—	amortización f
ammortamento del valore di libro (I)	Buchwert-abschreibung f	declining balance depreciation	amortissement dé-gressif au prorata de la valeur restante m	—	amortización del valor contable f
ammortamento speciale (I)	Sonderabschreibung f	special depreciation	amortissement extraordinaire m	—	amortización extraordinaria f
ammortamento straordinario (I)	außerordentliche Abschreibung f	extraordinary depreciation	amortissement extraordinaire m	—	amortización extraordinaria f
Amortisation (D)	—	amortization	amortissement m	ammortamento m	amortización f
Amortisations-hypothek (D)	—	instalment mortgage	hypothèque amortissable f	ipoteca ammortizzabile f	hipoteca de amortización f
amortissement (F)	Amortisation f	amortization	—	ammortamento m	amortización f
amortissement (F)	Abschreibung f	writing off	—	ammortamento m	amortización f
amortissement (F)	Tilgung f	redemption	—	rimborso m	amortización f
amortissement dé-gressif au prorata de la valeur restante (F)	Buchwert-abschreibung f	declining balance depreciation	—	ammortamento del valore di libro m	amortización del valor contable f
amortissement en nature (F)	Naturaltilgung f	redemption in kind	—	rimborso del credito ipotecario pattuito m	amortización en especie f
amortissement extraordinaire (F)	außerordentliche Abschreibung f	extraordinary depreciation	—	ammortamento straordinario m	amortización extraordinaria f

	D	E	F	I	Es
amortissement extraordinaire (F)	Sonderabschreibung f	special depreciation	—	ammortamento speciale m	amortización extraordinaria f
amortizable mortgage loan (E)	Tilgungshypothek f	—	hypothèque garantissant une cránce remboursable à termes périodiques f	ipoteca ammortizzabile f	hipoteca amortizable f
amortización (Es)	Tilgung f	redemption	amortissement m	rimborso m	—
amortización (Es)	Amortisation f	amortization	amortissement m	ammortamento m	—
amortización (Es)	Abschreibung f	writing off	amortissement m	ammortamento m	—
amortización del valor contable (Es)	Buchwertabschreibung f	declining balance depreciation	amortissement dégressif au prorata de la valeur restante m	ammortamento del valore di libro m	—
amortización en especie (Es)	Naturaltilgung f	redemption in kind	amortissement en nature m	rimborso del credito ipotecario pattuito m	—
amortizaciones pendientes (Es)	Tilgungsrückstände m/pl	redemption in arrears	arriérés d'amortissement m/pl	rate di rimborso arretrate f/pl	—
amortización extraordinaria (Es)	außerordentliche Abschreibung f	extraordinary depreciation	amortissement extraordinaire m	ammortamento straordinario m	—
amortización extraordinaria (Es)	Sonderabschreibung f	special depreciation	amortissement extraordinaire m	ammortamento speciale m	—
amortization (E)	Amortisation f	—	amortissement m	ammortamento m	amortización f
amortization instalment (E)	Tilgungsrate f	—	annuité f	rata di rimborso f	tasa de amortización f
ampiezza d'ordinazione (I)	Auftragsgröße f	size of an order	importance de la commande f	—	volumen de pedido m
amtlicher Handel (D)	—	official trading	négociations en bourse f/pl	contrattazione ufficiale f	cotización oficial f
amtlicher Markt (D)	—	official market	marché officiel m	mercato ufficiale m	mercado oficial m
amtlich nicht notierte Werte (D)	—	unquoted securities	titres non cotés officiellement m/pl	valori non quotati m/pl	valores no cotizados oficialmente m/pl
analisi (I)	Analyse f	analysis	analyse f	—	análisis m
analisi (I)	Auswertung f	evaluation	évaluation f	—	evaluación f
analisi dei flussi monetari (I)	Geldstromanalyse f	flow-of-funds analysis	analyse des courants monétaires f	—	análisis de flujos monetarios m
analisi del capitale (I)	Kapitalanalyse f	capital analysis	analyse de capital f	—	análisis de capital m
analisi di azioni (I)	Aktienanalyse f	analysis of shares	analyse d'actions f	—	análisis de acciones m
analisi di bilancio (I)	Bilanzanalyse f	balance sheet analysis	analyse du bilan f	—	análisis de balance m
analisi di mercato (I)	Marktanalyse f	market analysis	analyse du marché f	—	análisis del mercado m
analisi di portafoglio (I)	Portfolio-Analyse f	portfolio analysis	analyse du portefeuille f	—	análisis de cartera m
analisi di tendenza (I)	Trendanalyse f	trend analysis	analyse de la tendance générale f	—	análisis de la tendencia m
analisi di titoli (I)	Wertpapieranalyse f	securities research	analyse des valeurs mobilières f	—	análisis de inversiones m
analisi finanziaria (I)	Finanzanalyse f	financial analysis	analyse financière f	—	análisis financiero m
analisi fondamentale (I)	Fundamentalanalyse f	portfolio analysis	analyse fondamentale f	—	análisis fundamental m
analisi marginale (I)	Marginalanalyse f	marginal analysis	analyse marginale f	—	análisis marginal m
análisis (Es)	Analyse f	analysis	analyse f	analisi f	—
análisis de acciones (Es)	Aktienanalyse f	analysis of shares	analyse d'actions f	analisi di azioni f	—
análisis de acciones técnico (Es)	technische Aktienanalyse f	technical analysis	analyse technique f	analisi tecnica f	—
análisis de balance (Es)	Bilanzanalyse f	balance sheet analysis	analyse du bilan f	analisi di bilancio m	—
análisis de capital (Es)	Kapitalanalyse f	capital analysis	analyse de capital f	analisi del capitale f	—
análisis de cartera (Es)	Portfolio-Analyse f	portfolio analysis	analyse du portefeuille f	analisi di portafoglio f	—
análisis de flujos monetarios (Es)	Geldstromanalyse f	flow-of-funds analysis	analyse des courants monétaires f	analisi dei flussi monetari m	—
análisis de inversiones (Es)	Wertpapieranalyse f	securities research	analyse des valeurs mobilières f	analisi di titoli f	—

	D	E	F	I	Es
análisis de la tendencia (Es)	Trendanalyse f	trend analysis	analyse de la tendance générale f	analisi di tendenza f	—
análisis del desarrollo de una acción (Es)	Chartanalyse f	chart analysis	analyse du développement d'une action f	analisi tecnica f	—
análisis del mercado (Es)	Marktanalyse f	market analysis	analyse du marché f	analisi di mercato f	—
análisis financiero (Es)	Finanzanalyse f	financial analysis	analyse financière f	analisi finanziaria f	—
análisis fundamental (Es)	Fundamentalanalyse f	portfolio analysis	analyse fondamentale f	analisi fondamentale m	—
análisis marginal (Es)	Marginalanalyse f	marginal analysis	analyse marginale f	analisi marginale f	—
analisi statistica dei bilanci (I)	Bilanzstatistik f	balance sheet statistics	statistique des bilans f	—	estadística de balances f
analisi tecnica (I)	technische Aktienanalyse f	technical analysis	analyse technique f	—	análisis de acciones técnico m
analisi tecnica (I)	Chartanalyse f	chart analysis	analyse du développement d'une action f	—	análisis del desarrollo de una acción m
Analyse (D)	—	analysis	analyse f	analisi f	análisis m
analyse (F)	Analyse f	analysis	—	analisi f	análisis m
analyse d'actions (F)	Aktienanalyse f	analysis of shares	—	analisi di azioni f	análisis de acciones m
analyse de capital (F)	Kapitalanalyse f	capital analysis	—	analisi del capitale f	análisis de capital m
analyse de la tendance générale (F)	Trendanalyse f	trend analysis	—	analisi di tendenza f	análisis de la tendencia m
analyse des courants monétaires (F)	Geldstromanalyse f	flow-of-funds analysis	—	analisi dei flussi monetari m	análisis de flujos monetarios m
analyse des valeurs mobilières (F)	Wertpapieranalyse f	securities research	—	analisi di titoli f	análisis de inversiones m
analyse du bilan (F)	Bilanzkritik f	balance sheet analysis	—	esame critico del bilancio m	crítica del balance f
analyse du développement d'une action (F)	Chartanalyse f	chart analysis	—	analisi tecnica f	análisis del desarrollo de una acción m
analyse du marché (F)	Marktanalyse f	market analysis	—	analisi di mercato f	análisis del mercado m
analyse du portefeuille (F)	Portfolio-Analyse f	portfolio analysis	—	analisi di portafoglio f	análisis de cartera m
analyse financière (F)	Finanzanalyse f	financial analysis	—	analisi finanziaria f	análisis financiero m
analyse fondamentale (F)	Fundamentalanalyse f	portfolio analysis	—	analisi fondamentale m	análisis fundamental m
analyse marginale (F)	Marginalanalyse f	marginal analysis	—	analisi marginale f	análisis marginal m
analyse technique (F)	technische Aktienanalyse f	technical analysis	—	analisi tecnica f	análisis de acciones técnico m
analysis (E)	Analyse f	—	analyse f	analisi f	análisis m
analysis of shares (E)	Aktienanalyse f	—	analyse d'actions f	analisi di azioni f	análisis de acciones m
anatocismo (I)	Zinseszins m	compound interest	intérêt composé m	—	interés compuesto m
andamento dei prezzi (I)	Preisentwicklung f	trend in prices	évolution des prix f	—	evolución de los precios f
Anderdepot (D)	—	fiduciary deposit	dépôt de consignation m	deposito altrui m	depósito por cuenta de terceros m
Anderkonto (D)	—	fiduciary account	compte de tiers m	conto altrui m	cuenta fiduciaria f
Anderskosten (D)	—	costing expenditures	coût précalculé m	costi calcolatori m/pl	costes calculatorios m/pl
Angebotssteuerung (D)	—	supply control	régulation des offres f	controllo dell'offerta f	control de oferta m
Angebotsstruktur (D)	—	supply structure	structure d'offres f	struttura dell'offerta f	estructura de ofertas f
animado (Es)	freundlich	buoyant	ferme	favorevole	—
Ankaufsrecht (D)	—	purchase right	droit d'achat m	opzione f	derecho de compra m
Anlage (D)	—	investment	investissement m	investimento m	inversión f
Anlageausschuß (D)	—	investment committee	comité d'investissements m	comitato consulenza investimenti m	comité de inversión m
Anlageberatung (D)	—	investment counseling	orientation en matière de placement f	consulenza in investimenti f	asesoramiento en materia de inversiones m
Anlagekapital (D)	—	investment capital	capital d'investissement m	capitale d'investimento m	capital de inversión m

	D	E	F	I	Es
Anlagekonten (D)	—	investment accounts	comptes d'investissement *m/pl*	conti degli investimenti *m/pl*	cuentas de inversión *f/pl*
Anlagenfinanzierung (D)	—	financing of investment in fixed assets	financement du renouvellement des immobilisations *m*	finanziamento di investimenti *m*	financiación de inversión *f*
Anlagepapiere (D)	—	investment securities	valeurs de placement *f/pl*	titoli d'investimento *m/pl*	valores de inversión *m/pl*
Anlagevermögen (D)	—	fixed assets	valeurs immobilisées *f/pl*	attivo fisso *m*	activo fijo *m*
Anlagevorschriften (D)	—	rules for investment of resources	prescriptions d'investissement *f/pl*	disposizioni d'investimento *f/pl*	normas de inversión *f/pl*
Anlagewagnis (D)	—	investment risk	risque de l'investisseur *m*	rischio d'investimento *m*	riesgo del inversor *m*
Anlagewährung (D)	—	currency of investment	monnaie d'investissement *f*	valuta d'investimento *f*	moneda de inversión *f*
Anlaufkosten (D)	—	launching costs	frais de mise en marche *m/pl*	spese d'avviamento *f/pl*	gastos de instalación *m/pl*
Anlegerschutz (D)	—	protection for the investor	protection de l'investisseur *f*	tutela degli investori *f*	protección del inversor *f*
Anleihegeschäft (D)	—	loan business	opération de placement de titres d'emprunt *f*	operazione di prestito *f*	operación crediticia *f*
Anleiherechnung (D)	—	loan calculation	décompte des emprunts *m*	calcolo rimborso e interessi *m*	cálculo de empréstito *m*
Anleiheschein (D)	—	bond certificate	certificat d'emprunt *m*	certificato di prestito *m*	certificado de empréstito *m*
Anleihetreuhänderschaft (D)	—	loan custodianship	fidéicommis d'emprunts *m*	amministrazione fiduciaria prestiti *f*	fideicomiso de empréstitos *m*
annacquamento della quotazione (I)	Kursverwässerung *f*	price watering	baisse du cours par émission d'action gratuites *f*	—	caída de cotización *f*
annacquamento di capitali (I)	Kapitalverwässerung *f*	watering of capital stock	augmentation du capital par émission d'actions gratuites ou par incorporation des réserves au fonds social *f*	—	depreciación del capital *f*
anno d'esercizio (I)	Geschäftsjahr *n*	financial year	exercice commercial *m*	—	ejercicio *m*
annotazione di controllo (I)	Prüfungsvermerk *m*	certificate of audit	mention de vérification *f*	—	certificado de revisión *m*
annual balance sheet (E)	Jahresbilanz *f*	—	bilan de fin d'année *m*	bilancio d'esercizio *m*	balance anual *m*
annualità (I)	Annuität *f*	annuity	annuité *f*	—	anualidad *f*
annualità perpetua (I)	ewige Rente *f*	perpetual annuity	rente perpétuelle *f*	—	anualidad perpetua *f*
annual statement of accounts (E)	Jahresabschluß *m*	—	clôture annuelle des comptes *f*	bilancio d'esercizio *m*	balance anual *m*
Annuität (D)	—	annuity	annuité *f*	annualità *f*	anualidad *f*
Annuitätenanleihe (D)	—	annuity bond	emprunt amortissable par annuités *m*	prestito rimborsabile in annualità *m*	obligación sin vencimiento *f*
annuité (F)	Tilgungsrate *f*	amortization instalment	—	rata di rimborso *f*	tasa de amortización *f*
annuité (F)	Annuität *f*	annuity	—	annualità *f*	anualidad *f*
annuity (E)	Rente *f*	—	rente *f*	titolo a reddito fisso *m*	renta *f*
annuity (E)	Annuität *f*	—	annuité *f*	annualità *f*	anualidad *f*
annuity bond (E)	Annuitätenanleihe *f*	—	emprunt amortissable par annuités *m*	prestito rimborsabile in annualità *m*	empréstito por anualidades *m*
annuity certificate (E)	Rentenbrief *m*	—	titre de rente foncière *m*	titolo di rendita *m*	título de renta *m*
annuity department (E)	Rentenabteilung *f*	—	service des titres à revenu fixe *m*	ufficio per titoli a reddito fisso *m*	sección de títulos de renta fija *f*
annul (E)	annullieren	—	annuler	annullare	anular
annulation (F)	Löschung *f*	cancellation	—	cancellazione *f*	cancelación *f*
annulation (F)	Streichung *f*	deletion	—	mancata quotazione *f*	anulación *f*

	D	E	F	I	Es
annulation de la cotation (F)	Kursstreichung *f*	non-quotation	—	mancata quotazione *f*	no cotización *f*
annuler (F)	annullieren	to annul	—	annullare	anular
annullare (I)	annullieren	to annul	annuler	—	anular
annullieren (D)	—	to annul	annuler	annullare	anular
annuncio (I)	Bekanntmachung *f*	notification	publication *f*	—	publicación *f*
anonyme Sparkonten (D)	—	anonymous savings accounts	comptes d'épargne anonymes *m/pl*	conti di risparmio cifrati *m/pl*	cuentas de ahorro anónimas *f/pl*
anonymous savings accounts (E)	anonyme Sparkonten *n/pl*	—	comptes d'épargne anonymes *m/pl*	conti di risparmio cifrati *m/pl*	cuentas de ahorro anónimas *f/pl*
Anpassungsinflation (D)	—	adaptive inflation	inflation adaptive *f*	inflazione di adattamento *f*	inflación adaptiva *f*
Anpassungs-investition (D)	—	adjustment project	investissement d'ajustement *m*	investimento di aggiornamento *m*	inversión de ajuste *f*
Anrechtscheine (D)	—	intermediate share certificate	certificats provisoires *m/pl*	certificati provvisori *m/pl*	certificados provisionales *m/pl*
Ansa (I)	Hanse *f* ·	Hanseatic League	Hansa *f*	—	Hansa *f*
Anschaffungs-geschäft (D)	—	buying or selling for customers	opérations d'achat *f/pl*	operazione d'acquisto *f*	operaciones de compra *f/pl*
Anschaffungswert (D)	—	acquisition value	valeur d'acquisition *f*	valore d'acquisto *m*	valor de adquisición *m*
Anteil (D)	—	share	part *f*	aliquota *f*	parte alícuota *f*
Anteilseigner (D)	—	shareholder	porteur de parts *m*	azionista *m*	titular de acciones *m*
Anteilspapiere (D)	—	equity security	titres de participation *m/pl*	cedole azionarie *f/pl*	títulos de participación *m/pl*
anticipare (I)	eskomptieren	to discount	escompter	—	descontar
anticipation term (E)	Erwartungswert *m*	—	valeur escomptée *f*	valore stimato *m*	valor esperado *m*
anticipazione su cambiali (I)	Wechsellombard *m*	collateral loan based on a bill of exchange	avance sur effet nanti *f*	—	letra de cambio tomada en prenda *f*
anticipazione su crediti (I)	Lombardkredit *m*	collateral credit	crédit garanti par nantissement *m*	—	crédito pignoraticio *m*
anticipazione su titoli (I)	Effektenlombard *m*	advances against securities	prêt sur tites *m*	—	adelanto sobre valores *m*
anticipazione su titoli straordinaria (I)	Sonderlombard *m*	special lombard facility	facilités spéciales de prêts sur nantissement *f/pl*	—	préstamo pignoraticio especial *m*
anticipo (Es)	Vorschuß *m*	advance	avance *f*	anticipo *m*	—
anticipo (Es)	Vorleistung *f*	advance performance	prestation exécutée avant l'échéance *f*	prestazione anticipata *f*	—
anticipo (I)	Vorschuß *m*	advance	avance *f*	—	anticipo *m*
anticyclical reserve (E)	Konjunkturausgleichs-rücklage *f*	—	réserve anticyclique *f*	fondo compensazione congiuntura negativa *m*	reserva de compensa-ción coyuntural *f*
antizyklisches Verhalten (D)	—	countercyclical development	comportement anticyclique *m*	comportamento anticiclico *m*	comportamiento anticíclico *m*
anualidad (Es)	Annuität *f*	annuity	annuité *f*	annualità *f*	—
anualidad perpetua (Es)	ewige Rente *f*	perpetual annuity	rente perpétuelle *f*	annualità perpetua *f*	—
anulación (Es)	Streichung *f*	deletion	annulation *f*	mancata quotazione *f*	—
anular (Es)	annullieren	to annul	annuler	annullare	—
anuncio bursátil (Es)	Börsenaushang *m*	stock market notice board	affiche de bourse *f*	affissione in borsa *f*	—
Anwartschafts-deckungsverfahren (D)	—	expectancy cover procedure	système de la capitalisation *m*	sistema di capitalizzazione *m*	sistema de capitalización *m*
Anweisung (D)	—	payment order	mandat *m*	ordine di pagamento *m*	orden de pago *f*
Anzahlung (D)	—	deposit	acompte *m*	acconto *m*	pago a cuenta *m*
Anzahlungs-bürgschaft (D)	—	payment guarantee	garantie de payement *f*	garanzia rimborso acconto *f*	garantía de pago *f*
an Zahlungs Statt (D)	—	in lieu of payment	à titre de payement	pro soluto	a título de pago
Anzeigepflicht (D)	—	legal obligation to disclose one's results	obligation de publier *f*	obbligo di denuncia *m*	obligación de declarar *m*
apelación al crédito (Es)	Kreditaufnahme *f*	raising of credits	recours à l'emprunt *m*	accensione di credito *f*	—

	D	E	F	I	Es
apertura (Es)	Erschließung f	development	ouverture f	apertura f	—
apertura (I)	Erschließung f	development	ouverture f	—	apertura f
apertura de la quiebra (Es)	Konkurseröffnung f	commencement of bankruptcy proceedings	ouverture de la faillite f	apertura del fallimento f	—
apertura del fallimento (I)	Konkurseröffnung f	commencement of bankruptcy proceedings	ouverture de la faillite f	—	apertura de la quiebra f
apertura del mercado (Es)	Markterschließung f	opening of new markets	ouverture du marché f	penetrazione del mercato f	—
apertura de una cuenta (Es)	Kontoeröffnung f	opening of an account	ouverture d'un compte f	apertura di un conto f	—
apertura di credito documentario (I)	Bar-Akkreditiv m	clean credit	accréditif payable en espèce m	—	crédito simple m
apertura di un conto (I)	Kontoeröffnung f	opening of an account	ouverture d'un compte f	—	apertura de una cuenta f
apoderado (Es)	Bevollmächtigter m	authorized person	fondé de pouvoir m	delegato m	—
apoderado general (Es)	Prokurist m	authorized clerk	fondé de procuration m	procuratore commerciale m	—
aportación (Es)	Einzahlung f	payment	payement m	versamento m	—
aportación en especie (Es)	Sacheinlage f	investment in kind	apport en nature m	apporto in natura m	—
aportación suplementaria (Es)	Nachschuß m	subsequent payment	versement complémentaire m	apporto supplemetare m	—
à porter en compte (F)	nur zur Verrechnung	for account only	—	da accreditare	sólo para compensación
apoyo de la cotización (Es)	Kursstützung f	price pegging	soutien des cours m	sostegno delle quotazioni m	—
appalto (I)	Ausschreibung f	invitation to tender	soumission f	—	subasta f
apport en nature (F)	Sacheinlage f	investment in kind	—	apporto in natura m	aportación en especie f
apportionment (E)	Repartierung f	—	répartition f	ripartizione f	repartición f
apportionment between accounting periods (E)	Rechnungs-abgrenzung f	—	délimitation des comptes non encore soldés en fin d'exercice f	ratei e risconti m/pl	ajustes por periodificación m/pl
apport obligatoire (F)	Pflichteinlage f	compulsory contribution	—	deposito obbligatorio m	depósito obligatorio m
apporto in denaro (I)	Bareinlage f	cash deposit	dépôt en numéraire m	—	depósito en efectivo m
apporto in natura (I)	Sacheinlage f	investment in kind	apport en nature m	—	aportación en especie f
apporto supplemetare (I)	Nachschuß m	subsequent payment	versement complémentaire m	—	aportación suplementaria f
appréciation des résultats des succursales bancaires (F)	Filialkalkulation f	branch office accounting	—	calcolo delle filiali m	cálculos de sucursal m/pl
appropriazione indebita (I)	Unterschlagung f	embezzlement	détournement m	—	defraudación f
appropriazione indebita di depositi (I)	Depotunterschlagung f	misapplication of deposit	détournement de titres en dépôt m	—	defraudación de depósito f
approvazione (I)	Zustimmung f	consent	accord m	—	consentimiento m
approvazione estratto deposito (I)	Depotanerkenntnis f	deposit acknowledgement	reconnaissance de dépôt f	—	reconocimiento de depósito m
Arbeitgeberanteil (D)	—	employer's share	part patronale f	quota del datore di lavoro f	cuota patronal f
Arbeitgeber-zuschüsse (D)	—	employer's contributions	compléments patronaux m/pl	contributi del datore di lavoro m/pl	suplementos patronales m/pl
Arbeitnehmeraktie (D)	—	employees' shares	action de travail f	azione di lavoro f	acción de trabajo f
Arbeitnehmer-sparzulage (D)	—	employees' savings premium	prime d'épargne en faveur de l'employée f	indennità di risparmio dipendenti f	prima de ahorro del empleado f
Arbeitseinkommen (D)	—	earned income	revenu du travail m	reddito di lavoro m	ingresos del trabajo m/pl
Arbeitsentgelt (D)	—	remuneration	rémunération du travail m	remunerazione f	remuneración del trabajo f
Arbeitslosengeld (D)	—	unemployment benefit	indemnité de chômage f	indennità di disoccupazione f	subsidio de desempleo m

	D	E	F	I	Es
Arbeitsproduktivität (D)	—	productivity of labour	productivité du travail *m*	produttività del lavoro *f*	productividad por hora de trabajo *f*
Arbitrage (D)	—	arbitrage	arbitrage *m*	arbitraggio *m*	arbitraje *m*
arbitrage (E)	Arbitrage *f*	—	arbitrage *m*	arbitraggio *m*	arbitraje *m*
arbitrage (F)	Arbitrage *f*	arbitrage	—	arbitraggio *m*	arbitraje *m*
arbitrage clause (E)	Arbitrageklausel *f*	—	clause d'arbitrage *f*	clausola arbitrale *f*	cláusula de arbitraje *f*
arbitrage dealings (E)	Arbitragegeschäft *n*	—	opération d'arbitrage *f*	operazione di arbitraggio *f*	operación de arbitraje *f*
arbitrage d'or (F)	Goldarbitrage *f*	arbitrage in bullion	—	arbitraggio sull'oro *m*	arbitraje de oro *m*
Arbitragegeschäft (D)	—	arbitrage dealings	opération d'arbitrage *f*	operazione di arbitraggio *f*	operación de arbitraje *f*
arbitrage in bullion (E)	Goldarbitrage *f*	—	arbitrage d'or *m*	arbitraggio sull'oro *m*	arbitraje de oro *m*
arbitrage in securities (E)	Wertpapierarbitrage *f*	—	arbitrage sur les cours des valeurs mobilières *m*	arbitraggio su titoli *m*	arbitraje de valores *m*
Arbitrageklausel (D)	—	arbitrage clause	clause d'arbitrage *f*	clausola arbitrale *f*	cláusula de arbitraje *f*
arbitrage par compensation (F)	Ausgleichs-Arbitrage *f*	offsetting arbitrage	—	arbitraggio di rimborso *m*	arbitraje de divisas *m*
arbitrager (E)	Arbitrageur *m*	—	arbitragiste *m*	arbitraggista *m*	arbitrajista *m*
Arbitragerechnung (D)	—	arbitrage voucher	calcul d'arbitrage *m*	calcolo arbitrale *m*	nota arbitral *f*
arbitrage sur les cours des valeurs mobilières (F)	Wertpapierarbitrage *f*	arbitrage in securities	—	arbitraggio su titoli *m*	arbitraje de valores *m*
arbitrage sur les devises (F)	Devisenarbitrage *f*	arbitration in foreign exchange	—	arbitraggio in cambio *m*	arbitraje de divisas *m*
arbitrage sur les taux de l'intérêt (F)	Zinsarbitrage *f*	interest rate arbitrage	—	arbitraggio sui tassi d'interesse *m*	arbitraje en materia de tipos de interés *m*
arbitrage triangulaire (F)	Dreiecksarbitrage *f*	triangular arbitrage	—	arbitraggio triangolare *m*	arbitraje triangular *m*
Arbitrageur (D)	—	arbitrager	arbitragiste *m*	arbitraggista *m*	arbitrajista *m*
arbitrage value (E)	Arbitragewert *m*	—	valeur d'arbitrage *f*	titolo arbitrale *m*	valor de arbitraje *m*
arbitrage voucher (E)	Arbitragerechnung *f*	—	calcul d'arbitrage *m*	calcolo arbitrale *m*	nota arbitral *f*
Arbitragewert (D)	—	arbitrage value	valeur d'arbitrage *f*	titolo arbitrale *m*	valor de arbitraje *m*
arbitraggio (I)	Arbitrage *f*	arbitrage	arbitrage *m*	—	arbitraje *m*
arbitraggio di rimborso (I)	Ausgleichs-Arbitrage *f*	offsetting arbitrage	arbitrage par compensation *m*	—	arbitraje de divisas *m*
arbitraggio in cambio (I)	Devisenarbitrage *f*	arbitration in foreign exchange	arbitrage sur les devises *m*	—	arbitraje de divisas *m*
arbitraggio sui tassi d'interesse (I)	Zinsarbitrage *f*	interest rate arbitrage	arbitrage sur les taux de l'intérêt *m*	—	arbitraje en materia de tipos de interés *m*
arbitraggio sull'oro (I)	Goldarbitrage *f*	arbitrage in bullion	arbitrage d'or *m*	—	arbitraje de oro *m*
arbitraggio su titoli (I)	Wertpapierarbitrage *f*	arbitrage in securities	arbitrage sur les cours des valeurs mobilières *m*	—	arbitraje de valores *m*
arbitraggio triangolare (I)	Dreiecksarbitrage *f*	triangular arbitrage	arbitrage triangulaire *m*	—	arbitraje triangular *m*
arbitraggista (I)	Arbitrageur *m*	arbitrager	arbitragiste *m*	—	arbitrajista *m*
arbitragiste (F)	Arbitrageur *m*	arbitrager	—	arbitraggista *m*	arbitrajista *m*
arbitraje (Es)	Arbitrage *f*	arbitrage	arbitrage *m*	arbitraggio *m*	—
arbitraje de divisas (Es)	Devisenarbitrage *f*	arbitration in foreign exchange	arbitrage sur les devises *m*	arbitraggio in cambio *m*	—
arbitraje de divisas (Es)	Ausgleichs-Arbitrage *f*	offsetting arbitrage	arbitrage par compensation *m*	arbitraggio di rimborso *m*	—
arbitraje de oro (Es)	Goldarbitrage *f*	arbitrage in bullion	arbitrage d'or *m*	arbitraggio sull'oro *m*	—
arbitraje de valores (Es)	Wertpapierarbitrage *f*	arbitrage in securities	arbitrage sur les cours des valeurs mobilières *m*	arbitraggio su titoli *m*	—
arbitraje en materia de tipos de interés (Es)	Zinsarbitrage *f*	interest rate arbitrage	arbitrage sur les taux de l'intérêt *m*	arbitraggio sui tassi d'interesse *m*	—
arbitraje triangular (Es)	Dreiecksarbitrage *f*	triangular arbitrage	arbitrage triangulaire *m*	arbitraggio triangolare *m*	—

	D	E	F	I	Es
arbitrajista (Es)	Arbitrageur *m*	arbitrager	arbitragiste *m*	arbitraggista *m*	—
arbitration in foreign exchange (E)	Devisenarbitrage *f*	—	arbitrage sur les devises *m*	arbitraggio in cambio *m*	arbitraje de divisas *m*
archivio d'informazioni (I)	Auskunftdatei *f*	information file	fichier de renseignements *m*	—	archivo de datos con fines de información *m*
archivo de datos con fines de información (Es)	Auskunftdatei *f*	information file	fichier de renseignements *m*	archivio d'informazioni *m*	—
area del dollaro (I)	Dollarblock *m*	dollar area	bloc dollar *m*	—	zona del dólar *f*
area delle valute libere (I)	freier Währungsraum *m*	free currency area	zone monétaire libre *f*	—	área monetaria libre *f*
area monetaria (I)	Währungsgebiet *n*	currency area	zone monétaire *f*	—	área monetaria *f*
área monetaria (Es)	Währungsgebiet *n*	currency area	zone monétaire *f*	area monetaria *f*	—
área monetaria libre (Es)	freier Währungsraum *m*	free currency area	zone monétaire libre *f*	area delle valute libere *f*	—
a reddito fisso (I)	festverzinslich	with a fixed rate of interest	à revenu fixe	—	de renta fija
à revenu fixe (F)	festverzinslich	with a fixed rate of interest	—	a reddito fisso	de renta fija
argent (F)	Geld *n*	money	—	denaro *m*	dinero *m*
argent au jour le jour (F)	Tagesgeld *n*	day-to-day money	—	prestito giornaliero *m*	dinero de día a día *m*
argent à un mois (F)	Monatsgeld *n*	one month money	—	deposito vincolato ad un mese *m*	dinero a 30 días *m*
argent comptant (F)	Bargeld *n*	ready money	—	denaro contante *m*	efectivo *m*
argent de consomption (F)	Schwundgeld *n*	scalage	—	bollatura di monete *f*	dinero de consunción *m*
argent de crédit (F)	Kreditgeld *n*	credit money	—	credito *m*	dinero crediticio *m*
argent en nature (F)	Naturalgeld *n*	commodity money	—	oggetto di baratto *m*	dinero en especie *m*
argent exogène (F)	exogenes Geld *n*	exogenous money base	—	denaro esogeno *m*	dinero exógeno *m*
argent facultatif (F)	fakultatives Geld *n*	facultative money	—	denaro facoltativo *m*	dinero facultativo *m*
argent fiduciaire (F)	fiduziäres Geld *n*	fiduciary funds	—	denaro fiduciario *m*	dinero fiduciario *m*
argent fin (F)	Feinsilber *n*	fine silver	—	argento fino *m*	plata fina *f*
argent gardé dans le bas de laine (F)	Strumpfgeld *n*	hoarded notes and coins	—	denaro tesaurizzato *m*	dinero en el calcetín *m*
argent immobilisé (F)	Festgeld *n*	fixed deposit	—	deposito a termine *m*	depósito a plazo *m*
argent liquide potentiel (F)	potentielles Bargeld *n*	potential cash	—	contanti potenziali *m/pl*	dinero efectivo potencial *m*
argent métallique (F)	Metallgeld *n*	metallic money	—	moneta metallica *f*	moneda metálica *f*
argent neutre (F)	neutrales Geld *n*	neutral money	—	moneta neutrale *f*	dinero neutral *m*
argento fino (I)	Feinsilber *n*	fine silver	argent fin *m*	—	plata fina *f*
argent remboursable à vue (F)	Call-Geld *n*	call money	—	prestito giornaliero *m*	dinero exigible a la vista *m*
arithmetical average (E)	arithmetische Mittel *n*	—	moyenne arithmétique *f*	media aritmeticha *f*	media aritmética *f*
arithmetische Mittel (D)	—	arithmetical average	moyenne arithmétique *f*	media aritmeticha *f*	media aritmética *f*
armonizzazione (I)	Harmonisierung *f*	harmonization	harmonisation *f*	—	harmonisación *f*
arrangement (E)	Disposition *f*	—	disposition *f*	disponibilità *f*	disposición *f*
arrangement stand-by (F)	Bereitschaftskreditabkommen *n*	stand-by arrangement	—	stand-by agreement *m*	préstamo de ayuda *m*
arrastre de beneficios (Es)	Gewinnvortrag *m*	profit carried forward	report du solde excédentaire *m*	avanzo utile *m*	—
arrear on interests (E)	Zinsrückstand *m*	—	intérêt arriéré *m*	interessi arretrati *m/pl*	interés retrasado *m*
arrendamiento (Es)	Pachtzins *m*	rent	prix du bail *m*	canone d'affitto *m*	—
arrendamiento con opción de compra (Es)	Mietkauf *m*	lease with option to purchase	location-vente *f*	locazione finanziaria *f*	—
arrêt (F)	Erlaß *m*	decree	—	decreto *m*	decreto *m*
arrêté quotidien de compte (F)	Tagesbilanz *f*	daily trial balance sheet	—	bilancio giornaliero *m*	balance diario *m*

	D	E	F	I	Es
arriérés d'amortissement (F)	Tilgungsrückstände *m/pl*	redemption in arrears	—	rate di rimborso arretrate *f/pl*	amortizaciones pendientes *f/pl*
arrondieren (D)	—	to round off	arrondir	arrotondare	redondear
arrondir (F)	arrondieren	to round off	—	arrotondare	redondear
arrotondare (I)	arrondieren	to round off	arrondir	—	redondear
asesoramiento (Es)	Beratung *f*	counseling	consultation *f*	consulenza *f*	—
asesoramiento de clientes (Es)	Kundenberatung *f*	consumer advice	orientation de la clientèle *f*	servizio d'assistenza *m*	—
asesor en materia de divisas (Es)	Devisenberater *m*	foreign exchange advisor	conseiller en matière de devises *m*	consulente di cambio *m*	—
asesoramiento en materia de inversiones (Es)	Anlageberatung *f*	investment counseling	orientation en matière de placement *f*	consulenza in investimenti *f*	—
asesor en materia de inversiones (Es)	Vermögensberater *m*	investment advisor	conseiller en investissement *m*	consulente patrimoniale *m*	—
asesor en materia de títulos de renta fija (Es)	Rentenberater *m*	consultant on pensions	conseiller en matière de pensions *m*	consulente titoli a reddito fisso *m*	—
as guarantor of payment (E)	per aval	—	bon pour aval	per buon fine	por aval
Asian Dollar market (E)	Asiendollarmarkt *m*	—	marché du dollar asiatique *m*	mercato del dollaro asiatico *m*	mercado del dólar asiático *m*
Asiendollarmarkt (D)	—	Asian Dollar market	marché du dollar asiatique *m*	mercato del dollaro asiatico *m*	mercado del dólar asiático *m*
asiento activo (Es)	Aktivposten *m*	credit item	poste de l'actif *m*	attività *f*	—
asiento en el pasivo (Es)	Passivierung *f*	inclusion on the liabilities side	inscription au passif *f*	passività *f*	—
asiento en otra cuenta (Es)	Umbuchung *f*	transfer of an entry	jeu d'écritures *m*	giro di partite *m*	—
asignación (Es)	Allokation *f*	aliocation	allocation *f*	allocazione *f*	—
asignación de pérdidas (Es)	Verlustzuweisung *f*	loss allocation	assignation des pertes *f*	assegnazione perdite *f*	—
asked price (E)	Briefkurs *m*	—	cours de vente *m*	prezzo d'offerta *m*	cotización ofrecida *f*
asociación (Es)	Verband *m*	association	association *f*	federazione *f*	—
asociación bancaria (Es)	Bankenverband *m*	banking association	association des banques *f*	associazione bancaria *f*	—
asociación de ahorro (Es)	Sparverein *m*	savings club	association d'épargne *f*	società di risparmio *f*	—
asociación de bancos de giro (Es)	Giroverband *m*	giro association	association des banques de virement *f*	associazione di banche di giro *f*	—
Asociación de Banqueros Estadounidenses (Es)	American Bankers Association *f*	American Bankers Association	Association des banquiers américains *f*	American Bankers Association *f*	—
Asociación Internacional de las Bolsas de Valores (Es)	Internationale Vereinigung der Wertpapierbörsen *f*	International Federation of Stock Exchanges	Association internationale des bourses de titres et valeurs mobilières *f*	Associazione internazionale delle borse valori *f*	—
aspettativa d'inflazione (I)	Inflationserwartung *f*	expected inflation	inflation prévue *f*	—	inflación pronostizada *f*
aspettative razionali (I)	rationale Erwartungen *f/pl*	rational	expectatives rationnelles *f/pl*	—	expectativas racionales *f/pl*
assainissement (F)	Sanierung *f*	reconstruction	—	risanamento *m*	saneamiento *m*
assegnazione perdite (I)	Verlustzuweisung *f*	loss allocation	assignation des pertes *f*	—	asignación de pérdidas *f*
assegno (I)	Scheck *m*	cheque	chèque *m*	—	cheque *m*
assegno all'ordine (I)	Orderscheck *m*	order cheque	chèque à ordre *m*	—	cheque a la orden *m*
assegno al portatore (I)	Inhaberscheck *m*	cheque to bearer	chèque au porteur *m*	—	cheque al portador *m*
assegno al portatore (I)	Überbringerscheck *m*	bearer cheque	chèque au porteur *m*	—	cheque al portador *m*
assegno coperto (I)	gedeckter Scheck *m*	covered cheque	chèque provisionné *m*	—	cheque cubierto *m*
assegno da accreditare (I)	Verrechnungsscheck *m*	crossed cheque	chèque à porter en compte *m*	—	cheque cruzado *m*
assegno fuori piazza (I)	Versandscheck *m*	out-of-town cheque	chèque déplacé *m*	—	cheque sobre otra plaza *m*

	D	E	F	I	Es
assegno garantito per acquisti (I)	Kaufscheck *m*	purchasing cheque	chèque d'achat *m*	—	cheque de compra *m*
assegno in bianco (I)	Blanko-Scheck *m*	blank cheque	chèque en blanc *m*	—	cheque en blanco *m*
assegno integrativo di risparmio (I)	Sparzulage *f*	savings bonus	prime d'épargne *f*	—	subvención de ahorro *f*
assegno postale (I)	Postscheck *m*	postal giro	chèque postal *m*	—	cheque postal *m*
assegno ritornato (I)	Rückscheck *m*	returned cheque	chèque retourné *m*	—	cheque devuelto *m*
assegno sbarrato (I)	gekreuzter Scheck *m*	crossed cheque	chèque barré *m*	—	cheque cruzado *m*
assegno senza copertura (I)	ungedeckter Scheck *m*	uncovered cheque	chèque sans provision *m*	—	cheque descubierto *m*
assegno sostitutivo (I)	Ersatzscheck *m*	substitute cheque	chèque de substitution *m*	—	cheque de sustitución *m*
assegno standardizzato (I)	Einheitsscheck *m*	standard cheque	formule de chèque normalisée *f*	—	cheque estándar *m*
assegno su filiale (I)	Filialscheck *m*	house cheque	chèque interne *m*	—	cheque de sucursal *m*
assegno sull'estero (I)	Auslandsscheck *m*	foreign cheque	chèque payable à l'étranger *m*	—	cheque sobre el extranjero *m*
assegno tratto su se stesso (I)	trassiert-eigener Scheck *m*	cheque drawn by the drawer himself	chèque tiré sur soi-même *m*	—	cheque girado a su propio cargo *m*
assegno turistico (I)	Reisescheck *m*	traveller's cheque	chèque de voyage *m*	—	cheque de viaje *m*
Assekuranz (D)	—	insurance system	assurance *f*	assicurazione *f*	seguro *m*
assemblea dei creditori (I)	Gläubiger- versammlung *f*	creditors' meeting	assemblée des créanciers *f*	—	junta de acreedores *f*
assemblea generale (I)	General- versammlung *f*	general assembly	assemblée générale *f*	—	junta general *f*
assemblée des actionnaires (F)	Aktionärs- vereinigungen *f/pl*	associations of shareholders	—	associazioni di azionisti *f/pl*	juntas de accionistas *f/pl*
assemblée des créanciers (F)	Gläubiger- versammlung *f*	creditors' meeting	—	assemblea dei creditori *f*	junta de acreedores *f*
assemblée générale (F)	General- versammlung *f*	general assembly	—	assemblea generale *f*	junta general *f*
assessment basis (E)	Bemessungs- grundlage *f*	—	base de calcul *f*	base imponibile *f*	base de cálculo *f*
Assessment Center (D)	—	assessment center	assessment center *m*	assessment center *m*	assessment center *m*
assessment center (E)	Assessment Center *n*	—	assessment center *m*	assessment center *m*	assessment center *m*
assessment center (Es)	Assessment Center *n*	assessment center	assessment center *m*	assessment center *m*	—
assessment center (F)	Assessment Center *n*	assessment center	—	assessment center *m*	assessment center *m*
assessment center (I)	Assessment Center *n*	assessment center	assessment center *m*	—	assessment center *m*
asset and liability statement (E)	Vermögensbilanz *f*	—	état du patrimoine *m*	bilancio patrimoniale *m*	balance patrimonial *m*
Asset market (D)	—	asset market	asset market *m*	asset market *m*	asset market *m*
asset market (E)	Asset market *m*	—	asset market *m*	asset market *m*	asset market *m*
asset market (Es)	Asset market *m*	asset market	asset market *m*	asset market *m*	—
asset market (F)	Asset market *m*	asset market	—	asset market *m*	asset market *m*
asset market (I)	Asset market *m*	asset market	asset market *m*	—	asset market *m*
assets (E)	Aktiva *n/pl*	—	masse active *f*	attività di bilancio *f/pl*	activo *m*
assicurazione (I)	Assekuranz *f*	insurance system	assurance *f*	—	seguro *m*
assicurazione (I)	Versicherung *f*	insurance	assurance *f*	—	seguro *m*
assicurazione collettiva (I)	Sammelinkasso- versicherung *f*	group collection security	assurance d'encais- sement groupé *f*	—	seguro de cobro colectivo *m*
assicurazione crediti individuali (I)	Einzelkredit- versicherung *f*	individual credit insurance	assurance crédit individuelle *f*	—	seguro de crédito individual *m*
assicurazione credito d'investimento (I)	Investitionskredit- versicherung *f*	investment credit insurance	assurance de crédits d'investissement *f*	—	seguro de crédito de inversión *m*
assicurazione del debito residuo (I)	Restschuld- versicherung *f*	residual debt insurance	assurance solde de dette *f*	—	seguro de deuda restante *m*
assicurazione dell'ipoteca (I)	Hypotheken- versicherung *f*	mortgage insurance	assurance hypothécaire *f*	—	seguro de hipotecas *m*
assicurazione di credito (I)	Kreditversicherung *f*	credit insurance	assurance crédit *f*	—	seguro crediticio *m*

	D	E	F	I	Es
assicurazione sulla vita con garanzia reale (I)	Fondsgebundene Lebensversicherung *f*	fund-linked life insurance	assurance-vie liée à un fonds *f*	—	seguro de vida vinculado a fondos *m*
assiette de l'imposition (F)	Besteuerungs-grundlage *f*	tax basis	—	base d'imposizione *f*	base imponible *f*
assignation (F)	Zuweisung *f*	assignment	—	conferimento *m*	atribución *f*
assignation des pertes (F)	Verlustzuweisung *f*	loss allocation	—	assegnazione perdite *f*	asignación de pérdidas *f*
assignment (E)	Zuweisung *f*	—	assignation *f*	conferimento *m*	atribución *f*
assignment by way of security (E)	Sicherungsabtretung *f*	—	cession d'une sûreté *f*	cessione a titolo di garanzia *f*	cesión fiduciaria *f*
assistenza (I)	Beihilfe *f*	financial aid	subside *m*	—	ayuda *f*
assistenza finanziario (I)	finanzieller Beistand *m*	financial assistance	aide financière *f*	—	ayuda financiera *f*
association (E)	Verband *m*	—	association *f*	federazione *f*	asociación *f*
association (F)	Verband *m*	association	—	federazione *f*	asociación *f*
association commerciale en participation (F)	stille Gesellschaft *f*	dormant partnership	—	società di diritto *f*	sociedad en participación *f*
association d'épargne (F)	Sparverein *m*	savings club	—	società di risparmio *f*	asociación de ahorro *f*
association des banques (F)	Bankenverband *m*	banking association	—	associazione bancaria *f*	asociación bancaria *f*
association des banques de virement (F)	Giroverband *m*	giro association	—	associazione di banche di giro *f*	asociación de bancos de giro *f*
Association des banquiers américains (F)	American Bankers Association *f*	American Bankers Association	—	American Bankers Association *f*	Asociación de Banqueros Estadounidenses *f*
association de vérification des comptes (F)	Prüfungsverband *f*	auditing association	—	associazione di controllo *f*	sociedad de revisión *f*
Association internationale des bourses de titres et valeurs mobilières (F)	Internationale Vereinigung der Wertpapierbörsen *f*	International Federation of Stock Exchanges	—	Associazione internazionale delle borse valori *f*	Asociación Internacional de las Bolsas de Valores *f*
association of stockbrokers (E)	Maklerkammer *f*	—	chambre syndicale des courtiers *f*	comitato degli agenti di cambio *m*	colegio de agentes de cambio y bolsa *m*
associations of shareholders (E)	Aktionärs-vereinigungen *f/pl*	—	assemblée des actionnaires *f*	associazioni di azionisti *f/pl*	juntas de accionistas *f/pl*
associazione bancaria (I)	Bankenverband *m*	banking association	association des banques *f*	—	asociación bancaria *f*
associazione di banche di giro (I)	Giroverband *m*	giro association	association des banques de virement *f*	—	asociación de bancos de giro *f*
associazione di controllo (I)	Prüfungsverband *f*	auditing association	association de vérification des comptes *f*		sociedad de revisión *f*
Associazione internazionale delle borse valori (I)	Internationale Vereinigung der Wertpapierbörsen *f*	International Federation of Stock Exchanges	Association internationale des bourses de titres et valeurs mobilières *f*	—	Asociación Internacional de las Bolsas de Valores *f*
associazioni di azionisti (I)	Aktionärs-vereinigungen *f/pl*	associations of shareholders	assemblée des actionnaires *f*	—	juntas de accionistas *f/pl*
associé (F)	Teilhaber *m*	partner	—	socio *m*	socio *m*
assorbimento di mercato (I)	Aufnahmefähigkeit des Marktes *f*	absorptive capacity of the market	capacité d'absorption du marché *f*	—	capacidad de ab-sorción del mercado *f*
assortiment (F)	Sortiment *n*	assortment	—	assortimento *m*	surtido *m*
assortimento (I)	Sortiment *n*	assortment	assortiment *m*	—	surtido *m*
assortment (E)	Sortiment *n*	—	assortiment *m*	assortimento *m*	surtido *m*
assumption of an obligation (E)	Schuldübernahme *f*	—	reprise de dette *f*	espromissione *f*	aceptación de deuda *f*
assunzione di garanzia per terzi (I)	Garantiegeschäft *n*	guarantee business	opération de garantie *f*	—	operación de garantía *f*
assurance (F)	Assekuranz *f*	insurance system	—	assicurazione *f*	seguro *m*
assurance (F)	Versicherung *f*	insurance	—	assicurazione *f*	seguro *m*

	D	E	F	I	Es
assurance crédit (F)	Kreditversicherung f	credit insurance	—	assicurazione di credito f	seguro crediticio m
assurance crédit individuelle (F)	Einzelkreditversicherung f	individual credit insurance	—	assicurazione crediti individuali f	seguro de crédito individual m
assurance de crédits d'investissement (F)	Investitionskreditversicherung f	investment credit insurance	—	assicurazione credito d'investimento f	seguro de crédito de inversión m
assurance d'encaissement groupé (F)	Sammelinkassoversicherung f	group collection security	—	assicurazione collettiva f	seguro de cobro colectivo m
assurance hypothécaire (F)	Hypothekenversicherung f	mortgage insurance	—	assicurazione dell'ipoteca f	seguro de hipotecas m
assurance solde de dette (F)	Restschuldversicherung f	residual debt insurance	—	assicurazione del debito residuo f	seguro de deuda restante m
assurance-vie liée à un fonds (F)	Fondsgebundene Lebensversicherung f	fund-linked life insurance	—	assicurazione sulla vita con garanzia reale f	seguro de vida vinculado a fondos m
asta dell'oro (I)	Goldauktion f	gold auction	vente à l'enchère d'or f	—	subasta de oro f
asta marginale (I)	Tenderverfahren n	tender procedure	offre d'emprunts pour la régulation monétaire f	—	sistema de ofertas m
asta non competitiva (I)	Mengentender m	quantity tender	offre d'emprunts par quantités pour la régulation monétaire f	—	subasta de préstamos de regulación monetaria por cantidades f
asta olandese (I)	Einschreibung f	registration	enregistrement m	—	inscripción f
at best (E)	bestens	—	au mieux	al meglio	al mejor cambio
atentismo (Es)	Attentismus m	wait-and-see attitude	attentisme m	attentismo m	—
atesoramiento (Es)	Thesaurierung f	accumulation of capital	thésauration f	tesaurizzazione f	—
à titre de payement (F)	an Zahlungs Statt	in lieu of payment	—	pro soluto	a título de pago
a título de pago (Es)	an Zahlungs Statt	in lieu of payment	à titre de payement	pro soluto	—
at lowest (E)	billigst	—	au meilleur prix	al meglio	al cambio más barato
atmosfera di crisi (I)	Krisenstimmung f	crisis feeling	climat de crise m	—	ambiente de crisis m
atribución (Es)	Zuweisung f	assignment	assignation f	conferimento m	—
atteinte au crédit (F)	Kreditgefährdung f	endangering the credit of a person or a firm	—	pregiudizio della capacità creditizia m	amenaza del crédito f
attendance stock exchange (E)	Präsenzbörse f	—	bourse de présence f	borsa di presenza f	bolsa de presencia f
attentisme (F)	Attentismus m	wait-and-see attitude	—	attentismo m	atentismo m
attentismo (I)	Attentismus m	wait-and-see attitude	attentisme m	—	atentismo m
Attentismus (D)	—	wait-and-see attitude	attentisme m	attentismo m	atentismo m
attivi e passivi contabili (I)	Buchbestände m/pl	book value	existences comptables f/pl	—	existencias inventariadas f/pl
attività (I)	Aktivposten m	credit item	poste de l'actif m	—	asiento activo m
attività terziaria (I)	Dienstleistung f	service	prestation de service f	—	servicio m
attività vincolata (I)	Regelbindung f	rule-bound policy	affectation à des règles f	—	vinculación a reglas f
attivo (I)	Aktiva n/pl	assets	masse active f	—	activo m
attivo fisso (I)	Anlagevermögen n	fixed assets	valeurs immobilisées f/pl	—	activo fijo m
attivo immobilitato (I)	Sachanlagevermögen n	tangible fixed assets	immobilisations corporelles f/pl	—	inmovilizado m
attivo netto (I)	Reinvermögen n	net assets	avoir net m	—	patrimonio neto m
attivo sociale (I)	Gesellschaftsvermögen n	partnership assets	patrimoine social m	—	activo social m
atto costitutivo (I)	Gesellschaftsvertrag m	shareholder's agreement	contrat de société m	—	contrato social m
atto di pegno (I)	Pfandschein m	certificate of pledge	bulletin de gage m	—	resguardo de prenda m
audit (E)	Revision f	—	vérification f	revisione f	revisión f
audit department (E)	Revisionsabteilung f	—	service de vérification m	ufficio revisioni m	sección de revisión f

	D	E	F	I	Es
auditing (E)	Buchprüfung f	—	vérification des livres f	ispezione contabile f	revisión contable f
auditing association (E)	Prüfungsverband m	—	association de vérification des comptes f	associazione di controllo f	sociedad de revisión f
auditing requirements (E)	Revisionspflicht f	—	obligation de vérification f	obbligo di revisione m	obligación de revisión f
audit of prospectus (E)	Prospektprüfung f	—	vérification du prospectus f	controllo del prospetto m	examinación del prospecto f
audit of the bank balance sheet (E)	Bankprüfung f	—	vérification du bilan bancaire f	esame del bilancio m	revisión de cuentas del banco f
audit report (E)	Prüfungsbericht m	—	compte rendu de vérification m	relazione d'ispezione f	informe de auditoría m
Aufbaukonto (D)	—	build-up account	compte d'installation m	conto accumulativo m	cuenta de financiación de desarrollo f
Aufbewahrung (D)	—	deposit	garde en dépôt f	custodia f	conservación f
Aufbewahrungsfrist (D)	—	retention period	délai de dépôt m	periodo di custodia m	plazo de conservación m
Auffanggesellschaft (D)	—	recipient company	consortium de renflouement m	società finanziaria f	sociedad holding f
Aufgabegeschäft (D)	—	name transaction	opération de médiation f	contratto intermediato m	contrato intermediado m
Aufgeld (D)	—	agio	agio m	aggio d'emissione m	agio m
aufgenommene Gelder (D)	—	borrowed funds	fonds empruntés m/pl	mezzi presi a prestito m/pl	fondos recogidos m/pl
aufgerufene Wertpapiere (D)	—	securities publicly notified as lost	titres appelés au remboursement m/pl	titoli colpiti da ammortamento m/pl	títulos retirados de la circulación con aviso m/pl
Aufkaufspekulation (D)	—	take-over speculation	accaparement spéculatif m	speculazione in accaparramenti f	especulación de acaparamiento f
Aufnahmefähigkeit des Marktes (D)	—	absorptive capacity of the market	capacité d'absorption du marché f	assorbimento di mercato m	capazidad de absorción del mercado f
Aufrechnung (D)	—	set-off	compensation f	compensazione f	compensación f
Aufschwung (D)	—	recovery	reprise f	ripresa f	auge m
Aufsichtsamt (D)	—	control board	office de surveillance m	ispettorato m	oficina de inspección f
Aufsichtsrat (D)	—	supervisory board	conseil de surveillance m	consiglio di sorveglianza m	consejo de administración m
Aufsichtsratsteuer (D)	—	directors' fees tax	impôt sur les jetons de présence et les tantièmes m	imposta consiglio di vigilanza f	impuesto sobre la remuneración de los miembros del consejo de administración m
Auftrag (D)	—	order	commande f	ordine m	pedido m
Auftragsbestätigung (D)	—	confirmation of the order	confirmation de commande f	conferma di ordinazione f	confirmación de un pedido f
Auftragseingang (D)	—	incoming order	entrée de commandes f	afflusso di ordini m	entrada de pedidos f
Auftragsgröße (D)	—	size of an order	importance de la commande f	ampiezza d'ordinazione f	volumen de pedido m
Aufwandsausgleichkonto (D)	—	account for reimbursements of expenses	compte de frais à reporter m	conto compensazione spese m	cuenta de compensación de gastos f
Aufwandskonto (D)	—	expense account	compte de frais m	conto spesa m	cuenta de gastos f
Aufwandskosten (D)	—	expenses incurred	frais de représentation m/pl	spese di rappresentanza f/pl	gastos originados m/pl
Aufwands- und Ertragsrechnung (D)	—	profit and loss account	compte de profits et pertes m	conto economico m	cuenta de beneficios y pérdidas f
Aufwertung (D)	—	revaluation	revalorisation f	rivalutazione f	revalorización f
Aufzinsung (D)	—	addition of accrued interest	addition des intérêts accumulés f	capitalizzazione f	adición de los intereses acumulados f
auge (Es)	Aufschwung m	recovery	reprise f	ripresa f	—
auge (Es)	Boom m	boom	boom m	boom m	—
augmentation de capital (F)	Kapitalerhöhung f	increase of the share capital	—	aumento del capitale m	aumento de capital m

	D	E	F	I	Es
augmentation de capital ordinaire (F)	ordentliche Kapitalerhöhung f	ordinary increase in capital	—	aumento di capitale a pagamento m	aumento de capital ordinario m
augmentation du capital par élargissement des immobilisations corporelles (F)	Sachkapitalerhöhung f	capital increase through contribution in kind	—	aumento del capitale reale m	aumento del capital real m
augmentation du capital par émission d'actions gratuites ou par incorporation des réserves au fonds social (F)	Kapitalverwässerung f	watering of capital stock	—	annacquamento di capitali m	depreciación del capital f
augmentation du capital propre (F)	Eigenkapitalerhöhung f	increase in own capital	—	aumento del capitale proprio m	aumento del capital propio m
au meilleur prix (F)	billigst	at lowest	—	al meglio	al cambio más barato
aumento de capital (Es)	Kapitalerhöhung f	increase of the share capital	augmentation de capital f	aumento del capitale m	—
aumento de capital condicional (Es)	bedingte Kapitalerhöhung f	conditional capital increase	restriction à l'augmentation du capital social f	aumento di capitale condizionato m	—
aumento de capital ordinario (Es)	ordentliche Kapitalerhöhung f	ordinary increase in capital	augmentation de capital ordinaire f	aumento di capitale a pagamento m	—
aumento dei prezzi (I)	Preissteigerung f	price increase	hausse des prix f	—	subida de precios f
aumento del capitale (I)	Kapitalerhöhung f	increase of the share capital	augmentation de capital f	—	aumento de capital m
aumento del capitale proprio (I)	Eigenkapitalerhöhung f	increase in own capital	augmentation du capital propre f	—	aumento del capital propio m
aumento del capitale reale (I)	Sachkapitalerhöhung f	capital increase through contribution in kind	augmentation du capital par élargissement des immobilisations corporelles f	—	aumento del capital real m
aumento del capital propio (Es)	Eigenkapitalerhöhung f	increase in own capital	augmentation du capital propre f	aumento del capitale proprio m	—
aumento del capital real (Es)	Sachkapitalerhöhung f	capital increase through contribution in kind	augmentation du capital par élargissement des immobilisations corporelles f	aumento del capitale reale m	—
aumento di capitale a pagamento (I)	ordentliche Kapitalerhöhung f	ordinary increase in capital	augmentation de capital ordinaire f	—	aumento de capital ordinario m
aumento di capitale condizionato (I)	bedingte Kapitalerhöhung f	conditional capital increase	restriction à l'augmentation du capital social f	—	aumento de capital condicional m
au mieux (F)	bestens	at best	—	al meglio	al mejor cambio
Ausbrechen des Kurses (D)	—	erratic price movements	fortes fluctuations des cours f/pl	oscillazione inattesa della quotazione f	fuertes movimientos en las cotizaciones m/pl
Ausbringung (D)	—	out-put	volume de la production m	gettito m	volumen de la producción m
Ausfallbürgschaft (D)	—	deficiency guarantee	garantie de bonne fin f	garanzia di sostituzione f	fianza de indemnidad f
Ausfallforderung (D)	—	bad debt loss	créance prioritaire f	credito per l'ammanco m	impagados m/pl
Ausfolgungsprotest (D)	—	protest for non-delivery	acte de protêt pour non-restitution d'effet m	protesto mancata consegna cambiale m	protesta de incumplimiento f
Ausfuhrabgaben (D)	—	export duties	taxes à l'exportation f/pl	tasse all'esportazione f/pl	exacciones de exportación f/pl
Ausfuhrbürgschaften (D)	—	export credit guarantee	garanties à l'exportation f/pl	cauzioni d'esportazione f/pl	garantías para la exportación f/pl
Ausfuhrfinanzierung (D)	—	export financing	financement de l'exportation m	finanziamento all'esportazione m	financiación de la exportación f
Ausfuhrgarantie (D)	—	export credit guarantee	garantie en faveur de l'exportateur f	garanzia d'esportazione f	garantía de exportación f
Ausfuhrgenehmigung (D)	—	export license	autorisation d'exportation f	autorizzazione all'esportazione f	licencia de exportación f
Ausfuhrkontrolle (D)	—	export control	contrôle des exportations m	controllo delle esportazioni m	control de las exportaciónes m

	D	E	F	I	Es
Ausfuhrüberschuß (D)	—	export surplus	excédent d'exportation *m*	eccedenza delle esportazioni *f*	excedente de exportación *m*
Ausfuhrzoll (D)	—	export duty	taxe de sortie *m*	dazio all'esportazione *m*	derechos de exportación *m/pl*
Ausgaben (D)	—	expenses	dépenses *f/pl*	spese *f/pl*	gastos *m/pl*
Ausgabenplan (D)	—	plan of expenditure	état prévisionnel des dépenses *m*	piano di spesa *m*	presupuesto de ğastos *m*
Ausgabensteuer (D)	—	outlay tax	taxe de débours *f*	imposta di consumo *f*	impuesto de emisión *m*
ausgabenwirksame Kosten (D)	—	spending costs	coût créant des dépenses *m*	costi comportanti spese *m/pl*	gastos de desembolso *m/pl*
Ausgabepreis (D)	—	issuing price	prix d'émission *m*	prezzo d'emissione *m*	precio de emisión *m*
Ausgabewert (D)	—	nominal value	cours d'émission *m*	valore d'emissione *m*	valor de emisión *m*
Ausgleichsabgabe (D)	—	countervailing duty	taxe de compensation *f*	tassa di compensazione *f*	tasa de compensación *f*
Ausgleichs-Arbitrage (D)	—	offsetting arbitrage	arbitrage par compensation *m*	arbitraggio di rimborso *m*	arbitraje de divisas *m*
Ausgleichsfonds (D)	—	compensation fund	fonds de compensation *m*	fondo di compensazione *m*	fondo de compensación *m*
Ausgleichs-forderung (D)	—	equalization claim	droit à une indemnité compensatoire *f*	credito di compensazione *m*	reclamación de indemnización contra la administración pública *f*
Ausgleichsfunktion des Preises (D)	—	invisible hand	main invisible *f*	meccanismo dei prezzi *m*	mano invisible *f*
Ausgleichsrecht (D)	—	equalization right	droit à une compensation *m*	diritto di compensazione *m*	derecho a compensación *m*
Ausgleichs- und Deckungsforderung (D)	—	equalization and covering claim	demande de dédom-magement et de couverture *f*	credito di compensazione *m*	crédito de igualación y cobertura *m*
Ausgleichs-verfahren (D)	—	composition proceedings	procédé de la compensation *m*	metodo di compensazione *m*	procedimiento de compensación *m*
Ausgleichszahlung (D)	—	compensation payment	payement pour solde de compte *m*	compensazione *f*	pago de compensación *m*
Aushang (D)	—	notice board	tableau de signalisation *m*	affisso *m*	tablilla *f*
Auskunftdatei (D)	—	information file	fichier de renseignements *m*	archivio d'informazioni *m*	archivo de datos con fines de información *m*
Auskunftei (D)	—	commercial agency	agence de renseignements *f*	agenzia d'informazioni *f*	agencia de información *f*
Auskunftspflicht (D)	—	obligation to give information	obligation de fournir des renseignements *f*	obbligo d'informazione *m*	obligación de información *f*
ausländischer Anteilseigner (D)	—	foreign shareholder	actionnaire étranger *m*	azionista estero *m*	titular de acciones extranjero *m*
ausländisches Wertpapier (D)	—	foreign security	valeurs étrangères *f/pl*	titolo estero *m*	título extranjero *m*
Auslandsakzept (D)	—	foreign acceptance	traite tirée sur l'étranger *f*	accettazione estera *f*	acceptación extranjera *f*
Auslandsanleihe (D)	—	foreign bond	emprunt extérieur *m*	prestito estero *m*	empréstito exterior *m*
Auslandsbank (D)	—	foreign bank	banque extérieure *f*	banca estera *f*	banco exterior *m*
Auslandsbonds (D)	—	foreign currency bonds	titres d'emprunt émis en monnaie étrangère *m/pl*	obbligazioni in valuta estera *f/pl*	bonos en moneda extranjera *m/pl*
Auslandsbonds-bereinigung (D)	—	external bonds validation	validation des titres d'emprunt émis en monnaie étrangère *f*	correzione bonds in valuta estera *f*	convalidación de obligaciones en el exterior *f*
Auslandsgeschäft (D)	—	business in foreign countries	opération avec l'étranger *f*	affare all'estero *m*	negocio de exportación *m*
Auslandsinvestition (D)	—	foreign investment	investissement à l'étranger *m*	investimento estero *m*	inversión exterior *f*
Auslandskapital (D)	—	foreign capital	capital étranger *m*	capitale estero *m*	capital extranjero *m*
Auslandskonto (D)	—	foreign account	compte entretenu à l'étranger *f*	conto estero *m*	cuenta en el extranjero *f*
Auslandskredit (D)	—	foreign credit	crédit extérieur *m*	credito estero *m*	crédito extranjero *m*

	D	E	F	I	Es
Auslands-niederlassung (D)	—	branch abroad	succursale à l'étranger f	filiale all'estero f	sucursal en el extranjero f
Auslandspatente (D)	—	foreign patents	brevets à l'étranger m/pl	brevetti esteri m/pl	patentes extranjeras f/pl
Auslandsscheck (D)	—	foreign cheque	chèque payable à l'étranger m	assegno sull'estero m	cheque sobre el extranjero m
Auslandsschulden (D)	—	foreign debts	dettes à l'étranger f/pl	debiti esteri m/pl	deudas exteriores f/pl
Auslandsstatus (D)	—	foreign assets and liabilities	avoirs et obligations extérieurs m/pl	posizione verso l'estero f	créditos activos y pasivos en el extranjero m/pl
Auslandsvermögen (D)	—	foreign assets	avoirs à l'étranger m/pl	beni all'estero m/pl	patrimonio en el extranjero m
Auslands-verschuldung (D)	—	external indebtedness	dette extérieure f	indebitamento verso l'estero m	deuda exterior f
Auslandswechsel (D)	—	foreign bill of exchange	traite tirée sur l'étranger f	cambiale sull'estero f	letra sobre el exterior f
Auslosungsanleihe (D)	—	lottery bond	emprunt amortissable par séries tirées au sort m	prestito rimborsabile mediante per sorteggio m	empréstito de sorteo m
ausmachender Betrag (D)	—	actual amount	montant calculé m	controvalore della contrattazione m	importe calculado m
Ausnahmeregelung (D)	—	provision	mesure dérogatoire f	regolamento d'eccezione m	disposición excepcional f
Ausnahmetarif (D)	—	preferential rate	tarif exceptionnel m	tariffa d'eccezione f	tarifa excepcional f
Ausprägung (D)	—	coinage	monnayage m	coniazione f	acuñación f
Ausschließlichkeits-erklärung (D)	—	undertaking to deal exclusively with one bank or firm	déclaration d'exclusivité f	dichiarazione d'esclusività f	contrato de exclusividad m
Ausschlußprinzip (D)	—	exclusion principle	principe d'exclusion m	principio d'esclusione m	principio de exclusión del precio m
Ausschreibung (D)	—	invitation to tender	soumission f	appalto m	subasta f
Außenfinanzierung (D)	—	external financing	financement externe m	finanziamento esterno m	financiación externa f
Außenhandel (D)	—	foreign trade	commerce extérieur m	commercio estero m	comercio exterior m
Außenhandels-abteilung (D)	—	export department	service étranger m	ufficio commercio estero m	sección de comercio exterior f
Außenhandels finanzierung (D)	—	foreign trade financing	aide financière à l'exportation f	finanziamento commercio estero m	financiación del comercio exterior f
Außenhandels-gewinn (D)	—	gains from trade	excédent du com-merce extérieur m	saldo attivo bilancia commerciale m	excedente del comercio exterior m
Außenhandels-monopol (D)	—	foreign trade monopoly	monopole du com-merce extérieur m	monopolio del commercio estero m	monopolio del comercio exterior m
Außenhandels-rahmen (D)	—	foreign trade structure	structure du com-merce extérieur m	quadro commercio estero m	estructura del comercio exterior f
Außenhandels-statistik (D)	—	foreign trade statistics	statistique du com-merce extérieur f	statistica del commercio estero f	estadística del comercio exterior f
Außenmarkt (D)	—	external market	marché extérieur m	mercato estero m	mercado externo m
Außenstände (D)	—	outstanding accounts	dettes actives f/pl	crediti pendenti m/pl	cobros pendientes m/pl
Außenwerbung (D)	—	outdoor advertising	publicité extérieure f	pubblicità esterna f	propaganda al aire libre f
Außenwert der Währung (D)	—	external value of the currency	valeur externe de la monnaie f	valore esterno della valuta m	valor de la moneda en el exterior m
Außenwirtschaft (D)	—	foreign trade and payments	économie des échanges extérieurs f	commercio estero m	economía exterior f
außenwirtschaftliches Gleichgewicht (D)	—	external balance	équilibre de l'écono-mie extérieure m	equilibrio del commercio estero m	equilibrio de la eco-nomía exterior m
Außenwirtschafts-gesetz (D)	—	Act on Foreign Trade and Payments	loi sur le commerce extérieur f	legge sul commercio estero f	ley de transacciones exteriores f
außerordentliche Abschreibung (D)	—	extraordinary depreciation	amortissement extraordinaire m	ammortamento straordinario m	amortización extraordinaria f
außerordentliche Erträge (D)	—	extraordinary income	profits exceptionnels m/pl	sopravvenienze attive f/pl	ingresos extraordinarios m/pl
Aussetzung (D)	—	suspension	suspension f	rinvio m	suspensión f

	D	E	F	I	Es
Aussonderung (D)	—	separation of property belonging to a third party from the bankrupt's estate	distraction f	separazione f	tercería de dominio f
Ausverkauf (D)	—	clearance sale	soldes f	liquidazione f	venta de liquidación f
Auswahlverfahren (D)	—	selection procedure	méthode de sélection f	campionamento m	procedimiento de selección m
Ausweichkurs (D)	—	fictitious security price	cours nominal m	quotazione evasiva f	precio ficticio de acciones m
Ausweis der Kapitalherabsetzung (D)	—	return of capital reduction	situation de la réduction du capital f	dichiarazione di riduzione capitale f	devolución de la disminución de capital f
Ausweisung (D)	—	statement	publication f	pubblicazione f	registrar un importe m
Auswertung (D)	—	evaluation	évaluation f	analisi f	evaluación f
Auszahlung (D)	—	payment	payement m	esborso m	pago m
Auszählung (D)	—	counting	comptage m	scrutinio m	cómputo m
autarchia (I)	Autarkie f	autarky	autarcie f	—	autarquía f
autarcie (F)	Autarkie f	autarky	—	autarchia f	autarquía f
Autarkie (D)	—	autarky	autarcie f	autarchia f	autarquía f
autarky (E)	Autarkie f	—	autarcie f	autarchia f	autarquía f
autarquía (Es)	Autarkie f	autarky	autarcie f	autarchia f	—
autenticazione (I)	Beglaubigung f	certification	légalisation f	—	legalización f
autenticazione pubblica (I)	öffentliche Beurkundung f	public authentication	authentification f	—	formalización en escritura pública f
authentification (F)	öffentliche Beurkundung f	public authentication	—	autenticazione pubblica f	formalización en escritura pública f
authority (E)	Behörde f	—	autorité f	autorità f	autoridad f
authorized balance sheet (E)	genehmigte Bilanz f	—	bilan approuvé m	bilancio approvato m	balance aprobado m
authorized capital (E)	genehmigtes Kapital n	—	capital autorisé m	capitale approvato m	capital concedido m
authorized capital (E)	autorisiertes Kapital n	—	capital autorisé m	capitale autorizzato m	capital autorizado m
authorized clerk (E)	Prokurist m	—	fondé de procuration m	procuratore commerciale m	apoderado general m
authorized deposit (E)	Ermächtigungsdepot n	—	dépôt d'usage m	deposito con permesso di permuta m	depósito de autorización m
authorized person (E)	Bevollmächtigter m	—	fondé de pouvoir m	delegato m	apoderado m
autocorrelación (Es)	Autokorrelation f	autocorrelation	autocorrélation f	autocorrelazione f	—
autocorrelation (E)	Autokorrelation f	—	autocorrélation f	autocorrelazione f	autocorrelación f
autocorrélation (F)	Autokorrelation f	autocorrelation	—	autocorrelazione f	autocorrelación f
autocorrelazione (I)	Autokorrelation f	autocorrelation	autocorrélation f	—	autocorrelación f
auto de adhesión (Es)	Beitrittsbeschluß m	decision of accession	jugement déclaratif d'admission de la créance m	decreto di adesione all'asta coattiva m	—
autofinancement (F)	Eigenfinanzierung f	self-financing	—	autofinanziamento m	autofinanciación f
autofinanciación (Es)	Eigenfinanzierung f	self-financing	autofinancement m	autofinanziamento m	—
autofinanziamento (I)	Eigenfinanzierung f	self-financing	autofinancement m	—	autofinanciación f
Autokorrelation (D)	—	autocorrelation	autocorrélation f	autocorrelazione f	autocorrelación f
automación (Es)	Automation f	automation	automation f	automazione f	—
automación bancaria (Es)	Bankautomation f	bank automation	automation bancaire f	automazione bancaria f	—
automatic quotation (E)	automatische Kursanzeige f	—	indication automatique des cotations m	indicatore automatico quotazioni m	tablero electrónico m
Automatic Transfer Service (E)	Automatic Transfer Service [ATS] m	—	service de virements automatiques m	Automatic Transfer Service m	servicio de transferencia automático [STA] m
Automatic Transfer Service (I)	Automatic Transfer Service [ATS] m	—	Automatic Transfer Service	service de virements automatiques m	servicio de transferencia automático [STA] m
Automatic Transfer Service [ATS] (D)	—	Automatic Transfer Service	service de virements automatiques m	Automatic Transfer Service m	servicio de transferencia automático [STA] m
Automation (D)	—	automation	automation f	automazione f	automación f

	D	E	F	I	Es
automation (E)	Automation f	—	automation f	automazione f	automación f
automation (F)	Automation f	automation	—	automazione f	automación f
automation bancaire (F)	Bankautomation f	bank automation	—	automazione bancaria f	automación bancaria f
automation degree (E)	Automatisationsgrad m	—	dégré d'automation m	grado di automazione m	grado de automación m
Automatisationsgrad (D)	—	automation degree	dégré d'automation m	grado di automazione m	grado de automación m
automatische Kursanzeige (D)	—	automatic quotation	indication automatique des cotations m	indicatore automatico quotazioni m	tablero electrónico m
automatism (E)	Automatismus m	—	automatisme m	automatismo m	automatismo m
automatisme (F)	Automatismus m	automatism	—	automatismo m	automatismo m
automatismo (Es)	Automatismus m	automatism	automatisme m	automatismo m	—
automatismo (I)	Automatismus m	automatism	automatisme m	—	automatismo m
Automatismus (D)	—	automatism	automatisme m	automatismo m	automatismo m
automazione (I)	Automation f	automation	automation f	—	automación f
automazione bancaria (I)	Bankautomation f	bank automation	automation bancaire f	—	automación bancaria f
autonome Größen (D)	—	autonomous variables	magnitudes autonomes f/pl	grandezze autonome f/pl	magnitudes autónomas f/pl
autonomía (Es)	Autonomie f	autonomy	autonomie f	autonomia f	—
autonomía (I)	Autonomie f	autonomy	autonomie f	—	autonomía f
Autonomie (D)	—	autonomy	autonomie f	autonomia f	autonomía f
autonomie (F)	Autonomie f	autonomy	—	autonomia f	autonomía f
autonomous variables (E)	autonome Größen f/pl	—	magnitudes autonomes f/pl	grandezze autonome f/pl	magnitudes autónomas f/pl
autonomy (E)	Autonomie f	—	autonomie f	autonomia f	autonomía f
autoridad (Es)	Behörde f	authority	autorité f	autorità f	—
autorisation de disposer (F)	Ermächtigung zur Verfügung f	proxy for disposal	—	autorizzazione di disporre dei titoli depositati f	autorización a disponer f
autorisation de l'émission (F)	Emissionsgenehmigung f	issue permit	—	permesso d'emissione m	autorización de emisión f
autorisation d'exportation (F)	Ausfuhrgenehmigung f	export license	—	autorizzazione all'esportazione f	licencia de exportación f
autorisiertes Kapital (D)	—	authorized capital	capital autorisé m	capitale autorizzato m	capital autorizado m
autorità (I)	Behörde f	authority	autorité f	—	autoridad f
autorità di vigilanza sul credito (I)	Kreditaufsicht f	state supervision of credit institutions	office de surveillance des établissements de crédit f	—	supervisión crediticia f
autorité (F)	Behörde f	authority	—	autorità f	autoridad f
autorización a disponer (Es)	Ermächtigung zur Verfügung f	proxy for disposal	autorisation de disposer f	autorizzazione di disporre dei titoli depositati f	—
autorización de emisión (Es)	Emissionsgenehmigung f	issue permit	autorisation de l'émission f	permesso d'emissione m	—
autorización para el cobro (Es)	Einziehungsauftrag m	direct debit order	ordre de recouvrement m	mandato di incasso m	—
autorizzazione (I)	Bewilligung f	allowance	consentement m	—	concesión f
autorizzazione alla riscossione (I)	Einziehungsermächtigung f	direct debit authorization	mandat de prélèvement automatique m	—	comisión de cobranza f
autorizzazione alla riscossione (I)	Einzugsermächtigungsverfahren n	collection procedure	système du mandat de prélèvement automatique m	—	proceso de cobro bancario m
autorizzazione all'esportazione (I)	Ausfuhrgenehmigung f	export license	autorisation d'exportation f	—	licencia de exportación f
autorizzazione di disporre dei titoli depositati (I)	Ermächtigung zur Verfügung f	proxy for disposal	autorisation de disposer f	—	autorización a disponer f
au total (F)	unter dem Strich	in total	—	fuori bilancio	en total

	D	E	F	I	Es
autres obligations (F)	sonstige Verbindlichkeiten f/pl	other liabilities	—	debiti diversi m/pl	acreedores varios m/pl
auxiliar mercantil (Es)	Handlungsgehilfe m	commercial employee	commis du commerce m	commesso m	—
availability date (E)	Wertstellung f	—	datation de la valeur en compte f	valuta f	valuta f
available funds (E)	Finanzdecke f	—	fonds disponibles m/pl	disponibilità di mezzi liquidi f	previsión financiera f
Aval (D)	—	guarantee of a bill	aval m	avallo m	aval m
aval (Es)	Aval m	guarantee of a bill	aval m	avallo m	—
aval (F)	Aval m	guarantee of a bill	—	avallo m	aval m
aval bancario (Es)	Bankaval m	bank guarantee	aval de banque m	avallo bancario m	—
aval de banque (F)	Bankaval m	bank guarantee	—	avallo bancario m	aval bancario m
Aval-Kredit (D)	—	credit by way of bank guarantee	crédit d'escompte sur traite avalisée m	credito d'avallo m	crédito de aval m
avallo (I)	Aval m	guarantee of a bill	aval m	—	aval m
avallo bancario (I)	Bankaval m	bank guarantee	aval de banque m	—	aval bancario m
Aval-Provision (D)	—	commission on bank guarantee	commission pour aval f	provvigione d'avallo f	comisión por aval f
avance (F)	Vorschuß m	advance	—	anticipo m	anticipo m
avance en compte (F)	Buchkredit m	book credit	—	credito contabile m	crédito en cuenta m
avancement (F)	Beförderung f	promotion	—	promozione f	promoción m
avance sur compte courant (F)	Überziehungskredit m	credit by way of overdraft	—	credito su base scoperta m	crédito en descubierto m
avance sur effet nanti (F)	Wechsellombard m	collateral loan based on a bill of exchange	—	anticipazione su cambiali f	letra de cambio tomada en prenda f
avance sur marchandises (F)	Warenkredit m	trade credit	—	credito su merci m	crédito sobre mercancías m
avance sur vente payée à tempérament (F)	Teilzahlungskredit m	instalment credit	—	finanziamento di acquisti rateali m	crédito para la financiación a plazo m
avantage en nature (F)	Deputat n	payment in kind	—	compenso in natura m	remuneración en especie f
avant bourse (I)	Vorbörse f	before hours dealing	marché avant le marché officiel m	—	operaciones antes de la apertura f/pl
avanzo utile (I)	Gewinnvortrag m	profit carried forward	report du solde excédentaire m	—	arrastre de beneficios m
average price (E)	Durchschnittspreis m	—	prix moyen m	prezzo medio m	precio medio m
average rate (E)	Durchschnittssatz m	—	taux moyen m	tasso medio m	tasa media f
average value (E)	Mittelwert m	—	valeur moyenne f	valore medio m	valor medio m
average value date (E)	Durchschnittsvaluta f	—	datation moyenne de la valeur en compte f	valuta media f	cambio medio m
average yield (E)	Durchschnittsertrag m	—	rendement moyen m	reddito medio m	rendimiento medio m
avere (I)	Haben n	credit side	avoir m	—	haber m
avere (I)	Guthaben n	credit balance	avoir m	—	activo m
avere bloccato (I)	Sperrguthaben n	blocked balance	avoir bloqué m	—	fondos bloqueados m/pl
avere loro (I)	Loroguthaben n	loro balance	avoirs de clients bancaires m	—	haberes de clientes bancarios m/pl
avere nostro (I)	Nostroguthaben n	nostro balance	avoir dans une autre banque m	—	haber a nuestro favor m
averiguación de los beneficios (Es)	Gewinnermittlung f	determination of profits	détermination du bénéfice f	determinazione degli utili f	—
avis de non-payement (F)	Notanzeige f	notice of dishonour	—	occorrendo m	notificación de no aceptación f
avis d'exécution (F)	Schlußnote f	broker's note	—	fissato bollato m	póliza de negociación f
aviso (Es)	Benachrichtigung f	notification	notification f	avviso m	—
aviso bancario (Es)	Bankavis m	bank's confirmation of a letter of credit	confirmation bancaire f	avviso bancario m	—
avoir (F)	Guthaben n	credit balance	—	avere m	activo m
avoir (F)	Haben n	credit side	—	avere m	haber m

	D	E	F	I	Es
avoir auprès de la Banque fédérale (F)	Bundesbankguthaben n	Federal Bank assets	—	fondo banca centrale m	saldo activo del Banco Federal m
avoir bloqué (F)	Sperrguthaben n	blocked balance	—	avere bloccato m	fondos bloqueados m/pl
avoir commercial (F)	Geschäftsguthaben n	proprietor's capital holding	—	capitale da soci di una cooperativa m	saldo activo de la empresa m
avoir dans une autre banque (F)	Nostroguthaben n	nostro balance	—	avere nostro m	haber a nuestro favor m
avoir en banque (F)	Bankguthaben n	bank balance	—	deposito bancario m	haber bancario m
avoir en monnaie étrangère (F)	Fremdwährungsguthaben n	foreign currency balance	—	disponibilità in valuta estera f	haberes de moneda extranjera m/pl
avoir net (F)	Reinvermögen n	net assets	—	attivo netto m	patrimonio neto m
avoirs à l'étranger (F)	Auslandsvermögen n	foreign assets	—	beni all'estero m/pl	patrimonio en el extranjero m
avoirs de clients bancaires (F)	Loroguthaben n	loro balance	—	avere loro m	haberes de clientes bancarios m/pl
avoirs et obligations extérieurs (F)	Auslandsstatus m	foreign assets and liabilities	—	posizione verso l'estero f	créditos activos y pasivos en el extranjero m/pl
avoir sur un compte d'épargne (F)	Sparguthaben n	savings account	—	deposito a risparmio m	depósito de ahorro m
avoir total (F)	Gesamtvermögen n	aggregate property	—	patrimonio complessivo m	totalidad del patrimonio f
avviamento (I)	Geschäftswert m	value of the subject matter at issue	valeur commerciale f	—	valor comercial m
avviso (I)	Benachrichtigung f	notification	notification f	—	aviso m
avviso bancario (I)	Bankavis m	bank's confirmation of a letter of credit	confirmation bancaire f	—	aviso bancario m
avviso di addebito (I)	Lastschriftkarte f	debit card	carte de débit f	—	nota de cargo f
ayuda (Es)	Beihilfe f	financial aid	subside m	assistenza f	—
ayuda de inversión (Es)	Investitionshilfe f	investment assistance	subvention en faveur des investissements f	aiuti agli investimenti m/pl	—
ayuda financiera (Es)	Kapitalhilfe f	capital aid	aide financière f	aiuto finanziario m	—
ayuda financiera (Es)	finanzieller Beistand m	financial assistance	aide financière f	assistenza finanziaria f	—
azione (I)	Aktie f	share	action f	—	acción f
azione al portatore (I)	Inhaberaktie f	bearer share	action au porteur f	—	acción al portador f
azione assicurativa (I)	Versicherungsaktie f	insurance company share	action d'une société d'assurance f	—	acción de compañías de seguros f
azione a valore nominale (I)	Nennwertaktie f	par value share	action nominale f	—	acción de suma f
azione a valore nominale determinato (I)	Summenaktie f	share at a fixed amount	action d'un montant fixe f	—	acción de valor determinado f
azione a voto plurimo (I)	Mehrstimmrechtsaktie f	multiple voting share	action à droit de vote plural f	—	acción de voto plural f
azione con diritto di voto (I)	Stimmrechtsaktie f	voting share	action à droit de vote simple f	—	acción con derecho a voto f
azione con possibilità di sviluppo (I)	Wuchsaktie f	growth share	action avec possibilité d'acroissement f	—	acción con posibilidad de incremento f
azione danneggiata (I)	beschädigte Aktie f	damaged share certificates	certificat d'action endommagé m	—	acción deteriorada f
azione di lavoro (I)	Arbeitnehmeraktie f	employees' shares	action de travail f	—	acción de trabajo f
azione di miniere d'oro (I)	Goldaktie f	gold share	action-or f	—	acción de oro f
azione di riserva (I)	Vorratsaktie f	disposable share	action en réserve f	—	acción de provisión f
azione globale (I)	Sammelaktie f	global share	titre représentant globalement un paquet d'actions m	—	acción global f
azione gratuita (I)	Berichtigungsaktie f	bonus share	action gratuite f	—	acción de reajuste f
azione gratuita (I)	Gratisaktie f	bonus share	action gratuite f	—	acción gratuita f
azione gratuita (I)	Zusatzaktie f	bonus share	action supplémentaire f	—	acción suplementaria f
azione in deposito (I)	Depotaktie f	deposited share	action déposée en compte courant f	—	acción de depósito f

	D	E	F	I	Es
azione industriale (I)	Industrieaktie f	industrial shares	action industrielle f	—	acción industrial f
azione mineraria (I)	Kux m	mining share	part de mines f	—	acción minera f
azione nominativa (I)	Namensaktie f	registered share	action nominative f	—	acción nominal f
azione non interamente versata (I)	Leeraktie f	shares not fully paid up	action non entièrement libérée f	—	acción al descubierto f
azione non quotata ufficialmente (I)	nichtnotierte Aktie f	unquoted share	action non cotée f	—	acción no cotizada f
azione ordinaria (I)	Stammaktie f	ordinary share	action ordinaire f	—	acción ordinaria f
azione per dipendenti (I)	Belegschaftsaktie f	staff shares	action de travail f	—	acción de personal f
azione popolare (I)	Volksaktie f	low-denomination share for small savers	action populaire f	—	acción popular f
azione preferita dai risparmiatori (I)	Publikumsaktie f	popular share	action populaire f	—	acción al público f
azione privilegiata (I)	Vorzugsaktie f	preference share	action privilégiée f	—	acción preferente f
azione privilegiata senza diritto di voto (I)	stimmrechtslose Vorzugsaktie f	non-voting share	action privilégiée sans droit de vote f	—	acción preferente sin derecho a voto f
azione senza valore nominale (I)	nennwertlose Aktie f	no par value share	action sans valeur nominale f	—	acción sin valor nominal f
azione sostitutiva (I)	Ersatzaktie f	replacement share certificate	action supplétive en remplacement d'un titre adiré f	—	acción de sustitución f
azione vincolata (I)	vinkulierte Aktie f	restricted share	action négociable sous réserve f	—	acción vinculada f
azioni amministrate (I)	Verwaltungsaktien f/pl	treasury stock	actions de Trésor f/pl	—	acciones de tesorería f
azioni privilegiate (I)	Prioritätsaktien f/pl	preference shares	actions de priorité f/pl	—	acciónes de preferencia f/pl
azioni sociali (I)	eigene Aktien f/pl	company-owned shares	actions propres f/pl	—	acciones propias f/pl
azionista (I)	Aktionär m	shareholder	actionnaire m	—	accionista m
azionista (I)	Anteilseigner m	shareholder	porteur de parts m	—	titular de acciones m
azionista estero (I)	ausländischer Anteilseigner m	foreign shareholder	actionnaire étranger m	—	titular de acciones extranjero m
azionista non permanente (I)	Zwischenaktionär m	interim shareholder	actionnaire intermédiaire m	—	accionista intermedio m
azionista permanente (I)	Daueraktionär m	permanent shareholder	actionnaire permanent m	—	accionista permanente m
Baby-Bonds (D)	—	baby bonds	bons de petite valeur nominale m/pl	baby-bonds m/pl	bonos de pequeño valor nominal m/pl
baby bonds (E)	Baby-Bonds m/pl	—	bons de petite valeur nominale m/pl	baby-bonds m/pl	bonos de pequeño valor nominal m/pl
baby-bonds (I)	Baby-Bonds m/pl	baby bonds	bons de petite valeur nominale m/pl	—	bonos de pequeño valor nominal m/pl
back-to-back letter of credit (E)	Gegenakkreditiv n	—	contrecrédit m	controcredito m	contracrédito m
Backwardation (D)	—	backwardation	déport m	backwardation f	tasa de prolongación del bajista f
backwardation (E)	Backwardation f	—	déport m	backwardation f	tasa de prolongación del bajista f
backwardation (I)	Backwardation f	backwardation	déport m	—	tasa de prolongación del bajista f
bad debt loss (E)	Ausfallforderung f	—	créance prioritaire f	credito per l'ammanco m	impagados m/pl
Baisse (D)	—	bear market	baisse f	ribasso m	baja f
baisse (F)	Baisse f	bear market	—	ribasso m	baja f
baisse du cours par émission d'action gratuites (F)	Kursverwässerung f	price watering	—	annacquamento della quotazione m	caída de cotización f
Baisseklausel (D)	—	bear clause	clause de baisse f	clausola di ribasso f	cláusula de baja f
Baisser (D)	—	bear	baissier m	ribassista m	bajista m
baissier (F)	bearish	bearish	—	bearish	bajista

	D	E	F	I	Es
baissier (F)	Baisser *m*	bear	—	ribassista *m*	bajista *m*
baja (Es)	Baisse *f*	bear market	baisse *f*	ribasso *m*	—
bajista (Es)	Baisser *m*	bear	baissier *m*	ribassista *m*	—
bajista (Es)	bearish	bearish	baissier	bearish	—
balance (E)	Saldo *m*	—	solde *m*	saldo *m*	saldo *m*
balance (E)	Gleichgewicht *n*	—	équilibre *m*	equilibrio *m*	equilibrio *m*
balance (Es)	Bilanz *f*	balance sheet	bilan *m*	bilancio *m*	—
balance (E)	saldieren	—	solder	saldare	saldar
balance anual (Es)	Jahresabschluß *m*	annual statement of accounts	clôture annuelle des comptes *f*	bilancio d'esercizio *m*	—
balance anual (Es)	Jahresbilanz *f*	annual balance sheet	bilan de fin d'année *m*	bilancio d'esercizio *m*	—
balance aprobado (Es)	genehmigte Bilanz *f*	authorized balance sheet	bilan approuvé *m*	bilancio approvato *m*	—
balance bancario (Es)	Bankbilanz *f*	bank balance sheet	bilan bancaire *m*	bilancio di banca *m*	—
balance bruto (Es)	Rohbilanz *f*	rough balance	bilan brut *m*	progetto di bilancio *m*	—
balance consolidado (Es)	konsolidierte Bilanz *f*	consolidated balance sheet	bilan consolidé *m*	bilancio consolidato *m*	—
balance de cierre (Es)	Schlußbilanz *f*	closing balance	bilan de clôture *m*	bilancio di chiusura *m*	—
balance de comparación (Es)	Vergleichsbilanz *f*	comparative balance sheet	bilan au moment de l'ouverture du règlement judiciare *m*	situazione patrimoniale di concordato *f*	—
balance de débitos (Es)	Überschuldungsbilanz *f*	statement of overindebtedness	bilan de l'endettement *m*	stato di disavanzo patrimoniale *m*	—
balance deficitario (Es)	Unterbilanz *f*	deficit balance	bilan déficitaire *m*	bilancio in deficit *m*	—
balance del consorcio (Es)	Konzernbilanz *f*	group balance sheet	bilan consolidé d'un groupement de sociétés *m*	bilancio consolidato *m*	—
balance del presupuesto (Es)	Budgetausgleich *m*	balancing of the budget	solde de budget *m*	equilibrio del bilancio pubblico *m*	—
balance de saldos (Es)	Saldenbilanz *f*	list of balances	balance des soldes des comptes généraux *f*	conto saldi contabili *m*	—
balance des opérations courantes (F)	Leistungsbilanz *f*	balance of goods and services	—	bilancia delle partite correnti *f*	balanza por cuenta corriente *f*
balance des opérations courantes en services (F)	Dienstleistungsbilanz *f*	balance of service transactions	—	bilancia dei servizi *f*	balanza de servicios *f*
balance des opérations en capital (F)	Kapitalbilanz *f*	balance of capital transactions	—	bilancia dei capitali *f*	balanza de capital *f*
balance des opérations en marchandises (F)	Handelsbilanz *f*	commercial balance sheet	—	bilancia commerciale *f*	balanza comercial *f*
balance des payements (F)	Zahlungsbilanz *f*	balance of payments	—	bilancia dei pagamenti *f*	balanza de pagos *f*
balance des soldes des comptes généraux (F)	Saldenbilanz *f*	list of balances	—	conto saldi contabili *m*	balance de saldos *m*
balance de sumas (Es)	Summenbilanz *f*	turnover balance	relevé des comptes généraux *m*	bilancio generale *m*	—
balance diario (Es)	Tagesbilanz *f*	daily trial balance sheet	arrêté quotidien de compte *m*	bilancio giornaliero *m*	—
balance inicial (Es)	Eröffnungsbilanz *f*	opening balance sheet	bilan d'ouverture *m*	bilancio d'apertura *m*	—
balance intermedio (Es)	Zwischenbilanz *f*	interim balance sheet	bilan intermédiaire *m*	bilancio intermedio *m*	—
balance mensual (Es)	Monatsbilanz *f*	monthly balance sheet	situation comptable mensuelle *f*	bilancio mensile *m*	—
balance mundial (Es)	Weltbilanz *f*	worldwide fincancial statements	bilan mondial *m*	bilancio internazionale *m*	—
balance no compensado (Es)	unkompensierte Bilanz *f*	unoffset balance sheet	bilan non compensé *m*	bilancio senza compensazioni *m*	—
balance of capital transactions (E)	Kapitalbilanz *f*	—	balance des opérations en capital *f*	bilancia dei capitali *f*	balanza de capital *f*

	D	E	F	I	Es
balance of goods and services (E)	Leistungsbilanz f	—	balance des opérations courantes f	bilancia delle partite correnti f	balanza por cuenta corriente f
balance of payments (E)	Zahlungsbilanz f	—	balance des payements f	bilancia dei pagamenti f	balanza de pagos f
balance of service transactions (E)	Dienstleistungsbilanz f	—	balance des opérations courantes en services f	bilancia dei servizi f	balanza de servicios f
balance patrimonial (Es)	Vermögensbilanz f	asset and liability statement	état du patrimoine m	bilancio patrimoniale m	—
balance semanal (Es)	Wochenausweis m	weekly return	bilan hebdomadaire m	situazione settimanale f	—
balance semestral (Es)	Halbjahresbilanz f	semi-annual balance sheet	bilan semestriel m	bilancio semestrale m	—
balance sheet (E)	Bilanz f	—	bilan m	bilancio m	balance m
balance sheet account (E)	Bilanzkonto n	—	compte de bilan m	conto di bilancio m	cuenta permanente f
balance sheet analysis (E)	Bilanzanalyse f	—	analyse du bilan f	analisi di bilancio m	análisis de balance m
balance sheet audit (E)	Bilanzprüfung f	—	contrôle du bilan m	revisione del bilancio f	revisión del balance f
balance sheet consistency (E)	Bilanzkontinuität f	—	identité des bilans successifs f	continuità di bilancio f	continuidad de balance f
balance sheet statistics (E)	Bilanzstatistik f	—	statistique des bilans f	analisi statistica dei bilanci f	estadística de balances f
balance sheet total (E)	Bilanzsumme f	—	total du bilan m	totale del bilancio m	suma del balance f
balance sheet value (E)	Bilanzwert m	—	valeur portée au bilan f	valore di bilancio m	valor de balance m
balance unitario (Es)	Einheitsbilanz f	unified balance sheet	bilan unique m	bilancio unico m	—
balancing of the budget (E)	Budgetausgleich m	—	solde de budget m	equilibrio del bilancio pubblico m	balance del presupuesto m
balanza comercial (Es)	Handelsbilanz f	commercial balance sheet	balance des opérations en marchandises f	bilancia commerciale f	—
balanza de capital (Es)	Kapitalbilanz f	balance of capital transactions	balance des opérations en capital f	bilancia dei capitali f	—
balanza de divisas (Es)	Devisenbilanz f	net movement of foreign exchange	compte de devises m	bilancia valutaria f	—
balanza de pagos (Es)	Zahlungsbilanz f	balance of payments	balance des payements f	bilancia dei pagamenti f	—
balanza de servicios (Es)	Dienstleistungsbilanz f	balance of service transactions	balance des opérations courantes en services f	bilancia dei servizi f	—
balanza por cuenta corriente (Es)	Leistungsbilanz f	balance of goods and services	balance des opérations courantes f	bilancia delle partite correnti f	—
balzo delle quotazioni (I)	Kursprung m	jump in prices	hausse sensible des cours f	—	alza considerable de las cotizaciones f
banca (Es)	Bankgewerbe n	banking business	banque f	settore bancario m	—
banca (I)	Bank f	bank	banque f	—	banco m
banca centrale (I)	Zentralbank f	central bank	banque centrale f	—	banco central m
banca coloniale (I)	Kolonialbank f	colonial bank	banque coloniale f	—	banco colonial m
banca commerciale (I)	Geschäftsbank f	commercial bank	banque commerciale f	—	banco comercial m
banca comunale (I)	Kommunalbank f	local authorities bank	banque communale f	—	banco comunal m
banca comune (I)	Gemeinschaftsbank f	combination bank	banque combinée f	—	banco de combinación m
banca consorziale garanzia liquidità (I)	Liquiditätskonsortialbank f	liquidity syndicate bank	syndicat bancaire de liquidité m	—	banco asegurador de liquidez m
banca corrispondente (I)	Korrespondenzbank f	correspondent bank	banque de correspondance f	—	banco corresponsal m
Banca dei Regolamenti Internazionali (I)	Bank für internationalen Zahlungsausgleich [BIZ] f	Bank for International Settlements [BIS]	Banque pour les Règlements Internationaux B.R.I. f	—	Banco Internacional de Compensación de Pagos [BIP] m
banca del lavoro (I)	Gewerkschaftsbank f	trade union bank	banque de syndicat f	—	banco sindical m
banca d'emissione (I)	Notenbank f	central bank	banque d'émission f	—	banco emisor m

	D	E	F	I	Es
banca d'emissione (I)	Emissionsbank f	issuing bank	banque d'affaires f	—	banco emisor m
banca di credito (I)	Kreditbank f	commercial bank	banque de crédit f	—	banco de crédito m
banca di credito agrario (I)	Bodenkreditinstitut n	mortgage bank	institut de crédit foncier m	—	instituto de crédito inmobiliario m
banca di credito industriale (I)	Industriekreditbank f	industrial credit bank	banque de crédit à l'industrie f	—	banco de crédito industrial m
banca di deposito di titoli (I)	Wertpapiersammel-bank f	central depository for securities	banque de dépôts et de virements de titres f	—	banco de depósito de valores mobiliarios m
banca di diritto pubblico (I)	öffentliche Bank f	public bank	banque publique f	—	banco público m
banca di giro (I)	Girobank f	deposit clearing bank	banque de dépôts et de virements f	—	banco de giros m
banca di sconto (I)	Diskontbank f	discount bank	banque d'escompte f	—	banco de descuento m
banca di speculazione (I)	Spekulationsbank f	speculation bank	banque de spéculation f	—	banco de especulación m
banca di Stato (I)	Staatsbank f	state bank	banque d'Etat f	—	banco del Estado m
banca emittente (I)	Emissionshaus n	issuing house	établissement d'émission m	—	casa emisora f
banca estera (I)	Auslandsbank f	foreign bank	banque extérieure f	—	banco exterior m
Banca Europea per gli Investimenti (I)	Europäische Investitionsbank f	European Investment Bank	banque européenne d'investissement f	—	Banco Europeo de Inversiones f
banca importante (I)	Großbank f	big bank	grande banque f	—	gran banco m
banca industriale (I)	Gewerbebank f	industrial bank	banque industrielle et artisanale f	—	banco industrial m
banca intermediaria (I)	Maklerbank f	brokerage bank	banque de courtiers f	—	banco corredor m
banca ipotecaria (I)	Hypothekenbank f	mortgage bank	banque hypothécaire f	—	banco hipotecario m
Banca mondiale (I)	Weltbank f	World Bank	banque mondiale f	—	Banco Mundial m
banca perequazione oneri (I)	Lastenausgleichs-bank f	equalization of burdens bank	banque de péréqua-tion des charges f	—	banco de compensa-ción de cargas m
banca per lo sviluppo (I)	Entwicklungsbank f	development bank	banque de développement f	—	banco de desarrollo m
banca preferita (I)	Hausbank f	firm's bank	banque habituelle f	—	banco con que trata generalmente el cliente m
banca provinciale (I)	Provinzbank f	country bank	banque provinciale f	—	banco provincial m
banca regionale (I)	Regionalbank f	regional bank	banque régionale f	—	banco regional m
bancarotta (I)	Bankrott m	bankruptcy	banqueroute f	—	bancarrota f
bancarrota (Es)	Bankrott m	bankruptcy	banqueroute f	bancarotta f	—
banca universale (I)	Universalbank f	all-round bank	banque universelle f	—	banco mixto m
banca valori (I)	Effektenbank f	issuing bank	banque d'affaires f	—	banco de inversiones m
banche centrali cooperative (I)	genossenschaftliche Zentralbanken f/pl	cooperative central banks	banques coopératives centrales f/pl	—	bancos centrales cooperativos m/pl
banche di riserva (I)	Reservebanken f/pl	reserve banks	banques de réserve f/pl	—	banco de reserva m
banche fiduciarie (I)	Treuhandbanken f/pl	trust banks	banques dépositaires f/pl	—	bancos fiduciarios m/pl
banche locali (I)	Lokalbanken f/pl	local banks	banques locales f/pl	—	bancos locales m/pl
banche per azioni (I)	Aktienbanken f/pl	joint stock banks	banques par actions f/pl	—	bancos por acciones m/pl
banchiere (I)	Bankier m	banker	banquier m	—	banquero m
banco (Es)	Bank f	bank	banque f	banca f	—
banco asegurador de liquidez (Es)	Liquiditätskonsortial-bank f	liquidity syndicate bank	syndicat bancaire de liquidité m	banca consorziale garanzia liquidità f	—
banco central (Es)	Zentralbank f	central bank	banque centrale f	banca centrale f	—
banco colonial (Es)	Kolonialbank f	colonial bank	banque coloniale f	banca coloniale f	—
banco comercial (Es)	Geschäftsbank f	commercial bank	banque commerciale f	banca commerciale f	—
banco comunal (Es)	Kommunalbank f	local authorities bank	banque communale f	banca comunale f	—

	D	E	F	I	Es
banco con que trata generalmente el cliente (Es)	Hausbank *f*	firm's bank	banque habituelle *f*	banca preferita *f*	—
banco corredor (Es)	Maklerbank *f*	brokerage bank	banque de courtiers *f*	banca intermediaria *f*	—
banco corresponsal (Es)	Korrespondenzbank *f*	correspondent bank	banque de correspondance *f*	banca corrispondente *f*	—
banco de combinación (Es)	Gemeinschaftsbank *f*	combination bank	banque combinée *f*	banca comune *f*	—
banco de compensación de cargas (Es)	Lastenausgleichs-bank *f*	equalization of burdens bank	banque de péréquation des charges *f*	banca perequazione oneri *f*	
banco de crédito (Es)	Kreditbank *f*	commercial bank	banque de crédit *f*	banca di credito *f*	—
banco de crédito industrial (Es)	Industriekreditbank *f*	industrial credit bank	banque de crédit à l'industrie *f*	banca di credito industriale *f*	—
banco de depósto de valores mobiliarios (Es)	Wertpapiersammel-bank *f*	central depository for securities	banque de dépôts et de virements de titres *f*	banca di deposito di titoli *f*	—
banco de desarrollo (Es)	Entwicklungsbank *f*	development bank	banque de développement *f*	banca per lo sviluppo *f*	—
banco de descuento (Es)	Diskontbank *f*	discount bank	banque d'escompte *f*	banca di sconto *f*	—
banco de especulación (Es)	Spekulationsbank *f*	speculation bank	banque de spéculation *f*	banca di speculazione *f*	—
banco de giros (Es)	Girobank *f*	deposit clearing bank	banque de dépôts et de virements *f*	banca di giro *f*	—
banco de inversiones (Es)	Effektenbank *f*	issuing bank	banque d'affaires *f*	banca valori *f*	—
banco del Estado (Es)	Staatsbank *f*	state bank	banque d'Etat *f*	banca di Stato *f*	—
banco de reserva (Es)	Reservebanken *f/pl*	reserve banks	banques de réserve *f/pl*	banche di riserva *f/pl*	—
banco emisor (Es)	Emissionsbank *f*	issuing bank	banque d'affaires *f*	banca d'emissione *f*	—
banco emisor (Es)	Notenbank *f*	central bank	banque d'émission *f*	banca d'emissione *f*	—
banco especializado (Es)	Spezialbank *f*	specialized commercial bank	banque spécialisée *f*	istituto di credito speciale *m*	—
banco europeo (Es)	Euro-Bank *f*	Eurobank	banque européenne *f*	eurobanca *f*	—
Banco Europeo de Inversiones (Es)	Europäische Investitionsbank *f*	European Investment Bank	banque européenne d'investissement *f*	Banca Europea per gli Investimenti *f*	—
banco exterior (Es)	Auslandsbank *f*	foreign bank	banque extérieure *f*	banca estera *f*	—
bancogiro (I)	Überweisungsverkehr *m*	money transfer transactions	virements *m/pl*	—	transferencias *f/pl*
bancogiro (I)	Giroverkehr *m*	transfer of money by means of a clearing system	opérations de virement *f/pl*	—	giro de valores *m*
bancogiro della banca centrale (I)	Überweisungs-scheck *m*	transfer cheque	chèque postal de virement *m*	—	cheque de transferencia *m*
banco hipotecario (Es)	Hypothekenbank *f*	mortgage bank	banque hypothécaire *f*	banca ipotecaria *f*	—
banco hipotecario (Es)	Pfandbriefanstalt *f*	mortgage bank	banque hypothécaire *f*	istituto di credito fondiario *m*	—
banco hipotecario (Es)	Grundkreditanstalt *f*	mortgage bank	établissement de crédit foncier *m*	istituto di credito fondiario *m*	—
banco industrial (Es)	Gewerbebank *f*	industrial bank	banque industrielle et artisanale *f*	banca industriale *f*	—
Banco Internacional de Compensación de Pagos [BIP] (Es)	Bank für internationalen Zahlungsausgleich [BIZ] *f*	Bank for International Settlements [BIS]	Banque pour les Règlements Internationaux B.R.I. *f*	Banca dei Regolamenti Internazionali *f*	—
bancomat (I)	Geldautomat *m*	cash dispenser	distribanque *m*	—	cajero automático *m*
banco mixto (Es)	Universalbank *f*	all-round bank	banque universelle *f*	banca universale *f*	—
Banco Mundial (Es)	Weltbank *f*	World Bank	banque mondiale *f*	Banca mondiale *f*	—
banconota (I)	Banknote *f*	bank note	billet de banque *m*	—	billete *m*
banconote (I)	Noten *f/pl*	bank notes	billets *m/pl*	—	billetes *m/pl*
banco postal (Es)	Postbank *f*	Postal Savings Bank	banque postale *f*	servizio bancario postale *m*	—
banco provincial (Es)	Provinzbank *f*	country bank	banque provinciale *f*	banca provinciale *f*	—

	D	E	F	I	Es
banco público (Es)	öffentliche Bank *f*	public bank	banque publique *f*	banca di diritto pubblico *f*	—
banco regional (Es)	Regionalbank *f*	regional bank	banque régionale *f*	banca regionale *f*	—
bancos centrales cooperativos (Es)	genossenschaftliche Zentralbanken *f/pl*	cooperative central banks	banques coopératives centrales *f/pl*	banche centrali cooperative *f/pl*	—
bancos de aceptación (Es)	Akzepthäuser *n/pl*	acceptance banks	banques d'acceptation *f/pl*	acceptance banks *f/pl*	—
bancos fiduciarios (Es)	Treuhandbanken *f/pl*	trust banks	banques dépositaires *f/pl*	banche fiduciarie *f/pl*	—
banco sindical (Es)	Gewerkschaftsbank *f*	trade union bank	banque de syndicat *f*	banca del lavoro *f*	—
bancos locales (Es)	Lokalbanken *f/pl*	local banks	banques locales *f/pl*	banche locali *f/pl*	—
bancos por acciones (Es)	Aktienbanken *f/pl*	joint stock banks	banques par actions *f/pl*	banche per azioni *f/pl*	—
banda di oscillazione (I)	Bandbreite *f*	margin	marge *f*	—	margen de fluctuación *m*
Bandbreite (D)	—	margin	marge *f*	banda di oscillazione *f*	margen de fluctuación *m*
Bandwaggon-Effekt (D)	—	bandwaggon effect	effet bandwaggon *m*	effetto bandwaggon *m*	efecto bandwaggon *m*
bandwaggon effect (E)	Bandwaggon-Effekt *m*	—	effet bandwaggon *m*	effetto bandwaggon *m*	efecto bandwaggon *m*
Bank (D)	—	bank	banque *f*	banca *f*	banco *m*
bank (E)	Bank *f*	—	banque *f*	banca *f*	banco *m*
bank acceptance (E)	Bankakzept *n*	—	acceptation de banque *f*	accettazione bancaria *f*	aceptación bancaria *f*
bank account (E)	Bankkonto *n*	—	compte en banque *m*	conto bancario *m*	cuenta bancaria *f*
Bankakademie (D)	—	banking academy	académie de banquiers *f*	accademia bancaria *f*	academia de banqueros *f*
Bankakzept (D)	—	bank acceptance	acceptation de banque *f*	accettazione bancaria *f*	aceptación bancaria *f*
Bankangestellter (D)	—	bank clerk	employé de banque *m*	impiegato di banca *m*	empleado de banco *m*
Bankanleihen (D)	—	bank bonds	emprunt émis par une banque *m*	mutuo bancario *m*	empréstito bancario *m*
Bankanweisung (D)	—	bank money order	mandat de payement bancaire *m*	vaglia bancario *m*	pago bancario *m*
bank audit (E)	Bankrevision *f*	—	contrôle du bilan d'une banque *m*	ispezione bancaria *f*	censura de cuentas del banco *f*
Bankauftrag (D)	—	remunerated order to effect a transaction	ordre bancaire *m*	ordine di banca *m*	orden bancaria remunerada *f*
Bankauskunft (D)	—	banker's reference	renseignement par la banque *m*	informazione bancaria *f*	información bancaria *f*
Bankausweis (D)	—	bank return	situation de banque *f*	bollettino bancario *m*	documento bancario *m*
Bankauszug (D)	—	bank statement	relevé de compte *m*	estratto bancario *m*	relación *f*
Bankautomation (D)	—	bank automation	automation bancaire *f*	automazione bancaria *f*	automación bancaria *f*
bank automation (E)	Bankautomation *f*	—	automation bancaire *f*	automazione bancaria *f*	automación bancaria *f*
Bankaval (D)	—	bank guarantee	aval de banque *m*	avallo bancario *m*	aval bancario *m*
Bankavis (D)	—	bank's confirmation of a letter of credit	confirmation bancaire *f*	avviso bancario *m*	aviso bancario *m*
bank balance (E)	Bankguthaben *n*	—	avoir en banque *m*	deposito bancario *m*	haber bancario *m*
bank balance sheet (E)	Bankbilanz *f*	—	bilan bancaire *m*	bilancio di banca *m*	balance bancario *m*
Bankbetriebslehre (D)	—	science of banking	science bancaire *f*	tecnica bancaria *f*	ciencias bancarias *f/pl*
Bankbeziehungen (D)	—	bank relations	relations bancaires *f/pl*	relazioni bancarie *f/pl*	relaciones bancarias *f/pl*
Bankbilanz (D)	—	bank balance sheet	bilan bancaire *m*	bilancio di banca *m*	balance bancario *m*
bank bond (E)	Bankschuldverschreibung *f*	—	obligation bancaire *f*	obbligazione bancaria *f*	obligación bancaria *f*
bank bond (E)	Bankobligation *f*	—	obligation de banque *f*	obbligazione bancaria *f*	obligación bancaria *f*
bank bonds (E)	Bankanleihen *f/pl*	—	emprunt émis par une banque *m*	mutuo bancario *m*	empréstito bancario *m*

	D	E	F	I	Es
bank branch numbering (E)	Bankennumerierung f	—	classification numérique des succursales bancaires f	codice bancario m	numeración de las filiales bancarias f
Bankbuchhaltung (D)	—	bank's accounting	comptabilité bancaire f	contabilità bancaria f	contabilidad bancaria f
bank charges (E)	Bankspesen pl	—	frais de banque m/pl	spese bancarie f/pl	gastos bancarios m/pl
bank clerk (E)	Bankkaufmann m	—	employé bancaire m	impiegato di banca m	empleado bancario m
bank clerk (E)	Bankangestellter m	—	employé de banque m	impiegato di banca m	empleado de banco m
bank conditions (E)	Bankkonditionen f/pl	—	conditions bancaires f/pl	condizioni bancarie f/pl	condiciones bancarias f/pl
bank costing (E)	Bankkalkulation f	—	calcul des coûts bancaires m	calcolo bancario m	calculación bancaria f
bank credit (E)	Bankkredit m	—	crédit bancaire m	credito bancario m	crédito bancario m
Bank Custody Act (E)	Bankdepotgesetz n	—	loi sur dépôts en banque f	legge sui depositi bancari f	ley sobre depósitos bancarios f
bank customer (E)	Bankkunde m	—	client bancaire m	cliente bancario m	cliente bancario m
bank debts (E)	Bankschulden f/pl	—	dettes bancaires f/pl	debiti verso banche m/pl	deudas bancarias f/pl
Bankdeckung (D)	—	banking cover	couverture de garantie d'une banque f	copertura bancaria f	cobertura bancaria f
bank deposit (E)	Bankdepositen f/pl	—	fonds déposés en banque m/pl	depositi bancari m/pl	depósitos bancarios m/pl
Bankdepositen (D)	—	bank deposits	fonds déposés en banque m/pl	depositi bancari m/pl	depósitos bancarios m/pl
bank deposits (E)	Bankeinlage f	—	dépôt en banque m	deposito bancario m	imposición en un banco f
Bankdepotgesetz (D)	—	Bank Custody Act	loi sur dépôts en banque f	legge sui depositi bancari f	ley sobre depósitos bancarios f
Bankeinlage (D)	—	bank deposit	dépôt en banque m	deposito bancario m	imposición en un banco f
Bankeinzugsverfahren (D)	—	direct debiting	encaissements bancaires m/pl	procedimento d'incasso bancario m	cobranzas bancarias f/pl
Bankenaufsicht (D)	—	public supervision of banking	contrôle des banques m	controllo sulle banche m	superintendencia bancaria f
bank endorsed bill (E)	bankgirierter Warenwechsel m	—	traite endossée par une banque f	effetto commerciale girato da banche m	letra comercial con endoso bancario f
Bankenerlaß (D)	—	banking decree	décret bancaire m	decreto sul segreto bancario m	decreto bancario m
Bankengesetzgebung (D)	—	banking legislation	législation bancaire f	legislazione bancaria f	legislación bancaria f
Bankenkonsortium (D)	—	banking syndicate	consortium de banques m	consorzio bancario m	sindicato bancario m
Bankenkonzentration (D)	—	concentration of banks	concentration bancaire f	concentrazione bancaria f	concentración bancaria f
Bankenkrise (D)	—	banking crisis	crise bancaire f	crisi bancaria f	crisis bancaria f
Bankennummerierung (D)	—	bank branch numbering	classification numérique des succursales bancaires f	codice bancario m	numeración de las filiales bancarias f
Bankenquete (D)	—	banking inquiry	demande de renseignements par la banque f	inchiesta bancaria f	demanda de informe por el banco f
Bankenstatistik (D)	—	banking statistics	statistique bancaire f	statistica bancaria f	estadística bancaria f
Bankenstimmrecht (D)	—	banks' voting rights	droit de vote de la banque m	diritto di voto bancario m	derecho de voto del banco m
Bankensystem (D)	—	banking system	système bancaire m	sistema bancario m	sistema bancario m
Bankenverband (D)	—	banking association	association des banques f	associazione bancaria f	asociación bancaria f
banker (E)	Bankier m	—	banquier m	banchiere m	banquero m
banker's commission (E)	Bankprovision f	—	commission de banque f	commissione bancaria f	comisión bancaria f
banker's duty of secrecy (E)	Bankgeheimnis n	—	secret bancaire m	segreto bancario m	secreto bancario m
banker's guarantee (E)	Bankgarantie f	—	garantie de banque f	garanzia bancaria f	garantía bancaria f

	D	E	F	I	Es
banker's note (E)	Dispositionsschein m	—	reconnaissance bancaire f	certificato di disponibilità m	fianza de disposición de banquero f
banker's reference (E)	Bankauskunft f	—	renseignement par la banque m	informazione bancaria f	información bancaria f
banker's rule (E)	Bankregel f	—	règle bancaire f	norma bancaria f	regla bancaria f
Bankfeiertage (D)	—	bank holidays	jours de fête bancaires m/pl	giorni festivi delle banche m/pl	días de fiesta bancarios m/pl
Bank for International Settlements [BIS] (E)	Bank für Internationalen Zahlungsausgleich [BIZ] f	—	Banque pour les Règlements Internationaux B.R.I. f	Banca dei Regolamenti Internazionali f	Banco Internacional de Compensación de Pagos [BIP] m
Bank für Internationalen Zahlungsausgleich [BIZ] (D)	—	Bank for International Settlements [BIS]	Banque pour les Règlements Internationaux B.R.I. f	Banca dei Regolamenti Internazionali f	Banco Internacional de Compensación de Pagos [BIP] m
Bankgarantie (D)	—	banker's guarantee	garantie de banque f	garanzia bancaria f	garantía bancaria f
Bankgeheimnis (D)	—	banker's duty of secrecy	secret bancaire m	segreto bancario m	secreto bancario m
Bankgewerbe (D)	—	banking business	banque f	settore bancario m	banca f
bankgirierter Warenwechsel (D)	—	bank endorsed bill	traite endossée par une banque f	effetto commerciale girato da banche m	letra comercial con endoso bancario f
bank guarantee (E)	Bankaval m	—	aval de banque m	avallo bancario m	aval bancario m
Bankguthaben (D)	—	bank balance	avoir en banque m	deposito bancario m	haber bancario m
bank holidays (E)	Bankfeiertage m/pl	—	jours de fête bancaires m/pl	giorni festivi delle banche m/pl	días de fiesta bancarios m/pl
bank identification number (E)	Bankleitzahl f	—	numéro de code bancaire m	codice bancario m	codigo de identificación bancaria m
Bankior (D)		banker	banquier m	banchiere m	banquero m
Bankierbonifikation (D)	—	placing commission	commission de placement f	provvigione bancaria f	comisión de mediación bancaria f
banking academy (E)	Bankakademie f	—	académie de banquiers f	accademia bancaria f	academia de banqueros f
banking association (E)	Bankenverband m	—	association des banques f	associazione bancaria f	asociación bancaria f
banking business (E)	Bankgewerbe n	—	banque f	settore bancario m	banca f
banking cover (E)	Bankdeckung f	—	couverture de garantie d'une banque f	copertura bancaria f	cobertura bancaria f
banking crisis (E)	Bankenkrise f	—	crise bancaire f	crisi bancaria f	crisis bancaria f
banking decree (E)	Bankenerlaß m	—	décret bancaire m	decreto sul segreto bancario m	decreto bancario m
banking inquiry (E)	Bankenquete f	—	demande de renseignements par la banque f	inchiesta bancaria f	demanda de informe por el banco f
banking interest (E)	Bankzinsen m/pl	—	intérêts bancaires m/pl	interessi bancari m/pl	intereses bancarios m/pl
Banking Law (E)	Kreditwesengesetz n	—	loi sur le crédit f	legge sul sistema creditizio f	ley sobre el régimen de créditos f
banking legislation (E)	Bankengesetzgebung f	—	législation bancaire f	legislazione bancaria f	legislación bancaria f
banking organization (E)	Bankorganisation f	—	organisation bancaire f	organizzazione bancaria f	organisación bancaria f
banking statistics (E)	Bankenstatistik f	—	statistique bancaire f	statistica bancaria f	estadística bancaria f
banking statistics (E)	Bankstatistik f	—	statistique bancaire f	statistica bancaria f	estadística bancaria f
banking syndicate (E)	Bankenkonsortium n	—	consortium de banques m	consorzio bancario m	sindicato bancario m
banking system (E)	Bankensystem n	—	système bancaire m	sistema bancario m	sistema bancario m
Bankkalkulation (D)	—	bank costing	calcul des coûts bancaires m	calcolo bancario m	calculación bancaria f
Bankkapital (D)	—	bank stock	capital bancaire m	capitale bancario m	capital bancario m
Bankkaufmann (D)	—	bank clerk	employé bancaire m	impiegato di banca m	empleado bancario m
Bankkonditionen (D)	—	bank conditions	conditions bancaires f/pl	condizioni bancarie f/pl	condiciones bancarias f/pl
Bankkonto (D)	—	bank account	compte en banque m	conto bancario m	cuenta bancaria f
Bankkontokorrent (D)	—	current account with a bank	compte courant de banque m	conto corrente bancario m	cuenta corriente bancaria f

	D	E	F	I	Es
Bankkontrolle (D)	—	bank supervision	surveillance des banques f	controllo bancario m	control bancario m
Bankkredit (D)	—	bank credit	crédit bancaire m	credito bancario m	crédito bancario m
Bankkunde (D)	—	bank customer	client bancaire m	cliente bancario m	cliente bancario m
Bankleitzahl (D)	—	bank identification number	numéro de code bancaire m	codice bancario m	codigo de identificación bancaria m
Bankliquidität (D)	—	bank liquidity	liquidité de banque f	liquidità bancaria f	liquidez bancaria f
bank liquidity (E)	Bankliquidität f	—	liquidité de banque f	liquidità bancaria f	liquidez bancaria f
bank money order (E)	Bankanweisung f	—	mandat de payement bancaire m	vaglia bancario m	pago bancario m
Banknote (D)	—	bank note	billet de banque m	banconota f	billete m
bank note (E)	Banknote f	—	billet de banque m	banconota f	billete m
bank notes (E)	Noten f/pl	—	billets m/pl	banconote f/pl	billetes m/pl
Bankobligation (D)	—	bank bond	obligation de banque f	obbligazione bancaria f	obligación bancaria f
bank office network (E)	Bankstellennetz n	—	réseau bancaire m	rete di sportelli bancari f	red bancaria f
Bankorganisation (D)	—	banking organization	organisation bancaire f	organizzazione bancaria f	organisación bancaria f
bank place (E)	Bankplatz m	—	place bancable f	piazza bancaria f	plaza bancable f
Bankplatz (D)	—	bank place	place bancable f	piazza bancaria f	plaza bancable f
Bankprovision (D)	—	banker's commission	commission de banque f	commissione bancaria f	comisión bancaria f
Bankprüfung (D)	—	audit of the bank balance sheet	vérification du bilan bancaire f	esame del bilancio m	revisión de cuentas del banco f
Bankpublizität (D)	—	banks' duty to publish	publication obligatoire des bilans bancaires f	pubblicazione obligatoria dei bilanci bancari f	obligación de publicidad bancaria f
bankrate for advances against collateral (E)	Lombardsatz m	—	taux lombard m	tasso lombard m	tipo de pignoración m
bank rate policy (E)	Diskontpolitik f	—	politique d'escompte f	politica di sconto f	política de descuento f
Bankregel (D)	—	banker's rule	règle bancaire f	norma bancaria f	regla bancaria f
bank relations (E)	Bankbeziehungen f/pl	—	relations bancaires f/pl	relazioni bancarie f/pl	relaciones bancarias f/pl
bank return (E)	Bankausweis m	—	situation de banque f	bollettino bancario m	documento bancario m
Bankrevision (D)	—	bank audit	contrôle du bilan d'une banque m	ispezione bancaria f	censura de cuentas del banco f
Bankrott (D)	—	bankruptcy	banqueroute f	bancarotta f	bancarrota f
bankruptcy (E)	Konkurs m	—	faillite f	fallimento m	quiebra f
bankruptcy (E)	Bankrott m	—	banqueroute f	bancarotta f	bancarrota f
Bankruptcy Act (E)	Konkursordnung f	—	régime juridique de la faillite m	legge fallimentare f	ley de las quiebras f
bankruptcy offence (E)	Konkursdelikt n	—	fraude en matière de faillite f	reato fallimentare m	delito concursal m
bankrupt's creditor (E)	Konkursgläubiger m	—	créancier de la faillite m	creditore della massa fallimentare m	acreedor de la quiebra m
bankrupt's estate (E)	Konkursmasse f	—	masse de la faillite f	massa fallimentare f	masa de la quiebra f
bank's accounting (E)	Bankbuchhaltung f	—	comptabilité bancaire f	contabilità bancaria f	contabilidad bancaria f
Bankschulden (D)	—	bank debts	dettes bancaires f/pl	debiti verso banche m/pl	deudas bancarias f/pl
Bankschuldverschreibung (D)	—	bank bond	obligation bancaire f	obbligazione bancaria f	obligación bancaria f
bank's confirmation of a letter of credit (E)	Bankavis m	—	confirmation bancaire f	avviso bancario m	aviso bancario m
banks' duty to publish (E)	Bankpublizität f	—	publication obligatoire des bilans bancaires f	pubblicazione obligatoria dei bilanci bancari f	obligación de publicidad bancaria f
Bankspesen (D)	—	bank charges	frais de banque m/pl	spese bancarie f/pl	gastos bancarios m/pl
bank statement (E)	Bankauszug m	—	relevé de compte m	estratto bancario m	relación f

	D	E	F	I	Es
Bankstatistik (D)	—	banking statistics	statistique bancaire f	statistica bancaria f	estadística bancaria f
Bankstatus (D)	—	bank status	état bancaire m	situazione di banca f	estado bancario m
bank status (E)	Bankstatus m	—	état bancaire m	situazione di banca f	estado bancario m
Bankstellennetz (D)	—	bank office network	réseau bancaire m	rete di sportelli bancari f	red bancaria f
Bankstichtage (D)	—	settling days	jours de règlement fixés m/pl	date di resoconto settimanale della banca centrale f/pl	días de referencia de los bancos m/pl
bank stock (E)	Bankkapital n	—	capital bancaire m	capitale bancario m	capital bancario m
bank's transaction dealing with cashless transactions (E)	Girogeschäft n	—	opération de virement f	trasferimento di giro m	operación de giro f
bank supervision (E)	Bankkontrolle f	—	surveillance des banques f	controllo bancario m	control bancario m
banks' voting rights (E)	Bankenstimmrecht n	—	droit de vote de la banque m	diritto di voto bancario m	derecho de voto del banco m
bank transfer (E)	Banküberweisung f	—	virement bancaire m	trasferimento bancario m	giro bancario m
bank turnover (E)	Bankumsätze m/pl	—	chiffres d'affaires d'une banque m/pl	movimento bancario m	facturación bancaria f
Banküberweisung (D)	—	bank transfer	virement bancaire m	trasferimento bancario m	giro bancario m
Bankumsätze (D)	—	bank turnover	chiffres d'affaires d'une banque m/pl	movimento bancario m	facturación bancaria f
Bankzinsen (D)	—	banking interest	intérêts bancaires m/pl	interessi bancari m/pl	intereses bancarios m/pl
ban on new issues (E)	Emissionssperre f	—	blocage des émissions d'actions et d'obligations m	blocco delle emissioni m	restricción de emisión f
banque (F)	Bankgewerbe n	banking business	—	settore bancario m	banca f
banque (F)	Bank f	bank	—	banca f	banco m
banque centrale (F)	Zentralbank f	central bank	—	banca centrale f	banco central m
banque centrale de virement (F)	Girozentrale f	central giro institution	—	centrale di bancogiro f	central de giros m
banque chargée d'opérations sur titres (F)	Effekten- kommissionär m	securities commission agent	—	commissionario di borsa m	comisionista de valores m
banque coloniale (F)	Kolonialbank f	colonial bank	—	banca coloniale f	banco colonial m
banque combinée (F)	Gemeinschaftsbank f	combination bank	—	banca comune f	banco de combinación m
banque commerciale (F)	Geschäftsbank f	commercial bank	—	banca commerciale f	banco comercial m
banque communale (F)	Kommunalbank f	local authorities bank	—	banca comunale f	banco comunal m
banque d'affaires (F)	Effektenbank f	issuing bank	—	banca valori f	banco de inversiones m
banque d'affaires (F)	Emissionsbank f	issuing bank	—	banca d'emissione f	banco emisor m
banque de correspondance (F)	Korrespondenzbank f	correspondent bank	—	banca corrispondente f	banco corresponsal m
banque de courtiers (F)	Maklerbank f	brokerage bank	—	banca intermediaria f	banco corredor m
banque de crédit (F)	Kreditbank f	commercial bank	—	banca di credito f	banco de crédito m
banque de crédit à l'industrie (F)	Industriekreditbank f	industrial credit bank	—	banca di credito industriale f	banco de crédito industrial m
banque de dépôts et de virements (F)	Girobank f	deposit clearing bank	—	banca di giro f	banco de giros m
banque de dépôts et de virements de titres (F)	Wertpapier- sammelbank f	central depository for securities	—	banca di deposito di titoli f	banco de depósito de valores mobiliarios m
banque de développement (F)	Entwicklungsbank f	development bank	—	banca per lo sviluppo f	banco de desarrollo m
banque d'émission (F)	Notenbank f	central bank	—	banca d'emissione f	banco emisor m
banque d'épargne- construction (F)	Bausparkasse f	building society	—	cassa di risparmio edilizio f	caja de ahorros para la construcción f

	D	E	F	I	Es
banque de péréquation des charges (F)	Lastenausgleichs-bank *f*	equalization of burdens bank	—	banca perequazione oneri *f*	banco de compensación de cargas *m*
banque d'escompte (F)	Diskontbank *f*	discount bank	—	banca di sconto *f*	banco de descuento *m*
banque de spéculation (F)	Spekulationsbank *f*	speculation bank	—	banca di speculazione *f*	banco de especulación *m*
banque de syndicat (F)	Gewerkschaftsbank *f*	trade union bank	—	banca del lavoro *f*	banco sindical *m*
banque d'Etat (F)	Staatsbank *f*	state bank	—	banca di Stato *f*	banco del Estado *m*
banque européenne (F)	Euro-Bank *f*	Eurobank	—	eurobanca *f*	banco europeo *m*
banque européenne d'investissement (F)	Europäische Investitionsbank *f*	European Investment Bank	—	Banca Europea per gli Investimenti *f*	Banco Europeo de Inversiones *m*
banque extérieure (F)	Auslandsbank *f*	foreign bank	—	banca estera *f*	banco exterior *m*
banque habituelle (F)	Hausbank *f*	firm's bank	—	banca preferita *f*	banco con que trata generalmente el cliente *m*
banque hypothécaire (F)	Pfandbriefanstalt *f*	mortgage bank		istituto di credito fondiario *m*	banco hipotecario *m*
banque hypothécaire (F)	Hypothekenbank *f*	mortgage bank	—	banca ipotecaria *f*	banco hipotecario *m*
banque industrielle et artinsanale (F)	Gewerbebank *f*	industrial bank	—	banca industriale *f*	banco industrial *m*
banque mondiale (F)	Weltbank *f*	World Bank	—	Banca mondiale *f*	Banco Mundial *m*
banque postale (F)	Postbank *f*	Postal Savings Bank	—	servizio bancario postale *m*	banco postal *m*
Banque pour les Règlements Inter-nationaux B.R.I. (F)	Bank für Inter-nationalen Zahlungs-ausgleich [BIZ] *f*	Bank for International Settlements [BIS]	—	Banca dei Regolamenti Internazionali *f*	Banco Internacional de Compensación de Pagos [BIP] *m*
banque provinciale (F)	Provinzbank *f*	country bank	—	banca provinciale *f*	banco provincial *m*
banque publique (F)	öffentliche Bank *f*	public bank	—	banca di diritto pubblico *f*	banco público *m*
banque régionale (F)	Regionalbank *f*	regional bank	—	banca regionale *f*	banco regional *m*
banquero (Es)	Bankier *m*	banker	banquier *m*	banchiere *m*	—
banqueroute (F)	Bankrott *m*	bankruptcy	—	bancarotta *f*	bancarrota *f*
banques coopératives centrales (F)	genossenschaftliche Zentralbanken *f/pl*	cooperative central banks	—	banche centrali cooperative *f/pl*	bancos centrales cooperativos *m/pl*
banques d'acceptation (F)	Akzepthäuser *n/pl*	acceptance banks	—	acceptance banks *f/pl*	bancos de aceptación *m/pl*
banques dépositaires (F)	Treuhandbanken *f/pl*	trust banks	—	banche fiduciarie *f/pl*	bancos fiduciarios *m/pl*
banques de réserve (F)	Reservebanken *f/pl*	reserve banks	—	banche di riserva *f/pl*	banco de reserva *m*
banques locales (F)	Lokalbanken *f/pl*	local banks	—	banche locali *f/pl*	bancos locales *m/pl*
banques par actions (F)	Aktienbanken *f/pl*	joint stock banks	—	banche per azioni *f/pl*	bancos por acciones *m/pl*
banque spécialisée (F)	Spezialbank *f*	specialized commercial bank	—	istituto di credito speciale *m*	banco especializado *m*
banque universelle (F)	Universalbank *f*	all-round bank	—	banca universale *f*	banco mixto *m*
banquier (F)	Bankier *m*	banker	—	banchiere *m*	banquero *m*
bar (D)	—	cash	comptant	in contanti	al contado
Barabfindung (D)	—	settlement in cash	indemnité en espèces *f*	indennità in contanti *f*	compensación en efectivo *f*
Bar-Akkreditiv (D)	—	cash letter of credit	accréditif payable en espèce *m*	apertura di credito documentario *f*	crédito simple *m*
bar chart (E)	Blockdiagramm *n*	—	ordinogramme *m*	diagramma a blocchi *m*	diagrama de bloque *m*
Bardeckung (D)	—	cash cover	couverture en espèces *f*	copertura in contanti *f*	cobertura en efectivo *f*
Bardividende (D)	—	cash dividend	dividende payé en espèces *m*	dividendo in contanti *m*	dividendo en efectivo *m*
Bareinlage (D)	—	cash deposit	dépôt en numéraire *m*	apporto in denaro *m*	depósito en efectivo *m*
Bareinschuß (D)	—	cash loss payment	payement en espèces *m*	versamento in contanti *m*	reserva en efectivo *m*
barème des intérêts (F)	Zinsstaffel *f*	interest rate table	—	scaletta *f*	escala de intereses *f*

	D	E	F	I	Es
Bargeld (D)	—	ready money	argent comptant *m*	denaro contante *m*	efectivo *m*
bargeldlose Kassensysteme (D)	—	point of sale system POS	payements scripturaux au point de vente *m/pl*	sistemi di cass non in contanti *m/pl*	sistemas de caja por transferencia *m/pl*
Bargeschäft (D)	—	cash transactions	marché au comptant *m*	affare in contanti *m*	operación al contado *f*
Barkauf (D)	—	cash purchase	achat au comptant *m*	acquisto in contanti *m*	compra en efectivo *f*
Barkredit (D)	—	cash credit	crédit de caisse *m*	credito in contanti *m*	crédito en efectivo *m*
Barlohn (D)	—	wage in cash	salaire en espèces *m*	paga in contanti *f*	salario en efectivo *m*
Barrengold (D)	—	gold in bars	or en lingot *m*	oro in barre *m*	oro en lingotes *m*
barter (E)	Tausch *m*	—	troc *m*	cambio *m*	trueque *m*
Bartergeschäft (D)	—	barter transactions	troc *m*	operazione switch *f*	transacciones de trueque *f/pl*
barter transactions (E)	Bartergeschäft *n*	—	troc *m*	operazione switch *f*	transacciones de trueque *f/pl*
Barverkauf (D)	—	cash sale	vente au comptant *f*	vendita a contanti *f*	venta al contado *f*
Barvermögen (D)	—	cash assets	valeurs réalisables à court terme ou disponibles *f/pl*	capitale liquido *m*	activo efectivo *m*
Barwert (D)	—	value in cash	valeur actuelle *f*	valore di cassa *m*	valor efectivo *m*
Barzahlung (D)	—	cash payment	payement comptant *m*	pagamento in contanti *m*	pago al contado *m*
base (E)	Basis *f*	—	base *f*	base *f*	base *f*
base (Es)	Basis *f*	base	base *f*	base *f*	—
base (F)	Basis *f*	base	—	base *f*	base *f*
base (I)	Basis *f*	base	base *f*	—	base *f*
base de calcul (F)	Bemessungs-grundlage *f*	assessment basis	—	base imponibile *f*	base de cálculo *f*
base de cálculo (Es)	Bemessungs-grundlage *f*	assessment basis	base de calcul *f*	base imponibile *f*	—
base del negocio (Es)	Geschäftsgrundlage *f*	implicit basis of a contract	base implicite d'un contrat *f*	base negoziale *f*	—
base d'imposizione (I)	Besteuerungs-grundlage *f*	tax basis	assiette de l'imposition *f*	—	base imponible *f*
base implicite d'un contrat (F)	Geschäftsgrundlage *f*	implicit basis of a contract	—	base negoziale *f*	base del negocio *f*
base imponibile (I)	Bemessungs-grundlage *f*	assessment basis	base de calcul *f*	—	base de cálculo *f*
base imponible (Es)	Besteuerungs-grundlage *f*	tax basis	assiette de l'imposition *f*	base d'imposizione *f*	—
base monétaire (F)	Geldbasis *f*	monetary base	—	base monetaria *f*	base monetaria *f*
base monetaria (Es)	Geldbasis *f*	monetary base	base monétaire *f*	base monetaria *f*	—
base monetaria (I)	Geldbasis *f*	monetary base	base monétaire *f*	—	base monetaria *f*
base monetaria (I)	Geldmenge *f*	money stock	quantité de monnaie en circulation *f*	—	masa monetaria *f*
base monetaria programmata (I)	Geldmengenziel *n*	money supply target	fourchette de crois-sance monétaire *f*	—	objetivo del volumen monetario *m*
base negoziale (I)	Geschäftsgrundlage *f*	implicit basis of a contract	base implicite d'un contrat *f*	—	base del negocio *f*
basic price (E)	Basispreis *m*	—	prix de base *m*	prezzo base *m*	precio de base *m*
basic rate of interest (E)	Eckzins *m*	—	taux d'intérêt de base *m*	interesse di riferimento *m*	tipo base *m*
basic savings rate (E)	Spareckzins *m*	—	taux-clé d'intérêt bancaire sur les dépôts d'épargne *m*	interesse di riferimento per il risparmio *m*	tipo de referencia *m*
basic trend (E)	Basistrend *m*	—	tendance de base *f*	trend di base *m*	tendencia de base *f*
Basis (D)	—	base	base *f*	base *f*	base *f*
Basispreis (D)	—	basic price	prix de base *m*	prezzo base *m*	precio de base *m*
Basistrend (D)	—	basic trend	tendance de base *f*	trend di base *m*	tendencia de base *f*
basket currency (E)	Korbwährung *f*	—	monnaie de panier *f*	valuta paniere *f*	moneda de cesta *f*

	D	E	F	I	Es
Baudarlehen (D)	—	building loan	prêt à la construction *m*	mutuo edilizio *m*	crédito para la construcción *m*
Baufinanzierung (D)	—	building financing	financement à la construction *m*	finanziamento all'edilizia *m*	financiación de la construcción *f*
Baukostenzuschuß (D)	—	tenant's contribution to the construction costs	participation financière à la construction *f*	contributo alla costruzione *m*	contribución a los costes de construcción *f*
Baumwollbörse (D)	—	Cotton Exchange	bourse de coton *f*	borsa del cotone *f*	bolsa de algodón *f*
Bauspardarlehen (D)	—	loan granted for building purposes	prêt d'épargne-construction *m*	mutuo edilizio *m*	préstamo ahorro-vivienda *m*
bausparen (D)	—	saving through building societies	épargner pour la construction	risparmiare per l'edilizia	ahorrar para la construcción
Bauspar-finanzierung (D)	—	building society funding	financement d'égargne-construction *m*	finanziamento edilizio *m*	financiación de ahorros para la construcción *f*
Bausparförderung (D)	—	promotion of saving through building societies	promotion de l'épargne-construction *f*	promozione del risparmio edilizio *f*	fomento de ahorros para la construcción *m*
Bausparkasse (D)	—	building society	banque d'épargne-construction *f*	cassa di risparmio edilizio *f*	caja de ahorros para la construcción *f*
Bausparkassen-beiträge (D)	—	contributions paid to the building society	contributions payées à la banque d'épargne *f/pl*	contributi di risparmio edilizio *m/pl*	cuotas de ahorro *f/pl*
Bausparvertrag (D)	—	savings agreement with the building society	contrat d'épargne-construction *m*	contratto di risparmio edilizio *m*	contrato de ahorro para la construcción *m*
Bauträger (D)	—	builder	promoteur constructeur *m*	costruttore *m*	promotor de construcción *m*
Bauzinsen (D)	—	fixed-interest coupons	coupons d'intérêt fixe *m/pl*	interessi intercalari *m/pl*	cupones de interés fijo *m/pl*
bear (E)	Baisser *m*	—	baissier *m*	ribassista *m*	bajista *m*
bear clause (E)	Baisseklausel *f*	—	clause de baisse *f*	clausola di ribasso *f*	cláusula de baja *f*
bearer bond (E)	Inhaberschuld-verschreibung *f*	—	obligation au porteur *f*	obbligazione al portatore *f*	obligación al portador *f*
bearer cheque (E)	Überbringerscheck *m*	—	chèque au porteur *m*	assegno al portatore *m*	cheque al portador *m*
bearer clause (E)	Inhaberklausel *f*	—	clause au porteur *f*	clausola al portatore *f*	cláusula al portador *f*
bearer securities (E)	Inhaberpapier *n*	—	titre souscrit au porteur *m*	titolo al portatore *m*	título al portador *m*
bearer share (E)	Inhaberaktie *f*	—	action au porteur *f*	azione al portatore *f*	acción al portador *f*
bearish (D)	—	bearish	baissier	bearish	bajista
bearish (E)	bearish	—	baissier	bearish	bajista
bearish (I)	bearish	bearish	baissier	—	bajista
bear market (E)	Baisse *f*	—	baisse *f*	ribasso *m*	baja *f*
bear seller (E)	Fixer *m*	—	vendeur à découvert *m*	scopertista *m*	vendedor al descubierto *m*
bear selling (E)	Leerverkauf *m*	—	vente à découvert *f*	vendita allo scoperto *f*	venta al descubierto *f*
bear selling position (E)	Leerposition *f*	—	découvert *m*	scoperto *m*	descubierto *m*
Bedarfsdeckungs-prinzip (D)	—	principle of satisfaction of needs	principe de la satisfactions des besoins *m*	principio copertura fabbisogno *m*	principio de cober-tura de demanda *m*
bedingte Kapitalerhöhung (D)	—	conditional capital increase	restriction à l'augmentation du capital social *f*	aumento di capitale condizionato *m*	aumento de capital condicional *m*
Bedingung (D)	—	condition	condition *f*	clausola *f*	condición *f*
Beförderung (D)	—	promotion	avancement *m*	promozione *f*	promoción *m*
before hours dealing (E)	Vorbörse *f*	—	marché avant le marché officiel *m*	avant bourse *m*	operaciones antes de la apertura *f/pl*
befristete Einlagen (D)	—	fixed deposits	bons et comptes à échéance fixe *m/pl*	depositi a scadenza fissa *m/pl*	imposiciones a plazo *f/pl*
Befristung (D)	—	time limit	fixation d'un délai *f*	fissazione di un termine *f*	condición de plazo *f*
Begebung (D)	—	issue	émission *f*	emissione *f*	emisión *f*

	D	E	F	I	Es
Beglaubigung (D)	—	certification	légalisation f	autenticazione f	legalización f
Beherrschungs-vertrag (D)	—	control agreement	accord de contrôle m	contratto di controllo m	contrato de dominación m
Behörde (D)	—	authority	autorité f	autorità f	autoridad f
Beihilfe (D)	—	financial aid	subside m	assistenza f	ayuda f
be in the market (E)	im Markt sein	—	être sur le marché	essere presente sul mercato	estar en el mercado
Beistandskredit (D)	—	standby credit	crédit de soutien m	credito di sostegno m	crédito de ayuda m
Beiträge (D)	—	contributions	contributions f/pl	contributi m/pl	cuotas f/pl
Beitragsbemessungs-grenze (D)	—	income limit for the assessment of contributions	plafond d'assujettis-sement servant au calcul de la cotisation à l'assurance invali-dité-vieillesse m	massimale di contributo m	tope de la base de cotización m
Beitragserstattung (D)	—	contribution refund	remboursement des cotisations m	rimborso di contributi m	reintegro de las cuotas m
Beitritt (D)	—	joining	adhésion f	adesione f	adhesión f
Beitrittsbeschluß (D)	—	decision of accession	jugement déclaratif d'admission de la créance m	decreto di adesione all'asta coattiva m	auto de adhesión m
Bekanntmachung (D)	—	notification	publication f	annuncio m	publicación f
Belassungsgebühr (D)	—	prolongation charge	frais de prolongation m/pl	tassa prolungamento ipoteche f	derechos de prolongación m/pl
Beleg (D)	—	receipt	document justificatif m	ricevuta f	justificante m
Belegschaftsaktie (D)	—	staff shares	action de travail f	azione per dipendenti f	acción de personal f
beleihen (D)	—	to lend money on something	nantir	ipotecare	pignorar
Bemessungs-grundlage (D)	—	assessment basis	base de calcul f	base imponibile f	base de cálculo f
Benachrichtigung (D)	—	notification	notification f	avviso m	aviso m
Benachrichtigungs-pflicht (D)	—	duty of notification	obligation de notification f	obbligo d'avviso m	obligación de aviso f
bene (I)	Gut n	property	bien m	—	bienes m
bénéfice (F)	Gewinn m	profit	—	utile m	beneficio m
bénéfice brut (F)	Bruttogewinn m	gross profit	—	utile lordo m	beneficio bruto m
bénéfice comptable (F)	Buchgewinn m	book profit	—	utile contabile m	beneficio contable m
bénéfice d'aliénation (F)	Veräußerungsgewinn m	gain on disposal	—	plusvalenza f	beneficio de la venta m
bénéfice d'amortissement (F)	Tilgungsgewinn m	gain of redemption	—	utile di rimborso m	beneficio de amortización m
bénéfice de discussion (F)	Vorausklage f	preliminary injunction	—	citazione preventiva f	excusión f
bénéfice imaginaire (F)	imaginärer Gewinn m	imaginary profit	—	lucro cessante m	beneficio imaginario m
bénéfice intermédiaire des groupements de sociétés (F)	Konzernzwischen-gewinn m	group interim benefits	—	margine d'utile di gruppo m	beneficio intermedio consolidado m
beneficencia (Es)	Wohlfahrt f	welfare	bienfaisance f	benessere m	—
beneficiario (I)	Remittent m	payee	remettant m	—	remitente m
beneficiario di una cambiale (I)	Wechselnehmer m	payee of a bill of exchange	preneur d'un effet m	—	endosado m
beneficio (Es)	Gewinn m	profit	bénéfice m	utile m	—
beneficio bruto (Es)	Bruttogewinn m	gross profit	bénéfice brut m	utile lordo m	—
beneficio contable (Es)	Buchgewinn m	book profit	bénéfice comptable m	utile contabile m	—
beneficio de amortización (Es)	Tilgungsgewinn m	gain of redemption	bénéfice d'amortissement m	utile di rimborso m	—
beneficio de la venta (Es)	Veräußerungs-gewinn m	gain on disposal	bénéfice d'aliénation m	plusvalenza f	—
beneficio especulativo (Es)	Spekulationsgewinn m	speculative profit	gain spéculatif m	utile di speculazione m	—

	D	E	F	I	Es
beneficio imaginario (Es)	imaginärer Gewinn *m*	imaginary profit	bénéfice imaginaire *m*	lucro cessante *m*	—
beneficio intermedio consolidado (Es)	Konzernzwischen-gewinn *m*	group interim benefits	bénéfice intermédiaire des groupements de sociétés *m*	margine d'utile di gruppo *m*	—
beneficio marginal (Es)	Grenzerlös *m*	marginal earnings	produit marginal *m*	ricavo marginale *m*	—
beneficio real (Es)	bereinigter Gewinn *m*	actual profit	produit net d'exploitation *m*	utile rettificato *m*	—
beneficio simulado (Es)	Scheingewinn *m*	fictitious profit	gain fictif *m*	utile fittizio *m*	—
bene immobile (I)	Liegenschaft *f*	immovable property	bien foncier *m*	—	inmuebles *m/pl*
benessere (I)	Wohlfahrt *f*	welfare	bienfaisance *f*	—	beneficencia *f*
beni all'estero (I)	Auslandsvermögen *n*	foreign assets	avoirs à l'étranger *m/pl*	—	patrimonio en el extranjero *m*
beni di consumo (I)	Konsumgüter *n/pl*	consumer goods	biens de consommation *m/pl*	—	bienes de consumo *m/pl*
beni immobili (I)	Immobilien *f/pl*	immovables	biens immobiliers *m/pl*	—	bienes inmuebles *m/pl*
beni materiali (I)	Sachvermögen *n*	material assets	biens corporels *m/pl*	—	patrimonio real *m*
beni mobili (I)	Mobilien *f/pl*	movable goods	biens mobiliers *m/pl*	—	bienes muebles *m/pl*
Benutzungsrecht (D)	—	right to use	droit d'usage *m*	diritto d'uso *m*	derecho de uso *m*
Beratung (D)	—	counseling	consultation *f*	consulenza *f*	asesoramiento *m*
bereinigter Gewinn (D)	—	actual profit	produit net d'exploitation *m*	utile rettificato *m*	beneficio real *m*
Bereitschaftskredit-abkommen (D)	—	stand-by arrangement	arrangement stand-by *m*	stand-by agreement *m*	préstamo de ayuda *m*
Berichtigung (D)	—	correction	rectification *f*	correzione *f*	rectificación *f*
Berichtigungsaktie (D)	—	bonus share	action gratuite *f*	azione gratuita *f*	acción de reajuste *f*
Berichtsperiode (D)	—	period under review	période de référence *f*	periodo in esame *m*	período considerado *m*
BERI-Index (D)	—	business environ-ment risk index	indice BERI *m*	indice BERI *m*	índice BERI *m*
Berufshändler (D)	—	professional trader	agent professionnel *m*	operatore professionale *m*	agente profesional *m*
beschädigte Aktie (D)	—	damaged share certificates	certificat d'action endommagé *m*	azione danneggiata *f*	acción deteriorada *f*
Beschäftigten-struktur (D)	—	employment structure	structure d'emploi *f*	struttura dell'occupazione *f*	estructura de empleo *f*
Beschluß (D)	—	decision	décision *f*	delibera *f*	decisión *f*
beschränkte Geschäftsfähigkeit (D)	—	limited capacity to enter into legal transactions	capacité restreinte d'accomplir des actes juridiques *f*	capacità giuridica limitata *f*	incapacidad jurídica parcial *f*
Besicherungswert (D)	—	collateral value	valeur du gage *f*	valore di garanzia di credito *m*	valor colateral *m*
Besitzeinkommen (D)	—	property income	revenu du patrimoine *m*	reddito del patrimonio *m*	renta de la propiedad *f*
Besitzwechsel (D)	—	bills receivable	effet à recevoir *m*	cambiale attiva *f*	efecto a cobrar *m*
besoin en capital (F)	Kapitalbedarf *m*	capital requirement	—	fabbisogno di capitale *m*	necesidad de capital *f*
besoin en crédits (F)	Kreditbedarf *m*	credit demand	—	fabbisogno creditizio *m*	necesidad de crédito *f*
besoins de trésorerie (F)	Finanzbedarf *m*	financial requirements	—	fabbisogno finanziario *m*	necesidad financiera *f*
Besoldung (D)	—	payment	salaire *m*	retribuzione *f*	salario *m*
Besserungsschein (D)	—	debtor warrant	surenchère au concordat *f*	certificato di rim-borso in caso di miglioramento della situazione finanziaria *m*	certificado de mejora *m*
Bestand (D)	—	stocks	inventaire *m*	inventario *m*	inventario *m*
Bestandsaufnahme (D)	—	stock-taking	établissement de l'inventaire *m*	redazione d'inventario *f*	formación de un inventario *f*
Bestandskonto (D)	—	real account	compte d'existences *m*	conto magazzino *m*	cuenta de existencia *f*
Bestands-veränderung (D)	—	inventory change	variation des existences *f*	movimento di scorte *m*	variaciones de las partidas *f/pl*

	D	E	F	I	Es
Bestätigung (D)	—	confirmation	confirmation f	conferma f	certificado m
Bestätigungs-schreiben (D)	—	letter of confirmation	lettre de confirmation f	lettera di conferma f	carta confirmadora f
beste Adresse (D)	—	prime name	client de première catégorie m	società di prim'ordine f	cliente de primera categoría f
Bestellung (D)	—	order	commande f	ordinazione f	pedido m
bestens (D)	—	at best	au mieux	al meglio	al mejor cambio
Besteuerung (D)	—	taxation	taxation f	tassazione f	imposición f
Besteuerungs-grundlage (D)	—	tax basis	assiette de l'imposition f	base d'imposizione f	base imponible f
Besteuerungs-verfahren (D)	—	taxation procedure	régime de taxation m	procedura d'imposizione f	procedimiento tributario m
Bestimmtheitsmaß (D)	—	determination coefficient	coefficient de détermination m	coefficiente di determinazione m	coeficiente de determinación m
beta factor (E)	Betafaktor m	—	coefficient beta m	indice beta m	factor beta de regresión m
Betafaktor (D)	—	beta factor	coefficient beta m	indice beta m	factor beta de regresión m
Beteiligung (D)	—	participation	participation f	partecipazione f	participación f
Beteiligungs-darlehen (D)	—	loan with profit participation	prêt de participation m	partecipazione a forma di anticipo f	préstamo participativo m
Beteiligungs-finanzierung (D)	—	equity financing	financement par participation m	finanziamento di portafoglio m	financiación de participación f
Beteiligungshandel (D)	—	equity financing transactions	opérations de financement par participation f/pl	commercio in partecipazioni m	operaciones de financiación de participación f/pl
Beteiligungs-vermittlung (D)	—	agency of equity financing transactions	agence d'opérations de financement par participation f	mediazione di partecipazioni f	mediación en las operaciones de financiación de participación f
Betongold (D)	—	real estate property	patrimoine immobilier m	proprietà immobiliare f	propiedad inmobiliaria f
betriebliches Rechnungswesen (D)	—	operational accountancy	comptabilité industrielle f	ragioneria aziendale f	contabilidad empresarial f
Betriebskosten (D)	—	working expenses	charges d'exploitation f/pl	costi d'esercizio m/pl	gastos de explotación m
Betriebsmittel (D)	—	working funds	équipement d'exploitation m	fondi d'esercizio m/pl	fondos de explotación m/pl
Betriebsprüfung (D)	—	investigation by the tax authorities	vérification des livres de l'entreprise f	revisione aziendale f	revisión f
Betriebsrentabilität (D)	—	operational profitability	rentabilité d'exploitation f	redditività aziendale f	rentabilidad de la actividad de la empresa f
Betriebsvermögen (D)	—	operating assets	capital d'exploitation m	capitale d'esercizio m	patrimonio empresarial m
Betriebs-wirtschaftslehre (D)	—	business economics	gestion industrielle et commerciale f	scienza dell'economia aziendale f	teoría de la empresa f
Betrug (D)	—	fraud	fraude f	truffa f	fraude m
Bevollmächtigter (D)	—	authorized person	fondé de pouvoir m	delegato m	apoderado m
Beweismittel (D)	—	evidence	moyen de preuve m	prova f	medio probatorio m
Bewertung (D)	—	valuation	valorisation f	valutazione f	evaluación f
Bewilligung (D)	—	allowance	consentement m	autorizzazione f	concesión f
bezahlt (D)	—	paid	équilibre entre offre et demande m	pagato	equilibrio entre papel y dinero m
bezahlt Brief (D)	—	more sellers than buyers	comptant vendeur	offerta eccedente la domanda f	la oferta fue mayor que la demanda f
bezahlt Geld (D)	—	more buyers than sellers	comptant acheteur	domanda parzialmen-te insoddisfatta f	compra limitada f
Bezogener (D)	—	drawee	tiré m	trattario m	librado m
Bezugsangebot (D)	—	right issue	offre de souscription f	offerta in opzione f	oferta de suscripción f
Bezugs-bedingungen (D)	—	subscription conditions	conditions de souscription f/pl	condizioni d'acquisto f/pl	condiciones de suscripción f/pl

	D	E	F	I	Es
Bezugsfrist (D)	—	subscription period	délai de souscription *m*	termine d'opzione *m*	plazo de suscripción *m*
Bezugskurs (D)	—	subscription price	prix de souscription *m*	corso d'acquisto *m*	cotización de emisión *f*
Bezugsrecht (D)	—	subscription right	droit de souscription *m*	diritto d'opzione *m*	derecho de opción *m*
Bezugsrecht-abschlag (D)	—	ex-rights markdown	cours moins le droit de souscription *m*	stacco del diritto d'opzione *m*	deducción del derecho de suscripción *f*
Bezugsrecht-erklärung (D)	—	declaration to exercise the subscription right	déclaration d'exercer le droit de souscription *f*	dichiarazione diritto d'opzione *f*	declaración de ejercer el derecho de suscripción *f*
Bezugsrechthandel (D)	—	trading in suscription rights	marché des droits de souscription *m*	trattazione di diritti d'opzione *f*	comercio de derechos de suscripción *m*
Bezugsrecht-notierung (D)	—	subscription price	cotation des droits de souscription *f*	prezzo del diritto d'opzione *m*	cotización de derechos de suscripción *f*
Bezugsrechts-bewertung (D)	—	subscription rights evaluation	évaluation des droits de souscription *f*	valutazione del diritto d'opzione *f*	evaluación del derecho de suscripción *f*
Bezugsrechts-disposition (D)	—	subscription rights disposition	disposition des droits de souscription *f*	esercizio del diritto d'opzione *m*	disposición del derecho de suscripción *f*
Bezugsrechtskurs (D)	—	subscription price	prix de souscription *m*	prezzo del diritto d'opzione *m*	precio de suscripción *m*
Bezugsrechtsparität (D)	—	subscription rights parity	parité des droits de souscription *f*	valore aritmetico diritto d'opzione *m*	paridad de derecho de suscripción *f*
Bezugsschein (D)	—	subscription warrant	certificat de souscription *m*	buono d'opzione *m*	boletín de suscripción *m*
Bezugstag (D)	—	subscription day	jour de souscription *m*	giorno di scadenza opzione *m*	día de la emisión *m*
bid (E)	Gebot *n*	—	offre *f*	offerta *f*	oferta *f*
bid price (E)	Geldkurs *m*	—	cours de la demande *m*	corso di domanda *m*	cotización demandada *f*
bien (F)	Gut *n*	property	—	bene *m*	bienes *m*
bienes (Es)	Gut *n*	property	bien *m*	bene *m*	—
bienes de consumo (Es)	Konsumgüter *n/pl*	consumer goods	biens de consommation *m/pl*	beni di consumo *m/pl*	—
bienes inmuebles (Es)	Immobilien *f/pl*	immovables	biens immobiliers *m/pl*	beni immobili *m/pl*	—
bienes muebles (Es)	Mobilien *f/pl*	movable goods	biens mobiliers *m/pl*	beni mobili *m/pl*	—
bienes patrimoniales (Es)	Kapitalvermögen *n*	capital assets	capital *m*	impieghi di capitale *m/pl*	—
bienfaisance (F)	Wohlfahrt *f*	welfare	—	benessere *m*	beneficencia *f*
bien foncier (F)	Liegenschaft *f*	immovable property	—	bene immobile *m*	inmuebles *m/pl*
biens corporels (F)	Sachvermögen *n*	material assets	—	beni materiali *m/pl*	patrimonio real *m*
biens de consommation (F)	Konsumgüter *n/pl*	consumer goods	—	beni di consumo *m/pl*	bienes de consumo *m/pl*
biens immobiliers (F)	Immobilien *f/pl*	immovables	—	beni immobili *m/pl*	bienes inmuebles *m/pl*
biens mobiliers (F)	Mobilien *f/pl*	movable goods	—	beni mobili *m/pl*	bienes muebles *m/pl*
big bank (E)	Großbank *f*	—	grande banque *f*	banca importante *f*	gran banco *m*
bilan (F)	Bilanz *f*	balance sheet	—	bilancio *m*	balance *m*
bilan approuvé (F)	genehmigte Bilanz *f*	authorized balance sheet	—	bilancio approvato *m*	balance aprobado *m*
bilan au moment de l'ouverture du règlement judiciare (F)	Vergleichsbilanz *f*	comparative balance sheet	—	situazione patrimoniale di concordato *f*	balance de comparación *m*
bilan bancaire (F)	Bankbilanz *f*	bank balance sheet	—	bilancio di banca *m*	balance bancario *m*
bilan brut (F)	Rohbilanz *f*	rough balance	—	progetto di bilancio *m*	balance bruto *m*
bilancia commerciale (I)	Handelsbilanz *f*	commercial balance sheet	balance des opérations en marchandises *f*	—	balanza comercial *f*
bilancia dei capitali (I)	Kapitalbilanz *f*	balance of capital transactions	balance des opérations en capital *f*	—	balanza de capital *f*
bilancia dei pagamenti (I)	Zahlungsbilanz *f*	balance of payments	balance des payements *f*	—	balanza de pagos *f*

	D	E	F	I	Es
bilancia dei servizi (I)	Dienstleistungsbilanz f	balance of service transactions	balance des opérations courantes en services f	—	balanza de servicios f
bilancia delle partite correnti (I)	Leistungsbilanz f	balance of goods and services	balance des opérations courantes f	—	balanza por cuenta corriente f
bilancia valutaria (I)	Devisenbilanz f	net movement of foreign exchange	compte de devises m	—	balanza de divisas f
bilancio (I)	Bilanz f	balance sheet	bilan m	—	balance m
bilancio (I)	Haushalt m	budget	budget m	—	presupuesto m
bilancio approvato (I)	genehmigte Bilanz f	authorized balance sheet	bilan approuvé m	—	balance aprobado m
bilancio consolidato (I)	Konzernbilanz f	group balance sheet	bilan consolidé d'un groupement de sociétés m	—	balance del consorcio m
bilancio consolidato (I)	konsolidierte Bilanz f	consolidated balance sheet	bilan consolidé m	—	balance consolidado m
bilancio d'apertura (I)	Eröffnungsbilanz f	opening balance sheet	bilan d'ouverture m	—	balance inicial m
bilancio d'esercizio (I)	Jahresabschluß m	annual statement of accounts	clôture annuelle des comptes f	—	balance anual m
bilancio d'esercizio (I)	Jahresbilanz f	annual balance sheet	bilan de fin d'année m	—	balance anual m
bilancio di banca (I)	Bankbilanz f	bank balance sheet	bilan bancaire m	—	balance bancario m
bilancio di chiusura (I)	Schlußbilanz f	closing balance	bilan de clôture m	—	balance de cierre m
bilancio generale (I)	Summenbilanz f	turnover balance	relevé des comptes généraux m	—	balance de sumas m
bilancio giornaliero (I)	Tagesbilanz f	daily trial balance sheet	arrêté quotidien de compte m	—	balance diario m
bilancio in deficit (I)	Unterbilanz f	deficit balance	bilan déficitaire m	—	balance deficitario m
bilancio intermedio (I)	Zwischenbilanz f	interim balance sheet	bilan intermédiaire m	—	balance intermedio m
bilancio internazionale (I)	Weltbilanz f	worldwide financial statements	bilan mondial m	—	balance mundial m
bilancio mensile (I)	Monatsbilanz f	monthly balance sheet	situation comptable mensuelle f	—	balance mensual m
bilancio mensile (I)	Monatsausweis m	monthly return	situation mensuelle f	—	resumen mensual m
bilancio patrimoniale (I)	Vermögensbilanz f	asset and liability statement	état du patrimoine m	—	balance patrimonial m
bilancio preventivo (I)	Haushaltsplan m	budget	budget m	—	presupuesto m
bilancio pubblico (I)	öffentlicher Haushalt m	public budget	budget public m	—	presupuesto público m
bilancio semestrale (I)	Halbjahresbilanz f	semi-annual balance sheet	bilan semestriel m	—	balance semestral m
bilancio senza compensazioni (I)	unkompensierte Bilanz f	unoffset balance sheet	bilan non compensé m	—	balance no compensado m
bilancio unico (I)	Einheitsbilanz f	unified balance sheet	bilan unique m	—	balance unitario m
bilan consolidé (F)	konsolidierte Bilanz f	consolidated balance sheet	—	bilancio consolidato m	balance consolidado m
bilan consolidé d'un groupement de sociétés (F)	Konzernbilanz f	group balance sheet	—	bilancio consolidato m	balance del consorcio m
bilan de clôture (F)	Schlußbilanz f	closing balance	—	bilancio di chiusura m	balance de cierre m
bilan déficitaire (F)	Unterbilanz f	deficit balance	—	bilancio in deficit m	balance deficitario m
bilan de fin d'année (F)	Jahresbilanz f	annual balance sheet	—	bilancio d'esercizio m	balance anual m
bilan de l'endettement (F)	Überschuldungsbilanz f	statement of overindebtedness	—	stato di disavanzo patrimoniale m	balance de débitos m
bilan d'ouverture (F)	Eröffnungsbilanz f	opening balance sheet	—	bilancio d'apertura m	balance inicial m
bilan hebdomadaire (F)	Wochenausweis m	weekly return	—	situazione settimanale f	balance semanal m
bilan intermédiaire (F)	Zwischenbilanz f	interim balance sheet	—	bilancio intermedio m	balance intermedio m
bilan mondial (F)	Weltbilanz f	worldwide financial statements	—	bilancio internazionale m	balance mundial m
bilan non compensé (F)	unkompensierte Bilanz f	unoffset balance sheet	—	bilancio senza compensazioni m	balance no compensado m

	D	E	F	I	Es
bilan semestriel (F)	Halbjahresbilanz *f*	semi-annual balance sheet	—	bilancio semestrale *m*	balance semestral *m*
bilan unique (F)	Einheitsbilanz *f*	unified balance sheet	—	bilancio unico *m*	balance unitario *m*
Bilanz (D)	—	balance sheet	bilan *m*	bilancio *m*	balance *m*
Bilanzanalyse (D)	—	balance sheet analysis	analyse du bilan *f*	analisi di bilancio *m*	análisis de balance *m*
Bilanzänderung (D)	—	alteration of a balance sheet	modification apportée au bilan *f*	modifica del bilancio *f*	alteración del balance *f*
Bilanzfälschung (D)	—	falsification of the balance sheet	falsification du bilan *f*	falsificazione del bilancio *f*	falsificación del balance *f*
Bilanzgliederung (D)	—	format of the balance sheet	présentation du bilan *f*	struttura di bilancio *f*	estructura del balance *f*
Bilanzierung (D)	—	procedure to draw up a balance sheet	établissement du bilan *m*	redazione del bilancio *f*	formación del balance *f*
Bilanzierungsvorschriften (D)	—	accounting regulations	prescriptions concernant l'établissement du bilan *f/pl*	norme per la redazione del bilancio *f/pl*	normas sobre balances *f/pl*
Bilanzklarheit (D)	—	accounting transparency	clarté du bilan *f*	chiarezza del bilancio *f*	transparencia del balance *f*
Bilanzkontinuität (D)	—	balance sheet consistency	identité des bilans successifs *f*	continuità di bilancio *f*	continuidad de balance *f*
Bilanzkonto (D)	—	balance sheet account	compte de bilan *m*	conto di bilancio *m*	cuenta permanente *f*
Bilanzkritik (D)	—	balance sheet analysis	analyse du bilan *f*	esame critico del bilancio *m*	crítica del balance *f*
Bilanzkurs (D)	—	book value	valeur comptable *f*	prezzo di bilancio *m*	valor contable *m*
bilanzpolitische Instrumente (D)	—	instruments of balance sheet policy	instruments de la politique en matière de bilans *m/pl*	strumenti di politica del bilancio *m/pl*	instrumentos en materia de política de balances *m/pl*
Bilanzprüfung (D)	—	balance sheet audit	contrôle du bilan *m*	revisione del bilancio *f*	revisión del balance *f*
Bilanzrichtliniengesetz (D)	—	Accounting and Reporting Law	loi sur les directives de l'établissement du bilan *f*	legge sulla formazione del bilancio *f*	ley sobre directivas en materia de balances *f*
Bilanzstatistik (D)	—	balance sheet statistics	statistique des bilans *f*	analisi statistica dei bilanci *f*	estadística de balances *f*
Bilanzstichtag (D)	—	date of the balance	jour du bilan *m*	giorno chiusura bilancio *m*	fecha del balance *f*
Bilanzstruktur (D)	—	structure of the balance sheet	structure du bilan *f*	struttura del bilancio *f*	estructura del balance *f*
Bilanzsumme (D)	—	balance sheet total	total du bilan *m*	totale del bilancio *m*	suma del balance *f*
Bilanzverlängerung (D)	—	increase in total assets and liabilities	extension du bilan *f*	allungamento del bilancio *m*	extensión del balance *f*
Bilanzverlust (D)	—	net loss	perte comptable *f*	perdita di bilancio *f*	pérdida de balance *f*
Bilanzwert (D)	—	balance sheet value	valeur portée au bilan *f*	valore di bilancio *m*	valor de balance *m*
bill drawn by the drawer himself (E)	trassiert-eigener Wechsel *m*	—	traite tirée sur soi-même *f*	cambiale tratta su se stesso *f*	letra girada a su propio cargo *f*
billet à ordre (F)	trockener Wechsel *m*	negotiable promissory note	—	pagherò *m*	pagaré *m*
billet de banque (F)	Banknote *f*	bank note	—	banconota *f*	billete *m*
billete (Es)	Banknote *f*	bank note	billet de banque *m*	banconota *f*	—
billetes (Es)	Noten *f/pl*	bank notes	billets *m/pl*	banconote *f/pl*	—
billets (F)	Noten *f/pl*	bank notes	—	banconote *f/pl*	billetes *m/pl*
bill for collection (E)	Inkassowechsel *m*	—	traite donnée au recouvrement *f*	cambiale all'incasso *f*	letra al cobro *f*
billigst (D)	—	at lowest	au meilleur prix	al meglio	al cambio más barato
bill in foreign currency (E)	Devisen-Wechsel *m*	—	lettre de change libellée en monnaie étrangère *f*	cambiale in valuta estera *f*	letra en moneda extranjera *f*
bill in foreign currency (E)	Auslandsakzept *n*	—	traite tirée sur l'étranger *f*	accettazione estera *f*	letra sobre el extranjero *f*
bill of exchange (E)	Wechsel *m*	—	lettre de change *f*	cambiale *f*	letra *f*
bill of exchange drawn for third-party account (E)	Kommissionstratte *f*	—	traite pour compte d'autrui *f*	tratta per conto terzi *f*	giro por cuenta *m*

	D	E	F	I	Es
bill of receipts and expenditures (E)	Einnahmen-Ausgabenrechnung *f*	—	état des recettes et des dépenses *m*	conto entrate e uscite *m*	cuenta de gastos-ingresos *f*
bill on deposit (E)	Depotwechsel *m*	—	lettre de change déposée en garantie d'un prêt *f*	cambiale depositata in garanzia *f*	efecto cambial en depósito *m*
bill payable (E)	Schuldwechsel *m*	—	effet à payer *m*	cambiale passiva *f*	efecto a pagar *m*
bill payable in instalments (E)	Ratenwechsel *m*	—	effet à échéances multiples *m*	cambiale di pagamento rateale *f*	letra de vencimientos sucesivos *f*
bills discounted (E)	Diskonten *m/pl*	—	effets escomptés *f/pl*	effetti nazionali *m/pl*	letras de cambio descontados *f/pl*
bills discounted ledger (E)	Obligobuch *n*	—	livre des traites escomptées *m*	libro rischi *m*	libro de aceptaciones *m*
bills drawn on debtors (E)	Debitorenziehung *f*	—	traite tirée sur débiteur *f*	cambiale tratta sul debitore *f*	letra librada *f*
bills receivable (E)	Besitzwechsel *m*	—	effet à recevoir *m*	cambiale attiva *f*	efecto a cobrar *m*
bills rediscountable at the Federal Bank (E)	bundesbankfähige Wertpapiere *n/pl*	—	titres escomptables auprès de la Banque fédérale *m/pl*	titoli riscontabili presso la banca centrale *m/pl*	títulos redescontables en el Banco Federal *m/pl*
bimetallismo (I)	Parallelwährung *f*	parallel currency	monnaie parallèle *f*	—	moneda paralela *f*
bimetallismo (I)	Doppelwährung *f*	double currency	double étalon *m*	—	moneda doble *f*
Binnenmarkt (D)	—	domestic market	marché national *m*	mercato interno *m*	mercado interior *m*
black bourse (E)	schwarze Liste *f*	—	liste noire *f*	elenco dei debitori *m*	lista negra *f*
Black Friday (E)	Schwarzer Freitag *m*	—	vendredi noir *m*	venerdì nero *m*	viernes negro *m*
black market (E)	schwarzer Markt *m*	—	marché noir *m*	mercato nero *m*	mercado negro *m*
black stock exchange (E)	schwarze Börse *f*	—	bourse noire *f*	borsa nera *f*	bolsín *m*
blank bill (E)	Blanko-Wechsel *m*	—	traite en blanc *f*	cambiale in bianco *f*	letra en blanco *f*
blank cheque (E)	Blanko-Scheck *m*	—	chèque en blanc *m*	assegno in bianco *m*	cheque en blanco *m*
Blankett (D)	—	blank form	imprimé en blanc *m*	foglio in bianco *m*	carta blanca *f*
blank form (E)	Blankett *n*	—	imprimé en blanc *m*	foglio in bianco *m*	carta blanca *f*
blank indorsement (E)	Blanko-Indossament *n*	—	endossement en blanc *m*	girata in bianco *f*	endoso en blanco *m*
Blanko-Akzept (D)	—	acceptance in blank	acceptation en blanc *f*	accettazione in bianco *f*	aceptación en blanco *f*
Blanko-Indossament (D)	—	blank indorsement	endossement en blanc *m*	girata in bianco *f*	endoso en blanco *m*
Blanko-Kredit (D)	—	open credit	crédit en compte courant *m*	fido in bianco *m*	crédito en blanco *m*
Blanko-Scheck (D)	—	blank cheque	chèque en blanc *m*	assegno in bianco *m*	cheque en blanco *m*
Blanko-Verkauf (D)	—	short sale	vente à découvert *f*	vendita allo scoperto *f*	venta al descubierto *f*
Blanko-Wechsel (D)	—	blank bill	traite en blanc *f*	cambiale in bianco *f*	letra en blanco *f*
Blankozession (D)	—	transfer in blank	cession en blanc *f*	cessione allo scoperto *f*	cesión en blanco *f*
Blitzgiro (D)	—	direct telex transfer system	virement transmis par le système de virements de télex direct *m*	bonifico telegrafico *m*	giro transmitido por el sistema de transferencia de télex directo *m*
blocage des émissions d'actions et d'obligations (F)	Emissionssperre *f*	ban on new issues	—	blocco delle emissioni *m*	restricción de emisión *f*
blocage des prix (F)	Preisstopp *m*	price stop	—	blocco dei prezzi *m*	congelación de precios *f*
bloccare (I)	sperren	to block	bloquer	—	bloquear
blocco dei prezzi (I)	Preisstopp *m*	price stop	blocage des prix *m*	—	congelación de precios *f*
blocco delle emissioni (I)	Emissionssperre *f*	ban on new issues	blocage des émissions d'actions et d'obligations *m*	—	restricción de emisión *f*
blocco monetario (I)	Währungsblock *m*	monetary block	bloc monétaire *m*	—	bloque monetario *m*
bloc dollar (F)	Dollarblock *m*	dollar area	—	area del dollaro *f*	zona del dólar *f*
block (E)	sperren	—	bloquer	bloccare	bloquear

	D	E	F	I	Es
Blockdiagramm (D)	—	bar chart	ordinogramme *m*	diagramma a blocchi *m*	diagrama de bloque *m*
blocked account (E)	Sperrkonto *n*	—	compte bloqué *m*	conto bloccato *m*	cuenta bloqueada *f*
blocked balance (E)	Sperrguthaben *n*	—	avoir bloqué *m*	avere bloccato *m*	fondos bloqueados *m/pl*
blocked deposit (E)	gesperrtes Depot *n*	—	dépôt bloqué *m*	deposito bloccato *m*	depósito congelado *m*
blocked safe-deposit (E)	Sperrdepot *n*	—	dépôt bloqué *m*	deposito bloccato *m*	depósito bloqueado *m*
blocked shares (E)	gesperrte Stücke *n/pl*	—	titres bolqués *m/pl*	titoli colpiti da fermo *m/pl*	títulos congelados *m/pl*
Blockfloating (D)	—	block floating	cours flottant commun adopté par plusieurs pays *m*	fluttuazione congiunta *f*	flotación en bloque *f*
block floating (E)	Blockfloating *n*	—	cours flottant commun adopté par plusieurs pays *m*	fluttuazione congiunta *f*	flotación en bloque *f*
block of shares (E)	Aktienpaket *n*	—	paquet d'actions *m*	pacchetto azionario *m*	paquete de acciones *m*
block sale (E)	Blockverkauf *m*	—	vente en bloc *f*	vendita di pacchetti azionari *f*	venta en bloque *f*
Blockverkauf (D)	—	block sale	vente en bloc *f*	vendita di pacchetti azionari *f*	venta en bloque *f*
bloc monétaire (F)	Währungsblock *m*	monetary block	—	blocco monetario *m*	bloque monetario *m*
bloquear (Es)	sperren	to block	bloquer	bloccare	—
bloque monetario (Es)	Währungsblock *m*	monetary block	bloc monétaire *m*	blocco monetario *m*	—
bloqueo de un cheque (Es)	Scheckssperre *f*	stopping payment of cheque	opposition au payement d'un chèque *f*	fermo su assegno *m*	—
bloquer (F)	sperren	to block	—	bloccare	bloquear
Blue Chips (D)	—	blue chips	blue chips *m/pl*	blue chips *m/pl*	valores punteros *m/pl*
blue chips (E)	Blue Chips *m/pl*	—	blue chips *m/pl*	blue chips *m/pl*	valores punteros *m/pl*
blue chips (F)	Blue Chips *m/pl*	blue chips	—	blue chips *m/pl*	valores punteros *m/pl*
blue chips (I)	Blue Chips *m/pl*	blue chips	blue chips *m/pl*	—	valores punteros *m/pl*
board (E)	Vorstand *m*	—	comité directeur *m*	consiglio d'amministrazione *m*	junta directiva *f*
board of trustees (E)	Kuratorium *n*	—	charge de curateur *f*	consiglio di gestione *m*	curatorio *m*
Bodenkredit (D)	—	loan on landed property	crédit foncier *m*	credito fondario *m*	crédito inmobiliario *m*
Bodenkreditinstitut (D)	—	mortgage bank	institut de crédit foncier *m*	banca di credito agrario *f*	instituto de crédito inmobiliario *m*
Bodensatz (D)	—	undeclared securities	titres non déclarés *m/pl*	giacenza media di depositi a vista *f*	títulos no declarados *m/pl*
bogus firm (E)	Scheinfirma *f*	—	raison sociale imaginaire *f*	impresa fittizia *f*	casa ficticia *f*
boicot (Es)	Boykott *m*	boycott	boycottage *m*	boicottaggio *m*	—
boicottaggio (I)	Boykott *m*	boycott	boycottage *m*	—	boicot *m*
Boletín de Bolsa (Es)	Cote *n*	share list	bulletin officiel de la cote *m*	cote *m*	—
boletín de bolsa (Es)	Kurszettel *m*	stock exchange list	bulletin des cours *m*	listino di borsa *m*	—
boletín de suscripción (Es)	Bezugsschein *m*	subscription warrant	certificat de souscription *m*	buono d'opzione *m*	—
boletín de suscripción (Es)	Zeichnungsschein *m*	subscription form	certificat de souscription *m*	bollettino di sottoscrizione *m*	—
boletín oficial (Es)	offizielles Kursblatt *n*	offical stock exchange list	cote de la bourse officielle *f*	listino ufficiale *m*	—
bollatura (I)	Abstempelung *f*	stamping	estampillage *m*	—	estampillado *m*
bollatura di monete (I)	Schwundgeld *n*	scalage	argent de consomption *m*	—	dinero de consunción *m*
bollettino bancario (I)	Bankausweis *m*	bank return	situation de banque *f*	—	documento bancario *m*
bollettino di borsa (I)	Börsenbericht *m*	stock exchange report	bulletin de la bourse *m*	—	informe bursátil *m*
bollettino di sottoscrizione (I)	Zeichnungsschein *m*	subscription form	certificat de souscription *m*	—	boletín de suscripción *m*

	D	E	F	I	Es
bollo (I)	Marke f	brand trademark	marque f	—	marca f
bolsa (Es)	Börse f	exchange	bourse f	borsa f	—
bolsa de algodón (Es)	Baumwollbörse f	Cotton Exchange	bourse de coton f	borsa del cotone f	—
bolsa de cambios (Es)	Devisenbörse f	foreign exchange market	bourse de devises f	borsa dei cambi f	—
bolsa de cereales (Es)	Getreidebörse f	grain exchange	bourse aux grains f	borsa dei cereali f	—
bolsa de fletes (Es)	Frachtbörse f	shipping exchange	bourse de fret f	borsa dei noli f	—
bolsa de hierro (Es)	Eisenbörse f	iron exchange	bourse de fer f	borsa del ferro f	—
bolsa de mercancías (Es)	Warenbörse f	commodity exchange	bourse de marchandises f	borsa merci f	—
bolsa de metales (Es)	Metallbörse f	Metal Exchange	bourse des métaux f	borsa metalli f	—
bolsa de petróleo a término (Es)	Ölterminbörse f	oil futures exchange	bourse à terme des valeurs pétrolières f	mercato petrolifero a termine m	—
bolsa de presencia (Es)	Präsenzbörse f	attendance stock exchange	bourse de présence f	borsa di presenza f	—
bolsa de tabaco (Es)	Tabakbörse f	tobacco exchange	bourse de tabacs f	borsa tabacchi f	—
bolsa de valores (Es)	Effektenbörse f	stock exchange	bourse des titres et valeurs mobilières f	borsa valori f	—
bolsa de valores (Es)	Wertpapierbörse f	securities market	bourse des titres et valeurs f	borsa valori f	—
bolsa de valores a término (Es)	Terminbörse f	futures market	bourse à terme f	mercato a termine m	—
bolsa extraoficial (Es)	Kulisse f	unofficial stock market	coulisse f	operatori di borsa m/pl	—
bolsa industrial (Es)	Industrieborse f	industrial stock exchange	bourse des valeurs industrielles f	borsa industriale f	—
bolsa local (Es)	Lokalbörse f	local stock exchange	bourse de province f	borsa locale f	—
bolsa naval (Es)	Schiffahrtsbörse f	shipping exchange	bourse maritime f	borsa dei noli marittimi f	—
bolsa nocturna (Es)	Abendbörse f	evening stock exchange	bourse nocturne f	borsa pomeridiana f	—
bolsa provincial (Es)	Provinzbörse f	regional stock exchange	bourse provinciale f	borsa provinciale f	—
bolsín (Es)	schwarze Börse f	black stock exchange	bourse noire f	borsa nera f	—
bolsín (Es)	Winkelbörse f	bucket shop	bourse du marché en banque f	borsa clandestina f	—
bolsín oficial (Es)	Nebenplatz m	place without a Federal Bank office	place non bancaire f	piazza secondaria f	—
bon (F)	Bond m	bond	—	bond m	bono m
Bond (D)	—	bond	bon m	bond m	bono m
bond (E)	Bond m	—	bon m	bond m	bono m
bond (E)	Obligation f	—	obligation f	obbligazione f	obligación f
bond (I)	Bond m	bond	bon m	—	bono m
bond and share certificate vault (E)	Manteltresor m	—	coffre-fort de titres m	cassaforte dei mantelli f	caja fuerte para certificados de bonos y acciones f
bond certificate (E)	Anleiheschein m	—	certificat d'emprunt m	certificato di prestito m	certificado de empréstito m
bon d'épargne (F)	Sparbrief m	savings certificate	—	lettera di risparmio f	cédula de ahorro f
bon d'épargne (F)	Spargeschenkgutschein m	savings gift credit voucher	—	buono regalo di risparmio m	vale de ahorro m
bondholder (E)	Obligationär m	—	obligataire m	obbligazionista m	obligacionista m
bond issue (E)	Obligationsausgabe f	—	émission d'obligations f	emissione di obbligazioni f	emisión de obligaciones f
bond market (E)	Rentenmarkt m	—	marché obligataire m	mercato del reddito fisso m	mercado de renta fija m
Bond-Option (D)	—	bond option	option de bond f	opzione bond f	opción bono f
bond option (E)	Bond-Option f	—	option de bond f	opzione bond f	opción bono f
bond trading (E)	Rentenhandel m	—	négociation des valeurs à revenu fixe f	commercio titoli a reddito fisso m	contratación de títulos de renta fija f
bon du Trésor (F)	Schatzanweisung f	treasury bond	—	buono del tesoro m	bono del tesoro m

	D	E	F	I	Es
bonification (F)	Bonus *m*	extra dividend	—	dividendo *m*	bono *m*
bonifico da una piazza all'altra (I)	Ferngiro *m*	long distance giro	virement entre deux places bancaires *m*	—	transferencia de una plaza a otra *f*
bonifico sulla piazza (I)	Platzanweisung *f*	cheques and orders payable at a certain place	mandat de place *m*	—	cheques y órdenes a pagar en plaza *m/pl*
bonifico telegrafico (I)	Blitzgiro *m*	direct telex transfer system	virement transmis par le système de virements de télex direct *m*	—	giro transmitido por el sistema de transferencia de télex directo *m*
Bonität (D)	—	financial soundness	solvabilité *f*	solvibilità *f*	solvencia *f*
Bonitätsprüfung (D)	—	credit check	vérification de la solvabilité *f*	esame di solvibilità *m*	inspección de solvencia *f*
Bonitätsrisiko (D)	—	credit solvency risk	risque de rendement douteux *m*	rischio di solvibilità *m*	riesgo de solvencia *f*
bonne foi (F)	guter Glauben *m*	good faith	—	buona fede *f*	buena fe *f*
bono (Es)	Bonus *m*	extra dividend	bonification *f*	dividendo *m*	—
bono (Es)	Bond *m*	bond	bon *m*	bond *m*	—
bono cero (Es)	Zerobond *m*	zero bond	obligation à coupon zéro *f*	zero coupon bond *m*	—
bono de disfrute (Es)	Genußschein *m*	participating certificate	certificat de jouissance *m*	buono di godimento *m*	—
bono de liquidación (Es)	Liquidationsschuldverschreibung *f*	liquidation bond	obligation de liquidation *f*	titolo obbligazionario di liquidazione *m*	—
bono del tesoro (Es)	Schatzanweisung *f*	treasury bond	bon du Trésor *f*	buono del tesoro *m*	—
bono de participación (Es)	Partizipationsschein *m*	participating receipt	récépissé de participation *m*	buono di partecipazione *m*	—
bono opcional (Es)	Optionsanleihe *f*	option bond	titre d'emprunt convertible *m*	prestito convertibile *m*	—
bonos certificados (Es)	zertifizierte Bonds *m/pl*	certified bonds	bons certifiés *m/pl*	titoli a reddito fisso in valuta estera *m/pl*	—
bonos de caja (Es)	Kassenobligationen *f/pl*	medium-term bonds	obligations à moyen terme *f/pl*	obbligazioni di cassa *f/pl*	—
bonos del Estado (Es)	Staatsanleihen *f/pl*	public bonds	emprunts d'Etat *m/pl*	titoli di Stato *m/pl*	—
bonos del tesoro (Es)	Schätze *m/pl*	treasury bonds	obligations du Trésor *f/pl*	buoni del tesoro *m/pl*	—
bonos de pequeño valor nominal (Es)	Baby-Bonds *m/pl*	baby bonds	bons de petite valeur nominale *m*	baby-bonds *m/pl*	—
bonos en moneda extranjera (Es)	Auslandsbonds *m*	foreign currency bonds	titres d'emprunt émis en monnaie étrangère *m/pl*	obbligazioni in valuta estera *f/pl*	—
bono sobre beneficios (Es)	Gewinnobligation *f*	participating debenture	obligation indexée *f*	obbligazione a premio *f*	—
bon pour aval (F)	per aval	as guarantor of payment	—	per buon fine	por aval
bons certifiés (F)	zertifizierte Bonds	certified bonds *m/pl*	—	titoli a reddito fisso in valuta estera *m/pl*	bonos certificados *m/pl*
bons de petite valeur nominale (F)	Baby-Bonds *m/pl*	baby bonds	—	baby-bonds *m/pl*	bonos de pequeño valor nominal *m/pl*
bons et comptes à échéance fixe (F)	befristete Einlagen *f/pl*	fixed deposits	—	depositi a scadenza fissa *m/pl*	imposiciones a plazo *f/pl*
Bonus (D)	—	extra dividend	bonification *f*	dividendo *m*	bono *m*
bonus (E)	Prämie *f*	—	prime *f*	premio *m*	prima *f*
bonus (E)	Gratifikation *f*	—	gratification *f*	gratificazione *f*	gratificación *f*
bonus-aided saving (E)	Prämiensparen *n*	—	épargne à primes *f*	risparmio a premi *m*	ahorro con primas *m*
bonus savings contract (E)	Prämiensparvertrag *m*	—	contrat d'épargne à primes *m*	contratto di risparmio a premi *m*	contrato de ahorro con primas *m*
bonus share (E)	Zusatzaktie *f*	—	action supplémentaire *f*	azione gratuita *f*	acción suplementaria *f*
bonus share (E)	Gratisaktie *f*	—	action gratuite *f*	azione gratuita *f*	acción gratuita *f*
book credit (E)	Buchkredit *m*	—	avance en compte *f*	credito contabile *m*	crédito en cuenta *m*
book debt (E)	Buchschuld *f*	—	dette comptable *f*	debito contabile *m*	pasivo exigible *m*

	D	E	F	I	Es
bookkeeping error (E)	Buchungsfehler *m*	—	erreur de comptabilité *f*	errore di contabilità *m*	error contable *m*
book profit (E)	Buchgewinn *m*	—	bénéfice comptable *m*	utile contabile *m*	beneficio contable *m*
book value (E)	Bilanzkurs *m*	—	valeur comptable *f*	prezzo di bilancio *m*	valor contable *m*
book value (E)	Buchbestände *m/pl*	—	existences comptables *f/pl*	attivi e passivi contabili *m/pl*	existencias inventariadas *f/pl*
Boom (D)	—	boom	boom *m*	boom *m*	auge *m*
boom (E)	Boom *m*	—	boom *m*	boom *m*	auge *m*
boom (E)	Hochkonjunktur *f*	—	haute conjoncture *f*	alta congiuntura *f*	alta coyuntura *f*
boom (F)	Boom *m*	boom	—	boom *m*	auge *m*
boom (I)	Boom *m*	boom	boom *m*	—	auge *m*
borrowed funds (E)	fremde Mittel *n/pl*	—	capitaux prêtés *m/pl*	denaro da terzi *m*	fondos de terceros *m/pl*
borrowed funds (E)	aufgenommene Gelder *n/pl*	—	fonds empruntés *m/pl*	mezzi presi a prestito *m/pl*	fondos recogidos *m/pl*
borrower's under- taking to create no new charge ranking ahead of lender (E)	Negativhypothek *f*	—	hypothèque négative *f*	ipoteca negativa *f*	hipoteca negativa *f*
borrowing (E)	Passivkredit *m*	—	crédit passif *m*	finanziamento passivo *m*	crédito pasivo *m*
borrowing customers' card index (E)	Kreditkartei *f*	—	fichier des opérations d'avances et de crédit *m*	schedario dei crediti *m*	fichero de operacio- nes de crédito *m*
borsa (I)	Börse *f*	exchange	bourse *f*	—	bolsa *f*
borsa clandestina (I)	Winkelbörse *f*	bucket shop	bourse du marché en banque *f*	—	bolsín *m*
borsa dei cambi (I)	Devisenbörse *f*	foreign exchange market	bourse de devises *f*	—	bolsa de cambios *f*
borsa dei cereali (I)	Getreidebörse *f*	grain exchange	bourse aux grains *f*	—	bolsa de cereales *f*
borsa dei noli (I)	Frachtbörse *f*	shipping exchange	bourse de fret *f*	—	bolsa de fletes *f*
borsa dei noli marittimi (I)	Schiffahrtsbörse *f*	shipping exchange	bourse maritime *f*	—	bolsa naval *f*
borsa del cotone (I)	Baumwollbörse *f*	Cotton Exchange	bourse de coton *f*	—	bolsa de algodón *f*
borsa del ferro (I)	Eisenbörse *f*	iron exchange	bourse de fer *f*	—	bolsa de hierro *f*
borsa delle valute (I)	Geldbörse *f*	money market	bourse des valeurs *f*	—	mercado monetario *m*
borsa di presenza (I)	Präsenzbörse *f*	attendance stock exchange	bourse de présence *f*	—	bolsa de presencia *f*
borsa industriale (I)	Industriebörse *f*	industrial stock exchange	bourse des valeurs industrielles *f*	—	bolsa industrial *f*
borsa locale (I)	Lokalbörse *f*	local stock exchange	bourse de province *f*	—	bolsa local *f*
borsa merci (I)	Produktenbörse *f*	produce exchange	bourse de marchandises *f*	—	lonja *f*
borsa merci (I)	Warenbörse *f*	commodity exchange	bourse de marchandises *f*	—	bolsa de mercancías *f*
borsa metalli (I)	Metallbörse *f*	Metal Exchange	bourse des métaux *f*	—	bolsa de metales *f*
borsa nera (I)	schwarze Börse *f*	black stock exchange	bourse noire *f*	—	bolsín *m*
borsa pomeridiana (I)	Abendbörse *f*	evening stock exchange	bourse nocturne *f*	—	bolsa nocturna *f*
borsa provinciale (I)	Provinzbörse *f*	regional stock exchange	bourse provinciale *f*	—	bolsa provincial *f*
borsa tabacchi (I)	Tabakbörse *f*	tobacco exchange	bourse de tabacs *f*	—	bolsa de tabaco *f*
borsa valori (I)	Wertpapierbörse *f*	securities market	bourse des titres et valeurs *f*	—	bolsa de valores *f*
borsa valori (I)	Effektenbörse *f*	stock exchange	bourse des titres et valeurs mobilières *f*	—	bolsa de valores *m*
Börse (D)	—	exchange	bourse *f*	borsa *f*	bolsa *f*
Börsenabteilung (D)	—	exchange department	service des valeurs en bourse *m*	ufficio borsa *m*	sección de bolsa *f*
Börsenaufsicht (D)	—	stock exchange supervision	surveillance de la bourse *f*	sorveglianza della borsa *f*	control estatal de bolsas *m*

bourse de marchandises

	D	E	F	I	Es
Börsenauftrag (D)	—	stock exchange order	ordre de bourse *m*	ordine di borsa *m*	orden de bolsa *f*
Börsenaushang (D)	—	stock market notice board	affiche de bourse *f*	affissione in borsa *f*	anuncio bursátil *m*
Börsenauskunft (D)	—	stock market information	service des renseignements de la bourse *m*	informazioni borsa *f/pl*	información bursátil *f*
Börsenausschuß (D)	—	stock committee	conseil de la bourse *m*	comitato di borsa *m*	comité de las bolsas *m*
Börsenbericht (D)	—	stock exchange report	bulletin de la bourse *m*	bollettino di borsa *m*	informe bursátil *m*
börsengängige Wertpapiere (D)	—	quoted securities	valeurs négociées en bourse *f/pl*	titoli ammessi in borsa *m/pl*	títulos cotizados en bolsa *m/pl*
Börsengeschäfte (D)	—	stock exchange operations	opération de bourse *f*	operazioni di borsa *f/pl*	operaciones bursátiles *f/pl*
Börsengesetz (D)	—	Stock Exchange Act	loi en matière de bourse *f*	legge sulla borsa *f*	ley sobre las operaciones bursátiles *f*
Börsenindex (D)	—	stock exchange index	indice des cours des actions *m*	indice di borsa *m*	índice bursátil *m*
Börsenkurs (D)	—	stock exchange price	cours de bourse *m*	quotazione di borsa *f*	cotización bursátil *f*
Börsenmakler (D)	—	stockbroker	courtier en bourse *m*	agente di borsa *m*	agente de bolsa *m*
Börsennotierung (D)	—	quotation	cotation des cours en bourse *f*	quotazione di borsa *f*	cotización bursátil *f*
Börsenordnung (D)	—	stock exchange regulations	règlement de la bourse *m*	regolamento della borsa *m*	reglamento de bolsa *m*
Börsenorganisation (D)	—	stock exchange organization	organisation boursière *f*	organizzazione della borsa *f*	organización bursátil *f*
Börsenplatz (D)	—	stock exchange centre	place boursière *f*	sede di borsa *f*	plaza bursátil *f*
Börsenrecht (D)	—	stock exchange rules	régime de bourse *m*	diritto della borsa *m*	derecho de la bolsa *m*
Börsenreform (D)	—	reorganization of the stock exchange	réforme de la bourse *f*	riforma della borsa *f*	reforma de bolsa *f*
Börsenschluß (D)	—	close of stock exchange business	clôture de la bourse *f*	fine della riunione di borsa *f*	cierre de la bolsa *m*
Börsensegmente (D)	—	sectors of the stock exchange	segments de bourse *m/pl*	segmenti di borsa *m/pl*	segmentos bursátiles *m/pl*
Börsentendenz (D)	—	stock market trend	tendance de la bourse *f*	tendenza borsistica *f*	tendencia bursátil *f*
Börsentermingeschäfte (D)	—	trading in futures on a stock exchange	opérations boursières à terme *f/pl*	contratti di borsa a termine *m/pl*	operaciones bursátiles a término *f/pl*
Börsenumsätze (D)	—	stock exchange	volume d'opérations boursières *m*	scambi borsistici *m/pl*	volumen de operaciones bursátiles *m*
Börsenumsatzsteuer (D)	—	stock exchange turnover tax	taxe de transaction sur les opérations boursières *f*	imposta sui contratti di borsa *f*	impuesto sobre la negociación bursátil *m*
Börsenusancen (D)	—	stock exchange customs	usages de la bourse *m/pl*	usanze borsistiche *f/pl*	usos bursátiles *m/pl*
Börsenzeit (D)	—	official trading hours	heures d'ouverture de la bourse *f/pl*	orario di borsa *m*	sesión de bolsa *f*
Börsenzulassung (D)	—	admission to the stock exchange	admission en bourse *f*	ammissione alla quotazione di borsa *f*	admisión en la bolsa *f*
bottle-neck factor (E)	Engpaßfaktor *m*	—	facteur de goulot d'étranglement *m*	fattore di stretta *m*	factor de escasez *m*
bourse (F)	Börse *f*	exchange	—	borsa *f*	bolsa *f*
bourse à terme (F)	Terminbörse *f*	futures market	—	mercato a termine *m*	bolsa de valores a término *f*
bourse à terme des valeurs pétrolières (F)	Ölterminbörse *f*	oil futures exchange	—	mercato petrolifero a termine *m*	bolsa de petróleo a término *f*
bourse aux grains (F)	Getreidebörse *f*	grain exchange	—	borsa dei cereali *f*	bolsa de cereales *f*
bourse de coton (F)	Baumwollbörse *f*	Cotton Exchange	—	borsa del cotone *f*	bolsa de algodón *f*
bourse de devises (F)	Devisenbörse *f*	foreign exchange market	—	borsa dei cambi *f*	bolsa de cambios *f*
bourse de fer (F)	Eisenbörse *f*	iron exchange	—	borsa del ferro *f*	bolsa de hierro *f*
bourse de fret (F)	Frachtbörse *f*	shipping exchange	—	borsa dei noli *f*	bolsa de fletes *f*
bourse de marchandises (F)	Produktenbörse *f*	produce exchange	—	borsa merci *f*	lonja *f*

	D	E	F	I	Es
bourse de marchandises (F)	Warenbörse f	commodity exchange	—	borsa merci f	bolsa de mercancías f
bourse de présence (F)	Präsenzbörse f	attendance stock exchange	—	borsa di presenza f	bolsa de presencia f
bourse de province (F)	Lokalbörse f	local stock exchange	—	borsa locale f	bolsa local f
bourse des métaux (F)	Metallbörse f	Metal Exchange	—	borsa metalli f	bolsa de metales f
bourse des titres et valeurs (F)	Wertpapierbörse f	securities market	—	borsa valori f	bolsa de valores f
bourse des titres et valeurs mobilières (F)	Effektenbörse f	stock exchange	—	borsa valori f	bolsa de valores m
bourse des valeurs (F)	Geldbörse f	money market	—	borsa delle valute f	mercado monetario m
bourse des valeurs industrielles (F)	Industriebörse f	industrial stock exchange	—	borsa industriale f	bolsa industrial f
bourse de tabacs (F)	Tabakbörse f	tobacco exchange	—	borsa tabacchi f	bolsa de tabaco f
bourse du marché en banque (F)	Winkelbörse f	bucket shop	—	borsa clandestina f	bolsín m
bourse maritime (F)	Schiffahrtsbörse f	shipping exchange	—	borsa dei noli marittimi f	bolsa naval f
bourse nocturne (F)	Abendbörse f	evening stock exchange	—	borsa pomeridiana f	bolsa nocturna f
bourse noire (F)	schwarze Börse f	black stock exchange	—	borsa nera f	bolsín m
bourse provinciale (F)	Provinzbörse f	regional stock exchange	—	borsa provinciale f	bolsa provincial f
boycott (E)	Boykott m	—	boycottage m	boicottaggio m	boicot m
boycottage (F)	Boykott m	boycott	—	boicottaggio m	boicot m
Boykott (D)	—	boycott	boycottage m	boicottaggio m	boicot m
branch (E)	Zweigstelle f	—	agence f	filiale f	sucursal f
branch abroad (E)	Auslandsniederlassung f	—	succursale à l'étranger f	filiale all'estero f	sucursal en el extranjero f
branch office (E)	Filiale f	—	succursale f	filiale f	filial f
branch office accounting (E)	Filialkalkulation f	—	appréciation des résultats des succursales bancaires f	calcolo delle filiali m	cálculos de sucursal m/pl
brand trademark (E)	Marke f	—	marque f	bollo m	marca f
break-even point (E)	Gewinnschwelle f	—	seuil de rentabilité m	soglia dell'utile f	umbral de la rentabilidad m
brevets à l'étranger (F)	Auslandspatente n/pl	foreign patents	—	brevetti esteri m/pl	patentes extranjeras f/pl
brevetti esteri (I)	Auslandspatente n/pl	foreign patents	brevets à l'étranger m/pl	—	patentes extranjeras f/pl
bridging loan (E)	Überbrückungskredit m	—	crédit transitoire m	credito per necessità di cassa m	crédito transitorio m
Briefkurs (D)	—	ask(ed) price	cours de vente m	prezzo d'offerta m	cotización ofrecida f
broken period interest (E)	Stückzinsen m/pl	—	intérêts courus m/pl	interessi maturati m/pl	intereses por fracción de período m/pl
Broker (D)	—	broker	courtier m	broker m	corredor m
broker (E)	Broker m	—	courtier m	broker m	corredor m
broker (I)	Broker m	broker	courtier m	—	corredor m
brokerage (E)	Courtage f	—	courtage m	courtage f	corretaje m
brokerage bank (E)	Maklerbank f	—	banque de courtiers f	banca intermediaria f	banco corredor m
brokerage business (E)	Vermittlungsgeschäft n	—	affaire de médiation f	operazione di intermediazione f	transacción de mediación f
brokers' code of conduct (E)	Maklerordnung f	—	régime des courtiers m	codice degli agenti di cambio m	régimen de corredores m
broker's note (E)	Schlußnote f	—	avis d'exécution m	fissato bollato m	póliza de negociación f
Bruchteilseigentum (D)	—	ownership in fractional shares	propriété d'une quote-part indivise f	comproprietà di quota ideale f	propiedad por fracciones f
brut (F)	Brutto	gross	—	lordo	bruto
bruto (Es)	Brutto	gross	brut	lordo	—
Brutto (D)	—	gross	brut	lordo	bruto

builder

	D	E	F	I	Es
Brutto-Dividende (D)	—	gross dividend	dividende brut *m*	dividendo lordo *m*	dividendo bruto *m*
Bruttoeinkommen (D)	—	gross income	revenu brut *m*	reddito lordo *m*	renta bruta *f*
Bruttoertrag (D)	—	gross return	gain brut *m*	ricavo lordo *m*	producto bruto *m*
Bruttogewinn (D)	—	gross profit	bénéfice brut *m*	utile lordo *m*	beneficio bruto *m*
Bruttoinlands-produkt (D)	—	gross domestic product	produit intérieur brut *m*	prodotto interno lordo *m*	producto interior bruto *m*
Bruttolohn (D)	—	gross wage	salaire brut *m*	retribuzione lorda *f*	salario bruto *m*
Bruttosozialprodukt (D)	—	gross national product	produit national brut *m*	prodotto nazionale lordo *m*	producto nacional bruto *m*
Bruttoverdienst (D)	—	gross earnings	salaire brut *m*	guadagno lordo *m*	remuneración bruta *f*
Bruttowährungs-reserve (D)	—	gross monetary reserve	réserves monétaires brutes *f/pl*	riserva monetaria lorda *f*	reserva monetaria brutas *f*
Buchbestände (D)	—	book value	existences comptables *f/pl*	attivi e passivi contabili *m/pl*	existencias inventariadas *f/pl*
Buchforderung (D)	—	account receivable	créance en compte *f*	credito contabile *m*	crédito en cuenta *m*
Buchführung (D)	—	accounting	comptabilité *f*	contabilità *f*	contabilidad *f*
Buchgeld (D)	—	money in account	monnaie de crédit *f*	moneta bancaria *f*	dinero bancario *m*
Buchgeldschöpfungs-multiplikator (D)	—	deposit money creation multiplier	multiplicateur de création de monnaie scripturale *m*	moltiplicatore di moneta contabile *m*	multiplicador de creación de dinero giral *m*
Buchgewinn (D)	—	book profit	bénéfice comptable *m*	utile contabile *m*	beneficio contable *m*
Buchgrundschuld (D)	—	uncertificated land charge	dette foncière inscrite au bureau foncier *f*	debito iscritto nel libro fondiario *m*	deuda inmobiliaria registrada *f*
Buchhypothek (D)	—	uncertificated mortgage	hypothèque inscrite au livre foncier *f*	ipoteca iscritta *f*	hipoteca de registro *f*
Buchkredit (D)	—	book credit	avance en compte *f*	credito contabile *m*	crédito en cuenta *m*
Buchprüfung (D)	—	auditing	vérification des livres *f*	ispezione contabile *f*	revisión contable *f*
Buchschuld (D)	—	book debt	dette comptable *f*	debito contabile *m*	pasivo exigible *m*
Buchungsbeleg (D)	—	accounting voucher	pièce comptable *f*	documento contabile *m*	comprobante de asiento *m*
Buchungsfehler (D)	—	bookkeeping error	erreur de comptabilité *f*	errore di contabilità *m*	error contable *m*
Buchwert (D)	—	accounting value	valeur comptable *f*	valore di libro *m*	valor contable *m*
Buchwert-abschreibung (D)	—	declining balance depreciation	amortissement dé-gressif au prorata de la valeur restante *m*	ammortamento del valore di libro *m*	amortización del valor contable *f*
bucket shop (E)	Winkelbörse *f*	—	bourse du marché en banque *f*	borsa clandestina *f*	bolsín *m*
Budget (D)	—	budget	budget *m*	budget *m*	presupuesto *m*
budget (E)	Haushaltsplan *m*	—	budget *m*	bilancio preventivo *m*	presupuesto *m*
budget (E)	Budget *n*	—	budget *m*	budget *m*	presupuesto *m*
budget (F)	Haushalt *m*	budget	—	bilancio *m*	presupuesto *m*
budget (E)	Haushalt *m*	—	budget *m*	bilancio *m*	presupuesto *m*
budget (F)	Budget *n*	budget	—	budget *m*	presupuesto *m*
budget (F)	Haushaltsplan *m*	budget	—	bilancio preventivo *m*	presupuesto *m*
budget (I)	Budget *n*	budget	budget *m*	—	presupuesto *m*
Budgetausgleich (D)	—	balancing of the budget	solde de budget *m*	equilibrio del bilancio pubblico *m*	balance del presupuesto *m*
budget credit (E)	Haushaltskredit *m*	—	crédit budgétaire *m*	credito di finanzia-mento bilancio *m*	crédito presupuestario *m*
Budgetierung (D)	—	drawing up of a budget	établissement du budget *m*	formazione del bilancio pubblico *f*	establecimiento del presupuesto *m*
budgeting (E)	Finanzplanung *f*	—	planification financière *f*	pianificazione finanziaria *f*	planificación financiera *f*
budget public (F)	öffentlicher Haushalt *m*	public budget	—	bilancio pubblico *m*	presupuesto público *m*
buena fe (Es)	guter Glauben *m*	good faith	bonne foi *f*	buona fede *f*	—
builder (E)	Bauträger *m*	—	promoteur constructeur *m*	costruttore *m*	promotor de construcción *m*

	D	E	F	I	Es
building financing (E)	Baufinanzierung f	—	financement à la construction m	finanziamento all'edilizia m	financiación de la construcción f
building loan (E)	Baudarlehen n	—	prêt à la construction m	mutuo edilizio m	crédito para la construcción m
building society (E)	Bausparkasse f	—	banque d'épargne-construction f	cassa di risparmio edilizio f	caja de ahorros para la construcción f
building society funding (E)	Bausparfinanzierung f	—	financement d'épargne-construction m	finanziamento edilizio m	financiación de ahorros para la construcción f
build-up account (E)	Aufbaukonto n	—	compte d'installation m	conto accumulativo m	cuenta de financiación de desarrollo f
bull (E)	Haussier m	—	haussier m	rialzista m	alcista m
bulletin de contrôle (F)	Kontrollmitteilung f	tracer note	—	communicazione di revisione f	control cruzado m
bulletin de gage (F)	Pfandschein m	certificate of pledge	—	atto di pegno m	resguardo de prenda m
bulletin de la bourse (F)	Börsenbericht m	stock exchange report	—	bollettino di borsa m	informe bursátil m
bulletin des cours (F)	Kurszettel f	stock exchange list	—	listino di borsa m	boletín de bolsa m
bulletin officiel de la cote (F)	Cote n	share list	—	cote m	Boletín de Bolsa m
Bullion (D)	—	bullion	lingot de métal précieux m	bullion m	lingote de metal fino m
bullion (E)	Bullion m	—	lingot de métal précieux m	bullion m	lingote de metal fino m
bullion (I)	Bullion m	bullion	lingot de métal précieux m	—	lingote de metal fino m
Bullionbroker (D)	—	bullion broker	courtier de métaux précieux m	bullionbroker m	corredor de metales finos m
bullionbroker (I)	Bullionbroker m	bullion broker	courtier de métaux précieux m	—	corredor de metales finos m
bullion broker (E)	Bullionbroker m	—	courtier de métaux précieux m	bullionbroker m	corredor de metales finos m
bullion trade (E)	Edelmetallgeschäft n	—	opérations de métaux précieux f/pl	operazione in metalli pregiati f	operaciones de metales preciosos f/pl
Bullish (D)	—	bullish	haussier m	bullish m	alcista
bullish (E)	Bullish n	—	haussier m	bullish m	alcista
bullish (I)	Bullish n	bullish	haussier m	—	alcista
bull market (E)	Hausse f	—	hausse f	contegno rialzistico m	alza f
Bundesanleihe (D)	—	Federal loan	titre de dette publique m	titolo di Stato m	empréstito de la Federación m
Bundesanleihe-konsortium (D)	—	Federal loan syndicate	syndicat fédéral d'emprunts m	consorzio emissione titoli pubblici m	consorcio de empréstitos federales m
bundesbankfähige Wertpapiere (D)	—	bills rediscountable at the Federal Bank	titres escomptables auprès de la Banque fédérale m/pl	titoli riscontabili presso la banca centrale m/pl	títulos redescontables en el Banco Federal m/pl
Bundesbank-guthaben (D)	—	Federal Bank assets	avoir auprès de la Banque fédérale m	fondo banca centrale m	saldo activo del Banco Federal m
Bundesbürgschaft (D)	—	Federal guarantee	garantie fédérale f	garanzia federale f	garantía federal f
Bundeskartellamt (D)	—	Federal Cartel Authority	administration fédérale pour la réglementation des cartels f	ufficio federale dei cartelli m	oficina federal de cártel f
Bundesobligation (D)	—	Federal bonds	obligation fédérale f	prestito pubblico m	obligación federal f
Bundesschuldbuch (D)	—	Federal Debt Register	grand-livre de la dette publique m	libro del debito pubblico m	registro de deudas federales m
buona fede (I)	guter Glauben m	good faith	bonne foi f	—	buena fe f
buoni del tesoro (I)	Schätze m/pl	treasury bonds	obligations du Trésor f/pl	—	bonos del tesoro m/pl
buoni del tesoro (I)	Finanzierungsschätze m/pl	financing bonds	effets du Trésor m/pl	—	letras del Tesoro f/pl
buoni del tesoro infruttiferi (I)	U-Schätze m/pl	non-interest bearing Treasury bond	obligations du Trésor ne produisant pas d'intérêts f/pl	—	letras del Tesoro sin interés f/pl

	D	E	F	I	Es
buono del tesoro (I)	Schatzanweisung f	treasury bond	bon du Trésor f	—	bono del tesoro m
buono del tesoro (I)	Schatzwechsel m	Treasury bill	effet du Trésor m	—	letra de tesorería f
buono di godimento (I)	Genußschein m	participating certificate	certificat de jouissance m	—	bono de disfrute m
buono di partecipazione (I)	Partizipationsschein m	participating receipt	récépissé de participation m	—	bono de participación m
buono d'opzione (I)	Bezugsschein m	subscription warrant	certificat de souscription m	—	boletín de suscripción m
buono frazionario (I)	Teilrechte n/pl	partial rights	droits partiels m/pl	—	derechos de partición m/pl
buono regalo di risparmio (I)	Spargeschenk-gutschein m	savings gift credit voucher	bon d'épargne m	—	vale de ahorro m
buoyant (E)	freundlich	—	ferme	favorevole	animado
bureau de change (F)	Wechselstube f	exchange office	—	ufficio cambi m	casa cambiaria f
bureau de chèques postaux (F)	Postscheckamt n	postal giro centre	—	ufficio conto correnti postali m	oficina de cheques postales f
bureau de liquidation (F)	Abrechnungsstelle f	clearing house	—	stanza di compensazione f	oficina de compensación f
bureau payeur (F)	Zahlstelle f	payments office	—	cassa di pagamento f	pagaduría f
Bürge (D)	—	guarantor	garant m	fidefaciente m	fiador m
Bürgschaft (D)	—	guarantee	caution f	fideiussione f	fianza f
Bürgschaftskredit (D)	—	credit by way of bank guarantee	crédit cautionné m	credito di fideiussione m	crédito de fianza m
Bürgschaftsplafond (D)	—	guarantee limit	plafond de garantie m	plafond di fideiussione m	límite de garantía m
business category costing (E)	Geschäftssparten-kalkulation f	—	calcul des coûts des catégories commerciales m	calcolo dei rami d'attività m	cálculos de costes de las categorías comerciales m/pl
business concentration (E)	Unternehmens-konzentration f	—	concentration d'entreprises f	concentrazione industriale f	concentración empresarial f
business cycle (E)	Konjunktur f	—	conjoncture f	congiuntura f	coyuntura f
business economics (E)	Betriebs-wirtschaftslehre f	—	gestion industrielle et commerciale f	scienza dell'economia aziendale f	teoría de la empresa f
business environment risk index (E)	BERI-Index m	—	indice BERI m	indice BERI m	índice BERI m
business income (E)	Erwerbseinkünfte pl	—	revenus d'une activité professionelle m/pl	redditi di lavoro m/pl	ingresos procedentes de una actividad remunerada m/pl
business in foreign countries (E)	Auslandsgeschäft n	—	opération avec l'étranger f	affare all'estero m	negocio de exportación m
business letter (E)	Handelsbrief m	—	lettre commerciale f	lettera commerciale f	carta comercial f
business over the counter (E)	Schaltergeschäft n	—	opération de guichet f	operazione a contanti f	operación al contado f
business report (E)	Geschäftsbericht m	—	rapport de gestion m	rapporto di gestione m	informe anual m
business risk (E)	Investitionsrisiko n	—	risque d'investissement m	rischio d'investimento m	riesgo de inversión m
business set-up loan (E)	Existenzaufbau-darlehen n	—	prêt de premier établissement m	mutuo inizio attività imprenditoriale m	préstamo de fundación m
buyer's market (E)	Käufermarkt m	—	marché d'acheteurs m	mercato degli acquisti m	mercado del comprador m
buying of shares to secure the controlling interest in a company (E)	Majoritätskäufe m/pl	—	achats majoritaires m/pl	acquisti di maggioranza m/pl	compras mayoritarias f/pl
buying or selling for customers (E)	Anschaffungs-geschäft n	—	opérations d'achat f/pl	operazione d'acquisto f	operaciones de compra f/pl
cadre comptable (F)	Kontenrahmen m	standard form of accounts	—	quadro dei conti m	sistema de cuentas m
caducidad (Es)	Kaduzierung f	forfeiture of shares	caducité f	decadenza del socio moroso f	—
caducité (F)	Kaduzierung f	forfeiture of shares	—	decadenza del socio moroso f	caducidad f

	D	E	F	I	Es
caída de cotización (Es)	Kursverwässerung f	price watering	baisse du cours par émission d'action gratuites f	annacquamento della quotazione m	—
caisse centrale (F)	Zentralkasse f	central credit institution	—	cassa centrale f	caja central f
caisse coopérative de crédit (F)	Kreditgenossenschaft f	credit cooperative	—	cooperativa di credito f	cooperativa de crédito f
caisse d'épargne (F)	Sparkasse f	savings bank	—	cassa di risparmio f	caja de ahorros f
caisse de retraite (F)	Pensionskasse f	staff pension fund	—	fondo di previdenza m	caja de jubilaciones f
caisse de valeurs mobilières (F)	Effektenkasse f	security department counter	—	cassa titoli f	caja de valores f
caja central (Es)	Zentralkasse f	central credit institution	caisse centrale f	cassa centrale f	—
caja de ahorros (Es)	Sparkasse f	savings bank	caisse d'épargne f	cassa di risparmio f	—
caja de ahorros para la construcción (Es)	Bausparkasse f	building society	banque d'épargne-construction f	cassa di risparmio edilizio f	—
caja de jubilaciones (Es)	Pensionskasse f	staff pension fund	caisse de retraite f	fondo di previdenza m	—
caja de transacción (Es)	Transaktionskasse f	transaction balance	solde des transactions m	domanda di moneta per transazioni f	—
caja de valores (Es)	Effektenkasse f	security department counter	caisse de valeurs mobilières f	cassa titoli f	—
caja fuerte (Es)	Tresor m	safe	coffre-fort m	cassaforte f	—
caja fuerte para certificados de bonos y acciones (Es)	Manteltresor m	bond and share certificate vault	coffre-fort de titres m	cassaforte dei mantelli f	—
caja nocturna (Es)	Nachttresor m	night safe	dépôt de nuit m	cassa continua f	—
cajero automático (Es)	Geldautomat m	cash dispenser	distribanque m	bancomat m	—
calcolare (I)	rechnen	calculate	calculer	—	calcular
calcolazione (I)	Kalkulation f	calculation	calcul m	—	calculación f
calcolo arbitrale (I)	Arbitragerechnung f	arbitrage voucher	calcul d'arbitrage m	—	nota arbitral f
calcolo bancario (I)	Bankkalkulation f	bank costing	calcul des coûts bancaires m	—	calculación bancaria f
calcolo capitalizzazione composta (I)	Zinseszinsrechnung f	calculation of compound interest	calcul des intérêts composés m	—	cálculo de interés compuesto m
calcolo dei conti (I)	Kontenkalkulation f	account costing	calcul des comptes m	—	calculación por cuentas f
calcolo dei costi (I)	Kostenrechnung f	statement of costs	compte de frais m	—	cálculo de costes m
calcolo dei rami d'attività (I)	Geschäftssparten-kalkulation f	business category costing	calcul des coûts des catégories commerciales m	—	cálculos de costes de las categorías comerciales m/pl
calcolo del fabbisogno di capitale (I)	Kapitalbedarfs-rechnung f	capital requirement calculation	calcul du besoin en capital m	—	cálculo de necesidad de capital m
calcolo del flusso di capitale (I)	Kapitalflußrechnung f	funds statement	tableau de financement m	—	tabla de financiación f
calcolo delle filiali (I)	Filialkalkulation f	branch office accounting	appréciation des résultats des succur-sales bancaires f	—	cálculos de sucursal m/pl
calcolo d'investimento (I)	Investitionsrechnung f	investment appraisal	calcul des investissements m	—	cálculo de inversiones m
calcolo di sconto (I)	Diskontrechnung f	discount calculation	calcul de l'escompte f	—	cálculo de descuento m
calcolo d'utilità di cliente (I)	Kundenkalkulation f	customer costing	calcul des résultats obtenus par chaque client m	—	calculación de participación por cliente f
calcolo margine d'interesse (I)	Gesamtzinsspannen-rechnung f	whole-bank interest margin calculation	calcul du total de la marge entre les taux d'intérêt créditeur et débiteur m	—	cálculo del margen de beneficio por intereses total m
calcolo rimborso e interessi (I)	Anleiherechnung f	loan calculation	décompte des emprunts m	—	cálculo de empréstito m
calcolo valutario (I)	Devisenrechnung f	foreign exchange calculation	calcul des changes m	—	cálculo de divisas m
calcul (F)	Kalkulation f	calculation	—	calcolazione f	calculación f

	D	E	F	I	Es
calculación (Es)	Kalkulation *f*	calculation	calcul *m*	calcolazione *f*	—
calculación bancaria (Es)	Bankkalkulation *f*	bank costing	calcul des coûts bancaires *m*	calcolo bancario *m*	—
calculación de participación por cliente (Es)	Kundenkalkulation *f*	customer costing	calcul des résultats obtenus par chaque client *m*	calcolo d'utilità di cliente *m*	—
calculación por cuentas (Es)	Kontenkalkulation *f*	account costing	calcul des comptes *m*	calcolo dei conti *m*	—
calcular (Es)	rechnen	calculate	calculer	calcolare	—
calculate (E)	rechnen	—	calculer	calcolare	calcular
calculation (E)	Kalkulation *f*	—	calcul *m*	calcolazione *f*	calculación *f*
calculation interest rate (E)	Kalkulationszinssatz *m*	—	taux d'intérêt de calcul *m*	tasso d'interesse desiderato minimo *m*	tipo de interés calculado *m*
calculation of compound interest (E)	Zinseszinsrechnung *f*	—	calcul des intérêts composés *m*	calcolo capitalizzazione composta *m*	cálculo de interés compuesto *m*
calculation of price of shares (E)	Effektenrechnung *f*	—	calcul du prix des titres *m*	conto titoli *m*	cálculo del precio de valores *m*
calcul d'arbitrage (F)	Arbitragerechnung *f*	arbitrage voucher	—	calcolo arbitrale *m*	nota arbitral *f*
calcul de l'escompte (F)	Diskontrechnung *f*	discount calculation	—	calcolo di sconto *m*	cálculo de descuento *m*
calcul des changes (F)	Devisenrechnung *f*	foreign exchange calculation	—	calcolo valutario *m*	cálculo de divisas *m*
calcul des comptes (F)	Kontenkalkulation *f*	account costing	—	calcolo dei conti *m*	calculación por cuentas *f*
calcul des coûts bancaires (F)	Bankkalkulation *f*	bank costing	—	calcolo bancario *m*	calculación bancaria *f*
calcul des coûts des catégories commerciales (F)	Geschäftssparten-kalkulation *f*	business category costing	—	calcolo dei rami d'attività *m*	cálculos de costes de las categorías comerciales *m/pl*
calcul des intérêts composés (F)	Zinseszinsrechnung *f*	calculation of compound interest	—	calcolo capitalizzazione composta *m*	cálculo de interés compuesto *m*
calcul des investissements (F)	Investitionsrechnung *f*	investment appraisal	—	calcolo d'investimento *m*	cálculo de inversiones *m*
calcul des résultats obtenus par chaque client (F)	Kundenkalkulation *f*	customer costing	—	calcolo d'utilità di cliente *m*	calculación de participación por cliente *f*
calcul du besoin en capital (F)	Kapitalbedarfs-rechnung *f*	capital requirement calculation	—	calcolo del fabbisogno di capitale *m*	cálculo de necesidad de capital *m*
calcul du prix des titres (F)	Effektenrechnung *f*	calculation of price of shares	—	conto titoli *m*	cálculo del precio de valores *m*
calcul du total de la marge entre les taux d'intérêt créditeur et débiteur (F)	Gesamtzinsspannen-rechnung *f*	whole-bank interest margin calculation	—	calcolo margine d'interesse *m*	cálculos del margen de beneficio por intereses total *m*
calculer (F)	rechnen	calculate	—	calcolare	calcular
cálculo de costes (Es)	Kostenrechnung *f*	statement of costs	compte de frais *m*	calcolo dei costi *m*	—
cálculo de descuento (Es)	Diskontrechnung *f*	discount calculation	calcul de l'escompte *m*	calcolo di sconto *m*	—
cálculo de divisas (Es)	Devisenrechnung *f*	foreign exchange calculation	calcul des changes *m*	calcolo valutario *m*	—
cálculo de empréstito (Es)	Anleiherechnung *f*	loan calculation	décompte des emprunts *m*	calcolo rimborso e interessi *m*	—
cálculo de interés compuesto (Es)	Zinseszinsrechnung *f*	calculation of compound interest	calcul des intérêts composés *m*	calcolo capitalizzazione composta *m*	—
cálculo de inversiones (Es)	Investitionsrechnung *f*	investment appraisal	calcul des investissements *m*	calcolo d'investimento *m*	—
cálculo del margen de beneficio por intereses total (Es)	Gesamtzinsspannen-rechnung *f*	whole-bank interest margin calculation	calcul du total de la marge entre les taux d'intérêt créditeur et débiteur *m*	calcolo margine d'interesse *m*	—
cálculo del precio de valores (Es)	Effektenrechnung *f*	calculation of price of shares	calcul du prix des titres *m*	conto titoli *m*	—
cálculo del valor neto (Es)	Vermögensrechnung *f*	capital account	compte de capital *m*	situazione patrimoniale *f*	—
cálculo de necesidad de capital (Es)	Kapitalbedarfs-rechnung *f*	capital requirement calculation	calcul du besoin en capital *m*	calcolo del fabbisognodi capitale *m*	—

	D	E	F	I	Es
cálculos de costes de las categorías comerciales (Es)	Geschäftssparten-kalkulation f	business category costing	calcul des coûts des catégories commerciales m	calcolo dei rami d'attività m	—
cálculos de sucursal (Es)	Filialkalkulation f	branch office accounting	appréciation des résultats des succursales bancaires f	calcolo delle filiali m	—
calendario de emisión (Es)	Emissionskalender m	issue calendar	calendrier d'émission m	calendario delle emissioni m	—
calendario delle emissioni (I)	Emissionskalender m	issue calendar	calendrier d'émission m	—	calendario de emisión m
calendrier d'émission (F)	Emissionskalender m	issue calendar	—	calendario delle emissioni m	calendario de emisión m
Call (D)	—	option to buy	call m	call m	call m
call (Es)	Call m	option to buy	call m	call m	—
call (F)	Call m	option to buy	—	call m	call m
call (I)	Call m	option to buy	call m	—	call m
callable forward transaction (E)	Wandelgeschäft n	—	marché à option m	contratto a termine con opzione di adempimento anticipato m	operación de opción f
Call-Geld (D)	—	call money	argent remboursable à vue m	prestito giornaliero m	dinero exigible a la vista m
Call-Geschäft (D)	—	call transaction	cotation par opposition f	operazione call f	operaciones call f/pl
call money (E)	Call-Geld n	—	argent remboursable à vue m	prestito giornaliero m	dinero exigible a la vista m
call option (E)	Kaufoption f	—	option d'achat f	opzione d'acquisto f	opción de compra f
call transaction (E)	Call-Geschäft n	—	cotation par opposition f	operazione call f	operaciones call f/pl
calme (F)	still	slack	—	fiacco	flojo
cámara de industria y comercio (Es)	Industrie- und Handelskammer f	Chamber of Industry and Commerce	chambre de commerce et d'industrie f	camera di commercio f	—
cambiale (I)	Wechsel m	bill of exchange	lettre de change f	—	letra f
cambiale a certo tempo data (I)	Datowechsel m	after-date bill	effet payable à un certain délai de date m	—	letra a tantos días fecha f
cambiale a certo tempo vista (I)	Nachsichtwechsel m	after-sight bill	traite à un certain délai de vue f	—	letra a tantos días vista f
cambiale all'incasso (I)	Inkassowechsel m	bill for collection	traite donnée au recouvrement f	—	letra al cobro f
cambiale a scadenza fissa (I)	Tageswechsel m	day bill	traite à jour fixe f	—	letra al día fijo f
cambiale attiva (I)	Besitzwechsel m	bills receivable	effet à recevoir m	—	efecto a cobrar m
cambiale a vista (I)	Sichtwechsel m	demand bill	traite à vue f	—	letra a la vista f
cambiale commerciale (I)	Warenwechsel m	commercial bill	traite commerciale f	—	letra comercial f
cambiale depositata in garanzia (I)	Depotwechsel m	bill on deposit	lettre de change déposée en garantie d'un prêt f		efecto cambial en depósito m
cambiale di pagamento rateale (I)	Ratenwechsel m	bill payable in instalments	effet à échéances multiples m	—	letra de vencimientos sucesivos f
cambiale di ritorno (I)	Rückwechsel m	unpaid bill of exchange	traite retournée f	—	letra de recambio f
cambiale finanziaria (I)	Finanzwechsel m	finance bill	traite financière f	—	letra bancaria f
cambiale fittizia (I)	Kellerwechsel m	fictitious bill	traite fictive f	—	letra de cambio ficticia f
cambiale in bianco (I)	Blanko-Wechsel m	blank bill	traite en blanc f	—	letra en blanco f
cambiale incrociata (I)	Reitwechsel m	windbill	traite de cavalerie f	—	letra cruzada f
cambiale in valuta estera (I)	Devisen-Wechsel m	bill in foreign currency	lettre de change libellée en monnaie étrangère f	—	letra en moneda extranjera f
cambiale marittima (I)	Seewechsel m	sea bill	lettre de prêt à la grosse f	—	letra de cambio marítima f

	D	E	F	I	Es
cambiale non all'ordine (I)	Rektawechsel *m*	non-negotiable bill of exchange	traite non à ordre *f*	—	letra nominativa *f*
cambiale pagabile sul posto (I)	Platzwechsel *m*	local bill	effet sans change de place *m*	—	letra de plaza *f*
cambiale passiva (I)	Schuldwechsel *m*	bill payable	effet à payer *m*	—	efecto a pagar *m*
cambiale passiva (I)	Wechselobligo *n*	customer's liability on bills	engagement par lettre de change *m*	—	obligación en letras de cambio *f*
cambiale pregiudicata (I)	präjudizierter Wechsel *m*	void bill	traite protestée hors des délais *f*	—	letra prejudicada *f*
cambiale protestata (I)	Protestwechsel *m*	protested bill	traite protestée *f*	—	letra protestada *f*
cambiale standardizzata (I)	Einheitswechsel *m*	standard bill	lettre de change normalisée *f*	—	letra de cambio estándar *f*
cambiale sull'estero (I)	Auslandswechsel *m*	foreign bill of exchange	traite tirée sur l'étranger *f*	—	letra sobre el exterior *f*
cambiale tratta (I)	gezogener Wechsel *m*	drawn bill	traite tirée *f*	—	letra girada *f*
cambiale tratta sul debitore (I)	Debitorenziehung *f*	bills drawn on debtors	traite tirée sur débiteur *f*	—	letra librada *f*
cambiale tratta su se stesso (I)	trassiert-eigener Wechsel *m*	bill drawn by the drawer himself	traite tirée sur soi-même *f*	—	letra girada a su propio cargo *f*
cambiale vuota (I)	Leerwechsel *m*	finance bill	traite financière *f*	—	letra al descubierto *f*
cambi a pronti (I)	Devisenkassa-geschäft *n*	foreign exchange spot dealings	opérations de change au comptant *f/pl*	—	operación de divisas al contado *f*
cambio (Es)	Devisenkurs *m*	foreign exchange rate	taux de change *m*	cambio *m*	—
cambio (I)	Tausch *m*	barter	troc *m*	—	trueque *m*
cambio (I)	Devisennotierung *f*	foreign exchange quotations	cotation des devises *f*	—	cotización de cambio *f*
cambio (I)	Devisenkurs *m*	foreign exchange rate	taux de change *m*	—	cambio *m*
cambio (I)	Wechselkurs *m*	exchange rate	cours du change *m*	—	tipo de cambio *m*
cambio a la par (Es)	Parikurs *m*	par price	cours au pair *m*	corso alla pari *m*	—
cambio a la vista (Es)	Sichtkurs *m*	sight rate	cours à vue *m*	cambio a vista *m*	—
cambio al contado (Es)	Kassakurs *m*	spot price	cours au comptant *m*	prezzo a pronti *m*	—
cambio a vista (I)	Sichtkurs *m*	sight rate	cours à vue *m*	—	cambio a la vista *m*
cambio certo per incerto (I)	Mengennotierung *f*	fixed exchange rate	cotation au certain *f*	—	cotización real *f*
cambio de acciones (Es)	Aktienumtausch *m*	exchange of share certificates for new ones	échange d'actions *m*	cambio di azioni *m*	—
cambio de adquisición por el banco emisor (Es)	Übernahmekurs *m*	underwriting price	cours de souscription d'un emprunt *m*	corso d'acquisto per il consorzio *m*	—
cambio de asientos en el pasivo (Es)	Passivtausch *m*	accounting exchange on the liabilities side	écritures entre postes de passif *f/pl*	rettifica del passivo *f*	—
cambio de compensación (Es)	Kompensationskurs *m*	making-up price	cours de compensation *m*	corso di compensazione *m*	—
cambio de divisas a término (Es)	Devisenterminkurs *m*	forward exchange rate	cours des devises négociées à terme *m*	quotazione dei cambi a termine *f*	—
cambio de estructura (Es)	Strukturwandel *m*	structural change	changement dans les structures *m*	adeguamento di struttura *m*	—
cambio de liquidación (Es)	Liquidationskurs *m*	making-up price	cours de liquidation *m*	corso di compensazione *m*	—
cambio di azioni (I)	Aktienumtausch *m*	exchange of share certificates for new ones	échange d'actions *m*	—	cambio de acciones *m*
cambio fisso (I)	starrer Wechselkurs *m*	fixed exchange rate	taux de change fixe *m*	—	tipo de cambio fijo *m*
cambio flessibile (I)	flexibler Wechselkurs *m*	flexible exchange rate	taux de change flottant *m*	—	cambio variable *m*
cambio libero (I)	freier Wechselkurs *m*	freely fluctuating exchange rate	taux de change libre *m*	—	tipo de cambio libre *m*
cambio limitado (Es)	Kurslimit *n*	price limit	cours limité *m*	limite di prezzo *m*	—
cambio manual (Es)	Geldwechsel-geschäft *n*	currency exchange business	opération de change *f*	operazione di cambio *f*	—

	D	E	F	I	Es
cambio medio (Es)	Durchschnittsvaluta *f*	average value date	datation moyenne de la valeur en compte *f*	valuta media *f*	—
cambio multiplo (I)	gespaltener Wechselkurs *m*	multiple exchange rates	cours du change multiple *m*	—	tipo de cambio múltiple *m*
cambio neto (Es)	Nettokurs *m*	net price	cours net *m*	quotazione netta *f*	
cambio valuta (I)	Devisenhandel *m*	foreign exchange dealings	marché des changes *m*	—	operaciones de divisas *f/pl*
cambio variable (Es)	flexibler Wechselkurs *m*	flexible exchange rate	taux de change flottant *m*	cambio flessibile *m*	—
cambista (Es)	Devisenhändler *m*	foreign exchange dealer	courtier en devises *m*	cambista *m*	—
cambista (I)	Devisenhändler *m*	foreign exchange dealer	courtier en devises *m*	—	cambista *m*
camera di commercio (I)	Industrie- und Handelskammer *f*	Chamber of Industry and Commerce	chambre de commerce et d'industrie *f*	—	cámara de industria y comercio *f*
campionamento (I)	Auswahlverfahren *n*	selection procedure	méthode de sélection *f*	—	procedimiento de selección *m*
cancelación (Es)	Storno *n*	counter entry	écriture de contre-passation *f*	storno *m*	—
cancelación (Es)	Löschung *f*	cancellation	annulation *f*	cancellazione *f*	—
cancellation (E)	Löschung *f*	—	annulation *f*	cancellazione *f*	cancelación *f*
cancellazione (I)	Löschung *f*	cancellation	annulation *f*	—	cancelación *f*
canje de acciones (Es)	Aktienaustausch *m*	exchange of shares	échange d'actions *f*	scambio di azioni *m*	—
canone (I)	Gebühr *f*	fee	taxe *f*	—	derechos *m/pl*
canone d'affitto (I)	Pachtzins *m*	rent	prix du bail *m*	—	arrendamiento *m*
canone di leasing (I)	Leasingrate *f*	leasing rate	taux de leasing *m*	—	tasa de leasing *f*
Cap (D)	—	cap	plafond d'intérêt *m*	cap *m*	techo de interés *m*
cap (E)	Cap *n*	—	plafond d'intérêt *m*	cap *m*	techo de interés *m*
cap (I)	Cap *n*	cap	plafond d'intérêt *m*	—	techo de interés *m*
capacidad de absorción del mercado (Es)	Aufnahmefähigkeit des Marktes *f*	absorptive capacity of the market	capacité d'absorption du marché *f*	assorbimento di mercato *m*	—
capacidad de girar cheques (Es)	Scheckfähigkeit *f*	capacity to draw cheques	habilité en matière de chèque *f*	capacità di obbligarsi per assegno *f*	—
capacidad de ser pignorable (Es)	Lombardfähigkeit *f*	acceptability as collateral	capacité d'être dé-posé à titre de gage *f*	idoneità di titoli all'anticipazione *f*	—
capacidad dispositiva (Es)	Verfügungsrecht *n*	right of disposal	droit de disposition *m*	diritto di disporre *m*	—
capacidad jurídica (Es)	Rechtsfähigkeit *f*	legal capacity	capacité de jouis-sance de droits *f*	capacità giuridica *f*	—
capacità di obbligarsi per assegno (I)	Scheckfähigkeit *f*	capacity to draw cheques	habilité en matière de chèque *f*	—	capacidad de girar cheques *f*
capacità finanziaria (I)	Finanzkraft *f*	financial strength	capacité financière *f*	—	potencial financiero *m*
capacità giuridica (I)	Rechtsfähigkeit *f*	legal capacity	capacité de jouis-sance de droits *f*	—	capacidad jurídica *f*
capacità giuridica limitata (I)	beschränkte Geschäftsfähigkeit *f*	limited capacity to enter into legal transactions	capacité restreinte d'accomplir des actes juridiques *f*	—	incapacidad jurídica parcial *f*
capacité d'absorption du marché (F)	Aufnahmefähigkeit des Marktes *f*	absorptive capacity of the market	—	assorbimento di mercato *m*	capacidad de absor-ción del mercado *f*
capacité de jouissance de droits (F)	Rechtsfähigkeit *f*	legal capacity	—	capacità giuridica *f*	capacidad jurídica *f*
capacité d'être déposé à titre de gage (F)	Lombardfähigkeit *f*	acceptability as collateral	—	idoneità di titoli all'anticipazione *f*	capacidad de ser pignorable *f*
capacité financière (F)	Finanzkraft *f*	financial strength	—	capacità finanziaria *f*	potencial financiero *m*
capacité restreinte d'accomplir des actes juridiques (F)	beschränkte Geschäftsfähigkeit *f*	limited capacity to enter into legal transactions	—	capacità giuridica limitata *f*	incapacidad jurídica parcial *f*
capacity to draw cheques (E)	Scheckfähigkeit *f*	—	habilité en matière de chèque *f*	capacità di obbligarsi per assegno *f*	capacidad de girar cheques *f*
capitación (Es)	Kopfsteuer *f*	per capita tax	impôt personnel *m*	capitazione *f*	

	D	E	F	I	Es
capital (E)	Kapital *n*	—	capital *m*	capitale *m*	capital *m*
capital (Es)	Kapital *n*	capital	capital *m*	capitale *m*	—
capital (F)	Kapitalvermögen *n*	capital assets	—	impieghi di capitale *m/pl*	bienes patrimoniales *m/pl*
capital (F)	Kapital *n*	capital	—	capitale *m*	capital *m*
capital account (E)	Kapitalkonto *n*	—	compte de capital *m*	conto capitale *m*	cuenta de capital *f*
capital account (E)	Vermögensrechnung *f*	—	compte de capital *m*	situazione patrimoniale *f*	cálculo del valor neto *m*
capital aid (E)	Kapitalhilfe *f*	—	aide financière *f*	aiuto finanziario *m*	ayuda financiera *f*
capital ajeno (Es)	Fremdkapital *n*	debt capital	capital de tiers *m*	capitale di credito *m*	—
capital analysis (E)	Kapitalanalyse *f*	—	analyse de capital *f*	analisi del capitale *f*	análisis de capital *m*
capital-apport (F)	Dotationskapital *n*	endowment funds	—	capitale di dotazione *m*	capital de dotación *m*
capital assets (E)	Kapitalvermögen *n*	—	capital *m*	impieghi di capitale *m/pl*	bienes patrimoniales *m/pl*
capital autorisé (F)	genehmigtes Kapital *n*	authorized capital	—	capitale approvato *m*	capital concedido *m*
capital autorisé (F)	autorisiertes Kapital *n*	authorized capital	—	capitale autorizzato *m*	capital autorizado *m*
capital autorizado (Es)	autorisiertes Kapital *n*	authorized capital	capital autorisé *m*	capitale autorizzato *m*	—
capital bancaire (F)	Bankkapital *n*	bank stock	—	capitale bancario *m*	capital bancario *m*
capital bancario (Es)	Bankkapital *n*	bank stock	capital bancaire *m*	capitale bancario *m*	—
capital bénéficiaire (F)	Genußrechtskapital *n*	participating rights capital	—	capitale da buoni di godimento *m*	capital de bono de disfrute *m*
capital circulante (Es)	Umlaufvermögen *n*	current assets	capital de roulement *m*	circolante *m*	—
capital concedido (Es)	genehmigtes Kapital *n*	authorized capital	capital autorisé *m*	capitale approvato *m*	—
capital constituant le fonds (F)	Fondsvermögen *n*	fund assets	—	patrimonio del fondo *m*	activo en fondos públicos *m*
capital de bono de disfrute (Es)	Genußrechtskapital *n*	participating rights capital	capital bénéficiaire *m*	capitale da buoni di godimento *m*	—
capital déclaré dans le pays où l'assujetti à sa résidence (F)	Inlandsvermögen *n*	domestic capital	—	capitale nazionale *m*	patrimonio interno *m*
capital de cobertura (Es)	Deckungskapital *n*	capital sum required as cover	capital de couverture *m*	capitale di copertura *m*	—
capital de couverture (F)	Deckungskapital *n*	capital sum required as cover	—	capitale di copertura *m*	capital de cobertura *m*
capital de dotación (Es)	Dotationskapital *n*	endowment funds	capital-apport *m*	capitale di dotazione *m*	—
capital de garantía (Es)	Garantiekapital *n*	capital serving as a guarantee	capital de garantie *m*	capitale di garanzia *m*	—
capital de garantie (F)	Garantiekapital *n*	capital serving as a guarantee	—	capitale di garanzia *m*	capital de garantía *m*
capital de inversión (Es)	Anlagekapital *n*	investment capital	capital d'investissement *m*	capitale d'investimento *m*	—
capital de riesgo (Es)	Venture Kapital *n*	venture capital	capital de risque *m*	capitale di rischio *m*	—
capital de risque (F)	Venture Kapital *n*	venture capital	—	capitale di rischio *m*	capital de riesgo *m*
capital de roulement (F)	Umlaufvermögen *n*	current assets	—	circolante *m*	capital circulante *m*
capital de tiers (F)	Leihkapital *n*	debt capital	—	capitale di prestito *m*	capital prestado *m*
capital de tiers (F)	Fremdkapital *n*	debt capital	—	capitale di credito *m*	capital ajeno *m*
capital d'exploitation (F)	Betriebsvermögen *n*	operating assets	—	capitale d'esercizio *m*	patrimonio empresarial *m*
capital d'investissement (F)	Anlagekapital *n*	investment capital	—	capitale d'investimento *m*	capital de inversión *m*
capitale (I)	Kapital *n*	capital	capital *m*	—	capital *m*
capitale addizionale (I)	Zusatzkapital *n*	additional capital	capital supplémentaire *m*	—	capital suplementario *m*
capitale approvato (I)	genehmigtes Kapital *n*	authorized capital	capital autorisé *m*	—	capital concedido *m*
capitale autorizzato (I)	autorisiertes Kapital *n*	authorized capital	capital autorisé *m*	—	capital autorizado *m*
capitale azionario (I)	Aktienkapital *n*	share capital	fonds social *m*	—	capital en acciones *m*
capitale bancario (I)	Bankkapital *n*	bank stock	capital bancaire *m*	—	capital bancario *m*

	D	E	F	I	Es
capitale da buoni di godimento (I)	Genußrechtskapital n	participating rights capital	capital bénéficiaire m	—	capital de bono de disfrute m
capitale da soci di una cooperativa (I)	Geschäftsguthaben n	proprietor's capital holding	avoir commercial m	—	saldo activo de la empresa m
capitale del minore (I)	Mündelgeld n	money held in trust for a ward	deniers de pupille m/pl	—	dinero pupilar m
capitale d'esercizio (I)	Betriebsvermögen n	operating assets	capital d'exploitation m	—	patrimonio empresarial m
capitale di copertura (I)	Deckungskapital n	capital sum required as cover	capital de couverture m	—	capital de cobertura m
capitale di credito (I)	Fremdkapital n	debt capital	capital de tiers m	—	capital ajeno m
capitale di dotazione (I)	Dotationskapital n	endowment funds	capital-apport m	—	capital de dotación m
capitale di garanzia (I)	Garantiekapital n	capital serving as a guarantee	capital de garantie m	—	capital de garantía m
capitale d'investimento (I)	Anlagekapital n	investment capital	capital d'investissement m	—	capital de inversión m
capitale di prestito (I)	Leihkapital n	debt capital	capital de tiers m	—	capital prestado m
capitale di rischio (I)	Venture Kapital n	venture capital	capital de risque m	—	capital de riesgo m
capitale estero (I)	Auslandskapital n	foreign capital	capital étranger m	—	capital extranjero m
capitale finanziario (I)	Finanzkapital n	financial capital	capital financier m	—	capital financiero m
capitale immobilizzato netto (I)	Netto-Anlagevermögen n	net fixed assets	capital fixe net m	—	activo fijo neto m
capitale investito (I)	investiertes Kapital n	invested capital	capital investi m	—	capital invertido m
capitale liquido (I)	Barvermögen n	cash assets	valeurs réalisables à court terme ou disponibles f/pl	—	activo efectivo m
capitale minimo (I)	Mindestkapital n	minimum capital	capital minimum m	—	capital mínimo m
capitale monetario (I)	Geldkapital n	monetary capital	capital monétaire m	—	capital monetario m
capital en acciones (Es)	Aktienkapital n	share capital	fonds social m	capitale azionario m	—
capitale nazionale (I)	Inlandsvermögen n	domestic capital	capital déclaré dans le pays où l'assujetti à sa résidence m	—	patrimonio interno m
capital encouragement treaty (E)	Kapitalförderungsvertrag m	—	accord sur l'encouragement de la formation de capital m	accordo sulla formazione di capitale m	contrato de fomento de capital m
capitale nominale (I)	Nominalkapital n	nominal capital	capital nominal m	—	fondo capital m
capitale nominale (I)	gezeichnetes Kapital n	subscribed capital	capital souscrit m	—	capital suscrito m
capitale proprio (I)	Eigenkapital n	one's own capital	capital propre m	—	capital propio m
capitale proprio nominale (I)	nominelles Eigenkapital n	nominal capital borrowed	capital propre nominal m	—	capital propio nominal m
capitale reale (I)	Sachkapital n	real capital	immobilisations corporelles f/pl	—	capital real m
capitale sociale (I)	Stammkapital n	share capital	capital social m	—	capital social m
capital étranger (F)	Auslandskapital n	foreign capital	—	capitale estero m	capital extranjero m
capital extranjero (Es)	Auslandskapital n	foreign capital	capital étranger m	capitale estero m	—
capital financier (F)	Finanzkapital n	financial capital	—	capitale finanziario m	capital financiero m
capital financiero (Es)	Finanzkapital n	financial capital	capital financier m	capitale finanziario m	—
capital fixe net (F)	Netto-Anlagevermögen n	net fixed assets	—	capitale immobilizzato netto m	activo fijo neto m
capital flow (E)	Kapitalfluß m	—	fluidité des capitaux f	flusso dei fondi m	flujo de capital m
capital formation (E)	Vermögensbildung f	—	formation de capital f	formazione del patrimonio f	formación de capital f
capital forming payment (E)	vermögenswirksame Leistungen f/pl	—	prestations primées f/pl	prestazioni con effetti patrimoniali f/pl	prestaciones que fomentan la formación de capital f/pl
capital increase through contribution in kind (E)	Sachkapitalerhöhung f	—	augmentation du capital par élargissement des immobilisations corporelles f	aumento del capitale reale m	aumento del capital real m
capital invertido (Es)	investiertes Kapital n	invested capital	capital investi m	capitale investito m	—

	D	E	F	I	Es
capital investi (F)	investiertes Kapital *n*	invested capital	—	capitale investito *m*	capital invertido *m*
capital investment (E)	Kapitalanlage *f*	—	investissement de capitaux *m*	impiego di capitale *m*	inversión de capital *f*
capital investment company (E)	Kapitalanlage-gesellschaft *f*	—	société d'investissement *f*	società d'investimento *f*	compañía de inversiones *f*
Capital Investment Law (E)	Kapitalanlagegesetz *n*	—	loi sur les investisse-ment de capital *f*	legge sugli investi-menti di capitale *f*	ley sobre la inversión de capital *f*
capitali ripartiti (I)	Streubesitz *m*	diversified holdings	propriété disséminée *f*	—	propiedad dispersa *f*
capitalisation (F)	Kapitalisierung *f*	capitalization	—	capitalizzazione *f*	capitalización *f*
capitalisme de valeurs mobilières (F)	Effektenkapitalismus *m*	securities capitalism	—	capitalismo (basato su) titoli *m*	capitalismo por títulos-valores *m*
capitalismo (basato su) titoli (I)	Effektenkapitalismus *m*	securities capitalism	capitalisme de valeurs mobilières *m*	—	capitalismo por títulos-valores *m*
capitalismo por títulos-valores (Es)	Effektenkapitalismus *m*	securities capitalism	capitalisme de valeurs mobilières *m*	capitalismo (basato su) titoli *m*	—
capitalización (Es)	Kapitalisierung *f*	capitalization	capitalisation *f*	capitalizzazione *f*	—
capitalization (E)	Kapitalisierung *f*	—	capitalisation *f*	capitalizzazione *f*	capitalización *f*
capitalized value (E)	Ertragswert *m*	—	valeur d'une chose mesurée à son rendement *f*	valore del reddito *m*	valor de la renta *m*
capitalizzazione (I)	Kapitalisierung *f*	capitalization	capitalisation *f*	—	capitalización *f*
capitalizzazione (I)	Aufzinsung *f*	addition of accrued interest	addition des intérêts accumulés *f*	—	adición de los inter-eses acumulados *f*
capital majority (E)	Kapitalmehrheit *f*	—	majorité de capital *f*	maggioranza del capitale *f*	mayoría de capital *f*
capital market (E)	Kapitalmarkt *m*	—	marché des capitaux *m*	mercato finanziario *m*	mercado de capitales *m*
capital market committee (E)	Kapitalmarkt-kommission *f*	—	commission du marché des capitaux *f*	commissione mercato finanziario *f*	comité de mercado de capital *m*
capital market efficiency (E)	Kapitalmarkteffizienz *f*	—	efficience du marché des capitaux *f*	efficienza del mercato finanziario *f*	eficiencia del mercado de capitales *f*
Capital Market Encouragement Law (E)	Kapitalmarkt-förderungsgesetz *n*	—	loi sur la stimulation du marché des capitaux *f*	legge sulla promo-zione del mercato finanziario *f*	ley sobre el fomento del mercado de capital
capital market interest rate (E)	Kapitalmarktzins *m*	—	intérêt pratiqué sur le marché des capitaux *m*	tasso d'interesse del mercato finanziario *m*	interés pagado en el mercado de capital *m*
capital market research (E)	Kapitalmarkt-forschung *f*	—	étude du marché des capitaux *f*	ricerca del mercato finanziario *f*	investigación del mercado de capital *f*
capital mínimo (Es)	Mindestkapital *n*	minimum capital	capital minimum *m*	capitale minimo *m*	—
capital minimum (F)	Mindestkapital *n*	minimum capital	—	capitale minimo *m*	capital mínimo *m*
capital monétaire (F)	Geldkapital *n*	monetary capital	—	capitale monetario *m*	capital monetario *m*
capital monetario (Es)	Geldkapital *n*	monetary capital	capital monétaire *m*	capitale monetario *m*	—
capital movements (E)	Kapitalbewegungen *f/pl*	—	mouvements de capital *m/pl*	movimento di capitali *m*	movimientos de capital *m/pl*
capital nominal (F)	Nominalkapital *n*	nominal capital	—	capitale nominale *m*	fondo capital *m*
capital outflows (E)	Kapitalabfluß *m*	—	sortie de capital *f*	deflusso di capitale *m*	salida de capital *f*
capital prestado (Es)	Leihkapital *n*	debt capital	capital de tiers *m*	capitale di prestito *m*	—
capital productivity (E)	Kapitalproduktivität *f*	—	productivité du capital *f*	produttività del capitale *f*	productividad del capital *f*
capital propio (Es)	Eigenkapital *n*	one's own capital	capital propre *m*	capitale proprio *m*	—
capital propio nominal (Es)	nominelles Eigenkapital *n*	nominal capital borrowed	capital propre nominal *m*	capitale proprio nominale *m*	—
capital propio respondiente (Es)	haftendes Eigenkapital *n*	liable funds	capital propre de garantie *m*	patrimonio netto *m*	—
capital propre (F)	Eigenkapital *n*	one's own capital	—	capitale proprio *m*	capital propio *m*
capital propre de garantie (F)	haftendes Eigenkapital *n*	liable funds	—	patrimonio netto *m*	capital propio respondiente *f*
capital propre nominal (F)	nominelles Eigenkapital *n*	nominal capital borrowed	—	capitale proprio nominale *m*	capital propio nominal *m*
capital protection (E)	Kapitalschutz *m*	—	protection de capital *f*	tutela dei capitali *m*	protección del capital *f*

	D	E	F	I	Es
capital protection agreement (E)	Kapitalschutzvertrag *m*	—	accord sur la protection de capital *m*	accordo di tutela degli investimenti *m*	contrato de protección del capital *m*
capital real (Es)	Sachkapital *n*	real capital	immobilisations corporelles *f/pl*	capitale reale *m*	—
capital reduction (E)	Kapitalherabsetzung *f*	—	diminution du capital *f*	riduzione del capitale sociale *f*	reducción de capital *f*
capital requirement (E)	Kapitalbedarf *m*	—	besoin en capital *m*	fabbisogno di capitale *m*	necesidad de capital *f*
capital requirement calculation (E)	Kapitalbedarfsrechnung *f*	—	calcul du besoin en capital *m*	calcolo del fabbisogno di capitale *m*	cálculo de necesidad de capital *m*
capital serving as a guarantee (E)	Garantiekapital *n*	—	capital de garantie *m*	capitale di garanzia *m*	capital de garantía *m*
capital social (Es)	Stammkapital *n*	share capital	capital social *m*	capitale sociale *m*	—
capital social (F)	Stammkapital *n*	share capital	—	capitale sociale *m*	capital social *m*
capital social occulte (F)	verdecktes Stammkapital *n*	quasi-equity capital	—	conferimento di un socio *m*	capital social oculto *m*
capital social oculto (Es)	verdecktes Stammkapital *n*	quasi-equity capital	capital social occulte *m*	conferimento di un socio *m*	—
capital souscrit (F)	gezeichnetes Kapital *n*	subscribed capital	—	capitale nominale *m*	capital suscrito *m*
capital sum required as cover (E)	Deckungskapital *n*	—	capital de couverture *m*	capitale di copertura *m*	capital de cobertura *m*
capital suplementario (Es)	Zusatzkapital *n*	additional capital	capital supplémentaire *m*	capitale addizionale *m*	—
capital supplémentaire (F)	Zusatzkapital *n*	additional capital	—	capitale addizionale *m*	capital suplementario *m*
capital susorito (Es)	gezeichnetes Kapital *n*	subscribed capital	capital souscrit *m*	capitale nominale *m*	—
capital tie-up (E)	Kapitalbindung *f*	—	immobilisation de capitaux *f*	vincolamento di capitale *m*	vinculación de capital *f*
capital transaction tax (E)	Kapitalverkehrssteuer *f*	—	taxe sur les mutations du capital *f*	imposta sulla circolazione dei capitali *f*	impuesto sobre transacciones *m*
capitaux de tiers (F)	fremde Gelder *n/pl*	external funds	—	fondi di terzi *m/pl*	fondos ajenos *m/pl*
capitaux fébriles (F)	heißes Geld *n*	hot money	—	hot money *m*	dinero caliente *m*
capitaux liquides (F)	flüssige Mittel *n/pl*	liquid assets	—	fondi liquidi *m/pl*	fondos líquidos *m/pl*
capitaux prêtés (F)	fremde Mittel *n/pl*	borrowed funds	—	denaro da terzi *m*	fondos de terceros *m/pl*
capitazione (I)	Kopfsteuer *f*	per capital tax	impôt personnel *m*	—	capitación *f*
Capped Warrants (D)	—	capped warrants	options frappées d'une saisie-arrêt *f/pl*	capped warrants *m/pl*	talón de opción combinado *m*
capped warrants (E)	Capped Warrants *m/pl*	—	options frappées d'une saisie-arrêt *f/pl*	capped warrants *m/pl*	talón de opción combinado *m*
capped warrants (I)	Capped Warrants *m/pl*	capped warrants	options frappées d'une saisie-arrêt *f/pl*		talón de opción combinado *m*
cap rate of interest (E)	Zinskappe *f*	—	plafond de l'intérêt *m*	tetto interessi *m*	plafón de interés *m*
cap rate of interest agreement (E)	Zinskappenvereinbahrung *f*	—	accord d'un plafond d'intérêt *m*	accordo sul tetto interessi *m*	acuerdo de un plafón de interés *m*
caractères de l'or (F)	Goldeigenschaften *f/pl*	gold characteristics	—	caratteristiche dell'oro *f/pl*	características del oro *m/pl*
características de financiación interna (Es)	Innenfinanzierungskennzahl *f*	self-generated financing ratio	ratio de financement interne *m*	codice di finanziamento interno *m*	—
características del oro (Es)	Goldeigenschaften *f/pl*	gold characteristics	caractères de l'or *m/pl*	caratteristiche dell'oro *f/pl*	—
caratteristiche dell'oro (I)	Goldeigenschaften *f/pl*	gold characteristics	caractères de l'or *m/pl*	—	características del oro *m/pl*
cargo en cuenta (Es)	Lastschrift *f*	debit entry	note de débit *f*	addebitamento *m*	—
carnet des négociations (F)	Maklerbuch *n*	dealings book of the stockbroker	—	libro giornale dell'agente di cambio *m*	libro de corredores *m*
carrera de desvalorización (Es)	Abwertungswettlauf *m*	devaluation race	course de dévaluation *f*	corsa alla svalutazione *f*	—
carry-forward of the losses (E)	Verlustvortrag *m*	—	report des pertes *m*	riporto delle perdite *m*	traslación de pérdidas *f*
carta blanca (Es)	Blankett *n*	blank form	imprimé en blanc *m*	foglio in bianco *m*	—
carta comercial (Es)	Handelsbrief *m*	business letter	lettre commerciale *f*	lettera commerciale *f*	—

cash letter of credit

	D	E	F	I	Es
carta commerciale di prim'ordine (I)	Privatdiskont *m*	prime acceptance	escompte hors banque *m*	—	descuento privado *m*
carta confirmadora (Es)	Bestätigungs- schreiben *n*	letter of confirmation	lettre de confirmation *f*	lettera di conferma *f*	—
carta de crédito (Es)	Kreditbrief *m*	letter of credit	lettre de crédit *f*	lettera di credito *f*	—
carta de crédito viajero (Es)	Reisekreditbrief *m*	traveller's letter of credit	lettre de crédit circulaire *f*	titolo di credito turistico *m*	—
carta di credito (I)	Kreditkarte *f*	credit card	carte de crédit *f*	—	tarjeta de crédito *f*
carta eurocheque (I)	Eurocheck-Karte *f*	Eurocheque card	carte d'identité eurochèque *f*	—	tarjeta eurocheque *f*
carta hipotecaria (Es)	Hypothekenbrief *m*	mortgage deed	cédule hypothécaire *f*	titolo ipotecario *m*	—
carta intestata (I)	Geschäftspapier *n*	commercial papers	papier d'affaires *m*	—	documento comercial *m*
carte commerciali di prim'ordine (I)	Primapapiere *n/pl*	prime papers	effets de tout premier ordre *m/pl*	—	valores de primera clase *m/pl*
carte de crédit (F)	Kreditkarte *f*	credit card	—	carta di credito *f*	tarjeta de crédito *f*
carte de débit (F)	Lastschriftkarte *f*	debit card	—	avviso di addebito *m*	nota de cargo *f*
carte d'identité eurochèque (F)	Eurocheck-Karte *f*	Eurocheque card	—	carta eurocheque *f*	tarjeta eurocheque *f*
cartel de contingentement (F)	Quotenkartell *f*	commodity restriction scheme	—	cartello di contingentamento *m*	cartel de contingentes *m*
cartel de contingentes (Es)	Quotenkartell *f*	commodity restriction scheme	cartel de contingentement *m*	cartello di contingentamento *m*	—
cartella debito pubblico collettiva (I)	Sammelschuldbuch- forderung *f*	collective debt register claim	créance collective inscrite dans le livre de la dette *f*	—	crédito contabilizado colectivo *m*
cartella del debito pubblico (I)	Schuldbuch- forderung *f*	debt-register claim	créance inscrite dans le livre de la dette *f*	—	deuda inscrita en el libro de deudas *f*
cartella di credito (I)	Kreditakte *f*	credit folder	dossier de crédit *m*	—	expediente de crédito *m*
cartello di contingentamento (I)	Quotenkartell *f*	commodity restriction scheme	cartel de contingentement *m*	—	cartel de contingentes *m*
cartera (Es)	Portfolio *n*	portfolio	portefeuille *m*	portafoglio *m*	—
cartera inmobiliaria (Es)	Immobilienfonds *m*	real estate fund	fonds immobilier *m*	fondo di titoli immobiliari *m*	—
casa cambiaria (Es)	Wechselstube *f*	exchange office	bureau de change *m*	ufficio cambi *m*	—
casa de aceptación (Es)	Diskonthäuser *n/pl*	discount houses	établissements d'escompte *m/pl*	discount houses *m/pl*	—
casa emisora (Es)	Emissionshaus *n*	issuing house	établissement d'émission *m*	banca emittente *f*	—
casa ficticia (Es)	Scheinfirma *f*	bogus firm	raison sociale imaginaire *f*	impresa fittizia *f*	—
cash (E)	bar	—	comptant	in contanti	al contado
cash accountancy (E)	Kassenhaltung *f*	—	tenue de la caisse *f*	tenuta di cassa *f*	contabilidad de caja *f*
cash assets (E)	Barvermögen *n*	—	valeurs réalisables à court terme ou disponibles *f/pl*	capitale liquido *m*	activo efectivo *m*
cash cover (E)	Bardeckung *f*	—	couverture en espèces *f*	copertura in contanti *f*	cobertura en efectivo *f*
cash credit (E)	Barkredit *m*	—	crédit de caisse *m*	credito in contanti *m*	crédito en efectivo *m*
cash credit (E)	Kassenkredite *m/pl*	—	crédit à court terme *m*	crediti di cassa *m/pl*	créditos a corto plazo *m/pl*
cash deposit (E)	Bareinlage *f*	—	dépôt en numéraire *m*	apporto in denaro *m*	depósito en efectivo *m*
cash dispenser (E)	Geldautomat *m*	—	distribanque *m*	bancomat *m*	cajero automático *m*
cash dividend (E)	Bardividende *f*	—	dividende payé en espèces *m*	dividendo in contanti *m*	dividendo en efectivo *m*
cash in hand (E)	Kassenbestand *m*	—	montant des espèces en caisse *m*	consistenza di cassa *f*	dinero en caja *m*
cash lending (E)	Kassenverstärkungs- kredit *m*	—	crédit pour augmenter la liquidité *m*	credito per elasticità di cassa *m*	crédito con fines de aumentar la liquidez *m*
cash letter of credit (E)	Bar-Akkreditiv *m*	—	accréditif payable en espèce *m*	apertura di credito per cassa *f*	crédito simple *m*

	D	E	F	I	Es
cash loss payment (E)	Bareinschuß m	—	payement en espèces m	versamento in contanti m	reserva en efectivo m
cash payment (E)	Barzahlung f	—	payement comptant m	pagamento in contanti m	pago al contado m
cash purchase (E)	Barkauf m	—	achat au comptant m	acquisto in contanti m	compra en efectivo f
cash sale (E)	Barverkauf m	—	vente au comptant f	vendita a contanti f	venta al contado f
cash transactions (E)	Kassageschäft n	—	opération au comptant f	operazione a pronti f	operaciones al contado f/pl
cash transactions (E)	Bargeschäft n	—	marché au comptant m	affare in contanti m	operación al contado f
cassa cedolare (I)	Kuponkasse f	coupon collection department	service de payement des coupons m	—	sección de cobro por cupones f
cassa centrale (I)	Zentralkasse f	central credit institution	caisse centrale f	—	caja central f
cassa continua (I)	Spätschalter m	night safe deposit	guichet extérieur de permanence m	—	taquilla de noche f
cassa continua (I)	Nachttresor m	night safe	dépôt de nuit m	—	caja nocturna f
cassa di pagamento (I)	Zahlstelle f	payments office	bureau payeur m	—	pagaduría f
cassa di risparmio (I)	Sparkasse f	savings bank	caisse d'épargne f	—	caja de ahorros f
cassa di risparmio edilizio (I)	Bausparkasse f	building society	banque d'épargne-construction f	—	caja de ahorros para la construcción f
cassaforte (I)	Tresor m	safe	coffre-fort m	—	caja fuerte f
cassaforte dei mantelli (I)	Manteltresor m	bond and share certificate vault	coffre-fort de titres m	—	caja fuerte para certificados de bonos y acciones f
cassa titoli (I)	Effektenkasse f	security department counter	caisse de valeurs mobilières f	—	caja de valores f
catasto (I)	Grundbuch n	register of land titles	livre foncier m	—	registro de la propiedad m
catégories de patrimoine (F)	Vermögensarten f/pl	types of property	—	tipi di patrimonio m/pl	clases de patrimonio f/pl
caution (F)	Kaution f	security	—	cauzione f	fianza f
caution (F)	Bürgschaft f	guarantee	—	fideiussione f	fianza f
cautionary land charge (E)	Sicherungs-grundschuld f	—	dette foncière de garantie f	debito fondiario di garanzia m	deuda inmobiliaria de seguridad f
cautionary mortgage (E)	Sicherungshypothek f	—	hypothèque constituée dans le but de garantir une créance f	ipoteca di garanzia f	hipoteca de seguridad f
cauzione (I)	Kaution f	security	caution f	—	fianza f
cauzioni d'esportazione (I)	Ausfuhrbürgschaften f/pl	export credit guarantee	garanties à l'exportation f/pl	—	garantías para la exportación f/pl
cedola (I)	Gewinnanteilsschein m	dividend coupon	coupon de dividende m	—	cupón m
cedola d'interessi (I)	Zinsschein m	coupon	coupon d'intérêts m	—	cupón de intereses m
cedola di riaffogliamento (I)	Stichkupon m	renewal coupon	coupon de renouvellement m	—	cupón de renovación m
cedola di riaffoglimento (I)	Erneuerungsschein m	talon for renewal of coupon sheet	talon de recouponnement m	—	talón de renovación m
cedola di un titolo estero (I)	Valutakupon m	foreign currency coupon	coupon payable en monnaie étrangère m	—	cupón de divisas m
cedolario (I)	Kuponbogen m	coupon sheet	feuille de coupons f	—	hoja de cupones f
cedole azionarie (I)	Anteilspapiere n/pl	equity security	titres de participation m/pl	—	títulos de participación m/pl
cedole di titoli esteri (I)	Valuten f/pl	foreign exchange	coupons de titres étrangers m/pl	—	moneda extranjera f
cédula de ahorro (Es)	Sparbrief m	savings certificate	bon d'épargne m	lettera di risparmio f	—
cédula de deuda inmobiliaria (Es)	Grundschuldbrief m	land charge certificate	cédule foncière f	certificato di debito fondiario m	—
cédula hipotecaria (Es)	Pfandbrief m	mortgage bond	obligation hypothécaire f	obbligazione fondiaria f	—
cédula hipotecaria agrícola (Es)	Landwirtschaftsbrief m	agricultural mortgage bond	cédule hypothécaire agricole f	obbligazione di una banca agrícola f	—

	D	E	F	I	Es
cédula hipotecaria con fines sociales (Es)	Sozialpfandbrief n	mortgage bond serving a social purpose	obligation hypothécaire pour financer des projets sociaux f	obbligazione ipotecaria edilizia sociale f	—
cédulas hipotecarias de mobilización (Es)	Mobilisierungs-pfandbriefe m/pl	mobilization mortgage bond	obligations hypothécaires de mobilisation f/pl	obbligazioni fondiarie di smobilizzo f/pl	—
cédule foncière (F)	Grundschuldbrief m	land charge certificate	—	certificato di debito fondiario m	cédula de deuda inmobiliaria f
cédule hypothécaire (F)	Hypothekenbrief m	mortgage deed	—	titolo ipotecario m	carta hipotecaria f
cédule hypothécaire agricole (F)	Landwirtschaftsbrief m	agricultural mortgage bond	—	obbligazione di una banca agricola f	cédula hipotecaria agrícola f
ceiling (E)	Plafond m	—	plafond m	plafond m	límite máximo m
censura de cuentas del banco (Es)	Bankrevision f	bank audit	contrôle du bilan d'une banque m	ispezione bancaria f	—
central (Es)	Zentrale f	head office	centrale f	centrale f	—
central bank (E)	Zentralbank f	—	banque centrale f	banca centrale f	banco central m
central bank (E)	Notenbank f	—	banque d'émission f	banca d'emissione f	banco emisor m
Central Bank Council (E)	Zentralbankrat m	—	Conseil de la banque centrale m	consiglio centrale banca centrale m	Consejo del Banco Central m
central bank money (E)	Zentralbankgeld n	—	monnaie de banque centrale f	moneta creata dalla banca centrale f	dinero legal m
central credit institution (E)	Zentralkasse f	—	caisse centrale f	cassa centrale f	caja central f
central de evidencia (Es)	Evidenzzentrale f	information centre	centre de déclaration m	centrale dei rischi f	—
central de giros (Es)	Girozentrale f	central giro institution	banque centrale de virement f	centrale di bancogiro f	—
central depository for securities (E)	Wertpapier-sammelbank f	—	banque de dépôts et de virements de titres f	banca di deposito di titoli f	banco de depósito de valores mobiliarios m
centrale (F)	Zentrale f	head office	centrale f	centrale f	central f
centrale (I)	Zentrale f	head office	centrale f	—	central f
centrale dei rischi (I)	Evidenzzentrale f	information centre	centre de déclaration m	—	central de evidencia f
centrale di bancogiro (I)	Girozentrale f	central giro institution	banque centrale de virement f	—	central de giros m
central giro institution (E)	Girozentrale f	—	banque centrale de virement f	centrale di bancogiro f	central de giros m
central rate (E)	Leitkurs m	—	taux central m	parità centrale f	tipo de pivote m
centre de déclaration (F)	Evidenzzentrale f	information centre	—	centrale dei rischi f	central de evidencia f
centres off shore (F)	Offshore-Zentren n/pl	offshore centres	—	centri off-shore m/pl	centros offshore m/pl
centri off-shore (I)	Offshore-Zentren n/pl	offshore centres	centres off shore m/pl	—	centros offshore m/pl
centro de acumula-ción de capitales (Es)	Kapitalsammelstelle f	institutional investors	organisme collecteur de fonds m	investitore istituzionale m	—
centro di costo (I)	Kostenstelle f	cost centre	compte de frais par secteur m	—	sección de gastos f
centros offshore (Es)	Offshore-Zentren n/pl	offshore centres	centres off shore m/pl	centri off-shore m/pl	—
certain (F)	Quantitätsnotierung f	fixed exchange	—	quotazione del certo f	cotización cuantitativa f
certificado (Es)	Bestätigung f	confirmation	confirmation f	conferma f	—
certificado (Es)	Zertifikat n	certificate	certificat m	certificato m	—
certificado de acción (Es)	Zwischenschein m	provisional receipt	certificat provisoire m	certificato provvisorio m	—
certificado de acciones (Es)	Aktienzertifikat n	share certificate	certificat d'actions m	certificato azionario m	—
certificado de control (Es)	Sicherungsschein m	security note	certificat de contrôle m	certificato di controllo m	—
certificado de depósito (Es)	Depotschein m	deposit receipt	récépissé de dépôt m	certificato di deposito m	—
certificado de depósito (Es)	Einlagenzertifikat n	certificates of deposit	certificat de dépôt m	certificato di deposito m	—

	D	E	F	I	Es
certificado de disponibilidad (Es)	Lieferbarkeits-bescheinigung f	certificate of good delivery	certificat de négociabilité m	certificato di negoziabilità m	—
certificado de empréstito (Es)	Anleiheschein m	bond certificate	certificat d'emprunt m	certificato di prestito m	
certificado de inversión (Es)	Investmentzertifikate n/pl	investment fund certificates	parts de fonds d'investissement f/pl	certificato d'investimento m	—
certificado de mejora (Es)	Besserungsschein m	debtor warrant	surenchère au concordat f	certificato di rimborso in caso di miglio-ramento della situa-zione finanziaria f	—
certificado de participación en un programa de inversión (Es)	Programmzertifikat n	certificate of participation in an investment program	certificat d'un programme d'investissement m	certificato di parteci-pazione ad un programma d'investimento m	—
certificado de revisión (Es)	Prüfungsvermerk m	certificate of audit	mention de vérification f	annotazione di controllo f	—
certificado oro (Es)	Goldzertifikat n	gold certificate	certificat d'or m	certificato oro m	—
certificados de depósito (Es)	Warrants m/pl	warrants	warrant m	warrants m/pl	—
certificados provisionales (Es)	Anrechtscheine m/pl	warrants	certificats provisoires m/pl	certificati provvisori m/pl	—
certificat (F)	Zertifikat n	certificate	—	certificato m	certificado m
certificat d'action endommagé (F)	beschädigte Aktie f	damaged share certificates	—	azione danneggiata f	acción deteriorada f
certificat d'actions (F)	Aktienzertifikat n	share certificate	—	certificato azionario m	certificado de acciones m
certificat de contrôle (F)	Sicherungsschein m	security note	—	certificato di controllo m	certificado de control m
certificat de dépôt (F)	Einlagenzertifikat n	certificates of deposit	—	certificato di deposito m	certificado de depósito m
certificat de jouissance (F)	Genußschein m	participating certificate	—	buono di godimento m	bono de disfrute m
certificat de liquidation (F)	Liquidations-anteilsschein m	liquidation certificate	—	certificato di quota liquidazione m	cupón de parte de liquidación m
certificat d'emprunt (F)	Anleiheschein m	bond certificate	—	certificato di prestito m	certificado de empréstito m
certificat de négociabilité (F)	Lieferbarkeits-bescheinigung f	certificate of good delivery	—	certificato di negoziabilità m	certificado de disponibilidad m
certificat de souscription (F)	Bezugsschein m	subscription warrant	—	buono d'opzione m	boletín de suscripción m
certificat de souscription (F)	Zeichnungsschein m	subscription form	—	bollettino di sottoscrizione m	boletín de suscripción m
certificat d'or (F)	Goldzertifikat n	gold certificate	—	certificato oro m	certificado oro m
certificat d'un programme d'investissement (F)	Programmzertifikat n	certificate of participation in an investment program	—	certificato di partecipazione ad un programma d'investimento m	certificado de participación en un programa de inversión m
certificate (E)	Zertifikat n	—	certificat m	certificato m	certificado m
certificate of audit (E)	Prüfungsvermerk m	—	mention de vérification f	annotazione di controllo f	certificado de revisión m
certificate of good delivery (E)	Lieferbarkeits-bescheinigung f	—	certificat de négociabilité m	certificato di negoziabilità m	certificado de disponibilidad m
certificate of indebtedness (E)	Schuldschein m	—	reconnaissance de dette f	certificato di debito m	pagaré m
certificate of indebtedness (E)	Schuldbrief m	—	titre d'obligation m	titolo di debito m	título de deuda m
certificate of participation in an investment program (E)	Programmzertifikat n	—	certificat d'un programme d'investissement m	certificato di partecipazione ad un programma d'investimento m	certificado de participación en un programa de inversión m
certificate of pledge (E)	Pfandschein m	—	bulletin de gage m	atto di pegno m	resguardo de prenda m
certificates of deposit (E)	Einlagenzertifikat n	—	certificat de dépôt m	certificato di deposito m	certificado de depósito m
certification (E)	Beglaubigung f	—	légalisation f	autenticazione f	legalización f
certificati provvisori (I)	Anrechtscheine m/pl	warrants	certificats provisoires m/pl	—	certificados provisionales m/pl

	D	E	F	I	Es
certificato (I)	Zertifikat *n*	certificate	certificat *m*	—	certificado *m*
certificato azionario (I)	Aktienzertifikat *n*	share certificate	certificat d'actions *m*	—	certificado de acciones *m*
certificato di comproprietà al deposito collettivo di titoli (I)	Neugiro *m*	new endorsement	nouvel endossement *m*	—	nuevo endoso *m*
certificato di controllo (I)	Sicherungsschein *m*	security note	certificat de contrôle *m*	—	certificado de control *m*
certificato di debito (I)	Schuldschein *m*	certificate of indebtedness	reconnaissance de dette *f*	—	pagaré *m*
certificato di debito fondiario (I)	Grundschuldbrief *m*	land charge certificate	cédule foncière *f*	—	cédula de deuda inmobiliaria *f*
certificato d'identità (I)	Identitätsnachweis *m*	proof of identity	preuve de l'identité *f*	—	prueba de la identidad *f*
certificato d'investimento (I)	Investment-zertifikate *n/pl*	investment fund certificates	parts de fonds d'investissement *f/pl*	—	certificado de inversión *m*
certificato di deposito (I)	Einlagenzertifikat *n*	certificates of deposit	certificat de dépôt *m*	—	certificado de depósito *m*
certificato di deposito (I)	Depotschein *m*	deposit receipt	récépissé de dépôt *m*	—	certificado de depósito *m*
certificato di disponibilità (I)	Dispositionsschein *m*	banker's note	reconnaissance bancaire *f*	—	fianza de disposición de banquero *f*
certificato di negoziabilità (I)	Lieferbarkeits-bescheinigung *f*	certificate of good delivery	certificat de négociabilité *m*	—	certificado de disponibilidad *m*
certificato di partecipazione ad un programma d'investimento (I)	Programmzertifikat *n*	certificate of participation in an investment program	certificat d'un programme d'investissement *m*	—	certificado de participación en un programa de inversión *m*
certificato di prestito (I)	Anleiheschein *m*	bond certificate	certificat d'emprunt *m*	—	certificado de empréstito *m*
certificato di quota liquidazione (I)	Liquidations-anteilsschein *m*	liquidation certificate	certificat de liquidation *m*	—	cupón de parte de liquidación *m*
certificato di rimborso in caso di miglioramento della situazione finanziaria (I)	Besserungsschein *m*	debtor warrant	surenchère au concordat *f*	—	certificado de mejora *m*
certificato oro (I)	Goldzertifikat *n*	gold certificate	certificat d'or *m*	—	certificado oro *m*
certificato provvisorio (I)	Zwischenschein *m*	provisional receipt	certificat provisoire *m*	—	certificado de acción *m*
certificat provisoire (F)	Zwischenschein *m*	provisional receipt	—	certificato provvisorio *m*	certificado de acción *m*
certificats provisoires (F)	Anrechtscheine *m/pl*	warrants	—	certificati provvisori *m/pl*	certificados provisionales *m/pl*
certified bonds (E)	zertifizierte Bonds *m/pl*	—	bons certifiés *m/pl*	titoli a reddito fisso in valuta estera *m/pl*	bonos certificados *m/pl*
cesión en blanco (Es)	Blankozession *f*	transfer in blank	cession en blanc *f*	cessione allo scoperto *f*	—
cesión en bloque (Es)	Globalzession *f*	overall assignment	cession globale *f*	cessione globale *f*	—
cesión fiduciaria (Es)	Sicherungsabtretung *f*	assignment by way of security	cession d'une sûreté *f*	cessione a titolo di garanzia *f*	—
cesión tácita (Es)	stille Zession *f*	undisclosed assignment	cession occulte *f*	cessione tacita *f*	—
cesión temporal de valores (Es)	Effekten-pensionierung *f*	raising money on securities by cash sale coupled with contract for subsequent repurchase	mise en pension d'effets *f*	sconto di titoli in pensione *m*	—
cessation of payments (E)	Zahlungseinstellung *f*	—	suspension de payement *f*	cessazione di pagamento *f*	suspensión de pagos *f*
cessazione di pagamento (I)	Zahlungseinstellung *f*	cessation of payments	suspension de payement *f*	—	suspensión de pagos *f*
cession d'une sûreté (F)	Sicherungsabtretung *f*	assignment by way of security	—	cessione a titolo di garanzia *f*	cesión fiduciaria *f*
cessione allo scoperto (I)	Blankozession *f*	transfer in blank	cession en blanc *f*	—	cesión en blanco *f*
cessione a titolo di garanzia (I)	Sicherungsabtretung *f*	assignment by way of security	cession d'une sûreté *f*	—	cesión fiduciaria *f*

	D	E	F	I	Es
cessione degli utili ipotecari (I)	Hypotheken-gewinnabgabe f	levy on mortgage profits	impôt sur des bénéfices hypothécaires m	—	impuesto sobre ganancias hipotecarias m
cessione fiduciaria (I)	Sicherungs-übereignung f	transfer of ownership by way of security	transfert à titre de sûreté m	—	transmisión en garantía f
cessione globale (I)	Globalzession f	overall assignment	cession globale f	—	cesión en bloque f
cession en blanc (F)	Blankozession f	transfer in blank	—	cessione allo scoperto f	cesión en blanco f
cessione tacita (I)	stille Zession f	undisclosed assignment	cession occulte f	—	cesión tácita f
cession globale (F)	Globalzession f	overall assignment	—	cessione globale f	cesión en bloque f
cession occulte (F)	stille Zession f	undisclosed assignment	—	cessione tacita f	cesión tácita f
cesta de monedas (Es)	Währungskorb m	currency basket	panier des monnaies m	paniere monetario m	—
Chamber of Industry and Commerce (E)	Industrie- und Handelskammer f	—	chambre de commerce et d'industrie f	camera di commercio f	cámara de industria y comercio f
chambre de commerce et d'industrie (F)	Industrie- und Handelskammer f	Chamber of Industry and Commerce	—	camera di commercio f	cámara de industria y comercio f
chambre syndicale des courtiers (F)	Maklerkammer f	association of stockbrokers	—	comitato degli agenti di cambio m	colegio de agentes de cambio y bolsa m
change de place (F)	Platzspesen pl	local expenses	—	spese d'incasso di piazza f/pl	gastos locales m/pl
changement dans les structures (F)	Strukturwandel m	structural change	—	adeguamento di struttura m	cambio de estructura m
charge de curateur (F)	Kuratorium n	board of trustees	—	consiglio di gestione m	curatorio m
charges d'exploitation (F)	Betriebskosten pl	working expenses	—	costi d'esercizio m/pl	gastos de explotación m/pl
Chartanalyse (D)	—	chart analysis	analyse du développement d'une action f	analisi tecnica f	análisis del desarrollo de una acción m
chart analysis (E)	Chartanalyse f	—	analyse du développement d'une action f	analisi tecnica f	análisis del desarrollo de una acción m
chart of accounts (E)	Kontenplan m	—	plan comptable m	piano dei conti m	plan contable m
cheque (E)	Scheck m	—	chèque m	assegno m	cheque m
cheque (Es)	Scheck m	cheque	chèque m	assegno m	—
chèque (F)	Scheck m	cheque	—	assegno m	cheque m
cheque a la orden (Es)	Orderscheck m	order cheque	chèque à ordre m	assegno all'ordine m	—
cheque al portador (Es)	Überbringerscheck m	bearer cheque	chèque au porteur m	assegno al portatore m	—
cheque al portador (Es)	Inhaberscheck m	cheque to bearer	chèque au porteur m	assegno al portatore m	—
chèque à ordre (F)	Orderscheck m	order cheque	—	assegno all'ordine m	cheque a la orden m
chèque à porter en compte (F)	Verrechnungsscheck m	crossed cheque	—	assegno da accreditare m	cheque cruzado m
chèque au porteur (F)	Überbringerscheck m	bearer cheque	—	assegno al portatore m	cheque al portador m
chèque au porteur (F)	Inhaberscheck m	cheque to bearer	—	assegno al portatore m	cheque al portador m
chèque barré (F)	gekreuzter Scheck m	crossed cheque	—	assegno sbarrato m	cheque cruzado m
cheque clause (E)	Scheckklausel f	—	mention sur un chèque f	indicazione di assegno bancario f	cláusula de cheque f
cheque clearance (E)	Scheckabrechnung f	—	règlement des chèques par voie de compensation m	compensazione degli assegni f	liquidación de cheques f
cheque collection (E)	Scheckeinzug m	—	recouvrement de chèques m	incasso di assegno m	cobro del cheque m
cheque cruzado (Es)	Verrechnungs-scheck m	crossed cheque	chèque à porter en compte m	assegno da accreditare m	—
cheque cruzado (Es)	gekreuzter Scheck m	crossed cheque	chèque barré m	assegno sbarrato m	—
cheque cubierto (Es)	gedeckter Scheck m	covered cheque	chèque provisionné m	assegno coperto m	—
chèque d'achat (F)	Kaufscheck m	purchasing cheque	—	assegno garantito per acquisti m	cheque de compra m

	D	E	F	I	Es
cheque de compra (Es)	Kaufscheck *m*	purchasing cheque	chèque d'achat *m*	assegno garantito per acquisti *m*	—
cheque department (E)	Scheckabteilung *f*	—	service des chèques *m*	ufficio assegni *m*	sección de cheques *f*
chèque déplacé (F)	Versandscheck *m*	out-of-town cheque	—	assegno fuori piazza *m*	cheque sobre otra plaza *m*
cheque descubierto (Es)	ungedeckter Scheck *m*	uncovered cheque	chèque sans provision *m*	assegno senza copertura *m*	—
chèque de substitution (F)	Ersatzscheck *m*	substitute cheque	—	assegno sostitutivo *m*	cheque de sustitución *m*
cheque de sucursal (Es)	Filialscheck *m*	house cheque	chèque interne *m*	assegno su filiale *m*	—
cheque de sustitución (Es)	Ersatzscheck *m*	substitute cheque	chèque de substitution *m*	assegno sostitutivo *m*	—
cheque de transferencia (Es)	Überweisungsscheck *m*	transfer cheque	chèque postal de virement *m*	bancogiro della banca centrale *m*	—
cheque de viaje (Es)	Reisescheck *m*	traveller's cheque	chèque de voyage *m*	assegno turistico *m*	—
chèque de voyage (F)	Reisescheck *m*	traveller's cheque	—	assegno turistico *m*	cheque de viaje *m*
cheque devuelto (Es)	Rückscheck *m*	returned cheque	chèque retourné *m*	assegno ritornato *m*	—
cheque drawn by the drawer himself (E)	trassiert-eigener Scheck *m*	—	chèque tiré sur soi-même *m*	assegno tratto su se stesso *m*	cheque girado a su propio cargo *m*
chèque en blanc (F)	Blanko-Scheck *m*	blank cheque	—	assegno in bianco *m*	cheque en blanco *m*
cheque en blanco (Es)	Blanko-Scheck *m*	blank cheque	chèque en blanc *m*	assegno in bianco *m*	—
cheque estándar (Es)	Einheitsscheck *m*	standard cheque	formule de chèque normalisée *f*	assegno standardizzato *m*	—
cheque girado a su propio cargo (Es)	trassiert-eigener Scheck *m*	cheque drawn by the drawer himself	chèque tiré sur soi-même *m*	assegno tratto su se stesso *m*	—
chèque interne (F)	Filialscheck *m*	house cheque	—	assegno su filiale *m*	cheque de sucursal *m*
chèque payable à l'étranger (F)	Auslandsscheck *m*	foreign cheque	—	assegno sull'estero *m*	cheque sobre el extranjero *m*
chèque postal (Es)	Postscheck *m*	postal giro	chèque postal *m*	assegno postale *m*	—
chèque postal (F)	Postscheck *m*	postal giro	—	assegno postale *m*	cheque postal *m*
chèque postal de virement (F)	Überweisungsscheck *m*	transfer cheque	—	bancogiro della banca centrale *m*	cheque de transferencia *m*
chèque provisionné (F)	gedeckter Scheck *m*	covered cheque	—	assegno coperto *m*	cheque cubierto *m*
cheque recourse (E)	Scheckregreß *m*	—	recours en matière de chèque *m*	regresso d'assegno *m*	regreso de cheque *m*
chèque retourné (F)	Rückscheck *m*	returned cheque	—	assegno ritornato *m*	cheque devuelto *m*
cheques and orders payable at a certain place (E)	Platzanweisung *f*	—	mandat de place *m*	bonifico sulla piazza *m*	cheques y órdenes a pagar en plaza *m/pl*
chèque sans provision (F)	ungedeckter Scheck *m*	uncovered cheque	—	assegno senza copertura *m*	cheque descubierto *m*
cheque sobre el extranjero (Es)	Auslandsscheck *m*	foreign cheque	chèque payable à l'étranger *m*	assegno sull'estero *m*	—
cheque sobre otra plaza (Es)	Versandscheck *m*	out-of-town cheque	chèque déplacé *m*	assegno fuori piazza *m*	—
cheque stopping (E)	Scheckwiderruf *m*	—	contremandement de l'ordre de payement d'un chèque *m*	revoca dell'assegno *f*	revocación de la orden de pago de un cheque *f*
cheques y órdenes a pagar en plaza (Es)	Platzanweisung *f*	cheques and orders payable at a certain place	mandat de place *m*	bonifico sulla piazza *m*	—
chèque tiré sur soi-même (F)	trassiert-eigener Scheck *m*	cheque drawn by the drawer himself	—	assegno tratto su se stesso *m*	cheque girado a su propio cargo *m*
cheque to bearer (E)	Inhaberscheck *m*	—	chèque au porteur *m*	assegno al portatore *m*	cheque al portador *m*
cheque transactions (E)	Scheckverkehr *m*	—	opérations par chèque *f/pl*	pagamenti mediante assegno *m/pl*	operaciones de cheques *f/pl*
chiarezza del bilancio (I)	Bilanzklarheit *f*	accounting transparency	clarté du bilan *f*	—	transparencia del balance *f*
chief accountancy (E)	Hauptbuchhaltung *f*	—	comptabilité générale *f*	ufficio di contabilità generale *m*	contabilidad principal *f*
chiffre (F)	Zahl *f*	figure	—	cifra *f*	número *m*

	D	E	F	I	Es
chiffre d'affaires (F)	Umsatz *m*	turnover	—	fatturato *m*	cifra de facturación *f*
chiffres d'affaires d'une banque (F)	Bankumsätze *m/pl*	bank turnover	—	movimento bancario *m*	facturación bancaria *f*
chi sostiene le spese (I)	Kostenträger *m*	cost unit	poste de production absorbant des coûts *m*	—	portador de costes *m*
chiusura (I)	Schluß *m*	closure	clôture *f*	—	cierre *m*
chiusura (I)	Abschluß *m*	conclusion	conclusion *f*	—	conclusión *f*
chiusura dei conti (I)	Rechnungslegung *f*	accounting	reddition des comptes *f*	—	rendición de cuentas *f*
chômage caché (F)	versteckte Arbeitslosigkeit *f*	hidden unemployment	—	disoccupazione camuffata *f*	desempleo disfrazado *m*
ciencia financiera (Es)	Finanzwissenschaft *f*	public finance	science financière *f*	scienza delle finanze *f*	—
ciencias bancarias (Es)	Bankbetriebslehre *f*	science of banking	science bancaire *f*	tecnica bancaria *f*	—
ciencias económicas (Es)	Volkswirtschaftslehre *f*	economics	économie politique *f*	economia politica *f*	—
cierre (Es)	Schluß *m*	closure	clôture *f*	chiusura *f*	—
cierre de la bolsa (Es)	Börsenschluß *m*	close of stock exchange business	clôture de la bourse *f*	fine della riunione di borsa *f*	—
cifra (I)	Zahl *f*	figure	chiffre *m*	—	número *m*
cifra de facturación (Es)	Umsatz *m*	turnover	chiffre d'affaires *m*	fatturato *m*	
cifra nominal (Es)	Merkposten *m*	memorandum item	poste pour mémoire *m*	voce per memoria *f*	—
circolante (I)	Umlaufvermögen *n*	current assets	capital de roulement *m*	—	capital circulante *m*
circolazione di capitali internazionale (I)	internationaler Kapitalverkehr *m*	international capital transactions	mouvement international des capitaux *m*	—	movimiento de capitales internacional *m*
circolazione di mezzi di pagamento (I)	Zahlungsmittel-umlauf *m*	notes and coins in circulation	circulation monétaire *f*	—	medios de pago en circulación *m/pl*
circolazione monetaria (I)	Geldumsatz *m*	turnover of money	roulement de l'argent *m*	—	giro monetario *m*
circolazione monetaria (I)	Geldumlauf *m*	circulation of money	circulation monétaire *f*	—	circulación de dinero *m*
circuit économique (F)	Wirtschaftskreislauf *m*	economic circulation	—	circuito economico *m*	circuito económico *m*
circuito económico (Es)	Wirtschaftskreislauf *m*	economic circulation	circuit économique *m*	circuito economico *m*	—
circuito economico (I)	Wirtschaftskreislauf *m*	economic circulation	circuit économique *m*	—	circuito económico *m*
circulación de dinero (Es)	Geldumlauf *m*	circulation of money	circulation monétaire *f*	circolazione monetaria *f*	—
circulaire d'actionnaires (F)	Aktionärsbrief *m*	circular letter from board to shareholders	—	lettera degli azionisti *f*	circular de accionistas *m*
circular de accionistas (Es)	Aktionärsbrief *m*	circular letter from board to shareholders	circulaire d'actionnaires *f*	lettera degli azionisti *f*	—
circular letter from board to shareholders (E)	Aktionärsbrief *m*	—	circulaire d'actionnaires *f*	lettera degli azionisti *f*	circular de accionistas *m*
circulation monétaire (F)	Geldumlauf *m*	circulation of money	—	circolazione monetaria *f*	circulación de dinero *m*
circulation monétaire (F)	Zahlungsmittel-umlauf *m*	notes and coins in circulation	—	circolazione di mezzi di pagamento *f*	medios de pago en circulación *m/pl*
citazione preventiva (I)	Vorausklage *f*	preliminary injunction	bénéfice de discussion *m*	—	excusión *f*
claim (E)	Forderung *f*	—	créance *f*	credito *m*	crédito *m*
claim for return (E)	Herausgabeanspruch *m*	—	prétention à restitution *f*	diritto alla restituzione *m*	pretensión de entrega *f*
claim in default (E)	notleidende Forderung *f*	—	créance irrécupérable *f*	credito in sofferenza *m*	crédito dudoso *m*
clarté du bilan (F)	Bilanzklarheit *f*	accounting transparency	—	chiarezza del bilancio *f*	transparencia del balance *f*
clase de costes (Es)	Kostenart *f*	cost type	coût par nature *m*	tipo di costo *m*	—
clases de patrimonio (Es)	Vermögensarten *f/pl*	types of property	catégories de patrimoine *f/pl*	tipi di patrimonio *m/pl*	—

	D	E	F	I	Es
classification numérique des succursales bancaires (F)	Bankennumerierung f	bank branch numbering	—	codice bancario m	numeración de las filiales bancarias f
classificazione dei conti (I)	Kontennumerierung f	account numbering	numérotage des comptes m	—	numeración de cuentas f
clause à ordre (F)	Orderklausel f	order clause	—	clausola "all'ordine" f	cláusula a la orden f
clause au porteur (F)	Inhaberklausel f	bearer clause	—	clausola al portatore f	cláusula al portador f
clause d'arbitrage (F)	Arbitrageklausel f	arbitrage clause	—	clausola arbitrale f	cláusula de arbitraje f
clause de baisse (F)	Baisseklausel f	bear clause	—	clausola di ribasso f	cláusula de baja f
clause de couverture (F)	Deckungsklausel f	cover clause	—	clausola di garanzia f	cláusula de cobertura f
clause de dépôt (F)	Depositenklausel f	deposit clause	—	clausola di deposito f	cláusula de depósito f
clause de payement effectif en une monnaie étrangère (F)	Kursklausel f	currency clause	—	clausola di cambio f	cláusula de tipo de cambio f
clause de payement en monnaie étrangère (F)	Effektivvermerk m	actual currency clause	—	clausola di pagamento effettivo in moneta estera f	cláusula de efectividad f
clause de présentation (F)	Präsentationsklausel f	presentation clause	—	clausola di presentazione f	cláusula de presentación f
clause de prix mobile (F)	Gleitklausel f	escalation clause	—	clausola della scala mobile f	cláusula de escala móvil f
clause d'indexation (F)	Indexklausel f	index clause	—	clausola numeri indici f	cláusula de índice variable f
clause d'indexation (F)	Geldwertsicherungsklausel f	money guarantee clause	—	clausola di garanzia monetaria f	cláusula de garantía sobre el valor monetario f
clause d'option (F)	Fakultativklausel f	option clause	—	clausola facoltativa f	cláusula potestativa f
clause non à ordre (F)	negative Orderklausel f	negative wording	—	clausola all'ordine negativa f	cláusula de no negociabilidad f
clause prohibitive (F)	Negativklausel f	negative clause	—	clausola negativa f	cláusula negativa f
clausola (I)	Bedingung f	condition	condition f	—	condición f
clausola "all'ordine" (I)	Orderklausel f	order clause	clause à ordre f	—	cláusula a la orden f
clausola al portatore (I)	Inhaberklausel f	bearer clause	clause au porteur f	—	cláusula al portador f
clausola arbitrale (I)	Arbitrageklausel f	arbitrage clause	clause d'arbitrage f	—	cláusula de arbitraje f
clausola della scala mobile (I)	Gleitklausel f	escalation clause	clause de prix mobile f	—	cláusula de escala móvil f
clausola di cambio (I)	Kursklausel f	currency clause	clause de payement effectif en une monnaie étrangère f	—	cláusula de tipo de cambio f
clausola di deposito (I)	Depositenklausel f	deposit clause	clause de dépôt f	—	cláusula de depósito f
clausola di garanzia (I)	Deckungsklausel f	cover clause	clause de couverture f	—	cláusula de cobertura f
clausola di garanzia monetaria (I)	Geldwertsicherungsklausel f	money guarantee clause	clause d'indexation f	—	cláusula de garantía sobre el valor monetario f
clausola di pagamento effettivo in moneta estera (I)	Effektivvermerk m	actual currency clause	clause de payement en monnaie étrangère f	—	cláusula de efectividad f
clausola di presentazione (I)	Präsentationsklausel f	presentation clause	clause de présentation f	—	cláusula de presentación f
clausola di ribasso (I)	Baisseklausel f	bear clause	clause de baisse f	—	cláusula de baja f
clausola facoltativa (I)	Fakultativklausel f	option clause	clause d'option f	—	cláusula potestativa f
clausola negativa (I)	Negativklausel f	negative clause	clause prohibitive f	—	cláusula negativa f
clausola negativa (I)	Negativerklärung f	negative declaration	déclaration négative f	—	declaración negativa f
clausola numeri indici (I)	Indexklausel f	index clause	clause d'indexation f	—	cláusula de índice variable f
clausola valutaria (I)	Valutaklausel f	foreign currency clause	mention de la valeur fournie f	—	cláusula de valuta f
cláusula a la orden (Es)	Orderklausel f	order clause	clause à ordre f	clausola "all'ordine" f	—
cláusula al portador (Es)	Inhaberklausel f	bearer clause	clause au porteur f	clausola al portatore f	—

	D	E	F	I	Es
cláusula de arbitraje (Es)	Arbitrageklausel f	arbitrage clause	clause d'arbitrage f	clausola arbitrale f	—
cláusula de baja (Es)	Baisseklausel f	bear clause	clause de baisse f	clausola di ribasso f	—
cláusula de cheque (Es)	Scheckklausel f	cheque clause	mention sur un chèque f	indicazione di assegno bancario f	—
cláusula de cobertura (Es)	Deckungsklausel f	cover clause	clause de couverture f	clausola di garanzia f	—
cláusula de depósito (Es)	Depositenklausel f	deposit clause	clause de dépôt f	clausola di deposito f	—
cláusula de efectividad (Es)	Effektivvermerk m	actual currency clause	clause de payement en monnaie étrangère f	clausola di pagamento effettivo in moneta estera f	—
cláusula de escala móvil (Es)	Gleitklausel f	escalation clause	clause de prix mobile f	clausola della scala mobile f	—
cláusula de garantía sobre el valor monetario (Es)	Geldwertsicherungs-klausel f	money guarantee clause	clause d'indexation f	clausola di garanzia monetaria f	—
cláusula de incumplimiento (Es)	Default Clause f	default clause	default clause f	default clause f	—
cláusula de índice variable (Es)	Indexklausel f	index clause	clause d'indexation f	clausola numeri indici f	—
cláusula de presentación (Es)	Präsentationsklausel f	presentation clause	clause de présentation f	clausola di presentazione f	—
cláusula de tipo de cambio (Es)	Kursklausel f	currency clause	clause de payement effectif en une monnaie étrangère f	clausola di cambio f	—
cláusula de valuta (Es)	Valutaklausel f	foreign currency clause	mention de la valeur fournie f	clausola valutaria f	—
cláusula negativa (Es)	Negativklausel f	negative clause	clause prohibitive f	clausola negativa f	—
cláusula potestativa (Es)	Fakultativklausel f	option clause	clause d'option f	clausola facoltativa f	—
clean bill of lading (E)	reines Konossement n	—	connaissement sans réserve m	polizza di carico netta f	conocimiento limpio m
clean factoring (E)	echtes Factoring n	—	factoring authentique m	factoring pro soluto m	factoring auténtico m
clearance sale (E)	Ausverkauf m	—	soldes f/pl	liquidazione f	venta de liquidación f
clearing (I)	Abrechnungsverkehr m	clearing system	opérations de compensation f/pl	—	operaciones de compensación f/pl
clearing department (E)	Giroabteilung f	—	service des virements m	reparto giro m	sección de giros f
clearing house (E)	Abrechnungsstelle f	—	bureau de liquidation m	stanza di compensazione f	oficina de compensación f
clearing system (E)	Abrechnungsverkehr m	—	opérations de compensation f/pl	clearing m	operaciones de compensación f/pl
clearing system (E)	Gironetz n	—	réseau des banques de virement m	rete di giro f	red de bancos de giros f
clearing unit (E)	Verrechnungseinheit f	—	unité de compte f	unità di conto f	unidad de compensación f
client bancaire (F)	Bankkunde m	bank customer	—	cliente bancario m	cliente bancario m
client de première catégorie (F)	beste Adresse f	prime name	—	società di prim'ordine f	cliente de primera categoría f
cliente abituale (I)	Stammkunde m	regular customer	client habituel m	—	cliente habitual m
cliente bancario (Es)	Bankkunde m	bank customer	client bancaire m	cliente bancario m	—
cliente bancario (I)	Bankkunde m	bank customer	client bancaire m	—	cliente bancario m
cliente de primera categoría (Es)	beste Adresse f	prime name	client de première catégorie m	società di prim'ordine f	—
cliente habitual (Es)	Stammkunde m	regular customer	client habituel m	cliente abituale m	—
client habituel (F)	Stammkunde m	regular customer	—	cliente abituale m	cliente habitual m
climat de crise (F)	Krisenstimmung f	crisis feeling	—	atmosfera di crisi f	ambiente de crisis m
closed-end real estate fund (E)	geschlossener Immobilienfonds m	—	fonds de placement immobilier fermé m	fondo immobiliare chiuso m	fondo inmobiliario cerrado m
close of stock exchange business (E)	Börsenschluß m	—	clôture de la bourse f	fine della riunione di borsa f	cierre de la bolsa m

	D	E	F	I	Es
closing balance (E)	Schlußbilanz *f*	—	bilan de clôture *m*	bilancio di chiusura *m*	balance de cierre *m*
closing price (E)	Schlußkurs *m*	—	dernier cours *m*	quotazione di chiusura *f*	cotización de cierre *f*
closure (E)	Schluß *m*	—	clôture *f*	chiusura *f*	cierre *m*
clôture (F)	Schluß *m*	closure	—	chiusura *f*	cierre *m*
clôture annuelle des comptes (F)	Jahresabschluß *m*	annual statement of accounts	—	bilancio d'esercizio *m*	balance anual *m*
clôture de la bourse (F)	Börsenschluß *m*	close of stock exchange business	—	fine della riunione di borsa *f*	cierre de la bolsa *m*
cobertura (Es)	Deckung *f*	coverage	couverture *f*	copertura *f*	—
cobertura (Es)	Sicherungsgeschäft *n*	security transaction	couverture *f*	garanzia *f*	—
cobertura bancaria (Es)	Bankdeckung *f*	banking cover	couverture de garantie d'une banque *f*	copertura bancaria *f*	—
cobertura en efectivo (Es)	Bardeckung *f*	cash cover	couverture en espèces *f*	copertura in contanti *f*	—
cobertura en metálico (Es)	Metalldeckung *f*	metal cover	couverture métallique *f*	copertura metallica *f*	—
cobertura monetaria (Es)	Notendeckung *f*	cover of note circulation	couverture en billets de banque *f*	copertura di emissione di banconote *f*	—
cobertura-oro (Es)	Golddeckung *f*	gold cover	couverture or *f*	copertura oro *f*	—
cobranza (Es)	Inkasso *n*	collection	encaissement *m*	incasso *m*	—
cobranzas bancarias (Es)	Bankeinzugsverfahren *n*	direct debiting	encaissements bancaires *m/pl*	procedimento d'incasso bancario *m*	—
cobro del cheque (Es)	Scheckeinzug *m*	cheque collection	recouvrement de chèques *m*	incasso di assegno *m*	—
cobro de letras (Es)	Wechselinkasso *n*	collection of bills of exchange	encaissement d'un effet *m*	incasso di cambiale *m*	—
cobros pendientes (Es)	Außenstände *m/pl*	outstanding accounts	dettes actives *f/pl*	crediti pendenti *m/pl*	—
code (F)	Kennzahl *f*	code number	—	indice *m*	índice *m*
code des impôts (F)	Abgabenordnung *f*	fiscal code	—	legislazione tributaria *f*	ordenanza tributaria *f*
code number (E)	Kennzahl *f*	—	code *m*	indice *m*	índice *m*
code speculative (I)	Schwänze *f/pl*	corners	corners *m/pl*	—	corners *m*
codice bancario (I)	Bankleitzahl *f*	bank identification number	numéro de code bancaire *m*	—	codigo de identificación bancaria *m*
codice bancario (I)	Bankennumerierung *f*	bank branch numbering	classification numérique des succursales bancaires *f*	—	numeración de las filiales bancarias *f*
codice degli agenti di cambio (I)	Maklerordnung *f*	brokers' code of conduct	régime des courtiers *m*	—	régimen de corredores *m*
codice di finanziamento interno (I)	Innenfinanzierungskennzahl *f*	self-generated financing ratio	ratio de financement interne *m*	—	características de financiación interna *f/pl*
codigo de identificación bancaria (Es)	Bankleitzahl *f*	bank identification number	numéro de code bancaire *m*	codice bancario *m*	—
coefficient bêta (F)	Betafaktor *m*	beta factor	—	indice beta *m*	factor beta de regresión *m*
coefficient de détermination (F)	Bestimmtheitsmaß *n*	determination coefficient	—	coefficiente di determinazione *m*	coeficiente de determinación *m*
coefficient de liquidité (F)	Liquiditätsquote *f*	liquidity ratio	—	tasso di liquiditá *m*	coeficiente de liquidez *m*
coefficient d'investissement (F)	Investitionskennzahl *f*	investment index	—	indice di investimento *m*	índice de inversión *m*
coefficiente di determinazione (I)	Bestimmtheitsmaß *n*	determination coefficient	coefficient de détermination *m*	—	coeficiente de determinación *m*
coeficiente de determinación (Es)	Bestimmtheitsmaß *n*	determination coefficient	coefficient de détermination *m*	coefficiente di determinazione *m*	—
coeficiente de liquidez (Es)	Liquiditätsquote *f*	liquidity ratio	coefficient de liquidité *m*	tasso di liquiditá *m*	—
coffre-fort (F)	Tresor *m*	safe	—	cassaforte *f*	caja fuerte *f*
coffre-fort de titres (F)	Manteltresor *m*	bond and share certificate vault	—	cassaforte dei mantelli *f*	caja fuerte para certificados de bonos y acciones *f*

	D	E	F	I	Es
colegio de agentes de cambio y bolsa (Es)	Maklerkammer *f*	association of stockbrokers	chambre syndicale des courtiers *f*	comitato degli agenti di cambio *m*	—
collapse (E)	Deroute *f*	—	déroute *f*	tracollo dei prezzi di borsa *m*	fuga desbaratada *f*
collateral credit (E)	Lombardkredit *m*	—	crédit garanti par nantissement *m*	anticipazione su crediti *f*	crédito pignoraticio *m*
collateral deposit (E)	Lombarddepot *n*	—	dépôt de titres remis en nantissement *m*	deposito lombard *m*	depósito de valores pignoraticios *m*
collateral guarantee (E)	Nachbürgschaft *f*	—	garantie du certifica-teur de la caution *f*	fideiussione per il fideiussore *f*	subfianza *f*
collateral loan based on a bill of exchange (E)	Wechsellombard *m*	—	avance sur effet nanti *f*	anticipazione su cambiali *f*	letra de cambio tomada en prenda *f*
collateral value (E)	Besicherungswert *m*	—	valeur du gage *f*	valore di garanzia di credito *m*	valor colateral *m*
collection (E)	Inkasso *n*	—	encaissement *m*	incasso *m*	cobranza *f*
collection business (E)	Einziehungsgeschäft *n*	—	opération d'encaissement *f*	operazione d'incasso *f*	operaciones de cobranza *f/pl*
collection business (E)	Inkassogeschäft *n*	—	opération de recouvrement *f*	operazione d'incasso *f*	operación de cobro *f*
collection commission (E)	Inkassoprovision *f*	—	commission d'encaissement *f*	provvigione d'incasso *f*	comisión *f*
collection department (E)	Inkasso-Abteilung *f*	—	service des encaissements *m*	ufficio incassi *m*	sección de cobranza *f*
collection fee (E)	Inkassogebühr *f*	—	frais de recouvrement *m/pl*	commissione d'incasso *f*	comisión de cobro *f*
collection of bills of exchange (E)	Wechselinkasso *n*	—	encaissement d'un effet *m*	incasso di cambiale *m*	cobro de letras *m*
collection procedure (E)	Einzugs-ermächtigungs-verfahren *n*	—	système du mandat de prélèvement automatique *m*	autorizzazione alla riscossione *f*	proceso de cobro bancario *m*
collection procedure (E)	Forderungseinzugs-verfahren *n*	—	système de recouvrement de créances *m*	procedimento d'incasso crediti *m*	procedimiento de cobro de créditos *m*
collection receipt (E)	Einzugsquittung *f*	—	quittance d'encaissement *f*	ricevuta di riscossione *f*	recibo de cobro *m*
collective account (E)	Sammelkonto *n*	—	compte collectif *m*	conto collettivo *m*	cuenta colectiva *f*
collective bill (E)	Sammeltratte *f*	—	traite globale *f*	tratta collettiva *f*	libranza colectiva *f*
collective debt register claim (E)	Sammelschuldbuch-forderung *f*	—	créance collective inscrite dans le livre de la dette *f*	cartella debito pubblico collettiva *f*	crédito contabilizado colectivo *m*
collective deposit (E)	Sammeldepot *n*	—	dépôt collectif de titres *m*	deposito collettivo di titoli *m*	depósito colectivo *m*
collective order (E)	Sammelauftrag *m*	—	ordre groupé *m*	ordine cumulativo *m*	orden colectiva *f*
collective saving (E)	Kollektivsparen *n*	—	épargne collective *f*	risparmio collettivo *m*	ahorro colectivo *m*
collective securities deposit operations (E)	Girosammel-verkehr *m*	—	opérations de vire-ments collectives *f/pl*	trasferimenti collettivi di giro *m/pl*	giro central de valores *m*
collectivité (F)	Körperschaft *f*	corporation	—	ente *m*	corporación *f*
collectivité territoriale (F)	Gebietskörperschaft *f*	regional authority	—	ente locale *m*	corporación territorial *f*
collocamento (I)	Placierung *f*	placing	placement *m*	—	colocación *f*
colocación (Es)	Placierung *f*	placing	placement *m*	collocamento *m*	—
colonial bank (E)	Kolonialbank *f*	—	banque coloniale *f*	banca coloniale *f*	banco colonial *m*
comanditario (Es)	Kommanditist *m*	limited partner	commanditaire *m*	accomandante *m*	—
combinación de coste mínimo (Es)	Minimalkosten-kombination *f*	minimum cost combination	combinaison du coût minimal *f*	combinazione di costi minimi *f*	—
combinaison du coût minimal (F)	Minimalkosten-kombination *f*	minimum cost combination	—	combinazione di costi minimi *f*	combinación de coste mínimo *f*
combination bank (E)	Gemeinschaftsbank *f*	—	banque combinée *f*	banca comune *f*	banco de combinación *m*
combinazione di costi minimi (I)	Minimalkosten-kombination *f*	minimum cost combination	combinaison du coût minimal *f*	—	combinación de coste mínimo *f*
combined bank transfer (E)	Sammelüberweisung *f*	—	virement global *m*	trasferimento cumulativo *m*	transferencia colectiva *f*

	D	E	F	I	Es
comercialización (Es)	Vermarktung f	marketing	commercialisation f	vendibilità f	—
comerciante (Es)	Händler m	dealer	commerçant m	commerciante m	—
comerciante pleno (Es)	Vollkaufmann m	registered trader	commerçant de plein droit m	imprenditore a pieno titolo m	—
comercio (Es)	Handel m	trade	commerce m	commercio m	—
comercio al por menor (Es)	Einzelhandel m	retail trade	commerce de détail m	commercio al dettaglio m	—
comercio con monedas (Es)	Münzhandel m	dealings in gold and silver coins	commerce des pièces de monnaie m	commercio monete pregiate m	—
comercio de cambio (Es)	Usancenhandel m	trading in foreign exchange	commerce de change m	commercio delle valute m	—
comercio de derechos de suscripción (Es)	Bezugsrechthandel m	trading in subscription rights	marché des droits de souscription m	trattazione di diritti d'opzione f	—
comercio de oro (Es)	Goldhandel m	gold trade	commerce de l'or m	commercio dell'oro m	—
comercio de ultramarinos (Es)	Produktenhandel m	produce trade	commerce des produits agricoles m	commercio delle derrate m	—
comercio exterior (Es)	Außenhandel m	foreign trade	commerce extérieur m	commercio estero m	—
comercio multilateral (Es)	multilateraler Handel m	multilateral trade	commerce multilatéral m	commercio multilaterale m	—
comercio por cuenta propia (Es)	Eigenhandel m	trading on own account	commerce à propre compte m	commercio in proprio m	—
comisión (Es)	Inkassoprovision f	collection commission	commission d'encaissement f	provvigione d'incasso f	—
comisión (Es)	Provision f	commission	commission f	commissione f	—
comisión al contado (Es)	Schalterprovision f	selling commission	commission de vente f	commissione di collocamento f	—
comisión bancaria (Es)	Bankprovision f	banker's commission	commission de banque f	commissione bancaria f	—
comisión de aceptación (Es)	Akzeptprovision f	commission for acceptance	commission bancaire sur crédit d'acceptation f	commissione d'accettazione f	—
comisión de alta dirección (Es)	Führungsprovision f	managers commission	commission d'apériteur f	provvigione di gestione f	—
comisión de apertura de crédito (Es)	Kreditprovision f	credit commission	frais de commission d'ouverture de crédit m/pl	provvigione di credito f	—
comisión de cheque devuelto (Es)	Rückscheckprovision f	commision on returned cheque	commission de chèque retourné f	provvigione di rigresso f	—
comisión de cobranza (Es)	Einziehungsermächtigung f	direct debit authorization	mandat de prélèvement automatique m	autorizzazione alla riscossione f	—
comisión de cobro (Es)	Inkassogebühr f	collection fee	frais de recouvrement m/pl	commissione d'incasso f	—
comisión de descuento (Es)	Diskontprovision f	discount commission	commission d'escompte f	provvigione di sconto f	—
comisión de giro en descubierto (Es)	Überziehungsprovision f	overdraft commission	commission de découvert f	provvigione di scoperta f	—
comisión de los acreedores (Es)	Gläubigerausschuß m	committee of inspection	commission des contrôleurs f	comitato dei creditori m	—
comisión de mediación bancaria (Es)	Bankierbonifikation f	placing commission	commission de placement f	provvigione bancaria f	—
comisión de monopolios (Es)	Monopolkommission f	Monopolies Commission	commission de monopoles f	commissione antitrust f	—
comisión de revisión de cuentas (Es)	Prüfungskommission f	examining commission	commission de contrôle f	giuria f	—
comisionista (Es)	Kommissionär m	commission agent	commissionnaire m	commissionario m	—
comisionista de valores (Es)	Effektenkommissionär m	securities commission agent	banque chargée d'opérations sur titres f	commissionario di borsa m	—
comisión por aval (Es)	Aval-Provision f	commission on bank guarantee	commission pour aval f	provvigione d'avallo f	—
comisión sobre la cifra de facturación (Es)	Umsatzprovision f	commission on turnover	commission sur le chiffre d'affaires f	provvigione sul fatturato f	—
comitato consulenza investimenti (I)	Anlageausschuß m	investment committee	comité d'investissements m	—	comité de inversión m

	D	E	F	I	Es
comitato degli agenti di cambio (I)	Maklerkammer f	association of stockbrokers	chambre syndicale des courtiers f	—	colegio de agentes de cambio y bolsa m
comitato dei creditori (I)	Gläubigerausschuß m	committee of inspection	commission des contrôleurs f	—	comisión de los acreedores f
comitato di borsa (I)	Börsenausschuß m	stock committee	conseil de la bourse m	—	comité de las bolsas m
comitato di credito (I)	Kreditausschuß m	credit committee	commission d'étude des dossiers de crédit f	—	comité de crédito m
comité de crédito (Es)	Kreditausschuß m	credit committee	commission d'étude des dossiers de crédit f	comitato di credito m	—
comité de inversión (Es)	Anlageausschuß m	investment committee	comité d'investissements m	comitato consulenza investimenti m	—
comité de las bolsas (Es)	Börsenausschuß m	stock committee	conseil de la bourse m	comitato di borsa m	—
comité de mercado de capital (Es)	Kapitalmarkt-kommission f	capital market committee	commission du marché des capitaux f	commissione mercato finanziario f	—
comité de mercado libre (Es)	Freiverkehrs-ausschuß m	unofficial dealings committee	comité du marché libre m	commissione operazioni fuori borsa f	—
comité d'investissements (F)	Anlageausschuß m	investment committee	—	comitato consulenza investimenti m	comité de inversión m
comité directeur (F)	Vorstand m	board	—	consiglio d'amministrazione m	junta directiva f
comité du marché libre (F)	Freiverkehrs-ausschuß m	unofficial dealings committee	—	commissione operazioni fuori borsa f	comité de mercado libre m
commande (F)	Auftrag m	order	—	ordine m	pedido m
commande (F)	Bestellung f	order	—	ordinazione f	pedido m
commandes placées par un groupement de sociétés (F)	Konzernaufträge m/pl	group orders	—	ordini di gruppo m/pl	órdenes de grupos f/pl
commanditaire (F)	Kommanditist m	limited partner	—	accomandante m	comanditario m
commandité (F)	Komplementär m	general partner	—	accomandatario m	socio colectivo m
commencement of bankruptcy proceedings (E)	Konkurseröffnung f	—	ouverture de la faillite f	apertura del fallimento f	apertura de la quiebra f
commerçant (F)	Händler m	dealer	—	commerciante m	comerciante m
commerçant de plein droit (F)	Vollkaufmann m	registered trader	—	imprenditore a pieno titolo m	comerciante pleno m
commerce (F)	Handel m	trade	—	commercio m	comercio m
commerce à propre compte (F)	Eigenhandel m	trading on own account	—	commercio in proprio m	comercio por cuenta propia m
commerce de change (F)	Usancenhandel m	trading in foreign exchange	—	commercio delle valute m	comercio de cambio m
commerce de change (F)	Sortengeschäft n	dealings in foreign notes and coins	—	operazione di cambio f	operación de moneda extranjera f
commerce de change (F)	Sortenhandel m	dealing in foreign notes and coins	—	commercio delle valute m	negociación de moneda extranjera f
commerce de détail (F)	Einzelhandel m	retail trade	—	commercio al dettaglio m	comercio al por menor m
commerce de l'or (F)	Goldhandel m	gold trade	—	commercio dell'oro m	comercio de oro m
commerce des pièces de monnaie (F)	Münzhandel m	dealings in gold and silver coins	—	commercio monete pregiate m	comercio con monedas m
commerce des produits agricoles (F)	Produktenhandel m	produce trade	—	commercio delle derrate m	comercio de ultramarinos m
commerce des valeurs mobilières (F)	Effektengeschäft n	securities business	—	operazione in titoli f	operación con valores f
commerce extérieur (F)	Außenhandel m	foreign trade	—	commercio estero m	comercio exterior m
commerce libre (F)	Freihandel m	over-the-counter trade	—	libero scambio m	librecambio m
commerce multilatéral (F)	multilateraler Handel m	multilateral trade	—	commercio multilaterale m	comercio multilateral m
commercial agency (E)	Auskunftei f	—	agence de renseignements f	agenzia d'informazioni f	agencia de información f
commercial agent (E)	Handelsvertreter m	—	représentant de commerce m	agente di commercio m	representante comercial m

	D	E	F	I	Es
commercial balance sheet (E)	Handelsbilanz f	—	balance des opérations en marchandises f	bilancia commerciale f	balanza comercial f
commercial bank (E)	Kreditbank f	—	banque de crédit f	banca di credito f	banco de crédito m
commercial bank (E)	Geschäftsbank f	—	banque commerciale f	banca commerciale f	banco comercial m
commercial bill (E)	Warenwechsel m	—	traite commerciale f	cambiale commerciale f	letra comercial f
commercial book (E)	Handelsbuch n	—	livre de commerce m	libro di commercio m	libro comercial m
commercial broker (E)	Handelsmakler m	—	agent commercial m	mediatore di commercio m	corredor de comercio m
commercial credits (E)	Handelskredite m/pl	—	crédits commerciaux m/pl	crediti al commercio m/pl	créditos comerciales m/pl
commercial employee (E)	Handlungsgehilfe m	—	commis du commerce m	commesso m	auxiliar mercantil m
commercial instruments to order (E)	kaufmännische Orderpapiere n/pl	—	effets de commerce à ordre m/pl	effetti commerciali all'ordine m/pl	títulos comerciales a la orden m/pl
commercialisation (F)	Vermarktung f	marketing	—	vendibilità f	comercialización f
commercial law (E)	Handelsrecht n	—	droit commercial m	diritto commerciale m	derecho comercial m
Commercial Paper (D)	—	commercial paper	effet de commerce m	commercial paper m	documento mercantil m
commercial paper (E)	Commercial Paper n	—	effet de commerce m	commercial paper m	documento mercantil m
commercial paper (I)	Commercial Paper n	commercial paper	effet de commerce m	—	documento mercantil m
commercial papers (E)	Handelspapiere n/pl	—	effets de commerce m/pl	effetti commerciali m/pl	documentos m/pl
commercial papers (E)	Geschäftspapier n	—	papier d'affaires m	carta intestata f	documento comercial m
commercial power of attorney (E)	Handlungsvollmacht f	—	pouvoir commercial m	mandato commerciale m	poder mercantil m
commercial register (E)	Handelsregister n	—	registre de commerce m	registro commerciale m	registro comercial m
commercial transactions (E)	Handelsgeschäfte n/pl	—	affaires commerciales f/pl	affari commerciali m/pl	negocio m
commerciante (I)	Händler m	dealer	commerçant m	—	comerciante m
commercio (I)	Handel m	trade	commerce m	—	comercio m
commercio al dettaglio (I)	Einzelhandel m	retail trade	commerce de détail m	—	comercio al por menor m
commercio delle derrate (I)	Produktenhandel m	produce trade	commerce des produits agricoles m	—	comercio de ultramarinos m
commercio delle valute (I)	Usancenhandel m	trading in foreign exchange	commerce de change m	—	comercio de cambio m
commercio delle valute (I)	Sortenhandel m	dealing in foreign notes and coins	commerce de change m	—	negociación de moneda extranjera f
commercio dell'oro (I)	Goldhandel m	gold trade	commerce de l'or m	—	comercio de oro m
commercio estero (I)	Außenwirtschaft f	foreign trade and payments	économie des échanges extérieurs f	—	economía exterior f
commercio estero (I)	Außenhandel m	foreign trade	commerce extérieur m	—	comercio exterior m
commercio in partecipazioni (I)	Beteiligungshandel m	equity financing transactions	opérations de financement par participation f/pl	—	operaciones de financiación de participación f/pl
commercio in proprio (I)	Eigenhandel m	trading on own account	commerce à propre compte m	—	comercio por cuenta propia m
commercio monete pregiate (I)	Münzhandel m	dealings in gold and silver coins	commerce des pièces de monnaie m	—	comercio con monedas m
commercio multilaterale (I)	Multilateraler Handel m	multilateral trade	commerce multilatéral m	—	comercio multilateral m
commercio petrolifero a termine (I)	Ölterminhandel m	oil futures dealings	opérations pétrolières à terme f/pl	—	negociación de petróleo a término f
commercio titoli a reddito fisso (I)	Rentenhandel m	bond trading	négociation des valeurs à revenu fixe f	—	contratación de títulos de renta fija f
commesso (I)	Handlungsgehilfe m	commercial employee	commis du commerce m	—	auxiliar mercantil m

	D	E	F	I	Es
commis du commerce (F)	Handlungsgehilfe *m*	commercial employee	—	commesso *m*	auxiliar mercantil *m*
commission (E)	Provision *f*	—	commission *f*	commissione *f*	comisión *f*
commission (F)	Provision *f*	commission	—	commissione *f*	comisión *f*
commission agent (E)	Kommissionär *m*	—	commissionnaire *m*	commissionario *m*	comisionista *m*
commissionario (I)	Untermakler *m*	intermediate broker	sous-agent *m*	—	subagente *m*
commissionario (I)	Kommissionär *m*	commission agent	commissionnaire *m*	—	comisionista *m*
commissionario di borsa (I)	Effekten-kommissionär *m*	securities commission agent	banque chargée d'opérations sur titres *f*	—	comisionista de valores *m*
commission bancaire sur crédit d'acceptation (F)	Akzeptprovision *f*	commission for acceptance	—	commissione d'accettazione *f*	comisión de aceptación *f*
commission-bearing account (E)	provisionspflichtiges Konto *n*	—	compte de débiteurs *m*	conto soggetto a provvigione *m*	cuenta sujeto al pago de una comisión *f*
commission business (E)	Kommissions-geschäft *n*	—	affaire en commission *f*	contratto di commissione *m*	operación de comisión *f*
commission d'apériteur (F)	Führungsprovision *f*	managers commission	—	provvigione di gestione *f*	comisión de alta dirección *f*
commission de banque (F)	Bankprovision *f*	banker's commission	—	commissione bancaria *f*	comisión bancaria *f*
commission de chèque retourné (F)	Rückscheckprovision *f*	commision on returned cheque	—	provvigione di rigresso *f*	comisión de cheque devuelto *f*
commission de contrôle (F)	Prüfungskommission *f*	examining commission	—	giuria *f*	comisión de revisión de cuentas *f*
commission de découvert (F)	Überziehungs provision *f*	overdraft commission	—	provvigione di scoperta *f*	comisión de giro en descubierto *f*
commission d'émission (F)	Emissionsvergütung *f*	issue commission	—	commissione d'emissione *f*	remuneración emisora *f*
commission de monopoles (F)	Monopolkommission *f*	Monopolies Commission	—	commissione antitrust *f*	comisión de monopolios *f*
commission d'encaissement (F)	Inkassoprovision *f*	collection commission	—	provvigione d'incasso *f*	comisión *f*
commission de placement (F)	Bankierbonifikation *f*	placing commission	—	provvigione bancaria *f*	comisión de mediación bancaria *f*
commission d'escompte (F)	Diskontprovision *f*	discount commission	—	provvigione di sconto *f*	comisión de descuento *f*
commission d'étude des dossiers de crédit (F)	Kreditausschuß *m*	credit committee	—	comitato di credito *m*	comité de crédito *m*
commission des contrôleurs (F)	Gläubigerausschuß *m*	committee of inspection	—	comitato dei creditori *m*	comisión de los acreedores *f*
commission de vente (F)	Schalterprovision *f*	selling commission	—	commissione di collocamento *f*	comisión al contado *f*
commission du marché des capitaux (F)	Kapitalmarkt-kommission *f*	capital market committee	—	commissione mercato finanziario *f*	comité de mercado de capital *m*
commissione (I)	Provision *f*	commission	commission *f*	—	comisión *f*
commissione antitrust (I)	Monopol-kommission *f*	Monopolies Commission	commission de monopoles *f*	—	comisión de monopolios *f*
commissione bancaria (I)	Bankprovision *f*	banker's commission	commission de banque *f*	—	comisión bancaria *f*
commissione d'accettazione (I)	Akzeptprovision *f*	commission for acceptance	commission bancaire sur crédit d'acceptation *f*	—	comisión de aceptación *f*
commissione d'emissione (I)	Emissionsvergütung *f*	issue commission	commission d'émission *f*	—	remuneración emisora *f*
commissione di collocamento (I)	Schalterprovision *f*	selling commission	commission de vente *f*	—	comisión al contado *f*
commissione di liquidazione (I)	Liquidationsgebühr *f*	liquidation fee	frais de liquidation *m/pl*	—	derechos de liquidación *m/pl*
commissione d'incasso (I)	Inkassogebühr *f*	collection fee	frais de recouvrement *m/pl*	—	comisión de cobro *f*
commissione mercato finanziario (I)	Kapitalmarkt-kommission *f*	capital market committee	commission du marché des capitaux *f*	—	comité de mercado de capital *m*

	D	E	F	I	Es
commissione operazioni fuori borsa (I)	Freiverkehrsausschuß m	unofficial dealings committee	comité du marché libre m	—	comité de mercado libre m
commission for acceptance (E)	Akzeptprovision f	—	commission bancaire sur crédit d'acceptation f	commissione d'accettazione f	comisión de aceptación f
commission-free account (E)	provisionsfreies Konto n	—	compte de créditeurs m	conto franco di provvigione m	cuenta sin comisión f
commissionnaire (F)	Kommissionär m	commission agent	—	commissionario m	comisionista m
commission on bank guarantee (E)	Aval-Provision f	—	commission pour aval f	provvigione d'avallo f	comisión por aval f
commission on returned cheque (E)	Rückscheckprovision f	—	commission de chèque retourné f	provvigione di rigresso f	comisión de cheque devuelto f
commission on turnover (E)	Umsatzprovision f	—	commission sur le chiffre d'affaires f	provvigione sul fatturato f	comisión sobre la cifra de facturación f
commission pour aval (F)	Aval-Provision f	commission on bank guarantee	—	provvigione d'avallo f	comisión por aval f
commission pour l'admission des valeurs à la cote (F)	Zulassungsstelle f	admission board	—	ufficio d'ammissione m	oficina de matrícula f
commission sur le chiffre d'affaires (F)	Umsatzprovision f	commission on turnover	—	provvigione sul fatturato f	comisión sobre la cifra de facturación f
commitment (E)	Engagement n	—	engagement m	impegno m	compromiso m
committee of inspection (E)	Gläubigerausschuß m	—	commission des contrôleurs f	comitato dei creditori m	comisión de los acreedores f
commodity exchange (E)	Warenbörse f	—	bourse de marchandises f	borsa merci f	bolsa de mercancías f
commodity future (E)	Commodity futures f/pl	—	opérations à livrer m	commodity futures m/pl	operaciones de mercancías a plazo f/pl
Commodity futures (D)	—	commodity future	opérations à livrer m	commodity futures m/pl	operaciones de mercancías a plazo f/pl
commodity futures (I)	Commodity futures f/pl	commodity future	opérations à livrer m	—	operaciones de mercancías a plazo f/pl
commodity futures trading (E)	Warentermingeschäft n	—	opération à livrer f	operazione a termine su merci f	operación a plazo f
commodity market (E)	Gütermarkt m	—	marché des biens m	mercato delle merci m	mercado de bienes m
commodity money (E)	Naturalgeld n	—	argent en nature m	oggetto di baratto m	dinero en especie m
commodity restriction scheme (E)	Quotenkartell f	—	cartel de contingentement m	cartello di contingentamento m	cartel de contingentes m
communauté d'intérêts (F)	Interessengemeinschaft f	pooling of interests	—	comunione d'interessi f	comunidad de intereses f
Communauté Européene (F)	Europäische Gemeinschaft f	European Community	—	Comunità Europea f	Comunidad Europea f
communicazione di revisione (I)	Kontrollmitteilung f	tracer note	bulletin de contrôle m	—	control cruzado m
compañía colectiva (Es)	offene Handelsgesellschaft f	general partnership	société en nom collectif f	società in nome collettivo f	—
compañía de inversiones (Es)	Kapitalanlagegesellschaft f	capital investment company	société d'investissement f	società d'investimento f	—
company (E)	Gesellschaft f	—	société f	società f	sociedad f
Company Law (E)	Aktiengesetz n	—	loi sur des sociétés par actions f	legge sulle società per azioni f	ley sobre régimen jurídico de las sociedades anónimas f
company law (E)	Aktienrecht n	—	loi sur les sociétés anonymes f	diritto delle società per azioni m	derecho de sociedades anónimas m
company limited by shares (E)	Kapitalgesellschaft f	—	société de capitaux f	società di capitali f	sociedad de capital f
company-owned shares (E)	eigene Aktien f/pl	—	actions propres f/pl	azioni sociali f/pl	acciones propias f/pl
company's debts (E)	Gesellschaftsschulden f/pl	—	dettes sociales f/pl	debiti della società m/pl	deudas sociales f/pl
comparative balance sheet (E)	Vergleichsbilanz f	—	bilan au moment de l'ouverture du règlement judiciare m	situazione patrimoniale di concordato f	balance de comparación m
compensación (Es)	Aufrechnung f	set-off	compensation f	compensazione f	—
compensación (Es)	Abfindung f	compensation	indemnité f	indennizzo m	—

	D	E	F	I	Es
compensación (Es)	Verrechnung *f*	compensation	compensation *f*	compensazione *f*	—
compensación (Es)	Kompensation *f*	compensation	compensation *f*	compensazione *f*	—
compensación ajena (Es)	Fremdkompensation *f*	offset transaction with resale to a third party	intervention d'un tiers dans une affaire de compensation *f*	compensazione per conto altrui *f*	—
compensación de cambios (Es)	Währungsausgleich *m*	currency conversion compensation	alignement des monnaies *m*	conguaglio dei cambi *m*	—
compensación de cargas (Es)	Lastenausgleich *m*	equalization of burdens	péréquation des charges *f*	perequazione degli oneri *f*	—
compensación de cuentas (Es)	Skontration *f*	settlement of time bargains	inventaire mouvementé *m*	compensazione *f*	—
compensación de pérdidas (Es)	Verlustausgleich *m*	loss compensation	compensation des pertes *f*	conguaglio dei passivi *m*	—
compensación en efectivo (Es)	Barabfindung *f*	settlement in cash	indemnité en espèces *f*	indennità in contanti *f*	—
compensation (E)	Verrechnung *f*	—	compensation *f*	compensazione *f*	compensación *f*
compensation (E)	Kompensation *f*	—	compensation *f*	compensazione *f*	compensación *f*
compensation (E)	Abfindung *f*	—	indemnité *f*	indennizzo *m*	compensación *f*
compensation (F)	Verrechnung *f*	compensation	—	compensazione *f*	compensación *f*
compensation (F)	Kompensation *f*	compensation	—	compensazione *f*	compensación *f*
compensation (F)	Aufrechnung *f*	set-off	—	compensazione *f*	compensación *f*
compensation des pertes (F)	Verlustausgleich *m*	loss compensation	—	conguaglio dei passivi *m*	compensación de pérdidas *f*
compensation financière (F)	Finanzausgleich *m*	financial equalization	—	conguaglio finanziario *m*	ajuste financiero *m*
compensation for loss suffered (E)	Schadensersatz *m*	—	dommages-intérêts *m/pl*	risarcimento dei danni *m*	indemnización por daños y perjuicios *f*
compensation fund (E)	Ausgleichsfonds *m*	—	fonds de compensation *m*	fondo di compensazione *m*	fondo de compensación *m*
compensation offer (E)	Abfindungsangebot *n*	—	offre d'indemnité *f*	offerta di riscatto *f*	oferta de compensación *f*
compensation payment (E)	Ausgleichszahlung *f*	—	payement pour solde de compte *m*	compensazione *f*	pago de compensación *m*
compensazione (I)	Ausgleichszahlung *f*	compensation payment	payement pour solde de compte *m*	—	pago de compensación *m*
compensazione (I)	Aufrechnung *f*	set-off	compensation *f*	—	compensación *f*
compensazione (I)	Verrechnung *f*	compensation	compensation *f*	—	compensación *f*
compensazione (I)	Skontration *f*	settlement of time bargains	inventaire mouvementé *m*	—	compensación de cuentas *f*
compensazione (I)	Kompensation *f*	compensation	compensation *f*	—	compensación *f*
compensazione degli assegni (I)	Scheckabrechnung *f*	cheque clearance	règlement des chèques par voie de compensation *m*	—	liquidación de cheques *f*
compensazione per conto altrui (I)	Fremdkompensation *f*	offset transaction with resale to a third party	intervention d'un tiers dans une affaire de compensation *f*	—	compensación ajena *f*
compenso in natura (I)	Deputat *n*	payment in kind	avantage en nature *m*	—	remuneración en especie *f*
competencia desleal (Es)	unlauterer Wettbewerb *m*	unfair competition	concurrence déloyale *f*	concorrenza sleale *f*	—
complacencia (Es)	Kulanz *f*	fairness in trade	souplesse en affaires *f*	correntezza *f*	—
complaint (E)	Reklamation *f*	—	réclamation *f*	reclamo *m*	reclamación *f*
compléments patronaux (F)	Arbeitgeber-zuschüsse *m/pl*	employer's contributions	—	contributi del datore di lavoro *m/pl*	suplementos patronales *m/pl*
comportamento anticiclico (I)	antizyklisches Verhalten *n*	countercyclical development	comportement anticyclique *m*	—	comportamiento anticíclico *m*
comportamiento anticíclico (Es)	antizyklisches Verhalten *n*	countercyclical development	comportement anticyclique *m*	comportamento anticiclico *m*	—
comportement anticyclique (F)	antizyklisches Verhalten *n*	countercyclical development	—	comportamento anticiclico *m*	comportamiento anticíclico *m*
composition proceedings (E)	Vergleichsverfahren *n*	—	procédure de conciliation *f*	procedura di concordato *f*	procedimiento conciliatorio *m*

	D	E	F	I	Es
composition proceedings (E)	Ausgleichsverfahren *n*	—	procédé de la compensation *m*	metodo di compensazione *m*	procedimiento de compensación *m*
compound interest (E)	Zinseszins *m*	—	intérêt composé *m*	anatocismo *m*	interés compuesto *m*
compra (Es)	Kauf *m*	purchase	achat *m*	acquisto *m*	—
compra de crédito (Es)	Kreditkauf *m*	credit purchase	achat à crédit *m*	acquisto di credito *m*	—
compra de créditos (Es)	Forderungskauf *m*	purchase of accounts receivable	vente d'une créance *f*	acquisizione di crediti *f*	—
compra de valores (Es)	Effektenkauf *m*	purchase of securities	achat de titres *m*	acquisto di titoli *m*	—
compra en efectivo (Es)	Barkauf *m*	cash purchase	achat au comptant *m*	acquisto in contanti *m*	—
compra limitada (Es)	bezahlt Geld	more buyers than sellers	comptant acheteur	domanda parzial-mente insoddisfatta *f*	—
compra para sostener precios (Es)	Stützungskauf *m*	support buying	achat de soutien *m*	acquisto di sostegno *m*	—
compras de sostén (Es)	Kurspflege *f*	price nursing	régulation des cours *f*	sostegno delle quotazioni *m*	—
compras mayoritarias (Es)	Majoritätskäufe *m/pl*	buying of shares to secure the controlling interest in a company	achats majoritaires *m/pl*	acquisti di maggioranza *m/pl*	—
compras offshore (Es)	Offshore-Käufe *m/pl*	offshore purchases	achats off shore *m/pl*	acquisti off-shore *m/pl*	—
compravendita titoli su commissione (I)	Effekten-kommissions-geschäft *n*	securities transactions on commission	opération sur titres *f*	—	operaciones de valores a base de comisión *f/pl*
comprobante de asiento (Es)	Buchungsbeleg *m*	accounting voucher	pièce comptable *f*	documento contabile *m*	—
compromiso (Es)	Engagement *n*	commitment	engagement *m*	impegno *m*	—
comproprietà (I)	Miteigentum *n*	co-ownership	copropriété *f*	—	copropiedad *f*
comproprietà di quota ideale (I)	Bruchteilseigentum *n*	ownership in fractional shares	propriété d'une quote-part indivise *f*	—	propiedad por fracciones *f*
comptabilité (F)	Buchführung *f*	accounting	—	contabilità *f*	contabilidad *f*
comptabilité bancaire (F)	Bankbuchhaltung *f*	bank's accounting	—	contabilità bancaria *f*	contabilidad bancaria *f*
comptabilité de devises (F)	Devisenbuchhaltung *f*	currency accounting	—	contabilità dei cambi *f*	contabilidad de divisas *f*
comptabilité de postes ouverts (F)	Offene-Posten-Buchhaltung *f*	open-item accounting	—	contabilità a partite sospese *f*	contabilidad de partidas abiertas *f*
comptabilité des dépôts (F)	Depotbuchhaltung *f*	security deposit account	—	contabilità dei depositi *f*	contabilidad de depósitos *f*
comptabilité dite américaine (F)	amerikanisches Rechnungswesen *n*	American accounting system	—	contabilità americana *f*	contabilidad americana *f*
comptabilité en partie double (F)	doppelte Buchführung *f*	double entry bookkeeping	—	partita doppia *f*	contabilidad de partida doble *f*
comptabilité financière (F)	Finanzbuchhaltung *f*	financial accounting	—	contabilità finanziaria *f*	contabilidad financiera *f*
comptabilité générale (F)	Hauptbuchhaltung *f*	chief accountancy	—	ufficio di contabilità generale *m*	contabilidad principal *f*
comptabilité nationale (F)	Volkswirtschaftliche Gesamtrechnung *f*	national accounting	—	contabilità nazionale *f*	contabilidad nacional *f*
comptabité industrielle (F)	betriebliches Rechnungswesen *n*	operational accountancy	—	ragioneria aziendale *f*	contabilidad empresarial *f*
comptage (F)	Auszählung *f*	counting	—	scrutinio *m*	cómputo *m*
comptant (F)	bar	cash	—	in contanti	al contado
comptant acheteur (F)	bezahlt Geld	more buyers than sellers	—	domanda parzial-mente insoddisfatta *f*	compra limitada *f*
comptant vendeur (F)	bezahlt Brief	more sellers than buyers	—	offerta eccedente la domanda *f*	la oferta fue mayor que la demanda *f*
compte (F)	Konto *n*	account	—	conto *m*	cuenta *f*
compte à intérêt fixe (F)	Festzinskonto *n*	fixed-interest bearing account	—	conto ad interesse fisso *m*	cuenta de interés fijo *f*
compte anonyme (F)	Nummernkonto *n*	numbered account	—	conto cifrato *m*	cuenta anónima *f*
compte bloqué (F)	Sperrkonto *n*	blocked account	—	conto bloccato *m*	cuenta bloqueada *f*
compte capital (F)	Eigenkapitalkonto *n*	equity account	—	conto del capitale proprio *m*	cuenta de capital propio *f*

	D	E	F	I	Es
compte collectif (F)	Sammelkonto *n*	collective account	—	conto collettivo *m*	cuenta colectiva *f*
compte commun (F)	Gemeinschaftskonto *n*	joint account	—	conto congiunto *m*	cuenta conjunta *f*
compte courant (F)	Kontokorrent *m*	current account	—	conto corrente *m*	cuenta corriente *f*
compte courant de banque (F)	Bankkontokorrent *n*	current account with a bank	—	conto corrente bancario *m*	cuenta corriente bancaria *f*
compte dans une autre banque (F)	Nostrokonto *n*	nostro account	—	conto nostro *m*	nuestra cuenta *f*
compte de bilan (F)	Bilanzkonto *n*	balance sheet account	—	conto di bilancio *m*	cuenta permanente *f*
compte de capital (F)	Kapitalkonto *n*	capital account	—	conto capitale *m*	cuenta de capital *f*
compte de capital (F)	Vermögensrechnung *f*	capital account	—	situazione patrimoniale *f*	cálculo del valor neto *m*
compte de choses (F)	totes Depot *n*	dormant deposit	—	deposito inattivo *m*	depósito muerto *m*
compte de créances à recevoir (F)	Debitorenkonto *n*	customer account	—	conto debitori *m*	cuenta deudor *f*
compte de créditeur (F)	provisionsfreies Konto *n*	commission-free account	—	conto franco di provvigione *m*	cuenta sin comisión *f*
compte de débiteur (F)	provisionspflichtiges Konto *n*	commission-bearing account	—	conto soggetto a provvigione *m*	cuenta sujeto al pago de una comisión *f*
compte de dépôt (F)	Depotkonto *n*	security deposit account	—	conto di deposito *m*	cuenta de depósitos *f*
compte de devises (F)	Devisenbilanz *f*	net movement of foreign exchange	—	bilancia valutaria *f*	balanza de divisas *f*
compte de fournisseurs (F)	Lieferkonto *n*	accounts payable	—	conto fornitori *m*	cuenta de suministradores *f*
compte de frais (F)	Kostenrechnung *f*	statement of costs	—	calcolo dei costi *m*	cálculo de costes *m*
compte de frais (F)	Aufwandskonto *n*	expense account	—	conto spesa *m*	cuenta de gastos *f*
compte de frais (F)	Spesenrechnung *f*	statement of expenses	—	conto delle spese *m*	cuenta de gastos *f*
compte de frais à reporter (F)	Aufwands- ausgleichkonto *n*	account for reimbursements of expenses	—	conto compensazione spese *m*	cuenta de compen- sación de gastos *f*
compte de frais par secteur (F)	Kostenstelle *f*	cost centre	—	centro di costo *m*	sección de gastos *f*
compte d'épargne (F)	Sparkonto *n*	savings account	—	conto a risparmio *m*	cuenta de ahorros *f*
compte de profits et pertes (F)	Aufwands- und Ertragsrechnung *f*	profit and loss account	—	conto economico *m*	cuenta de beneficios y pérdidas *f*
compte de résultat (F)	Gewinn- und Verlustrechnung *f*	profit and loss account	—	conto profitti e perdite *m*	cuenta de pérdidas y ganancias *f*
compte des titres de participation (F)	Effektenkonto *n*	securities account	—	conto titoli *m*	cuenta de valores *f*
compte de syndicat (F)	Syndikatskonto *n*	syndicate account	—	conto sindacale *m*	cuenta de cártel *f*
compte de tiers (F)	Anderkonto *n*	fiduciary account	—	conto altrui *m*	cuenta fiduciaria *f*
compte de titres (F)	Stückekonto *n*	shares account	—	conto titoli *m*	cuenta de valores *f*
compte de ventes (F)	Verkaufskonto *n*	trading account	—	conto vendite *m*	cuenta de ventas *f*
compte de virement (F)	Girokonto *n*	current account	—	giroconto *m*	cuenta corriente *f*
compte d'existences (F)	Bestandskonto *n*	real account	—	conto magazzino *m*	cuenta de existencia *f*
compte d'installation (F)	Aufbaukonto *n*	build-up account	—	conto accumulativo *m*	cuenta de financiación de desarrollo *f*
compte du marché monétaire (F)	Geldmarktkonto *n*	money market account	—	conto monetario *m*	cuenta de mercado monetario *f*
compte d'un client bancaire (F)	Lorokonto *n*	loro account	—	conto loro *m*	cuenta de un cliente bancario *f*
compte en banque (F)	Bankkonto *n*	bank account	—	conto bancario *m*	cuenta bancaria *f*
compte en monnaie étrangère (F)	Fremdwährungs- konto *n*	account in foreign currency	—	conto in valuta estera *m*	cuenta de moneda extranjera *f*
compte en monnaie étrangère (F)	Valutakonto *n*	foreign currency account	—	conto valutario *m*	cuenta de moneda extranjera *f*
compte en monnaies étrangères (F)	Währungskonto *n*	currency account	—	conto valutario *m*	cuenta de moneda extranjera *f*
compte entretenu à l'étranger (F)	Auslandskonto *n*	foreign account	—	conto estero *m*	cuenta en el extranjero *f*

concentration of banks

	D	E	F	I	Es
compte financier (F)	Finanzkonto *n*	financial account	—	conto finanziario *m*	cuenta financiera *f*
compte joint (F)	Und-Konto *n*	joint account where all signatories must sign	—	conto comune *m*	cuenta colectiva *f*
compte joint (F)	Oderkonten *n/pl*	joint account	—	conti a firme disgiunte *m/pl*	cuentas indistintas *f/pl*
compte libellé en devises (F)	Devisenkonto *n*	foreign exchange account	—	conto in valuta estera *m*	cuenta en divisas *f*
compte ouvert (F)	offenes Konto *n*	open account	—	conto aperto *m*	cuenta abierta *f*
compte privé (F)	Privatkonto *n*	personal account	—	conto particolare *m*	cuenta privada *f*
compte rendu (F)	Rechenschaft *f*	rendering of account	—	conto *m*	cuenta *f*
compte rendu de vérification (F)	Prüfungsbericht *m*	audit report	—	relazione d'ispezione *f*	informe de auditoría *m*
compte sans mouvement (F)	totes Konto *n*	inoperative account	—	conto inattivo *m*	cuenta muerta *f*
comptes d'épargne anonymes (F)	anonyme Sparkonten *n/pl*	anonymous savings accounts	—	conti di risparmio cifrati *m/pl*	cuentas de ahorro anónimas *f/pl*
comptes de personne (F)	Personenkonten *n/pl*	personal accounts	—	conti di persone *m/pl*	cuentas personas *f/pl*
comptes de résultats intermédiaires (F)	Kurzfristige Erfolgsrechnung *f*	monthly income statement	—	conto economico a breve termine *m*	estado de resultados a corto plazo *m*
comptes d'investissement (F)	Anlagekonten *n/pl*	investment accounts	—	conti degli investimenti *m/pl*	cuentas de inversión *f/pl*
compte spécial (F)	Sonderkonto *n*	separate account	—	conto particolare *m*	cuenta especial *f*
compte vidéotex (F)	Tele-Konto *n*	videotext account	—	conto videotel *m*	cuenta videotexto *f*
compulsory contribution (E)	Pflichteinlage *f*	—	apport obligatoire *m*	deposito obbligatorio *m*	depósito obligatorio *m*
compulsory disclosure (E)	Publikationspflicht *f*	—	obligation de publication *f*	obbligo di pubblicazione *m*	obligación de publicación *f*
compulsory loan (E)	Zwangsanleihe *f*	—	emprunt forcé *m*	prestito forzato *m*	empréstito forzoso *m*
compulsory safe custody (E)	Depotzwang *m*	—	dépôt obligatoire *m*	obbligo di deposito *m*	depósito obligatorio *m*
compulsory saving (E)	Zwangssparen *n*	—	épargne forcée *f*	risparmio forzato *m*	ahorro forzoso *m*
cómputo (Es)	Auszählung *f*	counting	comptage *m*	scrutinio *m*	—
comunidad de intereses (Es)	Interessen- gemeinschaft *f*	pooling of interests	communauté d'intérêts *f*	comunione d'interessi *f*	—
comunidad de obtención de beneficios (Es)	Gewinngemeinschaft *f*	profit pool	pool de profit *m*	comunione degli utili *f*	—
Comunidad Europea (Es)	Europäische Gemeinschaft *f*	European Community	Communauté Européene	Comunità Europea *f*	—
comunione degli utili (I)	Gewinngemeinschaft *f*	profit pool	pool de profit *m*	—	comunidad de obten- ción de beneficios *f*
comunione d'interessi (I)	Interessen- gemeinschaft *f*	pooling of interests	communauté d'intérêts *f*	—	comunidad de intereses *f*
Comunità Europea (I)	Europäische Gemeinschaft *f*	European Community	Communauté Européene	—	Comunidad Europea *f*
concedere una moratoria (I)	stillhalten	to sell an option	vendre une option	—	prorrogar
concentración bancaria (Es)	Bankenkonzentration *f*	concentration of banks	concentration bancaire *f*	concentrazione bancaria *f*	—
concentración de capital (Es)	Kapitalkonzentration *f*	concentration of capital	concentration de capital *f*	concentrazione di capitali *f*	—
concentración empresarial (Es)	Unternehmens- konzentration *f*	business concentration	concentration d'entreprises *f*	concentrazione industriale *f*	—
concentration bancaire (F)	Bankenkonzentration *f*	concentration of banks	—	concentrazione bancaria *f*	concentración bancaria *f*
concentration de capital (F)	Kapitalkonzentration *f*	concentration of capital	—	concentrazione di capitali *f*	concentración de capital *f*
concentration d'entreprises (F)	Unternehmens- konzentration *f*	business concentration	—	concentrazione industriale *f*	concentración empresarial *f*
concentration of banks (E)	Bankenkonzentration *f*	—	concentration bancaire *f*	concentrazione bancaria *f*	concentración bancaria *f*

	D	E	F	I	Es
concentration of capital (E)	Kapitalkonzentration f	—	concentration de capital f	concentrazione di capitali f	concentración de capital f
concentrazione bancaria (I)	Bankenkonzentration f	concentration of banks	concentration bancaire f	—	concentración bancaria f
concentrazione di capitali (I)	Kapitalkonzentration f	concentration of capital	concentration de capital f	—	concentración de capital f
concentrazione industriale (I)	Unternehmens-konzentration f	business concentration	concentration d'entreprises f	—	concentración empresarial f
concesión (Es)	Konzession f	license	concession f	licenza f	—
concesión (Es)	Bewilligung f	allowance	consentement m	autorizzazione f	—
concession (F)	Konzession f	license	—	licenza f	concesión f
conclusion (E)	Abschluß m	—	conclusion f	chiusura f	conclusión f
conclusion (F)	Abschluß m	conclusion	—	chiusura f	conclusión f
conclusión (Es)	Abschluß m	conclusion	conclusion f	chiusura f	—
conclusion d'un contrat (F)	Kontrahierung f	contraction	—	conclusione di contratto f	contratación f
conclusione di contratto (I)	Kontrahierung f	contraction	conclusion d'un contrat f	—	contratación f
concordance of maturities (E)	Fristenkongruenz f	—	congruence d'échéances f	congruenza dei termini di scadenza f	congruencia de plazos f
concorrenza sleale (I)	unlauterer Wettbewerb m	unfair competition	concurrence déloyale f	—	competencia desleal f
concurrence déloyale (F)	unlauterer Wettbewerb m	unfair competition	—	concorrenza sleale f	competencia desleal f
condición (Es)	Bedingung f	condition	condition f	clausola f	—
condición de pago (Es)	Zahlungsbedingung f	terms of payment	condition de payement f	condizione di pagamento f	—
condición de plazo (Es)	Befristung f	time limit	fixation d'un délai f	fissazione di un termine f	—
condiciones (Es)	Konditionen f/pl	conditions	conditions f/pl	condizioni f/pl	—
condiciones bancarias (Es)	Bankkonditionen f/pl	bank conditions	conditions bancaires f/pl	condizioni bancarie f/pl	—
condiciones comerciales (Es)	Geschäfts-bedingungen f/pl	terms and conditions of business	conditions commerciales f/pl	condizioni contrattuali f/pl	—
condiciones de emisión (Es)	Emissions-bedingungen f/pl	terms and conditions of issue	conditions de l'émission f/pl	condizioni d'emissione f/pl	—
condiciones de suscripción (Es)	Bezugsbedingungen f/pl	subscription conditions	conditions de souscription f/pl	condizioni d'acquisto f/pl	—
condiciones preliminares (Es)	Vorschaltkonditionen f/pl	preliminary conditions	conditions préliminaires f/pl	condizioni preliminari f/pl	—
condition (E)	Bedingung f	—	condition f	clausola f	condición f
condition (F)	Bedingung f	condition	—	clausola f	condición f
conditional capital increase (E)	bedingte Kapitalerhöhung f	—	restriction à l'augmentation du capital social f	aumento di capitale condizionato m	aumento de capital condicional m
condition de payement (F)	Zahlungsbedingung f	terms of payment	—	condizione di pagamento f	condición de pago f
conditions (E)	Konditionen f/pl	—	conditions f/pl	condizioni f/pl	condiciones f/pl
conditions (F)	Konditionen f/pl	conditions	—	condizioni f/pl	condiciones f/pl
conditions bancaires (F)	Bankkonditionen f/pl	bank conditions	—	condizioni bancarie f/pl	condiciones bancarias f/pl
conditions commerciales (F)	Geschäfts-bedingungen f/pl	terms and conditions of business	—	condizioni contrattuali f/pl	condiciones comerciales f/pl
conditions de l'émission (F)	Emissions-bedingungen f/pl	terms and conditions of issue	—	condizioni d'emissione f/pl	condiciones de emisión f/pl
conditions de souscription (F)	Bezugsbedingungen f/pl	subscription conditions	—	condizioni d'acquisto f/pl	condiciones de suscripción f/pl
conditions préliminaires (F)	Vorschaltkonditionen f/pl	preliminary conditions	—	condizioni preliminari f/pl	condiciones preliminares f/pl
condizione di pagamento (I)	Zahlungsbedingung f	terms of payment	condition de payement f	—	condición de pago f
condizioni (I)	Konditionen f/pl	conditions	conditions f/pl	—	condiciones f/pl

	D	E	F	I	Es
condizioni bancarie (I)	Bankkonditionen *f/pl*	bank conditions	conditions bancaires *f/pl*	—	condiciones bancarias *f/pl*
condizioni contrattuali (I)	Geschäfts-bedingungen *f/pl*	terms and conditions of business	conditions commerciales *f/pl*	—	condiciones comerciales *f/pl*
condizioni d'acquisto (I)	Bezugsbedingungen *f/pl*	subscription conditions	conditions de souscription *f/pl*	—	condiciones de suscripción *f/pl*
condizioni d'emissione (I)	Emissions-bedingungen *f/pl*	terms and conditions of issue	conditions de l'émission *f/pl*	—	condiciones de emisión *f/pl*
condizioni preliminari (I)	Vorschaltkonditionen *f/pl*	preliminary conditions	conditions préliminaires *f/pl*	—	condiciones preliminares *f/pl*
conferimento (I)	Zuweisung *f*	assignment	assignation *f*	—	atribución *f*
conferimento di un socio (I)	Gesellschafter-Darlehen *n*	proprietor's loan	prêt d'un associé à la société *m*	—	préstamo concedido a socios *m*
conferimento di un socio (I)	verdecktes Stammkapital *n*	quasi-equity capital	capital social occulte *m*	—	capital social oculto *m*
conferma (I)	Bestätigung *f*	confirmation	confirmation *f*	—	certificado *m*
conferma di ordinazione (I)	Auftragsbestätigung *f*	confirmation of the order	confirmation de commande *f*	—	confirmación de un pedido *f*
confirmación de un pedido (Es)	Auftragsbestätigung *f*	confirmation of the order	confirmation de commande *f*	conferma di ordinazione *f*	—
confirmation (E)	Bestätigung *f*	—	confirmation *f*	conferma *f*	certificado *m*
confirmation (F)	Bestätigung *f*	confirmation	—	conferma *f*	certificado *m*
confirmation bancaire (F)	Bankavis *m*	bank's confirmation of a letter of credit	—	avviso bancario *m*	aviso bancario *m*
confirmation de commande (F)	Auftragsbestätigung *f*	confirmation of the order	—	conferma di ordinazione *f*	confirmación de un pedido *f*
confirmation of the order (E)	Auftragsbestätigung *f*	—	confirmation de commande *f*	conferma di ordinazione *f*	confirmación de un pedido *f*
congelación de precios (Es)	Preisstopp *m*	price stop	blocage des prix *m*	blocco dei prezzi *m*	—
congiuntura (I)	Konjunktur *f*	business cycle	conjoncture *f*	—	coyuntura *f*
congruence d'échéances (F)	Fristenkongruenz *f*	concordance of maturities	—	congruenza dei termini di scadenza *f*	congruencia de plazos *f*
congruencia de plazos (Es)	Fristenkongruenz *f*	concordance of maturities	congruence d'échéances *f*	congruenza dei termini di scadenza *f*	—
congruenza dei termini di scadenza (I)	Fristenkongruenz *f*	concordance of maturities	congruence d'échéances *f*	—	congruencia de plazos *f*
conguaglio dei cambi (I)	Währungsausgleich *m*	currency conversion compensation	alignement des monnaies *m*	—	compensación de cambios *f*
conguaglio dei passivi (I)	Verlustausgleich *m*	loss compensation	compensation des pertes *f*	—	compensación de pérdidas *f*
conguaglio finanziario (I)	Finanzausgleich *m*	financial equalization	compensation financière *f*	—	ajuste financiero *m*
coniatura (I)	Prägung *f*	minting	frappe *f*	—	acuñación *f*
coniazione (I)	Ausprägung *f*	markedness	monnayage *m*	—	acuñación *f*
conjoncture (F)	Konjunktur *f*	business cycle	—	congiuntura *f*	coyuntura *f*
connaissement à ordre (F)	Orderkonnossement *n*	order bill of lading	—	polizza di carico all'ordine *f*	conocimiento a la orden *m*
connaissement partiel (F)	Teilkonnossement *n*	partial bill of lading	—	polizza di carico parziale *f*	recibo parcial *m*
connaissement sans réserve (F)	reines Konossement *n*	clean bill of lading	—	polizza di carico netta *f*	conocimiento limpio *m*
conocimiento a la orden (Es)	Orderkonnossement *n*	order bill of lading	connaissement à ordre *m*	polizza di carico all'ordine *f*	—
conocimiento limpio (Es)	reines Konossement *n*	clean bill of lading	connaissement sans réserve *m*	polizza di carico netta *f*	—
conseil (F)	Rat *m*	advice	—	consiglio *m*	consejo *m*
conseil d'experts (F)	Sachverständigenrat *m*	panel of experts	—	consiglio degli esperti *m*	consejo de asesores económicos *m*
Conseil de la banque centrale (F)	Zentralbankrat *m*	Central Bank Council	—	consiglio centrale banca centrale *m*	Consejo del Banco Central *m*
conseil de la bourse (F)	Börsenausschuß *m*	stock committee	—	comitato di borsa *m*	comité de las bolsas *m*

	D	E	F	I	Es
conseil de surveillance (F)	Aufsichtsrat *m*	supervisory board	—	consiglio di sorveglianza *m*	consejo de administración *m*
conseiller en investissement (F)	Vermögensberater *m*	investment advisor	—	consulente patrimoniale *m*	asesor en materia de inversiones *m*
conseiller en matière de devises (F)	Devisenberater *m*	foreign exchange advisor	—	consulente di cambio *m*	asesor en materia de divisas *m*
conseiller en matière de pensions (F)	Rentenberater *m*	consultant on pensions	—	consulente titoli a reddito fisso *m*	asesor en materia de títulos de renta fija *m*
consejo (Es)	Rat *m*	advice	conseil *m*	consiglio *m*	—
consejo de administración (Es)	Aufsichtsrat *m*	supervisory board	conseil de surveillance *m*	consiglio di sorveglianza *m*	—
consejo de asesores económicos (Es)	Sachverständigenrat *m*	panel of experts	conseil d'experts *m*	consiglio degli esperti *m*	—
Consejo del Banco Central (Es)	Zentralbankrat *m*	Central Bank Council	Conseil de la banque centrale *m*	consiglio centrale banca centrale *m*	—
consent (E)	Zustimmung *f*	—	accord *m*	approvazione *f*	consentimiento *m*
consentement (F)	Bewilligung *f*	allowance	—	autorizzazione *f*	concesión *f*
consentimiento (Es)	Zustimmung *f*	consent	accord *m*	approvazione *f*	—
conservación (Es)	Aufbewahrung *f*	deposit	garde en dépôt *f*	custodia *f*	—
conservación de capital (Es)	Kapitalerhaltung *f*	maintenance of capital	maintien du capital *m*	stabilità del valore del capitale *f*	—
consiglio (I)	Rat *m*	advice	conseil *m*	—	consejo *m*
consiglio centrale banca centrale (I)	Zentralbankrat *m*	Central Bank Council	Conseil de la banque centrale *m*	—	Consejo del Banco Central *m*
consiglio d'amministrazione (I)	Vorstand *m*	board	comité directeur *m*	—	junta directiva *f*
consiglio degli esperti (I)	Sachverständigenrat *m*	panel of experts	conseil d'experts *m*	—	consejo de asesores económicos *m*
consiglio di gestione (I)	Kuratorium *n*	board of trustees	charge de curateur *f*	—	curatorio *m*
consiglio di sorveglianza (I)	Aufsichtsrat *m*	supervisory board	conseil de surveillance *m*	—	consejo de administración *m*
consistenza di cassa (I)	Kassenbestand *m*	cash in hand	montant des espèces en caisse *m*	—	dinero en caja *m*
consoles (E)	Konsols *m/pl*	—	dettes consolidées *f/pl*	prestiti consolidati *m/pl*	deudas consolidadas *f/pl*
consolidación (Es)	Unifizierung *f*	consolidation	consolidation *f*	unificazione *f*	—
consolidar (Es)	fundieren	to fund	fonder	consolidare	—
consolidare (I)	fundieren	to fund	fonder	—	consolidar
consolidated balance sheet (E)	konsolidierte Bilanz *f*	—	bilan consolidé *m*	bilancio consolidato *m*	balance consolidado *m*
consolidation (E)	Unifizierung *f*	consolidation	consolidation *f*	unificazione *f*	consolidación *f*
consolidation (F)	Unifizierung *f*	consolidation	—	unificazione *f*	consolidación *f*
consolidation of shares (E)	Aktien-zusammenlegung *f*	—	regroupement d'actions *m*	raggruppamento di azioni *m*	fusión de acciones *f*
consorcio (Es)	Konsortium *n*	syndicate	consortium *m*	consorzio *m*	—
consorcio de empréstitos federales (Es)	Bundesanleihe-konsortium *n*	Federal loan syndicate	syndicat fédéral d'emprunts *m*	consorzio emissione titoli pubblici *m*	—
consorcio de garantía (Es)	Garantiekonsortium *n*	underwriting syndicate	syndicat bancaire de garantie *m*	consorzio di garanzia *m*	—
consorcio de suscripción (Es)	Übernahme-konsortium *n*	security-taking syndicate	syndicat bancaire de garantie *m*	consorzio di collocamento *m*	—
consorcio emisor (Es)	Emissions-konsortium *n*	underwriting syndicate	syndicat bancaire appuyant une émission *m*	consorzio d'emissione *m*	—
consorcio industrial (Es)	Industriekonsortium *n*	industrial syndicate	consortium industriel *m*	consorzio industriale *m*	—
consorcio interior (Es)	Innenkonsortium *n*	internal syndicate	consortium intérieur *m*	consorzio interno *m*	—
consorcios de comercialización (Es)	Verwertungs-konsortien *n/pl*	marketing syndicates	consortium de commercialisation *f*	consorzi di utilizzazione *m/pl*	—

	D	E	F	I	Es
consortium (F)	Konsortium *n*	syndicate	—	consorzio *m*	consorcio *m*
consortium de banques (F)	Bankenkonsortium *n*	banking syndicate	—	consorzio bancario *m*	sindicato bancario *m*
consortium de commercialisation (F)	Verwertungs konsortien *n/pl*	marketing syndicates	—	consorzi di utilizzazione *m/pl*	consorcios de comercialización *m/pl*
consortium de renflouement (F)	Auffanggesellschaft *f*	recipient company	—	società finanziaria *f*	sociedad holding *f*
consortium industriel (F)	Industriekonsortium *n*	industrial syndicate	—	consorzio industriale *m*	consorcio industrial *m*
consortium intérieur (F)	Innenkonsortium *n*	internal syndicate	—	consorzio interno *m*	consorcio interior *m*
consorzi di utilizzazione (I)	Verwertungs-konsortien *n/pl*	marketing syndicates	consortium de commercialisation *f*	—	consorcios de comercialización *m/pl*
consorzio (I)	Konsortium *n*	syndicate	consortium *m*	—	consorcio *m*
consorzio bancario (I)	Bankenkonsortium *n*	banking syndicate	consortium de banques *m*	—	sindicato bancario *m*
consorzio d'emissione (I)	Emissions-konsortium *n*	underwriting syndicate	syndicat bancaire appuyant une émission *m*	—	consorcio emisor *m*
consorzio di collocamento (I)	Übernahme-konsortium *n*	security-taking syndicate	syndicat bancaire de garantie *m*	—	consorcio de suscripción *m*
consorzio di garanzia (I)	Garantiekonsortium *n*	underwriting syndicate	syndicat bancaire de garantie *m*	—	consorcio de garantía *m*
consorzio emissione titoli pubblici (I)	Bundesanleihe-konsortium *n*	Federal loan syndicate	Syndicat fédéral d'emprunts *m*	—	consorcio de emprés-titos federales *m*
consorzio industriale (I)	Industriekonsortium *n*	industrial syndicate	consortium industriel *m*	—	consorcio industrial *m*
consorzio interno (I)	Innenkonsortium *n*	internal syndicate	consortium intérieur *m*	—	consorcio interior *m*
constant issuer (E)	Dauerremittent *m*	—	émetteur permanent *m*	emittente continuo *m*	remitente permanente *m*
constitución financiera (Es)	Finanzverfassung *f*	financial system	système financier *m*	ordinamento finanziario *f*	—
constitution de capital (F)	Kapitalbeschaffung *f*	procurement of capital	—	raccolta di capitali *f*	obtención de capital *f*
constitution de capital par apport de tiers (F)	Fremdfinanzierung *f*	debt financing	—	finanziamento esterno *m*	financiación con capital ajeno *f*
constitution d'opportunité (F)	Scheingründung *f*	fictitious formation	—	costituzione fittizia *f*	fundación simulada *f*
constitution par apports en nature (F)	Illationsgründung *f*	formation by founders' non-cash capital contributions	—	costituzione di una società mediante con-ferimento in natura *f*	formación por aportaciones en especie *f*
consulente di cambio (I)	Devisenberater *m*	foreign exchange advisor	conseiller en matière de devises *m*	—	asesor en materia de divisas *m*
consulente patrimoniale (I)	Vermögensberater *m*	investment advisor	conseiller en investissement *m*	—	asesor en materia de inversiones *m*
consulente titoli a reddito fisso (I)	Rentenberater *m*	consultant on pensions	conseiller en matière de pensions *m*	—	asesor en materia de títulos de renta fija *m*
consulenza (I)	Beratung *f*	counseling	consultation *f*	—	asesoramiento *m*
consulenza in investimenti (I)	Anlageberatung *f*	investment counseling	orientation en matière de placement *f*	—	asesoramiento en ma-teria de inversiones *m*
consultant on pensions (E)	Rentenberater *m*	—	conseiller en matière de pensions *m*	consulente titoli a reddito fisso *m*	asesor en materia de títulos de renta fija *m*
consultation (F)	Beratung *f*	counseling	—	consulenza *f*	asesoramiento *m*
consumer advice (E)	Kundenberatung *f*	—	orientation de la clientèle *f*	servizio d'assistenza *m*	asesoramiento de clientes *m*
consumer cooperative (E)	Konsum-genossenschaft *f*	—	société coopérative de consommation *f*	cooperativa di consumo *f*	cooperativa de consumo *f*
consumer credit (E)	Konsumentenkredit *m*	—	crédit à la consommation *m*	credito al consumo *m*	crédito al consumidor *m*
consumer credit act (E)	Verbraucherkredit-gesetz *n*	—	loi sur les crédits à la consommation *f*	legge sul credito al consumo *f*	ley sobre créditos al consumidor *f*
consumer goods (E)	Konsumgüter *n/pl*	—	biens de consommation *m/pl*	beni di consumo *m/pl*	bienes de consumo *m/pl*
consumption financing (E)	Konsumfinanzierung *f*	—	financement de la vente à crédit *m*	finanziamento di vendite rateali *m*	financiación al consumo *f*

	D	E	F	I	Es
contabilidad (Es)	Buchführung f	accounting	comptabilité f	contabilità f	—
contabilidad americana (Es)	amerikanisches Rechnungswesen n	American accounting system	comptabilité dite américaine f	contabilità americana f	—
contabilidad bancaria (Es)	Bankbuchhaltung f	bank's accounting	comptabilité bancaire f	contabilità bancaria f	—
contabilidad de caja (Es)	Kassenhaltung f	cash accountancy	tenue de la caisse f	tenuta di cassa f	—
contabilidad de depósitos (Es)	Depotbuchhaltung f	security deposit account	comptabilité des dépôts m	contabilità dei depositi f	—
contabilidad de divisas (Es)	Devisenbuchhaltung f	currency accounting	comptabilité de devises f	contabilità dei cambi f	—
contabilidad de partida doble (Es)	doppelte Buchführung f	double entry bookkeeping	comptabilité en partie double f	partita doppia f	—
contabilidad de partidas abiertas (Es)	Offene-Posten-Buchhaltung f	open-item accounting	comptabilité de postes ouverts f	contabilità a partite sospese f	—
contabilidad empresarial (Es)	betriebliches Rechnungswesen n	operational accountancy	comptabité industrielle f	ragioneria aziendale f	—
contabilidad financiera (Es)	Finanzbuchhaltung f	financial accounting	comptabilité financière f	contabilità finanziaria f	—
contabilidad nacional (Es)	Volkswirtschaftliche Gesamtrechnung f	national accounting	comptabilité nationale f	contabilitá nazionale f	—
contabilidad principal (Es)	Hauptbuchhaltung f	chief accountancy	comptabilité générale f	ufficio di contabilità generale m	—
contabilità (I)	Buchführung f	accounting	comptabilité f	—	contabilidad f
contabilità americana (I)	amerikanisches Rechnungswesen n	American accounting system	comptabilité dite américaine f	—	contabilidad americana f
contabilità a partite sospese (I)	Offene-Posten-Buchhaltung f	open-item accounting	comptabilité de postes ouverts f	—	contabilidad de partidas abiertas f
contabilità bancaria (I)	Bankbuchhaltung f	bank's accounting	comptabilité bancaire f	—	contabilidad bancaria f
contabilità dei cambi (I)	Devisenbuchhaltung f	currency accounting	comptabilité de devises f	—	contabilidad de divisas f
contabilità dei depositi (I)	Depotbuchhaltung f	security deposit account	comptabilité des dépôts m	—	contabilidad de depósitos f
contabilità finanziaria (I)	Finanzbuchhaltung f	financial accounting	comptabilité financière f	—	contabilidad financiera f
contabilitá nazionale (I)	Volkswirtschaftliche Gesamtrechnung f	national accounting	comptabilité nationale f	—	contabilidad nacional f
contabilización (Es)	Verbuchung f	entry	inscription en compte f	registrazione f	—
contango (E)	Report m	—	report en bourse m	riporto m	reporte m
contango securities (E)	Reporteffekten pl	—	titres reportés m/pl	titoli dati a riporto m/pl	efectos de reporte m/pl
contango transaction (E)	Reportgeschäft n	—	opération de report f	operazione di riporto f	operación de reporte f
contanti potenziali (I)	potentielles Bargeld n	potential cash	argent liquide potentiel m	—	dinero efectivo potencial m
contegno rialzistico (I)	Hausse f	bull market	hausse f	—	alza f
con tendencia alcesta (Es)	im Aufwind	under upward pressure	en progrès	con tendenza ascendente	—
con tendenza ascendente (I)	im Aufwind	under upward pressure	en progrès	—	con tendencia alcesta
contenido de oro (Es)	Goldgehalt m	gold content	teneur en or f	contenuto aureo m	—
contenido empírico (Es)	empirischer Gehalt m	empirical contents	contenu empirique m	contenuto empirico m	—
contenu empirique (F)	empirischer Gehalt m	empirical contents	—	contenuto empirico m	contenido empírico m
contenuto aureo (I)	Goldgehalt m	gold content	teneur en or f	—	contenido de oro m
contenuto empirico (I)	empirischer Gehalt m	empirical contents	contenu empirique m	—	contenido empírico m
conti a firme disgiunte (I)	Oderkonten n/pl	joint account	compte joint m	—	cuentas indistintas f/pl
conti degli investimenti (I)	Anlagekonten n/pl	investment accounts	comptes d'investissement m/pl	—	cuentas de inversión f/pl
conti di persone (I)	Personenkonten n/pl	personal accounts	comptes de personne m/pl	—	cuentas personales f/pl

	D	E	F	I	Es
conti di risparmio cifrati (I)	anonyme Sparkonten *n/pl*	anonymous savings accounts	comptes d'épargne anonymes *m/pl*	—	cuentas de ahorro anónimas *f/pl*
contingent (F)	Kontingent *n*	quota	—	contingente *m*	contingente *m*
contingentamento (I)	Kontingentierung *f*	fixing of a quota	contingentement *m*	—	imposición de contingentes *f*
contingente (Es)	Kontingent *n*	quota	contingent *m*	contingente *m*	—
contingente (I)	Kontingent *n*	quota	contingent *m*	—	contingente *m*
contingente de emisión fiduciaria (Es)	Notenkontingent *n*	fixed issue of notes	maximum toléré à l'émission des billets de banque *m*	contingente di banconote *m*	—
contingente di banconote (I)	Notenkontingent *n*	fixed issue of notes	maximum toléré à l'émission des billets de banque *m*	—	contingente de emisión fiduciaria *m*
contingentement (F)	Kontingentierung *f*	fixing of a quota	—	contingentamento *m*	imposición de contingentes *f*
contingent liability (E)	Eventual-verbindlichkeit *f*	—	obligation éventuelle *f*	obbligazione contingenziale *f*	obligación eventual *f*
continuidad de balance (Es)	Bilanzkontinuität *f*	balance sheet consistency	identité des bilans successifs *f*	continuità di bilancio *f*	—
continuità di bilancio (I)	Bilanzkontinuität *f*	balance sheet consistency	identité des bilans successifs *f*	—	continuidad de balance *f*
conto (I)	Rechenschaft *f*	rendering of account	compte rendu *m*	—	cuenta *f*
conto (I)	Konto *n*	account	compte *m*	—	cuenta *f*
conto accumulativo (I)	Aufbaukonto *n*	build-up account	compte d'installation *m*	—	cuenta de financiación de desarrollo *f*
conto ad interesse fisso (I)	Festzinskonto *n*	fixed-interest bearing account	compte à intérêt fixe *m*	—	cuenta de interés fijo *f*
conto altrui (I)	Anderkonto *n*	fiduciary account	compte de tiers *m*	—	cuenta fiduciaria *f*
conto aperto (I)	offenes Konto *n*	open account	compte ouvert *m*	—	cuenta abierta *f*
conto aperto (I)	offene Rechnung *f*	unsettled account	facture pas encore payée *f*	—	factura pendiente *f*
conto a risparmio (I)	Sparkonto *n*	savings account	compte d'épargne *m*	—	cuenta de ahorros *f*
conto bancario (I)	Bankkonto *n*	bank account	compte en banque *m*	—	cuenta bancaria *f*
conto bloccato (I)	Sperrkonto *n*	blocked account	compte bloqué *m*	—	cuenta bloqueada *f*
conto capitale (I)	Kapitalkonto *n*	capital account	compte de capital *m*	—	cuenta de capital *f*
conto cifrato (I)	Nummernkonto *n*	numbered account	compte anonyme *m*	—	cuenta anónima *f*
conto collettivo (I)	Sammelkonto *n*	collective account	compte collectif *m*	—	cuenta colectiva *f*
conto compensazione spese (I)	Aufwands-ausgleichkonto *n*	account for reimbursements of expenses	compte de frais à reporter *m*	—	cuenta de compensación de gastos *f*
conto comune (I)	Und-Konto *n*	joint account where all signatories must sign	compte joint *m*	—	cuenta colectiva *f*
conto congiunto (I)	Gemeinschaftskonto *n*	joint account	compte commun *m*	—	cuenta conjunta *f*
conto corrente (I)	Kontokorrent *n*	current account	compte courant *m*	—	cuenta corriente *f*
conto corrente bancario (I)	Bankkontokorrent *n*	current account with a bank	compte courant de banque *m*	—	cuenta corriente bancaria *f*
conto debitori (I)	Debitorenkonto *n*	customer account	compte de créances à recevoir *m*	—	cuenta deudor *f*
conto del capitale proprio (I)	Eigenkapitalkonto *n*	equity account	compte capital *m*	—	cuenta de capital propio *f*
conto delle spese (I)	Spesenrechnung *f*	statement of expenses	compte de frais *m*	—	cuenta de gastos *f*
conto di bilancio (I)	Bilanzkonto *n*	balance sheet account	compte de bilan *m*	—	cuenta permanente *f*
conto di deposito (I)	Depotkonto *n*	security deposit account	compte de dépôt *m*	—	cuenta de depósitos *f*
conto economico (I)	Aufwands- und Ertragsrechnung *f*	profit and loss account	compte de profits et pertes *m*	—	cuenta de beneficios y pérdidas *f*
conto economico a breve termine (I)	Kurzfristige Erfolgsrechnung *f*	monthly income statement	comptes de résultats intermédiaires *m/pl*	—	estado de resultados a corto plazo *m*
conto entrate e uscite (I)	Einnahmen-Ausgabenrechnung *f*	bill of receipts and expenditures	état des recettes et des dépenses *m*	—	cuenta de gastos-ingresos *f*

	D	E	F	I	Es
conto estero (I)	Auslandskonto n	foreign account	compte entretenu à l'étranger m	—	cuenta en el extranjero f
conto finanziario (I)	Finanzkonto n	financial account	compte financier m	—	cuenta financiera f
conto fornitori (I)	Lieferkonto n	accounts payable	compte de fournisseurs m	—	cuenta de suministradores f
conto franco di provvigione (I)	provisionsfreies Konto n	commission-free account	compte de créditeurs m	—	cuenta sin comisión f
conto inattivo (I)	totes Konto n	inoperative account	compte sans mouvement m	—	cuenta muerta f
conto in valuta estera (I)	Devisenkonto n	foreign exchange account	compte libellé en devises m	—	cuenta en divisas f
conto in valuta estera (I)	Fremdwährungs-konto n	account in foreign currency	compte en monnaie étrangère m	—	cuenta de moneda extranjera f
conto loro (I)	Lorokonto n	loro account	compte d'un client bancaire m	—	cuenta de un cliente bancario f
conto magazzino (I)	Bestandskonto n	real account	compte d'existences m	—	cuenta de existencia f
conto monetario (I)	Geldmarktkonto n	money market account	compte du marché monétaire m	—	cuenta de mercado monetario f
conto nostro (I)	Nostrokonto n	nostro account	compte dans une autre banque m	—	nuestra cuenta f
conto particolare (I)	Privatkonto n	personal account	compte privé m	—	cuenta privada f
conto particolare (I)	Sonderkonto n	separate account	compte spécial m	—	cuenta especial f
conto profitti e perdite (I)	Gewinn- und Verlustrechnung f	profit and loss account	compte de résultat m	—	cuenta de pérdidas y ganancias f
conto saldi contabili (I)	Saldenbilanz f	list of balances	balance des soldes des comptes généraux f	—	balance de saldos m
conto sindacale (I)	Syndikatskonto n	syndicate account	compte de syndicat m	—	cuenta de cártel f
conto soggetto a provvigione (I)	provisionspflichtiges Konto n	commission-bearing account	compte de débiteur m	—	cuenta sujeto al pago de una comisión f
conto spesa (I)	Aufwandskonto n	expense account	compte de frais m	—	cuenta de gastos f
conto titoli (I)	Effektenrechnung f	calculation of price of shares	calcul du prix des titres m	—	cálculo del precio de valores m
conto titoli (I)	Stückekonto n	shares account	compte de titres m	—	cuenta de valores f
conto valutario (I)	Währungskonto n	currency account	compte en monnaies étrangères m	—	cuenta de moneda extranjera f
conto valutario (I)	Valutakonto n	foreign currency account	compte en monnaie étrangère m	—	cuenta de moneda extranjera f
conto vendite (I)	Verkaufskonto n	trading account	compte de ventes m	—	cuenta de ventas f
conto videotel (I)	Tele-Konto n	videotext account	compte vidéotex m	—	cuenta videotexto f
conto vostro (I)	Vostrokonto n	vostro account	votre compte en notre établissement m	—	su cuenta f
contracrédito (Es)	Gegenakkreditiv n	back-to-back letter of credit	contrecrédit m	controcredito m	—
contract (E)	Vertrag m	—	contrat m	contratto m	contrato m
contraction (E)	Kontrahierung f	—	conclusion d'un contrat f	conclusione di contratto f	contratación f
contract of pledge (E)	Pfandvertrag m	—	contrat pignoratif m	contratto di pegno m	contrato de prenda m
contracts on capital collecting (E)	Kapitalsammlungs-verträge m/pl	—	contrats de réunion de capitaux m/pl	contratti di accumula-zione di capitale m/pl	contratos de acumula-ción de capitales m/pl
contractual obligation (E)	Vertragsbindung f	—	obligation de respecter le contrat f	vincolo di contratto m	vínculo contractual m
contractual penalty (E)	Vertragsstrafe f	—	pénalité f	convenzionale f	pena contractual f
contractual penalty (E)	Konventionalstrafe f	—	pénalité f	pena convenzionale f	pena convencional f
contrapartida (Es)	Gegenbuchung f	counter entry	contrepartie f	registrazione in contropartita f	—
contra-reclamación (Es)	Gegenforderung f	counterclaim	contre-prétention f	contropretesa f	—
contrat (F)	Vertrag m	contract	—	contratto m	contrato m

	D	E	F	I	Es
contratación (Es)	Kontrahierung *f*	contraction	conclusion d'un contrat *f*	conclusione di contratto *f*	—
contratación a término sobre divisas (Es)	Currency future *m*	currency future	opération à terme sur les changes *f*	currency future *m*	—
contratación de títulos de renta fija (Es)	Rentenhandel *m*	bond trading	négociation des valeurs à revenu fixe *f*	commercio titoli a reddito fisso *m*	—
contratación forzosa (Es)	Kontrahierungszwang *m*	obligation to contract	obligation de contracter *f*	obbligo di contrarre *m*	—
contrat de dépôt (F)	Depotvertrag *m*	securities deposit contract	—	contratto di deposito *m*	contrato de depósito *m*
contrat de gestion d'affaires (F)	Geschäftsbesorgungsvertrag *m*	agency agreement	—	contratto d'agenzia *m*	contrato de mandato *m*
contrat de marché à primes (F)	Prämienbrief *m*	option contract	—	contratto a premio *m*	documento de una operación con prima *m*
contrat d'épargne à dépôts multiples (F)	Ratensparvertrag *m*	saving-by-instalments contract	—	risparmio contrattuale *m*	contrato de ahorro a plazos *m*
contrat d'épargne à primes (F)	Prämiensparvertrag *m*	bonus savings contract	—	contratto di risparmio a premi *m*	contrato de ahorro con primas *m*
contrat d'épargne-construction (F)	Bausparvertrag *m*	savings agreement with the building society	—	contratto di risparmio edilizio *m*	contrato de ahorro para la construcción *m*
contrat d'épargne mobilière (F)	Wertpapiersparvertrag *m*	securities-linked savings scheme	—	contratto di risparmio in titoli *m*	contrato de ahorro en forma de valores *m*
contrat de société (F)	Gesellschaftsvertrag *m*	shareholder's agreement	—	atto costitutivo *m*	contrato social *m*
contrat de vente (F)	Kaufvertrag *m*	agreement of purchase and sale	—	contratto di compravendita *m*	contrato de compraventa *m*
contrat de vente à crédit (F)	Kreditvertrag *f*	credit agreement	—	contratto di credito *m*	contrato de crédito *m*
contrat d'ouverture de crédit (F)	Krediteröffnungsvertrag *m*	credit agreement	—	contratto d'apertura di credito *m*	contrato de apertura de crédito *m*
contrat financier à terme (F)	Finanzterminkontrakt *m*	financial futures contract	—	financial futures *m/pl*	contrato a plazo financiero *m*
contrato (Es)	Vertrag *m*	contract	contrat *m*	contratto *m*	—
contrato a plazo financiero (Es)	Finanzterminkontrakt *m*	financial futures contract	contrat financier à terme *m*	financial futures *m/pl*	—
contrato de ahorro a plazos (Es)	Ratensparvertrag *m*	saving-by-instalments contract	contrat d'épargne à dépôts multiples *m*	risparmio contrattuale *m*	—
contrato de ahorro con primas (Es)	Prämiensparvertrag *m*	bonus savings contract	contrat d'épargne à primes *m*	contratto di risparmio a premi *m*	—
contrato de ahorro en forma de valores (Es)	Wertpapiersparvertrag *m*	securities-linked savings scheme	contrat d'épargne mobilière *m*	contratto di risparmio in titoli *m*	—
contrato de ahorro para la construcción (Es)	Bausparvertrag *m*	savings agreement with the building society	contrat d'épargne-construction *m*	contratto di risparmio edilizio *m*	—
contrato de apertura de crédito (Es)	Krediteröffnungsvertrag *m*	credit agreement	contrat d'ouverture de crédit *m*	contratto d'apertura di credito *m*	—
contrato de compraventa (Es)	Kaufvertrag *m*	agreement of purchase and sale	contrat de vente *m*	contratto di compravendita *m*	—
contrato de crédito (Es)	Kreditvertrag *f*	credit agreement	contrat de vente à crédit *m*	contratto di credito *m*	—
contrato de depósito (Es)	Depotvertrag *m*	securities deposit contract	contrat de dépôt *m*	contratto di deposito *m*	—
contrato de dominación (Es)	Beherrschungsvertrag *m*	control agreement	accord de contrôle *m*	contratto di controllo *m*	—
contrato de exclusividad (Es)	Ausschließlichkeitserklärung *f*	undertaking to deal exclusively with one bank or firm	déclaration d'exclusivité *f*	dichiarazione d'esclusività *f*	—
contrato de fomento de capital (Es)	Kapitalförderungsvertrag *m*	capital encouragement treaty	accord sur l'encouragement de la formation de capital *m*	accordo sulla formazione di capitale *m*	—
contrato de mandato (Es)	Geschäftsbesorgungsvertrag *m*	agency agreement	contrat de gestion d'affaires *m*	contratto d'agenzia *m*	—
contrato de prenda (Es)	Pfandvertrag *m*	contract of pledge	contrat pignoratif *m*	contratto di pegno *m*	—

contrato de protección

	D	E	F	I	Es
contrato de protección del capital (Es)	Kapitalschutzvertrag *m*	capital protection agreement	accord sur la protection de capital *m*	accordo di tutela degli investimenti *m*	—
contrato intermediado (Es)	Aufgabegeschäft *n*	name transaction	opération de médiation *f*	contratto intermediato *m*	—
contrato recíproco (Es)	gegenseitiger Vertrag *m*	reciprocal contract	accord de réciprocité *m*	contratto bilaterale *m*	—
contratos de acumulación de capitales (Es)	Kapitalsammlungsverträge *m/pl*	contracts on capital collecting	contrats de réunion de capitaux *m/pl*	contratti di accumulazione di capitale *m/pl*	—
contrato social (Es)	Gesellschaftsvertrag *m*	shareholder's agreement	contrat de société *m*	atto costitutivo *m*	—
contrat pignoratif (F)	Pfandvertrag *m*	contract of pledge	—	contratto di pegno *m*	contrato de prenda *m*
contrats de réunion de capitaux (F)	Kapitalsammlungsverträge *m/pl*	contracts on capital collecting	—	contratti di accumulazione di capitale *m/pl*	contratos de acumulación de capitales *m/pl*
contrattazione a fermo (I)	Fixgeschäft *n*	transaction for delivery by a fixed date	opération à terme fixe *f*	—	negocio fijo *m*
contrattazione a fermo (I)	Festgeschäft *n*	firm deal	opération à terme fixe *f*	—	operaciones a plazo fijo *f/pl*
contrattazione ufficiale (I)	amtlicher Handel *m*	official trading	négociations en bourse *f/pl*	—	cotización oficial *f*
contrattazioni fuori borsa (I)	Freiverkehr *m*	unofficial dealings	marché libre *m*	—	mercado libre *m*
contratti di accumulazione di capitale (I)	Kapitalsammlungsverträge *m/pl*	contracts on capital collecting	contrats de réunion de capitaux *m/pl*	—	contratos de acumulación de capitales *m/pl*
contratti di borsa a termine (I)	Börsentermingeschäfte *n/pl*	trading in futures on a stock exchange	opérations boursières à terme *f/pl*	—	operaciones bursátiles a término *f/pl*
contratto (I)	Vertrag *m*	contract	contrat *m*	—	contrato *m*
contratto (I)	Geschäft *n*	exchange operation	opération *f*	—	negocio *m*
contratto a fine ultimo (I)	Ultimogeschäft *n*	last-day business	opération à liquider en fin de mois *f*	—	operación a término con vencimiento a fin de mes *f*
contratto a premio (I)	Prämienbrief *m*	option contract	contrat de marché à primes *m*	—	documento de una operación con prima *m*
contratto a termine (I)	Termingeschäft *n*	time bargain	opération à terme *f*	—	operación a plazo *f*
contratto a termine con opzione di adempimento anticipato (I)	Wandelgeschäft *n*	callable forward transaction	marché à option *m*	—	operación de opción *f*
contratto a termine outright (I)	Outright-Termingeschäft *n*	outright futures transactions	opération à terme outright *f*	—	operación a término outright *f*
contratto ad opzione (I)	Optionsgeschäft *n*	option dealing	marché à option *m*	—	operación de opción *f*
contratto bilaterale (I)	gegenseitiger Vertrag *m*	reciprocal contract	accord de réciprocité *m*	—	contrato recíproco *m*
contratto d'agenzia (I)	Geschäftsbesorgungsvertrag *m*	agency agreement	contrat de gestion d'affaires *m*	—	contrato de mandato *m*
contratto d'apertura di credito (I)	Krediteröffnungsvertrag *m*	credit agreement	contrat d'ouverture de crédit *m*	—	contrato de apertura de crédito *m*
contratto di commissione (I)	Kommissionsgeschäft *n*	commission business	affaire en commission *f*	—	operación de comisión *f*
contratto di compravendita (I)	Kaufvertrag *m*	agreement of purchase and sale	contrat de vente *m*	—	contrato de compraventa *m*
contratto di controllo (I)	Beherrschungsvertrag *m*	control agreement	accord de contrôle *m*	—	contrato de dominación *m*
contratto di credito (I)	Kreditvertrag *m*	credit agreement	contrat de vente à crédit *m*	—	contrato de crédito *m*
contratto di deposito (I)	Depotvertrag *m*	securities deposit contract	contrat de dépôt *m*	—	contrato de depósito *m*
contratto di pegno (I)	Pfandvertrag *m*	contract of pledge	contrat pignoratif *m*	—	contrato de prenda *m*
contratto di proroga (I)	Prolongationsgeschäft *n*	prolongation business	opération de report *f*	—	operación de prolongación *f*
contratto di risparmio a premi (I)	Prämiensparvertrag *m*	bonus savings contract	contrat d'épargne a primes *m*	—	contrato de ahorro con primas *m*

control de emisión

	D	E	F	I	Es
contratto di risparmio edilizio (I)	Bausparvertrag *m*	savings agreement with the building society	contrat d'épargne-construction *m*	—	contrato de ahorro para la construcción *m*
contratto di risparmio in titoli (I)	Wertpapierspar-vertrag *m*	securities-linked savings scheme	contrat d'épargne mobilière *m*	—	contrato de ahorro en forma de valores *m*
contratto di trasferi-mento profitto (I)	Ergebnisabführungs-vertrag *m*	profit and loss transfer agreement	accord de transfer des résultats *m*	—	acuerdo de pago del resultado *m*
contratto spot (I)	Spotgeschäft *n*	spot transactions	opération en disponible *m*	—	operaciones al contado y de entrega inmediata *f/pl*
contratto stellage (I)	Stellgeschäft *n*	put and call	opération de stellage *f*	—	operación de doble opción *f*
contratto stellage (I)	Stellagegeschäft *n*	double option operation	marché à double option *m*	—	operación de doble prima *f*
contratto swap (I)	Swapabkommen *n*	swap agreement	accord swap *m*	—	acuerdo de swap *m*
contrecrédit (F)	Gegenakkreditiv *n*	back-to-back letter of credit	—	controcredito *m*	contracrédito *m*
contremandement de l'ordre de paye-ment d'un chèque (F)	Scheckwiderruf *m*	cheque stopping	—	revoca dell'assegno *f*	revocación de la orden de pago de un cheque *f*
contrepartie (F)	Gegenbuchung *f*	counter entry	—	registrazione in contropartita *f*	contrapartida *f*
contre-prétention (F)	Gegenforderung *f*	counterclaim	—	contropretesa *f*	contrarreclamación *f*
contribución a los costes de construcción (Es)	Baukostenzuschuß *m*	tenant's contribution to the construction costs	participation financière à la construction *f*	contributo alla costruzione	—
contributi (I)	Beiträge *m/pl*	contributions	contributions *f/pl*	—	cuotas *f/pl*
contributi del datore di lavoro (I)	Arbeitgeber-zuschüsse *m/pl*	employer's contributions	compléments patronaux *m/pl*	—	suplementos patronales *m/pl*
contributi di risparmio edilizio (I)	Bausparkassen-beiträge *m/pl*	contributions paid to the building society	contributions payées à la banque d'épargne *f/pl*	—	cuotas de ahorro *f/pl*
contribution receipt (E)	Einschußquittung *f*	—	quittance de contribution *f*	ricevuta di apporto *f*	recibo de la inyección de dinero *m*
contribution refund (E)	Beitragserstattung *f*	—	remboursement des cotisations *m*	rimborso di contributi *m*	reintegro de las cuotas *m*
contributions (E)	Beiträge *m/pl*	—	contributions *f/pl*	contributi *m/pl*	cuotas *f/pl*
contributions (F)	Beiträge *m/pl*	contributions	—	contributi *m/pl*	cuotas *f/pl*
contributions paid to the building society (E)	Bausparkassen-beiträge *m/pl*	—	contributions payées à la banque d'épargne *f/pl*	contributi di risparmio edilizio *m/pl*	cuotas de ahorro *f/pl*
contributions payées à la banque d'épargne (F)	Bausparkassen-beiträge *m/pl*	contributions paid to the building society	—	contributi di risparmio edilizio *m/pl*	cuotas de ahorro *f/pl*
contributo alla costruzione (I)	Baukostenzuschuß *m*	tenant's contribution to the construction costs	participation financière à la construction *f*	—	contribución a los costes de construcción *f*
controcredito (I)	Gegenakkreditiv *n*	back-to-back letter of credit	contrecrédit *m*	—	contracrédito *m*
control agreement (E)	Beherrschungs-vertrag *m*	—	accord de contrôle *m*	contratto di controllo *m*	contrato de dominación *m*
control bancario (Es)	Bankkontrolle *f*	bank supervision	surveillance des banques *f*	controllo bancario *m*	—
control board (E)	Aufsichtsamt *n*	—	office de surveillance *m*	ispettorato *m*	oficina de inspección *f*
control by foreign capital (E)	Überfremdung *f*	—	envahissement de capitaux étrangers *m*	inforestieramento *m*	extranjerización *f*
control crediticio (Es)	Kreditkontrolle *f*	credit control	contrôle de crédit *m*	controllo del credito *m*	—
control cruzado (Es)	Kontrollmitteilung *f*	tracer note	bulletin de contrôle *m*	comunicazione di revisione *f*	—
control de cambio (Es)	Devisenkontrolle *f*	foreign exchange control	contrôle des changes *m*	controllo dei cambi *m*	—
control de emisión (Es)	Emissionskontrolle *f*	security issue control	contrôle en matière d'émission d'actions et d'obligations *m*	controllo delle emissioni *m*	—

control de éxito

	D	E	F	I	Es
control de éxito (Es)	Erfolgskontrolle f	efficiency review	contrôle du rendememt m	controllo del risultato m	—
control de las exportaciónes (Es)	Ausfuhrkontrolle f	export control	contrôle des exportations m	controllo delle esportazioni m	—
control de las inversiones de cartera (Es)	Portfeuillesteuerung f	portfolio controlling	régulation du portefeuille f	controllo di portafoglio m	—
control de oferta (Es)	Angebotssteuerung f	supply control	régulation des offres f	controllo dell'offerta m	—
control de precios (Es)	Preiskontrolle f	price control	contrôle des prix m	controllo concordato dei prezzi m	—
contrôle de crédit (F)	Kreditkontrolle f	credit control	—	controllo del credito m	control crediticio m
contrôle des banques (F)	Bankenaufsicht f	public supervision of banking	—	controllo sulle banche m	superintendencia bancaria f
contrôle des changes (F)	Devisenkontrolle f	foreign exchange control	—	controllo dei cambi m	control de cambio m
contrôle des établissements dépositaires de titres (F)	Depotprüfung f	securities deposit audit		revisione dei depositi	revisión de depósito f
contrôle des exportations (F)	Ausfuhrkontrolle f	export control	—	controllo delle esportazioni m	control de las exportaciónes m
contrôle des prix (F)	Preiskontrolle f	price control	—	controllo concordato dei prezzi m	control de precios m
contrôle du bilan (F)	Bilanzprüfung f	balance sheet audit	—	revisione del bilancio f	revisión del balance f
contrôle du bilan d'une banque (F)	Bankrevision f	bank audit	—	ispezione bancaria f	censura de cuentas del banco f
contrôle du rendememt (F)	Erfolgskontrolle f	efficiency review	—	controllo del risultato m	control de éxito m
contrôle en matière d'émission d'actions et d'obligations (F)	Emissionskontrolle f	security issue control	—	controllo delle emissioni m	control de emisión m
contrôle global (F)	Globalsteuerung f	global control	—	controllo della domanda globale m	control global m
control estatal de bolsas (Es)	Börsenaufsicht f	stock exchange supervision	surveillance de la bourse f	sorveglianza della borsa f	—
control global (Es)	Globalsteuerung f	global control	contrôle global f	controllo della domanda globale m	—
controlled company (E)	Organgesellschaft f	—	entreprise dominée f	società legata contrattualmente f	sociedad órgano f
controller (E)	Controller m	—	contrôleur m	controller m	interventor m
controllo (I)	Prüfung f	examination	vérification f	—	revisión f
controllo bancario (I)	Bankkontrolle f	bank supervision	surveillance des banques f	—	control bancario m
controllo concordato dei prezzi (I)	Preiskontrolle f	price control	contrôle des prix m	—	control de precios m
controllo dei cambi (I)	Devisenkontrolle f	foreign exchange control	contrôle des changes m	—	control de cambio m
controllo dei crediti (I)	Kreditprüfung f	credit status investigation	enquête sur la solvabilité f	—	investigación de crédito y solvencia de un cliente f
controllo del credito (I)	Kreditkontrolle f	credit control	contrôle de crédit m	—	control crediticio m
controllo della domanda globale (I)	Globalsteuerung f	global control	contrôle global f	—	control global m
controllo delle emissioni (I)	Emissionskontrolle f	security issue control	contrôle en matière d'émission d'actions et d'obligations m	—	control de emisión m
controllo delle esportazioni (I)	Ausfuhrkontrolle f	export control	contrôle des exportations m	—	control de las exportaciónes m
controllo dell'offerta (I)	Angebotssteuerung f	supply control	régulation des offres f	—	control de oferta m
controllo del prospetto (I)	Prospektprüfung	audit of prospectus	vérification du prospectus f	—	examinación del prospecto f
controllo del risultato (I)	Erfolgskontrolle f	efficiency review	contrôle du rendememt m		control de éxito m

	D	E	F	I	Es
controllo di portafoglio (I)	Portfeuillesteuerung f	portfolio controlling	régulation du portefeuille f	—	control de las inversiones de cartera m
controllo sulle banche (I)	Bankenaufsicht f	public supervision of banking	contôle des banques m	—	superintendencia bancaria f
contropretesa (I)	Gegenforderung f	counterclaim	contre-prétention f	—	contrareclamación f
controvalore della contrattazione (I)	ausmachender Betrag m	actual amount	montant calculé m	—	importe calculado m
convalidación de obligaciones en el exterior (Es)	Auslandsbonds- bereinigung f	external bonds validation	validation des titres d'emprunt émis en monnaie étrangère f	correzione bonds in valuta estera f	—
convention de salaire aux pièces (F)	Geldakkord m	money piece rate	—	cottimo al pezzo m	destajo m
convenzionale (I)	Vertragsstrafe f	contractual penalty	pénalité f	—	pena contractual f
conversion (E)	Konvertierung f	—	conversion f	conversione f	conversión f
conversión (Es)	Konvertierung f	conversion	conversion f	conversione f	—
conversion (F)	Konvertierung f	conversion	—	conversione f	conversión f
conversion charge (E)	Transaktionskosten pl	—	frais de transaction m/pl	costi di transazione m/pl	gastos de transacción m/pl
conversion de dette (F)	Umschuldung f	debt rescheduling	—	conversione del debito f	conversión de la deuda f
conversión de la deuda (Es)	Umschuldung f	debt rescheduling	conversion de dette f	conversione del debito f	—
conversione (I)	Konvertierung f	conversion	conversion f	—	conversión f
conversione del debito (I)	Umschuldung f	debt rescheduling	conversion de dette f	—	conversión de la deuda f
convertibilidad (Es)	Konvertibilität f	convertibility	convertibilité f	convertibilità f	—
convertibilidad de oro (Es)	Goldkonvertibilität f	gold convertibility	convertibilité d'or f	convertibilità in oro f	—
convertibilidad interna (Es)	Inländer- konvertibilität f	convertibility for residents	convertibilité intérieure f	convertibilità interna f	—
convertibilità (I)	Konvertibilität f	convertibility	convertibilité f	—	convertibilidad f
convertibilità delle banconote (I)	Noteneinlösungs- pflicht f	obligation to redeem notes	obligation de remboursement de billets f	—	obligación de convertibilidad monetaria f
convertibilità in oro (I)	Goldkonvertibilität f	gold convertibility	convertibilité d'or f	—	convertibilidad de oro f
convertibilità interna (I)	Inländer- konvertibilität f	convertibility for residents	convertibilité intérieure f	—	convertibilidad interna f
convertibilité (F)	Konvertibilität f	convertibility	—	convertibilità f	convertibilidad f
convertibilité d'or (F)	Goldkonvertibilität f	gold convertibility	—	convertibilità in oro f	convertibilidad de oro f
convertibilité intérieure (F)	Inländer- konvertibilität f	convertibility for residents	—	convertibilità interna f	convertibilidad interna f
convertibility (E)	Konvertibilität f	—	convertibilité f	convertibilità f	convertibilidad f
convertibility for residents (E)	Inländer- konvertibilität f	—	convertibilité intérieure f	convertibilità interna f	convertibilidad interna f
convertible bonds (E)	Wandelanleihen f/pl	—	obligation convertible f	prestiti convertibili m/pl	empréstitos convertibles m/pl
cooperación (Es)	Kooperation f	cooperation	coopération f	cooperazione f	—
cooperation (E)	Kooperation f	—	coopération f	cooperazione f	cooperación f
coopération (F)	Kooperation f	cooperation	—	cooperazione f	cooperación f
cooperation loan (E)	Kooperations- darlehen n	—	prêt de coopération m	prestito di cooperazione m	préstamo de cooperación m
cooperativa (Es)	Genossenschaft f	cooperative	société coopérative f	cooperativa f	—
cooperativa (I)	Genossenschaft f	cooperative	société coopérative f	—	cooperativa f
cooperativa de consumo (Es)	Konsum- genossenschaft f	consumer cooperative	société coopérative de consommation f	cooperativa di consumo f	—
cooperativa de crédito (Es)	Kreditgenossenschaft f	credit cooperative	caisse coopérative de crédit f	cooperativa di credito f	—
cooperativa di consumo (I)	Konsum- genossenschaft f	consumer cooperative	société coopérative de consommation f	—	cooperativa de consumo f

	D	E	F	I	Es
cooperativa di credito (I)	Kreditgenossenschaft f	credit cooperative	caisse coopérative de crédit f	—	cooperativa de crédito f
cooperative (E)	Genossenschaft f	—	société coopérative f	cooperativa f	cooperativa f
cooperative banking sector (E)	genossenschaftlicher Bankensektor m	—	activités bancaires coopératives f/pl	settore bancario cooperativo m	actividades bancarias cooperativas f/pl
cooperative central banks (E)	genossenschaftliche Zentralbanken f/pl	—	banques coopératives centrales f/pl	banche centrali cooperative f/pl	bancos centrales cooperativos m/pl
cooperazione (I)	Kooperation f	cooperation	coopération f	—	cooperación f
coordinamento dei depositi (I)	Depotabstimmung f	securities deposit reconciliation	vote de titres en dépôt m	—	voto de título en depósito m
co-ownership (E)	Miteigentum n	—	copropriété f	comproprietà f	copropiedad f
copertura (I)	Deckung f	coverage	couverture f	—	cobertura f
copertura bancaria (I)	Bankdeckung f	banking cover	couverture de garantie d'une banque f	—	cobertura bancaria f
copertura delle spese (I)	Kostendeckung f	cost recovery	couverture des coûts f	—	dotación f
copertura di emissione di banconote (I)	Notendeckung f	cover of note circulation	couverture en billets de banque f	—	cobertura monetaria f
copertura in contanti (I)	Bardeckung f	cash cover	couverture en espèces f	—	cobertura en efectivo f
copertura metallica (I)	Metalldeckung f	metal cover	couverture métallique f	—	cobertura en metálico f
copertura metallica (I)	Gelddeckung f	monetary standard	couverture monétaire f	—	reserva-metales finos f
copertura oro (I)	Golddeckung f	gold cover	couverture or f	—	cobertura-oro f
copertura sostitutiva (I)	Ersatzdeckung f	substitute cover	garantie de substitution f	—	garantía adicional f
copiacambiale (I)	Wechselkopie f	copy of a bill	copie de traite f	—	copia de una letra f
copia de una letra (Es)	Wechselkopie f	copy of a bill	copie de traite f	copiacambiale f	—
copie de traite (F)	Wechselkopie f	copy of a bill	—	copiacambiale f	copia de una letra f
copropiedad (Es)	Miteigentum n	co-ownership	copropriété f	comproprietà f	—
copropriété (F)	Miteigentum n	co-ownership	—	comproprietà f	copropiedad f
copy of a bill (E)	Wechselkopie f	—	copie de traite f	copiacambiale f	copia de una letra f
corners (E)	Schwänze f/pl	—	corners m/pl	code speculative f/pl	corners m
corners (Es)	Schwänze f/pl	corners	corners m/pl	code speculative f/pl	—
corners (F)	Schwänze f/pl	corners	—	code speculative f/pl	corners m
corporación (Es)	Körperschaft f	corporation	collectivité f	ente m	—
corporación territorial (Es)	Gebietskörperschaft f	regional authority	collectivité territoriale f	ente locale m	—
corporate value (E)	Unternehmungswert m	—	valeur de l'entreprise f	valutazione del capitale f	valor de la empresa m
corporation (E)	Körperschaft f	—	collectivité f	ente m	corporación f
corporation tax (E)	Körperschaftssteuer f	—	taxe sur les sociétés m	imposta sul reddito delle società f	impuesto de sociedades m
correction (E)	Berichtigung f	—	rectification f	correzione f	rectificación f
correction des variations saisonnières (F)	Saisonbereinigung f	seasonal adjustment	—	destagionalizzazione f	desestacionalización f
corredor (Es)	Broker m	broker	courtier m	broker m	—
corredor de bolsa (Es)	Effektenmakler m	stockbroker	courtier en valeurs mobilières m	agente di cambio m	—
corredor de bolsa (Es)	Effektenhändler m	dealer in securities	courtier en valeurs mobilières m	agente in valori m	—
corredor de cambios (Es)	Devisenkursmakler m	exchange broker	courtier en devises m	agente di cambio m	—
corredor de comercio (Es)	Handelsmakler m	commercial broker	agent commercial m	mediatore di commercio m	—
corredor de metales finos (Es)	Bullionbroker m	bullion broker	courtier de métaux précieux m	bullionbroker m	—
corredor de parqué (Es)	Parkettmakler m	official market broker	agent de change m	agente di cambio m	—

	D	E	F	I	Es
corredor no colegiado (Es)	freier Makler *m*	floor trader	courtier en valeurs mobilières *m*	mediatore libero *m*	—
correlación (Es)	Korrelation *f*	correlation	corrélation *f*	correlazione *f*	
correlation (E)	Korrelation *f*	—	corrélation *f*	correlazione *f*	correlación *f*
corrélation (F)	Korrelation *f*	correlation	—	correlazione *f*	correlación *f*
correlazione (I)	Korrelation *f*	correlation	corrélation *f*	—	correlación *f*
correntezza (I)	Kulanz *f*	fairness in trade	souplesse en affaires *f*	—	complacencia *f*
correspondent bank (E)	Korrespondenzbank *f*	—	banque de correspondance *f*	banca corrispondente *f*	banco corresponsal *m*
corretaje (Es)	Courtage *f*	brokerage	courtage *m*	courtage *f*	—
correzione (I)	Berichtigung *f*	correction	rectification *f*	—	rectificación *f*
correzione bonds in valuta estera (I)	Auslandsbonds-bereinigung *f*	external bonds validation	validation des titres d'emprunt émis en monnaie étrangère *f*	—	convalidación de obligaciones en el exterior *f*
corsa alla svalutazione (I)	Abwertungswettlauf *m*	devaluation race	course de dévaluation *f*	—	carrera de desvalorización *f*
corso alla pari (I)	Parikurs *m*	par price	cours au pair *m*	—	cambio a la par *m*
corso certo per incerto (I)	Mengenkurs *m*	direct exchange	cours de change indirect *m*	—	precio por cantidad *m*
corso d'acquisto (I)	Bezugskurs *m*	subscription price	prix de souscription *m*	—	cotización de emisión *f*
corso d'acquisto per il consorzio (I)	Übernahmekurs *m*	underwriting price	cours payé par le souscripteur au syndicat des banquiers *m*	—	cambio de adquisición por el banco emisor *m*
corso d'apertura (I)	Eröffnungskurs *m*	opening price	cours d'ouverture *m*	—	cotización de apertura *f*
corso dei cambi (I)	Sortenkurs *m*	rate for foreign notes and coins	cours des monnaies étrangères *m*	—	tipo de cambio de billetes y monedas extranjeras *m*
corso dei cambi a pronti (I)	Devisenkassakurs *m*	foreign exchange spot operations	taux de change au comptant *m*	—	tipo de cambio al contado *m*
corso del giorno (I)	Tageskurs *m*	current quotation	cote du jour *f*	—	cotización del día *f*
corso d'emissione (I)	Emissionskurs *m*	issue price	cours d'émission *m*	—	tipo de emisión *m*
corso di compensazione (I)	Liquidationskurs *m*	making-up price	cours de liquidation *m*	—	cambio de liquidación *m*
corso di compensazione (I)	Kompensationskurs *m*	making-up price	cours de compensation *m*	—	cambio de compensación *m*
corso di compensazione (I)	Liquidations-auszahlungskurs *m*	liquidation outpayment rate	cours de compensation *m*	—	cotización de compensación *f*
corso di domanda (I)	Geldkurs *m*	bid price	cours de la demande *m*	—	cotización demandada *f*
corso di stima (I)	Taxkurs *m*	estimated quotation	cours d'estimation *m*	—	precio de tasación *m*
corso estratto a sorte (I)	Loskurs *m*	lottery quotation	cotation de tirage au sort *f*	—	cotización de sorteo *f*
corso medio (I)	Mittelkurs *m*	medium price	cours moyen *m*	—	cotización media *f*
corso preferenziale (I)	Vorzugskurs *m*	preferential price	cours de faveur *m*	—	curso preferencial *m*
corso unitario (I)	Stückkurs *m*	price per share	cours coté au prix unitaire du titre *m*	—	cotización por unidad *f*
corso variabile (I)	variabler Kurs *m*	variable price	cours variable *m*	—	cotización variable *f*
cost centre (E)	Kostenstelle *f*	—	compte de frais par secteur *m*	centro di costo *m*	sección de gastos *f*
coste de capital ajeno (Es)	Fremdkapitalkosten *pl*	costs of loan capital	coût de l'argent emprunté *m*	costi del capitale di credito *m/pl*	—
coste de oportunidad (Es)	Opportunitätskosten *pl*	opportunity costs	coût d'opportunité *m*	costi opportunità *m/pl*	—
costes (Es)	Kosten *pl*	costs	coût *m*	costi *m/pl*	—
costes calculatorios (Es)	Anderskosten *pl*	costing expenditures	coût précalculé *m*	costi calcolatori *m/pl*	—
costes totales (Es)	Gesamtkosten *pl*	overall costs	coût total *m*	costi complessivi *m/pl*	—
cost factor (E)	Kostenfaktor *m*	—	facteur de coûts *m*	fattore di costo *m*	tipo de coste *m*

	D	E	F	I	Es
costi (I)	Kosten *pl*	costs	coût *m*	—	costes *m/pl*
costi aziendali (I)	Betriebsaufwand *m*	operating expenses	dépenses d'exploitation *f/pl*	—	gastos de explotación *m/pl*
costi calcolatori (I)	Anderskosten *pl*	costing expenditures	coût précalculé *m*	—	costes calculatorios *m/pl*
costi complessivi (I)	Gesamtkosten *pl*	overall costs	coût total *m*	—	costes totales *m/pl*
costi comportanti spese (I)	ausgabenwirksame Kosten *pl*	spending costs	coût créant des dépenses *m*	—	gastos de desembolso *m/pl*
costi decrescenti (I)	degressive Kosten *pl*	degressive costs	coût dégressif *m*	—	gastos degresivos *m/pl*
costi dei fattori (I)	Faktorkosten *pl*	factor costs	coût des facteurs *m*	—	gastos de los factores *m/pl*
costi del capitale (I)	Kapitalkosten *pl*	cost of capital	frais financiers *m/pl*	—	gastos de capital *m/pl*
costi del capitale di credito (I)	Fremdkapitalkosten *pl*	costs of loan capital	coût de l'argent emprunté *m*	—	coste de capital ajeno *m*
costi del credito (I)	Kreditkosten *f*	cost of credit	coût de crédit *m*	—	gastos de crédito *m/pl*
costi d'esercizio (I)	Betriebskosten *pl*	working expenses	charges d'exploitation *f/pl*	—	gastos de explotación *m/pl*
costi di rischio (I)	Risikokosten *pl*	risk-induced costs	coût hasardeux *m*	—	gastos de riesgo *m/pl*
costi di transazione (I)	Transaktionskosten *pl*	conversion charge	frais de transaction *m/pl*	—	gastos de transacción *m/pl*
costi fissi (I)	fixe Kosten *pl*	standing costs	coûts fixes *m/pl*	—	gastos fijos *m/pl*
costing expenditures (E)	Anderskosten *pl*	—	coût précalculé *m*	costi calcolatori *m/pl*	costes calculatorios *m/pl*
costi opportunità (I)	Opportunitätskosten *pl*	opportunity costs	coût d'opportunité *m*	—	coste de oportunidad *m*
costituzione di una società mediante conferimento in natura (I)	Illationsgründung *f*	formation by founders' non-cash capital contributions	constitution par apports en nature *f*		formación por aportaciones en especie *f*
costituzione fittizia (I)	Scheingründung *f*	fictitious formation	constitution d'opportunité *f*		fundación simulada *f*
costituzione fraudolenta (I)	Schwindelgründung *f*	fraud foundation	fondation fictive *f*		fundación ficticia *f*
costituzione qualificata (I)	qualifizierte Gründung *f*	formation involving subscription in kind	fondation par apports en nature *f*	—	fundación calificada *f*
costituzione simulatanea (I)	Übernahmegründung *f*	foundation in which founders take all shares	fondation simultanée *f*	—	fundación de adquisición *f*
costituzione successiva (I)	Nachgründung *f*	post-formation acquisition	acquisitions complémentaires de la société *f/pl*	—	adquisición de instalaciones por una sociedad después de su fundación *f*
cost of capital (E)	Kapitalkosten *pl*	—	frais financiers *m/pl*	costi del capitale *m/pl*	gastos de capital *m/pl*
cost of credit (E)	Kreditkosten *f*	—	coût de crédit *m*	costi del credito *m/pl*	gastos de crédito *m/pl*
cost pressure (E)	Kostendruck *m*	—	poids des coûts *m*	pressione dei costi *f*	tensiones sobre los gastos *f/pl*
cost price (E)	Einstandspreis *m*	—	prix coûtant *m*	prezzo d'acquisto *m*	precio de coste *m*
cost recovery (E)	Kostendeckung *f*	—	couverture des coûts *f*	copertura delle spese *f*	dotación *f*
costruttore (I)	Bauträger *m*	builder	promoteur constructeur *m*	—	promotor de construcción *m*
costs (E)	Kosten *pl*	—	coût *m*	costi *m/pl*	costes *m/pl*
costs of loan capital (E)	Fremdkapitalkosten *pl*	—	coût de l'argent emprunté *m*	costi del capitale di credito *m/pl*	coste de capital ajeno *m*
cost type (E)	Kostenart *f*	—	coût par nature *m*	tipo di costo *m*	clase de costes *f*
costumbre de pago (Es)	Zahlungssitte *f*	payment habit	habitude de payement *f*	usanza di pagamento *f*	—
cost unit (E)	Kostenträger *m*	—	poste de production absorbant des coûts *m*	chi sostiene le spese	portador de costes *m*
cotation (F)	Kursanzeige *f*	quotation	—	indicazione delle quotazioni *f*	indicación de las cotizaciones *f*
cotation (F)	Kotierung *f*	admission of shares to official quotation	—	ammissione alla quotazione *f*	cotización *f*

	D	E	F	I	Es
cotation (F)	Quotation f	quotation	—	quotazione f	prorrateo m
cotation au certain (F)	Mengennotierung f	fixed exchange rate	—	cambio certo per incerto m	cotización real f
cotation des cours en bourse (F)	Börsennotierung f	quotation	—	quotazione di borsa f	cotización bursátil f
cotation des devises (F)	Devisennotierung f	foreign exchange quotations	—	cambio m	cotización de cambio f
cotation des droits de souscription (F)	Bezugsrecht-notierung f	subscription price	—	prezzo del diritto d'opzione m	cotización de derechos de suscripción f
cotation des prix (F)	Preisnotierung f	prices quoted	—	quotazione dei prezzi f	cotización de precios f
cotation de tirage au sort (F)	Loskurs m	lottery quotation	—	corso estratto a sorte m	cotización de sorteo f
cotation par opposition (F)	Call-Geschäft n	call transaction	—	operazione call f	operaciones call f/pl
cotation variable (F)	fortlaufende Notierung f	variable price quoting	—	libere contrattazioni f/pl	cotización variable f
Cote (D)	—	share list	bulletin officiel de la cote m	cote m	Boletín de Bolsa m
cote (I)	Cote n	share list	bulletin officiel de la cote m	—	Boletín de Bolsa m
cote de la bourse (F)	Kursblatt n	stock exchange list	—	listino di borsa m	listín de bolsa m
cote de la bourse officielle (F)	offizielles Kursblatt n	offical stock exchange list	—	listino ufficiale m	boletín oficial m
cote du jour (F)	Tageskurs m	current quotation	—	corso del giorno m	cotización del día f
cotización (Es)	Kursfestsetzung f	fixing of prices	détermination des cours f	fissazione dei corsi f	—
cotización (Es)	Kotierung f	admission of shares to official quotation	cotation f	ammissione alla quotazione f	—
cotización (Es)	Kurs m	market price	cours m	quotazione f	—
cotización ajustable (Es)	Adjustable Peg m	adjustable peg	cours adaptable m	adjustable peg m	—
cotización bursátil (Es)	Börsenkurs m	stock exchange price	cours de bourse m	quotazione di borsa f	—
cotización bursátil (Es)	Börsennotierung f	quotation	cotation des cours en bourse f	quotazione di borsa f	—
cotización colectiva (Es)	Gesamtkurs m	total market value	cours total m	quotazione accordata f	—
cotización cuantitativa (Es)	Quantitätsnotierung f	fixed exchange	certain m	quotazione del certo f	—
cotización de apertura (Es)	Einführungskurs m	introductory price	cours d'ouverture m	prima quotazione f	—
cotización de apertura (Es)	Eröffnungskurs m	opening price	cours d'ouverture m	corso d'apertura m	—
cotización de cambio (Es)	Devisennotierung f	foreign exchange quotations	cotation des devises f	cambio m	—
cotización de cierre (Es)	Schlußkurs m	closing price	dernier cours m	quotazione di chiusura f	—
cotización de compensación (Es)	Liquidations-auszahlungskurs m	liquidation outpayment rate	cours de compensation m	corso di compensazione m	—
cotización de derechos de suscripción (Es)	Bezugsrechtnotierung f	subscription price	cotation des droits de souscription f	prezzo del diritto d'opzione m	—
cotización de doble opción (Es)	Stellkurs m	put and call price	cours du stellage m	prezzo giorno di risposta premi m	—
cotización de emisión (Es)	Bezugskurs m	subscription price	prix de souscription m	corso d'acquisto m	—
cotización de las acciones (Es)	Aktienkurs m	share price	cours des actions f	quotazione azionaria f	—
cotización del día (Es)	Tageskurs m	current quotation	cote du jour f	corso del giorno m	—
cotización del día de referencia (Es)	Stichtagskurs m	market price on reporting date	cours offert à la date de référence m	quotazione del giorno di riferimento f	—
cotización demandada (Es)	Geldkurs m	bid price	cours de la demande m	corso di domande m	—

	D	E	F	I	Es
cotización de precios (Es)	Preisnotierung f	prices quoted	cotation des prix f	quotazione dei prezzi f	—
cotización de sorteo (Es)	Loskurs m	lottery quotation	cotation de tirage au sort f	corso estratto a sorte m	—
cotización de un cupón (Es)	Kuponkurs m	coupon price	prix des coupons m	quotazione della cedola f	—
cotización de valores (Es)	Effektenkurs m	securities price	cours des valeurs mobilières m	quotazione di titoli f	—
cotización en un tanto porciento del valor nominal (Es)	Prozentkurs m	price expressed as a percentage of the nominal value	cours coté en pour-cent de la valeur nominale m	quotazione percentuale f	—
cotización ficticia (Es)	Scheinkurs m	fictitious quotation price	cours nominal m	quotazione evasiva f	—
cotización máxima (Es)	Stoppkurs m	stop price	cours maximum m	quotazione bloccata f	—
cotización media (Es)	Mittelkurs m	medium price	cours moyen m	corso medio m	—
cotización oficial (Es)	amtlicher Handel m	official trading	négociations en bourse f/pl	contrattazione ufficiale f	—
cotización ofrecida (Es)	Briefkurs m	ask(ed) price	cours de vente m	prezzo d'offerta m	—
cotización por unidad (Es)	Stückkurs m	price per share	cours coté au prix unitaire du titre m	corso unitario m	—
cotización real (Es)	Mengennotierung f	fixed exchange rate	cotation au certain f	cambio certo per incerto m	—
cotización variable (Es)	variabler Kurs m	variable price	cours variable m	corso variabile m	—
cotización variable (Es)	fortlaufende Notierung f	variable price quoting	cotation variable f	libere contrattazioni f/pl	—
cottimo al pezzo (I)	Geldakkord m	money piece rate	convention de salaire aux pièces f	—	destajo m
Cotton Exchange (E)	Baumwollbörse f	—	bourse de coton f	borsa del cotone f	bolsa de algodón f
coulisse (F)	Kulisse f	unofficial stock market	—	operatori di borsa m/pl	bolsa extraoficial f
counseling (E)	Beratung f	—	consultation f	consulenza f	asesoramiento m
counterclaim (E)	Gegenforderung f	—	contre-prétention f	contropretesa f	contrareclamación f
countercyclical development (E)	antizyklisches Verhalten n	—	comportement anticyclique m	comportamento anticiclico m	comportamiento anticíclico m
counter entry (E)	Gegenbuchung f	—	contrepartie f	registrazione in contropartita f	contrapartida f
counter entry (E)	Storno n	—	écriture de contre-passation f	storno m	cancelación f
counterfeiting (E)	Falschmünzerei f	—	faux-monnayage m	fabbricazione di monete false f	fabricación de moneda falsa f
counterfeit money (E)	Falschgeld n	—	fausse monnaie f	moneta contraffatta f	moneda falsa f
counter stock (E)	Schalterstücke n/pl	—	titres de guichet m/pl	titoli venduti allo sportello m/pl	títulos al contado m/pl
countertrade (E)	Gegengeschäft n	—	affaire en contrepartie f	operazione di compensazione f	transacción en contra f
countervailing duty (E)	Ausgleichsabgabe f	—	taxe de compensation f	tassa di compensazione f	tasa de compensación f
counting (E)	Auszählung f	—	comptage m	scrutinio m	cómputo m
country bank (E)	Provinzbank f	—	banque provinciale f	banca provinciale f	banco provincial m
country risk (E)	Länderrisiko n	—	risque de pays m	rischio paese m	riesgo nacional m
coupon (E)	Zinsschein m	—	coupon d'intérêts m	cedola d'interessi f	cupón de intereses m
coupon collection department (E)	Kuponkasse f	—	service de payement des coupons m	cassa cedolare f	sección de cobro por cupones f
coupon de dividende (F)	Gewinnanteilsschein m	dividend coupon	—	cedola f	cupón m
coupon de renouvellement (F)	Stichkupon m	renewal coupon	—	cedola di riaffogliamento f	cupón de renovación m
coupon d'intérêts (F)	Zinsschein m	coupon	—	cedola d'interessi f	cupón de intereses m
coupon d'option (F)	Optionsschein m	share purchase warrant	—	warrant m	documento de opción m
coupon market (E)	Kuponmarkt m	—	marché des coupons m	mercato delle cedole m	mercado de cupones m

	D	E	F	I	Es
coupon payable en monnaie étrangère (F)	Valutakupon *m*	foreign currency coupon	—	cedola di un titolo estero *f*	cupón de divisas *m*
coupon price (E)	Kuponkurs *m*	—	prix des coupons *m*	quotazione della cedola *f*	cotización de un cupón *f*
coupons de titres étrangers (F)	Valuten *f/pl*	foreign exchange	—	cedole di titoli esteri *m/pl*	moneda extranjera *f*
coupons d'intérêt fixe (F)	Bauzinsen *m/pl*	fixed-interest coupons	—	interessi intercalari *m/pl*	cupones de interés fijo *m/pl*
coupon sheet (E)	Kuponbogen *m*	—	feuille de coupons *f*	cedolario *m*	hoja de cupones *f*
coupon tax (E)	Kuponsteuer *f*	—	impôt sur les coupons *m*	imposta sulle cedole *f*	impuesto sobre cupones *m*
cours (F)	Kurs *m*	market price	—	quotazione *f*	cotización *f*
cours adaptable (F)	Adjustable Peg *m*	adjustable peg	—	adjustable peg *m*	cotización ajustable *f*
cours au comptant (F)	Kassakurs *m*	spot price	—	prezzo a pronti *m*	cambio al contado *m*
cours au pair (F)	Parikurs *m*	par price	—	corso alla pari *m*	cambio a la par *m*
cours à vue (F)	Sichtkurs *m*	sight rate	—	cambio a vista *m*	cambio a la vista *m*
cours coté au prix unitaire du titre (F)	Stückkurs *m*	price per share	—	corso unitario *m*	cotización por unidad *f*
cours coté en pour-cent de la valeur nominale (F)	Prozentkurs *m*	price expressed as a percentage of the nominal value	—	quotazione percentuale *f*	cotización en un tanto porciento del valor nominal *f*
cours de bourse (F)	Börsenkurs *m*	stock exchange price	—	quotazione di borsa *f*	cotización bursátil *f*
cours de change indirect (F)	Mengenkurs *m*	direct exchange	—	corso certo per incerto *m*	precio por cantidad *m*
cours de compensation (F)	Liquidations-auszahlungskurs *m*	liquidation outpayment rate	—	corso di compensazione *m*	cotización de compensación *f*
cours de compensation (F)	Kompensationskurs *m*	making-up price	—	corso di compensazione *m*	cambio de compensación *m*
cours de faveur (F)	Vorzugskurs *m*	preferential price	—	corso preferenziale *m*	curso preferencial *m*
cours de la demande (F)	Geldkurs *m*	bid price	—	corso di domanda *m*	cotización demandada *f*
cours de liquidation (F)	Liquidationskurs *m*	making-up price	—	corso di compensazione *m*	cambio de liquidación *m*
cours d'émission (F)	Emissionskurs *m*	issue price	—	corso d'emissione *m*	tipo de emisión *m*
cours d'émission (F)	Ausgabewert *m*	nominal value	—	valore d'emissione *m*	valor de emisión *m*
cours des actions (F)	Aktienkurs *m*	share price	—	quotazione azionaria *f*	cotización de las acciones *f*
cours des devises négociés à terme (F)	Devisenterminkurs *m*	forward exchange rate	—	quotazione dei cambi a termine *f*	cambio de divisas a término *m*
cours des monnaies étrangères (F)	Sortenkurs *m*	rate for foreign notes and coins	—	corso dei cambi *m*	tipo de cambio de billetes y monedas extranjeras *m*
cours d'estimation (F)	Taxkurs *m*	estimated quotation	—	corso di stima *m*	precio de tasación *m*
cours des valeurs mobilières (F)	Effektenkurs *m*	securities price	—	quotazione di titoli *f*	cotización de valores *f*
cours de vente (F)	Briefkurs *m*	ask(ed) price	—	prezzo d'offerta *m*	cotización ofrecida *f*
cours d'ouverture (F)	Eröffnungskurs *m*	opening price	—	corso d'apertura *m*	cotización de apertura *f*
cours d'ouverture (F)	Einführungskurs *m*	introductory price	—	prima quotazione *f*	cotización de apertura *f*
cours du change (F)	Wechselkurs *m*	exchange rate	—	cambio *m*	tipo de cambio *m*
cours du change multiple (F)	gespaltener Wechselkurs *m*	multiple exchange rates	—	cambio multiplo *m*	tipo de cambio múltiple *m*
cours du stellage (F)	Stellkurs *m*	put and call price	—	prezzo giorno di risposta premi *m*	cotización de doble opción *f*
course de dévaluation (F)	Abwertungswettlauf *m*	devaluation race	—	corsa alla svalutazione *f*	carrera de desvalorización *f*
course des prix et des salaires (F)	Lohn-Preis-Spirale *f*	wage-price spiral	—	spirale dei salari e dei prezzi *f*	espiral precios-salarios *m*
cours extrême (F)	Extremkurs *m*	peak quotation	—	quotazione estrema *f*	curso extremo *m*
cours flottant commun adopté par plusieurs pays (F)	Blockfloating *n*	block floating	—	fluttuazione congiunta *f*	flotación en bloque *f*

	D	E	F	I	Es
cours limité (F)	Kurslimit *n*	price limit	—	limite di prezzo *m*	cambio limitado *m*
cours maximum (F)	Stoppkurs *m*	stop price	—	quotazione bloccata *f*	cotización máxima *f*
cours moins le dividende (F)	Dividendenabschlag *m*	quotation ex dividend	—	ex dividendo *m*	disagio de dividendo *m*
cours moins le droit de souscription (F)	Bezugsrechtabschlag *m*	ex-rights markdown	—	stacco del diritto d'opzione *m*	deducción del derecho de suscripción *f*
cours moyen (F)	Mittelkurs *m*	medium price	—	corso medio *m*	cotización media *f*
cours net (F)	Nettokurs *m*	net price	—	quotazione netta *f*	cambio neto *m*
cours nominal (F)	Scheinkurs *m*	fictitious quotation price	—	quotazione evasiva *f*	cotización ficticia *f*
cours nominal (F)	Ausweichkurs *m*	fictitious security price	—	quotazione evasiva *f*	precio ficticio de acciones *m*
cours offert à la date de référence (F)	Stichtagskurs *m*	market price on reporting date	—	quotazione del giorno di riferimento *f*	cotización del día de referencia *f*
cours payé par le souscripteur au syndicat des banquiers (F)	Übernahmekurs *m*	underwriting price	—	corso d'acquisto per il consorzio *m*	cambio de adquisición por el banco emisor *m*
cours total (F)	Gesamtkurs *m*	total market value	—	quotazione accordata *f*	cotización colectiva *f*
cours variable (F)	variabler Kurs *m*	variable price	—	corso variabile *m*	cotización variable *f*
Courtage (D)	—	brokerage	courtage *m*	courtage *f*	corretaje *m*
courtage (F)	Courtage *f*	brokerage	—	courtage *f*	corretaje *m*
courtage (I)	Courtage *f*	brokerage	courtage *m*	—	corretaje *m*
courtier (F)	Broker *m*	broker	—	broker *m*	corredor *m*
courtier de métaux précieux (F)	Bullionbroker *m*	bullion broker	—	bullionbroker *m*	corredor de metales finos *m*
courtier en bourse (F)	Kursmakler *m*	stockbroker	—	agente di borsa *m*	agente de cambio y bolsa *m*
courtier en bourse (F)	Börsenmakler *m*	stockbroker	—	agente di borsa *m*	agente de bolsa *m*
courtier en devises (F)	Devisenkursmakler *m*	exchange broker	—	agente di cambio *m*	corredor de cambios *m*
courtier en devises (F)	Devisenhändler *m*	foreign exchange dealer	—	cambista *m*	cambista *m*
courtier en valeurs mobilières (F)	Effektenmakler *m*	stockbroker	—	agente di cambio *m*	corredor de bolsa *m*
courtier en valeurs mobilières (F)	freier Makler *m*	floor trader	—	mediatore libero *m*	corredor no colegiado *m*
courtier en valeurs mobilières (F)	Effektenhändler *m*	dealer in securities	—	agente in valori *m*	corredor de bolsa *m*
coût (F)	Kosten *pl*	costs	—	costi *m/pl*	costes *m/pl*
coût créant des dépenses (F)	ausgabenwirksame Kosten *pl*	spending costs	—	costi comportanti spese *m/pl*	gastos de desembolso *m/pl*
coût de crédit (F)	Kreditkosten *f*	cost of credit	—	costi del credito *m*	gastos de crédito *m/pl*
coût de garde (F)	Verwahrungskosten *pl*	custody fee	—	spese di custodia *f/pl*	gastos de depósito *m/pl*
coût dégressif (F)	degressive Kosten *pl*	degressive costs	—	costi decrescenti *m/pl*	gastos degresivos *m/pl*
coût de l'argent emprunté (F)	Fremdkapitalkosten *pl*	costs of loan capital	—	costi del capitale di credito *m/pl*	coste de capital ajeno *m*
coût des facteurs (F)	Faktorkosten *pl*	factor costs	—	costi dei fattori *m/pl*	gastos de los factores *m/pl*
coût d'opportunité (F)	Opportunitätskosten *pl*	opportunity costs	—	costi opportunità *m/pl*	coste de oportunidad *m*
coût fixe (F)	fixe Kosten *pl*	standing costs	—	costi fissi *m/pl*	gastos fijos *m/pl*
coût hasardeux (F)	Risikokosten *pl*	risk-induced costs	—	costi di rischio *m/pl*	gastos de riesgo *m/pl*
coût par nature (F)	Kostenart *f*	cost type	—	tipo di costo *m*	clase de costes *f*
coût précalculé (F)	Anderskosten *pl*	costing expenditures	—	costi calcolatori *m/pl*	costes calculatorios *m/pl*
coût total (F)	Gesamtkosten *pl*	overall costs	—	costi complessivi *m/pl*	costes totales *m/pl*
couverture (F)	Deckung *f*	coverage	—	copertura *f*	cobertura *f*

	D	E	F	I	Es
couverture (F)	Sicherungsgeschäft *n*	security transaction	—	garanzia *f*	cobertura *f*
couverture de garantie d'une banque (F)	Bankdeckung *f*	banking cover	—	copertura bancaria *f*	cobertura bancaria *f*
couverture des coûts (F)	Kostendeckung *f*	cost recovery	—	copertura delle spese *f*	dotación *f*
couverture en billets de banque (F)	Notendeckung *f*	cover of note circulation	—	copertura di emissione di banconote *f*	cobertura monetaria *f*
couverture en espèces (F)	Bardeckung *f*	cash cover	—	copertura in contanti *f*	cobertura en efectivo *f*
couverture métallique (F)	Metalldeckung *f*	metal cover	—	copertura metallica *f*	cobertura en metálico *f*
couverture monétaire (F)	Gelddeckung *f*	monetary standard	—	copertura metallica *f*	reserva-metales finos *f*
couverture or (F)	Golddeckung *f*	gold cover	—	copertura oro *f*	cobertura-oro *f*
coverage (E)	Deckung *f*	—	couverture *f*	copertura *f*	cobertura *f*
coverage interest rate (E)	Deckungszinsen *m/pl*	—	intérêts de couverture *m/pl*	interessi di copertura *m/pl*	intereses de cobertura *m/pl*
coverage loan (E)	Deckungsdarlehen *n*	—	prêt de couverture *m*	mutuo destinato a copertura *m*	préstamo de cobertura *m*
cover clause (E)	Deckungsklausel *f*	—	clause de couverture *f*	clausola di garanzia *f*	cláusula de cobertura *f*
covered cheque (E)	gedeckter Scheck *m*	—	chèque provisionné *m*	assegno coperto *m*	cheque cubierto *m*
covered credit (E)	gedeckter Kredit *m*	—	crédit garanti *m*	credito garantito *m*	crédito cubierto *m*
covering claim (E)	Deckungsforderung *f*	—	créance de couverture *f*	richiesta di copertura *f*	crédito de cobertura *m*
covering operation (E)	Deckungsgeschäft *n*	—	opération de couverture *f*	operazione di copertura *f*	operación de cobertura *f*
cover of note circulation (E)	Notendeckung *f*	—	couverture en billets de banque *f*	copertura di emissione di banconote *f*	cobertura monetaria *f*
coyuntura (Es)	Konjunktur *f*	business cycle	conjoncture *f*	congiuntura *f*	—
crans variables (F)	Crawling peg *m*	crawling peg	—	crawling peg *m*	sistema de paridad flotante *m*
crawling exchange rate adjustment (E)	gleitende Paritätsanpassung *f*	—	ajustement continu de parités *m*	adattamento delle parità flessibile *m*	ajuste continuado de paridades *m*
Crawling peg (D)	—	crawling peg	crans variables *m*	crawling peg *m*	sistema de paridad flotante *m*
crawling peg (E)	Crawling peg *m*	—	crans variables *m*	crawling peg *m*	sistema de paridad flotante *m*
crawling peg (I)	Crawling peg *m*	crawling peg	crans variables *m*	—	sistema de paridad flotante *m*
creación de créditos (Es)	Kreditschöpfung *f*	creation of credit	création de crédit *f*	creazione di credito *f*	—
creación de depósitos bancarios (Es)	Giralgeldschöpfung *f*	creation of deposit money	création de monnaie scripturale *f*	creazione di moneta bancaria *f*	—
creación de dinero (Es)	Geldschöpfung *f*	creation of money	création d'argent *f*	creazione di denaro *f*	—
créance (F)	Forderung *f*	claim	—	credito *m*	crédito *m*
créance collective inscrite dans le livre de la dette (F)	Sammelschuldbuchforderung *f*	collective debt register claim	—	cartella debito pubblico collettiva *f*	crédito contabilizado colectivo *m*
créance de couverture (F)	Deckungsforderung *f*	covering claim	—	richiesta di copertura *f*	crédito de cobertura *m*
créance douteuse (F)	dubiose Forderung *f*	doubtful debts	—	credito controverso *m*	crédito dudoso *m*
créance d'un associé d'une société par intérêts (F)	Gesamthandforderung *f*	jointly owned claim	—	credito comunione a mani unite *m*	crédito en mano común *m*
créance en compte (F)	Buchforderung *f*	account receivable	—	credito contabile *m*	crédito en cuenta *m*
créance inscrite dans le livre de la dette (F)	Schuldbuchforderung *f*	debt-register claim	—	cartella del debito pubblico *f*	deuda inscrita en el libro de deudas *f*
créance irrécupérable (F)	notleidende Forderung *f*	claim in default	—	credito in sofferenza *m*	crédito dudoso *m*
créance partielle (F)	Teilforderung *f*	partial claim	—	credito parziale *m*	crédito parcial *m*
créance prioritaire (F)	Ausfallforderung *f*	bad debt loss	—	credito per l'ammanco *m*	impagados *m/pl*

	D	E	F	I	Es
créances irrécupérables (F)	uneinbringliche Forderung *f*	uncollectible	—	credito irrecuperabile *m*	crédito incobrable *m*
créance totale (F)	Gesamtforderung *f*	total claim	—	credito complessivo *m*	crédito total *m*
créancier (F)	Gläubiger *m*	creditor	—	creditore *m*	acreedor *m*
créancier de la faillite (F)	Konkursgläubiger *m*	bankrupt's creditor	—	creditore della massa fallimentare *m*	acreedor de la quiebra *m*
créancier de la masse (F)	Massegläubiger *m*	preferential creditor	—	creditore della massa *m*	acreedor sin garantía *m*
création d'argent (F)	Geldschöpfung *f*	creation of money	—	creazione di denaro *f*	creación de dinero *f*
création de crédit (F)	Kreditschöpfung *f*	creation of credit	—	creazione di credito *f*	creación de créditos *f*
création de monnaie scripturale (F)	Giralgeldschöpfung *f*	creation of deposit money	—	creazione di moneta bancaria *f*	creación de depósitos bancarios *f*
creation of credit (E)	Kreditschöpfung *f*	—	création de crédit *f*	creazione di credito *f*	creación de créditos *f*
creation of deposit money (E)	Giralgeldschöpfung *f*	—	création de monnaie scripturale *f*	creazione di moneta bancaria *f*	creación de depósitos bancarios *f*
creation of money (E)	Geldschöpfung *f*	—	création d'argent *f*	creazione di denaro *f*	creación de dinero *f*
creazione di credito (I)	Kreditschöpfung *f*	creation of credit	création de crédit *f*	—	creación de créditos *f*
creazione di denaro (I)	Geldschöpfung *f*	creation of money	création d'argent *f*	—	creación de dinero *f*
creazione di moneta bancaria (I)	Giralgeldschöpfung *f*	creation of deposit money	création de monnaie scripturale *f*	—	creación de depósitos bancarios *f*
credit (E)	Kredit *m*	—	crédit *m*	credito *m*	crédito *m*
crédit (F)	Kreditwesen *n*	credit system	—	sistema creditizio *m*	régimen de creditos *m*
crédit (F)	Kredit *m*	credit	—	credito *m*	crédito *m*
crédit accordé à la clientèle (F)	Kundschaftskredit *m*	customers' credit	—	credito alla clientela *m*	crédito al consumidor *m*
crédit accordé par une banque à ses membres du directoire (F)	Organkredit *m*	loans granted to members of a managing board	—	credito concesso all'organico *m*	crédito interconsorcial *m*
crédit accordé sur le marché monétaire (F)	Geldmarktkredit *m*	money market credit	—	credito monetario *m*	crédito de mercado monetario *m*
crédit à court terme (F)	Saisonkredit *m*	seasonal loan	—	credito stagionale *m*	crédito estacional *m*
crédit à court terme (F)	Kassenkredite *m/pl*	cash credit	—	crediti di cassa *m/pl*	créditos a corto plazo *m/pl*
credit agreement (E)	Krediteröffnungs-vertrag *m*	—	contrat d'ouverture de crédit *m*	contratto d'apertura di credito *m*	contrato de apertura de crédito *m*
credit agreement (E)	Kreditvertrag *f*	—	contrat de vente à crédit *m*	contratto di credito *m*	contrato de crédito *m*
crédit agricole (F)	Hofkredit *m*	farm credit	—	credito agricolo *m*	crédito agropecuario *m*
crédit agricole (F)	Landwirtschafts-kredit *m*	agricultural loan	—	credito all'agricoltura *m*	crédito agrario *m*
crédit agricole aux fermiers (F)	Pächterkredit *m*	tenant's credit	—	credito ai fittavoli *m*	crédito agrícola a favor de los arrendatarios *m*
crédit à l'industrie (F)	Industriekredit *m*	industrial credit	—	credito industriale *m*	crédito industrial *m*
crédit à long terme (F)	langfristiger Kredit *m*	long-term credit	—	credito a lunga scadenza *m*	crédito a largo plazo *m*
crédit à tempéraments (F)	Ratenkredit *m*	instalment sales credit	—	finanziamento di acquisti rateali *m*	crédito a plazos *m*
credit authorizing negotiation of bills (E)	Negoziationskredit *m*	—	crédit autorisant à la négociation de traites *m*	credito di negoziazione *m*	crédito de negociación *m*
crédit autorisant à la négociation de traites (F)	Negoziationskredit *m*	credit authorizing negotiation of bills	—	credito di negoziazione *m*	crédito de negociación *m*
crédit-bail (F)	Leasing *n*	leasing	—	leasing *m*	leasing *m*
credit balance (E)	Guthaben *n*	—	avoir *m*	avere *m*	activo *m*
crédit bancaire (F)	Bankkredit *m*	bank credit	—	credito bancario *m*	crédito bancario *m*
crédit bancaire sur documents (F)	Trassierungskredit *m*	acceptance credit	—	credito di traenza *m*	crédito de reembolso *m*
credit based on collateral security (E)	Sachkredit *m*	—	crédit réel *m*	credito reale *m*	crédito real *m*

	D	E	F	I	Es
crédit budgétaire (F)	Haushaltskredit *m*	budget credit	—	credito di finanziamento bilancio *m*	crédito presupuestario *m*
credit business (E)	Kreditgeschäft *n*	—	opérations d'avances sur crédit *f/pl*	operazione di credito *f*	operación crediticia *f*
credit by way of bank guarantee (E)	Bürgschaftskredit *m*	—	crédit cautionné *m*	credito di fideiussione *m*	crédito de fianza *m*
credit by way of bank guarantee (E)	Aval-Kredit *m*	—	crédit d'escompte sur traite avalisée *m*	credito d'avallo *m*	crédito de aval *m*
credit by way of discount of bills (E)	Wechseldiskontkredit *m*	—	crédit sur effets escomptés *m*	credito per sconto effetti *m*	crédito de descuento cambial *m*
credit by way of overdraft (E)	Überziehungskredit *m*	—	avance sur compte courant *f*	credito su base scoperta *m*	crédito en descubierto *m*
crédit-cadre (F)	Rahmenkredit *m*	credit line	—	linea di credito *f*	línea de crédito *f*
credit card (E)	Kreditkarte *f*	—	carte de crédit *f*	carta di credito *f*	tarjeta de crédito *f*
crédit cautionné (F)	Bürgschaftskredit *m*	credit by way of bank guarantee	—	credito di fideiussione *m*	crédito de fianza *m*
credit ceiling (E)	Kreditplafond *n*	—	plafond du crédit accordé *m*	limite massimo di fido *m*	plafón de crédito *m*
credit check (E)	Bonitätsprüfung *f*	—	vérification de la solvabilité *f*	esame di solvibilità *m*	inspección de solvencia *f*
credit checking sheets (E)	Kreditprüfungsblätter *n/pl*	—	feuilles d'enquête sur la solvabilité *f/pl*	fogli di controllo crediti *m/pl*	hojas de investigación crediticia *f/pl*
credit commission (E)	Kreditprovision *f*	—	frais de commission d'ouverture de crédit *m/pl*	provvigione di credito *f*	comisión de apertura de crédito *f*
credit committee (E)	Kreditausschuß *m*	—	commission d'étude des dossiers de crédit *f*	comitato di credito *m*	comité de crédito *m*
credit control (E)	Kreditkontrolle *f*	—	contrôle de crédit *m*	controllo del credito *m*	control crediticio *m*
credit cooperative (E)	Kreditgenossenschaft *f*	—	caisse coopérative de crédit *f*	cooperativa di credito *f*	cooperativa de crédito *f*
credit culture (E)	Kreditkultur *f*	—	culture de crédit *f*	panorama creditizio *m*	cultura crediticia *f*
crédit d'achat (F)	Kaufkredit *m*	purchasing credit	—	credito finanziamento acquisti *m*	crédito de compra *m*
crédit de caisse (F)	Barkredit *m*	cash credit	—	credito in contanti *m*	crédito en efectivo *m*
crédit de financement (F)	Finanzkredit *m*	financial credit	—	credito di finanziamento *m*	crédito financiero *m*
credit demand (E)	Kreditbedarf *m*	—	besoin en crédits *m*	fabbisogno creditizio *m*	necesidad de crédito *f*
credit department (E)	Kreditabteilung *f*	—	service du crédit et des prêts *m*	ufficio crediti *m*	sección de crédito *f*
crédit d'escompte (F)	Diskontkredit *m*	discount credit	—	credito di sconto *m*	crédito de descuento *m*
crédit d'escompte sur traite avalisée (F)	Aval-Kredit *m*	credit by way of bank guarantee	—	credito d'avallo *m*	crédito de aval *m*
crédit de soutien (F)	Beistandskredit *m*	standby credit	—	credito di sostegno *m*	crédito de ayuda *m*
crédit destiné à un objet déterminé (F)	Objektkredit *m*	loan for special purposes	—	credito per specifico oggetto *m*	crédito destinado a un determinado objeto *m*
crédit de structure (F)	Strukturkredit *m*	structural loan	—	credito strutturale *m*	crédito de estructura *m*
crédit d'infrastructure (F)	Infrastrukturkredit *m*	infrastructural credit	—	credito per l'infrastruttura *m*	crédito de infraestructura *m*
crédit d'investissement (F)	Investitionskredit *m*	investment credit	—	credito d'investimento *m*	crédito de inversión *m*
crédit d'un million (F)	Millionenkredit *m*	multimillion credit	—	credito di un milione e più *m*	crédito de millones *m*
crédit en compte courant (F)	Kontokorrentkredit *m*	current account credit	—	credito in conto corrente *m*	crédito en cuenta corriente *m*
crédit en compte courant (F)	Blanko-Kredit *m*	open credit	—	fido in bianco *m*	crédito en blanco *m*
crédit en faveur de l'exportation (F)	Exportkredit *m*	export credits	—	credito d'esportazione *m*	crédito a la exportación *m*
crédit en monnaie étrangère (F)	Valutakredit *m*	foreign currency loan	—	credito in valuta estera *m*	crédito en divisas *m*

	D	E	F	I	Es
crédit en nature (F)	Naturalkredit *m*	credit granted in kind	—	prestito ipotecario a obbligazione fondiaria *m*	crédito en especie *m*
créditeurs (F)	Kreditoren *m/pl*	creditors	—	creditori *m/pl*	acreedores *m/pl*
crédit extérieur (F)	Auslandskredit *m*	foreign credit	—	credito estero *m*	crédito extranjero *m*
credit facilities (E)	Kreditfazilität *f*	—	facilité de crédit *f*	facilitazione creditizia *f*	facilidades crediticias *f/pl*
crédit fiduciaire (F)	Treuhandkredit *m*	loan on a trust basis	—	credito indiretto *m*	crédito fiduciario *m*
crédit financier accordé par les banques à l'émetteur (F)	Emissionskredit *m*	credit granted to the issuer by the bank by underwriting the issue	—	credito d'emissione *m*	crédito de emisión *m*
credit financing register (E)	Teilzahlungsbuch *n*	—	livre de payements partiels *m*	libro di pagamento parziale *m*	libro de pagos parciales *m*
credit folder (E)	Kreditakte *f*	—	dossier de crédit *m*	cartella di credito *f*	expediente de crédito *m*
crédit foncier (F)	Bodenkredit *m*	loan on landed property	—	credito fondario *m*	crédito inmobiliario *m*
credit fraud (E)	Kreditschwindel *m*	—	obtention de crédits par duperie *f*	frode creditizia *f*	fraude crediticio *m*
crédit garanti (F)	gedeckter Kredit *m*	covered credit	—	credito garantito *m*	crédito cubierto *m*
crédit garanti par nantissement (F)	Lombardkredit *m*	collateral credit	—	anticipazione su crediti *f*	crédito pignoraticio *m*
crédit garanti par un consortium bancaire (F)	Konsortialkredit *m*	syndicated credit	—	credito consorziale *m*	crédito consorcial *m*
credit granted in kind (E)	Naturalkredit *m*	—	crédit en nature *m*	prestito ipotecario a obbligazione fondiaria *m*	crédito en especie *m*
credit granted to a local authority (E)	Kommunalkredit *m*	—	prêt aux communes *m*	credito comunale *m*	crédito municipal *m*
credit granted to the issuer by the bank by underwriting the issue (E)	Emissionskredit *m*	—	crédit financier accordé par les banques à l'émetteur *m*	credito d'emissione *m*	crédito de emisión *m*
credit guarantee (E)	Kreditgarantie *f*	—	garantie de crédit *f*	garanzia di credito *f*	garantía de crédito *f*
crédit hypothécaire (F)	Hypothekarkredit *m*	mortgage loan	—	credito ipotecario *m*	crédito hipotecario *m*
crediti al commercio (I)	Handelskredite *m/pl*	commercial credits	crédits commerciaux *m/pl*	—	créditos comerciales *m/pl*
crediti di cassa (I)	Kassenkredite *m/pl*	cash credit	crédit à court terme *m*	—	créditos a corto plazo *m/pl*
crédit immobilier (F)	Immobiliarkredit *m*	real estate credit	—	credito immobiliare *m*	crédito inmobiliario *m*
crédit important (F)	Großkredit *m*	large-scale lending	—	grosso credito *m*	crédito importante *m*
crediti indiretti (I)	durchlaufende Kredite *m/pl*	transmitted loans	crédits en consignation *m/pl*	—	crédito transitorio *m*
credit inflation (E)	Kreditinflation *f*	—	inflation de crédit *f*	inflazione creditizia *f*	inflación crediticia *f*
credit information (E)	Kreditauskunft *f*	—	reseignement sur la solvabilité du demandeur d'un crédit *m*	informazione creditizia *f*	información de crédito *f*
credit institution (E)	Kreditinstitut *n*	—	établissement de crédit *m*	istituto di credito *m*	instituto de crédito *m*
credit insurance (E)	Kreditversicherung *f*	—	assurance crédit *f*	assicurazione di credito *f*	seguro crediticio *m*
credit interest (E)	Habenzinsen *m/pl*	—	intérêts créditeurs *m/pl*	interessi attivi *m/pl*	intereses acreedores *m/pl*
crédit intermédiare (F)	Zwischenkredit *m*	interim loan	—	credito transitorio *m*	crédito interino *m*
crediti pendenti (I)	Außenstände *m/pl*	outstanding accounts	dettes actives *f/pl*	—	cobros pendientes *m/pl*
crediti pubblici (I)	öffentliche Kredite *m/pl*	credits extended to public authorities	crédits publics *m/pl*	—	créditos público *m/pl*
crediti speciali all'esportazione (I)	AKA-Kredite *m/pl*	export credits	crédits en faveur de l'exportation *m/pl*	—	créditos a la exportación *m/pl*
credit item (E)	Aktivposten *m*	—	poste de l'actif *m*	attività *f*	asiento activo *m*
credit limit (E)	Kreditlimit *n*	—	plafond du crédit alloué *m*	limite di credito *m*	límite de crédito *m*

	D	E	F	I	Es
credit limitation (E)	Kreditplafondierung *f*	—	fixation d'une limite de crédit *f*	fissazione del fido *f*	volumen máximo de crédito disponible *m*
credit line (E)	Rahmenkredit *m*	—	crédit-cadre *m*	linea di credito *f*	línea de crédito *f*
credit line (E)	Kreditlinie *f*	—	plafond du crédit accordé *m*	linea di credito *f*	línea de crédito *f*
credit money (E)	Kreditgeld *n*	—	argent de crédit *m*	credito *m*	dinero crediticio *m*
crédit moratoire (F)	Stillhalte-Kredit *m*	standstill credit	—	credito inattivo *m*	crédito inmovilizado *m*
crédito (Es)	Kreditwürdigkeit *f*	creditworthiness	solvabilité *f*	fido *m*	—
crédito (Es)	Forderung *f*	claim	créance *f*	credito *m*	—
crédito (Es)	Kredit *m*	credit	crédit *m*	credito *m*	—
credito (I)	Kredit *m*	credit	crédit *m*	—	crédito *m*
credito (I)	Kreditgeld *n*	credit money	argent de crédit *m*	—	dinero crediticio *m*
credito (I)	Forderung *f*	claim	créance *f*	—	crédito *m*
credito (I)	Darlehen *n*	loan	prêt *m*	—	préstamo *m*
crédito agrario (Es)	Landwirtschafts-kredit *m*	agricultural loan	crédit agricole *m*	credito all'agricoltura *m*	—
credito agrario (I)	Bodenkredit *m*	loan on landed property	crédit foncier *m*	—	crédito inmobiliario *m*
crédito agrícola a favor de los arrendatarios (Es)	Pächterkredit *m*	tenant's credit	crédit agricole aux fermiers *m*	credito ai fittavoli *m*	—
credito agricolo (I)	Hofkredit *m*	farm credit	crédit agricole *m*	—	crédito agropecuario *m*
crédito agropecuario (Es)	Hofkredit *m*	farm credit	crédit agricole *m*	credito agricolo *m*	—
credito ai fittavoli (I)	Pächterkredit *m*	tenant's credit	crédit agricole aux fermiers *m*	—	crédito agrícola a favor de los arrendatarios *m*
crédito a la exportación (Es)	Exportkredit *m*	export credits	crédit en faveur de l'exportation *m*	credito d'esportazione *m*	—
crédito a largo plazo (Es)	langfristiger Kredit *m*	long-term credit	crédit à long terme *m*	credito a lunga scadenza *m*	—
crédito al consumidor (Es)	Kundschaftskredit *m*	customers' credit	crédit accordé à la clientèle *m*	credito alla clientela *m*	—
credito alla clientela (I)	Kundschaftskredit *m*	customers' credit	crédit accordé à la clientèle *m*	—	crédito al consumidor *m*
credito all'agricoltura (I)	Landwirtschafts-kredit *m*	agricultural loan	crédit agricole *m*	—	crédito agrario *m*
credito allo scoperto (I)	ungedeckter Kredit *m*	uncovered credit	crédit sur notoriété *m*	—	crédito descubierto *m*
credito a lunga scadenza (I)	langfristiger Kredit *m*	long-term credit	crédit à long terme *m*	—	crédito a largo plazo *m*
crédito a plazos (Es)	Ratenkredit *m*	instalment sales credit	crédit à tempéraments *m*	finanziamento di acquisti rateali *m*	—
crédito bancario (Es)	Bankkredit *m*	bank credit	crédit bancaire *m*	credito bancario *m*	—
credito bancario (I)	Bankkredit *m*	bank credit	crédit bancaire *m*	—	crédito bancario *m*
credito bimonetario (I)	Doppelwährungs-anleihe *f*	double currency loan	emprunt à double étalon *m*	—	empréstito de moneda dual *m*
credito complessivo (I)	Gesamtforderung *f*	total claim	créance totale *f*	—	crédito total *m*
credito comunale (I)	Kommunalkredit *m*	credit granted to a local authority	prêt aux communes *m*	—	crédito municipal *m*
credito comunione a mani unite (I)	Gesamthand-forderung *f*	jointly owned claim	créance d'un associé d'une société par intérêts *f*	—	crédito en mano común *m*
credito concesso all'organico (I)	Organkredit *m*	loans granted to members of a managing board	crédit accordé par une banque à ses membres du directoire *m*	—	crédito interconsorcial *m*
crédito con fines de aumentar la liquidez (Es)	Kassenverstärkungs-kredit *m*	cash lending	crédit pour augmenter la liquidité *m*	credito per elasticità di cassa *m*	—
crédito consorcial (Es)	Konsortialkredit *m*	syndicated credit	crédit garanti par un consortium bancaire *m*	credito consorziale *m*	—

	D	E	F	I	Es
credito consorziale (I)	Konsortialkredit *m*	syndicated credit	crédit garanti par un consortium bancaire *m*	—	crédito consorcial *m*
credito contabile (I)	Buchforderung *f*	account receivable	créance en compte *f*	—	crédito en cuenta *m*
credito contabile (I)	Buchkredit *m*	book credit	avance en compte *f*	—	crédito en cuenta *m*
crédito contabilizado colectivo (Es)	Sammelschuldbuchforderung *f*	collective debt register claim	créance collective inscrite dans le livre de la dette *f*	cartella debito pubblico collettiva *f*	—
credito controverso (I)	dubiose Forderung *f*	doubtful debts	créance douteuse *f*	—	crédito dudoso *m*
crédito cubierto (Es)	gedeckter Kredit *m*	covered credit	crédit garanti *m*	credito garantito *m*	—
credito d'accettazione (I)	Akzeptkredit *m*	acceptance credit	crédit par traite acceptée *m*	—	crédito de aceptación *m*
credito d'avallo (I)	Aval-Kredit *m*	credit by way of bank guarantee	crédit d'escompte sur traite avalisée *f*	—	crédito de aval *m*
crédito de aceptación (Es)	Akzeptkredit *m*	acceptance credit	crédit par traite acceptée *m*	credito d'accettazione *m*	—
crédito de aval (Es)	Aval-Kredit *m*	credit by way of bank guarantee	crédit d'escompte sur traite avalisée *m*	credito d'avallo *m*	—
crédito de ayuda (Es)	Beistandskredit *m*	standby credit	crédit de soutien *m*	credito di sostegno *m*	—
crédito de cobertura (Es)	Deckungsforderung *f*	covering claim	créance de couverture *f*	richiesta di copertura *f*	—
crédito de compra (Es)	Kaufkredit *m*	purchasing credit	crédit d'achat *m*	credito finanziamento acquisti *m*	—
crédito de descuento (Es)	Diskontkredit *m*	discount credit	crédit d'escompte *m*	credito di sconto *m*	—
crédito de descuento cambial (Es)	Wechseldiskontkredit *m*	credit by way of discount of bills	crédit sur effets escomptés *m*	credito per sconto effetti *m*	—
crédito de emisión (Es)	Emissionskredit *m*	credit granted to the issuer by the bank by underwriting the issue	crédit financier accordé par les banques à l'émetteur *m*	credito d'emissione *m*	—
crédito de estructura (Es)	Strukturkredit *m*	structural loan	crédit de structure *m*	credito strutturale *m*	—
crédito de fianza (Es)	Bürgschaftskredit *m*	credit by way of bank guarantee	crédit cautionné *m*	credito di fideiussione *m*	—
crédito de igualación y cobertura (Es)	Ausgleichs- und Deckungsforderung *f*	equalization and covering claim	demande de dédommagement et de couverture *f*	credito di compensazione *m*	—
crédito de infraestructura (Es)	Infrastrukturkredit *m*	infrastructural credit	crédit d'infrastructure *m*	credito per l'infrastruttura *m*	—
crédito de inversión (Es)	Investitionskredit *m*	investment credit	crédit d'investissement *m*	credito d'investimento *m*	—
crédito de mercado monetario (Es)	Geldmarktkredit *m*	money market credit	crédit accordé sur le marché monétaire *m*	credito monetario *m*	—
crédito de millones (Es)	Millionenkredit *m*	multimillion credit	crédit d'un million *m*	credito di un milione e più *m*	—
credito d'emissione (I)	Emissionskredit *m*	credit granted to the issuer by the bank by underwriting the issue	crédit financier accordé par les banques à l'émetteur *m*	—	crédito de emisión *m*
crédito de negociación (Es)	Negoziationskredit *m*	credit authorizing negotiation of bills	crédit autorisant à la négociation de traites *m*	credito di negoziazione *m*	—
crédito de reembolso (Es)	Trassierungskredit *m*	acceptance credit	crédit bancaire sur documents *m*	credito di traenza *m*	—
crédito descubierto (Es)	ungedeckter Kredit *m*	uncovered credit	crédit sur notoriété *m*	credito allo scoperto *m*	—
credito d'esportazione (I)	Exportkredit *m*	export credits	crédit en faveur de l'exportation *m*	—	crédito a la exportación *m*
crédito destinado a un determinado objeto (Es)	Objektkredit *m*	loan for special purposes	crédit destiné à un objet déterminé *m*	credito per specifico oggetto *m*	—
credito di compensazione (I)	Ausgleichsforderung *f*	equalization claim	droit à une indemnité compensatoire *f*	—	reclamación de indemnización contra la administración pública *f*

	D	E	F	I	Es
credito di compensazione (I)	Ausgleichs- und Deckungsforderung f	equalization and covering claim	demande de dédommagement et de couverture f	—	crédito de igualación y cobertura m
credito di fideiussione (I)	Bürgschaftskredit m	credit by way of bank guarantee	crédit cautionné m	—	crédito de fianza m
credito di finanziamento (I)	Finanzkredit m	financial credit	crédit de financement m	—	crédito financiero m
credito di finanziamento bilancio (I)	Haushaltskredit m	budget credit	crédit budgétaire m	—	crédito presupuestario m
credito di firma (I)	Kreditleihe f	loan of credit	prêt de crédit m	—	préstamo de crédito m
credito di negoziazione (I)	Negoziationskredit m	credit authorizing negotiation of bills	crédit autorisant à la négociation de traites m	—	crédito de negociación m
credito d'investimento (I)	Investitionskredit m	investment credit	crédit d'investissement m	—	crédito de inversión m
credito di sconto (I)	Diskontkredit m	discount credit	crédit d'escompte m	—	crédito de descuento m
credito di sostegno (I)	Beistandskredit m	standby credit	crédit de soutien m	—	crédito de ayuda m
credito di traenza (I)	Trassierungskredit m	acceptance credit	crédit bancaire sur documents m	—	crédito de reembolso m
credito di un milione e più (I)	Millionenkredit m	multimillion credit	crédit d'un million m	—	crédito de millones m
crédito documentario (Es)	Akkreditiv n	letter of credit	accréditif m	lettera di credito f	—
credito documentario (I)	Akkreditiv n	letter of credit	accréditif m	—	crédito documentario m
crédito dudoso (Es)	dubiose Forderung f	doubtful debts	créance douteuse f	credito controverso m	—
crédito dudoso (Es)	notleidende Forderung f	claim in default	créance irrécupérable f	credito in sofferenza m	—
crédito en blanco (Es)	Blanko-Kredit m	open credit	crédit en compte courant m	fido in bianco m	—
crédito en cuenta (Es)	Buchforderung f	account receivable	créance en compte f	credito contabile m	—
crédito en cuenta (Es)	Buchkredit m	book credit	avance en compte f	credito contabile m	—
crédito en cuenta corriente (Es)	Kontokorrentkredit m	current account credit	crédit en compte courant m	credito in conto corrente m	—
crédito en descubierto (Es)	Überziehungskredit m	credit by way of overdraft	avance sur compte courant f	credito su base scoperta m	—
crédito en divisas (Es)	Valutakredit m	foreign currency loan	crédit en monnaie étrangère m	credito in valuta estera m	—
crédito en efectivo (Es)	Barkredit m	cash credit	crédit de caisse m	credito in contanti m	—
crédito en especie (Es)	Naturalkredit m	credit granted in kind	crédit en nature m	prestito ipotecario a obbligazione fondiaria m	—
crédito en mano común (Es)	Gesamthand-forderung f	jointly owned claim	créance d'un associé d'une société par intérêts f	credito comunione a mani unite m	—
crédito estacional (Es)	Saisonkredit m	seasonal loan	crédit à court terme m	credito stagionale m	—
credito estero (I)	Auslandskredit m	foreign credit	crédit extérieur m	—	crédito extranjero m
crédito extranjero (Es)	Auslandskredit m	foreign credit	crédit extérieur m	credito estero m	—
crédito fiduciario (Es)	Treuhandkredit m	loan on a trust basis	crédit fiduciaire m	credito indiretto m	—
crédito financiero (Es)	Finanzkredit m	financial credit	crédit de financement m	credito di finanziamento m	—
credito finanziamento acquisti (I)	Kaufkredit m	purchasing credit	crédit d'achat m	—	crédito de compra m
credito garantito (I)	gedeckter Kredit m	covered credit	crédit garanti m	—	crédito cubierto m
credito globale (I)	Global-Anleihe f	all-share certificate	titre représentant globalement un paquet d'emprunts m	—	empréstito global m
crédito hipotecario (Es)	Hypothekarkredit m	mortgage loan	crédit hypothécaire m	credito ipotecario m	—
credito immobiliare (I)	Immobiliarkredit m	real estate credit	crédit immobilier m	—	crédito inmobiliario m
crédito importante (Es)	Großkredit m	large-scale lending	crédit important m	grosso credito m	—
credito inattivo (I)	Stillhalte-Kredit m	standstill credit	crédit moratoire m	—	crédito inmovilizado m

	D	E	F	I	Es
crédito incobrable (Es)	uneinbringliche Forderung f	uncollectible	créances irrécupérables f/pl	credito irrecuperabile m	—
credito in contanti (I)	Barkredit m	cash credit	crédit de caisse m	—	crédito en efectivo m
credito in conto corrente (I)	Kontokorrentkredit m	current account credit	crédit en compte courant m	—	crédito en cuenta corriente m
credito indiretto (I)	Treuhandkredit m	loan on a trust basis	crédit fiduciaire m	—	crédito fiduciario m
crédito industrial (Es)	Industriekredit m	industrial credit	crédit à l'industrie m	credito industriale m	—
credito industriale (I)	Industriekredit m	industrial credit	crédit à l'industrie m	—	crédito industrial m
crédito inmobiliario (Es)	Bodenkredit m	loan on landed property	crédit foncier m	credito fondario m	—
crédito inmobiliario (Es)	Immobiliarkredit m	real estate credit	crédit immobilier m	credito immobiliare m	—
crédito inmovilizado (Es)	Stillhalte-Kredit m	standstill credit	crédit moratoire m	credito inattivo m	—
credito in sofferenza (I)	notleidende Forderung f	claim in default	créance irrécupérable f	—	crédito dudoso m
crédito interconsorcial (Es)	Organkredit m	loans granted to members of a managing board	crédit accordé par une banque à ses membres du directoire m	credito concesso all'organico m	—
crédito interino (Es)	Zwischenkredit m	interim loan	crédit intermédiare m	credito transitorio m	—
credito in valuta estera (I)	Valutakredit m	foreign currency loan	crédit en monnaie étrangère m	—	crédito en divisas m
credito ipotecario (I)	Hypothekarkredit m	mortgage loan	crédit hypothécaire m	—	crédito hipotecario m
credito irrecuperabile (I)	uneinbringliche Forderung f	uncollectible	créances irrécupérables f/pl	—	crédito incobrable m
credito monetario (I)	Geldmarktkredit m	money market credit	crédit accordé sur le marché monétaire m	—	crédito de mercado monetario m
crédito municipal (Es)	Kommunalkredit m	credit granted to a local authority	prêt aux communes m	credito comunale m	—
crédito para la construcción (Es)	Baudarlehen n	building loan	prêt à la construction m	mutuo edilizio m	—
crédito para la financiación a plazo (Es)	Teilzahlungskredit m	instalment credit	avance sur vente payée à tempérament f	finanziamento di acquisti rateali m	—
crédito parcial (Es)	Teilforderung f	partial claim	créance partielle f	credito parziale m	—
credito parziale (I)	Teilforderung f	partial claim	créance partielle f	—	crédito parcial m
crédito pasivo (Es)	Passivkredit m	borrowing	crédit passif m	finanziamento passivo m	—
credito per elasticità di cassa (I)	Kassenverstärkungskredit m	cash lending	crédit pour augmentar la liquidité m	—	crédito con fines de aumentar la liquidez m
credito per l'ammanco (I)	Ausfallforderung f	bad debt loss	créance prioritaire f	—	impagados m/pl
credito per l'infrastruttura (I)	Infrastrukturkredit m	infrastructural credit	crédit d'infrastructure m	—	crédito de infraestructura m
credito per necessità di cassa (I)	Überbrückungskredit m	bridging loan	crédit transitoire m	—	crédito transitorio m
credito per sconto effetti (I)	Wechseldiskontkredit m	credit by way of discount of bills	crédit sur effets escomptés m	—	crédito de descuento cambial m
crédito personal (Es)	Personalkredit m	personal loan	crédit personnel m	credito personale m	—
credito personale (I)	Personalkredit m	personal loan	crédit personnel m	—	crédito personal m
credito per specifico oggetto (I)	Objektkredit m	loan for special purposes	crédit destiné à un objet déterminé m	—	crédito destinado a un determinado objeto m
crédito pignoraticio (Es)	Lombardkredit m	collateral credit	crédit garanti par nantissement m	anticipazione su crediti f	—
crédito presupuestario (Es)	Haushaltskredit m	budget credit	crédit budgétaire m	credito di finanziamento bilancio m	—
creditor (E)	Gläubiger m	—	créancier m	creditore m	acreedor m
creditore (I)	Gläubiger m	creditor	créancier m	—	acreedor m
crédito real (Es)	Sachkredit m	credit based on collateral security	crédit réel m	credito reale m	—
credito reale (I)	Sachkredit m	credit based on collateral security	crédit réel m	—	crédito real m

	D	E	F	I	Es
creditore della massa (I)	Massegläubiger *m*	preferential creditor	créancier de la masse *m*	—	acreedor sin garantía *m*
creditore della massa fallimentare (I)	Konkursgläubiger *m*	bankrupt's creditor	créancier de la faillite *m*	—	acreedor de la quiebra *m*
creditori (I)	Kreditoren *m/pl*	creditors	créditeurs *m/pl*	—	acreedores *m/pl*
credito rinnovabile (I)	revolvierendes Akkreditiv *n*	revolving letter of credit	accréditif rotatif *m*	—	crédito rotativo *m*
crédito roll over (Es)	Roll-over-Kredit *m*	roll-over credit	crédit roll-over *m*	credito roll-over *m*	—
credito roll-over (I)	Roll-over-Kredit *m*	roll-over credit	crédit roll-over *m*	—	crédito roll over *m*
crédito rotativo (Es)	revolvierendes Akkreditiv *n*	revolving letter of credit	accréditif rotatif *m*	credito rinnovabile *m*	—
creditor paper (E)	Gläubigerpapier *n*	—	titre créditeur *m*	titolo di credito *m*	título acreedor *m*
creditors (E)	Kreditoren *m/pl*	—	créditeurs *m/pl*	creditori *m/pl*	acreedores *m/pl*
creditors' meeting (E)	Gläubiger-versammlung *f*	—	assemblée des créanciers *f*	assemblea dei creditori *f*	junta de acreedores *f*
créditos a corto plazo (Es)	Kassenkredite *m/pl*	cash credit	crédit à court terme *m*	crediti di cassa *m/pl*	—
créditos activos y pasivos en el extranjero (Es)	Auslandsstatus *m*	foreign assets and liabilities	avoirs et obligations extérieurs *m/pl*	posizione verso l'estero *f*	—
créditos a la exportación (Es)	AKA-Kredite *m/pl*	export credits	crédits en faveur de l'exportation *m/pl*	crediti speciali all'esportazione *m/pl*	—
créditos comerciales (Es)	Handelskredite *m/pl*	commercial credits	crédits commerciaux *m/pl*	crediti al commercio *m/pl*	—
crédito simple (Es)	Bar-Akkreditiv *m*	clean credit	accréditif payable en espèce *m*	apertura di credito per cassa *f*	—
crédito sobre mercancías (Es)	Warenkredit *m*	trade credit	avance sur marchandises *f*	credito su merci *m*	—
créditos públicos (Es)	öffentliche Kredite *m/pl*	credits extended to public authorities	crédits publics *m/pl*	crediti pubblici *m/pl*	—
credito stagionale (I)	Saisonkredit *m*	seasonal loan	crédit à court terme *m*	—	crédito estacional *m*
crédito stand-by (Es)	Stand-by-Kredit *m*	stand-by credit	crédit stand-by *m*	credito stand-by *m*	—
credito stand-by (I)	Stand-by-Kredit *m*	stand-by credit	crédit stand-by *m*	—	crédito stand-by *m*
credito strutturale (I)	Strukturkredit *m*	structural loan	crédit de structure *m*	—	crédito de estructura *m*
credito su base scoperta (I)	Überziehungskredit *m*	credit by way of overdraft	avance sur compte courant *f*	—	crédito en descubierto *m*
credito su merci (I)	Warenkredit *m*	trade credit	avance sur marchandises *f*	—	crédito sobre mercancías *m*
crédito total (Es)	Gesamtforderung *f*	total claim	créance totale *f*	credito complessivo *m*	—
crédito transitorio (Es)	Überbrückungs-kredit *m*	bridging loan	crédit transitoire *m*	credito per necessità di cassa *m*	—
crédito transitorio (Es)	durchlaufende Kredite *m/pl*	transmitted loans	crédits en consignation *m/pl*	crediti indiretti *m/pl*	—
credito transitorio (I)	Zwischenkredit *m*	interim loan	crédit intermédiare *m*	—	crédito interino *m*
crédit par traite acceptée (F)	Akzeptkredit *m*	acceptance credit	—	credito d'accettazione *m*	crédito de aceptación *m*
crédit passif (F)	Passivkredit *m*	borrowing	—	finanziamento passivo *m*	crédito pasivo *m*
credit period (E)	Kreditfrist *f*	—	délai de rembourse-ment des avances sur crédit *m*	scadenza del credito *f*	plazo de vencimiento del crédito *m*
crédit personnel (F)	Personalkredit *m*	personal loan	—	credito personale *m*	crédito personal *m*
crédit pour augmen-ter la liquidité (F)	Kassenverstärkungs-kredit *m*	cash lending	—	credito per elasticità di cassa *m*	crédito con fines de aumentar la liquidez *m*
credit purchase (E)	Kreditkauf *m*	—	achat à crédit *m*	acquisto di credito *m*	compra de crédito *f*
crédit réel (F)	Sachkredit *m*	credit based on collateral security	—	credito reale *m*	crédito real *m*
credit restriction (E)	Kreditrestriktion *f*	—	restriction du crédit *f*	restrizione creditizia *f*	restricción de créditos *f*
credit risk (E)	Kreditrisiko *n*	—	risque inhérent aux opérations de crédit *m*	rischio inerente al credito *m*	riesgo del crédito *m*

	D	E	F	I	Es
crédit roll-over (F)	Roll-over-Kredit *m*	roll-over credit	—	credito roll-over *m*	crédito roll over *m*
crédits commerciaux (F)	Handelskredite *m/pl*	commercial credits	—	crediti al commercio *m/pl*	créditos comerciales *m/pl*
crédits en consignation (F)	durchlaufende Kredite *m/pl*	transmitted loans	—	crediti indiretti *m/pl*	crédito transitorio *m*
crédits en faveur de l'exportation (F)	AKA-Kredite *m/pl*	export credits	—	crediti speciali all'esportazione *m/pl*	créditos a la exportación *m/pl*
credits extended to public authorities (E)	öffentliche Kredite *m/pl*	—	crédits publics *m/pl*	crediti pubblici *m/pl*	créditos públicos *m/pl*
credit share (E)	Kreditaktie *f*	—	titre de crédit *m*	titolo di credito *m*	título de crédito *m*
credit side (E)	Haben *n*	—	avoir *m*	avere *m*	haber *m*
credit solvency risk (E)	Bonitätsrisiko *n*	—	risque de rendement douteux *m*	rischio di solvibilità *m*	riesgo de solvencia *f*
crédits publics (F)	öffentliche Kredite *m/pl*	credits extended to public authorities	—	crediti pubblici *m/pl*	créditos públicos *m/pl*
crédit stand-by (F)	Stand-by-Kredit *m*	stand-by credit	—	credito stand-by *m*	crédito stand-by *m*
credit standing (E)	Kreditstatus *m*	—	état de l'endettement *m*	situazione creditizia *f*	estado del endeudamiento *m*
credit status investigation (E)	Kreditprüfung *f*	—	enquête sur la solvabilité *f*	controllo dei crediti *m*	investigación de crédito y solvencia de un cliente *f*
crédit sur effets escomptés (F)	Wechseldiskont-kredit *m*	credit by way of discount of bills	—	credito per sconto effetti *m*	crédito de descuento cambial *m*
crédit sur notoriété (F)	ungedeckter Kredit *m*	uncovered credit	—	credito allo scoperto *m*	crédito descubierto *m*
credit system (E)	Kreditwesen *n*	—	crédit *m*	sistema creditizio *m*	régimen de creditos *m*
credit tranche (E)	Kredittranche *f*	—	tranche de crédit *f*	quota di credito *f*	fracción de crédito *f*
credit transaction (E)	Aktivgeschäft *n*	—	opération de prêt *f*	operazione attiva *f*	operación activa *f*
credit transaction under repurchase agreement of securities (E)	Wertpapierpensions-geschäft *n*	—	prise en pension de valeurs mobilières *f*	operazione pronti contro termine *f*	operación de reporte de valores *f*
credit transfer (E)	Giro *n*	—	virement *m*	girata *f*	giro *m*
crédit transitoire (F)	Überbrückungs-kredit *m*	bridging loan	—	credito per necessità di cassa *m*	crédito transitorio *m*
creditworthiness (E)	Kreditwürdigkeit *f*	—	solvabilité *f*	fido *m*	crédito *m*
crise (F)	Krise *f*	crisis	—	crisi *f*	crisis *f*
crise bancaire (F)	Bankenkrise *f*	banking crisis	—	crisi bancaria *f*	crisis bancaria *f*
crise économique (F)	Wirtschaftskrise *f*	economic crisis	—	crisi economica *f*	crisis económica *f*
crise économique mondiale (F)	Weltwirtschaftskrise *f*	worldwide economic crisis	—	crisi economica internazionale *f*	crisis económica mundial *f*
crise monétaire (F)	Währungskrise *f*	monetary crisis	—	crisi monetaria *f*	crisis monetaria *f*
crisi (I)	Krise *f*	crisis	crise *f*	—	crisis *f*
crisi bancaria (I)	Bankenkrise *f*	banking crisis	crise bancaire *f*	—	crisis bancaria *f*
crisi economica (I)	Wirtschaftskrise *f*	economic crisis	crise économique *f*	—	crisis económica *f*
crisi economica internazionale (I)	Weltwirtschaftskrise *f*	worldwide economic crisis	crise économique mondiale *f*	—	crisis económica mundial *f*
crisi monetaria (I)	Währungskrise *f*	monetary crisis	crise monétaire *f*	—	crisis monetaria *f*
crisis (E)	Krise *f*	—	crise *f*	crisi *f*	crisis *f*
crisis (Es)	Krise *f*	crisis	crise *f*	crisi *f*	—
crisis bancaria (Es)	Bankenkrise *f*	banking crisis	crise bancaire *f*	crisi bancaria *f*	—
crisis económica (Es)	Wirtschaftskrise *f*	economic crisis	crise économique *f*	crisi economica *f*	—
crisis económica mundial (Es)	Weltwirtschaftskrise *f*	worldwide economic crisis	crise économique mondiale *f*	crisi economica internazionale *f*	—
crisis feeling (E)	Krisenstimmung *f*	—	climat de crise *m*	atmosfera di crisi *f*	ambiente de crisis *m*
crisis monetaria (Es)	Währungskrise *f*	monetary crisis	crise monétaire *f*	crisi monetaria *f*	—
crossed cheque (E)	gekreuzter Scheck *m*	—	chèque barré *m*	assegno sbarrato *m*	cheque cruzado *m*
crossed cheque (E)	Verrechnungs-scheck *m*	—	chèque à porter en compte *m*	assegno da accreditare *m*	cheque cruzado *m*
cross rate (E)	Kreuzparität *f*	—	parité indirecte *f*	parità incrociata *f*	paridad cruzada *f*

	D	E	F	I	Es
cuenta (Es)	Konto *n*	account	compte *m*	conto *m*	—
cuenta (Es)	Rechenschaft *f*	rendering of account	compte rendu *m*	conto *m*	—
cuenta abierta (Es)	offenes Konto *n*	open account	compte ouvert *m*	conto aperto *m*	—
cuenta anónima (Es)	Nummernkonto *n*	numbered account	compte anonyme *m*	conto cifrato *m*	—
cuenta bancaria (Es)	Bankkonto *n*	bank account	compte en banque *m*	conto bancario *m*	—
cuenta bloqueada (Es)	Sperrkonto *n*	blocked account	compte bloqué *m*	conto bloccato *m*	—
cuenta colectiva (Es)	Sammelkonto *n*	collective account	compte collectif *m*	conto collettivo *m*	—
cuenta colectiva (Es)	Und-Konto *n*	joint account where all signatories must sign	compte joint *m*	conto comune *m*	—
cuenta conjunta (Es)	Gemeinschaftskonto *n*	joint account	compte commun *m*	conto congiunto *m*	—
cuenta corriente (Es)	Girokonto *n*	current account	compte de virement *m*	giroconto *m*	—
cuenta corriente (Es)	Kontokorrent *m*	current account	compte courant *m*	conto corrente *m*	—
cuenta corriente bancaria (Es)	Bankkontokorrent *m*	current account with a bank	compte courant de banque *m*	conto corrente bancario *m*	—
cuenta de ahorros (Es)	Sparkonto *n*	savings account	compte d'épargne *m*	conto a risparmio *m*	—
cuenta de beneficios y pérdidas (Es)	Aufwands- und Ertragsrechnung *f*	profit and loss account	compte de profits et pertes *m*	conto economico *m*	—
cuenta de capital (Es)	Kapitalkonto *n*	capital account	compte de capital *m*	conto capitale *m*	—
cuenta de capital propio (Es)	Eigenkapitalkonto *n*	equity account	compte capital *m*	conto del capitale proprio *m*	—
cuenta de cártel (Es)	Syndikatskonto *n*	syndicate account	compte de syndicat *m*	conto sindacale *m*	—
cuenta de compensación de gastos (Es)	Aufwands- ausgleichkonto *n*	account for reimbursements of expenses	compte de frais à reporter *m*	conto compensazione spese *m*	—
cuenta de depósitos (Es)	Depotkonto *n*	security deposit account	compte de dépôt *m*	conto di deposito *m*	—
cuenta de existencia (Es)	Bestandskonto *n*	real account	compte d'existences *m*	conto magazzino *m*	—
cuenta de financia- ción de desarrollo (Es)	Aufbaukonto *n*	build-up account	compte d'installation *m*	conto accumulativo *m*	—
cuenta de gastos (Es)	Spesenrechnung *f*	statement of expenses	compte de frais *m*	conto delle spese *m*	—
cuenta de gastos (Es)	Aufwandskonto *n*	expense account	compte de frais *m*	conto spesa *m*	—
cuenta de gastos-ingresos (Es)	Einnahmen- Ausgabenrechnung *f*	bill of receipts and expenditures	état des recettes et des dépenses *m*	conto entrate e uscite *m*	—
cuenta de interés fijo (Es)	Festzinskonto *n*	fixed-interest bearing account	compte à intérêt fixe *m*	conto ad interesse fisso *m*	—
cuenta de mercado monetario (Es)	Geldmarktkonto *n*	money market account	compte du marché monétaire *m*	conto monetario *m*	—
cuenta de moneda extranjera (Es)	Valutakonto *n*	foreign currency account	compte en monnaie étrangère *m*	conto valutario *m*	—
cuenta de moneda extranjera (Es)	Fremdwährungs- konto *n*	account in foreign currency	compte en monnaie étrangère *m*	conto in valuta estera *m*	—
cuenta de moneda extranjera (Es)	Währungskonto *n*	currency account	compte en monnaies étrangères *m*	conto valutario *m*	—
cuenta de pérdidas y ganancias (Es)	Gewinn- und Verlustrechnung *f*	profit and loss account	compte de pertes et profits *m*	conto profitti e perdite *m*	—
cuenta de suministradores (Es)	Lieferkonto *n*	accounts payable	compte de fournisseurs *m*	conto fornitori *m*	—
cuenta deudor (Es)	Debitorenkonto *n*	customer account	compte de créances à recevoir *m*	conto debitori *m*	—
cuenta de un cliente bancario (Es)	Lorokonto *n*	loro account	compte d'un client bancaire *m*	conto loro *m*	—
cuenta de valores (Es)	Effektenkonto *n*	securities account	compte des titres de participation *m*	conto titoli *m*	—
cuenta de valores (Es)	Stückekonto *n*	shares account	compte de titres *m*	conto titoli *m*	—
cuenta de ventas (Es)	Verkaufskonto *n*	trading account	compte de ventes *m*	conto vendite *m*	—
cuenta en divisas (Es)	Devisenkonto *n*	foreign exchange account	compte libellé en devises *m*	conto in valuta estera *m*	—
cuenta en el extranjero (Es)	Auslandskonto *n*	foreign account	compte entretenu à l'étranger *m*	conto estero *m*	—

	D	E	F	I	Es
cuenta especial (Es)	Sonderkonto n	separate account	compte spécial m	conto particolare m	—
cuenta fiduciaria (Es)	Anderkonto n	fiduciary account	compte de tiers m	conto altrui m	—
cuenta financiera (Es)	Finanzkonto n	financial account	compte financier m	conto finanziario m	—
cuenta muerta (Es)	totes Konto n	inoperative account	compte sans mouvement m	conto inattivo m	—
cuenta permanente (Es)	Bilanzkonto n	balance sheet account	compte de bilan m	conto di bilancio m	—
cuentas personales (Es)	Personenkonten n/pl	personal accounts	comptes de personne m/pl	conti di persone m/pl	—
cuenta privada (Es)	Privatkonto n	personal account	compte privé m	conto particolare m	—
cuentas de ahorro anónimas (Es)	anonyme Sparkonten n/pl	anonymous savings accounts	comptes d'épargne anonymes m/pl	conti di risparmio cifrati m/pl	—
cuentas de inversión (Es)	Anlagekonten n/pl	investment accounts	comptes d'investissement m/pl	conti degli investimenti m/pl	—
cuenta sin comisión (Es)	provisionsfreies Konto n	commission-free account	compte de créditeur m	conto franco di provvigione m	—
cuentas indistintas (Es)	Oderkonten n/pl	joint account	compte joint m	conti a firme disgiunte m/pl	—
cuenta sujeto al pago de una comisión (Es)	provisionspflichtiges Konto n	commission-bearing account	compte de débiteur m	conto soggetto a provvigione m	—
cuenta videotexto (Es)	Tele-Konto n	videotext account	compte vidéotex m	conto videotel m	—
cultura crediticia (Es)	Kreditkultur f	credit culture	culture de crédit f	panorama creditizio m	—
culture de crédit (F)	Kreditkultur f	credit culture	—	panorama creditizio m	cultura crediticia f
Cumbre Económica Occidental (Fs)	Weltwirtschaftsgipfel m	world economic summit	sommet économique international m	vertice internazionale di economia m	—
cumplimiento (Es)	Erfüllung f	performance	accomplissement m	adempimento m	—
cumulative dividend (E)	kumulative Dividende f	—	dividende cumulé m	dividendo cumulativo m	dividendo acumulativo m
cuota de ahorro (Es)	Sparquote f	savings ratio	quote-part de revenu réservé à des fins d'épargne f	aliquota di risparmio f	—
cuota de ahorro (Es)	Sparmarke f	savings stamp	timbre d'épargne m	marca di risparmio f	—
cuota de capital propio (Es)	Eigenkapitalquote f	equity ratio	quote-part du capital propre f	percentuale dei mezzi propri f	—
cuota del activo de la quiebra (Es)	Konkursquote f	dividend in bankruptcy	pour-cent accordé aux créanciers dans la masse m	quota di riparto f	—
cuota de pérdidas (Es)	Verlustanteil m	share in the loss	participation aux pertes f	quota alle perdite f	—
cuota patronal (Es)	Arbeitgeberanteil m	employer's share	part patronale f	quota del datore di lavoro f	—
cuota restante (Es)	Restquote f	residual quota	quote-part restante f	pagamento residuale m	—
cuotas (Es)	Beiträge m/pl	contributions	contributions f/pl	contributi m/pl	—
cuotas de ahorro (Es)	Bausparkassen-beiträge m/pl	contributions paid to the building society	contributions payées à la banque d'épargne f/pl	contributi di risparmio edilizio m/pl	—
cupo de redescuento (Es)	Rediskontkontingent n	rediscount quota	quota de réescompte m	plafond di risconto m	—
cupón (Es)	Gewinnanteilsschein m	dividend coupon	coupon de dividende m	cedola f	—
cupón de divisas (Es)	Valutakupon m	foreign currency coupon	coupon payable en monnaie étrangère m	cedola di un titolo estero f	—
cupón de intereses (Es)	Zinsschein m	coupon	coupon d'intérêts m	cedola d'interessi f	—
cupón de parte de liquidación (Es)	Liquidations-anteilsschein m	liquidation certificate	certificat de de liquidation m	certificato di quota liquidazione m	—
cupón de renovación (Es)	Stichkupon m	renewal coupon	coupon de renouvellement m	cedola di riaffogliamento f	—
cupones de interés fijo (Es)	Bauzinsen m/pl	fixed-interest coupons	coupons d'intérêt fixe m/pl	interessi intercalari m/pl	—
curatore del fallimento (I)	Konkursverwalter m	administrator in bankruptcy proceedings	liquidateur de la faillite m	—	síndico de quiebra m

	D	E	F	I	Es
curatorio (Es)	Kuratorium *n*	board of trustees	charge de curateur *f*	consiglio di gestione *m*	—
currency (E)	Devisen *f/pl*	—	devises *f/pl*	valuta estera *f*	divisas *f/pl*
currency (E)	Währung *f*	—	monnaie *f*	moneta *f*	moneda *f*
currency account (E)	Währungskonto *n*	—	compte en monnaies étrangères *m*	conto valutario *m*	cuenta de moneda extranjera *f*
currency accounting (E)	Devisenbuchhaltung *f*	—	comptabilité de devises *f*	contabilità dei cambi *f*	contabilidad de divisas *f*
currency area (E)	Währungsgebiet *n*	—	zone monétaire *f*	area monetaria *f*	área monetaria *f*
currency basket (E)	Währungskorb *m*	—	panier des monnaies *m*	paniere monetario *m*	cesta de monedas *f*
currency clause (E)	Kursklausel *f*	—	clause de payement effectif en une monnaie étrangère *f*	clausola di cambio *f*	cláusula de tipo de cambio *f*
currency conversion (E)	Währungs-umstellung *f*	—	adaptation d'une monnaie *f*	riforma monetaria *f*	reforma monetaria *f*
currency conversion compensation (E)	Währungs-ausgleich *m*	—	alignement des monnaies *m*	conguaglio dei cambi *m*	compensación de cambios *f*
currency dumping (E)	Währungsdumping *n*	—	dumping du change *m*	dumping di valuta *m*	dumping monetario *m*
currency erosion (E)	Geldwertschwund *m*	—	érosion monétaire *f*	deprezzamento monetario *m*	erosión monetaria *f*
currency exchange business (E)	Geldwechselgeschäft *n*	—	opération de change *f*	operazione di cambio *f*	cambio manual *m*
Currency future (D)	—	currency future	opération à terme sur les changes *f*	currency future *m*	contratación a término sobre divisas *f*
currency future (E)	Currency future *m*	—	opération à terme sur les changes *f*	currency future *m*	contratación a término sobre divisas *f*
currency future (I)	Currency future *m*	currency future	opération à terme sur les changes *f*	—	contratación a término sobre divisas *f*
currency of investment (E)	Anlagewährung *f*	—	monnaie d'investissement *f*	valuta d'investimento *f*	moneda de inversión *f*
currency policy (E)	Valutapolitik *f*	—	politique monétaire *f*	politica valutaria *f*	política de divisas *f*
currency pool (E)	Währungspool *m*	—	pool monétaire *m*	pool monetario *m*	pool monetario *m*
currency substitution (E)	Währungssubstitution *f*	—	substitution monétaire *f*	sostituzione monetaria *f*	substitución monetaria *f*
currency swap (E)	Währungsswap *m*	—	swap de devises *m*	currency swap *m*	swap en moneda extranjera *m*
currency swap (I)	Währungsswap *m*	currency swap	swap de devises *m*	—	swap en moneda extranjera *m*
currency transactions (E)	Valutageschäft *n*	—	opération de change *f*	operazione di cambio *f*	operación de divisas *f*
current account (E)	Kontokorrent *m*	—	compte courant *m*	conto corrente *m*	cuenta corriente *f*
current account (E)	Girokonto *n*	—	compte de virement *m*	giroconto *m*	cuenta corriente *f*
current account credit (E)	Kontokorrentkredit *m*	—	crédit en compte courant *m*	credito in conto corrente *m*	crédito en cuenta corriente *m*
current account with a bank (E)	Bankkontokorrent *n*	—	compte courant de banque *m*	conto corrente bancario *m*	cuenta corriente bancaria *m*
current assets (E)	Umlaufvermögen *n*	—	capital de roulement *m*	circolante *m*	capital circulante *m*
current quotation (E)	Tageskurs *m*	—	cote du jour *f*	corso del giorno *m*	cotización del día *f*
curso extremo (Es)	Extremkurs	peak quotation	cours extrême *m*	quotazione estrema *f*	—
curso preferencial (Es)	Vorzugskurs *m*	preferential price	cours de faveur *m*	corso preferenziale *m*	—
custodia (Es)	Verwahrung *f*	custody	dépôt *m*	custodia *f*	—
custodia (I)	Verwahrung *f*	custody	dépôt *m*	—	custodia *f*
custodia (I)	Aufbewahrung *f*	deposit	garde en dépôt *f*	—	conservación *f*
custodia de valores (Es)	Wertpapier-verwahrung *f*	safe custody and administration of securities	garde de titres *f*	custodia di titoli *f*	—
custodia di titoli (I)	Wertpapier-verwahrung *f*	safe custody and administration of securities	garde de titres *f*	—	custodia de valores *f*
custody (E)	Verwahrung *f*	—	dépôt *m*	custodia *f*	custodia *f*

	D	E	F	I	Es
custody fee (E)	Verwahrungskosten *pl*	—	coût de garde *m*	spese di custodia *f/pl*	gastos de depósito *m/pl*
custody ledger (E)	Verwahrungsbuch *n*	—	registre des dépôts *m*	libretto di deposito *m*	libro de custodia *f*
customary law (E)	Stammrecht *n*	—	droit habituel *m*	diritto principale *m*	derecho habitual *m*
customer account (E)	Debitorenkonto *n*	—	compte de créances à recevoir *m*	conto debitori *m*	cuenta deudor *f*
customer costing (E)	Kundenkalkulation *f*	—	calcul des résultats obtenus par chaque client *m*	calcolo d'utilità di cliente *m*	calculación de participación por cliente *f*
customers' credit (E)	Kundschaftskredit *m*	—	crédit accordé à la clientèle *m*	credito alla clientela *m*	crédito al consumidor *m*
customer's liability on bills (E)	Wechselobligo *n*	—	engagement par lettre de change *m*	cambiale passiva *f*	obligación en letras de cambio *f*
customer's order (E)	Kundenauftrag *m*	—	ordre d'un client *m*	ordinazione *f*	orden de cliente *f*
customer's security deposit (E)	Personendepot *n*	—	dépôt de personne *m*	libretto personale di deposito titoli *m*	depósito personal *m*
custom of trade (E)	Handelsusancen *f/pl*	—	usages commerciaux *m/pl*	usanze commerciali *f/pl*	uso comercial *m*
customs duty (E)	Zoll *m*	—	droit de douane *m*	dazio *m*	aduana *f*
customs union (E)	Zollunion *f*	—	union douanière *f*	unione doganale *f*	unión aduanera *f*
da accreditare (I)	nur zur Verrechnung	for account only	à porter en compte	—	sólo para compensación
Dachfonds (D)	—	holding fund	fonds d'une société holding *m/pl*	fondo che tratta quote di altri fondi *m*	fondos de una sociedad holding *m/pl*
Dachgesellschaft (D)	—	holding company	holding *m*	società madre *f*	sociedad cúpula *f*
daily statement (E)	Tagesauszug *m*	—	relevé quotidien de compte *m*	estratto giornaliero *m*	extracto de cuenta diario *m*
daily trial balance sheet (E)	Tagesbilanz *f*	—	arrêté quotidien de compte *m*	bilancio giornaliero *m*	balance diario *m*
damaged share certificates (E)	beschädigte Aktie *f*	—	certificat d'action endommagé *m*	azione danneggiata *f*	acción deteriorada *f*
Damnum (D)	—	debt discount	différence en moins *f*	disaggio *m*	disagio de préstamo *m*
Darlehen (D)	—	loan	prêt *m*	credito *m*	préstamo *m*
Darlehens- finanzierung (D)	—	loan financing	financement par capitaux prêtés *m*	finanziamento mediante mutuo *m*	financiación de préstamo *f*
Darlehenshypothek (D)	—	mortgage as security for a loan	hypothèque de sûreté constituée pour garantir un prêt *f*	ipoteca su prestiti *f*	préstamo hipotecario *m*
data di godimento (I)	Zinstermin *m*	interest payment date	délai de payement de l'intérêt *m*	—	vencimiento de intereses *m*
data di riferimento (I)	Stichtag *m*	reporting date	jour fixé *m*	—	día de liquidación *m*
datation de la valeur en compte (F)	Wertstellung *f*	availability date	—	valuta *f*	valuta *f*
datation moyenne de la valeur en compte (F)	Durchschnittsvaluta *f*	average value date	—	valuta media *f*	cambio medio *m*
date d'échéance (F)	Verfallzeit *f*	time of expiration	—	scadenza *f*	plazo de vencimiento *m*
date di resoconto settimanale della banca centrale (I)	Bankstichtage *m/pl*	settling days	jours de règlement fixés *m/pl*	—	días de referencia de los bancos *m/pl*
date of the balance sheet (E)	Bilanzstichtag *m*	—	jour du bilan *m*	giorno chiusura bilancio *m*	fecha del balance *f*
Datowechsel (D)	—	after-date bill	effet payable à un certain délai de date *m*	cambiale a certo tempo data *f*	letra a tantos días fecha *f*
Daueraktionär (D)	—	permanent share- holder	actionnaire permanent *m*	azionista permanente *m*	accionista permanente *m*
Dauerauftrag (D)	—	standing order	ordre régulier *m*	incarico permanente *m*	orden permanente *f*
Dauerbesitz (D)	—	permanent holding	possession permanente *f*	detenzione permanente *f*	posesión permanente *f*
Dauerremittent (D)	—	constant issuer	émetteur permanent *m*	emittente continuo *m*	remitente permanente *m*

	D	E	F	I	Es
Dauerschuldzinsen (D)	—	interest on long-term debts	intérêts concernant une dette permanente *m/pl*	interessi debitori permanenti *m/pl*	intereses de obligación permanente *m/pl*
DAX-Index (D)	—	DAX-index	indice boursier DAX *m*	indice DAX *m*	índice DAX *m*
DAX-index (E)	DAX-Index *m*	—	indice boursier DAX *m*	indice DAX *m*	índice DAX *m*
day bill (E)	Tageswechsel *m*	—	traite à jour fixe *f*	cambiale a scadenza fissa *f*	letra al día fijo *f*
day of expiry (E)	Verfalltag *m*	—	jour de l'échéance *m*	giorno di scadenza *m*	día de vencimiento *m*
day-to-day money (E)	Tagesgeld *n*	—	argent au jour le jour *m*	prestito giornaliero *m*	dinero de día a día *m*
dazio (I)	Zoll *m*	customs duty	droit de douane *m*	—	aduana *f*
dazio all'esportazione (I)	Ausfuhrzoll *m*	export duty	taxe de sortie *m*	—	derechos de exportación *m/pl*
dealer (E)	Händler *m*	—	commerçant *m*	commerciante *m*	comerciante *m*
dealer in securities (E)	Effektenhändler *m*	—	courtier en valeurs mobilières *m*	agente in valori *m*	corredor de bolsa *m*
dealer transaction (E)	Händlergeschäft *n*	—	opération pour propre compte *f*	operazioni tra agenti di borsa *f/pl*	operaciones de corridor bursátil *f/pl*
dealing in foreign notes and coins (E)	Sortenhandel *m*	—	commerce de change *m*	commercio delle valute *m*	negociación de moneda extranjera *f*
dealing in large lots (E)	Pakethandel *m*	—	négociation de lots importants *f*	negoziazione di pacchetti azionari *f*	transacciones de paquetes mayores de acciones *f/pl*
dealings book of the stockbroker (E)	Maklerbuch *n*	—	carnet des négociations *m*	libro giornale dell'agente di cambio *m*	libro de corredores *m*
dealings in foreign notes and coins (E)	Sortengeschäft *n*	—	commerce de change *m*	operazione di cambio *f*	operación de moneda extranjera *f*
dealings in gold and silver coins (E)	Münzhandel *m*	—	commerce des pièces de monnaie *m*	commercio monete pregiate *m*	comercio con monedas *m*
debe (Es)	Debet *n*	debit	débit *m*	addebito *m*	—
debenture stock (E)	Schuldverschreibung *f*	—	obligation *f*	titolo obbligazionario *m*	obligación *f*
deber de canje (Es)	Einlösungspflicht *f*	obligation to redeem	obligation de rachat *f*	obbligo di pagamento *m*	—
deber de liberación de acciones (Es)	Einzahlungspflicht *f*	obligation to pay subscription	obligation de libérer une action *f*	obbligo di versamento *m*	—
Debet (D)	—	debit	débit *m*	addebito *m*	debe *m*
debit (E)	Soll *n*	—	doit *m*	debito *m*	débito *m*
debit (E)	Debet *n*	—	débit *m*	addebito *m*	debe *m*
débit (F)	Debet *n*	debit	—	addebito *m*	debe *m*
debit card (E)	Lastschriftkarte *f*	—	carte de débit *f*	avviso di addebito *m*	nota de cargo *f*
debit entry (E)	Lastschrift *f*	—	note de débit *f*	addebitamento *m*	cargo en cuenta *m*
débiteur (F)	Schuldner *m*	debtor	—	debitore *m*	deudor *m*
débiteur en failli (F)	Gemeinschuldner *m*	adjudicated bankrupt	—	debitore fallito *m*	deudor común *m*
débiteur solidaire (F)	Gesamtschuldner *m*	joint and several debtor	—	debitore solidale *m*	deudor solidario *m*
debiti consolidati (I)	fundierte Schulden *f/pl*	funded debts	dette consolidée *f*	—	deudas consolidadas *f/pl*
debiti della società (I)	Gesellschafts-schulden *f/pl*	company's debts	dettes sociales *f/pl*	—	deudas sociales *f/pl*
debiti diversi (I)	sonstige Verbindlichkeiten *f/pl*	other liabilities	autres obligations *f/pl*	—	acreedores varios *m/pl*
debiti esteri (I)	Auslandsschulden *f/pl*	foreign debts	dettes à l'étranger *f/pl*	—	deudas exteriores *f/pl*
debiti verso banche (I)	Bankschulden *f/pl*	bank debts	dettes bancaires *f/pl*	—	deudas bancarias *f/pl*
débito (Es)	Soll *n*	debit	doit *m*	debito *m*	—
debito (I)	Verbindlichkeit *f*	liability	obligation *f*	—	obligación *f*
debito (I)	Schuld *f*	debt	dette *f*	—	deuda *f*
debito (I)	Soll *n*	debit	doit *m*	—	débito *m*

	D	E	F	I	Es
debito comunione a mani unite (I)	Gesamthandschuld f	joint debt	dette d'un associé d'une société par intérêts f	—	deuda en mano común f
debito contabile (I)	Buchschuld f	book debt	dette comptable f	—	pasivo exigible m
debito fluttuante (I)	schwebende Schuld f	floating debt	dette flottante f	—	deuda flotante f
debito fondiario (I)	Grundschuld f	land charge	dette foncière f	—	hipoteca f
debito fondiario al proprietario (I)	Eigentümergrundschuld f	land charge in favour of the owner	dette foncière constituée par le propriétaire à son profit f	—	deuda inmobiliaria del propietario f
debito fondiario a scadenza (I)	Fälligkeitsgrundschuld f	fixed-date land charge	dette foncière remboursable à terme fixe f	—	deuda inmobiliaria de vencimiento f
debito fondiario di garanzia (I)	Sicherungsgrundschuld f	cautionary land charge	dette foncière de garantie f	—	deuda inmobiliaria de seguridad f
debito in valuta estera (I)	Fremdwährungsschuld f	foreign currency debt	dette exprimée en monnaie étrangère f	—	deuda en moneda extranjera f
debito iscritto nel libro fondiario (I)	Buchgrundschuld f	uncertificated land charge	dette foncière inscrite au bureau foncier f	—	deuda inmobiliaria registrada f
debito pubblico (I)	öffentliche Schuld f	public debt	dette publique f	—	deuda pública f
debitore (I)	Schuldner m	debtor	débiteur m	—	deudor m
debitore fallito (I)	Gemeinschuldner m	adjudicated bankrupt	débiteur en failli m	—	deudor común m
Debitorenkonto (D)	—	customer account	compte de créances à recevoir m	conto debitori m	cuenta deudor f
Debitorenziehung (D)	—	bills drawn on debtors	traite tirée sur débiteur f	cambiale tratta sul debitore f	letra librada f
debitore solidale (I)	Gesamtschuldner m	joint and several debtor	débiteur solidaire m	—	deudor solidario m
débitos a nuestro cargo (Es)	Nostroverbindlichkeit f	nostro liability	obligations vis-à-vis d'une autre banque f/pl	impegno nostro m	—
debito solidale (I)	Gesamtschuld f	total debt	dette solidaire f	—	obligación solidaria f
debole (I)	schwach	slack	faible	—	flojo
debt (E)	Schuld f	—	dette f	debito m	deuda f
debt capital (E)	Fremdkapital n	—	capital de tiers m	capitale di credito m	capital ajeno m
debt capital (E)	Leihkapital n	—	capital de tiers m	capitale di prestito m	capital prestado m
debt discount (E)	Damnum m	—	différence en moins f	disaggio m	disagio de préstamo m
debt financing (E)	Fremdfinanzierung f	—	constitution de capital par apport de tiers f	finanziamento esterno m	financiación con capital ajeno f
debtor (E)	Schuldner m	—	débiteur m	debitore m	deudor m
debtor interest rates (E)	Sollzinsen m/pl	—	intérêts débiteurs m/pl	interessi passivi m/pl	intereses deudores m/pl
debtor warrant (E)	Besserungsschein m	—	surenchère au concordat f	certificato di rimborso in caso di miglioramento della situazione finanziaria m	certificado de mejora m
debt-register claim (E)	Schuldbuchforderung f	—	créance inscrite dans le livre de la dette f	cartella del debito pubblico f	deuda inscrita en el libro de deudas f
debt rescheduling (E)	Umschuldung f	—	conversion de dette f	conversione del debito f	conversión de la deuda f
debt service (E)	Schuldendienst m	—	service de la dette m	servizio dei debiti m	servicio de deudas m
debts profit levy (E)	Kreditgewinnabgabe f	—	taxe sur les bénéfices de crédit m	ritenuta sugli utili dei crediti f	tributo sobre beneficios del crédito m
decadenza del socio moroso (I)	Kaduzierung f	forfeiture of shares	caducité f	—	caducidad f
decision (E)	Beschluß m	—	décision f	delibera f	decisión f
decisión (Es)	Beschluß m	decision	décision f	delibera f	—
décision (F)	Beschluß m	decision	—	delibera f	decisión f
decision of accession (E)	Beitrittsbeschluß m	—	jugement déclaratif d'admission de la créance m	decreto di adesione all'asta coattiva m	auto de adhesión m
decision rule (E)	Entscheidungsregel f	—	règle de décision f	regola di decisione f	regla de decisión f
Deckung (D)	—	coverage	couverture f	copertura f	cobertura f

	D	E	F	I	Es
Deckungsdarlehen (D)	—	coverage loan	prêt de couverture *m*	mutuo destinato a copertura *m*	préstamo de cobertura *m*
deckungsfähige Devisen (D)	—	foreign currencies eligible as cover	devises aptes à servir de couverture *f/pl*	valute pregiate *f/pl*	divisas cubiertas por el banco emisor *f/pl*
deckungsfähige Wertpapiere (D)	—	securities eligible as cover	titres susceptibles d'être déposé en couverture *m/pl*	titoli riscontabili *m/pl*	títulos cubiertos por el banco emisor *m/pl*
Deckungsforderung (D)	—	covering claim	créance de couverture *f*	richiesta di copertura *f*	crédito de cobertura *m*
Deckungsgeschäft (D)	—	covering operation	opération de couverture *f*	operazione di copertura *f*	operación de cobertura *f*
Deckungskapital (D)	—	capital sum required as cover	capital de couverture *m*	capitale di copertura *m*	capital de cobertura *m*
Deckungsklausel (D)	—	cover clause	clause de couverture *f*	clausola di garanzia *f*	cláusula de cobertura *f*
Deckungszinsen (D)	—	coverage interest rate	intérêts de couverture *m/pl*	interessi di copertura *m/pl*	intereses de cobertura *m/pl*
declaración (Es)	Erklärung *f*	explanation	déclaration *f*	dichiarazione *f*	—
declaración de ejercer el derecho de suscripción (Es)	Bezugsrechterklärung *f*	declaration to exercise the subscription right	déclaration d'exercer le droit de souscription *f*	dichiarazione diritto d'opzione *f*	—
declaración negativa (Es)	Negativerklärung *f*	negative declaration	déclaration négative *f*	clausola negativa *f*	—
déclaration (F)	Erklärung *f*	explanation	—	dichiarazione *f*	declaración *f*
déclaration d'exclusivité (F)	Ausschließlichkeitserklärung *f*	undertaking to deal exclusively with one bank or firm	—	dichiarazione d'esclusività *f*	contrato de exclusividad *m*
déclaration d'exercer le droit de souscription (F)	Bezugsrechterklärung *f*	declaration to exercise the subscription right	—	dichiarazione diritto d'opzione *f*	declaración de ejercer el derecho de suscripción *f*
déclaration négative (F)	Negativerklärung *f*	negative declaration	—	clausola negativa *f*	declaración negativa *f*
déclaration obligatoire (F)	Meldepflicht *f*	obligation to register	—	obbligo di dichiarazione *m*	obligación de comunicar *f*
declaration to exercise the subscription right (E)	Bezugsrechterklärung *f*	—	déclaration d'exercer le droit de souscription *f*	dichiarazione diritto d'opzione *f*	declaración de ejercer el derecho de suscripción *f*
declaratory protest (E)	Deklarationsprotest *m*	—	protêt d'une traite dont le porteur et l'intervenant sont identiques *m*	protesto per identità del portatore della cambiale col protestato *m*	protesto de declaración *m*
declining balance depreciation (E)	Buchwertabschreibung *f*	—	amortissement dégressif au prorata de la valeur restante *m*	ammortamento del valore di libro *m*	amortización del valor contable *f*
décompte des emprunts (F)	Anleiherechnung *f*	loan calculation	—	calcolo rimborso e interessi *m*	cálculo de empréstito *m*
découvert (F)	Leerposition *f*	bear selling position	—	scoperto *m*	descubierto *m*
découvert de compte (F)	Überziehen eines Kontos *n*	overdraft	—	mandare un conto allo scoperto *m*	descubierto *m*
decree (E)	Erlaß *m*	—	arrêt *m*	decreto *m*	decreto *m*
décret bancaire (F)	Bankenerlaß *m*	banking decree	—	decreto sul segreto bancario *m*	decreto bancario *m*
decreto (Es)	Erlaß *m*	decree	arrêt *m*	decreto *m*	—
decreto (I)	Erlaß *m*	decree	arrêt *m*	—	decreto *m*
decreto bancario (Es)	Bankenerlaß *m*	banking decree	décret bancaire *m*	decreto sul segreto bancario *m*	—
decreto di adesione all'asta coattiva (I)	Beitrittsbeschluß *m*	decision of accession	jugement déclaratif d'admission de la créance *m*	—	auto de adhesión *m*
decreto sul segreto bancario (I)	Bankenerlaß *m*	banking decree	décret bancaire *m*	—	decreto bancario *m*
decurtazione (I)	Dekort *n*	deduction	rabais *m*	—	descuento *m*
deducción de intereses no acumulados (Es)	Abzinsung *f*	discounting	déduction des intérêts non courus *f*	deduzione di interessi *f*	—

	D	E	F	I	Es
deducción del derecho de suscripción (Es)	Bezugsrecht-abschlag *m*	ex-rights markdown	cours moins le droit de souscription *f*	stacco del diritto d'opzione *m*	—
deduction (E)	Dekort *n*	—	rabais *m*	decurtazione *f*	descuento *m*
déduction des intérêts non courus (F)	Abzinsung *f*	discounting	—	deduzione di interessi *f*	deducción de intereses no acumulados *f*
deduzione di interessi (I)	Abzinsung *f*	discounting	déduction des intérêts non courus *f*	—	deducción de intereses no acumulados *f*
default interest (E)	Verzugszinsen *m/pl*	—	intérêts moratoires *m/pl*	interessi moratori *m/pl*	intereses de demora *m/pl*
defence of fraud (E)	Einrede der Arglist *f*	—	exception du dol *f*	eccezione di dolo *f*	excepción de dolo *f*
defence of lack of prosecution (E)	Einrede der Vorausklage *f*	—	exception de la discussion *f*	preescussione *f*	excepción de excusión *f*
défense de cession (F)	Abtretungsverbot *n*	prohibition of assignment	—	divieto di cessione *m*	prohibición de cesión *f*
défense d'usure (F)	Wucherverbot *n*	prohibition of usurious money-lending	—	proibizione di usura *f*	prohibición de usura *f*
deficiency guarantee (E)	Ausfallbürgschaft *f*	—	garantie de bonne fin *f*	garanzia di sostituzione *f*	fianza de indemnidad *f*
deficit (E)	Defizit *n*	—	déficit *m*	deficit *m*	déficit *m*
déficit (Es)	Defizit *n*	deficit	déficit *m*	deficit *m*	—
déficit (Es)	Fehlbetrag *m*	shortfall	déficit *m*	disavanzo *m*	—
déficit (F)	Fehlbetrag *m*	shortfall	—	disavanzo *m*	déficit *m*
déficit (F)	Defizit *n*	deficit	—	deficit *m*	déficit *m*
deficit (I)	Defizit *n*	deficit	déficit *m*	—	déficit *m*
deficit balance (E)	Unterbilanz *f*	—	bilan déficitaire *m*	bilancio in deficit *m/pl*	balance deficitario *m*
déficit de financiación (Es)	Finanzierungsdefizit *n*	finance deficit	déficit de financement *m*	deficit di finanziamento *m*	—
déficit de financement (F)	Finanzierungsdefizit *n*	finance deficit	—	deficit di finanziamento *m*	déficit de financiación *f*
deficit di finanziamento (I)	Finanzierungsdefizit *n*	finance deficit	déficit de financement *m*	—	déficit de financiación *f*
deficit financing (E)	Defizit-Finanzierung *f*	—	financement du déficit *m*	deficit financing *m*	financiación del déficit *f*
deficit financing (I)	Defizit-Finanzierung *f*	deficit financing	financement du déficit *m*	—	financiación del déficit *f*
Deficit Spending (D)	—	deficit spending	deficit spending *m*	deficit spending *m*	gastos deficitarios *m/pl*
deficit spending (E)	Deficit Spending *n*	—	deficit spending *m*	deficit spending *m*	gastos deficitarios *m/pl*
deficit spending (F)	Deficit Spending *n*	deficit spending	—	deficit spending *m*	gastos deficitarios *m/pl*
deficit spending (I)	Deficit Spending *n*	deficit spending	deficit spending *m*	—	gastos deficitarios *m/pl*
Defizit (D)	—	deficit	déficit *m*	deficit *m*	déficit *m*
Defizit-Finanzierung (D)	—	deficit financing	financement du déficit *m*	deficit financing *m*	financiación del déficit *f*
deflación (Es)	Deflation *f*	deflation	déflation *f*	deflazione *f*	—
Deflation (D)	—	deflation	déflation *f*	deflazione *f*	deflación *f*
deflation (E)	Deflation *f*	—	déflation *f*	deflazione *f*	deflación *f*
déflation (F)	Deflation *f*	deflation	—	deflazione *f*	deflación *f*
deflazione (I)	Deflation *f*	deflation	déflation *f*	—	deflación *f*
deflusso di capitale (I)	Kapitalabfluß *m*	capital outflows	sortie de capital *f*	—	salida de capital *f*
defraudación (Es)	Unterschlagung *f*	embezzlement	détournement *m*	appropriazione indebita *f*	—
defraudación de depósito (Es)	Depotunter-schlagung *f*	misapplication of deposit	détournement de titres en dépôt *m*	appropriazione indebita di depositi *f*	—
degré d'automation (F)	Automatisations-grad *m*	automation degree	—	grado di automazione *m*	grado de automación *m*
degressive costs (E)	degressive Kosten *pl*	—	coût dégressif *m*	costi decrescenti *m/pl*	gastos degresivos *m/pl*

	D	E	F	I	Es
degressive Kosten (D)	—	degressive costs	coût dégressif *m*	costi decrescenti *m/pl*	gastos degresivos *m/pl*
Deklarationsprotest (D)	—	declaratory protest	protêt d'une traite dont le porteur et l'intervenant sont identiques *m*	protesto per identità del portatore della cambiale col protestato *m*	protesto de declaración *m*
Dekort (D)	—	deduction	rabais *m*	decurtazione *f*	descuento *m*
délai de blocage de dénonciation (F)	Kündigungssperrfrist *f*	non-calling period	—	termine di preavviso *m*	plazo de suspensión de preaviso *m*
délai de dépôt (F)	Aufbewahrungsfrist *f*	retention period	—	periodo di custodia *m*	plazo de conservación *m*
délai de payement (F)	Zahlungsziel *n*	period for payment	—	dilazione di pagamento *f*	plazo de pago *m*
délai de payement de l'intérêt (F)	Zinstermin *m*	interest payment date	—	data di godimento *f*	vencimiento de intereses *m*
délai de présentation (F)	Präsentationsfrist *f*	presentation period	—	termine di presentazione *m*	tiempo útil para la presentación *m*
délai de remboursement des avances sur crédit (F)	Kreditfrist *f*	credit period	—	scadenza del credito *f*	plazo de vencimiento del crédito *m*
délai de souscription (F)	Bezugsfrist *f*	subscription period	—	termine d'opzione *m*	plazo de suscripción *m*
delay (E)	Verzug *m*	—	demeure *f*	mora *f*	demora *f*
delcrédere (Es)	Delkredere *n*	reserve for bad debts	ducroire *m*	star del credere *m*	—
del credere global (Es)	Pauschaldelkredere *n*	global delcredere	ducroire forfaitaire *m*	star del credere forfettario	—
delegación de pago (Es)	Zahlungsauftrag *m*	order for payment	ordre de payement *m*	ordine di pagamento *m*	—
delegated authority (E)	Untervollmacht *f*	—	sous-délégation *f*	procura rilasciata dal procuratore *f*	subpoder *m*
delegato (I)	Bevollmächtigter *m*	authorized person	fondé de pouvoir *m*	—	apoderado *m*
deletion (E)	Streichung *f*	—	annulation *f*	mancata quotazione *f*	anulación *f*
delibera (I)	Beschluß *m*	decision	décision *f*	—	decisión *f*
délimitation des comptes non encore soldés en fin d'exercice (F)	Rechnungsabgrenzung *f*	apportionment between accounting periods	—	ratei e risconti *m/pl*	ajustes por periodificación *m/pl*
delito concursal (Es)	Konkursdelikt *n*	bankruptcy offence	fraude en matière de faillite *f*	reato fallimentare *m*	—
deliverable security (E)	lieferbares Wertpapier *n*	—	valeur négociable *f*	titolo negoziabile *m*	título de buena entrega *m*
Delkredere (D)	—	reserve for bad debts	ducroire *m*	star del credere *m*	delcrédere *m*
demand (E)	Nachfrage *f*	—	demande *f*	domanda *f*	demanda *f*
demanda (Es)	Nachfrage *f*	demand	demande *f*	domanda *f*	—
demanda de informe por el banco (Es)	Bankenquete *f*	banking inquiry	demande de renseignements par la banque *f*	inchiesta bancaria *f*	—
demanda final (Es)	Endnachfrage *f*	final demand	demande finale *f*	domanda aggregata effettiva *f*	—
demanda monetaria (Es)	Geldnachfrage *f*	money demand	demande d'argent *f*	domanda monetaria *f*	—
demand bill (E)	Sichtwechsel *m*	—	traite à vue *f*	cambiale a vista *f*	letra a la vista *f*
demande (F)	Nachfrage *f*	demand	—	domanda *f*	demanda *f*
demande d'argent (F)	Geldnachfrage *f*	money demand	—	domanda monetaria *f*	demanda monetaria *f*
demande de dédommagement et de couverture (F)	Ausgleichs- und Deckungsforderung *f*	equalization and covering claim	—	credito di compensazione *m*	crédito de igualación y cobertura *m*
demande de renseignements par la banque (F)	Bankenquete *f*	banking inquiry	—	inchiesta bancaria *f*	demanda de informe por el banco *f*
demande finale (F)	Endnachfrage *f*	final demand	—	domanda aggregata effettiva *f*	demanda final *f*
demeure (F)	Verzug *m*	delay	—	mora *f*	demora *f*
demeure du débiteur (F)	Zahlungsverzug *m*	failure to pay on due date	—	mora nel pagamento *f*	retraso en el pago *m*

	D	E	F	I	Es
demora (Es)	Verzug *m*	delay	demeure *f*	mora *f*	—
denaro (I)	Geld *n*	money	argent *m*	—	dinero *m*
denaro altrui (I)	hereingenommene Gelder *n/pl*	money taken on deposit	fonds mis en dépôt *m/pl*	—	fondos ingresados *m/pl*
denaro contante (I)	Bargeld *n*	ready money	argent comptant *m*	—	efectivo *m*
denaro da terzi (I)	fremde Mittel *n/pl*	borrowed funds	capitaux prêtés *m/pl*	—	fondos de terceros *m/pl*
denaro d'ordine (I)	durchlaufende Gelder *n/pl*	transmitted accounts	fonds en consignation *m/pl*	—	dinero en tránsito *m*
denaro esogeno (I)	exogenes Geld *n*	exogenous money base	argent exogène *m*	—	dinero exógeno *m*
denaro facoltativo (I)	fakultatives Geld *n*	facultative money	argent facultatif *m*	—	dinero facultativo *m*
denaro fiduciario (I)	fiduziäres Geld *n*	fiduciary funds	argent fiduciaire *m*	—	dinero fiduciario *m*
denaro fluttuante (I)	fluktuierende Gelder *n/pl*	fluctuating funds	fonds soumis à des fluctuations *m/pl*	—	fondos sujetos a fluctuaciones *m/pl*
denaro monetato (I)	Münzgeld *n*	species	monnaie métallique *f*	—	moneda acuñada *f*
denaro tesaurizzato (I)	Strumpfgeld *n*	hoarded notes and coins	argent gardé dans le bas de laine *m*	—	dinero en el calcetín *m*
dénationalisation (F)	Reprivatisierung *f*	reversion to private ownership	—	riprivatizzazione *f*	desnacionalización *f*
deniers de pupille (F)	Mündelgeld *n*	money held in trust for a ward	—	capitale del minore *m*	dinero pupilar *m*
departamento (Es)	Ressort *n*	department	ressort *m*	sezione *f*	—
department (E)	Ressort *n*	—	ressort *m*	sezione *f*	departamento *m*
dépenses (F)	Ausgaben *f/pl*	expenses	—	spese *f/pl*	gastos *m/pl*
dépenses publiques (F)	Staatsausgaben *f/pl*	public spending	—	spese pubbliche *f/pl*	gastos públicos *m/pl*
Deponent (D)	—	depositor	déposant *m*	depositante *m*	depositante *m*
deponieren (D)	—	to deposit	déposer	depositare	depositar
Deport (D)	—	discount	déport *m*	deporto *m*	deport *m*
deport (Es)	Deport *m*	discount	déport *m*	deporto *m*	—
déport (F)	Deport *m*	discount	—	deporto *m*	deport *m*
déport (F)	Backwardation *f*	backwardation	—	backwardation *f*	tasa de prolongación del bajista *f*
deporto (I)	Deport *m*	discount	déport *m*	—	deport *m*
déposant (F)	Deponent *m*	depositor	—	depositante *m*	depositante *m*
déposer (F)	deponieren	to deposit	—	depositare	depositar
deposit (E)	deponieren	—	déposer	depositare	depositar
deposit (E)	Anzahlung *f*	—	acompte *m*	acconto *m*	pago a cuenta *m*
deposit (E)	Aufbewahrung *f*	—	garde en dépôt *f*	custodia *f*	conservación *f*
deposit (E)	Depot *n*	—	dépôt *m*	deposito *m*	depósito *m*
deposit acknowledgement (E)	Depotanerkenntnis *n*	—	reconnaissance de dépôt *f*	approvazione estratto deposito *f*	reconocimiento de depósito *m*
depositante (Es)	Deponent *m*	depositor	déposant *m*	depositante *m*	—
depositante (I)	Deponent *m*	depositor	déposant *m*	—	depositante *m*
depositar (Es)	deponieren	to deposit	déposer	depositare	—
depositare (I)	deponieren	to deposit	déposer	—	depositar
deposit at notice (E)	Kündigungsgeld *n*	—	sommes disponibles avec préavis *f/pl*	deposito ritirabile dietro preavviso *m*	depósitos con preaviso *m/pl*
deposit banking (E)	Depotgeschäft *n*	—	garde des titres *f*	operazione di deposito *f*	custodia de valores *f*
deposit banking (E)	Depositengeschäft *n*	—	opération de garde de fonds *f*	operazione di deposito *f*	operación de depósito *f*
deposit book (E)	Depotbuch *n*	—	registre des valeurs en dépôt *m*	libretto di deposito *m*	libreta de depósito *f*
deposit business (E)	Einlagengeschäft *n*	—	opération de garde de fonds *f/pl*	operazione di deposito *f*	operaciones de depósito *f/pl*
deposit clause (E)	Depositenklausel *f*	—	clause de dépôt *f*	clausola di deposito *f*	cláusula de depósito *f*
deposit clearing bank (E)	Girobank *f*	—	banque de dépôts et de virements *f*	banca di giro *f*	banco de giros *m*

	D	E	F	I	Es
deposited share (E)	Depotaktie *f*	—	action déposée en compte courant *f*	azione in deposito *f*	acción de depósito *f*
Depositen (D)	—	deposits	dépôts *m/pl*	depositi *m/pl*	depósitos *m/pl*
Depositenbank (D)	—	bank of deposit	banque de dépôts *f*	banca di depositi *f*	banco depositario *m*
Depositengeschäft (D)	—	deposit banking	opération de garde de fonds *f*	operazione di deposito *f*	operación de depósito *f*
Depositenklausel (D)	—	deposit clause	clause de dépôt *f*	clausola di deposito *f*	cláusula de depósito *f*
deposit for insurance payments (E)	Prämiendepot *n*	—	dépôt de titres à primes *f*	deposito di premio *m*	depósito de primas *m*
deposit guarantee fund (E)	Einlagensicherungs- fonds *m*	—	fonds de sûreté en garantie de dépôts *m*	fondo di garanzia dei depositi *m*	fondos de garantía de depósitos *m/pl*
depositi (I)	Depositen *f/pl*	deposits	dépôts *m/pl*	—	depósitos *m/pl*
depositi a lunga scadenza (I)	langfristige Einlagen *f/pl*	long-term deposits	placements à long terme *m/pl*	—	imposiciones a largo plazo *f/pl*
depositi a scadenza fissa (I)	befristete Einlagen *f/pl*	fixed deposits	bons et comptes à échéance fixe *m/pl*	—	imposiciones a plazo *f/pl*
depositi bancari (I)	Bankdepositen *pl*	bank deposit	fonds déposés en banque *m/pl*	—	depósitos bancarios *m/pl*
depositi per conto altrui (I)	Treuhanddepots *n/pl*	trust deposits	dépôts de consignation *m/pl*	—	depósitos fiduciarios *m/pl*
deposit money creation multiplier (E)	Buchgeldschöpfungs- multiplikator *m*	—	multiplicateur de création de monnaie scripturale *m*	moltiplicatore di moneta contabile *m*	multiplicador de creación de dinero giral *m*
depósito (Es)	Depot *n*	deposit	dépôt *m*	deposito *m*	
deposito (I)	Depot *n*	deposit	dépôt *m*	—	depósito *m*
deposito (I)	Einlage *f*	money deposited	dépôt *m*	—	imposición *f*
depósito abierto (Es)	offenes Depot *n*	safe custody account	dépôt collectif *m*	deposito aperto *m*	—
deposito a dossier (I)	Streifbanddepot *n*	individual deposit of securities	dépôt individuel avec mandat de gestion *m*	—	depósito separado *m*
deposito a dossier (I)	Sonderdepot *n*	separate deposit	dépôt individuel avec mandat de gestion *m*	—	depósito específico *m*
deposito a garanzia (I)	Pfanddepot *n*	pledged securities deposit	dépôt de titres remis en nantissement *m*	—	depósito de prenda *m*
depósito ajeno (Es)	Fremddepot *n*	fiduciary deposit	dépôt d'autrui *m*	deposito presso terzi *m*	—
deposito altrui (I)	Anderdepot *n*	fiduciary deposit	dépôt de consignation *m*	—	depósito por cuenta de terceros *m*
deposito aperto (I)	offenes Depot *n*	safe custody account	dépôt collectif *m*	—	depósito abierto *m*
depósito a plazo (Es)	Festgeld *n*	fixed deposit	argent immobilisé *m*	deposito a termine *m*	—
deposito a risparmio (I)	Sparguthaben *n*	savings account	avoir sur un compte d'épargne *m*	—	depósito de ahorro *m*
deposito a risparmio (I)	Spareinlage *f*	savings deposit	dépôt d'épargne *m*	—	imposición de ahorro *f*
depositi a scadenza (I)	Termineinlagen *f/pl*	time deposit	dépôt à échéance convenue *m*	—	depósitos a plazo *m/pl*
deposito a termine (I)	Festgeld *n*	fixed deposit	argent immobilisé *m*	—	depósito a plazo *m*
deposito attivo (I)	lebendes Depot *n*	customers' security deposit	dépôt de personne *m*	—	depósito animado *m*
deposito a vista (I)	Sichteinlagen *f/pl*	sight deposits	dépôts à vue *m/pl*	—	depósitos a la vista *m/pl*
deposito bancario (I)	Bankguthaben *n*	bank balance	avoir en banque *m*	—	haber bancario *m*
deposito bancario (I)	Bankeinlage *f*	bank deposits	dépôt en banque *m*	—	imposición en un banco *f*
deposito bloccato (I)	Sperrdepot *n*	blocked safe-deposit	dépôt bloqué *m*	—	depósito bloqueado *m*
deposito bloccato (I)	gesperrtes Depot *n*	blocked deposit	dépôt bloqué *m*	—	depósito congelado *m*
depósito bloqueado (Es)	Sperrdepot *n*	blocked safe-deposit	dépôt bloqué *m*	deposito bloccato *m*	—
depósito cerrado (Es)	verschlossenes Depot *n*	safe deposit	dépôt fermé *m*	deposito chiuso *m*	—
deposito chiuso (I)	verschlossenes Depot *n*	safe deposit	dépôt fermé *m*	—	depósito cerrado *m*
depósito colectivo (Es)	Sammeldepot *n*	collective deposit	dépôt collectif de titres *m*	deposito collettivo di titoli *m*	—

	D	E	F	I	Es
deposito collettivo di titoli (I)	Sammeldepot *n*	collective deposit	dépôt collectif de titres *m*	—	depósito colectivo *m*
depósito común (Es)	Gemeinschaftsdepot *n*	joint security deposit	dépôt en commun *m*	deposito congiunto *m*	—
deposito comune (I)	Oderdepot *n*	joint deposit	dépôt joint *m*	—	depósito indistinto *m*
depósito congelado (Es)	gesperrtes Depot *n*	blocked deposit	dépôt bloqué *m*	deposito bloccato *m*	—
deposito congiunto (I)	Gemeinschaftsdepot *n*	joint security deposit	dépôt en commun *m*	—	depósito común *m*
deposito con permesso di permuta (I)	Ermächtigungs- depot *n*	authorized deposit	dépôt d'usage *m*	—	depósito de autorización *m*
depósito de ahorro (Es)	Sparguthaben *n*	savings account	avoir sur un compte d'épargne *m*	deposito a risparmio *m*	—
depósito de autorización (Es)	Ermächtigungs- depot *n*	authorized deposit	dépôt d'usage *m*	deposito con permes- so di permuta *m*	—
deposito dei titoli (I)	Effektendepot *n*	deposit of securities	dépôt de titres *m*	—	depósito irregular de títulos *m*
depósito de prenda (Es)	Pfanddepot *n*	pledged securities deposit	dépôt de titres remis en nantissement *m*	deposito a garanzia *m*	—
depósito de primas (Es)	Prämiendepot *n*	deposit for insurance payments	dépôt de titres à primes *m*	deposito di premio *m*	—
depósito de títulos fungibles (Es)	Aberdepot *n*	fungible security deposit	dépôt de choses fongibles *m*	deposito irregolare di titoli *m*	—
depósito de trueque (Es)	Tauschdepot *n*	security deposit	dépôt de titres-gestion *m*	deposito di custodia scambiabile *m*	—
depósito de valores pignoraticios (Es)	Lombarddepot *n*	collateral deposit	dépôt de titres remis en nantissement *m*	deposito lombard *m*	—
depósito de valores propio (Ec)	Eigendepot *n*	own security deposit	dépôt personnel *m*	depósito proprio *m*	—
deposito di custodia scambiabile (I)	Tauschdepot *n*	security deposit	dépôt de titres-gestion *m*	—	depósito de trueque *m*
deposito di denaro (I)	Summendepot *n*	collective deposit	dépôt irrégulier *m*	—	depósito de uso *m*
deposito di premio (I)	Prämiendepot *n*	deposit for insurance payments	dépôt de titres à primes *m*	—	depósito de primas *m*
depósito en cuenta de giros (Es)	Giroeinlage *f*	deposits on a current account	dépôt de virement *m*	deposito in giroconto *m*	—
depósito en efectivo (Es)	Bareinlage *f*	cash deposit	dépôt en numéraire *m*	apporto in denaro *m*	—
depósito específico (Es)	Sonderdepot *n*	separate deposit	dépôt individuel avec mandat de gestion *m*	deposito a dossier *m*	—
deposit of securities (E)	Effektendepot *n*	—	dépôt de titres *m*	deposito dei titoli *m*	depósito irregular de títulos *m*
depósito impersonal de títulos (Es)	Sachdepot *n*	impersonal security deposit	dépôt de choses *m*	libretto di deposito titoli *m*	—
deposito inattivo (I)	totes Depot *n*	dormant deposit	compte de choses *m*	—	depósito muerto *m*
depósito indistinto (Es)	Oderdepot *n*	joint deposit	dépôt joint *m*	deposito comune *m*	—
deposito in giroconto (I)	Giroeinlage *f*	deposits on a current account	dépôt de virement *m*	—	depósito en cuenta de giros *m*
deposito irregolare di titoli (I)	Aberdepot *n*	fungible security desposit	dépôt de choses fongibles *m*	—	depósito de títulos fungibles *m*
depósito irregular de títulos (Es)	Effektendepot *n*	deposit of securities	dépôt de titres *m*	deposito dei titoli *m*	—
deposito lombard (I)	Lombarddepot *n*	collateral deposit	dépôt de titres remis en nantissement *m*	—	depósito de valores pignoraticios *m*
depósito mínimo (Es)	Mindesteinlage *f*	minimum investment	dépôt initial minimum *m*	deposito minimo *m*	—
deposito minimo (I)	Mindesteinlage *f*	minimum investment	dépôt initial minimum *m*	—	depósito mínimo *m*
depósito muerto (Es)	totes Depot *n*	dormant deposit	compte de choses *m*	deposito inattivo *m*	—
deposito obbligatorio (I)	Pflichteinlage *f*	compulsory contribution	apport obligatoire *m*	—	depósito obligatorio *m*
depósito obligatorio (Es)	Pflichteinlage *f*	compulsory contribution	apport obligatoire *m*	deposito obbligatorio *m*	—
depósito obligatorio (Es)	Depotzwang *m*	compulsory safe custody	dépôt obligatoire *m*	obbligo di deposito *m*	—

	D	E	F	I	Es
depósito personal (Es)	Personendepot *n*	customer's security deposit	dépôt de personne *m*	libretto personale di deposito titoli *m*	—
depósito por cuenta de terceros (Es)	Anderdepot *n*	fiduciary deposit	dépôt de consignation *m*	deposito altrui *m*	—
deposito presso terzi (I)	Fremddepot *n*	fiduciary deposit	dépôt d'autrui *m*	—	depósito ajeno *m*
deposito proprio (I)	Eigendepot *n*	own security deposit	dépôt personnel *m*	—	depósito de valores propio *m*
depositor (E)	Depotkunde *m*	—	déposant *m*	cliente depositante *m*	depositante *m*
depositor (E)	Deponent *m*	—	déposant *m*	depositante *m*	depositante *m*
deposito ritirabile dietro preavviso (I)	Kündigungsgeld *n*	deposit at notice	sommes disponibles avec préavis *f/pl*	—	depósitos con preaviso *m/pl*
depósitos (Es)	Depositen *f/pl*	deposits	dépôts *m/pl*	depositi *m/pl*	—
depósitos a la vista (Es)	Sichteinlagen *f/pl*	sight deposits	dépôts à vue *m/pl*	deposito a vista *m*	—
depósitos a plazo (Es)	Termineinlagen *f/pl*	time deposit	dépôt à échéance convenue *m*	deposito a scadenza *m*	—
depósitos bancarios (Es)	Bankdepositen *pl*	bank deposit	fonds déposés en banque *m/pl*	depositi bancari *m/pl*	—
depósitos con preaviso (Es)	Kündigungsgeld *n*	deposit at notice	sommes disponibles avec préavis *f/pl*	deposito ritirabile dietro preavviso *m*	—
depósito separado (Es)	Streifbanddepot *n*	individual deposit of securities	dépôt individuel avec mandat de gestion *m*	deposito a dossier *m*	—
depósitos fiduciarios (Es)	Treuhanddepots *n/pl*	trust deposits	dépôts de consignation *m/pl*	depositi per conto altrui *m/pl*	—
deposito vincolato ad un mese (I)	Monatsgeld *n*	one month money	argent à un mois *m*	—	dinero a 30 días *m*
deposit policy (E)	Einlagenpolitik *f*	—	politique de dépôts *f*	politica dei depositi *f*	política de depositos *f*
deposit receipt (E)	Depotschein *m*	—	récépissé de dépôt *m*	certificato di deposito *m*	certificado de depósito *m*
deposits (E)	Depositen *f/pl*	—	dépôts *m/pl*	depositi *m/pl*	depósitos *m/pl*
deposits on a current account (E)	Giroeinlage *f*	—	dépôt de virement *m*	deposito in giro-conto *m*	depósito en cuenta de giros *m*
Depot (D)	—	deposit	dépôt *m*	deposito *m*	depósito *m*
dépôt (F)	Verwahrung *f*	custody	—	custodia *f*	custodia *f*
dépôt (F)	Depot *n*	deposit	—	deposito *m*	depósito *m*
dépôt (F)	Einlage *f*	money deposited	—	deposito *m*	imposición *f*
Depotabstimmung (D)	—	securities deposit reconciliation	vote de titres en dépôt *m*	coordinamento dei depositi *m*	voto de título en depósito *m*
Depotabteilung (D)	—	safe custody department	service des dépôts *m*	reparto depositi *m*	sección de depósito *f*
dépôt à échéance convenue (F)	Termineinlagen *f/pl*	time deposit	—	depositi a scadenza *m/pl*	depósitos a plazo *m/pl*
Depotaktie (D)	—	deposited share	action déposée en compte courant *f*	azione in deposito *f*	acción de depósito *f*
Depotaner-kenntnis (D)	—	deposit acknowledgement	reconnaissance de dépôt *f*	approvazione estratto deposito *f*	reconocimiento de depósito *m*
Depotarten (D)	—	types of deposit	sortes de dépôts *f/pl*	tipi di deposito *m/pl*	tipos de depósito *m/pl*
Depotaufstellung (D)	—	list of securities deposited	liste des valeurs déposées *f*	distinta di deposito *f*	lista de depósito *f*
Depotauszug (D)	—	statement of securities	relevé de compte-titres *m*	estratto deposito *m*	extracto de depósito *m*
Depotbank (D)	—	bank holding securities on deposit	banque de dépôts *f*	banca depositaria *f*	banco depositario *m*
dépôt bloqué (F)	gesperrtes Depot *n*	blocked deposit	—	deposito bloccato *m*	depósito congelado *m*
dépôt bloqué (F)	Sperrdepot *n*	blocked safe-deposit	—	deposito bloccato *m*	depósito bloqueado *m*
Depotbuch (D)	—	deposit book	registre des valeurs en dépôt *m*	libretto di deposito *m*	libreta de depósito *f*
Depotbuchhaltung (D)	—	security deposit account	comptabilité des dépôts *m*	contabilità dei depositi *f*	contabilidad de depósitos *f*
dépôt collectif (F)	offenes Depot *n*	safe custody account	—	deposito aperto *m*	depósito abierto *m*
dépôt collectif de titres (F)	Sammeldepot *n*	collective deposit	—	deposito collettivo di titoli *m*	depósito colectivo *m*

	D	E	F	I	Es
dépôt d'autrui (F)	Fremddepot *n*	fiduciary deposit	—	deposito presso terzi *m*	depósito ajeno *m*
dépôt de choses (F)	Sachdepot *n*	impersonal security deposit	—	libretto di deposito titoli *m*	depósito impersonal de títulos *m*
dépôt de choses fongibles (F)	Aberdepot *n*	fungible security deposit	—	deposito irregolare di titoli *m*	depósito de títulos fungibles *m*
dépôt de consignation (F)	Anderdepot *n*	fiduciary deposit	—	deposito altrui *m*	depósito por cuenta de terceros *m*
dépôt de nuit (F)	Nachttresor *m*	night safe	—	cassa continua *f*	caja nocturna *f*
dépôt d'épargne (F)	Spareinlage *f*	savings deposit	—	deposito a risparmio *m*	imposición de ahorro *f*
dépôt de personne (F)	Personendepot *n*	customer's security deposit	—	libretto personale di deposito titoli *m*	depósito personal *m*
dépôt de titres (F)	Effektendepot *n*	deposit of securities	—	deposito dei titoli *m*	depósito irregular de títulos *m*
dépôt de titres à primes (F)	Prämiendepot *n*	deposit for insurance payments	—	deposito di premio *m*	depósito de primas *m*
dépôt de titres-gestion (F)	Tauschdepot *n*	security deposit	—	deposito di custodia scambiabile *m*	depósito de trueque *m*
dépôt de titres remis en nantissement (F)	Lombarddepot *n*	collateral deposit	—	deposito lombard *m*	depósito de valores pignoraticios *m*
dépôt de titres remis en nantissement (F)	Pfanddepot *n*	pledged securities deposit	—	deposito a garanzia *m*	depósito de prenda *m*
dépôt de virement (F)	Giroeinlage *f*	deposits on a current account	—	deposito in giro-conto *m*	depósito en cuenta de giros *m*
dépôt d'usage (F)	Ermächtigungsdepot *n*	authorized deposit	—	deposito con permesso di permuta *m*	depósito de autorización *m*
dépôt en banque (F)	Bankeinlage *f*	bank deposits	—	deposito bancario *m*	imposición en un banco *f*
dépôt en commun (F)	Gemeinschaftsdepot *n*	joint security deposit	—	deposito congiunto *m*	depósito común *m*
dépôt en numéraire (F)	Bareinlage *f*	cash deposit	—	apporto in denaro *m*	depósito en efectivo *m*
dépôt fermé (F)	verschlossenes Depot *n*	safe deposit	—	deposito chiuso *m*	depósito cerrado *m*
Depotgebühren (D)	—	safe custody charges	frais de garde *m/pl*	diritti di deposito *m/pl*	derechos de custodia *m/pl*
Depotgesetz (D)	—	Securities Deposit Act	législation sur les dépôts et achats de valeurs par les banques *f*	legge sui depositi *f*	ley de depósitos *f*
dépôt individuel avec mandat de gestion (F)	Streifbanddepot *n*	individual deposit of securities	—	deposito a dossier *m*	depósito separado *m*
dépôt individuel avec mandat de gestion (F)	Sonderdepot *n*	separate deposit	—	deposito a dossier *m*	depósito específico *m*
dépôt initial minimum (F)	Mindesteinlage *f*	minimum investment	—	deposito minimo *m*	depósito mínimo *m*
Depotkonto (D)	—	security deposit account	compte de dépôt *m*	conto di deposito *m*	cuenta de depósitos *f*
dépôt joint (F)	Oderdepot *n*	joint deposit	—	deposito comune *m*	depósito indistinto *m*
dépôt obligatoire (F)	Depotzwang *m*	compulsory safe custody	—	obbligo di deposito *m*	depósito obligatorio *m*
dépôt personnel (F)	Eigendepot *n*	own security deposit	—	deposito proprio *m*	depósito de valores propio *m*
Depotprüfung (D)	—	securities deposit audit	contrôle des établissements dépositaires de titres *m*	revisione dei depositi *f*	revisión de depósito *f*
dépôts (F)	Depositen *f/pl*	deposits	—	depositi *m/pl*	depósitos *m/pl*
dépôts à trois mois (F)	Dreimonatsgeld *n*	three months' money	—	prestito a tre mesi *m*	imposición a un plazo de 3 meses *f*
dépôts à vue (F)	Sichteinlagen *f/pl*	sight deposits	—	depositi a vista *m/pl*	depósitos a la vista *m/pl*
Depotschein (D)	—	deposit receipt	récépissé de dépôt *m*	certificato di deposito *m*	certificado de depósito *m*

	D	E	F	I	Es
dépôts de consignation (F)	Treuhanddepots *n/pl*	trust deposits	—	depositi per conto altrui *m/pl*	depósitos fiduciario *m/pl*
Depotstimmrecht (D)	—	voting rights of nominee shareholders	droit de vote d'une banque dépositaire d'actions en compte courant *m*	diritto di voto azioni in deposito *m*	derecho de voto de título en depósito *m*
Depotunter-schlagung (D)	—	misapplication of deposit	détournement de titres en dépôt *m*	appropriazione indebita di depositi *f*	defraudación de depósito *f*
Depotvertrag (D)	—	securities deposit contract	contrat de dépôt *m*	contratto di deposito *m*	contrato de depósito *m*
Depotverwaltung (D)	—	portfolio management	administration des titres déposés *f*	amministrazione di un deposito *f*	administración de depósito *f*
Depotwechsel (D)	—	bill on deposit	lettre de change déposée en garantie d'un prêt *f*	cambiale depositata in garanzia *f*	efecto cambial en depósito *m*
Depotzwang (D)	—	compulsory safe custody	dépôt obligatoire *m*	obbligo di deposito *m*	depósito obligatorio *m*
depreciación del capital (Es)	Kapitalverwässerung *f*	watering of capital stock	augmentation du capital par émission d'actions gratuites ou par incorporation des réserves au fonds social *f*	annacquamento di capitali *m*	—
depreciation (E)	Entwertung *f*	—	dévaluation *f*	svalutazione *f*	desvalorización *f*
dépréciation (F)	Geldentwertung *f*	monetary devaluation	—	svalutazione monetaria *f*	devaluación del dinero *f*
deprezzamento monetario (I)	Geldwertschwund *m*	currency erosion	érosion monétaire *f*	—	erosión monetaria *f*
Deputat (D)	—	payment in kind	avantage en nature *m*	compenso in natura *m*	remuneración en especie *f*
derecho a compensación (Es)	Ausgleichsrecht *n*	equalization right	droit à une compensation *m*	diritto di compensazione *m*	—
derecho a un divi-dendo cumulativo (Es)	Nachbezugsrecht *n*	right to a cumulative dividend	droit à un dividende cumulatif *m*	diritto di dividendo cumulativo *m*	—
derecho a voto (Es)	Stimmrecht *n*	right to vote	droit de vote *m*	diritto di voto *m*	—
derecho comercial (Es)	Handelsrecht *n*	commercial law	droit commercial *m*	diritto commerciale *m*	—
derecho de cheque (Es)	Scheckrecht *n*	negotiable instruments law concerning cheques	législation en matière de chèque *f*	disciplina degli assegni *f*	—
derecho de compra (Es)	Ankaufsrecht *n*	purchase right	droit d'achat *m*	opzione *f*	—
derecho de crédito (Es)	Forderungsrecht *n*	right to claim	droit issu d'une créance *m*	diritto di credito *m*	—
derecho de disfrute (Es)	Genußrecht *n*	participation rights	droit de jouissance *m*	diritto di godimento *m*	—
derecho de dividendo de años precedentes (Es)	Nachdividende *f*	dividend payable for previous years	droit aux dividendes des années précédentes *m*	dividendo cumulativo *m*	—
derecho de giro especial (Es)	Sonderziehungs-recht *n*	special drawing right	droit de tirage spécial *m*	diritto speciale di prelievo *m*	—
derecho de la bolsa (Es)	Börsenrecht *n*	stock exchange rules	régime de bourse *m*	diritto della borsa *m*	—
derecho de obligaciones (Es)	Schuldrecht *n*	law of obligations	droit des obligations et contrats *m*	diritto delle obbligazioni *m*	—
derecho de opción (Es)	Optionsrecht *n*	option right	droit d'option *m*	diritto d'opzione *m*	—
derecho de opción (Es)	Bezugsrecht *n*	subscription right	droit de souscription *m*	diritto d'opzione *m*	—
derecho de preferencia (Es)	Vorkaufsrecht *n*	preemption right	droit de préemption *m*	diritto di prelazione *m*	—
derecho de prenda (Es)	Pfandrecht *n*	lien	droit de gage *m*	diritto di pegno *m*	—
derecho de sociedades anónimas (Es)	Aktienrecht *n*	company law	loi sur les sociétés anonymes *f*	diritto delle società per azioni *f*	—
derecho de superficie (Es)	Erbbaurecht *n*	hereditary building right	droit de superficie héréditaire *m*	diritto d'enfiteusi *m*	—
derecho de uso (Es)	Benutzungsrecht *n*	right to use	droit d'usage *m*	diritto d'uso *m*	—
derecho de uso (Es)	Nutzungsrecht *n*	usufructury right	droit de jouissance *m*	diritto di godimento *m*	—
derecho de voto del banco (Es)	Bankenstimmrecht *n*	banks' voting rights	droit de vote de la banque *m*	diritto di voto bancario *m*	—

	D	E	F	I	Es
derecho de voto de título en depósito (Es)	Depotstimmrecht n	voting rights of nominee shareholders	droit de vote d'une banque dépositaire d'actions en compte courant m	diritto di voto azioni in deposito m	—
derecho de voto plural (Es)	Mehrstimmrecht n	multiple voting right	droit de vote plural m	diritto di voto plurimo m	—
derecho habitual (Es)	Stammrecht n	customary law	droit habituel m	diritto principale m	—
derechos (Es)	Gebühr f	fee	taxe f	canone m	—
derechos administrativos (Es)	Verwaltungsgebühr f	official fees	taxe administrative f	tassa amministrativa f	—
derechos de acceso (Es)	Zuteilungsrechte n/pl	allotment right	droits de répartition m/pl	diritti d'assegnazione m/pl	—
derechos de custodia (Es)	Depotgebühren f/pl	safe custody charges	frais de garde m/pl	diritti di deposito m/pl	—
derechos de exportación (Es)	Ausfuhrzoll m	export duty	taxe de sortie m	dazio all'esportazione m	—
derechos de giro (Es)	Ziehungsrechte n/pl	drawing rights	droits de tirage m/pl	diritti di prelievo m/pl	—
derechos de liquidación (Es)	Liquidationsgebühr f	liquidation fee	frais de liquidation m/pl	commissione di liquidazione f	—
derechos de partición (Es)	Teilrechte n/pl	partial rights	droits partiels m/pl	buono frazionario m	—
derechos de prolongación (Es)	Belassungsgebühr f	prolongation charge	frais de prolongation m/pl	tassa prolungamento ipoteche f	—
derechos de propiedad (Es)	Eigentumsrechte n/pl	property rights	droits de propriété m/pl	diritti di proprietà m/pl	—
déréglementation (F)	Deregulierung f	deregulation	—	diregolazione f	deregulación f
deregulación (Es)	Deregulierung f	deregulation	déréglementation f	diregolazione f	—
deregulation (E)	Deregulierung f	—	déréglementation f	diregolazione f	deregulación f
Deregulierung (D)	—	deregulation	déréglementation f	diregolazione f	deregulación f
de renta fija (Es)	festverzinslich	with a fixed rate of interest	à revenu fixe	a reddito fisso	—
dernier cours (F)	Schlußkurs m	closing price	—	quotazione di chiusura f	cotización de cierre f
Deroute (D)	—	collapse	déroute f	tracollo dei prezzi di borsa m	fuga desbaratada f
déroute (F)	Deroute f	collapse	—	tracollo dei prezzi di borsa m	fuga desbaratada f
descontar (Es)	eskomptieren	to discount	escompter	anticipare	—
descubierto (Es)	Überziehen eines Kontos n	overdraft	découvert de compte m	mandare un conto allo scoperto m	—
descubierto (Es)	Leerposition f	bear selling position	découvert m	scoperto m	—
descuento (Es)	Diskont m	discount	escompte m	sconto m	—
descuento (Es)	Skonto n	discount	escompte m	sconto m	—
descuento (Es)	Diskontierung f	discounting	escompte m	operazione di sconto f	—
descuento (Es)	Dekort n	deduction	rabais m	decurtazione f	—
descuento de letras (Es)	Wechseldiskont m	discount of bills	escompte d'un effet m	sconto cambiario m	—
descuento de valores (Es)	Effektendiskont m	securities discount	escompte sur achat de titres m	sconto di titoli m	—
descuento directo (Es)	Direktdiskont m	direct discount	escompte direct m	sconto diretto m	—
descuento privado (Es)	Privatdiskont m	prime acceptance	escompte hors banque m	carta commerciale di prim'ordine f	—
desembolso parcial (Es)	Teilauszahlung f	partial payment	payement partiel m	pagamento parziale m	—
desembolso telegráfico (Es)	telegrafische Auszahlung f	telegraphic transfer	payement télégraphique m	trasferimento telegrafico m	—
desempleo disfrazado (Es)	versteckte Arbeitslosigkeit f	hidden unemployment	chômage caché m	disoccupazione camuffata f	—
désendettement (F)	Entschuldung f	disencumberment	—	pagamento dei debiti m	desgravamen m
desestacionalización (Es)	Saisonbereinigung f	seasonal adjustment	correction des variations saisonnières f	destagionalizzazione f	—

	D	E	F	I	Es
desgravamen (Es)	Entschuldung f	disencumberment	désendettement m	pagamento dei debiti m	—
designación (Es)	Designation f	designation	désignation f	designazione f	—
Designation (D)	—	designation	désignation f	designazione f	designación f
designation (E)	Designation f	—	désignation f	designazione f	designación f
désignation (F)	Designation f	designation	—	designazione f	designación f
designazione (I)	Designation f	designation	désignation f	—	designación f
desinversión (Es)	Desinvestition f	disinvestment	désinvestissement m	disinvestimento m	—
désinvestissement (F)	Desinvestition f	disinvestment	—	disinvestimento m	desinversión f
Desinvestition (D)	—	disinvestment	désinvestissement m	disinvestimento m	desinversión f
desnacio- nalización (Es)	Reprivatisierung f	reversion to private ownership	dénationalisation f	riprivatizzazione f	—
destagio- nalizzazione (I)	Saisonbereinigung f	seasonal adjustment	correction des varia- tions saisonnières f	—	desestacionalización f
destajo (Es)	Geldakkord m	money piece rate	convention de salaire aux pièces f	cottimo al pezzo m	—
destroyed securities (E)	vernichtete Wertpapiere n/pl	—	titres détruits m/pl	titoli annullati m/pl	títulos destruidos m/pl
destrucción de dinero (Es)	Geldvernichtung f	reduction of the volume of money	destruction d'argent f	distruzione di denaro f	—
destruction d'argent (F)	Geldvernichtung f	reduction of the volume of money	—	distruzione di denaro f	destrucción de dinero f
desvalorización (Es)	Abwertung f	devaluation	dévaluation f	svalutazione f	—
desvalorización (Es)	Entwertung f	depreciation	dévaluation f	svalutazione f	—
detenzione permanente (I)	Dauerbesitz m	permanent holding	possession permanente f	—	posesión permanente f
determination coefficient (E)	Bestimmtheitsmaß n	—	coefficient de détermination m	coefficiente di determinazione m	coeficiente de determinación m
détermination des cours (F)	Kursfestsetzung f	fixing of prices	—	fissazione dei corsi f	cotización f
détermination du bénéfice (F)	Gewinnermittlung f	determination of profits	—	determinazione degli utili f	averiguación de los beneficios f
determination of profits (E)	Gewinnermittlung f	—	détermination du bénéfice f	determinazione degli utili f	averiguación de los beneficios f
determination of the value (E)	Wertermittlung f	—	évaluation f	valutazione f	evaluación del valor f
determinazione degli utili (I)	Gewinnermittlung f	determination of profits	détermination du bénéfice f	—	averiguación de los beneficios f
détournement (F)	Unterschlagung f	embezzlement	—	appropriazione indebita f	defraudación f
détournement de titres en dépôt (F)	Depotunter- schlagung f	misapplication of deposit	—	appropriazione indebita di depositi f	defraudación de depósito f
dette (F)	Schuld f	debt	—	debito m	deuda f
dette comptable (F)	Buchschuld f	book debt	—	debito contabile m	pasivo exigible m
dette consolidée (F)	fundierte Schulden f/pl	funded debts	—	debiti consolidati m/pl	deudas consolidadas f/pl
dette d'argent exprimée en unité mo- nétaire étrangère (F)	Währungsschuld f	foreign currency debt	—	debito in valuta estera m	deuda en moneda extranjera f
dette d'un associé d'une société par intérêts (F)	Gesamthandschuld f	joint debt	—	debito comunione a mani unite m	deuda en mano común f
dette extérieure (F)	Auslands- verschuldung f	external indebtedness	—	indebitamento verso l'estero m	deuda exterior f
dette flottante (F)	schwebende Schuld f	floating debt	—	debito fluttuante m	deuda flotante f
dette foncière (F)	Grundschuld f	land charge	—	debito fondiario m	hipoteca f
dette foncière constituée avec une cédule au porteur (F)	Inhabergrundschuld f	land charge with a deed issued to the bearer	—	debito fondiario al portatore m	deuda inmobiliaria al portador f
dette foncière de garantie (F)	Sicherungsgrund- schuld f	cautionary land charge	—	debito fondiario di garanzia m	deuda inmobiliaria de seguridad f
dette foncière inscrite au bureau foncier (F)	Buchgrundschuld f	uncertificated land charge	—	debito iscritto nel libro fondiario m	deuda inmobiliaria registrada f

dette foncière   144

	D	E	F	I	Es
dette foncière remboursable à terme fixe (F)	Fälligkeitsgrundschuld f	fixed-date land charge	—	debito fondiario a scadenza m	deuda inmobiliaria de vencimiento f
dette foncière remboursable avec préavis (F)	Kündigungsgrundschuld f	land charge not repayable until called	—	termine di preavviso m	deuda inmobiliaria con preaviso f
dette perpétuelle (F)	ewige Schuld f	perpetual debt	—	prestito perpetuo m	deuda perpetua f
dette publique (F)	öffentliche Schuld f	public debt	—	debito pubblico m	deuda pública f
dettes actives (F)	Außenstände m/pl	outstanding accounts	—	crediti pendenti m/pl	cobros pendientes m/pl
dettes à l'étranger (F)	Auslandsschulden f/pl	foreign debts		debiti esteri m/pl	deudas exteriores f/pl
dettes bancaires (F)	Bankschulden f/pl	bank debts	—	debiti verso banche m/pl	deudas bancarias f/pl
dettes consolidées (F)	Konsols m/pl	consoles	—	prestiti consolidati m/pl	deudas consolidadas f/pl
dette solidaire (F)	Gesamtschuld f	total debt	—	debito solidale m	obligación solidaria f
dettes sociales (F)	Gesellschaftsschulden f/pl	company's debts	—	debiti della società m/pl	deudas sociales f/pl
deuda (Es)	Schuld f	debt	dette f	debito m	—
deuda en mano común (Es)	Gesamthandschuld f	joint debt	dette d'un associé d'une société par intérêts f	debito comunione a mani unite m	—
deuda en moneda extranjera (Es)	Währungsschuld f	foreign currency debt	dette d'argent exprimée en unité monétaire étrangère f	debito in valuta estera m	—
deuda exterior (Es)	Auslandsverschuldung f	external indebtedness	dette extérieure f	indebitamento verso l'estero m	—
deuda flotante (Es)	schwebende Schuld f	floating debt	dette flottante f	debito fluttuante m	—
deuda inmobiliaria con preaviso (Es)	Kündigungsgrundschuld f	land charge not repayable until called	dette foncière remboursable avec préavis f	termine di preavviso m	—
deuda inmobiliaria del propietario (Es)	Eigentümergrundschuld f	land charge in favour of the owner	dette foncière constituée par le propriétaire à son profit f	redebito fondiario al proprietario m	—
deuda inmobiliaria de seguridad (Es)	Sicherungsgrundschuld f	cautionary land charge	dette foncière de garantie f	debito fondiario di garanzia m	—
deuda inmobiliaria de vencimiento (Es)	Fälligkeitsgrundschuld f	fixed-date land charge	dette foncière remboursable à terme fixe f	debito fondiario a scadenza m	—
deuda inmobiliaria registrada (Es)	Buchgrundschuld f	uncertificated land charge	dette foncière inscrite au bureau foncier f	debito iscritto nel libro fondiario m	—
deuda inscrita en el libro de deudas (Es)	Schuldbuchforderung f	debt-register claim	créance inscrite dans le livre de la dette f	cartella del debito pubblico f	—
deuda perpetua (Es)	ewige Schuld f	perpetual debt	dette perpétuelle f	prestito perpetuo m	—
deuda pública (Es)	öffentliche Schuld f	public debt	dette publique f	debito pubblico m	—
deudas bancarias (Es)	Bankschulden f/pl	bank debts	dettes bancaires f/pl	debiti verso banche m/pl	—
deudas consolidadas (Es)	Konsols m/pl	consoles	dettes consolidées f/pl	prestiti consolidati m/pl	—
deudas consolidadas (Es)	fundierte Schulden f/pl	funded debts	dette consolidée f	debiti consolidati m/pl	—
deudas exteriores (Es)	Auslandsschulden f/pl	foreign debts	dettes à l'étranger f/pl	debiti esteri m/pl	—
deudas sociales (Es)	Gesellschaftsschulden f/pl	company's debts	dettes sociales f/pl	debiti della società m/pl	—
deudor (Es)	Schuldner m	debtor	débiteur m	debitore m	—
deudor común (Es)	Gemeinschuldner m	adjudicated bankrupt	débiteur en failli m	debitore fallito m	—
deudor solidario (Es)	Gesamtschuldner m	joint and several debtor	débiteur solidaire m	debitore solidale m	—
devaluación del dinero (Es)	Geldentwertung f	monetary devaluation	dépréciation f	svalutazione monetaria f	—
devaluation (E)	Abwertung f	—	dévaluation f	svalutazione f	desvalorización f
dévaluation (F)	Abwertung f	devaluation	—	svalutazione f	desvalorización f
dévaluation (F)	Entwertung f	depreciation	—	svalutazione f	desvalorización f

	D	E	F	I	Es
devaluation race (E)	Abwertungs-wettlauf *m*	—	course de dévaluation *f*	corsa alla svalutazione *f*	carrera de desvalorización *f*
development (E)	Erschließung *f*	—	ouverture *f*	apertura *f*	apertura *f*
development bank (E)	Entwicklungsbank *f*	—	banque de développement *f*	banca per lo sviluppo *f*	banco de desarrollo *m*
development fund (E)	Entwicklungsfonds *m*	—	fonds de développement *m*	fondo di sviluppo *m*	fondo de desarrollo *m*
devinculación (Es)	Devinkulierung *f*	unrestricted transferability	transférabilité illimitée *f*	svincolamento *m*	—
Devinkulierung (D)	—	unrestricted transferability	transférabilité illimitée *f*	svincolamento *m*	devinculación *f*
devise (F)	Sorte *f*	foreign notes and coins	—	valuta estera *f*	moneda extranjera *f*
Devisen (D)	—	currency	devises *f/pl*	valuta estera *f*	divisas *f/pl*
Devisenabteilung (D)	—	foreign exchange department	service des devises *m*	ufficio cambi *m*	sección de divisas *f*
Devisenarbitrage (D)	—	arbitration in foreign exchange	arbitrage sur les devises *m*	arbitraggio in cambio *m*	arbitraje de divisas *m*
Devisenausländer (D)	—	non-resident	non-résident *m*	non residente *m*	no residente *m*
Devisenberater (D)	—	foreign exchange advisor	conseiller en matière de devises *m*	consulente di cambio *m*	asesor en materia de divisas *m*
Devisenbilanz (D)	—	net movement of foreign exchange	compte de devises *m*	bilancia valutaria *f*	balanza de divisas *f*
Devisenbörse (D)	—	foreign exchange market	bourse de devises *f*	borsa dei cambi *f*	bolsa de cambios *f*
Devisenbuchhaltung (D)	—	currency accounting	comptabilité de devises *f*	contabilità dei cambi *f*	contabilidad de divisas *f*
Devisengeschäft (D)	—	foreign exchange business	opération en devises *f*	operazione di cambio *f*	operación de divisas *f*
Devisenhandel (D)	—	foreign exchange dealings	marché des changes *m*	cambio valuta *m*	operaciones de divisas *f/pl*
Devisenhändler (D)	—	foreign exchange dealer	courtier en devises *m*	cambista *m*	cambista *m*
Deviseninländer (D)	—	resident	résident *m*	residente *m*	residente *m*
Devisenkassa-geschäft (D)	—	foreign exchange spot dealings	opérations de change au comptant *f/pl*	cambi a pronti *m/pl*	operación de divisas al contado *f*
Devisenkassakurs (D)	—	foreign exchange spot operations	taux de change au comptant *m*	corso dei cambi a pronti *m*	tipo de cambio al contado *m*
Devisenkassamarkt (D)	—	foreign exchange spot market	marché des changes au comptant *m*	mercato dei cambi a pronti *m*	mercado de divisas al contado *m*
Devisenkommissions-geschäft (D)	—	foreign exchange transactions for customers	opérations de change en commission *f/pl*	operazione di cambio su commissione *f*	operaciones de divisas a base de comisión *f/pl*
Devisenkonto (D)	—	foreign exchange account	compte libellé en devises *m*	conto in valuta estera *m*	cuenta en divisas *f*
Devisenkontrolle (D)	—	foreign exchange control	contrôle des changes *m*	controllo dei cambi *m*	control de cambio *m*
Devisenkurs (D)	—	foreign exchange rate	taux de change *m*	cambio *m*	cambio *m*
Devisenkursbildung (D)	—	exchange rate formation	formation du taux de change *f*	formazione dei cambi *f*	formación del tipo de cambio *f*
Devisenkursmakler (D)	—	exchange broker	courtier en devises *m*	agente di cambio *m*	corredor de cambios *m*
Devisenmarkt (D)	—	foreign exchange market	marché des changes *m*	mercato dei cambi *m*	mercado de divisas *m*
Devisenmarkt-interventionen (D)	—	exchange market intervention	intervention dans le marché des devises *f*	interventi sul mercato dei cambi *m/pl*	intervención en el mercado de divisas *f*
Devisennotierung (D)	—	foreign exchange quotations	cotation des devises *f*	cambio *m*	cotización de cambio *f*
Devisenoption (D)	—	exchange option	option de change *f*	opzione di cambio *f*	opción de divisas *f*
Devisenpensions-geschäft (D)	—	purchase of foreign exchange for later sale	opération de mise en pension de devises *f*	sconto di valuta in pensione *f*	operación de reporte en divisas *f*
Devisenrechnung (D)	—	foreign exchange calculation	calcul des changes *m*	calcolo valutario *m*	cálculo de divisas *m*

	D	E	F	I	Es
Devisenreserve (D)	—	foreign exchange reserves	réserve de devises f	disponibilità in valuta f	reserva de divisas f
Devisenspekulation (D)	—	speculation in foreign currency	spéculation sur les changes f	speculazione in cambi f	especulación de divisas f
Devisentermin-geschäft (D)	—	forward exchange dealings	opération à terme sur les changes f	operazione di cambio a termine f	transacción a término en divisas f
Devisentermin-handel (D)	—	forward exchange trading	marché des changes à terme m	operazione di cambio a termine f	mercado de cambios a plazo m
Devisenterminkurs (D)	—	forward exchange rate	cours des devises négociées à terme m	quotazione dei cambi a termine f	cambio de divisas a término m
Devisentermin-markt (D)	—	forward exchange market	marché des changes à terme m	mercato a termine delle divise m	mercado de divisas a plazo m
Devisenüberschuß (D)	—	foreign exchange surplus	excédent de devises m	eccedenza di valuta estera f	excedente de divisas m
Devisen-Wechsel (D)	—	bill in foreign currency	lettre de change libellée en monnaie étrangère f	cambiale in valuta estera f	letra en moneda extranjera f
devises (F)	Devisen f/pl	currency	—	valuta estera f	divisas f/pl
devises aptes à servir de couverture (F)	deckungsfähige Devisen f/pl	foreign currencies eligible as cover	—	valute pregiate f/pl	divisas cubiertas por el banco emisor f/pl
devises négociées en bourse à terme (F)	Termindevisen f/pl	exchange for forward delivery	—	divise a termine f/pl	divisas a plazo f/pl
devises négociées en bourse au comptant (F)	Kassadevisen f/pl	spot exchange	—	divisa a contanti f	divisas al contado f/pl
devises obtenues par l'exportation (F)	Exportdevisen f/pl	export exchange	—	valuta estera da esportazioni f	divisas obtenidas mediante la exportación f/pl
devolución (Es)	Erstattung f	reimbursement	restitution f	rimborso m	—
devolución de la dis-minución de capital (Es)	Ausweis der Kapital-herabsetzung m	return of capital reduction	situation de la ré-duction du capital f	dichiarazione di riduzione capitale f	—
devoluciones (Es)	Returen f/pl	returns	retours m/pl	merci di ritorno f/pl	—
día de la emisión (Es)	Bezugstag m	subscription day	jour de souscription m	giorno di scadenza opzione m	—
día de liquidación (Es)	Stichtag m	reporting date	jour fixé m	data di riferimento f	—
día de pago (Es)	Zahltag m	payday	jour de paye m	giorno di pagamento m	—
día de vencimiento (Es)	Verfalltag m	day of expiry	jour de l'échéance m	giorno di scadenza m	—
diagrama de bloque (Es)	Blockdiagramm n	bar chart	ordinogramme m	diagramma a blocchi m	—
diagramma a blocchi (I)	Blockdiagramm n	bar chart	ordinogramme m	—	diagrama de bloque m
diario (Es)	Primanota f	journal	mémorial m	prima nota f	—
días de fiesta bancarios (Es)	Bankfeiertage m/pl	bank holidays	jours de fête bancaires m/pl	giorni festivi delle banche m/pl	—
días de referencia de los bancos (Es)	Bankstichtage m/pl	settling days	jours de règlement fixés m/pl	date di resoconto settimanale della banca centrale f/pl	—
dichiarazione (I)	Erklärung f	explanation	déclaration f	—	declaración f
dichiarazione d'esclusività (I)	Ausschließlichkeits-erklärung f	undertaking to deal exclusively with one bank or firm	déclaration d'exclusivité f	—	contrato de exclusividad m
dichiarazione di riduzione capitale (I)	Ausweis der Kapital-herabsetzung m	return of capital reduction	situation de la réduction du capital f	—	devolución de la disminución de capital f
dichiarazione diritto d'opzione (I)	Bezugsrechter-klärung f	declaration to exercise the subscription right	déclaration d'exercer le droit de souscription f	—	declaración de ejercer el derecho de suscripción f
Dienstleistung (D)	—	service	prestation de service f	attività terziaria f	servicio m
Dienstleistungs-bilanz (D)	—	balance of service transactions	balance des opérations courantes en services f	bilancia dei servizi f	balanza de servicios f
diferencial de intereses (Es)	Zinsgefälle n	margin between interest rates	disparité des niveaux d'intérêts f	differenza di interessi f	—
difference between purchase and hedging price (E)	Kursspanne f	—	écart de cours m	margine di cambio m	margen de cotización m

	D	E	F	I	Es
différence en moins (F)	Damnum *m*	debt discount	—	disaggio *m*	disagio de préstamo *m*
differentiated tariffs (E)	gespaltener Tarif *m*	—	tarif différencié *m*	tariffa multipla *f*	tarifa múltiple *f*
differenza di interessi (I)	Zinsgefälle *n*	margin between interest rates	disparité des niveaux d'intérêts *f*	—	diferencial de intereses *m*
differimento di rimborso (I)	Tilgungsaussetzung *f*	suspension of redemption payments	suspension d'amortissement *f*	—	suspensión de la amortización *f*
dilazione di pagamento (I)	Zahlungsaufschub *m*	extension of time for payment	sursis de payement *m*	—	pago aplazado *m*
dilazione di pagamento (I)	Zahlungsziel *n*	period for payment	délai de payement *m*	—	plazo de pago *m*
diminution de capital simplifiée (F)	vereinfachte Kapitalherabsetzung *f*	simplified capital reduction	—	riduzione di *f* capitale semplice	reducción de capital simplificada *f*
diminution du capital (F)	Kapitalherabsetzung *f*	capital reduction	—	riduzione del capitale sociale *f*	reducción de capital *f*
diminuzione dei risparmi accumulati (I)	Entsparen *n*	dissaving	épargne négative *f*	—	ahorro negativo *m*
dimissione (I)	Rücktritt *m*	rescission	résolution du contrat *f*	—	rescisión *f*
dinero (Es)	Geld *n*	money	argent *m*	denaro *m*	—
dinero a fin de mes (Es)	Ultimogeld *n*	last-day money	fonds remboursables à fin de mois *m/pl*	prestito per fine mese *m*	—
dinero a 30 días (Es)	Monatsgeld *n*	one month money	argent à un mois *m*	deposito vincolato ad un mese *m*	—
dinero bancario (Es)	Buchgeld *n*	money in account	monnaie de crédit *f*	moneta bancaria *f*	—
dinero bancario (Es)	Giralgeld *n*	money in account	monnaie scripturale *f*	moneta scritturale *f*	—
dinero caliente (Es)	heißes Geld *n*	hot money	capitaux fébriles *m/pl*	hot money *m*	—
dinero crediticio (Es)	Kreditgeld *n*	credit money	argent de crédit *m*	credito *m*	—
dinero de consunción (Es)	Schwundgeld *n*	scalage	argent de consomption *m*	bollatura di monete *f*	—
dinero de día a día (Es)	Tagesgeld *n*	day-to-day money	argent au jour le jour *m*	prestito giornaliero *m*	—
dinero de urgencia (Es)	Notgeld *n*	emergency money	monnaie obsidionale *f*	moneta d'emergenza *f*	—
dinero efectivo potencial (Es)	potentielles Bargeld *n*	potential cash	argent liquide potentiel *m*	contanti potenziali *m/pl*	—
dinero en caja (Es)	Kassenbestand *m*	cash in hand	montant des espèces en caisse *m*	consistenza di cassa *f*	—
dinero en el calcetín (Es)	Strumpfgeld *n*	hoarded notes and coins	argent gardé dans le bas de laine *m*	denaro tesaurizzato *m*	—
dinero en especie (Es)	Naturalgeld *n*	commodity money	argent en nature *m*	oggetto di baratto *m*	—
dinero en tránsito (Es)	durchlaufende Gelder *n/pl*	transmitted accounts	fonds en consignation *m/pl*	denaro d'ordine *m*	—
dinero exigible a la vista (Es)	Call-Geld *n*	call money	argent remboursable à vue *m*	prestito giornaliero *m*	—
dinero exógeno (Es)	exogenes Geld *n*	exogenous money base	argent exogène *m*	denaro esogeno *m*	—
dinero facultativo (Es)	fakultatives Geld *n*	facultative money	argent facultatif *m*	denaro facoltativo *m*	—
dinero fiduciario (Es)	fiduziäres Geld *n*	fiduciary funds	argent fiduciaire *m*	denaro fiduciario *m*	—
dinero inactivo (Es)	Spekulationskasse *f*	speculative balance	solde de spéculation *m*	domanda speculativa di moneta *f*	—
dinero legal (Es)	Zentralbankgeld *n*	central bank money	monnaie de banque centrale *f*	moneta creata dalla banca centrale *f*	—
dinero metálico (Es)	Hartgeld *n*	metallic currency	monnaie métallique *f*	moneta metallica *f*	—
dinero neutral (Es)	neutrales Geld *n*	neutral money	argent neutre *m*	moneta neutrale *f*	—
dinero-papel (Es)	Papiergeld *n*	paper money	monnaie de papier *f*	moneta cartacea *f*	—
dinero pupilar (Es)	Mündelgeld *n*	money held in trust for a ward	deniers de pupille *m/pl*	capitale del minore *m*	—
dipolio (Es)	Dyopol *n*	duopoly	duopole *m*	dipolio *m*	—
dipolio (I)	Dyopol *n*	duopoly	duopole *m*	—	dipolio *m*
dirección (Es)	Geschäftsleitung *f*	managerial staff	direction commerciale *f*	direzione *f*	—
dirección propia en caso necesario (Es)	Nostronotadresse *f*	nostro address in case of need	notre adresse au besoin *f*	indicazione al bisogno nostro *f*	—

	D	E	F	I	Es
direct debit authorization (E)	Einziehungs-ermächtigung f	—	mandat de prélève-ment automatique m	autorizzazione alla riscossione f	comisión de cobranza f
direct debiting (E)	Lastschrifteinzugs-verfahren n	—	système de prélèvement automatique m	incasso tramite addebitamento m	procedimiento de cobro en cuenta m
direct debiting (E)	Bankeinzugs-verfahren n	—	encaissements bancaires m/pl	procedimento d'incasso bancario m	cobranzas bancarias f/pl
direct debiting transactions (E)	Lastschriftverkehr m	—	prélèvements automatiques m/pl	addebiti m/pl	sistema de cargo en cuenta m
direct debit order (E)	Einziehungsauftrag m	—	ordre de recouvrement m	mandato di incasso m	autorización para el cobro f
direct debit procedure (E)	Abbuchungs-verfahren n	—	système de prélèvement automatique m	procedimento di addebito m	procedimiento de adeudo en cuenta m
direct discount (E)	Direktdiskont m	—	escompte direct m	sconto diretto m	descuento directo m
direct exchange (E)	Mengenkurs m	—	cours de change indirect m	corso certo per incerto m	precio por cantidad m
direct investments (E)	Direktinvestitionen f/pl	—	investissements directs m/pl	investimenti diretti m/pl	inversiones directas f/pl
direction commerciale (F)	Geschäftsleitung f	managerial staff	—	direzione f	dirección f
directives boursières européennes (F)	europäische Börsen-richtlinien f/pl	European stock exchange guide-lines	—	regolamenti europei di borsa m/pl	normas bursátiles europeas f/pl
directors' fees tax (E)	Aufsichtsratsteuer f	—	impôt sur les jetons de présence et les tantièmes m	imposta consiglio di vigilanza f	impuesto sobre la remuneración de los miembros del consejo de administración m
direct selling (E)	Direktverkauf m	—	vente directe au consommateur f	vendita diretta f	venta directa f
direct taxes (E)	direkte Steuer f	—	impôts directs m/pl	imposta diretta f	impuesto directo m
direct telex transfer system (E)	Blitzgiro m	—	virement transmis par le système de virements de télex direct m	bonifico telegrafico m	giro transmitido por el sistema de transferencia de télex directo m
diregolazione (I)	Deregulierung f	deregulation	déréglementation f	—	deregulación f
Direktdiskont (D)	—	direct discount	escompte direct m	sconto diretto m	descuento directo m
direkte Steuer (D)	—	direct taxes	impôts directs m/pl	imposta diretta f	impuesto directo m
Direktinvestitionen (D)	—	direct investments	investissements directs m/pl	investimenti diretti m/pl	inversiones directas f/pl
Direktverkauf (D)	—	direct selling	vente directe au consommateur f	vendita diretta f	venta directa f
direzione (I)	Geschäftsleitung f	managerial staff	direction commerciale f	—	dirección f
diritti d'assegnazione (I)	Zuteilungsrechte n/pl	allotment right	droits de répartition m/pl	—	derechos de acceso m/pl
diritti di deposito (I)	Depotgebühren f/pl	safe custody charges	frais de garde m/pl	—	derechos de custodia m/pl
diritti di prelievo (I)	Ziehungsrechte n/pl	drawing rights	droits de tirage m/pl	—	derechos de giro m/pl
diritti di proprietà (I)	Eigentumsrechte n/pl	property rights	droits de propriété m/pl	—	derechos de propiedad m/pl
diritto alla restituzione (I)	Herausgabean-spruch m	claim for return	prétention à restitution f	—	pretensión de entrega f
diritto commerciale (I)	Handelsrecht n	commercial law	droit commercial m	—	derecho comercial m
diritto della borsa (I)	Börsenrecht n	stock exchange rules	régime de bourse m	—	derecho de la bolsa m
diritto delle obbligazioni (I)	Schuldrecht n	law of obligations	droit des obligations et contrats m	—	derecho de obligaciones m
diritto delle società per azioni (I)	Aktienrecht n	company law	loi sur les sociétés anonymes f	—	derecho de socie-dades anónimas m
diritto d'enfiteusi (I)	Erbbaurecht n	hereditary building right	droit de superficie héréditaire m	—	derecho de superficie m
diritto di compensazione (I)	Ausgleichsrecht n	equalization right	droit à une compensation m	—	derecho a compensación m
diritto di credito (I)	Forderungsrecht n	right to claim	droit issu d'une créance m	—	derecho de crédito m

	D	E	F	I	Es
diritto di disporre (I)	Verfügungsrecht *n*	right of disposal	droit de disposition *m*	—	capacidad dispositiva *f*
diritto di dividendo cumulativo (I)	Nachbezugsrecht *n*	right to a cumulative dividend	droit à un dividende cumulatif *m*	—	derecho a un dividendo cumulativo *m*
diritto di godimento (I)	Genußrecht *n*	participation rights	droit de jouissance *m*	—	derecho de disfrute *m*
diritto di godimento (I)	Nutzungsrecht *n*	usufructury right	droit de jouissance *m*	—	derecho de uso *m*
diritto di pegno (I)	Pfandrecht *n*	lien	droit de gage *m*	—	derecho de prenda *m*
diritto di prelazione (I)	Aktienoption *f*	share stock option	option d'échanger des titres convertibles en actions *f*	—	opción de cambiar títulos convertibles en acciones *f*
diritto di prelazione (I)	Vorkaufsrecht *n*	preemption right	droit de préemption *m*	—	derecho de preferencia *m*
diritto di riservato dominio (I)	Eigentumsvorbehalt *m*	reservation of title	réserve de propriété *f*	—	reserva de propiedad *f*
diritto di voto (I)	Stimmrecht *n*	right to vote	droit de vote *m*	—	derecho a voto *m*
diritto di voto azioni in deposito (I)	Depotstimmrecht *n*	voting rights of nominee shareholders	droit de vote d'une banque dépositaire d'actions en compte courant *m*	—	derecho de voto de título en depósito *m*
diritto di voto bancario (I)	Bankenstimmrecht *n*	banks' voting rights	droit de vote de la banque *m*	—	derecho de voto del banco *m*
diritto di voto plurimo (I)	Mehrstimmrecht *n*	multiple voting right	droit de vote plural *m*	—	derecho de voto plural *m*
diritto d'opzione (I)	Optionsrecht *n*	option right	droit d'option *m*	—	derecho de opción *m*
diritto d'opzione (I)	Bezugsrecht *n*	subscription right	droit de souscription *m*	—	derecho de opción *f*
diritto d'uso (I)	Benutzungsrecht *n*	right to use	droit d'usage *m*	—	derecho de uso *m*
diritto principale (I)	Stammrecht *n*	customary law	droit habituel *m*	—	derecho habitual *m*
diritto speciale di prelievo (I)	Sonderziehungsrecht *n*	special drawing right	droit de tirage spécial *m*	—	derecho de giro especial *m*
disaggio (I)	Disagio *n*	disagio	disagio *m*	—	disagio *m*
disaggio (I)	Damnum *m*	debt discount	différence en moins *f*	—	disagio de préstamo *m*
Disagio (D)	—	disagio	disagio *m*	disaggio *m*	disagio *m*
disagio (E)	Disagio *n*	—	disagio *m*	disaggio *m*	disagio *m*
disagio (Es)	Disagio *n*	disagio	disagio *m*	disaggio *m*	—
disagio (F)	Disagio *n*	disagio	disagio *m*	disaggio *m*	disagio *m*
disagio de dividendo (Es)	Dividendenabschlag *m*	quotation ex dividend	cours moins le dividende *f*	ex dividendo *m*	disagio *m*
disagio de préstamo (Es)	Damnum *m*	debt discount	différence en moins *f*	disaggio *m*	
disagio de recompra (Es)	Rückkaufdisagio *n*	discount on repurchase	perte de rachat *f*	scarto di rimborso su obbligazione *m*	
disavanzo (I)	Fehlbetrag *m*	shortfall	déficit *m*	—	déficit *m*
disciplina degli assegni (I)	Scheckrecht *n*	negotiable instruments law concerning cheques	législation en matière de chèque *f*	—	derecho de cheque *m*
disciplina del mercato (I)	Marktordnung *f*	market organization	organisation du marché *f*	—	organización del mercado *f*
disclosed reserves (E)	offene Rücklagen *f/pl*	—	réserves déclarées *f/pl*	riserve dichiarate *f/pl*	reservas declaradas *f/pl*
discount (E)	eskomptieren	—	escompter	anticipare	descontar
discount (E)	Rabatt *m*	—	remise *f*	sconto *m*	rebaja *f*
discount (E)	Diskont *m*	—	escompte *m*	sconto *m*	descuento *m*
discount (E)	Deport *m*	—	déport *m*	deporto *m*	deport *m*
discount (E)	Skonto *n*	—	escompte *m*	sconto *m*	descuento *m*
discountable paper (E)	Diskontpapier *n*	—	titre escomptable *m*	titolo di sconto *m*	título de descuento *m*
discount bank (E)	Diskontbank *f*	—	banque d'escompte *f*	banca di sconto *f*	banco de descuento *m*
discount business (E)	Diskontgeschäft *n*	—	opération d'escompte *f*	operazione di sconto *m*	negocio de descuento *m*
discount calculation (E)	Diskontrechnung *f*	—	calcul de l'escompte *f*	calcolo di sconto *m*	cálculo de descuento *m*

	D	E	F	I	Es
discount commission (E)	Diskontprovision *f*	—	commission d'escompte *f*	provvigione di sconto *f*	comisión de descuento *f*
discount credit (E)	Diskontkredit *m*	—	crédit d'escompte *m*	credito di sconto *m*	crédito de descuento *m*
discount factor (E)	Diskontierungs-faktor *m*	—	facteur d'escompte *m*	fattore di sconto *m*	factor de descuento *m*
discount houses (E)	Diskonthäuser *n/pl*	—	établissements d'escompte *m/pl*	discount houses *m/pl*	casa de aceptación *f*
discount houses (I)	Diskonthäuser *n/pl*	discount houses	établissements d'escompte *m/pl*	—	casa de aceptación *f*
discounting (E)	Diskontierung *f*	—	escompte *m*	operazione di sconto *f*	descuento *m*
discounting (E)	Abzinsung *f*	—	déduction des intérêts non courus *f*	deduzione di interessi *f*	deducción de intereses no acumulados *f*
discount market (E)	Diskontmarkt *m*	—	marché de l'escompte *m*	mercato di sconto *m*	mercado de descuento *m*
discount of bills (E)	Wechseldiskont *m*	—	escompte d'un effet *m*	sconto cambiario *m*	descuento de letras *m*
discount on repurchase (E)	Rückkaufdisagio *n*	—	perte de rachat *f*	scarto di rimborso su obbligazione *m*	disagio de recompra *m*
discount rate (E)	Diskontsatz *m*	—	taux d'escompte *m*	saggio di sconto *m*	tipo de descuento *m*
disencumberment (E)	Entschuldung *f*	—	désendettement *m*	pagamento dei debiti *m*	desgravamen *m*
disguido di capitale (I)	Kapitalfehlleitung *f*	misguided investment	faux investissements *m/pl*	—	extravío de capital *m*
disinvestimento (I)	Desinvestition *f*	disinvestment	désinvestissement *m*	—	desinversión *f*
disinvestimento di capitale (I)	Kapitalfreisetzung *f*	liberation of capital	libération de capital *f*	—	liberación de capital *f*
disinvestment (E)	Desinvestition *f*	—	désinvestissement *m*	disinvestimento *m*	desinversión *f*
Diskont (D)	—	discount	escompte *m*	sconto *m*	descuento *m*
Diskontbank (D)	—	discount bank	banque d'escompte *f*	banca di sconto *f*	banco de descuento *m*
Diskonten (D)	—	bills discounted	effets escomptés *f/pl*	effetti nazionali *m/pl*	letras de cambio descontados *f/pl*
Diskontgeschäft (D)	—	discount business	opération d'escompte *f*	operazione di sconto *f*	negocio de descuento *m*
Diskonthäuser (D)	—	discount houses	établissements d'escompte *m/pl*	discount houses *m/pl*	casa de aceptación *f*
Diskontierung (D)	—	discounting	escompte *m*	operazione di sconto *f*	descuento *m*
Diskontierungs-faktor (D)	—	discount factor	facteur d'escompte *m*	fattore di sconto *m*	factor de descuento *m*
Diskontkredit (D)	—	discount credit	crédit d'escompte *m*	credito di sconto *m*	crédito de descuento *m*
Diskontmarkt (D)	—	discount market	marché de l'escompte *m*	mercato di sconto *m*	mercado de descuento *m*
Diskontpapier (D)	—	discountable paper	titre escomptable *m*	titolo di sconto *m*	título de descuento *m*
Diskontpolitik (D)	—	bank rate policy	politique d'escompte *f*	politica di sconto *f*	política de descuento *f*
Diskontprovision (D)	—	discount commission	commission d'escompte *f*	provvigione di sconto *f*	comisión de descuento *f*
Diskontrechnung (D)	—	discount calculation	calcul de l'escompte *f*	calcolo di sconto *m*	cálculo de descuento *m*
Diskontsatz (D)	—	discount rate	taux d'escompte *m*	saggio di sconto *m*	tipo de descuento *m*
disloyalty (E)	Untreue *f*	—	abus de confiance *m*	infedeltà *f*	infidelidad *f*
disoccupazione camuffata (I)	versteckte Arbeits-losigkeit *f*	hidden unemployment	chômage caché *m*	—	desempleo disfrazado *m*
disparité des niveaux d'intérêts (F)	Zinsgefälle *n*	margin between interest rates	—	differenza di interessi *f*	diferencial de intereses *m*
disponibilità (I)	Disposition *f*	arrangement	disposition *f*	—	disposición *f*
disponibilità di mezzi liquidi (I)	Finanzdecke *f*	available funds	fonds disponibles *m/pl*	—	previsión financiera *f*
disponibilità in valuta (I)	Devisenreserve *f*	foreign exchange reserves	réserve de devises *f*	—	reserva de divisas *f*
disponibilità in valuta estera (I)	Fremdwährungs-guthaben *n*	foreign currency balance	avoir en monnaie étrangère *m*	—	haberes de moneda extranjera *m/pl*

	D	E	F	I	Es
disponibilités (F)	Finanzvermögen *n*	financial assets	—	patrimonio finanziario *m*	patrimonio financiero *m*
disposable income (E)	verfügbares Einkommen *n*	—	revenu disponible *m*	reddito disponibile *f*	renta disponible *f*
disposable share (E)	Vorratsaktie *f*	—	action en réserve *f*	azione di riserva *f*	acción de provisión *f*
disposición (Es)	Disposition *f*	arrangement	disposition *f*	disponibilità *f*	—
disposición (Es)	Verfügung *f*	disposition	disposition *f*	disposizione *f*	—
disposición del derecho de suscripción (Es)	Bezugsrechtsdisposition *f*	subscription rights disposition	disposition des droits de souscription *f*	esercizio del diritto d'opzione *m*	—
disposición excepcional (Es)	Ausnahmeregelung *f*	provision	mesure dérogatoire *f*	regolamento d'eccezione *m*	—
disposición financiera (Es)	Finanzdisposition *f*	financial arrangement	disposition financière *f*	disposizioni finanziarie *f/pl*	—
disposición monetaria (Es)	Gelddisposition *f*	monetary arrangement	disposition monétaire *f*	disposizione di moneta *f*	—
Disposition (D)	—	arrangement	disposition *f*	disponibilità *f*	disposición *f*
disposition (E)	Verfügung *f*	—	disposition *f*	disposizione *f*	disposición *f*
disposition (F)	Disposition *f*	arrangement	—	disponibilità *f*	disposición *f*
disposition (F)	Verfügung *f*	disposition	—	disposizione *f*	disposición *f*
disposition des droits de souscription (F)	Bezugsrechtsdisposition *f*	subscription rights disposition	—	esercizio del diritto d'opzione *m*	disposición del derecho de suscripción *f*
disposition financière (F)	Finanzdisposition *f*	financial arrangement	—	disposizioni finanziarie *f/pl*	disposición financiera *f*
disposition monétaire (F)	Gelddisposition *f*	monetary arrangement	—	disposizione di moneta *f*	disposición monetaria *f*
Dispositionsfonds (D)	—	reserve funds	fonds de réserves *m/pl*	fondi segreti *m/pl*	fondo disponible *m*
Dispositionsschein (D)	—	banker's note	reconnaissance bancaire *f*	certificato di disponibilità *m*	fianza de disposición de banquero *f*
disposizione (I)	Verfügung *f*	disposition	disposition *f*	—	disposición *f*
disposizione di moneta (I)	Gelddisposition *f*	monetary arrangement	disposition monétaire *f*	—	disposición monetaria *f*
disposizioni d'investimento (I)	Anlagevorschriften *f/pl*	rules for investment of resources	prescriptions d'investissement *f/pl*	—	normas de inversión *f/pl*
disposizioni finanziarie (I)	Finanzdisposition *f*	financial arrangement	disposition financière *f*	—	disposición financiera *f*
dissaving (E)	Entsparen *n*	—	épargne négative *f*	diminuzione dei risparmi accumulati *f*	ahorro negativo *m*
distinta di deposito (I)	Depotaufstellung *f*	list of securities deposited	liste des valeurs déposées *f*	—	lista de depósito *f*
distraction (F)	Aussonderung *f*	separation of property belonging to a third party from the bankrupt's estate	—	separazione *f*	tercería de dominio *f*
distribanque (F)	Geldautomat *m*	cash dispenser	—	bancomat *m*	cajero automático *m*
distribución de la renta (Es)	Einkommensverteilung *f*	distribution of income	distribution du revenu *f*	distribuzione dei redditi *f*	—
distribución exclusiva (Es)	Alleinvertrieb *m*	sole distribution	distribution exclusive *f*	esclusiva *f*	—
distribución oculta (Es)	verdeckte Gewinnausschüttung *f*	hidden profit distribution	distribution occulte de bénéfices *f*	partecipazione agli utili velata *f*	—
distribution de bénéfices (F)	Gewinnausschüttung *f*	distribution of profit	—	ripartizione degli utili *f*	reparto de beneficios *m*
distribution du revenu (F)	Einkommensverteilung *f*	distribution of income	—	distribuzione dei redditi *f*	distribución de la renta *f*
distribution empirique exclusive (F)	Alleinvertrieb *m*	sole distribution	—	esclusiva *f*	distribución exclusiva *f*
distribution occulte de bénéfices (F)	verdeckte Gewinnausschüttung *f*	hidden profit distribution	—	partecipazione agli utili velata *f*	distribución oculta *f*
distribution of income (E)	Einkommensverteilung *f*	—	distribution du revenu *f*	distribuzione dei redditi *f*	distribución de la renta *f*

	D	E	F	I	Es
distribution of profit (E)	Gewinnausschüttung *f*	—	distribution de bénéfices *f*	ripartizione degli utili *f*	reparto de beneficios *m*
distribuzione dei redditi (I)	Einkommensverteilung *f*	distribution of income	distribution du revenu *f*	—	distribución de la renta *f*
distribuzione straordinaria (I)	Sonderausschüttung *f*	extra dividend	répartition extraordinaire *f*	—	reparto extraordinario *m*
distruzione di denaro (I)	Geldvernichtung *f*	reduction of the volume of money	destruction d'argent *f*	—	destrucción de dinero *f*
diversified holdings (E)	Streubesitz *m*	—	propriété disséminée *f*	capitali ripartiti *m/pl*	propiedad dispersa *f*
dividend (E)	Dividende *f*	—	dividende *m*	dividendo *m*	dividendo *m*
dividend coupon (E)	Gewinnanteilsschein *m*	—	coupon de dividende *m*	cedola *f*	cupón *m*
Dividende (D)	—	dividend	dividende *m*	dividendo *m*	dividendo *m*
dividende (F)	Dividende *f*	dividend	—	dividendo *m*	dividendo *m*
dividende brut (F)	Brutto-Dividende *f*	gross dividend	—	dividendo lordo *m*	dividendo bruto *m*
dividende cumulé (F)	kumulative Dividende *f*	cumulative dividend	—	dividendo cumulativo *m*	dividendo acumulativo *m*
dividende distribué sous forme de titres (F)	Stockdividende *f*	stock dividend	—	dividendo in azioni *m*	dividendo por acciones *m*
dividende final (F)	Schlußdividende *f*	final dividend	—	saldo di dividendo *m*	dividendo final *m*
dividende limité (F)	limitierte Dividende *f*	limited dividend	—	dividendo limitato *m*	dividendo limitado *m*
Dividendenabgabe (D)	—	dividend tax	impôt sur les dividendes *m*	imposta sui dividendi *f*	impuesto sobre dividendos *m*
Dividendenabschlag (D)	—	quotation ex dividend	cours moins le dividende *f*	ex dividendo *m*	disagio de dividendo *m*
dividende net (F)	Netto-Dividende *f*	net dividend	—	dividendo netto *m*	dividendo neto *m*
Dividendengarantie (D)	—	dividend guarantee	garantie de distribution d'un dividende *f*	dividendo garantito *m*	garantía de dividendos *f*
dividende payé en espèces (F)	Bardividende *f*	cash dividend	—	dividendo in contanti *m*	dividendo en efectivo *m*
dividende prioritaire (F)	Vorzugsdividende *f*	preferential dividend	—	dividendo privilegiato *m*	dividendo preferente *m*
dividend guarantee (E)	Dividendengarantie *f*	—	garantie de distribution d'un dividende *f*	dividendo garantito *m*	garantía de dividendos *f*
dividend in bankruptcy (E)	Konkursquote *f*	—	pour-cent accordé aux créanciers dans la masse *m*	quota di riparto *f*	cuota del activo de la quiebra *f*
dividendo (Es)	Dividende *f*	dividend	dividende *m*	dividendo *m*	—
dividendo (I)	Bonus *m*	extra dividend	bonification *f*	—	bono *m*
dividendo (I)	Dividende *f*	dividend	dividende *m*	—	dividendo *m*
dividendo a cuenta (Es)	Abschlagsdividende *f*	dividend on account	acompte sur dividende *m*	acconto dividendo *m*	—
dividendo acumulativo (Es)	kumulative Dividende *f*	cumulative dividend	dividende cumulé *m*	dividendo cumulativo *m*	—
dividendo addizionale (I)	Überdividende *f*	super-dividend	superdividende *m*	—	dividendo adicional *m*
dividendo adicional (Es)	Überdividende *f*	super-dividend	superdividende *m*	dividendo addizionale *m*	—
dividendo bruto (Es)	Brutto-Dividende *f*	gross dividend	dividende brut *m*	dividendo lordo *m*	—
dividendo cumulativo (I)	Nachdividende *f*	dividend payable for previous years	droit aux dividendes des années précédentes *m*	—	derecho de dividendo de años precedentes *m*
dividendo cumulativo (I)	kumulative Dividende *f*	cumulative dividend	dividende cumulé *m*	—	dividendo acumulativo *m*
dividendo en efectivo (Es)	Bardividende *f*	cash dividend	dividende payé en espèces *m*	dividendo in contanti *m*	—
dividendo final (Es)	Schlußdividende *f*	final dividend	dividende final *m*	saldo di dividendo *m*	—
dividendo garantito (I)	Dividendengarantie *f*	dividend guarantee	garantie de distribution d'un dividende *f*	—	garantía de dividendos *f*
dividendo in azioni (I)	Stockdividende *f*	stock dividend	dividende distribué sous forme de titres *m*	—	dividendo por acciones *m*

	D	E	F	I	Es
dividendo in contanti (I)	Bardividende *f*	cash dividend	dividende payé en espèces *m*	—	dividendo en efectivo *m*
dividendo limitado (Es)	limitierte Dividende *f*	limited dividend	dividende limité *m*	dividendo limitato *m*	—
dividendo limitato (I)	limitierte Dividende *f*	limited dividend	dividende limité *m*	—	dividendo limitado *m*
dividendo lordo (I)	Brutto-Dividende *f*	gross dividend	dividende brut *m*	—	dividendo bruto *m*
dividend on account (E)	Abschlagsdividende *f*	—	acompte sur dividende *m*	acconto dividendo *m*	dividendo a cuenta *m*
dividendo neto (Es)	Netto-Dividende *f*	net dividend	dividende net *m*	dividendo netto *m*	—
dividendo netto (I)	Netto-Dividende *f*	net dividend	dividende net *m*	—	dividendo neto *m*
dividendo por acciones (Es)	Stockdividende *f*	stock dividend	dividende distribué sous forme de titres *m*	dividendo in azioni *m*	—
dividendo preferente (Es)	Vorzugsdividende *f*	preferential dividend	dividende prioritaire *m*	dividendo privilegiato *m*	—
dividendo privilegiato (I)	Vorzugsdividende *f*	preferential dividend	dividende prioritaire *m*	—	dividendo preferente *m*
dividend payable for previous years (E)	Nachdividende *f*	—	droit aux dividendes des années précédentes *m*	dividendo cumulativo *m*	derecho de dividendo de años precedentes *m*
dividend tax (E)	Dividendenabgabe *f*	—	impôt sur les dividendes *m*	imposta sui dividendi *f*	impuesto sobre dividendos *m*
divieto (I)	Verbot *n*	prohibition	prohibition *f*	—	prohibición *f*
divieto del cumulo delle agevolazioni (I)	Kumulierungsverbot *n*	rule against accumulation	prohibition de cumuler *f*	—	prohibición de acumulación *f*
divieto di accensione di credito (I)	Kreditaufnahmeverbot *n*	prohibition of raising of credits	prohibition d'emprunt *f*	—	prohibición de apelación al crédito *f*
divieto di cessione (I)	Abtretungsverbot *n*	prohibition of assignment	défense de cession *f*	—	prohibición de cesión *f*
divieto d'investimento (I)	Investitionsverbot *n*	prohibition of investment	prohibition d'investissement *f*	—	prohibición de inversión *f*
divisa a contanti (I)	Kassadevisen *f/pl*	spot exchange	devises négociées en bourse au comptant *f/pl*	—	divisas al contado *f/pl*
divisa circolante aurea (I)	Goldumlaufswährung *f*	gold specie standard	monnaie or *f*	—	moneda de oro en circulación *f*
divisas (Es)	Devisen *f/pl*	currency	devises *f/pl*	valuta estera *f*	—
divisas al contado (Es)	Kassadevisen *f/pl*	spot exchange	devises négociées en bourse au comptant *f/pl*	divisa a contanti *f*	—
divisas a plazo (Es)	Termindevisen *f/pl*	exchange for forward delivery	devises négociées en bourse à terme *f/pl*	divise a termine *f/pl*	—
divisas cubiertas por el banco emisor (Es)	deckungsfähige Devisen *f/pl*	foreign currencies eligible as cover	devises aptes à servir de couverture *f/pl*	valute pregiate *f/pl*	—
divisas obtenidas mediante la exportación (Es)	Exportdevisen *f/pl*	export exchange	devises obtenues par l'exportation *f/pl*	valuta estera da esportazioni *f*	—
divise a termine (I)	Termindevisen *f/pl*	exchange for forward delivery	devises négociées en bourse à terme *f/pl*	—	divisas a plazo *f/pl*
divisional coin (E)	Scheidemünze *f*	—	monnaie divisionnaire *f*	moneta divisionale *f*	moneda fraccionaria *f*
doble imposición (Es)	Doppelbesteuerung *f*	double taxation	double imposition *f*	doppia imposizione *f*	—
documenti di legittimazione (I)	Legitimationspapiere *n/pl*	title-evidencing instrument	titre nominatif *m*	—	títulos de legitimación *m/pl*
document justificatif (F)	Beleg *m*	receipt	—	ricevuta *f*	justificante *m*
documento bancario (Es)	Bankausweis *m*	bank return	situation de banque *f*	bollettino bancario *m*	—
documento comercial (Es)	Geschäftspapier *n*	commercial papers	papier d'affaires *m*	carta intestata *f*	—
documento contabile (I)	Buchungsbeleg *m*	accounting voucher	pièce comptable *f*	—	comprobante de asiento *m*
documento de opción (Es)	Optionsschein *m*	share purchase	coupon d'option *m* warrant	warrant *m*	—

	D	E	F	I	Es
documento de una operación con prima (Es)	Prämienbrief *m*	option contract	contrat de marché à primes *m*	contratto a premio *m*	—
document of title (E)	Warenpapier *n*	—	effet de commerce *m*	titolo rappresentativo di merci *m*	valor comercial *m*
documento mercantil (Es)	Commercial Paper *n*	commercial paper	effet de commerce *m*	commercial paper *m*	—
documentos comerciales (Es)	Handelspapiere *n/pl*	commercial papers	effets de commerce *m/pl*	effetti commerciali *m/pl*	—
doit (F)	Soll *n*	debit	—	debito *m*	débito *m*
Dokumententratte (D)	—	acceptance bill	traite documentaire *f*	tratta documentaria *f*	letra documentaria *f*
dólar verde (Es)	grüner Dollar *m*	green dollar	dollar vert *m*	dollaro verde *m*	—
Dollaranleihe (D)	—	dollar bond	emprunt en dollars *m*	prestito in dollari *m*	empréstito en dólares *m*
dollar area (E)	Dollarblock *m*	—	bloc dollar *m*	area del dollaro *f*	zona del dólar *f*
Dollarblock (D)	—	dollar area	bloc dollar *m*	area del dollaro *f*	zona del dólar *f*
dollar bond (E)	Dollaranleihe *f*	—	emprunt en dollars *m*	prestito in dollari *m*	empréstito en dólares *m*
dollaro verde (I)	grüner Dollar *m*	green dollar	dollar vert *m*	—	dólar verde *m*
Dollar-Standard (D)	—	dollar standard	étalon dollar *m*	dollar standard *m*	patrón-dólar *m*
dollar standard (E)	Dollar-Standard *m*	—	étalon dollar *m*	dollar standard *m*	patrón-dólar *m*
dollar standard (I)	Dollar-Standard *m*	dollar standard	étalon dollar *m*	—	patrón-dólar *m*
dollar vert (F)	grüner Dollar *m*	green dollar	—	dollaro verde *m*	dólar verde *m*
domanda (I)	Nachfrage *f*	demand	demande *f*	—	demanda *f*
domanda aggregata effettiva (I)	Endnachfrage *f*	final demand	demande finale *f*	—	demanda final *f*
domanda di moneta per transazioni (I)	Transaktionskasse *f*	transaction balance	solde des transactions *m*	—	caja de transacción *f*
domanda monetaria (I)	Geldnachfrage *f*	money demand	demande d'argent *f*	—	demanda monetaria *f*
domanda parzialmente insoddisfatta (I)	bezahlt Geld	more buyers than sellers	comptant acheteur	—	compra limitada *f*
domanda precauzionale di moneta (I)	Vorsichtskasse *f*	precautionary holding	fonds de réserve *m/pl*	—	existencias de precaución *f/pl*
domanda speculativa di moneta (I)	Spekulationskasse *f*	speculative balance	solde de spéculation *m*	—	dinero inactivo *m*
domestic capital (E)	Inlandsvermögen *n*	—	capital déclaré dans le pays où l'assujetti à sa résidence *m*	capitale nazionale *m*	patrimonio interno *m*
domestic market (E)	Binnenmarkt *m*	—	marché national *m*	mercato interno *m*	mercado interior *m*
dommages-intérêts (F)	Schadensersatz *m*	compensation for loss suffered	—	risarcimento dei danni *m*	indemnización por daños y perjuicios *f*
dopolistino (I)	Nachbörse *f*	after-hours dealing	après-Bourse *f*	—	operaciones después del cierre de la bolsa *f/pl*
Doppelbesteuerung (D)	—	double taxation	double imposition *f*	doppia imposizione *f*	doble imposición *f*
doppelte Buchführung (D)	—	double entry bookkeeping	comptabilité en partie double *f*	partita doppia *f*	contabilidad de partida doble *f*
Doppelwährung (D)	—	double currency	double étalon *m*	bimetallismo *m*	moneda doble *f*
Doppelwährungsanleihe (D)	—	double currency loan	emprunt à double étalon *m*	credito bimonetario *m*	empréstito de moneda dual *m*
doppia imposizione (I)	Doppelbesteuerung *f*	double taxation	double imposition *f*	—	doble imposición *f*
dormant deposit (E)	totes Depot *n*	—	compte de choses *m*	deposito inattivo *m*	depósito muerto *m*
dormant partnership (E)	stille Gesellschaft *f*	—	association commerciale en participation *f*	società di diritto *f*	sociedad en participación *f*
dossier de crédit (F)	Kreditakte *f*	credit folder	—	cartella di credito *f*	expediente de crédito *m*
dotación (Es)	Dotation *f*	endowment	dotation *f*	dotazione *f*	—
dotación (Es)	Kostendeckung *f*	cost recovery	couverture des coûts *f*	copertura delle spese *f*	—
Dotation (D)	—	endowment	dotation *f*	dotazione *f*	dotación *f*

	D	E	F	I	Es
dotation (F)	Dotation f	endowment	—	dotazione f	dotación f
dotation initiale (F)	Erstausstattung f	initial allowance set	—	dotazione iniziale f	primer establecimiento m
Dotationskapital (D)	—	endowment funds	capital-apport m	capitale di dotazione m	capital de dotación m
dotazione (I)	Dotation f	endowment	dotation f	—	dotación f
dotazione iniziale (I)	Erstausstattung f	initial allowance set	dotation initiale f	—	primer establecimiento m
double currency (E)	Doppelwährung f	—	double étalon m	bimetallismo m	moneda doble f
double currency loan (E)	Doppelwährungs-anleihe f	—	emprunt à double étalon m	credito bimonetario m	empréstito de moneda dual m
double entry bookkeeping (E)	doppelte Buch-führung f	—	comptabilité en partie double f	partita doppia f	contabilidad de partida doble f
double étalon (F)	Doppelwährung f	double currency	—	bimetallismo m	moneda doble f
double imposition (F)	Doppelbesteuerung f	double taxation	—	doppia imposizione f	doble imposición f
double option operation (E)	Stellagegeschäft n	—	marché à double option m	contratto stellage m	operación de doble prima f
double taxation (E)	Doppelbesteuerung f	—	double imposition f	doppia imposizione f	doble imposición f
doubtful debts (E)	dubiose Forderung f	—	créance douteuse f	credito controverso m	crédito dudoso m
down payment (E)	Abschlagszahlung f	—	acompte m	acconto m	pago a cuenta m
draft (E)	Tratte f	—	traite f	tratta f	letra girada f
drawee (E)	Trassat n	—	tiré m	trattario m	girado m
drawee (E)	Bezogener m	—	tiré m	trattario m	librado m
drawer (E)	Trassant m	—	tireur m	traente m	girador m
drawer of a bill (E)	Wechselaussteller m	—	tireur d'une traite m	traente di una cambiale m	librador m
drawing (E)	Trassierung f	—	tirage m	traenza f	giro m
drawing (E)	Ziehung f	—	tirage m	estrazione f	giro m
drawing rights (E)	Ziehungsrechte n/pl	—	droits de tirage m/pl	diritti di prelievo m/pl	derechos de giro m/pl
drawing up of a budget (E)	Budgetierung f	—	établissement du budget m	formazione del bilancio pubblico m	establecimiento del presupuesto m
drawn bill (E)	gezogener Wechsel m	—	traite tirée f	cambiale tratta f	letra girada f
Dreiecksarbitrage (D)	—	triangular arbitrage	arbitrage triangulaire m	arbitraggio triangolare m	arbitraje triangular m
Dreimonatsgeld (D)	—	three months' money	dépôts à trois mois m/pl	prestito a tre mesi m	imposición a un plazo de 3 meses m
Drittpfändung (D)	—	garnishee proceedings	saisie de tiers débiteurs f	subpegno di titoli m	embargo del tercer deudor m
Drittschuldner (D)	—	third-party debtor	tiers débiteur m	terzo debitore m	tercer deudor m
droit à un dividende cumulatif (F)	Nachbezugsrecht n	right to a cumulative dividend	—	diritto di dividendo cumulativo m	derecho a un divi-dendo cumulativo m
droit à une compensation (F)	Ausgleichsrecht n	equalization right	—	diritto di compensazione m	derecho a compensación m
droit à une indemnité compensatoire (F)	Ausgleichsforderung f	equalization claim	—	credito di compensazione m	reclamación de indemnización contra la administración pública f
droit aux dividendes des années précédentes (F)	Nachdividende f	dividend payable for previous years	—	dividendo cumulativo m	derecho de dividendo de años precedentes m
droit commercial (F)	Handelsrecht n	commercial law	—	diritto commerciale m	derecho comercial m
droit d'achat (F)	Ankaufsrecht n	purchase right	—	opzione f	derecho de compra m
droit de disposition (F)	Verfügungsrecht n	right of disposal	—	diritto di disporre m	capacidad dispositiva f
droit de douane (F)	Zoll m	customs duty	—	dazio m	aduana f
droit de gage (F)	Pfandrecht n	lien	—	diritto di pegno m	derecho de prenda m
droit de jouissance (F)	Genußrecht n	participation rights	—	diritto di godimento m	derecho de disfrute m
droit de jouissance (F)	Nutzungsrecht n	usufructury right	—	diritto di godimento m	derecho de uso m
droit de préemption (F)	Vorkaufsrecht n	preemption right	—	diritto di prelazione m	derecho de preferencia m
droit des obligations et contrats (F)	Schuldrecht n	law of obligations	—	diritto delle obbligazioni m	derecho de obligaciones m

	D	E	F	I	Es
droit de souscription (F)	Bezugsrecht n	subscription right	—	diritto d'opzione m	derecho de opción f
droit de superficie héréditaire (F)	Erbbaurecht n	hereditary building right	—	diritto d'enfiteusi m	derecho de superficie m
droit de timbre (F)	Stempelsteuer f	stamp duty	—	imposta di bollo f	impuesto del timbre m
droit de tirage spécial (F)	Sonderziehungsrecht n	special drawing right	—	diritto speciale di prelievo m	derecho de giro especial m
droit de vote (F)	Stimmrecht n	right to vote	—	diritto di voto m	derecho a voto m
droit de vote de la banque (F)	Bankenstimmrecht n	banks' voting rights	—	diritto di voto bancario m	derecho de voto del banco m
droit de vote d'une banque dépositaire d'actions en compte courant (F)	Depotstimmrecht n	voting rights of nominee shareholders	—	diritto di voto azioni in deposito m	derecho de voto de título en depósito m
droit de vote maximum (F)	Höchststimmrecht n	maximum voting right	—	valore massimo di voto m	límite máximo de votos m
droit de vote plural (F)	Mehrstimmrecht n	multiple voting right	—	diritto di voto plurimo m	derecho de voto plural m
droit d'option (F)	Optionsrecht n	option right	—	diritto d'opzione m	derecho de opción m
droit d'usage (F)	Benutzungsrecht n	right to use	—	diritto d'uso m	derecho de uso m
droit habituel (F)	Stammrecht n	customary law	—	diritto principale m	derecho habitual m
droit issu d'une créance (F)	Forderungsrecht n	right to claim	—	diritto di credito m	derecho de crédito m
droits de propriété (F)	Eigentumsrechte n/pl	property rights	—	diritti di proprietà m/pl	derechos de propiedad m/pl
drnits de répartition (F)	Zuteilungsrechte n/pl	allotment right	—	dirittl d'assegnazione m/pl	derechos de acceso m/pl
droits de tirage (F)	Ziehungsrechte n/pl	drawing rights	—	diritti di prelievo m/pl	derechos de giro m/pl
droits partiels (F)	Teilrechte n/pl	partial rights	—	buono frazionario m	derechos de partición m/pl
dualidad (Es)	Dualität f	duality	dualité f	dualità f	—
dualità (I)	Dualität f	duality	dualité f	—	dualidad
Dualität (D)	—	duality	dualité f	dualità f	dualidad
dualité (F)	Dualität f	duality	—	dualità f	dualidad
duality (E)	Dualität f	—	dualité f	dualità f	dualidad
dubiose Forderung (D)	—	doubtful debts	créance douteuse f	credito controverso m	crédito dudoso m
ducroire (F)	Delkredere n	reserve for bad debts	—	star del credere m	delcrédere m
ducroire forfaitaire (F)	Pauschaldelkredere n	global delcredere	—	star del credere forfettario	del credere global m
dumping di valuta (I)	Währungsdumping n	currency dumping	dumping du change m	—	dumping monetario m
dumping du change (F)	Währungsdumping n	currency dumping	—	dumping di valuta m	dumping monetario m
dumping monetario (Es)	Währungsdumping n	currency dumping	dumping du change m	dumping di valuta m	—
duopole (F)	Dyopol n	duopoly	—	dipolio m	dipolio m
duopoly (E)	Dyopol n	—	duopole m	dipolio m	dipolio m
duración (Es)	Duration f	duration	durée f	duration f	—
durata di godimento (I)	Nutzungsdauer f	service life	durée normale d'utilisation f	—	tiempo de utilización m
Duration (D)	—	duration	durée f	duration f	duración f
duration (E)	Duration f	—	durée f	duration f	duración f
duration (I)	Duration f	duration	durée f	—	duración f
duration of capital tie-up (E)	Kapitalbindungsdauer f	—	durée de l'immobilisation de capitaux f	vincolo del capitale m	plazo de vinculación de capital m
durchlaufende Gelder (D)	—	transmitted accounts	fonds en consignation m/pl	denaro d'ordine m	dinero en tránsito m
durchlaufende Kredite (D)	—	transmitted loans	crédits en consignation m/pl	crediti indiretti m/pl	crédito transitorio m
Durchschnittsertrag (D)	—	average yield	rendement moyen m	reddito medio m	rendimiento medio m

	D	E	F	I	Es
Durchschnittspreis (D)	—	average price	prix moyen *m*	prezzo medio *m*	precio medio *m*
Durchschnittssatz (D)	—	average rate	taux moyen *m*	tasso medio *m*	tasa media *f*
Durchschnittsvaluta (D)	—	average value date	datation moyenne de la valeur en compte *f*	valuta media *f*	cambio medio *m*
durée (F)	Duration *f*	duration	—	duration *f*	duración *f*
durée de l'immobilisation de capitaux (F)	Kapitalbindungs- dauer *f*	duration of capital tie-up	—	vincolo del capitale *m*	plazo de vinculación de capital *m*
durée normale d'utilisation (F)	Nutzungsdauer *f*	service life	—	durata di godimento *f*	tiempo de utilización *m*
duty of notification (E)	Benachrichtigungs- pflicht *f*	—	obligation de notification *f*	obbligo d'avviso *m*	obligación de aviso *f*
duty to disclose one's financial conditions (E)	Offenlegungspflicht *f*	—	obligation d'réveler les derniers bilans du postulant d'un prêt *f*	obbligo di rendere pubblico *m*	obligación de declarar *f*
duty to obtain a permit (E)	Genehmigungs- pflicht *f*	—	obligation de solliciter une permission *f*	obbligo d'auto- rizzazione *m*	régimen de autorización *m*
Dyopol (D)	—	duopoly	duopole *m*	dipolio *m*	dipolio *m*
earned income (E)	Arbeitseinkommen *n*	—	revenu du travail *m*	reddito di lavoro *m*	ingresos del trabajo *m/pl*
earnings (E)	Einkünfte *pl*	—	revenus *m/pl*	entrate *f/pl*	rentas *f/pl*
earnings retention (E)	Gewinnthesaurierung *f*	—	rétention de bénéfices *f*	tesaurizzazione degli utili *f*	retención de beneficios *f*
écart de cours (F)	Kursspanne *f*	difference between purchase and hedging price	—	margine di cambio *m*	margen de cotización *m*
eccedenza da liquidazione (I)	Liquidation- überschuß *m*	realization profit	excédent de liquidation *m*	—	exceso de liquidación *m*
eccedenza degli interessi (I)	Zinsüberschuß *m*	interest surplus	excédent d'intérèts *m*	—	excedente de interés *m*
eccedenza delle esportazioni (I)	Ausfuhrüberschuß *m*	export surplus	excédent d'exportation *m*	—	excedente de exportación *m*
eccedenza di valuta estera (I)	Devisenüberschuß *m*	foreign exchange surplus	excédent de devises *m*	—	excedente de divisas *m*
eccedenza finanziaria (I)	Geldüberhang *m*	excessive supply of money	excédent des moyens de payement *m*	—	exceso de dinero *m*
eccezione di dolo (I)	Einrede der Arglist *f*	defence of fraud	exception du dol *f*	—	excepción de dolo *f*
échange d'acceptations (F)	Akzeptaustausch *m*	exchange of acceptances	—	scambio di accettazioni *m*	intercambio de acceptaciones *m*
échange d'actions (F)	Aktienumtausch *m*	exchange of share certificates for new ones	—	cambio di azioni *m*	cambio de acciones *m*
échange d'actions (F)	Aktienaustausch *m*	exchange of shares	—	scambio di azioni *m*	canje de acciones *m*
échéance (F)	Fälligkeit *f*	maturity	—	scadenza *f*	vencimiento *m*
échéance à moyen terme (F)	mittlere Verfallszeit *f*	mean due date	—	scadenza media *f*	vencimiento a medio plazo *m*
échéance longue (F)	lange Sicht *f*	long run	—	a lunga scadenza	a largo plazo
echtes Factoring (D)	—	clean factoring	factoring authentique *m*	factoring pro soluto *m*	factoring auténtico *m*
Eckzins (D)	—	basic rate of interest	taux d'intérêt de base *m*	interesse di riferimento *m*	tipo base *m*
economía colectiva (Es)	Gemeinwirtschaft *f*	sociai economy	économie sociale *f*	economia collettiva *f*	—
economia collettiva (I)	Gemeinwirtschaft *f*	social economy	économie sociale *f*	—	economía colectiva *f*
economía de mercado (Es)	Marktwirtschaft *f*	market economy	économie de marché *f*	economia di mercato *f*	—
economia di mercato (I)	Marktwirtschaft *f*	market economy	économie de marché *f*	—	economía de mercado *m*
economía exterior (Es)	Außenwirtschaft *f*	foreign trade and payments	économie des échanges extérieurs *f*	commercio estero *m*	—
economía financiera (Es)	Geldwirtschaft *f*	money economy	économie monétaire *f*	economia monetaria *f*	—
economia monetaria (I)	Geldwirtschaft *f*	money economy	économie monétaire *f*	—	economía financiera *f*

	D	E	F	I	Es
economía nacional (Es)	Volkswirtschaft f	national economy	économie nationale f	economia politica f	—
economía pianificata (I)	Planwirtschaft f	planned economy	économie planifiée f	—	economía planificada f
economía planificada (Es)	Planwirtschaft f	planned economy	économie planifiée f	economia pianificata f	—
economia politica (I)	Volkswirtschaft f	national economy	économie nationale f	—	economía nacional f
economia politica (I)	Volkswirtschaftslehre f	economics	économie politique f	—	ciencias económicas f/pl
economic circulation (E)	Wirtschaftskreislauf m	—	circuit économique m	circuito economico m	circuito económico m
economic crisis (E)	Wirtschaftskrise f	—	crise économique f	crisi economica f	crisis económica f
economic miracle (E)	Wirtschaftswunder n	—	miracle économique m	miracolo economico m	milagro económico m
economic order (E)	Wirtschaftsordnung f	—	ordre économique m	ordinamento economico m	orden económico m
economic plan (E)	Wirtschaftsplan m	—	plan économique m	piano economico m	plan económico m
economic policy (E)	Wirtschaftspolitik f	—	politique économique f	politica economica f	política económica f
economics (E)	Volkswirtschaftslehre f	—	économie politique f	economia politica f	ciencias económicas f/pl
économie de marché (F)	Marktwirtschaft f	market economy	—	economia di mercato f	economía de mercado f
économie des échanges extérieurs (F)	Außenwirtschaft f	foreign trade and payments	—	commercio estero m	economía exterior f
économie monétaire (F)	Geldwirtschaft f	money economy	—	economia monetaria f	economía financiera f
économie nationale (F)	Volkswirtschaft f	national economy	—	economia politica f	economía nacional f
économie planifiée (F)	Planwirtschaft f	planned economy	—	economia pianificata f	economía planificada f
économie politique (F)	Volkswirtschaftslehre f	economics	—	economia politica f	ciencias económicas f/pl
économie sociale (F)	Gemeinwirtschaft f	social economy	—	economia collettiva f	economía colectiva f
économiser (F)	sparen	saving	—	risparmiare	ahorrar
economist (E)	Volkswirt m	—	économiste m	esperto di economia politica m	economista m
economista (Es)	Volkswirt m	economist	économiste m	esperto di economia politica m	—
économiste (F)	Volkswirt m	economist	—	esperto di economia politica m	economista m
écriture de contre-passation (F)	Storno n	counter entry	—	storno m	cancelación f
écritures entre postes de passif (F)	Passivtausch m	accounting exchange on the liabilities side	—	rettifica del passivo f	cambio de asientos en el pasivo m
ecuación cuantitativa (Es)	Quantitätsgleichung f	quantity equation	équation quantitative f	equazione degli scambi f	—
Edelmetalle (D)	—	precious metal	métaux précieux m/pl	metalli pregiati m/pl	metales preciosos m/pl
Edelmetallgeschäft (D)	—	bullion trade	opérations de métaux précieux f/pl	operazione in metalli pregiati f	operaciones de metales preciosos f/pl
efectivo (Es)	Bargeld n	ready money	argent comptant m	denaro contante m	—
efecto a cobrar (Es)	Besitzwechsel m	bills receivable	effet à recevoir m	cambiale attiva f	—
efecto a pagar (Es)	Schuldwechsel m	bill payable	effet à payer m	cambiale passiva f	—
efecto bandwaggon (Es)	Bandwaggon-Effekt m	bandwaggon effect	effet bandwaggon m	effetto bandwaggon m	—
efecto cambial en depósito (Es)	Depotwechsel m	bill on deposit	lettre de change déposée en garantie d'un prêt f	cambiale depositata in garanzia f	—
efectos (Es)	Effekten pl	securities	valeurs mobilières f/pl	titoli m/pl	—
efectos a nuestro cargo (Es)	Nostroeffekten pl	securities held by a bank at another bank	effets dans une autre banque m/pl	titoli nostri m/pl	—
efectos de reporte (Es)	Reporteffekten pl	contango securities	titres reportés m/pl	titoli dati a riporto m/pl	—

	D	E	F	I	Es
efectos patrimoniales (Es)	Vermögenseffekten *pl*	real balance effect	effets patrimoniaux *m/pl*	effetti patrimoniali *m/pl*	—
effective interest (E)	Effektivzins *m*	—	intérêt effectif *m*	interesse effettivo *m*	interés efectivo *m*
effective interest yield (E)	Effektivverzinsung *f*	—	taux effectif *m*	reddito effettivo *m*	interés efectivo *m*
Effekten (D)	—	securities	valeurs mobilières *f/pl*	titoli *m/pl*	efectos *m/pl*
Effektenabteilung (D)	—	securities department	service des titres *m*	ufficio titoli *m*	sección de efectos *f*
Effektenbank (D)	—	issuing bank	banque d'affaires *f*	banca valori *f*	banco de inversiones *m*
Effektenbörse (D)	—	stock exchange	bourse des titres et valeurs mobilières *f*	borsa valori *f*	bolsa de valores *m*
Effektenbuch (D)	—	stockbook	registre des titres *m*	registro dei titoli *m*	libro de valores *m*
Effektendepot (D)	—	deposit of securities	dépôt de titres *m*	deposito dei titoli *m*	depósito irregular de títulos *m*
Effektendiskont (D)	—	securities discount	escompte sur achat de titres *m*	sconto di titoli *m*	descuento de valores *m*
Effekteneigengeschäft (D)	—	security trading for own account	opérations sur titres à propre compte *f/pl*	operazione in proprio in titoli *f*	operaciones de valores por cuenta propia *f/pl*
Effektenemission (D)	—	issue of securities	émission de valeurs mobilières *f*	emissione di titoli *f*	emisión de valores *f*
Effektenfinanzierung (D)	—	security financing	financement de valeurs mobilières *m*	finanziamento tramite titoli *m*	financiación de valores *f*
Effektengeschäft (D)	—	securities business	commerce des valeurs mobilières *m*	operazione in titoli *f*	operación con valores *f*
Effektenhändler (D)	—	dealer in securities	courtier en valeurs mobilières *m*	agente in valori *m*	corredor de bolsa *m*
Effektenkapitalismus (D)	—	securities capitalism	capitalisme de valeurs mobilières *m*	capitalismo (basato su) titoli *m*	capitalismo por títulos-valores *m*
Effektenkasse (D)	—	security department counter	caisse de valeurs mobilières *f*	cassa titoli *f*	caja de valores *f*
Effektenkauf (D)	—	purchase of securities	achat de titres *m*	acquisto di titoli *m*	compra de valores *f*
Effektenkommissionär (D)	—	securities commission agent	banque chargée d'opérations sur titres *f*	commissionario di borsa *m*	comisionista de valores *m*
Effektenkommissionsgeschäft (D)	—	securities transactions on commission	opération sur titres *f*	compravendita titoli su commissione *f*	operaciones de valores a base de comisión *f/pl*
Effektenkonto (D)	—	securities account	compte des titres de participation *m*	conto titoli *m*	cuenta de valores *f*
Effektenkurs (D)	—	securities price	cours des valeurs mobilières *m*	quotazione di titoli *f*	cotización de valores *f*
Effektenlombard (D)	—	advances against securities	prêt sur titres *m*	anticipazione su titoli *f*	adelanto sobre valores *m*
Effektenmakler (D)	—	stockbroker	courtier en valeurs mobilières *m*	agente di cambio *m*	corredor de bolsa *m*
Effektenpensionierung (D)	—	raising money on securities by cash sale coupled with contract for subsequent repurchase	mise en pension d'effets *f*	sconto di titoli in pensione *m*	cesión temporal de valores *f*
Effektenpensionsgeschäft (D)	—	security transactions under repurchase agreement	opération de mise en pension d'effets *f*	sconto di titoli in pensione *m*	operaciones de cesión temporal de valores *f/pl*
Effektenplazierung (D)	—	securities placing	placement de titres *m*	emissione di titoli *f*	emisión de valores *f*
Effektenrechnung (D)	—	calculation of price of shares	calcul du prix des titres *m*	conto titoli *m*	cálculo del precio de valores *m*
Effektenstatistik (D)	—	securities statistics	statistique de titres *f*	statistica dei titoli *f*	estadística de valores *f*
Effektensubstitution (D)	—	securities substitution	substitution de titres *f*	sostituzione di titoli *f*	sustitución de valores *f*
Effektenverkauf (D)	—	over-the-counter trading	vente de titres *f*	vendita di titoli *f*	venta de valores *f*
Effektenverwaltung (D)	—	portfolio management	administration de titres *f*	amministrazione di titoli *f*	administración de valores *f*

	D	E	F	I	Es
Effektivgeschäft (D)	—	actual transaction	marché en disponible *m*	operazione in effettivo *f*	operación al contado *f*
Effektivvermerk (D)	—	actual currency clause	clause de payement en monnaie étrangère *f*	clausola di pagamento effettivo in moneta estera *f*	cláusula de efectividad *f*
Effektivverzinsung (D)	—	effective interest yield	taux effectif *m*	reddito effettivo *m*	interés efectivo *m*
Effektivzins (D)	—	effective interest	intérêt effectif *m*	interesse effettivo *m*	interés efectivo *m*
effet à échéances multiples (F)	Ratenwechsel *m*	bill payable in instalments	—	cambiale di pagamento rateale *f*	letra de vencimientos sucesivos *f*
effet à payer (F)	Schuldwechsel *m*	bill payable	—	cambiale passiva *f*	efecto a pagar *m*
effet à recevoir (F)	Besitzwechsel *m*	bills receivable	—	cambiale attiva *f*	efecto a cobrar *m*
effet bandwaggon (F)	Bandwaggon-Effekt *m*	bandwaggon effect	—	effetto bandwaggon *m*	efecto bandwaggon *m*
effet de commerce (F)	Commercial Paper *n*	commercial paper	—	commercial paper *m*	documento mercantil *m*
effet de commerce (F)	Warenpapier *n*	document of title	—	titolo rappresentativo di merci *m*	valor comercial *m*
effets de commerce à ordre (F)	kaufmännische Orderpapiere *n/pl*	commercial instruments to order	—	effetti commerciali all'ordine *m/pl*	títulos comerciales a la orden *m/pl*
effet du Trésor (F)	Schatzwechsel *m*	Treasury bill	—	buono del tesoro *m*	letra de tesorería *f*
effet payable à un certain délai de date (F)	Datowechsel *m*	after-date bill	—	cambiale a certo tempo data *f*	letra a tantos días fecha *f*
effet sans change de place (F)	Platzwechsel *m*	local bill	—	cambiale pagabile sul posto *f*	letra de plaza *f*
effets dans une autre banque (F)	Nostroeffekten *pl*	securities held by a bank at another bank		titoli nostri *m/pl*	efectos a nuestro cargo *m/pl*
effets de commerce (F)	Handelspapiere *n/pl*	commercial papers	—	effetti commerciali *m/pl*	documentos comerciales *m/pl*
effets de tout premier ordre (F)	Primapapiere *n/pl*	prime papers	—	carte commerciali di prim'ordine *f/pl*	valores de primera clase *m/pl*
effets du Trésor (F)	Finanzierungsschätze *m/pl*	financing bonds	—	buoni del tesoro *m/pl*	letras del Tesoro *f/pl*
effets escomptés (F)	Diskonten *m/pl*	bills discounted	—	effetti nazionali *m/pl*	letras de cambio descontados *f/pl*
effets patrimoniaux (F)	Vermögenseffekten *pl*	real balance effect	—	effetti patrimoniali *m/pl*	efectos patrimoniales *m/pl*
effets publics (F)	Staatspapiere *n/pl*	public securities	—	titoli di Stato *m/pl*	papeles del Estado *m/pl*
effetti commerciali (I)	Handelspapiere *n/pl*	commercial papers	effets de commerce *m/pl*	—	documentos comerciales *m/pl*
effetti commerciali all'ordine (I)	kaufmännische Orderpapiere *n/pl*	commercial instruments to order	effets de commerce à ordre *m/pl*	—	títulos comerciales a la orden *m/pl*
effetti nazionali (I)	Diskonten *m/pl*	bills discounted	effets escomptés *m/pl*	—	letras de cambio descontados *f/pl*
effetti patrimoniali (I)	Vermögenseffekten *pl*	real balance effect	effets patrimoniaux *m/pl*	—	efectos patrimoniales *m/pl*
effetto bandwaggon (I)	Bandwaggon-Effekt *m*	bandwaggon effect	effet bandwaggon *m*	—	efecto bandwaggon *m*
effetto commerciale girato da banche (I)	bankgirierter Warenwechsel *m*	bank endorsed bill	traite endossée par une banque *f*	—	letra comercial con endoso bancario *f*
effetto di smobilizzo (I)	Mobilisierungstratte *f*	mobilization draft	traite de mobilisation *f*	—	letra de mobilización *f*
effetto passivo (I)	Akzeptverbindlichkeit *f*	acceptance liability	engagement par acceptation *m*	—	obligación de aceptación *f*
efficience du marché des capitaux (F)	Kapitalmarkteffizienz *f*	capital market efficiency	—	efficienza del mercato finanziario *f*	eficiencia del mercado de capitales *f*
efficience marginale du capital (F)	Grenzleistungsfähigkeit des Kapitals *f*	marginal efficiency of capital	—	efficienza marginale del capitale *f*	eficiencia marginal del capital *f*
efficiency review (E)	Erfolgskontrolle *f*	—	contrôle du rendememt *m*	controllo del risultato *m*	control de éxito *m*
efficienza del mercato finanziario (I)	Kapitalmarkteffizienz *f*	capital market efficiency	efficience du marché des capitaux *f*	—	eficiencia del mercado de capitales *f*
efficienza marginale del capitale (I)	Grenzleistungsfähigkeit des Kapitals *f*	marginal efficiency of capital	efficience marginale du capital *f*	—	eficiencia marginal del capital *f*
Effizienzregeln (D)	—	performance regulations	régulation d'efficience *f*	regole per l'efficienza *f/pl*	normas de eficacia *f/pl*

	D	E	F	I	Es
eficiencia del mercado de capitales (Es)	Kapitalmarkteffizienz f	capital market efficiency	efficience du marché des capitaux f	efficienza del mercato finanziario f	—
eficiencia marginal del capital (Es)	Grenzleistungsfähigkeit des Kapitals f	marginal efficiency of capital	efficience marginale du capital f	efficienza marginale del capitale f	—
Eigendepot (D)	—	own security deposit	dépôt personnel m	deposito proprio m	depósito de valores propio m
eigene Aktien (D)	—	company-owned shares	actions propres f/pl	azioni sociali f/pl	acciones propias f/pl
eigene Effekten (D)	—	own security holdings	titres propres m/pl	titoli propri m/pl	valores propios m/pl
Eigenfinanzierung (D)	—	self-financing	autofinancement m	autofinanziamento m	autofinanciación f
Eigengeschäft (D)		transactions on own account	opération en nom personnel et à propre compte f	affare in proprio m	operación por cuenta propia f
Eigenhandel (D)	—	trading on own account	commerce à propre compte m	commercio in proprio m	comercio por cuenta propia m
Eigenkapital (D)	—	one's own capital	capital propre m	capitale proprio m	capital propio m
Eigenkapitalentzug (D)	—	own capital withdrawal	retrait du capital propre m	ritiro del capitale proprio m	retiro del capital propio m
Eigenkapitalerhöhung (D)	—	increase in own capital	augmentation du capital propre f	aumento del capitale proprio m	aumento del capital propio m
Eigenkapitalgrundsätze (D)	—	principles on own capital	principes de capital propre m/pl	principi sul capitale proprio m/pl	principios sobre el capital propio m/pl
Eigenkapitalkonto (D)	—	equity account	compte capital m	conto del capitale proprio m	cuenta de capital propio f
Eigenkapitalquote (D)	—	equity ratio	quote-part du capital propre f	percentuale dei mezzi propri f	cuota de capital propio f
Eigenkapitalrentabilität (D)	—	equity return	rentabilité du capital propre f	redditività del capitale proprio f	rédito del capital propio m
Eigenleistungen (D)	—	own contributions	prestations propres f/pl	prestazioni proprie f/pl	producciones propias f/pl
Eigentum (D)	—	property	propriété f	proprietà f	propiedad f
Eigentümer-Grundschuld (D)	—	land charge in favour of the owner	dette foncière constituée par le propriétaire à son profit f	debito fondiario al proprietario m	deuda inmobiliaria del propietario f
Eigentümer-Hypothek (D)	—	mortgage for the benefit of the owner	hypothèque revenant au propriétaire du fonds grevé f	ipoteca a favore del proprietario f	hipoteca de propietario f
Eigentumsrechte (D)		property rights	droits de propriété m/pl	diritti di proprietà m/pl	derechos de propiedad m/pl
Eigentumsvorbehalt (D)	—	reservation of title	réserve de propriété f	diritto di riservato dominio m	reserva de propiedad f
Eilüberweisung (D)	—	rapid money transfer	virement accéléré m	vaglia espresso m	giro urgente m
Einführungskurs (D)	—	introductory price	cours d'ouverture m	prima quotazione f	cotización de apertura f
Einheitsbilanz (D)	—	unified balance sheet	bilan unique m	bilancio unico m	balance unitario m
Einheitsgesellschaft (D)	—	unified company	société unitaire f	società unitaria f	sociedad unitaria f
Einheitsmarkt (D)	—	single-price market	marché unique m	mercato unico m	mercado único m
Einheitsscheck (D)	—	standard cheque	formule de chèque normalisée f	assegno standardizzato m	cheque estándar m
Einheitswechsel (D)	—	standard bill	lettre de change normalisée f	cambiale standardizzata f	letra de cambio estándar f
Einheitswert (D)	—	standard value	valeur globale intrinsèque f	titolo unitario m	valor unitario m
Einkommensteuer (D)	—	income tax	impôt sur le revenu m	tassa sul reddito f	impuesto sobre la renta m
Einkommenstheorie (D)	—	theory of income determination	théorie de la détermination du revenu f	teoria del reddito f	teoría de la determinación de la renta f
Einkommensumverteilung (D)	—	redistribution of income	redistribution des revenus f	ridistribuzione dei redditi f	redistribución de la renta f
Einkommensverteilung (D)	—	distribution of income	distribution du revenu f	distribuzione dei redditi f	distribución de la renta f
Einkünfte (D)	—	earnings	revenus m/pl	entrate f/pl	rentas f/pl
Einlage (D)	—	money deposited	dépôt m	deposito m	imposición f

	D	E	F	I	Es
Einlagengeschäft (D)	—	deposit business	opération de garde de fonds f/pl	operazione di deposito f	operaciones de depósito f/pl
Einlagenpolitik (D)	—	deposit policy	politique de dépôts f	politica dei depositi f	política de depositos f
Einlagensicherung (D)	—	guarantee of deposit	sûreté en garantie de dépôts f	garanzia dei depositi f	garantía de depositos f
Einlagensicherungsfonds (D)	—	deposit guarantee fund	fonds de sûreté en garantie de dépôts m	fondo di garanzia dei depositi m	fondos de garantía de depósitos m/pl
Einlagenzertifikat (D)	—	certificates of deposit	certificat de dépôt m	certificato di deposito m	certificado de depósito m
Einlösungspflicht (D)	—	obligation to redeem	obligation de rachat f	obbligo di pagamento m	deber de canje m
Einnahmen (D)	—	receipts	recettes f/pl	entrate f/pl	ingresos m/pl
Einnahmen-Ausgabenrechnung (D)	—	bill of receipts and expenditures	état des recettes et des dépenses m	conto entrate e uscite m	cuenta de gastos-ingresos f
Einrede der Arglist (D)	—	defence of fraud	exception du dol f	eccezione di dolo f	excepción de dolo f
Einrede der Vorausklage (D)	—	defence of lack of prosecution	exception de la discussion f	preescussione f	excepción de excusión f
Einschreibung (D)	—	registration	enregistrement m	asta olandese f	inscripción f
Einschußquittung (D)	—	contribution receipt	quittance de contribution f	ricevuta di apporto f	recibo de la inyección de dinero m
Einstandspreis (D)	—	cost price	prix coûtant m	prezzo di costo m	precio de coste m
Einstimmigkeitsregel (D)	—	unanimity rule	règle d'unanimité f	regola dell'unanimità f	regla de la unanimidad f
Eintragung im Handelsregister (D)	—	registration in the Commercial Register	inscription au registre du commerce f	iscrizione nel registro commerciale f	inscripción en el registro comercial f
Einzahlung (D)	—	payment	payement m	versamento m	aportación f
Einzahlungspflicht (D)	—	obligation to pay subscription	obligation de libérer une action f	obbligo di versamento m	deber de liberación de acciones m
Einzelhandel (D)	—	retail trade	commerce de détail m	commercio al dettaglio m	comercio al por menor m
Einzelkreditversicherung (D)	—	individual credit insurance	assurance crédit individuelle f	assicurazione crediti individuali f	seguro de crédito individual m
Einziehungsauftrag (D)	—	direct debit order	ordre de recouvrement m	mandato di incasso m	autorización para el cobro f
Einziehungsermächtigung (D)	—	direct debit authorization	mandat de prélèvement automatique m	autorizzazione alla riscossione f	comisión de cobranza f
Einziehungsgeschäft (D)	—	collection business	opération d'encaissement f	operazione d'incasso f	operaciones de cobranza f/pl
Einzugsermächtigungsverfahren (D)	—	collection procedure	système du mandat de prélèvement automatique m	autorizzazione alla riscossione f	proceso de cobro bancario m
Einzugsquittung (D)	—	collection receipt	quittance d'encaissement f	ricevuta di riscossione f	recibo de cobro m
Eisenbörse (D)	—	iron exchange	bourse de fer f	borsa del ferro f	bolsa de hierro f
eisenschaffende Industrie (D)	—	iron and steel producing industry	sidérurgie f	industria siderurgica f	industria metalúrgica f
ejecución (Es)	Vollstreckung f	enforcement	exécution f	esecuzione f	—
ejecución (Es)	Abwicklung f	settlement	exécution f	esecuzione f	—
ejercicio (Es)	Geschäftsjahr n	financial year	exercice commercial m	anno d'esercizio m	—
elasticidad de los intereses (Es)	Zinselastizität f	interest elasticity	élasticité des intérêts f	elasticità degli interessi f	—
elasticità degli interessi (I)	Zinselastizität f	interest elasticity	élasticité des intérêts f	—	elasticidad de los intereses f
elasticité des intérêts (F)	Zinselastizität f	interest elasticity	—	elasticità degli interessi f	elasticidad de los intereses f
electricity and fuels fonds (E)	Energiefonds m	—	fonds d'énergie m	fondo per il settore energetico m	fondo de energía f
Electronic Banking (D)	—	electronic banking	electronic banking m	electronic banking m	operaciones bancarias electrónicas f/pl
electronic banking (E)	Electronic Banking n	—	electronic banking m	electronic banking m	operaciones bancarias electrónicas f/pl
electronic banking (F)	Electronic Banking n	electronic banking	—	electronic banking m	operaciones bancarias electrónicas f/pl

	D	E	F	I	Es
electronic banking (I)	Electronic Banking n	electronic banking	electronic banking m	—	operaciones bancarias electrónicas f/pl
electronic fund transfer (E)	elektronischer Zahlungsverkehr m	—	règlements électroniques m/pl	operazioni di pagamento elettronici f/pl	servicio de pagos electrónico m
elektronischer Zahlungsverkehr (D)	—	electronic fund transfer	règlements électroniques m/pl	operazioni di pagamento elettronici f/pl	servicio de pagos electrónico m
elenco dei debitori (I)	schwarze Liste f	black bourse	liste noire f	—	lista negra f
elenco dei debitori (I)	Schuldnerverzeichnis n	list of insolvent debtors	liste des personnes ayant été poursuivies pour dettes f	—	lista de deudores f
elenco dei protesti (I)	Protestliste m	list of firms whose bills and notes have been protested	liste des protêts f	—	lista de protesta f
elenco numerico (I)	Nummernverzeichnis n	list of serial numbers of securities purchased or deposited	liste numérique f	—	escritura numérica f
elenco titoli ammessi ad anticipazioni (I)	Lombardverzeichnis n	list of securities eligible as collateral	liste des titres remis en gage f	—	lista de títulos pignorados f
eligible title-evidencing instrument (E)	qualifizierte Legitimationspapiere n/pl	—	titre établi à personne dénommée ou à tout autre porteur m	titoli al portatore qualificati m/pl	títulos de legitimación calificados m/pl
Embargo (D)	—	embargo	embargo m	embargo m	embargo m
embargo (E)	Embargo n	—	embargo m	embargo m	embargo m
embargo (Es)	Pfändung f	seizure	saisie f	pignoramento m	—
embargo (Es)	Embargo n	embargo	embargo m	embargo m	—
embargo (F)	Embargo n	embargo	—	embargo m	embargo m
embargo (I)	Embargo n	embargo	embargo m	—	embargo m
embargo del tercer deudor (Es)	Drittpfändung f	garnishee proceedings	saisie de tiers débiteurs f	subpegno di titoli m	—
embargo total (Es)	Kahlpfändung f	seizure of all the debtor's goods	saisie de tous les biens f	pignoramento totale m	—
embezzlement (E)	Unterschlagung f	—	détournement m	appropriazione indebita f	defraudación f
emergency money (E)	Notgeld n	—	monnaie obsidionale f	moneta d'emergenza f	dinero de urgencia m
émetteur d'un accréditif (F)	Akkreditivsteller m	person opening a credit in favour of somebody	—	ordinante il credito m	acreditante m
émetteur permanent (F)	Dauerremittent m	constant issuer	—	emittente continuo m	remitente permanente m
emisión (Es)	Begebung f	issue	émission f	emissione f	—
emisión (Es)	Erscheinen n	issuing	émission f	emissione f	—
emisión (Es)	Emission f	issuing	émission f	emissione f	—
emisión ajena (Es)	Fremdemission f	security issue for third account	émission de valeurs pour compte de tiers f	emissione per conto terzi f	—
emisión a la par (Es)	Pariemission f	issue at par	émission au pair f	emissione alla pari f	—
emisión común (Es)	Gemeinschaftsemission f	joint issue	émission en commun f	emissione comune f	—
emisión de acciones (Es)	Aktienausgabe f	issuing of shares	émission d'actions f	emissione di azioni f	—
emisión de acciones prohibida (Es)	verbotene Aktienausgabe f	prohibited share issue	émission d'actions interdite f	emissione vietata di azioni f	—
emisión de billetes (Es)	Notenausgabe f	note issue	émission de billets f	emissione di banconote f	—
emisión de obligaciones (Es)	Obligationsausgabe f	bond issue	émission d'obligations f	emissione di obbligazioni f	—
emisión de valores (Es)	Effektenplazierung f	securities placing	placement de titres m	emissione di titoli f	—
emisión de valores (Es)	Effektenemission f	issue of securities	émission de valeurs mobilières f	emissione di titoli f	—
emisión de valores (Es)	Wertpapieremission f	issue of securities	émission de titres f	emissione di titoli f	—
emisión por debajo de la par (Es)	Unter-Pari-Emission f	issue below par	émission au-dessous du pair f	emissione sotto la pari f	—
Emission (D)	—	issuing	émission f	emissione f	emisión f

	D	E	F	I	Es
émission (F)	Emission *f*	issuing	—	emissione *f*	emisión *f*
émission (F)	Begebung *f*	issue	—	emissione *f*	emisión *f*
émission (F)	Erscheinen *n*	issuing	—	emissione *f*	emisión *f*
émission au-dessous du pair (F)	Unter-Pari-Emission *f*	issue below par	—	emissione sotto la pari *f*	emisión por debajo de la par *f*
émission au pair (F)	Pariemission *f*	issue at par	—	emissione alla pari *f*	emisión a la par *f*
émission d'actions (F)	Aktienausgabe *f*	issuing of shares	—	emissione di azioni *f*	emisión de acciones *f*
émission d'actions interdite (F)	verbotene Aktienausgabe *f*	prohibited share issue	—	emissione vietata di azioni *f*	emisión de acciones prohibida *f*
émission de billets (F)	Notenausgabe *f*	note issue	—	emissione di banconote *f*	emisión de billetes *f*
émission de titres (F)	Wertpapieremission *f*	issue of securities	—	emissione di titoli *f*	emisión de valores *f*
émission de valeurs mobilières (F)	Effektenemission *f*	issue of securities	—	emissione di titoli *f*	emisión de valores *f*
émission de valeurs pour compte de tiers (F)	Fremdemission *f*	security issue for third account	—	emissione per conto terzi *f*	emisión ajena *f*
émission d'obligations (F)	Obligationsausgabe *f*	bond issue	—	emissione di obbligazioni *f*	emisión de obligaciones *f*
emissione (I)	Begebung *f*	issue	émission *f*	—	emisión *f*
emissione (I)	Emission *f*	issuing	émission *f*	—	emisión *f*
emissione (I)	Erscheinen *n*	issuing	émission *f*	—	emisión *f*
emissione alla pari (I)	Pariemission *f*	issue at par	émission au pair *f*	—	emisión a la par *f*
emissione comune (I)	Gemeinschafts-emission *f*	joint issue	émission en commun *f*	—	emisión común *f*
emissione di azioni (I)	Aktienausgabe *f*	issuing of shares	émission d'actions *f*	—	emisión de acciones *f*
emissione di banconote (I)	Notenausgabe *f*	note issue	émission de billets *f*	—	emisión de billetes *f*
emissione di obbligazioni (I)	Obligationsausgabe *f*	bond issue	émission d'obligations *f*	—	emisión de obligaciones *f*
emissione di titoli (I)	Wertpapieremission *f*	issue of securities	émission de titres *f*	—	emisión de valores *f*
emissione di titoli (I)	Effektenplazierung *f*	securities placing	placement de titres *m*	—	emisión de valores *f*
emissione di titoli (I)	Effektenemission *f*	issue of securities	émission de valeurs mobilières *f*	—	emisión de valores *f*
émission en commun (F)	Gemeinschafts-emission *f*	joint issue	—	emissione comune *f*	emisión común *f*
emissione per conto terzi (I)	Fremdemission *f*	security issue for third account	émission de valeurs pour compte de tiers *f*	—	emisión ajena *f*
emissione sotto la pari (I)	Unter-Pari-Emission *f*	issue below par	émission au-dessous du pair *f*	—	emisión por debajo de la par *f*
emissione vietata di azioni (I)	verbotene Aktienausgabe *f*	prohibited share issue	émission d'actions interdite *f*	—	emisión de acciones prohibida *f*
Emissionsabteilung (D)	—	issue department	service d'émission *m*	ufficio emissioni *m*	sección de emisión *f*
Emissionsagio (D)	—	issue premium	prime d'émission *f*	premio d'emissione *m*	prima de emisión *f*
Emissionsarten (D)	—	types of issuing	sortes d'émission *f/pl*	tipi di emissione *m/pl*	tipos de emisión *m/pl*
Emissionsbank (D)	—	issuing bank	banque d'affaires *f*	banca d'emissione *f*	banco emisor *m*
Emissions-bedingungen (D)	—	terms and conditions of issue	conditions de l'émission *f/pl*	condizioni d'emissione *f/pl*	condiciones de emisión *f/pl*
Emissions-genehmigung (D)	—	issue permit	autorisation de l'émission *f*	permesso d'emissione *m*	autorización de emisión *f*
Emissionsgeschäft (D)	—	underwriting business	opération de place-ment de parts *f*	operazione d'emissione *f*	operación de emisión *f*
Emissionsgesetz (D)	—	Issue Law	loi sur l'émission des billets de banque *f*	legge sulle emissioni *f*	ley de emisión *f*
Emissionshaus (D)	—	issuing house	établissement d'émission *m*	banca emittente *f*	casa emisora *f*
Emissionskalender (D)	—	issue calendar	calendrier d'émission *m*	calendario delle emissioni *m*	calendario de emisión *m*
Emissions-konsortium (D)	—	underwriting syndicate	syndicat bancaire appuyant une émission *m*	consorzio d'emissione *m*	consorcio emisor *m*

	D	E	F	I	Es
Emissionskontrolle (D)	—	security issue control	contrôle en matière d'émission d'actions et d'obligations *m*	controllo delle emissioni *m*	control de emisión *m*
Emissionskosten (D)	—	underwriting costs	frais de l'émission *m/pl*	spese d'emissione *f/pl*	gastos de emisión *m/pl*
Emissionskredit (D)	—	credit granted to the issuer by the bank by underwriting the issue	crédit financier accordé par les banques à l'émetteur *m*	credito d'emissione *m*	crédito de emisión *m*
Emissionskurs (D)	—	issue price	cours d'émission *m*	corso d'emissione *m*	tipo de emisión *m*
Emissionsmarkt (D)	—	primary market	marché des valeurs émises *m*	mercato d'emissione *m*	mercado de emisión *m*
Emissionsrendite (D)	—	issue yield	rapport de l'émission *m*	rendita di nuovi titoli *f*	rédito de emisión *m*
Emissionsreste (D)	—	residual securities of an issue	titres restant d'une émission	titoli rimanenti di un'emissione *m/pl*	títulos restantes de una emisión *m/pl*
Emissionssperre (D)	—	ban on new issues	blocage des émissions d'actions et d'obligations *m*	blocco delle emissioni *m*	restricción de emisión *f*
Emissionsstatistik (D)	—	new issue statistics	statistique d'émission *f*	statistica delle nuove emissioni *f*	estadística de emisión *f*
Emissionssyndikat (D)	—	underwriting syndicate	syndicat bancaire de garantie *m*	sindacato d'emissione *m*	sindicato de emisión *m*
Emissions-verfahren (D)	—	issuing procedure	procédure d'émission *f*	procedimento di emissione *m*	procedimiento de emisión *m*
Emissions-vergütung (D)	—	issue commission	commission d'émission *f*	commissione d'emissione *f*	remuneración emisora *f*
emittente continuo (I)	Dauerremittent *m*	constant issuer	émetteur permanent *m*	—	remitente permanente *m*
empirical contents (E)	empirischer Gehalt *m*	—	contenu empirique *m*	contenuto empirico *m*	contenido empírico *m*
empirical economic research (E)	empirische Wirt-schaftsforschung *f*	—	études économiques empiriques *f/pl*	ricerca economica empirica *f*	investigación econó-mica empírica *f*
empirischer Gehalt (D)	—	empirical contents	contenu empirique *m*	contenuto empirico *m*	contenido empírico *m*
empirische Wirt-schaftsforschung (D)	—	empirical economic research	études économiques empiriques *f/pl*	ricerca economica empirica *f*	investigación econó-mica empírica *f*
empleado bancario (Es)	Bankkaufmann *m*	bank clerk	employé bancaire *m*	impiegato di banca *m*	—
empleado de banco (Es)	Bankangestellter *m*	bank clerk	employé de banque *m*	impiegato di banca *m*	—
employé bancaire (F)	Bankkaufmann *m*	bank clerk	—	impiegato di banca *m*	empleado bancario *m*
employé de banque (F)	Bankangestellter *m*	bank clerk	—	impiegato di banca *m*	empleado de banco *m*
employees' savings premium (E)	Arbeitnehmer-sparzulage *f*	—	prime d'épargne en faveur de l'employé *f*	indennità di risparmio dipendenti *f*	prima de ahorro del empleado *f*
employees' shares (E)	Arbeitnehmeraktie *f*	—	action de travail *f*	azione di lavoro *f*	acción de trabajo *f*
employer's contributions (E)	Arbeitgeberzuschüsse *m/pl*	—	compléments patronaux *m/pl*	contributi del datore di lavoro *m/pl*	suplementos patronales *m/pl*
employer's share (E)	Arbeitgeberanteil *m*	—	part patronale *f*	quota del datore di lavoro *f*	cuota patronal *f*
employment structure (E)	Beschäftigtenstruktur *f*	—	structure d'emploi *f*	struttura dell'occupazione *f*	estructura de empleo *f*
empresa (Es)	Unternehmen *n*	enterprise	entreprise *f*	impresa *f*	—
empréstito amortizable (Es)	Tilgungsanleihe *f*	redemption loan	emprunt d'amortissement *m*	prestito ammortizzabile *m*	—
empréstito bancario (Es)	Bankanleihen *f/pl*	bank bonds	emprunt émis par une banque *m*	mutuo bancario *m*	—
empréstito colectivo (Es)	Sammelanleihe *f*	joint loan issue	emprunt collectif *m*	obbligazione comunale *f*	—
empréstito comunitario (Es)	Gemeinschafts-anleihe *f*	joint loan	prêt commun *f*	prestito collettivo *m*	—
empréstito con garantía-oro (Es)	Goldanleihe *f*	loan on a gold basis	emprunt or *m*	prestito oro *m*	—
empréstito con prima (Es)	Prämienanleihe *f*	lottery loan	emprunt à primes *m*	prestito a premi *m*	—
empréstito consolidado (Es)	Fundierungsanleihe *f*	funding loan	emprunt consolidé *m*	prestito consolidato *m*	—

	D	E	F	I	Es
empréstito con un tipo de interés variable (Es)	zinsvariable Anleihe f	loan at variable rates	emprunt d'un taux d'intérêt variable m	prestito a tasso d'interesse variabile m	—
empréstito de amortización (Es)	Ablösungsanleihe f	redemption loan	emprunt de revalorisation m	prestito di ammortamento m	—
empréstito de guerra (Es)	Kriegsanleihe f	war loan	emprunt de guerre m	prestito di guerra m	—
empréstito de la Federación (Es)	Bundesanleihe f	Federal loan	titre de dette publique m	titolo di Stato m	—
empréstito del Estado inscrito en el libro de la deuda (Es)	Wertrechtanleihe f	government-inscribed debt	emprunt de l'Etat inscrit dans le livre de la dette m	obbligazione contabile f	—
empréstito de liquidez (Es)	Liquiditätsanleihe f	liquidity loan	emprunt de liquidité m	obbligazione di liquidità f	—
empréstito de moneda dual (Es)	Doppelwährungs-anleihe f	double currency loan	emprunt à double étalon m	credito bimonetario m	—
empréstito de sorteo (Es)	Auslosungsanleihe f	lottery bond	emprunt amortissable par séries tirées au sort m	prestito rimborsabile mediante per sorteggio m	—
empréstito en dólares (Es)	Dollaranleihe f	dollar bond	emprunt en dollars m	prestito in dollari m	—
empréstito en especie (Es)	Naturadarlehen n	loan granted in form of a mortgage bond	prêt en nature m	prestito ipotecario a obbligazione fondiaria m	—
empréstito en especie (Es)	Sachwertanleihen f/pl	material value loans	emprunt de valeurs réelles m	prestito indicizzato m	—
empréstito escalonado (Es)	Staffelanleihe f	graduated-interest loan	emprunt à taux progressif m	prestito a interesse scalare m	—
empréstito exterior (Es)	Auslandsanleihe f	foreign bond	emprunt extérieur m	prestito estero m	—
empréstito forzoso (Es)	Zwangsanleihe f	compulsory loan	emprunt forcé m	prestito forzato m	—
empréstito global (Es)	Global-Anleihe f	all-share certificate	titre représentant globalement un paquet d'emprunts m	credito globale m	—
empréstito municipal (Es)	Kommunaldarlehen n	loan granted to a local authority	prêt aux communes m	mutuo comunale m	—
empréstito municipal (Es)	Kommunalanleihe f	local authorities loan	emprunt communal m	prestito comunale m	—
empréstito paralelo (Es)	Parallelanleihe f	parallel loan	emprunt parallèle m	obbligazione parallela f	—
empréstito perpétuo (Es)	ewige Anleihe f	perpetual loan	emprunt perpétuel m	prestito perpetuo m	—
empréstito por anualidades (Es)	Annuitätenanleihe f	annuity bond	emprunt amortis-sable par annuités m	prestito rimborsabile in annualità m	—
empréstito produciendo interés (Es)	Zinsanleihe f	loan repayable in full at a due date	emprunt produisant des intérêts m	prestito non ammortizzabile m	—
empréstitos a plazos (Es)	Ratenanleihen f/pl	instalment loans	emprunt remboursable par annuités constantes m	prestiti ammortizzabili m/pl	—
empréstitos convertibles (Es)	Wandelanleihen f/pl	convertible bonds	obligation convertible f	prestiti convertibili m/pl	—
empréstitos de lotería (Es)	Lotterieanleihen f/pl	lottery bonds	emprunts à lots m/pl	prestiti a premi m/pl	—
empréstitos en moneda extranjera (Es)	Valuta-Anleihen f/pl	loan in foreign currency	emprunt émis en monnaie étrangère m	prestiti in valuta estera m/pl	—
empréstito sinodal (Es)	Synodalanleihe f	synodal loan	emprunt synodal m	obbligazione sinodale f	—
empréstitos libor (Es)	Liboranleihen f/pl	Libor loans	emprunts Libor m	obbligazioni libor f/pl	—
emprunt à double étalon (F)	Doppelwährungs-anleihe f	double currency loan	—	credito bimonetario m	empréstito de moneda dual m
emprunt amortissable par annuités (F)	Annuitätenanleihe f	annuity bond	—	prestito rimborsabile in annualità m	obligación sin vencimiento f
emprunt amortissable par séries tirées au sort (F)	Auslosungsanleihe f	lottery bond	—	prestito rimborsabile mediante per sorteggio m	empréstito de sorteo m
emprunt à primes (F)	Prämienanleihe f	lottery loan	—	prestito a premi m	empréstitos con prima m/pl

	D	E	F	I	Es
emprunt à taux progressif (F)	Staffelanleihe f	graduated-interest loan	—	prestito a interesse scalare m	empréstito escalonado m
emprunt collectif (F)	Sammelanleihe f	joint loan issue	—	obbligazione comunale f	empréstito colectivo m
emprunt communal (F)	Kommunalanleihe f	local authorities loan	—	prestito comunale m	empréstito municipal m
emprunt consolidé (F)	Fundierungsanleihe f	funding loan	—	prestito consolidato m	empréstito consolidado m
emprunt d'amortissement (F)	Tilgungsanleihe f	redemption loan	—	prestito ammortizzabile m	empréstito amortizable m
emprunt de guerre (F)	Kriegsanleihe f	war loan	—	prestito di guerra m	empréstito de guerra m
emprunt de l'Etat inscrit dans le livre de la dette (F)	Wertrechtanleihe f	government-inscribed debt	—	obbligazione contabile f	empréstito del Estado inscrito en el libro de la deuda m
emprunt de liquidité (F)	Liquiditätsanleihe f	liquidity loan	—	obbligazione di liquidità f	empréstito de liquidez m
emprunt de revalorisation (F)	Ablösungsanleihe f	redemption loan	—	prestito di ammortamento m	empréstito de amortización m
emprunt de valeurs réelles (F)	Sachwertanleihen f/pl	material value loans	—	prestito indicizzato m	empréstito en especie m
emprunt d'un taux d'intérêt variable (F)	zinsvariable Anleihe f	loan at variable rates	—	prestito a tasso d'interesse variabile m	empréstito con un tipo de interés variable m
emprunt émis en monnaie étrangère (F)	Valuta-Anleihen f/pl	loan in foreign currency	—	prestiti in valuta estera m/pl	empréstitos en moneda extranjera m/pl
emprunt émis par une banque (F)	Bankanleihen f/pl	bank bonds	—	mutuo bancario m	empréstito bancario m
emprunt en dollars (F)	Dollaranleihe f	dollar bond	—	prestito in dollari m	empréstito en dólares m
emprunt extérieur (F)	Auslandsanleihe f	foreign bond	—	prestito estero m	empréstito exterior m
emprunt forcé (F)	Zwangsanleihe f	compulsory loan	—	prestito forzato m	empréstito forzoso m
emprunt indexé (F)	Indexanleihe f	index-linked loan	—	prestito indicizzato m	préstamo provisto de una cláusula de valor estable m
emprunt libellé en monnaie étrangère (F)	Euro-Bond m	Eurobond	—	eurobond m	euroobligación f
emprunt net (F)	Nettokreditaufnahme f	net borrowing	—	indebitamento netto m	toma de crédito neta f
emprunt or (F)	Goldanleihe f	loan on a gold basis	—	prestito oro m	empréstito con garantía-oro m
emprunt parallèle (F)	Parallelanleihe f	parallel loan	—	obbligazione parallela f	empréstito paralelo m
emprunt perpétuel (F)	ewige Anleihe f	perpetual loan	—	prestito perpetuo m	empréstito perpétuo m
emprunt produisant des intérêts (F)	Zinsanleihe f	loan repayable in full at a due date	—	prestito non ammortizzabile m	empréstito produciendo interés m
emprunt remboursable par annuités constantes (F)	Ratenanleihen f/pl	instalment loans	—	prestiti ammortizzabili m/pl	empréstitos a plazos m/pl
emprunts à lots (F)	Lotterieanleihen f/pl	lottery bonds	—	prestiti a premi m/pl	empréstitos de lotería m/pl
emprunts d'Etat (F)	Staatsanleihen f/pl	public bonds	—	titoli di Stato m/pl	bonos del Estado m/pl
emprunts Libor (F)	Liboranleihen f/pl	Libor loans	—	obbligazioni libor f/pl	empréstitos libor m/pl
emprunt sur marchandises (F)	Warenbeleihung f	lending on goods	—	prestito su merci m	préstamo sobre mercancías m
emprunt synodal (F)	Synodalanleihe f	synodal loan	—	obbligazione sinodale f	empréstito sinodal m
encaissement (F)	Inkasso n	collection	—	incasso m	cobranza f
encaissement d'un effet (F)	Wechselinkasso n	collection of bills of exchange	—	incasso di cambiale m	cobro de letras m
encaissements bancaires (F)	Bankeinzugs-verfahren n	direct debiting	—	procedimento d'incasso bancario m	cobranzas bancarias f/pl
encouragement à l'exportation (F)	Exportförderung f	export promotion	—	agevolazione all'esportazione f	fomento de la exportación m
endangering the credit of a person or a firm (E)	Kreditgefährdung f	—	atteinte au crédit f	pregiudizio della capacità creditizia m	amenaza del crédito f

	D	E	F	I	Es
endettement (F)	Verschuldung f	indebtedness	—	indebitamento m	endeudamiento m
endeudamiento (Es)	Verschuldung f	indebtedness	endettement m	indebitamento m	—
endeudamiento neto (Es)	Netto-neuverschuldung f	net new indebtedness	nouveaux emprunts en termes nets m	indebitamento netto m	—
Endnachfrage (D)	—	final demand	demande finale f	domanda aggregata effettiva f	demanda final f
end of the month (E)	Ultimo m	—	fin de mois f	fine mese m	fin de mes m
endogene Variable (D)	—	endogenous variable	variable endogène f	variabile endogena f	variable endógena f
endogenous variable (E)	endogene Variable f	—	variable endogène f	variabile endogena f	variable endógena f
endorsable securities (E)	indossable Wertpapiere n/pl	—	valeurs endossables f/pl	titoli girabili m/pl	títulos endosables m/pl
endorsee (E)	Indossatar m	—	endossataire m	giratario m	endosatario m
endorsement (E)	Indossament n	—	endossement m	girata f	endoso m
endorsement for collection (E)	Inkasso-Indossament n	—	endossement pour encaissement m	girata "per incasso" f	endoso al cobro m
endorsement liabilities (E)	Indossament-verbindlichkeiten f/pl	—	obligations par endossement f/pl	impegni di girata m/pl	obligaciones por endoso f/pl
endorsement made out to bearer (E)	Inhaberindossament n	—	endossement du porteur m	girata al portatore f	endoso al portador m
endorsement of an overdue bill of exchange (E)	Nachindossament n	—	endossement après la date de l'échéance de la lettre de change m	girata posteriore alla scadenza f	endoso de letra vencida m
endorser (E)	Indossant m	—	endosseur m	girante m	endosador m
endorser (E)	Girant m	—	endosseur m	girante m	endosador m
endosado (Es)	Wechselnehmer m	payee of a bill of exchange	preneur d'un effet m	beneficiario di una cambiale m	—
endosador (Es)	Girant m	endorser	endosseur m	girante m	—
endosador (Es)	Indossant m	endorser	endosseur m	girante m	—
endosatario (Es)	Indossatar m	endorsee	endossataire m	giratario m	—
endoso (Es)	Indossament n	endorsement	endossement m	girata f	—
endoso al cobro (Es)	Inkasso-Indossament n	endorsement for collection	endossement pour encaissement m	girata "per incasso" f	—
endoso al portador (Es)	Inhaberindossament n	endorsement made out to bearer	endossement du porteur m	girata al portatore f	—
endoso de favor (Es)	Gefälligkeitsgiro m	accommodation endorsement	endossement de complaisance m	girata di favore f	—
endoso de letra vencida (Es)	Nachindossament n	endorsement of an overdue bill of exchange	endossement après la date de l'échéance de la lettre de change m	girata posteriore alla scadenza f	—
endoso en blanco (Es)	Blanko-Indossament n	blank endorsement	endossement en blanc m	girata in bianco f	—
endoso en prenda (Es)	Pfandindossament n	pledge endorsement	endossement pignoratif m	girata "valuta in pegno" f	—
endoso intransferible (Es)	Rektaindossament n	restrictive endorsement	endossement non à ordre m	girata non all'ordine f	—
endoso parcial (Es)	Teilindossament n	partial endorsement	endossement partiel m	girata parziale f	—
endoso por procuración (Es)	Prokuraindossament n	per procuration endorsement	endossement de procuration m	girata "per procura" f	—
endossataire (F)	Indossatar m	endorsee	—	giratario m	endosatario m
endossement (F)	Indossament n	endorsement	—	girata f	endoso m
endossement après la date de l'échéance de la lettre de change (F)	Nachindossament n	endorsement of an overdue bill of exchange	—	girata posteriore alla scadenza f	endoso de letra vencida m
endossement de complaisance (F)	Gefälligkeitsgiro m	accommodation endorsement	—	girata di favore f	endoso de favor m
endossement de procuration (F)	Prokuraindossament n	per procuration endorsement	—	girata "per procura" f	endoso por procuración m
endossement du porteur (F)	Inhaberindossament n	endorsement made out to bearer	—	girata al portatore f	endoso al portador m

	D	E	F	I	Es
endossement en blanc (F)	Blanko-Indossament *n*	blank endorsement	—	girata in bianco *f*	endoso en blanco *m*
endossement non à ordre (F)	Rektaindossament *n*	restrictive endorsement	—	girata non all'ordine *f*	endoso intransferible *m*
endossement partiel (F)	Teilindossament *n*	partial endorsement	—	girata parziale *f*	endoso parcial *m*
endossement pignoratif (F)	Pfandindossament *n*	pledge endorsement	—	girata "valuta in pegno" *f*	endoso en prenda *m*
endossement pour encaissement (F)	Inkasso-- Indossament *n*	endorsement for collection	—	girata "per incasso" *f*	endoso al cobro *m*
endosseur (F)	Indossant *m*	endorser	—	girante *m*	endosador *m*
endosseur (F)	Girant *m*	endorser	—	girante *m*	endosador *m*
endowment (E)	Dotation *f*	—	dotation *f*	dotazione *f*	dotación *f*
endowment funds (E)	Dotationskapital *n*	—	capital-apport *m*	capitale di dotazione *m*	capital de dotación *m*
en el año (Es)	Anno *n*	in the year	en l'année	anno *m*	—
Energiefonds (D)	—	electricity and fuels fonds	fonds d'énergie *m*	fondo per il settore energetico *m*	fondo de energía *f*
enforcement (E)	Vollstreckung *f*	—	exécution *f*	esecuzione *f*	ejecución *f*
Engagement (D)	—	commitment	engagement *m*	impegno *m*	compromiso *m*
engagement (F)	Obligo *n*	liability	—	garanzia *f*	obligación *f*
engagement (F)	Promesse *f*	promissory note	—	promessa *f*	pagaré *m*
engagement (F)	Engagement *n*	commitment	—	impegno *m*	compromiso *m*
engagement par acceptation (F)	Akzeptverbindlichkeit *f*	acceptance liability	—	effetto passivo *m*	obligación de aceptación *f*
engagement par lettre de change (F)	Wechselobligo *n*	customer's liability on bills	—	cambiale passiva *f*	obligación en letras de cambio *f*
engagement sur le taux d'intérêt accordé (F)	Zinsbindung *f*	interest rate control	—	prescrizione sui tassi *f*	vinculación al tipo de interés pactado *m*
enger Markt (D)	—	restricted market	marché restreint *m*	mercato a scarso flottante *m*	mercado de valores poco flexible *m*
Engpaßfaktor (D)	—	bottle-neck factor	facteur de goulot d'étranglement *m*	fattore di stretta *m*	factor de escasez *m*
en l'année (F)	Anno *n*	in the year	—	anno *m*	en el año
en liquidación (Es)	in Liquidation	in liquidation	en liquidation	in liquidazione	—
en liquidation (F)	in Liquidation	in liquidation	—	in liquidazione	en liquidación
en progrès (F)	im Aufwind	under upward pressure	—	con tendenza ascendente	contendencia alcesta
enquête sur la solvabilité (F)	Kreditprüfung *f*	credit status investigation	—	controllo dei crediti *m*	investigación de crédito y solvencia de un cliente *f*
enregistrement (F)	Einschreibung *f*	registration	—	asta olandese *f*	inscripción *f*
ente (I)	Körperschaft *f*	corporation	collectivité *f*	—	corporación *f*
Enteignung (D)	—	expropriation	expropriation *f*	espropriazione *f*	expropiación *f*
ente locale (I)	Gebietskörperschaft *f*	regional authority	collectivité territoriale *f*	—	corporación territorial *f*
enterprise (E)	Unternehmen *n*	—	entreprise *f*	impresa *f*	empresa *f*
Entgeld (D)	—	remuneration	rémunération *f*	corrispettivo *m*	remuneración *f*
Entlohnung (D)	—	paying off	rétribution *f*	retribuzione *f*	retribución *f*
Entnahme (D)	—	withdrawal	prélèvement *m*	prelevamento *m*	retirada de dinero *f*
en total (Es)	unter dem Strich	in total	au total	fuori bilancio	—
entrada de dinero (Es)	Geldeingang *m*	receipt of money	rentrée de fonds *f*	entrata di denaro *f*	—
entrada de pedidos (Es)	Auftragseingang *m*	incoming order	entrée de commandes *f*	afflusso di ordini *m*	—
entrata di denaro (I)	Geldeingang *m*	receipt of money	rentrée de fonds *f*	—	entrada de dinero *f*
entrate (I)	Einnahmen *f/pl*	receipts	recettes *f/pl*	—	ingresos *m/pl*
entrate (I)	Einkünfte *pl*	earnings	revenus *m/pl*	—	rentas *f/pl*
entrate pubbliche (I)	Staatseinnahmen *f/pl*	public revenue	recettes de l'Etat *f/pl*	—	ingresos públicos *m/pl*
entrée de commandes (F)	Auftragseingang *m*	incoming order	—	afflusso di ordini *m*	entrada de pedidos *f*

	D	E	F	I	Es
entreprise (F)	Unternehmen n	enterprise	—	impresa f	empresa f
entreprise dominée (F)	Organgesellschaft f	controlled company	—	società legata contrattualmente f	sociedad órgano f
entry (E)	Verbuchung f	—	inscription en compte f	registrazione f	contabilización f
Entschädigung (D)	—	indemnification	indemnité f	indennità f	indemnización f
Entscheidungsregel (D)	—	decision rule	règle de décision f	regola di decisione f	regla de decisión f
Entschuldung (D)	—	disencumberment	désendettement m	pagamento dei debiti m	desgravamen m
Entsparen (D)	—	dissaving	épargne négative f	diminuzione dei risparmi accumulati f	ahorro negativo m
Entwertung (D)	—	depreciation	dévaluation f	svalutazione f	desvalorización f
Entwicklungsbank (D)	—	development bank	banque de développement f	banca per lo sviluppo f	banco de desarrollo m
Entwicklungsfonds (D)	—	development fund	fonds de développement m	fondo di sviluppo m	fondo de desarrollo m
envahissement de capitaux étrangers (F)	Überfremdung f	control by foreign capital	—	inforestieramento m	extranjerización f
épargnant (F)	Sparer m	saver	—	risparmiatore m	ahorrador m
épargne (F)	Ersparnis f	savings	—	risparmio m	ahorros m/pl
épargne à lots (F)	Gewinnsparen n	lottery premium saving	—	risparmio a premi m	ahorro de beneficios m
épargne à primes (F)	Prämiensparen n	bonus-aided saving	—	risparmio a premi m	ahorro con primas m
épargne à un but déterminé (F)	Zwecksparen n	target saving	—	risparmio ad investimento vincolato m	ahorro con un fin determinado m
épargne collective (F)	Kollektivsparen n	collective saving	—	risparmio collettivo m	ahorro colectivo m
épargne collective (F)	Gemeinschaftssparen n	joint saving	—	risparmio collettivo m	ahorro común m
épargne d'excédents (F)	Überschuß-Sparen n	surplus saving	—	risparmio con ordine permanente m	ahorro de los importes excesivos m
épargne d'excédents (F)	Plus-Sparen n	surplus saving	—	risparmio restanti del conto corrente m	ahorro de excedentes m
épargne forcée (F)	Zwangssparen n	compulsory saving	—	risparmio forzato m	ahorro forzoso m
épargne individuelle (F)	individuelles Sparen n	saving by private households	—	risparmio individuale m	ahorro individual m
épargne jouissant d'avantages fiscaux (F)	steuerbegünstigtes Sparen n	tax-privileged saving	—	risparmio con privilegi fiscali m	ahorro favorecido por ventajas fiscales m
épargne libéralisée (F)	freizügiger Sparverkehr m	system by which savings depositor can effect inpayments and withdrawals at all savings banks or post offices	—	libertà per l'intestatario del libretto di risparmio di effettuare versamenti e esborsi in tutte le casse di risparmio tedesche f	movimiento de ahorros liberalizado m
épargne négative (F)	Entsparen n	dissaving	—	diminuzione dei risparmi accumulati f	ahorro negativo m
épargner pour la construction (F)	bausparen	saving through building societies	—	risparmiare per l'edilizia	ahorrar para la construcción
equalization and covering claim (E)	Ausgleichs- und Deckungsforderung f	—	demande de dédommagement et de couverture f	credito di compensazione m	crédito de igualación y cobertura m
equalization claim (E)	Ausgleichsforderung f	—	droit à une indemnité compensatoire m	credito di compensazione m	reclamación de indemnización contra la administración pública f
equalization of burdens (E)	Lastenausgleich m	—	péréquation des charges f	perequazione degli oneri f	compensación de cargas f
equalization of burdens bank (E)	Lastenausgleichsbank f	—	banque de péréquation des charges f	banca perequazione oneri f	banco de compensación de cargas m
Equalization of Burdens Fund (E)	Lastenausgleichsfonds m	—	fonds de péréquation des charges m	fondo perequazione oneri m	fondo de compensación de cargas m
equalization right (E)	Ausgleichsrecht n	—	droit à une compensation m	diritto di compensazione m	derecho a compensación m
équation quantitative (F)	Quantitätsgleichung f	quantity equation	—	equazione degli scambi f	ecuación cuantitativa f

	D	E	F	I	Es
equazione degli scambi (I)	Quantitätsgleichung f	quantity equation	équation quantitative f	—	ecuación cuantitativa f
équilibre (F)	Gleichgewicht n	balance	—	equilibrio m	equilibrio m
équilibre de l'économie extérieure (F)	außenwirtschaftliches Gleichgewicht n	external balance	—	equilibrio del commercio estero m	equilibrio de la economía exterior m
équilibre entre offre et demande (F)	bezahlt	paid	—	pagato	equilibrio entre papel y dinero m
equilibrio (Es)	Gleichgewicht n	balance	équilibre m	equilibrio m	—
equilibrio (I)	Gleichgewicht n	balance	équilibre m	—	equilibrio m
equilibrio de la economía exterior (Es)	außenwirtschaftliches Gleichgewicht n	external balance	équilibre de l'économie extérieure m	equilibrio del commercio estero m	—
equilibrio del bilancio pubblico (I)	Budgetausgleich m	balancing of the budget	solde de budget m	—	balance del presupuesto m
equilibrio del commercio estero (I)	außenwirtschaftliches Gleichgewicht n	external balance	équilibre de l'économie extérieure m	—	equilibrio de la economía exterior m
equilibrio entre papel y dinero (Es)	bezahlt	paid	équilibre entre offre et demande m	pagato	—
equilibrium interest rate (E)	Gleichgewichtszins m	—	intérêt équilibré m	interesse d'equilibrio m	interés de equilibrio m
equilibrium price (E)	Gleichgewichtspreis m	—	prix équilibré m	prezzo di equilibrio m	precio de equilibrio m
équipement d'exploitation (F)	Betriebsmittel n	working funds	—	fondi d'esercizio m/pl	fondos de explotación m/pl
equity account (E)	Eigenkapitalkonto n	—	compte capital m	conto del capitale proprio m	cuenta de capital propio f
equity financing (E)	Beteiligungsfinanzierung f	—	financement par participation m	finanziamento di partecipazione m	financiación de participación f
equity financing transactions (E)	Beteiligungshandel m	—	opérations de financement par participation f/pl	commercio in partecipazioni m	operaciones de financiación de participación f/pl
equity participation (E)	Kapitalbeteiligung f	—	participation par apport de capital f	partecipazione al capitale f	intervención financiera f
equity ratio (E)	Eigenkapitalquote f	—	quote-part du capital propre f	percentuale dei mezzi propri f	cuota de capital propio f
equity return (E)	Eigenkapitalrentabilität f	—	rentabilité du capital propre f	redditività del capitale proprio f	rédito del capital propio m
equity security (E)	Anteilspapiere n/pl	—	titres de participation m/pl	cedole azionarie f/pl	títulos de participación m/pl
Erbbaurecht (D)	—	hereditary building right	droit de superficie héréditaire m	diritto d'enfiteusi m	derecho de superficie m
Erfolgsbeteiligung (D)	—	profit-sharing	participation aux résultats f	partecipazione agli utili f	participación en el beneficio f
Erfolgskontrolle (D)	—	efficiency review	contrôle du rendememt m	controllo del risultato m	control de éxito m
Erfüllung (D)	—	performance	accomplissement m	adempimento m	cumplimiento m
Erfüllungsort (D)	—	place of performance	lieu de l'exécution de la prestation m	luogo d'adempimento m	lugar del cumplimiento m
Ergänzungsabgabe (D)	—	supplementary levy	taxe complémentaire f	imposta complementare f	tasa complementaria f
Ergebnisabführungsvertrag (D)	—	profit and loss transfer agreement	accord de transfer des résultats m	contratto di trasferimento profitto m	acuerdo de pago del resultado m
Ergebnisbeteiligung (D)	—	participating in yield	participation aux résultats f	partecipazione agli utili f	participación en los beneficios f
Erholung (D)	—	recovery	rétablissement m	rianimazione f	recuperación f
Erkenntnisobjekt (D)	—	object of discernment	objet de discernement m	oggetto di cognizione m	objeto de conocimiento m
Erklärung (D)	—	explanation	déclaration f	dichiarazione f	declaración f
Erlaß (D)	—	decree	arrêt m	decreto m	decreto m
Ermächtigungsdepot (D)	—	authorized deposit	dépôt d'usage m	deposito con permesso di permuta m	depósito de autorización m
Ermächtigung zur Verfügung (D)	—	proxy for disposal	autorisation de disposer f	autorizzazione di disporre dei titoli depositati f	autorización a disponer f

	D	E	F	I	Es
Ermattung (D)	—	exhaust	léthargie f	indebolimento delle quotazioni m	letargía f
Erneuerungsfonds (D)	—	renewal reserve	fonds de renouvellement m	fondo di rinnovamento m	fondo de renovación m
Erneuerungsschein (D)	—	talon for renewal of coupon sheet	talon de recouponnement m	cedola di riaffoglimento f	talón de renovación m
Eröffnungsbilanz (D)	—	opening balance sheet	bilan d'ouverture m	bilancio d'apertura m	balance inicial m
Eröffnungskurs (D)	—	opening price	cours d'ouverture m	corso d'apertura m	cotización de apertura f
érosion monétaire (F)	Geldwertschwund m	currency erosion	—	deprezzamento monetario m	erosión monetaria f
erosión monetaria (Es)	Geldwertschwund m	currency erosion	érosion monétaire f	deprezzamento monetario m	—
erratic price movements (E)	Ausbrechen des Kurses n	—	fortes fluctuations des cours f/pl	oscillazione inattesa della quotazione f	fuertes movimientos en las cotizaciones m/pl
erreur de comptabilité (F)	Buchungsfehler m	bookkeeping error	—	errore di contabilità m	error contable m
error contable (Es)	Buchungsfehler m	bookkeeping error	erreur de comptabilité f	errore di contabilità m	—
errore di contabilità (I)	Buchungsfehler m	bookkeeping error	erreur de comptabilité f	—	error contable m
Ersatzaktie (D)	—	replacement share certificate	action supplétive en remplacement d'un titre adiré f	azione sostitutiva f	acción de sustitución f
Ersatzdeckung (D)	—	substitute cover	garantie de substitution f	copertura sostitutiva f	garantía adicional f
Ersatzinvestition (D)	—	replacement of capital assets	investissement pour remplacmenet des moyens de production m	Investimento sostitutivo m	inversión de reposición f
Ersatzscheck (D)	—	substitute cheque	chèque de substitution m	assegno sostitutivo m	cheque de sustitución m
Ersatzüberweisung (D)	—	substitute transfer	virement de substitution m	trasferimento sostitutivo m	transferencia sustitutiva f
Erscheinen (D)	—	issuing	émission f	emissione f	emisión f
Erschließung (D)	—	development	ouverture f	apertura f	apertura f
Ersparnis (D)	—	savings	épargne f	risparmio m	ahorros m/pl
Erstattung (D)	—	reimbursement	restitution f	rimborso m	devolución f
Erstausstattung (D)	—	initial allowance set	dotation initiale f	dotazione iniziale f	primer establecimiento m
Ersterwerb (D)	—	first acquisition	première acquisition f	primo acquisto m	adquisición original f
Ertrag (D)	—	profits	rendement m	ricavo m	rendimiento m
Ertragssteuer (D)	—	tax on income	impôt assis sur le produit m	imposta cedolare f	impuesto sobre las ganancias m
Ertragswert (D)	—	capitalized value	valeur d'une chose mesurée à son rendement m	valore del reddito m	valor de la renta m
Erwartungswert (D)	—	anticipation term	valeur escomptée f	valore stimato m	valor esperado m
Erweiterungs-investition (D)	—	expansion investment	investissement d'expansion m	investimento d'ampliamento m	inversión de ampliación f
Erwerbermodell (D)	—	acquirer model	modèle d'acquéreur m	acquisto di immobili affittati m	modelo de adquirente m
Erwerbseinkommen (D)	—	income from gainful employment	revenu du travail m	reddito di lavoro m	remuneración de los asalariados f
Erwerbseinkünfte (D)	—	business income	revenus d'une activité professionelle m	redditi di lavoro m/pl	ingresos procenden-tes de una actividad remunerada m/pl
Erwerbsperson (D)	—	gainfully employed person	personne active f	persona abile al lavoro f	persona activa f
Erzeuger (D)	—	manufacturer	producteur m	produttore m	productor m
esame del bilancio (I)	Bankprüfung f	audit of the bank balance sheet	vérification du bilan bancaire f	—	revisión de cuentas del banco f
esame di solvibilità (I)	Bonitätsprüfung f	credit check	vérification de la solvabilité f	—	inspección de solvencia f

	D	E	F	I	Es
esborso (I)	Auszahlung f	payment	payement m	—	pago m
escala de intereses (Es)	Zinsstaffel f	interest rate table	barème des intérêts m	scaletta f	—
escalation clause (E)	Gleitklausel f	—	clause de prix mobile f	clausola della scala mobile f	cláusula de escala móvil f
escalation parity (E)	Gleitparität f	—	parité mobile f	parità variabile f	paridad móvil f
esclusiva (I)	Alleinvertrieb m	sole distribution	distribution exclusive f	—	distribución exclusiva f
escompte (F)	Diskont m	discount	—	sconto m	descuento m
escompte (F)	Skonto n	discount	—	sconto m	descuento m
escompte (F)	Diskontierung f	discounting	—	operazione di sconto f	descuento m
escompte direct (F)	Direktdiskont m	direct discount	—	sconto diretto m	descuento directo m
escompte d'un effet (F)	Wechseldiskont m	discount of bills	—	sconto cambiario m	descuento de letras m
escompte hors banque (F)	Privatdiskont m	prime acceptance	—	carta commerciale di prim'ordine f	descuento privado m
escompter (F)	eskomptieren	to discount	—	anticipare	descontar
escompte sur achat de titres (F)	Effektendiskont m	securities discount	—	sconto di titoli m	descuento de valores m
escritura numérica (Es)	Nummernverzeichnis n	list of serial numbers of securities purchased or deposited	liste numérique f	elenco numerico m	—
esecuzione (I)	Abwicklung f	settlement	exécution f	—	ejecución f
esecuzione (I)	Vollstreckung f	enforcement	exécution f	—	ejecución f
esercizio del diritto d'opzione (I)	Bezugsrechtsdisposition f	subscription rights disposition	disposition des droits de souscription f	—	disposición del derecho de suscripción f
eskomptieren (D)	—	to discount	escompter	anticipare	descontar
espansione del credito (I)	Kreditausweitung f	expansion of credit	expansion du crédit f	—	expansión del crédito f
especulación (Es)	Spekulation f	speculation	spéculation f	speculazione f	—
especulación de acaparamiento (Es)	Aufkaufspekulation f	take-over speculation	accaparement spéculatif m	speculazione in accaparramenti f	—
especulación de divisas (Es)	Devisenspekulation f	speculation in foreign currency	spéculation sur les changes f	speculazione in cambi f	—
esperto di economia politica (I)	Volkswirt m	economist	économiste m	—	economista m
espiral precio-salario (Es)	Preis-Lohn-Spirale f	wage-price spiral	course des prix et des salaires f	spirale dei prezzi e dei salari f	—
esportazione di capitale (I)	Kapitalausfuhr f	export of capital	exportation de capitaux f	—	exportación de capital f
esportazione di valuta (I)	Geldexport m	money export	exportation monétaire f	—	exportación monetaria f
espromissione (I)	Schuldübernahme f	assumption of an obligation	reprise de dette f	—	aceptación de deuda f
espropriazione (I)	Enteignung f	expropriation	expropriation f	—	expropiación f
essere presente sul mercato (I)	im Markt sein	to be in the market	être sur le marché	—	estar en el mercado
estabilidad (Es)	Stabilität f	stability	stabilité f	stabilità f	—
estabilidad monetaria (Es)	Geldwertstabilität f	monetary stability	stabilité monétaire f	stabilità monetaria f	—
estabilización (Es)	Stabilisierung f	stabilization	stabilisation f	stabilizzazione f	—
estable (Es)	stabil	stable	stable	stabile	—
establecimiento del presupuesto (Es)	Budgetierung f	drawing up of a budget	établissement du budget m	formazione del bilancio pubblico f	—
estadística (Es)	Statistik f	statistics	statistique f	statistica f	—
estadística bancaria (Es)	Bankenstatistik f	banking statistics	statistique bancaire f	statistica bancaria f	—
estadística bancaria (Es)	Bankstatistik f	banking statistics	statistique bancaire f	statistica bancaria f	—
estadística de balances (Es)	Bilanzstatistik f	balance sheet statistics	statistique des bilans f	analisi statistica dei bilanci f	—

	D	E	F	I	Es
estadística de emisión (Es)	Emissionsstatistik f	new issue statistics	statistique d'émission f	statistica delle nuove emissioni f	—
estadística del comercio exterior (Es)	Außenhandelsstatistik f	foreign trade statistics	statistique du commerce extérieur f	statistica del commercio estero f	—
estadística de valores (Es)	Effektenstatistik f	securities statistics	statistique de titres f	statistica dei titoli f	—
estado bancario (Es)	Bankstatus m	bank status	état bancaire m	situazione di banca f	—
estado de estancamiento (Es)	geschäftslos	slack	stagnant	inattivo	—
estado del endeudamiento (Es)	Kreditstatus m	credit standing	état de l'endettement m	situazione creditizia f	—
estado de resultados a corto plazo (Es)	kurzfristige Erfolgsrechnung f	monthly income statement	comptes de résultats intermédiaires m/pl	conto economico a breve termine m	—
estampillado (Es)	Abstempelung f	stamping	estampillage m	bollatura f	—
estampillado de billetes (Es)	Notenabstempelung f	stamping of bank notes	estampillage des billets de banque m	timbratura di banconote f	—
estampillage (F)	Abstempelung f	stamping	—	bollatura f	estampillado m
estampillage des billets de banque (F)	Notenabstempelung f	stamping of bank notes	—	timbratura di banconote f	estampillado de billetes m
estandardización (Es)	Standardisierung f	standardization	standardisation f	standardizzazione f	—
estanflación (Es)	Stagflation f	stagflation	stagflation f	stagflazione f	—
estar en el mercado (Es)	im Markt sein	to be in the market	être sur le marché	essere presente sul mercato	—
estatutos (Es)	Satzung f	statutes	statut m	statuto m	—
estimated quotation (E)	Taxkurs m	—	cours d'estimation m	corso di stima m	precio de tasación m
estratto bancario (I)	Bankauszug m	bank statement	relevé de compte m	—	relación f
estratto conto (I)	Kontoauszug m	statement of account	relevé de compte m	—	extracto de cuenta m
estratto deposito (I)	Depotauszug m	statement of securities	relevé de compte-titres m	—	extracto de depósito m
estratto giornaliero (I)	Tagesauszug m	daily statement	relevé quotidien de compte m	—	extracto de cuenta diario m
estrazione (I)	Ziehung f	drawing	tirage m	—	giro m
estructura de empleo (Es)	Beschäftigtenstruktur f	employment structure	structure d'emploi f	struttura dell'occupazione f	—
estructura de interés inversa (Es)	inverse Zinsstruktur f	inverse interest rate structure	structure inverse des intérêts f	struttura degli interessi inversa f	—
estructura del balance (Es)	Bilanzstruktur f	structure of the balance sheet	structure du bilan f	struttura del bilancio f	—
estructura del balance (Es)	Bilanzgliederung f	format of the balance sheet	présentation du bilan f	struttura del bilancio f	—
estructura del comercio exterior (Es)	Außenhandelsrahmen m	foreign trade structure	structure du commerce extérieur f	quadro commercio estero m	—
estructura del mercado (Es)	Marktstruktur f	market structure	structure du marché f	struttura del mercato f	—
estructura de los intereses (Es)	Zinsstruktur f	interest rate structure	structure des intérêts f	struttura degli interessi f	—
estructura de ofertas (Es)	Angebotsstruktur f	supply structure	structure d'offres f	struttura dell'offerta f	—
estructura monetaria (Es)	Geldverfassung f	monetary structure	structure monétaire f	sistema monetario m	—
établissement de crédit (F)	Kreditinstitut n	credit institution	—	istituto di credito m	instituto de crédito m
établissement de crédit foncier (F)	Grundkreditanstalt f	mortgage bank	—	istituto di credito fondiario m	banco hipotecario m
établissement de l'inventaire (F)	Bestandsaufnahme f	stock-taking	—	redazione d'inventario f	formación de un inventario f
établissement d'émission (F)	Emissionshaus n	issuing house	—	banca emittente f	casa emisora f
établissement du bilan (F)	Bilanzierung f	procedure to draw up a balance sheet	—	redazione del bilancio f	formación del balance f
établissement du budget (F)	Budgetierung f	drawing up of a budget	—	formazione del bilancio pubblico f	establecimiento del presupuesto m

	D	E	F	I	Es
établissement financier (F)	Geldinstitut *n*	financial institution	—	istituto di credito *m*	instituto monetario *m*
établissements d'escompte (F)	Diskonthäuser *n/pl*	discount houses	—	discount houses *m/pl*	casa de aceptación *f*
étalon dollar (F)	Dollar-Standard *m*	dollar standard	—	dollar standard *m*	patrón-dólar *m*
étalon or (F)	Gold-Standard *m*	gold standard	—	gold standard *m*	patrón-oro *m*
etalon-or (F)	Goldwährung *f*	gold currency	—	valuta aurea *f*	moneda oro *f*
étalon or et devises (F)	Gold-Devisen-Standard *m*	gold exchange standard	—	gold exchange standard *m*	patrón de divisas en oro *m*
état bancaire (F)	Bankstatus *m*	bank status	—	situazione di banca *f*	estado bancario *m*
état de la liquidité (F)	Liquiditätsstatus *m*	liquidity status	—	situazione di liquidità *f*	situación de liquidez *f*
état de l'endettement (F)	Kreditstatus *m*	credit standing	—	situazione creditizia *f*	estado del endeudamiento *m*
état des recettes et des dépenses (F)	Einnahmen--Ausgabenrechnung *f*	bill of receipts and expenditures	—	conto entrate e uscite *m*	cuenta de gastos-ingresos *f*
état du patrimoine (F)	Vermögensbilanz *f*	asset and liability statement	—	bilancio patrimoniale *m*	balance patrimonial *m*
état prévisionnel des dépenses (F)	Ausgabenplan *m*	plan of expenditure	—	piano di spesa *m*	presupuesto de gastos *m*
être sur le marché (F)	im Markt sein	to be in the market	—	essere presente sul mercato	estar en el mercado
étude du marché des capitaux (F)	Kapitalmarkt-forschung *f*	capital market research	—	ricerca del mercato finanziario *f*	investigación del mercado de capital *f*
études économiques empiriques (F)	empirische Wirt-schaftsforschung *f*	empirical economic research	—	ricerca economica empirica *f*	investigación eco-nómica empírica *f*
Euro-Aktienmarkt (D)	—	Euro share market	marché de l'euroaction *m*	euromercato azionario *m*	mercado de euroacciones *m*
Euro-Anleihe (D)	—	Eurocurrency loans	euroémission *f*	europrestito *m*	euroemisión *f*
Euro-Anleihen-markt (D)	—	Eurocurrency loan market	marché de l'euroémission *m*	mercato degli europrestiti *m*	mercado de euroemisiones *m*
eurobanca (I)	Euro-Bank *f*	Eurobank	banque européenne *f*	—	banco europeo *m*
Euro-Bank (D)	—	Eurobank	banque européenne *f*	eurobanca *f*	banco europeo *m*
Eurobank (E)	Euro-Bank *f*	—	banque européenne *f*	eurobanca *f*	banco europeo *m*
Euro-Bond (D)	—	Eurobond	emprunt libellé en monnaie étrangère *m*	eurobond *m*	euroobligación *f*
Eurobond (E)	Euro-Bond *m*	—	emprunt libellé en monnaie étrangère *m*	eurobond *m*	euroobligación *f*
eurobond (I)	Euro-Bond *m*	Eurobond	emprunt libellé en monnaie étrangère *m*	—	euroobligación *f*
Eurobond market (E)	Euro-Bondmarkt *m*	—	marché de l'euroémission *m*	mercato degli eurobond *m*	mercado de euroobligaciones *m*
Euro-Bondmarkt (D)	—	Eurobond market	marché de l'euroémission *m*	mercato degli eurobond *m*	mercado de euroobligaciones *m*
Eurocapital market (E)	Euro-Kapitalmarkt *m*	—	marché européen financier *m*	euromercato finanziario *m*	mercado de las euroobligaciones *m*
eurocheque (E)	Euroscheck *m*	—	eurochèque *m*	eurocheque *m*	eurocheque *m*
eurocheque (Es)	Euroscheck *m*	eurocheque	eurochèque *m*	eurocheque *m*	—
eurochèque (F)	Euroscheck *m*	eurocheque	—	eurocheque *m*	eurocheque *m*
eurocheque (I)	Euroscheck *m*	eurocheque	eurochèque *m*	—	eurocheque *m*
Eurocheque card (E)	Euroscheck-Karte *f*	—	carte d'identité eurochèque *f*	carta eurocheque *f*	tarjeta eurocheque *f*
Eurocurrency loan market (E)	Euro-Anleihenmarkt *m*	—	marché de l'euroémission *m*	mercato degli europrestiti *m*	mercado de euroemisiones *m*
Eurocurrency loans (E)	Euro-Anleihe *f*	—	euroémission *f*	europrestito *m*	euroemisión *f*
Eurocurrency market (E)	Euro-Geldmarkt *m*	—	marché des eurodevises *m*	euromercato monetario *m*	mercado de eurodivisas *m*
Euro-DM (D)	—	Euro mark	euromark *m*	euromarco *m*	euromarco *m*
Euro-DM-Markt (D)	—	Euro mark market	marché de l'euromark *m*	mercato dell'euromarco *m*	mercado de euromarcos *m*
eurodólar (Es)	Euro-Dollar *m*	Eurodollar	eurodollar *m*	eurodollaro *m*	—
Euro-Dollar (D)	—	Eurodollar	eurodollar *m*	eurodollaro *m*	eurodólar *m*

	D	E	F	I	Es
Eurodollar (E)	Euro-Dollar *m*	—	eurodollar *m*	eurodollaro *m*	eurodólar *m*
eurodollar (F)	Euro-Dollar *m*	Eurodollar	—	eurodollaro *m*	eurodólar *m*
Eurodollar market (E)	Euro-Dollarmarkt *m*	—	marché de l'eurodollar *m*	mercato dell'eurodollaro *m*	mercado de eurodólares *m*
Euro-Dollarmarkt (D)	—	Eurodollar market	marché de l'eurodollar *m*	mercato dell'eurodollaro *m*	mercado de eurodólares *m*
eurodollaro (I)	Euro-Dollar *m*	Eurodollar	eurodollar *m*	—	eurodólar *m*
euroemisión (Es)	Euro-Emission *f*	Euro security issue	euroémission *f*	euroemissione *f*	—
euroemisión (Es)	Euro-Anleihe *f*	Eurocurrency loans	euroémission *f*	europrestito *m*	—
Euro-Emission (D)	—	Euro security issue	euroémission *f*	euroemissione *f*	euroemisión *f*
euroémission (F)	Euro-Anleihe *f*	Eurocurrency loans	—	europrestito *m*	euroemisión *m*
euroémission (F)	Euro-Emission *f*	Euro security issue	—	euroemissione *f*	euroemisión *f*
euroemissione (I)	Euro-Emission *f*	Euro security issue	euroémission *f*	—	euroemisión *f*
Euro-Geldmarkt (D)	—	Eurocurrency market	marché des eurodevises *m*	euromercato monetario *m*	mercado de eurodivisas *m*
Euro-Kapitalmarkt (D)	—	Eurocapital market	marché européen financier *m*	euromercato finanziario *m*	mercado de las euroobligaciones *m*
euromarché (F)	Euro-Markt *m*	Euromarket	—	euromercato *m*	euromercado *m*
euromarco (Es)	Euro-DM *f*	Euro mark	euromark *m*	euromarco *m*	—
euromarco (I)	Euro-DM *f*	Euro mark	euromark *m*	—	euromarco *m*
euromark (F)	Euro-DM *f*	Euro mark	—	euromarco *m*	euromarco *m*
Euro mark (E)	Euro-DM *f*	—	euromark *m*	euromarco *m*	euromarco *m*
Euromarket (E)	Euro-Markt *m*	—	euromarché *m*	euromercato *m*	euromercado *m*
Euro mark market (E)	Euro-DM-Markt *m*	—	marché de l'euromark *m*	mercato dell'euromarco *m*	mercado de euromarcos *m*
Euro-Markt (D)	—	Euromarket	euromarché *m*	euromercato *m*	euromercado *m*
euromercado (Es)	Euro-Markt *m*	Euromarket	euromarché *m*	euromercato *m*	—
euromercato (I)	Euro-Markt *m*	Euromarket	euromarché *m*	—	euromercado *m*
euromercato azionario (I)	Euro-Aktienmarkt *m*	Euro share market	marché de l'euroaction *m*	—	mercado de euroacciones *m*
euromercato finanziario (I)	Euro-Kapitalmarkt *m*	Eurocapital market	marché européen financier *m*	—	mercado de las euroobligaciones *m*
euromercato monetario (I)	Euro-Geldmarkt *m*	Eurocurrency market	marché des eurodevises *m*	—	mercado de eurodivisas *m*
euroobligación (Es)	Euro-Bond *m*	Eurobond	emprunt libellé en monnaie étrangère *m*	eurobond *m*	—
europäische Börsenrichtlinien (D)	—	European stock exchange guide-lines	directives boursières européennes *f/pl*	regolamenti europei di borsa *m/pl*	normas bursátiles europeas *f/pl*
Europäische Gemeinschaft (D)	—	European Community	Communauté Européenne	Comunità Europea *f*	Comunidad Europea *f*
Europäische Handelsgesellschaft (D)	—	European trading company	Société commerciale européenne *f*	società per azioni europea *f*	Sociedad Comercial Europea *f*
Europäische Investitionsbank (D)	—	European Investment Bank	Banque européenne d'investissement *f*	Banca Europea per gli Investimenti *f*	Banco Europeo de Inversiones *m*
Europäischer Entwicklungsfonds (D)	—	European Development Fund [EDF]	Fonds européen de développement *m*	Fondo europeo di sviluppo *m*	Fondo de Desarrollo y Saneamiento *m*
Europäischer Fonds für Währungspolitische Zusammenarbeit [EFWZ] (D)	—	European Monetary Cooperation Fund [EMCF]	Fonds Européen de Coopération Monétaire (FECOM) *m*	Fondo Europeo di cooperazione monetaria *m*	Fondo Europeo de Cooperación Monetaria [FECOM] *m*
Europäisches Währungsabkommen (D)	—	European Monetary Agreement	Accord monétaire européen *m*	Accordo Monetario Europeo *m*	Acuerdo Monetario Europeo *m*
Europäisches Währungssystem [EWS] (D)	—	European Monetary System [EMS]	Système Monétaire Européen S.M.E. *m*	Sistema monetario europeo *m*	Sistema Monetario Europeo [SME] *m*
Europäische Union (D)	—	European Union	Union Européenne *f*	Unione Europea *f*	Unión Europea *f*
Europäische Währungseinheit [ECU] (D)	—	European Currency Unit [ECU]	Unité monétaire européenne *f*	Unità Monetaria Europea *f*	Unidad Monetaria Europea [UME] *f*
European Community (E)	Europäische Gemeinschaft *f*	—	Communauté Européenne	Comunità Europea *f*	Comunidad Europea *f*
European Currency Unit [ECU] (E)	Europäische Währungseinheit [ECU] *f*	—	Unité monétaire européenne *f*	Unità Monetaria Europea *f*	Unidad Monetaria Europea [UME] *f*

	D	E	F	I	Es
European Development Fund [EDF] (E)	Europäischer Entwicklungsfonds *m*	—	Fonds européen de développement *m*	Fondo europeo di sviluppo *m*	Fondo de Desarrollo y Saneamiento *m*
European Investment Bank (E)	Europäische Investitionsbank *f*	—	Banque européenne d'investissement *f*	Banca Europea per gli Investimenti *f*	Banco Europeo de Inversiones *m*
European Monetary Agreement (E)	Europäisches Währungsabkommen *n*	—	Accord monétaire européen *m*	Accordo Monetario Europeo *m*	Acuerdo Monetario Europeo *m*
European Monetary Cooperation Fund [EMCF] (E)	Europäischer Fonds für Währungspolitische Zusammenarbeit [EFWZ] *m*	—	Fonds européen de coopération monétaire (FECOM) *m*	Fondo Europeo di cooperazione monetaria *m*	Fondo Europeo de Cooperación Monetaria [FECOM] *m*
European Monetary System [EMS] (E)	Europäisches Währungssystem [EWS] *n*	—	Système monétaire européen S.M.E. *m*	Sistema monetario europeo *m*	Sistema Monetario Europeo [SME] *m*
European stock exchange guide-lines (E)	europäische Börsenrichtlinien *f/pl*	—	directives boursières européennes *f/pl*	regolamenti europei di borsa *m/pl*	normas bursátiles europeas *f/pl*
European trading company (E)	Europäische Handelsgesellschaft *f*	—	Société commerciale européenne *f*	società per azioni europea *f*	Sociedad Comercial Europea *f*
European Union (E)	Europäische Union *f*	—	Union européenne *f*	Unione Europea *f*	Unión Europea *f*
europrestito (I)	Euro-Anleihe *f*	Eurocurrency loans	euroémission *f*	—	euroemisión *m*
Euroscheck (D)	—	eurocheque	eurochèque *m*	eurocheque *m*	eurocheque *m*
Euroscheck-Karte (D)	—	Eurocheque card	carte d'identité eurochèque *f*	carta eurocheque *f*	tarjeta eurocheque *f*
Euro security issue (E)	Euro-Emission *f*	—	euroémission *f*	euroemissione *f*	euroemisión *f*
Euro share market (E)	Euro-Aktienmarkt *m*	—	marché de l'euroaction *m*	euromercato azionario *m*	mercado de euroacciones *m*
evaluación (Es)	Bewertung *f*	valuation	valorisation *f*	valutazione *f*	—
evaluación (Es)	Auswertung *f*	evaluation	évaluation *f*	analisi *f*	—
evaluación del derecho de suscripción (Es)	Bezugsrechtsbewertung *f*	subscription rights evaluation	évaluation des droits de souscription *f*	valutazione del diritto d'opzione *f*	—
evaluación del valor (Es)	Wertermittlung *f*	determination of the value	évaluation *f*	valutazione *f*	—
evaluation (E)	Auswertung *f*	—	évaluation *f*	analisi *f*	evaluación *f*
évaluation (F)	Auswertung *f*	evaluation	—	analisi *f*	evaluación *f*
évaluation (F)	Wertermittlung *f*	determination of the value	—	valutazione *f*	evaluación del valor *f*
évaluation des droits de souscription (F)	Bezugsrechtsbewertung *f*	subscription rights evaluation	—	valutazione del diritto d'opzione *f*	evaluación del derecho de suscripción *f*
evasión al patrimonio real (Es)	Flucht in die Sachwerte *f*	flight into real assets	fuite vers les biens réels *f*	fuga nei beni materiali *f*	—
évasion des capitaux (F)	Kapitalflucht *f*	exodus of capital	—	fuga dei capitali *f*	fuga de capital *f*
evening stock exchange (E)	Abendbörse *f*	—	bourse nocturne *f*	borsa pomeridiana *f*	bolsa nocturna *f*
Eventualverbindlichkeit (D)	—	contingent liability	obligation éventuelle *f*	obbligazione contingenziale *f*	obligación eventual *f*
evidence (E)	Beweismittel *n*	—	moyen de preuve *m*	prova *f*	medio probatorio *m*
Evidenzzentrale (D)	—	information centre	centre de déclaration *m*	centrale dei rischi *f*	central de evidencia *f*
evolución de los precios (Es)	Preisentwicklung *f*	trend in prices	évolution des prix *f*	andamento dei prezzi *m*	—
évolution des prix (F)	Preisentwicklung *f*	trend in prices	—	andamento dei prezzi *m*	evolución de los precios *f*
ewige Anleihe (D)	—	perpetual loan	emprunt perpétuel *m*	prestito perpetuo *m*	empréstito perpétuo *m*
ewige Rente (D)	—	perpetual annuity	rente perpétuelle *f*	annualità perpetua *f*	anualidad perpetua *f*
ewige Schuld (D)	—	perpetual debt	dette perpétuelle *f*	prestito perpetuo *m*	deuda perpetua *f*
exacciones de exportación (Es)	Ausfuhrabgaben *f/pl*	export duties	taxes à l'exportation *f/pl*	tasse all'esportazione *f/pl*	—
examinación del prospecto (Es)	Prospektprüfung *f*	audit of prospectus	vérification du prospectus *f*	controllo del prospetto *m*	—
examination (E)	Prüfung *f*	—	vérification *f*	controllo *m*	revisión *f*
examining commission (E)	Prüfungskommission *f*	—	commission de contrôle *f*	giuria *f*	comisión de revisión de cuentas *f*
Ex-ante (D)	—	in prospect	ex ante	ex-ante	por anticipado

	D	E	F	I	Es
ex ante (F)	Ex-ante	in prospect	—	ex-ante	por anticipado
ex-ante (I)	Ex-ante	in prospect	ex ante	—	por anticipado
excédent de devises (F)	Devisenüberschuß *m*	foreign exchange surplus	—	eccedenza di valuta estera *f*	excedente de divisas *m*
excédent de liquidation (F)	Liquidationsüberschuß *m*	realization profit	—	eccedenza da liquidazione *f*	exceso de liquidación *m*
excédent des moyens de payement (F)	Geldüberhang *m*	excessive supply of money	—	eccedenza finanziaria *f*	exceso de dinero *m*
excédent d'exportation (F)	Ausfuhrüberschuß *m*	export surplus	—	eccedenza delle esportazioni *f*	excedente de exportación *m*
excédent d'intérêts (F)	Zinsüberschuß *m*	interest surplus	—	eccedenza degli interessi *f*	excedente de interés *m*
excédent du commerce extérieur (F)	Außenhandelsgewinn *m*	gains from trade	—	saldo attivo bilancia commerciale *m*	excedente del comercio exterior *m*
excedente de divisas (Es)	Devisenüberschuß *m*	foreign exchange surplus	excédent de devises *m*	eccedenza di valuta estera *f*	—
excedente de exportación (Es)	Ausfuhrüberschuß *m*	export surplus	excédent d'exportation *m*	eccedenza delle esportazioni *f*	—
excedente de interés (Es)	Zinsüberschuß *m*	interest surplus	excédent d'intérêts *m*	eccedenza degli interessi *f*	—
excedente del comercio exterior (Es)	Außenhandelsgewinn *m*	gains from trade	excédent du commerce extérieur *m*	saldo attivo bilancia commerciale *m*	—
ex cedola (I)	ohne Kupon	ex coupon	sans coupon	—	sin cupón
excepción de dolo (Es)	Einrede der Arglist *f*	defence of fraud	exception du dol *f*	eccezione di dolo *f*	—
excepción de excusión (Es)	Einrede der Vorausklage *f*	defence of lack of prosecution	exception de la discussion *f*	preescussione *f*	—
exception de la discussion (F)	Einrede der Vorausklage *f*	defence of lack of prosecution	—	preescussione *f*	excepción de excusión *f*
exception du dol (F)	Einrede der Arglist *f*	defence of fraud	—	eccezione di dolo *f*	excepción de dolo *f*
exceso de deudas (Es)	Überschuldung *f*	excessive indebtedness	surendettement *m*	indebitamento eccessivo *m*	—
exceso de dinero (Es)	Geldüberhang *m*	excessive supply of money	excédent des moyens de payement *m*	eccedenza finanziaria *f*	—
exceso de liquidación (Es)	Liquidationsüberschuß *m*	realization profit	excédent de liquidation *m*	eccedenza da liquidazione *f*	—
excessive indebtedness (E)	Überschuldung *f*	—	surendettement *m*	indebitamento eccessivo *m*	exceso de deudas *m*
excessive supply of money (E)	Geldüberhang *m*	—	excédent des moyens de payement *m*	eccedenza finanziaria *f*	exceso de dinero *m*
exchange (E)	Börse *f*	—	bourse *f*	borsa *f*	bolsa *f*
exchange broker (E)	Devisenkursmakler *m*	—	courtier en devises *m*	agente di cambio *m*	corredor de cambios *m*
exchange department (E)	Börsenabteilung *f*	—	service des valeurs en bourse *m*	ufficio borsa *m*	sección de bolsa *f*
exchange for forward delivery (E)	Termindevisen *f/pl*	—	devises négociées en bourse à terme *f/pl*	divise a termine *f/pl*	divisas a plazo *f/pl*
exchange function of money (E)	Tauschmittelfunktion des Geldes *f*	—	fonction de l'argent de moyen d'échange *f*	funzione di scambio della moneta *f*	función de medio de cambio del dinero *f*
exchange market intervention (E)	Devisenmarktinterventionen *f/pl*	—	intervention dans le marché des devises *f*	interventi sul mercato dei cambi *m/pl*	intervención en el mercado de divisas *f*
exchange of acceptances (E)	Akzeptaustausch *m*	—	échange d'acceptations *m*	scambio di accettazioni *m*	intercambio de aceptaciones *m*
exchange office (E)	Wechselstube *f*	—	bureau de change *m*	ufficio cambi *m*	casa cambiaria *f*
exchange of share certificates for new ones (E)	Aktienumtausch *m*	—	échange d'actions *m*	cambio di azioni *m*	cambio de acciones *m*
exchange of shares (E)	Aktienaustausch *m*	—	échange d'actions *m*	scambio di azioni *m*	canje de acciones *m*
exchange operation (E)	Geschäft *n*	—	opération *f*	contratto *m*	negocio *m*
exchange option (E)	Devisenoption *f*	—	option de change *f*	opzione di cambio *f*	opción de divisas *f*
exchange rate (E)	Wechselkurs *m*	—	cours du change *m*	cambio *m*	tipo de cambio *m*
exchange rate formation (E)	Devisenkursbildung *f*	—	formation du taux de change *f*	formazione dei cambi *f*	formación del tipo de cambio *f*

	D	E	F	I	Es
exchange rate mechanism (E)	Wechselkurs-mechanismus *m*	—	mécanisme du cours du change *m*	meccanismo di cambio *m*	mecanismo de cambio *m*
exchange risk (E)	Valutarisiko *n*	—	risque de perte au change *m*	rischio di cambio *m*	riesgo en el cambio *m*
exclusion principle (E)	Ausschlußprinzip *n*	—	principe d'exclusion *m*	principio d'esclusione *m*	principio de exclusión del precio *m*
exclusive right of coinage (E)	Münzregal *n*	—	monopole de la frappe *m*	privilegio di battere moneta *m*	regalía de acuñación *f*
ex coupon (E)	ohne Kupon	—	sans coupon	ex cedola	sin cupón
excusión (Es)	Vorausklage *f*	preliminary injunction	bénéfice de discussion *m*	citazione preventiva *f*	—
ex dividendo (I)	Dividendenabschlag *m*	quotation ex dividend	cours moins le dividende *f*	—	disagio de dividendo *m*
ex drawing (E)	Ex Ziehung *f*	—	sans tirage	ex tratta	ex giro
exécution (F)	Abwicklung *f*	settlement	—	esecuzione *f*	ejecución *f*
exécution (F)	Vollstreckung *f*	enforcement	—	esecuzione *f*	ejecución *f*
exercice commercial (F)	Geschäftsjahr *n*	financial year	—	anno d'esercizio *m*	ejercicio *m*
ex giro (Es)	Ex Ziehung *f*	ex drawing	sans tirage	ex tratta	—
exhaust (E)	Ermattung *f*	—	léthargie *f*	indebolimento delle quotazioni *m*	letargía *f*
existences accumulées (F)	Stapelbestand *m*	stockpile	—	portafoglio stivato *m*	existencias de títulos almacenadas *f/pl*
existences comptables (F)	Buchbestände *m/pl*	book value	—	attivi e passivi contabili *m/pl*	existencias inventariadas *f/pl*
existencias de precaución (Es)	Vorsichtskasse *f*	precautionary holding	fonds de réserve *m/pl*	domanda precauzionale di moneta *f*	—
existencias de títulos almacenadas (Es)	Stapelbestand *m*	stockpile	existences accumulées *f/pl*	portafoglio stivato *m*	—
existencias inventariadas (Es)	Buchbestände *m/pl*	book value	existences comptables *f/pl*	attivi e passivi contabili *m/pl*	—
Existenzaufbau-darlehen (D)	—	business set-up loan	prêt de premier établissement *m*	mutuo inizio attività imprenditoriale *m*	préstamo de fundación *m*
Existenzminimum (D)	—	subsistence minimum	minimum vital *m*	minimo d'esistenza *m*	mínimo vital *m*
exodus of capital (E)	Kapitalflucht *f*	—	évasion des capitaux *f*	fuga dei capitali *f*	fuga de capital *f*
exogenes Geld (D)	—	exogenous money base	argent exogène *m*	denaro esogeno *m*	dinero exógeno *m*
exogenous money base (E)	exogenes Geld *n*	—	argent exogène *m*	denaro esogeno *m*	dinero exógeno *m*
Exoten (D)	—	highly speculative securities	valeurs extrêmement spéculatives *f/pl*	titoli provenienti da paesi esotici *m/pl*	valores especulativos *m/pl*
expansión del crédito (Es)	Kreditausweitung *f*	expansion of credit	expansion du crédit *f*	espansione del credito *f*	—
expansion du crédit (F)	Kreditausweitung *f*	expansion of credit	—	espansione del credito *f*	expansión del crédito *f*
expansion investment (E)	Erweiterungs-investition *f*	—	investissement d'expansion *m*	investimento d'ampliamento *m*	inversión de ampliación *f*
expansion of credit (E)	Kreditausweitung *f*	—	expansion du crédit *f*	espansione del credito *f*	expansión del crédito *f*
expectancy cover procedure (E)	Anwartsschafts-deckungsverfahren *n*	—	système de la capitalisation *m*	sistema di capitalizzazione *m*	sistema de capitalización *m*
expectativas racionales (Es)	rationale Erwartungen *f/pl*	rational	expectatives rationnelles *f/pl*	aspettative razionali *f/pl*	—
expectatives rationnelles (F)	rationale Erwartungen *f/pl*	rational	—	aspettative razionali *f/pl*	expectativas racionales *f/pl*
expected inflation (E)	Inflationserwartung *f*	—	inflation prévue *f*	aspettativa d'inflazione *f*	inflación pronostizada *f*
expediente de crédito (Es)	Kreditakte *f*	credit folder	dossier de crédit *m*	cartella di credito *f*	—
expense account (E)	Aufwandskonto *n*	—	compte de frais *m*	conto spesa *m*	cuenta de gastos *f*
expenses (E)	Spesen *pl*	—	frais *m/pl*	spese *f/pl*	gastos *m/pl*
expenses (E)	Ausgaben *f/pl*	—	dépenses *f/pl*	spese *f/pl*	gastos *m/pl*

	D	E	F	I	Es
expenses incurred (E)	Aufwandskosten f	—	frais de représentation m/pl	spese di rappresentanza f/pl	gastos originados m/pl
expertise (F)	Gutachten n	expert opinion	—	perizia f	peritaje m
expert opinion (E)	Gutachten n	—	expertise f	perizia f	peritaje m
explanation (E)	Erklärung f	—	déclaration f	dichiarazione f	declaración f
exportación monetaria (Es)	Geldexport m	money export	exportation monétaire f	esportazione di valuta f	—
exportation de capitaux (F)	Kapitalausfuhr f	export of capital	—	esportazione di capitale f	exportación de capital f
exportation monétaire (F)	Geldexport m	money export	—	esportazione di valuta f	exportación monetaria f
export control (E)	Ausfuhrkontrolle f	—	contrôle des exportations m	controllo delle esportazioni m	control de las exportaciónes m
export credit guarantee (E)	Ausfuhr-bürgschaften f/pl	—	garanties à l'exportation f/pl	cauzioni d'esportazione f/pl	garantías para la exportación f/pl
export credit guarantee (E)	Ausfuhrgarantie f	—	garantie en faveur de l'exportateur f	garanzia d'esportazione f	garantía de exportación f
export credits (E)	Exportkredit m	—	crédit en faveur de l'exportation f	credito d'esportazione m	crédito a la exportación m
export credits (E)	AKA-Kredite m/pl	—	crédits en faveur de l'exportation m/pl	crediti speciali all'esportazione m/pl	créditos a la exportación m/pl
export department (E)	Außenhandels-abteilung f	—	service étranger m	ufficio commercio estero m	sección de comercio exterior f
Exportdevisen (D)	—	export exchange	devises obtenues par l'exportation f/pl	valuta estera da esportazioni f	divisas obtenidas mediante la exportación f/pl
export duties (E)	Ausfuhrabgaben f/pl	—	taxes à l'exportation f/pl	tasse all'esportazione f/pl	exacciones de exportación f/pl
export duty (E)	Ausfuhrzoll m	—	taxe de sortie f	dazio all'esportazione m	derechos de exportación m/pl
export exchange (E)	Exportdevisen f/pl	—	devises obtenues par l'exportation f/pl	valuta estera da esportazioni f	divisas obtenidas mediante la exportación f/pl
export financing (E)	Ausfuhrfinanzierung f	—	financement de l'exportation m	finanziamento all'esportazione m	finanziación de la exportación f
Exportfinanzierung (D)	—	financing of exports	financement d'opérations d'exportation m	finanziamento all'esportazione m	financiación de la exportación f
Exportförderung (D)	—	export promotion	encouragement à l'exportation m	agevolazione all'esportazione f	fomento de la exportación m
Exportkredit (D)	—	export credits	crédit en faveur de l'exportation m	credito d'esportazione m	crédito a la exportación m
export license (E)	Ausfuhrgenehmigung f	—	autorisation d'exportation f	autorizzazione all'esportazione f	licencia de exportación f
export of capital (E)	Kapitalausfuhr f	—	exportation de capitaux f	esportazione di capitale f	exportación de capital f
Exportprämie (D)	—	export premium	prime à l'exportation f	premio all'esportazione m	prima de exportación f
export premium (E)	Exportprämie f	—	prime à l'exportation f	premio all'esportazione m	prima de exportación f
export promotion (E)	Exportförderung f	—	encouragement à l'exportation m	agevolazione all'esportazione f	fomento de la exportación m
export surplus (E)	Ausfuhrüberschuß m	—	excédent d'exportation m	eccedenza delle esportazioni f	excedente de exportación m
Ex-post (Es)	ex-post	in retrospect	ex post	ex-post	—
ex post (F)	ex-post	in retrospect	—	ex-post	Ex-post
ex-post (D)	—	in retrospect	ex post	ex-post	Ex-post
ex-post (I)	ex-post	in retrospect	ex post	—	Ex-post
expropiación (Es)	Enteignung f	expropriation	expropriation f	espropriazione f	—
expropriation (E)	Enteignung f	—	expropriation f	espropriazione f	expropiación f
expropriation (F)	Enteignung f	expropriation	—	espropriazione f	expropiación f
ex-rights markdown (E)	Bezugsrecht-abschlag m	—	cours moins le droit de souscription f	stacco del diritto d'opzione m	deducción del derecho de suscripción f

	D	E	F	I	Es
extensión del balance (Es)	Bilanzverlängerung *f*	increase in total assets and liabilities	extension du bilan *f*	allungamento del bilancio *m*	—
extensión del plazo de reintegración (Es)	Tilgungsstreckung *f*	repayment extension	prolongation du délai de remboursement *f*	proroga di rimborso *f*	—
extension du bilan (F)	Bilanzverlängerung *f*	increase in total assets and liabilities	—	allungamento del bilancio *m*	extensión del balance *f*
extension of time for payment (E)	Zahlungsaufschub *m*	—	sursis de payement *m*	dilazione di pagamento *f*	pago aplazado *m*
external balance (E)	außenwirtschaftliches Gleichgewicht *n*	—	équilibre de l'économie extérieure *m*	equilibrio del commercio estero *m*	equilibrio de la economía exterior *m*
external bonds validation (E)	Auslandsbondsbereinigung *f*	—	validation des titres d'emprunt émis en monnaie étrangère *f*	correzione bonds in valuta estera *f*	convalidación de obligaciones en el exterior *f*
external financing (E)	Außenfinanzierung *f*	—	financement externe *m*	finanziamento esterno *m*	financiación externa *f*
external funds (E)	Fremde Gelder *n/pl*	—	capitaux de tiers *m/pl*	fondi di terzi *m/pl*	fondos ajenos *m/pl*
external indebtedness (E)	Auslandsverschuldung *f*	—	dette extérieure *f*	indebitamento verso l'estero *m*	deuda exterior *f*
external investment (E)	Fremdinvestition *f*	—	investissement de capitaux étrangers *m*	investimento in imprese altrui *m*	inversión de capitales extranjeros *f*
external market (E)	Außenmarkt *m*	—	marché extérieur *m*	mercato estero *m*	mercado externo *m*
external procurement (E)	Fremdbezug *m*	—	matériel acheté au-dehors *m*	acquisto di beni e servizi da terzi *m*	suministro externo *m*
external value of the currency (E)	Außenwert der Währung *m*	—	valeur externe de la monnaie *f*	valore esterno della valuta *m*	valor de la moneda en el exterior *m*
extracto de cuenta (Es)	Kontoauszug *m*	statement of account	relevé de compte *f*	estratto conto *m*	—
extracto de cuenta diario (Es)	Tagesauszug *m*	daily statement	relevé quotidien de compte *m*	estratto giornaliero *m*	—
extracto de depósito (Es)	Depotauszug *m*	statement of securities	relevé de compte-titres *m*	estratto deposito *m*	—
extra dividend (E)	Bonus *m*	—	bonification *f*	dividendo *m*	bono *m*
extra dividend (E)	Sonderausschüttung *f*	—	répartition extraordinaire *f*	distribuzione straordinaria *f*	reparto extraordinario *m*
extranjerización (Es)	Überfremdung *f*	control by foreign capital	envahissement de capitaux étrangers *m*	inforestieramento *m*	—
extraordinary depreciation (E)	außerordentliche Abschreibung *f*	—	amortissement extraordinaire *m*	ammortamento straordinario *m*	amortización extraordinaria *f*
extraordinary income (E)	außerordentliche Erträge *m/pl*	—	profits exceptionnels *m/pl*	sopravvenienze attive *f/pl*	ingresos extraordinarios *m/pl*
extraordinary trend (E)	Sonderbewegung *f*	—	tendance extraordinaire *f*	movimento divergente *m*	oscilación extraordinaria *f*
ex tratta (I)	Ex Ziehung *f*	ex drawing	sans tirage	—	ex giro
extravío de capital (Es)	Kapitalfehlleitung *f*	misguided investment	faux investissements *m/pl*	disguido di capitale *m*	—
Extremkurs (D)	—	peak quotation	cours extrême *m*	quotazione estrema *f*	curso extremo *m*
Ex Ziehung (D)	—	ex drawing	sans tirage	ex tratta	ex giro
fabbisogno creditizio (I)	Kreditbedarf *m*	credit demand	besoin en crédits *m*	—	necesidad de crédito *f*
fabbisogno di capitale (I)	Kapitalbedarf *m*	capital requirement	besoin en capital *m*	—	necesidad de capital *f*
fabbisogno finanziario (I)	Finanzbedarf *m*	financial requirements	besoins de trésorerie *m/pl*	—	necesidad financiera *f*
fabbricazione di monete false (I)	Falschmünzerei *f*	counterfeiting	faux-monnayage *m*	—	fabricación de moneda falsa *f*
fabricación de moneda falsa (Es)	Falschmünzerei *f*	counterfeiting	faux-monnayage *m*	fabbricazione di monete false *f*	—
face value (E)	Nominalwert *m*	—	valeur nominale *f*	valore nominale *m*	valor nominal *m*
facilidad (Es)	Fazilität *f*	facilities	facilités *f/pl*	facilitazione creditizia *f*	—
facilidades crediticias (Es)	Kreditfazilität *f*	credit facilities	facilité de crédit *f*	facilitazione creditizia *f*	—
facilidades especiales (Es)	Sonderfazilitäten *f/pl*	special credit facilities	facilités spéciales *f/pl*	facilitazioni creditizie speciali *f/pl*	—

	D	E	F	I	Es
facilitazione creditizia (I)	Kreditfazilität f	credit facilities	facilité de crédit f	—	facilidades crediticias f/pl
facilitazione creditizia (I)	Fazilität f	facilities	facilités f/pl	—	facilidad f
facilitazioni creditizie speciali (I)	Sonderfazilitäten f/pl	special credit facilities	facilités spéciales f/pl	—	facilidades especiales f/pl
facilité de crédit (F)	Kreditfazilität f	credit facilities	—	facilitazione creditizia f	facilidades crediticias f/pl
facilités (F)	Fazilität f	facilities	—	facilitazione creditizia f	facilidad f
facilités spéciales (F)	Sonderfazilitäten f/pl	special credit facilities	—	facilitazioni creditizie speciali f/pl	facilidades especiales f/pl
facilités spéciales de prêts sur nantissement (F)	Sonderlombard m	special lombard facility	—	anticipazione su titoli straordinaria f	préstamo pignoraticio especial m
facilities (E)	Fazilität f	—	facilités f/pl	facilitazione creditizia f	facilidad f
facteur de coûts (F)	Kostenfaktor m	cost factor	—	fattore di costo m	tipo de coste m
facteur de goulot d'étranglement (F)	Engpaßfaktor m	bottle-neck factor	—	fattore di stretta m	factor de escasez m
facteur d'escompte (F)	Diskontierungsfaktor m	discount factor	—	fattore di sconto m	factor de descuento m
facteur monétaire (F)	Geldfaktor m	monetary factor	—	fattore monetario m	factor monetario m
factor beta de regresión (Es)	Betafaktor m	beta factor	coefficient bêta m	indice beta m	—
factor costs (E)	Faktorkosten pl	—	coût des facteurs m	costi dei fattori m/pl	gastos de los factores m/pl
factor de descuento (Es)	Diskontierungsfaktor m	discount factor	facteur d'escompte m	fattore di sconto m	—
factor de escasez (Es)	Engpaßfaktor m	bottle-neck factor	facteur de goulot d'étranglement m	fattore di stretta m	—
factoring auténtico (Es)	echtes Factoring n	clean factoring	factoring authentique m	factoring pro soluto m	—
factoring authentique (F)	echtes Factoring n	clean factoring	—	factoring pro soluto m	factoring auténtico m
factoring falso (Es)	unechtes Factoring n	false factoring	factoring non authentique m	factoring pro solvendo m	—
factoring non authentique (F)	unechtes Factoring n	false factoring	—	factoring pro solvendo m	factoring falso m
factoring pro soluto (I)	echtes Factoring n	clean factoring	factoring authentique m	—	factoring auténtico m
factoring pro solvendo (I)	unechtes Factoring n	false factoring	factoring non authentique m	—	factoring falso m
factor monetario (Es)	Geldfaktor m	monetary factor	facteur monétaire m	fattore monetario m	—
facturación bancaria (Es)	Bankumsätze m/pl	bank turnover	chiffres d'affaires d'une banque m/pl	movimento bancario m	—
factura pendiente (Es)	offene Rechnung f	unsettled account	facture pas encore payée f	conto aperto m	—
facture pas encore payée (F)	offene Rechnung f	unsettled account	—	conto aperto m	factura pendiente f
facultative money (E)	fakultatives Geld n	—	argent facultatif m	denaro facoltativo m	dinero facultativo m
faible (F)	schwach	slack	—	debole	flojo
faillite (F)	Konkurs m	bankruptcy	—	fallimento m	quiebra f
failure to pay on due date (E)	Zahlungsverzug m	—	demeure du débiteur f	mora nel pagamento f	retraso en el pago m
fair market value (E)	Marktwert m	—	valeur sur le marché f	valore di mercato m	valor de mercado m
fairness in trade (E)	Kulanz f	—	souplesse en affaires f	correttezza f	complacencia f
Faktorkosten (D)	—	factor costs	coût des facteurs m	costi dei fattori m/pl	gastos de los factores m/pl
fakultatives Geld (D)	—	facultative money	argent facultatif m	denaro facoltativo m	dinero facultativo m
Fakultativklausel (D)	—	option clause	clause d'option f	clausola facoltativa f	cláusula potestativa f
Fälligkeit (D)	—	maturity	échéance f	scadenza f	vencimiento m

	D	E	F	I	Es
Fälligkeits-grundschuld (D)	—	fixed-date land charge	dette foncière remboursable à terme fixe *f*	debito fondiario a scadenza *m*	deuda inmobiliaria de vencimiento *f*
Fälligkeitshypothek (D)	—	fixed-date land mortgage	hypothèque consti-tuée sur la base d'un remboursement du capital à terme fixe sans dénonciation préalable *f*	ipoteca a scadenza determinata *f*	hipoteca de vencimiento *f*
fallimento (I)	Konkurs *m*	bankruptcy	faillite *f*	—	quiebra *f*
Falschgeld (D)	—	counterfeit money	fausse monnaie *f*	moneta contraffatta *f*	moneda falsa *f*
Falschmünzerei (D)	—	counterfeiting	faux-monnayage *m*	fabbricazione di monete false *f*	fabricación de moneda falsa *f*
false factoring (E)	unechtes Factoring *n*	—	factoring non authentique *m*	factoring pro solvendo *m*	factoring falso *m*
falsificación (Es)	Falsifikat *n*	falsification	falsification *f*	falsificazione *f*	—
falsificación del balance (Es)	Bilanzfälschung *f*	falsification of the balance sheet	falsification du bilan *f*	falsificazione del bilancio *f*	—
falsification (E)	Falsifikat *n*	—	falsification *f*	falsificazione *f*	falsificación *f*
falsification (F)	Falsifikat *n*	falsification	—	falsificazione *f*	falsificación *f*
falsification du bilan (F)	Bilanzfälschung *f*	falsification of the balance sheet	—	falsificazione del bilancio *f*	falsificación del balance *f*
falsification of the balance sheet (E)	Bilanzfälschung *f*	—	falsification du bilan *f*	falsificazione del bilancio *f*	falsificación del balance *f*
falsificazione (I)	Falsifikat *n*	falsification	falsification *f*	—	falsificación *f*
falsificazione del bilancio (I)	Bilanzfälschung *f*	falsification of the balance sheet	falsification du bilan *f*	—	falsificación del balance *f*
Falsifikat (D)	—	falsification	falsification *f*	falsificazione *f*	falsificación *f*
falta de liquidez (Es)	Illiquidität *f*	illiquidity	manque de liquidité *m*	illiquidità *f*	—
farm credit (E)	Hofkredit *m*	—	crédit agricole *m*	credito agricolo *m*	crédito agropecuario *m*
fattore di costo (I)	Kostenfaktor *m*	cost factor	facteur de coûts *m*	—	tipo de coste *m*
fattore di sconto (I)	Diskontierungsfaktor *m*	discount factor	facteur d'escompte *m*	—	factor de descuento *m*
fattore di stretta (I)	Engpaßfaktor *m*	bottle-neck factor	facteur de goulot d'étrangelement *m*	—	factor de escasez *m*
fattore monetario (I)	Geldfaktor *m*	monetary factor	facteur monétaire *m*	—	factor monetario *m*
fatturato (I)	Umsatz *m*	turnover	chiffre d'affaires *m*	—	cifra de facturación *f*
fausse monnaie (F)	Falschgeld *n*	counterfeit money	—	moneta contraffatta *f*	moneda falsa *f*
Faustpfand (D)	—	pawn	gage mobilier *m*	pegno mobile *m*	prenda mobiliaria *f*
faux investissements (F)	Kapitalfehlleitung *f*	misguided investment	—	disguido di capitale *m*	extravío de capital *m*
faux-monnayage (F)	Falschmünzerei *f*	counterfeiting	—	fabbricazione di monete false *f*	fabricación de moneda falsa *f*
favorevole (I)	freundlich	buoyant	ferme	—	animado
favoris (F)	Favoriten *m/pl*	seasoned securities	—	titoli molto richiesti *m/pl*	favoritos *m/pl*
Favoriten (D)	—	seasoned securities	favoris *m/pl*	titoli molto richiesti *m/pl*	favoritos *m/pl*
favoritos (Es)	Favoriten *m/pl*	seasoned securities	favoris *m/pl*	titoli molto richiesti *m/pl*	—
Fazilität (D)	—	facilities	facilités *f/pl*	facilitazione creditizia *f*	facilidad *f*
fecha del balance (Es)	Bilanzstichtag *m*	date of the balance sheet	jour du bilan *m*	giorno chiusura bilancio *m*	—
Federal Bank assets (E)	Bundesbank-guthaben *n*	—	avoir auprès de la Banque fédérale *m*	fondo banca centrale *m*	saldo activo del Banco Federal *m*
Federal bonds (E)	Bundesobligation *f*	—	obligation fédérale *f*	prestito pubblico *m*	obligación federal *f*
Federal Cartel Authority (E)	Bundeskartellamt *n*	—	administration fédérale pour la réglementation des cartels *f*	ufficio federale dei cartelli *m*	Oficina Federal de Cártel *f*
Federal Debt Register (E)	Bundesschuldbuch *n*	—	grand-livre de la dette publique *m*	libro del debito pubblico *m*	Registro de Deudas Federales *m*

	D	E	F	I	Es
Federal guarantee (E)	Bundesbürgschaft f	—	garantie fédérale f	garanzia federale f	garantía federal f
Federal loan (E)	Bundesanleihe f	—	titre de dette publique m	titolo di Stato m	empréstito de la Federación m
Federal loan syndicate (E)	Bundesanleihe-konsortium n	—	Syndicat fédéral d'emprunts m	consorzio emissione titoli pubblici m	consorcio de emprés-titos federales m
federazione (I)	Verband m	association	association f	—	asociación f
fee (E)	Gebühr f	—	taxe f	canone m	derechos m/pl
Fehlbetrag (D)	—	shortfall	déficit m	disavanzo m	déficit m
Feingehalt (D)	—	standard	titre m	titolo m	ley f
Feingewicht (D)	—	standard	poids de métal fin m	titolo m	peso fino m
Feingold (D)	—	fine gold	or fin m	oro fino m	oro fino m
Feinsilber (D)	—	fine silver	argent fin m	argento fino m	plata fina f
Feinunze (D)	—	troy ounce	once fine f	oncia f	onza fina f
ferme (F)	freundlich	buoyant	—	favorevole	animado
fermo su assegno (I)	Schecksperre f	stopping payment of cheque	opposition au paye-ment d'un chèque f	—	bloqueo de un cheque m
Ferngiro (D)	—	long distance giro	virement entre deux places bancaires m	bonifico da una piazza all'altra m	transferencia de una plaza a otra f
fester Verrechnungspreis (D)	—	standard price	prix standard m	prezzo unico m	precio estándar m
Festgeld (D)	—	fixed deposit	argent immobilisé m	deposito a termine m	depósito a plazo m
Festgeschäft (D)	—	firm deal	opération à terme fixe f	contrattazione a fermo f	operaciones a plazo fijo f/pl
Festpreis (D)	—	fixed price	prix fixe m	prezzo fisso m	precio firme m
festverzinslich (D)	—	with a fixed rate of interest	à revenu fixe	a reddito fisso	de renta fija
Festwert (D)	—	fixed value	valeur fixe f	valore costante m	precio fijo m
Festzins (D)	—	fixed interest	intérêt fixe m	interesse fisso m	interés fijo m
Festzinshypothek (D)	—	fixed-rate mortgage	hypothèque à intérêt fixe f	ipoteca ad interesse fisso f	hipoteca de interés fijo f
Festzinskonto (D)	—	fixed-interest bearing account	compte à intérêt fixe m	conto ad interesse fisso m	cuenta de interés fijo f
feuille de coupons (F)	Kuponbogen m	coupon sheet	—	cedolario m	hoja de cupones f
feuilles d'enquête sur la solvabilité (F)	Kreditprüfungsblätter n/pl	credit checking sheets	—	fogli di controllo crediti m/pl	hojas de investigación crediticia f/pl
fiacco (I)	lustlos	slack	inactif m	—	poco animado
fiacco (I)	still	slack	calme	—	flojo
fiador (Es)	Bürge m	guarantor	garant m	fidefaciente m	—
fianza (Es)	Kaution f	security	caution f	cauzione f	—
fianza (Es)	Bürgschaft f	guarantee	caution f	fideiussione f	—
fianza de contratista (Es)	Leistungsgarantie f	performance guarantee	garantie de prestation f	garanzia di esecuzione f	—
fianza de disposición de banquero (Es)	Dispositionsschein m	banker's note	reconnaissance bancaire f	certificato di disponibilità m	—
finanza de indemnidad (Es)	Ausfallbürgschaft f	deficiency guarantee	garantie de bonne fin f	garanzia di sostituzione f	—
Fibor (D)	—	Fibor	Fibor m	fibor m	fibor m
Fibor (E)	Fibor m	—	Fibor m	fibor m	fibor m
Fibor (F)	Fibor m	Fibor	—	fibor m	fibor m
fibor (Es)	Fibor m	Fibor	Fibor m	fibor m	—
fibor (I)	Fibor m	Fibor	Fibor m	—	fibor m
fichero de operaciones de crédito (Es)	Kreditkartei f	borrowing customers' card index	fichier des opérations d'avances et de crédit m	—	schedario dei crediti m
fichier de renseignements (F)	Auskunftdatei f	information file	—	archivio d'informazioni m	archivo de datos con fines de información m
fichier des opérations d'avances et de crédit (F)	Kreditkartei f	borrowing customers' card index	—	schedario dei crediti m	fichero de operaciones de crédito m

	D	E	F	I	Es
fictitious bill (E)	Kellerwechsel m	—	traite fictive f	cambiale fittizia f	letra de cambio ficticia f
fictitious formation (E)	Scheingründung f	—	constitution d'opportunité f	costituzione fittizia f	fundación simulada f
fictitious order (E)	fingierte Order f	—	ordre simulé m	ordinazione fittizia f	orden fingida f
fictitious profit (E)	Scheingewinn m	—	gain fictif m	utile fittizio m	beneficio simulado m
fictitious quotation price (E)	Scheinkurs m	—	cours nominal m	quotazione evasiva f	cotización ficticia f
fictitious security price (E)	Ausweichkurs m	—	cours nominal m	quotazione evasiva f	precio ficticio de acciones m
fidefaciente (I)	Bürge m	guarantor	garant m	—	fiador m
fideicomiso de empréstitos (Es)	Anleihetreu-händerschaft f	loan custodianship	fidéicommis d'emprunts m	amministrazione fiduciaria prestiti f	—
fidéicommis d'emprunts (F)	Anleihetreu-händerschaft f	loan custodianship	—	amministrazione fiduciaria prestiti f	fideicomiso de empréstitos m
fideiussione (I)	Bürgschaft f	guarantee	caution f	—	fianza f
fideiussione per il fideiussore (I)	Nachbürgschaft f	collateral guarantee	garantie du certifica-teur de la caution f	—	subfianza f
fido (I)	Kreditwürdigkeit f	creditworthiness	solvabilité f	—	crédito m
fido in bianco (I)	Blanko-Kredit m	open credit	crédit en compte courant m	—	crédito en blanco m
fiduciaire (F)	Treuhänder m	trustee	—	fiduciario m	fiduciario m
fiduciaire institué (F)	Treuhandanstalt f	institutional trustee	—	istituto fiduciario m	instituto fiduciario m
fiduciario (Es)	Treuhänder m	trustee	fiduciaire m	fiduciario m	—
fiduciario (I)	Treuhänder m	trustee	fiduciaire m	—	fiduciario m
fiduciary account (E)	Anderkonto n	—	compte de tiers m	conto altrui m	cuenta fiduciaria f
fiduciary deposit (E)	Fremddepot n	—	dépôt d'autrui m	deposito presso terzi m	depósito ajeno m
fiduciary deposit (E)	Anderdepot n	—	dépôt de consignation m	deposito altrui m	depósito por cuenta de terceros m
fiduciary funds (E)	fiduziäres Geld n	—	argent fiduciaire m	denaro fiduciario m	dinero fiduciario m
fiduziäres Geld (D)	—	fiduciary funds	argent fiduciaire m	denaro fiduciario m	dinero fiduciario m
figure (E)	Zahl f	—	chiffre m	cifra f	número m
fijación de la cotización (Es)	Fixing n	fixing	fixation de la cotation f	fixing m	—
fijación del tipo de cambio (Es)	Valutierung f	fixing of exchange rate	fixation des cours de change f	valuta f	—
filial (Es)	Filiale f	branch office	succursale f	filiale f	—
Filiale (D)	—	branch office	succursale f	filiale f	filial f
filiale (I)	Filiale f	branch office	succursale f	—	filial f
filiale (I)	Zweigstelle f	branch	agence f	—	sucursal f
filiale all'estero (I)	Auslands-niederlassung f	branch abroad	succursale à l'étranger f	—	sucursal en el extranjero f
Filialkalkulation (D)	—	branch office accounting	appréciation des résultats des succur-sales bancaires f	calcolo delle filiali m	cálculos de sucursal m/pl
Filialscheck (D)	—	house cheque	chèque interne m	assegno su filiale m	cheque de sucursal m
final demand (E)	Endnachfrage f	—	demande finale f	domanda aggregata effettiva f	demanda final f
final dividend (E)	Schlußdividende f	—	dividende final m	saldo di dividendo m	dividendo final m
final order (E)	Abschlußauftrag m	—	ordre final f	operazione di chiusura f	orden final f
finance (E)	Finanzwesen n	—	finances f/pl	finanze f/pl	régimen financiero m
finance bill (E)	Finanzwechsel m	—	traite financière f	cambiale finanziaria f	letra bancaria f
finance bill (E)	Leerwechsel m	—	traite financière f	cambiale vuota f	letra al descubierto f
finance deficit (E)	Finanzierungsdefizit n	—	déficit de financement m	deficit di finanziamento m	déficit de financiación f
financement (F)	Finanzierung f	financing	—	finanziamento m	financiación f
financement à la construction (F)	Baufinanzierung f	building financing	—	finanziamento all'edilizia m	financiación de la construcción f

	D	E	F	I	Es
financement de l'exportation (F)	Ausfuhrfinanzierung *f*	export financing	—	finanziamento all'esportazione *m*	finanziación de la exportación *f*
financement de la vente à crédit (F)	Konsumfinanzierung *f*	consumption financing	—	finanziamento di vendite rateali *m*	financiación al consumo *f*
financement d'épargne-construction (F)	Bausparfinanzierung *f*	building society funding	—	finanziamento edilizio *m*	financiación de ahorros para la construcción *f*
financement de rang inférieur (F)	nachrangige Finanzierung *f*	junior financing	—	finanziamento subordinato *m*	financiación subordinada *f*
financement des importations (F)	Importfinanzierung *f*	import financing	—	finanziamento delle importazioni *m*	financiación de las importaciones *f*
financement de valeurs mobilières (F)	Effektenfinanzierung *f*	security financing	—	finanziamento tramite titoli *m*	financiación de valores *f*
financement d'opérations d'exportation (F)	Exportfinanzierung *f*	financing of exports	—	finanziamento all'esportazione *m*	financiación de la exportación *f*
financement du déficit (F)	Defizit-Finanzierung *f*	deficit financing	—	deficit financing *m*	financiación del déficit *f*
financement d'un projet (F)	Projektfinanzierung *f*	project financing	—	finanziamento di un progetto *m*	financiación de un proyecto *f*
financement du renouvellement des immobilisations (F)	Anlagenfinanzierung *f*	financing of investment in fixed assets	—	finanziamento di investimenti *m*	financiación de inversión *f*
financement exagéré (F)	Überfinanzierung *f*	overfinancing	—	sovraccapitalizzazione *f*	financiación excesiva *f*
financement externe (F)	Außenfinanzierung *f*	external financing	—	finanziamento esterno *m*	financiación externa *f*
financement insuffisant (F)	Unterfinanzierung *f*	underfinancing	—	sottocapitalizzazione *f*	financiación insuficiente *f*
financement intermédiaire (F)	Zwischenfinanzierung *f*	interim financing	—	finanziamento transitorio *m*	financiación interina *f*
financement interne (F)	Innenfinanzierung *f*	internal financing	—	finanziamento interno *m*	financiación interna *f*
financement par capitaux de tiers (F)	Kreditfinanzierung *f*	financing by way of credit	—	finanziamento mediante credito *m*	financiación mediante créditos *f*
financement par capitaux prêtés (F)	Darlehens-finanzierung *f*	loan financing	—	finanziamento mediante mutuo *m*	financiación de préstamo *f*
financement par participation (F)	Beteiligungs-finanzierung *f*	equity financing	—	finanziamento di partecipazione *m*	financiación de participación *f*
finances (F)	Finanzwesen *n*	finance	—	finanze *f/pl*	régimen financiero *m*
financiación (Es)	Finanzierung *f*	financing	financement *m*	finanziamento *m*	—
financiación al consumo (Es)	Konsumfinanzierung *f*	consumption financing	financement de la vente à crédit *m*	finanziamento di vendite rateali *m*	—
financiación anticipada (Es)	Vorfinanzierung *f*	prefinancing	préfinancement *m*	prefinanziamento *m*	—
financiación con capital ajeno (Es)	Fremdfinanzierung *f*	debt financing	constitution de capital par apport de tiers *f*	finanziamento esterno *m*	—
financiación de ahorros para la construcción (Es)	Bausparfinanzierung *f*	building society funding	financement d'épargne-construction *m*	finanziamento edilizio *m*	—
financiación de inversión (Es)	Anlagenfinanzierung *f*	financing of investment in fixed assets	financement du renouvellement des immobilisations *m*	finanziamento di investimenti *m*	—
financiación de la construcción (Es)	Baufinanzierung *f*	building financing	financement à la construction *m*	finanziamento all'edilizia *m*	—
financiación de la exportación (Es)	Exportfinanzierung *f*	financing of exports	financement d'opérations d'exportation *m*	finanziamento all'esportazione *m*	—
financiación de las importaciones (Es)	Importfinanzierung *f*	import financing	financement des importations *m*	finanziamento delle importazioni *m*	—
financiación del comercio exterior (Es)	Forfaitierung *f*	forfaiting	forfaitage *m*	forfaiting *m*	—
financiación del comercio exterior (Es)	Außenhandels-finanzierung *f*	foreign trade financing	aide financière à l'exportation *f*	finanziamento commercio estero *m*	—
financiación del déficit (Es)	Defizit-Finanzierung *f*	deficit financing	financement du déficit *m*	deficit financing *m*	—

	D	E	F	I	Es
financiación de participación (Es)	Beteiligungs-finanzierung f	equity financing	financement par participation m	finanziamento di participazione m	—
financiación de preexportación (Es)	Präexport-Finanzierung f	pre-export financing	préfinancement de l'exportation m	prefinanziamento delle esportazioni m	—
financiación de préstamo (Es)	Darlehens-finanzierung f	loan financing	financement par capitaux prêtés m	finanziamento mediante mutuo m	—
financiación de un proyecto (Es)	Projektfinanzierung f	project financing	financement d'un projet m	finanziamento di un progetto m	—
financiación de valores (Es)	Effektenfinanzierung f	security financing	financement de valeurs mobilières m	finanziamento tramite titoli m	—
financiación excesiva (Es)	Überfinanzierung f	overfinancing	financement exagéré m	sovraccapitalizzazione f	—
financiación externa (Es)	Außenfinanzierung f	external financing	financement externe m	finanziamento esterno m	—
financiación insuficiente (Es)	Unterfinanzierung f	underfinancing	financement insuffisant m	sottoccapitalizzazione f	—
financiación interina (Es)	Zwischenfinanzierung f	interim financing	financement intermédiaire m	finanziamento transitorio m	—
financiación interna (Es)	Innenfinanzierung f	internal financing	financement interne m	finanziamento interno m	—
financiación mediante créditos (Es)	Kreditfinanzierung f	financing by way of credit	financement par capitaux de tiers m	finanziamento mediante credito m	—
financiación subordinada (Es)	nachrangige Finanzierung f	junior financing	financement de rang inférieur m	finanziamento subordinato m	—
financial acceptance (E)	Kreditakzept n	—	traite tirée en garantie d'un crédit f	accettazione bancaria f	aceptación de crédito f
financial account (E)	Finanzkonto n	—	compte financier m	conto finanziario m	cuenta financiera f
financial accounting (E)	Finanzbuchhaltung f	—	comptabilité financière f	contabilità finanziaria f	contabilidad financiera f
financial aid (E)	Beihilfe f	—	subside m	assistenza f	ayuda f
financial analysis (E)	Finanzanalyse f	—	analyse financière f	analisi finanziaria f	análisis financiero m
financial arrangement (E)	Finanzdisposition f	—	disposition financière f	disposizioni finanziarie f/pl	disposición financiera f
financial assets (E)	Finanzanlage-vermögen n	—	valeurs immobilisées financières f/pl	investimenti finanziari m/pl	inversiones financieras f/pl
financial assets (E)	Finanzvermögen n	—	disponibilités f/pl	patrimonio finanziario m	patrimonio financiero m
financial assistance (E)	finanzieller Beistand m	—	aide financière f	assistenza finanziaria f	ayuda financiera f
financial capital (E)	Finanzkapital n	—	capital financier m	capitale finanziario m	capital financiero m
financial credit (E)	Finanzkredit m	—	crédit de financement m	credito di finanziamento m	crédito financiero m
financial equalization (E)	Finanzausgleich m	—	compensation financière f	conguaglio finanziario m	ajuste financiero m
financial futures (I)	Finanztermin-kontrakt m	financial futures contract	contrat financier à terme m	—	contrato a plazo financiero m
financial futures contract (E)	Finanztermin-kontrakt m	—	contrat financier à terme m	financial futures m/pl	contrato a plazo financiero m
financial hedging (E)	Finanzhedging n	—	hedging financier m	hedging finanziario m	hedging financiero m
financial innovation (E)	Finanzinnovationen f/pl	—	innovations financières f/pl	innovazioni finanziarie f/pl	innovaciones financieras f/pl
financial institution (E)	Geldinstitut n	—	établissement financier m	istituto di credito m	instituto monetario m
financial interlocking (E)	Finanzverflechtung f	—	interdépendance financière f	interferenza finanziaria f	vinculaciones financieras f/pl
financial market (E)	Finanzmarkt m	—	marché des capitaux m	mercato finanziario m	mercado financiero m
financial mathematics (E)	Finanzmathematik f	—	mathématiques financières f/pl	matematica finanziaria f	matemáticas financieras f/pl
financial plan (E)	Finanzplan m	—	plan financier m	piano finanziario m	plan financiero m
financial policy (E)	Finanzpolitik f	—	politique financière f	politica finanziaria f	política financiera f
financial press (E)	Finanzpresse f	—	presse financière f	stampa finanziaria f	prensa financiera f
financial reform (E)	Finanzreform f	—	réforme financière f	riforma finanziaria f	reforma financiera f

	D	E	F	I	Es
financial requirements (E)	Finanzbedarf *m*	—	besoins de trésorerie *m/pl*	fabbisogno finanziario *m*	necesidad financiera *f*
financial reserve (E)	Finanzierungsreserve *f*	—	réserves financières *f/pl*	riserve finanziarie *f/pl*	reserva de financiación *f*
financial sector (E)	Finanzsektor *m*		secteur financier *m*	settore della finanza *m*	sector financiero *m*
financial soundness (E)	Bonität *f*	—	solvabilité *f*	solvibilità *f*	solvencia *f*
financial strength (E)	Finanzkraft *f*	—	capacité financière *f*	capacità finanziaria *f*	potencial financiero *m*
financial system (E)	Finanzverfassung *f*	—	système financier *m*	ordinamento finanziario *f*	constitución financiera *f*
financial theory (E)	Finanztheorie *f*	—	théorie financière *f*	teoria finanziaria *f*	teoría financiera *f*
financial transaction (E)	Finanztransaktion *f*		transaction financière *f*	operazione finanziaria *f*	transacción financiera *f*
financial year (E)	Geschäftsjahr *n*	—	exercice commercial *m*	anno d'esercizio *m*	ejercicio *m*
financing (E)	Finanzierung *f*	—	financement *m*	finanziamento *m*	financiación *f*
financing bonds (E)	Finanzierungsschätze *m/pl*	—	effets du Trésor *m/pl*	buoni del tesoro *m/pl*	letras del Tesoro *f/pl*
financing by way of credit (E)	Kreditfinanzierung *f*		financement par capitaux de tiers *m*	finanziamento mediante credito *m*	financiación mediante créditos *f*
financing of exports (E)	Exportfinanzierung *f*	—	financement d'opérations d'exportation *m*	finanziamento all'esportazione *m*	financiación de la exportación *f*
financing of investment in fixed assets (E)	Anlagenfinanzierung *f*	—	financement du renouvellement des immobilisations *m*	finanziamento di investimenti *m*	financiación de inversión *f*
financing principles (E)	Finanzierungs-grundsätze *m/pl*	—	principes de financement *m/pl*	principi di finanziamento *m/pl*	normas de financiación *f/pl*
financing rules (E)	Finanzierungsregeln *f/pl*	—	règles de financement *f/pl*	regole di finanziamento *f/pl*	normas de financiación *f/pl*
financing theory (E)	Finanzierungstheorie *f*	—	théorie de financement *f*	teoria dei finanziamenti *f*	teoría de financiación *f*
Finanzakzept (D)	—	accepted finance bill	traite financière acceptée *f*	accettazione bancaria *f*	letra de cambio bancaria *f*
Finanzamt (D)	—	inland revenue office	service de contributions *m*	ufficio delle finanze *m*	hacienda *f*
Finanzanalyse (D)	—	financial analysis	analyse financière *f*	analisi finanziaria *f*	análisis financiero *m*
Finanzanlage-vermögen (D)	—	financial assets	valeurs immobilisées financières *f/pl*	investimenti finanziari *m/pl*	inversiones financieras *f/pl*
Finanzausgleich (D)	—	financial equalization	compensation financière *f*	conguaglio finanziario *m*	ajuste financiero *m*
Finanzbedarf (D)	—	financial requirements	besoins de trésorerie *m/pl*	fabbisogno finanziario *m*	necesidad financiera *f*
Finanzbuchhaltung (D)	—	financial accounting	comptabilité financière *f*	contabilità finanziaria *f*	contabilidad financiera *f*
Finanzdecke (D)	—	available funds	fonds disponibles *m/pl*	disponibilità di mezzi liquidi *f*	previsión financiera *f*
Finanzdisposition (D)	—	financial arrangement	disposition financière *f*	disposizioni finanziarie *f/pl*	disposición financiera
finanze (I)	Finanzwesen *n*	finance	finances *f/pl*	—	régimen financiero *m*
Finanzhedging (D)	—	financial hedging	hedging financier *m*	hedging finanziario *m*	hedging financiero *m*
financiación de la exportación (Es)	Ausfuhrfinanzierung *f*	export financing	financement de l'exportation *m*	finanziamento all'esportazione *m*	—
finanziamento (I)	Finanzierung *f*	financing	financement *m*	—	financiación *f*
finanziamento all'edilizia (I)	Baufinanzierung *f*	building financing	financement à la construction *m*	—	financiación de la construcción *f*
finanziamento all'esportazione (I)	Exportfinanzierung *f*	financing of exports	financement d'opérations d'exportation *m*	—	financiación de la exportación *f*
finanziamento all'esportazione (I)	Ausfuhrfinanzierung *f*	export financing	financement de l'exportation *m*	—	financiación de la exportación *f*
finanziamento commercio estero (I)	Außenhandels-finanzierung *f*	foreign trade financing	aide financière à l'exportation *f*	—	financiación del comercio exterior *f*

	D	E	F	I	Es
finanziamento delle importazioni (I)	Importfinanzierung *f*	import financing	financement des importations *m*	—	financiación de las importaciones *f*
finanziamento di acquisti rateali (I)	Teilzahlungskredit *m*	instalment credit	avance sur vente payée à tempérament *f*	—	crédito para la financiación a plazo *m*
finanziamento di acquisti rateali (I)	Ratenkredit *m*	instalment sales credit	crédit à tempéraments *m*	—	crédito a plazos *m*
finanziamento di investimenti (I)	Anlagenfinanzierung *f*	financing of investment in fixed assets	financement du renouvellement des immobilisations *m*	—	financiación de inversión *f*
finanziamento di portafoglio (I)	Beteiligungs-finanzierung *f*	equity financing	financement par participation *m*	—	financiación de participación *f*
finanziamento di un progetto (I)	Projektfinanzierung *f*	project financing	financement d'un projet *m*	—	financiación de un proyecto *f*
finanziamento di vendite rateali (I)	Konsumfinanzierung *f*	consumption financing	financement de la vente à crédit *m*	—	financiación al consumo *f*
finanziamento edilizio (I)	Bausparfinanzierung *f*	building society funding	financement d'épargne-construction *m*	—	financiación de ahorros para la construcción *f*
finanziamento esterno (I)	Außenfinanzierung *f*	external financing	financement externe *m*	—	financiación externa *f*
finanziamento esterno (I)	Fremdfinanzierung *f*	debt financing	constitution de capital par apport de tiers *f*	—	financiación con capital ajeno *f*
finanziamento interno (I)	Innenfinanzierung *f*	internal financing	financement interne *m*	—	financiación interna *f*
finanziamento mediante credito (I)	Kreditfinanzierung *f*	financing by way of credit	financement par capitaux de tiers *m*	—	financiación mediante créditos *f*
finanziamento mediante mutuo (I)	Darlehens-finanzierung *f*	loan financing	financement par capitaux prêtés *m*	—	financiación de préstamo *f*
finanziamento passivo (I)	Passivkredit *m*	borrowing	crédit passif *m*	—	crédito pasivo *m*
finanziamento subordinato (I)	nachrangige Finanzierung *f*	junior financing	financement de rang inférieur *m*	—	financiación subordinada *f*
finanziamento tramite titoli (I)	Effektenfinanzierung *f*	security financing	financement de valeurs mobilières *m*	—	financiación de valores *f*
finanziamento transitorio (I)	Zwischenfinanzierung	interim financing	financement intermédiaire *m*	—	financiación interina *f*
finanzieller Beistand (D)	—	financial assistance	aide financière *f*	assistenza finanziaria *f*	ayuda financiera *f*
Finanzierung (D)	—	financing	financement *m*	finanziamento *m*	financiación *f*
Finanzierungs-defizit (D)	—	finance deficit	déficit de financement *m*	deficit di finanziamento *m*	déficit de financiación *f*
Finanzierungs-grundsätze (D)	—	financing principles	principes de financement *m/pl*	principi di finanziamento *m/pl*	normas de financiación *f/pl*
Finanzierungs-papier (D)	—	funding paper	titres de financement *m/pl*	titolo di finanziamento *m*	título de financiación *m*
Finanzierungs-regeln (D)	—	financing rules	règles de financement *f/pl*	regole di finanziamento *f/pl*	normas de financiación *f/pl*
Finanzierungs-reserve (D)	—	financial reserve	réserves financières *f/pl*	riserve finanziarie *f/pl*	reserva de financiación *f*
Finanzierungssaldo (D)	—	net financial investment	investissement financier net *m*	saldo di finanziamento *m*	saldo de financiación *m*
Finanzierungs-schätze (D)	—	financing bonds	effets du Trésor *m/pl*	buoni del tesoro *m/pl*	letras del Tesoro *f/pl*
Finanzierungs-theorie (D)	—	financing theory	théorie de financement *f*	teoria dei finanziamenti *f*	teoría de financiación *f*
Finanzinnovationen (D)	—	financial innovation	innovations financières *f/pl*	innovazioni finanziarie *f/pl*	innovaciones financieras *f/pl*
Finanzkapital (D)	—	financial capital	capital financier *m*	capitale finanziario *m*	capital financiero *m*
Finanzkonto (D)	—	financial account	compte financier *m*	conto finanziario *m*	cuenta financiera *f*
Finanzkraft (D)	—	financial strength	capacité financière *f*	capacità finanziaria *f*	potencial financiero *m*
Finanzkredit (D)	—	financial credit	crédit de financement *m*	credito di finanziamento *m*	crédito financiero *m*

	D	E	F	I	Es
Finanzmakler (D)	—	money broker	intermédiaire de crédits à moyen et à long terme m	mediatore finanziario m	intermediario financiero m
Finanzmarkt (D)	—	financial market	marché des capitaux m	mercato finanziario m	mercado financiero m
Finanzmathematik (D)	—	financial mathematics	mathématiques financières f/pl	matematica finanziaria f	matemáticas financieras f/pl
Finanzmonopol (D)	—	fiscal monopoly	monopole fiscal m	monopolio fiscale m	monopolio financiero m
Finanzplan (D)	—	financial plan	plan financier m	piano finanziario m	plan financiero m
Finanzplanung (D)	—	budgeting	planification financière f	pianificazione finanziaria f	planificación financiera f
Finanzpolitik (D)	—	financial policy	politique financière f	politica finanziaria f	política financiera f
Finanzpresse (D)	—	financial press	presse financière f	stampa finanziaria f	prensa financiera f
Finanzreform (D)	—	financial reform	réforme financière f	riforma finanziaria f	reforma financiera f
Finanzsektor (D)	—	financial sector	secteur financier m	settore della finanza m	sector financiero m
Finanztermin-kontrakt (D)	—	financial futures contract	contrat financier à terme m	financial futures m/pl financiero m	contrato a plazo m
Finanztheorie (D)	—	financial theory	théorie financière f	teoria finanziaria f	teoría financiera f
Finanztransaktion (D)	—	financial transaction	transaction financière f	operazione finanziaria f	transacción financiera f
Finanzverfassung (D)	—	financial system	système financier m	ordinamento finanziario f	constitución financiera f
Finanzverflechtung (D)	—	financial interlocking	interdépendance financoièro f	interferenza finanziaria f	vinculaciones financieras f/pl
Finanzvermögen (D)	—	financial assets	disponibilités f/pl	patrimonio finanziario m	patrimonio financiero m
Finanzverwaltung (D)	—	administration of the finances	administration des finances f	amministrazione delle finanze f	administración fiscal f
Finanzwechsel (D)	—	finance bill	traite financière f	cambiale finanziaria f	letra bancaria f
Finanzwesen (D)	—	finance	finances f/pl	finanze f/pl	régimen financiero m
Finanzwissenschaft (D)	—	public finance	science financière f	scienza delle finanze f	ciencia financiera f
fin de mes (Es)	Ultimo m	end of the month	fin de mois f	fine mese m	—
fin de mois (F)	Ultimo m	end of the month	—	fine mese m	fin de mes m
fine della riunione di borsa (I)	Börsenschluß m	close of stock exchange business	clôture de la bourse f	—	cierre de la bolsa m
fine gold (E)	Feingold n	—	or fin m	oro fino m	oro fino m
fine gold content (E)	Goldfeingehalt m	—	poids d'or fin m	titolo aureo m	peso fino del oro m
fine mese (I)	Ultimo m	end of the month	fin de mois f	—	fin de mes m
fine silver (E)	Feinsilber n	—	argent fin m	argento fino m	plata fina f
fingierte Order (D)	—	fictitious order	ordre simulé m	ordinazione fittizia f	orden fingida f
firm deal (E)	Festgeschäft n	—	opération à terme fixe f	contrattazione a fermo f	operaciones a plazo fijo f/pl
firm's bank (E)	Hausbank f	—	banque habituelle f	banca preferita f	banco con que trata generalmente el cliente m
first acquisition (E)	Ersterwerb m	—	première acquisition f	primo acquisto m	adquisición original f
first come-first served principle (E)	Windhundverfahren n	—	principe du premier arrivé et le premier servi m	principio del primo offerente m	principio del primer venido, primer servido m
first of exchange (E)	Prima Warenwechsel m	—	première de change f	prima di cambio commerciale f	primera de cambio f
fisc (F)	Fiskus m	treasury	—	fisco m	fisco m
fiscal code (E)	Abgabenordnung f	—	code des impôts m	legislazione tributaria f	ordenanza tributaria f
fiscal illusion (E)	Fiskalillusion f	—	illusion fiscale f	illusione fiscale f	ilusión fiscal f
fiscal monopoly (E)	Finanzmonopol n	—	monopole fiscal m	monopolio fiscale m	monopolio financiero m
fiscal policy (E)	Fiskalpolitik f	—	politique fiscale f	politica fiscale f	política fiscal f

	D	E	F	I	Es
fisco (Es)	Fiskus *m*	treasury	fisc *m*	fisco *m*	—
fisco (I)	Fiskus *m*	treasury	fisc *m*	—	fisco *m*
Fiskalillusion (D)	—	fiscal illusion	illusion fiscale *f*	illusione fiscale *f*	ilusión fiscal *f*
Fiskalpolitik (D)	—	fiscal policy	politique fiscale *f*	politica fiscale *f*	política fiscal *f*
Fiskus (D)	—	treasury	fisc *m*	fisco *m*	fisco *m*
fissato bollato (I)	Schlußnote *f*	broker's note	avis d'exécution *m*	—	póliza de negociación *f*
fissazione dei corsi (I)	Kursfestsetzung *f*	fixing of prices	détermination des cours *f*	—	cotización *f*
fissazione del fido (I)	Kreditplafondierung *f*	credit limitation	fixation d'une limite de crédit *f*	—	volumen máximo de crédito disponible *m*
fissazione di un termine (I)	Befristung *f*	time limit	fixation d'un délai *f*	—	condición de plazo *f*
fixation (F)	Fixing *n*	fixing	—	fixing *m*	fijación de la cotización *f*
fixation des cours de change (F)	Valutierung *f*	fixing of exchange rate	—	valuta *f*	fijación del tipo de cambio *f*
fixation d'un délai (F)	Befristung *f*	time limit	—	fissazione di un termine *f*	condición de plazo *f*
fixation d'une limite de crédit (F)	Kreditplafondierung *f*	credit limitation	—	fissazione del fido *f*	volumen máximo de crédito disponible *m*
fixed assets (E)	Anlagevermögen *n*	—	valeurs immobilisées *f/pl*	attivo fisso *m*	activo fijo *m*
fixed-date land charge (E)	Fälligkeits-grundschuld *f*	—	dette foncière remboursable à terme fixe *f*	debito fondiario a scadenza *m*	deuda inmobiliaria de vencimiento *f*
fixed-date land mortgage (E)	Fälligkeitshypothek *f*	—	hypothèque constituée sur la base d'un remboursement du capital à terme fixe sans dénonciation préalable *f*	ipoteca a scadenza determinata *f*	hipoteca de vencimiento *f*
fixed deposit (E)	Festgeld *n*	—	argent immobilisé *m*	deposito a termine *m*	depósito a plazo *m*
fixed deposits (E)	befristete Einlagen *f/pl*	—	bons et comptes à échéance fixe *m/pl*	depositi a scadenza fissa *m/pl*	imposiciones a plazo *f/pl*
fixed exchange (E)	Quantitätsnotierung *f*	—	certain *m*	quotazione del certo *f*	cotización cuantitativa *f*
fixed exchange rate (E)	starrer Wechselkurs *m*	—	taux de change fixe *f*	cambio fisso *m*	tipo de cambio fijo *m*
fixed exchange rate (E)	Mengennotierung *f*	—	cotation au certain *f*	cambio certo per incerto *m*	cotización real *f*
fixed interest (E)	Festzins *m*	—	intérêt fixe *m*	interesse fisso *m*	interés fijo *m*
fixed-interest bearing account (E)	Festzinskonto *n*	—	compte à intérêt fixe *m*	conto ad interesse fisso *m*	cuenta de interés fijo *f*
fixed-interest coupons (E)	Bauzinsen *m/pl*	—	coupons d'intérêt fixe *m/pl*	interessi intercalari *m/pl*	cupones de interés fijo *m/pl*
fixed interest securities fund (E)	Rentenfonds *m*	—	fonds de placement en valeurs à revenu fixe *m*	fondo di obbligazioni *m*	fondo de títulos a renta fija *m*
fixed-interest security (E)	Rentenwert *m*	—	valeur à revenu fixe *f*	titolo a reddito fisso *m*	título de renta fija *m*
fixed issue of notes (E)	Notenkontingent *n*	—	maximum toléré à l'émission des billets de banque *m*	contingente di banconote *m*	contingente de emisión fiduciaria *m*
fixed price (E)	Festpreis *m*	—	prix fixe *m*	prezzo fisso *m*	precio firme *m*
fixed-rate mortgage (E)	Festzinshypothek *f*	—	hypothèque à intérêt fixe *f*	ipoteca ad interesse fisso *f*	hipoteca de interés fijo *f*
fixed value (E)	Festwert *m*	—	valeur fixe *f*	valore costante *m*	precio fijo *m*
fixe Kosten (D)	—	standing costs	coût fixe *m*	costi fissi *m/pl*	gastos fijos *m/pl*
fixen (D)	—	to speculate for a fall	vendre à découvert	vendere allo scoperto	vender al descubierto
Fixer (D)	—	bear seller	vendeur à découvert *m*	scopertista *m*	vendedor al descubierto *m*
Fixgeschäft (D)	—	transaction for delivery by a fixed date	opération à terme fixe *f*	contrattazione a fermo *f*	negocio fijo *m*

	D	E	F	I	Es
Fixing (D)	—	fixing	fixation f	fixing m	fijación de la cotización f
fixing (E)	Fixing n	—	fixation f	fixing m	fijación de la cotización f
fixing (I)	Fixing n	fixing	fixation f	—	fijación de la cotización f
fixing of a quota (E)	Kontingentierung f	—	contingentement m	contingentamento m	imposición de contingentes f
fixing of exchange rate (E)	Valutierung f	—	fixation des cours de change f	valuta f	fijación del tipo de cambio f
fixing of prices (E)	Kursfestsetzung f	—	détermination des cours f	fissazione dei corsi f	cotización f
flexible discount rate (E)	flexibler Diskontsatz m	—	taux d'escompte variable m	tasso di sconto flessibile m	tipo de descuento variable m
flexible exchange rate (E)	flexibler Wechselkurs m	—	taux de change flottant m	cambio flessibile m	cambio variable m
flexibler Diskontsatz (D)	—	flexible discount rate	taux d'escompte variable m	tasso di sconto flessibile m	tipo de descuento variable m
flexibler Wechselkurs (D)	—	flexible exchange rate	taux de change flottant m	cambio flessibile m	cambio variable m
flight into real assets (E)	Flucht in die Sachwerte f	—	fuite vers les biens réels f	fuga nei beni materiali f	evasión al patrimonio real f
Float (D)	—	float	float m	float m	valores pendientes de pago m/pl
float (E)	Float m	—	float m	float m	valores pendientes de pago m/pl
float (F)	Float m	float	—	float m	valores pendientes de pago m/pl
float (I)	Float m	float	float m	—	valores pendientes de pago m/pl
Floating (D)	—	floating	système des changes flottants m	floating m	flotación f
floating (E)	Floating n	—	floating m	floating m	flotación f
floating (E)	schwimmend	—	flottant	flottante	flotante
floating (I)	Floating n	floating	floating m	—	flotación f
floating debt (E)	schwebende Schuld f	—	dette flottante f	debito fluttuante m	deuda flotante f
Floating Rate Note (D)	—	floating rate note	floating rate note m	floating rate note m	nota de cambios flotantes f
floating rate note (E)	Floating Rate Note f	—	floating rate note m	floating rate note m	nota de cambios flotantes f
floating rate note (F)	Floating Rate Note f	floating rate note	—	floating rate note m	nota de cambios flotantes f
floating rate note (I)	Floating Rate Note f	floating rate note	floating rate note m	—	nota de cambios flotantes f
flojo (Es)	still	slack	calme	fiacco	—
flojo (Es)	schwach	slack	faible	debole	—
floor (E)	Parkett n	—	parquet m	recinto delle grida m	parqué m
floor trader (E)	freier Makler m	—	courtier en valeurs mobilières m	mediatore libero m	corredor no colegiado m
flotación (Es)	Floating n	floating	floating m	floating m	—
flotación en bloque (Es)	Blockfloating n	block floating	cours flottant commun adopté par plusieurs pays m	fluttuazione congiunta f	—
flotante (Es)	schwimmend	floating	flottant	flottante	—
flottant (F)	schwimmend	floating	—	flottante	flotante
flottante (I)	schwimmend	floating	flottant	—	flotante
flow-of-funds analysis (E)	Geldstromanalyse f	—	analyse des courants monétaires f	analisi dei flussi monetari f	análisis de flujos monetarios m
Flucht in die Sachwerte (D)	—	flight into real assets	fuite vers les biens réels f	fuga nei beni materiali f	evasión al patrimonio real f
fluctuating funds (E)	fluktuierende Gelder n/pl	—	fonds soumis à des fluctuations m/pl	denaro fluttuante m	fondos sujetos a fluctuaciones m/pl
fluidité des capitaux (F)	Kapitalfluß m	capital flow	—	flusso dei fondi m	flujo de capital m

	D	E	F	I	Es
flujo de capital (Es)	Kapitalfluß *m*	capital flow	fluidité des capitaux *f*	flusso dei fondi *m*	—
fluktuierende Gelder (D)	—	fluctuating funds	fonds soumis à des fluctuations *m/pl*	denaro fluttuante *m*	fondos sujetos a fluctuaciones *m/pl*
flüssige Mittel (D)	—	liquid assets	capitaux liquides *m/pl*	fondi liquidi *m/pl*	fondos líquidos *m/pl*
flüssiger Geldmarkt (D)	—	liquid money market	marché monétaire liquide *m*	mercato del denaro liquido *m*	mercado monetario líquido *m*
flusso dei fondi (I)	Kapitalfluß *m*	capital flow	fluidité des capitaux *f*	—	flujo de capital *m*
fluttuazione congiunta (I)	Blockfloating *n*	block floating	cours flottant commun adopté par plusieurs pays *m*	—	flotación en bloque *f*
fogli di controllo crediti (I)	Kreditprüfungs-blätter *n/pl*	credit checking sheets	feuilles d'enquête sur la solvabilité *f/pl*	—	hojas de investigación crediticia *f/pl*
foglio in bianco (I)	Blankett *n*	blank form	imprimé en blanc *m*	—	carta blanca *f*
follow-up order (E)	Nachorder *f*	—	nouveau ordre *m*	ordinazione successiva *f*	nueva orden *f*
fomento de ahorros para la construcción (Es)	Bausparförderung *f*	promotion of saving through building societies	promotion de l'épargne-construction *f*	promozione del risparmio edilizio *f*	—
fomento de la construcción de viviendas (Es)	Wohnungsbau-förderung *f*	promotion of housing construction	promotion de la construction de logements *f*	promozione edilizia residenziale *f*	—
fomento de la exportación (Es)	Exportförderung *f*	export promotion	encouragement à l'exportation *m*	agevolazione all'esportazione *f*	—
fomento del ahorro (Es)	Sparförderung *f*	savings promotion	promotion de l'épargne *f*	promozione del risparmio *f*	—
fonction de l'argent de moyen d'échange (F)	Tauschmittelfunktion des Geldes *f*	exchange function of money	—	funzione di scambio della moneta *f*	función de medio de cambio del dinero *f*
fonctions de la monnaie (F)	Geldfunktionen *f/pl*	functions of money	—	funzioni del denaro *f/pl*	funciones monetarias *f/pl*
fondation fictive (F)	Schwindelgründung *f*	fraud foundation	—	costituzione fraudolenta *f*	fundación ficticia *f*
fondation par apports en nature (F)	qualifizierte Gründung *f*	formation involving subscription in kind	—	costituzione qualificata *f*	fundación calificada *f*
fondation simultanée (F)	Übernahmegründung *f*	foundation in which founders take all shares	—	costituzione simultanea *f*	fundación de adquisición *f*
fondé de pouvoir (F)	Bevollmächtigter *m*	authorized person	—	delegato *m*	apoderado *m*
fondé de procuration (F)	Prokurist *m*	authorized clerk	—	procuratore commerciale *m*	apoderado general *m*
fonder (F)	fundieren	to fund	—	consolidare	consolidar
fondi d'esercizio (I)	Betriebsmittel *n*	working funds	équipement d'exploitation *m*	—	fondos de explotación *m/pl*
fondi di compensazione (I)	Saison-Reserven *f/pl*	seasonal reserves	provisions pour pertes inhérentes aux fluctuations saisonnières *f/pl*	—	reservas estacionales *f/pl*
fondi di terzi (I)	Fremde Gelder *n/pl*	external funds	capitaux de tiers *m/pl*	—	fondos ajenos *m/pl*
fondi liquidi (I)	flüssige Mittel *n/pl*	liquid assets	capitaux liquides *m/pl*	—	fondos líquidos *m/pl*
fondi monetari (I)	Geldmarktfonds *m*	money market funds	fonds du marché monétaire *m/pl*	—	fondos de mercado monetario *m/pl*
fondi segreti (I)	Dispositionsfonds *m*	reserve funds	fonds de réserves *m/pl*	—	fondo disponible *m*
fondo (Es)	Fonds *m*	funds	fonds *m*	fondo *m*	—
fondo (I)	Fonds *m*	funds	fonds *m*	—	fondo *m*
fondo abierto (Es)	offener Fonds *m*	open-end fund	fonds ouvert *m*	fondo d'investimento aperto *m*	—
fondo aperto al pubblico (I)	Publikumsfonds *m*	public fund	fonds de placement ouvert au public *m*	—	fondos ofrecidos al público *m/pl*
fondo a scadenza (I)	Laufzeitfonds *m*	term fund	fonds à terme *m*	—	fondos a plazo *m/pl*
fondo azionario (I)	Aktienfonds *m*	share fund	fonds d'actions *m*	—	fondo de acciones *m*
fondo banca centrale (I)	Bundesbankguthaben *n*	Federal Bank assets	avoir auprès de la Banque fédérale *m*	—	saldo activo del Banco Federal *m*
fondo capital (Es)	Nominalkapital *n*	nominal capital	capital nominal *m*	capitale nominale *m*	—

	D	E	F	I	Es
fondo che tratta quote di altri fondi (I)	Dachfonds *m*	holding fund	fonds d'une société holding *m/pl*	—	fondos de una sociedad holding *m/pl*
fondo compensazione congiuntura negativa (I)	Konjunkturausgleichsrücklage *f*	anticyclical reserve	réserve anticyclique *f*	—	reserva de compensación coyuntural *f*
fondo común (Es)	Gemeinschaftsfonds *m*	joint fund	fonds commun *m*	fondo comune *m*	—
fondo comune (I)	Gemeinschaftsfonds *m*	joint fund	fonds commun *m*	—	fondo común *m*
fondo d'ammortamento (I)	Tilgungsfonds *m*	redemption fund	fonds d'amortissement *m*	—	fondo de amortización *m*
fondo de acciones (Es)	Aktienfonds *m*	share fund	fonds d'actions *m*	fondo azionario *m*	—
fondo de amortización (Es)	Tilgungsfonds *m*	redemption fund	fonds d'amortissement *m*	fondo d'ammortamento *m*	—
fondo de atesoramiento (Es)	Thesaurierungsfonds *m*	accumulative investment fund	fonds de thésauration *m*	fondo di accumulazione *m*	—
fondo de compensación (Es)	Ausgleichsfonds *m*	compensation fund	fonds de compensation *m*	fondo di compensazione *m*	—
fondo de compensación de cargas (Es)	Lastenausgleichsfonds *m*	Equalization of Burdens Fund	fonds de péréquation des charges *m*	fondo perequazione oneri *m*	—
fondo de contrapartida (Es)	Gegenwertmittel *n/pl*	counterpart funds	fonds de contrepartie *m/pl*	mezzo controvalore *m*	—
fondo de crecimiento (Es)	Wachstumsfonds *m*	growth fund	fonds d'expansion *m*	fondo di accumulazione *m*	—
fondo de desarrollo (Es)	Entwicklungsfonds *m*	development fund	fonds de développement *m*	fondo di sviluppo *m*	—
Fondo de Desarrollo y Saneamiento (Es)	Europäischer Entwicklungsfonds *m*	European Development Fund [EDF]	fonds européen de développement *m*	Fondo europeo di sviluppo *m*	—
fondo de energía (Es)	Energiefonds *m*	electricity and fuels funds	fonds d'énergie *m*	fondo per il settore energetico *m*	—
fondo de inversión en valores reales (Es)	Sachwert-Investmentfonds *m*	material asset investment fund	fonds d'investissement en valeurs réelles *m*	fondo di valori reali *m*	—
fondo de inversión mobiliaria (Es)	Investmentfonds *m*	investment fund	fonds de placement *m*	fondo d'investimento *m*	—
fondo de las materias primas (Es)	Rohstoff-Fonds *m*	raw material fund	fonds de matières premières *m*	fondo titoli del settore primario *m*	—
fondo de renovación (Es)	Erneuerungsfonds *m*	renewal reserve	fonds de renouvellement *m*	fondo di rinnovamento *m*	—
fondo de reserva (Es)	Reservefonds *m*	reserve fund	fonds de réserve *m*	fondo di riserva *m*	—
fondo de retiros (Es)	Pensionsrückstellungen *f/pl*	pension reserve	provisions pour les retraites du personnel *f/pl*	fondo pensioni *m*	—
fondo de títulos a renta fija (Es)	Rentenfonds *m*	fixed interest securities fund	fonds de placement en valeurs à revenu fixe *m*	fondo di obbligazioni *m*	—
fondo di accumulazione (I)	Wachstumsfonds *m*	growth fund	fonds d'expansion *m*	—	fondo de crecimiento *m*
fondo di accumulazione (I)	Thesaurierungsfonds *m*	accumulative investment fund	fonds de thésauration *m*	—	fondo de atesoramiento *m*
fondo di compensazione (I)	Ausgleichsfonds *m*	compensation fund	fonds de compensation *m*	—	fondo de compensación *m*
fondo di garanzia dei depositi (I)	Einlagensicherungsfonds *m*	deposit guarantee fund	fonds de sûreté en garantie de dépôts *m*	—	fondo de garantía de depósitos *m*
fondo d'investimento (I)	Investmentfonds *m*	investment fund	fonds de placement *m*	—	fondo de inversión mobiliaria *m*
fondo d'investimento aperto (I)	offener Fonds *m*	open-end fund	fonds ouvert *m*	—	fondo abierto *m*
fondo d'investimento misto (I)	gemischter Fonds *m*	mixed fund	fonds mixte *m*	—	fondo mixto *m*
fondo di obbligazioni (I)	Rentenfonds *m*	fixed interest securities fund	fonds de placement en valeurs à revenu fixe *m*	—	fondo de títulos a renta fija *m*
fondo di previdenza (I)	Pensionskasse *f*	staff pension fund	caisse de retraite *f*	—	caja de jubilaciones *f*

	D	E	F	I	Es
fondo di rinnovamento (I)	Erneuerungsfonds *m*	renewal reserve	fonds de renouvellement *m*	—	fondo de renovación *m*
fondo di riserva (I)	Reservefonds *m*	reserve fund	fonds de réserve *m*	—	fondo de reserva *m*
fondo disponibile (Es)	Dispositionsfonds *m*	reserve fund	fonds de réserves *m/pl*	fondi segreti *m/pl*	—
fondo di sterilizzazione (I)	Sterilisierungsfonds *m*	sterilization fund	fonds de stérilisation *m*	—	fondo de esterilización *m*
fondo di sviluppo (I)	Entwicklungsfonds *m*	development fund	fonds de développement *m*	—	fondo de desarrollo *m*
fondo di titoli immobiliari (I)	Immobilienfonds *m*	real estate fund	fonds immobilier *m*	—	cartera inmobiliaria *f*
fondo di valori reali (I)	Sachwert-Investmentfonds *m*	material asset investment fund	fonds d'investissement en valeurs réelles *m*	—	fondo de inversión en valores reales *m*
Fondo Europeo de Cooperación Monetaria [FECOM] (Es)	Europäischer Fonds für Währungs-politische Zusammen-arbeit [EFWZ] *m*	European Monetary Cooperation Fund [EMCF]	Fonds Européen de Coopération Monétaire (FECOM) *m*	Fondo Europeo di cooperazione monetaria *m*	—
Fondo Europeo di cooperazione monetaria (I)	Europäischer Fonds für Währungs-politische Zusammen-arbeit [EFWZ] *m*	—	Fonds Européen de Coopération Monétaire (FECOM) *m*	Fondo Europeo di cooperazione monetaria *m*	Fondo Europeo de Cooperación Monetaria [FECOM] *m*
Fondo europeo di sviluppo (I)	Europäischer Entwicklungsfonds *m*	European Development Fund [EDF]	fonds européen de développement *m*	—	Fondo de Desarrollo y Saneamiento *m*
fondo immobiliare aperto (I)	offener Immobilienfonds *m*	open-end real estate fund	fonds de placement immobilier ouvert *m*	—	fondo inmobiliario abierto *m*
fondo immobiliare chiuso (I)	geschlossener Immobilienfonds *m*	closed-end real estate fund	fonds de placement immobilier fermé *m*	—	fondo inmobiliario cerrado *m*
fondo immobiliare fiduciario (I)	Treuhandfonds *m*	trust fund	fonds fiduciaire *m*	—	fondos fiduciarios *m/pl*
fondo inmobiliario abierto (Es)	offener Immobilienfonds *m*	open-end real estate fund	fonds de placement immobilier ouvert *m*	fondo immobiliare aperto *m*	—
fondo inmobiliario cerrado (Es)	geschlossener Immobilienfonds *m*	closed-end real estate fund	fonds de placement immobilier fermé *m*	fondo immobiliare chiuso *m*	—
fondo mixto (Es)	gemischter Fonds *m*	mixed fund	fonds mixte *m*	fondo d'investimento misto *m*	—
fondo monetario (Es)	Währungsfonds *m*	monetary fund	fonds monétaire *m*	fondo monetario *m*	—
fondo monetario (I)	Währungsfonds *m*	monetary fund	fonds monétaire *m*	—	fondo monetario *m*
fondo pensioni (I)	Pensions-rückstellungen *f/pl*	pension reserve	provisions pour les retraites du personnel *f/pl*	—	fondo de retiros *f*
fondo perequazione oneri (I)	Lastenausgleichs-fonds *m*	Equalization of Burdens Fund	fonds de péréquation des charges *m*	—	fondo de compensa-ción de cargas *m*
fondo per il settore energetico (I)	Energiefonds *m*	electricity and fuels funds	fonds d'énergie *m*	—	fondo de energía *f*
fondos ajenos (Es)	Fremde Gelder *n/pl*	external funds	capitaux de tiers *m/pl*	fondi di terzi *m/pl*	—
fondos a plazo (Es)	Laufzeitfonds *m*	term fund	fonds à terme *m*	fondo a scadenza *m*	—
fondos bloqueados (Es)	Sperrguthaben *n*	blocked balance	avoir bloqué *m*	avere bloccato *m*	—
fondos de esterilización (Es)	Sterilisierungsfonds *m*	sterilization fund	fonds de stérilisation *m*	fondo di sterilizzazione *m*	—
fondos de explotación (Es)	Betriebsmittel *n/pl*	working funds	équipement d'exploitation *m*	fondi d'esercizio *m/pl*	—
fondos de garantía de depósitos (Es)	Einlagensicherungs-fonds *m*	deposit guarantee fund	fonds de sûreté en garantie de dépôts *m*	fondo di garanzia dei depositi *m*	—
fondos de mercado monetario (Es)	Geldmarktfonds *m*	money market funds	fonds du marché monétaire *m/pl*	fondi monetari *m/pl*	—
fondos de terceros (Es)	fremde Mittel *n/pl*	borrowed funds	capitaux prêtés *m/pl*	denaro da terzi *m*	—
fondos de una sociedad holding (Es)	Dachfonds *m*	holding fund	fonds d'une société holding *m*	fondo che tratta quote di altri fondi *m*	—
fondos fiduciarios (Es)	Treuhandfonds *m*	trust funds	fonds fiduciaire *m*	fondo immobiliare fiduciario *m*	—
fondos ingresados (Es)	hereingenommene Gelder *n/pl*	money taken on deposit	fonds mis en dépôt *m/pl*	denaro altrui *m*	—
fondos líquidos (Es)	flüssige Mittel *n/pl*	liquid assets	capitaux liquides *m/pl*	fondi liquidi *m/pl*	—

	D	E	F	I	Es
fondo social (Es)	Sozialfonds *m*	social fund	fonds social *m*	fondo sociale *m*	—
fondo sociale (I)	Sozialfonds *m*	social fund	fonds social *m*	—	fondo social *m*
fondos ofrecidos al público (Es)	Publikumsfonds *m*	public fund	fonds de placement ouvert au public *m*	fondo aperto al pubblico *m*	—
fondos recogidos (Es)	aufgenommene Gelder *n/pl*	borrowed funds	fonds empruntés *m/pl*	mezzi presi a prestito *m/pl*	—
fondos sujetos a fluctuaciones (Es)	fluktuierende Gelder *n/pl*	fluctuating funds	fonds soumis à des fluctuations *m/pl*	denaro fluttuante *m*	—
fondo titoli del settore primario (I)	Rohstoff-Fonds *m*	raw material funds	fonds de matières premières *m*	—	fondo de las materias primas *m*
Fonds (D)	—	fund	fonds *m*	fondo *m*	fondo *m*
fonds (F)	Fonds *m*	fund	—	fondo *m*	fondo *m*
Fondsanlagen (D)	—	trust investment	placements en fonds *m/pl*	investimenti di fondo d'investimento *m/pl*	inversión de fondos *f*
fonds à terme (F)	Laufzeitfonds *m*	term fund	—	fondo a scadenza *m*	fondos a plazo *m/pl*
fonds commun (F)	Gemeinschaftsfonds *m*	joint fund	—	fondo comune	fondo común *m*
fonds d'actions (F)	Aktienfonds *m*	share fund	—	fondo azionario *m*	fondo de acciones *m*
fonds d'amortissement (F)	Tilgungsfonds *m*	redemption fund	—	fondo d'ammortamento *m*	fondo de amortización *m*
fonds de compensation (F)	Ausgleichsfonds *m*	compensation fund	—	fondo di compensazione *m*	fondo de compensación *m*
fonds de contrepartie (F)	Gegenwertmittel *n/pl*	counterpart fund	—	mezzo controvalore *m*	fondo de contrapartida *m*
fonds de développement (F)	Entwicklungsfonds *m*	development fund	—	fondo di sviluppo *m*	fondo de desarrollo *m*
fonds de matières premières (F)	Rohstoff-Fonds *m*	raw material funds	—	fondo titoli del settore primario *m*	fondo de las materias primas *m*
fonds d'énergie (F)	Energiefonds *m*	electricity and fuels fonds	—	fondo per il settore energetico *m*	fondo de energía *f*
fonds de péréquation des charges (F)	Lastenausgleichsfonds *m*	Equalization of Burdens Fund	—	fondo perequazione oneri *m*	fondo de compensación de cargas *m*
fonds de placement (F)	Investmentfonds *m*	investment fund	—	fondo d'investimento *m*	fondo de inversión mobiliaria *m*
fonds de placement en valeurs à revenu fixe (F)	Rentenfonds *m*	fixed interest securities fund	—	fondo di obbligazioni *m*	fondo de títulos a renta fija *m*
fonds de placement immobilier fermé (F)	geschlossener Immobilienfonds *m*	closed-end real estate fund	—	fondo immobiliare chiuso *m*	fondo inmobiliario cerrado *m*
fonds de placement immobilier ouvert (F)	offener Immobilienfonds *m*	open-end real estate fund	—	fondo immobiliare aperto *m*	fondo inmobiliario abierto *m*
fonds de placement ouvert au public (F)	Publikumsfonds *m*	public fund	—	fondo aperto al pubblico *m*	fondos ofrecidos al público *m/pl*
fonds déposés en banque (F)	Bankdepositen *pl*	bank deposit	—	depositi bancari *m/pl*	depósitos bancarios *m/pl*
fonds de renouvellement (F)	Erneuerungsfonds *m*	renewal reserve	—	fondo di rinnovamento *m*	fondo de renovación *m*
fonds de réserve (F)	Reservefonds *m*	reserve fund	—	fondo di riserva *m*	fondo de reserva *m*
fonds de réserve (F)	Vorsichtskasse *f*	precautionary holding	—	domanda precauzionale di moneta *f*	existencias de precaución *f/pl*
fonds de réserves (F)	Dispositionsfonds *m*	reserve fund	—	fondi segreti *m/pl*	fondo disponible *m*
fonds de stérilisation (F)	Sterilisierungsfonds *m*	sterilization fund	—	fondo di sterilizzazione *m*	fondo de esterilización *m*
fonds de sûreté en garantie de dépôts (F)	Einlagensicherungsfonds *m*	deposit guarantee fund	—	fondo di garanzia dei depositi *m*	fondos de garantía de depósitos *m/pl*
fonds de thésauration (F)	Thesaurierungsfonds *m*	accumulative investment fund	—	fondo di accumulazione *m*	fondo de atesoramiento *m*
fonds d'expansion (F)	Wachstumsfonds *m*	growth fund	—	fondo di accumulazione *m*	fondo de crecimiento *m*
fonds d'investissement en valeurs réelles (F)	Sachwert-Investmentfonds *m*	material asset investment funds	—	fondo di valori reali *m*	fondo de inversión en valores reales *m*
fonds disponibles (F)	Finanzdecke *f*	available funds	—	disponibilità di mezzi liquidi *f*	previsión financiera *f*

	D	E	F	I	Es
fonds du marché monétaire (F)	Geldmarktfonds *m*	money market funds	—	fondi monetari *m/pl*	fondos de mercado monetario *m/pl*
fonds d'une société holding (F)	Dachfonds *m*	holding fund	—	fondo che tratta quote di altri fondi *m*	fondos de una sociedad holding *m/pl*
fonds empruntés (F)	aufgenommene Gelder *n/pl*	borrowed funds	—	mezzi presi a prestito *m/pl*	fondos recogidos *m/pl*
fonds en consignation (F)	durchlaufende Gelder *n/pl*	transmitted accounts	—	denaro d'ordine *m*	dinero en tránsito *m*
Fonds Européen de Coopération Monétaire (FECOM) (F)	Europäischer Fonds für Währungs- politische Zusammen- arbeit [EFWZ] *m*	European Monetary Cooperation Fund [EMCF]	—	Fondo Europeo di cooperazione monetaria *m*	Fondo Europeo de Cooperación Monetaria [FECOM] *m*
fonds européen de développement (F)	Europäischer Entwicklungsfonds *m*	European Develop- ment Fund [EDF]	—	Fondo europeo di sviluppo *m*	Fondo de Desarrollo y Saneamiento *m*
fonds fiduciaire (F)	Treuhandfonds *m*	trust funds	—	fondo immobiliare fiduciario *m*	fondos fiduciarios *m/pl*
Fondsgebundene Lebensversiche- rung (D)	—	fund-linked life insurance	assurance-vie liée à un fonds *f*	assicurazione sulla vita con garanzia reale *f*	seguro de vida vinculado a fondos *m*
fonds immobilier (F)	Immobilienfonds *m*	real estate fund	—	fondo di titoli immobiliari *m*	cartera inmobiliaria *f*
fonds mis en dépôt (F)	hereingenommene Gelder *n/pl*	money taken on deposit	—	denaro altrui *m*	fondos ingresados *m/pl*
fonds mixte (F)	gemischter Fonds *m*	mixed fund	—	fondo d'investimento misto *m*	fondo mixto *m*
fonds monétaire (F)	Währungsfonds *m*	monetary fund	—	fondo monetario *m*	fondo monetario *m*
fonds ouvert (F)	offener Fonds *m*	open-end fund	—	fondo d'investimento aperto *m*	fondo abierto *m*
fonds remboursables à fin de mois (F)	Ultimogeld *n*	last-day money	—	prestito per fine mese *m*	dinero a fin de mes *m*
fonds social (F)	Aktienkapital *n*	share capital	—	capitale azionario *m*	capital en acciones *m*
fonds social (F)	Sozialfonds *m*	social fund	—	fondo sociale *m*	fondo social *m*
fonds soumis à des fluctuations (F)	fluktuierende Gelder *n/pl*	fluctuating funds	—	denaro fluttuante *m*	fondos sujetos a fluctuaciones *m/pl*
fonds spéciaux (F)	Sondervermögen *n*	special fund	—	patrimonio separato *m*	patrimonio especial *m*
Fondsvermögen (D)	—	fund assets	capital constituant le fonds *m*	patrimonio del fondo *m*	activo en fondos públicos *m*
for account only (E)	nur zur Verrechnung	—	à porter en compte	da accreditare	sólo para compensación
Forderung (D)	—	claim	créance *f*	credito *m*	crédito *m*
Forderungseinzugs- verfahren (D)	—	collection procedure	système de recouvre- ment de créances *m*	procedimento d'incasso crediti *m*	procedimiento de cobro de créditos *m*
Forderungskauf (D)	—	purchase of accounts receivable	vente d'une créance *f*	acquisizione di crediti *f*	compra de créditos *f*
Forderungspapiere (D)	—	instruments conferring title	titres de créance *m/pl*	titoli di credito *m/pl*	títulos de crédito *m/pl*
Forderungsrecht (D)	—	right to claim	droit issu d'une créance *m*	diritto di credito *m*	derecho de crédito *m*
forecast (E)	Prognose *f*	—	perspective *f*	previsione *f*	pronóstico *m*
foreign account (E)	Auslandskonto *n*	—	compte entretenu à l'étranger *m*	conto estero *m*	cuenta en el extranjero *f*
foreign assets (E)	Auslandsvermögen *n*	—	avoirs à l'étranger *m/pl*	beni all'estero *m/pl*	patrimonio en el extranjero *m*
foreign assets and liabilities (E)	Auslandsstatus *m*	—	avoirs et obligations extérieurs *m/pl*	posizione verso l'estero *f*	créditos activos y pasivos en el extranjero *m/pl*
foreign bank (E)	Auslandsbank *f*	—	banque extérieure *f*	banca estera *f*	banco exterior *m*
foreign bill of exchange (E)	Auslandswechsel *m*	—	traite tirée sur l'étranger *f*	cambiale sull'estero *f*	letra sobre el exterior *f*
foreign bond (E)	Auslandsanleihe *f*	—	emprunt extérieur *m*	prestito estero *m*	empréstito exterior *m*
foreign capital (E)	Auslandskapital *n*	—	capital étranger *m*	capitale estero *m*	capital extranjero *m*
foreign cheque (E)	Auslandsscheck *m*	—	chèque payable à l'étranger *m*	assegno sull'estero *m*	cheque sobre el extranjero *m*

	D	E	F	I	Es
foreign credit (E)	Auslandskredit m	—	crédit extérieur m	credito estero m	crédito extranjero m
foreign currencies eligible as cover (E)	deckungsfähige Devisen f/pl	—	devises aptes à servir de couverture f/pl	valute pregiate f/pl	divisas cubiertas por el banco emisor f/pl
foreign currency accept (E)	Valuta-Akzept n	—	traite libellée en monnaie étrangère f	accettazione in valuta estera f	aceptación en moneda extranjera f
foreign currency account (E)	Valutakonto n	—	compte en monnaie étrangère m	conto valutario m	cuenta de moneda extranjera f
foreign currency balance (E)	Fremdwährungs- guthaben n	—	avoir en monnaie étrangère m	disponibilità in valuta estera f	haberes de moneda extranjera m/pl
foreign currency bonds (E)	Auslandsbonds m	—	titres d'emprunt émis en monnaie étrangère m/pl	obbligazioni in valuta estera f/pl	bonos en moneda extranjera m/pl
foreign currency certificate of indebtedness (E)	Valutaschuldschein m	—	titre de créance en monnaie étrangère m	titolo di credito in valuta estera m	pagaré en moneda extranjera m
foreign currency clause (E)	Valutaklausel f	—	mention de la valeur fournie f	clausola valutaria f	cláusula de valuta f
foreign currency coupon (E)	Valutakupon m	—	coupon payable en monnaie étrangère m	cedola di un titolo estero f	cupón de divisas m
foreign currency debt (E)	Währungsschuld f	—	dette d'argent exprimée en unité monétaire étrangère f	debito in valuta estera m	deuda en moneda extranjera f
foreign currency loan (E)	Valutakredit m	—	crédit en monnaie étrangère m	credito in valuta estera m	crédito en divisas m
foreign debts (E)	Auslandsschulden f/pl	—	dettes à l'étranger f/pl	debiti esteri m/pl	deudas exteriores f/pl
foreign exchange (E)	Valuta f	—	monnaie étrangère f	valuta f	moneda extranjera f
foreign exchange (E)	Valuten f/pl	—	coupons de titres étrangers m/pl	cedole di titoli esteri m/pl	moneda extranjera f
foreign exchange account (E)	Devisenkonto n	—	compte libellé en devises m	conto in valuta estera m	cuenta en divisas f
foreign exchange advisor (E)	Devisenberater m	—	conseiller en matière de devises m	consulente di cambio m	asesor en materia de divisas m
foreign exchange business (E)	Devisengeschäft n	—	opération en devises f	operazione di cambio f	operación de divisas f
foreign exchange calculation (E)	Devisenrechnung f	—	calcul des changes m	calcolo valutario m	cálculo de divisas m
foreign exchange control (E)	Devisenkontrolle f	—	contrôle des changes m	controllo dei cambi m	control de cambio m
foreign exchange dealer (E)	Devisenhändler m	—	courtier en devises m	cambista m	cambista m
foreign exchange dealings (E)	Devisenhandel m	—	marché des changes m	cambio valuta m	operaciones de divisas f/pl
foreign exchange department (E)	Devisenabteilung f	—	service des devises m	ufficio cambi m	sección de divisas f
foreign exchange market (E)	Devisenbörse f	—	bourse de devises f	borsa dei cambi f	bolsa de cambios f
foreign exchange market (E)	Devisenmarkt m	—	marché des changes m	mercato dei cambi m	mercado de divisas m
foreign exchange quotations (E)	Devisennotierung f	—	cotation des devises f	cambio m	cotización de cambio f
foreign exchange rate (E)	Devisenkurs m	—	taux de change m	cambio m	cambio m
foreign exchange reserves (E)	Devisenreserve f	—	réserve de devises f	disponibilità in valuta f	reserva de divisas f
foreign exchange risk (E)	Wechselkursrisiko n	—	risque de change m	rischio di cambio m	riesgo de cambio m
foreign exchange spot dealings (E)	Devisenkassa- geschäft n	—	opérations de change au comptant f/pl	cambi a pronti m/pl	operación de divisas al contado f
foreign exchange spot market (E)	Devisenkassamarkt m	—	marché des changes au comptant m	mercato dei cambi a pronti m	mercado de divisas al contado m
foreign exchange spot operations (E)	Devisenkassakurs m	—	taux de change au comptant m	corso dei cambi a pronti m	tipo de cambio al contado m
foreign exchange surplus (E)	Devisenüberschuß m	—	excédent de devises m	eccedenza di valuta estera f	excedente de divisas m

	D	E	F	I	Es
foreign exchange transactions for customers (E)	Devisenkommissionsgeschäft *n*	—	opérations de change en commission *f/pl*	operazione di cambio su commissione *f*	operaciones de divisas a base de comisión *f/pl*
foreign investment (E)	Auslandsinvestition *f*	—	investissement à l'étranger *m*	investimento estero *m*	inversión exterior *f*
foreign notes and coins (E)	Sorte *f*	—	devise *f*	valuta estera *f*	moneda extranjera *f*
foreign patents (E)	Auslandspatente *n/pl*	—	brevets à l'étranger *m/pl*	brevetti esteri *m/pl*	patentes extranjeras *f/pl*
foreign security (E)	ausländisches Wertpapier *n*	—	valeurs étrangères *f/pl*	titolo estero *m*	título extranjero *m*
foreign shareholder (E)	ausländischer Anteilseigner *m*	—	actionnaire étranger *m*	azionista estero *m*	titular de acciones extranjero *m*
foreign trade (E)	Außenhandel *m*	—	commerce extérieur *m*	commercio estero *m*	comercio exterior *m*
foreign trade and payments (E)	Außenwirtschaft *f*	—	économie des échanges extérieurs *f*	commercio estero *m*	economía exterior *f*
foreign trade financing (E)	Außenhandelsfinanzierung *f*	—	aide financière à l'éxportation *f*	finanziamento commercio estero *m*	financiación del comercio exterior *f*
foreign trade monopoly (E)	Außenhandelsmonopol *n*	—	monopole du commerce extérieur *m*	monopolio del commercio estero *m*	monopolio del comercio exterior *m*
foreign trade statistics (E)	Außenhandelsstatistik *f*	—	statistique du commerce extérieur *f*	statistica del commercio estero *f*	estadística del comercio exterior *f*
foreign trade structure (E)	Außenhandelsrahmen *m*	—	structure du commerce extérieur *f*	quadro commercio estero *m*	estructura del comercio exterior *f*
forfaitage (F)	Forfaitierung *f*	forfaiting	—	forfaiting *m*	financiación del comercio exterior *f*
forfaitaire (F)	pauschal	global	—	a forfait	global
Forfaitierung (D)	—	forfaiting	forfaitage *m*	forfaiting *m*	financiación del comercio exterior *f*
forfaiting (E)	Forfaitierung *f*	—	forfaitage *m*	forfaiting *m*	financiación del comercio exterior *f*
forfaiting (I)	Forfaitierung *f*	forfaiting	forfaitage *m*	—	financiación del comercio exterior *f*
forfeiture of shares (E)	Kaduzierung *f*	—	caducité *f*	decadenza del socio moroso *f*	caducidad *f*
forma de mercado (Es)	Marktform *f*	market form	forme du marché *f*	sistema di mercato *m*	—
formación de capital (Es)	Vermögensbildung *f*	capital formation	formation de capital *f*	formazione del patrimonio *f*	—
formación de capital (Es)	Kapitalbildung *f*	formation of capital	formation de capital *f*	formazione di capitale *f*	—
formación del balance (Es)	Bilanzierung *f*	procedure to draw up a balance sheet	établissement du bilan *m*	redazione del bilancio *f*	—
formación del precio de oro (Es)	Goldpreisbildung *f*	gold pricing	formation du prix de l'or *f*	formazione del prezzo dell'oro *f*	—
formación del tipo de cambio (Es)	Devisenkursbildung *f*	exchange rate formation	formation du taux de change *f*	formazione dei cambi *f*	—
formación de un inventario (Es)	Bestandsaufnahme *f*	stock-taking	établissement de l'inventaire *m*	redazione d'inventario *f*	—
formación por aportaciones en especie (Es)	Illationsgründung *f*	formation by founders' non-cash capital contributions	constitution par apports en nature *f*	costituzione di una società mediante conferimento in natura *f*	—
formalización en escritura pública (Es)	öffentliche Beurkundung *f*	public authentication	authentification *f*	autenticazione pubblica *f*	—
formation by founders' non-cash capital contributions (E)	Illationsgründung *f*	—	constitution par apports en nature *f*	costituzione di una società mediante conferimento in natura *f*	formación por aportaciones en especie *f*
formation de capital (F)	Vermögensbildung *f*	capital formation	—	formazione del patrimonio *f*	formación de capital *f*
formation de capital (F)	Kapitalbildung *f*	formation of capital	—	formazione di capitale *f*	formación de capital *f*
formation du prix de l'or (F)	Goldpreisbildung *f*	gold pricing	—	formazione del prezzo dell'oro *f*	formación del precio de oro *f*

	D	E	F	I	Es
formation du taux de change (F)	Devisenkursbildung f	exchange rate formation	—	formazione dei cambi f	formación del tipo de cambio f
formation involving subscription in kind (E)	qualifizierte Gründung f	—	fondation par apports en nature f	costituzione qualificata f	fundación calificada f
formation of capital (E)	Kapitalbildung f	—	formation de capital f	formazione di capitale f	formación de capital f
format of the balance sheet (E)	Bilanzgliederung f	—	présentation du bilan f	struttura del bilancio f	estructura del balance f
formazione dei cambi (I)	Devisenkursbildung f	exchange rate formation	formation du taux de change f	—	formación del tipo de cambio f
formazione del bilancio pubblico (I)	Budgetierung f	drawing up of a budget	établissement du budget m	—	establecimiento del presupuesto m
formazione del patrimonio (I)	Vermögensbildung f	capital formation	formation de capital f	—	formación de capital f
formazione del prezzo dell'oro (I)	Goldpreisbildung f	gold pricing	formation du prix de l'or f	—	formación del precio de oro f
formazione di capitale (I)	Kapitalbildung f	formation of capital	formation de capital f	—	formación de capital f
forme du marché (F)	Marktform f	market form	—	sistema di mercato m	forma de mercado f
formulaire de virement (F)	Überweisungsträger m	remittance slip	—	nota d'accredito f	formulario de transferencia m
formulario de transferencia (Es)	Überweisungsträger m	remittance slip	formulaire de virement m	nota d'accredito f	—
formule de chèque normalisée (F)	Einheitsscheck m	standard cheque		assegno standardizzato m	cheque estándar m
fortes fluctuations des cours (F)	Ausbrechen des Kurses n	erratic price movements		oscillazione inattesa della quotazione f	fuertes movimientos en las cotizaciones m/pl
for the monthly settlement (E)	per Ultimo	—	à fin de mois	quotazione a fine corrente f	a fin de mes
fortlaufende Notierung (D)	—	variable price quoting	cotation variable f	libere contrattazioni f/pl	cotización variable f
forward exchange dealings (E)	Devisentermin-geschäft n	—	opération à terme sur les changes f	operazione di cambio a termine f	transacción a término en divisas f
forward exchange market (E)	Devisenterminmarkt m	—	marché des changes à terme m	mercato a termine delle divise m	mercado de divisas a plazo m
forward exchange rate (E)	Devisenterminkurs m	—	cours des devises négociés à terme m	quotazione dei cambi a termine f	cambio de divisas a término m
forward exchange	Devisentermin-handel m	—	marché des changes à terme m	operazione di cambio a termine f	mercado de cambios a plazo m
forward securities (E)	Terminpapiere n/pl	—	valeurs à terme f/pl	titoli ammessi a contratti future m/pl	títulos a plazo m/pl
foundation in which founders take all shares (E)	Übernahmegründung f	—	fondation simultanée f	costituzione simultanea f	fundación de adquisición f
fourchette de croissance monétaire (F)	Geldmengenziel n	money supply target	—	base monetaria programmata f	objetivo del volumen monetario m
fracción (Es)	Fraktion f	fractional order	ordre fractionné m	ordine di borsa frazionario f	—
fracción (Es)	Tranche f	tranche	tranche f	tranche f	—
fraccionamiento (Es)	Stückelung f	fragmentation	fractionnement m	frazionamento m	—
fracción de crédito (Es)	Kredittranche f	credit tranche	tranche de crédit f	quota di credito f	—
Frachtbörse (D)	—	shipping exchange	bourse de fret f	borsa dei noli f	bolsa de fletes f
fractional amount (E)	Kleinstücke n/pl	—	petits titres m/pl	titoli di importo modesto m/pl	títulos pequeños m/pl
fractional order (E)	Fraktion f	—	ordre fractionné m	ordine di borsa frazionario f	fracción f
fraction du revenu du travail disponible pour placements à long terme (F)	Investivlohn m	invested wages		risparmio contrattuale m	salario de inversión m
fractionnement (F)	Stückelung f	fragmentation	—	frazionamento m	fraccionamiento m
fragmentation (E)	Stückelung f	—	fractionnement m	frazionamento m	fraccionamiento m

	D	E	F	I	Es
frais (F)	Spesen *pl*	expenses	—	spese *f/pl*	gastos *m/pl*
frais de banque (F)	Bankspesen *pl*	bank charges	—	spese bancarie *f/pl*	gastos bancarios *m/pl*
frais de commission d'ouverture de crédit (F)	Kreditprovision *f*	credit commission	—	provvigione di credito *f*	comisión de apertura de crédito *f*
frais de garde (F)	Depotgebühren *f/pl*	safe custody charges	—	diritti di deposito *m/pl*	derechos de custodia *m/pl*
frais de l'émission (F)	Emissionskosten *pl*	underwriting costs	—	spese d'emissione *f/pl*	gastos de emisión *m/pl*
frais de liquidation (F)	Liquidationsgebühr *f*	liquidation fee	—	commissione di liquidazione *f*	derechos de liquidación *m/pl*
frais de mise en marche (F)	Anlaufkosten *pl*	launching costs	—	spese d'avviamento *f/pl*	gastos de instalación *m/pl*
frais de prolongation (F)	Belassungsgebühr *f*	prolongation charge	—	tassa prolungamento ipoteche *f*	derechos de prolongación *m/pl*
frais de recouvrement (F)	Inkassogebühr *f*	collection fee	—	commissione d'incasso *f*	comisión de cobro *f*
frais de représentation (F)	Aufwandskosten *pl*	expenses incurred	—	spese di rappresentanza *f/pl*	gastos originados *m/pl*
frais de transaction (F)	Transaktionskosten *pl*	conversion charge	—	costi di transazione *m/pl*	gastos de transacción *m/pl*
frais financiers (F)	Kapitalkosten *pl*	cost of capital	—	costi del capitale *m/pl*	gastos de capital *m/pl*
Fraktion (D)	—	fractional order	ordre fractionné *m*	ordine di borsa frazionario *f*	fracción *f*
franchigia (I)	Selbstbeteiligung *f*	retention	participation personnelle à la couverture du risque *f*	—	propia retención *f*
Frankoposten (D)	—	item free of charge	poste de port payé *m*	partita franco spese *f*	partida de porte pagado *f*
frappe (F)	Prägung *f*	minting	—	coniatura *f*	acuñación *f*
fraud (E)	Betrug *m*	—	fraude *f*	truffa *f*	fraude *m*
fraude (Es)	Betrug *m*	fraud	fraude *f*	truffa *f*	—
fraude (F)	Betrug *m*	fraud	—	truffa *f*	fraude *m*
fraude crediticio (Es)	Kreditschwindel *m*	credit fraud	obtention de crédits par duperie *f*	frode creditizia *f*	—
fraude en matière de faillite (F)	Konkursdelikt *n*	bankruptcy offence	—	reato fallimentare *m*	delito concursal *m*
fraud foundation (E)	Schwindelgründung *f*	—	fondation fictive *f*	costituzione fraudolenta *f*	fundación ficticia *f*
frazionamento (I)	Stückelung *f*	fragmentation	fractionnement *m*	—	fraccionamiento *m*
free access to the market (E)	freier Marktzutritt *m*	—	liberté d'accès au marché *f*	accesso libero al mercato *m*	libertad de acceso a un mercado *f*
free account (E)	Freikonto *n*	—	compte libre *m*	conto non vincolato *m*	cuenta libre *f*
free currency area (E)	freier Währungsraum *m*	—	zone monétaire libre *f*	area delle valute libere *f*	área monetaria libre *f*
free liquid reserves (E)	freie Liquiditäts-reserven *f/pl*	—	réserves de liquidités libres *f/pl*	riserve liquide a libera disposizione *f/pl*	reservas de liquidez libres *f/pl*
freely convertible (E)	frei konvertierbar	—	librement convertible	liberamente convertibile	libremente convertible
freely convertible currency (E)	freie Währung *f*	—	monnaie librement convertible *f*	valuta libera *f*	moneda libre *f*
freely fluctuating exchange rate (E)	freier Wechselkurs *m*	—	taux de change libre *m*	cambio libero *m*	tipo de cambio libre *m*
free of charge (E)	gratis	—	gratuit	gratis	gratuito
free trade area (E)	Freihandelszone *f*	—	zone de libre-échange *f*	zona di libero scambio *f*	zona de librecambio *f*
Freibetrag (D)	—	tax-free amount	montant exonéré *m*	importo esente *m*	importe exento *m*
freibleibend (D)	—	subject to confirmation	sans engagement	senza impegno	salvo venta
freie Liquiditäts-reserven (D)	—	free liquid reserves	réserves de liquidités libres *f/pl*	riserve liquide a libera disposizione *f/pl*	reservas de liquidez libres *f/pl*
freier Makler (D)	—	floor trader	courtier en valeurs mobilières *m*	mediatore libero *m*	corredor no colegiado *m*

	D	E	F	I	Es
freier Marktzutritt (D)	—	free access to the market	liberté d'accès au marché f	accesso libero al mercato m	libertad de acceso a un mercado f
freie Rücklage (D)	—	unrestricted retained earnings	réserve libre f	riserva non vincolata f	reservas libres f/pl
freier Währungsraum (D)	—	free currency area	zone monétaire libre f	area delle valute libere f	área monetaria libre f
freier Wechselkurs (D)	—	freely fluctuating exchange rate	taux de change libre m	cambio libero m	tipo de cambio libre m
freie Stücke (D)	—	negotiable securities	titres négociables m/pl	titoli non vincolati m/pl	títulos libres m/pl
freie Währung (D)	—	freely convertible currency	monnaie librement convertible f	valuta libera f	moneda libre f
Freihandel (D)	—	over-the-counter trade	commerce libre m	libero scambio m	librecambio m
Freihandelszone (D)	—	free trade area	zone de libre-échange f	zona di libero scambio f	zona de librecambio f
frei konvertierbar (D)	—	freely convertible	librement convertible	liberamente convertibile	libremente convertible
Freiverkehr (D)	—	unofficial dealings	marché libre m	contrattazioni fuori borsa f/pl	mercado libre m
Freiverkehrs-ausschuß (D)	—	unofficial dealings committee	comité du marché libre m	commissione operazioni fuori borsa f	comité de mercado libre m
freizügiger Sparverkehr (D)	—	system by which savings depositor can effect inpayments and withdrawals at all savings banks or post offices	épargne libéralisée f	libertà per l'intestatario del libretto di risparmio di effettuare versamenti e esborsi in tutte le casse di risparmio tedesche f	movimiento de ahorros liberalizado m
Fremdbezug (D)	—	external procurement	matériel acheté au-dehors m	acquisto di beni e servizi da terzi m	suministro externo m
Fremddepot (D)	—	fiduciary deposit	dépôt d'autrui m	deposito presso terzi m	depósito ajeno m
Fremde Gelder (D)	—	external funds	capitaux de tiers m/pl	fondi di terzi m/pl	fondos ajenos m/pl
Fremdemission (D)	—	security issue for third account	émission de valeurs pour compte de tiers f	emissione per conto terzi f	emisión ajena f
fremde Mittel (D)	—	borrowed funds	capitaux prêtés m/pl	denaro da terzi m	fondos de terceros m/pl
Fremdfinanzierung (D)	—	debt financing	constitution de capital par apport de tiers f	finanziamento esterno m	financiación con capital ajeno f
Fremdhypothek (D)	—	third-party mortgage	hypothèque constituée au profit d'un tiers f	ipoteca a favore di terzi f	hipoteca ajena f
Fremdinvestition (D)	—	external investment	investissement de capitaux étrangers m	investimento in imprese altrui m	inversión de capitales extranjeros f
Fremdkapital (D)	—	debt capital	capital de tiers m	capitale di credito m	capital ajeno m
Fremdkapitalkosten (D)	—	costs of loan capital	coût de l'argent emprunté m	costi del capitale di credito m/pl	coste de capital ajeno m
Fremdkapitalzins (D)	—	interest on borrowed capital	intérêt du capital prêté m	interessi per capitale di credito m/pl	intereses de capital ajeno m/pl
Fremd-kompensation (D)	—	offset transaction with resale to a third party	intervention d'un tiers dans une affaire de compensation f	compensazione per conto altrui f	compensación ajena f
Fremdvermutung (D)	—	presumption that securities deposited are fiduciary deposit	présomption que les valeurs déposées sont administrées à titre fiduciaire f	limitazione diritto di pegno e ritenzione su depositi di terzi f	suposición de depósito ajeno f
Fremdwährungs-guthaben (D)	—	foreign currency balance	avoir en monnaie étrangère m	disponibilità in valuta estera f	haberes de moneda extranjera m/pl
Fremdwährungs-konto (D)	—	account in foreign currency	compte en monnaie étrangère m	conto in valuta estera f	cuenta de moneda extranjera f
freundlich (D)	—	buoyant	ferme	favorevole	animado
Fristenkongruenz (D)	—	concordance of maturities	congruence d'échéances f	congruenza dei termini di scadenza f	congruencia de plazos f
Fristen-transformation (D)	—	maturity transformation	transformation d'échéances f	trasformazione termini di scadenza f	transformación de plazos f

	D	E	F	I	Es
frode creditizia (I)	Kreditschwindel m	credit fraud	obtention de crédits par duperie f	—	fraude crediticio m
fuertes movimientos en las cotizaciones (Es)	Ausbrechen des Kurses n	erratic price movements	fortes fluctuations des cours f/pl	oscillazione inattesa della quotazione f	
fuga de capital (Es)	Kapitalflucht f	exodus of capital	évasion des capitaux f	fuga dei capitali f	—
fuga dei capitali (I)	Kapitalflucht f	exodus of capital	évasion des capitaux f	—	fuga de capital f
fuga desbaratada (Es)	Deroute f	collapse	déroute f	tracollo dei prezzi di borsa m	—
fuga nei beni materiali (I)	Flucht in die Sachwerte f	flight into real assets	fuite vers les biens réels f	—	evasión al patrimonio real f
Führungs-grundsätze (D)	—	managerial principles	principes de gestion m/pl	principi amministrativi m/pl	principios de dirección m/pl
Führungsprovision (D)	—	managers commission	commission d'apériteur f	provvigione di gestione f	comisión de alta dirección f
fuite vers les biens réels (F)	Flucht in die Sachwerte f	flight into real assets	—	fuga nei beni materiali f	evasión al patrimonio real f
Fullarton reflux principle (E)	Fullartonsches Rückströmungs-prinzip n	—	principe de reflux de Fullarton m	legge di riflusso di Fullarton f	principio de reflujo de Fullarton m
Fullartonsches Rückströmungs-prinzip (D)	—	Fullarton reflux principle	principe de reflux de Fullarton m	legge di riflusso di Fullarton m	principio de reflujo de Fullarton m
full power of attorney (E)	Prokura f	—	procuration commer-ciale générale f	procura commerciale f	poder general m
función de medio de cambio del dinero (Es)	Tauschmittelfunktion des Geldes f	exchange function of money	fonction de l'argent de moyen d'échange f	funzione di scambio della moneta f	—
funciones monetarias (Es)	Geldfunktionen f/pl	functions of money	fonctions de la monnaie f	funzioni del denaro f/pl	
functions of money (E)	Geldfunktionen f/pl	—	fonctions de la monnaie f	funzioni del denaro f/pl	funciones monetarias f/pl
fund (E)	fundieren	—	fonder	consolidare	consolidar
fund (E)	Fonds m	—	fonds m	fondo m	fondo m
fundación calificada (Es)	qualifizierte Gründung f	formation involving subscription in kind	fondation par apports en nature f	costituzione qualificata f	—
fundación de adquisición (Es)	Übernahmegründung f	foundation in which founders take all shares	fondation simultanée f	costituzione simulatanea f	—
fundación ficticia (Es)	Schwindelgründung f	fraud foundation	fondation fictive f	costituzione fraudolenta f	—
fundación simulada (Es)	Scheingründung f	fictitious formation	constitution d'opportunité f	costituzione fittizia f	—
Fundamental-analyse (D)	—	portfolio analysis	analyse fondamentale f	analisi fondamentale m	análisis fundamental m
fund assets (E)	Fondsvermögen n	—	capital constituant le fonds m	patrimonio del fondo m	activo en fondos públicos m
funded debts (E)	fundierte Schulden f/pl	—	dette consolidée f	debiti consolidati m/pl	deudas consolidadas f/pl
fundieren (D)	—	to fund	fonder	consolidare	consolidar
fundierte Schulden (D)	—	funded debts	dette consolidée f	debiti consolidati m/pl	deudas consolidadas f/pl
Fundierungs-anleihe (D)	—	funding loan	emprunt consolidé m	prestito consolidato m	empréstito consolidado m
funding loan (E)	Fundierungsanleihe f	—	emprunt consolidé m	prestito consolidato m	empréstito consolidado m
funding paper (E)	Finanzierungspapier n	—	titres de financement m/pl	titolo di finanziamento m	título de financiación m
fund-linked life insurance (E)	Fondsgebundene Lebensversicherung f	—	assurance-vie liée à un fonds f	assicurazione sulla vita con garanzia reale f	seguro de vida vinculado a fondos m
funds statement (E)	Kapitalflußrechnung f	—	tableau de financement m	calcolo del flusso di capitale m	tabla de financiación f
fungibilidad (Es)	Fungibilität f	fungibility	qualité fongible d'un bien f	fungibilità f	—

	D	E	F	I	Es
fungibilità (I)	Fungilbilität f	fungibility	qualité fongible d'un bien f	—	fungibilidad f
Fungibilität (D)	—	fungibility	qualité fongible d'un bien f	fungibilità f	fungibilidad f
fungibility (E)	Fungilbilität f	—	qualité fongible d'un bien f	fungibilità f	fungibilidad f
fungible securities (E)	vertretbare Wertpapiere n/pl	—	titres fongibles m/pl	titoli fungibili m/pl	títulos fungibles m/pl
fungible security deposit (E)	Aberdepot n	—	dépôt de choses fongibles m	deposito irregolare di titoli m	depósito de títulos fungibles m
funzione di scambio della moneta (I)	Tauschmittelfunktion des Geldes f	exchange function of money	fonction de l'argent de moyen d'échange f	—	función de medio de cambio del dinero f
funzioni del denaro (I)	Geldfunktionen f/pl	functions of money	fonction de la monnaie f	—	funciones monetarias f/pl
fuori bilancio (I)	unter dem Strich	in total	au total	—	en total
Fusion (D)	—	amalgamation	fusion f	fusione f	fusión f
fusión (Es)	Fusion f	amalgamation	fusion f	fusione f	—
fusion (F)	Fusion f	amalgamation	—	fusione f	fusión f
fusión de acciones (Es)	Aktienzusammen-legung f	consolidation of shares	regroupement d'actions m	raggruppamento di azioni m	—
fusione (I)	Fusion f	amalgamation	fusion f	—	fusión f
Fusionssteuer (D)	—	amalgamation tax	impôt sur la fusion de sociétés m	tassa di fusione f	impuesto sobre la fusión de sociedades m
futures market (E)	Terminbörse f	—	bourse à terme f	mercato a termine m	bolsa de valores a término f
futures market (E)	Terminkontraktmarkt m	—	marché à terme m	mercato dei contratti a termine m	mercado de contratos de entrega futura m
futures market (E)	Futures-Markt m	—	marché des opéra-tions à terme m	mercato dei contratti future m	mercado de operaciones a plazo m
Futures-Markt (D)	—	futures market	marché des opéra-tions à terme m	mercato dei contratti future m	mercado de operaciones a plazo m
gage mobilier (F)	Faustpfand n	pawn	—	pegno mobile m	prenda mobiliaria f
gain brut (F)	Bruttoertrag m	gross return	—	ricavo lordo m	producto bruto m
gain fictif (F)	Scheingewinn m	fictitious profit	—	utile fittizio m	beneficio simulado m
gainfully employed person (E)	Erwerbsperson f	—	personne active f	persona abile al lavoro f	persona activa f
gain of redemption (E)	Tilgungsgewinn m	—	bénéfice d'amortissement m	utile di rimborso m	beneficio de amortización m
gain on disposal (E)	Veräußerungs-gewinn m	—	bénéfice d'aliénation m	plusvalenza f	beneficio de la venta m
gains from trade (E)	Außenhandelsgewinn m	—	excédent du commerce extérieur m	saldo attivo bilancia commerciale m	excedente del co-mercio exterior m
gain spéculatif (F)	Spekulationsgewinn m	speculative profit	—	utile di speculazione m	beneficio especulativo m
garant (F)	Bürge m	guarantor	—	fidefaciente m	fiador m
garantía (Es)	Haftsumme f	guarantee	garantie f	garanzia f	—
garantía adicional (Es)	Ersatzdeckung f	substitute cover	garantie de substitution f	copertura sostitutiva f	—
garantía bancaria (Es)	Bankgarantie f	banker's guarantee	garantie de banque f	garanzia bancaria f	—
garantía de cambio (Es)	Währungs-absicherung f	safeguarding of the currency	garantie de change f	sostegno di una moneta m	—
garantía de crédito (Es)	Kreditgarantie f	credit guarantee	garantie de crédit f	garanzia di credito f	—
garantía de depositos (Es)	Einlagensicherung f	guarantee of deposit	sûreté en garantie de dépôts f	garanzia dei depositi f	—
garantía de dividendos (Es)	Dividendengarantie f	dividend guarantee	garantie de distribu-tion d'un dividende f	dividendo garantito m	—
garantía de entrega (Es)	Liefergarantie f	guarantee of delivery	garantie de livraison f	garanzia di sostegno f	—
garantía de exportación (Es)	Ausfuhrgarantie f	export credit guarantee	garantie en faveur de l'exportateur f	garanzia d'esportazione f	—

	D	E	F	I	Es
garantía de intereses (Es)	Zinsgarantie *f*	guaranteed interest	garantie de l'intérêt *f*	garanzia d'interesse *f*	—
garantía de pago (Es)	Anzahlungsbürgschaft *f*	payment guarantee	garantie de payement *f*	garanzia rimborso acconto *f*	—
garantía de transferencia (Es)	Transfergarantie *f*	guarantee of foreign exchange transfer	garantie des transferts *f*	garanzia di trasferimento *f*	—
garantía de un crédito (Es)	Kreditsicherung *f*	safeguarding of credit	sûreté en garantie d'un crédit *f*	garanzia di credito *f*	—
garantía de un crédito (Es)	Kreditsicherheit *f*	security of credit	garantie concernant un crédit *m*	garanzia di credito *f*	—
garantía de valor (Es)	Wertsicherung *f*	value guarantee	garantie de valeur *f*	garanzia del valore *f*	—
garantía federal (Es)	Bundesbürgschaft *f*	Federal guarantee	garantie fédérale *f*	garanzia federale *f*	—
garantías para la exportación (Es)	Ausfuhrbürgschaften *f/pl*	export credit guarantee	garanties à l'exportation *f/pl*	cauzioni d'esportazione *f/pl*	—
garantie (F)	Haftsumme *f*	guarantee	—	garanzia *f*	garantía *f*
garantie concernant un crédit (F)	Kreditsicherheit *f*	security of credit	—	garanzia di credito *f*	garantía de un crédito *f*
garantie de banque (F)	Bankgarantie *f*	banker's guarantee	—	garanzia bancaria *f*	garantía bancaria *f*
garantie de bonne fin (F)	Ausfallbürgschaft *f*	deficiency guarantee	—	garanzia di sostituzione *f*	fianza de indemnidad *f*
garantie de change (F)	Währungsabsicherung *f*	safeguarding of the currency	—	sostegno di una moneta *m*	garantía de cambio *f*
garantie de crédit (F)	Kreditgarantie *f*	credit guarantee	—	garanzia di credito *f*	garantía de crédito *f*
garantie de distribution d'un dividende (F)	Dividendengarantie *f*	dividend guarantee	—	dividendo garantito *m*	garantía de dividendos *f*
garantie de l'intérêt (F)	Zinsgarantie *f*	guaranteed interest	—	garanzia d'interesse *f*	garantía de intereses *f*
garantie de livraison (F)	Liefergarantie *f*	guarantee of delivery	—	garanzia di sostegno *f*	garantía de entrega *f*
garantie de payement (F)	Anzahlungsbürgschaft *f*	payment guarantee	—	garanzia rimborso acconto *f*	garantía de pago *f*
garantie de prestation (F)	Leistungsgarantie *f*	performance guarantee	—	garanzia di esecuzione *f*	fianza de contratista *f*
garantie des créanciers (F)	Gläubigerschutz *m*	protection of creditors	—	protezione dei creditori *f*	protección de acreedores *f*
garantie des transferts (F)	Transfergarantie *f*	guarantee of foreign exchange transfer	—	garanzia di trasferimento *f*	garantía de transferencia *f*
garantie de substitution (F)	Ersatzdeckung *f*	substitute cover	—	copertura sostitutiva *f*	garantía adicional *f*
garantie de valeur (F)	Wertsicherung *f*	value guarantee	—	garanzia del valore *f*	garantía de valor *f*
garantie du certificateur de la caution (F)	Nachbürgschaft *f*	collateral guarantee	—	fideiussione per il fideiussore *f*	subfianza *f*
garantie en faveur de l'exportateur (F)	Ausfuhrgarantie *f*	export credit guarantee	—	garanzia d'esportazione *f*	garantía de exportación *f*
garantie fédérale (F)	Bundesbürgschaft *f*	Federal guarantee	—	garanzia federale *f*	garantía federal *f*
Garantiegeschäft (D)	—	guarantee business	opération de garantie *f*	assunzione di garanzia per terzi *f*	operación de garantía *f*
Garantiehaftung (D)	—	liability for breach of warranty	responsabilité de garantie *f*	responsabilità da garanzia *f*	responsabilidad de garantía *f*
Garantiekapital (D)	—	capital serving as a guarantee	capital de garantie *m*	capitale di garanzia *m*	capital de garantía *m*
Garantiekonsortium (D)	—	underwriting syndicate	syndicat bancaire de garantie *m*	consorzio di garanzia *m*	consorcio de garantía *m*
garanties à l'exportation (F)	Ausfuhrbürgschaften *f/pl*	export credit guarantee	—	cauzioni d'esportazione *f/pl*	garantías para la exportación *f*
garanzia (I)	Obligo *n*	liability	engagement *m*	—	obligación *f*
garanzia bancaria (I)	Bankgarantie *f*	banker's guarantee	garantie de banque *f*	—	garantía bancaria *f*
garanzia dei depositi (I)	Einlagensicherung *f*	guarantee of deposit	sûreté en garantie de dépôts *f*	—	garantía de depositos *f*
garanzia del valore (I)	Wertsicherung *f*	value guarantee	garantie de valeur *f*	—	garantía de valor *f*
garanzia d'esportazione (I)	Ausfuhrgarantie *f*	export credit guarantee	garantie en faveur de l'exportateur *f*	—	garantía de exportación *f*
garanzia di credito (I)	Kreditsicherung *f*	safeguarding of credit	sûreté en garantie d'un crédit *f*	—	garantía de un crédito *f*

	D	E	F	I	Es
garanzia di credito (I)	Kreditgarantie f	credit guarantee	garantie de crédit f	—	garantía de crédito f
garanzia di credito (I)	Kreditsicherheit f	security of credit	garantie concernant un crédit m	—	garantía de un crédito f
garanzia di esecuzione (I)	Leistungsgarantie f	performance guarantee	garantie de prestation f	—	fianza de contratista f
garanzia dei depositi (I)	Einlagensicherung f	guarantee of deposit	sûreté en garantie de dépôts f	—	garantía de depositos f
garanzia del valore (I)	Wertsicherung f	value guarantee	garantie de valeur f	—	garantía de valor f
garanzia d'interesse (I)	Zinsgarantie f	guaranteed interest	garantie de l'intérêt f	—	garantía de intereses f
garanzia di sostegno (I)	Liefergarantie f	guarantee of delivery	garantie de livraison f	—	garantía de entrega f
garanzia di sostituzione (I)	Ausfallbürgschaft f	deficiency guarantee	garantie de bonne fin f	—	fianza de indemnidad f
garanzia di trasferimento (I)	Transfergarantie f	guarantee of foreign exchange transfer	garantie des transferts f	—	garantía de transferencia f
garanzia federale (I)	Bundesbürgschaft f	Federal guarantee	garantie fédérale f	—	garantía federal f
garanzia rimborso acconto (I)	Anzahlungs-bürgschaft f	payment guarantee	garantie de payement f	—	garantía de pago f
garde en titres (F)	Depotverwahrung f	securities custody	—	custodia in deposito f	custodia de valores f
garde en dépôt (F)	Aufbewahrung f	deposit	—	custodia f	conservación f
garnishee procedings (E)	Drittpfändung f	—	saisie de tiers débiteurs f	subpegno di titoli m	embargo del tercer deudor m
gastos (Es)	Spesen pl	expenses	frais m/pl	spese f/pl	—
gastos (Es)	Ausgaben f/pl	expenses	dépenses f/pl	spese f/pl	—
gastos bancarios (Es)	Bankspesen pl	bank charges	frais de banque m/pl	spese bancarie f/pl	—
gastos de capital (Es)	Kapitalkosten pl	cost of capital	frais financiers m/pl	costi del capitale m/pl	—
gastos de crédito (Es)	Kreditkosten pl	cost of credit	coût de crédit m	costi del credito m/pl	—
gastos de depósito (Es)	Verwahrungskosten pl	custody fee	coût de garde m	spese di custodia f/pl	—
gastos de desembolso (Es)	ausgabenwirksame Kosten pl	spending costs	coût créant des dépenses m/pl	costi comportanti spese m/pl	—
gastos de emisión (Es)	Emissionskosten pl	underwriting costs	frais de l'émission m/pl	spese d'emissione f/pl	—
gastos de explotación (Es)	Betriebskosten pl	working expenses	charges d'exploitation f/pl	costi d'esercizio m/pl	—
gastos deficitarios (Es)	Deficit Spending n	deficit spending	deficit spending m	deficit spending m	—
gastos degresivos (Es)	degressive Kosten pl	degressive costs	coût dégressifs m	costi decrescenti m/pl	—
gastos de instalación (Es)	Anlaufkosten pl	launching costs	frais de mise en marche m/pl	spese d'avviamento f/pl	—
gastos de los factores (Es)	Faktorkosten pl	factor costs	coût des facteurs m	costi dei fattori m/pl	—
gastos de riesgo (Es)	Risikokosten pl	risk-induced costs	coût hasardeux m	costi di rischio m/pl	—
gastos de transacción (Es)	Transaktionskosten pl	conversion charge	frais de transaction m/pl	costi di transazione m/pl	—
gastos fijos (Es)	fixe Kosten pl	standing costs	coût fixes m	costi fissi m/pl	—
gastos locales (Es)	Platzspesen pl	local expenses	change de place m	spese d'incasso di piazza f/pl	—
gastos originados (Es)	Aufwandskosten pl	expenses incurred	frais de représentation m/pl	spese di rappresentanza f/pl	—
gastos públicos (Es)	Staatsausgaben f/pl	public spending	dépenses publiques f/pl	spese pubbliche f/pl	—
Gattungsvollmacht (D)	—	generic power	pouvoir générique m	procura specifica f	poder de género m
Gebietsansässiger (D)	—	resident	résident m	residente m	residente m
Gebietsfremder (D)	—	non-resident	non-résident m	non residente m	no residente m
Gebiets-körperschaft (D)	—	regional authority	collectivité territoriale f	ente locale m	corporación territorial f
geborene Orderpapiere (D)	—	instruments to order by law	titres à ordre par nature m/pl	titoli all'ordine per legge m/pl	valores a la orden por naturaleza m/pl
Gebot (D)	—	bid	offre f	offerta f	oferta f
Gebrauchswert (D)	—	value in use	valeur d'usage f	valore d'uso m	valor de uso m

	D	E	F	I	Es
gebrochener Schluß (D)	—	odd lot	lot ne pas négocié officiellement *m*	lotto senza quotazione ufficiale *m*	lote no negociado oficialmente *m*
Gebühr (D)	—	fee	taxe *f*	canone *m*	derechos *m/pl*
gebundene Währung (D)	—	linked currency	monnaie liée *f*	valuta a regime di controllo *f*	moneda vinculada *f*
gedeckter Kredit (D)	—	covered credit	crédit garanti *m*	credito garantito *m*	crédito cubierto *m*
gedeckter Scheck (D)	—	covered cheque	chèque provisionné *m*	assegno coperto *m*	cheque cubierto *m*
Gefälligkeitsakzept (D)	—	accommodation acceptance	acceptation de complaisance *f*	accettazione di favore *f*	aceptación de favor *f*
Gefälligkeitsgiro (D)	—	accommodation endorsement	endossement de complaisance *m*	girata di favore *f*	endoso de favor *m*
Gegenakkreditiv (D)	—	back-to-back letter of credit	contrecrédit *m*	controcredito *m*	contracrédito *m*
Gegenbuchung (D)	—	counter entry	contrepartie *f*	registrazione in contropartita *f*	contrapartida *f*
Gegenforderung (D)	—	counterclaim	contre-prétention *f*	contropretesa *f*	contrareclamación *f*
Gegengeschäft (D)	—	countertrade	affaire en contrepartie *f*	operazione di compensazione *f*	transacción en contra *f*
gegenseitiger Vertrag (D)	—	reciprocal contract	accord de réciprocité *m*	contratto bilaterale *m*	contrato recíproco *m*
Gegenwartswert (D)	—	present value	valeur actuelle *f*	valore attuale *m*	valor actual *m*
gekreuzter Scheck (D)	—	crossed cheque	chèque barré *m*	assegno sbarrato *m*	cheque cruzado *m*
Geld (D)	—	money	argent *m*	denaro *m*	dinero *m*
Geldakkord (D)	—	money piece rate	convention de salaire aux pièces *f*	cottimo al pezzo *m*	destajo *m*
Geldangebot (D)	—	supply of money	offre d'argent *f*	offerta monetaria *f*	oferta monetaria *f*
Geldanlage (D)	—	investment	placement d'argent *m*	investimento di denaro *m*	inversión *f*
Geldautomat (D)	—	cash dispenser	distribanque *m*	bancomat *m*	cajero automático *m*
Geldbasis (D)	—	monetary base	base monétaire *f*	base monetaria *f*	base monetaria *f*
Geldbasiskonzept (D)	—	monetary base principle	principe de la base monétaire *m*	principio della base monetaria *m*	principio de la base monetaria *m*
Geldbörse (D)	—	money market	bourse des valeurs *f*	borsa delle valute *f*	mercado monetario *m*
Gelddeckung (D)	—	monetary standard	couverture monétaire *f*	copertura metallica *f*	reserva-metales finos *f*
Gelddisposition (D)	—	monetary arrangement	disposition monétaire *f*	disposizione di moneta *f*	disposición monetaria *f*
Geldeingang (D)	—	receipt of money	rentrée de fonds *f*	entrata di denaro *f*	entrada de dinero *f*
Geldentwertung (D)	—	monetary devaluation	dépréciation *f*	svalutazione monetaria *f*	devaluación del dinero *f*
Geldexport (D)	—	money export	exportation monétaire *f*	esportazione di valuta *f*	exportación monetaria *f*
Geldfaktor (D)	—	monetary factor	facteur monétaire *m*	fattore monetario *m*	factor monetario *m*
Geldfunktionen (D)	—	functions of money	fonction de la monnaie *f*	funzioni del denaro *f/pl*	funciones monetarias *f/pl*
Geldhaltung (D)	—	money management	tenue d'argent *f*	tenuta di denaro *f*	tenencia de dinero *f*
Geldillusion (D)	—	money illusion	illusion monétaire *f*	illusione monetaria *f*	ilusión monetaria *f*
Geldimport (D)	—	money import	importation monétaire *f*	importazione di valuta *f*	importación monetaria *f*
Geldinstitut (D)	—	financial institution	établissement financier *m*	istituto di credito *m*	instituto monetario *m*
Geldkapital (D)	—	monetary capital	capital monétaire *m*	capitale monetario *m*	capital monetario *m*
Geldkurs (D)	—	bid price	cours de la demande *f*	corso di domanda *m*	cotización demandada *f*
Geldlohn (D)	—	money wage	salaire payé en argent *m*	salario in denaro *f*	salario en efectivo *m*
Geldmarkt (D)	—	money market	marché monétaire *m*	mercato monetario *m*	mercado monetario *m*
Geldmarktfonds (D)	—	money market funds	fonds du marché monétaire *m/pl*	fondi monetari *m/pl*	fondos de mercado monetario *m/pl*
Geldmarktkonto (D)	—	money market account	compte du marché monétaire *m*	conto monetario *m*	cuenta de mercado monetario *m*

	D	E	F	I	Es
Geldmarktkredit (D)	—	money market credit	crédit accordé sur le marché monétaire m	credito monetario m	crédito de mercado monetario m
Geldmarktpapier (D)	—	money market securities	titres du marché monétaire m/pl	portafoglio sconto m	título del mercado monetario m
Geldmarktpolitik (D)	—	money market policy	politique du marché monétaire f	politica del mercato monetario f	política monetaria f
Geldmarktsatz (D)	—	money market rate	taux d'intérêt sur le marché monétaire m	tasso del mercato monetario m	tipo de cambio del mercado monetario m
Geldmenge (D)	—	money stock	quantité de monnaie en circulation f	base monetaria f	masa monetaria f
Geldmengenziel (D)	—	money supply target	fourchette de croissance monétaire f	base monetaria programmata f	objetivo del volumen monetario m
Geldnachfrage (D)	—	money demand	demande d'argent f	domanda monetaria f	demanda monetaria f
Geldnutzen (D)	—	utility of funds	utilité monétaire f	utilità del denaro f	utilidad monetaria f
Geldpolitik (D)	—	monetary policy	politique monétaire f	politica monetaria f	política monetaria f
Geldsatz (D)	—	money rate	taux de l'argent m	tasso monetario m	tipo de interés m
Geldschleier (D)	—	veil of money	voile d'argent m	moneta-velo f	velo monetario m
Geldschöpfung (D)	—	creation of money	création d'argent f	creazione di denaro f	creación de dinero f
Geldschöpfungs-multiplikator (D)	—	money creation ratio	multiplicateur de crédit m	moltiplicatore di moneta m	multiplicador de crédito m
Geldsortier-maschine (D)	—	money sorting machine	trieuse d'argent f	macchina per la cernita delle monete f	máquina clasificadora de dinero f
Geldstromanalyse (D)	—	flow-of-funds analysis	analyse des courants monétaires f	analisi dei flussi monetari m	análisis de flujos monetarios m
Geldsubstitut (D)	—	money substitute	monnaie subrogée f	quasi moneta f	sustitutivo de dinero m
Geldüberhang (D)	—	excessive supply of money	excédent des moyens de payement m	eccedenza finanziaria f	exceso de dinero m
Geldumlauf (D)	—	circulation of money	circulation monétaire f	circolazione monetaria f	circulación de dinero f
Geldumlaufs-geschwindigkeit (D)	—	velocity of circulation of money	vitesse de la circulation de la monnaie f	velocità della circolazione monetaria f	ritmo de la circulación del dinero m
Geldumsatz (D)	—	turnover of money	roulement de l'argent m	circolazione monetaria f	giro monetario m
Geldverfassung (D)	—	monetary structure	structure monétaire f	sistema monetario m	estructura monetaria f
Geldvernichtung (D)	—	reduction of the volume of money	destruction d'argent f	distruzione di denaro f	destrucción de dinero f
Geldvolumen (D)	—	volume of money	masse monétaire f	massa monetaria f	volumen monetario m
Geldwechsel-geschäft (D)	—	currency exchange business	opération de change f	operazione di cambio f	cambio manual m
Geldwert (D)	—	value of money	valeur de l'argent f	valore monetario m	valor monetario m
Geldwertschwund (D)	—	currency erosion	érosion monétaire f	deprezzamento monetario m	erosión monetaria f
Geldwertsicherungs-klausel (D)	—	money guarantee clause	clause d'indexation f	clausola di garanzia monetaria f	cláusula de garantía sobre el valor monetario m
Geldwertstabilität (D)	—	monetary stability	stabilité monétaire f	stabilità monetaria f	estabilidad monetaria f
Geldwesen (D)	—	monetary system	système monétaire m	sistema monetario m	sistema monetario m
Geldwirtschaft (D)	—	money economy	économie monétaire f	economia monetaria f	economía financiera f
Geldzählautomat (D)	—	money counting machine	machine compte-monnaie f	macchina contadenaro f	máquina de contar dinero f
Geldzins (D)	—	interest on money	intérêt de l'argent prêté m	interesse del denaro m	interés del dinero m
gemeiner Wert (D)	—	market value	valeur habituelle f	prezzo teorico m	valor común m
Gemeinschafts-anleihe (D)	—	joint loan	prêt commun f	prestito collettivo m	empréstito comunitario m
Gemeinschafts-bank (D)	—	combination bank	banque combinée f	banca comune f	banco de combinación m
Gemeinschafts-depot (D)	—	joint security deposit	dépôt en commun m	deposito congiunto m	depósito común m
Gemeinschafts-emission (D)	—	joint issue	émission en commun f	emissione comune f	emisión común f

	D	E	F	I	Es
Gemeinschafts-fonds (D)	—	joint funds	fonds commun *m*	fondo comune *m*	fondo común *m*
Gemeinschafts-konto (D)	—	joint account	compte commun *m*	conto congiunto *m*	cuenta conjunta *f*
Gemeinschafts-sparen (D)	—	joint saving	épargne collective *f*	risparmio collettivo *m*	ahorro común *m*
Gemeinschuldner (D)	—	adjudicated bankrupt	débiteur en failli *m*	debitore fallito *m*	deudor común *m*
Gemeinwirtschaft (D)	—	social economy	économie sociale *f*	economia collettiva *f*	economía colectiva *f*
gemischter Fonds (D)	—	mixed fund	fonds mixte *m*	fondo d'investimento misto *m*	fondo mixto *m*
genannt (D)	—	indicated	indiqué	stimato	alias
genehmigte Bilanz (D)	—	authorized balance sheet	bilan approuvé *m*	bilancio approvato *m*	balance aprobado *m*
genehmigtes Kapital (D)	—	authorized capital	capital autorisé *m*	capitale approvato *m*	capital concedido *m*
Genehmigungs-pflicht (D)	—	duty to obtain a permit	obligation de solliciter une permission *f*	obbligo d'autorizzazione *m*	régimen de autorización *m*
general agent (E)	Handelsbevoll-mächtigter *m*	—	personne ayant le pouvoir commercial *f*	rappresentante commerciale *m*	agente comercial *m*
General Arrangements to Borrow (E)	allgemeine Kreditvereinbarung *f*	—	accord général de crédits *m*	accordo generale di credito *m*	acuerdo general de empréstito *m*
general assembly (E)	Generalversammlung *f*	—	assemblée générale *f*	assemblea generale *f*	junta general *f*
general mortgage (E)	Gesamthypothek *f*	—	hypothèque solidaire *f*	ipoteca generale *f*	hipoteca solidaria *f*
general partner (E)	Komplementär *m*	—	commandité *m*	accomandatario *m*	socio colectivo *m*
general partnership (E)	offene Handelsgesellschaft *f*	—	société en nom collectif *f*	società in nome collettivo *f*	compañía colectiva *f*
General-versammlung (D)	—	general assembly	assemblée générale *f*	assemblea generale *f*	junta general *f*
Generalvollmacht (D)	—	unlimited power	pouvoir général *m*	procura generale *f*	poder general *m*
generic power (E)	Gattungsvollmacht *f*	—	pouvoir générique *m*	procura specifica *f*	poder de género *m*
Genossenschaft (D)	—	cooperative	société coopérative *f*	cooperativa *f*	cooperativa *f*
genossenschaftlicher Bankensektor (D)	—	cooperative banking sector	activités bancaires coopératives *f/pl*	settore bancario cooperativo *m*	actividades bancarias cooperativas *f/pl*
genossenschaftliche Zentralbanken (D)	—	cooperative central banks	banques coopératives centrales *f/pl*	banche centrali cooperative *f/pl*	bancos centrales cooperativos *m/pl*
Genußrecht (D)	—	participation rights	droit de jouissance *m*	diritto di godimento *m*	derecho de disfrute *m*
Genußrechtskapital (D)	—	participating rights capital	capital bénéficiaire *m*	capitale da buoni di godimento *m*	capital de bono de disfrute *m*
Genußschein (D)	—	participating certificate	certificat de jouissance *m*	buono di godimento *m*	bono de disfrute *m*
geregelter Freiverkehr (D)	—	unofficial market	marché libre *m*	mercato libero disciplinato *m*	mercado de valores extrabursátil *m*
gerencia (Es)	Geschäftsführung *f*	management	gestion *f*	gestione *f*	—
Gesamtertrag (D)	—	total proceeds	produit global *m*	reddito totale *m*	renta total *f*
Gesamtforderung (D)	—	total claim	créance totale *f*	credito complessivo *m*	crédito total *m*
Gesamthand-eigentum (D)	—	joint tenancy	propriété d'un associé d'une société par intérêts *f*	proprietà indivisa *f*	propiedad en mano común *f*
Gesamthand-forderung (D)	—	jointly owned claim	créance d'un associé d'une société par intérêts *f*	credito comunione a mani unite *m*	crédito en mano común *m*
Gesamthandschuld (D)	—	joint debt	dette d'un associé d'une société par intérêts *f*	debito comunione a mani unite *m*	deuda en mano común *f*
Gesamthypothek (D)	—	general mortgage	hypothèque solidaire *f*	ipoteca generale *f*	hipoteca solidaria *f*
Gesamtkapital-rentabilität (D)	—	total capital profitability	rentabilité totale du capital *f*	redditività del capitale complessivo *f*	rédito del capital total *m*
Gesamtkosten (D)	—	overall costs	coût total *m*	costi complessivi *m/pl*	costes totales *m/pl*
Gesamtkurs (D)	—	total market value	cours total *m*	quotazione accordata *f*	cotización colectiva *f*

	D	E	F	I	Es
Gesamtplanung (D)	—	master planning	planification globale f	programmazione complessiva f	planificación global f
Gesamtschuld (D)	—	total debt	dette solidaire f	debito solidale m	obligación solidaria f
Gesamtschuldner (D)	—	joint and several debtor	débiteur solidaire m	debitore solidale m	deudor solidario m
Gesamtvermögen (D)	—	aggregate property	avoir total m	patrimonio complessivo m	totalidad del patrimonio f
Gesamtvollmacht (D)	—	joint power of attorney	procuration collective f	procura collettiva f	poder solidario m
Gesamtzinsspannen-rechnung (D)	—	whole-bank interest margin calculation	calcul du total de la marge entre les taux d'intérêt créditeur et débiteur m	calcolo margine d'interesse m	cálculo del margen de beneficio por intereses total m
Geschäft (D)	—	exchange operation	opération f	contratto m	negocio m
Geschäftsbank (D)	—	commercial bank	banque commerciale f	banca commerciale f	banco comercial m
Geschäfts-bedingungen (D)	—	terms and conditions of business	conditions commerciales f/pl	condizioni contrattuali f/pl	condiciones comerciales f/pl
Geschäftsbericht (D)	—	business report	rapport de gestion m	rapporto di gestione m	informe anual m
Geschäftsbesorgungs-vertrag (D)	—	agency agreement	contrat de gestion d'affaires m	contratto d'agenzia m	contrato de mandato m
Geschäftsführung (D)	—	management	gestion f	gestione f	gerencia f
Geschäfts-grundlage (D)	—	implicit basis of a contract	base implicite d'un contrat f	base negoziale f	base del negocio f
Geschäftsguthaben (D)	—	proprietor's capital holding	avoir commercial m	capitale da soci di una cooperativa m	saldo activo de la empresa m
Geschäftsjahr (D)	—	financial year	exercice commercial m	anno d'esercizio m	ejercicio m
Geschäftsleitung (D)	—	managerial staff	direction commerciale f	direzione f	dirección f
geschäftslos (D)	—	slack	stagnant	inattivo	estado de estancamiento m
Geschäftspapier (D)	—	commercial papers	papier d'affaires m	carta intestata f	documento comercial m
Geschäftssparten-kalkulation (D)	—	business category costing	calcul des coûts des catégories commerciales m	calcolo dei rami d'attività m	cálculos de costes de las categorías comerciales m/pl
Geschäftsvolumen (D)	—	volume of business	volume d'affaires m	volume d'affari m	volumen de negocios m
Geschäftswert (D)	—	value of the subject matter at issue	valeur commerciale f	avviamento m	valor comercial m
Geschenksparbuch (D)	—	gift savings book	livret d'épargne en cadeau m	libretto di risparmio in omaggio m	libreta de ahorros como regalo f
geschlossener Immobilienfonds (D)	—	closed-end real estate fund	fonds de placement immobilier fermé m	fondo immobiliare chiuso m	fondo inmobiliario cerrado m
geschlossener Markt (D)	—	self-contained market	marché fermé m	mercato chiuso m	mercado cerrado m
Gesellschaft (D)	—	company	société f	società f	sociedad f
Gesellschafter-Darlehen (D)	—	proprietor's loan	prêt d'un associé à la société m	conferimento di un socio m	préstamo concedido a socios m
Gesellschaft mit beschränkter Haftung [GmbH] (D)	—	limited liability company	société à respon-sabilité limitée S.A.R.L. f	società a responsabilità limitata f	sociedad de responsabilidad limitada f
Gesellschafts-schulden (D)	—	company's debts	dettes sociales f/pl	debiti della società m/pl	deudas sociales f/pl
Gesellschafts-vermögen (D)	—	partnership assets	patrimoine social m	attivo sociale m	activo social m
Gesellschafts-vertrag (D)	—	shareholder's agreement	contrat de société m	atto costitutivo m	contrato social m
gesetzliche Rücklage (D)	—	legally restricted retained earnings	réserves légales f/pl	riserva legale f	reservas legales f/pl
gesetzliches Zahlungsmittel (D)	—	legal tender	monnaie légale f	moneta legale f	medio de pago legal m

	D	E	F	I	Es
gespaltener Devisenmarkt (D)	—	two-tier foreign exchange market	marché des changes où existent deux taux de change pour une même monnaie *m*	mercato dei cambi multipli *m*	tipo de cambio múltiple *m*
gespaltener Tarif (D)	—	differentiated tariffs	tarif différencié *m*	tariffa multipla *f*	tarifa múltiple *f*
gespaltener Wechselkurs (D)	—	multiple exchange rates	cours du change multiple *m*	cambio multiplo *m*	tipo de cambio múltiple *m*
gesperrtes Depot (D)	—	blocked deposit	dépôt bloqué *m*	deposito bloccato *m*	depósito congelado *m*
gesperrte Stücke (D)	—	blocked shares	titres bloqués *m/pl*	titoli colpiti da fermo *m/pl*	títulos congelados *m/pl*
gestion (F)	Geschäftsführung *f*	management	—	gestione *f*	gerencia *f*
gestión de la cartera de valores (Es)	Portfolio-Management *n*	portfolio management	gestion du portefeuille *f*	gestione di portafoglio *f*	—
gestion du portefeuille (F)	Portfolio-Management *n*	portfolio management	—	gestione di portafoglio *f*	gestión de la cartera de valores *f*
gestione (I)	Geschäftsführung *f*	management	gestion *f*	—	gerencia *f*
gestione di portafoglio (I)	Portfolio-Management *n*	portfolio management	gestion du portefeuille *f*	—	gestión de la cartera de valores *f*
gestion industrielle et commerciale (F)	Betriebswirtschafts-lehre *f*	business economics	—	scienza dell'eco-nomia aziendale *f*	teoría de la empresa *f*
Getreidebörse (D)	—	grain exchange	bourse aux grains *f*	borsa dei cereali *f*	bolsa de cereales *f*
gettito (I)	Ausbringung *f*	output	volume de la production *m*	—	volumen de la producción *m*
Gewerbebank (D)	—	industrial bank	banque industrielle et artinsanale *f*	banca industriale *f*	banco industrial *m*
Gewerbesteuer (D)	—	trade tax	impôt sur les bénéfices des pro-fessions industrielles et commerciales *m*	tassa d'esercizio *f*	impuesto industrial *m*
Gewerkschaftsbank (D)	—	trade union bank	banque de syndicat *f*	banca del lavoro *f*	banco sindical *m*
gewillkürte Orderpapiere (D)	—	instruments to order by option	titres à ordre par destination *m/pl*	titoli all'ordine non per legge *m/pl*	valores a la orden por elección *m/pl*
Gewinn (D)	—	profit	bénéfice *m*	utile *m*	beneficio *m*
Gewinnabführung (D)	—	transfer of profits	transfert du bénéfice *m*	trasferimento degli utili *m*	transferencia de beneficios *f*
Gewinnanteil (D)	—	share in the profits	quote-part sur les bénéfices *f*	quota utile *f*	participación en los beneficios *f*
Gewinnanteils-schein (D)	—	dividend coupon	coupon de dividende *m*	cedola *f*	cupón *m*
Gewinn-ausschüttung (D)	—	distribution of profit	distribution de bénéfices *f*	ripartizione degli utili *f*	reparto de beneficios *m*
Gewinnbeteiligung (D)	—	participation in profits	participation aux bénéfices *f*	partecipazione agli utili *f*	participación en el beneficio *f*
Gewinndruck (D)	—	profit squeeze	pression de bénéfice *f*	profit push *m*	presión de beneficio *f*
Gewinnermittlung (D)	—	determination of profits	détermination du bénéfice *f*	determinazione degli utili *f*	averiguación de los beneficios *f*
Gewinn-gemeinschaft (D)	—	profit pool	pool de profit *m*	comunione degli utili *f*	comunidad de obten-ción de beneficios *f*
Gewinn-maximierung (D)	—	maximization of profits	maximisation du gain *f*	massimazione degli utili *f*	maximación de los beneficios *f*
Gewinnobligation (D)	—	participating debenture	obligation indexée *f*	obbligazione a premio *f*	bono sobre beneficios *m*
Gewinnpoolung (D)	—	profit-pooling	pool de bénéfices *m*	raggruppamento degli utili *m*	pool de beneficios *m*
Gewinnschwelle (D)	—	break-even point	seuil de rentabilité *m*	soglia dell'utile *f*	umbral de la rentabilidad *m*
Gewinnspanne (D)	—	margin of profit	marge de bénéfice *f*	margine di guadagno *m*	margen de beneficios *m*
Gewinnsparen (D)	—	lottery premium saving	épargne à lots *f*	risparmio a premi *m*	ahorro de beneficios *m*
Gewinn-thesaurierung (D)	—	earnings retention	retention de bénéfices *f*	tesaurizzazione degli utili *f*	retención de beneficios *f*
Gewinn- und Verlustrechnung (D)	—	profit and loss account	compte de pertes et profits *m*	conto profitti e perdite *m*	cuenta de pérdidas y ganancias *f*

	D	E	F	I	Es
Gewinnvortrag (D)	—	profit carried forward	report du solde excédentaire *m*	avanzo utile *m*	arrastre de beneficios *m*
gezeichnetes Kapital (D)	—	subscribed capital	capital souscrit *m*	capitale nominale *m*	capital suscrito *m*
gezogener Wechsel (D)	—	drawn bill	traite tirée *f*	cambiale tratta *f*	letra girada *f*
giacenza media di depositi a vista (I)	Bodensatz *m*	undeclared securities	titres non déclarés *m/pl*	—	títulos no declarados *m/pl*
gift savings book (E)	Geschenksparbuch *n*	—	livret d'épargne en cadeau *m*	libretto di risparmio in omaggio *m*	libreta de ahorros como regalo *f*
gilt-edged securities (E)	goldgeränderte Papiere *n/pl*	—	titres à marges dorées *m/pl*	titoli di prima classe *m/pl*	seguridades pupilares *f/pl*
giorni festivi delle banche (I)	Bankfeiertage *m/pl*	bank holidays	jours de fête bancaires *m/pl*	—	días de fiesta bancarios *m/pl*
giorni per il calcolo interessi (I)	Zinstage *m/pl*	quarter days	nombre de jours portant intérêt *m*	—	número de días devengado intereses *m*
giorno chiusura bilancio (I)	Bilanzstichtag *m*	date of the balance sheet	jour du bilan *m*	—	fecha del balance *f*
giorno di pagamento (I)	Zahltag *m*	payday	jour de paye *m*	—	día de pago *m*
giorno di scadenza (I)	Verfalltag *m*	day of expiry	jour de l'échéance *m*	—	día de vencimiento *m*
giorno di scadenza opzione (I)	Bezugstag *m*	subscription day	jour de souscription *m*	—	día de la emisión *m*
girado (Es)	Trassat *n*	drawee	tiré *m*	trattario *m*	—
girador (Es)	Trassant *m*	drawer	tireur *m*	traente *m*	—
Giralgeld (D)	—	money in account	monnaie scripturale *f*	moneta scritturale *f*	dinero bancario *m*
Giralgeldschöpfung (D)	—	creation of deposit money	création de monnaie scripturale *f*	creazione di moneta bancaria *f*	creación de depósitos bancarios *f*
Girant (D)	—	endorser	endosseur *m*	girante *m*	endosador *m*
girante (I)	Girant *m*	endorser	endosseur *m*	—	endosador *m*
girante (I)	Indossant *m*	endorser	endosseur *m*	—	endosador *m*
girata (I)	Giro *n*	credit transfer	virement *m*	—	giro *m*
girata (I)	Indossament *n*	endorsement	endossement *m*	—	endoso *m*
girata al portatore (I)	Inhaberindossament *n*	endorsement made out to bearer	endossement du porteur *m*	—	endoso al portador *m*
girata di favore (I)	Gefälligkeitsgiro *m*	accommodation endorsement	endossement de complaisance *m*	—	endoso de favor *m*
girata in bianco (I)	Blanko-Indossament *n*	blank endorsement	endossement en blanc *m*	—	endoso en blanco *m*
girata non all'ordine (I)	Rektaindossament *n*	restrictive endorsement	endossement non à ordre *m*	—	endoso intransferible *m*
girata parziale (I)	Teilindossament *n*	partial endorsement	endossement partiel *m*	—	endoso parcial *m*
girata "per incasso" (I)	Inkasso-Indossament *n*	endorsement for collection	endossement pour encaissement *m*	—	endoso al cobro *m*
girata "per procura" (I)	Prokuraindossament *n*	per procuration endorsement	endossement de procuration *m*	—	endoso por procuración *m*
girata posteriore alla scadenza (I)	Nachindossament *n*	endorsement of an overdue bill of exchange	endossement après la date de l'échéance de la lettre de change *m*	—	endoso de letra vencida *m*
giratario (I)	Indossatar *m*	endorsee	endossataire *m*	—	endosatario *m*
girata "valuta in pegno" (I)	Pfandindossament *n*	pledge endorsement	endossement pignoratif *m*	—	endoso en prenda *m*
Giro (D)	—	credit transfer	virement *m*	girata *f*	giro *m*
giro (Es)	Giro *n*	credit transfer	virement *m*	girata *f*	—
giro (Es)	Ziehung *f*	drawing	tirage *m*	estrazione *f*	—
giro (Es)	Trassierung *f*	drawing	tirage *m*	traenza *f*	—
Giroabteilung (D)	—	clearing department	service des virements *m*	reparto giro *m*	sección de giros *f*
giro association (E)	Giroverband *m*	—	association des banques de virement *f*	associazione di banche di giro *f*	asociación de bancos de giro *f*

	D	E	F	I	Es
giro bancario (Es)	Banküberweisung f	bank transfer	virement bancaire m	trasferimento bancario m	—
Girobank (D)	—	deposit clearing bank	banque de dépôts et de virements f	banca di giro f	banco de giros m
giro central de valores (Es)	Girosammelverkehr m	collective securities deposit operations	opérations de virements collectives f/pl	trasferimenti collettivi di giro m/pl	—
giroconto (I)	Girokonto n	current account	compte de virement m	—	cuenta corriente f
giro de valores (Es)	Giroverkehr m	transfer of money by means of a clearing system	opérations de virement f/pl	bancogiro m	—
giro di partite (I)	Umbuchung f	transfer of an entry	jeu d'écritures m	—	asiento en otra cuenta m
Giroeinlage (D)	—	deposits on a current account	dépôt de virement m	deposito in giroconto m	depósito en cuenta de giros m
Girogeschäft (D)	—	bank's transaction dealing with cashless transactions	opération de virement f	trasferimento di giro m	operación de giro f
Girokonto (D)	—	current account	compte de virement m	giroconto m	cuenta corriente f
giro monetario (Es)	Geldumsatz m	turnover of money	roulement de l'argent m	circolazione monetaria f	—
Gironetz (D)	—	clearing system	réseau des banques de virement m	rete di giro f	red de bancos de giros f
giro por cuenta (Es)	Kommissionstratte f	bill of exchange drawn for third-party account	traite pour compte d'autrui f	tratta per conto terzi f	—
giro postal (Es)	Postanweisung f	postal money order	mandat-poste m	vaglia postale m	—
Girosammeldepot- stück (D)	—	security held on giro-transferable deposit	titre en dépôt collectif m	titolo in deposito collettivo m	título en un depósito central de valores m
Girosammelstück (D)	—	security held on giro-transferable deposit	titre en dépôt collectif m	titolo in deposito collettivo m	título en depósito colectivo m
Girosammel- verkehr (D)	—	collective securities deposit operations	opérations de virements collectives f/pl	trasferimenti collettivi di giro m/pl	giro central de valores m
giro transmitido por el sistema de transferencia de télex directo (Es)	Blitzgiro m	direct telex transfer system	virement transmis par le système de virements de télex direct m	bonifico telegrafico m	—
giro urgente (Es)	Eilüberweisung f	rapid money transfer	virement accéléré m	vaglia espresso m	—
Giroverband (D)	—	giro association	association des banques de virement f	associazione di banche di giro f	asociación de bancos de giro f
Giroverkehr (D)	—	transfer of money by means of a clearing system	opérations de virement f/pl	bancogiro m	giro de valores m
Girozentrale (D)	—	central giro institution	banque centrale de virement f	centrale di bancogiro f	central de giros m
giuramento dichiarativo (I)	Offenbarungseid m	oath of disclosure	serment déclaratoire m	—	juramento declarativo m
giuria (I)	Prüfungskommission f	examining commission	commission de contrôle f	—	comisión de revisión de cuentas f
Glattstellen (D)	—	settlement	réalisation f	operazione di compensazione mediante trattazione titoli f	liquidación f
Gläubiger (D)	—	creditor	créancier m	creditore m	acreedor m
Gläubigerausschuß (D)	—	committee of inspection	commission des contrôleurs f	comitato dei creditori m	comisión de los acreedores f
Gläubigerpapier (D)	—	creditor paper	titre créditeur m	titolo di credito m	título acreedor m
Gläubigerschutz (D)	—	protection of creditors	garantie des créanciers f	protezione dei creditori f	protección de acreedores f
Gläubiger- versammlung (D)	—	creditors' meeting	assemblée des créanciers f	assemblea dei creditori f	junta de acreedores f
Gleichgewicht (D)	—	balance	équilibre m	equilibrio m	equilibrio m
Gleichgewichts- preis (D)	—	equilibrium price	prix équilibré m	prezzo di equilibrio m	precio de equilibrio m

	D	E	F	I	Es
Gleichgewichtszins (D)	—	equilibrium interest rate	intérêt équilibré *m*	interesse d'equilibrio *m*	interés de equilibrio *m*
gleitende Paritätsanpassung (D)	—	crawling exchange rate adjustment	ajustement continu de parités *m*	adattamento delle parità flessibile *m*	ajuste continuado de paridades *m*
Gleitklausel (D)	—	escalation clause	clause de prix mobile *f*	clausola della scala mobile *f*	cláusula de escala móvil *f*
Gleitparität (D)	—	escalation parity	parité mobile *f*	parità variabile *f*	paridad móvil *f*
global (E)	pauschal	—	forfaitaire	a forfait	global
global (Es)	pauschal	global	forfaitaire	a forfait	—
Global-Anleihe (D)	—	all-share certificate	titre représentant globalement un paquet d'emprunts *m*	credito globale *m*	empréstito global *m*
global control (E)	Globalsteuerung *f*	—	contrôle global *m*	controllo della domanda globale *m*	control global *m*
global delcredere (E)	Pauschaldelkredere *n*	—	ducroire forfaitaire *m*	star del credere forfettario	del credere global *m*
global share (E)	Sammelaktie *f*	—	titre représentant globalement un paquet d'actions *m*	azione globale *f*	acción global *f*
Globalsteuerung (D)	—	global control	contrôle global *m*	controllo della domanda globale *m*	control global *m*
global value adjustment (E)	Sammelwertberichtigung *f*	—	rajustement global *m*	rivalutazione forfettaria *f*	revaluación colectiva *f*
Globalwertberichtigung (D)	—	overall adjustment	rectification des valeurs globale *f*	rivalutazione globale *f*	rectificación de valor global *f*
Globalzession (D)	—	overall assignment	cession globale *f*	cessione globale *f*	cesión en bloque *f*
going concern value (E)	Firmenwert *m*	—	valeur commerciale *f*	avviamento *m*	valor comercial *m*
Gold (D)	—	gold	or *m*	oro *m*	oro *m*
gold (E)	Gold *n*	—	or *m*	oro *m*	oro *m*
Goldaktie (D)	—	gold share	action-or *f*	azione di miniere d'oro *f*	acción de oro *f*
Goldanleihe (D)	—	loan on a gold basis	emprunt or *m*	prestito oro *m*	empréstito con garantía-oro *m*
Goldarbitrage (D)	—	arbitrage in bullion	arbitrage d'or *m*	arbitraggio sull'oro *m*	arbitraje de oro *m*
gold auction (E)	Goldauktion *f*	—	vente à l'enchère d'or *f*	asta dell'oro *f*	subasta de oro *f*
Goldauktion (D)	—	gold auction	vente à l'enchère d'or *f*	asta dell'oro *f*	subasta de oro *f*
gold bar (E)	Goldbarren *m*	—	lingot d'or *m*	lingotto d'oro *m*	lingote de oro *m*
Goldbarren (D)	—	gold bar	lingot d'or *m*	lingotto d'oro *m*	lingote de oro *m*
gold certificate (E)	Goldzertifikat *n*	—	certificat d'or *m*	certificato oro *m*	certificado oro *m*
gold characteristics (E)	Goldeigenschaften *f*	—	caractères de l'or *m/pl*	caratteristiche dell'oro *f/pl*	características del oro *m/pl*
gold coin (E)	Goldmünze *f*	—	pièce d'or *f*	moneta aurea *f*	moneda de oro *f*
gold content (E)	Goldgehalt *m*	—	teneur en or *f*	contenuto aureo *m*	contenido de oro *m*
gold convertibility (E)	Goldkonvertibilität *f*	—	convertibilité d'or *f*	convertibilità in oro *f*	convertibilidad de oro *f*
gold cover (E)	Golddeckung *f*	—	couverture or *f*	copertura oro *f*	cobertura-oro *f*
gold currency (E)	Goldwährung *f*	—	étalon-or *m*	valuta aurea *f*	moneda oro *f*
Golddeckung (D)	—	gold cover	couverture or *f*	copertura oro *f*	cobertura-oro *f*
Gold-Devisen-Standard (D)	—	gold exchange standard	étalon or et devises *m*	gold exchange standard *m*	patrón de divisas en oro *m*
Goldeigenschaften (D)	—	gold characteristics	caractères de l'or *m/pl*	caratteristiche dell'oro *f/pl*	características del oro *m/pl*
gold exchange standard (E)	Gold-Devisen-Standard *m*	—	étalon or et devises *m*	gold exchange standard *m*	patrón de divisas en oro *m*
gold exchange standard (I)	Gold-Devisen-Standard *m*	gold exchange standard	étalon or et devises *m*	—	patrón de divisas en oro *m*
Goldfeingehalt (D)	—	fine gold content	poids d'or fin *m*	titolo aureo *m*	peso fino del oro *m*
Goldgehalt (D)	—	gold content	teneur en or *f*	contenuto aureo *m*	contenido de oro *m*
goldgeränderte Papiere (D)	—	gilt-edged securities	titres à marges dorées *m/pl*	titoli di prima classe *m/pl*	seguridades pupilares *f/pl*

	D	E	F	I	Es
Goldgeschäft (D)	—	gold transactions	transaction d'or *f*	operazione in oro *f*	transacción de oro *f*
Goldgewichte (D)	—	troy weights	poids de l'or *m/pl*	unità di misura per l'oro *f/pl*	pesos de oro *m/pl*
Goldhandel (D)	—	gold trade	commerce de l'or *m*	commercio dell'oro *m*	comercio de oro *m*
gold in bars (E)	Barrengold *n*	—	or en lingot *m*	oro in barre *m*	oro en lingotes *m*
Goldkonvertibilität (D)	—	gold convertibility	convertibilité d'or *f*	convertibilità in oro *f*	convertibilidad de oro *f*
gold market (E)	Goldmarkt *m*	—	marché de l'or *m*	mercato dell'oro *m*	mercado de oro *m*
Goldmarkt (D)	—	gold market	marché de l'or *m*	mercato dell'oro *m*	mercado de oro *m*
Goldmünze (D)	—	gold coin	pièce d'or *f*	moneta aurea *f*	moneda de oro *f*
Goldoption (D)	—	gold option	option d'or *f*	opzione oro *f*	opción de oro *f*
gold option (E)	Goldoption *f*	—	option d'or *f*	opzione oro *f*	opción de oro *f*
Goldparität (D)	—	gold parity	parité de l'or *f*	parità aurea *f*	paridad-oro *f*
gold parity (E)	Goldparität *f*	—	parité de l'or *f*	parità aurea *f*	paridad-oro *f*
gold point (E)	Goldpunkt *m*	—	point d'or *m*	punto dell'oro *m*	punto de oro *m*
Goldpool (D)	—	gold pool	pool d'or *m*	pool dell'oro *m*	pool de oro *m*
gold pool (E)	Goldpool *m*	—	pool d'or *m*	pool dell'oro *m*	pool de oro *m*
Goldpreis (D)	—	price of gold	prix de l'or *m*	prezzo dell'oro *m*	precio del oro *m*
Goldpreisbildung (D)	—	gold pricing	formation du prix de l'or *f*	formazione del prezzo dell'oro *f*	formación del precio de oro *f*
gold pricing (E)	Goldpreisbildung *f*	—	formation du prix de l'or *f*	formazione del prezzo dell'oro *f*	formación del precio de oro *f*
gold production (E)	Goldproduktion *f*	—	production d'or *f*	produzione dell'oro *f*	producción de oro *f*
Goldproduktion (D)	—	gold production	production d'or *f*	produzione dell'oro *f*	producción de oro *f*
Goldpunkt (D)	—	gold point	point d'or *m*	punto dell'oro *m*	punto de oro *m*
gold reserve (E)	Goldreserven *f/pl*	—	réserves d'or *f/pl*	riserve in oro *f/pl*	reservas de oro *f/pl*
Goldreserven (D)	—	gold reserve	réserves d'or *f/pl*	riserve in oro *f/pl*	reservas de oro *f/pl*
gold share (E)	Goldaktie *f*	—	action-or *f*	azione di miniere d'oro *f*	acción de oro *f*
gold specie standard (E)	Goldumlaufswährung *f*	—	monnaie or *f*	divisa circolante aurea *f*	moneda de oro en circulación *f*
Gold-Standard (D)	—	gold standard	étalon or *m*	gold standard *m*	patrón-oro *m*
gold standard (E)	Gold-Standard *m*	—	étalon or *m*	gold standard *m*	patrón-oro *m*
gold standard (I)	Gold-Standard *m*	gold standard	étalon or *m*	—	patrón-oro *m*
Goldswap (D)	—	gold swap	swap d'or *m*	goldswap *m*	swap de oro *m*
goldswap (I)	Goldswap *m*	gold swap	swap d'or *m*	—	swap de oro *m*
gold swap (E)	Goldswap *m*	—	swap d'or *m*	goldswap *m*	swap de oro *m*
gold trade (E)	Goldhandel *m*	—	commerce de l'or *m*	commercio dell'oro *m*	comercio de oro *m*
gold transactions (E)	Goldgeschäft *n*	—	transaction d'or *f*	operazione in oro *f*	transacción de oro *f*
Goldumlaufs-währung (D)	—	gold specie standard	monnaie or *f*	divisa circolante aurea *f*	moneda de oro en circulación *f*
Goldwährung (D)	—	gold currency	étalon-or *m*	valuta aurea *f*	moneda oro *f*
Goldzertifikat (D)	—	gold certificate	certificat d'or *m*	certificato oro *m*	certificado oro *m*
good faith (E)	guter Glauben *m*	—	bonne foi *f*	buona fede *f*	buena fe *f*
goods (E)	Ware *f*	—	marchandise *f*	merce *f*	mercancía *f*
government expendi-ture rate (E)	Staatsquote *f*	—	pourcentage des dé-penses publiques *m*	percentuale della spesa pubblica *f*	porcentaje de los gastos públicos *m*
government-inscribed debt (E)	Wertrechtanleihe *f*	—	emprunt de l'Etat inscrit dans le livre de la dette *m*	obbligazione contabile *f*	empréstito del Estado inscrito en el libro de la deuda *m*
grado de automación (Es)	Automatisationsgrad *m*	automation degree	degré d'automation *m*	grado di automazione *m*	—
grado di automazione (I)	Automatisationsgrad *m*	automation degree	degré d'automation *m*	—	grado de automación *m*
graduated-interest loan (E)	Staffelanleihe *f*	—	emprunt à taux progressif *m*	prestito a interesse scalare *m*	empréstito escalonado *m*
grain exchange (E)	Getreidebörse *f*	—	bourse aux grains *f*	borsa dei cereali *f*	bolsa de cereales *f*

	D	E	F.	I	Es
gran banco (Es)	Großbank f	big bank	grande banque f	banca importante f	—
grande banque (F)	Großbank f	big bank	—	banca importante f	gran banco m
grandezze autonome (I)	autonome Größen f/pl	autonomous variables	magnitudes autonomes f/pl	—	magnitudes autónomas f/pl
grand-livre de la dette publique (F)	Bundesschuldbuch n	Federal Debt Register	—	libro del debito pubblico m	Registro de Deudas Federales m
gratificación (Es)	Gratifikation f	bonus	gratification f	gratificazione f	—
gratification (F)	Gratifikation f	bonus	—	gratificazione f	gratificación f
gratificazione (I)	Gratifikation f	bonus	gratification f	—	gratificación f
Gratifikation (D)	—	bonus	gratification f	gratificazione f	gratificación f
gratis (D)	—	free of charge	gratuit	gratis	gratuito
gratis (I)	gratis	free of charge	gratuit	—	gratuito
Gratisaktie (D)	—	bonus share	action gratuite f	azione gratuita f	acción gratuita f
gratuit (F)	gratis	free of charge	—	gratis	gratuito
gratuito (Es)	gratis	free of charge	gratuit	gratis	—
green dollar (E)	grüner Dollar m	—	dollar vert m	dollaro verde m	dólar verde m
Grenzerlös (D)	—	marginal earnings	produit marginal m	ricavo marginale m	beneficio marginal m
Grenzleistungsfähigkeit des Kapitals (D)	—	marginal efficiency of capital	efficience marginale du capital f	efficienza marginale del capitale f	eficiencia marginal del capital f
Grenznutzen (D)	—	marginal utility	utilité marginale f	rendita marginale f	utilidad marginal f
Grenzproduktivität (D)	—	marginal productivity	productivité marginale f	produttività marginale f	productividad marginal f
Gresham'sches Gesetz (D)	—	Gresham Theory	loi de Gresham f	legge di Gresham f	Ley Gresham f
Gresham Theory (E)	Gresham'sches Gesetz n	—	loi de Gresham f	legge di Gresham f	Ley Gresham f
griglia delle parità (I)	Paritätengitter n	parity grid	table de parité f	—	parrilla de paridades f
gross (E)	Brutto	—	brut	lordo	bruto
Großbank (D)	—	big bank	grande banque f	banca importante f	gran banco m
gross dividend (E)	Brutto-Dividende f	—	dividende brut m	dividendo lordo m	dividendo bruto m
gross domestic product (E)	Bruttoinlandsprodukt n	—	produit intérieur brut m	prodotto interno lordo m	producto interior bruto m
gross earnings (E)	Bruttoverdienst m	—	salaire brut m	guadagno lordo m	remuneración bruta f
gross income (E)	Bruttoeinkommen n	—	revenu brut m	reddito lordo m	renta bruta f
Großkredit (D)	—	large-scale lending	crédit important m	grosso credito m	crédito importante m
gross monetary reserve (E)	Bruttowährungsreserve f	—	réserves monétaires brutes f/pl	riserva monetaria lorda f	reserva monetaria bruta f
gross national product (E)	Bruttosozialprodukt n	—	produit national brut m	prodotto nazionale lordo m	producto nacional bruto m
grosso credito (I)	Großkredit m	large-scale lending	crédit important m	—	crédito importante m
gross profit (E)	Bruttogewinn m	—	bénéfice brut m	utile lordo m	beneficio bruto m
gross return (E)	Bruttoertrag m	—	gain brut m	ricavo lordo m	producto bruto m
gross wage (E)	Bruttolohn m	—	salaire brut m	retribuzione lorda f	salario bruto m
group balance sheet (E)	Konzernbilanz f	—	bilan consolidé d'un groupement de sociétés m	bilancio consolidato m	balance del consorcio m
group collection security (E)	Sammelinkassoversicherung f	—	assurance d'encaissement groupé f	assicurazione collettiva f	seguro de cobro colectivo m
groupe des 77 (F)	Gruppe der 77 f	group of Seventy-Seven	—	gruppo dei 77 m	grupo de los 77 m
group interim benefits (E)	Konzernzwischengewinn m	—	bénéfice intermédiaire des groupements de sociétés m	margine d'utile di gruppo m	beneficio intermedio consolidado m
group of Seventy-Seven (E)	Gruppe der 77 f	—	groupe des 77 m	gruppo dei 77 m	grupo de los 77 m
group orders (E)	Konzernaufträge m/pl	—	commandes placées par un groupement de sociétés f	ordini di gruppo m/pl	órdenes de grupos f/pl

	D	E	F	I	Es
growth fund (E)	Wachstumsfonds *m*	—	fonds d'expansion *m*	fondo di accumulazione *m*	fondo de crecimiento *m*
growth share (E) ·	Wuchsaktie *f*	—	action avec possibilité d'accroissement *f*	azione con possibilità di sviluppo *f*	acción con posibilidad de incremento *f*
growth target (E)	Wachstumsziel *n*	—	objectif de croissance *m*	obiettivo di crescita *m*	objetivo de crecimiento *m*
Grundbuch (D)	—	register of land titles	livre foncier *m*	catasto *m*	registro de la propiedad *m*
Grundkreditanstalt (D)	—	mortage bank	établissement de crédit foncier *m*	istituto di credito fondiario *m*	banco hipotecario *m*
Grundsätze über das Eigenkapital und die Liquidität der Kreditinstitute (D)	—	principles of capital resources and the banks' liquid assets	principes de capital propre et de la liquidité des établissement de crédit *m/pl*	norme sul capitale proprio e la liquidità degli istituti di credito *f/pl*	principios de capital propio y de la liquidez de los institutos bancarios *m/pl*
Grundschuld (D)	—	land charge	dette foncière *f*	debito fondiario *m*	hipoteca *f*
Grundschuldbrief (D)	—	land charge certificate	cédule foncière *f*	certificato di debito fondiario *m*	cédula de deuda inmobiliaria *f*
grupo de los 77 (Es)	Gruppe der 77 *f*	group of Seventy-Seven	groupe des 77 *m*	gruppo dei 77 *m*	—
Gruppe der 77 (D)	—	group of Seventy-Seven	groupe des 77 *m*	gruppo dei 77 *m*	grupo de los 77 *m*
gruppo dei 77 (I)	Gruppe der 77 *f*	group of Seventy-Seven	groupe des 77 *m*	—	grupo de los 77 *m*
guadagno lordo (I)	Bruttoverdienst *m*	gross earnings	salaire brut *m*	—	remuneración bruta *f*
guarantee (E)	Bürgschaft *f*	—	caution *f*	fideiussione *f*	fianza *f*
guarantee (E)	Haftsumme *f*	—	garantie *f*	garanzia *f*	garantía *f*
guarantee business (E)	Garantiegeschäft *n*	—	opération de garantie *f*	assunzione di garanzia per terzi *f*	operación de garantía *f*
guaranteed interest (E)	Zinsgarantie *f*	—	garantie de l'intérêt *f*	garanzia d'interesse *f*	garantía de intereses *f*
guarantee limit (E)	Bürgschaftsplafond *n*	—	plafond de garantie *m*	plafond di fideiussione *m*	límite de garantía *m*
guarantee of a bill (E)	Aval *m*	—	aval *m*	avallo *m*	aval *m*
guarantee of delivery (E)	Liefergarantie *f*	—	garantie de livraison *f*	garanzia di sostegno *f*	garantía de entrega *f*
guarantee of deposit (E)	Einlagensicherung *f*	—	sûreté en garantie de dépôts *f*	garanzia dei depositi *f*	garantía de depositos *f*
guarantee of foreign exchange transfer (E)	Transfergarantie *f*	—	garantie des transferts *f*	garanzia di trasferimento *f*	garantía de transferencia *f*
guarantee securities (E)	Kautionseffekten *pl*	—	papiers de sûreté *m/pl*	titoli di deposito cauzionale *m/pl*	valores de fianza *m/pl*
guarantor (E)	Bürge *m*	—	garant *m*	fidefaciente *m*	fiador *m*
guichet extérieur de permanence (F)	Spätschalter *m*	night safe deposit	—	cassa continua *f*	taquilla de noche *f*
Gut (D)	—	property	bien *m*	bene *m*	bienes *m*
Gutachten (D)	—	expert opinion	expertise *f*	perizia *f*	peritaje *m*
guter Glauben (D)	—	good faith	bonne foi *f*	buona fede *f*	buena fe *f*
Gütermarkt (D)	—	commodity market	marché des biens *m*	mercato delle merci *m*	mercado de bienes *m*
Guthaben (D)	—	credit balance	avoir *m*	avere *m*	activo *m*
Haben (D)	—	credit side	avoir *m*	avere *m*	haber *m*
Habenzinsen (D)	—	credit interest	intérêts créditeurs *m/pl*	interessi attivi *m/pl*	intereses acreedores *m/pl*
haber (Es)	Haben *n*	credit side	avoir *m*	avere *m*	—
haber a nuestro favor (Es)	Nostroguthaben *n*	nostro balance	avoir dans une autre banque *m*	avere nostro *m*	—
haber bancario (Es)	Bankguthaben *n*	bank balance	avoir en banque *m*	deposito bancario *m*	—
haberes de clientes bancarios (Es)	Loroguthaben *n*	loro balance	avoirs de clients bancaires *m*	avere loro *m*	—
haberes de moneda extranjera (Es)	Fremdwährungsguthaben *n*	foreign currency balance	avoir en monnaie étrangère *m*	disponibilità in valuta estera *f*	—
habilité en matière de chèque (F)	Scheckfähigkeit *f*	capacity to draw cheques	—	capacità di obbligarsi per assegno *f*	capacidad de girar cheques *f*

	D	E	F	I	Es
habitude de payement (F)	Zahlungssitte f	payment habit	—	usanza di pagamento f	costumbre de pago f
hacienda (Es)	Finanzamt n	inland revenue office	service de contributions m	ufficio delle finanze m	—
haftendes Eigenkapital (D)	—	liable funds	capital propre de garantie m	patrimonio netto m	capital propio respondiente m
Haftsumme (D)	—	guarantee	garantie f	garanzia f	garantía f
Haftung (D)	—	responsibility	responsabilité f	responsabilità f	responsabilidad f
Halbjahresbilanz (D)	—	semi-annual balance sheet	bilan semestriel m	bilancio semestrale m	balance semestral m
Handel (D)	—	trade	commerce m	commercio m	comercio m
Handelsbevollmächtigter (D)	—	general agent	personne ayant le pouvoir commercial f	rappresentante commerciale m	agente comercial m
Handelsbilanz (D)	—	commercial balance sheet	balance des opérations en marchandises f	bilancia commerciale f	balanza comercial f
Handelsbrauch (D)	—	trade practice	usage commercial m	usanza commerciale f	uso comercial m
Handelsbrief (D)	—	business letter	lettre commerciale f	lettera commerciale f	carta comercial f
Handelsbuch (D)	—	commercial book	livre de commerce m	libro di commercio m	libro comercial m
Handelsgeschäfte (D)	—	commercial transactions	affaires commerciales f/pl	affari commerciali m/pl	negocio m
Handelskredite (D)	—	commercial credits	crédits commerciaux m/pl	crediti al commercio m/pl	crédito comercial m
Handelsmakler (D)	—	commercial broker	agent commercial m	mediatore di commercio m	corredor de comercio m
Handelspapiere (D)	—	commercial papers	effets de commerce m/pl	effetti commerciali m/pl	documentos comerciales m/pl
Handelsrecht (D)	—	commercial law	droit commercial m	diritto commerciale m	derecho comercial m
Handelsregister (D)	—	commercial register	registre de commerce m	registro commerciale m	registro comercial m
Handelsusancen (D)	—	custom of trade	usages commerciaux m/pl	usanze commerciali f/pl	uso comercial m
Handelsvertreter (D)	—	commercial agent	représentant de commerce m	agente di commercio m	representante comercial m
Händler (D)	—	dealer	commerçant m	commerciante m	comerciante m
Händlergeschäft (D)	—	dealer transaction	opération pour propre compte f	operazioni tra agenti di borsa f/pl	operaziones de corridor bursátil f/pl
Handlungsgehilfe (D)	—	commercial employee	commis du commerce m	commesso m	auxiliar mercantil m
Handlungsvollmacht (D)	—	commercial power of attorney	pouvoir commercial m	mandato commerciale m	poder mercantil m
Hansa (F)	Hanse f	Hanseatic League	—	Ansa f	Hansa f
Hansa (Es)	Hanse f	Hanseatic League	Hansa f	Ansa f	—
Hanse (D)	—	Hanseatic League	Hansa f	Ansa f	Hansa f
Hanseatic League (E)	Hanse f	—	Hansa f	Ansa f	Hansa f
hard currency (E)	harte Währung f	—	monnaie forte f	valuta forte f	moneda dura f
harmonisación (Es)	Harmonisierung f	harmonization	harmonisation f	armonizzazione f	—
harmonisation (F)	Harmonisierung f	harmonization	—	armonizzazione f	harmonisación f
Harmonisierung (D)	—	harmonization	harmonisation f	armonizzazione f	harmonisación f
harmonization (E)	Harmonisierung f	—	harmonisation f	armonizzazione f	harmonisación f
harte Währung (D)	—	hard currency	monnaie forte f	valuta forte f	moneda dura f
Hartgeld (D)	—	metallic currency	monnaie métallique f	moneta metallica f	dinero metálico m
Hauptbuchhaltung (D)	—	chief accountancy	comptabilité générale f	ufficio di contabilità generale m	contabilidad principal f
Hauptplätze (D)	—	main centers	places principales f/pl	sedi principali f/pl	plazas principales f/pl
Hauptvollmacht (D)	—	primary power	pouvoir principal m	procura principale f	poder principal m
Hausbank (D)	—	firm's bank	banque habituelle f	banca preferita f	banco con que trata generalmente el cliente m
Haushalt (D)	—	budget	budget m	bilancio m	presupuesto m

	D	E	F	I	Es
Haushaltskredit (D)	—	budget credit	crédit budgétaire m	credito di finanziamento bilancio m	crédito presupuestario m
Haushaltsplan (D)	—	budget	budget m	bilancio preventivo m	presupuesto m
Hausse (D)	—	bull market	hausse f	contegno rialzistico m	alza f
hausse (F)	Hausse f	bull market	—	contegno rialzistico m	alza f
hausse des prix (F)	Preissteigerung f	price increase	—	aumento dei prezzi m	subida de precios f
hausse sensible des cours (F)	Kurssprung m	jump in prices	—	balzo delle quotazioni m	alza considerable de las cotizaciones f
Haussier (D)	—	bull	haussier m	rialzista m	alcista m
haussier (F)	Bullish n	bullish	—	bullish m	alcista
haussier (F)	Haussier m	bull	—	rialzista m	alcista m
haute conjoncture (F)	Hochkonjunktur f	boom	—	alta congiuntura f	alta coyuntura f
head office (E)	Zentrale f	—	centrale f	centrale f	central f
heavy-priced securities (E)	schwere Papiere n/pl	—	titres chers m/pl	titoli pesanti m/pl	valores de alta cotización m/pl
Hedgegeschäft (D)	—	hedge operation	opération hedge f	operazione hedge f	negocio hedge m
hedge operation (E)	Hedgegeschäft n	—	opération hedge f	operazione hedge f	negocio hedge m
hedging financier (F)	Finanzhedging n	financial hedging	—	hedging finanziario m	hedging financiero m
hedging financiero (Es)	Finanzhedging n	financial hedging	hedging financier m	hedging finanziario m	—
hedging finanziario (I)	Finanzhedging n	financial hedging	hedging financier m	—	hedging financiero m
heißes Geld (D)	—	hot money	capitaux fébriles m/pl	hot money m	dinero caliente m
Herabsetzung des Grundkapitals (D)	—	reduction of the share capital	réduction de capital social f	riduzione del capitale sociale f	reducción del capital social f
Herausgabeanspruch (D)	—	claim for return	prétention à restitution f	diritto alla restituzione m	pretensión de entrega f
herauskommendes Material (D)	—	securities coming on to the market	titres lancés sur le marché m/pl	offerta di titoli f	material saliente m
hereditary building right (E)	Erbbaurecht n	—	droit de superficie héréditaire m	diritto d'enfiteusi m	derecho de superficie m
hereingenommene Gelder (D)	—	money taken on deposit	fonds mis en dépôt m/pl	denaro altrui m	fondos ingresados m/pl
heures de présentation du protêt (F)	Protestzeit f	period of protest	—	termine presentazione di protesto m	período de protesta m
heures d'ouverture de la bourse (F)	Börsenzeit f	official trading hours	—	orario di borsa m	sesión de bolsa f
heute gültig (D)	—	valid today	valable aujourd'hui	valido un giorno	válido hoy
hidden inflation (E)	versteckte Inflation f	—	inflation larvée f	inflazione mascherata f	inflación encubierta f
hidden profit distribution (E)	verdeckte Gewinnausschüttung f	—	distribution occulte de bénéfices f	partecipazione agli utili velata f	distribución oculta f
hidden reserves (E)	stille Reserve f	—	réserves cachées f/pl	riserva occulta f	reservas tácitas f/pl
hidden unemployment (E)	versteckte Arbeitslosigkeit f	—	chômage caché m	disoccupazione camuffata f	desempleo disfrazado m
Hifo-procedure (E)	Hifo-Verfahren n	—	méthode Hifo f	procedimento Hifo m	procedimiento hifo m
Hifo-Verfahren (D)	—	Hifo-procedure	méthode Hifo f	procedimento Hifo m	procedimiento hifo m
high interest rate policy (E)	Hochzinspolitik f	—	politique de taux d'intérêt élevés f	politica degli interessi alti f	política de tipos de interés elevados f
highly speculative securities (E)	Exoten m/pl	—	valeurs extrêmement spéculatives f/pl	titoli provenienti da paesi esotici m/pl	valores especulativos m/pl
hiperinflación (Es)	Hyperinflation f	hyperinflation	hyperinflation f	iperinflazione f	—
hipoteca (Es)	Grundschuld f	land charge	dette foncière f	debito fondiario m	—
hipoteca (Es)	Hypothek f	mortgage	hypothèque f	ipoteca f	—
hipoteca ajena (Es)	Fremdhypothek f	third-party mortgage	hypothèque constituée au profit d'un tiers f	ipoteca a favore di terzi f	—
hipoteca amortizable (Es)	Tilgungshypothek f	amortizable mortgage loan	hypothèque garantissant une créance remboursable à termes périodiques f	ipoteca ammortizzabile f	—
hipoteca a plazos (Es)	Abzahlungshypothek f	instalment mortgage	hypothèque réductible f	ipoteca di pagamento a rate f	—

	D	E	F	I	Es
hipoteca con preaviso (Es)	Kündigungshypothek f	mortgage loan repayable after having been duly called	hypothèque garantissant une dette remboursable avec préavis f	ipoteca rimborsabile dopo preavviso f	—
hipoteca de amortización (Es)	Amortisationshypothek f	instalment mortgage	hypothèque amortissable f	ipoteca ammortizzabile f	—
hipoteca de interés fijo (Es)	Festzinshypothek f	fixed-rate mortgage	hypothèque à intérêt fixe f	ipoteca ad interesse fisso f	—
hipoteca de propietario (Es)	Eigentümer-Hypothek f	mortgage for the benefit of the owner	hypothèque revenant au propriétaire du fonds grevé f	ipoteca a favore del proprietario f	—
hipoteca de registro (Es)	Buchhypothek f	uncertificated mortgage	hypothèque inscrite au livre foncier f	ipoteca iscritta f	—
hipoteca de seguridad (Es)	Sicherungshypothek f	cautionary mortgage	hypothèque constituée dans le but de garantir une créance f	ipoteca di garanzia f	—
hipoteca de vencimiento (Es)	Fälligkeitshypothek f	fixed-date land mortgage	hypothèque constituée sur la base d'un remboursement du capital à terme fixe sans dénonciation préalable f	ipoteca a scadenza determinata f	—
hipoteca naval (Es)	Schiffshypothek f	ship mortgage	hypothèque maritime f	ipoteca navale f	—
hipoteca negativa (Es)	Negativhypothek f	borrower's undertaking to create no new charge ranking ahead of lender	hypothèque négative f	ipoteca negativa f	—
hipoteca para la construcción de nuevas viviendas (Es)	Neubauhypothek f	mortgage loan to finance building of new dwelling-house	hypothèque pour financer la construction de logements neufs f	ipoteca su una nuova costruzione f	—
hipoteca solidaria (Es)	Gesamthypothek f	general mortgage	hypothèque solidaire f	ipoteca generale f	—
historical securities (E)	historische Wertpapiere n/pl	—	titres historiques m/pl	titoli a prezzo d'affezione m/pl	títulos históricos m/pl
historische Wertpapiere (D)	—	historical securities	titres historiques m/pl	titoli a prezzo d'affezione m/pl	títulos históricos m/pl
hoarded notes and coins (E)	Strumpfgeld n	—	argent gardé dans le bas de laine m	denaro tesaurizzato m	dinero en el calcetín m
Hochkonjunktur (D)	—	boom	haute conjoncture f	alta congiuntura f	alta coyuntura f
Höchstpreis (D)	—	maximum price	prix plafond m	prezzo massimo m	precio máximo m
Höchststimmrecht (D)	—	maximum voting right	droit de vote maximum m	valore massimo di voto m	límite máximo de votos m
Hochzinspolitik (D)	—	high interest rate policy	politique de taux d'intérêt élevés f	politica degli interessi alti f	política de tipos de interés elevados f
Hoffnungswert (D)	—	speculative security	titre spéculatif m	valore promettente reddito futuro m	título especulativo m
Hofkredit (D)	—	farm credit	crédit agricole m	credito agricolo m	crédito agropecuario m
hoja de cupones (Es)	Kuponbogen m	coupon sheet	feuille de coupons f	cedolario m	—
hojas de investigación crediticia (Es)	Kreditprüfungsblätter n/pl	credit checking sheets	feuilles d'enquête sur la solvabilité f/pl	fogli di controllo crediti m/pl	—
holding (F)	Holding Gesellschaft f	holding company	—	società finanziaria f	sociedad holding f
holding (F)	Dachgesellschaft f	holding company	—	società madre f	sociedad cúpula f
holding company (E)	Holding Gesellschaft f	—	holding m	società finanziaria f	sociedad holding f
holding company (E)	Dachgesellschaft f	—	holding m	società madre f	sociedad cúpula f
holding fund (E)	Dachfonds m	—	fonds d'une société holding m/pl	fondo che tratta quote di altri fondi m	fondos de una sociedad holding m/pl
Holding Gesellschaft (D)	—	holding company	holding m	società finanziaria f	sociedad holding f
holding of the majority (E)	Majorisierung f	—	obtention de la majorité f	messa in minoranza f	obtención de la mayoría f
honorar (Es)	honorieren	to remunerate	honorer	onorare	—
honorer (F)	honorieren	to remunerate	—	onorare	honorar
honorieren (D)	—	to remunerate	honorer	onorare	honorar
horizontal diversification (E)	horizontale Diversifikation f	—	diversification horizontale f	diversificazione orizzontale f	diversificación horizontal f

	D	E	F	I	Es
horizontale Diversifikation (D)	—	horizontal diversification	diversification horizontale *f*	diversificazione orizzontale *f*	diversificación horizontal *f*
horizontale Finanzierungsregeln (D)	—	horizontal financing rules	règles de financement horizontales *f/pl*	norme orizzontali di finanziamento *f/pl*	normas de financiación horizontal *f/pl*
horizontal financing rules (E)	horizontale Finanzierungsregeln *f/pl*	—	règles de financement horizontales *f/pl*	norme orizzontali di finanziamento *f/pl*	normas de financiación horizontal *f/pl*
hot money (E)	heißes Geld *n*	—	capitaux fébriles *m/pl*	hot money *m*	dinero caliente *m*
hot money (I)	heißes Geld *n*	hot money	capitaux fébriles *m/pl*	—	dinero caliente *m*
house cheque (E)	Filialscheck *m*	—	chèque interne *m*	assegno su filiale *m*	cheque de sucursal *m*
hybride Finanzierungsinstrumente (D)	—	hybrid financing instruments	instruments de financement hybrides *m/pl*	strumenti di finanziamento ibridi *m/pl*	instrumentos de financiación híbridos *m/pl*
hybrid financing instruments (E)	hybride Finanzierungsinstrumente *n/pl*	—	instruments de financement hybrides *m/pl*	strumenti di finanziamento ibridi *m/pl*	instrumentos de financiación híbridos *m/pl*
Hyperinflation (D)	—	hyperinflation	hyperinflation *f*	iperinflazione *f*	hiperinflación *f*
hyperinflation (E)	Hyperinflation *f*	—	hyperinflation *f*	iperinflazione *f*	hiperinflación *f*
hyperinflation (F)	Hyperinflation *f*	hyperinflation	—	iperinflazione *f*	hiperinflación *f*
Hypothek (D)	—	mortgage	hypothèque *f*	ipoteca *f*	hipoteca *f*
Hypothekarkredit (D)	—	mortgage loan	crédit hypothécaire *m*	credito ipotecario *m*	crédito hipotecario *m*
Hypothekenbank (D)	—	mortgage bank	banque hypothécaire *f*	banca ipotecaria *f*	banco hipotecario *m*
Hypothekenbankgesetz (D)	—	mortgage bank law	loi sur les banques de prêts hypothécaires *f*	legge sulle banche ipotecarie *f*	ley de bancos hipotecarios *f*
Hypothekenbrief (D)	—	mortgage deed	cédule hypothécaire *f*	titolo ipotecario *m*	carta hipotecaria *f*
Hypothekengewinnabgabe (D)	—	levy on mortgage profits	impôt sur les bénéfices hypothécaires *m*	cessione degli utili ipotecari *f*	impuesto sobre ganancias hipotecarias *m*
Hypothekenpfandbrief (D)	—	mortgage debenture	obligation foncière *f*	titolo di credito fondiario *m*	obligación hipotecaria *f*
Hypothekenregister (D)	—	mortgage register	livre foncier *m*	libro delle ipoteche *m*	registro hipotecario *m*
Hypothekenversicherung (D)	—	mortgage insurance	assurance hypothécaire *f*	assicurazione dell' ipoteca *f*	seguro de hipotecas *m*
hypothèque (F)	Hypothek *f*	mortgage	—	ipoteca *f*	hipoteca *f*
hypothèque à intérêt fixe (F)	Festzinshypothek *f*	fixed-rate mortgage	—	ipoteca ad interesse fisso *f*	hipoteca de interés fijo *f*
hypothèque amortissable (F)	Amortisationshypothek *f*	instalment mortgage	—	ipoteca ammortizzabile *f*	hipoteca de amortización *f*
hypothèque constituée au profit d'un tiers (F)	Fremdhypothek *f*	third-party mortgage	—	ipoteca a favore di terzi *f*	hipoteca ajena *f*
hypothèque constituée dans le but de garantir une créance (F)	Sicherungshypothek *f*	cautionary mortgage	—	ipoteca di garanzia *f*	hipoteca de seguridad *f*
hypothèque constituée sur la base d'un remboursement du capital à terme fixe sans dénonciation préalable (F)	Fälligkeitshypothek *f*	fixed-date land mortgage	—	ipoteca a scadenza determinata *f*	hipoteca de vencimiento *f*
hypothèque de sûreté constituée pour garantir un prêt (F)	Darlehenshypothek *f*	mortgage as security for a loan	—	ipoteca su prestiti *f*	préstamo hipotecario *m*
hypothèque garantissant une créance remboursable à termes périodiques (F)	Tilgungshypothek *f*	amortizable mortgage loan	—	ipoteca ammortizzabile *f*	hipoteca amortizable *f*
hypothèque garantissant une dette remboursable avec préavis (F)	Kündigungshypothek *f*	mortgage loan repayable after having been duly called	—	ipoteca rimborsabile dopo preavviso *f*	hipoteca con preaviso *f*
hypothèque inscrite au livre foncier (F)	Buchhypothek *f*	uncertificated mortgage	—	ipoteca iscritta *f*	hipoteca de registro *f*
hypothèque maritime (F)	Schiffshypothek *f*	ship mortgage	—	ipoteca navale *f*	hipoteca naval *f*
hypothèque négative (F)	Negativhypothek *f*	borrower's undertaking to create no new charge ranking ahead of lender	—	ipoteca negativa *f*	hipoteca negativa *f*

	D	E	F	I	Es
hypothèque pour financer la construction de logements neufs (F)	Neubauhypothek f	mortgage loan to finance building of new dwelling-house	—	ipoteca su una nuova costruzione f	hipoteca para la construcción de nuevas viviendas f
hypothèque réductible (F)	Abzahlungshypothek f	instalment mortgage	—	ipoteca di pagamento a rate f	hipoteca a plazos f
hypothèque revenant au propriétaire du fonds grevé (F)	Eigentümer-Hypothek f	mortgage for the benefit of the owner	—	ipoteca a favore del proprietario f	hipoteca de propietario f
hypothèque solidaire (F)	Gesamthypothek f	general mortgage	—	ipoteca generale f	hipoteca solidaria f
Identitätsnachweis (D)	—	proof of identity	preuve de l'identité f	certificato d'identità m	prueba de la identidad f
identité des bilans successifs (F)	Bilanzkontinuität f	balance sheet consistency	—	continuità di bilancio f	continuidad de balance f
idoneità di titoli all'anticipazione (I)	Lombardfähigkeit f	acceptability as collateral	capacité d'être déposé à titre de gage f	—	capacidad de ser pignorable f
Illationsgründung (D)	—	formation by founders' non-cash capital contributions	constitution par apports en nature f	costituzione di una società mediante conferimento in natura f	formación por aportaciones en especie f
illiquidità (I)	Illiquidität f	illiquidity	manque de liquidité m	—	falta de liquidez f
Illiquidität (D)	—	illiquidity	manque de liquidité m	illiquidità f	falta de liquidez f
illiquidity (E)	Illiquidität f	—	manque de liquidité m	illiquidità f	falta de liquidez f
illusione fiscale (I)	Fiskalillusion f	fiscal illusion	illusion fiscale f	—	ilusión fiscal f
illusione monetaria (I)	Geldillusion f	money illusion	illusion monétaire f	—	ilusión monetaria f
ilusión fiscal (Es)	Fiskalillusion f	fiscal illusion	illusion fiscale f	illusione fiscale f	—
illusion fiscale (F)	Fiskalillusion f	fiscal illusion	—	illusione fiscale f	ilusión fiscal f
illusion monétaire (F)	Geldillusion f	money illusion	—	illusione monetaria f	ilusión monetaria f
ilusión monetaria (Es)	Geldillusion f	money illusion	illusion monétaire f	illusione monetaria f	—
im Aufwind (D)	—	under upward pressure	en progrès	con tendenza ascendente	con tendencia alcesta
im Markt sein (D)	—	to be in the market	être sur le marché	essere presente sul mercato	estar en el mercado
imaginärer Gewinn (D)	—	imaginary profit	bénéfice imaginaire m	lucro cessante m	beneficio imaginario m
imaginary profit (E)	imaginärer Gewinn m	—	bénéfice imaginaire m	lucro cessante m	beneficio imaginario m
immaterielle Werte (D)	—	intangible assets	valeur des éléments incorporels f	valori immateriali m/pl	valores inmateriales m/pl
Immobiliarkredit (D)	—	real estate credit	crédit immobilier m	credito immobiliare m	crédito inmobiliario m
Immobilien (D)	—	immovables	biens immobiliers m/pl	beni immobili m/pl	bienes inmuebles m/pl
Immobilienfonds (D)	—	real estate fund	fonds immobilier m	fondo di titoli immobiliari m	cartera inmobiliaria f
immobilisation de capitaux (F)	Kapitalbindung f	capital tie-up	—	vincolamento di capitale m	vinculación de capital f
immobilisations corporelles (F)	Sachanlage-vermögen n	tangible fixed assets	—	attivo immobilitato m	inmovilizado m
immobilisations corporelles (F)	Sachkapital n	real capital	—	capitale reale m	capital real m
immovable property (E)	Liegenschaft f	—	bien foncier m	bene immobile m	inmuebles m/pl
immovables (E)	Immobilien f/pl	—	biens immobiliers m/pl	beni immobili m/pl	bienes inmuebles m/pl
impagados (Es)	Ausfallforderung f	bad debt loss	créance prioritaire f	credito per l'ammanco m	—
impegni di girata (I)	Indossament-verbindlichkeiten f/pl	endorsement liabilities	obligations par endossement f/pl	—	obligaciones por endoso f/pl
impegno (I)	Engagement n	commitment	engagement m	—	compromiso m
impegno nostro (I)	Nostroverbindlichkeit f	nostro liability	obligations vis-à-vis d'une autre banque f/pl	—	débitos a nuestro cargo m/pl
impersonal security deposit (E)	Sachdepot n	—	dépôt de choses m	libretto di deposito titoli m	depósito impersonal de títulos m

	D	E	F	I	Es
impiegato di banca (I)	Bankangestellter m	bank clerk	employé de banque m	—	empleado de banco m
impiegato di banca (I)	Bankkaufmann m	bank clerk	employé bancaire m	—	empleado bancario m
impieghi di capitale (I)	Kapitalvermögen n	capital assets	capital m	—	bienes patrimoniales m/pl
impiego di capitale (I)	Kapitalanlage f	capital investment	investissement de capitaux m	—	inversión de capital f
implicit basis of a contract (E)	Geschäftsgrundlage f	—	base implicite d'un contrat f	base negoziale f	base del negocio f
importación de capital (Es)	Kapitalimport m	import of capital	importation de capitaux f	importazione di capitale f	—
importación de inflación (Es)	Inflationsimport m	inflation import	importation d'inflation f	importazione dell'inflazione f	—
importación monetaria (Es)	Geldimport m	money import	importation monétaire f	importazione di valuta f	—
importance de la commande (F)	Auftragsgröße f	size of an order	—	ampiezza d'ordinazione f	volumen de pedido m
importation de capitaux (F)	Kapitalimport m	import of capital	—	importazione di capitale f	importación de capital f
importation d'inflation (F)	Inflationsimport m	inflation import	—	importazione dell'inflazione f	importación de inflación f
importation monétaire (F)	Geldimport m	money import	—	importazione di valuta f	importación monetaria f
importazione (I)	Einfuhr f	import	importation f	—	importación f
importazione (I)	Import m	import	importation f	—	importación f
importazione dell'inflazione (I)	Inflationsimport m	inflation import	importation d'inflation f	—	importación de inflación f
importazione di capitale (I)	Kapitalimport m	import of capital	importation de capitaux f	—	importación de capital f
importazione di valuta (I)	Geldimport m	money import	importation monétaire f	—	importación monetaria f
importe calculado (Es)	ausmachender Betrag m	actual amount	montant calculé m	controvalore della contrattazione m	—
importe de la opción (Es)	Kapitalabfindung f	lump-sum payment	indemnité en capital f	indennità in capitale f	—
imported inflation (E)	importierte Inflation f	—	inflation importée f	inflazione importata f	inflación importada f
importe exento (Es)	Freibetrag m	tax-free amount	montant exonéré m	importo esente m	—
import financing (E)	Importfinanzierung f	—	financement des importations m	finanziamento delle importazioni m	financiación de las importaciones f
Importfinanzierung (D)	—	import financing	financement des importations m	finanziamento delle importazioni m	financiación de las importaciones f
importierte Inflation (D)	—	imported inflation	inflation importée f	inflazione importata f	inflación importada f
importo di deposito (I)	Verwahrungsbetrag m	value of custody	valeur des fonds en dépôt f	—	valor de los fondos en depósito m
importo esente (I)	Freibetrag m	tax-free amount	montant exonéré m	—	importe exento m
import of capital (E)	Kapitalimport m	—	importation de capitaux f	importazione di capitale f	importación de capital f
import quota (E)	Importquote f	—	contingent d'importation m	contingente d'importazione m	cuota de importación f
imposición (Es)	Besteuerung f	taxation	taxation f	tassazione f	—
imposición (Es)	Einlage f	money deposited	dépôt m	deposito m	—
imposición a un plazo de 3 meses (Es)	Dreimonatsgeld n	three months' money	dépôts à trois mois m/pl	prestito a tre mesi m	—
imposición de ahorro (Es)	Spareinlage f	savings deposit	dépôt d'épargne m	deposito a risparmio m	—
imposición de contingentes (Es)	Kontingentierung f	fixing of a quota	contingentement m	contingentamento m	—
imposición en un banco (Es)	Bankeinlage f	bank deposits	dépôt en banque m	deposito bancario m	—
imposiciones a largo plazo (Es)	langfristige Einlagen f/pl	long-term deposits	placements à long terme m/pl	depositi a lunga scadenza m/pl	—
imposiciones a plazo (Es)	befristete Einlagen f/pl	fixed deposits	bons et comptes à échéance fixe m/pl	depositi a scadenza fissa m/pl	—
imposta (I)	Steuer f	tax	impôt m	—	impuesto m

	D	E	F	I	Es
imposta cedolare (I)	Ertragssteuer f	tax on income	impôt assis sur le produit m	—	impuesto sobre las ganancias m
imposta complementare (I)	Ergänzungsabgabe f	supplementary levy	taxe complémentaire f	—	tasa complementaria f
imposta consiglio di vigilanza (I)	Aufsichtsratsteuer f	directors' fees tax	impôt sur les jetons de présence et les tantièmes m	—	impuesto sobre la remuneración de los miembros del consejo de administración m
imposta di bollo (I)	Stempelsteuer f	stamp duty	droit de timbre m	—	impuesto del timbre m
imposta di consumo (I)	Ausgabensteuer f	outlay tax	taxe de débours f	—	impuesto de emisión m
imposta diretta (I)	direkte Steuer f	direct taxes	impôts directs m/pl	—	impuesto directo m
imposta sui contratti di borsa (I)	Börsenumsatzsteuer f	stock exchange turnover tax	taxe de transaction sur les opérations boursières f	—	impuesto sobre la negociación bursátil m
imposta sui dividendi (I)	Dividendenabgabe f	dividend tax	impôt sur les dividendes m	—	impuesto sobre dividendos m
imposta sul fatturato d'acquisto (I)	Vorsteuer f	input tax	impôt perçu en amont m	—	impuesto sobre el valor añadido deducible m
imposta sulla circolazione dei capitali (I)	Kapitalverkehrssteuer f	capital transaction tax	taxe sur les mutations du capital f	—	impuesto sobre transacciones m
imposta sulla speculazione (I)	Spekulationssteuer f	tax on speculative gains	impôt sur les gains spéculatifs m	—	impuesto sobre beneficios especulativos m
imposta sulle cedole (I)	Kuponsteuer f	coupon tax	impôt sur les coupons m	—	impuesto sobre cupones m
imposta sulle compensazioni (I)	Kompensationssteuer f	offset tax	impôt de compensation m	—	impuesto de compensación m
imposta sul patrimonio (I)	Vermögenssteuer f	wealth tax	impôt sur la fortune m	—	impuesto patrimonial m
imposta sul reddito dei capitali (I)	Kapitalertragssteuer f	tax on investment income	taxation des revenus du capital m	—	impuesto sobre la renta de capital m
imposta sul reddito delle società (I)	Körperschaftssteuer f	corporation tax	taxe sur les sociétés m	—	impuesto de sociedades m
imposta sul valore aggiunto (I)	Mehrwertsteuer f	value-added tax	taxe à la valeur ajoutée f	—	impuesto sobre el valor añadido m
impôt (F)	Steuer f	tax	—	imposta f	impuesto m
impôt assis sur le produit (F)	Ertragssteuer f	tax on income	—	imposta cedolare f	impuesto sobre las ganancias m
impôt de compensation (F)	Kompensationssteuer f	offset tax	—	imposta sulle compensazioni f	impuesto de compensación m
impôt perçu en amont (F)	Vorsteuer f	input tax	—	imposta sul fatturato d'acquisto f	impuesto sobre el valor añadido deducible m
impôt personnel (F)	Kopfsteuer f	per capita tax	—	capitazione f	capitación f
impôt retenu à la source (F)	Quellensteuer f	tax at source	—	ritenuta alla fonte f	impuesto deducido en la fuente m
impôts directs (F)	direkte Steuer f	direct taxes	—	imposta diretta f	impuesto directo m
impôt sur des bénéfices hypothécaires (F)	Hypothekengewinnabgabe f	levy on mortgage profits	—	cessione degli utili ipotecari f	impuesto sobre ganancias hipotecarias m
impôt sur la fortune (F)	Vermögenssteuer f	wealth tax	—	imposta sul patrimonio f	impuesto patrimonial m
impôt sur la fusion de sociétés (F)	Fusionssteuer f	amalgamation tax	—	tassa di fusione f	impuesto sobre la fusión de sociedades m
impôt sur le revenu (F)	Einkommensteuer f	income tax	—	tassa sul reddito f	impuesto sobre la renta m
impôt sur les bénéfices des professions industrielles et commerciales (F)	Gewerbesteuer f	trade tax	—	tassa d'esercizio f	impuesto industrial m
impôt sur les coupons (F)	Kuponsteuer f	coupon tax	—	imposta sulle cedole f	impuesto sobre cupones m
impôt sur les dividendes (F)	Dividendenabgabe f	dividend tax	—	imposta sui dividendi f	impuesto sobre dividendos m

	D	E	F	I	Es
impôt sur les gains spéculatifs (F)	Spekulationssteuer *f*	tax on speculative gains	—	imposta sulla speculazione *f*	impuesto sobre beneficios especulativos *m*
impôt sur les jetons de présence et les tantièmes (F)	Aufsichtsratsteuer *f*	directors' fees tax	—	imposta consiglio di vigilanza *f*	impuesto sobre la remuneración de los miembros del consejo de administración *m*
imprenditore a pieno titolo (I)	Vollkaufmann *m*	registered trader	commerçant de plein droit *m*	—	comerciante pleno *m*
impresa (I)	Unternehmen *n*	enterprise	entreprise *f*	—	empresa *f*
impresa fittizia (I)	Scheinfirma *f*	bogus firm	raison sociale imaginaire *f*	—	casa ficticia *f*
impreso para giro postal (Es)	Zahlschein *m*	payment slip	mandat-carte *m*	modulo di versamento *m*	—
imprimé en blanc (F)	Blankett *n*	blank form	—	foglio in bianco *m*	carta blanca *f*
impuesto (Es)	Steuer *f*	tax	impôt *m*	imposta *f*	—
impuesto de compensación (Es)	Kompensationssteuer *f*	offset tax	impôt de compensation *m*	imposta sulle compensazioni *f*	—
impuesto deducido en la fuente (Es)	Quellensteuer *f*	tax at source	impôt reçu à la source *m*	ritenuta alla fonte *f*	—
impuesto de emisión (Es)	Ausgabensteuer *f*	outlay tax	taxe de débours *f*	imposta di consumo *f*	—
impuesto del timbre (Es)	Stempelsteuer *f*	stamp duty	droit de timbre *m*	imposta di bollo *f*	—
impuesto de sociedades (Es)	Körperschaftssteuer *f*	corporation tax	taxe sur les sociétés *m*	imposta sul reddito delle società *f*	—
impuesto directo (Es)	direkte Steuer *f*	direct taxes	impôts directs *m/pl*	imposta diretta *f*	—
impuesto industrial (Es)	Gewerbesteuer *f*	trade tax	impôt sur les bénéfices des professions industrielles et commerciales *m*	tassa d'esercizio *f*	—
impuesto patrimonial (Es)	Vermögenssteuer *f*	wealth tax	impôt sur la fortune *m*	imposta sul patrimonio *f*	—
impuesto sobre beneficios especulativos (Es)	Spekulationssteuer *f*	tax on speculative gains	impôt sur les gains spéculatifs *m*	imposta sulla speculazione *f*	—
impuesto sobre cupones (Es)	Kuponsteuer *f*	coupon tax	impôt sur les coupons *m*	imposta sulle cedole *f*	—
impuesto sobre dividendos (Es)	Dividendenabgabe *f*	dividend tax	impôt sur les dividendes *m*	imposta sui dividendi *f*	—
impuesto sobre el valor añadido (Es)	Mehrwertsteuer *f*	value-added tax	taxe à la valeur ajoutée *f*	imposta sul valore aggiunto *f*	—
impuesto sobre el valor añadido deducible (Es)	Vorsteuer *f*	input tax	impôt perçu en amont *m*	imposta sul fatturato d'acquisto *f*	—
impuesto sobre ganancias hipotecarias (Es)	Hypothekengewinnabgabe *f*	levy on mortgage profits	impôt sur des bénéfices hypothécaires *m*	cessione degli utili ipotecari *f*	—
impuesto sobre la fusión de sociedades (Es)	Fusionssteuer *f*	amalgamation tax	impôt sur la fusion de sociétés *m*	tassa di fusione *f*	—
impuesto sobre la negociación bursátil (Es)	Börsenumsatzsteuer *f*	stock exchange turnover tax	taxe de transaction sur les opérations boursières *f*	imposta sui contratti di borsa *f*	—
impuesto sobre la remuneración de los miembros del consejo de administración (Es)	Aufsichtsratsteuer *f*	directors' fees tax	impôt sur les jetons de présence et les tantièmes *m*	imposta consiglio di vigilanza *f*	—
impuesto sobre la renta (Es)	Einkommensteuer *f*	income tax	impôt sur le revenu *m*	tassa sul reddito *f*	—
impuesto sobre la renta de capital (Es)	Kapitalertragssteuer *f*	tax on investment income	taxation des revenus du capital *f*	imposta sul reddito dei capitali *f*	—
impuesto sobre las ganancias (Es)	Ertragssteuer *f*	tax on income	impôt assis sur le produit *m*	imposta cedolare *f*	—
impuesto sobre transacciones (Es)	Kapitalverkehrssteuer *f*	capital transaction tax	taxe sur les mutations du capital *f*	imposta sulla circolazione dei capitali *f*	—

	D	E	F	I	Es
inactif (F)	lustlos	slack	—	fiacco	poco animado
inactive security (E)	totes Papier *n*	—	titre inactif *m*	titolo morto *m*	título muerto *m*
inattivo (I)	geschäftslos	slack	stagnant	—	estado de estancamiento *m*
incapacidad jurídica parcial (Es)	beschränkte Geschäftsfähigkeit *f*	limited capacity to enter into legal transactions	capacité restreinte d'accomplir des actes juridiques *f*	capacità giuridica limitata *f*	—
incarico permanente (I)	Dauerauftrag *m*	standing order	ordre régulier *m*	—	orden permanente *f*
incasso (I)	Inkasso *n*	collection	encaissement *m*	—	cobranza *f*
incasso di assegno (I)	Scheckeinzug *m*	cheque collection	recouvrement de chèques *m*	—	cobro del cheque *m*
incasso di cambiale (I)	Wechselinkasso *n*	collection of bills of exchange	encaissement d'un effet *m*	—	cobro de letras *m*
incasso tramite addebitamento (I)	Lastschrifteinzugsverfahren *n*	direct debiting	système de prélèvement automatique *m*	—	procedimiento de cobro en cuenta *m*
incentivos a la inversión (Es)	Investitionsförderung *f*	investment promotion	promotion de l'investissement *f*	promozione degli investimenti *f*	—
incertezza (I)	Unsicherheit *f*	uncertainty	insécurité *f*	—	inseguridad *f*
inchiesta bancaria (I)	Bankenquete *f*	banking inquiry	demande de renseignements par la banque *f*	—	demanda de informe por el banco *f*
inclusion on the liabilities side (E)	Passivierung *f*	—	inscription au passif *f*	passività *f*	asiento en el pasivo *m*
income from capital (E)	Kapitalertrag *m*	—	produit du capital *m*	reddito di capitale *m*	renta de capital *f*
income from gainful employment (E)	Erwerbseinkommen *n*	—	revenu du travail *m*	reddito di lavoro *m*	remuneración de los asalariados *f*
income from interests (E)	Zinsertrag *m*	—	intérêts perçus *m/pl*	provento d'interessi *m*	rédito *m*
income limit for the assessment of contributions (E)	Beitragsbemessungsgrenze *f*	—	plafond d'assujettissement servant au calcul de la cotisation à l'assurance invalidité-vieillesse *m*	massimale di contributo *m*	tope de la base de cotización *m*
income tax (E)	Einkommensteuer *f*	—	impôt sur le revenu *m*	tassa sul reddito *f*	impuesto sobre la renta *m*
incoming order (E)	Auftragseingang *m*	—	reentrée de commandes *f*	afflusso di ordini *m*	entrada de pedidos *f*
in contanti (I)	bar	cash	comptant	—	al contado
increase in own capital (E)	Eigenkapitalerhöhung *f*	—	augmentation du capital propre *f*	aumento del capitale proprio *m*	aumento del capital propio *m*
increase in total assets and liabilities (E)	Bilanzverlängerung *f*	—	extension du bilan *f*	allungamento del bilancio *m*	extensión del balance *f*
increase of the share capital (E)	Kapitalerhöhung *f*	—	augmentation de capital *f*	aumento del capitale *m*	aumento de capital *m*
indebitamento (I)	Verschuldung *f*	indebtedness	endettement *m*	—	endeudamiento *m*
indebitamento eccessivo (I)	Überschuldung *f*	excessive indebtedness	surendettement *m*	—	exceso de deudas *m*
indebitamento netto (I)	Nettokreditaufnahme	net borrowing	emprunt net *m*	—	toma de crédito neta *f*
indebitamento netto (I)	Nettoneuverschuldung *f*	net new indebtedness	nouveaux emprunts en termes nets *m*	—	endeudamiento neto *m*
indebitamento verso l'estero (I)	Auslandsverschuldung *f*	external indebtedness	dette extérieure *f*	—	deuda exterior *f*
indebolimento delle quotazioni (I)	Ermattung *f*	exhaust	léthargie *f*	—	letargía *f*
indebtedness (E)	Verschuldung *f*	—	endettement *m*	indebitamento *m*	endeudamiento *m*
indemnification (E)	Entschädigung *f*	—	indemnité *f*	indennità *f*	indemnización *f*
indemnité (F)	Abfindung *f*	compensation	—	indennizzo *m*	compensación *f*
indemnité (F)	Entschädigung *f*	indemnification	—	indennità *f*	indemnización *f*
indemnité de chômage (F)	Arbeitslosengeld *n*	unemployment benefit	—	indennità di disoccupazione *f*	subsidio de desempleo *m*
indemnité en capital (F)	Kapitalabfindung *f*	lump-sum payment	—	indennità in capitale *f*	importe de la opción *m*

	D	E	F	I	Es
indemnité en espèces (F)	Barabfindung f	settlement in cash	—	indennità in contanti f	compensación en efectivo f
indemnización (Es)	Entschädigung f	indemnification	indemnité f	indennità f	—
indemnización por daños y perjuicios (Es)	Schadensersatz m	compensation for loss suffered	dommages-intérêts m/pl	risarcimento dei danni m	—
indennità (I)	Entschädigung f	indemnification	indemnité f	—	indemnización f
indennità di disoccupazione (I)	Arbeitslosengeld n	unemployment benefit	indemnité de chômage f	—	subsidio de desempleo m
indennità di risparmio dipendenti (I)	Arbeitnehmer-sparzulage f	employees' savings premium	prime d'épargne en faveur de l'employée f	—	prima de ahorro del empleado f
indennità in capitale (I)	Kapitalabfindung f	lump-sum payment	indemnité en capital f	—	importe de la opción m
indennità in contanti (I)	Barabfindung f	settlement in cash	indemnité en espèces f	—	compensación en efectivo f
indennizzo (I)	Abfindung f	compensation	indemnité f	—	compensación f
Index (D)	—	index	indice m	indice m	índice m
index (E)	Index m	—	indice m	indice m	índice m
indexación (Es)	Indexierung f	indexation	indexation f	indicizzazione f	—
Indexanleihe (D)	—	index-linked loan	emprunt indexé m	prestito indicizzato m	préstamo provisto de una cláusula de valor estable m
indexation (E)	Indexierung f	—	indexation f	indicizzazione f	indexación f
indexation (F)	Indexierung f	indexation	—	indicizzazione f	indexación f
indexation (F)	Indexbindung f	index-linking	—	indicizzazione f	vinculación al índice f
Indexbindung (D)	—	index-linking	indexation f	indicizzazione f	vinculación al índice f
index clause (E)	Indexklausel f	—	clause d'indexation f	clausola numeri indici f	cláusula de índice variable f
Indexierung (D)	—	indexation	indexation f	indicizzazione f	indexación f
Indexklausel (D)	—	index clause	clause d'indexation f	clausola numeri indici f	cláusula de índice variable f
index-linked currency (E)	Indexwährung f	—	monnaie indexée f	moneta indice f	moneda-índice f
index-linked loan (E)	Indexanleihe f	—	emprunt indexé m	prestito indicizzato m	préstamo provisto de una cláusula de valor estable m
index-linking (E)	Indexbindung f	—	indexation f	indicizzazione f	vinculación al índice f
Indexwährung (D)	—	index-linked currency	monnaie indexée f	moneta indice f	moneda-índice f
indicación de las cotizaciones (Es)	Kursanzeige f	quotation	cotation f	indicazione delle quotazioni f	—
indicaciones explicativas de las cotizaciones (Es)	Kurszusätze m/pl	notes appended to quotation	indications supplémentaires de cotation f/pl	termini borsistici m/pl	—
indicador (Es)	Indikator m	indicator	indicateur m	indicatore m	—
indicated (E)	genannt	—	indiqué	stimato	alias
indicateur (F)	Indikator m	indicator	—	indicatore m	indicador m
indication automatique des cotations (F)	automatische Kursanzeige f	automatic quotation	—	indicatore automatico quotazioni m	tablero electrónico m
indications supplémentaires de cotation (F)	Kurszusätze m/pl	notes appended to quotation	—	termini borsistici m/pl	indicaciones explicativas de las cotizaciones f/pl
indicator (E)	Indikator m	—	indicateur m	indicatore m	indicador m
indicatore (I)	Indikator m	indicator	indicateur m	—	indicador m
indicatore automatico quotazioni (I)	automatische Kursanzeige f	automatic quotation	indication automa-tique des cotations m	—	tablero electrónico m
indicazione al bisogno nostro (I)	Nostronotadresse f	nostro address in case of need	notre adresse au besoin f	—	dirección propia en caso necesario f
indicazione delle quotazioni (I)	Kursanzeige f	quotation	cotation f	—	indicación de las cotizaciones f
indicazione di assegno bancario (I)	Scheckklausel f	cheque clause	mention sur un chèque f	—	cláusula de cheque f
índice (Es)	Index m	index	indice m	indice m	—

	D	E	F	I	Es
índice (Es)	Kennzahl *f*	code number	code *m*	indice *m*	—
indice (F)	Index *m*	index	—	indice *m*	índice *m*
indice (I)	Index *m*	index	indice *m*	—	índice *m*
indice (I)	Kennzahl *f*	code number	code *m*	—	índice *m*
indice azionario (I)	Aktienindex *m*	share index	indice du cours des actions *m*	—	índice de cotización *m*
índice BERI (Es)	BERI-Index *m*	business environment risk index	indice BERI *m*	indice BERI *m*	—
indice BERI (F)	BERI-Index *m*	business environment risk index	—	indice BERI *m*	índice BERI *m*
indice BERI (I)	BERI-Index *m*	business environment risk index	indice BERI *m*	—	índice BERI *m*
indice beta (I)	Betafaktor *m*	beta factor	coefficient bêta *m*	—	factor beta de regresión *m*
indice boursier DAX (F)	DAX-Index *m*	DAX-index	—	indice DAX *m*	índice DAX *m*
índice bursátil (Es)	Börsenindex *m*	stock exchange index	indice des cours des actions *m*	indice di borsa *m*	—
índice DAX (Es)	DAX-Index *m*	DAX-index	indice boursier DAX *m*	indice DAX *m*	—
indice DAX (I)	DAX-Index *m*	DAX-index	indice boursier DAX *m*	—	índice DAX *m*
índice de cotización (Es)	Aktienindex *m*	share index	indice du cours des actions *m*	indice azionario *m*	—
índice de cotizaciones (Es)	Kursindex *m*	stock exchange index	indice des cours *m*	indice di borsa *m*	—
índice de inversión (Es)	Investitionskennzahl *f*	investment index	coefficient d'investissement *m*	indice di investimento *m*	—
indice dei prezzi (I)	Preisindex *m*	price index	indice des prix *m*	—	índice de precios *m*
índice de precios (Es)	Preisindex *m*	price index	indice des prix *m*	indice dei prezzi *m*	—
indice des cours (F)	Kursindex *m*	stock exchange index	—	indice di borsa *m*	índice de cotizaciones *m*
indice des cours des actions (F)	Börsenindex *m*	stock exchange index	—	indice di borsa *m*	índice bursátil *m*
indice des prix (F)	Preisindex *m*	price index	—	indice dei prezzi *m*	índice de precios *m*
indice di borsa (I)	Börsenindex *m*	stock exchange index	indice des cours des actions *m*	—	índice bursátil *m*
indice di borsa (I)	Kursindex *m*	stock exchange index	indice des cours *m*	—	índice de cotizaciones *m*
indice di investimento (I)	Investitionskennzahl *f*	investment index	coefficient d'investissement *m*	—	índice de inversión *m*
indice du cours des actions (F)	Aktienindex *m*	share index	—	indice azionario *m*	índice de cotización *m*
indicizzazione (I)	Indexierung *f*	indexation	indexation *f*	—	indexación *f*
indicizzazione (I)	Indexbindung *f*	index-linking	indexation *f*	—	vinculación al índice *f*
Indikator (D)	—	indicator	indicateur *m*	indicatore *m*	indicador *m*
indiqué (F)	genannt	indicated	—	stimato	alias
indirekte Investition (D)	—	portfolio investments	investissement indirect *m*	investimento indiretto *m*	inversión indirecta *f*
individual credit insurance (E)	Einzelkreditversicherung *f*	—	assurance crédit individuelle *f*	assicurazione crediti individuali *f*	seguro de crédito individual *m*
individual deposit of securities (E)	Streifbanddepot *n*	—	dépôt individuel avec mandat de gestion *m*	deposito a dossier *m*	depósito separado *m*
individuelles Sparen (D)	—	saving by private households	épargne individuelle *f*	risparmio individuale *m*	ahorro individual *m*
indossable Wertpapiere (D)	—	endorsable securities	valeurs endossables *f/pl*	titoli girabili *m/pl*	títulos endosables *m/pl*
Indossament (D)	—	endorsement	endossement *m*	girata *f*	endoso *m*
Indossamentverbindlichkeiten (D)	—	endorsement liabilities	obligations par endossement *f/pl*	impegni di girata *m/pl*	obligaciones por endoso *f/pl*
Indossant (D)	—	endorser	endosseur *m*	girante *m*	endosador *m*
Indossatar (D)	—	endorsee	endossataire *m*	giratario *m*	endosatario *m*

	D	E	F	I	Es
industrial bank (E)	Gewerbebank *f*	—	banque industrielle et artinsanale *f*	banca industriale *f*	banco industrial *m*
industrial bonds (E)	Industrieobligationen *f/pl*	—	obligations de l'industrie *f/pl*	obbligazioni industriali *m/pl*	obligaciones industriales *f/pl*
industrial credit (E)	Industriekredit *m*	—	crédit à l'industrie *m*	credito industriale *m*	crédito industrial *m*
industrial credit bank (E)	Industriekreditbank *f*	—	banque de crédit à l'industrie *f*	banca di credito industriale *f*	banco de crédito industrial *m*
industrial shares (E)	Industrieaktie *f*	—	action industrielle *f*	azione industriale *f*	acción industrial *f*
industrial stock exchange (E)	Industriebörse *f*	—	bourse des valeurs industrielles *f*	borsa industriale *f*	bolsa industrial *f*
industrial syndicate (E)	Industriekonsortium *n*	—	consortium industriel *m*	consorzio industriale *m*	consorcio industrial *m*
industria metalúrgica (Es)	eisenschaffende Industrie *f*	iron and steel producing industry	sidérurgie *f*	industria siderurgica *f*	—
industria siderurgica (I)	eisenschaffende Industrie *f*	iron and steel producing industry	sidérurgie *f*	—	industria metalúrgica *f*
Industrieaktie (D)	—	industrial shares	action industrielle *f*	azione industriale *f*	acción industrial *f*
Industriebörse (D)	—	industrial stock exchange	bourse des valeurs industrielles *f*	borsa industriale *f*	bolsa industrial *f*
Industrie-konsortium (D)	—	industrial syndicate	consortium industriel *m*	consorzio industriale *m*	consorcio industrial *m*
Industriekredit (D)	—	industrial credit	crédit à l'industrie *m*	credito industriale *m*	crédito industrial *m*
Industriekreditbank (D)	—	industrial credit bank	banque de crédit à l'industrie *f*	banca di credito industriale *f*	banco de crédito industrial *m*
Industrie-obligationen (D)	—	industrial bonds	obligations de l'industrie *f/pl*	obbligazioni industriali *m/pl*	obligaciones industriales *f/pl*
Industrie- und Handelskammer (D)	—	Chamber of Industry and Commerce	chambre de commerce et d'industrie *f*	camera di commercio *f*	cámara de industria y comercio *f*
infedeltà (I)	Untreue *f*	disloyalty	abus de confiance *m*	—	infidelidad *f*
infidelidad (Es)	Untreue *f*	disloyalty	abus de confiance *m*	infedeltà *f*	—
inflación (Es)	Inflation *f*	inflation	inflation *f*	inflazione *f*	—
inflación adaptiva (Es)	Anpassungsinflation *f*	adaptive inflation	inflation adaptive *f*	inflazione di adattamento *f*	—
inflación crediticia (Es)	Kreditinflation *f*	credit inflation	inflation de crédit *f*	inflazione crediticia *f*	—
inflación detenida (Es)	zurückgestaute Inflation *f*	pent-up inflation	inflation refoulée *f*	inflazione arginata *f*	—
inflación encubierta (Es)	versteckte Inflation *f*	hidden inflation	inflation larvée *f*	inflazione mascherata *f*	—
inflación importada (Es)	importierte Inflation *f*	imported inflation	inflation importée *f*	inflazione importata *f*	—
inflación pronostizada (Es)	Inflationserwartung *f*	expected inflation	inflation prévue *f*	aspettativa d'inflazione *f*	—
Inflation (D)	—	inflation	inflation *f*	inflazione *f*	inflación *f*
inflation (E)	Inflation *f*	—	inflation *f*	inflazione *f*	inflación *f*
inflation (F)	Inflation *f*	inflation	—	inflazione *f*	inflación *f*
inflation adaptive (F)	Anpassungsinflation *f*	adaptive inflation	—	inflazione di adattamento *f*	inflación adaptiva *f*
inflation de crédit (F)	Kreditinflation *f*	credit inflation	—	inflazione crediticia *f*	inflación crediticia *f*
inflation import (E)	Inflationsimport *m*	—	importation d'inflation *f*	importazione dell'inflazione *f*	importación de inflación *f*
inflation importée (F)	importierte Inflation *f*	imported inflation	—	inflazione importata *f*	inflación importada *f*
inflation larvée (F)	versteckte Inflation *f*	hidden inflation	—	inflazione mascherata *f*	inflación encubierta *f*
inflation prévue (F)	Inflationserwartung *f*	expected inflation	—	aspettativa d'inflazione *f*	inflación pronostizada *f*
inflation refoulée (F)	zurückgestaute Inflation *f*	pent-up inflation	—	inflazione arginata *f*	inflación detenida *f*
Inflations-bekämpfung (D)	—	struggle against inflation	lutte contre l'inflation *f*	lotta all'inflazione *f*	lucha contra la inflación *f*
Inflations-beschleunigung (D)	—	acceleration of inflation	accélération de l'inflation *f*	accelerazione dell'inflazione *f*	aceleración de la inflación *f*

	D	E	F	I	Es
Inflationserwartung (D)	—	expected inflation	inflation prévue *f*	aspettativa d'inflazione *f*	inflación pronosticada *f*
Inflationsimport (D)	—	inflation import	importation d'inflation *f*	importazione dell'inflazione *f*	importación de inflación *f*
Inflationsrate (D)	—	rate of inflation	taux d'inflation *m*	tasso d'inflazione *m*	tasa de inflación *f*
inflazione (I)	Inflation *f*	inflation	inflation *f*	—	inflación *f*
inflazione arginata (I)	zurückgestaute Inflation *f*	pent-up inflation	inflation refoulée *f*	—	inflación detenida *f*
inflazione creditizia (I)	Kreditinflation *f*	credit inflation	inflation de crédit *f*	—	inflación crediticia *f*
inflazione di adattamento (I)	Anpassungsinflation *f*	adaptive inflation	inflation adaptive *f*	—	inflación adaptiva *f*
inflazione importata (I)	importierte Inflation *f*	imported inflation	inflation importée *f*	—	inflación importada *f*
inflazione mascherata (I)	versteckte Inflation *f*	hidden inflation	inflation larvée *f*	—	inflación encubierta *f*
inforestieramento (I)	Überfremdung *f*	control by foreign capital	envahissement de capitaux étrangers *m*	—	extranjerización *f*
información bancaria (Es)	Bankauskunft *f*	banker's reference	renseignement par la banque *m*	informazione bancaria *f*	—
información bursátil (Es)	Börsenauskunft *f*	stock market information	service des renseignements de la bourse *m*	informazioni borsa *f/pl*	—
información de crédito (Es)	Kreditauskunft *f*	credit information	reseignement sur la solvabilité du demandeur d'un crédit *m*	informazione creditizia *f*	—
información privilegiada (Es)	Insiderinformation *f*	insider information	information d'initiés *f*	insider information *f*	—
information centre (E)	Evidenzzentrale *f*	—	centre de déclaration *m*	centrale dei rischi *f*	central de evidencia *f*
information d'initiés (F)	Insiderinformation *f*	insider information	—	insider information *f*	información privilegiada *f*
information file (E)	Auskunftdatei *f*	—	fichier de renseignements *m*	archivio d'informazioni *m*	archivo de datos con fines de información *m*
Informationswert (D)	—	information value	valeur informative *f*	valore dell'informazione *m*	valor informativo *m*
information value (E)	Informationswert *m*	—	valeur informative *f*	valore dell'informazione *m*	valor informativo *m*
informazione bancaria (I)	Bankauskunft *f*	banker's reference	renseignement par la banque *m*	—	información bancaria *f*
informazione creditizia (I)	Kreditauskunft *f*	credit information	reseignement sur la solvabilité du demandeur d'un crédit *m*	—	información de crédito *f*
informazioni borsa (I)	Börsenauskunft *f*	stock market information	service des renseignements de la bourse *m*	—	información bursátil *f*
informe anual (Es)	Geschäftsbericht *m*	business report	rapport de gestion *m*	rapporto di gestione *m*	—
informe bursátil (Es)	Börsenbericht *m*	stock exchange report	bulletin de la bourse *m*	bollettino di borsa *m*	—
informe de auditoría (Es)	Prüfungsbericht *m*	audit report	compte rendu de vérification *m*	relazione d'ispezione *f*	—
informe trimestral (Es)	Quartalsbericht *m*	quarterly report	rapport trimestriel *m*	relazione trimestrale *f*	—
infrastructural credit (E)	Infrastrukturkredit *m*	—	crédit d'infrastructure *m*	credito per l'infrastruttura *m*	crédito de infraestructura *m*
Infrastrukturkredit (D)	—	infrastructural credit	crédit d'infrastructure *m*	credito per l'infrastruttura *m*	crédito de infraestructura *m*
ingresos (Es)	Einnahmen *f/pl*	receipts	recettes *f/pl*	entrate *f/pl*	—
ingresos del trabajo (Es)	Arbeitseinkommen *n*	earned income	revenu du travail *m*	reddito di lavoro *m*	—
ingresos extraordiarios (Es)	außerordentliche Erträge *m/pl*	extraordinary income	profits exceptionnels *m/pl*	sopravvenienze attive *f/pl*	—
ingresos por capital (Es)	Vermögenseinkommen *n*	real balance effect	revenu du capital *m*	reddito di capitale *m*	—

innovaciones financieras

	D	E	F	I	Es
ingresos por inversiones (Es)	Return on Investment *m*	return on investment	rentabilité du capital *f*	return on investment *m*	—
ingresos procedentes de una actividad remunerada (Es)	Erwerbseinkünfte *pl*	business income	revenu d'une activité professionelle *m*	redditi di lavoro *m/pl*	—
ingresos públicos (Es)	Staatseinnahmen *f/pl*	public revenue	recettes de l'Etat *f/pl*	entrate pubbliche *f/pl*	—
Inhaberaktie (D)	—	bearer share	action au porteur *f*	azione al portatore *f*	acción al portador *f*
Inhaber-indossament (D)	—	endorsement made out to bearer	endossement du porteur *m*	girata al portatore *f*	endoso al portador *m*
Inhaberklausel (D)	—	bearer clause	clause au porteur *f*	clausola al portatore *f*	cláusula al portador *f*
Inhaberpapier (D)	—	bearer securities	titre souscrit au porteur *m*	titolo al portatore *m*	título al portador *m*
Inhaberscheck (D)	—	cheque to bearer	chèque au porteur *m*	assegno al portatore *m*	cheque al portador *m*
Inhaberschuld-verschreibung (D)	—	bearer bond	obligation au porteur *f*	obbligazione al portatore *f*	obligación al portador *f*
iniezione di credito (I)	Kreditspritze *f*	injection of credit	injection de crédit *f*	—	inyección de crédito *f*
initial allowance set (E)	Erstausstattung *f*	—	dotation initiale *f*	dotazione iniziale *f*	primer establecimiento *m*
injection de crédit (F)	Kreditspritze *f*	injection of credit	—	iniezione di credito *f*	inyección de crédito *f*
injection of credit (E)	Kreditspritze *f*	—	injection de crédit *f*	iniezione di credito *f*	inyección de crédito *f*
Inkasso (D)	—	collection	encaissement *m*	incasso *m*	cobranza *f*
Inkasso-Abteilung (D)	—	collection department	service des encaissements *m*	ufficio incassi *m*	sección de cobranza *f*
Inkassoakzept (D)	—	acceptance for collection	acceptation pour encaissement *f*	accettazione in attesa d'incasso *f*	aceptación de cobranza *f*
Inkassogebühr (D)	—	collection fee	frais de recouvrement *m/pl*	commissione d'incasso *f*	comisión de cobro *f*
Inkassogeschäft (D)	—	collection business	opération de recouvrement *f*	operazione d'incasso *f*	operación de cobro *f*
Inkasso-Indossament (D)	—	endorsement for collection	endossement pour encaissement *m*	girata "per incasso" *f*	endoso al cobro *m*
Inkassoprovision (D)	—	collection commission	commission d'encaissement *f*	provvigione d'incasso *f*	comisión *f*
Inkassowechsel (D)	—	bill for collection	traite donnée au recouvrement *f*	cambiale all'incasso *f*	letra al cobro *f*
Inländer-konvertibilität (D)	—	convertibility for residents	convertibilité intérieure *f*	convertibilità interna *f*	convertibilidad interna *f*
inland revenue office (E)	Finanzamt *n*	—	service de contributions *m*	ufficio delle finanze *m*	hacienda *f*
Inlandsvermögen (D)	—	domestic capital	capital déclaré dans le pays où l'assujetti à sa résidence *m*	capitale nazionale *m*	patrimonio interno *m*
in lieu of payment (E)	an Zahlungs Statt	—	à titre de payement	pro soluto	a título de pago
in Liquidation (D)	—	in liquidation	en liquidation	in liquidazione	en liquidación
in liquidation (E)	in Liquidation	—	en liquidation	in liquidazione	en liquidación
in liquidazione (I)	in Liquidation	in liquidation	en liquidation	—	en liquidación
inmovilizado (Es)	Sachanlage-vermögen *n*	tangible fixed assets	immobilisations corporelles *f/pl*	attivo immobilitato *m*	—
inmuebles (Es)	Liegenschaft *f*	immovable property	bien foncier *m*	bene immobile *m*	—
Innenfinanzierung (D)	—	internal financing	financement interne *m*	finanziamento interno *m*	financiación interna *f*
Innenfinanzierungs-kennzahl (D)	—	self-generated financing ratio	ratio de financement interne *m*	codice di finanzia-mento interno *m*	características de financiación interna *f/pl*
Innengeld (D)	—	inside money	inside money *m*	inside money *m*	inside money *m*
Innenkonsortium (D)	—	internal syndicate	consortium intérieur *m*	consorzio interno *m*	consorcio interior *m*
innerer Wert (D)	—	intrinsic value	valeur intrinsèque *f*	valore intrinseco *m*	valor intrínseco *m*
innovaciones financieras (Es)	Finanzinnovationen *f/pl*	financial innovation	innovations financières *f/pl*	innovazioni finanziarie *f/pl*	—

	D	E	F	I	Es
innovations financières (F)	Finanzinnovationen *f/pl*	financial innovation	—	innovazioni finanziarie *f/pl*	innovaciones financieras *f/pl*
innovazioni finanziarie (I)	Finanzinnovationen *f/pl*	financial innovation	innovations financières *f/pl*	—	innovaciones financieras *f/pl*
inoperative account (E)	totes Konto *n*	—	compte sans mouvement *m*	conto inattivo *m*	cuenta muerta *f*
in prospect (E)	Ex-ante	—	ex ante	ex-ante	por anticipado
input tax (E)	Vorsteuer *f*	—	impôt perçu en amont *m*	imposta sul fatturato d'acquisto *f*	impuesto sobre el valor añadido deducible *m*
in retrospect (E)	ex-post	—	ex post	ex-post	Ex-post
inscripción (Es)	Einschreibung *f*	registration	enregistrement *m*	asta olandese *f*	—
inscripción en el registro comercial (Es)	Eintragung im Handelsregister *f*	registration in the Commercial Register	inscription au registre du commerce *f*	iscrizione nel registro commerciale *f*	—
inscription au passif (F)	Passivierung *f*	inclusion on the liabilities side	—	passività *f*	asiento en el pasivo *m*
inscription au registre du commerce (F)	Eintragung im Handelsregister *f*	registration in the Commercial Register	—	iscrizione nel registro commerciale *f*	inscripción en el registro comercial *f*
inscription en compte (F)	Verbuchung *f*	entry	—	registrazione *f*	contabilización *f*
insécurité (F)	Unsicherheit *f*	uncertainty	—	incertezza *f*	inseguridad *f*
inseguridad (Es)	Unsicherheit *f*	uncertainty	insécurité *f*	incertezza *f*	—
Insichgeschäft (D)	—	self-dealing	acte passé avec soi-même *m*	operazione fine a se stessa *f*	negocio consigo mismo *m*
inside money (E)	Innengeld *n*	—	inside money *m*	inside money *m*	inside money *m*
inside money (Es)	Innengeld *n*	Inside money	inside money *m*	inside money *m*	inside money *m*
inside money (F)	Innengeld *n*	inside money	—	inside money *m*	inside money *m*
inside money (I)	Innengeld *n*	inside money	inside money *m*	—	inside money *m*
Insiderhandel (D)	—	insider trading	opérations d'insider *f/pl*	insider trading *m*	transacciones realizadas utilizando información privilegiada *f/pl*
Insiderinformation (D)	—	insider information	information d'initiés *f*	insider information *f*	información privilegiada *f*
insider information (E)	Insiderinformation *f*	—	information d'initiés *f*	insider information *f*	información privilegiada *f*
insider information (I)	Insiderinformation *f*	insider information	information d'initiés *f*	—	información privilegiada *f*
Insiderpapier (D)	—	insider security	titre insider *m*	titolo insider *m*	título insider *m*
insider security (E)	Insiderpapier *n*	—	titre insider *m*	titolo insider *m*	título insider *m*
insider trading (E)	Insiderhandel *m*	—	opérations d'insider *f/pl*	insider trading *m*	transacciones realizadas utilizando información privilegiada *f/pl*
insider trading (I)	Insiderhandel *m*	insider trading	opérations d'insider *f/pl*	—	transacciones realizadas utilizando información privilegiada *f/pl*
insolvabilité (F)	Zahlungsunfähigkeit *f*	insolvency	—	insolvenza *f*	insolvencia *f*
insolvabilité (F)	Insolvenz *f*	insolvency	—	insolvenza *f*	insolvencia *f*
insolvencia (Es)	Zahlungsunfähigkeit *f*	insolvency	insolvabilité *f*	insolvenza *f*	—
insolvencia (Es)	Insolvenz *f*	insolvency	insolvabilité *f*	insolvenza *f*	—
insolvency (E)	Insolvenz *f*	—	insolvabilité *f*	insolvenza *f*	insolvencia *f*
insolvency (E)	Zahlungsunfähigkeit *f*	—	insolvabilité *f*	insolvenza *f*	insolvencia *f*
Insolvenz (D)	—	insolvency	insolvabilité *f*	insolvenza *f*	insolvencia *f*
insolvenza (I)	Zahlungsunfähigkeit *f*	insolvency	insolvabilité *f*	—	insolvencia *f*
insolvenza (I)	Insolvenz *f*	insolvency	insolvabilité *f*	—	insolvencia *f*
inspección de solvencia (Es)	Bonitätsprüfung *f*	credit check	vérification de la solvabilité *f*	esame di solvibilità *m*	—
instalment credit (E)	Teilzahlungskredit *m*	—	avance sur vente payée à tempérament *f*	finanziamento di acquisti rateali *m*	crédito para la financiación a plazo *m*

	D	E	F	I	Es
instalment loans (E)	Ratenanleihen *f/pl*	—	emprunt remboursable par annuités constantes *m*	prestiti ammortizzabili *m/pl*	empréstitos a plazos *m/pl*
instalment mortgage (E)	Abzahlungshypothek *f*	—	hypothèque réductible *f*	ipoteca di pagamento a rate *f*	hipoteca a plazos *f*
instalment mortgage (E)	Amortisationshypothek *f*	—	hypothèque amortissable *f*	ipoteca ammortizzabile *f*	hipoteca de amortización *f*
instalment sales credit (E)	Ratenkredit *m*	—	crédit à tempéraments *m*	finanziamento di acquisti rateali *m*	crédito a plazos *m*
instalment sale transaction (E)	Abzahlungsgeschäft *n*	—	vente a tempérament *f*	operazione con pagamento rateale *f*	operación a plazos *f*
institut de crédit foncier (F)	Bodenkreditinstitut *n*	mortgage bank	—	banca di credito agrario *f*	instituto de crédito inmobiliario *m*
institut de crédit foncier (F)	Realkreditinstitut *n*	real-estate credit institution	—	istituto di credito immobiliare *m*	instituto de crédito real *m*
institut de prêt (F)	Leihanstalt *f*	pawnshop	—	monte di pietà *m*	monte de piedad *m*
institute (E)	Institut *n*	—	institut *m*	istituto *m*	instituto *m*
institutional investors (E)	Kapitalsammelstelle *f*	—	organisme collecteur de fonds *m*	investitore istituzionale *m*	centro de acumulación de capitales *m*
institutional trustee (E)	Treuhandanstalt *f*	—	fiduciaire institué *m*	istituto fiduciario *m*	instituto fiduciario *m*
instituto de crédito (Es)	Kreditinstitut *n*	credit institution	établissement de crédit *m*	istituto di credito *m*	—
instituto de crédito inmobiliario (Es)	Bodenkreditinstitut *n*	mortgage bank	institut de crédit foncier *m*	banca di credito agrario *f*	—
instituto de crédito real (Es)	Realkreditinstitut *n*	real-estate credit institution	institut de crédit foncier *m*	istituto di credito immobiliare *m*	—
instituto fiduciario (Es)	Treuhandanstalt *f*	institutional trustee	fiduciaire institué *m*	istituto fiduciario *m*	—
instituto monetario (Es)	Geldinstitut *n*	financial institution	établissement financier *m*	istituto di credito *m*	—
instrument made out to order (E)	Orderpapier *n*	—	papier à ordre *m*	titolo all'ordine *m*	título a la orden *m*
instrumentos de financiación híbridos (Es)	hybride Finanzierungsinstrumente *n/pl*	hybrid financing instruments	instruments de financement hybrides *m/pl*	strumenti di finanziamento ibridi *m/pl*	—
instrumentos en materia de política de balances (Es)	bilanzpolitische Instrumente *n/pl*	instruments of balance sheet policy	instruments de la politique en matière de bilans *m/pl*	strumenti di politica del bilancio *m/pl*	—
instruments conferring title (E)	Forderungspapiere *n/pl*	—	titres de créance *m/pl*	titoli di credito *m/pl*	títulos de crédito *m/pl*
instruments de financement hybrides (F)	hybride Finanzierungsinstrumente *n/pl*	hybrid financing instruments	—	strumenti di finanziamento ibridi *m/pl*	instrumentos de financiación híbridos *m/pl*
instruments de la politique en matière de bilans (F)	bilanzpolitische Instrumente *n/pl*	instruments of balance sheet policy	—	strumenti di politica del bilancio *m/pl*	instrumentos en materia de política de balances *m/pl*
instruments of balance sheet policy (E)	bilanzpolitische Instrumente *n/pl*	—	instruments de la politique en matière de bilans *m/pl*	strumenti di politica del bilancio *m/pl*	instrumentos en materia de política de balances *m/pl*
instruments to order by law (E)	geborene Orderpapiere *n/pl*	—	titres à ordre par nature *m/pl*	titoli all'ordine per legge *m/pl*	valores a la orden por naturaleza *m/pl*
instruments to order by option (E)	gewillkürte Orderpapiere *n/pl*	—	titres à ordre par destination *m/pl*	titoli all'ordine non per legge *m/pl*	valores a la orden por elección *m/pl*
insuffisance de liquidité (F)	Unterliquidität *f*	lack of liquidity	—	liquidità insufficiente *f*	insuficiencia de liquidez *f*
insuficiencia de liquidez (Es)	Unterliquidität *f*	lack of liquidity	insuffisance de liquidité *f*	liquidità insufficiente *f*	—
insurance (E)	Versicherung *f*	—	assurance *f*	assicurazione *f*	seguro *m*
insurance company share (E)	Versicherungsaktie *f*	—	action d'une société d'assurance *f*	azione assicurativa *f*	acción de compañías de seguros *f*
insurance system (E)	Assekuranz *f*	—	assurance *f*	assicurazione *f*	seguro *m*
intangible assets (E)	immaterielle Werte *m/pl*	—	valeur des éléments incorporels *f*	valori immateriali *m/pl*	valores inmateriales *m/pl*
Interbankrate (D)	—	interbank rate	taux interbancaire *m*	tasso d'interesse interbancario *m*	tasa interbancaria *f*
interbank rate (E)	Interbankrate *f*	—	taux interbancaire *m*	tasso d'interesse interbancario *m*	tasa interbancaria *f*

	D	E	F	I	Es
intercambio de acceptaciones (Es)	Akzeptaustausch *m*	exchange of acceptances	échange d'acceptations *m*	scambio di accettazioni *m*	—
interconexión (Es)	Verbund *m*	union	union *f*	unione *f*	—
interdépendance (F)	Verschachtelung *f*	interlocking	—	partecipazione di società al capitale di altre società *f*	participación de una sociedad en el capital de otra *f*
interdépendance financière (F)	Finanzverflechtung *f*	financial interlocking	—	interferenza finanziaria *f*	vinculaciones financieras *f/pl*
interdipendenza internazionale dei prezzi (I)	internationaler Preiszusammenhang *m*	international price system	interrelation internationale en matière des prix *f*	—	vinculación de precios a nivel internacional *f*
interés (Es)	Zins *m*	interest	intérêt *m*	interesse *m*	—
interés (Es)	Verzinsung *f*	payment of interest	payement des intérêts *m*	tasso d'interesse *m*	—
interés a pagar (Es)	Passivzins *m*	interest payable	intérêt à payer par la banque *m*	interesse passivo *m*	—
interés compuesto (Es)	Zinseszins *m*	compound interest	intérêt composé *m*	anatocismo *m*	—
interés de equilibrio (Es)	Gleichgewichtszins *m*	equilibrium interest rate	intérêt équilibré *m*	interesse d'equilibrio *m*	—
interés del dinero (Es)	Geldzins *m*	interest on money	intérêt de l'argent prêté *m*	interesse del denaro *m*	—
interés efectivo (Es)	Effektivzins *m*	effective interest	intérêt effectif *m*	interesse effettivo *m*	—
interés efectivo (Es)	Effektivverzinsung *f*	effective interest yield	taux effectif *m*	reddito effettivo *m*	—
intereses acreedores (Es)	Habenzinsen *m/pl*	credit interest	intérêts créditeurs *m/pl*	interessi attivi *m/pl*	—
intereses bancarios (Es)	Bankzinsen *m/pl*	banking interest	intérêts bancaires *m/pl*	interessi bancari *m/pl*	—
intereses de capital ajeno (Es)	Fremdkapitalzins *m*	interest on borrowed capital	intérêt du capital prêté *m*	interessi per capitale di credito *m/pl*	—
intereses de cobertura (Es)	Deckungszinsen *m/pl*	coverage interest rate	intérêts de couverture *m/pl*	interessi di copertura *m/pl*	—
intereses de demora (Es)	Verzugszinsen *m/pl*	default interest	intérêts moratoires *m/pl*	interessi moratori *m/pl*	—
intereses de obligación permanente (Es)	Dauerschuldzinsen *m/pl*	interest on long-term debts	intérêts concernant une dette permanente *m*	interessi debitori permanenti *m/pl*	—
intereses deudores (Es)	Aktivzins *m*	interest receivable	intérêt demandé par la banque *m*	interessi attivi *m/pl*	—
intereses deudores (Es)	Sollzinsen *m/pl*	debtor interest rates	intérêts débiteurs *m/pl*	interessi passivi *m/pl*	—
intereses especiales (Es)	Sonderzinsen *m/pl*	special interest	intérêts spéciaux *m/pl*	saggio speciale di interesse *m*	—
intereses por fracción de período (Es)	Stückzinsen *m/pl*	broken period interest	intérêts courus *m/pl*	interessi maturati *m/pl*	—
intereses provisionales (Es)	Zwischenzinsen *m/pl*	interim interest	intérêts intermédiaires *m/pl*	interessi intercalari *m/pl*	—
interés fijo (Es)	Festzins *m*	fixed interest	intérêt fixe *m*	interesse fisso *m*	—
interés impuesto en el mercado (Es)	marktüblicher Zins *m*	interest rate customary in the market	intérêt pratiqué sur le marché *m*	tasso d'interesse corrente *m*	—
interés mínimo (Es)	Mindestzins *m*	minimum interest rate	intérêt minimum *m*	interesse minimo *m*	—
interés negativo (Es)	Negativzins *m*	negative interest	intérêt négatif *m*	interesse negativo *m*	—
interés negativo anticipado (Es)	Vorschußzinsen *m/pl*	negative advance interest	intérêts payés par anticipation *m/pl*	penalità interessi *f*	—
interés nominal (Es)	Nominalzins *m*	nominal rate of interest	intérêt nominal *m*	interesse nominale *m*	—
interés pagado en el mercado de capital (Es)	Kapitalmarktzins *m*	capital market interest rate	intérêt pratiqué sur le marché des capitaux *m*	tasso d'interesse del mercato finanziario *m*	—
interés punitivo (Es)	Strafzins *m*	penalty interest	intérêt punitif *m*	penalità *f*	—
interés real (Es)	Realzins *m*	real interest	rendement réel *m*	interesse reale *m*	—
interés retrasado (Es)	Zinsrückstand *m*	arrear on interests	intérêt arriéré *m*	interessi arretrati *m/pl*	—
interesse (I)	Leihzins *m*	interest rate on a loan	intérêt du capital prêté *m*	—	tipo de interés de un empréstito *m*

	D	E	F	I	Es
interesse (I)	Zins m	interest	intérêt m	—	interés m
interesse del capitale (I)	Kapitalzins m	interest on capital	intérêt du capital m	—	renta del capital f
interesse del denaro (I)	Geldzins m	interest on money	intérêt de l'argent prêté m	—	interés del dinero m
interesse d'equilibrio (I)	Gleichgewichtszins m	equilibrium interest rate	intérêt équilibré m	—	interés de equilibrio m
interesse di riferimento (I)	Eckzins m	basic rate of interest	taux d'intérêt de base m	—	tipo base m
interesse di riferimento per il risparmio (I)	Spareckzins m	basic savings rate	taux-clé d'intérêt bancaire sur les dépôts d'épargne m	—	tipo de referencia m
interesse effettivo (I)	Effektivzins m	effective interest	intérêt effectif m	—	interés efectivo m
interesse fisso (I)	Festzins m	fixed interest	intérêt fixe m	—	interés fijo m
interesse minimo (I)	Mindestzins m	minimum interest rate	intérêt minimum m	—	interés mínimo m
interesse negativo (I)	Negativzins m	negative interest	intérêt négatif m	—	interés negativo m
Interessen-gemeinschaft (D)	—	pooling of interests	communauté d'intérêts f	comunione d'interessi f	comunidad de intereses f
interesse nominale (I)	Nominalzins m	nominal rate of interest	intérêt nominal m	—	interés nominal m
Interessenwert (D)	—	vested interest stock	action qui fait l'objet d'un achat par un groupe intéressé f	titolo primario m	valor de interés m
interesse passivo (I)	Passivzins m	interest payable	intérêt à payer par la banque m	—	interés a pagar m
interesse reale (I)	Realzins m	real interest	rendement réel m	—	interés real m
interesse su debiti (I)	Schuldzins m	interest on debts	intérêt à payer m	—	interés sobre depósitos m
interesse usurario (I)	Zinswucher m	usury	usure en matière de prêt à intérêt f	—	interés usurario m
interesse variabile (I)	variabler Zins m	variable rate of interest	intérêt variable m	—	interés variable m
interessi arretrati (I)	Zinsrückstand m	arrear on interests	intérêt arriéré m	—	interés retrasado m
interessi attivi (I)	Habenzinsen m/pl	credit interest	intérêts créditeurs m/pl	—	intereses acreedores m/pl
interessi attivi (I)	Aktivzins m	interest receivable	intérêt demandé par la banque m	—	intereses deudores m/pl
interessi bancari (I)	Bankzinsen m/pl	banking interest	intérêts bancaires m/pl	—	intereses bancarios m/pl
interessi debitori permanenti (I)	Dauerschuldzinsen m/pl	interest on long-term debts	intérêts concernant une dette permanente m/pl	—	intereses de obligación permanente m/pl
interessi di copertura (I)	Deckungszinsen m/pl	coverage interest rate	intérêts de couverture m/pl	—	intereses de cobertura m/pl
interessi intercalari (I)	Zwischenzinsen m/pl	interim interest	intérêts intermédiaires m/pl	—	intereses provisionales m/pl
interessi intercalari (I)	Bauzinsen m/pl	fixed-interest coupons	coupons d'intérêt fixe m/pl	—	cupones de interés fijo m/pl
interessi maturati (I)	Stückzinsen m/pl	broken period interest	intérêts courus m/pl	—	intereses por fracción de período m/pl
interessi moratori (I)	Verzugszinsen m/pl	default interest	intérêts moratoires m/pl	—	intereses de demora m/pl
interessi passivi (I)	Sollzinsen m/pl	debtor interest rates	intérêts débiteurs m/pl	—	intereses deudores m/pl
interessi per capitale di credito (I)	Fremdkapitalzins m	interest on borrowed capital	intérêt du capital prêté m	—	intereses de capital ajeno m/pl
interés sobre depósitos (Es)	Schuldzins m	interest on debts	intérêt à payer m	interessi su debiti m/pl	—
interest (E)	Zins m	—	intérêt m	interesse m	interés m
interest elasticity (E)	Zinselastizität f	—	élasticité des intérêts f	elasticità degli interessi f	elasticidad de los intereses f
interest margin (E)	Zinsmarge f	—	marge entre les taux d'intérêt créditeur et débiteur f	margine d'interesse m	margen de interés m

	D	E	F	I	Es
interest margin (E)	Zinsspanne *f*	—	marge entre les taux d'intérêt créditeur et débiteur *f*	margine d'interesse *m*	margen de beneficio por intereses *m*
interest on borrowed capital (E)	Fremdkapitalzins *m*	—	intérêt du capital prêté *m*	interessi per capitale di credito *m/pl*	intereses de capital ajeno *m/pl*
interest on capital (E)	Kapitalzins *m*	—	intérêt du capital *m*	interesse del capitale *m*	renta del capital *f*
interest on debts (E)	Schuldzins *m*	—	intérêt à payer *m*	interesse su debiti *m*	interés sobre depósitos *m*
interest on long-term debts (E)	Dauerschuldzinsen *m/pl*	—	intérêts concernant une dette permanente *m/pl*	interessi debitori permanenti *m/pl*	intereses de obligación permanente *m/pl*
interest on money (E)	Geldzins *m*	—	intérêt de l'argent prêté *m*	interesse del denaro *m*	interés del dinero *m*
interest parity (E)	Zinsparität *f*	—	parité des intérêts *f*	parità dei tassi d'interesse *f*	paridad del interés *f*
interest payable (E)	Passivzins *m*	—	intérêt à payer par la banque *m*	interesse passivo *m*	interés a pagar *m*
interest payment date (E)	Zinstermin *m*	—	délai de payement de l'intérêt *m*	data di godimento *f*	vencimiento de intereses *m*
interest rate (E)	Zinssatz *m*	—	taux d'intérêt *m*	tasso d'interesse *m*	tipo de interés *m*
interest rate arbitrage (E)	Zinsarbitrage *f*	—	arbitrage sur les taux de l'intérêt *m*	arbitraggio sui tassi d'interesse *m*	arbitraje en materia de tipos de interés *m*
interest rate control (E)	Zinsbindung *f*	—	engagement sur le taux d'intérêt accordé *m*	prescrizione sui tassi *f*	vinculación al tipo de interés pactado *m*
interest rate customary in the market (E)	marktüblicher Zins *m*	—	intérêt pratiqué sur le marché *m*	tasso d'interesse corrente *m*	interés impuesto en el mercado *m*
Interest Rate Future (D)	—	interest rate future	interest rate future *m*	interest rate future *m*	término de tipo de interés *m*
interest rate future (E)	Interest Rate Future *m*	—	interest rate future *m*	interest rate future *m*	término de tipo de interés *m*
interest rate future (F)	Interest Rate Future *m*	interest rate future	—	interest rate future *m*	término de tipo de interés *m*
interest rate future (I)	Interest Rate Future *m*	interest rate future	interest rate future *m*	—	término de tipo de interés *m*
interest rate level (E)	Zinsniveau *n*	—	niveau du taux d'intérêt *m*	livello degli interessi *m*	nivel de los tipos de interés *m*
interest rate on a loan (E)	Leihzins *m*	—	intérêt du capital prêté *m*	interesse *m*	tipo de interés de un empréstito *m*
interest rate policy (E)	Zinspolitik *f*	—	politique en matière d'intérêts *f*	politica degli interessi *f*	política de intereses *f*
interest rate structure (E)	Zinsstruktur *f*	—	structure des intérêts *f*	struttura degli interessi *f*	estructura de los intereses *f*
interest rate swap (E)	Zinsswap *m*	—	swap d'intérêts *m*	interest swap *m*	swap de intereses *m*
interest rate table (E)	Zinsstaffel *f*	—	barème des intérêts *m*	scaletta *f*	escala de intereses *f*
interest receivable (E)	Aktivzins *m*	—	intérêt demandé par la banque *m*	interessi attivi *m/pl*	intereses deudores *m/pl*
interest service (E)	Zinsendienst *m*	—	service de l'intérêt *m*	servizio degli interessi *m*	servicio del interés *m*
interest surplus (E)	Zinsüberschuß *m*	—	excédent d'intérêts *m*	eccedenza degli interessi *f*	excedente de interés *m*
interest swap (I)	Zinsswap *m*	interest rate swap	swap d'intérêts *m*	—	swap de intereses *m*
interés usurario (Es)	Zinswucher *m*	usury	usure en matière de prêt à intérêt *f*	interesse usurario *m*	—
interés variable (Es)	variabler Zins *m*	variable rate of interest	intérêt variable *m*	interesse variabile *m*	—
intérêt (F)	Zins *m*	interest	—	interesse *m*	interés *m*
intérêt à payer (F)	Schuldzins *m*	interest on debts	—	interesse su debiti *m*	interés sobre depósitos *m*
intérêt à payer par la banque (F)	Passivzins *m*	interest payable	—	interesse passivo *m*	interés a pagar *m*
intérêt arriéré (F)	Zinsrückstand *m*	arrear on interests	—	interessi arretrati *m/pl*	interés retrasado *m*

	D	E	F	I	Es
intérêt composé (F)	Zinseszins m	compound interest	—	anatocismo m	interés compuesto m
intérêt de l'argent prêté (F)	Geldzins m	interest on money	—	interesse del denaro m	interés del dinero m
intérêt demandé par la banque (F)	Aktivzins m	interest receivable	—	interessi attivi m/pl	intereses deudores m/pl
intérêt du capital (F)	Kapitalzins m	interest on capital	—	interesse del capitale m	renta del capital f
intérêt du capital prêté (F)	Fremdkapitalzins m	interest on borrowed capital	—	interessi per capitale di credito m/pl	intereses de capital ajeno m/pl
intérêt du capital prêté (F)	Leihzins m	interest rate on a loan	—	interesse m	tipo de interés de un empréstito m
intérêt effectif (F)	Effektivzins m	effective interest	—	interesse effettivo m	interés efectivo m
intérêt équilibré (F)	Gleichgewichtszins m	equilibrium interest rate	—	interesse d'equilibrio m	interés de equilibrio m
intérêt fixe (F)	Festzins m	fixed interest	—	interesse fisso m	interés fijo m
intérêt minimum (F)	Mindestzins m	minimum interest rate	—	interesse minimo m	interés mínimo m
intérêt négatif (F)	Negativzins m	negative interest	—	interesse negativo m	interés negativo m
intérêt nominal (F)	Nominalzins m	nominal rate of interest	—	interesse nominale m	interés nominal m
intérêt pratiqué sur le marché (F)	marktüblicher Zins m	interest rate customary in the market	—	tasso d'interesse corrente m	interés impuesto en el mercado m
intérêt pratiqué sur le marché des capitaux (F)	Kapitalmarktzins m	capital market interest rate	—	tasso d'interesse del mercato finanziario m	interés pagado en el mercado de capital m
intérêt punitif (F)	Strafzins m	penalty interest	—	penalità f	interés punitivo m
intérêts bancaires (F)	Bankzinsen m/pl	banking interest	—	interessi bancari m/pl	intereses bancarios m/pl
intérêts concernant une dette permanete (F)	Dauerschuldzinsen m/pl	interest on long-term debts	—	interessi debitori permanenti m/pl	intereses de obligación permanente m/pl
intérêts courus (F)	Stückzinsen m/pl	broken period interest	—	interessi maturati m/pl	intereses por fracción de período m/pl
intérêts créditeurs (F)	Habenzinsen m/pl	credit interest	—	interessi attivi m/pl	intereses acreedores m/pl
intérêts débiteurs (F)	Sollzinsen m/pl	debtor interest rates	—	interessi passivi m/pl	intereses deudores m/pl
intérêts de couverture (F)	Deckungszinsen m/pl	coverage interest rate	—	interessi di copertura m/pl	intereses de cobertura m/pl
intérêts intermédiaires (F)	Zwischenzinsen m/pl	interim interest	—	interessi intercalari m/pl	intereses provisionales m/pl
intérêts moratoires (F)	Verzugszinsen m/pl	default interest	—	interessi moratori m/pl	intereses de demora m/pl
intérêts payés par anticipation (F)	Vorschußzinsen m/pl	negative advance interest	—	penalità interessi f	interés negativo anticipado m
intérêts perçus (F)	Zinsertrag m	income from interests	—	provento d'interessi m	rédito m
intérêts spéciaux (F)	Sonderzinsen m/pl	special interest	—	saggio speciale di interesse m	intereses especiales m/pl
intérêt variable (F)	variabler Zins m	variable rate of interest	—	interesse variabile m	interés variable m
interferenza finanziaria (I)	Finanzverflechtung f	financial interlocking	interdépendance financière f	—	vinculaciones financieras f/pl
interim balance sheet (E)	Zwischenbilanz f	—	bilan intermédiaire m	bilancio intermedio m	balance intermedio m
interim financing (E)	Zwischenfinanzierung f	—	financement intermédiaire m	finanziamento transitorio m	financiación interina f
interim interest (E)	Zwischenzinsen m/pl	—	intérêts intermédiaires m/pl	interessi intercalari m/pl	intereses provisionales m/pl
interim loan (E)	Zwischenkredit m	—	crédit intermédiare m	credito transitorio m	crédito interino m
interim shareholder (E)	Zwischenaktionär m	—	actionnaire intermédiaire m	azionista non permanente m	accionista intermedio m
interlocking (E)	Verschachtelung f	—	interdépendance f	partecipazione di società al capitale di altre società f	participación de una sociedad en el capital de otra f

	D	E	F	I	Es
intermédiaire de crédits à moyen et à long terme (F)	Finanzmakler *m*	money broker	—	mediatore finanziario *m*	intermediario financiero *m*
intermediario financiero (Es)	Finanzmakler *m*	money broker	intermédiaire de crédits à moyen et à long terme *m*	mediatore finanziario *m*	—
intermediario finanziario (I)	Kreditvermittler *f*	money broker	agent financier *m*	—	operador de negociación de créditos *m*
intermediate broker (E)	Untermakler *m*	—	sous-agent *m*	commissionario *m*	subagente *m*
internal financing (E)	Innenfinanzierung *f*	—	financement interne *m*	finanziamento interno *m*	financiación interna *f*
internal interest rate (E)	interner Zinsfuß *m*	—	taux d'intérêt interne *m*	saggio di rendimento interno *m*	tipo de interés interno *m*
internal syndicate (E)	Innenkonsortium *n*	—	consortium intérieur *m*	consorzio interno *m*	consorcio interior *m*
international capital transactions (E)	internationaler Kapitalverkehr *m*	—	mouvement international des capitaux *m*	circolazione di capitali internazionale *f*	movimiento de capitales internacional *m*
international cash position (E)	internationale Liquidität *f*	—	liquidité internationale *f*	liquidità internazionale *f*	liquidez internacional *f*
international credit markets (E)	internationale Kreditmärkte *m/pl*	—	marchés internationaux de crédit *m/pl*	mercati creditizi internazionali *m/pl*	mercados de créditos internacionales *m/pl*
internationale Kreditmärkte (D)	—	international credit markets	marchés internationaux de crédit *m/pl*	mercati creditizi internazionali *m/pl*	mercados de créditos internacionales *m/pl*
internationale Liquidität (D)	—	international cash position	liquidité internationale *f*	liquidità internazionale *f*	liquidez internacional *f*
internationaler Kapitalverkehr (D)	—	international capital transactions	mouvement international des capitaux *m*	circolazione di capitali internazionale	movimiento de capitales internacional *m*
internationaler Preiszusammenhang (D)	—	international price system	interrelation internationale en matière des prix *f*	interdipendenza internazionale dei prezzi *f*	vinculación de precios a nivel internacional *f*
Internationale Vereinigung der Wertpapierbörsen (D)	—	International Federation of Stock Exchanges	Association internationale des bourses de titres et valeurs mobilières *f*	Associazione internazionale delle borse valori *f*	Asociación Internacional de las Bolsas de Valores *f*
International Federation of Stock Exchanges (E)	Internationale Vereinigung der Wertpapierbörsen *f*	—	Association internationale des bourses de titres et valeurs mobilières *f*	Associazione internazionale delle borse valori *f*	Asociación Internacional de las Bolsas de Valores *f*
international price system (E)	internationaler Preiszusammenhang *m*	—	interrelation internationale en matière des prix *f*	interdipendenza internazionale dei prezzi *f*	vinculación de precios a nivel internacional *f*
interner Zinsfuß (D)	—	internal interest rate	taux d'intérêt interne *m*	saggio di rendimento interno *m*	tipo de interés interno *m*
interrelation internationale en matière des prix (F)	internationaler Preiszusammenhang *m*	international price system	—	interdipendenza internazionale dei prezzi *f*	vinculación de precios a nivel internacional *f*
intervención cambiaria (Es)	Kursintervention *f*	price intervention	intervention en matière des cours *f*	intervento di sostegno quotazioni *m*	—
intervención en el mercado de divisas (Es)	Devisenmarktinterventionen *f/pl*	exchange market intervention	intervention dans le marché des devises *f*	interventi sul mercato dei cambi *m/pl*	—
intervención financiera (Es)	Kapitalbeteiligung *f*	equity participation	participation par apport de capital *f*	partecipazione al capitale *f*	—
intervention dans le marché des devises (F)	Devisenmarktinterventionen *f/pl*	exchange market intervention	—	interventi sul mercato dei cambi *m/pl*	intervención en el mercado de divisas *f*
intervention d'un tiers dans une affaire de compensation (F)	Fremdkompensation *f*	offset transaction with resale to a third party	—	compensazione per conto altrui *f*	compensación ajena *f*
intervention en matière des cours (F)	Kursintervention *f*	price intervention	—	intervento di sostegno quotazioni *m*	intervención cambiaria *f*
intervention point (E)	Interventionspunkte *m/pl*	—	points d'intervention *m/pl*	punti d'intervento *m/pl*	puntos de intervención *m/pl*
Interventionspflicht (D)	—	obligation to intervene	obligation d'intervention *f*	obbligo all'intervento *m*	obligación de intervención *f*

	D	E	F	I	Es
Interventionspunkte (D)	—	intervention point	points d'intervention *m/pl*	punti d'intervento *m/pl*	puntos de intervención *m/pl*
interventi sul mercato dei cambi (I)	Devisenmarkt-interventionen *f/pl*	exchange market intervention	intervention dans le marché des devises *f*	—	intervención en el mercado de divisas *f*
intervento di sostegno quotazioni (I)	Kursintervention *f*	price intervention	intervention en matière des cours *f*	—	intervención cambiaria *f*
in the year (E)	Anno *n*	—	en l'année	anno *m*	en el año
in total (F)	unter dem Strich	—	au total	fuori bilancio	en total
intrinsic value (E)	innerer Wert *m*	—	valeur intrinsèque *f*	valore intrinseco *m*	valor intrínseco *m*
introductory price (E)	Einführungskurs *m*	—	cours d'ouverture *m*	prima quotazione *f*	cotización de apertura *f*
inventaire (F)	Bestand *m*	stocks	—	inventario *m*	inventario *m*
inventaire (F)	Inventar *n*	inventory	—	inventario *m*	inventario *m*
inventaire mouvementé (F)	Skontration *f*	settlement of time bargains	—	compensazione *f*	compensación de cuentas *f*
Inventar (D)	—	inventory	inventaire *m*	inventario *m*	inventario *m*
inventario (Es)	Bestand *m*	stocks	inventaire *m*	inventario *m*	—
inventario (Es)	Inventar *n*	inventory	inventaire *m*	inventario *m*	—
inventario (I)	Bestand *m*	stocks	inventaire *m*	—	inventario *m*
inventario (I)	Inventar *n*	inventory	inventaire *m*	—	inventario *m*
Inventarwert (D)	—	inventory value	valeur de l'inventaire *f*	valore d'inventario *m*	valor del inventario *m*
inventory (E)	Inventar *n*	—	inventaire *m*	inventario *m*	inventario *m*
inventory change (E)	Bestandsveränderung *f*	—	variation des existences *f*	movimento di scorte *m*	variaciones de las partidas *f/pl*
inventory value (E)	Inventarwert *m*	—	valeur de l'inventaire *f*	valore d'inventario *m*	valor del inventario *m*
inverse interest rate structure (E)	inverse Zinsstruktur *f*	—	structure inverse des intérêts *f*	struttura degli interessi inversa *f*	estructura de interés inversa *f*
inverse Zinsstruktur (D)	—	inverse interest rate structure	structure inverse des intérêts *f*	struttura degli interessi inversa *f*	estructura de interés inversa *f*
inversión (Es)	Anlage *f*	investment	investissement *m*	investimento *m*	—
inversión (Es)	Geldanlage *f*	investment	placement d'argent *m*	investimento di denaro *m*	—
inversión (Es)	Investition *f*	investment	investissement *m*	investimento *m*	—
inversión de ajuste (Es)	Anpassungs-investition *f*	adjustment project	investissement d'ajustement *m*	investimento di aggiornamento *m*	—
inversión de ampliación (Es)	Erweiterungs-investition *f*	expansion investment	investissement d'expansion *m*	investimento d'ampliamento *m*	—
inversión de capital (Es)	Kapitalanlage *f*	capital investment	investissement de capitaux *m*	impiego di capitale *m*	—
inversión de capital (Es)	Vermögensanlage *f*	investment	investissement de capital *m*	investimento patrimoniale *m*	—
inversión de capitales extranjeros (Es)	Fremdinvestition *f*	external investment	investissement de capitaux étrangers *m*	investimento in imprese altrui *m*	—
inversión de fondos (Es)	Fondsanlagen *f/pl*	trust investment	placements en fonds *m/pl*	investimenti di fondo d'investimento *m/pl*	—
inversión de reposición (Es)	Ersatzinvestition *f*	replacement of capital assets	investissement pour remplacmenet des moyens de production *m*	investimento sostitutivo *m*	—
inversión en valores (Es)	Wertpapieranlage *f*	investment in securities	placement en valeurs mobilières *m*	investimento in titoli *m*	—
inversiones directas (Es)	Direktinvestitionen *f/pl*	direct investments	investissements directs *m/pl*	investimenti diretti *m/pl*	—
inversiones financieras (Es)	Finanzanlage-vermögen *n*	financial assets	valeurs immobilisées financières *f/pl*	investimenti finanziari *m/pl*	—
inversión exterior (Es)	Auslandsinvestition *f*	foreign investment	investissement à l'étranger *m*	investimento estero *m*	—
inversión indirecta (Es)	indirekte Investition *f*	portfolio investments	investissement indirect *m*	investimento indiretto *m*	—
inversión neta (Es)	Nettoinvestition *f*	net investment	investissement net *m*	investimento netto *m*	—
inversor (Es)	Investor *m*	investor	investisseur *m*	investitore *m*	—

	D	E	F	I	Es
invested capital (E)	investiertes Kapital *n*	—	capital investi *m*	capitale investito *m*	capital invertido *m*
invested wages (E)	Investivlohn *m*	—	fraction du revenu du travail disponible pour placements à long terme *f*	risparmio contrattuale *m*	salario de inversión *m*
investiertes Kapital (D)	—	invested capital	capital investi *m*	capitale investito *m*	capital invertido *m*
investigación de crédito y solvencia de un cliente (Es)	Kreditprüfung *f*	credit status investigation	enquête sur la solvabilité *f*	controllo dei crediti *m*	—
investigación del mercado de capital (Es)	Kapitalmarkt-forschung *f*	capital market research	étude du marché des capitaux *f*	ricerca del mercato finanziario *f*	—
investigación económica empírica (Es)	empirische Wirtschaftsforschung *f*	empirical economic research	études économiques empiriques *f/pl*	ricerca economica empirica *f*	—
investigation by the tax authorities (E)	Betriebsprüfung *f*	—	vérification des livres de l'entreprise *f*	revisione aziendale *f*	revisión *f*
investimenti di fondo d'investimento (I)	Fondsanlagen *f/pl*	trust investment	placements en fonds *m/pl*	—	inversión de fondos *f*
investimenti diretti (I)	Direktinvestitionen *f/pl*	direct investments	investissements directs *m/pl*	—	inversiones directas *f/pl*
investimenti finanziari (I)	Finanzanlage-vermögen *n*	financial assets	valeurs immobilisées financières *f/pl*	—	inversiones financieras *f/pl*
investimento (I)	Anlage *f*	investment	investissement *m*	—	inversión *f*
investimento (I)	Investitionsobjekt *n*	object of capital expenditure	objet d'investissement *m*	—	objeto de inversión *m*
investimento (I)	Investition *f*	investment	investissement *m*	—	inversión *f*
investimento d'ampliamento (I)	Erweiterungs-investition *f*	expansion investment	investissement d'expansion *m*	—	inversión de ampliación *f*
investimento di aggiornamento (I)	Anpassungs-investition *f*	adjustment project	investissement d'ajustement *m*	—	inversión de ajuste *f*
investimento di denaro (I)	Geldanlage *f*	investment	placement d'argent *m*	—	inversión *f*
investimento estero (I)	Auslandsinvestition *f*	foreign investment	investissement à l'étranger *m*	—	inversión exterior *f*
investimento indiretto (I)	indirekte Investition *f*	portfolio investments	investissement indirect *m*	—	inversión indirecta *f*
investimento in imprese altrui (I)	Fremdinvestition *f*	external investment	investissement de capitaux étrangers *m*	—	inversión de capitales extranjeros *f*
investimento in titoli (I)	Wertpapieranlage *f*	investment in securities	placement en valeurs mobilières *m*	—	inversión en valores *f*
investimento netto (I)	Nettoinvestition *f*	net investment	investissement net *m*	—	inversión neta *f*
investimento patrimoniale (I)	Vermögensanlage *f*	investment	investissement de capital *m*	—	inversión de capital *f*
investimento sostitutivo (I)	Ersatzinvestition *f*	replacement of capital assets	investissement pour remplacment des moyens de production *m*		inversión de reposición *f*
investissement (F)	Investition *f*	investment	—	investimento *m*	inversión *f*
investissement (F)	Anlage *f*	investment	—	investimento *m*	inversión *f*
investissement à l'étranger (F)	Auslandsinvestition *f*	foreign investment	—	investimento estero *m*	inversión exterior *f*
investissement d'ajustement (F)	Anpassungs-investition *f*	adjustment project	—	investimento di aggiornamento *m*	inversión de ajuste *f*
investissement de capital (F)	Vermögensanlage *f*	investment	—	investimento patrimoniale *m*	inversión de capital *f*
investissement de capitaux (F)	Kapitalanlage *f*	capital investment	—	impiego di capitale *m*	inversión de capital *f*
investissement de capitaux étrangers (F)	Fremdinvestition *f*	external investment	—	investimento in imprese altrui *m*	inversión de capitales extranjeros *f*
investissement d'expansion (F)	Erweiterungs-investition *f*	expansion investment	—	investimento d'ampliamento *m*	inversión de ampliación *f*
investissement financier net (F)	Finanzierungssaldo *m*	net financial investment	—	saldo di finanziamento *m*	saldo de financiación *m*
investissement indirect (F)	indirekte Investition *f*	portfolio investments	—	investimento indiretto *m*	inversión indirecta *f*

	D	E	F	I	Es
investissement net (F)	Nettoinvestition f	net investment	—	investimento netto m	inversión neta f
investissement pour remplacement des moyens de production (F)	Ersatzinvestition f	replacement of capital assets	—	investimento sostitutivo m	inversión de reposición f
investissements directs (F)	Direktinvestitionen f/pl	direct investments	—	investimenti diretti m/pl	inversiones directas f/pl
investisseur (F)	Investor m	investor	—	investitore m	inversor m
Investition (D)	—	investment	investissement m	investimento m	inversión f
Investitionsförderung (D)	—	investment promotion	promotion de l'investissement f	promozione degli investimenti f	incentivos a la inversión m
Investitionshilfe (D)	—	investment assistance	subvention en faveur des investissements f	aiuti agli investimenti m/pl	ayuda de inversión f
Investitionskennzahl (D)	—	investment index	coefficient d'investissement m	indice di investimento m	índice de inversión m
Investitionskredit (D)	—	investment credit	crédit d'investissement m	credito d'investimento m	crédito de inversión m
Investitionskreditversicherung (D)	—	investment credit insurance	assurance de crédits d'investissement f	assicurazione credito d'investimento f	seguro de crédito de inversión f
Investitionsobjekt (D)	—	object of capital expenditure	objet d'investissement m	investimento m	objeto de inversión m
Investitionsplan (D)	—	investment scheme	plan des investissements m	piano d'investimento m	plan de inversión m
Investitionsrechnung (D)	—	investment appraisal	calcul des investissements m	calcolo d'investimento m	cálculo de inversiones m
Investitionsrisiko (D)	—	business risk	risque d'investissement m	rischio d'investimento m	riesgo de inversión m
Investitionsschutz (D)	—	protection of investment	protection de l'investisseur f	tutela degli investimenti f	protección del inversor f
Investitionsverbot (D)	—	prohibition of investment	prohibition d'investissement f	divieto d'investimento m	prohibición de inversión f
Investitionszulage (D)	—	investment grant	prime d'investissement f	premio d'investimento m	prima a la inversión f
investitore (I)	Investor m	investor	investisseur m	—	inversor m
investitore istituzionale (I)	Kapitalsammelstelle f	institutional investors	organisme collecteur de fonds m	—	centro de acumulación de capitales m
Investivlohn (D)	—	invested wages	fraction du revenu du travail disponible pour placements à long terme f	risparmio contrattuale m	salario de inversión m
investment (E)	Anlage f	—	investissement m	investimento m	inversión f
investment (E)	Vermögensanlage f	—	investissement de capital m	investimento patrimoniale m	inversión de capital f
investment (E)	Geldanlage f	—	placement d'argent m	investimento di denaro m	inversión f
investment (E)	Investition f	—	investissement m	investimento m	inversión f
investment accounts (E)	Anlagekonten n/pl	—	comptes d'investissement m/pl	conti degli investimenti m/pl	cuentas de inversión f/pl
investment advisor (E)	Vermögensberater m	—	conseiller en investissement m	consulente patrimoniale m	asesor en materia de inversiones m
Investmentanteil (D)	—	investment share	part de fonds d'investissement f	quota di fondo d'investimento f	participación en fondos de inversión mobiliaria f
investment appraisal (E)	Investitionsrechnung f	—	calcul des investissements m	calcolo d'investimento m	cálculo de inversiones m
investment assistance (E)	Investitionshilfe f	—	subvention en faveur des investissements f	aiuti agli investimenti m/pl	ayuda de inversión f
investment capital (E)	Anlagekapital n	—	capital d'investissement m	capitale d'investimento m	capital de inversión m
investment committee (E)	Anlageausschuß m	—	comité d'investissements m	comitato consulenza investimenti m	comité de inversión m
investment company (E)	Investmentgesellschaft f	—	société d'investissement f	società d'investimento f	sociedad de inversiones f
investment counseling (E)	Anlageberatung f	—	orientation en matière de placement f	consulenza in investimenti f	asesoramiento en materia de inversiones m

	D	E	F	I	Es
investment credit (E)	Investitionskredit *m*	—	crédit d'investissement *m*	credito d'investimento *m*	crédito de inversión *m*
investment credit insurance (E)	Investitionskredit-versicherung *f*	—	assurance de crédits d'investissement *f*	assicurazione credito d'investimento *f*	seguro de crédito de inversión *m*
Investmentfonds (D)	—	investment fund	fonds de placement *m*	fondo d'investimento *m*	fondo de inversión mobiliaria *m*
investment fund (E)	Investmentfonds *m*	—	fonds de placement *m*	fondo d'investimento *m*	fondo de inversión mobiliaria *m*
investment fund certificates (E)	Investmentzertifikate *n/pl*	—	parts de fonds d'investissement *f/pl*	certificato d'investimento *m*	certificado de inversión *m*
Investment-gesellschaft (D)	—	investment company	société d'investissement *f*	società d'investimento *f*	sociedad de inversiones *f*
investment grant (E)	Investitionszulage *f*	—	prime d'investissement *f*	premio d'investimento *m*	prima a la inversión *f*
investment index (E)	Investitionskennzahl *f*	—	coefficient d'investissement *m*	indice di investimento *m*	índice de inversión *m*
investment in kind (E)	Sacheinlage *f*	—	apport en nature *m*	apporto in natura *m*	aportación en especie *f*
investment in securities (E)	Wertpapieranlage *f*	—	placement en valeurs mobilières *m*	investimento in titoli *m*	inversión en valores *f*
investment program (E)	Programm-gesellschaft *f*	—	société de programmes d'investissement *f*	società con programmi d'investimento *f*	sociedad de programa de inversión *f*
investment promotion (E)	Investitions-förderung *f*	—	promotion de l'investissement *f*	promozione degli investimenti *f*	incentivos a la inversión *m*
investment risk (E)	Anlagewagnis *n*	—	risque de l'investisseur *m*	rischio d'investimento *m*	riesgo del inversor *m*
investment scheme (E)	Investitionsplan *m*	—	plan des investissements *m*	piano d'investimento *m*	plan de inversión *m*
investment securities (E)	Anlagepapiere *n/pl*	—	valeurs de placement *f/pl*	titoli d'investimento *m/pl*	valores de inversión *m/pl*
investment share (E)	Investmentanteil *m*	—	part de fonds d'investissement *f*	quota di fondo d'investimento *f*	participación en fondos de inversión mobiliaria *f*
Investment-zertifikate (D)	—	investment fund certificates	parts de fonds d'investissement *f/pl*	certificato d'investimento *m*	certificado de inversión *m*
Investor (D)	—	investor	investisseur *m*	investitore *m*	inversor *m*
investor (E)	Investor *m*	—	investisseur *m*	investitore *m*	inversor *m*
invisible hand (E)	Ausgleichsfunktion des Preises *f*	—	main invisible *f*	meccanismo dei prezzi *m*	mano invisible *f*
invitation to tender (E)	Ausschreibung *f*	—	soumission *f*	appalto *m*	subasta *f*
inyección de crédito (Es)	Kreditspritze *f*	injection of credit	injection de crédit *f*	iniezione di credito *f*	—
iperinflazione (I)	Hyperinflation *f*	hyperinflation	hyperinflation *f*	—	hiperinflación *f*
ipoteca (I)	Hypothek *f*	mortgage	hypothèque *f*	—	hipoteca *f*
ipoteca ad interesse fisso (I)	Festzinshypothek *f*	fixed-rate mortgage	hypothèque à intérêt fixe *f*	—	hipoteca de interés fijo *f*
ipoteca a favore del proprietario (I)	Eigentümer-Hypothek *f*	mortgage for the benefit of the owner	hypothèque revenant au propriétaire du fonds grevé *f*	—	hipoteca de propietario *f*
ipoteca a favore di terzi (I)	Fremdhypothek *f*	third party mortgage	hypothèque constituée au profit d'un tiers *f*	—	hipoteca ajena *f*
ipoteca ammortizzabile (I)	Tilgungshypothek *f*	amortizable mortgage loan	hypothèque garantissant une créance rem-boursable à termes périodiques *f*	—	hipoteca amortizable *f*
ipoteca ammortizzabile (I)	Amortisations-hypothek *f*	instalment mortgage	hypothèque amortissable *f*	—	hipoteca de amortización *f*
ipoteca a scadenza determinata (I)	Fälligkeitshypothek *f*	fixed-date land mortgage	hypothèque constituée sur la base d'un rem-boursement du capital à terme fixe sans dénonciation préalable *f*	—	hipoteca de vencimiento *f*

	D	E	F	I	Es
ipoteca di garanzia (I)	Sicherungshypothek *f*	cautionary mortgage	hypothèque constituée dans le but de garantir une créance *f*	—	hipoteca de seguridad *f*
ipoteca di pagamento a rate (I)	Abzahlungshypothek *f*	instalment mortgage	hypothèque réductible *f*	—	hipoteca a plazos *f*
ipoteca generale (I)	Gesamthypothek *f*	general mortgage	hypothèque solidaire *f*	—	hipoteca solidaria *f*
ipoteca iscritta (I)	Buchhypothek *f*	uncertificated mortgage	hypothèque inscrite au livre foncier *f*	—	hipoteca de registro *f*
ipoteca navale (I)	Schiffshypothek *f*	ship mortgage	hypothèque maritime *f*	—	hipoteca naval *f*
ipoteca negativa (I)	Negativhypothek *f*	borrower's undertaking to create no new charge ranking ahead of lender	hypothèque négative *f*	—	hipoteca negativa *f*
ipotecare (I)	beleihen	to lend money on something	nantir	—	pignorar
ipoteca rimborsabile dopo preavviso (I)	Kündigungshypothek *f*	mortgage loan repayable after having been duly called	hypothèque garantissant une dette remboursable avec préavis *f*	—	hipoteca con preaviso *f*
ipoteca su prestiti (I)	Darlehenshypothek *f*	mortgage as security for a loan	hypothèque de sûreté constituée pour garantir un prêt *f*	—	préstamo hipotecario *m*
ipoteca su una nuova costruzione (I)	Neubauhypothek *f*	mortgage loan to finance building of new dwelling-house	hypothèque pour financer la construction de logements neufs *f*	—	hipoteca para la construcción de nuevas viviendas *f*
iron and steel producing industry (E)	eisenschaffende Industrie *f*	—	sidérurgie *f*	industria siderurgica *f*	industria metalúrgica *f*
iron exchange (E)	Eisenbörse *f*	—	bourse de fer *f*	borsa del ferro *f*	bolsa de hierro *f*
iscrizione nel registro commerciale (I)	Eintragung im Handelsregister *f*	registration in the Commercial Register	inscription au registre du commerce *f*	—	inscripción en el registro comercial *f*
ispettorato (I)	Aufsichtsamt *n*	control board	office de surveillance *m*	—	oficina de inspección *f*
ispezione bancaria (I)	Bankrevision *f*	bank audit	contrôle du bilan d'une banque *m*	—	censura de cuentas del banco *f*
ispezione contabile (I)	Buchprüfung *f*	auditing	vérification des livres *f*	—	revisión contable *f*
issue (E)	Begebung *f*	—	émission *f*	emissione *f*	emisión *f*
issue at par (E)	Pariemission *f*	—	émission au pair *f*	emissione alla pari *f*	emisión a la par *f*
issue below par (E)	Unter-Pari-Emission *f*	—	émission au-dessous du pair *f*	emissione sotto la pari *f*	emisión por debajo de la par *f*
issue calendar (E)	Emissionskalender *m*	—	calendrier d'émission *m*	calendario delle emissioni *m*	calendario de emisión *m*
issue commission (E)	Emissionsvergütung *f*	—	commission d'émission *f*	commissione d'emissione *f*	remuneración emisora *f*
issue department (E)	Emissionsabteilung *f*	—	service d'émission *m*	ufficio emissioni *m*	sección de emisión *f*
Issue Law (E)	Emissionsgesetz *n*	—	loi sur l'émission des billets de banque *f*	legge sulle emissioni *f*	ley de emisión *f*
issue of securities (E)	Wertpapieremission *f*	—	émission de titres *f*	emissione di titoli *f*	emisión de valores *f*
issue of securities (E)	Effektenemission *f*	—	émission de valeurs mobilières *f*	emissione di titoli *f*	emisión de valores *f*
issue permit (E)	Emissionsgenehmigung *f*	—	autorisation de l'émission *f*	permesso d'emissione *m*	autorización de emisión *f*
issue premium (E)	Emissionsagio *n*	—	prime d'émission *f*	premio d'emissione *m*	prima de emisión *f*
issue price (E)	Emissionskurs *m*	—	cours d'émission *m*	corso d'emissione *m*	tipo de emisión *m*
issue yield (E)	Emissionsrendite *f*	—	rapport de l'émission *m*	rendita di nuovi titoli *f*	rédito de emisión *m*
issuing (E)	Emission *f*	—	émission *f*	emissione *f*	emisión *f*
issuing (E)	Erscheinen *n*	—	émission *f*	emissione *f*	emisión *f*
issuing bank (E)	Emissionsbank *f*	—	banque d'affaires *f*	banca d'emissione *f*	banco emisor *m*
issuing bank (E)	Effektenbank *f*	—	banque d'affaires *f*	banca valori *f*	banco de inversiones *m*
issuing house (E)	Emissionshaus *n*	—	établissement d'émission *m*	banca emittente *f*	casa emisora *f*

	D	E	F	I	Es
issuing of shares (E)	Aktienausgabe f	—	émission d'actions f	emissione di azioni f	emisión de acciones f
issuing price (E)	Ausgabepreis m	—	prix d'émission m	prezzo d'emissione m	precio de emisión m
issuing procedure (E)	Emissionsverfahren n	—	procédure d'émission f	procedimento di emissione m	procedimiento de emisión m
istituto di credito (I)	Kreditinstitut n	credit institution	établissement de crédit m	—	instituto de crédito m
istituto di credito (I)	Geldinstitut n	financial institution	établissement financier m	—	instituto monetario m
istituto di credito fondiario (I)	Grundkreditanstalt f	mortgage bank	établissement de crédit foncier m	—	banco hipotecario m
istituto di credito fondiario (I)	Pfandbriefanstalt f	mortgage bank	banque hypothécaire f	—	banco hipotecario m
istituto di credito immobiliare (I)	Realkreditinstitut n	real-estate credit institution	institut de crédit foncier m	—	instituto de crédito real m
istituto di credito speciale (I)	Spezialbank f	specialized commercial bank	banque spécialisée f	—	banco especializado m
istituto fiduciario (I)	Treuhandanstalt f	institutional trustee	fiduciaire institué m	—	instituto fiduciario m
Ist-Reserve (D)	—	actual reserve	réserve effective f	riserva effettiva f	reserva efectiva f
item free of charge (E)	Frankoposten m	—	poste de port payé m	partita franco spese f	partida de porte pagado f
Jahresabschluß (D)	—	annual statement of accounts	clôture annuelle des comptes f	bilancio d'esercizio m	balance anual m
Jahresbilanz (D)	—	annual balance sheet	bilan de fin d'année m	bilancio d'esercizio m	balance anual m
jeu d'écritures (F)	Umbuchung f	transfer of an entry	—	giro di partite m	asiento en otra cuenta m
joining (E)	Beitritt m	—	adhésion f	adesione f	adhesión f
joint account (E)	Oderkonten n/pl	—	compte joint m	conti a firme disgiunte m/pl	cuentas indistintas f/pl
joint account (E)	Gemeinschafts-konto n	—	compte commun m	conto congiunto m	cuenta conjunta f
joint account where all signatories must sign (E)	Und-Konto n	—	compte joint m	conto comune m	cuenta colectiva f
joint and several debtor (E)	Gesamtschuldner m	—	débiteur solidaire m	debitore solidale m	deudor solidario m
joint and several liability (E)	Solidarhaftung f	—	responsabilité solidaire f	responsabilità solidale f	responsabilidad solidaria f
joint debt (E)	Gesamthandschuld f	—	dette d'un associé d'une société par intérêts f	debito comunione a mani unite m	deuda en mano común f
joint deposit (E)	Oderdepot n	—	dépôt joint m	deposito comune m	depósito indistinto m
joint funds (E)	Gemeinschafts-fonds m	—	fonds commun m	fondo comune m	fondo común m
joint issue (E)	Gemeinschafts-emission f	—	émission en commun f	emissione comune f	emisión común f
joint loan (E)	Gemeinschafts-anleihe f	—	prêt commun f	prestito collettivo m	empréstito comunitario m
joint loan issue (E)	Sammelanleihe f	—	emprunt collectif m	obbligazione comunale f	empréstito colectivo m
jointly owned claim (E)	Gesamthand-forderung f	—	créance d'un associé d'une société par intérêts f	credito comunione a mani unite m	crédito en mano común m
joint power of attorney (E)	Gesamtvollmacht f	—	procuration collective f	procura collettiva f	poder solidario m
joint saving (E)	Gemeinschafts-sparen n	—	épargne collective f	risparmio collettivo m	ahorro común m
joint security deposit (E)	Gemeinschafts-depot n	—	dépôt en commun m	deposito congiunto m	depósito común m
joint stock banks (E)	Aktienbanken f/pl	—	banques par actions f/pl	banche per azioni f/pl	bancos por acciones m/pl
joint stock company (E)	Aktiengesellschaft f	—	société anonyme f	società per azioni f	sociedad anónima f
joint tenancy (E)	Gesamthand-eigentum n	—	propriété d'un associé d'une société par intérêts f	proprietà indivisa f	propiedad en mano común f

	D	E	F	I	Es
joint-venture company (E)	Projektgesellschaft *f*	—	société d'opération conjointe *f*	società ad hoc *f*	sociedad de operación conjunta *f*
jour de l'échéance (F)	Verfalltag *m*	day of expiry	—	giorno di scadenza *m*	día de vencimiento *m*
jour de paye (F)	Zahltag *m*	payday	—	giorno di pagamento *m*	día de pago *m*
jour de souscription (F)	Bezugstag *m*	subscription day	—	giorno di scadenza opzione *m*	día de la emisión *m*
jour du bilan (F)	Bilanzstichtag *m*	date of the balance sheet	—	giorno chiusura bilancio *m*	fecha del balance *f*
jour fixe (F)	Stichtag *m*	reporting date	—	data di riferimento *f*	día de liquidación *m*
journal (E)	Primanota *f*	—	mémorial *m*	prima nota *f*	diario *m*
jours de fête bancaires (F)	Bankfeiertage *m/pl*	bank holidays	—	giorni festivi delle banche *m/pl*	días de fiesta bancarios *m/pl*
jours de règlement fixés (F)	Bankstichtage *m/pl*	settling days	—	date di resoconto settimanale della banca centrale *f/pl*	días de referencia de los bancos *m/pl*
jugement déclaratif d'admission de la créance (F)	Beitrittsbeschluß *m*	decision of accession	—	decreto di adesione all'asta coattiva *m*	auto de adhesión *m*
jump in prices (E)	Kurssprung *m*	—	hausse sensible des cours *f*	balzo delle quotazioni *m*	alza considerable de las cotizaciones *f*
junge Aktien (D)	—	new shares	actions nouvelles *f/pl*	nuove azioni *f/pl*	acciones nuevas *f/pl*
Jungscheinverkehr (D)	—	new issue giro transfer system	système des certificats provisoires d'actions nouvelles *m*	sistema di certificato provvisorio *m*	sistema de certificados provisionales de acciones *f*
junior financing (E)	nachrangige Finanzierung *f*	—	financement de rang inférieur *m*	finanziamento subordinato *m*	financiación subordinada *f*
junta de acreedores (Es)	Gläubigerversammlung *f*	creditors' meeting	assemblée des créanciers *f*	assemblea dei creditori *f*	—
junta directiva (Es)	Vorstand *m*	board	comité directeur *m*	consiglio d'amministrazione *m*	—
junta general (Es)	Generalversammlung *f*	general assembly	assemblée générale *f*	assemblea generale *f*	—
juntas de accionistas (Es)	Aktionärsvereinigungen *f/pl*	associations of shareholders	assemblée des actionnaires *f*	associazioni di azionisti *f/pl*	—
juramento declarativo (Es)	Offenbarungseid *m*	oath of disclosure	serment déclaratoire *m*	giuramento dichiarativo *m*	—
juristische Person (D)	—	legal entity	personne juridique *f*	persona giuridica *f*	persona jurídica *f*
justificante (Es)	Beleg *m*	receipt	document justificatif *m*	ricevuta *f*	—
Kaduzierung (D)	—	forfeiture of shares	caducité *f*	decadenza del socio moroso *f*	caducidad *f*
Kahlpfändung (D)	—	seizure of all the debtor's goods	saisie de tous les biens *f*	pignoramento totale *m*	embargo total *m*
Kalkulation (D)	—	calculation	calcul *m*	calcolazione *f*	calculación *f*
Kalkulationszinssatz (D)	—	calculation interest rate	taux d'intérêt de calcul *m*	tasso d'interesse desiderato minimo *m*	tipo de interés calculado *m*
Kapital (D)	—	capital	capital *m*	capitale *m*	capital *m*
Kapitalabfindung (D)	—	lump-sum payment	indemnité en capital *f*	indennità in capitale *f*	importe de la opción *m*
Kapitalabfluß (D)	—	capital outflows	sortie de capital *f*	deflusso di capitale *m*	salida de capital *f*
Kapitalakkumulation (D)	—	accumulation of capital	accumulation de capital *f*	accumulazione di capitale *f*	acumulación de capital *f*
Kapitalallokation (D)	—	allocation of capital	allocation de capital *f*	allocazione di capitale *f*	alocación de capital *f*
Kapitalanalyse (D)	—	capital analysis	analyse de capital *f*	analisi del capitale *f*	análisis de capital *m*
Kapitalangebot (D)	—	supply of capital	offre de capital *f*	offerta di capitale *f*	oferta de capital *f*
Kapitalanlage (D)	—	capital investment	investissement de capitaux *m*	impiego di capitale *m*	inversión de capital *f*
Kapitalanlagegesellschaft (D)	—	capital investment company	société d'investissement *f*	società d'investimento *f*	compañía de inversiones *f*
Kapitalanlagegesetz (D)	—	capital investment law	loi sur les investissements de capital *f*	legge sugli investimenti di capitale *f*	ley sobre la inversión de capital *f*

	D	E	F	I	Es
Kapitalanlegearten (D)	—	types of capital investment	sortes d'investissement *f/pl*	tipi di investimento di capitale *m/pl*	tipos de inversión *m/pl*
Kapitalanteil (D)	—	share in capital	part de capital *f*	quota di capitale *f*	participación en el capital *f*
Kapitalausfuhr (D)	—	export of capital	exportation de capitaux *f*	esportazione di capitale *f*	exportación de capital *f*
Kapitalbedarf (D)	—	capital requirement	besoin en capital *m*	fabbisogno di capitale *m*	necesidad de capital *f*
Kapitalbedarfs- rechnung (D)	—	capital requirement calculation	calcul du besoin en capital *m*	calcolo del fabbisogno di capitale *m*	cálculo de necesidad de capital *m*
Kapitalbeschaffung (D)	—	procurement of capital	constitution de capital *f*	raccolta di capitali *f*	obtención de capital *f*
Kapitalbeteiligung (D)	—	equity participation	participation par apport de capital *f*	partecipazione al capitale *f*	intervención financiera *f*
Kapitalbewegungen (D)	—	capital movements	mouvements de capital *m/pl*	movimento di capitali *m*	movimientos de capital *m/pl*
Kapitalbilanz (D)	—	balance of capital transactions	balance des opéra- tions en capital *f*	bilancia dei capitali *f*	balanza de capital *f*
Kapitalbildung (D)	—	formation of capital	formation de capital *f*	formazione di capitale *f*	formación de capital *f*
Kapitalbindung (D)	—	capital tie-up	immobilisation de capitaux *f*	vincolamento di capitale *m*	vinculación de capital *f*
Kapitalbindungs- dauer (D)	—	duration of capital tie-up	durée de l'immobilisation de capitaux *f*	vincolo del capitale *m*	plazo de vinculación de capital *m*
Kapitaldienst (D)	—	service of capital	service du capital *m*	pagamento degli interessi *m*	servicio de capital *m*
Kapitalerhaltung (D)	—	maintenance of capital	maintien du capital *m*	stabilità del valore del capitale *f*	conservación de capital *f*
Kapitalerhöhung (D)	—	increase of the share capital	augmentation de capital *f*	aumento del capitale *m*	aumento de capital *m*
Kapitalertrag (D)	—	income from capital	produit du capital *m*	reddito di capitale *m*	renta de capital *f*
Kapitalertrags- steuer (D)	—	tax on investment income	taxation des revenus du capital *m*	imposta sul reddito dei capitali *f*	impuesto sobre la renta de capital *m*
Kapitalfehlleitung (D)	—	misguided investment	faux investissements *m/pl*	disguido di capitale *m*	extravío de capital *m*
Kapitalflucht (D)	—	exodus of capital	évasion des capitaux *f*	fuga dei capitali *f*	fuga de capital *f*
Kapitalfluß (D)	—	capital flow	fluidité des capitaux *f*	flusso dei fondi *m*	flujo de capital *m*
Kapitalfluß- rechnung (D)	—	funds statement	tableau de financement *m*	calcolo del flusso di capitale *m*	tabla de financiación *f*
Kapitalförderungs- vertrag (D)	—	capital encouragement treaty	accord sur l'encouragement de la formation de capital *m*	accordo sulla formazione di capitale *m*	contrato de fomento de capital *m*
Kapitalfreisetzung (D)	—	liberation of capital	libération de capital *f*	disinvestimento di capitale *m*	liberación de capital *f*
Kapitalgesellschaft (D)	—	company limited by shares	société de capitaux *f*	società di capitali *f*	sociedad de capital *f*
Kapitalherab- setzung (D)	—	capital reduction	diminution du capital *f*	riduzione del capitale sociale *f*	reducción de capital *f*
Kapitalhilfe (D)	—	capital aid	aide financière *f*	aiuto finanziario *m*	ayuda financiera *f*
Kapitalimport (D)	—	import of capital	importation de capitaux *f*	importazione di capitale *f*	importación de capital *f*
Kapitalisierung (D)	—	capitalization	capitalisation *f*	capitalizzazione *f*	capitalización *f*
Kapitalkonto (D)	—	capital account	compte de capital *m*	conto capitale *m*	cuenta de capital *f*
Kapitalkonzentration (D)	—	concentration of capital	concentration de capital *f*	concentrazione di capitali *f*	concentración de capital *f*
Kapitalkosten (D)	—	cost of capital	frais financiers *m/pl*	costi del capitale *m/pl*	gastos de capital *m/pl*
Kapitalmarkt (D)	—	capital market	marché des capitaux *m*	mercato finanziario *m*	mercado de capitales *m*
Kapitalmarkt- effizienz (D)	—	capital market efficiency	efficience du marché des capitaux *f*	efficienza del mercato finanziario *f*	eficiencia del mercado de capitales *f*
Kapitalmarktförde- rungsgesetz (D)	—	Capital Market Encouragement Law	loi sur la stimulation du marché des capitaux *f*	legge sulla promo- zione del mercato finanziario *f*	ley sobre el fomento del mercado de capital *f*

	D	E	F	I	Es
Kapitalmarkt-forschung (D)	—	capital market research	étude du marché des capitaux *f*	ricerca del mercato finanziario *f*	investigación del mercado de capital *f*
Kapitalmarkt-kommission (D)	—	capital market committee	commission du marché des capitaux *f*	commissione mercato finanziario *f*	comité de mercado de capital *m*
Kapitalmarktzins (D)	—	capital market interest rate	intérêt pratiqué sur le marché des capitaux *m*	tasso d'interesse del mercato finanziario *m*	interés pagado en el mercado de capital *m*
Kapitalmehrheit (D)	—	capital majority	majorité de capital *f*	maggioranza del capitale *f*	mayoría de capital *f*
Kapitalproduktivität (D)	—	capital productivity	productivité du capital *f*	produttività del capitale *f*	productividad del capital *f*
Kapitalrendite (D)	—	return on investment	rendement du capital *m*	rendimento del capitale *m*	rendimiento del capital *m*
Kapitalsammel-stelle (D)	—	institutional investors	organisme collecteur de fonds *m*	investitore istituzionale *m*	centro de acumulación de capitales *m*
Kapitalsammlungs-verträge (D)	—	contracts on capital collecting	contrats de réunion de capitaux *m/pl*	contratti di accumulazione di capitale *m/pl*	contratos de acumulación de capitales *m/pl*
Kapitalschutz (D)	—	capital protection	protection de capital *f*	tutela dei capitali *f*	protección del capital *f*
Kapitalschutzvertrag (D)	—	capital protection agreement	accord sur la pro-tection de capital *m*	accordo di tutela degli investimenti *m*	contrato de protección del capital *m*
Kapitalverkehrs-steuer (D)	—	capital transaction tax	taxe sur les mutations du capital *f*	imposta sulla circolazione dei capitali *f*	impuesto sobre transacciones *m*
Kapitalvermögen (D)	—	capital assets	capital *m*	impieghi di capitale *m/pl*	bienes patrimoniales *m/pl*
Kapitalver-wässerung (D)	—	watering of capital stock	augmentation du capital par émission d'actions gratuites ou par incorporation des réserves au fonds social *f*	annacquamento di capitali *m*	depreciación del capital *f*
Kapitalwert (D)	—	net present value	valeur en capital *f*	valore del capitale *m*	valor capitalizado *m*
Kapitalzins (D)	—	interest on capital	intérêt du capital *m*	interesse del capitale *m*	renta del capital *f*
Kassadevisen (D)	—	spot exchange	devises négociées en bourse au comptant *f/pl*	divisa a contanti *f*	divisas al contado *f/pl*
Kassageschäft (D)	—	cash transactions	opération au comptant *f*	operazione a pronti *f*	operaciones al contado *f/pl*
Kassakurs (D)	—	spot price	cours au comptant *m*	prezzo a pronti *m*	cambio al contado *m*
Kassamarkt (D)	—	spot market	marché au comptant *m*	mercato del pronto *m*	mercado al contado *m*
Kassenbestand (D)	—	cash in hand	montant des espèces en caisse *m*	consistenza di cassa *f*	dinero en caja *m*
Kassenhaltung (D)	—	cash accountancy	tenue de la caisse *f*	tenuta di cassa *f*	contabilidad de caja *f*
Kassenkredite (D)	—	cash credit	crédit à court terme *m*	crediti di cassa *m/pl*	créditos a corto plazo *m/pl*
Kassenobligationen (D)	—	medium-term bonds	obligations à moyen terme *f/pl*	obbligazioni di cassa *f/pl*	bonos de caja *m/pl*
Kassenverstärkungs-kredit (D)	—	cash lending	crédit pour augmenter la liquidité *m*	credito per elasticità di cassa *m*	crédito con fines de aumentar la liquidez *m*
Kauf (D)	—	purchase	achat *m*	acquisto *m*	compra *f*
Käufermarkt (D)	—	buyer's market	marché d'acheteurs *m*	mercato degli acquisti *m*	mercado del comprador *m*
Kaufkraft (D)	—	purchasing power	pouvoir d'achat *m*	potere d'acquisto *m*	poder adquisitivo *m*
Kaufkraftparität (D)	—	purchasing power parity	parité du pouvoir d'achat *f*	parità del potere d'acquisto *f*	paridad adquisitiva *f*
Kaufkredit (D)	—	purchasing credit	crédit d'achat *m*	credito finanziamento acquisti *m*	crédito de compra *m*
kaufmännische Order-papiere (D)	—	commercial instruments to order	effets de commerce à ordre *m/pl*	effetti commerciali all'ordine *m/pl*	títulos comerciales a la orden *m/pl*
Kaufoption (D)	—	call option	option d'achat *f*	opzione d'acquisto *f*	opción de compra *f*
Kaufpreis (D)	—	purchase price	prix d'achat *m*	prezzo d'acquisto *m*	precio de compra *m*
Kaufscheck (D)	—	purchasing cheque	chèque d'achat *m*	assegno garantito per acquisti *m*	cheque de compra *m*

	D	E	F	I	Es
Kaufvertrag (D)	—	agreement of purchase and sale	contrat de vente *m*	contratto di compravendita *m*	contrato de compraventa *m*
Kaution (D)	—	security	caution *f*	cauzione *f*	fianza *f*
Kautionseffekten (D)	—	guarantee securities	papiers de sûreté *m/pl*	titoli di deposito cauzionale *m/pl*	valores de fianza *m/pl*
Kellerwechsel (D)	—	fictitious bill	traite fictive *f*	cambiale fittizia *f*	letra de cambio ficticia *f*
Kennzahl (D)	—	code number	code *m*	indice *m*	índice *m*
key currency (E)	Leitwährung *f*	—	monnaie-clé *f*	moneta guida *f*	moneda de referencia *f*
Keynes Theory (E)	Keynes'sche Theorie *f*	—	théorie Keynésienne *f*	teoria di Keynes *f*	teoría keynesiana *f*
Keynes'sche Theorie (D)	—	Keynes Theory	théorie Keynésienne *f*	teoria di Keynes *f*	teoría keynesiana *f*
Kleinaktie (D)	—	share with low par value	action minimale *f*	piccola azione *f*	acción pequeña *f*
Kleinaktionär (D)	—	small shareholder	petit actionnaire *m*	piccolo azionista *m*	accionista pequeño *m*
Kleinkredit (D)	—	small personal loan	petit crédit *m*	piccolo credito *m*	préstamo pequeño *m*
Kleinsparer (D)	—	small saver	petit épargnant *m*	piccolo risparmiatore *m*	ahorrador de menor importancia *m*
Kleinstücke (D)	—	fractional amount	petits titres *m/pl*	titoli di importo modesto *m/pl*	títulos pequeños *m/pl*
Kollektivsparen (D)	—	collective saving	épargne collective *f*	risparmio collettivo *m*	ahorro colectivo *m*
Kolonialbank (D)	—	colonial bank	banque coloniale *f*	banca coloniale *f*	banco colonial *m*
Kommanditaktionär (D)	—	limited liability shareholder	actionnaire d'une société en commandite par actions *m*	socio di una società in accomandita per azioni *m*	accionista comanditario *m*
Kommandit-gesellschaft (D)	—	limited partnership	société en commandite *f*	società in accomandita semplice *f*	sociedad comanditaria *f*
Kommanditist (D)	—	limited partner	commandite *m*	accomandante *m*	comanditario *m*
Kommissionär (D)	—	commission agent	commissionnaire *m*	commissionario *m*	comisionista *m*
Kommissions-geschäft (D)	—	commission business	affaire en commission *f*	contratto di commissione *m*	operación de comisión *f*
Kommissionstratte (D)	—	bill of exchange drawn for third-party account	traite pour compte d'autrui *f*	tratta per conto terzi *f*	giro por cuenta *m*
Kommunalanleihe (D)	—	local authorities loan	emprunt communal *m*	prestito comunale *m*	empréstito municipal *m*
Kommunalbank (D)	—	local authorities bank	banque communale *f*	banca comunale *f*	banco comunal *m*
Kommunaldarlehen (D)	—	loan granted to a local authority	prêt aux communes *m*	mutuo comunale *m*	empréstito municipal *m*
Kommunalkredit (D)	—	credit granted to a local authority	prêt aux communes *m*	credito comunale *m*	crédito municipal *m*
Kommunal-obligation (D)	—	local bond	obligation communale *f*	obbligazione comunale *f*	obligación comunal *f*
Kompensation (D)	—	compensation	compensation *f*	compensazione *f*	compensación *f*
Kompensations-geschäft (D)	—	offset transaction	affaire de compensation *f*	operazione di compensazione *f*	operación de compensación *f*
Kompensationskurs (D)	—	making-up price	cours de compensation *m*	corso di compensazione *m*	cambio de compensación *m*
Kompensations-steuer (D)	—	offset tax	impôt de compensation *m*	imposta sulle compensazioni *f*	impuesto de compensación *m*
kompensierte Valuta (D)	—	value compensated	valeur compensée *f*	valuta compensata *f*	valuta compensada *f*
Komplementär (D)	—	general partner	commandité *m*	accomandatario *m*	socio colectivo *m*
Konditionen (D)	—	conditions	conditions *f/pl*	condizioni *f/pl*	condiciones *f/pl*
Konjunktur (D)	—	business cycle	conjoncture *f*	congiuntura *f*	coyuntura *f*
Konjunkturausgleichs-rücklage (D)	—	anticyclical reserve	réserve anticyclique *f*	fondo compensazione congiuntura negativa *m*	reserva de compensación coyuntural *f*
Konkurs (D)	—	bankruptcy	faillite *f*	fallimento *m*	quiebra *f*
Konkursdelikt (D)	—	bankruptcy offence	fraude en matière de faillite *f*	reato fallimentare *m*	delito concursal *m*
Konkurseröffnung (D)	—	commencement of bankruptcy proceedings	ouverture de la faillite *f*	apertura del fallimento *f*	apertura de la quiebra *f*

	D	E	F	I	Es
Konkursgläubiger (D)	—	bankrupt's creditor	créancier de la faillite *m*	creditore della massa fallimentare *m*	acreedor de la quiebra *m*
Konkursmasse (D)	—	bankrupt's estate	masse de la faillite *f*	massa fallimentare *f*	masa de la quiebra *f*
Konkursordnung (D)	—	Bankruptcy Act	régime juridique de la faillite *m*	legge fallimentare *f*	ley de las quiebras *f*
Konkursquote (D)	—	dividend in bankruptcy	pour-cent accordé aux créanciers dans la masse *m*	quota di riparto *f*	cuota del activo de la quiebra *f*
Konkursverfahren (D)	—	proceedings in bankruptcy	procédure de faillite *f*	procedura fallimentare *f*	procedimiento de quiebra *m*
Konkursverwalter (D)	—	administrator in bankruptcy proceedings	liquidateur de la faillite *m*	curatore del fallimento *m*	síndico de quiebra *m*
konsolidierte Bilanz (D)	—	consolidated balance sheet	bilan consolidé *m*	bilancio consolidato *m*	balance consolidado *m*
Konsols (D)	—	consoles	dettes consolidées *f/pl*	prestiti consolidati *m/pl*	deudas consolidadas *f/pl*
Konsortialabteilung (D)	—	syndicate department	service des syndicats *m*	ufficio consorzi *m*	sección de consorcios *f*
Konsortialgeschäft (D)	—	syndicate transaction	opération appuyée par plusieurs banques *f*	operazione consorziale *f*	negocio de consorcio *m*
Konsortialkredit (D)	—	syndicated credit	crédit garanti par un consortium bancaire *m*	credito consorziale *m*	crédito consorcial *m*
Konsortium (D)	—	syndicate	consortium *m*	consorzio *m*	consorcio *m*
Konsumfinanzierung (D)	—	consumption financing	financement de la vente à crédit *m*	finanziamento di vendite rateali *m*	financiación al consumo *f*
Konsumgenossen-schaft (D)	—	consumer cooperative	société coopérative de consommation *f*	cooperativa di consumo *f*	cooperativa de consumo *f*
Konsumgüter (D)	—	consumer goods	biens de consommation *m/pl*	beni di consumo *m/pl*	bienes de consumo *m/pl*
Kontenkalkulation (D)	—	account costing	calcul des comptes *m*	calcolo dei conti *m*	calculación por cuentas *f*
Konten-numerierung (D)	—	account numbering	numérotage des comptes *m*	classificazione dei conti *f*	numeración de cuentas *f*
Kontenplan (D)	—	chart of accounts	plan comptable *m*	piano dei conti *m*	plan contable *m*
Kontenrahmen (D)	—	standard form of accounts	cadre comptable *m*	quadro dei conti *m*	sistema de cuentas *m*
Kontingent (D)	—	quota	contingent *m*	contingente *m*	contingente *m*
Kontingentierung (D)	—	fixing of a quota	contingentement *m*	contingentamento *m*	imposición de contingentes *f*
Konto (D)	—	account	compte *m*	conto *m*	cuenta *f*
Kontoauszug (D)	—	statement of account	relevé de compte *m*	estratto conto *m*	extracto de cuenta *m*
Kontoeröffnung (D)	—	opening of an account	ouverture d'un compte *f*	apertura di un conto *f*	apertura de una cuenta *f*
Kontokorrent (D)	—	current account	compte courant *m*	conto corrente *m*	cuenta corriente *f*
Kontokorrentkredit (D)	—	current account credit	crédit en compte courant *m*	credito in conto corrente *m*	crédito en cuenta corriente *m*
Kontonummer (D)	—	account number	numéro de compte *m*	numero di conto *m*	número de la cuenta *m*
Kontovollmacht (D)	—	power to draw on an account	pouvoir de compte *m*	procura di disporre sul conto *f*	poder de cuenta *m*
Kontrahierung (D)	—	contraction	conclusion d'un contrat *f*	conclusione di contratto *f*	contratación *f*
Kontrahierungs-zwang (D)	—	obligation to contract	obligation de contracter *f*	obbligo di contrarre *m*	contratación forzosa *f*
Kontrollmitteilung (D)	—	tracer note	bulletin de contrôle *m*	comunicazione di revisione *f*	control cruzado *m*
Konventionalstrafe (D)	—	contractual penalty	pénalité *f*	pena convenzionale *f*	pena convencional *f*
Konvertibilität (D)	—	convertibility	convertibilité *f*	convertibilità *f*	convertibilidad *f*
Konvertierung (D)	—	conversion	conversion *f*	conversione *f*	conversión *f*
Konzernaufträge (D)	—	group orders	commandes placées par un groupement de sociétés *f/pl*	ordini di gruppo *m/pl*	órdenes de grupos *f/pl*

	D	E	F	I	Es
Konzernbilanz (D)	—	group balance sheet	bilan consolidé d'un groupement de sociétés *m*	bilancio consolidato *m*	balance del consorcio *m*
Konzernzwischen-gewinn (D)	—	group interim benefits	bénéfice intermédiaire des groupements de sociétés *m*	margine d'utile di gruppo *m*	beneficio intermedio consolidado *m*
Konzertzeichnung (D)	—	stagging	majorisation *f*	speculazione di borsa *f*	mayorización *f*
Konzession (D)	—	license	concession *f*	licenza *f*	concesión *f*
Kooperation (D)	—	cooperation	coopération *f*	cooperazione *f*	cooperación *f*
Kooperations-darlehen (D)	—	cooperation loan	prêt de coopération *m*	prestito di cooperazione *m*	préstamo de cooperación *m*
Kopfsteuer (D)	—	per capita tax	impôt personnel *m*	capitazione *f*	capitación *f*
Korbwährung (D)	—	basket currency	monnaie de panier *f*	valuta paniere *f*	moneda de cesta *f*
Ko (D)	—	corporation	collectivité *f*	ente *m*	corporación *f*
Körperschaftssteuer (D)	—	corporation tax	taxe sur les sociétés *m*	imposta sul reddito delle società *f*	impuesto de sociedades *m*
Korrelation (D)	—	correlation	corrélation *f*	correlazione *f*	correlación *f*
Korrespondenzbank (D)	—	correspondent bank	banque de correspondance *f*	banca corrispondente *f*	banco corresponsal *m*
Kosten (D)	—	costs	coût *m*	costi *m/pl*	costes *m/pl*
Kostenart (D)	—	cost type	coût par nature *m*	tipo di costo *m*	clase de costes *f*
Kostendeckung (D)	—	cost recovery	couverture des coûts *f*	copertura delle spese *f*	dotación *f*
Kostendruck (D)	—	cost pressure	poids des coûts *m*	pressione dei costi *f*	tensiones sobre los gastos *f/pl*
Kostenfaktor (D)	—	cost factor	facteur de coûts *m*	fattore di costo *m*	tipo de coste *m*
Kostenrechnung (D)	—	statement of costs	compte de frais *m*	calcolo dei costi *m*	cálculo de costes *m*
Kostenstelle (D)	—	cost centre	compte de frais par secteur *m*	centro di costo *m*	sección de gastos *f*
Kostenträger (D)	—	cost unit	poste de production absorbant des coûts *m*	chi sostiene le spese	portador de costes *m*
Kotierung (D)	—	admission of shares to official quotation	cotation *f*	ammissione alla quotazione *f*	cotización *f*
Kredit (D)	—	credit	crédit *m*	credito *m*	crédito *m*
Kreditabteilung (D)	—	credit department	service du crédit et des prêts *m*	ufficio crediti *m*	sección de crédito *f*
Kreditakte (D)	—	credit folder	dossier de crédit *m*	cartella di credito *f*	expediente de crédito *m*
Kreditaktie (D)	—	credit share	titre de crédit *m*	titolo di credito *m*	título de crédito *m*
Kreditakzept (D)	—	financial acceptance	traite tirée en garantie d'un crédit *f*	accettazione bancaria *f*	aceptación de crédito *f*
Kreditaufnahme (D)	—	raising of credits	recours à l'emprunt *m*	accensione di credito *f*	apelación al crédito *f*
Kreditaufnahme-verbot (D)	—	prohibition of raising of credits	prohibition d'emprunt *f*	divieto di accensione di credito *m*	prohibición de apelación al crédito *f*
Kreditaufsicht (D)	—	state supervision of credit institutions	office de surveillance des établissements de crédit *f*	autorità di vigilanza sul credito *f*	supervisión crediticia *f*
Kreditauftrag (D)	—	mandate to provide credit for a third party	ordre de crédit *m*	mandato di credito *m*	mandato crediticio *m*
Kreditauskunft (D)	—	credit information	renseignement sur la solvabilité du demandeur d'un crédit *m*	informazione creditizia *f*	información de crédito *f*
Kreditausschuß (D)	—	credit committee	commission d'étude des dossiers de crédit *f*	comitato di credito *m*	comité de crédito *m*
Kreditausweitung (D)	—	expansion of credit	expansion du crédit *f*	espansione del credito *f*	expansión del crédito *f*
Kreditbank (D)	—	commercial bank	banque de crédit *f*	banca di credito *f*	banco de crédito *m*
Kreditbedarf (D)	—	credit demand	besoin en crédits *m*	fabbisogno creditizio *m*	necesidad de crédito *f*
Kreditbrief (D)	—	letter of credit	lettre de crédit *f*	lettera di credito *f*	carta de crédito *f*

	D	E	F	I	Es
Krediteröffnungs-vertrag (D)	—	credit agreement	contrat d'ouverture de crédit *m*	contratto d'apertura di credito *m*	contrato de apertura de crédito *m*
Kreditfazilität (D)	—	credit facilities	facilité de crédit *f*	facilitazione creditizia *f*	facilidades crediticias *f/pl*
Kreditfinanzierung (D)	—	financing by way of credit	financement par capitaux de tiers *m*	finanziamento mediante credito *m*	financiación mediante créditos *f*
Kreditfrist (D)	—	credit period	délai de remboursement des avances sur crédit *m*	scadenza del credito *f*	plazo de vencimiento del crédito *m*
Kreditgarantie (D)	—	credit guarantee	garantie de crédit *f*	garanzia di credito *f*	garantía de crédito *f*
Kreditgefährdung (D)	—	endangering the credit of a person or a firm	atteinte au crédit *f*	pregiudizio della capacità creditizia *m*	amenaza del crédito *f*
Kreditgeld (D)	—	credit money	argent de crédit *m*	credito *m*	dinero crediticio *m*
Kreditgenossen-schaft (D)	—	credit cooperative	caisse coopérative de crédit *f*	cooperativa di credito *f*	cooperativa de crédito *f*
Kreditgeschäft (D)	—	credit business	opérations d'avances sur crédit *f/pl*	operazione di credito *f*	operación crediticia *f*
Kreditgewinnab-gabe (D)	—	debts profit levy	taxe sur les bénéfices de crédit *m*	ritenuta sugli utili dei crediti *f*	tributo sobre beneficios del crédito *m*
Kreditinflation (D)	—	credit inflation	inflation de crédit *f*	inflazione creditizia *f*	inflación crediticia *f*
Kreditinstitut (D)	—	credit institution	établissement de crédit *m*	istituto di credito *m*	instituto de crédito *m*
Kreditkarte (D)	—	credit card	carte de crédit *f*	carta di credito *f*	tarjeta de crédito *f*
Kreditkartei (D)	—	borrowing customers' card index	fichier des opérations d'avances et de crédit *m*	schedario dei crediti *m*	fichero de operaciones de crédito *m*
Kreditkauf (D)	—	credit purchase	achat à crédit *m*	acquisto di credito *m*	compra de crédito *f*
Kreditkontrolle (D)	—	credit control	contrôle de crédit *m*	controllo del credito *m*	control crediticio *m*
Kreditkosten (D)	—	cost of credit	coût de crédit *m*	costi del credito *m/pl*	gastos de crédito *m/pl*
Kreditkultur (D)	—	credit culture	culture de crédit *f*	panorama creditizio *m*	cultura crediticia *f*
Kreditleihe (D)	—	loan of credit	prêt de crédit *m*	credito di firma *m*	préstamo de crédito *m*
Kreditlimit (D)	—	credit limit	plafond du crédit alloué *m*	limite di credito *m*	límite de crédito *m*
Kreditlinie (D)		credit line	plafond du crédit accordé *m*	linea di credito *f*	línea de crédito *f*
Kreditmarkt (D)	—	money and capital market	marché financier *m*	mercato creditizio *m*	mercado de créditos *m*
Kreditoren (D)	—	creditors	créditeurs *m/pl*	creditori *m/pl*	acreedores *m/pl*
Kreditplafond (D)	—	credit ceiling	plafond du crédit accordé *m*	limite massimo di fido *m*	plafón de crédito *m*
Kreditplafondierung (D)	—	credit limitation	fixation d'une limite de crédit *f*	fissazione del fido *f*	volumen máximo de crédito disponible *m*
Kreditprovision (D)	—	credit commission	frais de commission d'ouverture de crédit *m/pl*	provvigione di credito *f*	comisión de apertura de crédito *f*
Kreditprüfung (D)	—	credit status investigation	enquête sur la solvabilité *f*	controllo dei crediti *m*	investigación de crédito y solvencia de un cliente *f*
Kreditprüfungs-blätter (D)	—	credit checking sheets	feuilles d'enquête sur la solvabilité *f/pl*	fogli di controllo crediti *m/pl*	hojas de investigación crediticia *f/pl*
Kreditrestriktion (D)	—	credit restriction	restriction du crédit *f*	restrizione creditizia *f*	restricción de créditos *f*
Kreditrisiko (D)	—	credit risk	risque inhérent aux opérations de crédit *m*	rischio inerente al credito *m*	riesgo del crédito *m*
Kreditschöpfung (D)	—	creation of credit	création de crédit *f*	creazione di credito *f*	creación de créditos *f*
Kreditschutz (D)	—	protection of credit	protection du crédit *f*	tutela del credito *f*	protección del crédito *f*
Kreditschwindel (D)	—	credit fraud	obtention de crédits par duperie *f*	frode creditizia *f*	fraude crediticio *m*
Kreditsicherheit (D)	—	security of credit	garantie concernant un crédit *f*	garanzia di credito *f*	garantía de un crédito *f*

	D	E	F	I	Es
Kreditsicherung (D)	—	safeguarding of credit	sûreté en garantie d'un crédit f	garanzia di credito f	garantía de un crédito f
Kreditspritze (D)	—	injection of credit	injection de crédit f	iniezione di credito f	inyección de crédito f
Kreditstatus (D)	—	credit standing	état de l'endettement m	situazione creditizia f	estado del endeudamiento m
Kredittranche (D)	—	credit tranche	tranche de crédit f	quota di credito f	fracción de crédito f
Kreditvermittler (D)	—	money broker	agent financier m	intermediario finanziario m	operador de negociación de créditos m
Kreditversicherung (D)	—	credit insurance	assurance crédit f	assicurazione di credito f	seguro crediticio m
Kreditvertrag (D)	—	credit agreement	contrat de vente à crédit m	contratto di credito m	contrato de crédito m
Kreditvolumen (D)	—	total credit outstanding	volume des crédits m	volume creditizio m	volumen de créditos m
Kreditwesen (D)	—	credit system	crédit m	sistema creditizio m	régimen de creditos m
Kreditwesengesetz (D)	—	Banking Law	loi sur le crédit f	legge sul sistema creditizio f	ley sobre el régimen de créditos f
Kreditwürdigkeit (D)	—	creditworthiness	solvabilité f	fido m	crédito m
Kreuzparität (D)	—	cross rate	parité indirecte f	parità incrociata f	paridad cruzada f
Kriegsanleihe (D)	—	war loan	emprunt de guerre m	prestito di guerra m	empréstito de guerra m
Krise (D)	—	crisis	crise f	crisi f	crisis f
Krisenstimmung (D)	—	crisis feeling	climat de crise m	atmosfera di crisi f	ambiente de crisis m
krummer Auftrag (D)	—	uneven order	ordre de lots irréguliers m	ordine irregolare m	orden de lotes irregulares f
Kulanz (D)	—	fairness in trade	souplesse en affaires f	correntezza f	complacencia f
Kulisse (D)	—	unofficial stock market	coulisse f	operatori di borsa m/pl	bolsa extraoficial f
Kulissenwert (D)	—	quotation on the unofficial market	valeur négociée sur le marché libre f	titolo del mercato ristretto m	valor de la bolsa extraoficial m
kumulative Dividende (D)	—	cumulative dividend	dividende cumulé m	dividendo cumulativo m	dividendo acumulativo m
Kumulierungsverbot (D)	—	rule against accumulation	prohibition de cumuler f	divieto del cumulo delle agevolazioni m	prohibición de acumulación f
Kundenauftrag (D)	—	customer's order	ordre d'un client m	ordinazione f	orden de cliente f
Kundenberatung (D)	—	consumer advice	orientation de la clientèle f	servizio d'assistenza m	asesoramiento de clientes m
Kundengeschäft (D)	—	transactions for third account	opération pour compte de client f	operazioni per la clientela f/pl	transacciones por cuenta ajena f/pl
Kundenkalkulation (D)	—	customer costing	calcul des résultats obtenus par chaque client m	calcolo d'utilità di cliente m	calculación de participación por cliente f
Kündigung (D)	—	termination	préavis m	preavviso m	preaviso m
Kündigungsgeld (D)	—	deposit at notice	sommes disponibles avec préavis f/pl	deposito ritirabile dietro preavviso m	depósitos con preaviso m/pl
Kündigungsgrundschuld (D)	—	land charge not repayable until called	dette foncière remboursable avec préavis f	termine di preavviso m	deuda inmobiliaria con preaviso f
Kündigungshypothek (D)	—	mortgage loan repayable after having been duly called	hypothèque garantissant une dette remboursable avec préavis f	ipoteca rimborsabile dopo preavviso f	hipoteca con preaviso f
Kündigungssperrfrist (D)	—	non-calling period	délai de blocage de dénonciation m	termine di preavviso m	plazo de suspensión de preaviso m
Kundschaftskredit (D)	—	customers' credit	crédit accordé à la clientèle m	credito alla clientela m	crédito al consumidor m
Kuponbogen (D)	—	coupon sheet	feuille de coupons f	cedolario m	hoja de cupones f
Kuponkasse (D)	—	coupon collection department	service de payement des coupons m	cassa cedolare f	sección de cobro por cupones f
Kuponkurs (D)	—	coupon price	prix des coupons m	quotazione della cedola f	cotización de un cupón f
Kuponmarkt (D)	—	coupon market	marché des coupons m	mercato delle cedole m	mercado de cupones m

	D	E	F	I	Es
Kuponsteuer (D)	—	coupon tax	impôt sur les coupons *m*	imposta sulle cedole *f*	impuesto sobre cupones *m*
Kurantmünze (D)	—	specie	monnaie courante *f*	moneta corrente *f*	moneda corriente *f*
Kuratorium (D)	—	board of trustees	charge de curateur *f*	consiglio di gestione *m*	curatorio *m*
Kurs (D)	—	market price	cours *m*	quotazione *f*	cotización *f*
Kursanzeige (D)	—	quotation	cotation *f*	indicazione delle quotazioni *f*	indicación de las cotizaciones *f*
Kursblatt (D)	—	stock exchange list	cote de la bourse *f*	listino di borsa *m*	listín de bolsa *m*
Kursfestsetzung (D)	—	fixing of prices	détermination des cours *f*	fissazione dei corsi *f*	cotización *f*
Kursgewinn (D)	—	price gain	plus-value sur les cours *f*	utile di borsa *m*	plusvalía de cotización *m*
Kurs-Gewinn-Verhältnis (D)	—	price-earnings ratio	relation cours-bénéfice *f*	rapporto corso-profitto *m*	relación cotización-ganancia *f*
Kursindex (D)	—	stock exchange index	indice des cours *m*	indice di borsa *m*	índice de cotizaciones *m*
Kursintervention (D)	—	price intervention	intervention en matière des cours *f*	intervento di sostegno quotazioni *m*	intervención cambiaria *f*
Kursklausel (D)	—	currency clause	clause de payement effectif en une monnaie étrangère *f*	clausola di cambio *f*	cláusula de tipo de cambio *f*
Kurslimit (D)	—	price limit	cours limité *m*	limite di prezzo *m*	cambio limitado *m*
Kursmakler (D)	—	stockbroker	courtier en bourse *m*	agente di borsa *m*	agente de cambio y bolsa *m*
Kursparität (D)	—	parity of rates	pair du change *m*	parità di scambio *f*	paridad cambiaria *f*
Kurspflege (D)	—	price nursing	régulation des cours *f*	sostegno delle quotazioni *m*	compras de sostén *f/pl*
Kursregulierung (D)	—	price regulation	régulation des cours *f*	sostegno delle quotazioni *m*	regulación de los tipos de cambio *f*
Kursrisiko (D)	—	price risk	risque de change *m*	rischio di quotazione *m*	riesgo del cambio *m*
Kursspanne (D)	—	difference between purchase and hedging price	écart de cours *m*	margine di cambio *m*	margen de cotización *m*
Kurssprung (D)	—	jump in prices	hausse sensible des cours *f*	balzo delle quotazioni *m*	alza considerable de las cotizaciones *f*
Kursstreichung (D)	—	non-quotation	annulation de la cotation *f*	mancata quotazione *f*	no cotización *f*
Kursstützung (D)	—	price pegging	soutien des cours *m*	sostegno delle quotazioni *m*	apoyo de la cotización *m*
Kursverwässerung (D)	—	price watering	baisse du cours par émission d'action gratuites *f*	annacquamento della quotazione *m*	caída de cotización *f*
Kurszettel (D)	—	stock exchange list	bulletin des cours *m*	listino di borsa *m*	boletín de bolsa *m*
Kurszusätze (D)	—	notes appended to quotation	indications supplémentaires de cotation *f/pl*	termini borsistici *m/pl*	indicaciones explicativas de las cotizaciones *f/pl*
Kurzfristige Erfolgs-rechnung (D)	—	monthly income statement	comptes de résultats intermédiaires *m/pl*	conto economico a breve termine *m*	estado de resultados a corto plazo *m*
Kux (D)	—	mining share	part de mines *f*	azione mineraria *f*	acción minera *f*
lack of liquidity (E)	Unterliquidität *f*	—	insufficance de liquidité *f*	liquidità insufficiente *f*	insuficiencia de liquidez *f*
land charge (E)	Grundschuld *f*	—	dette foncière *f*	debito fondiario *m*	hipoteca *f*
land charge certificate (E)	Grundschuldbrief *m*	—	cédule foncière *f*	certificato di debito fondiario *m*	cédula de deuda inmobiliaria *f*
land charge in favour of the owner (E)	Eigentümer-Grund-schuld *f*	—	dette foncière constituée par le propriétaire à son profit *f*	debito fondiario al proprietario *m*	deuda inmobiliaria del propietario *f*
land charge not re-payable until called (E)	Kündigungsgrund-schuld *f*	—	dette foncière rem-boursable avec préavis *f*	termine di preavviso *m*	deuda inmobiliaria con preaviso *f*
Länderrisiko (D)	—	country risk	risque de pays *m*	rischio paese *m*	riesgo nacional *m*
Landwirtschaftsbrief (D)	—	agricultural mortgage bond	cédule hypothéquaire agricole *f*	obbligazione di una banca agricola *f*	cédula hipotecaria agrícola *f*

	D	E	F	I	Es
Landwirtschafts-kredit (D)	—	agricultural loan	crédit agricole *m*	credito all'agricoltura *m*	crédito agrario *m*
lange Sicht (D)	—	long run	échéance longue *f*	a lunga scadenza	a largo plazo
langfristige Einlagen (D)	—	long-term deposits	placements à long terme *m/pl*	depositi a lunga scadenza *m/pl*	imposiciones a largo plazo *f/pl*
langfristiger Kredit (D)	—	long-term credit	crédit à long terme *m*	credito a lunga scadenza *m*	crédito a largo plazo *m*
la oferta fue mayor que la demanda (Es)	bezahlt Brief	more sellers than buyers	comptant vendeur *m*	offerta eccedente la domanda *f*	—
large-scale lending (E)	Großkredit *m*	—	crédit important *m*	grosso credito *m*	crédito importante *m*
last-day business (E)	Ultimogeschäft *n*	—	opération à liquider en fin de mois *f*	contratto a fine ultimo *m*	operación a término con vencimiento a fin de mes *f*
last-day money (E)	Ultimogeld *n*	—	fonds remboursables à fin de mois *m/pl*	prestito per fine mese *m*	dinero a fin de mes *m*
Lastenausgleich (D)	—	equalization of burdens	péréquation des charges *f*	perequazione degli oneri *f*	compensación de cargas *f*
Lastenausgleichs-bank (D)	—	equalization of burdens bank	banque de péréquation des charges *f*	banca perequazione oneri *f*	banco de compen-sación de cargas *m*
Lastenausgleichs-fonds (D)	—	Equalization of Burdens Fund	fonds de péréquation des charges *m*	fondo perequazione oneri *m*	fondo de compen-sación de cargas *m*
Lastschrift (D)	—	debit entry	note de débit *f*	addebitamento *m*	cargo en cuenta *m*
Lastschrifteinzugs-verfahren (D)	—	direct debiting	système de prélèvement automatique *m*	incasso tramite addebitamento *m*	procedimiento de cobro en cuenta *m*
Lastschriftkarte (D)	—	debit card	carte de débit *f*	avviso di addebito *m*	nota de cargo *f*
Lastschriftverkohr (D)	—	direct debiting transactions	prélèvements automatiques *m/pl*	addebiti *m/pl*	sistema de cargo en cuenta *m*
Laufzeitfonds (D)	—	term funds	fonds à terme *m*	fondo a scadenza *m*	fondos a plazo *m/pl*
launching costs (E)	Anlaufkosten *pl*	—	frais de mise en marche *m/pl*	spese d'avviamento *f/pl*	gastos de instalación *m/pl*
law of obligations (E)	Schuldrecht *n*	—	droit des obligations et contrats *m*	diritto delle obbligazioni *m*	derecho de obligaciones *m*
lease renewal option (E)	Mietverlängerungs-option *f*	—	option de prorogation du bail *f*	opzione proroga contratto di locazione *f*	opción de prorrogación de arrendamiento *f*
lease with option to purchase (E)	Mietkauf *m*	—	location-vente *f*	locazione finanziaria *f*	arrendamiento con opción de compra *m*
Leasing (D)	—	leasing	crédit-bail *m*	leasing *m*	leasing *m*
leasing (E)	Leasing *n*	—	crédit-bail *m*	leasing *m*	leasing *m*
leasing (Es)	Leasing *n*	leasing	crédit-bail *m*	leasing *m*	—
leasing (I)	Leasing *n*	leasing	crédit-bail *m*	—	leasing *m*
Leasingrate (D)	—	leasing rate	taux de leasing *m*	canone di leasing *m*	tasa de leasing *f*
leasing rate (E)	Leasingrate *f*	—	taux de leasing *m*	canone di leasing *m*	tasa de leasing *f*
Leeraktie (D)	—	shares not fully paid up	action non entièrement libérée *f*	azione non interamente versata *f*	acción al descubierto *f*
Leerlauf (D)	—	time wasted	temps creux *m*	tempo morto *m*	tiempo en vacío *m*
Leerposition (D)	—	bear selling position	découvert *m*	scoperto *m*	descubierto *m*
Leerverkauf (D)	—	bear selling	vente à découvert *f*	vendita allo scoperto *f*	venta al descubierto *f*
Leerwechsel (D)	—	finance bill	traite financière *f*	cambiale vuota *f*	letra al descubierto *f*
legal capacity (E)	Rechtsfähigkeit *f*	—	capacité de jouissance de droits *f*	capacità giuridica *f*	capacidad jurídica *f*
legal entity (E)	juristische Person *f*	—	personne juridique *f*	persona giuridica *f*	persona jurídica *f*
légalisation (F)	Beglaubigung *f*	certification	—	autenticazione *f*	legalización *f*
legalización (Es)	Beglaubigung *f*	certification	légalisation *f*	autenticazione *f*	—
legally restricted retained earnings (E)	gesetzliche Rücklage *f*	—	réserves légales *f/pl*	riserva legale *f*	reservas legales *f/pl*
legal obligation to disclose one's results (E)	Anzeigepflicht *f*	—	obligation de publier *f*	obbligo di denuncia *m*	obligación de declarar *f*

	D	E	F	I	Es
legal recourse for non-payment of a bill (E)	Wechselregress m	—	recours en matière de traite m	regresso cambiario m	recurso cambiario m
legal system (E)	Rechtsordnung f	—	ordre juridique m	ordinamento giuridico m	orden jurídico m
legal tender (E)	gesetzliches Zahlungsmittel n	—	monnaie légale f	moneta legale f	medio de pago legal m
legge di Gresham (I)	Gresham'sches Gesetz n	Gresham Theory	loi de Gresham f	—	Ley Gresham f
legge di riflusso di Fullarton (I)	Fullartonsches Rückströmungsprinzip n	Fullarton reflux principle	principe de reflux de Fullarton m	—	principio de reflujo de Fullarton m
legge fallimentare (I)	Konkursordnung f	Bankruptcy Act	régime juridique de la faillite m	—	ley de las quiebras f
legge sugli investimenti di capitale (I)	Kapitalanlagegesetz n	Capital Investment Law	loi sur les investissements de capital f	—	ley sobre la inversión de capital f
legge sui depositi (I)	Depotgesetz n	Securities Deposit Act	législation sur les dépôts et achats de valeurs par les banques f	—	ley de depósitos f
legge sui depositi bancari (I)	Bankdepotgesetz n	Bank Custody Act	loi sur les dépôts en banque f	—	ley sobre depósitos bancarios f
legge sul commercio estero (I)	Außenwirtschaftsgesetz n	Act on Foreign Trade and Payments	loi sur le commerce extérieur f	—	ley de transacciones exteriores f
legge sul credito al consumo (I)	Verbraucherkreditgesetz n	consumer credit act	loi sur les crédits à la consommation f	—	ley sobre créditos al consumidor f
legge sulla borsa (I)	Börsengesetz n	Stock Exchange Act	loi en matière de bourse f	—	ley sobre las operaciones bursátiles f
legge sulla formazione del bilancio (I)	Bilanzrichtliniengesetz n	Accounting and Reporting Law	loi sur les directives de l'établissement du bilan f	—	ley sobre directivas en materia de balances f
legge sulla promozione del mercato finanziario (I)	Kapitalmarktförderungsgesetz n	Capital Market Encouragement Law	loi sur la stimulation du marché des capitaux f	—	ley sobre el fomento del mercado de capital f
legge sulle banche ipotecarie (I)	Hypothekenbankgesetz n	mortgage bank law	loi sur les banques de prêts hypothécaires f	—	ley de bancos hipotecarios f
legge sulle emissioni (I)	Emissionsgesetz n	Issue Law	loi sur l'émission des billets de banque f	—	ley de emisión f
legge sulle obbligazioni ipotecarie (I)	Pfandbriefgesetz n	mortgage law	législation en matière d'hypothèques f	—	ley de pignoración f
legge sulle società per azioni (I)	Aktiengesetz n	Company Law	loi sur des sociétés par actions f	—	ley sobre régimen jurídico de las sociedades anónimas f
legge sul sistema creditizio (I)	Kreditwesengesetz n	Banking Law	loi sur le crédit f	—	ley sobre el régimen de créditos f
legislación bancaria (Es)	Bankengesetzgebung f	banking legislation	législation bancaire f	legislazione bancaria f	—
législation bancaire (F)	Bankengesetzgebung f	banking legislation	—	legislazione bancaria f	legislación bancaria f
législation en matière de chèque (F)	Scheckrecht n	negotiable instruments law concerning cheques	—	disciplina degli assegni f	derecho de cheque m
législation en matière d'hypothèques (F)	Pfandbriefgesetz n	mortgage law	—	legge sulle obbligazioni ipotecarie f	ley de pignoración f
législation sur les dépôts et achats de valeurs par les banques (F)	Depotgesetz n	Securities Deposit Act	—	legge sui depositi f	ley de depósitos f
legislazione bancaria (I)	Bankengesetzgebung f	banking legislation	législation bancaire f	—	legislación bancaria f
legislazione tributaria (I)	Abgabenordnung f	fiscal code	code des impôts m	—	ordenanza tributaria f
legitimación (Es)	Legitimation f	proof of identity	légitimation f	legittimazione f	—
Legitimation (D)	—	proof of identity	légitimation f	legittimazione f	legitimación f
légitimation (F)	Legitimation f	proof of identity	—	legittimazione f	legitimación f
Legitimationspapiere (D)	—	title-evidencing instrument	titre nominatif m	documenti di legittimazione m/pl	títulos de legitimación m/pl

	D	E	F	I	Es
legittimazione (I)	Legitimation f	proof of identity	légitimation f	—	legitimación f
leichte Papiere (D)	—	low-priced securities	titres de basse cotation m/pl	titoli leggeri m/pl	títulos de baja cotización m/pl
Leihanstalt (D)	—	pawnshop	institut de prêt m	monte di pietà m	monte de piedad m
Leihkapital (D)	—	debt capital	capital de tiers m	capitale di prestito m	capital prestado m
Leihzins (D)	—	interest rate on a loan	intérêt du capital prêté m	interesse m	tipo de interés de un empréstito m
Leistung (D)	—	performance	rendement m	prestazione f	prestación f
Leistungsbilanz (D)	—	balance of goods and services	balance des opérations courantes f	bilancia delle partite correnti f	balanza por cuenta corriente f
Leistungsgarantie (D)	—	performance guarantee	garantie de prestation f	garanzia di esecuzione f	fianza de contratista f
Leitkurs (D)	—	central rate	taux central m	parità centrale f	tipo pivote m
Leitwährung (D)	—	key currency	monnaie-clé f	moneta guida f	moneda de referencia f
lending on goods (E)	Warenbeleihung f	—	emprunt sur marchandises m	prestito su merci m	préstamo sobre mercancías m
lending on securities (E)	Wertpapierleihe f	—	prêt sur valeurs m	prestito per l'acquisto di titoli m	préstamo sobre títulos m
lending rate (E)	Lombardzinsfuß m	—	taux d'intérêt de l'argent prêté et garanti par un gage m	tasso anticipazioni m	tipo de interés para créditos pignoraticios m
lend money on something (E)	beleihen	—	nantir	ipotecare	pignorar
letargía (Es)	Ermattung f	exhaust	léthargie f	indebolimento delle quotazioni m	—
léthargie (F)	Ermattung f	exhaust	—	indebolimento delle quotazioni m	letargía f
letra (Es)	Wechsel m	bill of exchange	lettre de change f	cambiale f	—
letra a la vista (Es)	Sichtwechsel m	demand bill	traite à vue f	cambiale a vista f	—
letra al cobro (Es)	Inkassowechsel m	bill for collection	traite donnée au recouvrement f	cambiale all'incasso f	—
letra al descubierto (Es)	Leerwechsel m	finance bill	traite financière f	cambiale vuota f	—
letra al día fijo (Es)	Tageswechsel m	day bill	traite à jour fixe f	cambiale a scadenza fissa f	—
letra a tantos días fecha (Es)	Datowechsel m	after-date bill	effet payable à un certain délai de date m	cambiale a certo tempo data f	—
letra a tantos días vista (Es)	Nachsichtwechsel m	after-sight bill	traite à un certain délai de vue f	cambiale a certo tempo vista f	—
letra bancaria (Es)	Finanzwechsel m	finance bill	traite financière f	cambiale finanziaria f	—
letra comercial (Es)	Warenwechsel m	commercial bill	traite commerciale f	cambiale commerciale f	—
letra comercial con endoso bancario (Es)	bankgirierter Warenwechsel m	bank endorsed bill	traite endossée par une banque f	effetto commerciale girato da banche m	—
letra cruzada (Es)	Reitwechsel m	windbill	traite de cavalerie f	cambiale incrociata f	—
letra de cambio bancaria (Es)	Finanzakzept n	accepted finance bill	traite financière acceptée f	accettazione bancaria f	—
letra de cambio estándar (Es)	Einheitswechsel m	standard bill	lettre de change normalisée f	cambiale standardizzata f	—
letra de cambio ficticia (Es)	Kellerwechsel m	fictitious bill	traite fictive f	cambiale fittizia f	—
letra de cambio marítima (Es)	Seewechsel m	sea bill	lettre de prêt à la grosse f	cambiale marittima f	—
letra de cambio tomada en prenda (Es)	Wechsellombard m	collateral loan based on a bill of exchange	avance sur effet nanti f	anticipazione su cambiali f	—
letra de mobilización (Es)	Mobilisierungstratte f	mobilization draft	traite de mobilisation f	effetto di smobilizzo m	—
letra de plaza (Es)	Platzwechsel m	local bill	effet sans change de place m	cambiale pagabile sul posto f	—
letra de recambio (Es)	Rückwechsel m	unpaid bill of exchange	traite retournée f	cambiale di ritorno f	—
letra de tesorería (Es)	Schatzwechsel m	Treasury bill	effet du Trésor m	buono del tesoro m	—

	D	E	F	I	Es
letra de vencimientos sucesivos (Es)	Ratenwechsel *m*	bill payable in instalments	effet à échéances multiples *m*	cambiale di pagamento rateale *f*	—
letra documentaria (Es)	Dokumententratte *f*	acceptance bill	traite documentaire *f*	tratta documentaria *f*	—
letra en blanco (Es)	Blanko-Wechsel *m*	blank bill	traite en blanc *f*	cambiale in bianco *f*	—
letra en moneda extranjera (Es)	Devisen-Wechsel *m*	bill in foreign currency	lettre de change libellée en monnaie étrangère *f*	cambiale in valuta estera *f*	—
letra girada (Es)	Tratte *f*	draft	traite *f*	tratta *f*	—
letra girada (Es)	gezogener Wechsel *m*	drawn bill	traite tirée *f*	cambiale tratta *f*	—
letra girada a su propio cargo (Es)	trassiert-eigener Wechsel *m*	bill drawn by the drawer himself	traite tirée sur soi-même *f*	cambiale tratta su se stesso *f*	—
letra librada (Es)	Debitorenziehung *f*	bills drawn on debtors	traite tirée sur débiteur *f*	cambiale tratta sul debitore *f*	—
letra nominativa (Es)	Rektawechsel *m*	non-negotiable bill of exchange	traite non à ordre *f*	cambiale non all'ordine *f*	—
letra prejudicada (Es)	präjudizierter Wechsel *m*	void bill	traite protestée hors des délais *f*	cambiale pregiudicata *f*	—
letra protestada (Es)	Protestwechsel *m*	protested bill	traite protestée *f*	cambiale protestata *f*	—
letras de cambio descontados (Es)	Diskonten *m/pl*	bills discounted	effets escomptés *f/pl*	effetti nazionali *m/pl*	—
letras del Tesoro (Es)	Finanzierungsschätze *m/pl*	financing bonds	effets du Trésor *m/pl*	buoni del tesoro *m/pl*	—
letras del Tesoro sin interés (Es)	U-Schätze *m/pl*	non-interest bearing Treasury bond	obligations du Trésor ne produisant pas d'intérêts *f/pl*	buoni del tesoro infruttiferi *m/pl*	—
letra sobre el exterior (Es)	Auslandswechsel *m*	foreign bill of exchange	traite tirée sur l'étranger *f*	cambiale sull'estero *f*	—
letra sobre el extranjero (Es)	Auslandsakzept *n*	bill in foreign currency	traite tirée sur l'étranger *f*	accettazione estera *f*	—
lettera commerciale (I)	Handelsbrief *m*	business letter	lettre commerciale *f*	—	carta comercial *f*
lettera degli azionisti (I)	Aktionärsbrief *m*	circular letter from board to shareholders	circulaire d'actionnaires *f*	—	circular de accionistas *m*
lettera di conferma (I)	Bestätigungs-schreiben *n*	letter of confirmation	lettre de confirmation *f*	—	carta confirmadora *f*
lettera di credito (I)	Kreditbrief *m*	letter of credit	lettre de crédit *f*	—	carta de crédito *f*
lettera di risparmio (I)	Sparbrief *m*	savings certificate	bon d'épargne *m*	—	cédula de ahorro *f*
letter of confirmation (E)	Bestätigungs-schreiben *n*	—	lettre de confirmation *f*	lettera di conferma *f*	carta confirmadora *f*
letter of credit (E)	Kreditbrief *m*	—	lettre de crédit *f*	lettera di credito *f*	carta de crédito *f*
letter of credit (E)	Akkreditiv *n*	—	accréditif *m*	lettera di credito *f*	crédito documentario *m*
lettre commerciale (F)	Handelsbrief *m*	business letter	—	lettera commerciale *f*	carta comercial *f*
lettre de change (F)	Wechsel *m*	bill of exchange	—	cambiale *f*	letra *f*
lettre de change déposée en garantie d'un prêt (F)	Depotwechsel *m*	bill on deposit	—	cambiale depositata in garanzia *f*	efecto cambial en depósito *m*
lettre de change libellée en monnaie étrangère (F)	Devisen-Wechsel *m*	bill in foreign currency	—	cambiale in valuta estera *f*	letra en moneda extranjera *f*
lettre de change normalisée (F)	Einheitswechsel *m*	standard bill	—	cambiale standardizzata *f*	letra de cambio estándar *f*
lettre de confirmation (F)	Bestätigungs-schreiben *n*	letter of confirmation	—	lettera di conferma *f*	carta confirmadora *f*
lettre de crédit (F)	Kreditbrief *m*	letter of credit	—	lettera di credito *f*	carta de crédito *f*
lettre de crédit circulaire (F)	Reisekreditbrief *m*	traveller's letter of credit	—	titolo di credito turistico *m*	carta de crédito viajero *f*
lettre de prêt à la grosse (F)	Seewechsel *m*	sea bill	—	cambiale marittima *f*	letra de cambio marítima *f*
levy on mortgage profits (E)	Hypothekengewinn-abgabe *f*	—	impôt sur des bénéfices hypothécaires *m*	cessione degli utili ipotecari *f*	impuesto sobre ganancias hipotecarias *m*
ley (Es)	Feingehalt *n*	standard	titre *m*	titolo *m*	—

	D	E	F	I	Es
ley de bancos hipotecarios (Es)	Hypothekenbank-gesetz *n*	mortgage bank law	loi sur les banques de prêts hypothécaires *f*	legge sulle banche ipotecarie *f*	—
ley de depósitos (Es)	Depotgesetz *n*	Securities Deposit Act	législation sur les dépôts et achats de valeurs par les banques *f*	legge sui depositi *f*	—
ley de emisión (Es)	Emissionsgesetz *n*	Issue Law	loi sur l'émission des billets de banque *f*	legge sulle emissioni *f*	—
ley de las quiebras (Es)	Konkursordnung *f*	Bankruptcy Act	régime juridique de la faillite *m*	legge fallimentare *f*	—
ley de pignoración (Es)	Pfandbriefgesetz *n*	mortgage law	législation en matière d'hypothèques *f*	legge sulle obbligazioni ipotecarie *f*	—
ley de transacciones exteriores (Es)	Außenwirtschafts-gesetz *n*	Act on Foreign Trade and Payments	loi sur le le commerce extérieur *f*	legge sul commercio estero *f*	—
Ley Gresham (Es)	Gresham'sches Gesetz *n*	Gresham Theory	loi de Gresham *f*	legge di Gresham *f*	—
ley sobre créditos al consumidor (Es)	Verbraucherkredit-gesetz *n*	consumer credit act	loi sur les crédits à la consommation *f*	legge sul credito al consumo *f*	—
ley sobre depósitos bancarios (Es)	Bankdepotgesetz *n*	Bank Custody Act	loi sur dépôts en banque *f*	legge sui depositi bancari *f*	—
ley sobre directivas en materia de balances (Es)	Bilanzrichtlinien-gesetz *n*	Accounting and Reporting Law	loi sur les directives de l'établissement du bilan *f*	legge sulla formazione del bilancio *f*	—
ley sobre el fomento del mercado de capital (Es)	Kapitalmarktförde-rungsgesetz *n*	Capital Market Encouragement Law	loi sur la stimulation du marché des capitaux *f*	legge sulla promo-zione del mercato finanziario *f*	—
ley sobre el régimen de créditos (Es)	Kreditwesengesetz *n*	Banking Law	loi sur le crédit *f*	legge sul sistema creditizio *f*	—
ley sobre la inversión de capital (Es)	Kapitalanlagegesetz *n*	Capital Investment Law	loi sur les investissements de capital *f*	legge sugli investimenti di capitale *f*	—
ley sobre las operaciones bursátiles (Es)	Börsengesetz *n*	Stock Exchange Act	loi en matière de bourse *f*	legge sulla borsa *f*	—
ley sobre régimen jurídico de las sociedades anónimas (Es)	Aktiengesetz *n*	Company Law	loi sur des sociétés par actions *f*	legge sulle società per azioni *f*	—
liabilities (E)	Passiva *n/pl*	—	passif *m*	passività *f/pl*	pasivo *m*
liability (E)	Verbindlichkeit *f*	—	obligation *f*	debito *m*	obligación *f*
liability (E)	Obligo *n*	—	engagement *m*	garanzia *f*	obligación *f*
liability for breach of warranty (E)	Garantiehaftung *f*	—	responsabilité de garantie *f*	responsabilità da garanzia *f*	responsabilidad de garantía *f*
liable funds (E)	haftendes Eigen-kapital *n*	—	capital propre de garantie *f*	patrimonio netto *m*	capital propio respondiente *m*
liberación de capital (Es)	Kapitalfreisetzung *f*	liberation of capital	libération de capital *f*	disinvestimento di capitale *m*	—
liberamente convertibile (I)	frei konvertierbar	freely convertible	librement convertible	—	libremente convertible
libération de capital (F)	Kapitalfreisetzung *f*	liberation of capital	—	disinvestimento di capitale *m*	liberación de capital *f*
liberation of capital (E)	Kapitalfreisetzung *f*	—	libération de capital *f*	disinvestimento di capitale *m*	liberación de capital *f*
libere contrattazioni (I)	fortlaufende Notierung *f*	variable price quoting	cotation variable *f*	—	cotización variable *f*
libero scambio (I)	Freihandel *m*	over-the-counter trade	commerce libre *m*	—	librecambio *m*
libertad de acceso a un mercado (Es)	freier Marktzutritt *m*	free access to the market	liberté d'accès au marché *f*	accesso libero al mercato *m*	—
libertà per l'intestatario del libretto di risparmio di effettuare versamenti e esborsi in tutte le casse di risparmio tedesche (I)	freizügiger Spar-verkehr *m*	system by which savings depositor can effect inpayments and withdrawals at all savings banks or post offices	épargne libéralisée *f*	—	movimiento de ahorros liberalizado *m*
liberté d'accès au marché (F)	freier Marktzutritt *m*	free access to the market	—	accesso libero al mercato *m*	libertad de acceso a un mercado *f*

	D	E	F	I	Es
Liboranleihen (D)	—	Libor loans	emprunts Libor *m/pl*	obbligazioni libor *f/pl*	empréstitos libor *m/pl*
Libor loans (E)	Liboranleihen *f/pl*	—	emprunts Libor *m/pl*	obbligazioni libor *f/pl*	empréstitos libor *m/pl*
librado (Es)	Bezogener *m*	drawee	tiré *m*	trattario *m*	—
librador (Es)	Wechselaussteller *m*	drawer of a bill	tireur d'une traite *m*	traente di una cambiale *m*	—
libranza colectiva (Es)	Sammeltratte *f*	collective bill	traite globale *f*	tratta collettiva *f*	—
librecambio (Es)	Freihandel *m*	over-the-counter trade	commerce libre *m*	libero scambio *m*	—
librement convertible (F)	frei konvertierbar	freely convertible	—	liberamente convertibile	libremente convertible
libremente convertible (Es)	frei konvertierbar	freely convertible	librement convertible	liberamente convertibile	—
libreta de ahorro (Es)	Sparbuch *n*	savings-bank book	livret d'épargne *m*	libretto di risparmio *m*	—
libreta de ahorro de hojas intercambiables (Es)	Loseblattsparbuch *n*	loose-leaf savings book	livret d'épargne à feuilles mobiles *m*	libretto di risparmio a fogli mobili *m*	—
libreta de ahorros como regalo (Es)	Geschenksparbuch *n*	gift savings book	livret d'épargne en cadeau *m*	libretto di risparmio in omaggio *m*	—
libreta de depósito (Es)	Depotbuch *n*	deposit book	registre des valeurs en dépôt *m*	libretto di deposito *m*	—
libretto di deposito (I)	Verwahrungsbuch *n*	custody ledger	registre des dépôts *m*	—	libro de custodia *m*
libretto di deposito (I)	Depotbuch *n*	deposit book	registre des valeurs en dépôt *m*	—	libreta de depósito *f*
libretto di deposito titoli (I)	Sachdepot *n*	impersonal security deposit	dépôt de choses *m*	—	depósito impersonal de títulos *m*
libretto di risparmio (I)	Sparbuch *n*	savings-bank book	livret d'épargne *m*	—	libreta de ahorro *f*
libretto di risparmio a fogli mobili (I)	Loseblattsparbuch *n*	loose-leaf savings book	livret d'épargne à feuilles mobiles *m*	—	libreta de ahorro de hojas intercambiables *f*
libretto di risparmio in omaggio (I)	Geschenksparbuch *n*	gift savings book	livret d'épargne en cadeau *m*	—	libreta de ahorros como regalo *f*
libretto personale di deposito titoli (I)	Personendepot *n*	customer's security deposit	dépôt de personne *m*	—	depósito personal *m*
libro comercial (Es)	Handelsbuch *n*	commercial book	livre de commerce *m*	libro di commercio *m*	—
libro de acciones (Es)	Aktienbuch *n*	share register	registre des actions *m*	registro delle azioni *m*	—
libro de aceptaciones (Es)	Obligobuch *n*	bills discounted ledger	livre des traites escomptées *m*	libro rischi *m*	—
libro de corredores (Es)	Maklerbuch *n*	dealings book of the stockbroker	carnet des négociations *m*	libro giornale dell'agente di cambio *m*	—
libro de custodia (Es)	Verwahrungsbuch *n*	custody ledger	registre des dépôts *m*	libretto di deposito *m*	—
libro del debito pubblico (I)	Bundesschuldbuch *n*	Federal Debt Register	grand-livre de la dette publique *m*	—	registro de deudas federales *m*
libro delle ipoteche (I)	Hypothekenregister *n*	mortgage register	livre foncier *m*	—	registro hipotecario *m*
libro de pagos parciales (Es)	Teilzahlungsbuch *n*	credit financing register	livre de payements partiels *m*	libro di pagamento parziale *m*	—
libro de valores (Es)	Effektenbuch *n*	stockbook	registre des titres *m*	registro dei titoli *m*	—
libro di commercio (I)	Handelsbuch *n*	commercial book	livre de commerce *m*	—	libro comercial *m*
libro di pagamento parziale (I)	Teilzahlungsbuch *n*	credit financing register	livre de payements partiels *m*	—	libro de pagos parciales *m*
libro giornale dell'agente di cambio (I)	Maklerbuch *n*	dealings book of the stockbroker	carnet des négociations *m*	—	libro de corredores *m*
libro rischi (I)	Obligobuch *n*	bills discounted ledger	livre des traites escomptées *m*	—	libro de aceptaciones *m*
licencia de exportación (Es)	Ausfuhrgenehmigung *f*	export license	autorisation d'exportation *f*	autorizzazione all'esportazione *f*	—
license (E)	Konzession *f*	—	concession *f*	licenza *f*	concesión *f*
licenza (I)	Konzession *f*	license	concession *f*	—	concesión *f*
lieferbares Wertpapier (D)	—	deliverable security	valeur négociable *f*	titolo negoziabile *m*	título de buena entrega *m*
Lieferbarkeitsbescheinigung (D)	—	certificate of good delivery	certificat de négociabilité *m*	certificato di negoziabilità *m*	certificado de disponibilidad *m*

	D	E	F	I	Es
Liefergarantie (D)	—	guarantee of delivery	garantie de livraison f	garanzia di sostegno f	garantía de entrega f
Lieferkonto (D)	—	accounts payable	compte de fournisseurs m	conto fornitori m	cuenta de suministradores f
Liegenschaft (D)	—	immovable property	bien foncier m	bene immobile m	inmuebles m/pl
lien (E)	Pfandrecht n	—	droit de gage m	diritto di pegno m	derecho de prenda m
lieu de l'exécution de la prestation (F)	Erfüllungsort m	place of performance	—	luogo d'adempimento m	lugar del cumplimiento m
ligne de résistance (F)	Widerstandslinie f	line of resistance	—	linea di resistenza f	línea de resistencia f
ligne de soutien (F)	Unterstützunglinie f	support level	—	linea di sostegno f	línea de sostenimiento f
ligne de swap (F)	Swaplinie f	swap line	—	linea swap f	línea swap f
limitation of actions (E)	Verjährung f	—	prescription f	prescrizione f	prescripción f
limitazione della concorrenza (I)	Wettbewerbsbe-schränkung f	restraint of competition	restriction apportée à la concurrence f	—	restricción a la competencia f
limitazione diritto di pegno e ritenzione su depositi di terzi (I)	Fremdvermutung f	presumption that securities deposited are fiduciary deposit	présomption que les valeurs déposées sont administrées à titre fiduciaire f	—	suposición de depósito ajeno f
limited capacity to enter into legal transactions (E)	beschränkte Geschäftsfähigkeit f	—	capacité restreinte d'accomplir des actes juridiques f	capacità giudica limitata f	incapacidad jurídica parcial f
limited dividend (E)	limitierte Dividende f	—	dividende limité m	dividendo limitato m	dividendo limitado m
límite de crédito (Es)	Kreditlimit n	credit limit	plafond du crédit alloué m	limite di credito m	—
límite de garantía (Es)	Bürgschaftsplafond n	guarantee limit	plafond de garantie m	plafond di fideiussione m	—
limite di credito (I)	Kreditlimit n	credit limit	plafond du crédit alloué m	—	límite de crédito m
limite di prezzo (I)	Kurslimit n	price limit	cours limité m	—	cambio limitado m
limited liability company (E)	Gesellschaft mit be-schränkter Haftung [GmbH] f	—	société de re-sponsabilité limitée S.A.R.L. f	società a responsabilità limitata f	sociedad de responsabilidad limitada f
limited liability shareholder (E)	Kommanditaktionär m	—	actionnaire d'une société en commandite par actions m	socio di una società in accomandita per azioni m	accionista comanditario m
limited partner (E)	Kommanditist m	—	commanditaire m	accomandante m	comanditario m
limited partnership (E)	Kommanditge-sellschaft f	—	société en commandite f	società in accomandita semplice f	sociedad comanditaria f
limite massimo di fido (I)	Kreditplafond n	credit ceiling	plafond du crédit accordé m	—	plafón de crédito m
límite máximo (Es)	Plafond m	ceiling	plafond m	plafond m	—
límite máximo de votos (Es)	Höchststimmrecht n	maximum voting right	droit de vote maximum m	valore massimo di voto m	—
limitierte Dividende (D)	—	limited dividend	dividende limité m	dividendo limitato m	dividendo limitado m
línea de aceptación (Es)	Akzeptlinie f	line of acceptance	plafond des crédits sur effets acceptés m	linea di credito d'accettazione f	—
línea de crédito (Es)	Kreditlinie f	credit line	plafond du crédit accordé m	linea di credito f	—
línea de crédito (Es)	Rahmenkredit m	credit line	crédit-cadre m	linea di credito f	—
línea de resistencia (Es)	Widerstandslinie f	line of resistance	ligne de résistance f	linea di resistenza f	—
línea de sostenimiento (Es)	Unterstützunglinie f	support level	ligne de soutien f	linea di sostegno f	—
linea di credito (I)	Rahmenkredit m	credit line	crédit-cadre m	—	línea de crédito f
linea di credito (I)	Kreditlinie f	credit line	plafond du crédit accordé m	—	línea de crédito f
linea di credito d'accettazione (I)	Akzeptlinie f	line of acceptance	plafond des crédits sur effets acceptés m	—	línea de aceptación f
linea di resistenza (I)	Widerstandslinie f	line of resistance	ligne de résistance f	—	línea de resistencia f
linea di sostegno (I)	Unterstützunglinie f	support level	ligne de soutien f	—	línea de sostenimiento f

	D	E	F	I	Es
línea swap (Es)	Swaplinie *f*	swap line	ligne de swap *f*	linea swap *f*	—
linea swap (I)	Swaplinie *f*	swap line	ligne de swap *f*	—	línea swap *f*
line of acceptance (E)	Akzeptlinie *f*	—	plafond des crédits sur effets acceptés *m*	linea di credito d'accettazione *f*	línea de aceptación *f*
line of resistance (E)	Widerstandslinie *f*	—	ligne de résistance *f*	linea di resistenza *f*	línea de resistencia *f*
lingot de métal précieux (F)	Bullion *m*	bullion	—	bullion *m*	lingote de metal fino *m*
lingot d'or (F)	Goldbarren *m*	gold bar	—	lingotto d'oro *m*	lingote de oro *m*
lingote de metal fino (Es)	Bullion *m*	bullion	lingot de métal précieux *m*	bullion *m*	—
lingote de oro (Es)	Goldbarren *m*	gold bar	lingot d'or *m*	lingotto d'oro *m*	—
lingotto d'oro (I)	Goldbarren *m*	gold bar	lingot d'or *m*	—	lingote de oro *m*
linked currency (E)	gebundene Währung *f*	—	monnaie liée *f*	valuta a regime di controllo *f*	moneda vinculada *f*
liquidación (Es)	Liquidation *f*	liquidation	liquidation *f*	liquidazione *f*	—
liquidación (Es)	Glattstellen *n*	settlement	réalisation *f*	operazione di compensazione mediante trattazione titoli *f*	—
liquidación de cheques (Es)	Scheckabrechnung *f*	cheque clearance	règlement des chèques par voie de compensation *m*	compensazione degli assegni *f*	—
liquid assets (E)	flüssige Mittel *n/pl*	—	capitaux liquides *m/pl*	fondi liquidi *m/pl*	fondos líquidos *m/pl*
liquidateur de la faillite (F)	Konkursverwalter *m*	administrator in bankruptcy proceedings	—	curatore del fallimento *m*	síndico de quiebra *m*
liquidating dividend (E)	Liquidationsrate *f*	—	quote-part de la liquidation *f*	tasso di liquidazione *m*	tasa de liquidación *f*
Liquidation (D)	—	liquidation	liquidation *f*	liquidazione *f*	liquidación *f*
liquidation (E)	Liquidation *f*	—	liquidation *f*	liquidazione *f*	liquidación *f*
liquidation (F)	Liquidation *f*	liquidation	—	liquidazione *f*	liquidación *f*
liquidation bond (E)	Liquidationsschuldverschreibung *f*	—	obligation de liquidation *f*	titolo obbligazionario di liquidazione *m*	bono de liquidación *f*
liquidation certificate (E)	Liquidationsanteilsschein *m*	—	certificat de la liquidation *m*	certificato di quota liquidazione *m*	cupón de parte de liquidación *m*
liquidation fee (E)	Liquidationsgebühr *f*	—	frais de liquidation *m/pl*	commissione di liquidazione *f*	derechos de liquidación *m/pl*
liquidation outpayment rate (E)	Liquidationsauszahlungskurs *m*	—	cours de compensation *m*	corso di compensazione *m*	cotización de compensación *f*
Liquidationsanteilsschein (D)	—	liquidation certificate	certificat de liquidation *m*	certificato di quota liquidazione *m*	cupón de parte de liquidación *m*
Liquidationsauszahlungskurs (D)	—	liquidation outpayment rate	cours de compensation *m*	corso di compensazione *m*	cotización de compensación *f*
Liquidationserlös (D)	—	remaining assets after liquidation	produit de la liquidation *m*	ricavato dalla liquidazione *m*	producto de liquidación *m*
Liquidationsgebühr (D)	—	liquidation fee	frais de liquidation *m/pl*	commissione di liquidazione *f*	derechos de liquidación *m/pl*
Liquidationskurs (D)	—	making-up price	cours de liquidation *m*	corso di compensazione *m*	cambio de liquidación *m*
Liquidationsrate (D)	—	liquidating dividend	quote-part de la liquidation *f*	tasso di liquidazione *m*	tasa de liquidación *f*
Liquidationsschuldverschreibung (D)	—	liquidation bond	obligation de liquidation *f*	titolo obbligazionario di liquidazione *m*	bono de liquidación *f*
Liquidationsüberschuß (D)	—	realization profit	excédent de liquidation *m*	eccedenza da liquidazione *f*	exceso de liquidación *m*
liquidazione (I)	Liquidation *f*	liquidation	liquidation *f*	—	liquidación *f*
liquidazione (I)	Ausverkauf *m*	clearance sale	soldes *f*	—	venta de liquidación *f*
liquidez (Es)	Liquidität *f*	liquidity	liquidité *f*	liquidità *f*	—
liquidez bancaria (Es)	Bankliquidität *f*	bank liquidity	liquidité de banque *f*	liquidità bancaria *f*	—
liquidez internacional (Es)	internationale Liquidität *f*	international cash position	liquidité internationale *f*	liquidità internazionale *f*	—
liquidez secundaria (Es)	Sekundär-Liquidität *f*	secondary liquidity	liquidité secondaire *f*	liquidità secondaria *f*	—

	D	E	F	I	Es
liquidità (I)	Liquidität f	liquidity	liquidité f	—	liquidez f
liquidità bancaria (I)	Bankliquidität f	bank liquidity	liquidité de banque f	—	liquidez bancaria f
liquidità insufficiente (I)	Unterliquidität f	lack of liquidity	insuffisance de liquidité f	—	insuficiencia de liquidez f
liquidità internazionale (I)	internationale Liquidität f	international cash position	liquidité internationale f	—	liquidez internacional f
liquidità secondaria (I)	Sekundär-Liquidität f	secondary liquidity	liquidité secondaire f	—	liquidez secundaria f
Liquidität (D)	—	liquidity	liquidité f	liquidità f	liquidez f
Liquiditätsanleihe (D)	—	liquidity loan	emprunt de liquidité m	obbligazione di liquidità f	empréstito de liquidez m
Liquiditätskonsortial-bank (D)	—	liquidity syndicate bank	syndicat bancaire de liquidité m	banca consorziale garanzia liquidità f	banco asegurador de liquidez m
Liquiditätspapier (D)	—	liquidity papers	titre de liquidité m	titolo liquido m	título de liquidez m
Liquiditätsquote (D)	—	liquidity ratio	coefficient de liquidité m	tasso di liquidità m	coeficiente de liquidez m
Liquiditätsreserve (D)	—	liquid reserves	réserve de liquidité f	riserva liquida f	reserva de liquidez f
Liquiditätsstatus (D)	—	liquidity status	état de la liquidité m	situazione di liquidità f	situación de liquidez f
Liquiditätstheorie (D)	—	liquidity theory	théorie de la liquidité f	teoria della liquidità f	teoría de liquidez f
liquidité (F)	Liquidität f	liquidity	—	liquidità f	liquidez f
liquidité de banque (F)	Bankliquidität f	bank liquidity	—	liquidità bancaria f	liquidez bancaria f
liquidité internationale (F)	internationale Liquidität f	international cash position	—	liquidità internazionale f	liquidez internacional f
liquidité secondaire (F)	Sekundär-Liquidität f	secondary liquidity	—	liquidità secondaria f	liquidez secundaria f
liquidity (E)	Liquidität f	—	liquidité f	liquidità f	liquidez f
liquidity loan (E)	Liquiditätsanleihe f	—	emprunt de liquidité m	obbligazione di liquidità f	empréstito de liquidez m
liquidity papers (E)	Liquiditätspapier n	—	titre de liquidité m	titolo liquido m	título de liquidez m
liquidity ratio (E)	Liquiditätsquote f	—	coefficient de liquidité m	tasso di liquidità m	coeficiente de liquidez m
liquidity status (E)	Liquiditätsstatus m	—	état de la liquidité m	situazione di liquidità f	situación de liquidez f
liquidity syndicate bank (E)	Liquiditätskon-sortialbank f	—	syndicat bancaire de liquidité m	banca consorziale garanzia liquidità f	banco asegurador de liquidez m
liquidity theory (E)	Liquiditätstheorie f	—	théorie de la liquidité f	teoria della liquidità f	teoría de liquidez f
liquid money market (E)	flüssiger Geldmarkt m	—	marché monétaire liquide m	mercato del denaro liquido m	mercado monetario líquido m
liquid reserves (E)	Liquiditätsreserve f	—	réserve de liquidité f	riserva liquida f	reserva de liquidez f
list of balances (E)	Saldenbilanz f		balance des soldes des comptes généraux f	conto saldi contabili m	balance de saldos m
lista de depósito (Es)	Depotaufstellung f	list of securities deposited	liste des valeurs f	distinta di deposito déposées f	—
lista de deudores (Es)	Schuldnerverzeichnis n	list of insolvent debtors	liste des personnes ayant été poursuivies pour dettes f	elenco dei debitori m	—
lista de protesta (Es)	Protestliste f	list of firms whose bills and notes have been protested	liste des protêts f	elenco dei protesti m	—
lista de títulos pignorados (Es)	Lombardverzeichnis n	list of securities eligible as collateral	liste des titres remis en gage f	elenco titoli ammessi ad anticipazioni m	—
lista negra (Es)	schwarze Liste f	black bourse	liste noire f	elenco dei debitori m	—
liste des personnes ayant été poursuivies pour dettes (F)	Schuldnerverzeichnis n	list of insolvent debtors	—	elenco dei debitori m	lista de deudores f
liste des protêts (F)	Protestliste m	list of firms whose bills and notes have been protested	—	elenco dei protesti m	lista de protesta f
liste des titres remis en gage (F)	Lombardverzeichnis n	list of securities eligible as collateral	—	elenco titoli ammessi ad anticipazioni m	lista de títulos pignorados f
liste des valeurs déposées (F)	Depotaufstellung f	list of securities deposited	—	distinta di deposito f	lista de depósito f

	D	E	F	I	Es
liste noire (F)	schwarze Liste *f*	black bourse	—	elenco dei debitori *m*	lista negra *f*
liste numérique (F)	Nummernverzeichnis *n*	list of serial numbers of securities purchased or deposited	—	elenco numerico *m*	escritura numérica *f*
listín de bolsa (Es)	Kursblatt *n*	stock exchange list	cote de la bourse *f*	listino di borsa *m*	—
listino di borsa (I)	Kurszettel *m*	stock exchange list	bulletin des cours *m*	—	boletín de bolsa *m*
listino di borsa (I)	Kursblatt *n*	stock exchange list	cote de la bourse *f*	—	listín de bolsa *m*
listino ufficiale (I)	offizielles Kursblatt *n*	offical stock exchange list	cote de la bourse officielle *f*	—	boletín oficial *m*
list of firms whose bills and notes have been protested (E)	Protestliste *f*	—	liste des protêts *f*	elenco dei protesti *m*	lista de protesta *f*
list of insolvent debtors (E)	Schuldnerverzeichnis *n*	—	liste des personnes ayant été pousuivies pour dettes *f*	elenco dei debitori *m*	lista de deudores *f*
list of securities deposited (E)	Depotaufstellung *f*	—	liste des valeurs déposées *f*	distinta di deposito *f*	lista de depósito *f*
list of securities eligible as collateral (E)	Lombardverzeichnis *n*	—	liste des titres remis en gage *f*	elenco titoli ammessi ad anticipazioni *m*	lista de títulos pignorados *f*
list of serial numbers of securities purchased or deposited (E)	Nummernverzeichnis *n*	—	liste numérique *f*	elenco numerico *m*	escritura numérica *f*
livello degli interessi (I)	Zinsniveau *n*	interest rate level	niveau du taux d'intérêt *m*	—	nivel de los tipos de interés *m*
livello dei prezzi (I)	Preisniveau *n*	price level	niveau des prix *m*	—	nivel de precios *m*
livre de commerce (F)	Handelsbuch *n*	commercial book	—	libro di commercio *m*	libro comercial *m*
livre de payements partiels (F)	Teilzahlungsbuch *n*	credit financing register	—	libro di pagamento parziale *m*	libro de pagos parciales *m*
livre des traites escomptées (F)	Obligobuch *n*	bills discounted ledger	—	libro rischi *m*	libro de aceptaciones *m*
livre foncier (F)	Hypothekenregister *n*	mortgage register	—	libro delle ipoteche *m*	registro hipotecario *m*
livre foncier (F)	Grundbuch *n*	register of land titles	—	catasto *m*	registro de la propiedad *m*
livret d'épargne (F)	Sparbuch *n*	savings-bank book	—	libretto di risparmio *m*	libreta de ahorro *f*
livret d'épargne à feuilles mobiles (F)	Loseblattsparbuch *n*	loose-leaf savings book	—	libretto di risparmio a fogli mobili *m*	libreta de ahorro de hojas intercambiables *f*
livret d'épargne en cadeau (F)	Geschenksparbuch *n*	gift savings book	—	libretto di risparmio in omaggio *m*	libreta de ahorros como regalo *f*
loan (E)	Darlehen *n*		prêt *m*	credito *m*	préstamo *m*
loan at variable rates (E)	zinsvariable Anleihe *f*	—	emprunt d'un taux d'intérêt variable *m*	prestito a tasso d'interesse variabile *m*	empréstito con un tipo de interés variable *m*
loan business (E)	Anleihegeschäft *n*	—	opération de placement de titres d'emprunt *f*	operazione di prestito *f*	operación crediticia *f*
loan calculation (E)	Anleiherechnung *f*	—	décompte des emprunts *m*	calcolo rimborso e interessi *m*	cálculo de empréstito *m*
loan custodianship (E)	Anleihetreuhänderschaft *f*	—	fidéicommis d'emprunts *m*	amministrazione fiduciaria prestiti *f*	fideicomiso de empréstitos *m*
loan financing (E)	Darlehensfinanzierung *f*	—	financement par capitaux prêtés *m*	finanziamento mediante mutuo *m*	financiación de préstamo *f*
loan for special purposes (E)	Objektkredit *m*	—	crédit destiné à un objet déterminé *m*	credito per specifico oggetto *m*	crédito destinado a un determinado objeto *m*
loan granted for building purposes (E)	Bauspardarlehen *n*	—	prêt d'épargne-construction *m*	mutuo edilizio *m*	préstamo ahorro-vivienda *m*
loan granted in form of a mortgage bond (E)	Naturaldarlehen *n*	—	prêt en nature *m*	prestito ipotecario a obbligazione fondiaria *m*	empréstito en especie *m*
loan granted to a local authority (E)	Kommunaldarlehen *n*	—	prêt aux communes *m*	mutuo comunale *m*	empréstito municipal *m*
loan in foreign currency (E)	Valuta-Anleihen *f/pl*	—	emprunt émis en monnaie étrangère *m*	prestiti in valuta estera *m/pl*	empréstitos en moneda extranjera *m/pl*
loan of credit (E)	Kreditleihe *f*	—	prêt de crédit *m*	credito di firma *m*	préstamo de crédito *m*

	D	E	F	I	Es
loan on a gold basis (E)	Goldanleihe f	—	emprunt or m	prestito oro m	empréstito con garantía-oro m
loan on a trust basis (E)	Treuhandkredit m	—	crédit fiduciaire m	credito indiretto m	crédito fiduciario m
loan on landed property (E)	Bodenkredit m	—	crédit foncier m	credito fondario m	crédito inmobiliario m
loan repayable in full at a due date (E)	Zinsanleihe f	—	emprunt produisant des intérêts m	prestito non ammortizzabile m	empréstito produciendo interés m
loans granted to members of a managing board (E)	Organkredit m	—	crédit accordé par une banque à ses membres du directoire m	credito concesso all'organico m	crédito interconsorcial m
loan with profit participation (E)	Beteiligungsdarlehen n	—	prêt de participation m	partecipazione a forma di anticipo f	préstamo participativo m
local authorities bank (E)	Kommunalbank f	—	banque communale f	banca comunale f	banco comunal m
local authorities loan (E)	Kommunalanleihe f	—	emprunt communal m	prestito comunale m	empréstito municipal m
local banks (E)	Lokalbanken f/pl	—	banques locales f/pl	banche locali f/pl	bancos locales m/pl
local bill (E)	Platzwechsel m	—	effet sans change de place m	cambiale pagabile sul posto f	letra de plaza f
local bond (E)	Kommunalobligation f	—	obligation communale f	obbligazione comunale f	obligación comunal f
local expenses (E)	Platzspesen pl	—	change de place m	spese d'incasso di piazza f/pl	gastos locales m/pl
local stock exchange (E)	Lokalbörse f	—	bourse de province f	borsa locale f	bolsa local f
local transfer (E)	Platzübertragung f	—	virement de place m	trasferimento su piazza m	transferencia local f
location-vente (F)	Mietkauf m	lease with option to purchase	—	locazione finanziaria f	arrendamiento con opción de compra m
locazione finanziaria (I)	Mietkauf m	lease with option to purchase	location-vente f	—	arrendamiento con opción de compra m
Locogeschäft (D)	—	spot business	opération en disponible f	operazione a contanti f	operaciones de entrega inmediata f/pl
loi de Gresham (F)	Gresham'sches Gesetz n	Gresham Theory	—	legge di Gresham f	Ley Gresham f
loi en matière de bourse (F)	Börsengesetz n	Stock Exchange Act	—	legge sulla borsa f	ley sobre las operaciones bursátiles f
loi sur dépôts en banque (F)	Bankdepotgesetz n	Bank Custody Act	—	legge sui depositi bancari f	ley sobre depósitos bancarios f
loi sur des sociétés par actions (F)	Aktiengesetz n	Company Law	—	legge sulle società per azioni f	ley sobre régimen jurídico de las sociedades anónimas f
loi sur la stimulation du marché des capitaux (F)	Kapitalmarktförderungsgesetz n	Capital Market Encouragement Law	—	legge sulla promozione del mercato finanziario f	ley sobre el fomento del mercado de capital f
loi sur le commerce extérieur (F)	Außenwirtschaftsgesetz n	Act on Foreign Trade and Payments	—	legge sul commercio estero f	ley de transacciones exteriores f
loi sur le crédit (F)	Kreditwesengesetz n	Banking Law	—	legge sul sistema creditizio f	ley sobre el régimen de créditos f
loi sur l'émission des billets de banque (F)	Emissionsgesetz n	Issue Law	—	legge sulle emissioni f	ley de emisión f
loi sur les banques de prêts hypothécaires (F)	Hypothekenbankgesetz n	mortgage bank law	—	legge sulle banche ipotecarie f	ley de bancos hipotecarios f
loi sur les crédits à la consommation (F)	Verbraucherkreditgesetz n	consumer credit act	—	legge sul credito al consumo f	ley sobre créditos al consumidor f
loi sur les directives de l'établissement du bilan (F)	Bilanzrichtliniengesetz n	Accounting and Reporting Law	—	legge sulla formazione del bilancio f	ley sobre directivas en materia de balances f
loi sur les investissements de capital (F)	Kapitalanlagegesetz n	Capital Investment Law	—	legge sugli investimenti di capitale f	ley sobre la inversión de capital f
loi sur les sociétés anonymes (F)	Aktienrecht n	company law	—	diritto delle società per azioni m	derecho de sociedades anónimas m

	D	E	F	I	Es
Lokalbanken (D)	—	local banks	banques locales *f/pl*	banche locali *f/pl*	bancos locales *m/pl*
Lokalbörse (D)	—	local stock exchange	bourse de province *f*	borsa locale *f*	bolsa local *f*
Lokalpapier (D)	—	security only traded on a regional stock exchange	valeur régionale *f*	titolo locale *m*	título local *m*
Lokogeschäft (D)	—	spot transaction	opération en disponible *f*	operazione a contanti *f*	operaciones de entrega inmediata *f/pl*
Lombarddepot (D)	—	collateral deposit	dépôt de titres remis en nantissement *m*	deposito lombard *m*	depósito de valores pignoraticios *m*
Lombardeffekten (D)	—	securities serving as collateral	titres remis en nantissement *m/pl*	titoli lombard *m/pl*	títulos pignoraticios *m/pl*
Lombardfähigkeit (D)	—	acceptability as collateral	capacité d'être déposé à titre de gage *f*	idoneità di titoli all'anticipazione *f*	capacidad de ser pignorable *f*
Lombardkredit (D)	—	collateral credit	crédit garanti par nantissement *m*	anticipazione su crediti *f*	crédito pignoraticio *m*
Lombardsatz (D)	—	bankrate for advances against collateral	taux lombard *m*	tasso lombard *m*	tipo de pignoración *m*
Lombardverzeichnis (D)	—	list of securities eligible as collateral	liste des titres remis en gage *f*	elenco titoli ammessi ad anticipazioni *m*	lista de títulos pignorados *f*
Lombardzinsfuß (D)	—	lending rate	taux d'intérêt de l'argent prêté et garanti par un gage *m*	tasso anticipazioni *m*	tipo de interés para créditos pignoraticios *m*
long distance giro (E)	Ferngiro *m*	—	virement entre deux places bancaires *m*	bonifico da una piazza all'altra *m*	transferencia de una plaza a otra *f*
long run (E)	lange Sicht *f*	—	échéance longue *f*	a lunga scadenza	a largo plazo
long-term credit (E)	langfristiger Kredit *m*	—	crédit à long terme *m*	credito a lunga scadenza *m*	crédito a largo plazo *m*
long-term deposits (E)	langfristige Einlagen *f/pl*	—	placements à long terme *m/pl*	depositi a lunga scadenza *m/pl*	imposiciones a largo plazo *f/pl*
lonja (Es)	Produktenbörse *f*	produce exchange	bourse de marchandises *f*	borsa merci *f*	—
loose-leaf savings book (E)	Loseblattsparbuch *n*	—	livret d'épargne à feuilles mobiles *m*	libretto di risparmio a fogli mobili *m*	libreta de ahorro de hojas intercambiables *f*
lordo (I)	Brutto	gross	brut	—	bruto
loro account (E)	Lorokonto *n*	—	compte d'un client bancaire *m*	conto loro *m*	cuenta de un cliente bancario *f*
loro balance (E)	Loroguthaben *n*	—	avoirs de clients bancaires *m*	avere loro *m*	haberes de clientes bancarios *m/pl*
Loroguthaben (D)	—	loro balance	avoirs de clients bancaires *m*	avere loro *m*	haberes de clientes bancarios *m/pl*
Lorokonto (D)	—	loro account	compte d'un client bancaire *m*	conto loro *m*	cuenta de un cliente bancario *f*
Löschung (D)	—	cancellation	annulation *f*	cancellazione *f*	cancelación *f*
Loseblattsparbuch (D)	—	loose-leaf savings book	livret d'épargne à feuilles mobiles *m*	libretto di risparmio a fogli mobili *m*	libreta de ahorro de hojas intercambiables *f*
Loskurs (D)	—	lottery quotation	cotation de tirage au sort *f*	corso estratto a sorte *m*	cotización de sorteo *f*
loss (E)	Verlust *m*	—	perte *f*	perdita *f*	pérdida *f*
loss allocation (E)	Verlustzuweisung *f*	—	assignation des pertes *f*	assegnazione perdite *f*	asignación de pérdidas *f*
loss-compensation (E)	Verlustausgleich *m*	—	compensation des pertes *f*	conguaglio dei passivi *m*	compensación de pérdidas *f*
lote no negociado oficialmente (Es)	gebrochener Schluß *m*	odd lot	lot ne pas négocié officiellement *f*	lotto senza quotazione ufficiale *m*	—
lot ne pas négocié officiellement (F)	gebrochener Schluß *m*	odd lot	—	lotto senza quotazione ufficiale *m*	lote no negociado oficialmente *m*
lotta all'inflazione (I)	Inflationsbekämpfung *f*	struggle against inflation	lutte contre l'inflation *f*	—	lucha contra la inflación *f*
Lotterieanleihen (D)	—	lottery bonds	emprunts à lots *m/pl*	prestiti a premi *m/pl*	empréstitos de lotería *m/pl*
lottery bond (E)	Auslosungsanleihe *f*	—	emprunt amortissable par séries tirées au sort *m*	prestito rimborsabile mediante per sorteggio *m*	empréstito de sorteo *m*
lottery bonds (E)	Lotterieanleihen *f/pl*	—	emprunts à lots *m/pl*	prestiti a premi *m/pl*	empréstitos de lotería *m/pl*

	D	E	F	I	Es
lottery loan (E)	Prämienanleihe f	—	emprunt à primes m	prestito a premi m	empréstito con prima m
lottery premium saving (E)	Gewinnsparen n	—	épargne à lots f	risparmio a premi m	ahorro de beneficios m
lottery quotation (E)	Loskurs m	—	cotation de tirage au sort f	corso estratto a sorte m	cotización de sorteo f
lotto senza quotazione ufficiale (I)	gebrochener Schluß m	odd lot	lot ne pas négocié officiellement f	—	lote no negociado oficialmente m
low-denomination share for small savers (E)	Volksaktie f	—	action populaire f	azione popolare f	acción popular f
lowest value principle (E)	Niederstwertprinzip n	—	principe de la valeur minimale m	principio del valore minimo m	principio del valor mínimo m
low-priced securities (E)	leichte Papiere n/pl	—	titres de basse cotation m/pl	titoli leggeri m/pl	títulos de baja cotización m/pl
lucha contra la inflación (Es)	Inflationsbe-kämpfung f	struggle against inflation	lutte contre l'inflation f	lotta all'inflazione f	—
lucro cessante (I)	imaginärer Gewinn m	imaginary profit	bénéfice imaginaire m	—	beneficio imaginario m
lugar del cumplimiento (Es)	Erfüllungsort m	place of performance	lieu de l'exécution de la prestation m	luogo d'adempimento m	—
lump-sum payment (E)	Kapitalabfindung f	—	indemnité en capital f	indennità in capitale f	importe de la opción m
luogo d'adempimento (I)	Erfüllungsort m	place of performance	lieu de l'exécution de la prestation m	—	lugar del cumplimiento m
lustlos (D)	—	slack	inactif	fiacco	poco animado
lutte contre l'inflation (F)	Inflationsbe-kämpfung f	struggle against inflation	—	lotta all'inflazione f	lucha contra la inflación f
macchina contadenaro (I)	Geldzählautomat m	money counting machine	machine compte-monnaie f	—	máquina de contar dinero f
macchina per la cernita delle monete (I)	Geldsortiermaschine f	money sorting machine	trieuse d'argent f	—	máquina clasifi cadora de dinero f
machine compte-monnaie (F)	Geldzählautomat m	money counting machine	—	macchina contade-naro f	máquina de contar dinero f
maggioranza del capitale (I)	Kapitalmehrheit f	capital majority	majorité de capital f	—	mayoría de capital f
maggioranza qualificata (I)	qualifizierte Mehrheit	qualified majority	majorité qualifiée f	—	mayoría calificada f
magic polygon (E)	magisches Vieleck n	—	polygone magique m	poligono magico m	polígono mágico m
magisches Vieleck (D)	—	magic polygon	polygone magique m	poligono magico m	polígono mágico m
magnitudes autónomas (Es)	autonome Größen f/pl	autonomous variables f/pl	magnitudes autonomes f/pl	grandezze autonome	—
magnitudes autonome (F)	autonome Größen f/pl	autonomous variables f/pl	—	grandezze autonome	magnitudes autónomas f/pl
Mahnung (D)	—	reminder	mise en demeure f	sollecito m	monición f
main centers (E)	Hauptplätze m/pl	—	places principales f/pl	sedi principali f/pl	plazas principales f/pl
main invisible (F)	Ausgleichsfunktion des Preises f	invisible hand	—	meccanismo dei prezzi m	mano invisible f
maintenance of capital (E)	Kapitalerhaltung f	—	maintien du capital m	stabilità del valore del capitale f	conservación de capital f
maintien du capital (F)	Kapitalerhaltung f	maintenance of capital	—	stabilità del valore del capitale f	conservación de capi-tal f
majorisation (F)	Konzertzeichnung f	stagging	—'	speculazione di borsa f	mayorización f
Majorisierung (D)	—	holding of the majority	obtention de la majorité f	messa in minoranza f	obtención de la mayoría f
Majoritätskäufe (D)	—	buying of shares to secure the controlling interest in a company	achats majoritaires m/pl	acquisti di maggior anza m/pl	compras mayoritarias f/pl
majorité de capital (F)	Kapitalmehrheit f	capital majority	—	maggioranza del capitale f	mayoría de ca-pital f
majorité qualifiée (F)	qualifizierte Mehrheit f	qualified majority	—	maggioranza qualificata f	mayoría calificada f
majority participation (E)	Mehrheitsbeteiligung f	—	participation majoritaire f	partecipazione maggioritaria f	participación mayoritaria f

	D	E	F	I	Es
making-up price (E)	Kompensationskurs *m*	—	cours de compensation *m*	corso di compensazione *m*	cambio de compensación *m*
making-up price (E)	Liquidationskurs *m*	—	cours de liquidation *m*	corso di compensazione *m*	cambio de liquidación *m*
Maklerbank (D)	—	brokerage bank	banque de courtiers *f*	banca intermediaria *f*	banco corredor *m*
Maklerbuch (D)	—	dealings book of the stockbroker	carnet des négociations *m*	libro giornale dell' agente di cambio *m*	libro de corredores *m*
Maklerkammer (D)	—	association of stockbrokers	chambre syndicale des courtiers *f*	comitato degli agenti di cambio *m*	colegio de agentes de cambio y bolsa *m*
Maklerordnung (D)	—	brokers' code of conduct	régime des courtiers *m*	codice degli agenti di cambio *m*	régimen de corredores *m*
managed currency (E)	manipulierte Währung *f*		monnaie manipulée *f*	moneta manipulata *f*	moneda manipulada *f*
management (E)	Geschäftsführung *f*	—	gestion *f*	gestione *f*	gerencia *f*
managerial principles (E)	Führungsgrundsätze *m/pl*	—	principes de gestion *m/pl*	principi ammini-strativi *m/pl*	principios de dirección *m/pl*
managerial staff (E)	Geschäftsleitung *f*	—	direction commerciale *f*	direzione *f*	dirección *f*
managers commission (E)	Führungsprovision *f*	—	commission d'apériteur *f*	provvigione di gestione *f*	comisión de alta dirección *f*
mancata quotazione (I)	Streichung *f*	deletion	annulation *f*	—	anulación *f*
mancata quotazione (I)	Kursstreichung *f*	non-quotation	annulation de la cotation *f*	—	no cotización *f*
mandare un conto allo scoperto (I)	Überziehen eines Kontos *n*	overdraft	découvert de compte *m*	—	descubierto *m*
mandat (F)	Anweisung *f*	payment order	—	ordine di pagamento *m*	orden de pago *f*
mandat de payement (F)	Zahlungsanweisung *f*	order to pay	—	mandato di pagamento *m*	orden de pago *f*
mandat de payement bancaire (F)	Bankanweisung *f*	bank money order	—	vaglia bancario *m*	pago bancario *m*
mandat de place (F)	Platzanweisung *f*	cheques and orders payable at a certain place	—	bonifico sulla piazza *m*	cheques y órdenes a pagar en plaza *m/pl*
mandat de prélèvement automatique (F)	Einziehungser-mächtigung *f*	direct debit authorization	—	autorizzazione alla riscossione *f*	comisión de cobranza *f*
mandat-carte (F)	Zahlschein *m*	payment slip	—	modulo di versamento *m*	impreso para giro postal *m*
mandate to provide credit for a third party (E)	Kreditauftrag *m*	—	ordre de crédit *m*	mandato di credito *m*	mandato crediticio *m*
mandato commerciale (I)	Handlungsvollmacht *f*	commercial power of attorney	pouvoir commercial *m*	—	poder mercantil *m*
mandato crediticio (Es)	Kreditauftrag *m*	mandate to provide credit for a third party	ordre de crédit *m*	mandato di credito *m*	—
mandato di credito (I)	Kreditauftrag *m*	mandate to provide credit for a third party	ordre de crédit *m*	—	mandato crediticio *m*
mandato di incasso (I)	Einziehungsauftrag *m*	direct debit order	ordre de recouvrement *m*	—	autorización para el cobro *f*
mandato di pagamento (I)	Zahlungsanweisung *f*	order to pay	mandat de payement *m*	—	orden de pago *f*
mandat-poste (F)	Postanweisung *f*	postal money order	—	vaglia postale *m*	giro postal *m*
manifiesto de emisión (Es)	Prospekt bei Emissionen *m*	underwriting prospectus	prospectus d'émis-sion *m*	prospetto d'emissione *m*	—
manipulierte Währung (D)	—	managed currency	monnaie manipulée *f*	moneta manipulata *f*	moneda manipulada *f*
mano invisible (Es)	Ausgleichsfunktion des Preises *f*	invisible hand	main invisible *f*	meccanismo dei prezzi *m*	—
manque de liquidité (F)	Illiquidität *f*	illiquidity	—	illiquidità *f*	falta de liquidez *f*
Mantel (D)	—	share certificate	titre *m*	mantello *m*	título *m*
mantello (I)	Mantel *m*	share certificate	titre *m*	—	título *m*

	D	E	F	I	Es
Manteltresor (D)	—	bond and share certificate vault	coffre-fort de titres *m*	cassaforte dei mantelli *f*	caja fuerte para certificados de bonos y acciones *f*
manufacturer (E)	Erzeuger *m*	—	producteur *m*	produttore *m*	productor *m*
máquina clasificadora de dinero (Es)	Geldsortiermaschine *f*	money sorting machine	trieuse d'argent *f*	macchina per la cer nita delle monete *f*	—
máquina de contar dinero (Es)	Geldzählautomat *m*	money counting machine	machine compte-monnaie *f*	macchina con tadenaro *f*	—
marca (Es)	Marke *f*	brand trademark	marque *f*	bollo *m*	—
marca di risparmio (I)	Sparmarke *f*	savings stamp	timbre d'épargne *m*	—	cuota de ahorro *f*
marchandise (F)	Ware *f*	goods	—	merce *f*	mercancía *f*
marché (F)	Markt *m*	market	—	mercato *m*	mercado *m*
marché à cours variables (F)	variabler Markt *m*	variable market	—	mercato delle libere contrattazioni *m*	mercado variable *m*
marché à double option (F)	Stellagegeschäft *n*	double option operation	—	contratto stellage *m*	operación de doble prima *f*
marché à option (F)	Wandelgeschäft *n*	callable forward	—	contratto a termine con transaction opzione di adempimento anticipato *m*	operación de opción *f*
marché à option (F)	Optionsgeschäft *n*	option dealing	—	contratto ad opzione *m*	operación de opción *f*
marché après-bourse (F)	Nachbörse *f*	after-hours dealing	—	dopolistino *m*	operaciones después del cierre de la bolsa *f/pl*
marché à prime (F)	Prämiengeschäft *n*	option dealing	—	operazione a premio *f*	operación a prima *f*
morché à terme (F)	Termlnkontraktmarkt *m*	futures market	—	mercato dei contratti a termine *m*	mercado de contratos de entrega futura *m*
marché au comptant (F)	Kassamarkt *m*	spot market	—	mercato del pronto *m*	mercado al contado *m*
marché au comptant (F)	Bargeschäft *n*	cash transactions	—	affare in contanti *m*	operación al contado *f*
marché avant le marché officiel (F)	Vorbörse *f*	before hours dealing	—	avant bourse *m*	operaciones antes de la apertura *f/pl*
marché d'acheteurs (F)	Käufermarkt *m*	buyer's market	—	rnercato degli acquisti *m*	mercado del comprador *m*
marché d'actions (F)	Aktienmarkt *m*	share market	—	mercato azionario *m*	mercado de acciones *m*
marché de l'escompte (F)	Diskontmarkt *m*	discount market	—	mercato di sconto *m*	mercado de descuento *m*
marché de l' euroémission (F)	Euro-Bondmarkt *m*	Eurobond market	—	mercato degli eurobond *m*	mercado de eu roobligaciones *m*
marché de l'euroaction (F)	Euro-Aktienmarkt *m*	Euro share market	—	euromercato azionario *m*	mercado de eu roacciones *m*
marché de l'eurodollar (F)	Euro-Dollarmarkt *m*	Eurodollar market	—	mercato dell'euro-dollaro *m*	mercado de eu rodólares *m*
marché de l'euroémission (F)	Euro-Anleihenmarkt *m*	Eurocurrency loan market	—	mercato degli euro prestiti *m*	mercado de euroemi-siones *m*
marché de l' euromark (F)	Euro-DM-Markt *m*	Euro mark market	—	mercato dell'euro-marco *m*	mercado de eu romarcos *m*
marché de l'or (F)	Goldmarkt *m*	gold market	—	mercato dell'oro *m*	mercado de oro *m*
marché des biens (F)	Gütermarkt *m*	commodity market	—	mercato delle merci *m*	mercado de bienes *m*
marché des capitaux (F)	Finanzmarkt *m*	financial market	—	mercato finanziario *m*	mercado financiero *m*
marché des capitaux (F)	Kapitalmarkt *m*	capital market	—	mercato finanziario *m*	mercado de capitales *m*
marché des changes (F)	Devisenhandel *m*	foreign exchange dealings	—	cambio valuta *m*	operaciones de divisas *f/pl*
marché des changes (F)	Devisenmarkt *m*	foreign exchange market	—	mercato dei cambi *m*	mercado de divisas *m*
marché des changes à terme (F)	Devisenterminmarkt *m*	forward exchange market	—	mercato a termine delle divise *m*	mercado de divisas a plazo *m*
marché des changes à terme (F)	Devisenterminhandel *m*	forward exchange trading	—	operazione di cambio a termine *f*	mercado de cambios a plazo *m*
marché des changes au comptant (F)	Devisenkassamarkt *m*	foreign exchange spot market	—	mercato dei cambi a pronti *m*	mercado de divisas al contado *m*

	D	E	F	I	Es
marché des changes où existent deux taux de change pour une même monnaie (F)	gespaltener Devisenmarkt *m*	two-tier foreign exchange market	—	mercato dei cambi multipli *m*	tipo de cambio múltiple *m*
marché des coupons (F)	Kuponmarkt *m*	coupon market	—	mercato delle cedole *m*	mercado de cupones *m*
marché des droits de souscription (F)	Bezugsrechthandel *m*	trading in subscription rights	—	trattazione di diritti d'opzione *f*	comercio de derechos de suscripción *m*
marché des eurodevises (F)	Euro-Geldmarkt *m*	Eurocurrency market	—	euromercato monetario *m*	mercado de eurodivisas *m*
marché des opération à terme (F)	Futures-Markt *m*	futures market	—	mercato dei contratti future *m*	mercado de operaciones a plazo *m*
marché des valeurs à terme (F)	Wertpapier-Terminhandel *m*	trading in security futures	—	operazioni a termine in titoli *f/pl*	operaciones de valores a plazo *f/pl*
marché des valeurs émises (F)	Emissionsmarkt *m*	primary market	—	mercato d'emissione *m*	mercado de emisión *m*
marché des valeurs mobilières (F)	Wertpapiermarkt *m*	securities market	—	mercato mobiliare *m*	mercado de valores *m*
marché du dollar asiatique (F)	Asiendollarmarkt *m*	Asian Dollar market	—	mercato del dollaro asiatico *m*	mercado del dólar asiático *m*
marché en disponible (F)	Effektivgeschäft *n*	actual transaction	—	operazione in effettivo *f*	operación al contado *f*
marché européen financier (F)	Euro-Kapitalmarkt *m*	Eurocapital market	—	euromercato finanziario *m*	mercado de las euroobligaciones *m*
marché extérieur (F)	Außenmarkt *m*	external market	—	mercato estero *m*	mercado externo *m*
marché fermé (F)	geschlossener Markt *m*	self-contained market	—	mercato chiuso *m*	mercado cerrado *m*
marché financier (F)	Kreditmarkt *m*	money and capital market	—	mercato creditizio *m*	mercado de créditos *m*
marché libre (F)	Freiverkehr *m*	unofficial dealings	—	contrattazioni fuori borsa *f/pl*	mercado libre *m*
marché libre (F)	geregelter Freiverkehr *m*	unofficial market	—	mercato libero disciplinato *m*	mercado de valores extrabursátil *m*
marché mondial (F)	Weltmarkt *m*	world market	—	mercato internazionale *m*	mercado mundial *m*
marché monétaire (F)	Geldmarkt *m*	money market	—	mercato monetario *m*	mercado monetario *m*
marché monétaire liquide (F)	flüssiger Geldmarkt *m*	liquid money market	—	mercato del denaro liquido *m*	mercado monetario líquido *m*
marché national (F)	Binnenmarkt *m*	domestic market	—	mercato interno *m*	mercado interior *m*
marché noir (F)	schwarzer Markt *m*	black market	—	mercato nero *m*	mercado negro *m*
marché obligataire (F)	Rentenmarkt *m*	bond market	—	mercato del reddito fisso *m*	mercado de renta fija *m*
marché officiel (F)	amtlicher Markt *m*	official market	—	mercato ufficiale *m*	mercado oficial *m*
marché parallèle (F)	Parallelmarkt *m*	parallel market	—	mercato libero delle divise *m*	mercado paralelo *m*
marché primaire (F)	Primärmarkt *m*	primary market	—	mercato primario *m*	mercado primario *m*
marché restreint (F)	enger Markt *m*	restricted market	—	mercato a scarso flottante *m*	mercado de valores poco flexible *m*
marché secondaire (F)	Umlaufmarkt *m*	secondary market	—	mercato secondario *m*	mercado de circulación *m*
marché secondaire (F)	Sekundär-Markt *m*	secondary market	—	mercato secondario *m*	mercado secundario *m*
marchés internationaux de crédit (F)	internationale Kreditmärkte *m/pl*	international credit markets	—	mercati creditizi internazionali *m/pl*	mercados de créditos internacionales *m/pl*
marché unique (F)	Einheitsmarkt *m*	single-price market	—	mercato unico *m*	mercado único *m*
Marge (D)	—	margin	marge *f*	margine *m*	margen *m*
marge (F)	Bandbreite *f*	margin	—	banda di oscillazione *f*	margen de fluctuación *m*
marge (F)	Marge *f*	margin	—	margine *m*	margen *m*
marge de bénéfice (F)	Gewinnspanne *f*	margin of profit	—	margine di guadagno *m*	margen de beneficios *m*
marge entre les taux d'intérêt créditeur et débiteur (F)	Zinsmarge *f*	interest margin	—	margine d'interesse *m*	margen de interés *m*

	D	E	F	I	Es
marge entre les taux d'intérêt créditeur et débiteur (F)	Zinsspanne f	interest margin	—	margine d'interesse m	margen de beneficío por intereses m
margen (Es)	Marge f	margin	marge f	margine m	—
margen de beneficio por intereses (Es)	Zinsspanne f	interest margin	marge entre les taux d'intérêt créditeur et débiteur f	margine d'interesse m	—
margen de beneficios (Es)	Gewinnspanne f	margin of profit	marge de bénéfice f	margine di guadagno m	—
margen de cotización (Es)	Kursspanne f	difference between purchase and hedging price	écart de cours m	margine di cambio m	—
margen de fluctuación (Es)	Bandbreite f	margin	marge f	banda di oscillazione f	—
margen de interés (Es)	Zinsmarge f	interest margin	marge entre les taux d'intérêt créditeur et débiteur f	margine d'interesse m	—
margin (E)	Marge f	—	marge f	margine m	margen m
margin (E)	Bandbreite f	—	marge f	banda di oscillazione f	margen de fluctuación m
Marginalanalyse (D)	—	marginal analysis	analyse marginale f	analisi marginale f	análisis marginal m
marginal analysis (E)	Marginalanalyse f	—	analyse marginale f	analisi marginale f	análisis marginal m
marginal earnings (E)	Grenzerlös m	—	produit marginal m	ricavo marginale m	beneficio marginal m
marginal efficiency of capital (E)	Grenzleistungsfähigkeit des Kapitals f	—	efficience marginale du capital f	efficienza marginale del capitale f	eficiencia marginal del capital f
marginal productivity (F)	Grenzproduktivität f	—	productivité marginale f	produttività marginale f	productividad marginal f
marginal utility (E)	Grenznutzen m	—	utilité marginale f	rendita marginale f	utilidad marginal f
margin between interest rates (E)	Zinsgefälle n	—	disparité des niveaux d'intérêts f	differenza di interessi f	diferencial de intereses m
margine (I)	Marge f	margin	marge f	—	margen m
margine di cambio (I)	Kursspanne f	difference between purchase and hedging price	écart de cours m	—	margen de cotización m
margine di guadagno (I)	Gewinnspanne f	margin of profit	marge de bénéfice f	—	margen de beneficios m
margine d'interesse (I)	Zinsmarge f	interest margin	marge entre les taux d'intérêt créditeur et débiteur f	—	margen de interés m
margine d'interesse (I)	Zinsspanne f	interest margin	marge entre les taux d'intérêt créditeur et débiteur f	—	margen de beneficio por intereses m
margine d'utile di gruppo (I)	Konzernzwischengewinn m	group interim benefits	bénéfice intermédiaire des groupements des sociétés m	—	beneficio intermedio consolidado m
margin of profit (E)	Gewinnspanne f	—	marge de bénéfice f	margine di guadagno m	margen de beneficios f
Marke (D)	—	brand trademark	marque f	bollo m	marca f
markedness (E)	Ausprägung f	—	monnayage m	coniazione f	acuñación f
market (E)	Markt m	—	marché m	mercato m	mercado m
market adjustment (E)	Marktanpassung f	—	adaptation du marché f	adattamento del mercato m	ajuste de mercado m
market analysis (E)	Marktanalyse f	—	analyse du marché f	analisi di mercato f	análisis del mercado m
market economy (E)	Marktwirtschaft f	—	économie de marché f	economia di mercato f	economía de mercado f
market form (E)	Marktform f	—	forme du marché f	sistema di mercato m	forma de mercado f
marketing (E)	Vermarktung f	—	commercialisation f	vendibilità f	comercialización f
marketing syndicates (E)	Verwertungskonsortien n/pl	—	consortium de commercialisation f	consorzi di utilizzazione m/pl	consorcios de comercialización m/pl
market organization (E)	Marktordnung f	—	organisation du marché f	disciplina del mercato f	organización del mercado f
market performance (E)	Marktergebnis n	—	résultat du marché m	risultato sul mercato m	resultado de mercado m

	D	E	F	I	Es
market power (E)	Marktmacht *f*	—	pouvoir de marché *m*	potere di mercato *m*	poder de mercado *m*
market price (E)	Marktpreis *m*	—	prix du marché *m*	prezzo commerciale *m*	precio de mercado *m*
market price (E)	Kurs *m*	—	cours *m*	quotazione *f*	cotización *f*
market price on reporting date (E)	Stichtagskurs *m*	—	cours offert à la date de référence *m*	quotazione del giorno di riferimento *f*	cotización del día de referencia *f*
market rate of interest (E)	Marktzins *m*	—	taux du marché *m*	tasso d'interesse corrente *m*	tipo de interés del mercado *m*
market saturation (E)	Marktsättigung *f*	—	saturation du marché *f*	saturazione del mercato *f*	saturación del mercado *f*
market share (E)	Marktanteil *m*	—	participation au marché *f*	quota di mercato *f*	participación en el mercado *f*
market structure (E)*	Marktstruktur *f*	—	structure du marché *f*	struttura del mercato *f*	estructura del mercado *f*
market value (E)	gemeiner Wert *m*	—	valeur habituelle *f*	prezzo teorico *m*	valor común *m*
market volume (E)	Marktvolumen *n*	—	volume du marché *m*	volume di mercato *m*	volumen del mercado *m*
Markt (D)	—	market	marché *m*	mercato *m*	mercado *m*
Marktanalyse (D)	—	market analysis	analyse du marché *f*	analisi di mercato *f*	análisis del mercado *m*
Marktanpassung (D)	—	market adjustment	adaptation du marché *f*	adattamento del mercato *m*	ajuste de mercado *m*
Marktanteil (D)	—	market share	participation au marché *f*	quota di mercato *f*	participación en el mercado *f*
Marktergebnis (D)	—	market performance	résultat du marché *m*	risultato sul mercato *m*	resultado de mercado *m*
Markterschließung (D)	—	opening of new markets	ouverture du marché *f*	penetrazione del mercato *f*	apertura del mercado *f*
Marktform (D)	—	market form	forme du marché *f*	sistema di mercato *m*	forma de mercado *f*
Marktmacht (D)	—	market power	pouvoir de marché *m*	potere di mercato *m*	poder de mercado *m*
Marktordnung (D)	—	market organization	organisation du marché *f*	disciplina del mercato *f*	organización del mercado *f*
Marktpreis (D)	—	market price	prix du marché *m*	prezzo commerciale *m*	precio de mercado *m*
Marktsättigung (D)	—	market saturation	saturation du marché *f*	saturazione del mercato *f*	saturación del mercado *f*
Marktstruktur (D)	—	market structure	structure du marché *f*	struttura del mercato *f*	estructura del mercado *f*
marktüblicher Zins (D)	—	interest rate customary in the market	intérêt pratiqué sur le marché *m*	tasso d'interesse corrente *m*	interés impuesto en el mercado *m*
Marktvolumen (D)	—	market volume	volume du marché *m*	volume di mercato *m*	volumen del mercado *m*
Marktwert (D)	—	fair market value	valeur sur le marché *f*	valore di mercato *m*	valor de mercado *m*
Marktwirtschaft (D)	—	market economy	économie de marché *f*	economia di mercato *f*	economía de mercado *f*
Marktzins (D)	—	market rate of interest	taux du marché *m*	tasso d'interesse corrente *m*	tipo de interés del mercado *m*
marque (F)	Marke *f*	brand trademark	—	bollo *m*	marca *f*
más (Es)	plus	plus	plus	più	—
masa de la quiebra (Es)	Konkursmasse *f*	bankrupt's estate	masse de la faillite *f*	massa fallimentare *f*	—
masa monetaria (Es)	Geldmenge *f*	money stock	quantité de monnaie en circulation *f*	base monetaria *f*	—
massa fallimentare (I)	Konkursmasse *f*	bankrupt's estate	masse de la faillite *f*	—	masa de la quiebra *f*
massa monetaria (I)	Geldvolumen *n*	volume of money	masse monétaire *f*	—	volumen monetario *m*
masse active (F)	Aktiva *n/pl*	assets	—	attività di bilancio *f/pl*	activo *m*
masse de la faillite (F)	Konkursmasse *f*	bankrupt's estate	—	massa fallimentare *f*	masa de la quiebra *f*
Massegläubiger (D)	—	preferential creditor	créancier de la masse *m*	creditore della massa *m*	acreedor sin garantía *m*
masse monétaire (F)	Geldvolumen *n*	volume of money	—	massa monetaria *f*	volumen monetario *m*

	D	E	F	I	Es
massimale di contributo (I)	Beitragsbemessungs-grenze f	income limit for the assessment of contributions	plafond d'assujettisse-ment servant au cal-cul de la cotisation à l'assurance invalidité-vieillesse m	—	tope de la base de cotización m
massimazione degli utili (I)	Gewinnmaximierung f	maximization of profits	maximisation du gain f	—	maximación de los be-neficios f
master planning (E)	Gesamtplanung f	—	planification globale f	programmazione complessiva f	planificación global f
matematica finanziaria (I)	Finanzmathematik f	financial mathematics	mathématiques financières f/pl	—	matemáticas fi nancieras f/pl
mathmaticás financerias (Es)	Finanzmathematik f	financial mathematics	mathématiques financières f/pl	matematica finanziaria f	—
material asset investment funds (E)	Sachwert-Investment-fonds m	—	fonds d'investisse-ment en valeurs réelles m	fondo di valori reali m	fondo de inversión en valores reales m
material assets (E)	Sachvermögen n	—	biens corporels m/pl	beni materiali m/pl	patrimonio real m
material saliente (Es)	herauskommendes Material n	securities coming on to the market	titres lancés sur le marché m/pl	offerta di titoli f	—
material value loans (E)	Sachwertanleihen f/pl	—	emprunt de valeurs réelles m	prestito indicizzato m	empréstito en especie m
matériel acheté au-dehors (F)	Fremdbezug m	external procurement	—	acquisto di beni e servizi da terzi m	suministro externo m
mathématiques financières (F)	Finanzmathematik f	financial mathematics	—	matematica finanziaria f	matemáticas fi nancieras f/pl
maturity (E)	Fälligkeit f	—	échéance f	scadenza f	vencimiento m
maturity transfor-mation (E)	Fristentransformation f	—	trancformation d'échéances f	trasformazione ter-mini di scadenza f	transformación de plazos f
maximación de los beneficios (Es)	Gewinnmaximierung f	maximization of profits	maximisation du gain f	massimazione degli utili f	—
maximisation du gain (F)	Gewinnmaximierung f	maximization of profits	—	massimazione degli utili f	maximación de los beneficios f
maximization of profits (E)	Gewinnmaximierung f	—	maximisation du gain f	massimazione degli utili f	maximación de los beneficios f
maximum price (E)	Höchstpreis m	—	prix plafond m	prezzo massimo m	precio máximo m
maximum toléré à l'émission des billets de banque (F)	Notenkontingent n	fixed issue of notes	—	contingente di banconote m	contingente de emisión fiduciaria m
maximum voting right (E)	Höchststimmrecht n	—	droit de vote maximum m	valore massimo di voto m	límite máximo de votos m
mayoría calificada (Es)	qualifizierte Mehrheit f	qualified majority	majorité qualifiée f	maggioranza qualificata f	—
mayoría de capital (Es)	Kapitalmehrheit f	capital majority	majorité de capital f	maggioranza del capitale f	—
mayorización (Es)	Konzertzeichnung f	stagging	majorisation f	speculazione di borsa f	—
mean due date (E)	mittlere Verfallszeit f	—	échéance à moyen terme f	scadenza media f	vencimiento a medio plazo m
means of payment (E)	Zahlungsmittel n	—	moyen de payement m	mezzo di pagamento m	medio de pago m
mécanisme du cours du change (F)	Wechselkursmecha-nismus m	exchange rate mechanism	—	meccanismo di cambio m	mecanismo de cambio m
mecanismo de cambio (Es)	Wechselkursmecha-nismus m	exchange rate mechanism	mécanisme du cours du change m	meccanismo di cambio m	—
meccanismo dei prezzi (I)	Ausgleichsfunktion des Preises f	invisible hand	main invisible f	—	mano invisible f
meccanismo di cambio (I)	Wechselkursmecha-nismus m	exchange rate mechanism	mécanisme du cours du change m	—	mecanismo de cambio m
media aritmética (Es)	arithmetische Mittel n	arithmetical average	moyenne arithmétique f	media aritmetica f	—
media aritmetica (I)	arithmetische Mittel n	arithmetical average	moyenne arithmétique f	—	media aritmética f
mediación en las operaciones de financiación de participación (Es)	Beteiligungsvermitt-lung f	agency of equity financing transactions	agence d'opérations de financement par participation f	mediazione di partecipazioni f	—

	D	E	F	I	Es
mediatore di commercio (I)	Handelsmakler *m*	commercial broker	agent commercial *m*	—	corredor de comercio *m*
mediatore finanziario (I)	Finanzmakler *m*	money broker	intermédiaire de crédits à moyen et à long terme *m*	—	intermediario financiero *m*
mediatore libero (I)	freier Makler *m*	floor trader	courtier en valeurs mobilières *m*	—	corredor no colegiado *m*
mediazione di partecipazioni (I)	Beteiligungsvermittlung *f*	agency of equity financing transactions	agence d'opérations de financement par participation *f*	—	mediación en las operaciones de financiación de participación *f*
medio de pago (Es)	Zahlungsmittel *n*	means of payment	moyen de payement *m*	mezzo di pagamento *m*	—
medio de pago legal (Es)	gesetzliches Zahlungsmittel *n*	legal tender	monnaie légale *f*	moneta legale *f*	—
medio probatorio (Es)	Beweismittel *n*	evidence	moyen de preuve *m*	prova *f*	—
medios de pago en circulación (Es)	Zahlungsmittelumlauf *m*	notes and coins in circulation	circulation monétaire *f*	circolazione di mezzi di pagamento *f*	—
medium price (E)	Mittelkurs *m*	—	cours moyen *m*	corso medio *m*	cotización media *f*
medium-term bonds (E)	Kassenobligationen *f/pl*	—	obligations à moyen terme *f/pl*	obbligazioni di cassa *f/pl*	bonos de caja *m/pl*
Mehrheitsbeteiligung (D)	—	majority participation	participation majoritaire *f*	partecipazione maggioritaria *f*	participación mayoritaria *f*
Mehrstimmrecht (D)	—	multiple voting right	droit de vote plural *m*	diritto di voto plurimo *m*	derecho de voto plural *m*
Mehrstimmrechtsaktie (D)	—	multiple voting share	action à droit de vote plural *f*	azione a voto plurimo *f*	acción de voto plural *f*
Mehrwertsteuer (D)	—	value-added tax	taxe à la valeur ajoutée *f*	imposta sul valore aggiunto *f*	impuesto sobre el valor añadido *m*
Meistbegünstigung (D)	—	most-favoured nation treatment	régime de la nation la plus favorisée *m*	trattamento della nazione più favorita *m*	régimen de la nación más favorecida *m*
Meldepflicht (D)	—	obligation to register	déclaration obligatoire *f*	obbligo di dichiarazione *m*	obligación de comunicar *f*
memorandum item (E)	Merkposten *m*	—	poste pour mémoire *m*	voce per memoria *f*	cifra nominal *f*
mémorial (F)	Primanota *f*	journal	—	prima nota *f*	diario *m*
Mengenkurs (D)	—	direct exchange	cours de change indirect *m*	corso certo per incerto *m*	precio por cantidad *m*
Mengennotierung (D)	—	fixed exchange rate	cotation au certain *f*	cambio certo per incerto *m*	cotización real *f*
Mengentender (D)	—	quantity tender	offre d'emprunts par quantités pour la régulation monétaire *f*	asta non competitiva *f*	subasta de préstamos de regulación monetaria por cantidades *f*
mention de la valeur fournie (F)	Valutaklausel *f*	foreign currency clause	—	clausola valutaria *f*	cláusula de valuta *f*
mention de vérification (F)	Prüfungsvermerk *m*	certificate of audit	—	annotazione di controllo *f*	certificado de revisión *m*
mention sur un chèque (F)	Scheckklausel *f*	cheque clause	—	indicazione di assegno bancario *f*	cláusula de cheque *f*
mercado (Es)	Markt *m*	market	marché *m*	mercato *m*	—
mercado al contado (Es)	Kassamarkt *m*	spot market	marché au comptant *m*	mercato del pronto *m*	—
mercado cerrado (Es)	geschlossener Markt *m*	self-contained market	marché fermé *m*	mercato chiuso *m*	—
mercado de acciones (Es)	Aktienmarkt *m*	share market	marché d'actions *m*	mercato azionario *m*	—
mercado de bienes (Es)	Gütermarkt *m*	commodity market	marché des biens *m*	mercato delle merci *m*	—
mercado de cambios a plazo (Es)	Devisenterminhandel *m*	forward exchange trading	marché des changes à terme *m*	operazione di cambio a termine *f*	—
mercado de capitales (Es)	Kapitalmarkt *m*	capital market	marché des capitaux *m*	mercato finanziario *m*	—
mercado de circulación (Es)	Umlaufmarkt *m*	secondary market	marché secondaire *m*	mercato secondario *m*	—
mercado de contratos de entrega futura (Es)	Terminkontraktmarkt *m*	futures market	marché à terme *m*	mercato dei contratti a termine *m*	—

	D	E	F	I	Es
mercado de créditos (Es)	Kreditmarkt *m*	money and capital market	marché financier *m*	mercato creditizio *m*	—
mercado de cupones (Es)	Kuponmarkt *m*	coupon market	marché des coupons *m*	mercato delle cedole *m*	—
mercado de descuento (Es)	Diskontmarkt *m*	discount market	marché de l'escompte *m*	mercato di sconto *m*	—
mercado de divisas (Es)	Devisenmarkt *m*	foreign exchange market	marché des changes *m*	mercato dei cambi *m*	—
mercado de divisas al contado (Es)	Devisenkassamarkt *m*	foreign exchange spot market	marché des changes au comptant *m*	mercato dei cambi a pronti *m*	—
mercado de divisas a plazo (Es)	Devisenterminmarkt *m*	forward exchange market	marché des changes à terme *m*	mercato a termine delle divise *m*	—
mercado de emisión (Es)	Emissionsmarkt *m*	primary market	marché des valeurs émises *m*	mercato d'emissione *m*	—
mercado de euroacciones (Es)	Euro-Aktienmarkt *m*	Euro share market	marché de l'euroaction *m*	euromercato azionario *m*	—
mercado de eurodivisas (Es)	Euro-Geldmarkt *m*	Eurocurrency market	marché des eurodevises *m*	euromercato monetario *m*	—
mercado de eurodólares (Es)	Euro-Dollarmarkt *m*	Eurodollar market	marché de l'eurodollar *m*	mercato dell'euro-dollaro *m*	—
mercado de euroemisiones (Es)	Euro-Anleihenmarkt *m*	Eurocurrency loan market	marché de l'euro-émission *m*	mercato degli europrestiti *m*	—
mercado de euromarcos (Es)	Euro-DM-Markt *m*	Euro mark market	marché de l' euro-mark *m*	mercato dell'euro-marco *m*	—
mercado de euroobligaciones (Es)	Euro-Bondmarkt *m*	Eurobond market	marché de l' euro-émission *m*	mercato degli eurobond *m*	—
mercado de las euroobligaciones (Es)	Euro-Kapitalmarkt *m*	Eurocapital market	marché européen financier *m*	euromercato finanziario *m*	—
mercado del comprador (Es)	Käufermarkt *m*	buyer's market	marché d'acheteurs *m*	mercato degli acquisti *m*	—
mercado del dólar asiático (Es)	Asiendollarmarkt *m*	Asian Dollar market	marché du dollar asiatique *m*	mercato del dollaro asiatico *m*	—
mercado de operaciones a plazo (Es)	Futures-Markt *m*	futures market	marché des future *m*	mercato dei contratti opérations à terme *m*	—
mercado de operaciones de mostrador (Es)	Over-the-counter-market *m*	over-the-counter market	opérations de guichet *f/pl*	over-the-counter-market *m*	—
mercado de oro (Es)	Goldmarkt *m*	gold market	marché de l'or *m*	mercato dell'oro *m*	—
mercado de renta fjia (Es)	Rentenmarkt *m*	bond market	marché obligataire *m*	mercato del reddito fisso *m*	—
mercado de valores (Es)	Wertpapiermarkt *m*	securities market	marché des valeurs mobilières *m*	mercato mobiliare *m*	—
mercado de valores extrabursátil (Es)	Telefonverkehr *m*	telephone dealings	transactions par téléphone *f/pl*	negoziazione di titoli per telefono *f*	—
mercado de valores extrabursátil (Es)	geregelter Frei-verkehr *m*	unofficial market	marché libre *m*	mercato libero disciplinato *m*	—
mercado de valores poco flexible (Es)	enger Markt *m*	restricted market	marché restreint *m*	mercato a scarso flottante *m*	—
mercado externo (Es)	Außenmarkt *m*	external market	marché extérieur *m*	mercato estero *m*	—
mercado financiero (Es)	Finanzmarkt *m*	financial market	marché des capitaux *m*	mercato finanziario *m*	—
mercado interior (Es)	Binnenmarkt *m*	domestic market	marché national *m*	mercato interno *m*	—
mercado libre (Es)	Freiverkehr *m*	unofficial dealings	marché libre *m*	contrattazioni fuori borsa *f/pl*	—
mercado monetario (Es)	Geldmarkt *m*	money market	marché monétaire *m*	mercato monetario *m*	—
mercado monetario (Es)	Geldbörse *f*	money market	bourse des valeurs *f*	borsa delle valute *f*	—
mercado monetario líquido (Es)	flüssiger Geldmarkt *m*	liquid money market	marché monétaire liquide *m*	mercato del denaro liquido *m*	—
mercado mundial (Es)	Weltmarkt *m*	world market	marché mondial *m*	mercato internazionale *m*	—
mercado negro (Es)	schwarzer Markt *m*	black market	marché noir *m*	mercato nero *m*	—
mercado oficial (Es)	amtlicher Markt *m*	official market	marché officiel *m*	mercato ufficiale *m*	—

	D	E	F	I	Es
mercado paralelo (Es)	Parallelmarkt *m*	parallel market	marché parallèle *m*	mercato libero delle divise *m*	—
mercado primario (Es)	Primärmarkt *m*	primary market	marché primaire *m*	mercato primario *m*	—
mercados de créditos internacionales (Es)	internationale Kredit-märkte *m/pl*	international credit markets	marchés internationaux de crédit *m/pl*	mercati creditizi internazionali *m/pl*	—
mercado secundario (Es)	Sekundär-Markt *m*	secondary market	marché secondaire *m*	mercato secondario *m*	—
mercado único (Es)	Einheitsmarkt *m*	single-price market	marché unique *m*	mercato unico *m*	—
mercado variable (Es)	variabler Markt *m*	variable market	marché à cours variables *m*	mercato delle libere contrattazioni *m*	—
mercancía (Es)	Ware *f*	goods	marchandise *f*	merce *f*	—
mercati creditizi internazionali (I)	internationale Kredit-märkte *m/pl*	international credit markets	marchés internatio-naux de crédit *m/pl*	—	mercados de créditos internacionales *m/pl*
mercato (I)	Markt *m*	market	marché *m*	—	mercado *m*
mercato a scarso flottante (I)	enger Markt *m*	restricted market	marché restreint *m*	—	mercado de valores poco flexible *m*
mercato a termine (I)	Terminbörse *f*	futures market	bourse à terme *f*	—	bolsa de valores a término *f*
mercato a termine delle divise (I)	Devisenterminmarkt *m*	forward exchange market	marché des changes à terme *m*	—	mercado de divisas a plazo *m*
mercato azionario (I)	Aktienmarkt *m*	share market	marché d'actions *m*	—	mercado de acciones *m*
mercato chiuso (I)	geschlossener Markt *m*	self-contained market	marché fermé *m*	—	mercado cerrado *m*
mercato creditizio (I)	Kreditmarkt *m*	money and capital market	marché financier *m*	—	mercado de créditos *m*
mercato degli acquisti (I)	Käufermarkt *m*	buyer's market	marché d'acheteurs *m*	—	mercado del comprador *m*
mercato degli eurobond (I)	Euro-Bondmarkt *m*	Eurobond market	marché de l' euroémission *m*	—	mercado de euroobligaciones *m*
mercato degli europrestiti (I)	Euro-Anleihen-markt *m*	Eurocurrency loan market	marché de l'euroémission *m*	—	mercado de euroemisiones *m*
mercato dei cambi (I)	Devisenmarkt *m*	foreign exchange market	marché des changes *m*	—	mercado de divisas *m*
mercato dei cambi a pronti (I)	Devisenkassamarkt *m*	foreign exchange spot market	marché des changes au comptant *m*	—	mercado de divisas al contado *m*
mercato dei cambi multipli (I)	gespaltener Devisen-markt *m*	two-tier foreign exchange market	marché des changes où existent deux taux de change pour une même monnaie *m*	—	tipo de cambio múltiple *m*
mercato dei contratti a termine (I)	Terminkontrakt-markt *m*	futures market	marché à terme *m*	—	mercado de contratos de entrega futura *m*
mercato dei contratti future (I)	Futures-Markt *m*	futures market	marché des opération à terme *m*	—	mercado de operaciones a plazo *m*
mercato del denaro liquido (I)	flüssiger Geld-markt *m*	liquid money market	marché monétaire liquide *m*	—	mercado monetario líquido *m*
mercato del dollaro asiatico (I)	Asiendollarmarkt *m*	Asian Dollar market asiatique	marché du dollar *m*	—	mercado del dólar asiático *m*
mercato delle cedole (I)	Kuponmarkt *m*	coupon market	marché des coupons *m*	—	mercado de cupones *m*
mercato delle libere contrattazioni (I)	variabler Markt *m*	variable market	marché à cours variables *m*	—	mercado variable *m*
mercato delle merci (I)	Gütermarkt *m*	commodity market	marché des biens *m*	—	mercado de bienes *m*
mercato dell'eurodollaro (I)	Euro-Dollarmarkt *m*	Eurodollar market	marché de l'euro-dollar *m*	—	mercado de eurodólares *m*
mercato dell'euromarco (I)	Euro-DM-Markt *m*	Euro mark market	marché de l' euro-mark *m*	—	mercado de euromarcos *m*
mercato dell'oro (I)	Goldmarkt *m*	gold market	marché de l'or *m*	—	mercado de oro *m*
mercato del pronto (I)	Kassamarkt *m*	spot market	marché au comptant *m*	—	mercado al contado *m*
mercato del reddito fisso (I)	Rentenmarkt *m*	bond market	marché obligataire *m*	—	mercado de renta fija *m*
mercato d'emissione (I)	Emissionsmarkt *m*	primary market	marché des valeurs émises *m*	—	mercado de emisión *m*

	D	E	F	I	Es
mercato di quote di capitale (I)	Quotenhandel *m*	quota transactions	transactions sur les quotas *f/pl*	—	transacciones de cuotas *f/pl*
mercato di sconto (I)	Diskontmarkt *m*	discount market	marché de l'escompte *m*	—	mercado de descuento *m*
mercato estero (I)	Außenmarkt *m*	external market	marché extérieur *m*	—	mercado externo *m*
mercato finanziario (I)	Finanzmarkt *m*	financial market	marché des capitaux *m*	—	mercado financiero *m*
mercato finanziario (I)	Kapitalmarkt *m*	capital market	marché des capitaux *m*	—	mercado de capitales *m*
mercato internazionale (I)	Weltmarkt *m*	world market	marché mondial *m*	—	mercado mundial *m*
mercato interno (I)	Binnenmarkt *m*	domestic market	marché national *m*	—	mercado interior *m*
mercato libero delle divise (I)	Parallelmarkt *m*	parallel market	marché parallèle *m*	—	mercado paralelo *m*
mercato libero disciplinato (I)	geregelter Freiverkehr *m*	unofficial market	marché libre *m*	—	mercado de valores extrabursátil *m*
mercato mobiliare (I)	Wertpapiermarkt *m*	securities market	marché des valeurs mobilières *m*	—	mercado de valores *m*
mercato monetario (I)	Geldmarkt *m*	money market	marché monétaire *m*	—	mercado monetario *m*
mercato nero (I)	schwarzer Markt *m*	black market	marché noir *m*	—	mercado negro *m*
mercato petrolifero a termine (I)	Ölterminbörse *f*	oil futures exchange	bourse à terme des valeurs pétrolières *f*	—	bolsa de petróleo a término *f*
mercato primario (I)	Primärmarkt *m*	primary market	marché primaire *m*	—	mercado primario *m*
mercato secondario (I)	Umlaufmarkt *m*	secondary market	marché secondaire *m*	—	mercado de circulación *m*
mercato secondario (I)	Sekundär-Markt *m*	secondary market	marché secondaire *m*	—	mercado secundario *m*
mercato ufficiale (I)	amtlicher Markt *m*	official market	marché officiel *m*	—	mercado oficial *m*
mercato unico (I)	Einheitsmarkt *m*	single-price market	marché unique *m*	—	mercado único *m*
merce (I)	Ware *f*	goods	marchandise *f*	—	mercancía *f*
merci di ritorno (I)	Returen *f/pl*	returns	retours *m/pl*	—	devoluciones *f/pl*
Merkposten (D)	—	memorandum item	poste pour mémoire *m*	voce per memoria *f*	cifra nominal *f*
mesa redonda (Es)	runder Tisch *m*	round table	table ronde *f*	tavola rotonda *f*	—
messa in minoranza (I)	Majorisierung *f*	holding of the majority	obtention de la majorité *f*	—	obtención de la mayoría *f*
mesure dérogatoire (F)	Ausnahmeregelung *f*	provision	—	regolamento d'eccezione *m*	disposición excepcional *f*
metal cover (E)	Metalldeckung *f*	—	couverture métallique *f*	copertura metallica *f*	cobertura en metálico *f*
metales preciosos (Es)	Edelmetalle *n/pl*	precious metal	métaux précieux *m/pl*	metalli pregiati *m/pl*	—
Metal Exchange (E)	Metallbörse *f*	—	bourse des métaux *f*	borsa metalli *f*	bolsa de metales *f*
Metallbörse (D)	—	Metal Exchange	bourse des métaux *f*	borsa metalli *f*	bolsa de metales *f*
Metalldeckung (D)	—	metal cover	couverture métallique *f*	copertura metallica *f*	cobertura en metálico *f*
Metallgeld (D)	—	metallic money	argent métallique *m*	moneta metallica *f*	moneda metálica *f*
metallic currency (E)	Metallwährung *f*	—	monnaie métallique *f*	valuta metallica *f*	patrón metálico *m*
metallic currency (E)	Hartgeld *n*	—	monnaie métallique *f*	moneta metallica *f*	dinero metálico *m*
metallic money (E)	Metallgeld *n*	—	argent métallique *m*	moneta metallica *f*	moneda metálica *f*
metalli pregiati (I)	Edelmetalle *n/pl*	precious metal	métaux précieux *m/pl*	—	metales preciosos *m/pl*
Metallwährung (D)	—	metallic currency	monnaie métallique *f*	valuta metallica *f*	patrón metálico *m*
métaux précieux (F)	Edelmetalle *n/pl*	precious metal	—	metalli pregiati *m/pl*	metales preciosos *m/pl*
méthode de sélection (F)	Auswahlverfahren *n*	selection procedure	—	campionamento *m*	procedimiento de selección *m*
méthode Hifo (F)	Hifo-Verfahren *n*	Hifo-procedure	—	procedimento Hifo *m*	procedimiento hifo *m*
metodo di compensazione (I)	Ausgleichsverfahren *n*	composition proceedings	procédé de la compensation *m*	—	procedimiento de compensación *m*

	D	E	F	I	Es
mezzi presi a prestito (I)	aufgenommene Gelder n/pl	borrowed funds	fonds empruntés m/pl	—	fondos recogidos m/pl
mezzo controvalore (I)	Gegenwertmittel n/pl	counterpart funds	fonds de contrepartie m/pl	—	fondo de contrapartida m
mezzo di pagamento (I)	Zahlungsmittel n	means of payment	moyen de payement m	—	medio de pago m
Mietkauf (D)	—	lease with option to purchase	location-vente f	locazione finanziaria f	arrendamiento con opción de compra m
Mietverlängerungs- option (D)	—	lease renewal option	option de prorogation du bail f	opzione proroga contratto di locazione f	opción de prorroga- ción de arrenda- miento f
milagro económico (Es)	Wirtschaftswunder n	economic miracle	miracle économique m	miracolo economico m	—
Millionenkredit (D)	—	multimillion credit	crédit d'un million m	credito di un milione e più m	crédito de millones m
Minderkaufmann (D)	—	small trader	petit exploitant non soumis aux prescriptions générales du code de commerce m	piccolo imprenditore m	pequeño comerciante no registrable en el registro de comercio m
Mindesteinlage (D)	—	minimum investment	dépôt initial minimum m	deposito minimo m	depósito mínimo m
Mindestkapital (D)	—	minimum capital	capital minimum m	capitale minimo m	capital mínimo m
Mindestpreis (D)	—	minimum price	prix minimum m	prezzo minimo m	precio mínimo m
Mindestreserve (D)	—	minimum legal reserves	réserve minimum f	riserva obbligatoria f	reserva mínima f
Mindestreserve- politik (D)	—	minimum reserve policy	politique de réserve minimum f	politica delle riserve obbligatorie f	política de reservas mínimas f
Mindestreservesatz (D)	—	minimum reserve ratio	taux de réserve minimum m	tasso minimo di riserva m	porcentaje mínimo de reservas m
Mindestzins (D)	—	minimum interest rate	intérêt minimum m	interesse minimo m	interés mínimo m
Minimalkosten- kombination (D)	—	minimum cost combination	combinaison du coût minimal f	combinazione di costi minimi f	combinación de coste mínimo f
minimo d'esistenza (I)	Existenzminimum n	subsistence minimum	minimum vital m	—	mínimo vital m
mínimo vital (Es)	Existenzminimum n	subsistence minimum	minimum vital m	minimo d'esistenza m	—
minimum capital (E)	Mindestkapital n	—	capital minimum m	capitale minimo m	capital mínimo m
minimum cost combination (E)	Minimalkosten- kombination f	—	combinaison du coût minimal f	combinazione di costi minimi f	combinación de coste mínimo f
minimum interest rate (E)	Mindestzins m	—	intérêt minimum m	interesse minimo m	interés mínimo m
minimum investment (E)	Mindesteinlage f	—	dépôt initial minimum m	deposito minimo m	depósito mínimo m
minimum legal reserves (E)	Mindestreserve f	—	réserve minimum f	riserva obbligatoria f	reserva mínima f
minimum price (E)	Mindestpreis m	—	prix minimum m	prezzo minimo m	precio mínimo m
minimum reserve (E)	Pflichtreserve f	—	réserve légale f	riserva obbligatoria f	reserva obligatoria f
minimum reserve policy (E)	Mindestreserve- politik f	—	politique de réserve minimum f	politica delle riserve obbligatorie f	política de reservas mínimas f
minimum reserve ratio (E)	Mindestreservesatz m	—	taux de réserve minimum m	tasso minimo di riserva m	porcentaje mínimo de reservas m
minimum vital (F)	Existenzminimum n	subsistence minimum	—	minimo d'esistenza m	mínimo vital m
mining share (E)	Kux m	—	part de mines f	azione mineraria f	acción minera f
minoranza qualificata (I)	qualifizierte Minderheit f	right-conferring minority	minorité qualifiée f	—	minoría calificada f
minoría calificada (Es)	qualifizierte Minder- heit f	right-conferring minority	minorité qualifiée f	minoranza qualificata f	—
minorité qualifiée (F)	qualifizierte Minder- heit f	right-conferring minority	—	minoranza qualificata f	minoría calificada f
minting (E)	Prägung f	—	frappe f	coniatura f	acuñación f
miracle économique (F)	Wirtschaftswunder n	economic miracle	—	miracolo economico m	milagro económico m
miracolo economico (I)	Wirtschaftswunder n	economic miracle	miracle économique m	—	milagro económico m

	D	E	F	I	Es
misapplication of deposit (E)	Depotunterschlagung f	—	détournement de titres en dépôt m	appropriazione indebita di depositi f	defraudación de depósito f
mise en demeure (F)	Mahnung f	reminder	—	sollecito m	monición f
mise en gage (F)	Verpfändung f	pledge	—	pignoramento m	pignoración f
mise en pension d'effets (F)	Effektenpensionierung f	raising money on securities by cash sale coupled with contract for subsequent repurchase	—	sconto di titoli in pensione m	cesión temporal de valores f
misguided investment (E)	Kapitalfehlleitung f	—	faux investissements m/pl	disguido di capitale m	extravío de capital m
Miteigentum (D)	—	co-ownership	copropriété f	comproprietà f	copropiedad f
Mitteilungspflicht (D)	—	obligation to furnish information	obligation d'informer f	obbligo di rendere noto m	obligación de comunicación f
Mittelkurs (D)	—	medium price	cours moyen m	corso medio m	cotización media f
Mittelwert (D)	—	average value	valeur moyenne f	valore medio m	valor medio m
mittlere Verfallszeit (D)	—	mean due date	échéance à moyen terme f	scadenza media f	vencimiento a medio plazo m
mixed fund (E)	gemischter Fonds m	—	fonds mixte m	fondo d'investimento misto m	fondo mixto m
monnaie (F)	Münze f	coin	—	zecca f	casa de moneda f
Mobilien (D)	—	movable goods	biens mobiliers m/pl	beni mobili m/pl	bienes muebles m/pl
Mobilisierungspapiere (D)	—	mobilization papers	titres de mobilisation m/pl	titoli di smobilizzo m/pl	títulos de mobilización m/pl
Mobilisierungspfandbriefe (D)	—	mobilization mortgage bond	obligations hypothécaires de mobilisation f/pl	obbligazioni fondiarie di smobilizzo f/pl	cédulas hipotecarias de mobilización f/pl
Mobilisierungstratte (D)	—	mobilization draft	traite de mobilisation f	effetto di smobilizzo m	letra de mobilización f
mobilization draft (E)	Mobilisierungstratte f	—	traite de mobilisation f	effetto di smobilizzo m	letra de mobilización f
mobilization mortgage bond (E)	Mobilisierungspfandbriefe m/pl	—	obligations hypothécaires de mobilisation f/pl	obbligazioni fondiarie di smobilizzo f/pl	cédulas hipotecarias de mobilización f/pl
mobilization papers (E)	Mobilisierungspapiere n/pl	—	titres de mobilisation m/pl	titoli di smobilizzo m/pl	títulos de mobilización m/pl
modèle d'acquéreur (F)	Erwerbermodell n	acquirer model	—	acquisto di immobili affittati m	modelo de adquirente m
modelo de adquirente (Es)	Erwerbermodell n	acquirer model	modèle d'acquéreur m	acquisto di immobili affittati m	—
modifica del bilancio (I)	Bilanzänderung f	alteration of a balance sheet	modification apportée au bilan f	—	alteración del balance f
modification apportée au bilan (F)	Bilanzänderung f	alteration of a balance sheet	—	modifica del bilancio f	alteración del balance f
modulo di versamento (I)	Zahlschein m	payment slip	mandat-carte m	—	impreso para giro postal m
moltiplicatore di moneta (I)	Geldschöpfungsmultiplikator m	money creation ratio	multiplicateur de crédit m	—	multiplicador de crédito m
moltiplicatore di moneta contabile (I)	Buchgeldschöpfungsmultiplikator m	deposit money creation multiplier	multiplicateur de création de monnaie scripturale m	—	multiplicador de creación de dinero giral m
Monatsausweis (D)	—	monthly return	situation mensuelle f	bilancio mensile m	resumen mensual m
Monatsbilanz (D)	—	monthly balance sheet	situation comptable mensuelle f	bilancio mensile m	balance mensual m
Monatsgeld (D)	—	one month money	argent à un mois m	deposito vincolato ad un mese m	dinero a 30 días m
moneda (Es)	Währung f	currency	monnaie f	moneta f	—
moneda acuñada (Es)	Münzgeld n	species	monnaie métallique f	denaro monetato m	—
moneda corriente (Es)	Kurantmünze f	specie	monnaie courante f	moneta corrente f	—
moneda débil (Es)	Weichwährung f	soft currency	monnaie faible f	moneta debole f	—
moneda de cesta (Es)	Korbwährung f	basket currency	monnaie de panier f	valuta paniere f	—
moneda de inversión (Es)	Anlagewährung f	currency of investment	monnaie d'investissement f	valuta d'investimento f	—

	D	E	F	I	Es
moneda de oro (Es)	Goldmünze f	gold coin	pièce d'or f	moneta aurea f	—
moneda de oro en circulación (Es)	Goldumlaufswährung f	gold specie standard	monnaie or f	divisa circolante aurea f	—
moneda de plata (Es)	Silbermünze f	silver coin	pièce en argent f	moneta d'argento f	—
moneda de referencia (Es)	Leitwährung f	key currency	monnaie-clé f	moneta guida f	—
moneda de reserva (Es)	Reservewährung f	reserve currency	monnaie de réserve f	moneta di riserva f	—
moneda doble (Es)	Doppelwährung f	double currency	double étalon m	bimetallismo m	—
moneda dura (Es)	harte Währung f	hard currency	monnaie forte f	valuta forte f	—
moneda extranjera (Es)	Sorte f	foreign notes and coins	devise f	valuta estera f	—
moneda extranjera (Es)	Valuten f/pl	foreign exchange	coupons de titres étrangers m/pl	cedole di titoli esteri m/pl	—
moneda extranjera (Es)	Valuta f	foreign exchange	monnaie étrangère f	valuta f	—
moneda falsa (Es)	Falschgeld n	counterfeit money	fausse monnaie f	moneta contraffatta f	—
moneda fraccionaria (Es)	Scheidemünze f	divisional coin	monnaie divisionnaire f	moneta divisionale f	—
moneda-índice (Es)	Indexwährung f	index-linked currency	monnaie indexée f	moneta indice f	—
monedaje (Es)	Münzgewinn m	seignorage	monnayage m	utile di coniatura m	—
moneda libre (Es)	freie Währung f	freely convertible currency	monnaie librement convertible f	valuta libera f	—
moneda manipulada (Es)	manipulierte Währung f	managed currency	monnaie manipulée f	moneta manipulata f	—
moneda metálica (Es)	Metallgeld n	metallic money	argent métallique m	moneta metallica f	—
moneda oro (Es)	Goldwährung f	gold currency	monnaie à couverture or f	valuta aurea f	—
moneda paralela (Es)	Parallelwährung f	parallel currency	monnaie parallèle f	bimetallismo m	—
moneda vinculada (Es)	gebundene Währung f	linked currency	monnaie liée f	valuta a regime di controllo f	—
moneta (I)	Währung f	currency	monnaie f	—	moneda f
moneta aurea (I)	Goldmünze f	gold coin	pièce d'or f	—	moneda de oro f
moneta bancaria (I)	Buchgeld n	deposit money	monnaie scripturale f	—	moneda escritural f
moneta cartacea (I)	Papiergeld n	paper money	monnaie de papier f	—	dinero-papel m
moneta contraffatta (I)	Falschgeld n	counterfeit money	fausse monnaie f	—	moneda falsa f
moneta corrente (I)	Kurantmünze f	specie	monnaie courante f	—	moneda corriente f
moneta creata dalla banca centrale (I)	Zentralbankgeld n	central bank money	monnaie de banque centrale f	—	dinero legal m
moneta d'argento (I)	Silbermünze f	silver coin	pièce en argent f	—	moneda de plata f
moneta debole (I)	Weichwährung f	soft currency	monnaie faible f	—	moneda débil f
moneta d'emergenza (I)	Notgeld n	emergency money	monnaie obsidionale f	—	dinero de urgencia m
moneta di riserva (I)	Reservewährung f	reserve currency	monnaie de réserve f	—	moneda de reserva f
moneta divisionale (I)	Scheidemünze f	divisional coin	monnaie divisionnaire f	—	moneda fraccionaria f
moneta guida (I)	Leitwährung f	key currency	monnaie-clé f	—	moneda de referencia f
moneta indice (I)	Indexwährung f	index-linked currency	monnaie indexée f	—	moneda-índice f
moneta legale (I)	gesetzliches Zahlungsmittel n	legal tender	monnaie légale f	—	medio de pago legal m
moneta manipulata (I)	manipulierte Währung f	managed currency	monnaie manipulée f	—	moneda manipulada f
moneta metallica (I)	Metallgeld n	metallic money	argent métallique m	—	moneda metálica f
moneta metallica (I)	Hartgeld n	metallic currency	monnaie métallique f	—	dinero metálico m
moneta neutrale (I)	neutrales Geld n	neutral money	argent neutre m	—	dinero neutral m
monetary arrangement (E)	Gelddisposition f	—	disposition monétaire f	disposizione di moneta f	disposición monetaria f
monetary base (E)	Geldbasis f	—	base monétaire f	base monetaria f	base monetaria f

	D	E	F	I	Es
monetary base principle (E)	Geldbasiskonzept *n*	—	principe de la base monétaire *m*	principio della base monetaria *m*	principio de la base monetaria *m*
monetary block (E)	Währungsblock *m*	—	bloc monétaire *m*	blocco monetario *m*	bloque monetario *m*
monetary capital (E)	Geldkapital *n*	—	capital monétaire *m*	capitale monetario *m*	capital monetario *m*
monetary crisis (E)	Währungskrise *f*	—	crise monétaire *f*	crisi monetaria *f*	crisis monetaria *f*
monetary devaluation (E)	Geldentwertung *f*	—	dépréciation *f*	svalutazione monetaria *f*	devaluación del dinero *f*
monetary factor (E)	Geldfaktor *m*	—	facteur monétaire *m*	fattore monetario *m*	factor monetario *m*
monetary fund (E)	Währungsfonds *m*	—	fonds monétaire *m*	fondo monetario *m*	fondo monetario *m*
monetary parity (E)	Währungsparität *f*	—	parité des monnaies *f*	parità monetaria *f*	paridad monetaria *f*
monetary policy (E)	Währungspolitik *f*	—	politique monétaire *f*	politica monetaria *f*	política monetaria *f*
monetary policy (E)	Geldpolitik *f*	—	politique monétaire *f*	politica monetaria *f*	política monetaria *f*
monetary reform (E)	Währungsreform *f*	—	réforme monétaire *f*	riforma monetaria *f*	reforma monetaria *f*
monetary reserves (E)	Währungsreserven *f/pl*	—	réserves monétaires *f/pl*	riserve valutarie *f/pl*	reservas monetarias *f/pl*
monetary sovereignty (E)	Münzhoheit *f*	—	prérogative de la frappe *f*	privilegio di battere moneta *m*	soberanía de acuñación *f*
monetary stability (E)	Geldwertstabilität *f*	—	stabilité monétaire *f*	stabilità monetaria *f*	estabilidad monetaria *f*
monetary standard (E)	Gelddeckung *f*	—	couverture monétaire *f*	copertura metallica *f*	reserva-metales finos *m*
monetary structure (E)	Geldverfassung *f*	—	structure monétaire *f*	sistema monetario *m*	estructura monetaria *f*
monetary system (E)	Währungsordnung *f*	—	ordre monétaire *m*	ordinamento valutario *m*	ordenación monetaria *f*
monetary system (E)	Währungssystem *n*	—	système monétaire *m*	sistema monetario *m*	sistema monetario *m*
monetary system (E)	Geldwesen *n*	—	système monétaire *m*	sistema monetario *m*	sistema monetario *m*
monetary union (E)	Währungsunion *f*	—	union monétaire *f*	unione monetaria *f*	unión monetaria *f*
moneta scritturale (I)	Giralgeld *n*	money in account	monnaie scripturale *f*	—	dinero bancario *m*
moneta-velo (I)	Geldschleier *m*	veil of money	voile d'argent *m*	—	velo monetario *m*
monétisation (F)	Monetisierung *f*	monetization	—	monetizzazione *f*	monetización *f*
Monetisierung (D)	—	monetization	monétisation *f*	monetizzazione *f*	monetización *f*
monetización (Es)	Monetisierung *f*	monetization	monétisation *f*	monetizzazione *f*	—
monetization (E)	Monetisierung *f*	—	monétisation *f*	monetizzazione *f*	monetización *f*
monetizzazione (I)	Monetisierung *f*	monetization	monétisation *f*	—	monetización *f*
money (E)	Geld *n*	—	argent *m*	denaro *m*	dinero *m*
money and capital market (E)	Kreditmarkt *m*		marché financier *m*	mercato creditizio *m*	mercado de créditos *m*
money broker (E)	Finanzmakler *m*	—	intermédiaire de crédits à moyen et à long terme *m*	mediatore finanziario *m*	intermediario financiero *m*
money broker (E)	Kreditvermittler *f*	—	agent financier *m*	intermediario finanziario *m*	operador de negociación de créditos *m*
money counting machine (E)	Geldzählautomat *m*	—	machine compte-monnaie *f*	macchina contadenaro *f*	máquina de contar-dinero *f*
money creation ratio (E)	Geldschöpfungs-multiplikator *m*	—	multiplicateur de crédit *m*	moltiplicatore di moneta *m*	multiplicador de crédito *m*
money demand (E)	Geldnachfrage *f*	—	demande d'argent *f*	domanda monetaria *f*	demanda monetaria *f*
money deposited (E)	Einlage *f*	—	dépôt *m*	deposito *m*	imposición *f*
money economy (E)	Geldwirtschaft *f*	—	économie monétaire *f*	economia monetaria *f*	economía financiera *f*
money export (E)	Geldexport *m*	—	exportation monétaire *f*	esportazione di valuta *f*	exportación monetaria *f*
money guarantee clause (E)	Geldwertsicherungs-klausel *f*	—	clause d'indexation *f*	clausola di garanzia monetaria *f*	cláusula de garantía sobre el valor monetario *f*
money held in trust for a ward (E)	Mündelgeld *n*	—	deniers de pupille *m/pl*	capitale del minore *m*	dinero pupilar *m*
money illusion (E)	Geldillusion *f*	—	illusion monétaire *f*	illusione monetaria *f*	ilusión monetaria *f*
money import (E)	Geldimport *m*	—	importation monétaire *f*	importazione di valuta *f*	importación monetaria *f*

	D	E	F	I	Es
money in account (E)	Buchgeld *n*	—	monnaie de crédit *f*	moneta bancaria *f*	dinero bancario *m*
money in account (E)	Giralgeld *n*	—	monnaie scripturale *f*	moneta scritturale *f*	dinero bancario *m*
money management (E)	Geldhaltung *f*	—	tenue d'argent *f*	tenuta di denaro *f*	tenencia de dinero *f*
money market (E)	Geldmarkt *m*	—	marché monétaire *m*	mercato monetario *m*	mercado monetario *m*
money market (E)	Geldbörse *f*	—	bourse des valeurs *f*	borsa delle valute *f*	mercado monetario *m*
money market account (E)	Geldmarktkonto *n*	—	compte du marché monétaire *m*	conto monetario *m*	cuenta de mercado monetario *f*
money market credit (E)	Geldmarktkredit *m*	—	crédit accordé sur le marché monétaire *m*	credito monetario *m*	crédito de mercado monetario *m*
money market funds (E)	Geldmarktfonds *m*	—	fonds du marché monétaire *m/pl*	fondi monetari *m/pl*	fondos de mercado monetario *m/pl*
money market policy (E)	Geldmarktpolitik *f*	—	politique du marché monétaire *f*	politica del mercato monetario *f*	política monetaria *f*
money market rate (E)	Geldmarktsatz *m*	—	taux d'intérêt sur le marché monétaire *m*	tasso del mercato monetario *m*	tipo de cambio del mercado monetario *m*
money market securities (E)	Geldmarktpapier *n*	—	titres du marché monétaire *m/pl*	portafoglio sconto *m*	título del mercado monetario *m*
money piece rate (E)	Geldakkord *m*	—	convention de salaire aux pièces *f*	cottimo al pezzo *m*	destajo *m*
money rate (E)	Geldsatz *m*	—	taux de l'argent *m*	tasso monetario *m*	tipo de interés *m*
money sorting machine (E)	Geldsortiermaschine *f*	—	trieuse d'argent *f*	macchina per la cernita delle monete *f*	máquina clasificadora de dinero *f*
money stock (E)	Geldmenge *f*	—	quantité de monnaie en circulation *f*	base monetaria *f*	masa monetaria *f*
money substitute (E)	Geldsubstitut *n*	—	monnaie subrogée *f*	quasi moneta *f*	sustitutivo de dinero *m*
money supply target (E)	Geldmengenziel *n*	—	fourchette de croissance monétaire *f*	base monetaria programmata *f*	objetivo del volumen monetario *m*
money taken on deposit (E)	hereingenommene Gelder *n/pl*	—	fonds mis en dépôt *m/pl*	denaro altrui *m*	fondos ingresados *m/pl*
money transfer transactions (E)	Überweisungsverkehr *m*	—	virements *m/pl*	bancogiro *m*	transferencias *f/pl*
money wage (E)	Geldlohn *m*	—	salaire payé en argent *m*	salario in denaro *f*	salario en efectivo *m*
monición (Es)	Mahnung *f*	reminder	mise en demeure *f*	sollecito *m*	—
monnaie (F)	Währung *f*	currency	—	moneta *f*	moneda *f*
monnaie-clé (F)	Leitwährung *f*	key currency	—	moneta guida *f*	moneda de referencia *f*
monnaie courante (F)	Kurantmünze *f*	specie	—	moneta corrente *f*	moneda corriente *f*
monnaie de banque centrale (F)	Zentralbankgeld *n*	central bank money	—	moneta creata dalla banca centrale *f*	dinero legal *m*
monnaie de crédit (F)	Buchgeld *n*	money in account	—	moneta bancaria *f*	dinero bancario *m*
monnaie de panier (F)	Korbwährung *f*	basket currency	—	valuta paniere *f*	moneda de cesta *f*
monnaie de papier (F)	Papiergeld *n*	paper money	—	moneta cartacea *f*	dinero-papel *m*
monnaie de réserve (F)	Reservewährung *f*	reserve currency	—	moneta di riserva *f*	moneda de reserva *f*
monnaie d'investissement (F)	Anlagewährung *f*	currency of investment	—	valuta d'investimento *f*	moneda de inversión *f*
monnaie divisionnaire (F)	Scheidemünze *f*	divisional coin	—	moneta divisionale *f*	moneda fraccionaria *f*
monnaie en argent (F)	Silberwährung *f*	silver standard	—	valuta d'argento *f*	patrón plata *m*
monnaie étrangère (F)	Valuta *f*	foreign exchange	—	valuta *f*	moneda extranjera *f*
monnaie faible (F)	Weichwährung *f*	soft currency	—	moneta debole *f*	moneda débil *f*
monnaie forte (F)	harte Währung *f*	hard currency	—	valuta forte *f*	moneda dura *f*
monnaie indexée (F)	Indexwährung *f*	index-linked currency	—	moneta indice *f*	moneda-índice *f*
monnaie légale (F)	gesetzliches Zahlungsmittel *n*	legal tender	—	moneta legale *f*	medio de pago legal *m*
monnaie librement convertible (F)	freie Währung *f*	freely convertible currency	—	valuta libera *f*	moneda libre *f*

	D	E	F	I	Es
monnaie liée (F)	gebundene Währung f	linked currency	—	valuta a regime di controllo f	moneda vincu lada f
monnaie manipulée (F)	manipulierte Währung f	managed currency	—	moneta manipulata f	moneda manipulada f
monnaie métallique (F)	Hartgeld n	metallic currency	—	moneta metallica f	dinero metálico m
monnaie métallique (F)	Münzgeld n	species	—	denaro monetato m	moneda acuñada f
monnaie métallique (F)	Metallwährung f	metallic currency	—	valuta metallica f	patrón metálico m
monnaie obsidionale (F)	Notgeld n	emergency money	—	moneta d'emergenza f	dinero de urgencia m
monnaie or (F)	Goldumlaufswährung f	gold specie standard	—	divisa circolante aurea f	moneda de oro en circulación f
monnaie parallèle (F)	Parallelwährung f	parallel currency	—	bimetallismo m	moneda paralela f
monnaie scripturale (F)	Giralgeld n	money in account	—	moneta scritturale f	dinero bancario m
monnaie subrogée (F)	Geldsubstitut n	money substitute	—	quasi moneta f	sustitutivo de dinero m
monnayage (F)	Ausprägung f	markedness	—	coniazione f	acuñación f
monnayage (F)	Münzgewinn m	seignorage	—	utile di coniatura m	monedaje m
monopole de la frappe (F)	Münzregal n	exclusive right of coinage	—	privilegio di battere moneta m	regalía de acuñación f
monopole du commerce extérieur (F)	Außenhandels- monopol n	foreign trade monopoly	—	monopolio del commercio estero m	monopolio del comercio exterior m
monopole fiscal (F)	Finanzmonopol n	fiscal monopoly	—	monopolio fiscale m	monopolio financiero m
Monopolies Commission (E)	Monopolkommission f	—	commission de monopoles f	commissione antitrust f	comisión de monopolios f
monopolio del comercio exterior (Es)	Außenhandels- monopol n	foreign trade monopoly	monopole du commerce extérieur m	monopolio del commercio estero m	—
monopolio del commercio estero (I)	Außenhandels- monopol n	foreign trade monopoly	monopole du commerce extérieur m	—	monopolio del comercio exterior m
monopolio financiero (Es)	Finanzmonopol n	fiscal monopoly	monopole fiscal m	monopolio fiscale m	—
monopolio fiscale (I)	Finanzmonopol n	fiscal monopoly	monopole fiscal m	—	monopolio financiero m
Monopolkom- mission (D)	—	Monopolies Commission	commission de monopoles f	commissione antitrust f	comisión de monopolios f
montant calculé (F)	ausmachender Betrag m	actual amount	—	controvalore della contrattazione m	importe calculado m
montant des espèces en caisse (F)	Kassenbestand m	cash in hand	—	consistenza di cassa f	dinero en caja m
montant exonéré (F)	Freibetrag m	tax-free amount	—	importo esente m	importe exento m
monte de piedad (Es)	Leihanstalt f	pawnshop	institut de prêt m	monte di pietà m	—
monte di pietà (I)	Leihanstalt f	pawnshop	institut de prêt m	—	monte de piedad m
monthly balance sheet (E)	Monatsbilanz f	—	situation comptable mensuelle f	bilancio mensile m	balance mensual m
monthly income statement (E)	Kurzfristige Erfolgsrechnung f	—	comptes de résultats intermédiaires m/pl	conto economico a breve termine m	estado de resultados a corto plazo m
monthly return (E)	Monatsausweis m	—	situation mensuelle f	bilancio mensile m	resumen mensual m
mora (I)	Verzug m	delay	demeure f	—	demora f
mora nel pagamento (I)	Zahlungsverzug m	failure to pay on due date	demeure du débiteur f	—	retraso en el pago m
more buyers than sellers (E)	bezahlt Geld	—	comptant acheteur	domanda parzialmente insoddisfatta f	compra limitada f
more sellers than buyers (E)	bezahlt Brief	—	comptant vendeur	offerta eccedente la domanda f	la oferta fue mayor que la demanda f
mortgage (E)	Hypothek f	—	hypothèque f	ipoteca f	hipoteca f
mortgage as security for a loan (E)	Darlehenshypothek f	—	hypothèque de sûreté constituée pour garantir un prêt f	ipoteca su prestiti f	préstamo hipotecario m
mortgage bank (E)	Grundkreditanstalt f	—	établissement de crédit foncier m	istituto di credito fondiario m	banco hipotecario m

	D	E	F	I	Es
mortgage bank (E)	Hypothekenbank f	—	banque hypothécaire f	banca ipotecaria f	banco hipotecario m
mortgage bank (E)	Bodenkreditinstitut n	—	institut de crédit foncier m	banca di credito agrario f	instituto de crédito inmobiliario m
mortgage bank (E)	Pfandbriefanstalt f	—	banque hypothécaire f	istituto di credito fondiario m	banco hipotecario m
mortgage bank law (E)	Hypothekenbankgesetz n	—	loi sur les banques de prêts hypothécaires f	legge sulle banche ipotecarie f	ley de bancos hipotecarios f
mortgage bond (E)	Pfandbrief m	—	obligation hypothécaire f	obbligazione fondiaria f	cédula hipotecaria f
mortgage bond serving a social purpose (E)	Sozialpfandbrief n	—	obligation hypothécaire pour financer des projets sociaux f	obbligazione ipotecaria edilizia sociale f	cédula hipotecaria con fines sociales f
mortgage debenture (E)	Hypothekenpfandbrief m	—	obligation foncière f	titolo di credito fondiario m	obligación hipotecaria f
mortgage deed (E)	Hypothekenbrief m	—	cédule hypothécaire f	titolo ipotecario m	carta hipotecaria f
mortgage for the benefit of the owner (E)	Eigentümer-Hypothek f	—	hypothèque revenant au propriétaire du fonds grevé f	ipoteca a favore del proprietario f	hipoteca de propietario f
mortgage insurance (E)	Hypothekenversicherung f	—	assurance hypothécaire f	assicurazione dell'ipoteca f	seguro de hipotecas m
mortgage law (E)	Pfandbriefgesetz n	—	législation en matière d'hypothèques f	legge sulle obbligazioni ipotecarie f	ley de pignoración f
mortgage loan (E)	Pfandbriefdarlehen n	—	prêt hypothécaire m	prestito su pegno m	préstamo hipotecario m
mortgage loan (E)	Hypothekarkredit m	—	crédit hypothécaire m	credito ipotecario m	crédito hipotecario m
mortgage loan repayable after having been duly called (E)	Kündigungshypothek f		hypothèque garantissant une dette remboursable avec préavis f	ipoteca rimborsabile dopo preavviso f	hipoteca con preaviso f
mortgage loan to finance building of new dwelling-house (E)	Neubauhypothek f	—	hypothèque pour financer la construction de logements neufs f	ipoteca su una nuova costruzione f	hipoteca para la construcción de nuevas viviendas f
mortgage register (E)	Hypothekenregister n	—	livre foncier m	libro delle ipoteche m	registro hipotecario m
most-favoured nation treatment (E)	Meistbegünstigung f	—	régime de la nation la plus favorisée m	trattamento della nazione più favorita m	régimen de la nación más favorecida m
mouvement de panique (F)	Run m	run	—	run m	run m
mouvement international des capitaux (F)	internationaler Kapitalverkehr m	international capital transactions	—	circolazione di capitali internazionale f	movimiento de capitales internacional m
mouvements de capital (F)	Kapitalbewegungen f/pl	capital movements	—	movimenti di capitali m/pl	movimientos de capital m/pl
movable goods (E)	Mobilien f/pl	—	biens mobiliers m/pl	beni mobili m/pl	bienes muebles m/pl
movimenti di capitali (I)	Kapitalbewegungen f/pl	capital movements	mouvements de capital m/pl	—	movimientos de capital m/pl
movimento bancario (I)	Bankumsätze m/pl	bank turnover	chiffres d'affaires d'une banque m/pl	—	facturación bancaria f
movimento di scorte (I)	Bestandsveränderung f	inventory change	variation des existences f	—	variaciones de las partidas f/pl
movimento divergente (I)	Sonderbewegung f	extraordinary trend	tendance extraordinaire f	—	oscilación extraordinaria f
movimiento de ahorros liberalizado (Es)	freizügiger Sparverkehr m	system by which savings depositor can effect inpayments and withdrawals at all savings banks or post offices	épargne libéralisée f	libertà per l'intestatario del libretto di risparmio di effettuare versamenti e esborsi in tutte le casse di risparmio tedesche f	—
movimiento de capitales internacional (Es)	internationaler Kapitalverkehr m	international capital transactions	mouvement international des capitaux m	circolazione di capitali internazionale f	—
movimiento de pagos (Es)	Zahlungsverkehr m	payment transaction	règlements m/pl	pagamenti m/pl	—
movimientos de capital (Es)	Kapitalbewegungen f/pl	capital movements	mouvements de capital m/pl	movimenti di capitali m/pl	—

	D	E	F	I	Es
moyen de payement (F)	Zahlungsmittel *n*	means of payment	—	mezzo di pagamento *m*	medio de pago *m*
moyen de preuve (F)	Beweismittel *n*	evidence	—	prova *f*	medio probatorio *m*
moyenne arithmétique (F)	arithmetische Mittel *n*	arithmetical average	—	medie aritmetiche *f/pl*	media aritmética *f*
multilateraler Handel (D)	—	multilateral trade	commerce multilatéral *m*	commercio multilaterale *m*	comercio multilateral *m*
multilateral trade (E)	multilateraler Handel *m*	—	commerce multilatéral *m*	commercio multilaterale *m*	comercio multilateral *m*
multimillion credit (E)	Millionenkredit *m*	—	crédit d'un million *m*	credito di un milione e più *m*	crédito de millones *m*
multiple exchange rates (E)	gespaltener Wechselkurs *m*	—	cours du change multiple *m*	cambio multiplo *m*	tipo de cambio múltiple *m*
multiple voting right (E)	Mehrstimmrecht *n*	—	droit de vote plural *m*	diritto di voto plurimo *m*	derecho de voto plural *m*
multiple voting share (E)	Mehrstimmrechtsaktie *f*	—	action à droit de vote plural *f*	azione a voto plurimo *f*	acción de voto plural *f*
multiplicador de creación de dinero giral (Es)	Buchgeldschöpfungsmultiplikator *m*	deposit money creation multiplier	multiplicateur de création de monnaie scripturale *m*	moltiplicatore di moneta contabile *m*	—
multiplicador de crédito (Es)	Geldschöpfungsmultiplikator *m*	money creation ratio	multiplicateur de crédit *m*	moltiplicatore di moneta *m*	—
multiplicateur de création de monnaie scripturale (F)	Buchgeldschöpfungsmultiplikator *m*	deposit money creation multiplier	—	moltiplicatore di moneta contabile *m*	multiplicador de creación de dinero giral *m*
multiplicateur de crédit (F)	Geldschöpfungsmultiplikator *m*	money creation ratio	—	moltiplicatore di moneta *m*	multiplicador de crédito *m*
Mündelgeld (D)	—	money held in trust for a ward	deniers de pupille *m/pl*	capitale del minore *m*	dinero pupilar *m*
mündelsichere Papiere (D)	—	trustee securities	valeur de tout repos *f*	valori di tutto riposo *m/pl*	títulos pupilares *m/pl*
Münzgeld (D)	—	species	monnaie métallique *f*	denaro monetato *m*	moneda acuñada *f*
Münzgewinn (D)	—	seignorage	monnayage *m*	utile di coniatura *m*	monedaje *m*
Münzhandel (D)	—	dealings in gold and silver coins	commerce des pièces de monnaie *m*	commercio monete pregiate *m*	comercio con monedas *m*
Münzhoheit (D)	—	monetary sovereignty	prérogative de la frappe *f*	privilegio di battere moneta *m*	soberanía de acuñación *f*
Münzregal (D)	—	exclusive right of coinage	monopole de la frappe *m*	privilegio di battere moneta *m*	regalía de acuñación *f*
mutuo bancario (I)	Bankanleihen *f/pl*	bank bonds	emprunt émis par une banque *m*	—	empréstito bancario *m*
mutuo comunale (I)	Kommunaldarlehen *n*	loan granted to a local authority	prêt aux communes *m*	—	empréstito municipal *m*
mutuo convertibile (I)	Optionsdarlehen *n*	optional loan	prêt avec droit d'option *m*	—	préstamo de opción *m*
mutuo destinato a copertura (I)	Deckungsdarlehen *n*	coverage loan	prêt de couverture *m*	—	préstamo de cobertura *m*
mutuo edilizio (I)	Bauspardarlehen *n*	loan granted for building purposes	prêt d'épargne-construction *m*	—	préstamo ahorro-vivienda *m*
mutuo edilizio (I)	Baudarlehen *n*	building loan	prêt à la construction *m*	—	crédito para la construcción *m*
mutuo inizio attività imprenditoriale (I)	Existenzaufbaudarlehen *n*	business set-up loan	prêt de premier établissement *m*	—	préstamo de fundación *m*
Nachbezugsrecht (D)	—	right to a cumulative dividend	droit à un dividende cumulatif *m*	diritto di dividendo cumulativo *m*	derecho a un dividendo cumulativo *m*
Nachbörse (D)	—	after-hours dealing	marché après-bourse *m*	dopolistino *m*	operaciones después del cierre de la bolsa *f/pl*
Nachbürgschaft (D)	—	collateral guarantee	garantie du certificateur de la caution *f*	fideiussione per il fideiussore *f*	subfianza *f*
Nachdividende (D)	—	dividend payable for previous years	droit aux dividendes des années précédentes *m*	dividendo cumulativo *m*	derecho de dividendo de años precedentes *m*
Nachfrage (D)	—	demand	demande *f*	domanda *f*	demanda *f*

	D	E	F	I	Es
Nachgründung (D)	—	post-formation acquisition	acquisitions complémentaires de la société *f/pl*	costituzione successiva *f*	adquisición de instalaciones por una sociedad después de su fundación *f*
Nachindossament (D)	—	endorsement of an overdue bill of exchange	endossement après la date de l'échéance de la lettre de change *m*	girata posteriore alla scadenza *f*	endoso de letra vencida *m*
Nachorder (D)	—	follow-up order	nouveau ordre *m*	ordinazione successiva *f*	nueva orden *f*
nachrangige Finanzierung (D)	—	junior financing	financement de rang inférieur *m*	finanziamento subordinato *m*	financiación subordinada *f*
Nachricht (D)	—	news	avis *m*	communicazione *f*	noticia *f*
Nachschuß (D)	—	subsequent payment	versement complémentaire *m*	apporto supplemetare *m*	aportación suplementaria *f*
Nachschußpflicht (D)	—	obligation to make an additional contribution	obligation de faire un versement complémentaire *f*	obbligo di versamenti supplementari *m*	obligación de pago suplementario *m*
Nachsichtwechsel (D)	—	after-sight bill	traite à un certain délai de vue *f*	cambiale a certo tempo vista *f*	letra a tantos días vista *f*
Nachttresor (D)	—	night safe	dépôt de nuit *m*	cassa continua *f*	caja nocturna *f*
Namensaktie (D)	—	registered share	action nominative *f*	azione nominativa *f*	acción nominal *f*
Namenspapier (D)	—	registered securities	titre nominatif *m*	titolo nominativo *m*	título nominal *m*
name transaction (E)	Aufgabegeschäft *n*	—	opération de médiation *f*	contratto intermediato *m*	contrato intermediado *m*
nantir (F)	beleihen	lend money on something	—	ipotecare	pignorar
nantissement (F)	Pfand *n*	pledge	—	pegno *m*	prenda *f*
nasse Stücke (D)	—	unissued mortgage bonds still in trustee's hands	titres d'une émission pas encore placés *m/pl*	titoli rimanenti di un' emissione *m/pl*	títulos todavía no emitidos *m/pl*
national accounting (E)	volkswirtschaftliche Gesamtrechnung *f*	—	comptabilité nationale *f*	contabilitá nazionale *f*	contabilidad nacional *f*
national economy (E)	Volkswirtschaft *f*	—	économie nationale *f*	economia politica *f*	economía nacional *f*
national income (E)	Volkseinkommen *n*	—	revenu national *m*	reddito nazionale *m*	renta nacional *f*
national product (E)	Sozialprodukt *n*	—	produit national *m*	prodotto sociale *m*	producto nacional *m*
national wealth (E)	Volksvermögen *n*	—	patrimoine national *m*	ricchezza nazionale *f*	patrimonio nacional *m*
Naturadarlehen (D)	—	loan granted in form of a mortgage bond	prêt en nature *m*	prestito ipotecario a obbligazione fondiaria *m*	empréstito en especie *m*
Naturalgeld (D)	—	commodity money	argent en nature *m*	oggetto di baratto *m*	dinero en especie *m*
Naturalkredit (D)	—	credit granted in kind	crédit en nature *m*	prestito ipotecario a obbligazione fondiaria *m*	crédito en especie *m*
natural person (E)	natürliche Person *f*	—	personne physique *f*	persona fisica *f*	persona física *f*
Naturaltilgung (D)	—	redemption in kind	amortissement en nature *m*	rimborso del credito ipotecario pattuito *m*	amortización en especie *f*
natürliche Person (D)	—	natural person	personne physique *f*	persona fisica *f*	persona física *f*
Nebenplatz (D)	—	place without a Federal Bank office	place non bancaire *f*	piazza secondaria *f*	bolsín oficial *m*
necesidad de capital (Es)	Kapitalbedarf *m*	capital requirement	besoin en capital *m*	fabbisogno di capitale *m*	—
necesidad de crédito (Es)	Kreditbedarf *m*	credit demand	besoin en crédits *m*	fabbisogno creditizio *m*	—
necesidad financiera (Es)	Finanzbedarf *m*	financial requirements	besoins de trésorerie *m/pl*	fabbisogno finanziario *m*	—
negative advance interest (E)	Vorschußzinsen *m/pl*	—	intérêts payés par anticipation *m/pl*	penalità interessi *f*	interés negativo anticipado *m*
negative clause (E)	Negativklausel *f*	—	clause prohibitive *f*	clausola negativa *f*	cláusula negativa *f*
negative declaration (E)	Negativerklärung *f*	—	déclaration négative *f*	clausola negativa *f*	declaración negativa *f*
negative interest (E)	Negativzins *m*	—	intérêt négatif *m*	interesse negativo *m*	interés negativo *m*
Negativerklärung (D)	—	negative declaration	déclaration négative *f*	clausola negativa *f*	declaración negativa *f*
Negativhypothek (D)	—	borrower's undertaking to create no new charge ranking ahead of lender	hypothèque négative *f*	ipoteca negativa *f*	hipoteca negativa *f*

	D	E	F	I	Es
Negativklausel (D)	—	negative clause	clause prohibitive *f*	clausola negativa *f*	cláusula negativa *f*
Negativzins (D)	—	negative interest	intérêt négatif *m*	interesse negativo *m*	interés negativo *m*
negociación (Es)	Negotiation *f*	negotiation	négociation *f*	negoziazione *f*	—
negociación de moneda extranjera (Es)	Sortenhandel *m*	dealing in foreign notes and coins	commerce de change *m*	commercio delle valute *m*	—
negociación de petróleo a término (Es)	Ölterminhandel *m*	oil futures dealings	opérations pétrolières à terme *f/pl*	commercio petrolifero a termine *m*	—
negociaciones normales (Es)	Normalverkehr *m*	normal transactions	négociation normale *f*	operazioni normali *f/pl*	—
négociation (F)	Negotiation *f*	negotiation	—	negoziazione *f*	negociación *f*
négociation de lots importants (F)	Pakethandel *m*	dealing in large lots	—	negoziazione di pacchetti azionari *f*	transacciones de paquetes mayores de acciones *f/pl*
négociation des valeurs à revenu fixe (F)	Rentenhandel *m*	bond trading	—	commercio titoli a reddito fisso *m*	contratación de títulos de renta fija *f*
négociation normale (F)	Normalverkehr *m*	normal transactions	—	operazioni normali *f/pl*	negociaciones normales *f/pl*
négociations en bourse (F)	amtlicher Handel *m*	official trading	—	contrattazione ufficiale *f*	cotización oficial *f*
negocio (Es)	Handelsgeschäfte *n/pl*	commercial transactions	affaires commerciales *f/pl*	affari commerciali *m/pl*	—
negocio (Es)	Geschäft *n*	exchange operation	opération *f*	contratto *m*	—
negocio consigo mismo (Es)	Insichgeschäft *n*	self-dealing	acte passé avec soi-même *m*	operazione fine a se stessa *f*	—
negocio de consorcio (Es)	Konsortialgeschäft *n*	syndicate transaction	opération appuyée par plusieurs banques *f*	operazione consorziale *f*	—
negocio de descuento (Es)	Diskontgeschäft *n*	discount business	opération d'escompte *f*	operazione di sconto *f*	—
negocio de exportación (Es)	Auslandsgeschäft *n*	business in foreign countries	opération avec l'étranger *f*	affare all'estero *m*	—
negocio fijo (Es)	Fixgeschäft *n*	transaction for delivery by a fixed date	opération à terme fixe *f*	contrattazione a fermo *f*	—
negocio hedge (Es)	Hedgegeschäft *n*	hedge operation	opération hedge *f*	operazione hedge *f*	—
negocio neto (Es)	Nettogeschäft *n*	net-price transaction	opération nette de courtage et de commission *f*	operazione borsistica netta *f*	—
negocio offshore (Es)	Offshore-Geschäft *n*	offshore dealings	opération off shore *f*	operazione off-shore *f*	—
negocio onshore (Es)	Onshore-Geschäft *n*	onshore business	opération onshore *f*	operazione onshore *f*	—
negocios en curso (Es)	schwebende Geschäfte *n/pl*	pending transactions	affaires en suspens *f/pl*	affari pendenti *m/pl*	—
negotiable document of title (E)	Traditionspapier *n*	—	titre du type classique *m*	titolo di credito trasferibile *f*	título de tradición *m*
negotiable instruments law concerning cheques (E)	Scheckrecht *n*	—	législation en matière de chèque *f*	disciplina degli assegni *f*	derecho de cheque *m*
negotiable promissory note (E)	trockener Wechsel *m*	—	billet à ordre *m*	pagherò *m*	pagaré *m*
negotiable securities (E)	freie Stücke *n/pl*	—	titres négociables *m/pl*	titoli non vincolati *m/pl*	títulos libres *m/pl*
Negotiation (D)	—	negotiation	négociation *f*	negoziazione *f*	negociación *f*
negotiation (E)	Negotiation *f*	negotiation	négociation *f*	negoziazione *f*	negociación *f*
Negoziationskredit (D)	—	credit authorizing negotiation of bills	crédit autorisant à la négociation de traites *m*	credito di negoziazione *m*	crédito de negociación *m*
negoziazione (I)	Negotiation *f*	negotiation	négociation *f*	—	negociación *f*
negoziazione di pacchetti azionari (I)	Pakethandel *m*	dealing in large lots	négociation de lots importants *f*	—	transacciones de paquetes mayores de acciones *f/pl*
negoziazione di titoli per telefono (I)	Telefonverkehr *m*	telephone dealings	transactions par téléphone *f/pl*	—	mercado de valores extrabursátil *m*
Nennwert (D)	—	nominal value	valeur nominale *f*	valore nominale *m*	valor nominal *m*
Nennwertaktie (D)	—	par value share	action nominale *f*	azione a valore nominale *f*	acción de suma *f*

	D	E	F	I	Es
nennwertlose Aktie (D)	—	no par value share	action sans valeur nominale f	azione senza valore nominale f	acción sin valor nominal f
net (E)	Netto	—	net	netto	neto
net (F)	Netto	net	—	netto	neto
net assets (E)	Reinvermögen n	—	avoir net m	attivo netto m	patrimonio neto m
net borrowing (E)	Nettokreditaufnahme f	—	emprunt net m	indebitamento netto m	toma de crédito neta f
net dividend (E)	Netto-Dividende f	—	dividende net m	dividendo netto m	dividendo neto m
net financial investment (E)	Finanzierungssaldo m	—	investissement financier net m	saldo di finanziamento m	saldo de financiación m
net fixed assets (E)	Netto-Anlagevermögen n	—	capital fixe net m	capitale immobilizzato netto m	activo fijo neto m
net interest rate (E)	Nettozinssatz m	—	taux d'intérêt net m	tasso d'interesse netto m	tipo neto de intereses m
net investment (E)	Nettoinvestition f	—	investissement net m	investimento netto m	inversión neta f
net loss (E)	Bilanzverlust m	—	perte comptable f	perdita di bilancio f	pérdida de balance f
net movement of foreign exchange (E)	Devisenbilanz f	—	compte de devises m	bilancia valutaria f	balanza de divisas f
net national product (E)	Nettosozialprodukt n	—	produit national net m	prodotto nazionale netto m	producto nacional neto m
net new indebtedness (E)	Nettoneuverschuldung f	—	nouveaux emprunts en termes nets m	indebitamento netto m	endeudamiento neto m
neto (Es)	Netto	net	net	netto	—
net present value (E)	Kapitalwert m	—	valeur en capital f	valore del capitale m	valor capitalizado m
net price (E)	Nettokurs m	—	cours net m	quotazione netta f	cambio neto m
net-price transaction (E)	Nettogeschäft n	—	opération nette de courtage et de commission f	operazione borsistica netta f	negocio neto m
net profit ratio (E)	Umsatzrentabilität f	—	rendement du chiffre d'affaires m	rendimento del fatturato m	rentabilidad del volumen de negocios f
Netto (D)	—	net	net	netto	neto
netto (I)	Netto	net	net	—	neto
Netto-Anlagevermögen (D)	—	net fixed assets	capital fixe net m	capitale immobilizzato netto m	activo fijo neto m
Netto-Dividende (D)	—	net dividend	dividende net m	dividendo netto m	dividendo neto m
Nettogeschäft (D)	—	net-price transaction	opération nette de courtage et de commission f	operazione borsistica netta f	negocio neto m
Nettoinvestition (D)	—	net investment	investissement net m	investimento netto m	inversión neta f
Nettokreditaufnahme (D)	—	net borrowing	emprunt net m	indebitamento netto m	toma de crédito neta f
Nettokurs (D)	—	net price	cours net m	quotazione netta f	cambio neto m
Nettoneuverschuldung (D)	—	net new indebtedness	nouveaux emprunts en termes nets m	indebitamento netto m	endeudamiento neto m
Nettosozialprodukt (D)	—	net national product	produit national net m	prodotto nazionale netto m	producto nacional neto m
Nettozinssatz (D)	—	net interest rate	taux d'intérêt net m	tasso d'interesse netto m	tipo neto de intereses m
Neubauhypothek (D)	—	mortgage loan to finance building of new dwelling-house	hypothèque pour financer la construction de logements neufs f	ipoteca su una nuova costruzione f	hipoteca para la construcción de nuevas viviendas f
Neugiro (D)	—	new endorsement	nouvel endossement m	certificato di comproprietà al deposito collettivo di titoli m	nuevo endoso m
neutrales Geld (D)	—	neutral money	argent neutre m	moneta neutrale f	dinero neutral m
neutral money (E)	neutrales Geld n	—	argent neutre m	moneta neutrale f	dinero neutral m
Neuverschuldung (D)	—	new indebtedness	nouvel endettement m	nuovo debito m	nuevo endeudamiento m
new endorsement (E)	Neugiro m	—	nouvel endossement m	certificato di comproprietà al deposito collettivo di titoli m	nuevo endoso m
new indebtedness (E)	Neuverschuldung f	—	nouvel endettement m	nuovo debito m	nuevo endeudamiento m

	D	E	F	I	Es
new issue giro transfer system (E)	Jungscheinverkehr *m*	—	système des certificats provisoires d'actions nouvelles *m*	sistema di certificato provvisorio *f*	sistema de certificados provisionales de acciones *m*
new issue statistics (E)	Emissionsstatistik *f*	—	statistique d'émission *f*	statistica delle nuove emissioni *f*	estadística de emisión *f*
new shares (E)	junge Aktien *f/pl*	—	actions nouvelles *f/pl*	nuove azioni *f/pl*	acciones nuevas *f/pl*
nicht an Order (D)	—	not to order	non à ordre	non all'ordine	no a la orden
nichtnotierte Aktie (D)	—	unquoted share	action non cotée *f*	azione non quotata ufficialmente *f*	acción no cotizada *f*
Niederstwertprinzip (D)	—	lowest value principle	principe de la valeur minimale *m*	principio del valore minimo *m*	principio del valor mínimo *m*
Nießbrauch (D)	—	usufruct	usufruit *m*	usufrutto *m*	usufructo *m*
night safe (E)	Nachttresor *m*	—	dépôt de nuit *m*	cassa continua *f*	caja nocturna *f*
night safe deposit (E)	Spätschalter *m*	—	guichet extérieur de permanence *m*	cassa continua *f*	taquilla de noche *f*
niveau des prix (F)	Preisniveau *n*	price level	—	livello dei prezzi *m*	nivel de precios *m*
niveau du taux d'intérêt (F)	Zinsniveau *n*	interest rate level	—	livello degli interessi *m*	nivel de los tipos de interés *m*
nivel de los tipos de interés (Es)	Zinsniveau *n*	interest rate level	niveau du taux d'intérêt *m*	livello degli interessi *m*	—
nivel de precios (Es)	Preisniveau *n*	price level	niveau des prix *m*	livello dei prezzi *m*	—
no a la orden (Es)	nicht an Order	not to order	non à ordre	non all'ordine	—
no cotización (Es)	Kursstreichung *f*	non-quotation	annulation de la cotation *f*	mancata quotazione *f*	—
nombre de jours portant intérêt (F)	Zinstage *m/pl*	quarter days	—	giorni per il calcolo interessi *m/pl*	número de días devengado intereses *m*
nominal capital (E)	Nominalkapital *n*	—	capital nominal *m*	capitale nominale *m*	fondo capital *m*
nominal capital borrowed (E)	nominelles Eigenkapital *n*	—	capital propre nominal *m*	capitale proprio nominale *m*	capital propio nominal *m*
Nominalkapital (D)	—	nominal capital	capital nominal *m*	capitale nominale *m*	fondo capital *m*
nominal rate of interest (E)	Nominalzins *m*	—	intérêt nominal *m*	interesse nominale *m*	interés nominal *m*
nominal value (E)	Nennwert *m*	—	valeur nominale *f*	valore nominale *m*	valor nominal *m*
nominal value (E)	Ausgabewert *m*	—	cours d'émission *m*	valore d'emissione *m*	valor de emisión *m*
Nominalwert (D)	—	face value	valeur nominale *f*	valore nominale *m*	valor nominal *m*
Nominalzins (D)	—	nominal rate of interest	intérêt nominal *m*	interesse nominale *m*	interés nominal *m*
nominelles Eigenkapital (D)	—	nominal capital borrowed	capital propre nominal *m*	capitale proprio nominale *m*	capital propio nominal *m*
non all'ordine (I)	nicht an Order	not to order	non à ordre	—	no a la orden
non à ordre (F)	nicht an Order	not to order	—	non all'ordine	no a la orden
non-calling period (E)	Kündigungssperrfrist *f*	—	délai de blocage de dénonciation *m*	termine di preavviso *m*	plazo de suspensión de preaviso *m*
non-interest bearing Treasury bond (E)	U-Schätze *m/pl*	—	obligations du Trésor ne produisant pas d'intérêts *f/pl*	buoni del tesoro infruttiferi *m/pl*	letras del Tesoro sin interés *f/pl*
non-negotiable bill of exchange (E)	Rektawechsel *m*	—	traite non à ordre *f*	cambiale non all' ordine *f*	letra nominativa *f*
non-quotation (E)	Kursstreichung *f*	—	annulation de la cotation *f*	mancata quotazione *f*	no cotización *f*
non-resident (E)	Gebietsfremder *m*	—	non-résident *m*	non residente *m*	no residente *m*
non-resident (E)	Devisenausländer *m*	—	non-résident *m*	non residente *m*	no residente *m*
non-résident (F)	Gebietsfremder *m*	non-resident	—	non residente *m*	no residente *m*
non-résident (F)	Devisenausländer *m*	non-resident	—	non residente *m*	no residente *m*
non residente (I)	Gebietsfremder *m*	non-resident	non-résident *m*	—	no residente *m*
non residente (I)	Devisenausländer *m*	non-resident	non-résident *m*	—	no residente *m*
non-voting share (E)	stimmrechtslose Vorzugsaktie *f*	—	action privilégiée sans droit de vote *f*	azione privilegiata senza diritto di voto *f*	acción preferente sin derecho a voto *f*
no par value share (E)	nennwertlose Aktie *f*	—	action sans valeur nominale *f*	azione senza valore nominale *f*	acción sin valor nominal *f*
no residente (Es)	Devisenausländer *m*	non-resident	non-résident *m*	non residente *m*	—

	D	E	F	I	Es
no residente (Es)	Gebietsfremder *m*	non-resident	non-résident *m*	non residente *m*	—
norma bancaria (I)	Bankregel *f*	banker's rule	règle bancaire *f*	—	regla bancaria *f*
normal transactions (E)	Normalverkehr *m*	—	négociation normale *f*	operazioni normali *f/pl*	negociaciones normales *f/pl*
Normalverkehr (D)	—	normal transactions	négociation normale *f*	operazioni normali *f/pl*	negociaciones normales *f/pl*
normas bursátiles europeas (Es)	Europäische Börsenrichtlinien *f/pl*	European stock exchange guide-lines	directives boursières européennes *f/pl*	regolamenti europei di borsa *m/pl*	—
normas de eficacia (Es)	Effizienzregeln *f/pl*	performance regulations	régulation d'efficience *f*	regole per l'efficienza *f/pl*	—
normas de financiación (Es)	Finanzierungsregeln *f/pl*	financing rules	règles de financement *f/pl*	regole di finanziamento *f/pl*	—
normas de financiación (Es)	Finanzierungsgrundsätze *m/pl*	financing principles	principes de financement *m/pl*	principi di finanziamento *m/pl*	—
normas de financiación horizontal (Es)	horizontale Finanzierungsregeln *f/pl*	horizontal financing rules	règles de financement horizontales *f/pl*	norme orizzontali di finanziamento *f/pl*	—
normas de inversión (Es)	Anlagevorschriften *f/pl*	rules for investment of resources	prescriptions d'investissement *f/pl*	disposizioni d'investimento *f/pl*	—
normas sobre balances (Es)	Bilanzierungsvorschriften *f/pl*	accounting regulations	prescriptions concernant l'établissement du bilan *f/pl*	norme per la redazione del bilancio *f/pl*	—
norme orizzontali di finanziamento (I)	horizontale Finanzierungsregeln *f/pl*	horizontal financing rules	règles de financement horizontales *f/pl*	—	normas de financiación horizontal *f/pl*
norme per la redazione del bilancio (I)	Bilanzierungsvorschriften *f/pl*	accounting regulations	prescriptions concernant l'établissement du bilan *f/pl*	—	normas sobre balances *f/pl*
norme sul capitale proprio e la liquidità degli istituti di credito (I)	Grundsätze über das Eigenkapital und die Liquidität der Kreditinstitute *m/pl*	principles of capital resources and the banks' liquid assets	principes de capital propre et de la liquidité des établissement de crédit *m/pl*	—	principios de capital propio y de la liquidez de los institutos bancarios *m/pl*
nostro account (E)	Nostrokonto *n*	—	compte dans une autre banque *m*	conto nostro *m*	nuestra cuenta *f*
nostro address in case of need (E)	Nostronotadresse *f*	—	notre adresse au besoin *f*	indicazione al bisogno nostro *f*	dirección propia en caso necesario *f*
nostro balance (E)	Nostroguthaben *n*	—	avoir dans une autre banque *m*	avere nostro *m*	haber a nuestro favor *m*
Nostroeffekten (D)	—	securities held by a bank at another bank	effets dans une autre banque *m/pl*	titoli nostri *m/pl*	efectos a nuestro cargo *m/pl*
Nostroguthaben (D)	—	nostro balance	avoir dans une autre banque *m*	avere nostro *m*	haber a nuestro favor *m*
Nostrokonto (D)	—	nostro account	compte dans une autre banque *m*	conto nostro *m*	nuestra cuenta *f*
nostro liability (E)	Nostroverbindlichkeit *f*	—	obligations vis-à-vis d'une autre banque *f/pl*	impegno nostro *m*	débitos a nuestro cargo *m/pl*
Nostronotadresse (D)	—	nostro address in case of need	notre adresse au besoin *f*	indicazione al bisogno nostro *f*	dirección propia en caso necesario *f*
Nostroverbindlichkeit (D)	—	nostro liability	obligations vis-à-vis d'une autre banque *f/pl*	impegno nostro *m*	débitos a nuestro cargo *m/pl*
nota arbitral (Es)	Arbitragerechnung *f*	arbitrage voucher	calcul d'arbitrage *f*	calcolo arbitrale *m*	—
nota d'accredito (I)	Überweisungsträger *m*	remittance slip	formulaire de virement *m*	—	formulario de transferencia *m*
nota de cambios flotantes (Es)	Floating Rate Note *f*	floating rate note	floating rate note *f*	floating rate note *f*	—
nota de cargo (Es)	Lastschriftkarte *f*	debit card	carte de débit *f*	avviso di addebito *m*	—
Notanzeige (D)	—	notice of dishonour	avis de non-payement *m*	occorrendo *m*	notificación de no aceptación *f*
note de débit (F)	Lastschrift *f*	debit entry	—	addebitamento *m*	cargo en cuenta *m*
note issue (E)	Notenausgabe *f*	—	émission de billets *f*	emissione di banconote *f*	emisión de billetes *f*
Noten (D)	—	bank notes	billets *m/pl*	banconote *f/pl*	billetes *m/pl*
Notenabstempelung (D)	—	stamping of bank notes	estampillage des billets de banque *m*	timbratura di banconote *f*	estampillado de billetes *m*

	D	E	F	I	Es
Notenausgabe (D)	—	note issue	émission de billets *f*	emissione di banconote *f*	emisión de billetes *f*
Notenbank (D)	—	central bank	banque d'émission *f*	banca d'emissione *f*	banco emisor *m*
Notendeckung (D)	—	cover of note circulation	couverture en billets de banque *f*	copertura di emissione di banconote *f*	cobertura monetaria *f*
Noteneinlösungspflicht (D)	—	obligation to redeem notes	obligation de remboursement de billets *f*	convertibilità delle banconote *f*	obligación de convertibilidad monetaria *f*
Notenkontingent (D)	—	fixed issue of notes	maximum toléré à l'émission des billets de banque *m*	contingente di banconote *m*	contingente de emisión fiduciaria *m*
notes and coins in circulation (E)	Zahlungsmittelumlauf *m*	—	circulation monétaire *f*	circolazione di mezzi di pagamento *f*	medios de pago en circulación *m/pl*
notes appended to quotation (E)	Kurszusätze *m/pl*	—	indications supplémentaires de cotation *f/pl*	termini borsistici *m/pl*	indicaciones explicativas de las cotizaciones *f/pl*
Notgeld (D)	—	emergency money	monnaie obsidionale *f*	moneta d'emergenza *f*	dinero de urgencia *m*
notice board (E)	Aushang *m*	—	tableau de signalisation *m*	affisso *m*	tablilla *f*
notice of dishonour (E)	Notanzeige *f*	—	avis de non-payement *m*	occorrendo *m*	notificación de no aceptación *f*
notificación (Es)	Notifikation *f*	notification	notification *f*	notificazione *f*	—
notificación de no aceptación (Es)	Notanzeige *f*	notice of dishonour	avis de non-payement *m*	occorrendo *m*	—
notification (E)	Notifikation *f*	—	notification *f*	notificazione *f*	notificación *f*
notification (E)	Benachrichtigung *f*	—	notification *f*	avviso *m*	aviso *m*
notification (E)	Bekanntmachung *f*	—	publication *f*	annuncio *m*	publicación *f*
notification (F)	Notifikation *f*	notification	—	notificazione *f*	notificación *f*
notification (F)	Benachrichtigung *f*	notification	—	avviso *m*	aviso *m*
notificazione (I)	Notifikation *f*	notification	notification *f*	—	notificación *f*
Notifikation (D)	—	notification	notification *f*	notificazione *f*	notificación *f*
notleidende Forderung (D)	—	claim in default	créance irrécupérable *f*	credito in sofferenza *m*	crédito dudoso *m*
notre adresse au besoin (F)	Nostronotadresse *f*	nostro address in case of need	—	indicazione al bisogno nostro *f*	dirección propia en caso necesario *f*
not to order (E)	nicht an Order	—	non à ordre	non all'ordine	no a la orden
nouveau ordre (F)	Nachorder *f*	follow-up order	—	ordinazione successiva *f*	nueva orden *f*
nouveaux emprunts en termes nets (F)	Nettoneuverschuldung *f*	net new indebtedness	—	indebitamento netto *m*	endeudamiento neto *m*
nouvel endettement (F)	Neuverschuldung *f*	new indebtedness	—	nuovo debito *m*	nuevo endeudamiento *m*
nouvel endossement (F)	Neugiro *m*	new endorsement	—	certificato di comproprietà al deposito collettivo di titoli *m*	nuevo endoso *m*
nuestra cuenta (Es)	Nostrokonto *n*	nostro account	compte dans une autre banque *m*	conto nostro *m*	—
nueva orden (Es)	Nachorder *f*	follow-up order	nouveau ordre *m*	ordinazione successiva *f*	—
nuevo endeudamiento (Es)	Neuverschuldung *f*	new indebtedness	nouvel endettement *m*	nuovo debito *m*	—
nuevo endoso (Es)	Neugiro *m*	new endorsement	nouvel endossement *m*	certificato di comproprietà al deposito collettivo di titoli *m*	—
numbered account (E)	Nummernkonto *n*	—	compte anonyme *m*	conto cifrato *m*	cuenta anónima *f*
numbering (E)	Numerierung *f*	—	numérotage *m*	numerazione *f*	numeración *f*
numeración (Es)	Numerierung *f*	numbering	numérotage *m*	numerazione *f*	—
numeración de cuentas (Es)	Kontennumerierung *f*	account numbering	numérotage des comptes *m*	classificazione dei conti *f*	—
numeración de las filiales bancarias (Es)	Bankennumerierung *f*	bank branch numbering	classification numérique des succursales bancaires *f*	codice bancario *m*	—

	D	E	F	I	Es
numerazione (I)	Numerierung f	numbering	numérotage m	—	numeración f
Numerierung (D)	—	numbering	numérotage m	numerazione f	numeración f
número (Es)	Zahl f	figure	chiffre m	cifra f	—
numéro de code bancaire (F)	Bankleitzahl f	bank identification number	—	codice bancario m	codigo de identificación bancaria m
numéro de compte (F)	Kontonummer f	account number	—	numero di conto m	número de la cuenta m
número de días devengado intereses (Es)	Zinstage m/pl	quarter days	nombre de jours portant intérêt m	giorni per il calcolo interessi m	—
número de identificación personal (Es)	persönliche Identifikations-Nummer [PIN] f	personal identification number	numéro personnel d'identification m	numero di identificazione personale m	—
número de la cuenta (Es)	Kontonummer f	account number	numéro de compte m	numero di conto m	—
numero di conto (I)	Kontonummer f	account number	numéro de compte m	—	número de la cuenta m
numéro d'identification personnel (F)	persönliche Identifikations-Nummer [PIN] f	personal identification number	—	numero di identificazione personale m	número de identificación personal m
numero di identificazione personale (I)	persönliche Identifikations-Nummer [PIN] f	personal identification number	numéro d'identification personnel m	—	número de identificación personal m
numérotage (F)	Numerierung f	numbering	—	numerazione f	numeración f
numérotage des comptes (F)	Kontennumerierung f	account numbering	—	classificazione dei conti f	numeración de cuentas f
Nummernkonto (D)	—	numbered account	compte anonyme m	conto cifrato m	cuenta anónima f
Nummern-verzeichnis (D)	—	list of serial numbers of securities purchased or deposited	liste numérique f	elenco numerico m	escritura numérica f
nuove azioni (I)	junge Aktien f/pl	new shares	actions nouvelles f/pl	—	acciones nuevas f/pl
nuovo debito (I)	Neuverschuldung f	new indebtedness	nouvel endettement m	—	nuevo endeudamiento m
Nur zur Verrechnung (D)	—	for account only	à porter en compte	da accreditare	sólo para compensación
Nutzungsdauer (D)	—	service life	durée normale d'utilisation f	durata di godimento f	tiempo de utilización m
Nutzungsrecht (D)	—	usufructury right	droit de jouissance m	diritto di godimento m	derecho de uso m
oath of disclosure (E)	Offenbarungseid m	—	serment déclaratoire m	giuramento dichiarativo m	juramento declarativo m
obbligazione (I)	Obligation f	bond	obligation f	—	obligación f
obbligazione al portatore (I)	Inhaberschuld-verschreibung f	bearer bond	obligation au porteur f	—	obligación al portador f
obbligazione a premio (I)	Gewinnobligation f	participating debenture	obligation indexée f	—	bono sobre beneficios m
obbligazione bancaria (I)	Bankobligation f	bank bond	obligation de banque f	—	obligación bancaria f
obbligazione bancaria (I)	Bankschuld-verschreibung f	bank bond	obligation bancaire f	—	obligación bancaria f
obbligazione comunale (I)	Sammelanleihe f	joint loan issue	emprunt collectif m	—	empréstito colectivo m
obbligazione comunale (I)	Kommunalobligation f	local bond	obligation communale f	—	obligación comunal f
obbligazione contabile (I)	Wertrechtanleihe f	government-inscribed debt	emprunt de l'Etat inscrit dans le livre de la dette m	—	empréstito del Estado inscrito en el libro de la deuda m
obbligazione contingenziale (I)	Eventual-verbindlichkeit f	contingent liability	obligation éventuelle f	—	obligación eventual f
obbligazioni di cassa (I)	Kassenobligationen f/pl	medium-term bonds	obligations à moyen terme f/pl	—	bonos de caja m/pl
obbligazione di cassa di risparmio (I)	Sparobligation f	savings bond	obligation d'épargne f	—	obligación de ahorro f
obbligazione di liquidità (I)	Liquiditätsanleihe f	liquidity loan	emprunt de liquidité m	—	empréstito de liquidez m
obbligazione di una banca agricola (I)	Landwirtschafts-brief m	agricultural mortgage bond	cédule hypothéquaire agricole f	—	cédula hipotecaria agrícola f

	D	E	F	I	Es
obbligazione fondiaria (I)	Pfandbrief *m*	mortgage bond	obligation hypothécaire *f*	—	cédula hipotecaria *f*
obbligazione ipotecaria edilizia sociale (I)	Sozialpfandbrief *m*	mortgage bond serving a social purpose	obligation hypothécaire pour financer des projets sociaux *f*	—	cédula hipotecaria con fines sociales *f*
obbligazione parallela (I)	Parallelanleihe *f*	parallel loan	emprunt parallèle *m*	—	empréstito paralelo *m*
obbligazione privilegiata (I)	Vorzugsobligation *f*	preference bond	obligation assortie de droits réservés *f*	—	obligación preferente *f*
obbligazione sinodale (I)	Synodalanleihe *f*	synodal loan	emprunt synodal *m*	—	empréstito sinodal *m*
obbligazione sinodale (I)	Synodalobligation *f*	synodal bond	obligation synodale *f*	—	obligación sinodal *f*
obbligazioni fondiarie di smobilizzo (I)	Mobilisierungs- pfandbriefe *m/pl*	mobilization mortgage bond	obligations hypothécaires de mobilisation *f/pl*	—	cédulas hipotecarias de mobilización *f/pl*
obbligazioni industriali (I)	Industrieobligationen *f/pl*	industrial bonds	obligations de l'industrie *f/pl*	—	obligaciones industriales *f/pl*
obbligazioni in valuta estera (I)	Auslandsbonds *m/pl*	foreign currency bonds	titres d'emprunt émis en monnaie étrangère *m/pl*		bonos en moneda extranjera *m/pl*
obbligazioni libor (I)	Liboranleihen *f/pl*	Libor loans	emprunts Libor *m/pl*	—	empréstitos libor *m/pl*
obbligazioni privilegiate (I)	Prioritätsobligationen *f/pl*	priority bonds	obligation privilégié *f*	—	obligaciones preferentes *f/pl*
obbligazionista (I)	Obligationär *m*	bondholder	obligataire *m*	—	obligacionista *m*
obbligo all'intervento (I)	Interventionspflicht *f*	obligation to intervene	obligation d'intervention *f*	—	obligación de intervención *f*
obbligo d'autorizzazione (I)	Genehmigungspflicht *f*	duty to obtain a permit	obligation de solliciter une permission *f*	—	régimen de autorización *m*
obbligo d'avviso (I)	Benachrichtigungs- pflicht *f*	duty of notification	obligation de notification *f*	—	obligación de aviso *f*
obbligo d'informazione (I)	Auskunftspflicht *f*	obligation to give information	obligation de fournir des renseignements *f*		obligación de información *f*
obbligo di contrarre (I)	Kontrahierungs- zwang *m*	obligation to contract	obligation de contracter *f*		contratación forzosa *f*
obbligo di denuncia (I)	Anzeigepflicht *f*	legal obligation to disclose one's results	obligation de publier *f*	—	obligación de declarar *f*
obbligo di deposito (I)	Depotzwang *m*	compulsory safe custody	dépôt obligatoire *m*	—	depósito obligatorio *m*
obbligo di dichiarazione (I)	Meldepflicht *f*	obligation to register	déclaration obligatoire *f*	—	obligación de comunicar *f*
obbligo di pagamento (I)	Einlösungspflicht *f*	obligation to redeem	obligation de rachat *f*	—	deber de canje *m*
obbligo di pubblicazione (I)	Publikationspflicht *f*	compulsory disclosure	obligation de publication *f*	—	obligación de publicación *f*
obbligo di pubblicazione (I)	Veröffentlichungs- pflicht *f*	statutory public disclosure	obligation de publier *f*	—	publicación obligatoria *f*
obbligo di rendere noto (I)	Mitteilungspflicht *f*	obligation to furnish information	obligation d'informer *f*	—	obligación de comunicación *f*
obbligo di rendere pubblico (I)	Offenlegungspflicht *f*	duty to disclose one's financial conditions	obligation de révéler les derniers bilans du postulant d'un prêt *f*	—	obligación de declarar *f*
obbligo di revisione (I)	Revisionspflicht *f*	auditing requirements	obligation de vérification *f*	—	obligación de revisión *f*
obbligo di versamenti supplementari (I)	Nachdeckungspflicht *f*	obligation to provide further cover	obligation de mettre à disposition des fonds de couverture additionnaux *f*	—	obligación de poner a disposición fondos de cobertura *f*
obbligo di versamento (I)	Einzahlungspflicht *f*	obligation to pay subscription	obligation de libérer une action *f*	—	deber de liberación de acciones *m*
obiettivo di crescita (I)	Wachstumsziel *n*	growth target	objectif de croissance *m*	—	objetivo de crecimiento *m*
obiezione (I)	Widerspruch *m*	objection	objection *f*	—	objeción *f*
objeción (Es)	Widerspruch *m*	objection	objection *f*	obiezione *f*	—

	D	E	F	I	Es
objectif de croissance (F)	Wachstumsziel *n*	growth target	—	obiettivo di crescita *m*	objetivo de crecimiento *m*
objection (E)	Widerspruch *m*	—	objection *f*	obiezione *f*	objeción *f*
objection (F)	Widerspruch *m*	objection	—	obiezione *f*	objeción *f*
object of capital expenditure (E)	Investitionsobjekt *n*	—	objet d'investissement *m*	investimento *m*	objeto de inversión *m*
object of discernment (E)	Erkenntnisobjekt *n*	—	objet de discernement *m*	oggetto di cognizione *m*	objeto de conocimiento *m*
Objektkredit (D)	—	loan for special purposes	crédit destiné à un objet déterminé *m*	credito per specifico oggetto *m*	crédito destinado a un determinado objeto *m*
objet de discernement (F)	Erkenntnisobjekt *n*	object of discernment	—	oggetto di cognizione *m*	objeto de conocimiento *m*
objet d'investissement (F)	Investitionsobjekt *n*	object of capital expenditure	—	investimento *m*	objeto de inversión *m*
objetivo de crecimiento (Es)	Wachstumsziel *n*	growth target	objectif de croissance *m*	obiettivo di crescita *m*	—
objetivo del volumen monetario (Es)	Geldmengenziel *n*	money supply target	fourchette de croissance monétaire *f*	base monetaria programmata *f*	—
objeto de conocimiento (Es)	Erkenntnisobjekt *n*	object of discernment	objet de discernement *m*	oggetto di cognizione *m*	—
objeto de inversión (Es)	Investitionsobjekt *n*	object of capital expenditure	objet d'investissement *m*	investimento *m*	—
obligación (Es)	Obligation *f*	bond	obligation *f*	obbligazione *f*	—
obligación (Es)	Verbindlichkeit *f*	liability	obligation *f*	debito *m*	—
obligación (Es)	Schuldverschreibung *f*	debenture stock	obligation *f*	titolo obbligazionario *m*	—
obligación (Es)	Obligo *n*	liability	engagement *m*	garanzia *f*	—
obligación al portador (Es)	Inhaberschuld-verschreibung *f*	bearer bond	obligation au porteur *f*	obbligazione al portatore *f*	—
obligación bancaria (Es)	Bankschuld-verschreibung *f*	bank bond	obligation bancaire *f*	obbligazione bancaria *f*	—
obligación bancaria (Es)	Bankobligation *f*	bank bond	obligation de banque *f*	obbligazione bancaria *f*	—
obligación comunal (Es)	Kommunalobligation *f*	local bond	obligation communale *f*	obbligazione comunale *f*	—
obligación de aceptación (Es)	Akzeptverbindlichkeit *f*	acceptance liability	engagement par acceptation *m*	effetto passivo *m*	—
obligación de ahorro (Es)	Sparobligation *f*	savings bond	obligation d'épargne *f*	obbligazione di cassa di risparmio *f*	—
obligación de aviso (Es)	Benachrichtigungs-pflicht *f*	duty of notification	obligation de notification *f*	obbligo d'avviso *m*	—
obligación de comunicación (Es)	Mitteilungspflicht *f*	obligation to furnish information	obligation d'informer *f*	obbligo di rendere noto *m*	—
obligación de comunicar (Es)	Meldepflicht *f*	obligation to register	déclaration obligatoire *f*	obbligo di dichiarazione *m*	—
obligación de convertibilidad monetaria (Es)	Noteneinlösungs-pflicht *f*	obligation to redeem notes	obligation de remboursement de billets *f*	convertibilità delle banconote *f*	—
obligación de declarar (Es)	Offenlegungspflicht *f*	duty to disclose one's financial conditions	obligation de révéler les derniers bilans du postulant d'un prêt *f*	obbligo di rendere pubblico *m*	—
obligación de declarar (Es)	Anzeigepflicht *f*	legal obligation to disclose one's results	obligation de publier *f*	obbligo di denuncia *m*	—
obligación de información (Es)	Auskunftspflicht *f*	obligation to give information	obligation de fournir des renseignements *f*	obbligo d'informazione *m*	—
obligación de intervención (Es)	Interventionspflicht *f*	obligation to intervene	obligation d'intervention *f*	obbligo all'intervento *m*	—
obligación de pago suplementario (Es)	Nachschußpflicht *f*	obligation to make an additional contribution	obligation de faire un versement complémentaire *f*	obbligo di versamenti supplementari *m*	—
obligación de publicación (Es)	Publikationspflicht *f*	compulsory disclosure	obligation de publication à	obbligo di pubblicazione *m*	—
obligación de publicidad bancaria (Es)	Bankpublizität *f*	banks' duty to publish	publication obligatoire des bilans bancaires *f*	pubblicazione obbligatoria dei bilanci bancari *f*	—

	D	E	F	I	Es
obligación de revisión (Es)	Revisionspflicht f	auditing requirements	obligation de vérification f	obbligo di revisione m	—
obligación en letras de cambio (Es)	Wechselobligo n	customer's liability on bills	engagement par lettre de change m	cambiale passiva f	—
obligaciones industriales (Es)	Industrie-obligationen f/pl	industrial bonds	obligations de l'industrie f/pl	obbligazioni industriali m/pl	—
obligaciones por endoso (Es)	Indossament-verbindlichkeiten f/pl	endorsement liabilities	obligations par endossement f/pl	impegni di girata m/pl	—
obligaciones preferentes (Es)	Prioritätsobligationen f/pl	priority bonds	obligation privilégié f	obbligazioni privilegiate f/pl	—
obligación eventual (Es)	Eventual-verbindlichkeit f	contingent liability	obligation éventuelle f	obbligazione contingenziale f	—
obligación federal (Es)	Bundesobligation f	Federal bonds	obligation fédérale f	prestito pubblico m	—
obligación hipotecaria (Es)	Hypotheken-pfandbrief m	mortgage debenture	obligation foncière f	titolo di credito fondiario m	—
obligacionista (Es)	Obligationär m	bondholder	obligataire m	obbligazionista m	—
obligación preferente (Es)	Vorzugsobligation f	preference bond	obligation assortie de droits réservés f	obbligazione privilegiata f	—
obligación sinodal (Es)	Synodalobligation f	synodal bond	obligation synodale f	obbligazione sinodale f	—
obligación solidaria (Es)	Gesamtschuld f	total debt	dette solidaire f	debito solidale m	—
obligataire (F)	Obligationär m	bondholder	—	obbligazionista m	obligacionista m
obligatino de rachat (F)	Einlösungspflicht f	obligation to redeem	—	obbligo di pagamento m	deber de canje m
Obligation (D)	—	bond	obligation f	obbligazione f	obligación f
obligation (E)	Schuldverhältnis n	—	rapport d'obligation m	rapporto obbligatorio m	relación obligatoria f
obligation (F)	Schuldverschreibung f	debenture stock	—	titolo obbligazionario m	obligación f
obligation (F)	Obligation f	bond	—	obbligazione f	obligación f
obligation (F)	Verbindlichkeit f	liability	—	debito m	obligación f
obligation à coupon zéro (F)	Zerobond m	zero bond	—	zero coupon bond m	bono cero m
Obligationär (D)	—	bondholder	obligataire m	obbligazionista m	obligacionista m
obligation assortie de droits réservés (F)	Vorzugsobligation f	preference bond	—	obbligazione privilegiata f	obligación preferente f
obligation au porteur (F)	Inhaberschuld-verschreibung f	bearer bond	—	obbligazione al portatore f	obligación al portador f
obligation bancaire (F)	Bankschuld-verschreibung f	bank bond	—	obbligazione bancaria f	obligación bancaria f
obligation communale (F)	Kommunalobligation f	local bond	—	obbligazione comunale f	obligación comunal f
obligation convertible (F)	Wandelanleihen f/pl	convertible bonds	—	prestiti convertibili m/pl	empréstitos convertibles m/pl
obligation de banque (F)	Bankobligation f	bank bond	—	obbligazione bancaria f	obligación bancaria f
obligation de contracter (F)	Kontrahierungs-zwang m	obligation to contract	—	obbligo di contrarre m	contratación forzosa f
obligation de faire un versement complémentaire (F)	Nachschußpflicht f	obligation to make an additional contribution	—	obbligo di versamenti supplementari m	obligación de pago suplementario f
obligation de fournir des renseignements (F)	Auskunftspflicht f	obligation to give information	—	obbligo d'informazione m	obligación de información f
obligation de libérer une action (F)	Einzahlungspflicht f	obligation to pay subscription	—	obbligo di versamento m	deber de liberación de acciones m
obligation de liquidation (F)	Liquidationsschuld-verschreibung f	liquidation bond	—	titolo obbligazionario di liquidazione m	bono de liquidación f
obligation de notification (F)	Benachrichtigungs-pflicht f	duty of notification	—	obbligo d'avviso m	obligación de aviso f
obligation d'épargne (F)	Sparobligation f	savings bond	—	obbligazione di cassa di risparmio f	obligación de ahorro f
obligation de publication (F)	Publikationspflicht f	compulsory disclosure	—	obbligo di pubblicazione m	obligación de publicación f

	D	E	F	I	Es
obligation de publier (F)	Veröffentlichungspflicht *f*	statutory public disclosure	—	obbligo di pubblicazione *m*	publicación obligatoria *f*
obligation de publier (F)	Anzeigepflicht *f*	legal obligation to disclose one's results	—	obbligo di denuncia *m*	obligación de declarar *f*
obligation de remboursement de billets (F)	Noteneinlösungspflicht *f*	obligation to redeem notes	—	convertibilità delle banconote *f*	obligación de convertibilidad monetaria *f*
obligation de respecter le contrat (F)	Vertragsbindung *f*	contractual obligation	—	vincolo di contratto *m*	vínculo contractual *m*
obligation de révéler les derniers bilans du postulant d'un prêt (F)	Offenlegungspflicht *f*	duty to disclose one's financial conditions	—	obbligo di rendere pubblico *m*	obligación de declarar *f*
obligation de solliciter une permission (F)	Genehmigungspflicht *f*	duty to obtain a permit	—	obbligo d'autorizzazione *m*	régimen de autorización *m*
obligation de vérification (F)	Revisionspflicht *f*	auditing requirements	—	obbligo di revisione *m*	obligación de revisión *f*
obligation d'informer (F)	Mitteilungspflicht *f*	obligation to furnish information	—	obbligo di rendere noto *m*	obligación de comunicación *f*
obligation d'intervention (F)	Interventionspflicht *f*	obligation to intervene	—	obbligo all'intervento *m*	obligación de intervención *f*
obligation éventuelle (F)	Eventualverbindlichkeit *f*	contingent liability	—	obbligazione contingenziale *f*	obligación eventual *f*
obligation fédérale (F)	Bundesobligation *f*	Federal bonds	—	prestito pubblico *m*	obligación federal *f*
obligation foncière (F)	Hypothekenpfandbrief *m*	mortgage debenture	—	titolo di credito fondiario *m*	obligación hipotecaria *f*
obligation hypothécaire (F)	Pfandbrief *m*	mortgage bond	—	obbligazione fondiaria *f*	cédula hipotecaria *f*
obligation hypothécaire pour financer des projets sociaux (F)	Sozialpfandbrief *n*	mortgage bond serving a social purpose	—	obbligazione ipotecaria edilizia sociale *f*	cédula hipotecaria con fines sociales *f*
obligation indexée (F)	Gewinnobligation *f*	participating debenture	—	obbligazione a premio *f*	bono sobre beneficios *m*
obligation privilégiée (F)	Prioritätsobligationen *f/pl*	priority bonds	—	obbligazioni privilegiate *f/pl*	obligaciones preferentes *f/pl*
obligations à moyen terme (F)	Kassenobligationen *f/pl*	medium-term bonds	—	obbligazioni di cassa *f/pl*	bonos de caja *m/pl*
Obligationsausgabe (D)	—	bond issue	émission d'obligations *f*	emissione di obbligazioni *f*	emisión de obligaciones *f*
obligations de l'industrie (F)	Industrieobligationen *f/pl*	industrial bonds	—	obbligazioni industriali *m/pl*	obligaciones industriales *f/pl*
obligations du Trésor (F)	Schätze *m/pl*	treasury bonds	—	buoni del tesoro *m/pl*	bonos del tesoro *m/pl*
obligations du Trésor ne produisant pas d'intérêts (F)	U-Schätze *m/pl*	non-interest bearing Treasury bond	—	buoni del tesoro infruttiferi *m/pl*	letras del Tesoro sin interés *f/pl*
obligations hypothécaires de mobilisation (F)	Mobilisierungspfandbriefe *m/pl*	mobilization mortgage bond	—	obbligazioni fondiarie di smobilizzo *f/pl*	cédulas hipotecarias de mobilización *f/pl*
obligations par endossement (F)	Indossamentverbindlichkeiten *f/pl*	endorsement liabilities	—	impegni di girata *m/pl*	obligaciones por endoso *f/pl*
obligations remboursables avec prime (F)	Agiopapiere *n/pl*	securities redeemable at a premium	—	titoli a premio *m/pl*	valores de renta fija reembolsados con una prima *m/pl*
obligations vis-à-vis d'une autre banque (F)	Nostroverbindlichkeit *f*	nostro liability	—	impegno nostro *m*	débitos a nuestro cargo *m/pl*
obligation synodale (F)	Synodalobligation *f*	synodal bond	—	obbligazione sinodale *f*	obligación sinodal *f*
obligation to contract (E)	Kontrahierungszwang *m*	—	obligation de contracter *f*	obbligo di contrarre *m*	contratación forzosa *f*
obligation to furnish information (E)	Mitteilungspflicht *f*	—	obligation d'informer *f*	obbligo di rendere noto *m*	obligación de comunicación *f*
obligation to give information (E)	Auskunftspflicht *f*	—	obligation de fournir des renseignements *f*	obbligo d'informazione *m*	obligación de información *f*
obligation to intervene (E)	Interventionspflicht *f*	—	obligation d'intervention *f*	obbligo all'intervento *m*	obligación de intervención *f*

	D	E	F	I	Es
obligation to make an additional contribution (E)	Nachschußpflicht f	—	obligation de faire un versement complémentaire f	obbligo di versamenti supplementari m	obligación de pago suplementario f
obligation to pay subscription (E)	Einzahlungspflicht f	—	obligation de libérer une action f	obbligo di versamento m	deber de liberación de acciones m
obligation to redeem (E)	Einlösungspflicht f	—	obligation de rachat f	obbligo di pagamento m	deber de canje m
obligation to redeem notes (E)	Noteneinlösungspflicht f	—	obligation de remboursement de billets f	convertibilità delle banconote f	obligación de convertibilidad monetaria f
obligation to register (E)	Meldepflicht f	—	déclaration obligatoire f	obbligo di dichiarazione m	obligación de comunicar f
obliger (F)	Vinkulieren	restriction of transferability	—	vincolare m	vinculación f
Obligo (D)	—	liability	engagement m	garanzia f	obligación f
Obligobuch (D)	—	bills discounted ledger	livre des traites escomptées m	libro rischi m	libro de aceptaciones m
obtención de capital (Es)	Kapitalbeschaffung f	procurement of capital	constitution de capital f	raccolta di capitali f	—
obtención de la mayoría (Es)	Majorisierung f	holding of the majority	obtention de la majorité f	messa in minoranza f	—
obtention de crédits par duperie (F)	Kreditschwindel m	credit fraud	—	frode creditizia f	fraude crediticio m
obtention de la majorité (F)	Majorisierung f	holding of the majority	—	messa in minoranza f	obtención de la mayoría f
occorrendo (I)	Notanzeige f	notice of dishonour	avis de non-payement m	—	notificación de no aceptación f
odd lot (E)	gebrochener Schluß m	—	lot ne pas nécocié officiellement f	lotto senza quotazione ufficiale m	lote no negociado oficialmente m
Oderdepot (D)	—	joint deposit	dépôt joint m	deposito comune m	depósito indistinto m
Oderkonten (D)	—	joint account	compte joint m	conti a firme disgiunte m/pl	cuentas indistintas f/pl
oferta (Es)	Gebot n	bid	offre f	offerta f	—
oferta de capital (Es)	Kapitalangebot n	supply of capital	offre de capital f	offerta di capitale f	—
oferta de compensación (Es)	Abfindungsangebot n	compensation offer	offre d'indemnité f	offerta di riscatto f	—
oferta de suscripción (Es)	Bezugsangebot m	right issue	offre de souscription f	offerta in opzione f	—
oferta monetaria (Es)	Geldangebot n	supply of money	offre d'argent f	offerta monetaria f	—
Offenbarungseid (D)	—	oath of disclosure	serment déclaratoire m	giuramento dichiarativo m	juramento declarativo m
offene Handelsgesellschaft (D)	—	general partnership	société en nom collectif f	società in nome collettivo f	compañía colectiva f
offene Position (D)	—	open position	poste ouvert m	posizione scoperta f	partida abierta f
Offene-Posten-Buchhaltung (D)	—	open-item accounting	comptabilité de postes ouverts f	contabilità a partite sospese f	contabilidad de partidas abiertas f
offene Rechnung (D)	—	unsettled account	facture pas encore payée f	conto aperto m	factura pendiente f
offener Fonds (D)	—	open-end fund	fonds ouvert m	fondo d'investimento aperto m	fondo abierto m
offener Immobilienfonds (D)	—	open-end real estate fund	fonds de placement immobilier ouvert m	fondo immobiliare aperto m	fondo inmobiliario abierto m
offene Rücklagen (D)	—	disclosed reserves	réserves déclarées f/pl	riserve dichiarate f/pl	reservas declaradas f/pl
offenes Depot (D)	—	safe custody account	dépôt collectif m	deposito aperto m	depósito abierto m
offenes Konto (D)	—	open account	compte ouvert m	conto aperto m	cuenta abierta f
Offenlegungspflicht (D)	—	duty to disclose one's financial conditions	obligation de réveler les derniers bilans du postulant d'un prêt f	obbligo di rendere pubblico m	obligación de declarar f
Offenmarktpolitik (D)	—	open market policy	politique d'open market f	politica di mercato aperto f	política de mercado abierto f
öffentliche Bank (D)	—	public bank	banque publique f	banca di diritto pubblico f	banco público m

	D	E	F	I	Es
öffentliche Beglaubigung (D)	—	public certification	légalisation f	autenticazione f	legalización pública f
öffentliche Beurkundung (D)	—	public authentication	authentification f	autenticazione pubblica f	formalización en escritura pública f
öffentliche Kredite (D)	—	credits extended to public authorities	crédits publics m/pl	crediti pubblici m/pl	créditos públicos m/pl
öffentlicher Haushalt (D)	—	public budget	budget public m	bilancio pubblico m	presupuesto público m
öffentliche Schuld (D)	—	public debt	dette publique f	debito pubblico m	deuda pública f
offerta (I)	Gebot n	bid	offre f	—	oferta f
offerta di capitale (I)	Kapitalangebot n	supply of capital	offre de capital f	—	oferta de capital f
offerta di riscatto (I)	Abfindungsangebot n	compensation offer	offre d'indemnité f	—	oferta de compensación f
offerta di titoli (I)	herauskommendes Material n	securities coming on to the market	titres lancés sur le marché m/pl	—	material saliente m
offerta eccedente la domanda (I)	bezahlt Brief	more sellers than buyers	comptant vendeur	—	la oferta fue mayor que la demanda f
offerta in opzione (I)	Bezugsangebot m	right issue	offre de souscription f	—	oferta de suscripción f
offerta monetaria (I)	Geldangebot n	supply of money	offre d'argent f	—	oferta monetaria f
offical stock exchange list (E)	offizielles Kursblatt n	—	cote de la bourse officielle f	listino ufficiale m	boletín oficial m
office de surveillance (F)	Aufsichtsamt n	control board	—	ispettorato m	oficina de inspección f
office de surveillance des établissements de crédit (F)	Kreditaufsicht f	state supervision of credit institutions	—	autorità di vigilanza sul credito f	supervisión crediticia f
official fees (E)	Verwaltungsgebühr f	—	taxe administrative f	tassa amministrativa f	derechos administrativos m/pl
officially quoted security (E)	Schrankenwert m	—	valeur négociée au marché officiel f	valori ammessi alla quotazione ufficiale m/pl	título oficialmente cotizado m
official market (E)	amtlicher Markt m	—	marché officiel m	mercato ufficiale m	mercado oficial m
official market broker (E)	Parkettmakler m	—	agent de change m	agente di cambio m	corredor de parqué m
official trading (E)	amtlicher Handel m	—	négociations en bourse f/pl	contrattazione ufficiale f	cotización oficial f
official trading hours (E)	Börsenzeit f	—	heures d'ouverture de la bourse f/pl	orario di borsa m	sesión de bolsa f
offizielles Kursblatt (D)	—	offical stock exchange list	cote de la bourse officielle f	listino ufficiale m	boletín oficial m
offre (F)	Gebot n	bid	—	offerta f	oferta f
offre d'argent (F)	Geldangebot n	supply of money	—	offerta monetaria f	oferta monetaria f
offre de capital (F)	Kapitalangebot n	supply of capital	—	offerta di capitale f	oferta de capital f
offre d'emprunts par quantités pour la régulation monétaire (F)	Mengentender m	quantity tender	—	asta non competitiva f	subasta de préstamos de regulación monetaria por cantidades f
offre d'emprunts pour la régulation monétaire (F)	Tenderverfahren n	tender procedure	—	asta marginale f	sistema de ofertas m
offre de souscription (F)	Bezugsangebot m	right issue	—	offerta in opzione f	oferta de suscripción f
offre d'indemnité (F)	Abfindungsangebot n	compensation offer	—	offerta di riscatto f	oferta de compensación f
offset tax (E)	Kompensationssteuer f	—	impôt de compensation m	imposta sulle compensazioni f	impuesto de compensación m
offsetting arbitrage (E)	Ausgleichs-Arbitrage f	—	arbitrage par compensation m	arbitraggio di rimborso m	arbitraje de divisas m
offset transaction (E)	Kompensationsgeschäft n	—	affaire de compensation f	operazione di compensazione f	operación de compensación f
offset transaction with resale to a third party (E)	Fremdkompensation f	—	intervention d'un tiers dans une affaire de compensation f	compensazione per conto altrui f	compensación ajena f
offshore centres (E)	Offshore-Zentren n/pl	—	centres off shore m/pl	centri off-shore m/pl	centros offshore m/pl

	·D	E	F	I	Es
offshore dealings (E)	Offshore-Geschäft *n*	—	opération off shore *f*	operazione off-shore *f*	negocio offshore *m*
Offshore-Geschäft (D)	—	offshore dealings	opération off shore *f*	operazione off-shore *f*	negocio offshore *m*
Offshore-Käufe (D)	—	offshore purchases	achats off shore *m/pl*	acquisti off-shore *m/pl*	compras offshore *f/pl*
offshore purchases (E)	Offshore-Käufe *m/pl*	—	achats off shore *m/pl*	acquisti off-shore *m/pl*	compras offshore *f/pl*
Offshore-Zentren (D)	—	offshore centres	centres off shore *m/pl*	centri off-shore *m/pl*	centros offshore *m/pl*
oficina de cheques postales (Es)	Postscheckamt *n*	postal giro centre	bureau de chèques postaux *m*	ufficio conto correnti postali *m*	—
oficina de compensación (Es)	Abrechnungsstelle *f*	clearing house	bureau de liquidation *m*	stanza di compensazione *f*	—
oficina de inspección (Es)	Aufsichtsamt *n*	control board	office de surveillance *m*	ispettorato *m*	—
oficina de matrícula (Es)	Zulassungsstelle *f*	admission board	commission pour l'admission des valeurs à la cote *f*	ufficio d'ammissione *m*	—
oficina federal de cártel (Es)	Bundeskartellamt *n*	Federal Cartel Authority	administration fédérale pour la réglementation des cartels *f*	ufficio federale dei cartelli *m*	—
oggetto di baratto (I)	Naturalgeld *n*	commodity money	argent en nature *m*	—	dinero en especie *m*
oggetto di cognizione (I)	Erkenntnisobjekt *n*	object of discernment	objet de discernement *m*	—	objeto de conocimiento *m*
ohne Kupon (D)	—	ex coupon	sans coupon	ex cedola	sin cupón
oil futures dealings (E)	Ölterminhandel *m*	—	opérations pétrolières à terme *f/pl*	commercio petrolifero a termine *m*	negociación de petróleo a término *f*
oil futures exchange (E)	Ölterminbörse *f*	—	bourse à terme des valeurs pétrolières *f*	mercato petrolifero a termine *m*	bolsa de petróleo a término *f*
Ölterminbörse (D)	—	oil futures exchange	bourse à terme des valeurs pétrolières *f*	mercato petrolifero a termine *m*	bolsa de petróleo a término *f*
Ölterminhandel (D)	—	oil futures dealings	opérations pétrolières à terme *f/pl*	commercio petrolifero a termine *m*	negociación de petróleo a término *f*
once fine (F)	Feinunze *f*	troy ounce		oncia *f*	onza fina *f*
oncia (I)	Feinunze *f*	troy ounce	once fine *f*	—	onza fina *f*
one month money (E)	Monatsgeld *n*	—	argent à un mois *m*	deposito vincolato ad un mese *m*	dinero a 30 días *m*
one's own capital (E)	Eigenkapital *n*	—	capital propre *m*	capitale proprio *m*	capital propio *m*
onorare (I)	honorieren	to remunerate	honorer	—	honorar
onshore business (E)	Onshore-Geschäft *n*	—	opération onshore *f*	operazione onshore *f*	negocio onshore *m*
Onshore-Geschäft (D)	—	onshore business	opération onshore *f*	operazione onshore *f*	negocio onshore *m*
onza fina (Es)	Feinunze *f*	troy ounce	once fine *f*	oncia *f*	—
opción (Es)	Option *f*	option	option *f*	opzione *f*	—
opción bono (Es)	Bond-Option *f*	bond option	option de bond *f*	opzione bond *f*	—
opción de cambiar títulos convertibles en acciones (Es)	Aktienoption *f*	share stock option	option d'échanger des titres convertibles en actions *f*	diritto di prelazione *m*	—
opción de compra (Es)	Kaufoption *f*	call option	option d'achat *f*	opzione d'acquisto *f*	—
opción de divisas (Es)	Devisenoption *f*	exchange option	option de change *f*	opzione di cambio *f*	—
opción de oro (Es)	Goldoption *f*	gold option	option d'or *f*	opzione oro *f*	—
opción de prorrogación de arrendamiento (Es)	Mietverlängerungs-option *f*	lease renewal option	option de prorogation du bail *f*	opzione proroga contratto di locazione *f*	—
opción de venta (Es)	Verkaufsoption *f*	option to sell	option de vente *f*	opzione di vendita *f*	—
open account (E)	offenes Konto *n*	—	compte ouvert *m*	conto aperto *m*	cuenta abierta *f*
open a credit (E)	akkreditieren	—	accréditer	accreditare	acreditar
open credit (E)	Blanko-Kredit *m*	—	crédit en compte courant *m*	fido in bianco *m*	crédito en blanco *m*
open-end fund (E)	offener Fonds *m*	—	fonds ouvert *m*	fondo d'investimento aperto *m*	fondo abierto *m*

	D	E	F	I	Es
open-end real estate fund (E)	offener Immobilienfonds *m*	—	fonds de placement immobilier ouvert *m*	fondo immobiliare aperto *m*	fondo inmobiliario abierto *m*
opening balance sheet (E)	Eröffnungsbilanz *f*	—	bilan d'ouverture *m*	bilancio d'apertura *m*	balance inicial *m*
opening of an account (E)	Kontoeröffnung *f*	—	ouverture d'une compte *f*	apertura di un conto *f*	apertura de una cuenta *f*
opening of new markets (E)	Markterschließung *f*	—	ouverture du marché *f*	penetrazione del mercato *f*	apertura del mercado *f*
opening price (E)	Eröffnungskurs *m*	—	cours d'ouverture *m*	corso d'apertura *m*	cotización de apertura *f*
open-item accounting (E)	Offene-Posten-Buchhaltung *f*	—	comptabilité de postes ouverts *f*	contabilità a partite sospese *f*	contabilidad de partidas abiertas *f*
open market policy (E)	Offenmarktpolitik *f*	—	politique d'open market *f*	politica di mercato aperto *f*	política de mercado abierto *f*
open position (E)	offene Position *f*	—	poste ouvert *m*	posizione scoperta *f*	partida abierta *f*
operación activa (Es)	Aktivgeschäft *n*	credit transaction	opération de prêt *f*	operazione attiva *f*	—
operación al contado (Es)	Effektivgeschäft *n*	actual transaction	marché en disponible *m*	operazione in effettivo *f*	—
operación al contado (Es)	Bargeschäft *n*	cash transactions	marché au comptant *m*	affare in contanti *m*	—
operación al contado (Es)	Tafelgeschäft *n*	over-the-counter business	opération de guichet *f*	operazione a contanti *f*	—
operación al contado (Es)	Schaltergeschäft *n*	business over the counter	opération de guichet *f*	operazione a contanti *f*	—
operación a plazo (Es)	Termingeschäft *n*	time bargain	opération à terme *f*	contratto a termine *m*	—
operación a plazo (Es)	Warentermingeschäft *n*	commodity futures trading	opération à livrer *f*	operazione a termine su merci *f*	—
operación a plazos (Es)	Abzahlungsgeschäft *n*	instalment sale transaction	vente a tempérament *f*	operazione con pagamento rateale *f*	—
operación a prima (Es)	Prämiengeschäft *n*	option dealing	marché à prime *m*	operazione a premio *f*	—
operación a término con vencimiento a fin de mes (Es)	Ultimogeschäft *n*	last-day business	opération à liquider en fin de mois *f*	contratto a fine ultimo *m*	—
operación a término outright (Es)	Outright-Termingeschäft *n*	outright futures transactions	opération à terme outright *f*	contratto a termine outright *m*	—
operación con valores (Es)	Effektengeschäft *n*	securities business	commerce des valeurs mobilières *m*	operazione in titoli *f*	—
operación crediticia (Es)	Kreditgeschäft *n*	credit business	opérations d'avances sur crédit *f/pl*	operazione di credito *f*	—
operación crediticia (Es)	Anleihegeschäft *n*	loan business	operation de placement de titres d'emprunt *f*	operazione di prestito *f*	—
operación de arbitraje (Es)	Arbitragegeschäft *n*	arbitrage dealings	opération d'arbitrage *f*	operazione di arbitraggio *f*	—
operación de cobertura (Es)	Deckungsgeschäft *n*	covering operation	opération de couverture *f*	operazione di copertura *f*	—
operación de cobro (Es)	Inkassogeschäft *n*	collection business	opération de recouvrement *f*	operazione d'incasso *f*	—
operación de comisión (Es)	Kommissionsgeschäft *n*	commission business	affaire en commission *f*	contratto di commissione *m*	—
operación de compensación (Es)	Kompensationsgeschäft *n*	offset transaction	affaire de compensation *f*	operazione di compensazione *f*	—
operación de depósito (Es)	Depositengeschäft *n*	deposit banking	opération de garde de fonds *f*	operazione di deposito *f*	—
operación de divisas (Es)	Valutageschäft *n*	currency transactions	opération de change *f*	operazione di cambio *f*	—
operación de divisas (Es)	Devisengeschäft *n*	foreign exchange business	opération en devises *f*	operazione di cambio *f*	—
operación de divisas al contado (Es)	Devisenkassageschäft *n*	foreign exchange spot dealings	opérations de change au comptant *f/pl*	cambi a pronti *m/pl*	—
operación de doble opción (Es)	Stellgeschäft *n*	put and call	opération de stellage *f*	contratto stellage *m*	—
operación de doble prima (Es)	Stellagegeschäft *n*	double option operation	marché à double option *m*	contratto stellage *m*	—

operación de emisión

	D	E	F	I	Es
operación de emisión (Es)	Emissionsgeschäft *n*	underwriting business	opération de placement de parts *f*	operazione d'emissione *f*	—
operación de garantía (Es)	Garantiegeschäft *n*	guarantee business	opération de garantie *f*	assunzione di garanzia per terzi *f*	—
operación de giro (Es)	Girogeschäft *n*	bank's transaction dealing with cashless transactions	opération de virement *f*	trasferimento di giro *m*	—
operación de moneda extranjera (Es)	Sortengeschäft *n*	dealings in foreign notes and coins	commerce de change *m*	operazione di cambio *f*	—
operación de opción (Es)	Wandelgeschäft *n*	callable forward transaction	marché à option *m*	contratto a termine con opzione di adempimento anticipato *m*	—
operación de opción (Es)	Optionsgeschäft *n*	option dealing	marché à option *m*	contratto ad opzione *m*	—
operación de prolongación (Es)	Prolongationsgeschäft *n*	prolongation business	opération de report *f*	contratto di proroga *m*	—
operación de reporte (Es)	Pensionsgeschäft *n*	security transactions under repurchase agreement	opération de mise en pension d'effets *f*	sconto in pensione *m*	—
operación de reporte (Es)	Reportgeschäft *n*	contango transaction	opération de report *f*	operazione di riporto *f*	—
operación de reporte de letras (Es)	Wechselpensionsgeschäft *n*	pledging of bills of exchange against grant of a loan	opération de mise en pension d'effets *f*	pensione di effetti *f*	—
operación de reporte de valores (Es)	Wertpapierpensionsgeschäft *n*	credit transaction under repurchase agreement of securities	prise en pension de valeurs mobilières *f*	operazione pronti contro termine *f*	—
operación de reporte en divisas (Es)	Devisenpensionsgeschäft *n*	purchase of foreign exchange for later sale	opération de mise en pension de devises *f*	sconto di valuta in pensione *m*	—
operaciones al contado (Es)	Kassageschäft *n*	cash transactions	opération au comptant *f*	operazione a pronti *f*	—
operaciones al contado y de entrega inmediata (Es)	Spotgeschäft *n*	spot transactions	opération en disponible *m*	contratto spot *m*	—
operaciones antes de la apertura (Es)	Vorbörse *f*	before hours dealing	marché avant le marché officiel *m*	avant bourse *m*	—
operaciones a plazo fijo (Es)	Festgeschäft *n*	firm deal	opération à terme fixe *f*	contrattazione a fermo *f*	—
operaciones bancarias electrónicas (Es)	Electronic Banking *n*	electronic banking	electronic banking *m*	electronic banking *m*	—
operaciones bursátiles (Es)	Börsengeschäfte *n/pl*	stock exchange operations	opérations de bourse *f*	operazioni di borsa *f/pl*	—
operaciones bursátiles a término (Es)	Börsentermingeschäfte *n/pl*	trading in futures on a stock exchange	opérations boursières à terme *f/pl*	contratti di borsa a termine *m/pl*	—
operaciones call (Es)	Call-Geschäft *n*	call transaction	cotation par opposition *f*	operazione call *f*	—
operaciones de cesión temporal de valores (Es)	Effektenpensionsgeschäft *n*	security transactions under repurchase agreement	opération de mise en pension d'effets *f*	sconto di titoli in pensione *m*	—
operaciones de cheques (Es)	Scheckverkehr *m*	cheque transactions	opérations par chèque *f/pl*	pagamenti mediante assegno *m/pl*	—
operaciones de cobranza (Es)	Einziehungsgeschäft *n*	collection business	opération d'encaissement *f*	operazione d'incasso *f*	—
operaciones de compensación (Es)	Abrechnungsverkehr *m*	clearing system	opérations de compensation *f/pl*	clearing *m*	—
operaciones de compra (Es)	Anschaffungsgeschäft *n*	buying or selling for customers	opérations d'achat *f/pl*	operazione d'acquisto *f*	—
operaciones de corridor bursátil (Es)	Händlergeschäft *n*	dealer transaction	opération pour propre compte *f*	operazioni tra agenti di borsa *f/pl*	—
operaciones de depósito (Es)	Einlagengeschäft *n*	deposit business	opération de garde de fonds *f/pl*	operazione di deposito *f*	—
operaciones de divisas (Es)	Devisenhandel *m*	foreign exchange dealings	marché des changes *m*	cambio valuta *m*	—

	D	E	F	I	Es
operaciones de divisas a base de comisión (Es)	Devisenkommissionsgeschäft *n*	foreign exchange transactions for customers	opérations de change en commission *f/pl*	operazione di cambio su commissione *f*	—
operaciones de entrega inmediata (Es)	Locogeschäft *n*	spot business	opération en disponible *f*	operazione a contanti *f*	—
operaciones de entrega inmediata (Es)	Lokogeschäft *n*	spot transaction	opération en disponible *f*	operazione a contanti *f*	—
operaciones de financiación de participación (Es)	Beteiligungshandel *m*	equity financing transactions	opérations de financement par participation *f/pl*	commercio in partecipazione *m*	—
operaciones de mercancías a plazo (Es)	Commodity futures *f/pl*	commodity future	opérations à livrer *f/pl*	commodity futures *m/pl*	—
operaciones de metales preciosos (Es)	Edelmetallgeschäft *n*	bullion trade	opérations de métaux précieux *f/pl*	operazione in metalli pregiati *f*	—
operaciones después del cierre de la bolsa (Es)	Nachbörse *f*	after-hours dealing	marché après-bourse *m*	dopolistino *m*	—
operaciones de valores a base de comisión (Es)	Effektenkommissionsgeschäft *n*	securities transactions on commission	opération sur titres *f*	compravendita titoli su commissione *f*	—
operaciones de valores a plazo (Es)	Wertpapier-Terminhandel *m*	trading in security futures	marché des valeurs à terme *m*	operazioni a termine in titoli *f/pl*	—
operaciones de valores por cuenta propia (Es)	Effekteneigengeschäft *n*	security trading for own account	opérations sur titres à propre compte *f/pl*	operazione in proprio in titoli *f*	—
operación pasiva (Es)	Passivgeschäft *n*	passive deposit transactions	opération passive *f*	operazione di deposito *f*	—
operación por cuenta propia (Es)	Eigengeschäft *n*	transactions on own account	opération en nom personnel et à propre compte *f*	affare in proprio *m*	—
operación privada (Es)	Privatgeschäft *n*	private transaction	affaire privée *f*	transazione tra privati *f*	—
operación singular (Es)	Sologeschäft *n*	single operation	opération particulière *f*	operazione singola *f*	—
operación swap (Es)	Swapgeschäft *n*	swap transaction	opération swap *f*	operazione swap *f*	—
operación switch (Es)	Switch-Geschäft *n*	switch	opération switch *f*	operazione switch *f*	—
operador de negociación de créditos (Es)	Kreditvermittler *m*	money broker	agent financier *m*	intermediario finanziario *m*	—
operating assets (E)	Betriebsvermögen *n*	—	capital d'exploitation *m*	capitale d'esercizio *m*	patrimonio empresarial *m*
opération (F)	Geschäft *n*	exchange operation	—	contratto *m*	negocio *m*
operational accountancy (E)	betriebliches Rechnungswesen *n*	—	comptabilité industrielle *f*	ragioneria aziendale *f*	contabilidad empresarial *f*
operational profitability (E)	Betriebsrentabilität *f*	—	rentabilité d'exploitation *f*	redditività aziendale *f*	rentabilidad de la actividad de la empresa *f*
opération à liquider en fin de mois (F)	Ultimogeschäft *n*	last-day business	—	contratto a fine ultimo *m*	operación a término con vencimiento a fin de mes *f*
opération à livrer (F)	Warentermingeschäft *n*	commodity futures trading	—	operazione a termine su merci *f*	operación a plazo *f*
opération appuyée par plusieurs banques (F)	Konsortialgeschäft *n*	syndicate transaction	—	operazione consorziale *f*	negocio de consorcio *m*
opération à terme (F)	Termingeschäft *n*	time bargain	—	contratto a termine *m*	operación a plazo *f*
opération à terme fixe (F)	Festgeschäft *n*	firm deal	—	contrattazione a fermo *f*	operaciones a plazo fijo *f/pl*
opération à terme fixe (F)	Fixgeschäft *n*	transaction for delivery by a fixed date	—	contrattazione a fermo *f*	negocio fijo *m*
opération à terme outright (F)	Outright-Termingeschäft *n*	outright futures transactions	—	contratto a termine outright *m*	operación a término outright *f*
opération à terme sur les changes (F)	Devisentermingeschäft *n*	forward exchange dealings	—	operazione di cambio a termine *f*	transacción a término en divisas *f*
opération à terme sur les changes (F)	Currency future *m*	currency future	—	currency future *m*	contratación a término sobre divisas *f*

	D	E	F	I	Es
opération au comptant (F)	Kassageschäft n	cash transactions	—	operazione a pronti f	operaciones al contado f/pl
opération avec l'étranger (F)	Auslandsgeschäft n	business in foreign countries	—	affare all'estero m	negocio de exportación m
opération d'arbitrage (F)	Arbitragegeschäft n	arbitrage dealings		operazione di arbitraggio f	operación de arbitraje f
opération de change (F)	Geldwechselgeschäft n	currency exchange business		operazione di cambio f	cambio manual m
opération de change (F)	Valutageschäft n	currency transactions	—	operazione di cambio f	operación de divisas f
opération de couverture (F)	Deckungsgeschäft n	covering operation		operazione di copertura f	operación de cobertura f
opération de garantie (F)	Garantiegeschäft n	guarantee business	—	assunzione di garanzia per terzi f	operación de garantía f
opération de garde de fonds (F)	Depositengeschäft n	deposit banking		operazione di deposito f	operación de depósito f
opération de garde de fonds (F)	Einlagengeschäft n	deposit business	—	operazione di deposito f	operaciones de depósito f/pl
opération de guichet (F)	Schaltergeschäft n	business over the counter		operazione a contanti f	operación al contado f
opération de guichet (F)	Tafelgeschäft n	over-the-counter business		operazione a contanti f	operación al contado f
opération de médiation (F)	Aufgabegeschäft n	name transaction		contratto intermediato m	contrato intermediado m
opération de mise en pension d'effets (F)	Wechselpensionsgeschäft n	pledging of bills of exchange against grant of a loan		pensione di effetti f	operación de reporte de letras f
opération de mise en pension d'effets (F)	Effektenpensionsgeschäft n	security transactions under repurchase agreement	—	sconto di titoli in pensione m	operaciones de cesión temporal de valores f/pl
opération de mise en pension d'effets (F)	Pensionsgeschäft n	security transactions under repurchase agreement		sconto in pensione m	operación de reporte f
opération de mise en pension de devises (F)	Devisenpensionsgeschäft n	purchase of foreign exchange for later sale	—	sconto di valuta in pensione m	operación de reporte en divisas f
opération d'encaissement (F)	Einziehungsgeschäft n	collection business	—	operazione d'incasso f	operaciones de cobranza f/pl
opération de placement de parts (F)	Emissionsgeschäft n	underwriting business	—	operazione d'emissione f	operación de emisión f
opération de placement de titres d'emprunt (F)	Anleihegeschäft n	loan business	—	operazione di prestito f	operación crediticia f
opération de prêt (F)	Aktivgeschäft n	credit transaction	—	operazione attiva f	operación activa f
opération de recouvrement (F)	Inkassogeschäft n	collection business	—	operazione d'incasso f	operación de cobro f
opération de report (F)	Reportgeschäft n	contango transaction	—	operazione di riporto f	operación de reporte f
opération de report (F)	Prolongationsgeschäft n	prolongation business	—	contratto di proroga m	operación de prolongación f
opération d'escompte (F)	Diskontgeschäft n	discount business	—	operazione di sconto f	negocio de descuento m
opération de stellage (F)	Stellgeschäft n	put and call	—	contratto stellage m	operación de doble opción f
opération de virement (F)	Girogeschäft n	bank's transaction dealing with cashless transactions	—	trasferimento di giro m	operación de giro f
opération en devises (F)	Devisengeschäft n	foreign exchange business	—	operazione di cambio f	operación de divisas f
opération en disponible (F)	Lokogeschäft n	spot transaction	—	operazione a contanti f	operaciones de entrega inmediata f/pl
opération en disponible (F)	Spotgeschäft n	spot transactions	—	contratto spot m	operaciones al contado y de entrega inmediata f/pl
opération en disponible (F)	Locogeschäft n	spot business	—	operazione a contanti f	operaciones de entrega inmediata f/pl

	D	E	F	I	Es
opération en nom personnel et à propre compte (F)	Eigengeschäft n	transactions on own account	—	affare in proprio m	operación por cuenta propia f
opération hedge (F)	Hedgegeschäft n	hedge operation	—	operazione hedge f	negocio hedge m
opération nette de courtage et de commission (F)	Nettogeschäft n	net-price transaction	—	operazione borsistica netta f	negocio neto m
opération off shore (F)	Offshore-Geschäft n	offshore dealings	—	operazione off-shore f	negocio offshore m
opération onshore (F)	Onshore-Geschäft n	onshore business	—	operazione onshore f	negocio onshore m
opération particulière (F)	Sologeschäft n	single operation	—	operazione singola f	operación singular f
opération passive (F)	Passivgeschäft n	passive deposit transactions	—	operazione di deposito f	operación pasiva f
opération pour compte de client (F)	Kundengeschäft n	transactions for third account	—	operazioni per la clientela f/pl	transacciones por cuenta ajena f/pl
opération pour propre compte (F)	Händlergeschäft n	dealer transaction	—	operazioni tra agenti di borsa f/pl	contrato de ejecución instantánea f/pl
opérations à livrer (F)	Commodity futures f/pl	commodity future	—	commodity futures m/pl	operaciones de mercancías a plazo f/pl
opérations boursières à terme (F)	Börsentermin-geschäfte n/pl	trading in futures on a stock exchange	—	contratti di borsa a termine m/pl	operaciones bursátiles a término f/pl
opérations d'achat (F)	Anschaffungs-geschäft n	buying or selling for customers	—	operazione d'acquisto f	operaciones de compra f/pl
opérations d'avances sur crédit (F)	Kreditgeschäft n	credit business	—	operazione di credito f	operación crediticia f
opérations de bourse (F)	Börsengeschäfte n/pl	stock exchange operations	—	operazioni di borsa f/pl	operaciones bursátiles f/pl
opérations de change au comptant (F)	Devisenkassa-geschäft n	foreign exchange spot dealings	—	cambi a pronti m/pl	operación de divisas al contado f
opérations de change en commission (F)	Devisenkommissions-geschäft n	foreign exchange transactions for customers	—	operazione di cambio su commissione f	operaciones de divisas a base de comisión f/pl
opérations de compensation (F)	Abrechnungsverkehr m	clearing system	—	clearing m	operaciones de compensación f/pl
opérations de financement par participation (F)	Beteiligungshandel m	equity financing transactions	—	commercio in partecipazioni m	operaciones de financiación de participación f/pl
opérations de guichet (F)	Over-the-counter-market m	over-the-counter market	—	over-the-counter-market m	mercado de operaciones de mostrador m
opérations de métaux précieux (F)	Edelmetallgeschäft n	bullion trade	—	operazione in metalli pregiati f	operaciones de metales preciosos f/pl
opérations de virement (F)	Giroverkehr m	transfer of money by means of a clearing system	—	bancogiro m	giro de valores m
opérations de vire-ments collectives (F)	Girosammelverkehr m	collective securities deposit operations	—	trasferimenti collettivi di giro m/pl	giro central de valores m
opérations d'insider (F)	Insiderhandel m	insider trading	—	insider trading m	transacciones realizadas utilizando información privilegiada f/pl
opérations par chèque (F)	Scheckverkehr m	cheque transactions	—	pagamenti mediante assegno m/pl	operaciones de cheques f/pl
opérations pétrolières à terme (F)	Ölterminhandel m	oil futures dealings	—	commercio petrolifero a termine m	negociación de petróleo a término f
opération sur titres (F)	Effektenkommis-sionsgeschäft n	securities transactions on commission	—	compravendita titoli su commissione f	operaciones de valores a base de comisión f/pl
opérations sur titres à propre compte (F)	Effekteneigen-geschäft n	security trading for own account	—	operazione in proprio in titoli f	operaciones de valores por cuenta propia f/pl
opération swap (F)	Swapgeschäft n	swap transaction	—	operazione swap f	operación swap f
opération switch (F)	Switch-Geschäft n	switch	—	operazione switch f	operación switch f
operatore professionale (I)	Berufshändler m	professional trader	agent professionnel m	—	agente profesional m

	D	E	F	I	Es
operatori di borsa (I)	Kulisse f	unofficial stock market	coulisse f	—	bolsa extraoficial f
operazione a contanti (I)	Schaltergeschäft n	business over the counter	opération de guichet f	—	operación al contado f
operazione a contanti (I)	Lokogeschäft n	spot transaction	opération en disponible f	—	operaciones de entrega inmediata f/pl
operazione a contanti (I)	Tafelgeschäft n	over-the-counter business	opération de guichet f	—	operación al contado f
operazione a contanti (I)	Locogeschäft n	spot business	opération en disponible f	—	operaciones de entrega inmediata f/pl
operazione a premio (I)	Prämiengeschäft n	option dealing	marché à prime m	—	operación a prima f
operazione a pronti (I)	Kassageschäft n	cash transactions	opération au comptant f	—	operaciones al contado f/pl
operazione a termine su merci (I)	Warentermin-geschäft n	commodity futures trading	opération à livrer f	—	operación a plazo f
operazione attiva (I)	Aktivgeschäft n	credit transaction	opération de prêt f	—	operación activa f
operazione borsistica netta (I)	Nettogeschäft n	net-price transaction	opération nette de courtage et de commission f	—	negocio neto m
operazione call (I)	Call-Geschäft n	call transaction	cotation par opposition f	—	operaciones call f/pl
operazione con pagamento rateale (I)	Abzahlungsgeschäft n	instalment sale transaction	vente a tempérament f	—	operación a plazos f
operazione consorziale (I)	Konsortialgeschäft n	syndicate transaction	opération appuyée par plusieurs banques f	—	negocio de consorcio m
operazione d'acquisto (I)	Anschaffungs-geschäft n	buying or selling for customers	opérations d'achat f/pl	—	operaciones de compra f/pl
operazione d'emissione (I)	Emissionsgeschäft n	underwriting business	opération de place-ment de parts f	—	operación de emisión f
operazione di arbitraggio (I)	Arbitragegeschäft n	arbitrage dealings	opération d'arbitrage f	—	operación de arbitraje f
operazione di cambio (I)	Valutageschäft n	currency transactions	opération de change f	—	operación de divisas f
operazione di cambio (I)	Sortengeschäft n	dealings in foreign notes and coins	commerce de change m	—	operación de moneda extranjera f
operazione di cambio (I)	Geldwechsel-geschäft n	currency exchange business	opération de change f	—	cambio manual m
operazione di cambio (I)	Devisengeschäft n	foreign exchange business	opération en devises f	—	operación de divisas f
operazione di cambio a termine (I)	Devisentermin-handel m	forward exchange trading	marché des changes à terme m		mercado de cambios a plazo m
operazione di cambio a termine (I)	Devisentermin-geschäft n	forward exchange dealings	opération à terme sur les changes f		transacción a término en divisas f
operazione di cambio su commissione (I)	Devisenkommis-sionsgeschäft n	foreign exchange transactions for customers	opérations de change en commission f/pl		operaciones de divisas a base de comisión f/pl
operazione di chiusura (I)	Abschlußauftrag m	final order	ordre final f	—	orden final f
operazione di compensazione (I)	Gegengeschäft n	countertrade	affaire en contrepartie f	—	transacción en contra f
operazione di compensazione (I)	Kompensations-geschäft n	offset transaction	affaire de compensation f	—	operación de compensación f
operazione di compensazione mediante trattazione titoli (I)	Glattstellen n	settlement	réalisation f	—	liquidación f
operazione di copertura (I)	Deckungsgeschäft n	covering operation	opération de couverture f	—	operación de cobertura f
operazione di credito (I)	Kreditgeschäft n	credit business	opérations d'avances sur crédit f/pl	—	operación crediticia f
operazione di deposito (I)	Depositengeschäft n	deposit banking	opération de garde de fonds f	—	operación de depósito f
operazione di deposito (I)	Passivgeschäft n	passive deposit transactions	opération passive f	—	operación pasiva f

	D	E	F	I	Es
operazione di deposito (I)	Einlagengeschäft n	deposit business	opération de garde de fonds f	—	operaciones de depósito f/pl
operazione di intermediazione (I)	Vermittlungs- geschäft n	brokerage business	affaire de médiation f	—	transacción de mediación f
operazione d'incasso (I)	Inkassogeschäft n	collection business	opération de recouvrement f	—	operación de cobro f
operazione d'incasso (I)	Einziehungs- geschäft n	collection business	opération d'encaissement f	—	operaciones de cobranza f/pl
operazione di prestito (I)	Anleihegeschäft n	loan business	opération de placement de titres d'emprunt f	—	operación crediticia f
operazione di riporto (I)	Reportgeschäft n	contango transaction	opération de report f	—	operación de reporte f
operazione di sconto (I)	Diskontierung f	discounting	escompte m	—	descuento m
operazione di sconto (I)	Diskontgeschäft n	discount business	opération d'escompte f	—	negocio de descuento m
operazione finanziaria (I)	Finanztransaktion f	financial transaction	transaction financière f	—	transacción financiera f
operazione fine a se stessa (I)	Insichgeschäft n	self-dealing	acte passé avec soi-même m	—	negocio consigo mismo m
operazione hedge (I)	Hedgegeschäft n	hedge operation	opération hedge f	—	negocio hedge m
operazione in effettivo (I)	Effektivgeschäft n	actual transaction	marché en disponible m	—	operación al contado f
operazione in metalli pregiati (I)	Edelmetallgeschäft n	bullion trade	opérations de métaux précieux f/pl	—	operaciones de metales preciosos f/pl
operazione in oro (I)	Goldgeschäft n	gold transactions	transaction d'or f	—	transacción de oro f
operazione in proprio in titoli (I)	Effekteneigen- geschäft n	security trading for own account	opérations sur titres à propre compte f/pl	—	operaciones de valores por cuenta propia f/pl
operazione intermediato (I)	Aufgabegeschäft n	name transaction	opération de médiation f	—	contrato intermediado m
operazione in titoli (I)	Effektengeschäft n	securities business	commerce des valeurs mobilières m	—	operación con valores f
operazione off-shore (I)	Offshore-Geschäft n	offshore dealings	opération off shore f	—	negocio offshore m
operazione onshore (I)	Onshore-Geschäft n	onshore business	opération onshore f	—	negocio onshore m
operazione pronti contro termine (I)	Wertpapierpensions- geschäft n	credit transaction under repurchase agreement of securities	prise en pension de valeurs mobilières f	—	operación de reporte de valores f
operazione singola (I)	Sologeschäft n	single operacion	opération particulière f	—	operación singular f
operazione swap (I)	Swapgeschäft n	swap transaction	opération swap f	—	operación swap f
operazione swap (I)	Swap m	swap	swap m	—	swap m
operazione switch (I)	Switch-Geschäft n	switch	opération switch f	—	operación switch f
operazione switch (I)	Bartergeschäft n	barter transactions	troc m	—	transacciones de trueque f/pl
operazioni a termine in titoli (I)	Wertpapier- Terminhandel m	trading in security futures	marché des valeurs à terme m	—	operaciones de valores a plazo f/pl
operazioni di borsa (I)	Börsengeschäfte n/pl	stock exchange operations	opération de bourse f	—	operaciones bursátiles f/pl
operazioni di paga- mento elettronici (I)	elektronischer Zahlungsverkehr m	electronic fund transfer	règlements électroniques m/pl	—	servicio de pagos electrónico m
operazioni normali (I)	Normalverkehr m	normal transactions	négociation normale f	—	negociaciones normales f/pl
operazioni per la clientela (I)	Kundengeschäft n	transactions for third account	opération pour compte de client f	—	transacciones por cuenta ajena f/pl
operazioni tra agenti di borsa (I)	Händlergeschäft n	dealer transaction	opération pour propre compte f	—	operaciones de corridor bursátil f/pl
oposición (Es)	Opposition f	opposition	opposition f	opposizione f	—
Opportunitätskosten (D)	—	opportunity costs	coût d'opportunité m	costi opportunità m/pl	coste de oportunidad m
opportunity costs (E)	Opportunitätskosten pl	—	coût d'opportunité m	costi opportunità m/pl	coste de oportunidad m

	D	E	F	I	Es
Opposition (D)	—	opposition	opposition f	opposizione f	oposición f
opposition (E)	Opposition f	—	opposition f	opposizione f	oposición f
opposition (F)	Opposition f	opposition	—	opposizione f	oposición f
opposition au payement d'un chèque (F)	Schecksperre f	stopping payment of cheque	—	fermo su assegno m	bloqueo de un cheque m
opposizione (I)	Opposition f	opposition	opposition f	—	oposición f
Option (D)	—	option	option f	opzione f	opción f
option (E)	Option f	—	option f	opzione f	opción f
option (F)	Option f	option	—	opzione f	opción f
optional loan (E)	Optionsdarlehen n	—	prêt avec droit d'option m	mutuo convertibile m	préstamo de opción m
option bond (E)	Optionsanleihe f	—	titre d'emprunt convertible m	prestito convertibile m	bono opcional m
option clause (E)	Fakultativklausel f	—	clause d'option f	clausola facoltativa f	cláusula potestativa f
option contract (E)	Prämienbrief m	—	contrat de marché à primes m	contratto a premio m	documento de una operación con prima m
option d'achat (F)	Kaufoption f	call option	—	opzione d'acquisto f	opción de compra f
option dealing (E)	Optionsgeschäft n	—	marché à option m	contratto ad opzione m	operación de opción f
option dealing (E)	Prämiengeschäft n	—	marché à prime m	operazione a premio f	operación a prima f
option de bond (F)	Bond-Option f	bond option	—	opzione bond f	opción bono f
option de change (F)	Devisenoption f	exchange option	—	opzione di cambio f	opción de divisas f
option d'échanger des titres convertibles en actions (F)	Aktienoption f	share stock option	—	diritto di prelazione m	opción de cambiar títulos convertibles en acciones f
option de prorogation du bail (F)	Mietverlängerungsoption f	lease renewal option	—	opzione proroga contratto di locazione f	opción de prorrogación de arrendamiento f
option de vente (F)	Verkaufsoption f	option to sell	—	opzione di vendita f	opción de venta f
option d'or (F)	Goldoption f	gold option	—	opzione oro f	opción de oro f
option price (E)	Optionspreis m	—	prix d'option m	prezzo di opzione m	precio de opción m
option right (E)	Optionsrecht n	—	droit d'option m	diritto d'opzione m	derecho de opción m
Optionsanleihe (D)	—	option bond	titre d'emprunt convertible m	prestito convertibile m	bono opcional m
Optionsdarlehen (D)	—	optional loan	prêt avec droit d'option m	mutuo convertibile m	préstamo de opción m
option seller (E)	Stillhalter m	—	vendeur d'option m	venditore di un'opzione m	vendedor de opción m
options frappées d'une saisie-arrêt (F)	Capped Warrants m/pl	capped warrants	—	capped warrants m/pl	talón de opción combinado m
Optionsgeschäft (D)	—	option dealing	marché à option m	contratto ad opzione m	operación de opción f
Optionspreis (D)	—	option price	prix d'option m	prezzo di opzione m	precio de opción m
Optionsrecht (D)	—	option right	droit d'option m	diritto d'opzione m	derecho de opción m
Optionsschein (D)	—	share purchase warrant	coupon d'option m	warrant m	documento de opción m
option to buy (E)	Call m	—	call m	call m	call m
option to sell (E)	Verkaufsoption f	—	option de vente f	opzione di vendita f	opción de venta f
opzione (I)	Option f	option	option f	—	opción f
opzione (I)	Ankaufsrecht n	purchase right	droit d'achat m	—	derecho de compra m
opzione bond (I)	Bond-Option f	bond option	option de bond f	—	opción bono f
opzione d'acquisto (I)	Kaufoption f	call option	option d'achat f	—	opción de compra f
opzione di cambio (I)	Devisenoption f	exchange option	option de change f	—	opción de divisas f
opzione di vendita (I)	Verkaufsoption f	option to sell	option de vente f	—	opción de venta f
opzione oro (I)	Goldoption f	gold option	option d'or f	—	opción de oro f
opzione proroga contratto di locazione (I)	Mietverlängerungsoption f	lease renewal option	option de prorogation du bail f	—	opción de prorrogación de arrendamiento f

	D	E	F	I	Es
or (F)	Gold n	gold	—	oro m	oro m
orario di borsa (I)	Börsenzeit f	official trading hours	heures d'ouverture de la bourse f/pl	—	sesión de bolsa f
orden (Es)	Order f	order	ordre m	ordine m	—
ordenación monetaria (Es)	Währungsordnung f	monetary system	ordre monétaire m	ordinamento valutario m	—
ordenanza para la indicación de precios (Es)	Preisangabe- verordnung f	price marking ordinance	ordonnance de marquage des prix f	regolamento di indicazione dei prezzi m	—
ordenanza tributaria (Es)	Abgabenordnung f	fiscal code	code des impôts m	legislazione tributaria f	—
orden bancaria remunerada (Es)	Bankauftrag m	remunerated order to effect a transaction	ordre bancaire m	ordine di banca m	—
orden colectiva (Es)	Sammelauftrag m	collective order	ordre groupé m	ordine cumulativo m	—
orden de bolsa (Es)	Börsenauftrag m	stock exchange order	ordre de bourse m	ordine di borsa m	—
orden de cliente (Es)	Kundenauftrag m	customer's order	ordre d'un client m	ordinazione f	—
orden de lotes irregulares (Es)	krummer Auftrag m	uneven order	ordre des lots irréguliers m	ordine irregolare m	—
orden de pago (Es)	Anweisung f	payment order	mandat m	ordine di pagamento m	—
orden de pago (Es)	Zahlungsanweisung f	order to pay	mandat de payement m	mandato di pagamento m	—
orden económico m (Es)	Wirtschaftsordnung f	economic order	ordre économique m	ordinamento economico m	—
órdenes de grupos (Es)	Konzernaufträge m/pl	group orders	commandes placées par un groupement des sociétés f/pl	ordini di gruppo m/pl	—
orden final (Es)	Abschlußauftrag m	final order	ordre final f	operazione di chiusura f	—
orden fingida (Es)	fingierte Order f	fictitious order	ordre simulé m	ordinazioni fittizie f/pl	—
orden jurídico (Es)	Rechtsordnung f	legal system	ordre juridique m	ordinamento giuridico m	—
orden permanente (Es)	Dauerauftrag m	standing order	ordre régulier m	incarico permanente m	—
ordentliche Kapitalerhöhung (D)	—	ordinary increase in capital	augmentation de capital ordinaire f	aumento di capitale a pagamento m	aumento de capital ordinario m
Order (D)	—	order	ordre m	ordine m	orden f
order (E)	Order f	—	ordre m	ordine m	orden f
order (E)	Bestellung f	—	commande f	ordinazione f	pedido m
order (E)	Auftrag m	—	commande f	ordine m	pedido m
order bill of lading (E)	Orderkonnossement n	—	connaissement à ordre m	polizza di carico all'ordine f	conocimiento a la orden m
order cheque (E)	Orderscheck m	—	chèque à ordre m	assegno all'ordine m	cheque a la orden m
order clause (E)	Orderklausel f	—	clause à ordre f	clausola "all'ordine" f	cláusula a la orden f
order for payment (E)	Zahlungsauftrag m	—	ordre de payement m	ordine di pagamento m	delegación de pago f
Orderklausel (D)	—	order clause	clause à ordre f	clausola "all'ordine" f	cláusula a la orden f
Orderkonnossement (D)	—	order bill of lading	connaissement à ordre m	polizza di carico all'ordine f	conocimiento a la orden m
Orderpapier (D)	—	instrument made out to order	papier à ordre m	titolo all'ordine m	título a la orden m
Orderscheck (D)	—	order cheque	chèque à ordre m	assegno all'ordine m	cheque a la orden m
order to pay (E)	Zahlungsanweisung f	—	mandat de payement m	mandato di pagamento m	orden de pago f
ordinamento economico (I)	Wirtschaftsordnung f	economic order	ordre économique m	—	orden económico m
ordinamento finanziario (I)	Finanzverfassung f	financial system	système financier m	—	constitución financiera f
ordinamento giuridico (I)	Rechtsordnung f	legal system	ordre juridique m	—	orden jurídico m
ordinamento valutario (I)	Währungsordnung f	monetary system	ordre monétaire m	—	ordenación monetaria f

	D	E	F	I	Es
ordinante il credito (I)	Akkreditivsteller m	person opening a credit in favour of somebody	émetteur d'un accréditif m	—	acreditante m
ordinary increase in capital (E)	ordentliche Kapitalerhöhung f	—	augmentation de capital ordinaire f	aumento di capitale a pagamento m	aumento de capital ordinario m
ordinary reduction of capital (E)	ordentliche Kapital-herabsetzung f	—	réduction de capital ordinaire f	riduzione di capitale ordinaria f	disminución de capital ordinaria f
ordinary share (E)	Stammaktie f	—	action ordinaire f	azione ordinaria f	acción ordinaria f
ordinazione (I)	Bestellung f	order	commande f	—	pedido m
ordinazione (I)	Kundenauftrag m	customer's order	ordre d'un client m	—	orden de cliente f
ordinazione fittizia (I)	fingierte Order f	fictitious order	ordre simulé m	—	orden fingida f
ordinazione successiva (I)	Nachorder f	follow-up order	nouveau ordre m	—	nueva orden f
ordine (I)	Auftrag m	order	commande f	—	pedido m
ordine (I)	Order f	order	ordre m	—	orden f
ordine cumulativo (I)	Sammelauftrag m	collective order	ordre groupé m	—	orden colectiva f
ordine di banca (I)	Bankauftrag m	remunerated order to effect a transaction	ordre bancaire m	—	orden bancaria remunerada f
ordine di borsa (I)	Börsenauftrag m	stock exchange order	ordre de bourse m	—	orden de bolsa f
ordine di borsa frazionario (I)	Fraktion f	fractional order	ordre fractionné m	—	fracción f
ordine di pagamento (I)	Zahlungsauftrag m	order for payment	ordre de payement m	—	delegación de pago f
ordine di pagamento (I)	Anweisung f	payment order	mandat m	—	orden de pago f
ordine irregolare (I)	krummer Auftrag m	uneven order	ordre de lots irréguliers m	—	orden de lotes irregulares f
ordini di gruppo (I)	Konzernaufträge m/pl	group orders	commandes placées par un groupement des sociétés f/pl	—	órdenes de grupos f/pl
ordinogramme (F)	Blockdiagramm n	bar chart	—	diagramma a blocchi m	diagrama de bloque m
ordonnance de marquage des prix (F)	Preisangabe-verordnung f	price marking ordinance	—	regolamento di indicazione dei prezzi m	ordenanza para la indicación de precios f
ordre (F)	Order f	order	—	ordine m	orden f
ordre bancaire (F)	Bankauftrag m	remunerated order to effect a transaction	—	ordine di banca m	orden bancaria remunerada f
ordre d'un client (F)	Kundenauftrag m	customer's order	—	ordinazione f	orden de cliente f
ordre de bourse (F)	Börsenauftrag m	stock exchange order	—	ordine di borsa m	orden de bolsa f
ordre de crédit (F)	Kreditauftrag m	mandate to provide credit for a third party	—	mandato di credito m	mandato crediticio m
ordre de lots irréguliers (F)	krummer Auftrag m	uneven order	—	ordine irregolare m	orden de lotes irregulares f
ordre de payement (F)	Zahlungsauftrag m	order for payment	—	ordine di pagamento m	delegación de pago f
ordre de recouvrement (F)	Einziehungsauftrag m	direct debit order	—	mandato di incasso m	autorización para el cobro f
ordre économique (F)	Wirtschaftsordnung f	economic order	—	ordinamento economico m	orden económico m
ordre final (F)	Abschlußauftrag m	final order	—	operazione di chiusura f	orden final f
ordre fractionné (F)	Fraktion f	fractional order	—	ordine di borsa frazionario f	fracción f
ordre groupé (F)	Sammelauftrag m	collective order	—	ordine cumulativo m	orden colectiva f
ordre juridique (F)	Rechtsordnung f	legal system	—	ordinamento giuridico m	orden jurídico m
ordre monétaire (F)	Währungsordnung f	monetary system	—	ordinamento valutario m	ordenación monetaria f
ordre régulier (F)	Dauerauftrag m	standing order	—	incarico permanente m	orden permanente f
ordre simulé (F)	fingierte Order f	fictitious order	—	ordinazioni fittizie f/pl	orden fingida f
or en lingot (F)	Barrengold n	gold in bars	—	oro in barre m	oro en lingotes m

	D	E	F	I	Es
or fin (F)	Feingold *n*	fine gold	—	oro fino *m*	oro fino *m*
Organgesellschaft (D)	—	controlled company	entreprise dominée *f*	società legata contrattualmente *f*	sociedad órgano *f*
organisación bancaria (Es)	Bankorganisation *f*	banking organization	organisation bancaire *f*	organizzazione bancaria *f*	—
Organisation (D)	—	organization	organisation *f*	organizzazione *f*	organización *f*
organisation (F)	Organisation *f*	organization	—	organizzazione *f*	organización *f*
organisation bancaire (F)	Bankorganisation *f*	banking organization	—	organizzazione bancaria *f*	organisación bancaria *f*
organisation boursière (F)	Börsenorganisation *f*	stock exchange organization	—	organizzazione della borsa *f*	organización bursátil *f*
organisation du marché (F)	Marktordnung *f*	market organization	—	disciplina del mercato *f*	organización del mercado *f*
Organisations-abteilung (D)	—	organization and methods department	service d'organisation *m*	ufficio organizzazione *m*	sección de organización *f*
organisme collecteur de fonds (F)	Kapitalsammelstelle *f*	institutional investors	—	investitore istituzionale *m*	centro de acumulación de capitales *m*
organización (Es)	Organisation *f*	organization	organisation *f*	organizzazione *f*	—
organización bursátil (Es)	Börsenorganisation *f*	stock exchange organization	organisation boursière *f*	organizzazione della borsa *f*	—
organización del mercado (Es)	Marktordnung *f*	market organization	organisation du marché *f*	disciplina del mercato *f*	—
organization (E)	Organisation *f*	—	organisation *f*	organizzazione *f*	organización *f*
organization and methods department (E)	Organisations-abteilung *f*	—	service d'organisation *m*	ufficio organizzazione *m*	sección de organización *f*
organizzazione (I)	Organisation *f*	organization	organisation *f*	—	organización *f*
organizzazione bancaria (I)	Bankorganisation *f*	banking organization	organisation bancaire *f*	—	organisación bancaria *f*
organizzazione della borsa (I)	Börsenorganisation *f*	stock exchange organization	organisation boursière *f*	—	organización bursátil *f*
Organkredit (D)	—	loans granted to members of a managing board	crédit accordé par une banque à ses membres du directoire *m*	credito concesso all'organico *m*	crédito interconsorcial *m*
orientation de la clientèle (F)	Kundenberatung *f*	consumer advice	—	servizio d'assistenza *m*	asesoramiento de clientes *m*
orientation en matière de placement (F)	Anlageberatung *f*	investment counseling	—	consulenza in investimenti *f*	asesoramiento en materia de inversiones *m*
oro (Es)	Gold *n*	gold	or *m*	oro *m*	—
oro (I)	Gold *n*	gold	or *m*	—	oro *m*
oro en lingotes (Es)	Barrengold *n*	gold in bars	or en lingot *m*	oro in barre *m*	—
oro fino (Es)	Feingold *n*	fine gold	or fin *m*	oro fino *m*	—
oro fino (I)	Feingold *n*	fine gold	or fin *m*	—	oro fino *m*
oro in barre (I)	Barrengold *n*	gold in bars	or en lingot *m*	—	oro en lingotes *m*
oscilación extraordinaria (Es)	Sonderbewegung *f*	extraordinary trend	tendance extraordinaire *f*	movimento divergente *m*	—
oscillazione inattesa della quotazione (I)	Ausbrechen des Kurses *n*	erratic price movements	fortes fluctuations des cours *f/pl*	—	fuertes movimientos en las cotizaciones *m/pl*
other liabilities (E)	sonstige Verbindlichkeiten *f/pl*	—	autres obligations *f/pl*	debiti diversi *m/pl*	acreedores varios *m/pl*
outdoor advertising (E)	Außenwerbung *f*	—	publicité extérieure *f*	pubblicità esterna *f*	propaganda al aire libre *f*
outlay tax (E)	Ausgabensteuer *f*	—	taxe de débours *f*	imposta di consumo *f*	impuesto de emisión *m*
out-of-town cheque (E)	Versandscheck *m*	—	chèque déplacé *m*	assegno fuori piazza *m*	cheque sobre otra plaza *m*
output (E)	Ausbringung *f*	—	volume de la production *m*	gettito *m*	volumen de la producción *m*
outright futures transactions (E)	Outright-Termingeschäft *n*	—	opération à terme outright *f*	contratto a termine outright *m*	operación a término outright *f*

	D	E	F	I	Es
Outright-Termingeschäft (D)	—	outright futures transactions	opération à terme outright f	contratto a termine outright m	operación a término outright f
outstanding accounts (E)	Außenstände m/pl	—	dettes actives f/pl	crediti pendenti m/pl	cobros pendientes m/pl
ouverture (F)	Erschließung f	development	—	apertura f	apertura f
ouverture de la faillite (F)	Konkurseröffnung f	commencement of bankruptcy proceedings	—	apertura del fallimento f	apertura de la quiebra f
ouverture du marché (F)	Markterschließung f	opening of new markets	—	penetrazione del mercato f	apertura del mercado f
ouverture d'une compte (F)	Kontoeröffnung f	opening of an account	—	apertura di un conto f	apertura de una cuenta f
overall adjustment (E)	Globalwertberichtigung f	—	rectification des valeurs globale f	rivalutazione globale f	rectificación de valor global f
overall assignment (E)	Globalzession f	—	cession globale f	cessione globale f	cesión en bloque f
overall costs (E)	Gesamtkosten pl	—	coût total m	costi complessivi m/pl	costes totales m/pl
overcapitalization (E)	Überkapitalisierung f	—	surcapitalisation f	sovraccapitalizzazione f	sobrecapitalización f
overdraft (E)	Überziehen eines Kontos n	—	découvert de compte m	mandare un conto allo scoperto m	descubierto m
overdraft commission (E)	Überziehungsprovision f	—	commission de découvert f	provvigione di scoperta f	comisión de giro en descubierto f
overfinancing (E)	Überfinanzierung f	—	financement exagéré m	sovraccapitalizzazione f	financiación excesiva f
over-subscription (E)	Überzeichnung f	—	souscription surpassée f	sottoscrizione eccedente f	suscripción en exceso f
over-the-counter business (E)	Tafelgeschäft n	—	opération de guichet f	operazione a contanti f	operación al contado f
over-the-counter market (E)	Over-the-counter-market m	—	opérations de guichet f/pl	over-the-counter-market m	mercado de operaciones de mostrador m
over-the-counter trade (E)	Freihandel m	—	commerce libre m	libero scambio m	librecambio m
over-the-counter trading (E)	Effektenverkauf m	—	vente de titres f	vendita di titoli f	venta de valores f
Over-the-counter-market (D)	—	over-the-counter market	opérations de guichet f/pl	over-the-counter-market m	mercado de operaciones de mostrador m
over-the-counter-market (I)	Over-the-counter-market m	over-the-counter market	opérations de guichet f/pl	—	mercado de operaciones de mostrador m
own capital withdrawal (E)	Eigenkapitalentzug m	—	retrait du capital propre m	ritiro del capitale proprio m	retiro del capital propio m
own contributions (E)	Eigenleistungen f/pl	—	prestations propres f/pl	prestazioni proprie f/pl	producciones propias f/pl
ownership in fractional shares (E)	Bruchteilseigentum n	—	propriété d'une quote-part indivise f	comproprietà di quota ideale f	propiedad por fracciones f
own security deposit (E)	Eigendepot n	—	dépôt personnel m	deposito proprio m	depósito de valores propio m
own security holdings (E)	eigene Effekten pl	—	titres propres m/pl	titoli propri m/pl	valores propios m/pl
pacchetto azionario (I)	Aktienpaket n	block of shares	paquet d'actions m	—	paquete de acciones m
Pächterkredit (D)	—	tenant's credit	crédit agricole aux fermiers m	credito ai fittavoli m	crédito agrícola a favor de los arrendatarios m
Pachtzins (D)	—	rent	prix du bail m	canone d'affitto m	arrendamiento m
pagaduría (Es)	Zahlstelle f	payments office	bureau payeur m	cassa di pagamento f	—
paga in contanti (I)	Barlohn m	wage in cash	salaire en espèces m	—	salario en efectivo m
pagamenti (I)	Zahlungsverkehr m	payment transaction	règlements m/pl	—	movimiento de pagos m
pagamenti mediante assegno (I)	Scheckverkehr m	cheque transactions	opérations par chèque f/pl	—	operaciones de cheques f/pl
pagamento (I)	Zahlung f	payment	payement m	—	pago m

	D	E	F	I	Es
pagamento degli interessi (I)	Kapitaldienst m	service of capital	service du capital m	—	servicio de capital m
pagamento dei debiti (I)	Entschuldung f	disencumberment	désendettement m	—	desgravamen m
pagamento in acconto (I)	Teilzahlung f	partial payment	payement partiel m	—	pago parcial m
pagamento in contanti (I)	Barzahlung f	cash payment	payement comptant m	—	pago al contado m
pagamento parziale (I)	Teilauszahlung f	partial payment	payement partiel m	—	desembolso parcial m
pagamento residuale (I)	Restquote f	residual quota	quote-part restante f	—	cuota restante f
pagamento supplementare (I)	Zuzahlung f	additional contribution	payement supplémentaire m	—	pago suplementario m
pagaré (Es)	trockener Wechsel m	negotiable promissory note	seule de change f	pagherò m	—
pagaré (Es)	Promesse f	promissory note	engagement m	promessa f	—
pagaré (Es)	Schuldschein m	certificate of indebtedness	reconnaissance de dette f	certificato di debito m	—
pagaré en moneda extranjera (Es)	Valutaschuldschein m	foreign currency certificate of indebtedness	titre de créance en monnaie étrangère m	titolo di credito in valuta estera m	—
pagato (I)	bezahlt	paid	équilibre entre offre et demande m	—	equilibrio entre papel y dinero m
pagherò (I)	trockener Wechsel m	negotiable promissory note	billet à ordre m	—	pagaré m
pago (Es)	Zahlung f	payment	payement m	pagamento m	—
pago (Es)	Auszahlung f	payment	payement m	esborso m	—
pago a cuenta (Es)	Anzahlung f	deposit	acompte m	acconto m	—
pago a cuenta (Es)	Abschlagszahlung f	down payment	acompte m	acconto m	—
pago al contado (Es)	Barzahlung f	cash payment	payement comptant m	pagamento in contanti m	—
pago aplazado (Es)	Zahlungsaufschub m	extension of time for payment	sursis de payement m	dilazione di pagamento f	—
pago bancario (Es)	Bankanweisung f	bank money order	mandat de payement bancaire m	vaglia bancario m	—
pago de compensación (Es)	Ausgleichszahlung f	compensation payment	payement pour solde de compte m	compensazione f	—
pago parcial (Es)	Teilzahlung f	partial payment	payement partiel m	pagamento in acconto m	—
pago suplementario (Es)	Zuzahlung f	additional contribution	payement supplémentaire m	pagamento supplementare m	—
paid (E)	bezahlt	—	équilibre entre offre et demande m	pagato	equilibrio entre papel y dinero m
pair (F)	pari	par	—	pari	a la par
pair du change (F)	Kursparität f	parity of rates	—	parità di scambio f	paridad cambiaria f
Pakethandel (D)	—	dealing in large lots	négociation de lots importants f	negoziazione di pacchetti azionari f	transacciones de paquetes mayores de acciones f/pl
panel of experts (E)	Sachverständigenrat m	—	conseil d'experts m	consiglio degli esperti m	consejo de asesores económicos m
panier des monnaies (F)	Währungskorb m	currency basket	—	paniere monetario m	cesta de monedas f
paniere monetario (I)	Währungskorb m	currency basket	panier des monnaies m	—	cesta de monedas f
panorama creditizio (I)	Kreditkultur f	credit culture	culture de crédit f	—	cultura crediticia f
papeles del Estado (Es)	Staatspapiere n/pl	public securities	effets publics m/pl	titoli di Stato m/pl	—
paper money (E)	Papiergeld n	—	monnaie de papier f	moneta cartacea f	dinero-papel m
Papier (D)	—	security	titre m	titolo m	título m
papier à ordre (F)	Orderpapier n	instrument made out to order	—	titolo all'ordine m	título a la orden m
papier d'affaires (F)	Geschäftspapier n	commercial papers	—	carta intestata f	documento comercial m
Papiergeld (D)	—	paper money	monnaie de papier f	moneta cartacea f	dinero-papel m

	D	E	F	I	Es
papiers de sûreté (F)	Kautionseffekten *pl*	guarantee securities	—	titoli di deposito cauzionale *m/pl*	valores de fianza *m/pl*
paquet d'actions (F)	Aktienpaket *n*	block of shares	—	pacchetto azionario *m*	paquete de acciones *m*
paquete de acciones (Es)	Aktienpaket *n*	block of shares	paquet d'actions *m*	pacchetto azionario *m*	—
par (E)	pari	—	pair	pari	a la par
Parallelanleihe (D)	—	parallel loan	emprunt parallèle *m*	obbligazione parallela *f*	empréstito paralelo *m*
parallel currency (E)	Parallelwährung *f*	—	monnaie parallèle *f*	bimetallismo *m*	moneda paralela *f*
parallel loan (E)	Parallelanleihe *f*	—	emprunt parallèle *m*	obbligazione parallela *f*	empréstito paralelo *m*
parallel market (E)	Parallelmarkt *m*	—	marché parallèle *m*	mercato libero delle divise *m*	mercado paralelo *m*
Parallelmarkt (D)	—	parallel market	marché parallèle *m*	mercato libero delle divise *m*	mercado paralelo *m*
Parallelwährung (D)	—	parallel currency	monnaie parallèle *f*	bimetallismo *m*	moneda paralela *f*
pari (D)	—	par	pair	pari	a la par
pari (I)	pari	par	pair	—	a la par
paridad (Es)	Parität *f*	parity	parité *f*	parità *f*	—
paridad adquisitiva (Es)	Kaufkraftparität *f*	purchasing power parity	parité du pouvoir d'achat *f*	parità del potere d'acquisto *f*	—
paridad cambiaria (Es)	Kursparität *f*	parity of rates	pair du change *m*	parità di scambio *f*	—
paridad cruzada (Es)	Kreuzparität *f*	cross rate	parité indirecte *f*	parità incrociata *f*	—
paridad de derecho de suscripción (Es)	Bezugsrechtsparität *f*	subscription rights parity	parité des droits de souscription *f*	valore aritmetico diritto d'opzione *m*	—
paridad del interés (Es)	Zinsparität *f*	interest parity	parité des intérêts *f*	parità dei tassi d'interesse *f*	—
paridad monetaria (Es)	Währungsparität *f*	monetary parity	parité des monnaies *f*	parità monetaria *f*	—
paridad móvil (Es)	Gleitparität *f*	escalation parity	parité mobile *f*	parità variabile *f*	—
paridad-oro (Es)	Goldparität *f*	gold parity	parité de l'or *f*	parità aurea *f*	—
Pariemission (D)	—	issue at par	émission au pair *f*	emissione alla pari *f*	emisión a la par *f*
Parikurs (D)	—	par price	cours au pair *m*	corso alla pari *m*	cambio a la par *m*
Pariplätze (D)	—	places where cheques are collected by banks free of charge	places bancaires sans change de place *f/pl*	piazze alla pari *f/pl*	plazas donde los bancos cobran cheques a título gratuito *f/pl*
parità (I)	Parität *f*	parity	parité *f*	—	paridad *f*
parità aurea (I)	Goldparität *f*	gold parity	parité de l'or *f*	—	paridad-oro *f*
parità centrale (I)	Leitkurs *m*	central rate	taux central *m*	—	tipo de pivote *m*
parità dei tassi d'interesse (I)	Zinsparität *f*	interest parity	parité des intérêts *f*	—	paridad del interés *f*
parità del potere d'acquisto (I)	Kaufkraftparität *f*	purchasing power parity	parité du pouvoir d'achat *f*	—	paridad adquisitiva *f*
parità di scambio (I)	Kursparität *f*	parity of rates	pair du change *m*	—	paridad cambiaria *f*
parità incrociata (I)	Kreuzparität *f*	cross rate	parité indirecte *f*	—	paridad cruzada *f*
parità monetaria (I)	Währungsparität *f*	monetary parity	parité des monnaies *f*	—	paridad monetaria *f*
Parität (D)	—	parity	parité *f*	parità *f*	paridad *f*
Paritätengitter (D)	—	parity grid	table de parité *f*	griglia delle parità *f*	parrilla de paridades *f*
parità variabile (I)	Gleitparität *f*	escalation parity	parité mobile *f*	—	paridad móvil *f*
parité (F)	Parität *f*	parity	—	parità *f*	paridad *f*
parité de l'or (F)	Goldparität *f*	gold parity	—	parità aurea *f*	paridad-oro *f*
parité des droits de souscription (F)	Bezugsrechtsparität *f*	subscription rights parity	—	valore aritmetico diritto d'opzione *m*	paridad de derecho de suscripción *f*
parité des intérêts (F)	Zinsparität *f*	interest parity	—	parità dei tassi d'interesse *f*	paridad del interés *f*
parité des monnaies (F)	Währungsparität *f*	monetary parity	—	parità monetaria *f*	paridad monetaria *f*
parité du pouvoir d'achat (F)	Kaufkraftparität *f*	purchasing power parity	—	parità del potere d'acquisto *f*	paridad adquisitiva *f*
parité indirecte (F)	Kreuzparität *f*	cross rate	—	parità incrociata *f*	paridad cruzada *f*

	D	E	F	I	Es
parité mobile (F)	Gleitparität f	escalation parity	—	parità variabile f	paridad móvil f
parity (E)	Parität f	—	parité f	parità f	paridad f
parity grid (E)	Paritätengitter n	—	table de parité f	griglia delle parità f	parrilla de paridades f
parity of rates (E)	Kursparität f	—	pair du change m	parità di scambio f	paridad cambiaria f
Parkett (D)	—	floor	parquet m	recinto delle grida m	parqué m
Parkettmakler (D)	—	official market broker	agent de change m	agente di cambio m	corredor de parqué m
par price (E)	Parikurs m	—	cours au pair m	corso alla pari m	cambio a la par m
parqué (Es)	Parkett n	floor	parquet m	recinto delle grida m	—
parquet (F)	Parkett n	floor	—	recinto delle grida m	parqué m
parrilla de paridades (Es)	Paritätengitter n	parity grid	table de parité f	griglia delle parità f	—
part (F)	Anteil m	share	—	aliquota f	parte alícuota f
part de capital (F)	Kapitalanteil m	share in capital	—	quota di capitale f	participación en el capital f
part de fonds d'investissement (F)	Investmentanteil m	investment share	—	quota di fondo d'investimento f	participación en fondos de inversión mobiliaria f
part de mines (F)	Kux m	mining share	—	azione mineraria f	acción minera f
parte alícuota (Es)	Anteil m	share	part f	aliquota f	—
partecipazione (I)	Beteiligung f	participation	participation f	—	participación f
partecipazione a forma di anticipo (I)	Beteiligungsdarlehen n	loan with profit participation	prêt de participation m	—	préstamo participativo m
partecipazione agli utili (I)	Erfolgsbeteiligung f	profit-sharing	participation aux résultats f	—	participación en el beneficio f
partecipazione agli utili (I)	Gewinnbeteiligung f	participation in profits	participation aux bénéfices f	—	participación en el beneficio f
partecipazione agli utili (I)	Ergebnisbeteiligung f	participating in yield	participation aux résultats f	—	participación en los beneficios f
partecipazione agli utili velata (I)	verdeckte Gewinn-ausschüttung f	hidden profit distribution	distribution occulte de bénéfices f	—	distribución oculta f
partecipazione al capitale (I)	Kapitalbeteiligung f	equity participation	participation par apport de capital f	—	intervención financiera f
partecipazione di società al capitale di altre società (I)	Verschachtelung f	interlocking	interdépendance f	—	participación de una sociedad en el capital de otra f
partecipazione maggioritaria (I)	Mehrheitsbeteiligung f	majority participation	participation majoritaire f	—	participación mayoritaria f
parte di capitale (I)	Quotenaktie f	share of no par value	action de quotité f	—	acción de cuota f
partial acceptance (E)	Teilakzept n	—	acceptation partielle f	accettazione parziale f	aceptación parcial f
partial bill of lading (E)	Teilkonnossement n	—	connaissement partiel m	polizza di carico parziale f	recibo parcial m
partial claim (E)	Teilforderung f	—	créance partielle f	credito parziale m	crédito parcial m
partial endorsement (E)	Teilindossament n	—	endossement partiel m	girata parziale f	endoso parcial m
partial payment (E)	Teilzahlung f	—	payement partiel m	pagamento in acconto m	pago parcial m
partial payment (E)	Teilauszahlung f	—	payement partiel m	pagamento parziale m	desembolso parcial m
partial rights (E)	Teilrechte n/pl	—	droits partiels m/pl	buono frazionario m	derechos de partición m/pl
participación (Es)	Beteiligung f	participation	participation f	partecipazione f	—
participación de una sociedad en el capital de otra (Es)	Verschachtelung f	interlocking	interdépendance f	partecipazione di società al capitale di altre società f	—
participación en el beneficio (Es)	Erfolgsbeteiligung f	profit-sharing	participation aux résultats f	partecipazione agli utili f	—
participación en el beneficio (Es)	Gewinnbeteiligung f	participation in profits	participation aux bénéfices f	partecipazione agli utili f	—
participación en el capital (Es)	Kapitalanteil m	share in capital	part de capital f	quota di capitale f	—
participación en el mercado (Es)	Marktanteil m	market share	participation au marché f	quota di mercato f	—

	D	E	F	I	Es
participación en fondos de inversión mobiliaria (Es)	Investmentanteil *m*	investment share	part de fonds d'investissement *f*	quota di fondo d'investimento *f*	—
participación en los beneficios (Es)	Gewinnanteil *m*	share in the profits	quote-part sur les bénéfices *f*	quota utile *f*	—
participación en los beneficios (Es)	Ergebnisbeteiligung *f*	participating in yield	participation aux résultats *f*	partecipazione agli utili *f*	—
participación mayoritaria (Es)	Mehrheitsbe-teiligung *f*	majority participation	participation majoritaire *f*	partecipazione maggioritaria *f*	—
participating certificate (E)	Genußschein *m*	—	certificat de jouissance *m*	buono di godimento *m*	bono de disfrute *m*
participating debenture (E)	Gewinnobligation *f*	—	obligation indexée *f*	obbligazione a premio *f*	bono sobre beneficios *m*
participating in yield (E)	Ergebnisbeteiligung *f*	—	participation aux résultats *f*	partecipazione agli utili *f*	participación en los beneficios *f*
participating receipt (E)	Partizipationsschein *m*	—	récépissé de participation *m*	buono di partecipazione *m*	bono de participación *m*
participating rights capital (E)	Genußrechtskapital *n*	—	capital bénéficiaire *m*	capitale da buoni di godimento *m*	capital de bono de disfrute *m*
participation (E)	Beteiligung *f*	—	participation *f*	partecipazione *f*	participación *f*
participation (F)	Beteiligung *f*	participation	—	partecipazione *f*	participación *f*
participation au marché (F)	Marktanteil *m*	market share	—	quota di mercato *f*	participación en el mercado *f*
participation aux bénéfices (F)	Gewinnbeteiligung *f*	participation in profits	—	partecipazione agli utili *f*	participación en el beneficio *f*
participation aux pertes (F)	Verlustanteil *m*	share in the loss	—	quota alle perdite *f*	cuota de pérdidas *f*
participation aux résultats (F)	Erfolgsbeteiligung *f*	profit-sharing	—	partecipazione agli utili *f*	participación en el beneficio *f*
participation aux résultats (F)	Ergebnisbeteiligung *f*	participating in yield	—	partecipazione agli utili *f*	participación en los beneficios *f*
participation financière à la construction (F)	Baukostenzuschuß *m*	tenant's contribution to the construction costs	—	contributo alla costruzione *m*	contribución a los costes de construcción *f*
participation in profits (E)	Gewinnbeteiligung *f*	—	participation aux bénéfices *f*	partecipazione agli utili *f*	participación en el beneficio *f*
participation majoritaire (F)	Mehrheitsbeteiligung *f*	majority participation	—	partecipazione maggioritaria *f*	participación mayoritaria *f*
participation par apport de capital (F)	Kapitalbeteiligung *f*	equity participation	—	partecipazione al capitale *f*	intervención financiera *f*
participation personnelle à la couverture du risque (F)	Selbstbeteiligung *f*	retention	—	franchigia *f*	propia retención *f*
participation rights (E)	Genußrecht *n*	—	droit de jouissance *m*	diritto di godimento *m*	derecho de disfrute *m*
partida abierta (Es)	offene Position *f*	open position	poste ouvert *m*	posizione scoperta *f*	—
partida de porte pagado (Es)	Frankoposten *m*	item free of charge	poste de port payé *m*	partita franco spese *f*	—
partita doppia (I)	doppelte Buchführung *f*	double entry bookkeeping	comptabilité en partie double *f*	—	contabilidad de partida doble *f*
partida extraordinaria (Es)	Sonderposten *m*	separate item	poste spécial *m*	partita speciale *f*	—
partita franco spese (I)	Frankoposten *m*	item free of charge	poste de port payé *m*	—	partida de porte pagado *f*
partita speciale (I)	Sonderposten *m*	separate item	poste spécial *m*	—	partida extraordinaria *f*
Partizipationsschein (D)	—	participating receipt	récépissé de participation *m*	buono di partecipazione *m*	bono de participación *m*
partner (E)	Teilhaber *m*	—	associé *m*	socio *m*	socio *m*
partnership (E)	Personengesellschaft *f*	—	société de personnes *f*	società di persone *f*	sociedad personalista *f*
partnership assets (E)	Gesellschafts-vermögen *n*	—	patrimoine social *m*	attivo sociale *m*	activo social *m*
part patronale (F)	Arbeitgeberanteil *m*	employer's share	—	quota del datore di lavoro *f*	cuota patronal *f*

	D	E	F	I	Es
parts de fonds d'investissement (F)	Investmentzertifikate n/pl	investment fund certificates	—	certificato d'investimento m	certificado de inversión m
par value share (E)	Nennwertaktie f	—	action nominale f	azione a valore nominale f	acción de suma f
pasivo (Es)	Passiva n/pl	liabilities	passif m	passività f/pl	—
pasivo exigible (Es)	Buchschuld f	book debt	dette comptable f	debito contabile m	—
passif (F)	Passiva n/pl	liabilities	—	passività f/pl	pasivo m
Passiva (D)	—	liabilities	passif m	passività f/pl	pasivo m
passive deposit transactions (E)	Passivgeschäft n	—	opération passive f	operazione di deposito f	operación pasiva f
Passivgeschäft (D)	—	passive deposit transactions	opération passive f	operazione di deposito f	operación pasiva f
Passivierung (D)	—	inclusion on the liabilities side	inscription au passif f	passività f	asiento en el pasivo m
passività (I)	Passivierung f	inclusion on the liabilities side	inscription au passif f	—	asiento en el pasivo m
passività (I)	Passiva n/pl	liabilities	passif m	—	pasivo m
Passivkredit (D)	—	borrowing	crédit passif m	finanziamento passivo m	crédito pasivo m
Passivtausch (D)	—	accounting exchange on the liabilities side	écritures entre postes de passif f/pl	rettifica del passivo f	cambio de asientos en el pasivo m
Passivzins (D)	—	interest payable	intérêt à payer par la banque m	interesse passivo m	interés a pagar m
patentes extranjeras (Es)	Auslandspatente n/pl	foreign patents	brevets à l'étranger m/pl	brevetti esteri m/pl	—
patrimoine (F)	Vermögen n	property	—	patrimonio m	patrimonio m
patrimoine immobilier (F)	Betongold n	real estate property	—	proprietà immobiliare f	propiedad inmobiliaria f
patrimoine national (F)	Volksvermögen n	national wealth	—	ricchezza nazionale f	patrimonio nacional m
patrimoine réel (F)	Realvermögen n	real wealth	—	patrimonio reale m	activo inmobiliario m
patrimoine social (F)	Gesellschaftsvermögen n	partnership assets	—	attivo sociale m	activo social m
patrimonio (Es)	Vermögen n	property	patrimoine m	patrimonio m	—
patrimonio (I)	Vermögen n	property	patrimoine m	—	patrimonio m
patrimonio complessivo (I)	Gesamtvermögen n	aggregate property	avoir total m	—	totalidad del patrimonio f
patrimonio del fondo (I)	Fondsvermögen n	fund assets	capital constituant le fonds m	—	activo en fondos públicos m
patrimonio empresarial (Es)	Betriebsvermögen n	operating assets	capital d'exploitation m	capitale d'esercizio m	—
patrimonio en el extranjero (Es)	Auslandsvermögen n	foreign assets	avoirs à l'étranger m/pl	beni all'estero m/pl	—
patrimonio especial (Es)	Sondervermögen n	special fund	fonds spéciaux m/pl	patrimonio separato m	—
patrimonio financiero (Es)	Finanzvermögen n	financial assets	disponibilités f/pl	patrimonio finanziario m	—
patrimonio finanziario (I)	Finanzvermögen n	financial assets	disponibilités f/pl	—	patrimonio financiero m
patrimonio interno (Es)	Inlandsvermögen n	domestic capital	capital déclaré dans le pays où l'assujetti à sa résidence m	capitale nazionale m	—
patrimonio nacional (Es)	Volksvermögen n	national wealth	patrimoine national m	ricchezza nazionale f	—
patrimonio neto (Es)	Reinvermögen n	net assets	avoir net m	attivo netto m	—
patrimonio netto (I)	haftendes Eigenkapital n	liable funds	capital propre de garantie m	—	capital propio respondiente m
patrimonio real (Es)	Sachvermögen n	material assets	biens corporels m/pl	beni materiali m/pl	—
patrimonio reale (I)	Realvermögen n	real wealth	patrimoine réel m	—	activo inmobiliario m
patrimonio separato (I)	Sondervermögen n	special fund	fonds spéciaux m/pl	—	patrimonio especial m
patrón de divisas en oro (Es)	Gold-Devisen-Standard m	gold exchange standard	étalon or et devises m	gold exchange standard m	—
patrón-dólar (Es)	Dollar-Standard m	dollar standard	étalon dollar m	dollar standard m	—

	D	E	F	I	Es
patrón metálico (Es)	Metallwährung f	metallic currency	monnaie métallique f	valuta metallica f	—
patrón-oro (Es)	Gold-Standard m	gold standard	étalon or m	gold standard m	—
patrón plata (Es)	Silberwährung f	silver standard	monnaie en argent f	valuta d'argento f	—
pauschal (D)	—	global	forfaitaire	a forfait	global
Pauschaldelkredere (D)	—	global delcredere	ducroire forfaitaire m	star del credere forfettario m	del credere global m
pawn (E)	Faustpfand n	—	gage mobilier m	pegno mobile m	prenda mobiliaria f
pawnbroking (E)	Pfandleihe f	—	prêt sur gage m	prestito su pegno m	préstamo sobre prenda m
pawnshop (E)	Leihanstalt f	—	institut de prêt m	monte di pietà m	monte de piedad m
payday (E)	Zahltag m	—	jour de paye m	giorno di pagamento m	día de pago m
payee (E)	Remittent m	—	remettant m	beneficiario m	remitente m
payee of a bill of exchange (E)	Wechselnehmer m	—	preneur d'un effet m	beneficiario di una cambiale m	endosado m
payement (F)	Zahlung f	payment	—	pagamento m	pago m
payement (F)	Einzahlung f	payment	—	versamento m	aportación f
payement (F)	Auszahlung f	payment	—	esborso m	pago m
payement comptant (F)	Barzahlung f	cash payment	—	pagamento in contanti m	pago al contado m
payement des intérêts (F)	Verzinsung f	payment of interest	—	tasso d'interesse m	redito m
payement en espèces (F)	Bareinschuß m	cash loss payment	—	versamento in contanti m	reserva en efectivo m
payement partiel (F)	Teilauszahlung f	partial payment	—	pagamento parziale m	desembolso parcial m
payement partiel (F)	Teilzahlung f	partial payment	—	pagamento in acconto m	pago parcial m
payement pour solde de compte (F)	Ausgleichszahlung f	compensation payment	—	compensazione f	pago de compensación m
payements scripturaux au point de vente (F)	bargeldlose Kassensysteme n/pl	point of sale systems POS	—	sistemi di cassa non in contanti m/pl	sistemas de caja por transferencia m/pl
payement supplémentaire (F)	Zuzahlung f	additional contribution	—	pagamento supplementare m	pago suplementario m
payement télégraphique (F)	telegrafische Auszahlung f	telegraphic transfer	—	trasferimento telegrafico m	desembolso telegráfico m
paying off (E)	Entlohnung f	—	rétribution f	retribuzione f	retribución f
payment (E)	Auszahlung f	—	payement m	esborso m	pago m
payment (E)	Besoldung f	—	salaire m	retribuzione f	salario m
payment (E)	Zahlung f	—	payement m	pagamento m	pago m
payment (E)	Einzahlung f	—	payement f	versamento m	aportación f
payment guarantee (E)	Anzahlungs- bürgschaft f	—	garantie de payement f	garanzia rimborso acconto f	garantía de pago f
payment habit (E)	Zahlungssitte f	—	habitude de payement f	usanza di pagamento f	costumbre de pago f
payment in kind (E)	Deputat n	—	avantage en nature m	compenso in natura m	remuneración en especie f
payment of interest (E)	Verzinsung f	—	payement des intérêts m	tasso d'interesse m	interés m
payment order (E)	Anweisung f	—	mandat m	ordine di pagamento m	orden de pago f
payment slip (E)	Zahlschein m	—	mandat-carte m	modulo di versamento m	impreso para giro postal m
payments office (E)	Zahlstelle f	—	bureau payeur m	cassa di pagamento f	pagaduría f
payment transaction (E)	Zahlungsverkehr m	—	règlements m/pl	pagamenti m/pl	movimiento de pagos m
peak quotation (E)	Extremkurs m	—	cours extrême m	quotazione estrema f	curso extremo m
pécuniaire (F)	pekuniär	pecuniary	—	pecuniario	pecuniario
pecuniario (Es)	pekuniär	pecuniary	pécuniaire	pecuniario	—
pecuniario (I)	pekuniär	pecuniary	pécuniaire	—	pecuniario
pecuniary (E)	pekuniär	—	pécuniaire	pecuniario	pecuniario

	D	E	F	I	Es
pedido (Es)	Auftrag *m*	order	commande *f*	ordine *m*	—
pedido (Es)	Bestellung *f*	order	commande *f*	ordinazione *f*	—
pegno (I)	Pfand *n*	pledge	nantissement *m*	—	prenda *f*
pegno mobile (I)	Faustpfand *n*	pawn	gage mobilier *m*	—	prenda mobiliaria *f*
pekuniär (D)	—	pecuniary	pécuniaire	pecuniario	pecuniario
pena contractual (Es)	Vertragsstrafe *f*	contractual penalty	pénalité *f*	convenzionale *f*	—
pena convencional (Es)	Konventionalstrafe *f*	contractual penalty	penalité *f*	pena convenzionale *f*	—
pena convenzionale (I)	Konventionalstrafe *f*	contractual penalty	pénalité *f*	—	pena convencional *f*
penalità (I)	Strafzins *m*	penalty interest	intérêt punitif *m*	—	interés punitivo *m*
penalità interessi (I)	Vorschußzinsen *m/pl*	negative advance interest	intérêts payés par anticipation *m/pl*	—	interés negativo anticipado *m*
pénalité (F)	Konventionalstrafe *f*	contractual penalty	—	pena convenzionale *f*	pena convencional *f*
pénalité (F)	Vertragsstrafe *f*	contractual penalty	—	convenzionale *f*	pena contractual *f*
penalty (E)	Strafe *f*	—	peine *f*	punizione *f*	pena *f*
penalty interest (E)	Strafzins *m*	—	intérêt punitif *m*	penalità *f*	interés punitivo *m*
pending transactions (E)	schwebende Geschäfte *n/pl*	—	affaires en suspens *f/pl*	affari pendenti *m/pl*	negocios en curso *m/pl*
penetrazione del mercato (I)	Markterschließung *f*	opening of new markets	ouverture du marché *f*	—	apertura del mercado *f*
pensione di effetti (I)	Wechselpensionsgeschäft *n*	pledging of bills of exchange against grant of a loan	opération de mise en pension d'effets *f*	—	operación de reporte de letras *f*
pension reserve (E)	Pensionsrückstellungen *f/pl*	—	provisions pour les retraites du personnel *f/pl*	fondo pensioni *m*	fondo de retiros *f*
Pensionsgeschäft (D)	—	security transactions under repurchase agreement	opération de mise en pension d'effets *f*	sconto in pensione *m*	operación de reporte *f*
Pensionskasse (D)	—	staff pension fund	caisse de retraite *f*	fondo di previdenza *m*	caja de jubilaciones *f*
Pensionsrückstellungen (D)	—	pension reserve	provisions pour les retraites du personnel *f/pl*	fondo pensioni *m*.	fondo de retiros *f*
pent-up inflation (E)	zurückgestaute Inflation *f*	—	inflation refoulée *f*	inflazione arginata *f*	inflación detenida *f*
pequeño comerciante no registrable en el registro de comercio (Es)	Minderkaufmann *m*	small trader	petit exploitant non soumis aux prescriptions générales du code de commerce *m*	piccolo imprenditore *m*	—
per aval (D)	—	as guarantor of payment	bon pour aval	per buon fine	por aval
per buon fine (I)	per aval	as guarantor of payment	bon pour aval	—	por aval
per capita tax (E)	Kopfsteuer *f*	—	impôt personnel *m*	capitazione *f*	capitación *f*
per cent (E)	Prozent *n*	—	pour-cent *m*	percento *m*	por ciento *m*
percento (I)	Prozent *n*	per cent	pour-cent *m*	—	por ciento *m*
percentuale dei disoccupati (I)	Arbeitslosenquote *f*	rate of unemployment	taux de chômage *m*	—	tasa de paro *f*
percentuale dei mezzi propri (I)	Eigenkapitalquote *f*	equity ratio	quote-part du capital propre *f*	—	cuota de capital propio *f*
percentuale della spesa pubblica (I)	Staatsquote *f*	government expenditure rate	pourcentage des dépenses publiques *m*	—	porcentaje de los gastos públicos *m*
percepciones en especie (Es)	Sachbezüge *m/pl*	remuneration in kind	prestations en nature *f/pl*	retribuzioni in natura *f/pl*	—
pérdida (Es)	Verlust *m*	loss	perte *f*	perdita *f*	—
pérdida de balance (Es)	Bilanzverlust *m*	net loss	perte comptable *f*	perdita di bilancio *f*	—
perdita (I)	Verlust *m*	loss	perte *f*	—	pérdida *f*
perdita di bilancio (I)	Bilanzverlust *m*	net loss	perte comptable *f*	—	pérdida de balance *f*
péréquation des charges (F)	Lastenausgleich *m*	equalization of burdens	—	perequazione degli oneri *f*	compensación de cargas *f*
perequazione degli oneri (I)	Lastenausgleich *m*	equalization of burdens	péréquation des charges *f*	—	compensación de cargas *f*

performance

318

	D	E	F	I	Es
performance (E)	Erfüllung *f*	—	accomplissement *m*	adempimento *m*	cumplimiento *m*
performance (E)	Leistung *f*	—	rendement *f*	prestazione *f*	prestación *f*
performance guarantee (E)	Leistungsgarantie *f*	—	garantie de prestation *f*	garanzia di esecuzione *f*	fianza de contratista *f*
performance regulations (E)	Effizienzregeln *f/pl*	—	régulation d'efficience *f*	regole per l'efficienza *f/pl*	normas de eficacia *t/pl*
période de référence (F)	Berichtsperiode *f*	period under review	—	periodo in esame *m*	período considerado *m*
period for payment (E)	Zahlungsziel *n*	—	délai de payement *m*	dilazione di pagamento *f*	plazo de pago *m*
período considerado (Es)	Berichtsperiode *f*	period under review	période de référence *f*	periodo in esame *m*	—
período de protesta (Es)	Protestzeit *f*	period of protest	heures de présentation du protêt *f/pl*	termine presentazione di protesto *m*	—
periodo di custodia (I)	Aufbewahrungsfrist *f*	retention period	délai de dépôt *m*	—	plazo de conservación *m*
period of protest (E)	Protestzeit *f*	—	heures de présentation du protêt *f/pl*	termine presentazione di protesto *m*	período de protesta *m*
periodo in esame (I)	Berichtsperiode *f*	period under review	période de référence *f*	—	período considerado *m*
period under review (E)	Berichtsperiode *f*	—	période de référence *f*	periodo in esame *m*	período considerado *m*
permanent holding (E)	Dauerbesitz *m*	—	possession permanente *f*	detenzione permanente *f*	posesión permanente *f*
permanent shareholder (E)	Daueraktionär *m*	—	actionnaire permanent *m*	azionista permanente *m*	accionista permanente *m*
permesso d'emissione (I)	Emissions-genehmigung *f*	issue permit	autorisation de l'émission *f*	—	autorización de emisión *f*
perpetual annuity (F)	ewige Rente *f*	—	rente perpétuelle *f*	annualità porpetua *f*	anualidad perpetua *f*
perpetual debt (E)	ewige Schuld *f*	—	dette perpétuelle *f*	prestito perpetuo *m*	deuda perpetua *f*
perpetual loan (E)	ewige Anleihe *f*	—	emprunt perpétuel *m*	prestito perpetuo *m*	empréstito perpétuo *m*
per procuration endorsement (E)	Prokuraindossament *n*	—	endossement de procuration *m*	girata "per procura" *f*	endoso por procuración *m*
persona abile al lavoro (I)	Erwerbsperson *f*	gainfully employed person	personne active *f*	—	persona activa *f*
persona activa (Es)	Erwerbsperson *f*	gainfully employed person	personne active *f*	persona abile al lavoro *f*	—
persona física (Es)	natürliche Person *f*	natural person	personne physique *f*	persona fisica *f*	—
persona fisica (I)	natürliche Person *f*	natural person	personne physique *f*	—	persona física *f*
persona giuridica (I)	juristische Person *f*	legal entity	personne juridique *f*	—	persona jurídica *f*
persona jurídica (Es)	juristische Person *f*	legal entity	personne juridique *f*	persona giuridica *f*	—
personal account (E)	Privatkonto *n*	—	compte privé *m*	conto particolare *m*	cuenta privada *f*
personal accounts (E)	Personenkonten *n/pl*	—	comptes de personne	conti di persone *m/pl m/pl*	cuentas personales *f/pl*
personal identification number (E)	persönliche Identifikations-Nummer [PIN] *f*	—	numéro personnel d'identification *m*	numero di identificazione personale *m*	número de identificación personal *m*
Personalkredit (D)	—	personal loan	crédit personnel *m*	credito personale *m*	crédito personal *m*
personal loan (E)	Personalkredit *m*	—	crédit personnel *m*	credito personale *m*	crédito personal *m*
Personendepot (D)	—	customer's security deposit	dépôt de personne *m*	libretto personale di deposito titoli *m*	depósito personal *m*
Personen-gesellschaft (D)	—	partnership	société de personnes *f*	società di persone *f*	sociedad personalista *f*
Personenkonten (D)	—	personal accounts	comptes de personne *m/pl*	conti di persone *m/pl*	cuentas personales *f/pl*
persönliche Identifikations-Nummer [PIN] (D)	—	personal identification number	numéro d'identification personnel *m*	numero di identificazione personale *m*	número de identificación personal *m*
personne active (F)	Erwerbsperson *f*	gainfully employed person	—	persona abile al lavoro *f*	persona activa *f*
personne ayant le pouvoir commercial (F)	Handelsbevoll-mächtigter *m*	general agent	—	rappresentante commerciale *m*	agente comercial *m*
personne juridique (F)	juristische Person *f*	legal entity	—	persona giuridica *f*	persona jurídica *f*
personne physique (F)	natürliche Person *f*	natural person	—	persona fisica *f*	persona física *f*

	D	E	F	I	Es
person opening a credit in favour of somebody (E)	Akkreditivsteller *m*	—	émetteur d'un accréditif *m*	ordinante il credito *m*	acreditante *m*
perspective (F)	Prognose *f*	forecast	—	previsione *f*	pronóstico *m*
perte (F)	Verlust *m*	loss	—	perdita *f*	pérdida *f*
perte comptable (F)	Bilanzverlust *m*	net loss	—	perdita di bilancio *f*	pérdida de balance *f*
perte de rachat (F)	Rückkaufdisagio *n*	discount on repurchase	—	scarto di rimborso su obbligazione *m*	disagio de recompra *m*
per Ultimo (D)	—	for the monthly settlement	à fin de mois	quotazione a fine corrente *f*	a fin de mes
peso fino (Es)	Feingewicht *n*	standard	poids de métal fin *m*	titolo *m*	—
peso fino del oro (Es)	Goldfeingehalt *m*	fine gold content	poids d'or fin *m*	titolo aureo *m*	—
pesos de oro (Es)	Goldgewichte *n/pl*	troy weights	poids de l'or *m/pl*	unità di misura per l'oro *m*	—
petit actionnaire (F)	Kleinaktionär *m*	small shareholder	—	piccolo azionista *m*	accionista pequeño *m*
petit crédit (F)	Kleinkredit *m*	small personal loan	—	piccolo credito *m*	préstamo pequeño *m*
petit épargnant (F)	Kleinsparer *m*	small saver	—	piccolo risparmiatore *m*	ahorradores de menor importancia *m/pl*
petit exploitant non soumis aux prescriptions générales du code de commerce (F)	Minderkaufmann *m*	small trader	—	piccolo imprenditore *m*	pequeño comerciante no registrable en el registro de comercio *m*
petits titres (F)	Kleinstücke *n/pl*	fractional amount	—	titoli di importo modesto *m/pl*	títulos pequeños *m/pl*
petrodólar (Es)	Petrodollar *m*	petrodollar	pétrodollar *m*	petrodollaro *m*	—
Petrodollar (D)	—	petrodollar	pétrodollar *m*	petrodollaro *m*	petrodólar *m*
petrodollar (E)	Petrodollar *m*	—	pétrodollar *m*	petrodollaro *m*	petrodólar *m*
pétrodollar (F)	Petrodollar *m*	petrodollar	—	petrodollaro *m*	petrodólar *m*
petrodollaro (I)	Petrodollar *m*	petrodollar	pétrodollar *m*	—	petrodólar *m*
Pfand (D)	—	pledge	nantissement *m*	pegno *m*	prenda *f*
Pfandbrief (D)	—	mortgage bond	obligation hypothécaire *f*	obbligazione fondiaria *f*	cédula hipotecaria *f*
Pfandbriefanstalt (D)	—	mortgage bank	banque hypothécaire *f*	istituto di credito fondiario *m*	banco hipotecario *m*
Pfandbriefdarlehen (D)	—	mortgage loan	prêt hypothécaire *m*	prestito su pegno *m*	préstamo hipotecario *m*
Pfandbriefgesetz (D)	—	mortgage law	législation en matière d'hypothèques *f*	legge sulle obbligazioni ipotecarie *f*	ley de pignoración *f*
Pfanddepot (D)	—	pledged securities deposit	dépôt de titres remis en nantissement *m*	deposito a garanzia *m*	depósito de prenda *m*
Pfandindossament (D)	—	pledge endorsement	endossement pignoratif *m*	girata "valuta in pegno" *f*	endoso en prenda *m*
Pfandleihe (D)	—	pawnbroking	prêt sur gage *m*	prestito su pegno *m*	préstamo sobre prenda *m*
Pfandrecht (D)	—	lien	droit de gage *m*	diritto di pegno *m*	derecho de prenda *m*
Pfandschein (D)	—	certificate of pledge	bulletin de gage *m*	atto di pegno *m*	resguardo de prenda *m*
Pfändung (D)	—	seizure	saisie *f*	pignoramento *m*	embargo *m*
Pfandvertrag (D)	—	contract of pledge	contrat pignoratif *m*	contratto di pegno *m*	contrato de prenda *m*
Pfandverwertung (D)	—	realization of pledge	réalisation du gage *f*	realizzazione di un pegno *f*	realización de la prenda *f*
Pflichteinlage (D)	—	compulsory contribution	apport obligatoire *m*	deposito obbligatorio *m*	depósito obligatorio *m*
Pflichtreserve (D)	—	minimum reserve	réserve légale *f*	riserva obbligatoria *f*	reserva obligatoria *f*
pianificazione finanziaria (I)	Finanzplanung *f*	budgeting	planification financière *f*	—	planificación financiera *f*
piano dei conti (I)	Kontenplan *m*	chart of accounts	plan comptable *m*	—	plan contable *m*
piano d'investimento (I)	Investitionsplan *m*	investment scheme	plan des investissements *m*	—	plan de inversión *m*
piano di risparmio (I)	Sparpläne *m/pl*	savings plans	plans d'épargne *m/pl*	—	planes de ahorro *m/pl*
piano di spesa (I)	Ausgabenplan *m*	plan of expenditure	état prévisionnel des dépenses *m*	—	presupuesto de gastos *m*

	D	E	F	I	Es
piano economico (I)	Wirtschaftsplan *m*	economic plan	plan économique *m*	—	plan económico *m*
piano finanziario (I)	Finanzplan *m*	financial plan	plan financier *m*	—	plan financiero *m*
piazza bancaria (I)	Bankplatz *m*	bank place	place bancable *f*	—	plaza bancable *f*
piazza secondaria (I)	Nebenplatz *m*	place without a Federal Bank office	place non bancaire *f*	—	bolsín oficial *m*
piazze alla pari (I)	Pariplätze *m/pl*	places where cheques are collected by banks free of charge	places bancaires sans change de place *f/pl*	—	plazas donde los bancos cobran cheques a título gratuito *f/pl*
piccola azione (I)	Kleinaktie *f*	share with low par value	action minimale *f*	—	acción pequeña *f*
piccolo azionista (I)	Kleinaktionär *m*	small shareholder	petit actionnaire *m*	—	accionista pequeño *m*
piccolo credito (I)	Kleinkredit *m*	small personal loan	petit crédit *m*	—	préstamo pequeño *m*
piccolo imprenditore (I)	Minderkaufmann *m*	small trader	petit exploitant non soumis aux prescriptions générales du code de commerce *m*	—	pequeño comerciante no registrable en el registro de comercio *m*
piccolo risparmiatore (I)	Kleinsparer *m*	small saver	petit épargnant *m*	—	ahorradores de menor importancia *m/pl*
pièce comptable (F)	Buchungsbeleg *m*	accounting voucher	—	documento contabile *m*	comprobante de asiento *m*
pièce d'or (F)	Goldmünze *f*	gold coin	—	moneta aurea *f*	moneda de oro *f*
pièce en argent (F)	Silbermünze *f*	silver coin	—	moneta d'argento *f*	moneda de plata *f*
piggy bank (E)	Sparbüchse *f*	—	tirelire *f*	salvadanaio *m*	alcancía *f*
pignoración (Es)	Verpfändung *f*	pledge	mise en gage *f*	pignoramento *m*	—
pignoramento (I)	Verpfändung *f*	pledge	mise en gage *f*	—	pignoración *f*
pignoramento (I)	Pfändung *f*	seizure	saisie *f*	—	embargo *m*
pignoramento totale (I)	Kahlpfändung *f*	seizure of all the debtor's goods	saisie de tous les biens *f*	—	embargo total *m*
pignorar (Es)	beleihen	lend money on something	nantir	ipotecare	—
più (I)	plus	plus	plus	—	más
place bancable (F)	Bankplatz *m*	bank place	—	piazza bancaria *f*	plaza bancable *f*
place boursière (F)	Börsenplatz *m*	stock exchange centre	—	sede di borsa *f*	plaza bursátil *f*
placement (F)	Placierung *f*	placing	—	collocamento *m*	colocación *f*
placement d'argent (F)	Geldanlage *f*	investment	—	investimento di denaro *m*	inversión *f*
placement de titres (F)	Effektenplazierung *f*	securities placing	—	emissione di titoli *f*	emisión de valores *f*
placement en valeurs mobilières (F)	Wertpapieranlage *f*	investment in securities	—	investimento in titoli *m*	inversión en valores *f*
placements à long terme (F)	langfristige Einlagen *f/pl*	long-term deposits	—	depositi a lunga scadenza *m/pl*	imposiciones a largo plazo *f/pl*
placements en fonds (F)	Fondsanlagen *f/pl*	trust investment	—	investimenti di fondo d'investimento *m/pl*	inversión de fondos *f*
place non bancaire (F)	Nebenplatz *m*	place without a Federal Bank office	—	piazza secondaria *f*	bolsín oficial *m*
place of performance (E)	Erfüllungsort *m*	—	lieu de l'exécution de la prestation *m*	luogo d'adempimento *m*	lugar del cumplimiento *m*
places bancaires sans change de place (F)	Pariplätze *m/pl*	places where cheques are collected by banks free of charge	—	piazze alla pari *f/pl*	plazas donde los bancos cobran cheques a título gratuito *f/pl*
places principales (F)	Hauptplätze *m/pl*	main centers	—	sedi principali *f/pl*	plazas principales *f/pl*
places where cheques are collected by banks free of charge (E)	Pariplätze *m/pl*	—	places bancaires sans change de place *f/pl*	piazze alla pari *f/pl*	plazas donde los bancos cobran cheques a título gratuito *f/pl*
place without a Federal Bank office (E)	Nebenplatz *m*	—	place non bancaire *f*	piazza secondaria *f*	bolsín oficial *m*
Placierung (D)	—	placing	placement *m*	collocamento *m*	colocación *f*
placing (E)	Placierung *f*	—	placement *m*	collocamento *m*	colocación *f*
placing commission (E)	Bankierbonifikation *f*	—	commission de placement *f*	provvigione bancaria *f*	comisión de mediación bancaria *f*

	D	E	F	I	Es
Plafond (D)	—	ceiling	plafond *m*	plafond *m*	límite máximo *m*
plafond (F)	Plafond *m*	ceiling	—	plafond *m*	límite máximo *m*
plafond (I)	Plafond *m*	ceiling	plafond *m*	—	límite máximo *m*
plafond d'assujettissement servant au calcul de la cotisation à l'assurance invalidité-vieillesse (F)	Beitragsbemessungsgrenze *f*	income limit for the assessment of contributions	—	massimale di contributo *m*	tope de la base de cotización *m*
plafond de garantie (F)	Bürgschaftsplafond *n*	guarantee limit	—	plafond di fideiussione *m*	límite de garantía *m*
plafond de l'intérêt (F)	Zinskappe *f*	cap rate of interest	—	tetto interessi *m*	plafón de interés *m*
plafond des crédits sur effets acceptés (F)	Akzeptlinie *f*	line of acceptance	—	linea di credito d'accettazione *f*	línea de aceptación *f*
plafond di fideiussione (I)	Bürgschaftsplafond *n*	guarantee limit	plafond de garantie *m*	—	límite de garantía *m*
plafond d'intérêt (F)	Cap *n*	cap	—	cap *m*	techo de interés *m*
plafond di risconto (I)	Rediskontkontingent *n*	rediscount quota	quota de réescompte *m*	—	cupo de redescuento *m*
plafond du crédit accordé (F)	Kreditplafond *n*	credit ceiling	—	limite massimo di fido *m*	plafón de crédito *m*
plafond du crédit accordé (F)	Kreditlinie *f*	credit line	—	linea di credito *f*	línea de crédito *f*
plafond du crédit alloué (F)	Kreditlimit *n*	credit limit	—	limite di credito *m*	límite de crédito *m*
plafón de crédito (Es)	Kreditplafond *n*	credit ceiling	plafond du crédit accordé *m*	limite massimo di fido *m*	—
plafón de interés (Es)	Zinskappe *f*	cap rate of interest	plafond de l'intérêt *m*	tetto interessi *m*	—
plan comptable (F)	Kontenplan *m*	chart of accounts	—	piano dei conti *m*	plan contable *m*
plan contable (Es)	Kontenplan *m*	chart of accounts	plan comptable *m*	piano dei conti *m*	—
plan de inversión (Es)	Investitionsplan *m*	investment scheme	plan des investissements *m*	piano d'investimento *m*	—
plan des investissements (F)	Investitionsplan *m*	investment scheme	—	piano d'investimento *m*	plan de inversión *m*
plan económico (Es)	Wirtschaftsplan *m*	economic plan	plan économique *m*	piano economico *m*	—
plan économique (F)	Wirtschaftsplan *m*	economic plan	—	piano economico *m*	plan económico *m*
planes de ahorro (Es)	Sparpläne *m/pl*	savings plans	plans d'épargne *m/pl*	piano di risparmio *m*	—
plan financier (F)	Finanzplan *m*	financial plan	—	piano finanziario *m*	plan financiero *m*
plan financiero (Es)	Finanzplan *m*	financial plan	plan financier *m*	piano finanziario *m*	—
planificación financiera (Es)	Finanzplanung *f*	budgeting	planification financière *f*	pianificazione finanziaria *f*	—
planificación global (Es)	Gesamtplanung *f*	master planning	planification globale *f*	programmazione complessiva *f*	—
planification financière (F)	Finanzplanung *f*	budgeting	—	pianificazione finanziaria *f*	planificación financiera *f*
planification globale (F)	Gesamtplanung *f*	master planning	—	programmazione complessiva *f*	planificación global *f*
planned economy (E)	Planwirtschaft *f*	—	économie planifiée *f*	economia pianificata *f*	economía planificada *f*
plan of expenditure (E)	Ausgabenplan *m*	—	état prévisionnel des dépenses *m*	piano di spesa *m*	presupuesto de gastos *m*
plans d'épargne (F)	Sparpläne *m/pl*	savings plans	—	piano di risparmio *m*	planes de ahorro *m/pl*
Planwirtschaft (D)	—	planned economy	économie planifiée *f*	economia pianificata *f*	economía planificada *f*
plata fina (Es)	Feinsilber *n*	fine silver	argent fin *m*	argento fino *m*	—
Platzanweisung (D)	—	cheques and orders payable at a certain place	mandat de place *m*	bonifico sulla piazza *m*	cheques y órdenes a pagar en plaza *m/pl*
Platzspesen (D)	—	local expenses	change de place *m*	spese d'incasso di piazza *f/pl*	gastos locales *m/pl*
Platzübertragung (D)	—	local transfer	virement de place *m*	trasferimento su piazza *m*	transferencia local *f*
Platzwechsel (D)	—	local bill	effet sans change de place *m*	cambiale pagabile sul posto *f*	letra de plaza *f*

	D	E	F	I	Es
plaza bancable (Es)	Bankplatz *m*	bank place	place bancable *f*	piazza bancaria *f*	—
plaza bursátil (Es)	Börsenplatz *m*	stock exchange centre	place boursière *f*	sede di borsa *f*	—
plazas donde los bancos cobran cheques a título gratuito (Es)	Pariplätze *m/pl*	places where cheques are collected by banks free of charge	places bancaires sans change de place *f/pl*	piazze alla pari *f/pl*	—
plazas principales (Es)	Hauptplätze *m/pl*	main centers	places principales *f/pl*	sedi principali *f/pl*	—
plazo de conservación (Es)	Aufbewahrungsfrist *f*	retention period	délai de dépôt *m*	periodo di custodia *m*	—
plazo de pago (Es)	Zahlungsziel *n*	period for payment	délai de payement *m*	dilazione di pagamento *f*	—
plazo de suscripción (Es)	Bezugsfrist *f*	subscription period	délai de souscription *m*	termine d'opzione *m*	—
plazo de suspensión de preaviso (Es)	Kündigungssperrfrist *f*	non-calling period	délai de blocage de dénonciation *m*	termine di preavviso *m*	—
plazo de vencimiento (Es)	Verfallzeit *f*	time of expiration	époque de l'échéance *f*	scadenza *f*	—
plazo de vencimiento del crédito (Es)	Kreditfrist *f*	credit period	délai de rembourse-ment des avances sur crédit *m*	scadenza del credito *f*	—
plazo de vinculación de capital (Es)	Kapitalbindungsdauer *f*	duration of capital tie-up	durée de l'immobili-sation de capitaux *f*	vincolo del capitale *m*	—
pledge (E)	Pfand *n*	—	nantissement *m*	pegno *m*	prenda *f*
pledge (E)	Verpfändung *f*	—	mise en gage *f*	pignoramento *m*	pignoración *f*
pledged securities deposit (E)	Pfanddepot *n*	—	dépôt de titres remis en nantissement *m*	deposito a garanzia *m*	depósito de prenda *m*
pledge endorsement (E)	Pfandindossament *n*	—	endossement pignoratif *m*	girata "valuta in pegno" *f*	endoso en prenda *m*
pledging of bills of exchange against grant of a loan (E)	Wechselpensions-geschäft *n*	—	opération de mise en pension d'effets *f*	pensione di effetti *f*	operación de reporte de letras *f*
plein pouvoir (F)	Vollmacht *f*	power of attorney	—	procura *f*	poder *m*
plus (D)	—	plus	plus	più	más
plus (E)	plus	—	plus	più	más
plus (F)	plus	plus	—	più	más
Plus-Sparen (D)	—	surplus saving	épargne d'excédents *f*	risparmio restanti del conto corrente *m*	ahorro de excedentes *m*
plusvalenza (I)	Veräußerungsgewinn *m*	gain on disposal	bénéfice d'aliénation *m*	—	beneficio de la venta *m*
plusvalía de cotización (Es)	Kursgewinn *m*	price gain	plus-value sur les cours *f*	utile di borsa *m*	—
plus-value sur les cours (F)	Kursgewinn *m*	price gain	—	utile di borsa *m*	plusvalía de cotización *m*
poco animado (Es)	lustlos	slack	inactif *m*	fiacco	—
poder (Es)	Vollmacht *f*	power of attorney	plein pouvoir *m*	procura *f*	—
poder adquisitivo (Es)	Kaufkraft *f*	purchasing power	pouvoir d'achat *m*	potere d'acquisto *m*	—
poder de cuenta (Es)	Kontovollmacht *f*	power to draw on an account	pouvoir de compte *m*	procura di disporre sul conto *f*	—
poder de género (Es)	Gattungsvollmacht *f*	generic power	pouvoir générique *m*	procura specifica *f*	—
poder de mercado (Es)	Marktmacht *f*	market power	pouvoir de marché *m*	potere di mercato *m*	—
poder especial (Es)	Spezialvollmacht *f*	special power	pouvoir limité à un acte commercial déterminé *m*	procura speciale *f*	—
poder general (Es)	Prokura *f*	full power of attorney	procuration com-merciale générale *f*	procura commerciale *f*	—
poder general (Es)	Generalvollmacht *f*	unlimited power	pouvoir général *m*	procura generale *f*	—
poder mercantil (Es)	Handlungsvollmacht *f*	commercial power of attorney	pouvoir commercial *m*	mandato commerciale *m*	—
poder principal (Es)	Hauptvollmacht *f*	primary power	pouvoir principal *m*	procura principale *f*	—
poder solidario (Es)	Gesamtvollmacht *f*	joint power of attorney	procuration collective *f*	procura collettiva *f*	—

	D	E	F	I	Es
poids de l'or (F)	Goldgewichte *n/pl*	troy weights	—	unità di misura per l'oro *f/pl*	pesos de oro *m/pl*
poids de métal fin (F)	Feingewicht *n*	standard	—	titolo *m*	peso fino *m*
poids des coûts (F)	Kostendruck *m*	cost pressure	—	pressione dei costi *f*	tensiones sobre los gastos *f/pl*
poids d'or fin (F)	Goldfeingehalt *m*	fine gold content	—	titolo aureo *m*	peso fino del oro *m*
point d'or (F)	Goldpunkt *m*	gold point	—	punto dell'oro *m*	punto de oro *m*
point of sale systems POS (E)	bargeldlose Kassensysteme *n/pl*	—	payements scripturaux au point de vente *m/pl*	sistemi di cassa non in contanti *m/pl*	sistemas de caja por transferencia *m/pl*
points d'intervention (F)	Interventionspunkte *m/pl*	intervention point	—	punti d'intervento *m/pl*	puntos de intervención *m/pl*
policy of sterilization funds (E)	Sterilisierungspolitik *f*	—	politique de stérilisation *f*	politica di sterilizzazione *f*	política en materia de esterilización *f*
policy relating to capital formation (E)	Vermögenspolitik *f*	—	politique financière *f*	politica patrimoniale *f*	política de patrimonios *f*
polígono mágico (Es)	magisches Vieleck *n*	magic polygon	polygone magique *m*	poligono magico *m*	—
poligono magico (I)	magisches Vieleck *n*	magic polygon	polygone magique *m*	—	polígono mágico *m*
política de depositos (Es)	Einlagenpolitik *f*	deposit policy	politique de dépôts *f*	politica dei depositi *f*	—
política de descuento (Es)	Diskontpolitik *f*	bank rate policy	politique d'escompte *f*	politica di sconto *f*	—
política degli interessi (I)	Zinspolitik *f*	interest rate policy	politique en matière d'intérêts *f*	—	política de intereses *f*
política degli interessi alti (I)	Hochzinspolitik *f*	high interest rate policy	politique de taux d'intérêt élevés *f*	—	política de tipos de interés elevados *f*
política dei depositi (I)	Einlagenpolitik *f*	deposit policy	politique de dépôts *f*	—	política de depositos *f*
política de intereses (Es)	Zinspolitik *f*	interest rate policy	politique en matière d'intérêts *f*	politica degli interessi *f*	—
política delle riserve obbligatorie (I)	Mindestreservepolitik *f*	minimum reserve policy	politique de réserve minimum *f*	—	política de reservas mínimas *f*
política del mercato monetario (I)	Geldmarktpolitik *f*	money market policy	politique du marché monétaire *f*	—	política monetaria *f*
política de mercado abierto (Es)	Offenmarktpolitik *f*	open market policy	politique d'open market *f*	politica di mercato aperto *f*	—
política de patrimonios (Es)	Vermögenspolitik *f*	policy relating to capital formation	politique financière *f*	politica patrimoniale *f*	—
política de refinanciación (Es)	Refinanzierungs- politik *f*	refinancing policy	politique de refinancement *f*	politica di risconto *f*	—
política de reservas mínimas (Es)	Mindestreservepolitik *f*	minimum reserve policy	politique de réserve minimum *f*	politica delle riserve obbligatorie *f*	—
política de swap (Es)	Swappolitik *f*	swap policy	politique de swap *f*	politica swap *f*	—
política de tipos de interés elevados (Es)	Hochzinspolitik *f*	high interest rate policy	politique de taux d'intérêt élevés *f*	politica degli interessi alti *f*	—
política di mercato aperto (I)	Offenmarktpolitik *f*	open market policy	politique d'open market *f*	—	política de mercado abierto *f*
política di risconto (I)	Refinanzierungs- politik *f*	refinancing policy	politique de refinancement *f*	—	política de refinanciación *f*
política di sconto (I)	Diskontpolitik *f*	bank rate policy	politique d'escompte *f*	—	política de descuento *f*
política di sterilizzazione (I)	Sterilisierungspolitik *f*	policy of sterilization funds	politique de stérilisation *f*	—	política en materia de esterilización *f*
política económica (Es)	Wirtschaftspolitik *f*	economic policy	politique économique *f*	politica economica *f*	—
política economica (I)	Wirtschaftspolitik *f*	economic policy	politique économique *f*	—	política económica *f*
política en materia de esterilización (Es)	Sterilisierungspolitik *f*	policy of sterilization funds	politique de stérilisation *f*	politica di sterilizzazione *f*	—
política financiera (Es)	Finanzpolitik *f*	financial policy	politique financière *f*	politica finanziaria *f*	—
política finanziaria (I)	Finanzpolitik *f*	financial policy	politique financière *f*	—	política financiera *f*
política fiscal (Es)	Fiskalpolitik *f*	fiscal policy	politique fiscale *f*	politica fiscale *f*	—
política fiscale (I)	Fiskalpolitik *f*	fiscal policy	politique fiscale *f*	—	política fiscal *f*

	D	E	F	I	Es
política monetaria (Es)	Währungspolitik f	monetary policy	politique monétaire f	politica monetaria f	—
política monetaria (Es)	Geldmarktpolitik f	money market policy	politique du marché monétaire f	politica del mercato monetario f	—
política monetaria (Es)	Geldpolitik f	monetary policy	politique monétaire f	politica monetaria f	—
política monetaria (I)	Währungspolitik f	monetary policy	politique monétaire f	—	política monetaria f
política monetaria (I)	Geldpolitik f	monetary policy	politique monétaire f	—	política monetaria f
politica patrimoniale (I)	Vermögenspolitik f	policy relating to capital formation	politique financière f	—	política de patrimonios f
politica swap (I)	Swappolitik f	swap policy	politique de swap f	—	política de swap f
politica valutaria (I)	Valutapolitik f	currency policy	politique monétaire f	—	política de divisas f
politique de refinancement (F)	Refinanzierungspolitik f	refinancing policy	—	politica di risconto f	política de refinanciación f
politique de réserve minimum (F)	Mindestreservepolitik f	minimum reserve policy	—	politica delle riserve obbligatorie f	política de reservas mínimas f
politique d'escompte (F)	Diskontpolitik f	bank rate policy	—	politica di sconto f	política de descuento f
politique de stérilisation (F)	Sterilisierungspolitik f	policy of sterilization funds	—	politica di sterilizzazione f	política en materia de esterilización f
politique de swap (F)	Swappolitik f	swap policy	—	politica swap f	política de swap f
politique de taux d'intérêt élevés (F)	Hochzinspolitik f	high interest rate policy	—	politica degli interessi alti f	política de tipos de interés elevados f
politique d'open market (F)	Offenmarktpolitik f	open market policy	—	politica di mercato aperto f	política de mercado abierto f
politique du marché monétaire (F)	Geldmarktpolitik f	money market policy	—	politica del mercato monetario f	política monetaria f
politique économique (F)	Wirtschaftspolitik f	economic policy	—	politica economica f	política económica f
politique en matière d'intérêts (F)	Zinspolitik f	interest rate policy	—	politica degli interessi f	política de intereses f
politique financière (F)	Finanzpolitik f	financial policy	—	politica finanziaria f	política financiera f
politique financière (F)	Vermögenspolitik f	policy relating to capital formation	—	politica patrimoniale f	política de patrimonios f
politique fiscale (F)	Fiskalpolitik f	fiscal policy	—	politica fiscale f	política fiscal f
politique monétaire (F)	Geldpolitik f	monetary policy	—	politica monetaria f	política monetaria f
politique monétaire (F)	Währungspolitik f	monetary policy	—	politica monetaria f	política monetaria f
politique monétaire (F)	Valutapolitik f	currency policy	—	politica valutaria f	política de divisas f
póliza de negociación (Es)	Schlußnote f	broker's note	avis d'exécution m	fissato bollato m	—
polizza di carico all'ordine (I)	Orderkonnossement n	order bill of lading	connaissement à ordre m	—	conocimiento a la orden m
polizza di carico netta (I)	reines Konossement n	clean bill of lading	connaissement sans réserve m	—	conocimiento limpio m
polizza di carico parziale (I)	Teilkonnossement n	partial bill of lading	connaissement partiel m	—	recibo parcial m
polluter pays principle (E)	Verursacherprinzip n	—	principe du pollueur payeur m	principio di causalità m	principio contamina-dor-pagador m
polygone magique (F)	magisches Vieleck n	magic polygon	—	poligono magico m	polígono mágico m
pool de bénéfices (F)	Gewinnpoolung f	profit-pooling	—	raggruppamento degli utili m	pool de beneficios m
pool de beneficios (Es)	Gewinnpoolung f	profit-pooling	pool de bénéfices m	raggruppamento degli utili m	—
pool dell'oro (I)	Goldpool m	gold pool	pool d'or m	—	pool de oro m
pool de oro (Es)	Goldpool m	gold pool	pool d'or m	pool dell'oro m	—
pool de profit (F)	Gewinngemeinschaft f	profit pool	—	comunione degli utili f	comunidad de obten-ción de beneficios f
pool d'or (F)	Goldpool m	gold pool	—	pool dell'oro m	pool de oro m
pooling of interests (E)	Interessengemein-schaft f	—	communauté d'intérêts f	comunione d'interessi f	comunidad de intereses f
pool monétaire (F)	Währungspool m	currency pool	—	pool monetario m	pool monetario m
pool monetario (Es)	Währungspool m	currency pool	pool monétaire m	pool monetario m	—

	D	E	F	I	Es
pool monetario (I)	Währungspool *m*	currency pool	pool monétaire *m*	—	pool monetario *m*
popular share (E)	Publikumsaktie *f*	—	action populaire *f*	azione preferita dai risparmiatori *f*	acción al público *f*
por anticipado (Es)	Ex-ante	in prospect	ex ante	ex-ante	—
por aval (Es)	per aval	as guarantor of payment	bon pour aval	per buon fine	—
porcentaje de los gastos públicos (Es)	Staatsquote *f*	government expenditure rate	pourcentage des dépenses publiques *m*	percentuale della spesa pubblica *f*	—
porcentaje mínimo de reservas (Es)	Mindestreservesatz *m*	minimum reserve ratio	taux de réserve minimum *m*	tasso minimo di riserva *m*	—
por ciento (Es)	Prozent *n*	per cent	pour-cent *m*	percento *m*	—
portador de costes (Es)	Kostenträger *m*	cost unit	poste de production absorbant des coûts *m*	chi sostiene le spese	—
portafoglio sconto (I)	Geldmarktpapier *n*	money market securities	titres du marché monétaire *m/pl*	—	título del mercado monetario *m*
portafoglio stivato (I)	Stapelbestand *m*	stockpile	existences accumulées *f/pl*	—	existencias de títulos almacenadas *f/pl*
portefeuille (F)	Portfolio *n*	portfolio	—	portafoglio *m*	cartera *f*
porteur de parts (F)	Anteilseigner *m*	shareholder	—	azionista *m*	titular de acciones *m*
Portfeuillesteuerung (D)	—	portfolio controlling	régulation du portefeuille *f*	controllo di portafoglio *m*	control de las inversiones de cartera *m*
Portfolio (D)	—	portfolio	portefeuille *m*	portafoglio *m*	cartera *f*
portfolio (E)	Portfolio *n*	—	portefeuille *m*	portafoglio *m*	cartera *f*
Portfolio-Analyse (D)	—	portfolio analysis	analyse du portefeuille *f*	analisi di portafoglio *f*	análisis de cartera *m*
portfolio analysis (E)	Portfolio-Analyse *f*	—	analyse du portefeuille *f*	analisi di portafoglio *f*	análisis de cartera *m*
portfolio analysis (E)	Fundamentalanalyse *f*	—	analyse fondamentale *f*	analisi fondamentale *m*	análisis fundamental *m*
portfolio controlling (E)	Portfeuillesteuerung *f*	—	régulation du portefeuille *f*	controllo di portafoglio *m*	control de las inversiones de cartera *m*
portfolio investments (E)	indirekte Investition *f*	—	investissement indirect *m*	investimento indiretto *m*	inversión indirecta *f*
Portfolio-Management (D)	—	portfolio management	gestion du portefeuille *f*	gestione di portafoglio *f*	gestión de la cartera de valores *f*
portfolio management (E)	Depotverwaltung *f*	—	administration des titres déposés *f*	amministrazione di un deposito *f*	administración de depósito *f*
portfolio management (E)	Portfolio-Management *n*	—	gestion du portefeuille *f*	gestione di portafoglio *f*	gestión de la cartera de valores *f*
portfolio management (E)	Effektenverwaltung *f*	—	administration de titres *f*	amministrazione di titoli *f*	administración de valores *f*
Portfolio Selection (D)	—	portfolio selection	sélection du portefeuille *f*	selezione di portafoglio *f*	selección de cartera *f*
portfolio selection (E)	Portfolio Selection *f*	—	sélection du portefeuille *f*	selezione di portafoglio *f*	selección de cartera *f*
posesión permanente (Es)	Dauerbesitz *m*	permanent holding	possession permanente *f*	detenzione permanente *f*	—
posizione scoperta (I)	offene Position *f*	open position	poste ouvert *m*	—	partida abierta *f*
posizione verso l'estero (I)	Auslandsstatus *m*	foreign assets and liabilities	avoirs et obligations extérieurs *m/pl*	—	créditos activos y pasivos en el extranjero *m/pl*
possession permanente (F)	Dauerbesitz *m*	permanent holding	—	detenzione permanente *f*	posesión permanente *f*
postal giro (E)	Postscheck *m*	—	chèque postal *m*	assegno postale *m*	cheque postal *m*
postal giro centre (E)	Postscheckamt *n*	—	bureau de chèques postaux *m*	ufficio conto correnti postali *m*	oficina de cheques postales *f*
postal money order (E)	Postanweisung *f*	—	mandat-poste *m*	vaglia postale *m*	giro postal *m*
Postal Savings Bank (E)	Postbank *f*	—	banque postale *f*	servizio bancario postale *m*	banco postal *m*
Postanweisung (D)	—	postal money order	mandat-poste *m*	vaglia postale *m*	giro postal *m*
Postbank (D)	—	Postal Savings Bank	banque postale *f*	servizio bancario postale *m*	banco postal *m*

	D	E	F	I	Es
poste de l'actif (F)	Aktivposten *m*	credit item	—	attività *f*	asiento activo *m*
poste de port payé (F)	Frankoposten *m*	item free of charge	—	partita franco spese *f*	partida de porte pagado *f*
poste de production absorbant des coûts (F)	Kostenträger *m*	cost unit	—	chi sostiene le spese	portador de costes *m*
poste ouvert (F)	offene Position *f*	open position	—	posizione scoperta *f*	partida abierta *f*
poste pour mémoire (F)	Merkposten *m*	memorandum item	—	voce per memoria *f*	cifra nominal *f*
poste spécial (F)	Sonderposten *m*	separate item	—	partita speciale *f*	partida extraordinaria *f*
post-formation acquisition (E)	Nachgründung *f*		acquisitions commplémentaires de la société *f/pl*	costituzione successiva *f*	adquisición de instalaciones por una sociedad después de su fundación *f*
Postscheck (D)	—	postal giro	chèque postal *m*	assegno postale *m*	cheque postal *m*
Postscheckamt (D)	—	postal giro centre	bureau de chèques postaux *m*	ufficio conto correnti postali *m*	oficina de cheques postales *f*
potencial (Es)	Potential *n*	potential	potentiel *m*	potenziale *m*	—
potencial de producción (Es)	Produktionspotential *n*	production potential	potentiel de production *m*	potenzialità produttiva *f*	—
potencial financiero (Es)	Finanzkraft *f*	financial strength	capacité financière *f*	capacità finanziaria *f*	—
Potential (D)	—	potential	potentiel *m*	potenziale *m*	potencial *m*
potential (E)	Potential *n*	—	potentiel *m*	potenziale *m*	potencial *m*
potential cash (E)	potentielles Bargeld *n*	—	argent liquide potentiel *m*	contanti potenziali *m/pl*	dinero efectivo potencial *m*
potentiel (F)	Potential *n*	potontial	—	potenzlale *m*	potencial *m*
potentiel de production (F)	Produktionspotential *n*	production potential	—	potenzialità produttiva *f*	potencial de producción *m*
potentielles Bargeld (D)	—	potential cash	argent liquide potentiel *m*	contanti potenziali *m/pl*	dinero efectivo potencial *m*
potenziale (I)	Potential *n*	potential	potentiel *m*	—	potencial *m*
potenzialità produttiva (I)	Produktionspotential *n*	production potential	potentiel de production *m*	—	potencial de producción *m*
potere d'acquisto (I)	Kaufkraft *f*	purchasing power	pouvoir d'achat *m*	—	poder adquisitivo *m*
potere di mercato (I)	Marktmacht *f*	market power	pouvoir de marché *m*	—	poder de mercado *m*
pour-cent (F)	Prozent *n*	per cent	—	percento *m*	por ciento *m*
pour-cent accordé aux créanciers dans la masse (F)	Konkursquote *f*	dividend in bankruptcy	—	quota di riparto *f*	cuota del activo de la quiebra *f*
pourcentage des dépenses publiques (F)	Staatsquote *f*	government expenditure rate	—	percentuale della spesa pubblica *f*	porcentaje de los gastos públicos *m*
pouvoir commercial (F)	Handlungsvollmacht *f*	commercial power of attorney	—	mandato commerciale *m*	poder mercantil *m*
pouvoir d'achat (F)	Kaufkraft *f*	purchasing power	—	potere d'acquisto *m*	poder adquisitivo *m*
pouvoir de compte (F)	Kontovollmacht *f*	power to draw on an account	—	procura di disporre sul conto *f*	poder de cuenta *m*
pouvoir de marché (F)	Marktmacht *f*	market power	—	potere di mercato *m*	poder de mercado *m*
pouvoir général (F)	Generalvollmacht *f*	unlimited power	—	procura generale *f*	poder general *m*
pouvoir générique (F)	Gattungsvollmacht *f*	generic power	—	procura specifica *f*	poder de género *m*
pouvoir limité à un acte commercial déterminé (F)	Spezialvollmacht *f*	special power	—	procura speciale *f*	poder especial *m*
pouvoir principal (F)	Hauptvollmacht *f*	primary power	—	procura principale *f*	poder principal *m*
power of attorney (E)	Vollmacht *f*	—	plein pouvoir *m*	procura *f*	poder *m*
power to draw on an account (E)	Kontovollmacht *f*	—	pouvoir de compte *m*	procura di disporre sul conto *f*	poder de cuenta *m*
Präexport-Finanzierung (D)	—	pre-export financing	préfinancement de l'exportation *m*	prefinanziamento delle esportazioni *m*	financiación de preexportación *f*
Präferenz (D)	—	preference	préférence *f*	preferenza *f*	preferencia *f*
Prägung (D)	—	minting	frappe *f*	coniatura *f*	acuñación *f*

	D	E	F	I	Es
präjudizierter Wechsel (D)	—	void bill	traite protestée hors des délais *f*	cambiale pregiudicata *f*	letra prejudicada *f*
Prämie (D)	—	bonus	prime *f*	premio *m*	prima *f*
Prämienanleihe (D)	—	lottery loan	emprunt à primes *m*	prestito a premi *m*	empréstito con prima *m*
Prämienbrief (D)	—	option contract	contrat de marché à primes *m*	contratto a premio *m*	documento de una operación con prima *m*
Prämiendepot (D)	—	deposit for insurance payments	dépôt de titres à primes *m*	deposito di premio *m*	depósito de primas *m*
Prämiengeschäft (D)	—	option dealing	marché à prime *m*	operazione a premio *f*	operación a prima *f*
Prämiensparen (D)	—	bonus-aided saving	épargne à primes *f*	risparmio a premi *m*	ahorro con primas *m*
Prämiensparvertrag (D)	—	bonus savings contract	contrat d'épargne a primes *m*	contratto di risparmio a premi *m*	contrato de ahorro con primas *m*
Präsentationsfrist (D)	—	presentation period	délai de présentation *m*	termine di presentazione *m*	tiempo útil para la presentación *m*
Präsentationsklausel (D)	—	presentation clause	clause de présentation *f*	clausola di presentazione *f*	cláusula de presentación *f*
Präsenzbörse (D)	—	attendance stock exchange	bourse de présence *f*	borsa di presenza *f*	bolsa de presencia *f*
préavis (F)	Kündigung *f*	termination	—	preavviso *m*	preaviso *m*
preaviso (Es)	Kündigung *f*	termination	préavis *m*	preavviso *m*	—
preavviso (I)	Kündigung *f*	termination	préavis *m*	—	preaviso *m*
precautionary holding (E)	Vorsichtskasse *f*	—	fonds de réserve *m/pl*	domanda precauzionale di moneta *f*	existencias de precaución *f/pl*
precio (Es)	Preis *m*	price	prix *m*	prezzo *m*	—
precio de base (Es)	Basispreis *m*	basic price	prix de base *m*	prezzo base *m*	—
precio de compra (Es)	Kaufpreis *m*	purchase price	prix d'achat *m*	prezzo d'acquisto *m*	—
precio de coste (Es)	Einstandspreis *m*	cost price	prix coûtant *m*	prezzo d'acquisto *m*	—
precio de emisión (Es)	Ausgabepreis *m*	issuing price	prix d'émission *m*	prezzo d'emissione *m*	—
precio de equilibrio (Es)	Gleichgewichtspreis *m*	equilibrium price	prix équilibré *m*	prezzo di equilibrio *m*	—
precio del oro (Es)	Goldpreis *m*	price of gold	prix de l'or *m*	prezzo dell'oro *m*	—
precio de mercado (Es)	Marktpreis *m*	market price	prix du marché *m*	prezzo commerciale *m*	—
precio de opción (Es)	Optionspreis *m*	option price	prix d'option *m*	prezzo di opzione *m*	—
precio de suscripción (Es)	Bezugsrechtskurs *m*	subscription price	prix de souscription *m*	prezzo del diritto d'opzione *m*	—
precio de tasación (Es)	Taxkurs *m*	estimated quotation	cours d'estimation *m*	corso di stima *m*	—
precio estándar (Es)	fester Verrechnungspreis *m*	standard price	prix standard *m*	prezzo unico *m*	—
precio ficticio de acciones (Es)	Ausweichkurs *m*	fictitious security price	cours nominal *m*	quotazione evasiva *f*	—
precio fijo (Es)	Festwert *m*	fixed value	valeur fixe *f*	valore costante *m*	—
precio firme (Es)	Festpreis *m*	fixed price	prix fixe *m*	prezzo fisso *m*	—
precio indicativo (Es)	Richtpreis *m*	recommended retail price	prix indicatif *m*	prezzo indicativo *m*	—
precio máximo (Es)	Höchstpreis *m*	maximum price	prix plafond *m*	prezzo massimo *m*	—
precio medio (Es)	Durchschnittspreis *m*	average price	prix moyen *m*	prezzo medio *m*	—
precio mínimo (Es)	Mindestpreis *m*	minimum price	prix minimum *m*	prezzo minimo *m*	—
precio por cantidad (Es)	Mengenkurs *m*	direct exchange	cours de change indirect *m*	corso certo per incerto *m*	—
precio prohibitivo (Es)	Prohibitivpreis *m*	prohibitive price	prix prohibitif *m*	prezzo proibitivo *m*	—
precious metal (E)	Edelmetalle *n/pl*	—	métaux précieux *m/pl*	metalli pregiati *m/pl*	metales preciosos *m/pl*
preemption right (E)	Vorkaufsrecht *n*	—	droit de préemption *m*	diritto di prelazione *m*	derecho de preferencia *m*
preescussione (I)	Einrede der Vorausklage *f*	defence of lack of prosecution	exception de la discussion *f*	—	excepción de excusión *f*
pre-export financing (E)	Präexport-Finanzierung *f*	—	préfinancement de l'exportation *m*	prefinanziamento delle esportazioni *m*	financiación de preexportación *f*

	D	E	F	I	Es
preference (E)	Präferenz f	—	préférence f	preferenza f	preferencia f
préférence (F)	Präferenz f	preference	—	preferenza f	preferencia f
preference bond (E)	Vorzugsobligation f	—	obligation assortie de droits réservés f	obbligazione privilegiata f	obligación preferente f
preference share (E)	Vorzugsaktie f	—	action privilégiée f	azione privilegiata f	acción preferente f
preference shares (E)	Prioritätsaktien f/pl	—	actions de priorité f/pl	azioni privilegiate f/pl	acciones de preferencia f/pl
preferencia (Es)	Präferenz f	preference	préférence f	preferenza f	—
preferential creditor (E)	Massegläubiger m	—	créancier de la masse m	creditore della massa m	acreedor sin garantía m
preferential dividend (E)	Vorzugsdividende f	—	dividende prioritaire m	dividendo privilegiato m	dividendo preferente m
preferential price (E)	Vorzugskurs m	—	cours de faveur m	corso preferenziale m	curso preferencial m
preferential rate (E)	Ausnahmetarif m	—	tarif exceptionnel m	tariffa d'eccezione f	tarifa excepcional f
preferenza (I)	Präferenz f	preference	préférence f	—	preferencia f
préfinancement (F)	Vorfinanzierung f	prefinancing	—	prefinanziamento m	financiación anticipada f
préfinancement de l'exportation (F)	Präexport-Finanzierung f	pre-export financing	—	prefinanziamento delle esportazioni m	financiación de preexportación f
prefinancing (E)	Vorfinanzierung f	—	préfinancement m	prefinanziamento m	financiación anticipada f
prefinanziamento (I)	Vorfinanzierung f	prefinancing	préfinancement m	—	financiación anticipada f
prefinanziamento delle esportazioni (I)	Präexport-Finanzierung f	pre-export financing	préfinancement de l'exportation m	—	financiación de preexportación f
pregiudizio della capacità creditizia (I)	Kreditgefährdung f	endangering the credit of a person or a firm	atteinte au crédit f	—	amenaza del crédito f
Preis (D)	—	price	prix m	prezzo m	precio m
Preisangabe-verordnung (D)	—	price marking ordinance	ordonnance de marquage des prix f	regolamento di indicazione dei prezzi m	ordenanza para la indicación de precios f
Preisentwicklung (D)	—	trend in prices	évolution des prix f	andamento dei prezzi m	evolución de los precios f
Preisindex (D)	—	price index	indice des prix m	indice dei prezzi m	índice de precios m
Preiskontrolle (D)	—	price control	contrôle des prix m	controllo concordato dei prezzi m	control de precios m
Preis-Lohn-Spirale (D)	—	wage-price spiral	course des prix et des salaires f	spirale dei prezzi e dei salari f	espiral precio-salario f
Preisniveau (D)	—	price level	niveau des prix m	livello dei prezzi m	nivel de precios m
Preisnotierung (D)	—	prices quoted	cotation des prix f	quotazione dei prezzi f	cotización de precios f
Preissteigerung (D)	—	price increase	hausse des prix f	aumento dei prezzi m	subida de precios f
Preisstopp (D)	—	price stop	blocage des prix m	blocco dei prezzi m	congelación de precios f
prelevamento (I)	Entnahme f	withdrawal	prélèvement m	—	retirada de dinero f
prélèvement (F)	Entnahme f	withdrawal	—	prelevamento m	retirada de dinero f
prélèvements automatiques (F)	Lastschriftverkehr m	direct debiting transactions	—	addebiti m/pl	sistema de cargo en cuenta m
preliminary conditions (E)	Vorschaltkonditionen f/pl	—	conditions préliminaires f/pl	condizioni preliminari f/pl	condiciones preliminares f/pl
preliminary injunction (E)	Vorausklage f	—	bénéfice de discussion m	citazione preventiva f	excusión f
première acquisition (F)	Ersterwerb m	first acquisition	—	primo acquisto m	adquisición original f
première de change (F)	Prima Warenwechsel m	first of exchange	—	prima di cambio commerciale f	primera de cambio f
premio (I)	Prämie f	bonus	prime f	—	prima f
premio all'esportazione (I)	Exportprämie f	export premium	prime à l'exportation f	—	prima de exportación f
premio al risparmio (I)	Sparprämie f	savings premium	prime d'épargne f	—	prima de ahorro f

	D	E	F	I	Es
premio dello stellage (I)	Stellgeld n	premium for double option	prime de double option f	—	prima en operación de doble opción f
premio d'emissione (I)	Emissionsagio n	issue premium	prime d'émission f	—	prima de emisión f
premio d'investimento (I)	Investitionszulage f	investment grant	prime d'investissement f	—	prima a la inversión f
premio di rischio (I)	Risikoprämie f	risk premium	prime de risque f	—	prima de riesgo f
premi omaggio (I)	Spezialwerte m/pl	specialties	titres spéciaux m/pl	—	títulos especiales m/pl
Premium (D)	—	premium	prime f	premium m	prima f
premium (E)	Premium n	—	prime f	premium m	prima f
premium (I)	Premium n	premium	prime f	—	prima f
premium for double option (E)	Stellgeld n	—	prime de double option f	premio dello stellage m	prima en operación de doble opción f
premium payable on redemption (E)	Rückzahlungsagio n	—	prime de remboursement f	aggio di rimborso m	agio de reembolso m
prenda (Es)	Pfand n	pledge	nantissement m	pegno m	—
prenda mobiliaria (Es)	Faustpfand n	pawn	gage mobilier m	pegno mobile m	—
preneur d'un effet (F)	Wechselnehmer m	payee of a bill of exchange	—	beneficiario di una cambiale m	endosado m
prensa financiera (Es)	Finanzpresse f	financial press	presse financière f	stampa finanziaria f	—
prérogative de la frappe (F)	Münzhoheit f	monetary sovereignty	—	privilegio di battere moneta m	soberanía de acuñación f
prescripción (Es)	Verjährung f	limitation of actions	prescription f	prescrizione f	—
prescription (F)	Verjährung f	limitation of actions	—	prescrizione f	prescripción f
prescriptions concernant l'établissement du bilan (F)	Bilanzierungs-vorschriften f/pl	accounting regulations	—	norme per la redazione del bilancio f/pl	normas sobre balances f/pl
prescriptions d'investissement (F)	Anlagevorschriften f/pl	rules for investment of resources	—	disposizioni d'investimento f/pl	normas de inversión f/pl
prescrizione (I)	Verjährung f	limitation of actions	prescription f	—	prescripción f
prescrizione sui tassi (I)	Zinsbindung f	interest rate control	engagement sur le taux d'intérêt accordé m	—	vinculación al tipo de interés pactado m
presentation clause (E)	Präsentationsklausel f	—	clause de présentation f	clausola di presentazione f	cláusula de presentación f
présentation du bilan (F)	Bilanzgliederung f	format of the balance sheet	—	struttura del bilancio f	estructura del balance f
présentation d'un compte rendu (F)	Rechenschaftslegung f	rendering of account	—	resa dei conti f	rendición de cuentas f
presentation period (E)	Präsentationsfrist f	—	délai de présentation m	termine di presentazione m	tiempo útil para la presentación m
present value (E)	Gegenwartswert m	—	valeur actuelle f	valore attuale m	valor actual m
presión de beneficio (Es)	Gewinndruck m	profit squeeze	pression de bénéfice f	profit push m	—
présomption que les valeurs déposées sont administrées à titre fiduciaire (F)	Fremdvermutung f	presumption that securities deposited are fiduciary deposit	—	limitazione diritto di pegno e ritenzione su depositi di terzi f	suposición de depósito ajeno f
presse financière (F)	Finanzpresse f	financial press	—	stampa finanziaria f	prensa financiera f
pression de bénéfice (F)	Gewinndruck m	profit squeeze	—	profit push m	presión de beneficio f
pressione dei costi (I)	Kostendruck m	cost pressure	poids des coûts m	—	tensiones sobre los gastos f/pl
prestación (Es)	Leistung f	performance	rendement m	prestazione f	—
prestaciones que fomentan la formación de capital (Es)	vermögenswirksame Leistungen f/pl	capital forming payment	prestations primées f/pl	prestazioni con effetti patrimoniali f/pl	—
préstamo (Es)	Darlehen n	loan	prêt m	credito m	—
préstamo ahorro-vivienda (Es)	Bauspardarlehen n	loan granted for building purposes	prêt d'épargne-construction m	mutuo edilizio m	—
préstamo a título de pagaré (Es)	Schuldschein-darlehen n	promissory note bond	prêt en reconnais-sance de dette m	prestito obbligazionario m	—

	D	E	F	I	Es
préstamo concedido a socios (Es)	Gesellschafter-Darlehen *n*	proprietor's loan	prêt d'un associé à la société *m*	conferimento di un socio *m*	—
préstamo de ayuda (Es)	Bereitschaftskredit-abkommen *n*	stand-by arrangement	arrangement stand-by *m*	stand-by agreement *m*	—
préstamo de cobertura (Es)	Deckungsdarlehen *n*	coverage loan	prêt de couverture *m*	mutuo destinato a copertura *m*	—
préstamo de cooperación (Es)	Kooperations-darlehen *n*	cooperation loan	prêt de coopération *m*	prestito di cooperazione *m*	—
préstamo de crédito (Es)	Kreditleihe *f*	loan of credit	prêt de crédit *m*	credito di firma *m*	—
préstamo de fondación (Es)	Existenzaufbau-darlehen *n*	business set-up loan	prêt de premier établissement *m*	mutuo inizio attività imprenditoriale *m*	—
préstamo de opción (Es)	Optionsdarlehen *n*	optional loan	prêt avec droit d'option *m*	mutuo convertibile *m*	—
préstamo hipotecario (Es)	Darlehenshypothek *f*	mortgage as security for a loan	hypothèque de sûreté constituée pour garantir un prêt *f*	ipoteca su prestiti *f*	—
préstamo hipotecario (Es)	Pfandbriefdarlehen *n*	mortgage loan	prêt hypothécaire *m*	prestito su pegno *m*	—
préstamo participativo (Es)	Beteiligungsdarlehen *n*	loan with profit participation	prêt de participation *m*	partecipazione a forma di anticipo *f*	—
préstamo pequeño (Es)	Kleinkredit *m*	small personal loan	petit crédit *m*	piccolo credito *m*	—
préstamo pignoraticio especial (Es)	Sonderlombard *m*	special lombard facility	facilités spéciales de prêts sur nantissement *f/pl*	anticipazione su titoli straordinaria *f*	—
préstamo provisto de una cláusula de valor estable (Es)	Indexanleihe *f*	index-linked loan	emprunt indexé *m*	prestito indicizzato *m*	—
préstamo sobre mercancías (Es)	Warenbeleihung *f*	lending on goods	emprunt sur marchandises *m*	prestito su merci *m*	—
préstamo sobre prenda (Es)	Pfandleihe *f*	pawnbroking	prêt sur gage *m*	prestito su pegno *m*	—
préstamo sobre títulos (Es)	Wertpapierleihe *f*	lending on securities	prêt sur valeurs *m*	prestito per l'acquisto di titoli *m*	—
prestation de service (F)	Dienstleistung *f*	service	—	attività terziaria *f*	servicio *m*
prestation exécutée avant l'échéance (F)	Vorleistung *f*	advance performance	—	prestazione anticipata *f*	anticipo *m*
prestations en nature (F)	Sachbezüge *m/pl*	remuneration in kind	—	retribuzioni in natura *f/pl*	percepciones en especie *f/pl*
prestations primées (F)	vermögenswirksame Leistungen *f/pl*	capital forming payment	—	prestazioni con effetti patrimoniali *f/pl*	prestaciones que fomentan la formación de capital *f/pl*
prestations propres (F)	Eigenleistungen *f/pl*	own contributions	—	prestazioni proprie *f/pl*	producciones propias *f/pl*
prestazione (I)	Leistung *f*	performance	rendement *m*	—	prestación *f*
prestazione anticipata (I)	Vorleistung *f*	advance performance	prestation exécutée avant l'échéance *f*	—	anticipo *m*
prestazioni con effetti patrimoniali (I)	vermögenswirksame Leistungen *f/pl*	capital forming payment	prestations primées *f/pl*	—	prestaciones que fomentan la formación de capital *f/pl*
prestazioni proprie (I)	Eigenleistungen *f/pl*	own contributions	prestations propres *f/pl*	—	producciones propias *f/pl*
prestiti ammortizzabili (I)	Ratenanleihen *f/pl*	instalment loans	emprunt rembour-sable par annuités constantes *m*	—	empréstitos a plazos *m/pl*
prestiti a premi (I)	Lotterieanleihen *f/pl*	lottery bonds	emprunts à lots *m/pl*	—	empréstitos de lotería *m/pl*
prestiti consolidati (I)	Konsols *m/pl*	consoles	dettes consolidées *f/pl*	—	deudas consolidadas *f/pl*
prestiti convertibili (I)	Wandelanleihen *f/pl*	convertible bonds	obligation convertible *f*	—	empréstitos convertibles *m/pl*
prestiti in valuta estera (I)	Valuta-Anleihen *f/pl*	loan in foreign currency	emprunt émis en monnaie étrangère *m*	—	empréstitos en moneda extranjera *m/pl*

	D	E	F	I	Es
prestito a interesse scalare (I)	Staffelanleihe f	graduated-interest loan	emprunt à taux progressif m	—	empréstito escalonado m
prestito ammortizzabile (I)	Tilgungsanleihe f	redemption loan	emprunt d'amortissement m	—	empréstito amortizable m
prestito a premi (I)	Prämienanleihe f	lottery loan	emprunt à primes m	—	empréstito con prima m
prestito a tasso d'interesse variabile (I)	zinsvariable Anleihe f	loan at variable rates	emprunt d'un taux d'intérêt variable m	—	empréstito con un tipo de interés variable m
prestito a tre mesi (I)	Dreimonatsgeld n	three months' money	dépôts à trois mois m/pl	—	imposición a un plazo de 3 meses f
prestito collettivo (I)	Gemeinschafts-anleihe f	joint loan	prêt commun f	—	empréstito comunitario m
prestito comunale (I)	Kommunalanleihe f	local authorities loan	emprunt communal m	—	empréstito municipal m
prestito consolidato (I)	Fundierungsanleihe f	funding loan	emprunt consolidé m	—	empréstito consolidado m
prestito convertibile (I)	Optionsanleihe f	option bond	titre d'emprunt convertible m	—	bono opcional m
prestito di ammortamento (I)	Ablösungsanleihe f	redemption loan	emprunt de revalorisation m	—	empréstito de amortización m
prestito di cooperazione (I)	Kooperations-darlehen n	cooperation loan	prêt de coopération m	—	préstamo de cooperación m
prestito di guerra (I)	Kriegsanleihe f	war loan	emprunt de guerre m	—	empréstito de guerra m
prestito estero (I)	Auslandsanleihe f	foreign bond	emprunt extérieur m	—	empréstito exterior m
prestito forzato (I)	Zwangsanleihe f	compulsory loan	emprunt forcé m	—	empréstito forzoso m
prestito giornaliero (I)	Call-Geld n	call money	argent remboursable à vue m	—	dinero exigible a la vista m
prestito giornaliero (I)	Tagesgeld n	day-to-day money	argent au jour le jour m	—	dinero de día a día m
prestito indicizzato (I)	Sachwertanleihen f/pl	material value loans	emprunt de valeurs réelles m	—	empréstito en especie m
prestito indicizzato (I)	Indexanleihe f	index-linked loan	emprunt indexé m	—	préstamo provisto de una cláusula de valor estable m
prestito ipotecario a obbligazione fondiaria (I)	Naturadarlehen n	loan granted in form of a mortgage bond	prêt en nature m	—	empréstito en especie m
prestito in dollari (I)	Dollaranleihe f	dollar bond	emprunt en dollars m	—	empréstito en dólares m
prestito ipotecario a obbligazione fondiaria (I)	Naturalkredit m	credit granted in kind	crédit en nature m	—	crédito en especie m
prestito non ammortizzabile (I)	Zinsanleihe f	loan repayable in full at a due date	emprunt produisant des intérêts m	—	empréstito produ-ciendo interés m
prestito obbligazionario (I)	Schuldschein-darlehen n	promissory note bond	prêt en reconnais-sance de dette m	—	préstamo a título de pagaré m
prestito oro (I)	Goldanleihe f	loan on a gold basis	emprunt or m	—	empréstito con garantía-oro m
prestito per fine mese (I)	Ultimogeld n	last-day money	fonds remboursables à fin de mois m/pl	—	dinero a fin de mes m
prestito per l'acquisto di titoli (I)	Wertpapierleihe f	lending on securities	prêt sur valeurs m	—	préstamo sobre títulos m
prestito perpetuo (I)	ewige Anleihe f	perpetual loan	emprunt perpétuel m	—	empréstito perpétuo m
prestito perpetuo (I)	ewige Schuld f	perpetual debt	dette perpétuelle f	—	deuda perpetua f
prestito pubblico (I)	Bundesobligation f	Federal bonds	obligation fédérale f	—	obligación federal f
prestito rimborsabile in annualità (I)	Annuitätenanleihe f	annuity bond	emprunt amortis-sable par annuités m	—	obligación sin vencimiento f
prestito rimborsabile mediante per sorteggio (I)	Auslosungsanleihe f	lottery bond	emprunt amortis-sable par séries tirées au sort m	—	empréstito de sorteo m
prestito su merci (I)	Warenbeleihung f	lending on goods	emprunt sur marchandises m	—	préstamo sobre mercancías m
prestito su pegno (I)	Pfandleihe f	pawnbroking	prêt sur gage m	—	préstamo sobre prenda m

	D	E	F	I	Es
prestito su pegno (I)	Pfandbriefdarlehen *n*	mortgage loan	prêt hypothécaire *m*	—	préstamo hipotecario *m*
presumption that securities deposited are fiduciary deposit (E)	Fremdvermutung *f*	—	présomption que les valeurs déposées sont administrées à titre fiduciaire *f*	limitazione diritto di pegno e ritenzione su depositi di terzi *f*	suposición de depósito ajeno *f*
presupuesto (Es)	Budget *n*	budget	budget *m*	budget *m*	—
presupuesto (Es)	Haushalt *m*	budget	budget *m*	bilancio *m*	—
presupuesto (Es)	Haushaltsplan *m*	budget	budget *m*	bilancio preventivo *m*	—
presupuesto de gastos (Es)	Ausgabenplan *m*	plan of expenditure	état prévisionnel des dépenses *m*	piano di spesa *m*	—
presupuesto público (Es)	öffentlicher Haushalt *m*	public budget	budget public *m*	bilancio pubblico *m*	—
prêt (F)	Darlehen *n*	loan	—	credito *m*	préstamo *m*
prêt à la construction (F)	Baudarlehen *n*	building loan	—	mutuo edilizio *m*	crédito para la construcción *m*
prêt aux communes (F)	Kommunalkredit *m*	credit granted to a local authority	—	credito comunale *m*	crédito municipal *m*
prêt aux communes (F)	Kommunaldarlehen *n*	loan granted to a local authority	—	mutuo comunale *m*	empréstito municipal *m*
prêt avec droit d'option (F)	Optionsdarlehen *n*	optional loan	—	mutuo convertibile *m*	préstamo de opción *m*
prêt commun (F)	Gemeinschafts-anleihe *f*	joint loan	—	prestito collettivo *m*	empréstito comunitario *m*
prêt de coopération (F)	Kooperations-darlehen *n*	cooperation loan	—	prestito di cooperazione *m*	préstamo de cooperación *m*
prêt de oouverture (F)	Deckungsdarlehen *n*	coverage loan	—	mutuo destinato a copertura *m*	préstamo de cobertura *m*
prêt de crédit (F)	Kreditleihe *f*	loan of credit	—	credito di firma *m*	préstamo de crédito *m*
prêt d'épargne-construction (F)	Bauspardarlehen *n*	loan granted for building purposes	—	mutuo edilizio *m*	préstamo ahorro-vivienda *m*
prêt de participation (F)	Beteiligungs-darlehen *n*	loan with profit participation	—	partecipazione a forma di anticipo *f*	préstamo participativo *m*
prêt de premier établissement (F)	Existenzaufbau-darlehen *n*	business set-up loan	—	mutuo inizio attività imprenditoriale *m*	préstamo de fundación *m*
prêt d'un associé à la société (F)	Gesellschafter-Darlehen *n*	proprietor's loan	—	conferimento di un socio *m*	préstamo concedido a socios *m*
prêt en nature (F)	Naturadarlehen *n*	loan granted in form of a mortgage bond	—	prestito ipotecario a obbligazione fondiaria *m*	empréstito en especie *m*
prêt en reconnais-sance de dette (F)	Schuldschein-darlehen *n*	promissory note bond	—	prestito obbligazionario *m*	préstamo a título de pagaré *m*
pretensión de entrega (Es)	Herausgabe-anspruch *m*	claim for return	prétention à restitution *f*	diritto alla restituzione *m*	—
prétention à restitution (F)	Herausgabe-anspruch *m*	claim for return	—	diritto alla restituzione *m*	pretensión de entrega *f*
prêt hypothécaire (F)	Pfandbriefdarlehen *n*	mortgage loan	—	prestito su pegno *m*	préstamo hipotecario *m*
prêt sur gage (F)	Pfandleihe *f*	pawnbroking	—	prestito su pegno *m*	préstamo sobre prenda *m*
prêt sur titres (F)	Effektenlombard *m*	advances against securities	—	anticipazione su titoli *f*	adelanto sobre valores *m*
prêt sur valeurs (F)	Wertpapierleihe *f*	lending on securities	—	prestito per l'acquisto di titoli *m*	préstamo sobre títulos *m*
preuve de l'identité (F)	Identitätsnachweis *m*	proof of identity	—	certificato d'identità *m*	prueba de la identidad *f*
previsione (I)	Prognose *f*	forecast	perspective *f*	—	pronóstico *m*
previsión financiera (Es)	Finanzdecke *f*	available funds	fonds disponibles *m/pl*	disponibilità di mezzi liquidi *f*	—
prezzo (I)	Preis *m*	price	prix *m*	—	precio *m*
prezzo a pronti (I)	Kassakurs *m*	spot price	cours au comptant *m*	—	cambio al contado *m*
prezzo base (I)	Basispreis *m*	basic price	prix de base *m*	—	precio de base *m*
prezzo commerciale (I)	Marktpreis *m*	market price	prix du marché *m*	—	precio de mercado *m*

	D	E	F	I	Es
prezzo d'acquisto (I)	Kaufpreis *m*	purchase price	prix d'achat *m*	—	precio de compra *m*
prezzo del diritto d'opzione (I)	Bezugsrecht-notierung *f*	subscription price	cotation des droits de souscription *f*	—	cotización de derechos de suscripción *f*
prezzo del diritto d'opzione (I)	Bezugsrechtskurs *m*	subscription price	prix de souscription *m*	—	precio de suscripción *m*
prezzo dell'oro (I)	Goldpreis *m*	price of gold	prix de l'or *m*	—	precio del oro *m*
prezzo d'emissione (I)	Ausgabepreis *m*	issuing price	prix d'émission *m*	—	precio de emisión *m*
prezzo di bilancio (I)	Bilanzkurs *m*	book value	valeur comptable *f*	—	valor contable *m*
prezzo di costo (I)	Einstandspreis *m*	cost price	prix coûtant *m*	—	precio de coste *m*
prezzo di equilibrio (I)	Gleichgewichtspreis *m*	equilibrium price	prix équilibré *m*	—	precio de equilibrio *m*
prezzo di opzione (I)	Optionspreis *m*	option price	prix d'option *m*	—	precio de opción *m*
prezzo d'offerta (I)	Briefkurs *m*	ask(ed) price	cours de vente *m*	—	cotización ofrecida *f*
prezzo fisso (I)	Festpreis *m*	fixed price	prix fixe *m*	—	precio firme *m*
prezzo giorno di risposta premi (I)	Stellkurs *m*	put and call price	cours du stellage *m*	—	cotización de doble opción *f*
prezzo indicativo (I)	Richtpreis *m*	recommended retail price	prix indicatif *m*	—	precio indicativo *m*
prezzo massimo (I)	Höchstpreis *m*	maximum price	prix plafond *m*	—	precio máximo *m*
prezzo medio (I)	Durchschnittspreis *m*	average price	prix moyen *m*	—	precio medio *m*
prezzo minimo (I)	Mindestpreis *m*	minimum price	prix minimum *m*	—	precio mínimo *m*
prezzo proibitivo (I)	Prohibitivpreis *m*	prohibitive price	prix prohibitif *m*	—	precio prohibitivo *m*
prezzo teorico (I)	gemeiner Wert *m*	market value	valeur habituelle *f*	—	valor común *m*
prezzo unico (I)	fester Verrechnungspreis *m*	standard price	prix standard *m*	—	precio estándar *m*
price (E)	Preis *m*	—	prix *m*	prezzo *m*	precio *m*
price control (E)	Preiskontrolle *f*	—	contrôle des prix *m*	controllo concordato dei prezzi *m*	control de precios *m*
price-earning-rate (I)	Price-earning-ratio *f*	price-earnings ratio	relation cours-bénéfice *f*	—	relación cotización-beneficio *f*
Price-earning ratio (D)	—	price-earnings ratio	relation cours-bénéfice *f*	price-earning-rate *f*	relación cotización-beneficio *f*
price-earnings ratio (E)	Price-earning-ratio *f*	—	relation cours-bénéfice *f*	price-earning-rate *f*	relación cotización-beneficio *f*
price-earnings ratio (E)	Kurs-Gewinn-Verhältnis *n*	—	relation cours-bénéfice *f*	rapporto corso-profitto *m*	relación cotización-ganancia *f*
price expressed as a percentage of the nominal value (E)	Prozentkurs *m*	—	cours coté en pour-cent de la valeur nominale *m*	quotazione percentuale *f*	cotización en un tanto porciento del valor nominal *f*
price gain (E)	Kursgewinn *m*	—	plus-value sur les cours *f*	utile di borsa *m*	plusvalía de cotización *f*
price increase (E)	Preissteigerung *f*	—	hausse des prix *f*	aumento dei prezzi *m*	subida de precios *f*
price index (E)	Preisindex *m*	—	indice des prix *m*	indice dei prezzi *m*	índice de precios *m*
price intervention (E)	Kursintervention *f*	—	intervention en matière des cours *f*	intervento di sostegno quotazioni *m*	intervención cambiaria *f*
price level (E)	Preisniveau *n*	—	niveau des prix *m*	livello dei prezzi *m*	nivel de precios *m*
price limit (E)	Kurslimit *n*	—	cours limité *m*	limite di prezzo *m*	cambio limitado *m*
price marking ordinance (E)	Preisangabe-verordnung *f*	—	ordonnance de marquage des prix *f*	regolamento di indicazione dei prezzi *m*	ordenanza para la indicación de precios *f*
price nursing (E)	Kurspflege *f*	—	régulation des cours *f*	sostegno delle quotazioni *m*	compras de sostén *f/pl*
price of gold (E)	Goldpreis *m*	—	prix de l'or *m*	prezzo dell'oro *m*	precio del oro *m*
price pegging (E)	Kursstützung *f*	—	soutien des cours *m*	sostegno delle quotazioni *m*	apoyo de la cotización *m*
price per share (E)	Stückkurs *m*	—	cours coté au prix unitaire du titre *m*	corso unitario *m*	cotización por unidad *f*
price regulation (E)	Kursregulierung *f*	—	régulation des cours *f*	sostegno delle quotazioni *m*	regulación de los tipos de cambio *f*
price risk (E)	Kursrisiko *n*	—	risque de change *m*	rischio di quotazione *m*	riesgo del cambio *m*

	D	E	F	I	Es
price stop (E)	Preisstopp *m*	—	blocage des prix *m*	blocco dei prezzi *m*	congelación de precios *f*
prices quoted (E)	Preisnotierung *f*	—	cotation des prix *f*	quotazione dei prezzi *f*	cotización de precios *f*
price watering (E)	Kursverwässerung *f*	—	baisse du cours par émission d'action gratuites *f*	annacquamento della quotazione *m*	caída de cotización *f*
prima (Es)	Premium *n*	premium	prime *f*	premium *m*	—
prima (Es)	Prämie *f*	bonus	prime *f*	premio *m*	—
prima a la inversión (Es)	Investitionszulage *f*	investment grant	prime d'investissement *f*	premio d'investimento *m*	
prima de ahorro (Es)	Sparprämie *f*	savings premium	prime d'épargne *f*	premio al risparmio *m*	—
prima de ahorro del empleado (Es)	Arbeitnehmer-sparzulage *f*	employees' savings premium	prime d'épargne en faveur de l'employé *f*	indennità di risparmio dipendenti *f*	—
prima de emisión (Es)	Emissionsagio *n*	issue premium	prime d'émission *f*	premio d'emissione *m*	—
prima de riesgo (Es)	Risikoprämie *f*	risk premium	prime de risque *f*	premio di rischio *m*	—
prima di cambio commerciale (I)	Prima Warenwechsel *m*	first of exchange	première de change *f*	—	primera de cambio *f*
prima en operación de doble opción (Es)	Stellgeld *n*	premium for double option	prime de double option *f*	premio dello stellage *m*	—
Primanota (D)	—	journal	mémorial *m*	prima nota *f*	diario *m*
prima nota (I)	Primanota *f*	journal	mémorial *m*	—	diario *m*
Primapapiere (D)	—	prime papers	effets de tout premier ordre *m/pl*	carte commerciali di prim'ordine *f/pl*	valores de primera clase *m/pl*
prima quotazione (I)	Einführungskurs *m*	introductory price	cours d'ouverture *m*	—	cotización de apertura *f*
Primärmarkt (D)	—	primary market	marché primaire *m*	mercato primario *m*	mercado primario *m*
primary market (E)	Emissionsmarkt *m*	—	marché des valeurs émises *m*	mercato d'emissione *m*	mercado de emisión *m*
primary market (E)	Primärmarkt *m*	—	marché primaire *m*	mercato primario *m*	mercado primario *m*
primary power (E)	Hauptvollmacht *f*	—	pouvoir principal *m*	procura principale *f*	poder principal *m*
primas de exportación (Es)	Exportprämie *f*	export premium	prima à l'exportation *f*	premio all'esportazione *m*	—
Prima Warenwechsel (D)	—	first of exchange	première de change *f*	prima di cambio commerciale *f*	primera de cambio *f*
prime (F)	Premium *n*	premium	—	premium *m*	prima *f*
prime (F)	Prämie *f*	bonus	—	premio *m*	prima *f*
prime acceptance (E)	Privatdiskont *m*	—	escompte hors banque *m*	carta commerciale di prim'ordine *f*	descuento privado *m*
prime à l'exportation (F)	Exportprämie *f*	export premium	—	premio all'esportazione *m*	prima de exportación *f*
prime de double option (F)	Stellgeld *n*	premium for double option	—	premio dello stellage *m*	prima en operación de doble opción *f*
prime d'émission (F)	Emissionsagio *n*	issue premium	—	premio d'emissione *m*	prima de emisión *f*
prime d'épargne (F)	Sparprämie *f*	savings premium	—	premio al risparmio *m*	prima de ahorro *f*
prime d'épargne (F)	Sparzulage *f*	savings bonus	—	assegno integrativo di risparmio *m*	subvención de ahorro *f*
prime d'épargne en faveur de l'employée (F)	Arbeitnehmer-sparzulage *f*	employees' savings premium	—	indennità di risparmio dipendenti *f*	prima de ahorro del empleado *f*
prime de remboursement (F)	Rückzahlungsagio *n*	premium payable on redemption	—	aggio di rimborso *m*	agio de reembolso *m*
prime de risque (F)	Risikoprämie *f*	risk premium	—	premio di rischio *m*	prima de riesgo *f*
prime d'investissement (F)	Investitionszulage *f*	investment grant	—	premio d'investimento *m*	prima a la inversión *f*
prime name (E)	beste Adresse *f*	—	client de première catégorie *m*	società di prim'ordine *f*	cliente de primera categoría *f*
prime papers (E)	Primapapiere *n/pl*	—	effets de tout premier ordre *m/pl*	carte commerciali di prim'ordine *f/pl*	valores de primera clase *m/pl*
primera de cambio (Es)	Prima Warenwechsel *m*	first of exchange	première de change *f*	prima di cambio commerciale *f*	—

	D	E	F	I	Es
Prime Rate (D)	—	prime rate	taux d'intérêt préférentiel *m*	prime rate *m*	tasa de interés preferencial *f*
prime rate (E)	Prime Rate *f*	—	taux d'intérêt préférentiel *m*	prime rate *m*	tasa de interés preferencial *f*
prime rate (I)	Prime Rate *f*	prime rate	taux d'intérêt préférentiel *m*	—	tasa de interés preferencial *f*
primer establecimiento (Es)	Erstausstattung *f*	initial allowance set	dotation initiale *f*	dotazione iniziale *f*	—
primo acquisto (I)	Ersterwerb *m*	first acquisition	première acquisition *f*	—	adquisición original *f*
principe de la base monétaire (F)	Geldbasiskonzept *n*	monetary base principle	—	principio della base monetaria *m*	principio de la base monetaria *m*
principe de la satis- faction des besoins (F)	Bedarfsdeckungs- prinzip *n*	principle of satisfaction of needs	—	principio copertura fabbisogno *m*	principio de cobertura de demanda *m*
principe de la valeur minimale (F)	Niederstwertprinzip *n*	lowest value principle	—	principio del valore minimo *m*	principio del valor mínimo *m*
principe de reflux de Fullarton (F)	Fullartonsches Rückströmungs- prinzip *n*	Fullarton reflux principle	—	legge di riflusso di Fullarton *f*	principio de reflujo de Fullarton *m*
principe d'exclusion (F)	Ausschlußprinzip *n*	exclusion principle	—	principio d'esclusione *m*	principio de exclusión del precio *m*
principe d'imposition à la source (F)	Quellenprinzip *n*	source principle	—	principio della ritenuta alla fonte *m*	principio del grava- men en origen *m*
principe du pollueur payeur (F)	Verursacherprinzip *n*	polluter pays principle	—	principio di causalità *m*	principio contamina- dor-pagador *m*
principe du premier arrivé et le premier servi (F)	Windhundverfahren *n*	first come-first served principle	—	principio del primo offerente *m*	principio del primer venido, primer servido *m*
principes de capital propre (F)	Eigenkapital- grundsätze *m/pl*	principles on own capital	—	principi sul capitale proprio *m/pl*	principios sobre el capital propio *m/pl*
principes de financement (F)	Finanzierungs- grundsätze *m/pl*	financing principles	—	principi di finanziamento *m/pl*	normas de financiación *f/pl*
principes de gestion (F)	Führungsgrundsätze *m/pl*	managerial principles	—	principi amministrativi *m/pl*	principios de dirección *m/pl*
principi amministrativi (I)	Führungsgrundsätze *m/pl*	managerial principles	principes de gestion *m/pl*	—	principios de dirección *m/pl*
principi di finanziamento (I)	Finanzierungs- grundsätze *m/pl*	financing principles	principes de financement *m/pl*	—	normas de financiación *f/pl*
principio contamina- dor-pagador (Es)	Verursacherprinzip *n*	polluter pays principle	principe du pollueur payeur *m*	principio di causalità *m*	—
principio copertura fabbisogno (I)	Bedarfsdeckungs- prinzip *n*	principle of satis- faction of needs	principe de la satisfaction des besoins *m*	—	principio de cobertura de demanda *m*
principio de cobertura de demanda (Es)	Bedarfsdeckungs- prinzip *n*	principle of satis- faction of needs	principe de la satis- faction des besoins *m*	principio copertura fabbisogno *m*	—
principio de exclusión del precio (Es)	Ausschlußprinzip *n*	exclusion principle	principe d'exclusion *m*	principio d'esclusione *m*	—
principio d'esclusione (I)	Ausschlußprinzip *n*	exclusion principle	principe d'exclusion *m*	—	principio de exclusión del precio *m*
principio de la base monetaria (Es)	Geldbasiskonzept *n*	monetary base principle	principe de la base monétaire *m*	principio della base monetaria *m*	—
principio del grava- men en origen (Es)	Quellenprinzip *n*	source principle	principe d'imposition à la source *m*	principio della ritenuta alla fonte *m*	—
principio della base monetaria (I)	Geldbasiskonzept *n*	monetary base principle	principe de la base monétaire *m*	—	principio de la base monetaria *m*
principio della ritenuta alla fonte (I)	Quellenprinzip *n*	source principle	principe d'imposition à la source *m*	—	principio del grava- men en origen *m*
principio del primer venido, primer servido (Es)	Windhundverfahren *n*	first come-first served principle	principe du premier arrivé et le premier servi *m*	principio del primo offerente *m*	—
principio del primo offerente (I)	Windhundverfahren *n*	first come-first served principle	principe du premier arrivé et le premier servi *m*	—	principio del primer venido, primer servido *m*
principio del valore minimo (I)	Niederstwertprinzip *n*	lowest value principle	principe de la valeur minimale *m*	—	principio del valor mínimo *m*
principio del valor mínimo (Es)	Niederstwertprinzip *n*	lowest value principle	principe de la valeur minimale *m*	principio del valore minimo *m*	—

	D	E	F	I	Es
principio de reflujo de Fullarton (Es)	Fullartonsches Rückströmungsprinzip n	Fullarton reflux principle	principe de reflux de Fullarton m	legge di riflusso di Fullarton f	—
principio di causalità (I)	Verursacherprinzip n	polluter pays principle	principe du pollueur payeur m	—	principio contaminador-pagador m
principios de capital propio y de la liquidez de los institutos bancarios (Es)	Grundsätze über das Eigenkapital und die Liquidität der Kreditinstitute m/pl	principles of capital resources and the banks' liquid assets	principes de capital propre et de la liquidité des établissements de crédit m/pl	norme sul capitale proprio e la liquidità degli istituti di credito f/pl	—
principios de dirección (Es)	Führungsgrundsätze m/pl	managerial principles	principes de gestion m/pl	principi amministrativi m/pl	—
principios sobre el capital propio (Es)	Eigenkapitalgrundsätze m/pl	principles on own capital	principes de capital propre m/pl	principi sul capitale proprio m/pl	—
principi sul capitale proprio (I)	Eigenkapitalgrundsätze m/pl	principles on own capital	principes de capital propre m/pl	—	principios sobre el capital propio m/pl
principle of satisfaction of needs (E)	Bedarfsdeckungsprinzip n	—	principe de la satisfaction des besoins m	principio copertura fabbisogno m	principio de cobertura de demanda m
principles of capital resources and the banks' liquid assets (E)	Grundsätze über das Eigenkapital und die Liquidität der Kreditinstitute m/pl	—	principes de capital propre et de la liquidité des établissements de crédit m/pl	norme sul capitale proprio e la liquidità degli istituti di credito f/pl	principios de capital propio y de la liquidez de los institutos bancarios m/pl
principles on own capital (E)	Eigenkapitalgrundsätze m/pl	—	principes de capital propre m/pl	principi sul capitale proprio m/pl	principios sobre el capital propio m/pl
Prioritätsaktien (D)	—	preference shares	actions de priorité f/pl	azioni privilegiate f/pl	acciones de preferencia f/pl
Prioritätsobligationen (D)	—	priority bonds	obligation privilégié f	obbligazioni privilegiate f/pl	obligaciones preferentes f/pl
priority bonds (E)	Prioritätsobligationen f/pl	—	obligation privilégié f	obbligazioni privilegiate f/pl	obligaciones preferentes f/pl
prise en pension de valeurs mobilières (F)	Wertpapierpensionsgeschäft n	credit transaction under repurchase agreement of securities	—	operazione pronti contro termine f	operación de reporte de valores f
Privatdiskont (D)	—	prime acceptance	escompte hors banque m	carta commerciale di prim'ordine f	descuento privado m
private transaction (E)	Privatgeschäft n	—	affaire privée f	transazione tra privati f	operación privada f
Privatgeschäft (D)	—	private transaction	affaire privée f	transazione tra privati f	operación privada f
Privatkonto (D)	—	personal account	compte privé m	conto particolare m	cuenta privada f
privilegio di battere moneta (I)	Münzregal n	exclusive right of coinage	monopole de la frappe m	—	regalía de acuñación f
privilegio di battere moneta (I)	Münzhoheit f	monetary sovereignty	prérogative de la frappe f	—	soberanía de acuñación f
prix (F)	Preis m	price	—	prezzo m	precio m
prix coûtant (F)	Einstandspreis m	cost price	—	prezzo d'acquisto m	precio de coste m
prix d'achat (F)	Kaufpreis m	purchase price	—	prezzo d'acquisto m	precio de compra m
prix de base (F)	Basispreis m	basic price	—	prezzo base m	precio de base m
prix de l'or (F)	Goldpreis m	price of gold	—	prezzo dell'oro m	precio del oro m
prix d'émission (F)	Ausgabepreis m	issuing price	—	prezzo d'emissione m	precio de emisión m
prix des coupons (F)	Kuponkurs m	coupon price	—	quotazione della cedola f	cotización de un cupón f
prix de souscription (F)	Bezugsrechtskurs m	subscription price	—	prezzo del diritto d'opzione m	precio de suscripción m
prix de souscription (F)	Bezugskurs m	subscription price	—	corso d'acquisto m	cotización de emisión f
prix d'option (F)	Optionspreis m	option price	—	prezzo di opzione m	precio de opción m
prix du bail (F)	Pachtzins m	rent	—	canone d'affitto m	arrendamiento m
prix du marché (F)	Marktpreis m	market price	—	prezzo commerciale m	precio de mercado m
prix équilibré (F)	Gleichgewichtspreis m	equilibrium price	—	prezzo di equilibrio m	precio de equilibrio m
prix fixe (F)	Festpreis m	fixed price	—	prezzo fisso m	precio firme m

	D	E	F	I	Es
prix indicatif (F)	Richtpreis *m*	recommended retail price	—	prezzo indicativo *m*	precio indicativo *m*
prix minimum (F)	Mindestpreis *m*	minimum price	—	prezzo minimo *m*	precio mínimo *m*
prix moyen (F)	Durchschnittspreis *m*	average price	—	prezzo medio *m*	precio medio *m*
prix plafond (F)	Höchstpreis *m*	maximum price	—	prezzo massimo *m*	precio máximo *m*
prix prohibitif (F)	Prohibitivpreis *m*	prohibitive price	—	prezzo proibitivo *m*	precio prohibitivo *m*
prix standard (F)	fester Verrechnungspreis *m*	standard price	—	prezzo unico *m*	precio estándar *m*
procédé de la compensation (F)	Ausgleichsverfahren *n*	composition proceedings	—	metodo di compensazione *m*	procedimiento de compensación *m*
procedimento di addebito (I)	Abbuchungsverfahren *n*	direct debit procedure	système de prélèvement automatique *m*	—	procedimiento de adeudo en cuenta *m*
procedimento di emissione (I)	Emissionsverfahren *n*	issuing procedure	procédure d'émission *f*	—	procedimiento de emisión *m*
procedimento d'incasso bancario (I)	Bankeinzugsverfahren *n*	direct debiting	encaissements bancaires *m/pl*	—	cobranzas bancarias *f/pl*
procedimento d'incasso crediti (I)	Forderungseinzugsverfahren *n*	collection procedure	système de recouvrement de créances *m*	—	procedimiento de cobro de créditos *m*
procedimento d'incasso di fatture (I)	Rechnungseinzugsverfahren *n*	accounts collection method	système d'encaissement automatique de factures *m*	—	procedimiento de cobranza de pagos pendientes *m*
procedimento d'incasso di quietanza (I)	Quittungseinzugsverfahren *n*	receipt collection procedure	système d'encaissement de quittances *m*	—	procedimiento de cobro de recibos *m*
procedimento Hifo (I)	Hifo-Verfahren *n*	Hifo-procedure	méthode Hifo *f*	—	procedimiento hifo *m*
procedimiento conciliatorio (Es)	Vergleichsverfahren *n*	composition proceedings	procédure de conciliation *f*	procedura di concordato *f*	—
procedimiento de adeudo en cuenta (Es)	Abbuchungsverfahren *n*	direct debit procedure	système de prélèvement automatique *m*	procedimento di addebito *m*	—
procedimiento de cobranza de pagos pendientes (Es)	Rechnungseinzugsverfahren *n*	accounts collection method	système d'encaissement automatique de factures *m*	procedimento d'incasso di fatture *m*	—
procedimiento de cobro de créditos (Es)	Forderungseinzugsverfahren *n*	collection procedure	système de recouvrement de créances *m*	procedimento d'incasso crediti *m*	—
procedimiento de cobro de recibos (Es)	Quittungseinzugsverfahren *n*	receipt collection procedure	système d'encaissement de quittances *m*	procedimento d'incasso di quietanza *m*	—
procedimiento de cobro en cuenta (Es)	Lastschrifteinzugsverfahren *n*	direct debiting	système de prélèvement automatique *m*	incasso tramite addebitamento *m*	—
procedimiento de compensación (Es)	Ausgleichsverfahren *n*	composition proceedings	procédé de la compensation *m*	metodo di compensazione *m*	—
procedimiento de emisión (Es)	Emissionsverfahren *n*	issuing procedure	procédure d'émission *f*	procedimento di emissione *m*	—
procedimiento de quiebra (Es)	Konkursverfahren *n*	proceedings in bankruptcy	procédure de faillite *f*	procedura fallimentare *f*	—
procedimiento de selección (Es)	Auswahlverfahren *n*	selection procedure	méthode de sélection *f*	campionamento *m*	—
procedimiento hifo (Es)	Hifo-Verfahren *n*	Hifo-procedure	méthode Hifo *f*	procedimento Hifo *m*	—
procedimiento tributario (Es)	Besteuerungsverfahren *n*	taxation procedure	régime de taxation *m*	procedura d'imposizione *f*	
procedura di concordato (I)	Vergleichsverfahren *n*	composition proceedings	procédure de conciliation *f*	—	procedimiento conciliatorio *m*
procedura d'imposizione (I)	Besteuerungsverfahren *n*	taxation procedure	régime de taxation *m*	—	procedimiento tributario *m*
procedura fallimentare (I)	Konkursverfahren *n*	proceedings in bankruptcy	procédure de faillite *f*	—	procedimiento de quiebra *m*
procédure de conciliation (F)	Vergleichsverfahren *n*	composition proceedings	—	procedura di concordato *f*	procedimiento conciliatorio *m*
procédure de faillite (F)	Konkursverfahren *n*	proceedings in bankruptcy	—	procedura fallimentare *f*	procedimiento de quiebra *m*
procédure d'émission (F)	Emissionsverfahren *n*	issuing procedure	—	procedimento di emissione *m*	procedimiento de emisión *m*
procedure to draw up a balance sheet (E)	Bilanzierung *f*	—	établissement du bilan *m*	redazione del bilancio *f*	formación del balance *f*

	D	E	F	I	Es
proceedings in bankruptcy (E)	Konkursverfahren n	—	procédure de faillite f	procedura fallimentare f	procedimiento de quiebra m
proceso de cobro bancario (Es)	Einzugsermächtigungsverfahren n	collection procedure	système du mandat de prélèvement automatique m	autorizzazione alla riscossione f	—
procura (I)	Vollmacht f	power of attorney	plein pouvoir m	—	poder m
procura collettiva (I)	Gesamtvollmacht f	joint power of attorney	procuration collective f	—	poder solidario m
procura commerciale (I)	Prokura f	full power of attorney	procuration commerciale générale f	—	poder general m
procura di disporre sul conto (I)	Kontovollmacht f	power to draw on an account	pouvoir de compte m	—	poder de cuenta m
procura generale (I)	Generalvollmacht f	unlimited power	pouvoir général m	—	poder general m
procura principale (I)	Hauptvollmacht f	primary power	pouvoir principal m	—	poder principal m
procura rilasciata dal procuratore (I)	Untervollmacht f	delegated authority	sous-délégation f	—	subpoder m
procura specifica (I)	Gattungsvollmacht f	generic power	pouvoir générique m	—	poder de género m
procura speciale (I)	Spezialvollmacht f	special power	pouvoir limité à un acte commercial déterminé m	—	poder especial m
procuration collective (F)	Gesamtvollmacht f	joint power of attorney	—	procura collettiva f	poder solidario m
procuration commerciale générale (F)	Prokura f	full power of attorney	—	procura commerciale f	poder general m
procuratore commerciale (I)	Prokurist m	authorized clerk	fondé de procuration m	—	apoderado general m
procurement of capital (E)	Kapitalbeschaffung f	—	constitution de capital f	raccolta di capitali f	obtención de capital f
prodotto interno lordo (I)	Bruttoinlandsprodukt n	gross domestic product	produit intérieur brut m	—	producto interior bruto m
prodotto nazionale lordo (I)	Bruttosozialprodukt n	gross national product	produit national brut m	—	producto nacional bruto m
prodotto nazionale netto (I)	Nettosozialprodukt n	net national product	produit national net m	—	producto nacional neto m
prodotto sociale (I)	Sozialprodukt n	national product	produit national m	—	producto nacional m
producción de oro (Es)	Goldproduktion f	gold production	production d'or f	produzione dell'oro f	—
producciones propias (Es)	Eigenleistungen f/pl	own contributions	prestations propres f/pl	prestazioni proprie f/pl	—
produce exchange (E)	Produktenbörse f	—	bourse de marchandises f	borsa merci f	lonja f
produce trade (E)	Produktenhandel m	—	commerce des produits agricoles m	commercio delle derrate m	comercio de ultramarinos m
producteur (F)	Erzeuger m	manufacturer	—	produttore m	productor m
production d'or (F)	Goldproduktion f	gold production	—	produzione dell'oro f	producción de oro f
production potential (E)	Produktionspotential n	—	potentiel de production m	potenzialità produttiva f	potencial de producción m
productividad del capital (Es)	Kapitalproduktivität f	capital productivity	productivité du capital f	produttività del capitale f	—
productividad marginal (Es)	Grenzproduktivität f	marginal productivity	productivité marginale f	produttività marginale f	—
productividad por hora de trabajo (Es)	Arbeitsproduktivität f	productivity of labour	productivité du travail f	produttività del lavoro f	—
productivité du capital (F)	Kapitalproduktivität f	capital productivity	—	produttività del capitale f	productividad del capital f
productivité du travail (F)	Arbeitsproduktivität f	productivity of labour	—	produttività del lavoro f	productividad por hora de trabajo f
productivité marginale (F)	Grenzproduktivität f	marginal productivity	—	produttività marginale f	productividad marginal f
productivity of labour (E)	Arbeitsproduktivität f	—	productivité du travail f	produttività del lavoro f	productividad por hora de trabajo f
producto bruto (Es)	Bruttoertrag m	gross return	gain brut m	ricavo lordo m	—
producto de liquidación (Es)	Liquidationserlös m	remaining assets after liquidation	produit de la liquidation m	ricavato dalla liquidazione m	—

	D	E	F	I	Es
producto interior bruto (Es)	Bruttoinlands-produkt n	gross domestic product	produit intérieur brut m	prodotto interno lordo m	—
producto nacional (Es)	Sozialprodukt n	national product	produit national m	prodotto sociale m	—
producto nacional bruto (Es)	Bruttosozialprodukt n	gross national product	produit national brut m	prodotto nazionale lordo m	—
producto nacional neto (Es)	Nettosozialprodukt n	net national product	produit national net m	prodotto nazionale netto m	—
productor (Es)	Erzeuger m	manufacturer	producteur m	produttore m	—
produit de l' action (F)	Aktienrendite f	yield on shares	—	reddito effettivo di azioni m	rédito de las acciones m
produit de la liquidation (F)	Liquidationserlös m	remaining assets after liquidation	—	ricavato dalla liquidazione m	producto de liquidación m
produit du capital (F)	Kapitalertrag m	income from capital	—	reddito di capitale m	renta de capital f
produit global (F)	Gesamtertrag m	total proceeds	—	reddito totale m	renta total f
produit intérieur brut (F)	Bruttoinlandsprodukt n	gross domestic product	—	prodotto interno lordo m	producto interior bruto m
produit marginal (F)	Grenzerlös m	marginal earnings	—	ricavo marginale m	beneficio marginal m
produit national (F)	Sozialprodukt n	national product	—	prodotto sociale m	producto nacional m
produit national brut (F)	Bruttosozialprodukt n	gross national product	—	prodotto nazionale lordo m	producto nacional bruto m
produit national net (F)	Nettosozialprodukt n	net national product	—	prodotto nazionale netto m	producto nacional neto m
produit net d'exploitation (F)	bereinigter Gewinn m	actual profit	—	utile rettificato m	beneficio real m
Produktenbörse (D)	—	produce exchange	bourse de marchandises f	borsa merci f	lonja f
Produktenhandel (D)	—	produce trade	commerce des produits agricoles m	commercio delle derrate m	comercio de ultramarinos m
Produktions-potential (D)	—	production potential	potentiel de production m	potenzialità produttiva f	potencial de producción m
produttività del capitale (I)	Kapitalproduktivität f	capital productivity	productivité du capital f	—	productividad del capital f
produttività del lavoro (I)	Arbeitsproduktivität f	productivity of labour	productivité du travail m	—	productividad por hora de trabajo f
produttività marginale (I)	Grenzproduktivität f	marginal productivity	productivité marginale f	—	productividad marginal f
produttore (I)	Erzeuger m	manufacturer	producteur m	—	productor m
produzione dell'oro (I)	Goldproduktion f	gold production	production d'or f	—	producción de oro f
professional trader (E)	Berufshändler m	—	agent professionnel m	operatore professionale m	agente profesional m
profit and loss account (E)	Aufwands- und Ertragsrechnung f	—	compte de profits et pertes m	conto economico m	cuenta de beneficios y pérdidas f
profit and loss account (E)	Gewinn- und Verlustrechnung f	—	compte de pertes et de résultat m	conto profitti e perdite m	cuenta de pérdidas y ganancias f
profit and loss transfer agreement (E)	Ergebnisabführungs-vertrag m	—	accord de transfer des résultats m	contratto di trasferi-mento profitto m	acuerdo de pago del resultado m
profit carried forward (E)	Gewinnvortrag m	—	report du solde excédentaire m	avanzo utile m	arrastre de beneficios m
profit pool (E)	Gewinngemeinschaft f	—	pool de profit m	comunione degli utili f	comunidad de obten-ción de beneficios f
profit-pooling (E)	Gewinnpoolung f	—	pool de bénéfices m	raggruppamento degli utili m	pool de beneficios m
profit push (I)	Gewinndruck m	profit squeeze	pression de bénéfice f	—	presión de beneficio f
profits exceptionnels (F)	außerordentliche Erträge m/pl	extraordinary income	—	sopravvenienze attive f/pl	ingresos extraordinarios m/pl
profit-sharing (E)	Erfolgsbeteiligung f	—	participation aux résultats f	partecipazione agli utili f	participación en el beneficio f
profit squeeze (E)	Gewinndruck m	—	pression de bénéfice f	profit push m	presión de beneficio f
profits (E)	Ertrag m	—	rendement m	ricavo m	rendimiento m
progetto di bilancio (I)	Rohbilanz f	rough balance	bilan brut m	—	balance bruto m
Prognose (D)	—	forecast	perspective f	previsione f	pronóstico m

	D	E	F	I	Es
programmazione complessiva (I)	Gesamtplanung f	master planning	planification globale f	—	planificación global f
Programm-gesellschaft (D)	—	investment program	société de programmes d'investissement f	società con programmi d'investimento f	sociedad de programa de inversión f
Programmzertifikat (D)	—	certificate of participation in an investment program	certificat d'un programme d'investissement m	certificato di partecipazione ad un programma d'investimento m	certificado de participación en un programa de inversión m
progresión (Es)	Progression f	progression	progression f	progressione f	—
Progression (D)	—	progression	progression f	progressione f	progresión f
progression (E)	Progression f	—	progression f	progressione f	progresión f
progression (F)	Progression f	progression	—	progressione f	progresión f
progressione (I)	Progression f	progression	progression f	—	progresión f
prohibición (Es)	Verbot n	prohibition	prohibition f	divieto m	—
prohibición de acumulación (Es)	Kumulierungsverbot n	rule against accumulation	prohibition de cumuler f	divieto del cumulo delle agevolazioni m	—
prohibición de apelación al crédito (Es)	Kreditaufnahmeverbot n	prohibition of raising of credits	prohibition d'emprunt f	divieto di accensione di credito m	—
prohibición de cesión (Es)	Abtretungsverbot n	prohibition of assignment	défense de cession f	divieto di cessione m	—
prohibición de inversión (Es)	Investitionsverbot n	prohibition of investment	prohibition d'investissement f	divieto d'investimento m	—
prohibición de usura (Es)	Wucherverbot n	prohibition of usurious money-lending	défense d'usure f	proibizione di usura f	—
prohibited share issue (E)	verbotene Aktienausgabe f	—	émission d'actions interdite f	emissione vietata d'azioni f	emisión de acciones prohibida f
prohibition (E)	Verbot n	—	prohibition f	divieto m	prohibición f
prohibition (F)	Verbot n	prohibition	—	divieto m	prohibición f
prohibition de cumuler (F)	Kumulierungsverbot n	rule against accumulation	—	divieto del cumulo delle agevolazioni m	prohibición de acumulación f
prohibition d'emprunt (F)	Kreditaufnahmeverbot n	prohibition of raising of credits	—	divieto di accensione di credito m	prohibición de apelación al crédito f
prohibition d'investissement (F)	Investitionsverbot n	prohibition of investment	—	divieto d'investimento m	prohibición de inversión f
prohibition of assignment (E)	Abtretungsverbot n	—	défense de cession f	divieto di cessione m	prohibición de cesión f
prohibition of investment (E)	Investitionsverbot n	—	prohibition d'investissement f	divieto d'investimento m	prohibición de inversión f
prohibition of raising of credits (E)	Kreditaufnahmeverbot n	—	prohibition d'emprunt f	divieto di accensione di credito m	prohibición de apelación al crédito f
prohibition of usurious money-lending (E)	Wucherverbot n	—	défense d'usure f	proibizione di usura f	prohibición de usura f
prohibitive price (E)	Prohibitivpreis m	—	prix prohibitif m	prezzo proibitivo m	precio prohibitivo m
Prohibitivpreis (D)	—	prohibitive price	prix prohibitif m	prezzo proibitivo m	precio prohibitivo m
proibizione di usura (I)	Wucherverbot n	prohibition of usurious money-lending	défense d'usure f	—	prohibición de usura f
project financing (E)	Projektfinanzierung f	—	financement d'un projet m	finanziamento di un progetto m	financiación de un proyecto f
project write-off company (E)	Abschreibungsgesellschaft f	—	société d'amortissement f	società d'ammortamento f	sociedad de amortización f
Projektfinanzierung (D)	—	project financing	financement d'un projet m	finanziamento di un progetto m	financiación de un proyecto f
Projektgesellschaft (D)	—	joint-venture company	société d'opération conjointe f	società ad hoc f	sociedad de operación conjunta f
Prokura (D)	—	full power of attorney	procuration commerciale générale f	procura commerciale f	poder general m
Prokura-indossament (D)	—	per procuration endorsement	endossement de procuration m	girata "per procura" f	endoso por procuración m
Prokurist (D)	—	authorized clerc	fondé de procuration m	procuratore commerciale m	apoderado general m

	D	E	F	I	Es
prolongación (Es)	Prolongation f	prolongation	prolongation f	proroga f	—
Prolongation (D)	—	prolongation	prolongation f	proroga f	prolongación f
prolongation (E)	Prolongation f	—	prolongation f	proroga f	prolongación f
prolongation (F)	Prolongation f	prolongation	—	proroga f	prolongación f
prolongation business (E)	Prolongations-geschäft n	—	opération de report f	contratto di proroga m	operación de prolongación f
prolongation charge (E)	Belassungsgebühr f	—	frais de prolongation m/pl	tassa prolungamento ipoteche f	derechos de prolongación m/pl
prolongation de la traite (F)	Wechselprolongation f	renewal of a bill of exchange	—	proroga di cambiale f	renovación de la letra f
prolongation du délai de remboursement (F)	Tilgungsstreckung f	repayment extension	—	proroga di rimborso f	extensión del plazo de reintegración f
Prolongations-geschäft (D)	—	prolongation business	opération de report f	contratto di proroga m	operación de prolongación f
Prolongationssatz (D)	—	renewal rate	taux de report m	saggio di riporto m	tipo de prolongación m
promesa de deuda (Es)	Schuldversprechen n	promise to fulfil an obligation	reconnaissance fondant un rapport d'obligation f	promessa di debito f	—
promessa (I)	Promesse f	promissory note	engagement m	—	pagaré m
promessa di debito (I)	Schuldversprechen n	promise to fulfil an obligation	reconnaissance fondant un rapport d'obligation f	—	promesa de deuda f
Promesse (D)	—	promissory note	engagement m	promessa f	pagaré m
promise to fulfil an obligation (E)	Schuldversprechen n	—	reconnaissance fondant un rapport d'obligation f	promessa di debito f	promesa de deuda f
promissory note (E)	Promesse f	—	engagement m	promessa f	pagaré m
promissory note bond (E)	Schuldschein-darlehen n	—	prêt en reconnais-sance de dette m	prestito obbligazionario m	préstamo a título de pagaré m
promoción (Es)	Beförderung f	promotion	avancement m	promozione f	—
promoteur constructeur (F)	Bauträger m	builder	—	costruttore m	promotor de construcción m
promotion (E)	Beförderung f	—	avancement m	promozione f	promoción m
promotion de la construction de logements (F)	Wohnungsbau-Förderung f	promotion of housing construction	—	promozione edilizia residenziale f	fomento de la con-strucción de viviendas m
promotion de l'épargne (F)	Sparförderung f	savings promotion	—	promozione del risparmio f	fomento del ahorro m
promotion de l'épargne-construction (F)	Bausparförderung f	promotion of saving through building societies	—	promozione del risparmio edilizio f	fomento de ahorros para la construcción m
promotion de l'investissement (F)	Investitionsförderung f	investment promotion	—	promozione degli investimenti f	incentivos a la inversión m
promotion of housing construction (E)	Wohnungsbau-förderung f	—	promotion de la construction de logements f	promozione edilizia residenziale f	fomento de la construcción de viviendas m
promotion of saving through building societies (E)	Bausparförderung f	—	promotion de l'épargne-construction f	promozione del risparmio edilizio f	fomento de ahorros para la construcción m
promotor de construcción (Es)	Bauträger m	builder	promoteur constructeur m	costruttore m	—
promozione (I)	Beförderung f	promotion	avancement m	—	promoción m
promozione degli investimenti (I)	Investitionsförderung f	investment promotion	promotion de l'investissement f	—	incentivos a la inversión m
promozione del risparmio (I)	Sparförderung f	savings promotion	promotion de l'épargne f	—	fomento del ahorro m
promozione del risparmio edilizio (I)	Bausparförderung f	promotion of saving through building societies	promotion de l'épargne-construction f	—	fomento de ahorros para la construcción m
promozione edilizia residenziale (I)	Wohnungsbau-förderung f	promotion of housing construction	promotion de la construction de logements f	—	fomento de la con-strucción de viviendas m
pronóstico (Es)	Prognose f	forecast	perspective f	previsione f	—
proof of identity (E)	Legitimation f	—	légitimation f	legittimazione f	legitimación f

	D	E	F	I	Es
proof of identity (E)	Identitätsnachweis m	—	preuve de l'identité f	certificato d'identità m	prueba de la identidad f
propaganda al aire libre (Es)	Außenwerbung f	outdoor advertising	publicité extérieure f	pubblicità esterna f	—
property (E)	Eigentum n	—	propriété f	proprietà f	propiedad f
property (E)	Vermögen n	—	patrimoine m	patrimonio m	patrimonio m
property (E)	Gut n	—	bien m	bene m	bienes m
property income (E)	Besitzeinkommen n	—	revenu du patrimoine m	reddito del patrimonio m	renta de la propiedad f
property law securities (E)	Sachenrechtliche Wertpapiere n/pl	—	titres sur un droit réel m/pl	titoli di diritto reale m/pl	títulos jurídico-reales m/pl
property rights (E)	Eigentumsrechte n/pl	—	droits de propriété m/pl	diritti di proprietà n/pl	derechos de propiedad m/pl
propia retención (Es)	Selbstbeteiligung f	retention	participation personnelle à la couverture du risque f	franchigia f	—
propiedad (Es)	Eigentum n	property	propriété f	proprietà f	—
propiedad dispersa (Es)	Streubesitz m	diversified holdings	propriété disséminée f	capitali ripartiti m/pl	—
propiedad en mano común (Es)	Gesamthand-eigentum n	joint tenancy	propriété d'un associé d'une société par intérêts f	proprietà indivisa f	—
propiedad inmobiliaria (Es)	Betongold n	real estate property	patrimoine immobilier m	proprietà immobiliare f	—
propiedad por fracciones (Es)	Bruchteilseigentum n	ownership in fractional shares	propiété d'une quote-part indivise f	comproprietà di quota ideale f	—
proprietà (I)	Eigentum n	property	propriété f	—	propiedad f
proprietà immobiliare (I)	Betongold n	real estate property	patrimoine immobilier m	—	propiedad inmobiliaria f
proprietà indivisa (I)	Gesamthand-eigentum n	joint tenancy	propriété d'un associé d'une société par intérêts f	—	propiedad en mano común f
propriété (F)	Eigentum n	property	—	proprietà f	propiedad f
propriété disséminée (F)	Streubesitz m	diversified holdings	—	capitali ripartiti m/pl	propiedad dispersa f
propriété d'un associé d'une société par intérêts (F)	Gesamthand-eigentum n	joint tenancy	—	proprietà indivisa f	propiedad en mano común f
propriété d'une quote-part indivise (F)	Bruchteilseigentum n	ownership in fractional shares	—	comproprietà di quota ideale f	propiedad por fracciones f
proprietor's capital holding (E)	Geschäftsguthaben n	—	avoir commercial m	capitale da soci di una cooperativa m	saldo activo de la empresa m
proprietor's loan (E)	Gesellschafter--Darlehen m	—	prêt d'un associé à la société m	conferimento di un socio m	préstamo concedido a socios m
proroga (I)	Prolongation f	prolongation	prolongation f	—	prolongación f
proroga di cambiale (I)	Wechselprolongation f	renewal of a bill of exchange	prolongation de la traite f	—	renovación de la letra f
proroga di rimborso (I)	Tilgungsstreckung f	repayment extension	prolongation du délai de remboursement f	—	extensión del plazo de reintegración f
prorrateo (Es)	Quotation f	quotation	cotation f	quotazione f	—
prorrogar (Es)	stillhalten	to sell an option	vendre une option	concedere una moratoria	—
pro soluto (I)	an Zahlungs Statt	in lieu of payment	à titre de payement	—	a título de pago
prospectus d'émission (F)	Prospekt bei Emissionen m	underwriting prospectus	—	prospetto d'emissione m	manifiesto de emisión m
Prospekt bei Emissionen (D)	—	underwriting prospectus	prospectus d'émission m	prospetto d'emissione m	manifiesto de emisión m
Prospektprüfung (D)	—	audit of prospectus	vérification du prospectus f	controllo del prospetto m	examinación del prospecto f
prospetto d'emissione (I)	Prospekt bei Emissionen m	underwriting prospectus	prospectus d'émission m	—	manifiesto de emisión m
protección de acreedores (Es)	Gläubigerschutz m	protection of creditors	garantie des créanciers f	protezione dei creditori f	—

	D	E	F	I	Es
protección del capital (Es)	Kapitalschutz *m*	capital protection	protection de capital *f*	tutela dei capitali *f*	—
protección del crédito (Es)	Kreditschutz *m*	protection of credit	protection du crédit *f*	tutela del credito *f*	—
protección del inversor (Es)	Investitionsschutz *m*	protection of investment	protection de l'investisseur *f*	tutela degli investimenti *f*	—
protección del inversor (Es)	Anlegerschutz *m*	protection for the investor	protection de l'investisseur *f*	tutela degli investitori *f*	—
proteccionismo (Es)	Protektionismus *m*	protectionism	protectionnisme *m*	protezionismo *m*	—
protection de capital (F)	Kapitalschutz *m*	capital protection	—	tutela dei capitali *f*	protección del capital *f*
protection de l'investisseur (F)	Anlegerschutz *m*	protection for the investor	—	tutela degli investitori *f*	protección del inversor *f*
protection de l'investisseur (F)	Investitionsschutz *m*	protection of investment	—	tutela degli investimenti *f*	protección del inversor *f*
protection du crédit (F)	Kreditschutz *m*	protection of credit	—	tutela del credito *f*	protección del crédito *f*
protection for the investor (E)	Anlegerschutz *m*	—	protection de l'investisseur *f*	tutela degli investitori *f*	protección del inversor *f*
protectionism (E)	Protektionismus *m*	—	protectionnisme *m*	protezionismo *m*	proteccionismo *m*
protectionnisme (F)	Protektionismus *m*	protectionism	—	protezionismo *m*	proteccionismo *m*
protection of credit (E)	Kreditschutz *m*	—	protection du crédit *f*	tutela del credito *f*	protección del crédito *f*
protection of creditors (E)	Gläubigerschutz *m*	—	garantie des créanciers *f*	protezione dei creditori *f*	protección de acreedores *f*
protection of investment (E)	Investitionsschutz *m*	—	protection de l'investisseur *f*	tutela degli investimenti *f*	protección del inversor *f*
Protektionismus (D)	—	protectionism	protectionnisme *m*	protezionismo *m*	proteccionismo *m*
Protest (D)	—	protest	protêt *m*	protesto *m*	protesta *f*
protest (E)	Protest *m*	—	protêt *m*	protesto *m*	protesta *f*
protest (E)	Wechselprotest *m*	—	protêt de traite *m*	protesto cambiario *m*	protesto de una letra *m*
protesta (Es)	Protest *m*	protest	protêt *m*	protesto *m*	—
protesta de incumplimiento (Es)	Ausfolgungsprotest *m*	protest for non-delivery	acte de protêt pour non-restitution d'effet *m*	protesto mancata consegna cambiale *m*	—
protested bill (E)	Protestwechsel *m*	—	traite protestée *f*	cambiale protestata *f*	letra protestada *f*
protest for non-delivery (E)	Ausfolgungsprotest *m*	—	acte de protêt pour non-restitution d'effet *m*	protesto mancata consegna cambiale *m*	protesta de incumplimiento *f*
protesto de una letra (Es)	Wechselprotest *m*	protest	protêt de traite *m*	protesto cambiario *m*	—
Protestliste (D)	—	list of firms whose bills and notes have been protested	liste des protêts *f*	elenco dei protesti *m*	lista de protesta *f*
protesto (I)	Protest *m*	protest	protêt *m*	—	protesta *f*
protesto cambiario (I)	Wechselprotest *m*	protest	protêt de traite *m*	—	protesto de una letra *m*
protesto de declaración (Es)	Deklarationsprotest *m*	declaratory protest	protêt d'une traite dont le porteur et l'intervenant sont identiques *m*	protesto per identità del portatore della cambiale col protestato *m*	—
protesto mancata consegna cambiale (I)	Ausfolgungsprotest *m*	protest for non-delivery	acte de protêt pour non-restitution d'effet *m*	—	protesta de incumplimiento *f*
protesto per identità del portatore della cambiale col protestato (I)	Deklarationsprotest *m*	declaratory protest	protêt d'une traite dont le porteur et l'intervenant sont identiques *m*	—	protesto de declaración *m*
Protestwechsel (D)	—	protested bill	traite protestée *f*	cambiale protestata *f*	letra protestada *f*
Protestzeit (D)	—	period of protest	heures de présentation du protêt *f/pl*	termine presentazione di protesto *m*	período de protesta *m*
protêt (F)	Protest *m*	protest	—	protesto *m*	protesta *f*
protêt de traite (F)	Wechselprotest *m*	protest	—	protesto cambiario *m*	protesto de una letra *m*

	D	E	F	I	Es
protêt d'une traite dont le porteur et l'intervenant sont identiques (F)	Deklarationsprotest *m*	declaratory protest	—	protesto per identità del portatore della cambiale col protestato *m*	protesto de declaración *m*
protezione dei creditori (I)	Gläubigerschutz *m*	protection of creditors	garantie des créanciers *f*	—	protección de acreedores *f*
protezionismo (I)	Protektionismus *m*	protectionism	protectionnisme *m*	—	proteccionismo *m*
prova (I)	Beweismittel *n*	evidence	moyen de preuve *m*	—	medio probatorio *m*
provento d'interessi (I)	Zinsertrag *m*	income from interests	intérêts perçus *m/pl*	—	rédito *m*
Provinzbank (D)	—	country bank	banque provinciale *f*	banca provinciale *f*	banco provincial *m*
Provinzbörse (D)	—	regional stock exchange	bourse provinciale *f*	borsa provinciale *f*	bolsa provincial *f*
Provision (D)	—	commission	commission *f*	commissione *f*	comisión *f*
provision (E)	Ausnahmeregelung *f*	—	mesure dérogatoire *f*	regolamento d'eccezione *m*	disposición excepcional *f*
provisional receipt (E)	Zwischenschein *m*	—	certificat provisoire *m*	certificato provvisorio *m*	certificado de acción *m*
provisionsfreies Konto (D)	—	commission-free account	compte de créditeur *m*	conto franco di provvigione *m*	cuenta sin comisión *f*
provisionspflichtiges Konto (D)	—	commission-bearing account	compte de débiteur *m*	conto soggetto a provvigione *m*	cuenta sujeto al pago de una comisión *f*
provisions pour les retraites du personnel (F)	Pensionsrückstellungen *f/pl*	pension reserve	—	fondo pensioni *m*	fondo de retiros *f*
provisions pour pertes inhérentes aux fluctuations saisonnières (F)	Saison-Reserven *f/pl*	seasonal reserves	—	fondi di compensazione *m/pl*	reservas estacionales *f/pl*
provvigione bancaria (I)	Bankierbonifikation *f*	placing commission	commission de placement *f*	—	comisión de mediación bancaria *f*
provvigione d'avallo (I)	Aval-Provision *f*	commission on bank guarantee	commission pour aval *f*	—	comisión por aval *f*
provvigione di credito (I)	Kreditprovision *f*	credit commission	frais de commission d'ouverture de crédit *m/pl*	—	comisión de apertura de crédito *f*
provvigione di gestione (I)	Führungsprovision *f*	managers commission	commission d'apériteur *f*	—	comisión de alta dirección *f*
provvigione d'incasso (I)	Inkassoprovision *f*	collection commission	commission d'encaissement *f*	—	comisión *f*
provvigione d'incasso (I)	Inkasso-Kommission *f*	collecting commission	encaissement pour ordre d'autrui *m*	—	comisión de cobranza *f*
provvigione di rigresso (I)	Rückscheckprovision *f*	commission on returned cheque	commission de chèque retourné *f*	—	comisión de cheque devuelto *f*
provvigione di sconto (I)	Diskontprovision *f*	discount commission	commission d'escompte *f*	—	comisión de descuento *f*
provvigione di scoperta (I)	Überziehungsprovision *f*	overdraft commission	commission de découvert *f*	—	comisión de giro en descubierto *f*
provvigione sul fatturato (I)	Umsatzprovision *f*	commission on turnover	commission sur le chiffre d'affaires *f*	—	comisión sobre la cifra de facturación *f*
proxy for disposal (E)	Ermächtigung zur Verfügung *f*	—	autorisation de disposer *f*	autorizzazione di disporre dei titoli depositati *f*	autorización a disponer *f*
Prozent (D)	—	per cent	pour-cent *m*	percento *m*	por ciento *m*
Prozentkurs (D)	—	price expressed as a percentage of the nominal value	cours coté en pour-cent de la valeur nominale *m*	quotazione percentuale *f*	cotización en un tanto porciento del valor nominal *f*
prueba de la identidad (Es)	Identitätsnachweis *m*	proof of identity	preuve de l'identité *f*	certificato d'identità *m*	—
Prüfung (D)	—	examination	vérification *f*	controllo *m*	revisión *f*
Prüfungsbericht (D)	—	audit report	compte rendu de vérification *f*	relazione d'ispezione *f*	informe de auditoría *m*
Prüfungskommission (D)	—	examining commission	commission de contrôle *f*	giuria *f*	comisión de revisión de cuentas *f*
Prüfungsverband (D)	—	auditing association	association de vérification des comptes *f*	associazione di controllo *f*	sociedad de revisión *f*

	D	E	F	I	Es
Prüfungsvermerk (D)	—	certificate of audit	mention de vérification f	annotazione di controllo f	certificado de revisión m
pubblicazione (I)	Veröffentlichung f	publication	publication f	—	publicación f
pubblicazione (I)	Ausweisung f	statement	publication f	—	registrar un importe m
pubblicazione obligatoria dei bilanci bancari (I)	Bankpublizität f	banks' duty to publish	publication obligatoire des bilans bancaires f	—	obligación de publicidad bancaria f
pubblicità (I)	Publizität f	publicity	publicité f	—	publicidad f
pubblicità esterna (I)	Außenwerbung f	outdoor advertising	publicité extérieure f	—	propaganda al aire libre f
publicación (Es)	Bekanntmachung f	notification	publication f	annuncio m	—
publicación (Es)	Veröffentlichung f	publication	publication f	pubblicazione f	—
publicación obligatoria (Es)	Veröffentlichungs-pflicht f	statutory public disclosure	obligation de publier f	obbligo di pubblicazione m	—
publication (E)	Veröffentlichung f	—	publication f	pubblicazione f	publicación f
publication (F)	Veröffentlichung f	publication	—	pubblicazione f	publicación f
publication (F)	Ausweisung f	statement	—	pubblicazione f	registrar un importe m
publication (F)	Bekanntmachung f	notification	—	annuncio m	publicación f
publication obligatoire des bilans bancaires (F)	Bankpublizität f	banks' duty to publish	—	pubblicazione obbligatoria dei bilanci bancari f	obligación de publicidad bancaria f
public authentication (E)	öffentliche Beurkundung f	—	authentification f	autenticazione pubblica f	formalización en escritura pública f
public bank (E)	öffentliche Bank f	—	banque publique f	banca di diritto pubblico f	banco público m
public bonds (E)	Staatsanleihen f/pl	—	emprunts d'Etat m/pl	titoli di Stato m/pl	bonos del Estado m/pl
public budget (E)	öffentlicher Haushalt m	—	budget public m	bilancio pubblico m	presupuesto público m
public debt (E)	öffentliche Schuld f	—	dette publique f	debito pubblico m	deuda pública f
public finance (E)	Finanzwissenschaft f	—	science financière f	scienza delle finanze f	ciencia financiera f
public fund (E)	Publikumsfonds m	—	fonds de placement ouvert au public m	fondo aperto al pubblico m	fondos ofrecidos al público m/pl
publicidad (Es)	Publizität f	publicity	publicité f	pubblicità f	—
publicité (F)	Publizität f	publicity	—	pubblicità f	publicidad f
publicité extérieure (F)	Außenwerbung f	outdoor advertising	—	pubblicità esterna f	propaganda al aire libre f
publicity (E)	Publizität f	—	publicité f	pubblicità f	publicidad f
public revenue (E)	Staatseinnahmen f/pl	—	recettes de l'Etat f/pl	entrate pubbliche f/pl	ingresos públicos m/pl
public securities (E)	Staatspapiere n/pl	—	effets publics m/pl	titoli di Stato m/pl	papeles del Estado m/pl
public spending (E)	Staatsausgaben f/pl	—	dépenses publiques f/pl	spese pubbliche f/pl	gastos públicos m/pl
public supervision of banking (E)	Bankenaufsicht f	—	contrôle des banques m	controllo sulle banche m	superintendencia bancaria f
Publikationspflicht (D)	—	compulsory disclosure	obligation de publication f	obbligo di pubblicazione m	obligación de publicación f
Publikumsaktie (D)	—	popular share	action populaire f	azione preferita dai risparmiatori f	acción al público f
Publikumsfonds (D)	—	public fund	fonds de placement ouvert au public m	fondo aperto al pubblico m	fondos ofrecidos al público m/pl
Publizität (D)	—	publicity	publicité f	pubblicità f	publicidad f
punti d'intervento (I)	Interventionspunkte m/pl	intervention point	points d'intervention m/pl	—	puntos de intervención m/pl
punto dell'oro (I)	Goldpunkt m	gold point	point d'or m	—	punto de oro m
punto de oro (Es)	Goldpunkt m	gold point	point d'or m	punto dell'oro m	—
puntos de intervención (Es)	Interventionspunkte m/pl	intervention point	points d'intervention m/pl	punti d'intervento m/pl	—
purchase (E)	Kauf m	—	achat m	acquisto m	compra f
purchase of accounts receivable (E)	Forderungskauf m	—	vente d'une créance f	acquisizione di crediti f	compra de créditos f/pl

	D	E	F	I	Es
purchase of foreign exchange for later sale (E)	Devisenpensions-geschäft *n*	—	opération de mise en pension de devises *f*	sconto di valuta in pensione *m*	operación de reporte en divisas *f*
purchase of securities (E)	Effektenkauf *m*	—	achat de titres *m*	acquisto di titoli *m*	compra de valores *f*
purchase price (E)	Kaufpreis *m*	—	prix d'achat *m*	prezzo d'acquisto *m*	precio de compra *m*
purchase right (E)	Ankaufsrecht *n*	—	droit d'achat *m*	opzione *f*	derecho de compra *m*
purchasing cheque (E)	Kaufscheck *m*	—	chèque d'achat *m*	assegno garantito per acquisti *m*	cheque de compra *m*
purchasing credit (E)	Kaufkredit *m*	—	crédit d'achat *m*	credito finanziamento acquisti *m*	crédito de compra *m*
purchasing power (E)	Kaufkraft *f*	—	pouvoir d'achat *m*	potere d'acquisto *m*	poder adquisitivo *m*
purchasing power parity (E)	Kaufkraftparität *f*	—	parité du pouvoir d'achat *f*	parità del potere d'acquisto *f*	paridad adquisitiva *f*
put and call (E)	Stellgeschäft *n*	—	opération de stellage *f*	contratto stellage *m*	operación de doble opción *f*
put and call price (E)	Stellkurs *m*	—	cours du stellage *m*	prezzo giorno di risposta premi *m*	cotización de doble opción *f*
quadro commercio estero (I)	Außenhandels-rahmen *m*	foreign trade structure	structure du commerce extérieur *f*	—	estructura del comercio exterior *f*
quadro dei conti (I)	Kontenrahmen *m*	standard form of accounts	cadre comptable *m*	—	sistema de cuentas *m*
qualified majority (E)	qualifizierte Mehrheit *f*	—	majorité qualifiée *f*	maggioranza qualificata *f*	mayoría calificada *f*
qualifizierte Gründung (D)	—	formation involving subscription in kind	fondation par apports en nature *f*	costituzione qualificata *f*	fundación calificada *f*
qualifizierte Legitimations-papiere (D)	—	eligible title-evidencing instrument	titre établi à personne dénommée ou à tout autre porteur *m*	titoli al portatore qualificati *m/pl*	títulos de legitimación calificados *m/pl*
qualifizierte Mehrheit (D)	—	qualified majority	majorité qualifiée *f*	maggioranza qualificata *f*	mayoría calificada *f*
qualifizierte Minderheit (D)	—	right-conferring minority	minorité qualifiée *f*	minoranza qualificata *f*	minoría calificada *f*
qualité fongible d'un bien (F)	Fungilbilität *f*	fungibility	—	fungibilità *f*	fungibilidad *f*
Quantitäts-gleichung (D)	—	quantity equation	équation quantitative *f*	equazione degli scambi *f*	ecuación cuantitativa *f*
Quantitäts-notierung (D)	—	fixed exchange	certain *m*	quotazione del certo *f*	cotización cuantitativa *f*
Quantitätstheorie (D)	—	quantity theory	théorie quantitative *f*	teoria quantitativa *f*	teoría cuantitativa *f*
quantité de monnaie en circulation (F)	Geldmenge *f*	money stock	—	base monetaria *f*	masa monetaria *f*
quantity equation (E)	Quantitätsgleichung *f*	—	équation quantitative *f*	equazione degli scambi *f*	ecuación cuantitativa *f*
quantity tender (E)	Mengentender *m*	—	offre d'emprunts par quantités pour la régulation monétaire *f*	asta non competitiva *f*	subasta de préstamos de regulación monetaria por cantidades *f*
quantity theory (E)	Quantitätstheorie *f*	—	théorie quantitative *f*	teoria quantitativa *f*	teoría cuantitativa *f*
Quartalsbericht (D)	—	quarterly report	rapport trimestriel *m*	relazione trimestrale *f*	informe trimestral *m*
quarter days (E)	Zinstage *m/pl*	—	nombre de jours portant intérêt *m*	giorni per il calcolo interessi *m*	número de días devengado intereses *m*
quarterly report (E)	Quartalsbericht *m*	—	rapport trimestriel *m*	relazione trimestrale *f*	informe trimestral *m*
quasi-argent (F)	Quasigeld *n*	quasi money	—	quasi moneta *f*	activo casi líquido *m*
quasi-equity capital (E)	verdecktes Stammkapital *n*	—	capital social occulte *m*	conferimento di un socio *m*	capital social oculto *m*
Quasigeld (D)	—	quasi money	quasi-argent *m*	quasi moneta *f*	activo casi líquido *m*
quasi moneta (I)	Geldsubstitut *n*	money substitute	monnaie subrogée *f*	—	sustitutivo de dinero *m*
quasi moneta (I)	Quasigeld *n*	quasi money	quasi-argent *m*	—	activo casi líquido *m*
quasi money (E)	Quasigeld *n*	—	quasi-argent *m*	quasi moneta *f*	activo casi líquido *m*
Quellenprinzip (D)	—	source principle	principe d'imposition à la source *m*	principio della ritenuta alla fonte *m*	principio del gra-vamen en origen *m*

	D	E	F	I	Es
Quellensteuer (D)	—	tax at source	impôt retenu à la source *m*	ritenuta alla fonte *f*	impuesto deducido en la fuente *m*
quiebra (Es)	Konkurs *m*	bankruptcy	faillite *f*	fallimento *m*	—
quietanza (I)	Quittung *f*	receipt	quittance *f*	—	recibo *m*
quittance (F)	Quittung *f*	receipt	—	quietanza *f*	recibo *m*
quittance de contribution (F)	Einschußquittung *f*	contribution receipt	—	ricevuta di apporto *f*	recibo de la inyección de dinero *m*
quittance d'encaissement (F)	Einzugsquittung *f*	collection receipt	—	ricevuta di riscossione *f*	recibo de cobro *m*
Quittung (D)	—	receipt	quittance *f*	quietanza *f*	recibo *m*
Quittungseinzugs-verfahren (D)	—	receipt collection procedure	système d'encaissement de quittances *m*	procedimento d'incasso di quietanza *m*	procedimiento de cobro de recibos *m*
quorum azioni (I)	Aktienquorum *n*	share quorum	quorum d'actions *m*	—	quórum de acciones *m*
quorum d'actions (F)	Aktienquorum *n*	share quorum	—	quorum azioni *m*	quórum de acciones *m*
quórum de acciones (Es)	Aktienquorum *n*	share quorum	quorum d'actions *m*	quorum azioni *m*	—
quota (E)	Kontingent *n*	—	contingent *m*	contingente *m*	contingente *m*
quota alle perdite (I)	Verlustanteil *m*	share in the loss	participation aux pertes *f*	—	cuota de pérdidas *f*
quota del datore di lavoro (I)	Arbeitgeberanteil *m*	employer's share	part patronale *f*	—	cuota patronal *f*
quota de réescompte (F)	Rediskontkontingent *n*	rediscount quota	—	plafond di risconto *m*	cupo de redescuento *m*
quota di capitale (I)	Kapitalanteil *m*	share in capital	part de capital *f*	—	participación en el capital *f*
quota di credito (I)	Kredittranche *f*	credit tranche	tranche de crédit *f*	—	fracción de crédito *f*
quota di fondo d'investimento (I)	Investmentanteil *m*	investment share	part de fonds d'investissement *f*	—	participación en fondos de inversión mobiliaria *f*
quota di mercato (I)	Marktanteil *m*	market share	participation au marché *f*	—	participación en el mercado *f*
quota di riparto (I)	Konkursquote *f*	dividend in bankruptcy	pour-cent accordé aux créanciers dans la masse *m*	—	cuota del activo de la quiebra *f*
Quotation (D)	—	quotation	cotation *f*	quotazione *f*	prorrateo *m*
quotation (E)	Quotation *f*	—	cotation *f*	quotazione *f*	prorrateo *m*
quotation (E)	Kursanzeige *f*	—	cotation *f*	indicazione delle quotazioni *f*	indicación de las cotizaciones *f*
quotation (E)	Börsennotierung *f*	—	cotation des cours en bourse *f*	quotazione di borsa *f*	cotización bursátil *f*
quotation ex dividend (E)	Dividendenabschlag *m*	—	cours moins le dividende *f*	ex dividendo *m*	disagio de dividendo *m*
quotation on the unofficial market (E)	Kulissenwert *m*	—	valeur négociée sur le marché libre *f*	titolo del mercato ristretto *m*	valor de la bolsa extraoficial *m*
quota transactions (E)	Quotenhandel *m*	—	transactions sur les quotas *f/pl*	mercato di quote di capitale *m*	transacciones de cuotas *f/pl*
quota utile (I)	Gewinnanteil *n*	share in the profits	quote-part sur les bénéfices *f*	—	participación en los beneficios *f*
quotazione (I)	Kurs *m*	market price	cours *m*	—	cotización *f*
quotazione (I)	Quotation *f*	quotation	cotation *f*	—	prorrateo *m*
quotazione accordata (I)	Gesamtkurs *m*	total market value	cours total *m*	—	cotización colectiva *f*
quotazione a fine corrente (I)	per Ultimo	for the monthly settlement	à fin de mois	—	a fin de mes
quotazione azionaria (I)	Aktienkurs *m*	share price	cours des actions *m*	—	cotización de las acciones *f*
quotazione bloccata (I)	Stoppkurs *m*	stop price	cours maximum *m*	—	cotización máxima *f*
quotazione dei cambi a termine (I)	Devisenterminkurs *m*	forward exchange rate	cours des devises négociées à terme *m*	—	cambio de divisas a término *m*
quotazione dei prezzi (I)	Preisnotierung *f*	prices quoted	cotation des prix *f*	—	cotización de precios *f*

	D	E	F	I	Es
quotazione del certo (I)	Quantitätsnotierung *f*	fixed exchange	certain *m*	—	cotización cuantitativa *f*
quotazione del giorno di riferimento (I)	Stichtagskurs *m*	market price on reporting date	cours offert à la date de référence *m*	—	cotización del día de referencia *f*
quotazione della cedola (I)	Kuponkurs *m*	coupon price	prix des coupons *m*	—	cotización de un cupón *f*
quotazione di borsa (I)	Börsennotierung *f*	quotation	cotation des cours en bourse *f*	—	cotización bursátil *f*
quotazione di borsa (I)	Börsenkurs *m*	stock exchange price	cours de bourse *m*	—	cotización bursátil *f*
quotazione di chiusura (I)	Schlußkurs *m*	closing price	dernier cours *m*	—	cotización de cierre *f*
quotazione di titoli (I)	Effektenkurs *m*	securities price	cours des valeurs mobilières *m*	—	cotización de valores *f*
quotazione estrema (I)	Extremkurs	peak quotation	cours extrême *m*	—	curso extremo *m*
quotazione evasiva (I)	Scheinkurs *m*	fictitious quotation price	cours nominal *m*	—	cotización ficticia *f*
quotazione evasiva (I)	Ausweichkurs *m*	fictitious security price	cours nominal *m*	—	precio ficticio de acciones *m*
quotazione netta (I)	Nettokurs *m*	net price	cours net *m*	—	cambio neto *m*
quotazione percentuale (I)	Prozentkurs *m*	price expressed as a percentage of the nominal value	cours coté en pour-cent de la valeur nominale *m.*	—	cotización en un tanto porciento del valor nominal *f*
quoted securities (E)	börsengängige Wertpapiere *n/pl*	—	valeurs négociées en bourse *f/pl*	titoli ammessi in borsa *m/pl*	títulos cotizados en bolsa *m/pl*
Quotenaktie (D)	—	share of no par value	action de quotité *f*	parte di capitale *f*	acción de cuota *f*
Quotenhandel (D)	—	quota transactions	transactions sur les quotas *f/pl*	mercato di quote di capitale *m*	transacciones de cuotas *f/pl*
Quotenkartell (D)	—	commodity restriction scheme	entente imposant à ses membres des quotas de production *f*	cartello di contingentamento *m*	cartel de contingentes *m*
quote-part de la liquidation (F)	Liquidationsrate *f*	liquidating dividend	—	tasso di liquidazione *m*	tasa de liquidación *f*
quote-part de revenu réservé à des fins d'épargne (F)	Sparquote *f*	savings ratio	—	aliquota di risparmio *f*	cuota de ahorro *f*
quote-part du capital propre (F)	Eigenkapitalquote *f*	equity ratio	—	percentuale dei mezzi propri *f*	cuota de capital propio *f*
quote-part restante (F)	Restquote *f*	residual quota	—	pagamento residuale *m*	cuota restante *f*
quote-part sur les bénéfices (F)	Gewinnanteil *m*	share in the profits	—	quota utile *f*	participación en los beneficios *f*
rabais (F)	Dekort *n*	deduction	—	decurtazione *f*	descuento *m*
Rabatt (D)	—	discount	remise *f*	sconto *m*	rebaja *f*
raccolta di capitali (I)	Kapitalbeschaffung *f*	procurement of capital	constitution de capital *f*	—	obtención de capital *f*
rachat (F)	Rückkauf *m*	repurchase	—	riacquisto *m*	recompra *f*
raggruppamento degli utili (I)	Gewinnpoolung *f*	profit-pooling	pool de bénéfices *m*	—	pool de beneficios *m*
raggruppamento di azioni (I)	Aktienzusammenlegung *f*	consolidation of shares	regroupement d'actions *m*	—	fusión de acciones *f*
ragioneria aziendale (I)	betriebliches Rechnungswesen *n*	operational accountancy	comptablité industrielle *f*	—	contabilidad empresarial *f*
Rahmenkredit (D)	—	credit line	crédit-cadre *m*	linea di credito *f*	línea de crédito *f*
raising money on securities by cash sale coupled with contract for subsequent repurchase (E)	Effektenpensionierung *f*	—	mise en pension d'effets *f*	sconto di titoli in pensione *m*	cesión temporal de valores *f*
raising of credits (E)	Kreditaufnahme *f*	—	recours à l'emprunt *m*	accensione di credito *f*	apelación al crédito *f*
raison sociale imaginaire (F)	Scheinfirma *f*	bogus firm	—	impresa fittizia *f*	casa ficticia *f*
rajustement global (F)	Sammelwertberichtigung *f*	global value adjustment	—	rivalutazione forfettaria *f*	revaluación colectiva *f*

	D	E	F	I	Es
Random-Walk-Theorie (D)	—	random-walk theory	théorie d'imprévisibilité f	teoria Random-Walk f	teoría de imprevisibilidad f
random-walk theory (E)	Random-Walk-Theorie f	—	théorie d'imprévisibilité f	teoria Random-Walk f	teoría de imprevisibilidad f
rapid money transfer (E)	Eilüberweisung f	—	virement accéléré m	vaglia espresso f	giro urgente m
rapport de gestion (F)	Geschäftsbericht m	business report	—	rapporto di gestione m	informe anual m
rapport de l'émission (F)	Emissionsrendite f	issue yield	—	rendita di nuovi titoli f	rédito de emisión m
rapport d'obligation (F)	Schuldverhältnis n	obligation	—	rapporto obbligatorio m	relación obligatoria f
rapporto corso-profitto (I)	Kurs-Gewinn-Verhältnis n	price-earnings ratio	relation cours-bénéfice f	—	relación cotización-ganancia f
rapporto di gestione (I)	Geschäftsbericht m	business report	rapport de gestion m	—	informe anual m
rapporto obbligatorio (I)	Schuldverhältnis n	obligation	rapport d'obligation m	—	relación obligatoria f
rapport trimestriel (F)	Quartalsbericht m	quarterly report	—	relazione trimestrale f	informe trimestral m
rappresentante (I)	Repräsentant m	representative	représentant m	—	representante m
rappresentante commerciale (I)	Handelsbevollmächtigter m	general agent	personne ayant le pouvoir commercial f	—	agente comercial m
Rat (D)	—	advice	conseil m	consiglio m	consejo m
rata di rimborso (I)	Tilgungsrate f	amortization instalment	annuité f	—	tasa de amortización f
rate di rimborso arretrate (I)	Tilgungsrückstände m/pl	redemption in arrears	arriérés d'amortissement m/pl	—	amortizaciones pendientes f/pl
rate for foreign notes and coins (E)	Sortenkurs m	—	cours des monnaies étrangères m	corso dei cambi m	tipo de cambio de billetes y monedas extranjeras m
ratei e risconti (I)	Rechnungsabgrenzung f	apportionment between accounting periods	délimitation des comptes non encore soldés en fin d'exercice f	—	ajustes por periodificación m/pl
Ratenanleihen (D)	—	instalment loans	emprunt remboursable par annuités constantes m	prestiti ammortizzabile m/pl	empréstitos a plazos m/pl
Ratenkredit (D)	—	instalment sales credit	crédit à tempéraments m	finanziamento di acquisti rateali m	crédito a plazos m
Ratensparvertrag (D)	—	saving-by-instalments contract	contrat d'épargne à dépôts multiples m	risparmio contrattuale m	contrato de ahorro a plazos m
Ratenwechsel (D)	—	bill payable in instalments	effet à échéances multiples m	cambiale di pagamento rateale f	letra de vencimientos sucesivos f
rate of flow (E)	Stromgröße f	—	volume du flux m	variabile di flusso f	tasa de flujo f
rate of inflation (E)	Inflationsrate f	—	taux d'inflation m	tasso d'inflazione m	tasa de inflación f
ratio de financement interne (F)	Innenfinanzierungskennzahl f	self-generated financing ratio	—	codice di finanziamento interno m	características de financiación interna f/pl
rational (E)	rationale Erwartungen f/pl	—	expectatives rationnelles f/pl	aspettative razionali f/pl	expectativas racionales f/pl
rationale Erwartungen (D)	—	rational	expectatives rationnelles f/pl	aspettative razionali f/pl	expectativas racionales f/pl
raw material funds (E)	Rohstoff-Fonds m	—	fonds de matières premières m	fondo titoli del settore primario m	fondo de las materias primas m
ready money (E)	Bargeld n	—	argent comptant m	denaro contante m	efectivo m
real account (E)	Bestandskonto n	—	compte d'existences m	conto magazzino m	cuenta de existencia f
real balance effect (E)	Vermögenseffekten pl	—	effets patrimoniaux m/pl	effetti patrimoniali m/pl	efectos patrimoniales m/pl
real balance effect (E)	Vermögenseinkommen n	—	revenu du capital m	reddito di capitale m	ingresos por capital m/pl
real capital (E)	Sachkapital n	—	immobilisations corporelles f/pl	capitale reale m	capital real m
real estate credit (E)	Immobiliarkredit m	—	crédit immobilier m	credito immobiliare m	crédito inmobiliario m
real-estate credit institution (E)	Realkreditinstitut n	—	institut de crédit foncier m	istituto di credito immobiliare m	instituto de crédito real m

	D	E	F	I	Es
real estate fund (E)	Immobilienfonds *m*	—	fonds immobilier *m*	fondo di titoli immobiliari *m*	cartera inmobiliaria *f*
real estate property (E)	Betongold *n*	—	patrimoine immobilier *m*	proprietà immobiliare *f*	propiedad inmobiliaria *f*
real interest (E)	Realzins *m*	—	rendement réel *m*	interesse reale *m*	interés real *m*
Realisation (D)	—	realization	réalisation *f*	realizzazione *f*	realización *f*
réalisation (F)	Glattstellen *n*	settlement	—	operazione di compensazione mediante trattazione titoli *f*	liquidación *f*
réalisation (F)	Realisation *f*	realization	—	realizzazione *f*	realización *f*
réalisation du gage (F)	Pfandverwertung *f*	realization of pledge	—	realizzazione di un pegno *f*	realización de la prenda *f*
realización (Es)	Realisation *f*	realization	réalisation *f*	realizzazione *f*	—
realización de la prenda (Es)	Pfandverwertung *f*	realization of pledge	réalisation du gage *f*	realizzazione di un pegno *f*	—
realization (E)	Realisation *f*	—	réalisation *f*	realizzazione *f*	realización *f*
realization of pledge (E)	Pfandverwertung *f*	—	réalisation du gage *f*	realizzazione di un pegno *f*	realización de la prenda *f*
realization profit (E)	Liquidationsüberschuß *m*	—	excédent de liquidation *m*	eccedenza da liquidazione *f*	exceso de liquidación *m*
realizzazione (I)	Realisation *f*	realization	réalisation *f*	—	realización *f*
realizzazione di un pegno (I)	Pfandverwertung *f*	realization of pledge	réalisation du gage *f*	—	realización de la prenda *f*
Realkreditinstitut (D)	—	real-estate credit institution	institut de crédit foncier *m*	istituto di credito immobiliare *m*	instituto de crédito inmobiliario *m*
Realvermögen (D)	—	real wealth	patrimoine réel *m*	patrimonio reale *m*	activo inmobiliario *m*
real wealth (E)	Realvermögen *n*	—	patrimoine réel *m*	patrimonio reale *m*	activo inmobiliario *m*
Realzins (D)	—	real interest	rendement réel *m*	interesse reale *m*	interés real *m*
reato fallimentare (I)	Konkursdelikt *n*	bankruptcy offence	fraude en matière de faillite *f*	—	delito concursal *m*
rebaja (Es)	Rabatt *m*	discount	remise *f*	sconto *m*	—
recargo de riesgo (Es)	Risikozuschlag *m*	additional risk premium	surprime de risque *f*	soprappremio di rischio *m*	—
receipt (E)	Beleg *m*	—	document justificatif *m*	ricevuta *f*	justificante *m*
receipt (E)	Quittung *f*	—	quittance *f*	quietanza *f*	recibo *m*
receipt collection procedure (E)	Quittungseinzugsverfahren *n*	—	système d'encaissement de quittances *m*	procedimento d'incasso di quietanza *m*	procedimiento de cobro de recibos *m*
receipt of money (E)	Geldeingang *m*	—	rentrée de fonds *f*	entrata di denaro *f*	entrada de dinero *f*
receipts (E)	Einnahmen *f/pl*	—	recettes *f/pl*	entrate *f/pl*	ingresos *m/pl*
récépissé de dépôt (F)	Depotschein *m*	deposit receipt	—	certificato di deposito *m*	certificado de depósito *m*
récépissé de participation (F)	Partizipationsschein *m*	participating receipt	—	buono di partecipazione *m*	bono de participación *m*
recesión (Es)	Rezession *f*	recession	récession *f*	recessione *f*	—
recession (E)	Rezession *f*	—	récession *f*	recessione *f*	recesión *f*
récession (F)	Rezession *f*	recession	—	recessione *f*	recesión *f*
recessione (I)	Rezession *f*	recession	récession *f*	—	recesión *f*
recettes (F)	Einnahmen *f/pl*	receipts	—	entrate *f/pl*	ingresos *m/pl*
recettes de l'Etat (F)	Staatseinnahmen *f/pl*	public revenue	—	entrate pubbliche *f/pl*	ingresos públicos *m/pl*
Rechenschaft (D)	—	rendering of account	compte rendu *m*	conto *m*	cuenta *f*
Rechenschaftslegung (D)	—	rendering of account	présentation d'un compte rendu *f*	resa dei conti *f*	rendición de cuentas *f*
rechnen (D)	—	calculate	calculer	calcolare	calcular
Rechnungsabgrenzung (D)	—	apportionment between accounting periods	délimitation des comptes non encore soldés en fin d'exercice *f*	ratei e risconti *m/pl*	ajustes por periodificación *m/pl*
Rechnungseinheit (D)	—	unit of account	unité de compte *f*	unità di conto *f*	unidad de cuenta *f*

	D	E	F	I	Es
Rechnungseinzugsverfahren (D)	—	accounts collection method	système d'encaissement automatique de factures m	procedimento d'incasso di fatture m	procedimiento de cobranza de pagos pendientes m
Rechnungslegung (D)	—	accounting	reddition des comptes f	chiusura dei conti f	rendición de cuentas f
Rechtsfähigkeit (D)	—	legal capacity	capacité de jouissance de droits f	capacità giuridica f	capacidad jurídica f
Rechtsordnung (D)	—	legal system	ordre juridique m	ordinamento giuridico m	orden jurídico m
recibo (Es)	Quittung f	receipt	quittance f	quietanza f	—
recibo de cobro (Es)	Einzugsquittung f	collection receipt	quittance d'encaissement f	ricevuta di riscossione f	—
recibo de la inyección de dinero (Es)	Einschußquittung f	contribution receipt	quittance de contribution f	ricevuta di apporto f	—
recibo parcial (Es)	Teilkonnossement n	partial bill of lading	connaissement partiel m	polizza di carico parziale f	—
recinto delle grida (I)	Parkett n	floor	parquet m	—	parqué m
recipient company (E)	Auffanggesellschaft f	—	consortium de renflouement m	società finanziaria f	sociedad holding f
reciprocal contract (E)	gegenseitiger Vertrag m	—	accord de réciprocité m	contratto bilaterale m	contrato recíproco m
reclamación (Es)	Reklamation f	complaint	réclamation f	reclamo m	—
reclamación de indemnización contra la administración pública (Es)	Ausgleichsforderung f	equalization claim	droit à une indemnité compensatoire m	credito di compensazione m	—
réclamation (F)	Reklamation f	complaint	—	reclamo m	reclamación f
reclamo (I)	Reklamation f	complaint	réclamation f	—	reclamación f
recommended retail price (E)	Richtpreis m	—	prix indicatif m	prezzo indicativo m	precio indicativo m
recompra (Es)	Rückkauf m	repurchase	rachat m	riacquisto m	—
reconnaissance bancaire (F)	Dispositionsschein m	banker's note	—	certificato di disponibilità m	fianza de disposición de banquero f
reconnaissance de dépôt (F)	Depotanerkenntnis n	deposit acknowledgement	—	approvazione estratto deposito f	reconocimiento de depósito m
reconnaissance de dette (F)	Schuldanerkenntnis n	acknowledgement of a debt	—	ricognizione di debito f	reconocimiento de la deuda m
reconnaissance de dette (F)	Schuldschein m	certificate of indebtedness	—	certificato di debito m	pagaré m
reconnaissance fondant un rapport d'obligation (F)	Schuldversprechen n	promise to fulfil an obligation	—	promessa di debito f	promesa de deuda f
reconocimiento de depósito (Es)	Depotanerkenntnis n	deposit acknowledgement	reconnaissance de dépôt f	approvazione estratto deposito f	—
reconocimiento de la deuda (Es)	Schuldanerkenntnis n	acknowledgement of a debt	reconnaissance de dette f	ricognizione di debito f	—
reconstruction (E)	Sanierung f	—	assainissement m	risanamento m	saneamiento m
recours (F)	Regreß m	recourse	—	regresso m	regreso m
recours (F)	Rückgriff m	recourse	—	regresso m	regreso m
recours à l'emprunt (F)	Kreditaufnahme f	raising of credits	—	accensione di credito f	apelación al crédito f
recourse (E)	Rückgriff m	—	recours m	regresso m	regreso m
recourse (E)	Regreß m	—	recours m	regresso m	regreso m
recours en matière de chèque (F)	Scheckregreß m	cheque recourse	—	regresso d'assegno m	regreso de cheque m
recours en matière de traite (F)	Wechselregreß m	legal recourse for non-payment of a bill	—	regresso cambiario m	recurso cambiario m
recouvrement de chèques (F)	Scheckeinzug m	cheque collection	—	incasso di assegno m	cobro del cheque m
recovery (E)	Erholung f	—	rétablissement m	rianimazione f	recuperación f
recovery (E)	Aufschwung m	—	reprise f	ripresa f	auge m
rectificación (Es)	Berichtigung f	correction	rectification f	correzione f	—

	D	E	F	I	Es
rectificación de valor global (Es)	Globalwertberichtigung f	overall adjustment	rectification globale des valeurs f	rivalutazione globale f	—
rectification (F)	Berichtigung f	correction	—	correzione f	rectificación f
rectification globale des valeurs (F)	Globalwertberichtigung f	overall adjustment	—	rivalutazione globale f	rectificación de valor global f
recuperación (Es)	Erholung f	recovery	rétablissement m	rianimazione f	—
recuperación (Es)	Reprise f	reprise	tendance à la hausse f	ripresa f	—
recurso cambiario (Es)	Wechselregreß m	legal recourse for non-payment of a bill	recours en matière de traite m	regresso cambiario m	—
recursos (Es)	Ressourcen f/pl	resources	ressources f/pl	risorse f/pl	—
redazione del bilancio (I)	Bilanzierung f	procedure to draw up a balance sheet	établissement du bilan m	—	formación del balance f
redazione d'inventario (I)	Bestandsaufnahme f	stock-taking	établissement de l'inventaire m	—	formación de un inventario f
red bancaria (Es)	Bankstellennetz n	bank office network	réseau bancaire m	rete di sportelli bancari f	—
red de bancos de giros (Es)	Gironetz n	clearing system	réseau des banques de virement m	rete di giro f	—
redditi di lavoro (I)	Erwerbseinkünfte pl	business income	revenus d'une activité professionelle m/pl	—	procendentes de una actividad remunerada m/pl
reddition des comptes (F)	Rechnungslegung f	accounting	—	chiusura dei conti f	rendición de cuentas f
redditività aziendale (I)	Betriebsrentabilität f	operational profit-ability	rentabilité d'exploitation f	—	rentabilidad de la actividad de la empresa f
redditività del capitale complessivo (I)	Gesamtkapitalrentabilität f	total capital profit-ability	rentabilité totale du capital f	—	rédito del capital total m
redditività del capitale proprio (I)	Eigenkapitalrentabilität f	equity return	rentabilité du capital propre f	—	rédito del capital propio m
reddito del patrimonio (I)	Besitzeinkommen n	property income	revenu du patrimoine m	—	renta de la propiedad f
reddito di capitale (I)	Kapitalertrag m	income from capital	produit du capital m	—	renta de capital f
reddito di capitale (I)	Vermögenseinkommen n	real balance effect	revenu du capital m	—	ingresos por capital m/pl
reddito di lavoro (I)	Arbeitseinkommen n	earned income	revenu du travail m	—	ingresos del trabajo m/pl
reddito di lavoro (I)	Erwerbseinkommen n	income from gainful employment	revenu du travail m	—	remuneración de los asalariados f
reddito disponibile (I)	verfügbares Einkommen n	disposable income	revenu disponible m	—	renta disponible f
reddito effettivo (I)	Effektivverzinsung f	effective interest yield	taux effectif m	—	interés efectivo m
reddito effettivo di azioni (I)	Aktienrendite f	yield on shares	produit de l'action m	—	rédito de las acciones m
reddito lordo (I)	Bruttoeinkommen n	gross income	revenu brut m	—	renta bruta f
reddito medio (I)	Durchschnittsertrag m	average yield	rendement moyen m	—	rendimiento medio m
reddito nazionale (I)	Volkseinkommen n	national income	revenu national m	—	renta nacional f
reddito totale (I)	Gesamtertrag m	total proceeds	produit global m	—	renta total f
redemption (E)	Tilgung f	—	amortissement m	rimborso m	amortización f
redemption fund (E)	Tilgungsfonds m	—	fonds d'amortissement m	fondo d'amortamento m	fondo de amortización m
redemption in arears (E)	Tilgungsrückstände m/pl	—	arriérés d'amortissement m/pl	rate di rimborso arretrate f/pl	amortizaciones pendientes f/pl
redemption in kind (E)	Naturaltilgung f	—	amortissement en nature m	rimborso del credito ipotecario pattuito m	amortización en especie f
redemption loan (E)	Tilgungsanleihe f	—	emprunt d'amortissement m	prestito ammortizzabile m	empréstito amortizable m
redemption loan (E)	Ablösungsanleihe f	—	emprunt de revalorisation m	prestito di ammortamento m	empréstito de amortización m
redención de acciones (Es)	Aktieneinziehung f	withdrawal of shares	retrait d'actions m	ritiro di azioni m	—

	D	E	F	I	Es
redescuento (Es)	Rediskont *m*	rediscount	réescompte *m*	risconto *m*	—
redescuento (Es)	Rediskontierung *f*	rediscount	réescompte *m*	risconto *m*	—
rediscount (E)	Rediskontierung *f*	—	réescompte *m*	risconto *m*	redescuento *m*
rediscount (E)	Rediskont *m*	—	réescompte *m*	risconto *m*	redescuento *m*
rediscount quota (E)	Rediskontkontingent *n*	—	quota de réescompte *m*	plafond di risconto *m*	cupo de redescuento *m*
Rediskont (D)	—	rediscount	réescompte *m*	risconto *m*	redescuento *m*
Rediskontierung (D)	—	rediscount	réescompte *m*	risconto *m*	redescuento *m*
Rediskontkontingent (D)	—	rediscount quota	quota de réescompte *m*	plafond di risconto *m*	cupo de redescuento *m*
redistribución de la renta (Es)	Einkommensumverteilung *f*	redistribution of income	redistribution des revenus *f*	ridistribuzione dei redditi *f*	—
redistribution des revenus (F)	Einkommensumverteilung *f*	redistribution of income	—	ridistribuzione dei redditi *f*	redistribución de la renta *f*
redistribution of income (E)	Einkommensumverteilung *f*	—	redistribution des revenus *f*	ridistribuzione dei redditi *f*	redistribución de la renta *f*
rédito (Es)	Rendite *f*	yield	rendement *m*	rendimento *m*	—
rédito (Es)	Zinsertrag *m*	income from interests	intérêts perçus *m/pl*	provento d'interessi *m*	—
rédito de emisión (Es)	Emissionsrendite *f*	issue yield	rapport de l'émission *m*	rendita di nuovi titoli *f*	—
rédito de las acciones (Es)	Aktienrendite *f*	yield on shares	produit de l' action *m*	reddito effettivo di azioni *m*	—
rédito del capital propio (Es)	Eigenkapitalrentabilität *f*	equity return	rentabilité du capital propre *f*	redditività del capitale proprio *f*	—
rédito del capital total (Es)	Gesamtkapitalrentabilität *f*	total capital profitability	rentabilité totale du capital *f*	redditività del capitale complessivo *f*	—
redondear (Es)	arrondieren	to round off	arrondir	arrotondare	—
reducción de capital (Es)	Kapitalherabsetzung *f*	capital reduction	diminution du capital *f*	riduzione del capitale sociale *f*	—
reducción de capital simplificada (Es)	vereinfachte Kapitalherabsetzung *f*	simplified capital reduction	diminution de capital simplifiée *f*	riduzione di capitale semplice *f*	—
reducción del capital social (Es)	Herabsetzung des Grundkapitals *f*	reduction of the share capital	réduction de capital social *f*	riduzione del capitale sociale *f*	—
reducción del tipo de interés (Es)	Zinssenkung *f*	reduction of the interest rate	réduction des intérêts *f*	abbassamento del tasso d'interesse *m*	—
réduction de capital social (F)	Herabsetzung des Grundkapitals *f*	reduction of the share capital	—	riduzione del capitale sociale *f*	reducción del capital social *f*
réduction des intérêts (F)	Zinssenkung *f*	reduction of the interest rate	—	abbassamento del tasso d'interesse *m*	reducción del tipo de interés *f*
reduction of the interest rate (E)	Zinssenkung *f*	—	réduction des intérêts *f*	abbassamento del tasso d'interesse *m*	reducción del tipo de interés *f*
reduction of the share capital (E)	Herabsetzung des Grundkapitals *f*	—	réduction de capital social *f*	riduzione del capitale sociale *f*	reducción del capital social *f*
reduction of the volume of money (E)	Geldvernichtung *f*	—	destruction d'argent *f*	distruzione di denaro *f*	destrucción de dinero *f*
reembolsable (Es)	rückzahlbar	repayable	remboursable	rimborsabile	—
reembolso (Es)	Rückzahlung *f*	repayment	remboursement *m*	rimborso *m*	—
réescompte (F)	Rediskontierung *f*	rediscount	—	risconto *m*	redescuento *m*
réescompte (F)	Rediskont *m*	rediscount	—	risconto *m*	redescuento *m*
refinancement (F)	Refinanzierung *f*	refinancing	—	risconto *m*	refinanciación *f*
refinanciación (Es)	Refinanzierung *f*	refinancing	refinancement *m*	risconto *m*	—
refinancing (E)	Refinanzierung *f*	—	refinancement *m*	risconto *m*	refinanciación *f*
refinancing policy (E)	Refinanzierungspolitik *f*	—	politique de refinancement *f*	politica di risconto *f*	política de refinanciación *f*
Refinanzierung (D)	—	refinancing	refinancement *m*	risconto *m*	refinanciación *f*
Refinanzierungspolitik (D)	—	refinancing policy	politique de refinancement *f*	politica di risconto *f*	política de refinanciación *f*
reflujo (Es)	Rückfluß *m*	reflux	reflux *m*	riflusso *m*	—
reflux (E)	Rückfluß *m*	—	reflux *m*	riflusso *m*	reflujo *m*

	D	E	F	I	Es
reflux (F)	Rückfluß *m*	reflux	—	riflusso *m*	reflujo *m*
reforma de boisa (Es)	Börsenreform *f*	reorganization of the stock exchange	réforme de la bourse *f*	riforma della borsa *f*	—
reforma financiera (Es)	Finanzreform *f*	financial reform	réforme financière *f*	riforma finanziaria *f*	—
reforma monetaria (Es)	Währungsreform *f*	monetary reform	réforme monétaire *f*	riforma monetaria *f*	—
reforma monetaria (Es)	Währungsumstellung *f*	currency conversion	adaptation d'une monnaie *f*	riforma monetaria *f*	—
réforme de la bourse (F)	Börsenreform *f*	reorganization of the stock exchange	—	riforma della borsa *f*	reforma de bolsa *f*
réforme financière (F)	Finanzreform *f*	financial reform	—	riforma finanziaria *f*	reforma financiera *f*
réforme monétaire (F)	Währungsreform *f*	monetary reform	—	riforma monetaria *f*	reforma monetaria *f*
regalía de acuñación (Es)	Münzregal *n*	exclusive right of coinage	monopole de la frappe *m*	privilegio di battere moneta *m*	—
Regelbindung (D)	—	rule-bound policy	affectation à des règles *f*	attività vincolata *f*	vinculación a reglas *f*
Regelmäßigkeit (D)	—	regularity	régularité *f*	regolarità *f*	regularidad *f*
régime de bourse (F)	Börsenrecht *n*	stock exchange rules	—	diritto della borsa *m*	derecho de la bolsa *m*
regime dei cambi (I)	Wechselkurssystem *n*	system of exchange rates	système de change *m*	—	sistema de cambios *m*
régime de la nation la plus favorisée (F)	Meistbegünstigung *f*	most-favoured nation treatment	—	trattamento della nazione più favorita *m*	régimen de la nación más favorecida *m*
régime des courtiers (F)	Maklerordnung *f*	brokers' code of conduct	—	codice degli agenti di cambio *m*	régimen de corredores *m*
régime de taxation (F)	Besteuerungsverfahren *n*	taxation procedure	—	procedura d'imposizione *f*	procedimiento tributario *m*
régime juridique de la faillite (F)	Konkursordnung *f*	Bankruptcy Act	—	legge fallimentare *f*	ley de las quiebras *f*
régimen de autorización (Es)	Genehmigungspflicht *f*	duty to obtain a permit	obligation de solliciter une permission *f*	obbligo d'autorizzazione *m*	—
régimen de corredores (Es)	Maklerordnung *f*	brokers' code of conduct	régime des courtiers *m*	codice degli agenti di cambio *m*	—
régimen de creditos (Es)	Kreditwesen *n*	credit system	crédit *m*	sistema creditizio *m*	—
régimen de la nación más favorecida (Es)	Meistbegünstigung *f*	most-favoured nation treatment	régime de la nation la plus favorisée *m*	trattamento della nazione più favorita *m*	—
régimen financiero (Es)	Finanzwesen *n*	finance	finances *f/pl*	finanze *f/pl*	—
regional authority (E)	Gebietskörperschaft *f*	—	collectivité territoriale *f*	ente locale *m*	corporación territorial *f*
Regionalbank (D)	—	regional bank	banque régionale *f*	banca regionale *f*	banco regional *m*
regional bank (E)	Regionalbank *f*	—	banque régionale *f*	banca regionale *f*	banco regional *m*
regional stock exchange (E)	Provinzbörse *f*	—	bourse provinciale *f*	borsa provinciale *f*	bolsa provincial *f*
Register (D)	—	register	registre *m*	registro *m*	registro *m*
register (E)	Register *n*	—	registre *m*	registro *m*	registro *m*
registered securities (E)	Namenspapier *n*	—	titre nominatif *m*	titolo nominativo *m*	título nominal *m*
registered share (E)	Namensaktie *f*	—	action nominative *f*	azione nominativa *f*	acción nominal *f*
registered trader (E)	Vollkaufmann *m*	—	commerçant de plein droit *m*	imprenditore a pieno titolo *m*	comerciante pleno *m*
register of land titles (E)	Grundbuch *n*	—	livre foncier *m*	catasto *m*	registro de la propiedad *m*
registrar un importe (Es)	Ausweisung *f*	statement	publication *f*	pubblicazione *f*	—
registration (E)	Einschreibung *f*	—	enregistrement *m*	asta olandese *f*	inscripción *f*
registration in the Commercial Register (E)	Eintragung im Handelsregister *f*	—	inscription au registre du commerce *f*	iscrizione nel registro commerciale *f*	inscripción en el registro comercial *f*
registrazione (I)	Verbuchung *f*	entry	inscription en compte *f*	—	contabilización *f*
registrazione in contropartita (I)	Gegenbuchung *f*	counter entry	contrepartie *f*	—	contrapartida *f*

	D	E	F	I	Es
registre (F)	Register *n*	register	—	registro *m*	registro *m*
registre d'actions (F)	Aktienregister *n*	share register	—	registro delle azioni *m*	registro de acciones *m*
registre de commerce (F)	Handelsregister *n*	commercial register	—	registro commerciale *m*	registro comercial *m*
registre des actions (F)	Aktienbuch *n*	share register	—	registro delle azioni *m*	libro de acciones *m*
registre des dépôts (F)	Verwahrungsbuch *n*	custody ledger	—	libretto di deposito *m*	libro de custodia *f*
registre des titres (F)	Effektenbuch *n*	stockbook	—	registro dei titoli *m*	libro de valores *m*
registre des valeurs en dépôt (F)	Depotbuch *n*	deposit book	—	libretto di deposito *m*	libreta de depósito *f*
registro (Es)	Register *n*	register	registre *m*	registro *m*	—
registro (I)	Register *n*	register	registre *m*	—	registro *m*
registro comercial (Es)	Handelsregister *n*	commercial register	registre de commerce *m*	registro commerciale *m*	—
registro commerciale (I)	Handelsregister *n*	commercial register	registre de commerce *m*	—	registro comercial *m*
registro de acciones (Es)	Aktienregister *n*	share register	registre d'actions *m*	registro delle azioni *m*	—
Registro de Deudas Federales (Es)	Bundesschuldbuch *n*	Federal Debt Register	grand-livre de la dette publique *m*	libro del debito pubblico *m*	—
registro dei titoli (I)	Effektenbuch *n*	stockbook	registre des titres *m*	—	libro de valores *m*
registro de la propiedad (Es)	Grundbuch *n*	register of land titles	livre foncier *m*	catasto *m*	—
registro delle azioni (I)	Aktienbuch *n*	share register	registre des actions *m*	—	libro de acciones *m*
registro delle azioni (I)	Aktienregister *n*	share register	registre d'actions *m*	—	registro de acciones *m*
registro hipotecario (Es)	Hypothekenregister *n*	mortgage register	livre foncier *m*	libro delle ipoteche *m*	—
regla bancaria (Es)	Bankregel *f*	banker's rule	règle bancaire *f*	norma bancaria *f*	—
regla de decisión (Es)	Entscheidungsregel *f*	decision rule	règle de décision *f*	regola di decisione *f*	—
regla de la unanimidad (Es)	Einstimmigkeitsregel *f*	unanimity rule	règle d'unanimité *f*	regola dell'unanimità *f*	—
reglamento de bolsa (Es)	Börsenordnung *f*	stock exchange regulations	règlement de la bourse *m*	regolamento della borsa *m*	—
règle bancaire (F)	Bankregel *f*	banker's rule	—	norma bancaria *f*	regla bancaria *f*
règle de décision (F)	Entscheidungsregel *f*	decision rule	—	regola di decisione *f*	regla de decisión *f*
règle d'unanimité (F)	Einstimmigkeitsregel *f*	unanimity rule	—	regola dell'unanimità *f*	regla de la unanimidad *f*
règlement de la bourse (F)	Börsenordnung *f*	stock exchange regulations	—	regolamento della borsa *m*	reglamento de bolsa *m*
règlement des chèques par voie de compensation (F)	Scheckabrechnung *f*	cheque clearance	—	compensazione degli assegni *f*	liquidación de cheques *f*
règlements (F)	Zahlungsverkehr *m*	payment transaction	—	pagamenti *m/pl*	movimiento de pagos *m*
règlements électroniques (F)	elektronischer Zahlungsverkehr *m*	electronic fund transfer	—	operazioni di pagamento elettronici *f/pl*	servicio de pagos electrónico *m*
règles de financement (F)	Finanzierungsregeln *f/pl*	financing rules	—	regole di finanziamento *f/pl*	normas de financiación *f/pl*
règles de financement horizontales (F)	horizontale Finanzierungsregeln *f/pl*	horizontal financing rules	—	norme orizzontali di finanziamento *f/pl*	normas de financiación horizontal *f/pl*
regola dell'unanimità (I)	Einstimmigkeitsregel *f*	unanimity rule	règle d'unanimité *f*	—	regla de la unanimidad *f*
regola di decisione (I)	Entscheidungsregel *f*	decision rule	règle de décision *f*	—	regla de decisión *f*
regolamenti europei di borsa (I)	europäische Börsenrichtlinien *f/pl*	European stock exchange guide-lines	directives boursières européennes *f/pl*	—	normas bursátiles europeas *f/pl*
regolamento (I)	Regulierung *f*	regulation	régularisation *f*	—	regulación *f*
regolamento d'eccezione (I)	Ausnahmeregelung *f*	provision	mesure dérogatoire *f*	—	disposición excepcional *f*
regolamento della borsa (I)	Börsenordnung *f*	stock exchange regulations	règlement de la bourse *m*	—	reglamento de bolsa *m*

	D	E	F	I	Es
regolamento di indicazione dei prezzi (I)	Preisangabeverordnung f	price marking ordinance	ordonnance de marquage des prix f	—	ordenanza para la indicación de precios f
regolarità (I)	Regelmäßigkeit f	regularity	régularité f	—	regularidad f
regole di finanziamento (I)	Finanzierungsregeln f/pl	financing rules	règles de financement f/pl	—	normas de financiación f/pl
regole per l'efficienza (I)	Effizienzregeln f/pl	performance regulations	régulation d'efficience f	—	normas de eficacia f/pl
regresión (Es)	Regression f	regression	régression f	regressione f	—
regreso (Es)	Rückgriff m	recourse	recours m	regresso m	—
regreso (Es)	Regreß m	recourse	recours m	regresso m	—
regreso de cheque (Es)	Scheckregreß m	cheque recourse	recours en matière de chèque m	regresso d'assegno m	—
Regreß (D)	—	recourse	recours m	regresso m	regreso m
Regression (D)	—	regression	régression f	regressione f	regresión f
regression (E)	Regression f	—	régression f	regressione f	regresión f
régression (F)	Regression f	regression	—	regressione f	regresión f
regressione (I)	Regression f	regression	régression f	—	regresión f
regresso (I)	Regreß m	recourse	recours m	—	regreso m
regresso (I)	Rückgriff m	recourse	recours m	—	regreso m
regresso cambiario (I)	Wechselregreß m	legal recourse for non-payment of a bill	recours en matière de traite m	—	recurso cambiario m
regresso d'assegno (I)	Scheckregreß m	cheque recourse	recours en matière de chèque m	—	regreso de cheque m
regroupement d'actions (F)	Aktienzusammenlegung f	consolidation of shares	—	raggruppamento di azioni m	fusión de acciones f
regulación (Es)	Regulierung f	regulation	régularisation f	regolamento m	—
regulación de los tipos de cambio (Es)	Kursregulierung f	price regulation	régulation des cours f	sostegno delle quotazioni m	—
regular customer (E)	Stammkunde m	—	client habituel m	cliente abituale m	cliente habitual m
regularidad (Es)	Regelmäßigkeit f	regularity	régularité f	regolarità f	—
régularisation (F)	Regulierung f	regulation	—	regolamento m	regulación f
régularité (F)	Regelmäßigkeit f	regularity	—	regolarità f	regularidad f
regularity (E)	Regelmäßigkeit f	—	régularité f	regolarità f	regularidad f
regulation (E)	Regulierung f	—	régularisation f	regolamento m	regulación f
régulation d'efficience (F)	Effizienzregeln f/pl	performance regulations	—	regole per l'efficienza f/pl	normas de eficacia f/pl
régulation des cours (F)	Kursregulierung f	price regulation	—	sostegno delle quotazioni m	regulación de los tipos de cambio f
régulation des cours (F)	Kurspflege f	price nursing	—	sostegno delle quotazioni m	compras de sostén f/pl
régulation des offres (F)	Angebotssteuerung f	supply control	—	controllo dell'offerta m	control de oferta m
régulation du portefeuille (F)	Portfeuillesteuerung f	portfolio controlling	—	controllo di portafoglio m	control de las inversiones de cartera m
Regulierung (D)	—	regulation	régularisation f	regolamento m	regulación f
reich (D)	—	rich	riche	ricco	rico
reimbursement (E)	Erstattung f	—	restitution f	rimborso m	devolución f
reines Konossement (D)	—	clean bill of lading	connaissance sans réserve m	polizza di carico netta f	conocimiento limpio m
reintegración (Es)	Rückerstattung f	repayment	remboursement m	restituzione f	—
reintegro de las cuotas (Es)	Beitragserstattung f	contribution refund	remboursement des cotisations m	rimborso di contributi m	—
Reinvermögen (D)	—	net assets	avoir net m	attivo netto m	patrimonio neto m
reinversión (Es)	Wiederanlage f	reinvestment	réinvestissement m	reinvestimento m	—
reinvestimento (I)	Wiederanlage f	reinvestment	réinvestissement m	—	reinversión f
réinvestissement (F)	Wiederanlage f	reinvestment	—	reinvestimento m	reinversión f
reinvestment (E)	Wiederanlage f	—	réinvestissement m	reinvestimento m	reinversión f

	D	E	F	I	Es
Reisekreditbrief (D)	—	traveller's letter of credit	lettre de crédit circulaire f	titolo di credito turistico m	carta de crédito viajero f
Reisescheck (D)	—	traveller's cheque	chèque de voyage m	assegno turistico m	cheque de viaje m
Reitwechsel (D)	—	windbill	traite de cavalerie f	cambiale incrociata f	letra cruzada f
Reklamation (D)	—	complaint	réclamation f	reclamo m	reclamación f
Rektaindossament (D)	—	restrictive endorsement	endossement non à ordre m	girata non all'ordine f	endoso intransferible m
Rektawechsel (D)	—	non-negotiable bill of exchange	traite non à ordre f	cambiale non all'ordine f	letra nominativa f
relación (Es)	Bankauszug m	bank statement	relevé de compte m	estratto bancario m	—
relación cotización-beneficio (Es)	Price-earning-ratio f	price-earnings-ratio	relation cours-bénéfice f	price-earning-rate f	—
relación cotización-ganancia (Es)	Kurs-Gewinn-Verhältnis n	price-earnings ratio	relation cours-bénéfice f	rapporto corso-profitto m	—
relaciones bancarias (Es)	Bankbeziehungen f/pl	bank relations	relations bancaires f/pl	relazioni bancarie f/pl	—
relación obligatoria (Es)	Schuldverhältnis n	obligation	rapport d'obligation m	rapporto obbligatorio m	—
relation cours-bénéfice (F)	Kurs-Gewinn-Verhältnis n	price-earnings ratio	—	rapporto corso-profitto m	relación cotización-ganancia f
relation cours-bénéfice (F)	Price-earning-ratio f	price-earnings ratio	—	price-earning-rate f	relación cotización-beneficio f
relations bancaires (F)	Bankbeziehungen f/pl	bank relations	—	relazioni bancarie f/pl	relaciones bancarias f/pl
relazione d'ispezione (I)	Prüfungsbericht m	audit report	compte rendu de vérification m	—	informe de auditoría m
relazione trimestrale (I)	Quartalsbericht m	quarterly report	rapport trimestriel m	—	informe trimestral m
relazioni bancarie (I)	Bankbeziehungen f/pl	bank relations	relations bancaires f/pl	—	relaciones bancarias f/pl
relevé de compte (F)	Kontoauszug m	statement of account	—	estratto conto m	extracto de cuenta m
relevé de compte (F)	Bankauszug m	bank statement	—	estratto bancario m	relación f
relevé de compte-titres (F)	Depotauszug m	statement of securities	—	estratto deposito m	extracto de depósito m
relevé des comptes généraux (F)	Summenbilanz f	turnover balance	—	bilancio generale m	balance de sumas m
relevé quotidien de compte (F)	Tagesauszug m	daily statement	—	estratto giornaliero m	extracto de cuenta diario m
remaining assets after liquidation (E)	Liquidationserlös m	—	produit de la liquidation m	ricavato dalla liquidazione m	producto de liquidación m
remboursable (F)	rückzahlbar	repayable	—	rimborsabile	reembolsable
remboursement (F)	Rückerstattung f	repayment	—	restituzione f	reintegración f
remboursement (F)	Rückzahlung f	repayment	—	rimborso m	reembolso m
remboursement des cotisations (F)	Beitragserstattung f	contribution refund	—	rimborso di contributi m	reintegro de las cuotas m
remesa (Es)	Rimesse f	remittance	remise f	rimessa f	—
remettant (F)	Remittent m	payee	—	beneficiario m	remitente m
reminder (E)	Mahnung f	—	mise en demeure f	sollecito m	monición f
remise (F)	Rimesse f	remittance	—	rimessa f	remesa f
remise (F)	Rabatt m	discount	—	sconto m	rebaja f
remitente (Es)	Remittent m	payee	remettant m	beneficiario m	—
remitente permanente (Es)	Dauerremittent m	constant issuer	émetteur permanent m	emittente continuo m	—
remittance (E)	Überweisung f	—	virement m	trasferimento m	transferencia f
remittance (E)	Rimesse f	—	remise f	rimessa f	remesa f
remittance slip (E)	Überweisungsträger m	—	formulaire de virement m	nota d'accredito f	formulario de transferencia m
Remittent (D)	—	payee	remettant m	beneficiario m	remitente m
remuneración (Es)	Vergütung f	remuneration	rémunération f	remunerazione f	—
remuneración bruta (Es)	Bruttoverdienst m	gross earnings	salaire brut m	guadagno lordo m	—

	D	E	F	I	Es
remuneración de los asalariados (Es)	Erwerbseinkommen n	income from gainful employment	revenu du travail m	reddito di lavoro m	—
remuneración del trabajo (Es)	Arbeitsentgelt n	remuneration	rémunération du travail f	remunerazione f	—
remuneración emisora (Es)	Emissionsvergütung f	issue commission	commission d'émission f	commissione d'emissione f	—
remuneración en especie (Es)	Deputat n	payment in kind	avantage en nature m	compenso in natura m	—
remunerate (E)	honorieren	—	honorer	onorare	honorar
remunerated order to effect a transaction (E)	Bankauftrag m	—	ordre bancaire m	ordine di banca m	orden bancaria remunerada f
remuneration (E)	Vergütung f	—	rémunération f	remunerazione f	remuneración f
remuneration (E)	Arbeitsentgelt n	—	rémunération du travail f	remunerazione f	remuneración del trabajo f
rémunération (F)	Vergütung f	remuneration	—	remunerazione f	remuneración f
rémunération du travail (F)	Arbeitsentgelt n	remuneration	—	remunerazione f	remuneración del trabajo f
remuneration in kind (E)	Sachbezüge m/pl	—	prestations en nature f/pl	retribuzioni in natura f/pl	percepciones en especie f/pl
remunerazione (I)	Vergütung f	remuneration	rémunération f	—	remuneración f
remunerazione (I)	Arbeitsentgelt n	remuneration	rémunération du travail f	—	remuneración del trabajo f
rendement (F)	Rendite f	yield	—	rendimento m	rédito m
rendement (F)	Leistung f	performance	—	prestazione f	prestación f
rendement (F)	Ertrag m	profits	—	ricavo m	rendimiento m
rendement du capital (F)	Kapitalrendite f	return on investment	—	rendimento del capitale m	rendimiento del capital m
rendement du chiffre d'affaires (F)	Umsatzrentabilität f	net profit ratio	—	rendimento del fatturato m	rentabilidad del volumen de negocios f
rendement moyen (F)	Durchschnittsertrag m	average yield	—	reddito medio m	rendimiento medio m
rendement réel (F)	Realzins m	real interest	—	interesse reale m	interés real m
rendering of account (E)	Rechenschaftslegung f	—	présentation d'un compte rendu f	resa dei conti f	rendición de cuentas f
rendering of account (E)	Rechenschaft f	—	compte rendu m	conto m	cuenta f
rendición de cuentas (Es)	Rechenschaftslegung f	rendering of account	présentation d'un compte rendu f	resa dei conti f	—
rendición de cuentas (Es)	Rechnungslegung f	accounting	reddition des comptes f	chiusura dei conti f	—
rendimento (I)	Rendite f	yield	rendement m	—	rédito m
rendimento del capitale (I)	Kapitalrendite f	return on investment	rendement du capital m	—	rendimiento del capital m
rendimento del fatturato (I)	Umsatzrentabilität f	net profit ratio	rendement du chiffre d'affaires m	—	rentabilidad del volumen de negocios f
rendimiento (Es)	Ertrag m	profits	rendement m	ricavo m	—
rendimiento del capital (Es)	Kapitalrendite f	return on investment	rendement du capital m	rendimento del capitale m	—
rendimiento medio (Es)	Durchschnittsertrag m	average yield	rendement moyen m	reddito medio m	—
rendita di nuovi titoli (I)	Emissionsrendite f	issue yield	rapport de l'émission m	—	rédito de emisión m
rendita marginale (I)	Grenznutzen m	marginal utility	utilité marginale f	—	utilidad marginal f
Rendite (D)	—	yield	rendement m	rendimento m	rédito m
renewal coupon (E)	Stichkupon m	—	coupon de renouvellement m	cedola di riaffoglamento f	cupón de renovación m
renewal of a bill of exchange (E)	Wechselprolongation f	—	prolongation de la traite f	proroga di cambiale f	renovación de la letra f
renewal rate (E)	Prolongationssatz m	—	taux de report m	saggio di riporto m	tipo de prolongación m
renewal reserve (E)	Erneuerungsfonds m	—	fonds de renouvellement m	fondo di rinnovamento m	fondo de renovación m

	D	E	F	I	Es
renovación de la letra (Es)	Wechselprolongation f	renewal of a bill of exchange	prolongation de la traite f	proroga di cambiale f	—
renseignement par la banque (F)	Bankauskunft f	banker's reference	—	informazione bancaria f	información bancaria f
renseignement sur la solvabilité du demandeur d'un crédit (F)	Kreditauskunft f	credit information	—	informazione creditizia f	información de crédito f
rent (E)	Pachtzins m	—	prix du bail m	canone d'affitto m	arrendamiento m
renta (Es)	Rente f	annuity	rente f	titolo a reddito fisso m	—
rentabilidad de la actividad de la empresa (Es)	Betriebsrentabilität f	operational profitability	rentabilité d'exploitation f	redditività aziendale f	—
rentabilidad del volumen de negocios (Es)	Umsatzrentabilität f	net profit ratio	rendement du chiffre d'affaires m	rendimento del fatturato m	—
rentabilité d'exploitation (F)	Betriebsrentabilität f	operational profitability	—	redditività aziendale f	rentabilidad de la actividad de la empresa f
rentabilité du capital (F)	Return on Investment [ROI] m	return on investment	—	return on investment m	ingresos por inversiones m/pl
rentabilité du capital propre (F)	Eigenkapitalrentabilität f	equity return	—	redditività del capitale proprio f	rédito del capital propio m
rentabilité totale du capital (F)	Gesamtkapitalrentabilität f	total capital profitability	—	redditività del capitale complessivo f	rédito del capital total m
renta bruta (Es)	Bruttoeinkommen n	gross income	revenu brut m	reddito lordo m	—
renta de capital (Es)	Kapitalertrag m	income from capital	produit du capital m	reddito di capitale m	—
renta de la propiedad (Es)	Besitzeinkommen n	property income	revenu du patrimoine m	reddito del patrimonio m	—
renta del capital (Es)	Kapitalzins m	interest on capital	intérêt du capital m	interesse del capitale m	—
renta disponible (Es)	verfügbares Einkommen n	disposable income	revenu disponible m	reddito disponibile f	—
renta nacional (Es)	Volkseinkommen n	national income	revenu national m	reddito nazionale m	—
rentas (Es)	Einkünfte pl	earnings	revenus m/pl	entrate f/pl	—
renta total (Es)	Gesamtertrag m	total proceeds	produit global m	reddito totale m	—
Rente (D)	—	annuity	rente f	titolo a reddito fisso m	renta f
rente (F)	Rente f	annuity	—	titolo a reddito fisso m	renta f
Rentenabteilung (D)	—	annuity department	service des titres à revenu fixe m	ufficio per titoli a reddito fisso m	sección de títulos de renta fija f
Rentenberater (D)	—	consultant on pensions	conseiller en matière de pensions m	consulente titoli a reddito fisso m	asesor en materia de títulos de renta fija m
Rentenbrief (D)	—	annuity certificate	titre de rente foncière m	titolo di rendita m	título de renta m
Rentenfonds (D)	—	fixed interest securities fund	fonds de placement en valeurs à revenu fixe m	fondo di obbligazioni m	fondo de títulos a renta fija m
Rentenhandel (D)	—	bond trading	négociation des valeurs à revenu fixe f	commercio titoli a reddito fisso m	contratación de títulos de renta fija f
Rentenmarkt (D)	—	bond market	marché obligataire m	mercato del reddito fisso m	mercado de renta fija m
Rentenwert (D)	—	fixed-interest security	valeur à revenu fixe f	titolo a reddito fisso m	título de renta fija m
rente perpétuelle (F)	ewige Rente f	perpetual annuity	—	annualità perpetua f	anualidad perpetua f
rentrée de fonds (F)	Geldeingang m	receipt of money	—	entrata di denaro f	entrada de dinero f
réorganisation d'une société (F)	Umgründung f	reorganization	—	trasformazione f	reorganización f
reorganización (Es)	Umgründung f	reorganization	réorganisation d'une société f	trasformazione f	—
reorganization (E)	Umgründung f	—	réorganisation d'une société f	trasformazione f	reorganización f
reorganization of the stock exchange (E)	Börsenreform f	—	réforme de la bourse f	riforma della borsa f	reforma de bolsa f

	D	E	F	I	Es
repartición (Es)	Repartierung *f*	apportionment	répartition *f*	ripartizione *f*	—
Repartierung (D)	—	apportionment	répartition *f*	ripartizione *f*	repartición *f*
répartition (F)	Repartierung *f*	apportionment	—	ripartizione *f*	repartición *f*
répartition extraordinaire (F)	Sonderausschüttung *f*	extra dividend	—	distribuzione straordinaria *f*	reparto extraordinario *m*
reparto de beneficios (Es)	Gewinnausschüttung *f*	distribution of profit	distribution de bénéfices *f*	ripartizione degli utili *f*	—
reparto depositi (I)	Depotabteilung *f*	safe custody department	service des dépôts *m*	—	sección de depósito *f*
reparto extraordinario (Es)	Sonderausschüttung *f*	extra dividend	répartition extraordinaire *f*	distribuzione straordinaria *f*	—
reparto giro (I)	Giroabteilung *f*	clearing department	service des virements *m*	—	sección de giros *f*
repayable (E)	rückzahlbar	—	remboursable	rimborsabile	reembolsable
repayment (E)	Rückerstattung *f*	—	remboursement *m*	restituzione *f*	reintegración *f*
repayment (E)	Rückzahlung *f*	—	remboursement *m*	rimborso *m*	reembolso *m*
repayment extension (E)	Tilgungsstreckung *f*	—	prolongation du délai de remboursement *f*	proroga di rimborso *f*	extensión del plazo de reintegración *f*
replacement of capital assets (E)	Ersatzinvestition *f*	—	investissement pour remplacement des moyens de production *m*	investimento sostitutivo *m*	inversión de reposición *f*
replacement share certificate (E)	Ersatzaktie *f*	—	action supplétive en remplacement d'un titre adiré *f*	azione sostitutiva *f*	acción de sustitución *f*
Report (D)	—	contango	report en bourse *m*	riporto *m*	reporte *m*
report des pertes (F)	Verlustvortrag *m*	carry-forward of the losses	—	riporto delle perdite *m*	traslación de pérdidas *f*
report du solde excédentaire (F)	Gewinnvortrag *m*	profit carried forward	—	avanzo utile *m*	arrastre de beneficios *m*
reporte (Es)	Report *m*	contango	report en bourse *m*	riporto *m*	—
Reporteffekten (D)	—	contango securities	titres reportés *m/pl*	titoli dati a riporto *m/pl*	efectos de reporte *m/pl*
report en bourse (F)	Report *m*	contango	—	riporto *m*	reporte *m*
Reportgeschäft (D)	—	contango transaction	opération de report *f*	operazione di riporto *f*	operación de reporte *f*
reporting date (E)	Stichtag *m*	—	jour fixé *m*	data di riferimento *f*	día de liquidación *m*
Repräsentant (D)	—	representative	représentant *m*	rappresentante *m*	representante *m*
représentant (F)	Repräsentant *m*	representative	—	rappresentante *m*	representante *m*
représentant de commerce (F)	Handelsvertreter *m*	commercial agent	—	agente di commercio *m*	representante comercial *m*
representante (Es)	Repräsentant *m*	representative	représentant *m*	rappresentante *m*	—
representante comercial (Es)	Handelsvertreter *m*	commercial agent	représentant de commerce *m*	agente di commercio *m*	—
representative (E)	Repräsentant *m*	—	représentant *m*	rappresentante *m*	representante *m*
Reprise (D)	—	reprise	tendance à la hausse *f*	ripresa *f*	recuperación *f*
reprise (E)	Reprise *f*	—	tendance à la hausse *f*	ripresa *f*	recuperación *f*
reprise (F)	Aufschwung *m*	recovery	—	ripresa *f*	auge *m*
reprise de dette (F)	Schuldübernahme *f*	assumption of an obligation	—	espromissione *f*	aceptación de deuda *f*
Reprivatisierung (D)	—	reversion to private ownership	dénationalisation *f*	riprivatizzazione *f*	desnacionalización *f*
reproduction value (E)	Reproduktionswert *m*	—	valeur de remplacement *f*	valore reale *m*	valor de reproducción *m*
Reproduktionswert (D)	—	reproduction value	valeur de remplacement *f*	valore reale *m*	valor de reproducción *m*
repurchase (E)	Rückkauf *m*	—	rachat *m*	riacquisto *m*	recompra *f*
resa dei conti (I)	Rechenschaftslegung *f*	rendering of account	présentation d'un compte rendu *f*	—	rendición de cuentas *f*
rescisión (Es)	Rücktritt *m*	rescission	résolution du contrat *f*	dimissione *f*	—

	D	E	F	I	Es
rescission (E)	Rücktritt *m*	—	résolution du contrat *f*	dimissione *f*	rescisión *f*
réseau bancaire (F)	Bankstellennetz *n*	bank office network	—	rete di sportelli bancari *f*	red bancaria *f*
réseau des banques de virement (F)	Gironetz *n*	clearing system	—	rete di giro *f*	red de bancos de giros *f*
reserva de compensación coyuntural (Es)	Konjunkturausgleichsrücklage *f*	anticyclical reserve	réserve anticyclique *f*	fondo compensazione congiuntura negativa *m*	—
reserva de divisas (Es)	Devisenreserve *f*	foreign exchange reserves	réserve de devises *f*	disponibilità in valuta *f*	—
reserva de financiación (Es)	Finanzierungsreserve *f*	financial reserve	réserves financières *f/pl*	riserva finanziaria *f*	—
reserva de liquidez (Es)	Liquiditätsreserve *f*	liquid reserves	réserve de liquidité *f*	riserva liquida *f*	—
reserva de propiedad (Es)	Eigentumsvorbehalt *m*	reservation of title	réserve de propriété *f*	diritto di riservato dominio *m*	—
reserva efectiva (Es)	Ist-Reserve *f*	actual reserve	réserve effective *f*	riserva effettiva *f*	—
reserva en efectivo (Es)	Bareinschuß *m*	cash loss payment	payement en espèces *m*	versamento in contanti *m*	—
reserva en exceso (Es)	Überschußreserve *f*	surplus reserve	réserve excédentaire *f*	riserva liquida *f*	—
reserva-metales finos (Es)	Gelddeckung *f*	monetary standard	couverture monétaire *f*	copertura metallica *f*	—
reserva mínima (Es)	Mindestreserve *f*	minimum legal reserves	réserve minimum *f*	riserva obbligatoria *f*	—
reserva monetaria bruta (Es)	Bruttowährungsreserve *f*	gross monetary reserve	réserves monétaires brutes *f/pl*	riserva monetaria lorda *f*	—
reserva obligatoria (Es)	Pflichtreserve *f*	minimum reserve	réserve légale *f*	riserva obbligatoria *f*	—
reservas (Es)	Reserven *f/pl*	reserves	réserves *f/pl*	riserve *f/pl*	—
reservas (Es)	Rücklagen *f/pl*	reserves	réserves *f/pl*	accantonamenti *m/pl*	—
reservas declaradas (Es)	offene Rücklagen *f/pl*	disclosed reserves	réserves déclarées *f/pl*	riserve dichiarate *f/pl*	—
reservas de liquidez libres (Es)	freie Liquiditätsserven *f/pl*	free liquid reserves	réserves de liquidités libres *f/pl*	riserve liquide a libera disposizione *f/pl*	—
reservas de oro (Es)	Goldreserven *f/pl*	gold reserve	réserves d'or *f/pl*	riserve in oro *f/pl*	—
reservas estacionales (Es)	Saison-Reserven *f/pl*	seasonal reserves	provisions pour pertes inhérentes aux fluctuations saisonnières *f/pl*	fondi di compensazione *m/pl*	—
reservas legales (Es)	gesetzliche Rücklage *f*	legally restricted retained earnings	réserves legales *f/pl*	riserva legale *f*	—
reservas libres (Es)	freie Rücklage *f*	unrestricted retained earnings	réserve libre *f*	riserva non vincolata *f*	—
reservas monetarias (Es)	Währungsserven *f/pl*	monetary reserves	réserves monétaires *f/pl*	riserve valutarie *f/pl*	—
reservas tácitas (Es)	stille Reserve *f*	hidden reserves	réserves cachées *f/pl*	riserva occulta *f*	—
reservation of title (E)	Eigentumsvorbehalt *m*	—	réserve de propriété *f*	diritto di riservato dominio *m*	reserva de propiedad *f*
réserve anticyclique (F)	Konjunkturausgleichsrücklage *f*	anticyclical reserve	—	fondo compensazione congiuntura negativa *m*	reserva de compensación coyuntural *f*
Reservebanken (D)	—	reserve banks	banques de réserve *f/pl*	banche di riserva *f/pl*	banco de reserva *m*
reserve banks (E)	Reservebanken *f/pl*	—	banques de réserve *f/pl*	banche di riserva *f/pl*	banco de reserva *m*
reserve currency (E)	Reservewährung *f*	—	monnaie de réserve *f*	moneta di riserva *f*	moneda de reserva *f*
réserve de devises (F)	Devisenreserve *f*	foreign exchange reserves	—	disponibilità in valuta *f*	reserva de divisas *f*
réserve de liquidité (F)	Liquiditätsreserve *f*	liquid reserves	—	riserva liquida *f*	reserva de liquidez *f*
réserve de propriété (F)	Eigentumsvorbehalt *m*	reservation of title	—	diritto di riservato dominio *m*	reserva de propiedad *f*
réserve effective (F)	Ist-Reserve *f*	actual reserve	—	riserva effettiva *f*	reserva efectiva *f*

	D	E	F	I	Es
réserve excédentaire (F)	Überschußreserve *f*	surplus reserve	—	riserva liquida *f*	reserva en exceso *f*
Reservefonds (D)	—	reserve fund	fonds de réserve *m*	fondo di riserva *m*	fondo de reserva *m*
reserve for bad debts (E)	Delkredere *n*	—	ducroire *m*	star del credere *m*	delcrédere *m*
reserve fund (E)	Reservefonds *m*	—	fonds de réserve *m*	fondo di riserva *m*	fondo de reserva *m*
reserve funds (E)	Dispositionsfonds *m*	—	fonds de réserves *m/pl*	fondi segreti *m/pl*	fondo disponible *m*
réserve légale (F)	Pflichtreserve *f*	minimum reserve	—	riserva obbligatoria *f*	reserva obligatoria *f*
réserve libre (F)	freie Rücklage *f*	unrestricted retained earnings	—	riserva eventuale *f*	reservas libres *f/pl*
réserve minimum (F)	Mindestreserve *f*	minimum legal reserves	—	riserva obbligatoria *f*	reserva mínima *f*
Reserven (D)	—	reserves	réserves *f/pl*	riserve *f/pl*	reservas *f/pl*
reserves (E)	Rücklagen *f/pl*	—	réserves *f/pl*	accantonamenti *m/pl*	reservas *f/pl*
reserves (E)	Reserven *f/pl*	—	réserves *f/pl*	riserve *f/pl*	reservas *f/pl*
réserves (F)	Rücklagen *f/pl*	reserves	—	accantonamenti *m/pl*	reservas *f/pl*
réserves (F)	Reserven *f/pl*	reserves	—	riserve *f/pl*	reservas *f/pl*
réserves cachées (F)	stille Reserve *f*	hidden reserves	—	riserva occulta *f*	reservas tácitas *f/pl*
réserves déclarées (F)	offene Rücklagen *f/pl*	disclosed reserves	—	riserve dichiarate *f/pl*	reservas declaradas *f/pl*
réserves de liquidités libres (F)	freie Liquiditätsre- serven *f/pl*	free liquid reserves	—	riserve liquide a li- bera disposizione *f/pl*	reservas de liquidez libres *f/pl*
réserves d'or (F)	Goldreserven *f/pl*	gold reserve	—	riserve in oro *f/pl*	reservas de oro *f/pl*
réserves financières (F)	Finanzierungsre- serve *f*	financial reserve	—	riserve finanziarie *f/pl*	reserva de financiación *f*
réserves legales (F)	gesetzliche Rücklage *f*	legally restricted retained earnings	—	riserva legale *f*	reservas legales *f/pl*
réserves monétaires (F)	Währungsre- serven *f/pl*	monetary reserves	—	riserve valutarie *f/pl*	reservas monetarias *f/pl*
réserves monétaires brutes (F)	Bruttowährungsre- serve *f*	gross monetary reserve	—	riserva monetaria lorda *f*	reserva monetaria bruta *f*
Reservewährung (D)	—	reserve currency	monnaie de réserve *f*	moneta di riserva *f*	moneda de reserva *f*
resguardo de prenda (Es)	Pfandschein *m*	certificate of pledge	bulletin de gage *m*	atto di pegno *m*	—
resident (E)	Gebietsansässiger *m*	—	résident *m*	residente *m*	residente *m*
resident (E)	Deviseninländer *m*	—	résident *m*	residente *m*	residente *m*
résident (F)	Gebietsansässiger *m*	resident	—	residente *m*	residente *m*
résident (F)	Deviseninländer *m*	resident	—	residente *m*	residente *m*
residente (Es)	Gebietsansässiger *m*	resident	résident *m*	residente *m*	—
residente (Es)	Deviseninländer *m*	resident	résident *m*	residente *m*	—
residente (I)	Deviseninländer *m*	resident	résident *m*	—	residente *m*
residente (I)	Gebietsansässiger *m*	resident	résident *m*	—	residente *m*
residual debt insurance (E)	Restschuldver- sicherung *f*	—	assurance solde de dette *f*	assicurazione del debito residuo *f*	seguro de deuda restante *m*
residual quota (E)	Restquote *f*	—	quote-part restante *f*	pagamento residuale *m*	cuota restante *f*
residual securities of an issue (E)	Emissionsreste *m/pl*	—	titres restant d'une émission *m/pl*	titoli rimanenti di un'emissione *m/pl*	títulos restantes de una emisión *m/pl*
résolution du contrat (F)	Rücktritt *m*	rescission	—	dimissione *f*	rescisión *f*
resources (E)	Ressourcen *f/pl*	—	ressources *f/pl*	risorse *f/pl*	recursos *m/pl*
responsabilidad (Es)	Haftung *f*	responsibility	responsabilité *f*	responsabilità *f*	—
responsabilidad de garantía (Es)	Garantiehaftung *f*	liability for breach of warranty	responsabilité de garantie *f*	responsabilità da garanzia *f*	—
responsabilidad solidaria (Es)	Solidarhaftung *f*	joint and several liability	responsabilité solidaire *f*	responsabilità solidale *f*	—
responsabilità (I)	Haftung *f*	responsibility	responsabilité *f*	—	responsabilidad *f*
responsabilità da garanzia (I)	Garantiehaftung *f*	liability for breach of warranty	responsabilité de garantie *f*	—	responsabilidad de garantía *f*

	D	E	F	I	Es
responsabilità solidale (I)	Solidarhaftung f	joint and several liability	responsabilité solidaire f	—	responsabilidad solidaria f
responsabilité (F)	Haftung f	responsibility	—	responsabilità f	responsabilidad f
responsabilité de garantie (F)	Garantiehaftung f	liability for breach of warranty	—	responsabilità da garanzia f	responsabilidad de garantía f
responsabilité solidaire (F)	Solidarhaftung f	joint and several liability	—	responsabilità solidale f	responsabilidad solidaria f
responsibility (E)	Haftung f	—	responsabilité f	responsabilità f	responsabilidad f
Ressort (D)	—	department	ressort m	sezione f	departamento m
ressort (F)	Ressort n	department	—	sezione f	departamento m
Ressourcen (D)	—	resources	ressources f/pl	risorse f/pl	recursos m/pl
Ressourcentransfer (D)	—	transfer of resources	transfert de ressources m	trasferimento di risorse m	transferencia de recursos f
ressources (F)	Ressourcen f/pl	resources	—	risorse f/pl	recursos m/pl
restitution (F)	Erstattung f	reimbursement	—	rimborso m	devolución f
restituzione (I)	Rückerstattung f	repayment	remboursement m	—	reintegración f
Restquote (D)	—	residual quota	quote-part restante f	pagamento residuale m	cuota restante f
restraint of competition (E)	Wettbewerbsbeschränkung f	—	restriction apportée à la concurrence f	limitazione della concorrenza f	restricción a la competencia f
restricción (Es)	Restriktion f	restriction	restriction f	restrizione f	—
restricción a la competencia (Es)	Wettbewerbsbeschränkung f	restraint of competition	restriction apportée à la concurrence f	limitazione della concorrenza f	—
restricción de créditos (Es)	Kreditrestriktion f	credit restriction	restriction du crédit f	restrizione creditizia f	—
restricción de emisión (Es)	Emissionssperre f	ban on new issues	blocage des émissions d'actions et d'obligations m	blocco delle emissioni m	—
restricted market (E)	enger Markt m	—	marché restreint m	mercato a scarso flottante m	mercado de valores poco flexible m
restricted share (E)	vinkulierte Aktie f	—	action négociable sous réserve f	azione vincolata f	acción vinculada f
restriction (E)	Restriktion f	—	restriction f	restrizione f	restricción f
restriction (F)	Restriktion f	restriction	—	restrizione f	restricción f
restriction à l'augmentation du capital social (F)	bedingte Kapitalerhöhung f	conditional capital increase	—	aumento di capitale condizionato m	aumento de capital condicional m
restriction apportée à la concurrence (F)	Wettbewerbsbeschränkung f	restraint of competition	—	limitazione della concorrenza f	restricción a la competencia f
restriction du crédit (F)	Kreditrestriktion f	credit restriction	—	restrizione creditizia f	restricción de créditos f
restriction of transferability (E)	Vinkulieren	—	obliger	vincolare m	vinculación f
restrictive endorsement (E)	Rektaindossament n	—	endossement non à ordre m	girata non all'ordine f	endoso intransferible m
Restriktion (D)	—	restriction	restriction f	restrizione f	restricción f
restrizione (I)	Restriktion f	restriction	restriction f	—	restricción f
restrizione creditizia (I)	Kreditrestriktion f	credit restriction	restriction du crédit f	—	restricción de créditos f
Restschuldversicherung (D)	—	residual debt insurance	assurance solde de dette f	assicurazione del debito residuo f	seguro de deuda restante m
resultado de mercado (Es)	Marktergebnis n	market performance	résultat du marché m	risultato sul mercato m	—
résultat du marché (F)	Marktergebnis n	market performance	—	risultato sul mercato m	resultado de mercado m
resumen mensual (Es)	Monatsausweis m	monthly return	situation mensuelle f	bilancio mensile m	—
rétablissement (F)	Erholung f	recovery	—	rianimazione f	recuperación f
retail trade (E)	Einzelhandel m	—	commerce de détail m	commercio al dettaglio m	comercio al por menor m
rete di giro (I)	Gironetz n	clearing system	réseau des banques de virement m	—	red de bancos de giros f

	D	E	F	I	Es
rete di sportelli bancari (I)	Bankstellennetz n	bank office network	réseau bancaire m	—	red bancaria f
retención de beneficios (Es)	Gewinnthesaurierung f	earnings retention	rétention de bénéfices f	tesaurizzazione degli utili f	—
retention (E)	Selbstbeteiligung f	—	participation personnelle à la couverture du risque f	franchigia f	propia retención f
rétention de bénéfices (F)	Gewinnthesaurierung f	earnings retention	—	tesaurizzazione degli utili f	retención de beneficios f
retention period (E)	Aufbewahrungsfrist f	—	délai de dépôt m	periodo di custodia m	plazo de conservación m
retirada de dinero (Es)	Entnahme f	withdrawal	prélèvement m	prelevamento m	—
retiro del capital propio (Es)	Eigenkapitalentzug m	own capital withdrawal	retrait du capital propre m	ritiro del capitale proprio m	—
retours (F)	Returen f/pl	returns	—	merci di ritorno f/pl	devoluciones f/pl
retrait d'actions (F)	Aktieneinziehung f	withdrawal of shares	—	ritiro di azioni m	redención de acciones f
retrait du capital propre (F)	Eigenkapitalentzug m	own capital withdrawal	—	ritiro del capitale proprio m	retiro del capital propio m
retraso en el pago (Es)	Zahlungsverzug m	failure to pay on due date	demeure du débiteur f	mora nel pagamento f	—
retribución (Es)	Entlohnung f	paying off	rétribution f	retribuzione f	—
rétribution (F)	Entlohnung f	paying off	—	retribuzione f	retribución f
retribuzione (I)	Besoldung f	payment	salaire m	—	salario m
retribuzione (I)	Entlohnung f	paying off	rétribution f	—	retribución f
retribuzione lorda (I)	Bruttolohn m	gross wage	salaire brut m	—	salario bruto m
retribuzioni in natura (I)	Sachbezüge m/pl	remuneration in kind	prestations en nature f/pl	—	percepciones en especie f/pl
rettifica del passivo (I)	Passivtausch m	accounting exchange on the liabilities side	écritures entre postes de passif f/pl	—	cambio de asientos en el pasivo m
Returen (D)	—	returns	retours m/pl	merci di ritorno f/pl	devoluciones f/pl
returned cheque (E)	Rückscheck m	—	chèque retourné m	assegno ritornato m	cheque devuelto m
return of capital reduction (E)	Ausweis der Kapitalherabsetzung m	—	situation de la réduction du capital f	dichiarazione di riduzione capitale f	devolución de la disminución de capital f
Return on Investment [ROI] (D)	—	return on investment	rentabilité du capital f	return on investment m	ingresos por inversiones m/pl
return on investment (E)	Return on Investment [ROI] m	—	rentabilité du capital f	return on investment m	ingresos por inversiones m/pl
return on investment (E)	Kapitalrendite f	—	rendement du capital m	rendimento del capitale m	rendimiento del capital m
return on investment (I)	Return on Investment [ROI] m	return on investment	rentabilité du capital f	—	ingresos por inversiones m/pl
returns (E)	Returen f/pl	—	retours m/pl	merci di ritorno f/pl	devoluciones f/pl
revalorisation (F)	Aufwertung f	revaluation	—	rivalutazione f	revalorización f
revalorización (Es)	Aufwertung f	revaluation	revalorisation f	rivalutazione f	—
revaluación colectiva (Es)	Sammelwertberichtigung f	global value adjustment	rajustement global m	rivalutazione forfettaria f	—
revaluation (E)	Aufwertung f	—	revalorisation f	rivalutazione f	revalorización f
revenu brut (F)	Bruttoeinkommen n	gross income	—	reddito lordo m	renta bruta f
revenu disponible (F)	verfügbares Einkommen n	disposable income	—	reddito disponibile f	renta disponible f
revenu du capital (F)	Vermögenseinkommen n	real balance effect	—	reddito di capitale m	ingresos por capital m/pl
revenu du patrimoine (F)	Besitzeinkommen n	property income	—	reddito del patrimonio m	renta de la propiedad f
revenu du travail (F)	Arbeitseinkommen n	earned income	—	reddito di lavoro m	ingresos del trabajo m/pl
revenu du travail (F)	Erwerbseinkommen n	income from gainful employment	—	reddito di lavoro m	remuneración de los asalariados f
revenu national (F)	Volkseinkommen n	national income	—	reddito nazionale m	renta nacional f
revenus (F)	Einkünfte pl	earnings	—	entrate f/pl	rentas f/pl

	D	E	F	I	Es
revenus d'une activité professionelle (F)	Erwerbseinkünfte *pl*	business income	—	redditi di lavoro *m/pl*	ingresos procendentes de una actividad remunerada *m/pl*
reversion to private ownership (E)	Reprivatisierung *f*	—	dénationalisation *f*	riprivatizzazione *f*	desnacionalización *f*
Revision (D)	—	audit	vérification *f*	revisione *f*	revisión *f*
revisión (Es)	Prüfung *f*	examination	vérification *f*	controllo *m*	—
revisión (Es)	Betriebsprüfung *f*	investigation by the tax authorities	vérification des livres de l'entreprise *f*	revisione aziendale *f*	—
revisión (Es)	Revision *f*	audit	vérification *f*	revisione *f*	—
revisión contable (Es)	Buchprüfung *f*	auditing	vérification des livres *f*	ispezione contabile *f*	—
revisión de cuentas del banco (Es)	Bankprüfung *f*	audit of the bank balance sheet	vérification du bilan bancaire *f*	esame del bilancio *m*	—
revisión de depósito (Es)	Depotprüfung *f*	securities deposit audit	contrôle des établissements dépositaires de titres *m*	revisione dei depositi *f*	—
revisión del balance (Es)	Bilanzprüfung *f*	balance sheet audit	contrôle du bilan *m*	revisione del bilancio *f*	—
revisione (I)	Revision *f*	audit	vérification *f*	—	revisión *f*
revisione aziendale (I)	Betriebsprüfung *f*	investigation by the tax authorities	vérification des livres de l'entreprise *f*	—	revisión *f*
revisione dei depositi (I)	Depotprüfung *f*	securities deposit audit	contrôle des établissements dépositaires de titres *m*	—	revisión de depósito *f*
revisione del bilancio (I)	Bilanzprüfung *f*	balance sheet audit	contrôle du bilan *m*	—	revisión del balance *f*
Revisionsabteilung (D)	—	audit department	service de vérification *m*	ufficio revisioni *m*	sección de revisión *f*
Revisionspflicht (D)	—	auditing requirements	obligation de vérification *f*	obbligo di revisione *m*	obligación de revisión *f*
revocación de la orden de pago de un cheque (Es)	Scheckwiderruf *m*	cheque stopping	contremandement de l'ordre de payement d'un chèque *m*	revoca dell'assegno *f*	—
revoca dell'assegno (I)	Scheckwiderruf *m*	cheque stopping	contremandement de l'ordre de payement d'un chèque *m*	—	revocación de la orden de pago de un cheque *f*
revolvierendes Akkreditiv (D)	—	revolving letter of credit	accréditif rotatif *m*	credito rinnovabile *m*	crédito rotativo *m*
revolving letter of credit (E)	revolvierendes Akkreditiv *n*	—	accréditif rotatif *m*	credito rinnovabile *m*	crédito rotativo *m*
Rezession (D)	—	recession	récession *f*	recessione *f*	recesión *f*
riacquisto (I)	Rückkauf *m*	repurchase	rachat *m*	—	recompra *f*
rialzista (I)	Haussier *m*	bull	haussier *m*	—	alcista *m*
rianimazione (I)	Erholung *f*	recovery	rétablissement *m*	—	recuperación *f*
ribassista (I)	Baisser *m*	bear	baissier *m*	—	bajista *m*
ribasso (I)	Baisse *f*	bear market	baisse *f*	—	baja *f*
ricavato dalla liquidazione (I)	Liquidationserlös *m*	remaining assets after liquidation	produit de la liquidation *m*	—	producto de liquidación *m*
ricavo (I)	Ertrag *m*	profits	rendement *m*	—	rendimiento *m*
ricavo lordo (I)	Bruttoertrag *m*	gross return	gain brut *m*	—	producto bruto *m*
ricavo marginale (I)	Grenzerlös *m*	marginal earnings	produit marginal *m*	—	beneficio marginal *m*
ricchezza nazionale (I)	Volksvermögen *n*	national wealth	patrimoine national *m*	—	patrimonio nacional *m*
ricco (I)	reich	rich	riche	—	rico
ricerca del mercato finanziario (I)	Kapitalmarktforschung *f*	capital market research	étude du marché des capitaux *f*	—	investigación del mercado de capital *f*
ricerca economica empirica (I)	empirische Wirtschaftsforschung *f*	empirical economic research	études économiques empiriques *f/pl*	—	investigación económica empírica *f*
ricevuta (I)	Beleg *m*	receipt	document justificatif *m*	—	justificante *m*
ricevuta di apporto (I)	Einschußquittung *f*	contribution receipt	quittance de contribution *f*	—	recibo de la inyección de dinero *m*

	D	E	F	I	Es
ricevuta di riscossione (I)	Einzugsquittung f	collection receipt	quittance d'encaissement f	—	recibo de cobro m
rich (E)	reich	—	riche	ricco	rico
riche (F)	reich	rich	—	ricco	rico
richiesta di copertura (I)	Deckungsforderung f	covering claim	créance de couverture f	—	crédito de cobertura m
Richtpreis (D)	—	recommended retail price	prix indicatif m	prezzo indicativo m	precio indicativo m
rico (Es)	reich	rich	riche	ricco	—
ricognizione di debito (I)	Schuldaner-kenntnis n	acknowledgement of a debt	reconnaissance de dette f	—	reconocimiento de la deuda m
ridistribuzione dei redditi (I)	Einkommensumver-teilung f	redistribution of income	redistribution des revenus f	—	redistribución de la renta f
riduzione del capitale sociale (I)	Kapitalherab-setzung f	capital reduction	diminution du capital f	—	reducción de capital f
riduzione del capitale sociale (I)	Herabsetzung des Grundkapitals f	reduction of the share capital	réduction de capital social f	—	reducción del capital social f
riduzione di capitale semplice (I)	vereinfachte Kapital-herabsetzung f	simplified capital reduction	diminution de capital simplifiée f	—	reducción de capital simplificada m
riesgo (Es)	Risiko n	risk	risque m	rischio m	—
riesgo (Es)	Wagnis n	venture	risque m	rischio m	—
riesgo de cambio (Es)	Wechselkursrisiko n	foreign exchange risk	risque de change m	rischio di cambio m	—
riesgo de inversión (Es)	Investitionsrisiko n	business risk	risque d'investissement m	rischio d'investimento m	—
riesgo del cambio (Es)	Kursrisiko n	price risk	risque de change m	rischio di quotazione m	—
riesgo del cambio del tipo de interés (Es)	Zinsänderungs-risiko n	risk of change in interest rates	risque de fluctuations d'intérêts m	rischio variazione tassi d'interesse m	—
riesgo del crédito (Es)	Kreditrisiko n	credit risk	risque inhérent aux opérations de crédit m	rischio inerente al credito m	—
riesgo del inversor (Es)	Anlagewagnis n	investment risk	risque de l'investisseur m	rischio d'investimento m	—
riesgo de solvencia (Es)	Bonitätsrisiko n	credit solvency risk	risque de rendement douteux m	rischio di solvibilità m	—
riesgo en el cambio (Es)	Valutarisiko n	exchange risk	risque de perte au change m	rischio di cambio m	—
riesgo nacional (Es)	Länderrisiko n	country risk	risque de pays m	rischio paese m	—
riflusso (I)	Rückfluß m	reflux	reflux m	—	reflujo m
riforma della borsa (I)	Börsenreform f	reorganization of the stock exchange	réforme de la bourse f	—	reforma de bolsa f
riforma finanziaria (I)	Finanzreform f	financial reform	réforme financière f	—	reforma financiera f
riforma monetaria (I)	Währungsumstel-lung f	currency conversion	adaptation d'une monnaie f	—	reforma monetaria f
riforma monetaria (I)	Währungsreform f	monetary reform	réforme monétaire f	—	reforma monetaria f
right-conferring minority (E)	qualifizierte Minderheit f	—	minorité qualifiée f	minoranza qualificata f	minoría calificada f
right issue (E)	Bezugsangebot m	—	offre de souscription f	offerta in opzione f	oferta de suscripción f
right of disposal (E)	Verfügungsrecht n	—	droit de disposition m	diritto di disporre m	capacidad dispositiva f
right to a cumulative dividend (E)	Nachbezugsrecht n	—	droit à un dividende cumulatif m	diritto di dividendo cumulativo m	derecho a un divi-dendo cumulativo m
right to claim (E)	Forderungsrecht n	—	droit issu d'une créance f	diritto di credito m	derecho de crédito m
right to use (E)	Benutzungsrecht n	—	droit d'usage m	diritto d'uso m	derecho de uso m
right to vote (E)	Stimmrecht n	—	droit de vote m	diritto di voto m	derecho a voto m
rimborsabile (I)	rückzahlbar	repayable	remboursable	—	reembolsable
rimborso (I)	Tilgung f	redemption	amortissement m	—	amortización f
rimborso (I)	Rückzahlung f	repayment	remboursement m	—	reembolso m
rimborso (I)	Erstattung f	reimbursement	restitution f	—	devolución f

riserve finanziarie

	D	E	F	I	Es
rimborso del credito ipotecario pattuito (I)	Naturaltilgung f	redemption in kind	amortissement en nature m	—	amortización en especie f
rimborso di contributi (I)	Beitragserstattung f	contribution refund	remboursement des cotisations m	—	reintegro de las cuotas m
rimessa (I)	Rimesse f	remittance	remise f	—	remesa f
Rimesse (D)	—	remittance	remise f	rimessa f	remesa f
rinvio (I)	Aussetzung f	suspension	suspension f	—	suspensión f
ripartizione (I)	Repartierung f	apportionment	répartition f	—	repartición f
ripartizione degli utili (I)	Gewinnausschüttung f	distribution of profit	distribution de bénéfices f	—	reparto de beneficios m
riporto (I)	Report m	contango	report en bourse m	—	reporte m
riporto delle perdite (I)	Verlustvortrag m	carry-forward of the losses	report des pertes m	—	traslación de pérdidas f
ripresa (I)	Reprise f	reprise	tendance à la hausse f	—	recuperación f
ripresa (I)	Aufschwung m	recovery	reprise f	—	auge m
riprivatizzazione (I)	Reprivatisierung f	reversion to private ownership	dénationalisation f	—	desnacionalización f
risanamento (I)	Sanierung f	reconstruction	assainissement m	—	saneamiento m
risarcimento dei danni (I)	Schadensersatz m	compensation for loss suffered	dommages-intérêts m/pl	—	indemnización por daños y perjuicios f
rischio (I)	Wagnis n	venture	risque m	—	riesgo m
rischio (I)	Risiko n	risk	risque m	—	riesgo m
rischio di cambio (I)	Valutarisiko n	exchange risk	risque de perte au change m	—	riesgo en el cambio m
rischio di cambio (I)	Wechselkursrisiko n	foreign exchange risk	risque de change m	—	riesgo de cambio m
rischio d'investimento (I)	Investitionsrisiko n	business risk	risque d'investissement m	—	riesgo de inversión m
rischio d'investimento (I)	Anlagewagnis n	investment risk	risque de l'investisseur m	—	riesgo del inversor m
rischio di quotazione (I)	Kursrisiko n	price risk	risque de change m	—	riesgo del cambio m
rischio di solvibilità (I)	Bonitätsrisiko n	credit solvency risk	risque de rendement douteux m	—	riesgo de solvencia f
rischio inerente al credito (I)	Kreditrisiko n	credit risk	risque inhérent aux opérations de crédit m	—	riesgo del crédito m
rischio paese (I)	Länderrisiko n	country risk	risque de pays m	—	riesgo nacional m
rischio variazione tassi d'interesse (I)	Zinsänderungsrisiko n	risk of change in interest rates	risque de fluctuations d'intérêts m	—	riesgo del cambio del tipo de interés m
risconto (I)	Refinanzierung f	refinancing	refinancement m	—	refinanciación f
risconto (I)	Rediskont m	rediscount	réescompte m	—	redescuento m
risconto (I)	Rediskontierung f	rediscount	réescompte m	—	redescuento m
riserva effettiva (I)	Ist-Reserve f	actual reserve	réserve effective f	—	reserva efectiva f
riserva legale (I)	gesetzliche Rücklage f	legally restricted retained earnings	réserves legales f/pl	—	reservas legales f/pl
riserva liquida (I)	Liquiditätsreserve f	liquid reserves	réserve de liquidité f	—	reserva de liquidez f
riserva liquida (I)	Überschußreserve f	surplus reserve	réserve excédentaire f	—	reserva en exceso f
riserva monetaria lorda (I)	Bruttowährungsreserve f	gross monetary reserve	réserves monétaires brutes f/pl	—	reserva monetaria bruta f
riserva non vincolata (I)	freie Rücklage f	unrestricted retained earnings	réserve libre f	—	reservas libres f/pl
riserva obbligatoria (I)	Mindestreserve f	minimum legal reserves	réserve minimum f	—	reserva mínima f
riserva obbligatoria (I)	Pflichtreserve f	minimum reserve	réserve légale f	—	reserva obligatoria f
riserva occulta (I)	stille Reserve f	hidden reserves	réserves cachées f/pl	—	reservas tácitas f/pl
riserve (I)	Reserven f/pl	reserves	réserves f/pl	—	reservas f/pl
riserve dichiarate (I)	offene Rücklagen f/pl	disclosed reserves	réserves déclarées f/pl	—	reservas declaradas f/pl
riserve finanziarie (I)	Finanzierungsreserve f	financial reserve	réserves financières f/pl	—	reserva de financiación f

	D	E	F	I	Es
riserve in oro (I)	Goldreserven f/pl	gold reserve	réserves d'or f/pl	—	reservas de oro f/pl
riserve liquide a libera disposizione (I)	freie Liquiditätsreserven f/pl	free liquid reserves	réserves de liquidités libres f/pl	—	reservas de liquidez libres f/pl
riserve valutarie (I)	Währungsreserven f/pl	monetary reserves	réserves monétaires f/pl	—	reservas monetarias f/pl
Risiko (D)	—	risk	risque m	rischio m	riesgo m
Risikokosten (D)	—	risk-induced costs	coût hasardeux m	costi di rischio m/pl	gastos de riesgo m/pl
Risikoprämie (D)	—	risk premium	prime de risque f	premio di rischio m	prima de riesgo f
Risikozuschlag (D)	—	additional risk premium	surprime de risque f	soprappremio di rischio m	recargo de riesgo m
risk (E)	Risiko n	—	risque m	rischio m	riesgo m
risk-induced costs (E)	Risikokosten pl	—	coût hasardeux m	costi di rischio m/pl	gastos de riesgo m/pl
risk of change in interest rates (E)	Zinsänderungsrisiko n	—	risque de fluctuations d'intérêts m	rischio variazione tassi d'interesse m	riesgo del cambio di tipo de interés m
risk premium (E)	Risikoprämie f	—	prime de risque f	premio di rischio m	prima de riesgo f
risorse (I)	Ressourcen f/pl	resources	ressources f/pl	—	recursos m/pl
risparmiare (I)	sparen	saving	économiser	—	ahorrar
risparmiare per l'edilizia (I)	bausparen	saving through building societies	épargner pour la construction	—	ahorrar para la construcción
risparmiatore (I)	Sparer m	saver	épargnant m	—	ahorrador m
risparmio (I)	Ersparnis f	savings	épargne f	—	ahorros m/pl
risparmio ad investimento vincolato (I)	Zwecksparen n	target saving	épargne à un but déterminé f	—	ahorro con un fin determinado m
risparmio a premi (I)	Gewinnsparen n	lottery premium saving	épargne à lots f	—	ahorro de beneficios m
risparmio a premi (I)	Prämiensparen n	bonus-aided saving	épargne à primes f	—	ahorro con primas m
risparmio collettivo (I)	Kollektivsparen n	collective saving	épargne collective f	—	ahorro colectivo m
risparmio collettivo (I)	Gemeinschaftssparen n	joint saving	épargne collective f	—	ahorro común m
risparmio con ordine permanente (I)	Überschuß-Sparen n	surplus saving	épargne d'excédents f	—	ahorro de los importes excesivos m
risparmio con privilegi fiscali (I)	steuerbegünstigtes Sparen n	tax-privileged saving	épargne jouissant d'avantages fiscaux f	—	ahorro favorecido por ventajas fiscales m
risparmio contrattuale (I)	Ratensparvertrag m	saving-by-instalments contract	contrat d'épargne à dépôts multiples m	—	contrato de ahorro a plazos m
risparmio contrattuale (I)	Investivlohn m	invested wages	fraction du revenu du travail disponible pour placements à long terme f	—	salario de inversión m
risparmio forzato (I)	Zwangssparen n	compulsory saving	épargne forcée f	—	ahorro forzoso m
risparmio individuale (I)	individuelles Sparen n	saving by private households	épargne individuelle f	—	ahorro individual m
risparmi restanti del conto corrente (I)	Plus-Sparen n	surplus saving	épargne d'excédents f	—	ahorro de excedentes m
risque (F)	Risiko n	risk	—	rischio m	riesgo m
risque (F)	Wagnis n	venture	—	rischio m	riesgo m
risque de change (F)	Kursrisiko n	price risk	—	rischio di quotazione m	riesgo del cambio m
risque de change (F)	Wechselkursrisiko n	foreign exchange risk	—	rischio di cambio m	riesgo de cambio m
risque de fluctuations d'intérêts (F)	Zinsänderungsrisiko n	risk of change in interest rates	—	rischio variazione tassi d'interesse m	riesgo del cambio del tipo de interés m
risque de l'investisseur (F)	Anlagewagnis n	investment risk	—	rischio d'investimento m	riesgo del inversor m
risque de pays (F)	Länderrisiko n	country risk	—	rischio paese m	riesgo nacional m
risque de perte au change (F)	Valutarisiko n	exchange risk	—	rischio di cambio m	riesgo en el cambio m
risque de rendement douteux (F)	Bonitätsrisiko n	credit solvency risk	—	rischio di solvibilità m	riesgo de solvencia f
risque d'investissement (F)	Investitionsrisiko n	business risk	—	rischio d'investimento m	riesgo de inversión m

	D	E	F	I	Es
risque inhérent aux opérations de crédit (F)	Kreditrisiko *n*	credit risk	—	rischio inerente al credito *m*	riesgo del crédito *m*
risultato sul mercato (I)	Marktergebnis *n*	market performance	résultat du marché *m*	—	resultado de mercado *m*
ritenuta alla fonte (I)	Quellensteuer *f*	tax at source	impôt retenu à la source *m*	—	impuesto deducido en la fuente *m*
ritenuta sugli utili dei crediti (I)	Kreditgewinnabgabe *f*	debts profit levy	taxe sur les bénéfices de crédit *f*	—	tributo sobre beneficios del crédito *m*
ritiro del capitale proprio (I)	Eigenkapitalentzug *m*	own capital withdrawal	retrait du capital propre *m*	—	retiro del capital propio *m*
ritiro di azioni (I)	Aktieneinziehung *f*	withdrawal of shares	retrait d'actions *m*	—	redención de acciones *f*
ritmo de la circulación del dinero (Es)	Geldumlaufsgeschwindigkeit *f*	velocity of circulation of money	vitesse de la circulation de la monnaie *f*	velocità della circolazione monetaria *f*	—
rivalutazione (I)	Aufwertung *f*	revaluation	revalorisation *f*	—	revalorización *f*
rivalutazione forfettaria (I)	Sammelwertberichtigung *f*	global value adjustment	rajustement global *m*	—	revaluación colectiva *f*
rivalutazione globale (I)	Globalwertberichtigung *f*	overall adjustment	rectification globale des valeurs *f*	—	rectificación de valor global *f*
Rohbilanz (D)	—	rough balance	bilan brut *m*	progetto di bilancio *m*	balance bruto *m*
Rohstoff-Fonds (D)	—	raw material funds	fonds de matières premières *m*	fondo titoli del settore primario *m*	fondo de las materias primas *m*
roll-over credit (E)	Roll-over-Kredit *m*	—	crédit roll-over *m*	credito roll-over *m*	crédito roll over *m*
Roll-over-Kredit (D)	—	roll-over credit	crédit roll-over *m*	credito roll-over *m*	crédito roll over *m*
rough balance (E)	Rohbilanz *f*	—	bilan brut *m*	progetto di bilancio *m*	balance bruto *m*
roulement de l'argent (F)	Geldumsatz *m*	turnover of money	—	circolazione monetaria *f*	giro monetario *m*
round off (E)	arrondieren	—	arrondir	arrotondare	redondear
round table (E)	runder Tisch *m*	—	table ronde *f*	tavola rotonda *f*	mesa redonda *f*
Rückerstattung (D)	—	repayment	remboursement *m*	restituzione *f*	reintegración *f*
Rückfluß (D)	—	reflux	reflux *m*	riflusso *m*	reflujo *m*
Rückflußstücke (D)	—	securities repurchased	titres rachetés *m/pl*	titolo di riflusso *m*	títulos de reflujo *m/pl*
Rückgriff (D)	—	recourse	recours *m*	regresso *m*	regreso *m*
Rückkauf (D)	—	repurchase	rachat *m*	riacquisto *m*	recompra *f*
Rückkaufdisagio (D)	—	discount on repurchase	perte de rachat *f*	scarto di rimborso su obbligazione *m*	disagio de recompra *m*
Rücklagen (D)	—	reserves	réserves *f/pl*	accantonamenti *m/pl*	reservas *f/pl*
Rückscheck (D)	—	returned cheque	chèque retourné *m*	assegno ritornato *m*	cheque devuelto *m*
Rückscheckprovision (D)	—	commission on returned cheque	commission de chèque retourné *f*	provvigione di rigresso *f*	comisión de cheque devuelto *f*
Rücktritt (D)	—	rescission	résolution du contrat *f*	dimissione *f*	rescisión *f*
Rückwechsel (D)	—	unpaid bill of exchange	traite retournée *f*	cambiale di ritorno *f*	letra de recambio *f*
rückzahlbar (D)	—	repayable	remboursable	rimborsabile	reembolsable
Rückzahlung (D)	—	repayment	remboursement *m*	rimborso *m*	reembolso *m*
Rückzahlungsagio (D)	—	premium payable on redemption	prime de remboursement *f*	aggio di rimborso *m*	agio de reembolso *m*
rule against accumulation (E)	Kumulierungsverbot *n*	—	prohibition de cumuler *f*	divieto del cumulo delle agevolazioni *m*	prohibición de acumulación *f*
rule-bound policy (E)	Regelbindung *f*	—	affectation à des règles *f*	attività vincolata *f*	vinculación a reglas *f*
rules for investment of resources (E)	Anlagevorschriften *f/pl*	—	prescriptions d'investissement *f/pl*	disposizioni d'investimento *f/pl*	normas de inversión *f/pl*
Run (D)	—	run	mouvement de panique *m*	run *m*	run *m*
run (E)	Run *m*	—	mouvement de panique *m*	run *m*	run *m*

	D	E	F	I	Es
run (Es)	Run *m*	run	mouvement de panique *m*	run *m*	—
run (I)	Run *m*	run	mouvement de panique *m*	—	run *m*
runder Tisch (D)	—	round table	table ronde *f*	tavola rotonda *f*	mesa redonda *f*
Sachanlagever-mögen (D)	—	tangible fixed assets	immobilisations corporelles *f/pl*	attivo immobilitato *m*	inmovilizado *m*
Sachbezüge (D)	—	remuneration in kind	prestations en nature *f/pl*	retribuzioni in natura *f/pl*	percepciones en especie *f/pl*
Sachdepot (D)	—	impersonal security deposit	dépôt de choses *m*	libretto di deposito titoli *m*	depósito impersonal de títulos *m*
Sacheinlage (D)	—	investment in kind	apport en nature *m*	apporto in natura *m*	aportación en especie *f*
Sachenrechtliche Wertpapiere (D)	—	property law securities	titres sur un droit réel *m/pl*	titoli di diritto reale *m/pl*	títulos jurídico-reales *m/pl*
Sachkapital (D)	—	real capital	immobilisations corporelles *f/pl*	capitale reale *m*	capital real *m*
Sachkapitaler-höhung (D)	—	capital increase through contribution in kind	augmentation du capital par élargissement des immobilisations corporelles *f*	aumento del capitale reale *m*	aumento del capital real *m*
Sachkredit (D)	—	credit based on collateral security	crédit réel *m*	credito reale *m*	crédito real *m*
Sachvermögen (D)	—	material assets	biens corporels *m/pl*	beni materiali *m/pl*	patrimonio real *m*
Sachverständigenrat (D)	—	panel of experts	conseil d'experts *m*	consiglio degli esperti *m*	consejo de asesores económicos *m*
Sachwertanleihen (D)	—	material value loans	emprunt de valeurs réelles *m*	prestito indicizzato *m*	empréstito en especie *m*
Sachwert-Investment-fonds (D)	—	material asset investment funds	fonds d'investissement en valeurs réelles *m*	fondo di valori reali *m*	fondo de inversión en valores reales *m*
safe (E)	Tresor *m*	—	coffre-fort *m*	cassaforte *f*	caja fuerte *f*
safe custody account (E)	offenes Depot *n*	—	dépôt collectif *m*	deposito aperto *m*	depósito abierto *m*
safe custody and administration of securities (E)	Wertpapierver-wahrung *f*	—	garde de titres *f*	custodia di titoli *f*	custodia de valores *f*
safe custody charges (E)	Depotgebühren *f/pl*	—	frais de garde *m/pl*	diritti di deposito *m/pl*	derechos de custodia *m/pl*
safe custody department (E)	Depotabteilung *f*	—	service des dépôts *m*	reparto depositi *m*	sección de depósito *f*
safe deposit (E)	verschlossenes Depot *n*	—	dépôt fermé *m*	deposito chiuso *m*	depósito cerrado *m*
safeguarding of credit (E)	Kreditsicherung *f*	—	sûreté en garantie d'un crédit *f*	garanzia di credito *f*	garantía de un crédito *f*
safeguarding of the currency (E)	Währungsab-sicherung *f*	—	garantie de change *f*	sostegno di una moneta *m*	garantía de cambio *f*
saggio di rendimento interno (I)	interner Zinsfuß *m*	internal interest rate	taux d'intérêt interne *m*	—	tipo de interés interno *m*
saggio di riporto (I)	Prolongationssatz *m*	renewal rate	taux de report *m*	—	tipo de prolongación *m*
saggio di sconto (I)	Diskontsatz *m*	discount rate	taux d'escompte *m*	—	tipo de descuento *m*
saggio speciale di interesse (I)	Sonderzinsen *m/pl*	special interests	intérêts spéciaux *m/pl*	—	intereses especiales *m/pl*
saisie (F)	Pfändung *f*	seizure	—	pignoramento *m*	embargo *m*
saisie de tiers débiteurs (F)	Drittpfändung *f*	garnishee proceedings	—	subpegno di titoli *m*	embargo del tercer deudor *m*
saisie de tous les biens (F)	Kahlpfändung *f*	seizure of all the debtor's goods	—	pignoramento totale *m*	embargo total *m*
Saisonbereinigung (D)	—	seasonal adjustment	correction des varia-tions saisonnières *f*	destagionalizzazione *f*	desestacionalización *f*
Saisonkredit (D)	—	seasonal loan	crédit à court terme *m*	credito stagionale *m*	crédito estacional *m*
Saison-Reserven (D)	—	seasonal reserves	provisions pour pertes inhérentes aux fluctuations saisonnières *f/pl*	fondi di compensazione *m/pl*	reservas estacionales *f/pl*
salaire (F)	Besoldung *f*	payment	—	retribuzione *f*	salario *m*

	D	E	F	I	Es
salaire brut (F)	Bruttolohn *m*	gross wage	—	retribuzione lorda *f*	salario bruto *m*
salaire brut (F)	Bruttoverdienst *m*	gross earnings	—	guadagno lordo *m*	remuneración bruta *f*
salaire en espèces (F)	Barlohn *m*	wage in cash	—	paga in contanti *f*	salario en efectivo *m*
salaire payé en argent (F)	Geldlohn *m*	money wage	—	salario in denaro *f*	salario en efectivo *m*
salario (Es)	Besoldung *f*	payment	salaire *m*	retribuzione *f*	—
salario bruto (Es)	Bruttolohn *m*	gross wage	salaire brut *m*	retribuzione lorda *f*	—
salario de inversión (Es)	Investivlohn *m*	invested wages	fraction du revenu du travail disponible pour placements à long terme *f*	risparmio contrattuale *m*	—
salario en efectivo (Es)	Barlohn *m*	wage in cash	salaire en espèces *m*	paga in contanti *f*	—
salario en efectivo (Es)	Geldlohn *m*	money wage	salaire payé en argent *m*	salario in denaro *f*	—
salario in denaro (I)	Geldlohn *m*	money wage	salaire payé en argent *m*	—	salario en efectivo *m*
saldar (Es)	saldieren	to balance	solder	saldare	—
saldare (I)	saldieren	to balance	solder	—	saldar
Saldenbilanz (D)	—	list of balances	balance des soldes	conto saldi contabili *m*	balance de saldos *m*
saldieren (D)	—	to balance	solder	saldare	saldar
Saldo (D)	—	balance	solde *m*	saldo *m*	saldo *m*
saldo (Es)	Saldo *m*	balance	solde *m*	saldo *m*	—
saldo (I)	Saldo *m*	balance	solde *m*	—	saldo *m*
saldo activo de la empresa (Es)	Geschäftsguthaben *n*	proprietor's capital holding	avoir commercial *m*	capitale da soci di una cooperativa *m*	—
saldo activo del Banco Federal (Es)	Bundesbankgut-haben *n*	Federal Bank assets	avoir auprès de la Banque fédérale *m*	fondo banca centrale *m*	—
saldo attivo bilancia commerciale (I)	Außenhandels-gewinn *m*	gains from trade	excédent du commerce extérieur *m*	—	excedente del comercio exterior *m*
saldo de financiación (Es)	Finanzierungssaldo *m*	net financial investment	investissement financier net *m*	saldo di finanziamento *m*	—
saldo di dividendo (I)	Schlußdividende *f*	final dividend	dividende final *m*	—	dividendo final *m*
saldo di financiamento (I)	Finanzierungssaldo *m*	net financial investment	investissement financier net *m*	—	saldo de financiación *m*
sale (E)	Verkauf *m*	—	vente *f*	vendita *f*	venta *f*
salida de capital (Es)	Kapitalabfluß *m*	capital outflows	sortie de capital *f*	deflusso di capitale *m*	—
salvadanaio (I)	Sparbüchse *f*	piggy bank	tirelire *f*	—	alcancía *f*
salvo venta (Es)	freibleibend	subject to confirmation	sans engagement	senza impegno	—
Sammelaktie (D)	—	global share	titre représentant globalement un paquet d'actions *m*	azione globale *f*	acción global *f*
Sammelanleihe (D)	—	joint loan issue	emprunt collectif *m*	obbligazione comunale *f*	empréstito colectivo *m*
Sammelauftrag (D)	—	collective order	ordre groupé *m*	ordine cumulativo *m*	orden colectiva *f*
Sammeldepot (D)	—	collective deposit	dépôt collectif de titres *m*	deposito collettivo di titoli *m*	depósito colectivo *m*
Sammelinkasso-versicherung (D)	—	group collection security	assurance d'encaissement groupé *f*	assicurazione collettiva *f*	seguro de cobro colectivo *m*
Sammelkonto (D)	—	collective account	compte collectif *m*	conto collettivo *m*	cuenta colectiva *f*
Sammelschuldbuch-forderung (D)	—	collective debt register claim	créance collective inscrite dans le livre de la dette *f*	cartella debito pubblico collettiva *f*	crédito contabilizado colectivo *m*
Sammeltratte (D)	—	collective bill	traite globale *f*	tratta collettiva *f*	libranza colectiva *f*
Sammelüber-weisung (D)	—	combined bank transfer	virement global *m*	trasferimento cumulativo *m*	transferencia colectiva *f*
Sammelwert-berichtigung (D)	—	global value adjustment	rajustement global *m*	rivalutazione forfettaria *f*	revaluación colectiva *f*
saneamiento (Es)	Sanierung *f*	reconstruction	assainissement *m*	risanamento *m*	—
Sanierung (D)	—	reconstruction	assainissement *m*	risanamento *m*	saneamiento *m*

	D	E	F	I	Es
sans coupon (F)	ohne Kupon	ex coupon	—	ex cedola	sin cupón
sans engagement (F)	freibleibend	subject to confirmation	—	senza impegno	salvo venta
sans tirage (F)	Ex Ziehung f	ex drawing	—	ex tratta	ex giro
saturación del mercado (Es)	Marktsättigung f	market saturation	saturation du marché f	saturazione del mercato f	—
saturation du marché (F)	Marktsättigung f	market saturation	—	saturazione del mercato f	saturación del mercado f
saturazione del mercato (I)	Marktsättigung f	market saturation	saturation du marché f	—	saturación del mercado f
Satzung (D)	—	statutes	statut m	statuto m	estatutos m/pl
saver (E)	Sparer m	—	épargnant m	risparmiatore m	ahorrador m
saving (E)	sparen	—	économiser	risparmiare	ahorrar
saving-by-instalments contract (E)	Ratensparvertrag m		contrat d'épargne à dépôts multiples m	risparmio contrattuale m	contrato de ahorro a plazos m
saving by private households (E)	individuelles Sparen n		épargne individuelle f	risparmio individuale m	ahorro individual m
savings (E)	Ersparnis f	—	épargne f	risparmio m	ahorros m/pl
savings account (E)	Sparguthaben n	—	avoir sur un compte d'épargne m	deposito a risparmio m	depósito de ahorro m
savings account (E)	Sparkonto n	—	compte d'épargne m	conto a risparmio m	cuenta de ahorros f
savings agreement with the building society (E)	Bausparvertrag m	—	contrat d'épargne-construction m	contratto di risparmio edilizio m	contrato de ahorro para la construcción m
savings bank (E)	Sparkasse f	—	caisse d'épargne f	cassa di risparmio f	caja de ahorros f
savings-bank book (E)	Sparbuch n	—	livret d'épargne m	libretto di risparmio m	libreta de ahorro f
savings bond (E)	Sparobligation f	—	obligation d'épargne f	obbligazione di cassa di risparmio f	obligación de ahorro f
savings bonus (E)	Sparzulage f	—	prime d'épargne f	assegno integrativo di risparmio m	subvención de ahorro f
savings certificate (E)	Sparbrief m	—	bon d'épargne m	lettera di risparmio f	cédula de ahorro f
savings club (E)	Sparverein m	—	association d'épargne f	società di risparmio f	asociación de ahorro f
savings department (E)	Sparabteilung f	—	service d'épargne m	ufficio risparmi m	sección de ahorro f
savings deposit (E)	Spareinlage f	—	dépôt d'épargne m	deposito a risparmio m	imposición de ahorro f
savings gift credit voucher (E)	Spargeschenk-gutschein m	—	bon d'épargne m	buono regalo di risparmio m	vale de ahorro m
savings plans (E)	Sparpläne m/pl	—	plans d'épargne m/pl	piani di risparmio m/pl	planes de ahorro m/pl
savings premium (E)	Sparprämie f	—	prime d'épargne f	premio al risparmio m	prima de ahorro f
savings promotion (E)	Sparförderung f	—	promotion de l'épargne f	promozione del risparmio f	fomento del ahorro m
savings ratio (E)	Sparquote f	—	quote-part de revenu réservée à des fins d'épargne f	aliquota di risparmio f	cuota de ahorro f
savings stamp (E)	Sparmarke f	—	timbre d'épargne m	marca di risparmio f	cuota de ahorro f
saving through building societies (E)	bausparen	—	épargner pour la construction	risparmiare per l'edilizia m	ahorrar para la construcción
scadenza (I)	Fälligkeit f	maturity	échéance f	—	vencimiento m
scadenza (I)	Verfallzeit f	time of expiration	date de l'échéance f	—	plazo de vencimiento m
scadenza del credito (I)	Kreditfrist f	credit period	délai de remboursement des avances sur crédit m	—	plazo de vencimiento del crédito m
scadenza media (I)	mittlere Verfallszeit f	mean due date	échéance à moyen	— terme f	vencimiento a medio plazo m
scalage (E)	Schwundgeld n	—	argent de consomption m	bollatura di monete f	dinero de consunción m
scaletta (I)	Zinsstaffel f	interest rate table	barème des intérêts m	—	escala de intereses f
scambi borsistici (I)	Börsenumsätze m/pl	stock exchange turnover	volume d'opérations boursières m	—	volumen de operaciones bursátiles m

	D	E	F	I	Es
scambio di accettazioni (I)	Akzeptaustausch *m*	exchange of acceptances	échange d'acceptations *m*	—	intercambio de acceptaciones *m*
scambio di azioni (I)	Aktienaustausch *m*	exchange of shares	échange d'actions *f*	—	canje de acciones *m*
scarto di rimborso su obbligazione (I)	Rückkaufdisagio *n*	discount on repurchase	perte de rachat *f*	—	disagio de recompra *m*
Schadensersatz (D)	—	compensation for loss suffered	dommages-intérêts *m/pl*	risarcimento dei danni *m*	indemnización por daños y perjuicios *f*
Schaltergeschäft (D)	—	business over the counter	opération de guichet *f*	operazione a contanti *f*	operación al contado *f*
Schalterprovision (D)	—	selling commission	commission de vente *f*	commissione di collocamento *f*	comisión al contado *f*
Schalterstücke (D)	—	counter stock	titres de guichet m/pl	titoli venduti allo sportello m/pl	títulos al contado m/pl
Schatzanweisung (D)	—	treasury bond	bon du Trésor *f*	buono del tesoro *m*	bono del tesoro *m*
Schätze (D)	—	treasury bonds	obligations du Trésor *f/pl*	buoni del tesoro *m/pl*	bonos del tesoro *m/pl*
Schatzwechsel (D)	—	Treasury bill	effet du Trésor *m*	buono del tesoro *m*	letra de tesorería *f*
Scheck (D)	—	cheque	chèque *m*	assegno *m*	cheque *m*
Scheckabrechnung (D)	—	cheque clearance	règlement des chèques par voie de compensation *m*	compensazione degli assegni *f*	liquidación de cheques *f*
Scheckabteilung (D)	—	cheque department	service des chèques *m*	ufficio assegni *m*	sección de cheques *f*
Scheckeinzug (D)	—	cheque collection	recouvrement de chèques *m*	incasso di assegno *m*	cobro del cheque *m*
Scheckfähigkeit (D)	—	capacity to draw cheques	habilité en matière de chèque *f*	capacità di obbligarsi per assegno *f*	capacidad de girar cheques *f*
Scheckklausel (D)	—	cheque clause	mention sur un chèque *f*	indicazione di assegno bancario *f*	cláusula de cheque *f*
Scheckrecht (D)	—	negotiable instruments law concerning cheques	législation en matière de chèque *f*	disciplina degli assegni *f*	derecho de cheque *m*
Scheckregreß (D)	—	cheque recourse	recours en matière de chèque *m*	regresso d'assegno *m*	regreso de cheque *m*
Schecksperre (D)	—	stopping payment of cheque	opposition au paye-ment d'un chèque *f*	fermo su assegno *m*	bloqueo de un cheque *m*
Scheckverkehr (D)	—	cheque transactions	opérations par chèque *f/pl*	pagamenti mediante assegno *m/pl*	operaciones de cheques *f/pl*
Scheckwiderruf (D)	—	cheque stopping	contremandement de l'ordre de paye-ment d'un chèque *m*	revoca dell'assegno *f*	revocación de la orden de pago de un cheque *f*
schedario dei crediti (I)	Kreditkartei *f*	borrowing customers' card index	fichier des opérations d'avances et de crédit	—	fichero de operaciones de crédito *m*
Scheidemünze (D)	—	divisional coin	monnaie divisionnaire *f*	moneta divisionale *f*	moneda fraccionaria *f*
Scheinfirma (D)	—	bogus firm	raison sociale imaginaire *f*	impresa fittizia *f*	casa ficticia *f*
Scheingewinn (D)	—	fictitious profit	gain fictif *m*	utile fittizio *m*	beneficio simulado *m*
Scheingründung (D)	—	fictitious formation	constitution d'opportunité *f*	costituzione fittizia *f*	fundación simulada *f*
Scheinkurs (D)	—	fictitious quotation price	cours nominal *m*	quotazione evasiva *f*	cotización ficticia *f*
Schiffahrtsbörse (D)	—	shipping exchange	bourse maritime *f*	borsa dei noli marit-timi *f*	bolsa naval *f*
Schiffshypothek (D)	—	ship mortgage	hypothèque maritime *f*	ipoteca navale *f*	hipoteca naval *f*
Schluß (D)	—	closure	clôture *f*	chiusura *f*	cierre *m*
Schlußbilanz (D)	—	closing balance	bilan de clôture *m*	bilancio di chiusura *m*	balance de cierre *m*
Schlußdividende (D)	—	final dividend	dividende final *m*	saldo di dividendo *m*	dividendo final *m*
Schlußkurs (D)	—	closing price	dernier cours *m*	quotazione di chiusura *f*	cotización de cierre *f*
Schlußnote (D)	—	broker's note	avis d'exécution *m*	fissato bollato *m*	póliza de negociación *f*

	D	E	F	I	Es
Schrankenwert (D)	—	officially quoted security	valeur négociée au marché officiel *f*	valori amnessi alla quotazione ufficiale *m/pl*	título oficialmente cotizado *m*
Schuld (D)	—	debt	dette *f*	debito *m*	deuda *f*
Schuldanerkenntnis (D)	—	acknowledgement of a debt	reconnaissance de dette *f*	ricognizione di debito *f*	reconocimiento de la deuda *m*
Schuldbrief (D)	—	certificate of indebtedness	titre d'obligation *m*	titolo di debito *m*	título de deuda *m*
Schuldbuch-forderung (D)	—	debt-register claim	créance inscrite dans le livre de la dette *f*	cartella del debito pubblico *f*	deuda inscrita en el libro de deudas *f*
Schuldendienst (D)	—	debt service	service de la dette *m*	servizio dei debiti *m*	servicio de deudas *m*
Schuldner (D)	—	debtor	débiteur *m*	debitore *m*	deudor *m*
Schuldnerver-zeichnis (D)	—	list of insolvent debtors	liste des personnes ayant été pousuivies pour dettes *f*	elenco dei debitori *m*	lista de deudores *f*
Schuldrecht (D)	—	law of obligations	droit des obligations et contrats *m*	diritto delle obbligazioni *m*	derecho de obligaciones *m*
Schuldschein (D)	—	certificate of indebtedness	reconnaissance de dette *f*	certificato di debito *m*	pagaré *m*
Schuldschein-darlehen (D)	—	promissory note bond	prêt en reconnais-sance de dette *m*	prestito obbligazio-nario *m*	préstamo a título de pagaré *m*
Schuldübernahme (D)	—	assumption of an obligation	reprise de dette *f*	espromissione *f*	aceptación de deuda *f*
Schuldverhältnis (D)	—	obligation	rapport d'obligation *m*	rapporto obbligatorio *m*	relación obligatoria *f*
Schuldverschrei-bung (D)	—	debenture stock	obligation *f*	titolo obbligazionario *m*	obligación *f*
Schuldversprechen (D)	—	promise to fulfil an obligation	reconnaissance fondant un rapport d'obligation *f*	promessa di debito *f*	promesa de deuda *f*
Schuldwechsel (D)	—	bill payable	effet à payer *m*	cambiale passiva *f*	efecto a pagar *m*
Schuldzins (D)	—	interest on debts	intérêt à payer *m*	interesse su debiti *m*	interés sobre depósi tos *m*
schwach (D)	—	slack	faible	debole	flojo
Schwänze (D)	—	corners	corners *m/pl*	code speculative *f/pl*	corners *m*
schwarze Börse (D)	—	black stock exchange	bourse noire *f*	borsa nera *f*	bolsín *m*
schwarze Liste (D)	—	black bourse	liste noire *f*	elenco dei debitori *m*	lista negra *f*
Schwarzer Freitag (D)	—	black Friday	vendredi noir *m*	venerdì nero *m*	viernes negro *m*
schwarzer Markt (D)	—	black market	marché noir *m*	mercato nero *m*	mercado negro *m*
schwebende Geschäfte (D)	—	pending transactions	affaires en suspens *f/pl*	affari pendenti *m/pl*	negocios en curso *m/pl*
schwebende Schuld (D)	—	floating debt	dette flottante *f*	debito fluttuante *m*	deuda flotante *f*
schwere Papiere (D)	—	heavy-priced securities	titres chers *m/pl*	titoli pesanti *m/pl*	valores de alta cotización *m/pl*
schwimmend (D)	—	floating	flottant	flottante	flotante
Schwindelgründung (D)	—	fraud foundation	fondation fictive *f*	costituzione fraudolenta *f*	fundación ficticia *f*
Schwundgeld (D)	—	scalage	argent de consomption *m*	bollatura di monete *f*	dinero de consunción *m*
science bancaire (F)	Bankbetriebslehre *f*	science of banking	—	tecnica bancaria *f*	ciencias bancarias *f/pl*
science financière (F)	Finanzwissenschaft *f*	public finance	—	scienza delle finanze *f*	ciencia financiera *f*
science of banking (E)	Bankbetriebslehre *f*	—	science bancaire *f*	tecnica bancaria *f*	ciencias bancarias *f/pl*
scienza dell'economia aziendale (I)	Betriebswirtschafts-lehre *f*	business economics	gestion industrielle et commerciale *f*	—	teoría de la empresa *f*
scienza delle finanze (I)	Finanzwissenschaft *f*	public finance	science financière *f*	—	ciencia financiera *f*
sconto (I)	Rabatt *m*	discount	remise *f*	—	rebaja *f*
sconto (I)	Diskont *m*	discount	escompte *m*	—	descuento *m*
sconto (I)	Skonto *n*	discount	escompte *m*	—	descuento *m*
sconto cambiario (I)	Wechseldiskont *m*	discount of bills	escompte d'un effet *m*	—	descuento de letras *m*
sconto diretto (I)	Direktdiskont *m*	direct discount	escompte directe *m*	—	descuento directo *m*

	D	E	F	I	Es
sconto di titoli (I)	Effektendiskont *m*	securities discount	escompte sur achat de titres *m*	—	descuento de valores *m*
sconto di titoli in pensione (I)	Effektenpensionsgeschäft *n*	security transactions under repurchase agreement	opération de mise en pension d'effets *f*	—	operaciones de cesión temporal de valores *f/pl*
sconto di titoli in pensione (I)	Effektenpensionierung *f*	raising money on securities by cash sale coupled with contract for subsequent repurchase	mise en pension d'effets *f*	—	cesión temporal de valores *f*
sconto di valuta in pensione (I)	Devisenpensionsgeschäft *n*	purchase of foreign exchange for later sale	opération de mise en pension de devises *f*	—	operación de reporte en divisas *f*
sconto in pensione (I)	Pensionsgeschäft *n*	security transactions under repurchase agreement	opération de mise en pension d'effets *f*	—	operación de reporte *f*
scopertista (I)	Fixer *m*	bear seller	vendeur à découvert *m*	—	vendedor al descubierto *m*
scoperto (I)	Leerposition *f*	bear selling position	découvert *m*	—	descubierto *m*
scrutinio (I)	Auszählung *f*	counting	comptage *m*	—	cómputo *m*
sea bill (E)	Seewechsel *m*	—	lettre de prêt à la grosse *f*	cambiale marittima *f*	letra de cambio marítima *f*
seasonal adjustment (E)	Saisonbereinigung *f*	—	correction des variations saisonnières *f*	destagionalizzazione *f*	desestacionalización *f*
seasonal loan (E)	Saisonkredit *m*	—	crédit à court terme *m*	credito stagionale *m*	crédito estacional *m*
seasonal reserves (E)	Saison-Reserven *f/pl*	—	provisions pour pertes inhérentes aux fluctuations saisonnières *f/pl*	fondi di compensazione *m/pl*	reservas estacionales *f/pl*
seasoned securities (E)	Favoriten *m/pl*	—	favoris *m/pl*	titoli molto richiesti *m/pl*	favoritos *m/pl*
sección de ahorro (Es)	Sparabteilung *f*	savings department	service d'épargne *m*	ufficio risparmi *m*	—
sección de bolsa (Es)	Börsenabteilung *f*	exchange department	service des valeurs en bourse *m*	ufficio borsa *m*	—
sección de cheques (Es)	Scheckabteilung *f*	cheque department	service des chèques *m*	ufficio assegni *m*	—
sección de cobranza (Es)	Inkasso-Abteilung *f*	collection department	service des encaissements *m*	ufficio incassi *m*	—
sección de cobro por cupones (Es)	Kuponkasse *f*	coupon collection department	service de payement des coupons *m*	cassa cedolare *f*	—
sección de comercio exterior (Es)	Außenhandelsabteilung *f*	export department	service étranger *m*	ufficio commercio estero *m*	—
sección de consorcios (Es)	Konsortialabteilung *f*	syndicate department	service de syndicats *m*	ufficio consorzi *m*	—
sección de crédito (Es)	Kreditabteilung *f*	credit department	service du crédit et des prêts *m*	ufficio crediti *m*	—
sección de depósito (Es)	Depotabteilung *f*	safe custody department	service des dépôts *m*	reparto depositi *m*	—
sección de divisas (Es)	Devisenabteilung *f*	foreign exchange department	service des devises *m*	ufficio cambi *m*	—
sección de efectos (Es)	Effektenabteilung *f*	securities department	service des titres *m*	ufficio titoli *m*	—
sección de emisión (Es)	Emissionsabteilung *f*	issue department	service d'émission *m*	ufficio emissioni *m*	—
sección de gastos (Es)	Kostenstelle *f*	cost centre	compte de frais par secteur *m*	centro di costo *m*	—
sección de giro especial (Es)	Sonderziehungsabteilung *f*	Special Drawing Rights Department	service de tirage spécial *m*	ufficio prelievi speciali *m*	—
sección de giros (Es)	Giroabteilung *f*	clearing department	service des virements *m*	reparto giro *m*	—
sección de organización (Es)	Organisationsabteilung *f*	organization and methods department	service d'organisation *m*	ufficio organizzazione *m*	—
sección de revisión (Es)	Revisionsabteilung *f*	audit department	service de vérification *m*	ufficio revisioni *m*	—
sección de títulos de renta fija (Es)	Rentenabteilung *f*	annuity department	service des titres à revenu fixe *m*	ufficio per titoli a reddito fisso *m*	—
sección de valores (Es)	Wertpapierabteilung *f*	securities department	service des valeurs *m*	ufficio titoli *m*	—
seconda di cambio (I)	Sekunda-Wechsel *m*	second of exchange	seconde de change *f*	—	segunda de cambio *f*

	D	E	F	I	Es
secondary liquidity (E)	Sekundär-Liquidität f	—	liquidité secondaire f	liquidità secondaria f	liquidez secundaria f
secondary market (E)	Umlaufmarkt m	—	marché secondaire m	mercato secondario m	mercado de circulación m
secondary market (E)	Sekundär-Markt m	—	marché secondaire m	mercato secondario m	mercado secundario m
seconde de change (F)	Sekunda-Wechsel m	second of exchange	—	seconda di cambio f	segunda de cambio f
second of exchange (E)	Sekunda-Wechsel m	—	seconde de change f	seconda di cambio f	segunda de cambio f
secret bancaire (F)	Bankgeheimnis n	banker's duty of secrecy	—	segreto bancario m	secreto bancario m
secreto bancario (Es)	Bankgeheimnis n	banker's duty of secrecy	secret bancaire m	segreto bancario m	—
secteur financier (F)	Finanzsektor m	financial sector	—	settore della finanza m	sector financiero m
sector financiero (Es)	Finanzsektor m	financial sector	secteur financier m	settore della finanza m	—
sectors of the stock exchange (E)	Börsensegmente n/pl	—	segments de bourse m/pl	segmenti di borsa m/pl	segmentos bursátiles m/pl
sécurisation (F)	Sekurization f	securization	—	securizzazione f	segurización f
securities (E)	Effekten pl	—	valeurs mobilières f/pl	titoli m/pl	efectos m/pl
securities (E)	Stücke n/pl	—	titres m/pl	titoli m/pl	títulos m/pl
securities (E)	Valoren pl	—	valeurs f/pl	valori m/pl	valores m/pl
securities account (E)	Effektenkonto n	—	compte des titres de participation m	conto titoli m	cuenta de valores f
securities business (E)	Effektengeschäft n	—	commerce des valeurs mobilières m	operazione in titoli f	operación con valores f
securities capitalism (E)	Effektenkapitalismus m	—	capitalisme de valeurs mobilières m	capitalismo (basato su) titoli m	capitalismo por títulos-valores m
securities coming on to the market (E)	herauskommendes Material n	—	titres lancés sur le marché m/pl	offerta di titoli f	material saliente m
securities commission agent (E)	Effekten-kommissionär m	—	banque chargée d'opérations sur titres f	commissionario di borsa m	comisionista de valores m
securities department (E)	Effektenabteilung f	—	service des titres m	ufficio titoli m	sección de efectos f
securities department (E)	Wertpapierabteilung f	—	service des valeurs m	ufficio titoli m	sección de valores f
Securities Deposit Act (E)	Depotgesetz n	—	législation sur les dépôts et achats de valeurs par les banques f	legge sui depositi f	ley de depósitos f
securities deposit audit (E)	Depotprüfung f	—	contrôle des établissements dé-positaires de titres m	revisione dei depositi f	revisión de depósito f
securities deposit contract (E)	Depotvertrag m	—	contrat de dépôt m	contratto di deposito m	contrato de depósito m
securities deposit reconciliation (E)	Depotabstimmung f	—	vote de titres en dépôt m	coordinamento dei depositi m	voto de título en depósito m
securities discount (E)	Effektendiskont m	—	escompte sur achat de titres m	sconto di titoli m	descuento de valores m
securities eligible as cover (E)	deckungsfähige Wert-papiere n/pl	—	titres susceptibles d'être déposé en couverture m/pl	titoli riscontabili m/pl	títulos cubiertos por el banco emisor m/pl
securities held by a bank at another bank (E)	Nostroeffekten pl	—	effets dans une autre banque m/pl	titoli nostri m/pl	efectos a nuestro cargo m/pl
securities-linked savings scheme (E)	Wertpapierspar-vertrag m	—	contrat d'épargne mobilière m	contratto di risparmio in titoli m	contrato de ahorro en forma de valores m
securities market (E)	Wertpapierbörse f	—	bourse des titres et valeurs f	borsa valori f	bolsa de valores f
securities market (E)	Wertpapiermarkt m	—	marché des valeurs mobilières m	mercato mobiliare m	mercado de valores m
securities placing (E)	Effektenplazierung f	—	placement de titres m	emissione di titoli f	emisión de valores f
securities price (E)	Effektenkurs m	—	cours des valeurs mobilières m	quotazione di titoli f	cotización de valores f
securities publicly notified as lost (E)	aufgerufene Wert-papiere n/pl	—	titres appelés au remboursement m/pl	titoli colpiti da ammortamento m/pl	títulos retirados de la circulación con aviso m/pl

	D	E	F	I	Es
securities redeemable at a premium (E)	Agiopapiere *n/pl*	—	obligations remboursables avec prime *f/pl*	titoli a premio *m/pl*	valores de renta fija reembolsados con una prima *m/pl*
securities repurchased (E)	Rückflußstücke *n/pl*	—	titres rachetés *m/pl*	titolo di riflusso *m*	títulos de reflujo *m/pl*
securities research (E)	Wertpapieranalyse *f*	—	analyse des valeurs mobilières *f*	analisi di titoli *f*	análisis de inversiones *m*
securities serving as collateral (E)	Lombardeffekten *pl*	—	titres remis en nantissement *m/pl*	titoli lombard *m/pl*	títulos pignoraticios *m/pl*
securities statistics (E)	Effektenstatistik *f*	—	statistique de titres *f*	statistica dei titoli *f*	estadística de valores *f*
securities substitution (E)	Effektensubstitution *f*	—	substitution de titres *f*	sostituzione di titoli *f*	sustitución de valores *f*
securities taxed at the standard rate (E)	tarifbesteuerte Wertpapiere *n/pl*	—	titres soumis aux impôts en vigueur *m/pl*	titoli a tariffa d'imposizione *m/pl*	títulos sometidos a los impuestos en vigor *m/pl*
securities transactions on commission (E)	Effektenkommissionsgeschäft *n*	—	opération sur titres *f*	compravendita titoli su commissione *f*	operaciones de valores a base de comisión *f/pl*
security (E)	Papier *n*	—	titre *m*	titolo *m*	título *m*
security (E)	Wertpapier *n*	—	valeur *f*	titolo di credito *m*	valor *m*
security (E)	Kaution *f*	—	caution *f*	cauzione *f*	fianza *f*
security department counter (E)	Effektenkasse *f*	—	caisse de valeurs mobilières *f*	cassa titoli *f*	caja de valores *f*
security deposit (E)	Tauschdepot *n*	—	dépôt de titres-gestion *m*	deposito di custodia scambiabile *m*	depósito de trueque *m*
security deposit account (E)	Depotbuchhaltung *f*	—	comptabilité des dépôts *m*	contabilità dei depositi *f*	contabilidad de depósitos *f*
security deposit account (E)	Depotkonto *n*	—	compte de dépôt *m*	conto di deposito *m*	cuenta de depósitos *f*
security financing (E)	Effektenfinanzierung *f*	—	financement de valeurs mobilières *m*	finanziamento tramite titoli *m*	financiación de valores *f*
security held on giro-transferable deposit (E)	Girosammelstück *n*	—	titre en dépôt collectif *m*	titolo in deposito collettivo *m*	título en depósito colectivo *m*
security held on giro-transferable deposit (E)	Girosammeldepotstück *n*	—	titre en dépôt collectif *m*	titolo in deposito collettivo *m*	título en un depósito central de valores *m*
security issue control (E)	Emissionskontrolle *f*	—	contrôle en matière d'émission d'actions et d'obligations *m*	controllo delle emissioni *m*	control de emisión *m*
security issue for third account (E)	Fremdemission *f*	—	émission de valeurs pour compte de tiers *f*	emissione per conto terzi *f*	emisión ajena *f*
security note (E)	Sicherungsschein *m*	—	certificat de contrôle *m*	certificato di controllo *m*	certificado de control *m*
security of credit (E)	Kreditsicherheit *f*	—	garantie concernant un crédit *m*	garanzia di credito *f*	garantía de un crédito *f*
security only traded on a regional stock exchange (E)	Lokalpapier *n*	—	valeur régionale *f*	titolo locale *m*	título local *m*
security-taking syndicate (E)	Übernahmekonsortium *n*	—	syndicat bancaire de garantie *m*	consorzio di collocamento *m*	consorcio de suscripción *m*
security trading for own account (E)	Effekteneigengeschäft *n*	—	opérations sur titres à propre compte *f/pl*	operazione in proprio in titoli *f*	operaciones de valores por cuenta propia *f/pl*
security transaction (E)	Sicherungsgeschäft *n*	—	couverture *f*	garanzia *f*	cobertura *f*
security transactions under repurchase agreement (E)	Pensionsgeschäft *n*	—	opération de mise en pension d'effets *f*	sconto in pensione *m*	operación de reporte *f*
security transactions under repurchase agreement (E)	Effektenpensionsgeschäft *n*	—	opération de mise en pension d'effets *f*	sconto di titoli in pensione *m*	operaciones de cesión temporal de valores *f/pl*
securization (E)	Sekurization *f*	—	sécurisation *f*	securizzazione *f*	segurización *f*
securizzazione (I)	Sekurization *f*	securization	sécurisation *f*	—	segurización *f*
sede di borsa (I)	Börsenplatz *m*	stock exchange centre	place boursière *f*	—	plaza bursátil *f*
sedi principali (I)	Hauptplätze *m/pl*	main centers	places principales *f/pl*	—	plazas principales *f/pl*
Seewechsel (D)	—	sea bill	lettre de prêt à la grosse *f*	cambiale marittima *f*	letra de cambio marítima *f*

	D	E	F	I	Es
segmenti di borsa (I)	Börsensegmente *n/pl*	sectors of the stock exchange	segments de bourse *m/pl*	—	segmentos bursátiles *m/pl*
segmentos bursátiles (Es)	Börsensegmente *n/pl*	sectors of the stock exchange	segments de bourse *m/pl*	segmenti di borsa *m/pl*	—
segments de bourse (F)	Börsensegmente *n/pl*	sectors of the stock exchange	—	segmenti di borsa *m/p*	segmentos bursátil *m/pl*
segreto bancario (I)	Bankgeheimnis *n*	banker's duty of secrecy	secret bancaire *m*	—	secreto bancario *m*
segunda de cambio (Es)	Sekunda-Wechsel *m*	second of exchange	seconde de change *f*	seconda di cambio *f*	—
seguridades pupilares (Es)	goldgeränderte Papiere *n/pl*	gilt-edged securities	titres à marges dorées *m/pl*	titoli di prima classe *m/pl*	—
segurización (Es)	Sekurization *f*	securization	sécurisation *f*	securizzazione *f*	—
seguro (Es)	Versicherung *f*	insurance	assurance *f*	assicurazione *f*	—
seguro (Es)	Assekuranz *f*	insurance system	assurance *f*	assicurazione *f*	—
seguro crediticio (Es)	Kreditversicherung *f*	credit insurance	assurance crédit *f*	assicurazione di credito *f*	—
seguro de cobro colectivo (Es)	Sammelinkasso-versicherung *f*	group collection security	assurance d'encaissement groupé *f*	assicurazione collettiva *f*	—
seguro de crédito de inversión (Es)	Investitionskredit-versicherung *f*	investment credit insurance	assurance de crédits d'investissement *f*	assicurazione credito d'investimento *f*	—
seguro de crédito individual (Es)	Einzelkredit-versicherung *f*	individual credit insurance	assurance crédit individuelle *f*	assicurazione crediti individuali *f*	—
seguro de deuda restante (Es)	Restschuld-versicherung *f*	residual debt insurance	assurance solde de dette *f*	assicurazione del debito residuo *f*	—
seguro de hipotecas (Es)	Hypotheken-versicherung *f*	mortgage insurance	assurance hypothécaire *f*	assicurazione dell'ipoteca *f*	—
seguro de vida (Es)	fondsgebundene Lebensversicherung *f*	fund-linked life insurance	assurance-vie liée à un fonds *f*	assicurazione sulla vita con garanzia reale *f*	—
seignorage (E)	Münzgewinn *m*	—	monnayage *m*	utile di coniatura *m*	monedaje *m*
seizure (E)	Pfändung *f*	—	saisie *f*	pignoramento *m*	embargo *m*
seizure of all the debtor's goods (E)	Kahlpfändung *f*	—	saisie de tous les biens *f*	pignoramento totale *m*	embargo total *m*
Sekundär-Liquidität (D)	—	secondary liquidity	liquidité secondaire *f*	liquidità secondaria *f*	liquidez secundaria *f*
Sekundär-Markt (D)	—	secondary market	marché secondaire *m*	mercato secondario *m*	mercado secundario *m*
Sekunda-Wechsel (D)	—	second of exchange	seconde de change *f*	seconda di cambio *f*	segunda de cambio *f*
Sekurization (D)	—	securization	sécurisation *f*	securizzazione *f*	segurización *f*
Selbstbeteiligung (D)	—	retention	participation personnelle à la couverture du risque *f*	franchigia *f*	propia retención *f*
selección de cartera (Es)	Portfolio Selection *f*	portfolio selection	sélection du portefeuille *f*	selezione di portafoglio *f*	—
sélection du portefeuille (F)	Portfolio Selection *f*	portfolio selection	—	selezione di portafoglio *f*	selección de cartera *f*
selection procedure (E)	Auswahlverfahren *n*	—	méthode de sélection *f*	campionamento *m*	procedimiento de selección *m*
selezione di portafoglio (I)	Portfolio Selection *f*	portfolio selection	sélection du portefeuille *f*	—	selección de cartera *f*
self-contained market (E)	geschlossener Markt *m*	—	marché fermé *m*	mercato chiuso *m*	mercado cerrado *m*
self-financing (E)	Selbstfinanzierung *f*	—	autofinancement *m*	autofinanziamento *m*	autofinanciación *f*
self-financing (E)	Eigenfinanzierung *f*	—	autofinancement *m*	autofinanziamento *m*	autofinanciación *f*
self-generated financing ratio (E)	Innenfinanzierungs-kennzahl *f*	—	ratio de financement interne *m*	codice di finanziamento interno *m*	características de fi-nanciación interna *f/pl*
sell an option (E)	stillhalten	—	vendre une option	concedere una moratoria	prorrogar
selling commission (E)	Schalterprovision *f*	—	commission de vente *f*	commissione di collocamento *f*	comisión al contado *f*
selling value (E)	Verkaufswert *m*	—	valeur vénale *f*	valore di realizzo *m*	valor de venta *m*
semi-annual balance sheet (E)	Halbjahresbilanz *f*	—	bilan semestriel *m*	bilancio semestrale *m*	balance semestral *m*

	D	E	F	I	Es
senza impegno (I)	freibleibend	subject to confirmation	sans engagement	—	salvo venta
separate account (E)	Sonderkonto *n*	—	compte spécial *m*	conto particolare *m*	cuenta especial *f*
separate deposit (E)	Sonderdepot *n*	—	dépôt individuel avec mandat de gestion *m*	deposito a dossier *m*	depósito específico *m*
separate item (E)	Sonderposten *m*	—	poste spécial *m*	partita speciale *f*	partida extraordinaria *f*
separation of property belonging to a third party from the bankrupt's estate (E)	Aussonderung *f*	—	distraction *f*	separazione *f*	tercería de dominio *f*
separazione (I)	Aussonderung *f*	separation of property belonging to a third party from the bankrupt's estate	distraction *f*	—	tercería de dominio *f*
serment déclaratoire (F)	Offenbarungseid *m*	oath of disclosure	—	giuramento dichiarativo *m*	juramento declarativo *m*
service (E)	Dienstleistung *f*	—	prestation de service *f*	attività terziaria *f*	servicio *m*
service de contributions (F)	Finanzamt *n*	inland revenue office	—	ufficio delle finanze *m*	hacienda *f*
service de l'intérêt (F)	Zinsendienst *m*	interest service	—	servizio degli interessi *m*	servicio del interés *m*
service de la dette (F)	Schuldendienst *m*	debt service	—	servizio dei debiti *m*	servicio de deudas *m*
service d'émission (F)	Emissionsabteilung *f*	issue department	—	ufficio emissioni *m*	sección de emisión *f*
service d'épargne (F)	Sparabteilung *f*	savings department	—	ufficio risparmi *m*	sección de ahorro *f*
service de payement des coupons (F)	Kuponkasse *f*	coupon collection department	—	cassa cedolare *f*	sección de cobro por cupones *f*
service des chèques (F)	Scheckabteilung *f*	cheque department	—	ufficio assegni *m*	sección de cheques *f*
service des dépôts (F)	Depotabteilung *f*	safe custody department	—	reparto depositi *m*	sección de depósito *f*
service des devises (F)	Devisenabteilung *f*	foreign exchange department	—	ufficio cambi *m*	sección de divisas *f*
service des encaissements (F)	Inkasso-Abteilung *f*	collection department	—	ufficio incassi *m*	sección de cobranza *f*
service des renseignements de la bourse (F)	Börsenauskunft *f*	stock market information	—	informazioni borsa *f/pl*	información bursátil *f*
service des titres (F)	Effektenabteilung *f*	securities department	—	ufficio titoli *m*	sección de efectos *f*
service des titres à revenu fixe (F)	Rentenabteilung *f*	annuity department	—	ufficio per titoli a reddito fisso *m*	sección de títulos de renta fija *f*
service des valeurs (F)	Wertpapierabteilung *f*	securities department	—	ufficio titoli *m*	sección de valores *f*
service des valeurs en bourse (F)	Börsenabteilung *f*	exchange department	—	ufficio borsa *m*	sección de bolsa *f*
service des virements (F)	Giroabteilung *f*	clearing department	—	reparto giro *m*	sección de giros *f*
service de syndicats (F)	Konsortialabteilung *f*	syndicate department	—	ufficio consorzi *m*	sección de consorcios *f*
service de tirage spécial (F)	Sonderziehungs-abteilung *f*	Special Drawing Rights Department	—	ufficio prelievi speciali *m*	sección de giro especial *f*
service de vérification (F)	Revisionsabteilung *f*	audit department	—	ufficio revisioni *m*	sección de revisión *f*
service de virements automatiques (F)	Automatic Transfer Service [ATS] *m*	Automatic Transfer Service	—	Automatic Transfer Service *m*	servicio de transferencia automático [STA] *m*
service d'organisation (F)	Organisations-abteilung *f*	organization and methods department	—	ufficio organizzazione *m*	sección de organización *f*
service du capital (F)	Kapitaldienst *m*	service of capital	—	pagamento degli interessi *m*	servicio del capital *m*
service du crédit et des prêts (F)	Kreditabteilung *f*	credit department	—	ufficio crediti *m*	sección de crédito *f*
service étranger (F)	Außenhandels-abteilung *f*	export department	—	ufficio commercio estero *m*	sección de comercio exterior *f*
service life (E)	Nutzungsdauer *f*	—	durée normale d'utilisation *f*	durata di godimento *f*	tiempo de utilización *m*
service of capital (E)	Kapitaldienst *m*	—	service du capital *m*	pagamento degli interessi *m*	servicio del capital *m*

	D	E	F	I	Es
servicio (Es)	Dienstleistung *f*	service	prestation de service *f*	attività terziaria *f*	—
servicio de capital (Es)	Kapitaldienst *m*	service of capital	service du capital *m*	pagamento degli interessi *m*	—
servicio de deudas (Es)	Schuldendienst *m*	debt service	service de la dette *m*	servizio dei debiti *m*	—
servicio del interés (Es)	Zinsendienst *m*	interest service	service de l'intérêt *m*	servizio degli interessi *m*	—
servicio de pagos electrónico (Es)	elektronischer Zahlungsverkehr *m*	electronic fund transfer	règlements électroniques *m/pl*	operazioni di pagamento elettronici *f/pl*	—
servicio de transferencia automático [STA] (Es)	Automatic Transfer Service [ATS] *m*	Automatic Transfer Service	service de virements automatiques *m*	Automatic Transfer Service *m*	—
servizio bancario postale (I)	Postbank *f*	Postal Savings Bank	banque postale *f*	—	banco postal *m*
servizio d'assistenza (I)	Kundenberatung *f*	consumer advice	orientation de la clientèle *f*	—	asesoramiento de clientes *m*
servizio degli interessi (I)	Zinsendienst *m*	interest service	service de l'intérêt *m*	—	servicio del interés *m*
servizio dei debiti (I)	Schuldendienst *m*	debt service	service de la dette *m*	—	servicio de deudas *m*
sesión de bolsa (Es)	Börsenzeit *f*	official trading hours	heures d'ouverture de la bourse *f/pl*	orario di borsa *m*	—
set-off (E)	Aufrechnung *f*	—	compensation *f*	compensazione *f*	compensación *f*
settlement (E)	Abwicklung *f*	—	exécution *f*	esecuzione *f*	ejecución *f*
settlement (E)	Glattstellen *n*	—	réalisation *f*	operazione di compensazione mediante trattazione titoli *f*	liquidación *f*
settlement in cash (E)	Barabfindung *f*	—	indemnité en espèces *f*	indennità in contanti *f*	compensación en efectivo *f*
settlement of time bargains (E)	Skontration *f*	—	inventaire mouvementé *m*	compensazione *f*	compensación de cuentas *f*
settling days (E)	Bankstichtage *m/pl*	—	jours de règlement fixés *m/pl*	date di resoconto settimanale della banca centrale *f/pl*	días de referencia de los bancos *m/pl*
settore bancario (I)	Bankgewerbe *n*	banking business	banque *f*	—	banca *f*
settore bancario cooperativo (I)	genossenschaftlicher Bankensektor *m*	cooperative banking sector	activités bancaires coopératives *f/pl*	—	actividades bancarias cooperativas *f/pl*
settore della finanza (I)	Finanzsektor *m*	financial sector	secteur financier *m*	—	sector financiero *m*
seuil de rentabilité (F)	Gewinnschwelle *f*	break-even point	—	soglia dell'utile *f*	umbral de la rentabilidad *m*
sezione (I)	Ressort *n*	department	ressort *m*	—	departamento *m*
share (E)	Aktie *f*	—	action *f*	azione *f*	acción *f*
share (E)	Anteil *m*	—	part *f*	aliquota *f*	parte alícuota *f*
share at a fixed amount (E)	Summenaktie *f*	—	action d'un montant fixe *f*	azione a valore nominale determinato *f*	acción de valor determinado *f*
share capital (E)	Aktienkapital *n*	—	fonds social *m*	capitale azionario *m*	capital en acciones *m*
share capital (E)	Stammkapital *n*	—	capital social *m*	capitale sociale *m*	capital social *m*
share certificate (E)	Mantel *m*	—	titre *m*	mantello *m*	título *m*
share certificate (E)	Aktienzertifikat *n*	—	certificat d'actions *m*	certificato azionario *m*	certificado de acciones *m*
share fund (E)	Aktienfonds *m*	—	fonds d'actions *m*	fondo azionario *m*	fondo de acciones *m*
shareholder (E)	Aktionär *m*	—	actionnaire *m*	azionista *m*	accionista *m*
shareholder (E)	Anteilseigner *m*	—	porteur de parts *m*	azionista *m*	titular de acciones *m*
shareholder's agreement (E)	Gesellschaftsvertrag *m*	—	contrat de société *m*	atto costitutivo *m*	contrato social *m*
share in capital (E)	Kapitalanteil *m*	—	part de capital *f*	quota di capitale *f*	participación en el capital *f*
share index (E)	Aktienindex *m*	—	indice du cours des actions *m*	indice azionario *m*	índice de cotización *m*
share in the loss (E)	Verlustanteil *m*	—	participation aux pertes *f*	quota alle perdite *f*	cuota de pérdidas *f*
share in the profits (E)	Gewinnanteil *n*	—	quote-part sur les bénéfices *f*	quota utile *f*	participación en los beneficios *f*

sin cupón

	D	E	F	I	Es
share list (E)	Cote *n*	—	bulletin officiel de la cote *m*	cote *m*	Boletín de Bolsa *m*
share market (E)	Aktienmarkt *m*	—	marché d'actions *m*	mercato azionario *m*	mercado de acciones *m*
share of no par value (E)	Quotenaktie *f*	—	action de quotité *f*	parte di capitale *f*	acción de cuota *f*
share price (E)	Aktienkurs *m*	—	cours des actions *f*	quotazione azionaria *f*	cotización de las acciones *f*
share purchase warrant (E)	Optionsschein *m*	—	coupon d'option *m*	warrant *m*	documento de opción *m*
share quorum (E)	Aktienquorum *n*	—	quorum d'actions *m*	quorum azioni *m*	quórum de acciones *m*
share register (E)	Aktienbuch *n*	—	registre des actions *m*	registro delle azioni *m*	libro de acciones *m*
share register (E)	Aktienregister *n*	—	registre d'actions *m*	registro delle azioni *m*	registro de acciones *m*
shares account (E)	Stückekonto *n*	—	compte de titres *m*	conto titoli *m*	cuenta de valores *f*
shares not fully paid up (E)	Leeraktie *f*	—	action non entièrement libérée *f*	azione non interamente versata *f*	acción al descubierto *f*
share stock option (E)	Aktienoption *f*	—	option d'échanger des titres convertibles en actions *f*	diritto di prelazione *m*	opción de cambiar títulos convertibles en acciones *f*
share with low par value (E)	Kleinaktie *f*	—	action minimale *f*	piccola azione *f*	acción pequeña *f*
ship mortgage (E)	Schiffshypothek *f*	—	hypothèque maritime *f*	ipoteca navale *f*	hipoteca naval *f*
shipping exchange (E)	Frachtbörse *f*	—	bourse de fret *f*	borsa dei noli *f*	bolsa de fletes *f*
shipping exchange (E)	Schiffahrtsbörse *f*	—	bourse maritime *f*	borsa dei noli marittimi *f*	bolsa naval *f*
shortfall (E)	Fehlbetrag *m*	—	déficit *m*	disavanzo *m*	déficit *m*
short sale (E)	Blanko-Verkauf *m*	—	vente à découvert *f*	vendita allo scoperto *f*	venta al descubierto *f*
Sicherungs-abtretung (D)	—	assignment by way of security	cession d'une sûreté *f*	cessione a titolo di garanzia *f*	cesión fiduciaria *f*
Sicherungsgeschäft (D)	—	security transaction	couverture *f*	garanzia *f*	cobertura *f*
Sicherungsgrund-schuld (D)	—	cautionary land charge	dette foncière de garantie *f*	debito fondiario di garanzia *m*	deuda inmobiliaria de seguridad *f*
Sicherungshypothek (D)	—	cautionary mortgage	hypothèque constituée dans le but de garantir une créance *f*	ipoteca di garanzia *f*	hipoteca de seguridad *f*
Sicherungsschein (D)	—	security note	certificat de contrôle *m*	certificado di contollo *m*	certificado de control *m*
Sicherungsüber-eignung (D)	—	transfer of ownership by way of security	transfert à titre de sûreté *m*	cessione fiduciaria *f*	transmisión en garantía *f*
Sichteinlagen (D)	—	sight deposits	dépôts à vue *m/pl*	depositi a vista *m/pl*	depósitos a la vista *m/pl*
Sichtkurs (D)	—	sight rate	cours à vue *m*	cambio a vista *m*	cambio a la vista *m*
Sichtwechsel (D)	—	demand bill	traite à vue *f*	cambiale a vista *f*	letra a la vista *f*
sidérurgie (F)	eisenschaffende Industrie *f*	iron and steel producing industry	—	industria siderurgica *f*	industria metalúrgica *f*
sight deposits (E)	Sichteinlagen *f/pl*	—	dépôts à vue *m/pl*	depositi a vista *m/pl*	depósitos a la vista *m/pl*
sight rate (E)	Sichtkurs *m*	—	cours à vue *m*	cambio a vista *m*	cambio a la vista *m*
Silbermünze (D)	—	silver coin	pièce en argent *f*	moneta d'argento *f*	moneda de plata *f*
Silberwährung (D)	—	silver standard	monnaie en argent *f*	valuta d'argento *f*	patrón plata *m*
silver coin (E)	Silbermünze *f*	—	pièce en argent *f*	moneta d'argento *f*	moneda de plata *f*
silver standard (E)	Silberwährung *f*	—	monnaie en argent *f*	valuta d'argento *f*	patrón plata *m*
simplified capital reduction (E)	vereinfachte Kapitalherabsetzung *f*	—	diminution de capital simplifiée *f*	riduzione di capitale semplice *f*	reducción de capital simplificada *f*
simulación (Es)	Simulation *f*	simulation	simulation *f*	simulazione *f*	
Simulation (D)	—	simulation	simulation *f*	simulazione *f*	simulación *f*
simulation (E)	Simulation *f*	—	simulation *f*	simulazione *f*	simulación *f*
simulation (F)	Simulation *f*	simulation	—	simulazione *f*	simulación *f*
simulazione (I)	Simulation *f*	simulation	simulation *f*	—	simulación *f*
sin cupón (Es)	ohne Kupon	ex coupon	sans coupon	ex cedola	—

	D	E	F	I	Es
sindacato d'emissione (I)	Emissionssyndikat *f*	underwriting syndicate	syndicat bancaire de garantie *m*	—	sindicato de emisión *m*
sindicato bancario (Es)	Bankenkonsortium *n*	banking syndicate	consortium de banques *m*	consorzio bancario *m*	—
sindicato de emisión (Es)	Emissionssyndikat *f*	underwriting syndicate	syndicat bancaire de garantie *m*	sindacato d'emissione *m*	—
síndico de quiebra (Es)	Konkursverwalter *m*	administrator in bankruptcy proceedings	liquidateur de la faillite *m*	curatore del fallimento *m*	—
single operación (E)	Sologeschäft *n*	—	opération particulière *f*	operazione singola *f*	operación singular *f*
single-price market (E)	Einheitsmarkt *m*	—	marché unique *m*	mercato unico *m*	mercado único *m*
sistema bancario (Es)	Bankensystem *n*	banking system	système bancaire *m*	sistema bancario *m*	—
sistema bancario (I)	Bankensystem *n*	banking system	système bancaire *m*	—	sistema bancario *m*
sistema creditizio (I)	Kreditwesen *n*	credit system	crédit *m*	—	régimen de creditos *m*
sistema de bancos especializados (Es)	Trennbanksystem *n*	system of specialized banking	système des banques spécialisées *m*	sistema delle banche specializzate *m*	—
sistema de cambios (Es)	Wechselkurssystem *n*	system of exchange rates	système de change *m*	regime dei cambi *m*	—
sistema de capitalización (Es)	Anwartschafts-deckungsverfahren *n*	expectancy cover procedure	système de la capitalisation *m*	sistema di capitalizzazione *m*	—
sistema de cargo en cuenta (Es)	Lastschriftverkehr *m*	direct debiting transactions	prélèvements automatiques *m/pl*	addebiti *m/pl*	—
sistema de certificados provisionales de acciones (Es)	Jungscheinverkehr *m*	new issue giro transfer system	système des certificats provisoires d'actions nouvelles *m*	sistema di certificato provvisorio *f*	—
sistema de cuentas (Es)	Kontenrahmen *m*	standard form of accounts	cadre comptable *m*	quadro dei conti *m*	—
sistema delle banche specializzate (I)	Trennbanksystem *n*	system of specialized banking	système des banques spécialisées *m*	—	sistema de bancos especializados *m*
sistema de ofertas (Es)	Tenderverfahren *n*	tender procedure	offre d'emprunts pour la régulation monétaire *f*	asta marginale *f*	—
sistema de paridad flotante (Es)	Crawling peg *m*	crawling peg	crans variables *m*	crawling peg *m*	—
sistema di capitalizzazione (I)	Anwartschafts-deckungsverfahren *n*	expectancy cover procedure	système de la capitalisation *m*	—	sistema de capitalización *m*
sistema di certificato provvisorio (I)	Jungscheinverkehr *m*	new issue giro transfer system	système des certificats provisoires d'actions nouvelles —	—	sistema de certificados provisionales de acciones *m*
sistema di mercato (I)	Marktform *f*	market form	forme du marché *f*	—	forma de mercado *f*
sistema monetario (Es)	Geldwesen *n*	monetary system	système monétaire *m*	sistema monetario *m*	—
sistema monetario (Es)	Währungssystem *n*	monetary system	système monétaire *m*	sistema monetario *m*	—
sistema monetario (I)	Geldverfassung *f*	monetary structure	structure monétaire *f*	—	estructura monetaria *f*
sistema monetario (I)	Währungssystem *n*	monetary system	système monétaire *m*	—	sistema monetario *m*
sistema monetario (I)	Geldwesen *n*	monetary system	système monétaire *m*	—	sistema monetario *m*
Sistema monetario europeo (I)	Europäisches Währungssystem [EWS] *n*	European Monetary System [EMS]	Système Monétaire Européen [SME] *m*	—	Sistema Monetario Europeo [SME] *m*
Sistema Monetario Europeo [SME] (Es)	Europäisches Währungssystem [EWS] *n*	European Monetary System [EMS]	Système Monétaire Européen SME *m*	Sistema monetario europeo *m*	—
sistemas de caja por transferencia (Es)	bargeldlose Kassensysteme *n/pl*	point of sale systems POS	payements scripturaux au point de vente *m/pl*	sistemi di cassa non in contanti *m/pl*	—
sistemi di cassa non in contanti (I)	bargeldlose Kassensysteme *n/pl*	point of sale systems POS	payements scripturaux au point de vente *m/pl*	—	sistemas de caja por transferencia *m/pl*
situación de liquidez (Es)	Liquiditätsstatus *m*	liquidity status	état de la liquidité *m*	situazione di liquidità *f*	—
situation comptable mensuelle (F)	Monatsbilanz *f*	monthly balance sheet	—	bilancio mensile *m*	balance mensual *m*
situation de banque (F)	Bankausweis *m*	bank return	—	bollettino bancario *m*	documento bancario *m*
situation de la réduction du capital (F)	Ausweis der Kapitalherabsetzung *m*	return of capital reduction	—	dichiarazione di riduzione capitale *f*	devolución de la disminución de capital *f*

	D	E	F	I	Es
situation mensuelle (F)	Monatsausweis *m*	monthly return	—	bilancio mensile *m*	resumen mensual *m*
situazione creditizia (I)	Kreditstatus *m*	credit standing	état de l'endettement *m*	—	estado del endeudamiento *m*
situazione di banca (I)	Bankstatus *m*	bank status	état bancaire *m*	—	estado bancario *m*
situazione di liquidità (I)	Liquiditätsstatus *m*	liquidity status	état de la liquidité *m*	—	situación de liquidez *f*
situazione patrimoniale (I)	Vermögensrechnung *f*	capital account	compte de capital *m*	—	cálculo del valor neto *m*
situazione patrimoniale di concordato (I)	Vergleichsbilanz *f*	comparative balance sheet	bilan au moment de l'ouverture du règlement judiciare *m*	—	balance de comparación *m*
situazione settimanale (I)	Wochenausweis *m*	weekly return	bilan hebdomadaire *m*	—	balance semanal *m*
size of an order (E)	Auftragsgröße *f*	—	importance de la commande *f*	ampiezza d'ordinazione *f*	volumen de pedido *m*
Skonto (D)	—	discount	escompte *m*	sconto *m*	descuento *m*
Skontration (D)	—	settlement of time bargains	inventaire mouvementé *m*	compensazione *f*	compensación de cuentas *f*
slack (E)	geschäftslos	—	stagnant	inattivo	estado de estancamiento *m*
slack (E)	lustlos	—	inactif	fiacco	poco animado
slack (E)	still	—	calme	fiacco	flojo
slack (E)	schwach	—	faible	debole	flojo
small personal loan (E)	Kleinkredit *m*	—	petit crédit *m*	piccolo credito *m*	préstamo pequeño *m*
small saver (E)	Kleinsparer *m*	—	petit épargnant *m*	piccolo risparmiatore *m*	ahorradores de menor importancia *m/pl*
small shareholder (E)	Kleinaktionär *m*	—	petit actionnaire *m*	piccolo azionista *m*	accionista pequeño *m*
small trader (E)	Minderkaufmann *m*	—	petit exploitant non soumis aux prescriptions générales du code de commerce *m*	piccolo imprenditore *m*	pequeño comerciante no registrable en el registro de comercio *m*
soberanía de acuñación (Es)	Münzhoheit *f*	monetary sovereignty	prérogative de la frappe *f*	privilegio di battere moneta *m*	—
sobrecapitalización (Es)	Überkapitalisierung *f*	overcapitalization	surcapitalisation *f*	sovraccapitalizzazione *f*	—
social economy (E)	Gemeinwirtschaft *f*	—	économie sociale *f*	economia collettiva *f*	economía colectiva *f*
social fund (E)	Sozialfonds *m*	—	fonds social *m*	fondo sociale *m*	fondo social *m*
sociedad (Es)	Gesellschaft *f*	company	société *f*	società *f*	—
sociedad anónima (Es)	Aktiengesellschaft *f*	joint stock company	société anonyme *f*	società per azioni *f*	—
sociedad comanditaria (Es)	Kommanditgesellschaft *f*	limited partnership	société en commandite *f*	società in accomandita semplice *f*	—
Sociedad Comercial Europea (Es)	Europäische Handelsgesellschaft *f*	European trading company	société commerciale européenne *f*	società per azioni europea *f*	—
sociedad cúpula (Es)	Dachgesellschaft *f*	holding company	holding *m*	società madre *f*	—
sociedad de amortización (Es)	Abschreibungsgesellschaft *f*	project write-off company	société d'amortissement *f*	società d'ammortamento *f*	—
sociedad de capital (Es)	Kapitalgesellschaft *f*	company limited by shares	société de capitaux *f*	società di capitali *f*	—
sociedad de inversiones (Es)	Investmentgesellschaft *f*	investment company	société d'investissement *f*	società d'investimento *f*	—
sociedad de operación conjunta (Es)	Projektgesellschaft *f*	joint-venture company	société d'opération conjointe *f*	società ad hoc *f*	—
sociedad de programa de inversión (Es)	Programmgesellschaft *f*	investment program	société de programmes d'investissement *f*	società con programmi d'investimento *f*	—
sociedad de responsabilidad limitada (Es)	Gesellschaft mit beschränkter Haftung [GmbH] *f*	limited liability company	société de responsabilité limitée S.A.R.L. *f*	società a responsabilità limitata *f*	—
sociedad de revisión (Es)	Prüfungsverband *f*	auditing association	association de vérification des comptes *f*	associazione di controllo *f*	—

	D	E	F	I	Es
sociedad en participación (Es)	stille Gesellschaft *f*	dormant partnership	association commerciale en participation *f*	società di diritto *f*	—
sociedad fiduciaria (Es)	Treuhandgesellschaft *f*	trust company	société fiduciaire *f*	società fiduciaria *f*	—
sociedad holding (Es)	Holding Gesellschaft *f*	holding company	holding *m*	società finanziaria *f*	—
sociedad holding (Es)	Auffanggesellschaft *f*	recipient company	consortium de renflouement *m*	società finanziaria *f*	—
sociedad órgano (Es)	Organgesellschaft *f*	controlled company	entreprise dominée *f*	società legata contrattualmente *f*	—
sociedad personalista (Es)	Personengesellschaft *f*	partnership	société de personnes *f*	società di persone *f*	—
sociedad unitaria (Es)	Einheitsgesellschaft *f*	unified company	société unitaire *f*	società unitaria *f*	—
società (I)	Gesellschaft *f*	company	société *f*	—	sociedad *f*
società ad hoc (I)	Projektgesellschaft *f*	joint-venture company	société d'opération conjointe *f*	—	sociedad de operación conjunta *f*
società a responsabilità limitata (I)	Gesellschaft mit beschränkter Haftung [GmbH] *f*	limited liability company	société de responsabilité limitée S.A.R.L. *f*	—	sociedad de responsabilidad limitada *f*
società con programmi d'investimento (I)	Programmgesellschaft *f*	investment program	société de programmes d'investissement *f*	—	sociedad de programa de inversión *f*
società d'ammortamento (I)	Abschreibungsgesellschaft *f*	project write-off company	société d'amortissement *f*	—	sociedad de amortización *f*
società di capitali (I)	Kapitalgesellschaft *f*	company limited by shares	société de capitaux *f*	—	sociedad de capital *f*
società di diritto (I)	stille Gesellschaft *f*	dormant partnership	association commerciale en participation *f*	—	sociedad en participación *f*
società d'investimento (I)	Kapitalanlagegesellschaft *f*	capital investment company	société d'investissement *f*	—	compañía de inversiones *f*
società d'investimento (I)	Investmentgesellschaft *f*	investment company	société d'investissement *f*	—	sociedad de inversiones *f*
società di persone (I)	Personengesellschaft *f*	partnership	société de personnes *f*	—	sociedad personalista *f*
società di prim'ordine (I)	beste Adresse *f*	prime name	client de première catégorie *m*	—	cliente de primera categoría *f*
società di risparmio (I)	Sparverein *m*	savings club	association d'épargne *f*	—	asociación de ahorro *f*
società fiduciaria (I)	Treuhandgesellschaft *f*	trust company	société fiduciaire *f*	—	sociedad fiduciaria *f*
società finanziaria (I)	Auffanggesellschaft *f*	recipient company	consortium de renflouement *m*	—	sociedad holding *f*
società finanziaria (I)	Holding Gesellschaft *f*	holding company	holding *m*	—	sociedad holding *f*
società in accomandita semplice (I)	Kommanditgesellschaft *f*	limited partnership	société en commandite *f*	—	sociedad comanditaria *f*
società in nome collettivo (I)	offene Handelsgesellschaft *f*	general partnership	société en nom collectif *f*	—	compañía colectiva *f*
società legata contrattualmente (I)	Organgesellschaft *f*	controlled company	entreprise dominée *f*	—	sociedad órgano *f*
società madre (I)	Dachgesellschaft *f*	holding company	holding *m*	—	sociedad cúpula *f*
società per azioni (I)	Aktiengesellschaft *f*	joint stock company	société anonyme *f*	—	sociedad anónima *f*
società per azioni europea (I)	Europäische Handelsgesellschaft *f*	European trading company	société commerciale européenne *f*	—	Sociedad Comercial Europea *f*
società unitaria (I)	Einheitsgesellschaft *f*	unified company	société unitaire *f*	—	sociedad unitaria *f*
société (F)	Gesellschaft *f*	company	—	società *f*	sociedad *f*
société anonyme (F)	Aktiengesellschaft *f*	joint stock company	—	società per azioni *f*	sociedad anónima *f*
société commerciale européenne (F)	Europäische Handelsgesellschaft *f*	European trading company	—	società per azioni europea *f*	Sociedad Comercial Europea *f*
société coopérative (F)	Genossenschaft *f*	cooperative	—	cooperativa *f*	cooperativa *f*
société coopérative de consommation (F)	Konsumgenossenschaft *f*	consumer cooperative	—	cooperativa di consumo *f*	cooperativa de consumo *f*
société d'amortissement (F)	Abschreibungsgesellschaft *f*	project write-off company	—	società d'ammortamento *f*	sociedad de amortización *f*

	D	E	F	I	Es
société de capitaux (F)	Kapitalgesellschaft f	company limited by shares	—	società di capitali f	sociedad de capital f
société de personnes (F)	Personengesellschaft f	partnership	—	società di persone f	sociedad personalista f
société de programmes d'investissement (F)	Programmgesellschaft f	investment program		società con programmi d'investimento f	sociedad de programa de inversión f
société de responsabilité limité S.A.R.L. (F)	Gesellschaft mit beschränkter Haftung [GmbH] f	limited liability company	—	società a responsabilità limitata f	sociedad de responsabilidad limitada f
société d'investissement (F)	Investmentgesellschaft f	investment company	—	società d'investimento f	sociedad de inversiones f
société d'investissement (F)	Kapitalanlagegesellschaft f	capital investment company	—	società d'investimento f	compañía de inversiones f
société d'opération conjointe (F)	Projektgesellschaft f	joint-venture company	—	società ad hoc f	sociedad de operación conjunta f
société en commandite (F)	Kommanditgesellschaft f	limited partnership		società in accomandita semplice f	sociedad comanditaria f
société en nom collectif (F)	offene Handelsgesellschaft f	general partnership		società in nome collettivo f	compañía colectiva f
société fiduciaire (F)	Treuhandgesellschaft f	trust company	—	società fiduciaria f	sociedad fiduciaria f
société unitaire (F)	Einheitsgesellschaft f	unified company	—	società unitaria f	sociedad unitaria f
socio (Es)	Teilhaber m	partner	associé m	socio m	—
socio (I)	Teilhaber m	partner	associé m	—	socio m
socio colectivo (Es)	Komplementär m	general partner	commandité m	accomandatario m	—
socio di una società in accomandita per azioni (I)	Kommanditaktionär m	limited liability shareholder	actionnaire d'une société en commandite par actions f	—	accionista comanditario m
soft currency (E)	Weichwährung f	—	monnaie faible f	moneta debole f	moneda débil f
soglia dell'utile (I)	Gewinnschwelle f	break-even point	seuil de rentabilité m	—	umbral de la rentabilidad m
solde (F)	Saldo m	balance	—	saldo m	saldo m
solde de budget (F)	Budgetausgleich m	balancing of the budget	—	equilibrio del bilancio pubblico m	balance del presupuesto m
solde de spéculation (F)	Spekulationskasse f	speculative balance	—	domanda speculativa di moneta f	dinero inactivo m
solde des transactions (F)	Transaktionskasse f	transaction balance	—	domanda di moneta per transazioni f	caja de transacción f
solder (F)	saldieren	to balance	—	saldare	saldar
soldes (F)	Ausverkauf m	clearance sale	—	liquidazione f	venta de liquidación f
sole distribution (E)	Alleinvertrieb m	—	distribution exclusive f	esclusiva f	distribución exclusiva f
Solidarhaftung (D)	—	joint and several liability	responsabilité solidaire f	responsabilità solidale f	responsabilidad solidaria f
Soll (D)	—	debit	doit m	debito m	débito m
sollecito (I)	Mahnung f	reminder	mise en demeure f	—	monición f
Sollzinsen (D)	—	debtor interest rates	intérêts débiteurs m/pl	interessi passivi m/pl	intereses deudores m/pl
sólo para compensación (Es)	nur zur Verrechnung	for account only	à porter en compte	da accreditare	—
Sologeschäft (D)	—	single operacion	opération particulière f	operazione singola f	operación singular f
solvabilité (F)	Kreditwürdigkeit f	creditworthiness	—	fido m	crédito m
solvabilité (F)	Solvenz f	solvency	—	solvibilità f	solvencia f
solvabilité (F)	Bonität f	financial soundness	—	solvibilità f	solvencia f
solvencia (Es)	Bonität f	financial soundness	solvabilité f	solvibilità f	—
solvencia (Es)	Solvenz f	solvency	solvabilité f	solvibilità f	—
solvency (E)	Solvenz f	—	solvabilité f	solvibilità f	solvencia f
Solvenz (D)	—	solvency	solvabilité f	solvibilità f	solvencia f
solvibilità (I)	Solvenz f	solvency	solvabilité f	—	solvencia f

	D	E	F	I	Es
solvibilità (I)	Bonität *f*	financial soundness	solvabilité *f*	—	solvencia *f*
sommes disponibles avec préavis (F)	Kündigungsgeld *n*	deposit at notice	—	deposito ritirabile dietro preavviso *m*	depósitos con preaviso *m/pl*
sommet économique international (F)	Weltwirtschaftsgipfel *m*	world economic summit	—	vertice internazionale di economia *m*	Cumbre Económica Occidental *f*
Sonderabschreibung (D)	—	special depreciation	amortissement extraordinaire *m*	ammortamento speciale *m*	amortización extraordinaria *f*
Sonderausschüttung (D)	—	extra dividend	répartition extraordinaire *f*	distribuzione straordinaria *f*	reparto extraordinario *m*
Sonderbewegung (D)	—	extraordinary trend	tendance extraordinaire *f*	movimento divergente *m*	oscilación extraordinaria *f*
Sonderdepot (D)	—	separate deposit	dépôt individuel avec mandat de gestion *m*	deposito a dossier *m*	depósito específico *m*
Sonderfazilitäten (D)	—	special credit facilities	facilités spéciales *f/pl*	facilitazioni creditizie speciali *f/pl*	facilidades especiales *f/pl*
Sonderkonto (D)	—	separate account	compte spécial *m*	conto particolare *m*	cuenta especial *f*
Sonderlombard (D)	—	special lombard facility	facilités spéciales de prêts sur nantissement *f/pl*	anticipazione su titoli straordinaria *f*	préstamo pignoraticio especial *m*
Sonderposten (D)	—	separate item	poste spécial *m*	partita speciale *f*	partida extraordinaria *f*
Sondervermögen (D)	—	special fund	fonds spéciaux *m/pl*	patrimonio separato *m*	patrimonio especial *m*
Sonderziehungsabteilung (D)	—	Special Drawing Rights Department	service de tirage spécial *m*	ufficio prelievi speciali *m*	sección de giro especial *f*
Sonderziehungsrecht (D)	—	special drawing right	droit de tirage spécial *m*	diritto speciale di prelievo *m*	derecho de giro especial *m*
Sonderzinsen (D)	—	special interests	intérêts spéciaux *m/pl*	saggio speciale di interesse *m*	intereses especiales *m/pl*
sonstige Verbindlichkeiten (D)	—	other liabilities	autres obligations *f/pl*	debiti diversi *m/pl*	acreedores varios *m/pl*
soprappremio di rischio (I)	Risikozuschlag *m*	additional risk premium	surprime de risque *f*	—	recargo de riesgo *m*
sopravvenienze attive (I)	außerordentliche Erträge *m/pl*	extraordinary income	profits exceptionnels *m/pl*	—	ingresos extraordiarios *m/pl*
Sorte (D)	—	foreign notes and coins	devise *f*	valuta estera *f*	moneda extranjera *f*
Sortengeschäft (D)	—	dealings in foreign notes and coins	commerce de change *m*	operazione di cambio *f*	operación de moneda extranjera *f*
Sortenhandel (D)	—	dealing in foreign notes and coins	commerce de change *m*	commercio delle valute *m*	negociación de moneda extranjera *f*
Sortenkurs (D)	—	rate for foreign notes and coins	cours des monnaies étrangères *m*	corso dei cambi *m*	tipo de cambio de billetes y monedas extranjeras *m*
sortes de dépôts (F)	Depotarten *f/pl*	types of deposit	—	tipi di deposito *m/pl*	tipos de depósito *m/pl*
sortes d'émission (F)	Emissionsarten *f/pl*	types of issuing	—	tipi di emissione *m/pl*	tipos de emisión *m/pl*
sortes d'investissement (F)	Kapitalanlegearten *f/pl*	types of capital investment	—	tipi di investimento di capitale *m/pl*	tipos de inversión *m/pl*
sortie de capital (F)	Kapitalabfluß *m*	capital outflows	—	deflusso di capitale *m*	salida de capital *f*
Sortiment (D)	—	assortment	assortiment *m*	assortimento *m*	surtido *m*
sorveglianza della borsa (I)	Börsenaufsicht *f*	stock exchange supervision	surveillance de la bourse *f*	—	control estatal de bolsas *m*
sostegno delle quotazioni (I)	Kurspflege *f*	price nursing	régulation des cours *f*	—	compras de sostén *f/pl*
sostegno delle quotazioni (I)	Kursstützung *f*	price pegging	soutien des cours *m*	—	apoyo de la cotización *m*
sostegno delle quotazioni (I)	Kursregulierung *f*	price regulation	régulation des cours *f*	—	regulación de los tipos de cambio *f*
sostegno di una moneta (I)	Währungsabsicherung *f*	safeguarding of the currency	garantie de change *f*	—	garantía de cambio *f*
sostituzione di titoli (I)	Effektensubstitution *f*	securities substitution	substitution de titres *f*	—	sustitución de valores *f*
sostituzione monetaria (I)	Währungssubstitution *f*	currency substitution	substitution monétaire *f*	—	substitución monetaria *f*

	D	E	F	I	Es
sottoc-capitalizzazione (I)	Unterfinanzierung f	underfinancing	financement insuffisant m	—	financiación insuficiente f
sottoccupazione (I)	Unterbeschäftigung f	underemployment	sous-emploi m	—	subempleo m
sottoscrizione (I)	Subskription f	subscription	souscription f	—	suscripción f
sottoscrizione di azioni (I)	Aktienzeichnung f	subscription for shares	souscription d'actions f	—	suscripción de acciones f
sottoscrizione eccedente (I)	Überzeichnung f	over-subscription	souscription surpassée f	—	suscripción en exceso f
sottovalutazione (I)	Unterbewertung f	undervaluation	sous-estimation f	—	subvaloración f
soumission (F)	Ausschreibung f	invitation to tender	—	appalto m	subasta f
souplesse en affaires (F)	Kulanz f	fairness in trade	—	correntezza f	complacencia f
source principle (E)	Quellenprinzip n	—	principe d'imposition à la source m	principio della ritenuta alla fonte m	principio del gravamen en origen m
sous-agent (F)	Untermakler m	intermediate broker	—	commissionario m	subagente m
souscription (F)	Subskription f	subscription	—	sottoscrizione f	suscripción f
souscription d'actions (F)	Aktienzeichnung f	subscription for shares	—	sottoscrizione di azioni f	suscripción de acciones f
souscription surpassée (F)	Überzeichnung f	over-subscription	—	sottoscrizione eccedente f	suscripción en exceso f
sous-délégation (F)	Untervollmacht f	delegated authority	—	procura rilasciata dal procuratore f	subpoder m
sous-emploi (F)	Unterbeschäftigung f	underemployment	—	sottoccupazione f	subempleo m
sous-estimation (F)	Unterbewertung f	undervaluation	—	sottovalutazione f	subvaloración f
soutien des cours (F)	Kursstützung f	price pegging	—	sostegno delle quotazioni m	apoyo de la cotización m
sovraccapitaliz-zazione (I)	Überkapitalisierung f	overcapitalization	surcapitalisation f	—	sobrecapitalización f
sovraccapitaliz-zazione (I)	Überfinanzierung f	overfinancing	financement exagéré m	—	financiación excesiva f
sovvenzione (I)	Subvention f	subsidy	subvention f	—	subvención f
Sozialfonds (D)	—	social fund	fonds social m	fondo sociale m	fondo social m
Sozialpfandbrief (D)	—	mortgage bond serving a social purpose	obligation hypothécaire pour financer des projets sociaux f	obbligazione ipotecaria edilizia sociale f	cédula hipotecaria con fines sociales f
Sozialprodukt (D)	—	national product	produit national m	prodotto sociale m	producto nacional m
Sozius (D)	—	partner	associé m	socio m	socio m
Sparabteilung (D)	—	savings department	service d'épargne m	ufficio risparmi m	sección de ahorro f
Sparbrief (D)	—	savings certificate	bon d'épargne m	lettera di risparmio f	cédula de ahorro f
Sparbuch (D)	—	savings-bank book	livret d'épargne m	libretto di risparmio m	libreta de ahorro f
Sparbüchse (D)	—	piggy bank	tirelire f	salvadanaio m	alcancía f
Spareckzins (D)	—	basic savings rate	taux-clé d'intérêt bancaire sur les dépôts d'épargne m	interesse di riferimento per il risparmio m	tipo de referencia m
Spareinlage (D)	—	savings deposit	dépôt d'épargne m	deposito a risparmio m	imposición de ahorro f
sparen (D)	—	saving	économiser	risparmiare	ahorrar
Sparer (D)	—	saver	épargnant m	risparmiatore m	ahorrador m
Sparförderung (D)	—	savings promotion	promotion de l'épargne f	promozione del risparmio f	fomento del ahorro m
Spargeschenkgut-schein (D)	—	savings gift credit voucher	bon d'épargne m	buono regalo di risparmio m	vale de ahorro m
Sparguthaben (D)	—	savings account	avoir sur un compte d'épargne m	deposito a risparmio m	depósito de ahorro m
Sparkasse (D)	—	savings bank	caisse d'épargne f	cassa di risparmio f	caja de ahorros f
Sparkonto (D)	—	savings account	compte d'épargne m	conto a risparmio m	cuenta de ahorros f
Sparmarke (D)	—	savings stamp	timbre d'épargne m	marca di risparmio f	cuota de ahorro f
Sparobligation (D)	—	savings bond	obligation d'épargne f	obbligazione di cassa di risparmio f	obligación de ahorro f

Sparpläne 388

	D	E	F	I	Es
Sparpläne (D)	—	savings plans	plans d'épargne *m/pl*	piano di risparmio *m*	planes de ahorro *m/pl*
Sparprämie (D)	—	savings premium	prime d'épargne *f*	premio al risparmio *m*	prima de ahorro *f*
Sparquote (D)	—	savings ratio	quote-part de revenu réservé à des fins d'épargne *f*	aliquota di risparmio *f*	cuota de ahorro *f*
Sparverein (D)	—	savings club	association d'épargne *f*	società di risparmio *f*	asociación de ahorro *f*
Sparzulage (D)	—	savings bonus	prime d'épargne *f*	assegno integrativo di risparmio *m*	subvención de ahorro *f*
Spätschalter (D)	—	night safe deposit	guichet extérieur de permanence *m*	cassa continua *f*	taquilla de noche *f*
special credit facilities (E)	Sonderfazilitäten *f/pl*	—	facilités spéciales *f/pl*	facilitazioni creditizie speciali *f/pl*	facilidades especiales *f/pl*
special depreciation (E)	Sonderabschreibung *f*	—	amortissement extraordinaire *m*	ammortamento speciale *m*	amortización extraordinaria *f*
special drawing right (E)	Sonderziehungsrecht *n*	—	droit de tirage spécial *m*	diritto speciale di prelievo *m*	derecho de giro prelievo *m*
Special Drawing Rights Department (E)	Sonderziehungsabteilung *f*	—	service de tirage spécial *m*	ufficio prelievi speciali *m*	sección de giro especial *f*
special fund (E)	Sondervermögen *n*	—	fonds spéciaux *m/pl*	patrimonio separato *m*	patrimonio especial *m*
special interests (E)	Sonderzinsen *m/pl*	—	intérêts spéciaux *m/pl*	saggio speciale di interesse *m*	interese especial *m*
specialized commercial bank (E)	Spezialbank *f*	—	banque spécialilsée *f*	istituto di credito speciale *m*	banco especializado *m*
special lombard facility (E)	Sonderlombard *m*	—	facilités spéciales de prêts sur nantissement *f/pl*	anticipazione su titoli straordinaria *f*	préstamo pignoraticio especial *m*
special power (E)	Spezialvollmacht *f*	—	pouvoir limité à un acte commercial déterminé *m*	procura speciale *f*	poder especial *m*
specialties (E)	Spezialwerte *m/pl*	—	titres spéciaux *m/pl*	premi omaggio *m/pl*	títulos especiales *m/pl*
specie (E)	Kurantmünze *f*	—	monnaie courante *f*	moneta corrente *f*	moneda corriente *f*
species (E)	Münzgeld *n*	—	monnaie métallique *f*	denaro monetato *m*	moneda acuñada *f*
speculate for a fall (E)	fixen	—	vendre à découvert	vendere allo scoperto	vender al descubierto
speculation (E)	Spekulation *f*	—	spéculation *f*	speculazione *f*	especulación *f*
spéculation (F)	Spekulation *f*	speculation	—	speculazione *f*	especulación *f*
speculation bank (E)	Spekulationsbank *f*	—	banque de spéculation *f*	banca di speculazione *f*	banco de especulación *m*
speculation in foreign currency (E)	Devisenspekulation *f*	—	spéculation sur les changes *f*	speculazione in cambi *f*	especulación de divisas *f*
spéculation sur les changes (F)	Devisenspekulation *f*	speculation in foreign currency	—	speculazione in cambi *f*	especulación de divisas *f*
speculative balance (E)	Spekulationskasse *f*	—	solde de spéculation *m*	domanda speculativa di moneta *f*	dinero inactivo *m*
speculative profit (E)	Spekulationsgewinn *m*	—	gain spéculatif *m*	utile di speculazione *m*	beneficio especulativo *m*
speculative security (E)	Spekulationspapier *n*	—	valeur spéculative *f*	titolo speculativo *m*	título especulativo *m*
speculative security (E)	Hoffnungswert *m*	—	titre spéculatif *m*	valore promettente reddito futuro *m*	título especulativo *m*
speculazione (I)	Spekulation *f*	speculation	spéculation *f*	—	especulación *f*
speculazione di borsa (I)	Konzertzeichnung *f*	stagging	majorisation *f*	—	mayorización *f*
speculazione in accaparramenti (I)	Aufkaufspekulation *f*	take-over speculation	accaparement spéculatif *m*	—	especulación de acaparamiento *f*
speculazione in cambi (I)	Devisenspekulation *f*	speculation in foreign currency	spéculation sur les changes *f*	—	especulación de divisas *f*
Spekulation (D)	—	speculation	spéculation *f*	speculazione *f*	especulación *f*
Spekulationsbank (D)	—	speculation bank	banque de spéculation *f*	banca di speculazione *f*	banco de especulación *m*
Spekulationsgewinn (D)	—	speculative profit	gain spéculatif *m*	utile di speculazione *m*	beneficio especulación *m*

	D	E	F	I	Es
Spekulationskasse (D)	—	speculative balance	solde de spéculation *m*	domanda speculativa di moneta *f*	dinero inactivo *m*
Spekulationspapier (D)	—	speculative security	valeur spéculative *f*	titolo speculativo *m*	título especulativo *m*
Spekulationssteuer (D)	—	tax on speculative gains	impôt sur les gains spéculatifs *m*	imposta sulla speculazione *f*	impuesto sobre beneficios especulativos *m*
spending costs (E)	ausgabenwirksame Kosten *pl*	—	coût créant des dépenses *m*	costi comportanti spese *m/pl*	gastos de desembolso *m/pl*
Sperrdepot (D)	—	blocked safe-deposit	dépôt bloqué *m*	deposito bloccato *m*	depósito bloqueado *m*
sperren (D)	—	to block	bloquer	bloccare	bloquear
Sperrguthaben (D)	—	blocked balance	avoir bloqué *m*	avere bloccato *m*	fondos bloqueados *m/pl*
Sperrkonto (D)	—	blocked account	compte bloqué *m*	conto bloccato *m*	cuenta bloqueada *f*
spese (I)	Ausgaben *f/pl*	expenses	dépenses *f/pl*	—	gastos *m/pl*
spese (I)	Spesen *pl*	expenses	frais *m/pl*	—	gastos *m/pl*
spese bancarie (I)	Bankspesen *pl*	bank charges	frais de banque *m/pl*	—	gastos bancarios *m/pl*
spese d'avviamento (I)	Anlaufkosten *f*	launching costs	frais de mise en marche *m/pl*	—	gastos de instalación *m/pl*
spese d'emissione (I)	Emissionskosten *pl*	underwriting costs	frais de l'émission *m/pl*	—	gastos de emisión *m/pl*
spese d'emissione (I)	Ausgabekosten *pl*	issuing costs	coût d'émission *m*	—	gastos de emisión *m/pl*
spese di custodia (I)	Verwahrungs-kosten *pl*	custody fee	coût de garde *m*	—	gastos de depósito *m/pl*
spese d'incasso di piazza (I)	Platzspesen *pl*	local expenses	change de place *m*	—	gastos locales *m/pl*
spese di rappresentanza (I)	Aufwandskosten *f*	expenses incurred	frais de représentation *m/pl*	—	gastos originados *m/pl*
Spesen (D)	—	expenses	frais *m/pl*	spese *f/pl*	gastos *m/pl*
Spesenrechnung (D)	—	statement of expenses	compte de frais *m*	conto delle spese *m*	cuenta de gastos *f*
spese pubbliche (I)	Staatsausgaben *f/pl*	public spending	dépenses publiques *f/pl*	—	gastos públicos *m/pl*
Spezialbank (D)	—	specialized commercial bank	banque spécialisée *f*	istituto di credito speciale *m*	banco especializado *m*
Spezialvollmacht (D)	—	special power	pouvoir limité à un acte commercial déterminé *m*	procura speciale *f*	poder especial *m*
Spezialwerte (D)	—	specialties	titres spéciaux *m/pl*	premi omaggio *m/pl*	títulos especiales *m/pl*
spirale dei salari e dei prezzi (I)	Lohn-Preis-Spirale *f*	wage-price spiral	course des prix et des salaires *f*	—	espiral precios-salarios *m*
spot business (E)	Locogeschäft *n*	—	opération en disponible *f*	operazione a contanti *f*	operaciones de entrega inmediata *f/pl*
spot exchange (E)	Kassadevisen *f/pl*	—	devises négociées en bourse au comptant *f/pl*	divisa a contanti *f*	divisas al contado *f/pl*
Spotgeschäft (D)	—	spot transactions	opération en disponible *f*	operazione spot *f*	operaciones al contado y de entrega inmediata *f/pl*
spot market (E)	Kassamarkt *m*	—	marché au comptant *m*	mercato del pronto *m*	mercado al contado *m*
spot price (E)	Kassakurs *m*	—	cours au comptant *m*	prezzo a pronti *m*	cambio al contado *m*
spot transaction (E)	Lokogeschäft *n*	—	opération en disponible *f*	operazione a contanti *f*	operaciones de entrega inmediata *f/pl*
spot transactions (E)	Spotgeschäft *n*	—	opération en disponible *f*	operazione spot *f*	operaciones al contado y de entrega inmediata *f/pl*
Staatsanleihen (D)	—	public bonds	emprunts d'Etat *m/pl*	titoli di Stato *m/pl*	bonos del Estado *m/pl*
Staatsausgaben (D)	—	public spending	dépenses publiques *f/pl*	spese pubbliche *f/pl*	gastos públicos *m/pl*
Staatsbank (D)	—	state bank	banque d'Etat *f*	banca di Stato *f*	banco del Estado *m*
Staatseinnahmen (D)	—	public revenue	recettes de l'Etat *f/pl*	entrate pubbliche *f/pl*	ingresos públicos *m/pl*

	D	E	F	I	Es
Staatspapiere (D)	—	public securities	effets publics *m/pl*	titoli di Stato *m/pl*	papeles del Estado *m/pl*
Staatsquote (D)	—	government expenditure rate	pourcentage des dépenses publiques *m*	percentuale della spesa pubblica *f*	porcentaje de los gastos públicos *m*
stabil (D)	—	stable	stable	stabile	estable
stabile (I)	stabil	stable	stable	—	estable
stabilisation (F)	Stabilisierung *f*	stabilization	—	stabilizzazione *f*	estabilización *f*
Stabilisierung (D)	—	stabilization	stabilisation *f*	stabilizzazione *f*	estabilización *f*
stabilità (I)	Stabilität *f*	stability	stabilité *f*	—	estabilidad *f*
stabilità del valore del capitale (I)	Kapitalerhaltung *f*	maintenance of capital	maintien du capital *m*	—	conservación de capital *f*
stabilità monetaria (I)	Geldwertstabilität *f*	monetary stability	stabilité monétaire *f*	—	estabilidad monetaria *f*
Stabilität (D)	—	stability	stabilité *f*	stabilità *f*	estabilidad *f*
stabilité (F)	Stabilität *f*	stability	—	stabilità *f*	estabilidad *f*
stabilité monétaire (F)	Geldwertstabilität *f*	monetary stability	—	stabilità monetaria *f*	estabilidad monetaria *f*
stability (E)	Stabilität *f*	—	stabilité *f*	stabilità *f*	estabilidad *f*
stabilization (E)	Stabilisierung *f*	—	stabilisation *f*	stabilizzazione *f*	estabilización *f*
stabilizzazione (I)	Stabilisierung *f*	stabilization	stabilisation *f*	—	estabilización *f*
stable (E)	stabil	—	stable	stabile	estable
stable (F)	stabil	stable	—	stabile	estable
stacco del diritto d'opzione (I)	Bezugsrechtabschlag *m*	ex-rights markdown	cours moins le droit de souscription *m*	—	deducción del derecho de suscripción *f*
Staffelanleihe (D)	—	graduated-interest loan	emprunt à taux progressif *m*	prestito a interesse scalare *m*	empréstito escalonado *m*
staff pension fund (E)	Pensionskasse *f*	—	caisse de retraite *f*	fondo di previdenza *m*	caja de jubilaciones *f*
staff shares (E)	Belegschaftsaktie *f*	—	action de travail *f*	azione per dipendenti *f*	acción de personal *f*
Stagflation (D)	—	stagflation	stagflation *f*	stagflazione *f*	estanflación *f*
stagflation (E)	Stagflation *f*	—	stagflation *f*	stagflazione *f*	estanflación *f*
stagflation (F)	Stagflation *f*	stagflation	—	stagflazione *f*	estanflación *f*
stagflazione (I)	Stagflation *f*	stagflation	stagflation *f*	—	estanflación *f*
stagging (E)	Konzertzeichnung *f*	—	majorisation *f*	speculazione di borsa *f*	mayorización *f*
stagnant (F)	geschäftslos	slack	—	inattivo	estado de estancamiento *m*
Stammaktie (D)	—	ordinary share	action ordinaire *f*	azione ordinaria *f*	acción ordinaria *f*
Stammkapital (D)	—	share capital	capital social *m*	capitale sociale *m*	capital social *m*
Stammkunde (D)	—	regular customer	client habituel *m*	cliente abituale *m*	cliente habitual *m*
Stammrecht (D)	—	customary law	droit habituel *m*	diritto principale *m*	derecho habitual *m*
stampa finanziaria (I)	Finanzpresse *f*	financial press	presse financière *f*	—	prensa financiera *f*
stamp duty (E)	Stempelsteuer *f*	—	droit de timbre *m*	imposta di bollo *f*	impuesto del timbre *m*
stamping (E)	Abstempelung *f*	—	estampillage *m*	bollatura *f*	estampillado *m*
stamping of bank notes (E)	Notenabstempelung *f*	—	estampillage des billets de banque *m*	timbratura di banconote *f*	estampillado de billetes *m*
standard (E)	Feingewicht *n*	—	poids de métal fin *m*	titolo *m*	peso fino *m*
standard (E)	Feingehalt *n*	—	titre *m*	titolo *m*	ley *f*
standard bill (E)	Einheitswechsel *m*	—	lettre de change normalisée *f*	cambiale standardizzata *f*	letra de cambio estándar *f*
standard cheque (E)	Einheitsscheck *m*	—	formule de chèque normalisée *f*	assegno standardizzato *m*	cheque estándar *m*
standard form of accounts (E)	Kontenrahmen *m*	—	cadre comptable *m*	quadro dei conti *m*	sistema de cuentas *m*
standardisation (F)	Standardisierung *f*	standardization	—	standardizzazione *f*	estandarización *f*
Standardisierung (D)	—	standardization	standardisation *f*	standardizzazione *f*	estandarización *f*

statistique des bilans

	D	E	F	I	Es
standardization (E)	Standardisierung f	—	standardisation f	standardizzazione f	estandarización f
standardizzazione (I)	Standardisierung f	standardization	standardisation f	—	estandarización f
standard price (E)	fester Verrechnungs-preis m	—	prix standard m	prezzo unico m	precio estándar m
standard value (E)	Einheitswert m	—	valeur globale intrinsèque f	titolo unitario m	valor unitario m
stand-by agreement (I)	Bereitschaftskredit-abkommen n	stand-by arrangement	arrangement stand-by m	—	préstamo de ayuda m
stand-by arrangement (E)	Bereitschaftskredit-abkommen n	—	arrangement stand-by m	stand-by agreement m	préstamo de ayuda m
stand-by credit (E)	Stand-by-Kredit m	—	crédit stand-by m	credito stand-by m	crédito stand-by m
standby credit (E)	Beistandskredit m	—	crédit de soutien m	credito di sostegno m	crédito de ayuda m
Stand-by-Kredit (D)	—	stand-by credit	crédit stand-by m	credito stand-by m	crédito stand-by m
standing costs (E)	fixe Kosten pl	—	coût fixe m	costi fissi m/pl	gastos fijos m/pl
standing order (E)	Dauerauftrag m	—	ordre régulier m	incarico permanente m	orden permanente f
standstill credit (E)	Stillhalte-Kredit m	—	crédit moratoire m	credito inattivo m	crédito inmovilizado m
stanza di compensazione (I)	Abrechnungsstelle f	clearing house	bureau du clearing f	—	oficina de compensación f
Stapelbestand (D)	—	stockpile	existences accumulées f/pl	portafoglio stivato m	existencias de títulos almacenadas f/pl
star del credere (I)	Delkredere n	reserve for bad debts	ducroire m	—	delcrédere m
star del credere forfettario (I)	Pauschaldelkredere n	global delcredere	ducroire forfaitaire m	—	del credere global m
starrer Wechselkurs (D)	—	fixed exchange rate	taux de change fixe m	cambio fisso m	tipo de cambio fijo m
state bank (E)	Staatsbank f	—	banque d'Etat f	banca di Stato f	banco del Estado m
statement (E)	Ausweisung f	—	publication f	pubblicazione f	registrar un importe m
statement of account (E)	Kontoauszug m	—	relevé de compte m	estratto conto m	extracto de cuenta m
statement of costs (E)	Kostenrechnung f	—	compte des frais m	calcolo dei costi m	cálculo de costes m
statement of expenses (E)	Spesenrechnung f	—	compte de frais m	conto delle spese m	cuenta de gastos f
statement of overindebtedness (E)	Überschuldungs-bilanz f	—	bilan de l'endettement m	stato di disavanzo patrimoniale m	balance de débitos m
statement of securities (E)	Depotauszug m	—	relevé de compte-titres m	estratto deposito m	extracto de depósito m
state supervision of credit institutions (E)	Kreditaufsicht f	—	office de surveillance des établissements de crédit f	autorità di vigilanza sul credito f	supervisión crediticia f
statistica (I)	Statistik f	statistics	statistique f	—	estadística f
statistica bancaria (I)	Bankstatistik f	banking statistics	statistique bancaire f	—	estadística bancaria f
statistica bancaria (I)	Bankenstatistik f	banking statistics	statistique bancaire f	—	estadística bancaria f
statistica dei titoli (I)	Effektenstatistik f	securities statistics	statistique de titres f	—	estadística de valores f
statistica del commercio estero (I)	Außenhandels-statistik f	foreign trade statistics	statistique du commerce extérieur f	—	estadística del comercio exterior f
statistica delle nuove emissioni (I)	Emissionsstatistik f	new issue statistics	statistique d'émission f	—	estadística de emisión f
statistics (E)	Statistik f	—	statistique f	statistica f	estadística f
Statistik (D)	—	statistics	statistique f	statistica f	estadística f
statistique (F)	Statistik f	statistics	—	statistica f	estadística f
statistique bancaire (F)	Bankenstatistik f	banking statistics	—	statistica bancaria f	estadística bancaria f
statistique bancaire (F)	Bankstatistik f	banking statistics	—	statistica bancaria f	estadística bancaria f
statistique d'émission (F)	Emissionsstatistik f	new issue statistics	—	statistica delle nuove emissioni f	estadística de emisión f
statistique des bilans (F)	Bilanzstatistik f	balance sheet statistics	—	analisi statistica dei bilanci f	estadística de balances f

	D	E	F	I	Es
statistique de titres (F)	Effektenstatistik f	securities statistics	—	statistica dei titoli f	estadística de valores f
statistique du commerce extérieur (F)	Außenhandels- statistik f	foreign trade statistics	—	statistica del commercio estero f	estadística del comercio exterior f
stato di disavanzo patrimoniale (I)	Überschuldungs- bilanz f	statement of overindebtedness	bilan de l'endettement m	—	balance de débitos m
statut (F)	Satzung f	statutes	—	statuto m	estatutos m/pl
statutes (E)	Satzung f	—	statut m	statuto m	estatutos m/pl
statuto (I)	Satzung f	statutes	statut m	—	estatutos m/pl
statutory public disclosure (E)	Veröffentlichungs- pflicht f	—	obligation de publier f	obbligo di pubblicazione m	publicación obligatoria f
Stellagegeschäft (D)	—	double option operation	marché à double option m	contratto stellage m	operación de doble prima f
Stellgeld (D)	—	premium for double option	prime de double option f	premio dello stellage m	prima en operación de doble opción f
Stellgeschäft (D)	—	put and call	opération de stellage f	contratto stellage m	operación de doble opción f
Stellkurs (D)	—	put and call price	cours du stellage m	prezzo giorno di risposta premi m	cotización de doble opción f
Stempelsteuer (D)	—	stamp duty	droit de timbre m	imposta di bollo f	impuesto del timbre m
Sterilisierungs- fonds (D)	—	sterilization funds	fonds de stérilisation m	fondo di sterilizzazione m	fondos de esterilización m/pl
Sterilisierungs- politik (D)	—	policy of sterilization funds	politique de stérilisation f	politica di sterilizzazione f	política en materia de esterilización f
sterilization funds (E)	Sterilisierungs- fonds m	—	fonds de stérilisation m	fondo di sterilizzazione m	fondos de esterilización m/pl
Steuer (D)	—	tax	impôt m	imposta f	impuesto m
steuerbegünstigtes Sparen (D)	—	tax-privileged saving	épargne jouissant d'avantages fiscaux f	risparmio con privilegi fiscali m	ahorro favorecido por ventajas fiscales m
steuerbegünstigte Wertpapiere (D)	—	tax-privileged securities	titres assortis d'avan- tages fiscaux m/pl	titoli con privilegi fiscali m/pl	títulos favorecidos por ventajas fiscales m/pl
Stichkupon (D)	—	renewal coupon	coupon de renouvellement m	cedola di riaffogliamento f	cupón de renovación m
Stichtag (D)	—	reporting date	jour fixé m	data di riferimento f	día de liquidación m
Stichtagskurs (D)	—	market price on reporting date	cours offert à la date de référence m	quotazione del giorno di riferimento f	cotización del día de referencia f
still (D)	—	slack	calme	fiacco	flojo
stille Gesellschaft (D)	—	dormant partnership	association commerciale en participation f	società di diritto f	sociedad en participación f
stille Reserve (D)	—	hidden reserves	réserves cachées f/pl	riserva occulta f	reservas tácitas f/pl
stille Zession (D)	—	undisclosed assignment	cession occulte f	cessione tacita f	cesión tácita f
Stillhalte-Kredit (D)	—	standstill credit	crédit moratoire m	credito inattivo m	crédito inmovilizado m
stillhalten (D)	—	to sell an option	vendre une option	concedere una moratoria	prorrogar
Stillhalter (D)	—	option seller	vendeur d'option m	venditore di un'opzione m	vendedor de opción m
stimato (I)	genannt	indicated	indiqué	—	alias
Stimmrecht (D)	—	right to vote	droit de vote m	diritto di voto m	derecho a voto m
Stimmrechtsaktie (D)	—	voting share	action à droit de vote simple f	azione con diritto di voto f	acción con derecho a voto f
stimmrechtslose Vorzugsaktie (D)	—	non-voting share	action privilégiée sans droit de vote f	azione privilegiata senza diritto di voto f	acción preferente sin derecho a voto f
stockbook (E)	Effektenbuch n	—	registre des titres m	registro dei titoli m	libro de valores m
stockbroker (E)	Kursmakler m	—	courtier en bourse m	agente di borsa m	agente de cambio y bolsa m
stockbroker (E)	Effektenmakler m	—	courtier en valeurs mobilières m	agente di cambio m	corredor de bolsa m
stockbroker (E)	Börsenmakler m	—	courtier en bourse m	agente di borsa m	agente de bolsa m

	D	E	F	I	Es
stock committee (E)	Börsenausschuß *m*	—	conseil de la bourse *m*	comitato di borsa *m*	comité de las bolsas *m*
stock dividend (E)	Stockdividende *f*	—	dividende distribué sous forme de titres *m*	dividendo in azioni *m*	dividendo por acciones *m*
Stockdividende (D)	—	stock dividend	dividende distribué sous forme de titres *m*	dividendo in azioni *m*	dividendo por acciones *m*
stock exchange (E)	Effektenbörse *f*	—	bourse des titres et valeurs mobilières *f*	borsa valori *f*	bolsa de valores *m*
Stock Exchange Act (E)	Börsengesetz *n*	—	loi en matière de bourse *f*	legge sulla borsa *f*	ley sobre las operaciones bursátiles *f*
stock exchange centre (E)	Börsenplatz *m*	—	place boursière *f*	sede di borsa *f*	plaza bursátil *f*
stock exchange customs (E)	Börsenusancen *f/pl*	—	usages de la bourse *m/pl*	usanze borsistiche *f/pl*	usos bursátiles *m/pl*
stock exchange index (E)	Börsenindex *m*	—	indice des cours des actions *m*	indice di borsa *m*	índice bursátil *m*
stock exchange index (E)	Kursindex *m*	—	indice des cours *m*	indice di borsa *m*	índice de cotizaciones *m*
stock exchange list (E)	Kurszettel *m*	—	bulletin des cours *m*	listino di borsa *m*	boletín de bolsa *m*
stock exchange list (E)	Kursblatt *n*	—	cote de la bourse *f*	listino di borsa *m*	listín de bolsa *m*
stock exchange operations (E)	Börsengeschäfte *n/pl*	—	opération de bourse *f*	operazioni di borsa *f/pl*	operaciones bursátiles *f/pl*
stock exchange order (E)	Börsenauftrag *m*	—	ordre de bourse *m*	ordine di borsa *m*	orden de bolsa *f*
stock exchange organization (E)	Börsenorganisation *f*	—	organisation boursière *f*	organizzazione della borsa *f*	organización bursátil *f*
stock exchange price (E)	Börsenkurs *m*	—	cours de bourse *m*	quotazione di borsa *f*	cotización bursátil *f*
stock exchange regulations (E)	Börsenordnung *f*	—	règlement de la bourse *m*	regolamento della borsa *m*	reglamento de bolsa *m*
stock exchange report (E)	Börsenbericht *m*	—	bulletin de la bourse *m*	bollettino di borsa *m*	informe bursátil *m*
stock exchange rules (E)	Börsenrecht *n*	—	régime de bourse *m*	diritto della borsa *m*	derecho de la bolsa *m*
stock exchange supervision (E)	Börsenaufsicht *f*	—	surveillance de la bourse *f*	sorveglianza della borsa *f*	control estatal de bolsas *m*
stock exchange turnover (E)	Börsenumsätze *m/pl*	—	volume d'opérations boursières *m*	scambi borsistici *m/pl*	volumen de operaciones bursátiles *m*
stock exchange turnover tax (E)	Börsenumsatzsteuer *f*	—	taxe de transaction sur les opérations boursières *f*	imposta sui contratti di borsa *f*	impuesto sobre la negociación bursátil *m*
stock market information (E)	Börsenauskunft *f*	—	service des renseignements de la bourse *m*	informazioni borsa *f/pl*	información bursátil *f*
stock market notice board (E)	Börsenaushang *m*	—	affiche de bourse *f*	affissione in borsa *f*	anuncio bursátil *m*
stock market trend (E)	Börsentendenz *f*	—	tendance de la bourse *f*	tendenza borsistica *f*	tendencia bursátil *f*
stockpile (E)	Stapelbestand *m*	—	existences accumulées *f/pl*	portafoglio stivato *m*	existencias de títulos almacenadas *f/pl*
stocks (E)	Bestand *m*	—	inventaire *m*	inventario *m*	inventario *m*
stock-taking (E)	Bestandsaufnahme *f*	—	établissement de l'inventaire *m*	redazione d'inventario *f*	formación de un inventario *f*
stopping payment of cheque (E)	Schecksperre *f*	—	opposition au payement d'un chèque *f*	fermo su assegno *m*	bloqueo de un cheque *m*
Stoppkurs (D)	—	stop price	cours maximum *m*	quotazione bloccata *f*	cotización máxima *f*
stop price (E)	Stoppkurs *m*	—	cours maximum *m*	quotazione bloccata *f*	cotización máxima *f*
Storno (D)	—	counter entry	écriture de contre-passation *f*	storno *m*	cancelación *f*
storno (I)	Storno *n*	counter entry	écriture de contre-passation *f*	—	cancelación *f*
Strafzins (D)	—	penalty interest	intérêt punitif *m*	penalità *f*	interés punitivo *m*
Streichung (D)	—	deletion	annulation *f*	mancata quotazione *f*	anulación *f*

	D	E	F	I	Es
Streifbanddepot (D)	—	individual deposit of securities	dépôt individuel avec mandat de gestion m	deposito a dossier m	depósito separado m
Streubesitz (D)	—	diversified holdings	propriété disséminée f	capitali ripartiti m/pl	propiedad dispersa f
Stromgröße (D)	—	rate of flow	volume du flux m	variabile di flusso f	tasa de flujo f
structural change (E)	Strukturwandel m	—	changement dans les structures m	adeguamento di struttura m	cambio de estructura m
structural loan (E)	Strukturkredit m	—	crédit de structure m	credito strutturale m	crédito de estructura m
structure d'emploi (F)	Beschäftigtenstruktur f	employment structure	—	struttura dell'occupazione f	estructura de empleo f
structure des intérêts (F)	Zinsstruktur f	interest rate structure	—	struttura degli interessi f	estructura de los intereses f
structure d'offres (F)	Angebotsstruktur f	supply structure	—	struttura dell'offerta f	estructura de ofertas f
structure du bilan (F)	Bilanzstruktur f	structure of the balance sheet	—	struttura del bilancio f	estructura del balance f
structure du commerce extérieur (F)	Außenhandelsrahmen m	foreign trade structure	—	quadro commercio estero m	estructura del comercio exterior f
structure du marché (F)	Marktstruktur f	market structure	—	struttura del mercato f	estructura del mercado f
structure inverse des intérêts (F)	inverse Zinsstruktur f	inverse interest rate structure	—	struttura degli interessi inversa f	estructura de interés inversa f
structure monétaire (F)	Geldverfassung f	monetary structure	—	sistema monetario m	estructura monetaria f
structure of the balance sheet (E)	Bilanzstruktur f	—	structure du bilan f	struttura del bilancio f	estructura del balance f
struggle against inflation (E)	Inflationsbekämpfung f	—	lutte contre l'inflation f	lotta all'inflazione f	lucha contra la inflación f
Strukturkredit (D)	—	structural loan	crédit de structure m	credito strutturale m	crédito de estructura m
Strukturwandel (D)	—	structural change	changement dans les structures m	adeguamento di struttura m	cambio de estructura m
strumenti di finanziamento ibridi (I)	hybride Finanzierungsinstrumente n/pl	hybrid financing instruments	instruments de financement hybrides m/pl	—	instrumentos de financiación híbridos m/pl
strumenti di politica del bilancio (I)	bilanzpolitische Instrumente n/pl	instruments of balance sheet policy	instruments de la politique en matière de bilans m/pl	—	instrumentos en materia de política de balances m/pl
Strumpfgeld (D)	—	hoarded notes and coins	argent gardé dans le bas de laine m	denaro tesaurizzato m	dinero en el calcetín m
struttura degli interessi (I)	Zinsstruktur f	interest rate structure	structure des intérêts f	—	estructura de los intereses f
struttura degli interessi inversa (I)	inverse Zinsstruktur f	inverse interest rate structure	structure inverse des intérêts f	—	estructura de interés inversa f
struttura del bilancio (I)	Bilanzstruktur f	structure of the balance sheet	structure du bilan f	—	estructura del balance f
struttura del bilancio (I)	Bilanzgliederung f	format of the balance sheet	présentation du bilan f	—	estructura del balance f
struttura dell'occupazione (I)	Beschäftigtenstruktur f	employment structure	structure d'emploi f	—	estructura de empleo f
struttura dell'offerta (I)	Angebotsstruktur f	supply structure	structure d'offres f	—	estructura de ofertas f
struttura del mercato (I)	Marktstruktur f	market structure	structure du marché f	—	estructura del mercado f
Stücke (D)	—	securities	titres m/pl	titoli m/pl	títulos m/pl
Stückekonto (D)	—	shares account	compte de titres m	conto titoli m	cuenta de valores f
Stückelung (D)	—	fragmentation	fractionnement m	frazionamento m	fraccionamiento m
Stückkosten (D)	—	cost per unit	coût unitaire de production m	costo unitario m	costes específicos m/pl
Stückkurs (D)	—	price per share	cours coté au prix unitaire du titre m	corso unitario m	cotización por unidad f
Stückzinsen (D)	—	broken period interest	intérêts courus m/pl	interessi maturati m/pl	intereses por fracción de período m/pl
Stützungskauf (D)	—	support buying	achat de soutien m	acquisto di sostegno m	compra para sostener precios f

	D	E	F	I	Es
subagente (Es)	Untermakler *m*	intermediate broker	sous-agent *m*	commissionario *m*	—
subasta (Es)	Ausschreibung *f*	invitation to tender	soumission *f*	appalto *m*	—
subasta de oro (Es)	Goldauktion *f*	gold auction	vente à l'enchère d'or *f*	asta dell'oro *f*	—
subasta de préstamos de regulación monetaria por cantidades (Es)	Mengentender *m*	quantity tender	offre d'emprunts par quantités pour la *f* régulation monétaire	asta non competitiva *f*	—
subempleo (Es)	Unterbeschäftigung *f*	underemployment	sous-emploi *m*	sottoccupazione *f*	—
subfianza (Es)	Nachbürgschaft *f*	collateral guarantee	garantie du certificateur de la caution *f*	fideiussione per il fideiussore *f*	—
subida de precios (Es)	Preissteigerung *f*	price increase	hausse des prix *f*	aumento dei prezzi *m*	—
subject to confirmation (E)	freibleibend	—	sans engagement	senza impegno	salvo venta
subpegno di titoli (I)	Drittpfändung *f*	garnishee proceedings	saisie de tiers débiteurs *f*	—	embargo del tercer deudor *m*
subpoder (Es)	Untervollmacht *f*	delegated authority	sous-délégation *f*	procura rilasciata dal procuratore *f*	—
subscribed capital (E)	gezeichnetes Kapital *n*	—	capital souscrit *m*	capitale nominale *m*	capital suscrito *m*
subscription (E)	Subskription *f*	—	souscription *f*	sottoscrizione *f*	suscripción *f*
subscription arbitrage (E)	Bezugsrechtsarbitrage *f*	—	arbitrage de souscription *m*	arbitraggio sui diritti d'opzione *m*	arbitraje de derechos de suscripción *m*
subscription conditions (E)	Bezugsbedingungen *f/pl*	—	conditions de souscription *f/pl*	condizioni d'acquisto *f/pl*	condiciones de suscripción *f/pl*
subscription day (E)	Bezugstag *m*	—	jour de souscription *m*	giorno di scadenza opzione *m*	día de la emisión *m*
subscription form (E)	Zeichnungsschein *m*	—	certificat de souscription *m*	bollettino di sottoscrizione *m*	boletín de suscripción *m*
subscription for shares (E)	Aktienzeichnung *f*	—	souscription d'actions *f*	sottoscrizione di azioni *f*	suscripción de acciones *f*
subscription period (E)	Bezugsfrist *f*	—	délai de souscription *m*	termine d'opzione *m*	plazo de suscripción *m*
subscription price (E)	Bezugskurs *m*	—	prix de souscription *m*	corso d'acquisto *m*	cotización de emisión *f*
subscription price (E)	Bezugsrechtskurs *m*	—	prix de souscription *m*	prezzo del diritto d'opzione *m*	precio de suscripción *m*
subscription price (E)	Bezugsrechtnotierung *f*	—	cotation des droits de souscription *f*	prezzo del diritto d'opzione *m*	cotización de derechos de suscripción *f*
subscription right (E)	Bezugsrecht *n*	—	droit de souscription *m*	diritto d'opzione *m*	derecho de opción *f*
subscription rights disposition (E)	Bezugsrechtsdisposition *f*	—	disposition des droits de souscription *f*	esercizio del diritto d'opzione *m*	disposición del derecho de suscripción *f*
subscription rights evaluation (E)	Bezugsrechtsbewertung *f*	—	évaluation des droits de souscription *f*	valutazione del diritto d'opzione *f*	evaluación del derecho de suscripción *f*
subscription rights parity (E)	Bezugsrechtsparität *f*	—	parité des droits de souscription *f*	valore aritmetico diritto d'opzione *m*	paridad de derecho de suscripción *f*
subscription warrant (E)	Bezugsschein *m*	—	certificat de souscription *m*	buono d'opzione *m*	boletín de suscripción *m*
subsequent payment (E)	Nachschuß *m*	—	versement complémentaire *m*	apporto supplemetare *m*	aportación suplementaria *f*
subside (F)	Beihilfe *f*	financial aid	—	assistenza *f*	ayuda *f*
subsidio de desempleo (Es)	Arbeitslosengeld *n*	unemployment benefit	indemnité de chômage *f*	indennità di disoccupazione *f*	—
subsidy (E)	Subvention *f*	—	subvention *f*	sovvenzione *f*	subvención *f*
subsistence minimum (E)	Existenzminimum *n*	—	minimum vital *m*	minimo d'esistenza *m*	mínimo vital *m*
Subskription (D)	—	subscription	souscription *f*	sottoscrizione *f*	suscripción *f*
substitución monetaria (Es)	Währungssubstitution *f*	currency substitution	substitution monétaire *f*	sostituzione monetaria *f*	—
substitute cheque (E)	Ersatzscheck *m*	—	chèque de substitution *m*	assegno sostitutivo *m*	cheque de sustitución *m*

	D	E	F	I	Es
substitute cover (E)	Ersatzdeckung f	—	garantie de substitution f	copertura sostitutiva f	garantía adicional f
substitute transfer (E)	Ersatzüberweisung f	—	virement de substitution m	trasferimento sostitutivo m	transferencia sustitutiva f
substitution de titres (F)	Effektensubstitution f	securities substitution	—	sostituzione di titoli f	sustitución de valores f
substitution fidéicommissaire (F)	Treuhand f	trust	—	amministrazione fiduciaria f	administración fiduciaria f
substitution monétaire (F)	Währungssubstitution f	currency substitution	—	sostituzione monetaria f	sustitución monetaria f
subvaloración (Es)	Unterbewertung f	undervaluation	sous-estimation f	sottovalutazione f	—
subvención (Es)	Subvention f	subsidy	subvention f	sovvenzione f	—
subvención de ahorro (Es)	Sparzulage f	savings bonus	prime d'épargne f	assegno integrativo di risparmio m	—
Subvention (D)	—	subsidy	subvention f	sovvenzione f	subvención f
subvention (F)	Subvention f	subsidy	—	sovvenzione f	subvención f
subvention en faveur des investissements (F)	Investitionshilfe f	investment assistance	—	aiuti agli investimenti m/pl	ayuda de inversión f
succursale (F)	Filiale f	branch office	—	filiale f	filial f
succursale à l'étranger (F)	Auslandsniederlassung f	branch abroad	—	filiale all'estero f	sucursal en el extranjero f
su cuenta (Es)	Vostrokonto n	vostro account	votre compte en notre établissement m	conto vostro m	—
sucursal (Es)	Zweigstelle f	branch	agence f	filiale f	—
sucursal en el extranjero (Es)	Auslandsniederlassung f	branch abroad	succursale à l'étranger f	filiale all'estero f	—
suma del balance (Es)	Bilanzsumme f	balance sheet total	total du bilan m	totale del bilancio m	—
suministro externo (Es)	Fremdbezug m	external procurement	matériel acheté au-dehors m	acquisto di beni e servizi da terzi m	—
Summenaktie (D)	—	share at a fixed amount	action d'un montant fixe f	azione a valore nominale determinato f	acción de valor determinado f
Summenbilanz (D)	—	turnover balance	relevé des comptes généraux m	bilancio generale m	balance de sumas m
super-dividend (E)	Überdividende f	—	superdividende m	dividendo addizionale m	dividendo adicional m
superdividende (F)	Überdividende f	super-dividend	—	dividendo addizionale m	dividendo adicional m
superintendencia bancaria (Es)	Bankenaufsicht f	public supervision of banking	contrôle des banques m	controllo sulle banche m	—
supervisión crediticia (Es)	Kreditaufsicht f	state supervision of credit institutions	office de surveillance des établissements de crédit f	autorità di vigilanza sul credito f	—
supervisory board (E)	Aufsichtsrat m	—	conseil de surveillance m	consiglio di sorveglianza m	consejo de administración m
suplemento (Es)	Zuschuß m	allowance	allocation f	aggiunta f	—
suplementos patronales (Es)	Arbeitgeberzuschüsse m/pl	employer's contributions	compléments patronaux m/pl	contributi del datore di lavoro m/pl	—
suposición de depósito ajeno (Es)	Fremdvermutung f	presumption that securities deposited are fiduciary deposit	présomption que les valeurs déposées sont administrées à titre fiduciaire f	limitazione diritto di pegno e ritenzione su depositi di terzi f	—
supplementary levy (E)	Ergänzungsabgabe f	—	taxe complémentaire f	imposta complementare f	tasa complementaria f
supply control (E)	Angebotssteuerung f	—	régulation des offres f	controllo dell'offerta m	control de oferta m
supply of capital (E)	Kapitalangebot n	—	offre de capital f	offerta di capitale f	oferta de capital f
supply of money (E)	Geldangebot n	—	offre d'argent f	offerta monetaria f	oferta monetaria f
supply structure (E)	Angebotsstruktur f	—	structure d'offres f	struttura dell'offerta f	estructura de ofertas f
support buying (E)	Stützungskauf m	—	achat de soutien m	acquisto di sostegno m	compra para sostener precios f
support level (E)	Unterstützunglinie f	—	ligne de soutien f	linea di sostegno f	línea de sostenimiento f

	D	E	F	I	Es
surcapitalisation (F)	Überkapitalisierung f	overcapitalization	—	sovraccapitalizzazione f	sobrecapitalización f
surenchère au concordat (F)	Besserungsschein m	debtor warrant	—	certificato di rimborso in caso di miglioramento della situazione finanziaria m	certificado de mejora m
surendettement (F)	Überschuldung f	excessive indebtedness	—	indebitamento eccessivo m	exceso de deudas m
sûreté en garantie de dépôts (F)	Einlagensicherung f	guarantee of deposit	—	garanzia dei depositi f	garantía de depositos f
sûreté en garantie d'un crédit (F)	Kreditsicherung f	safeguarding of credit	—	garanzia di credito f	garantía de un crédito f
surplus reserve (E)	Überschußreserve f	—	réserve excédentaire f	riserva liquida f	reserva en exceso f
surplus saving (E)	Überschuß-Sparen n	—	épargne d'excédents f	risparmio con ordine permanente m	ahorro de los importes excesivos m
surplus saving (E)	Plus-Sparen n	—	épargne d'excédents f	risparmio restanti del conto corrente m	ahorro de excedentes m
surprime de risque (F)	Risikozuschlag m	additional risk premium	—	soprappremio di rischio m	recargo de riesgo m
sursis de payement (F)	Zahlungsaufschub m	extension of time for payment	—	dilazione di pagamento f	pago aplazado m
surtido (Es)	Sortiment n	assortment	assortiment m	assortimento m	—
surveillance de la bourse (F)	Börsenaufsicht f	stock exchange supervision	—	sorveglianza della borsa f	control estatal de bolsas m
surveillance des banques (F)	Bankkontrolle f	bank supervision	—	controllo bancario m	control bancario m
suscripción (Es)	Subskription f	subscription	souscription f	sottoscrizione f	—
suscripción de acciones (Es)	Aktienzeichnung f	subscription for shares	souscription d'actions f	sottoscrizione di azioni f	—
suscripción en exceso (Es)	Überzeichnung f	over-subscription	souscription surpassée f	sottoscrizione eccedente f	—
suspension (E)	Aussetzung f	—	suspension f	rinvio m	suspensión f
suspensión (Es)	Aussetzung f	suspension	suspension f	rinvio m	—
suspension (F)	Aussetzung f	suspension	—	rinvio m	suspensión f
suspension d'amortissement (F)	Tilgungsaussetzung f	suspension of redemption payments	—	differimento di rimborso m	suspensión de la amortización f
suspensión de la amortización (Es)	Tilgungsaussetzung f	suspension of redemption payments	suspension d'amortissement f	differimento di rimborso m	—
suspensión de pagos (Es)	Zahlungseinstellung f	cessation of payments	suspension de x payments	cessazione di pagamento f	—
suspension de payement (F)	Zahlungseinstellung f	cessation of payments	—	cessazione di pagamento f	suspensión de pagos f
suspension of redemption payments (E)	Tilgungsaussetzung f	—	suspension d'amortissement f	differimento di rimborso m	suspensión de la amortización f
sustitución de valores (Es)	Effektensubstitution f	securities substitution	substitution de titres f	sostituzione di titoli f	—
sustitutivo de dinero (Es)	Geldsubstitut n	money substitute	monnaie subrogée f	quasi moneta f	—
svalutazione (I)	Abwertung f	devaluation	dévaluation f	—	desvalorización f
svalutazione monetaria (I)	Geldentwertung f	monetary devaluation	dépréciation f	—	devaluación del dinero f
svincolamento (I)	Devinkulierung f	unrestricted transferability	transférabilité illimitée f	—	devinculación f
Swap (D)	—	swap	swap m	operazione swap f	swap m
swap (E)	Swap m	—	swap m	operazione swap f	swap m
swap (Es)	Swap m	swap	swap m	operazione swap f	—
swap (F)	Swap m	swap	—	operazione swap f	swap m
Swapabkommen (D)	—	swap agreement	accord swap m	contratto swap m	acuerdo de swap m
swap agreement (E)	Swapabkommen n	—	accord swap m	contratto swap m	acuerdo de swap m
swap de devises (F)	Währungsswap m	currency swap	—	currency swap m	swap en moneda extranjera m

	D	E	F	I	Es
swap de intereses (Es)	Zinsswap *m*	interest rate swap	swap d'intérêts *m*	interest swap *m*	—
swap de oro (Es)	Goldswap *m*	gold swap	swap d'or *m*	goldswap *m*	—
swap d'intérêts (F)	Zinsswap *m*	interest rate swap	—	interest swap *m*	swap de intereses *m*
swap d'or (F)	Goldswap *m*	gold swap	—	goldswap *m*	swap de oro *m*
swap en moneda extranjera (Es)	Währungsswap *m*	currency swap	swap de devises *m*	currency swap *m*	—
Swapgeschäft (D)	—	swap transaction	opération swap *f*	operazione swap *f*	operación swap *f*
swap line (E)	Swaplinie *f*	—	ligne de swap *f*	linea swap *f*	línea swap *f*
Swaplinie (D)	—	swap line	ligne de swap *f*	linea swap *f*	línea swap *f*
swap policy (E)	Swappolitik *f*	—	politique de swap *f*	politica swap *f*	política de swap *f*
Swappolitik (D)	—	swap policy	politique de swap *f*	politica swap *f*	política de swap *f*
swap rate (E)	Swapsatz *m*	—	taux de swap *m*	tasso swap *m*	tipo swap *m*
Swapsatz (D)	—	swap rate	taux de swap *m*	tasso swap *m*	tipo swap *m*
swap transaction (E)	Swapgeschäft *n*	—	opération swap *f*	operazione swap *f*	operación swap *f*
SWIFT (D)	—	swift	swift *m*	swift *m*	swift *m*
swift (E)	SWIFT *m*	—	swift *m*	swift *m*	swift *m*
swift (Es)	SWIFT *m*	swift	swift *m*	swift *m*	—
swift (F)	SWIFT *m*	swift	—	swift *m*	swift *m*
swift (I)	SWIFT *m*	swift	swift *m*	—	swift *m*
Swing (D)	—	swing	swing *m*	swing *m*	swing *m*
swing (E)	Swing *m*	—	swing *m*	swing *m*	swing *m*
swing (Es)	Swing *m*	swing	swing *m*	swing *m*	—
swing (F)	Swing *m*	swing	—	swing *m*	swing *m*
swing (I)	Swing *m*	swing	swing *m*	—	swing *m*
switch (E)	Switch-Geschäft *n*	—	opération switch *f*	operazione switch *f*	operación switch *f*
Switch-Geschäft (D)	—	switch	opération switch *f*	operazione switch *f*	operación switch *f*
syndicat bancaire appuyant une émission (F)	Emissionskonsortium *n*	underwriting syndicate	—	consorzio *m* d'emissione	consorcio emisor *m*
syndicat bancaire de garantie (F)	Emissionssyndikat *f*	underwriting syndicate	—	sindacato d'emissione *m*	sindicato de emisión *m*
syndicat bancaire de garantie (F)	Übernahmekonsortium *n*	security-taking syndicate	—	consorzio di collocamento *m*	consorcio de suscripción *m*
syndicat bancaire de garantie (F)	Garantiekonsortium *n*	underwriting syndicate	—	consorzio di garanzia *m*	consorcio de garantía *m*
syndicat bancaire de liquidité (F)	Liquiditätskonsortialbank *f*	liquidity syndicate bank	—	banca consorziale garanzia liquidità *f*	banco asegurador de liquidez *m*
syndicate (E)	Konsortium *n*	—	consortium *m*	consorzio *m*	consorcio *m*
syndicate account (E)	Syndikatskonto *n*	—	compte de syndicat *m*	conto sindacale *m*	cuenta de cártel *f*
syndicated credit (E)	Konsortialkredit *m*	—	crédit garanti par un consortium bancaire *m*	credito consorziale *m*	crédito consorcial *m*
syndicate department (E)	Konsortialabteilung *f*	—	service de syndicats *m*	ufficio consorzi *m*	sección de consorcios *f*
syndicate transaction (E)	Konsortialgeschäft *n*	—	opération appuyée par plusieurs banques *f*	operazione consorziale *f*	negocio de consorcio *m*
Syndicat fédéral d'emprunts (F)	Bundesanleihekonsortium *n*	Federal loan syndicate	—	consorzio emissione titoli pubblici *m*	consorcio de empréstitos federales *m*
Syndikatskonto (D)	—	syndicate account	compte de syndicat *m*	conto sindacale *m*	cuenta de cártel *f*
Synodalanleihe (D)	—	synodal loan	emprunt synodal *m*	obbligazione sinodale *f*	empréstito sinodal *m*
synodal bond (E)	Synodalobligation *f*	—	obligation synodale *f*	obbligazione sinodale *f*	obligación sinodal *f*
synodal loan (E)	Synodalanleihe *f*	—	emprunt synodal *m*	obbligazione sinodale *f*	empréstito sinodal *m*
Synodalobligation (D)	—	synodal bond	obligation synodale *f*	obbligazione sinodale *f*	obligación sinodal *f*

	D	E	F	I	Es
system by which savings depositor can effect inpayments and withdrawals at all savings banks or post offices (E)	freizügiger Sparverkehr *m*	—	épargne libéralisée *f*	libertà per l'intestatario del libretto di risparmio di effettuare versamenti e esborsi in tutte le cassé di risparmio tedesche *f*	movimiento de ahorros liberalizado *m*
système bancaire (F)	Bankensystem *n*	banking system	—	sistema bancario *m*	sistema bancario *m*
système de change (F)	Wechselkurssystem *n*	system of exchange rates	—	regime dei cambi *m*	sistema de cambios *m*
système de la capitalisation (F)	Anwartschaftsdeckungsverfahren *n*	expectancy cover procedure	—	sistema di capitalizzazione *m*	sistema de capitalización *m*
système de mandat de prélèvement automatique (F)	Einzugsermächtigungsverfahren *n*	collection procedure	—	autorizzazione alla riscossione *f*	proceso de cobro bancario *m*
système d'encaissement automatique de factures (F)	Rechnungseinzugsverfahren *n*	accounts collection method	—	procedimento d'incasso di fatture *m*	procedimiento de cobranza de pagos pendientes *m*
système d'encaissement de quittances (F)	Quittungseinzugsverfahren *n*	receipt collection procedure	—	procedimento d'incasso di quietanza *m*	procedimiento de cobro de recibos *m*
système de prélèvement automatique (F)	Abbuchungsverfahren *n*	direct debit procedure	—	procedimento di addebito *m*	procedimiento de adeudo en cuenta *m*
système de recouvrement de créances (F)	Forderungseinzugsverfahren *n*	collection procedure	—	procedimento d'incasso crediti *m*	procedimiento de cobro de créditos *m*
système des banques spécialisées (F)	Trennbanksystem *n*	system of specialized banking	—	sistema delle banche specializzate *m*	sistema de bancos especializados *m*
système des certificats provisoires d'actions nouvelles (F)	Jungscheinverkehr *m*	new issue giro transfer system	—	sistema di certificato provvisorio *f*	sistema de certificados provisionales de acciones *m*
système des changes flottants (F)	Floating *n*	floating	—	floating *m*	flotación *f*
système du prélèvement automatique (F)	Lastschrifteinzugsverfahren *n*	direct debiting	—	incasso tramite addebitamento *m*	procedimiento de cobro en cuenta *m*
système financier (F)	Finanzverfassung *f*	financial system	—	ordinamento finanziario *f*	constitución financiera *f*
système monétaire (F)	Währungssystem *n*	monetary system	—	sistema monetario *m*	sistema monetario *m*
système monétaire (F)	Geldwesen *n*	monetary system	—	sistema monetario *m*	sistema monetario *m*
Système Monétaire Européen SME (F)	Europäisches Währungssystem [EWS] *n*	European Monetary System [EMS]	—	Sistema monetario europeo *m*	Sistema Monetario Europeo [SME] *m*
system of exchange rates (E)	Wechselkurssystem *n*	—	système de change *m*	regime dei cambi *m*	sistema de cambios *m*
system of specialized banking (E)	Trennbanksystem *n*	—	système des banques spécialisées *m*	sistema delle banche specializzate *m*	sistema de bancos especializados *m*
Tabakbörse (D)	—	tobacco exchange	bourse de tabacs *f*	borsa tabacchi *f*	bolsa de tabaco *f*
tabla de financiación (Es)	Kapitalflußrechnung *f*	funds statement	tableau de financement *m*	calcolo del flusso di capitale *m*	—
tableau de financement (F)	Kapitalflußrechnung *f*	funds statement	—	calcolo del flusso di capitale *m*	tabla de financiación *f*
tableau de signalisation (F)	Aushang *m*	notice board	—	affisso *m*	tablilla *f*
table de parité (F)	Paritätengitter *n*	parity grid	—	griglia delle parità *f*	parrilla de paridades *f*
tablero electrónico (Es)	automatische Kursanzeige *f*	automatic quotation	indication automatique des cotations *f*	indicatore automatico quotazioni *m*	—
table ronde (F)	runder Tisch *m*	round table	—	tavola rotonda *f*	mesa redonda *f*
tablilla (Es)	Aushang *m*	notice board	tableau de signalisation *m*	affisso *m*	—
Tafelgeschäft (D)	—	over-the-counter business	opération de guichet *f*	operazione a contanti *f*	operación al contado *f*
Tagesauszug (D)	—	daily statement	relevé quotidien de compte *m*	estratto giornaliero *m*	extracto de cuenta diario *m*
Tagesbilanz (D)	—	daily trial balance sheet	arrêté quotidien de compte *m*	bilancio giornaliero *m*	balance diario *m*

	D	E	F	I	Es
Tagesgeld (D)	—	day-to-day money	argent au jour le jour m	prestito giornaliero m	dinero de día a día m
Tageskurs (D)	—	current quotation	cote du jour f	corso del giorno m	cotización del día f
Tageswechsel (D)	—	day bill	traite à jour fixe f	cambiale a scadenza fissa f	letra al día fijo f
take-over speculation (E)	Aufkaufspekulation f	—	accaparement spéculatif m	speculazione in accaparramenti f	especulación de acaparamiento f
talón de opción combinado (Es)	Capped Warrants m/pl	capped warrants	options frappées d'une saisie-arrêt f/pl	capped warrants m/pl	—
talon de recouponnement (F)	Erneuerungsschein m	talon for renewal of coupon sheet	—	cedola di riaffoglimento f	talón de renovación m
talón de renovación (Es)	Erneuerungsschein m	talon for renewal of coupon sheet	talon de recouponnement m	cedola di riaffoglimento f	—
talon for renewal of coupon sheet (E)	Erneuerungsschein m	—	talon de recouponnement m	cedola di riaffoglimento f	talón de renovación m
tangible fixed assets (E)	Sachanlagevermögen n	—	immobilisations corporelles f/pl	attivo immobilitato m	inmovilizado m
taquilla de noche (Es)	Spätschalter m	night safe deposit	guichet extérieur de permanence m	cassa continua f	—
target saving (E)	Zwecksparen n	—	épargne à un but déterminé f	risparmio ad investimento vincolato m	ahorro con un fin determinado m
Tarif (D)	—	tariff	tarif m	tariffa f	tarifa f
tarif (F)	Tarif m	tariff	—	tariffa f	tarifa f
tarifa (Es)	Tarif m	tariff	tarif m	tariffa f	—
tarifa excepcional (Es)	Ausnahmetarif m	preferential rate	tarif exceptionnel m	tariffa d'eccezione f	—
tarifa múltiple (Es)	gespaltener Tarif m	differentiated tariffs	tarif différencié m	tariffa multipla f	—
tarifbesteuerte Wertpapiere (D)	—	securities taxed at the standard rate	titres soumis aux impôts en vigueur m/pl	titoli a tariffa d'imposizione m/pl	titulos sometidos a los impuestos en vigor m/pl
tarif différencié (F)	gespaltener Tarif m	differentiated tariffs	—	tariffa multipla f	tarifa múltiple f
tarif exceptionnel (F)	Ausnahmetarif m	preferential rate	—	tariffa d'eccezione f	tarifa excepcional f
tariff (E)	Tarif m	—	tarif m	tariffa f	tarifa f
tariffa (I)	Tarif m	tariff	tarif m	—	tarifa f
tariffa d'eccezione (I)	Ausnahmetarif m	preferential rate	tarif exceptionnel m	—	tarifa excepcional f
tariffa multipla (I)	gespaltener Tarif m	differentiated tariffs	tarif différencié m	—	tarifa múltiple f
tariff value (E)	Tarifwert m	—	valeur au tarif f	titolo industria di pubblica utilità m	valor arancelario m
Tarifwert (D)	—	tariff value	valeur au tarif f	titolo industria di pubblica utilità m	valor arancelario m
tarjeta de crédito (Es)	Kreditkarte f	credit card	carte de crédit f	carta di credito f	—
tarjeta eurocheque (Es)	Euroscheck-Karte f	Eurocheque card	carte d'identité euro-chèque f	carta eurocheque f	—
tasa complementaria (Es)	Ergänzungsabgabe f	supplementary levy	taxe complémentaire f	imposta complementare f	—
tasa de amortización (Es)	Tilgungsrate f	amortization instalment	annuité f	rata di rimborso f	—
tasa de compensación (Es)	Ausgleichsabgabe f	countervailing duty	taxe de compensation f	tassa di compensazione f	—
tasa de flujo (Es)	Stromgröße f	rate of flow	volume du flux m	variabile di flusso f	—
tasa de inflación (Es)	Inflationsrate f	rate of inflation	taux d'inflation m	tasso d'inflazione m	—
tasa de interés preferencial (Es)	Prime Rate f	prime rate	taux d'intérêt préférentiel m	prime rate m	—
tasa de leasing (Es)	Leasingrate f	leasing rate	taux de leasing m	canone di leasing m	—
tasa de liquidación (Es)	Liquidationsrate f	liquidating dividend	quote-part de la liquidation f	tasso di liquidazione m	—
tasa de prolongación del bajista (Es)	Backwardation f	backwardation	déport m	backwardation f	—
tasa interbancaria (Es)	Interbankrate f	interbank rate	taux interbancaire m	tasso d'interesse interbancario m	—
tasa media (Es)	Durchschnittssatz m	average rate	taux moyen m	tasso medio m	—
tassa amministrativa (I)	Verwaltungsgebühr f	official fees	taxe administrative f	—	derechos administrativos m/pl

	D	E	F	I	Es
tassa d'esercizio (I)	Gewerbesteuer f	trade tax	impôt sur les bénéfices des professions industrielles et commerciales m	—	impuesto industrial m
tassa di compensazione (I)	Ausgleichsabgabe f	countervailing duty	taxe de compensation f	—	tasa de compensación f
tassa di fusione (I)	Fusionssteuer f	amalgamation tax	impôt sur la fusion de sociétés m	—	impuesto sobre la fusión de sociedades m
tassa prolungamento ipoteche (I)	Belassungsgebühr f	prolongation charge	frais de prolongation m/pl	—	derechos de prolongación m/pl
tassazione (I)	Besteuerung f	taxation	taxation f	—	imposición f
tassazione del reddito (I)	Einkommensbesteuerung f	income taxation	imposition du revenu f	—	impuestos sobre la renta m/pl
tasse all'esportazione (I)	Ausfuhrabgaben f/pl	export duties	taxes à l'exportation f/pl	—	exacciones de exportación f/pl
tasso anticipazioni (I)	Lombardzinsfuß m	lending rate	taux d'intérêt de l'argent prêté et garanti par un gage m	—	tipo de interés para créditos pignoraticios m
tasso del mercato monetario (I)	Geldmarktsatz m	money market rate	taux d'intérêt sur le marché monétaire m	—	tipo de cambio del mercado monetario m
tasso di liquidazione (I)	Liquidationsrate f	liquidating dividend	quote-part de la liquidation f	—	tasa de liquidación f
tasso di liquiditá (I)	Liquiditätsquote f	liquidity ratio	coefficient de liquidité m	—	coeficiente de liquidez m
tasso d'inflazione (I)	Inflationsrate f	rate of inflation	taux d'inflation m	—	tasa de inflación f
tasso d'interesse (I)	Zinssatz m	interest rate	taux d'intérêt m	—	tipo de interés m
tasso d'interesse (I)	Verzinsung f	payment of interest	payement des intérêts m	—	interés m
tasso d'interesse corrente (I)	Marktzins m	market rate of interest	taux du marché m	—	tipo de interés del mercado m
tasso d'interesse corrente (I)	marktüblicher Zins m	interest rate customary in the market	intérêt pratiqué sur le marché m	—	interés impuesto en el mercado m
tasso d'interesse del mercato finanziario (I)	Kapitalmarktzins m	capital market interest rate	intérêt pratiqué sur le marché des capitaux m	—	interés pagado en el mercado de capital m
tasso d'interesse desiderato minimo (I)	Kalkulationszinssatz m	calculation interest rate	taux d'intérêt de calcul m	—	tipo de interés calculado m
tasso d'interesse interbancario (I)	Interbankrate f	interbank rate	taux interbancaire m	—	tasa interbancaria f
tasso d'interesse netto (I)	Nettozinssatz m	net interest rate	taux d'intérêt net m	—	tipo neto de intereses m
tasso di sconto flessibile (I)	flexibler Diskontsatz m	flexible discount rate	taux d'escompte variable m	—	tipo de descuento variable m
tasso lombard (I)	Lombardsatz m	bankrate for advances against collateral	taux lombard m	—	tipo de pignoración m
tasso medio (I)	Durchschnittssatz m	average rate	taux moyen m	—	tasa media f
tasso minimo di riserva (I)	Mindestreservesatz m	minimum reserve ratio	taux de réserve minimum m	—	porcentaje mínimo de reservas m
tasso monetario (I)	Geldsatz m	money rate	taux de l'argent m	—	tipo de interés m
tasso swap (I)	Swapsatz m	swap rate	taux de swap m	—	tipo swap m
Tausch (D)	—	barter	troc m	cambio m	trueque m
Tauschdepot (D)	—	security deposit	dépôt de titres-gestion	deposito di custodia scambiabile m	depósito de trueque m
Tauschmittelfunktion des Geldes (D)	—	exchange function of money	fonction de l'argent de moyen d'échange f	funzione di scambio della moneta f	función de medio de cambio del dinero f
taux central (F)	Leitkurs m	central rate	—	parità centrale f	tipo de pivote m
taux-clé d'intérêt bancaire sur les dépôts d'épargne (F)	Spareckzins m	basic savings rate	—	interesse di riferimento per il risparmio m	tipo de referencia m
taux de change (F)	Devisenkurs m	foreign exchange rate	—	cambio m	cambio m
taux de change au comptant (F)	Devisenkassakurs m	foreign exchange spot operations	—	corso dei cambi a pronti m	tipo de cambio al contado m
taux de change fixe (F)	starrer Wechselkurs m	fixed exchange rate	—	cambio fisso m	tipo de cambio fijo m

	D	E	F	I	Es
taux de change flottant (F)	flexibler Wechselkurs m	flexible exchange rate	—	cambio flessibile m	cambio variable m
taux de change libre (F)	freier Wechselkurs m	freely fluctuating exchange rate	—	cambio libero m	tipo de cambio libre m
taux de l'argent (F)	Geldsatz m	money rate	—	tasso monetario m	tipo de interés m
taux de leasing (F)	Leasingrate f	leasing rate	—	canone di leasing m	tasa de leasing f
taux de report (F)	Prolongationssatz m	renewal rate	—	saggio di riporto m	tipo de prolongación m
taux de réserve minimum (F)	Mindestreservesatz m	minimum reserve ratio	—	tasso minimo di riserva m	porcentaje mínimo de reservas m
taux d'escompte (F)	Diskontsatz m	discount rate	—	saggio di sconto m	tipo de descuento m
taux d'escompte variable (F)	flexibler Diskontsatz m	flexible discount rate	—	tasso di sconto flessibile m	tipo de descuento variable m
taux de swap (F)	Swapsatz m	swap rate	—	tasso swap m	tipo swap m
taux d'inflation (F)	Inflationsrate f	rate of inflation	—	tasso d'inflazione m	tasa de inflación f
taux d'intérêt (F)	Zinssatz m	interest rate	—	tasso d'interesse m	tipo de interés m
taux d'intérêt de base (F)	Eckzins m	basic rate of interest	—	interesse di riferimento m	tipo base m
taux d'intérêt de calcul (F)	Kalkulationszinssatz m	calculation interest rate	—	tasso d'interesse desiderato minimo m	tipo de interés calculado m
taux d'intérêt de l'argent prêté et garanti par un gage (F)	Lombardzinsfuß m	lending rate	—	tasso anticipazioni m	tipo de interés para créditos pignoraticios m
taux d'intérêt interne (F)	interner Zinsfuß m	internal interest rate	—	saggio di rendimento interno m	tipo de interés interno m
taux d'intérêt net (F)	Nettozinssatz m	net interest rate	—	tasso d'interesse netto m	tipo neto de intereses m
taux d'intérêt préférentiel (F)	Prime Rate f	prime rate	—	prime rate m	tasa de interés preferencial f
taux d'intérêt sur le marché monétaire (F)	Geldmarktsatz m	money market rate	—	tasso del mercato monetario m	tipo de cambio del mercado monetario m
taux du marché (F)	Marktzins m	market rate of interest	—	tasso d'interesse corrente m	tipo de interés del mercado m
taux effectif (F)	Effektivverzinsung f	effective interest yield	—	reddito effettivo m	interés efectivo m
taux interbancaire (F)	Interbankrate f	interbank rate	—	tasso d'interesse interbancario m	tasa interbancaria f
taux lombard (F)	Lombardsatz m	bankrate for advances against collateral	—	tasso lombard m	tipo de pignoración m
taux moyen (F)	Durchschnittssatz m	average rate	—	tasso medio m	tasa media f
tavola rotonda (I)	runder Tisch m	round table	table ronde f	—	mesa redonda f
tax (E)	Steuer f	—	impôt m	imposta f	impuesto m
taxation (E)	Besteuerung f	—	taxation f	tassazione f	imposición f
taxation (F)	Besteuerung f	taxation		tassazione f	imposición f
taxation des revenus du capital (F)	Kapitalertragssteuer f	tax on investment income	—	imposta sul reddito dei capitali f	impuesto sobre la renta de capital m
taxation procedure (E)	Besteuerungsverfahren n	—	régime de taxation m	procedura d'imposizione f	procedimiento tributario m
tax at source (E)	Quellensteuer f	—	impôt retenu à la source m	ritenuta alla fonte f	impuesto deducido en la fuente m
tax basis (E)	Besteuerungsgrundlage f	—	assiette de l'imposition f	base d'imposizione f	base imponible f
taxe (F)	Gebühr f	fee	—	canone m	derechos m/pl
taxe administrative (F)	Verwaltungsgebühr f	official fees	—	tassa amministrativa f	derechos administrativos m/pl
taxe à la valeur ajoutée (F)	Mehrwertsteuer f	value-added tax	—	imposta sul valore aggiunto f	impuesto sobre el valor añadido m
taxe complémentaire (F)	Ergänzungsabgabe f	supplementary levy	—	imposta complementare f	tasa complementaria f
taxe de compensation (F)	Ausgleichsabgabe f	countervailing duty	—	tassa di compensazione f	tasas de compensación f/pl
taxe de débours (F)	Ausgabensteuer f	outlay tax	—	imposta di consumo f	impuesto de emisión m

	D	E	F	I	Es
taxe de sortie (F)	Ausfuhrzoll *m*	export duty	—	dazio all'esportazione *m*	derechos de exportación *m/pl*
taxe de transaction sur les opérations boursières (F)	Börsenumsatzsteuer *f*	stock exchange turn-over tax	—	imposta sui contratti di borsa *f*	impuesto sobre la negociación bursátil *m*
taxes à l'exportation (F)	Ausfuhrabgaben *f/pl*	export duties	—	tasse all'esportazione *f/pl*	exacciones de exportación *f/pl*
taxe sur les bénéfices de crédit (F)	Kreditgewinnabgabe *f*	debts profit levy	—	ritenuta sugli utili dei crediti *f*	tributo sobre beneficios del crédito *m*
taxe sur les mutations du capital (F)	Kapitalverkehrssteuer *f*	capital transaction tax	—	imposta sulla circolazione dei capitali *f*	impuesto sobre transacciones *m*
taxe sur les sociétés (F)	Körperschaftssteuer *f*	corporation tax	—	imposta sul reddito delle società *f*	impuesto de sociedades *m*
tax-free amount (E)	Freibetrag *m*	—	montant exonéré *m*	importo esente *m*	importe exento *m*
Taxkurs (D)	—	estimated quotation	cours d'estimation *m*	corso di stima *m*	precio de tasación *m*
tax on income (E)	Ertragssteuer *f*	—	impôt assis sur le produit *m*	imposta cedolare *f*	impuesto sobre las ganancias *m*
tax on investment income (E)	Kapitalertragssteuer *f*	—	taxation des revenus du capital *m*	imposta sul reddito dei capitali *f*	impuesto sobre la renta de capital *m*
tax on speculative gains (E)	Spekulationssteuer *f*	—	impôt sur les gains spéculatifs *m*	imposta sulla speculazione *f*	impuesto sobre beneficios especulativos *m*
tax-privileged saving (E)	steuerbegünstigtes Sparen *n*	—	épargne jouissant d'avantages fiscaux *f*	risparmio con privilegi fiscali *m*	ahorro favorecido por ventajas fiscales *m*
tax-privileged securities (E)	steuerbegünstigte Wertpapiere *n/pl*	—	titres assortis d'avantages fiscaux *m/pl*	titoli con privilegi fiscali *m/pl*	títulos favorecidos por ventajas fiscales *m/pl*
technical analysis (E)	technische Aktienanalyse *f*	—	analyse technique *f*	analisi tecnica *f*	análisis de acciones técnico *m*
technische Aktienanalyse (D)	—	technical analysis	analyse technique *f*	analisi tecnica *f*	análisis de acciones técnico *m*
techo de interés (Es)	Cap *n*	cap	plafond d'intérêt *m*	cap *m*	—
tecnica bancaria (I)	Bankbetriebslehre *f*	science of banking	science bancaire *f*	—	ciencias bancarias *f/pl*
Teilakzept (D)	—	partial acceptance	acceptation partielle *f*	accettazione parziale *f*	aceptación parcial *f*
Teilauszahlung (D)	—	partial payment	payement partiel *m*	pagamento parziale *m*	desembolso parcial *m*
Teilforderung (D)	—	partial claim	créance partielle *f*	credito parziale *m*	crédito parcial *m*
Teilhaber (D)	—	partner	associé *m*	socio *m*	socio *m*
Teilindossament (D)	—	partial endorsement	endossement partiel *m*	girata parziale *f*	endoso parcial *m*
Teilkonnossement (D)	—	partial bill of lading	connaissement partiel *m*	polizza di carico parziale *f*	recibo parcial *m*
Teilrechte (D)	—	partial rights	droits partiels *m/pl*	buono frazionario *m*	derechos de partición *m/pl*
Teilzahlung (D)	—	partial payment	payement partiel *m*	pagamento in acconto *m*	pago parcial *m*
Teilzahlungsbuch (D)	—	credit financing register	livre de payements partiels *m*	libro di pagamento parziale *m*	libro de pagos parciales *m*
Teilzahlungskredit (D)	—	instalment credit	avance sur vente payée à tempérament *f*	finanziamento di acquisti rateali *m*	crédito para la financiación a plazo *m*
Telefonverkehr (D)	—	telephone dealings	transactions par téléphone *f/pl*	negoziazione di titoli per telefono *f*	mercado de valores extrabursátil *m*
telegrafische Auszahlung (D)	—	telegraphic transfer	payement télégraphique *m*	trasferimento telegrafico *m*	desembolso telegráfico *m*
telegraphic transfer (E)	telegrafische Auszahlung *f*	—	payement télégraphique *m*	trasferimento telegrafico *m*	desembolso telegráfico *m*
teleimprenta (Es)	Ticker *m*	teleprinter	téléscripteur *m*	ticker *m*	—
Tele-Konto (D)	—	videotext account	compte vidéotex *m*	conto videotel *m*	cuenta videotexto *f*
telephone dealings (E)	Telefonverkehr *m*	—	transactions par téléphone *f/pl*	negoziazione di titoli per telefono *f*	mercado de valores extrabursátil *m*
teleprinter (E)	Ticker *m*	—	téléscripteur *m*	ticker *m*	teleimprenta *f*
téléscripteur (F)	Ticker *m*	teleprinter	—	ticker *m*	teleimprenta *f*
tempo morto (I)	Leerlauf *m*	time wasted	temps creux *m*	—	tiempo en vacío *m*
temps creux (F)	Leerlauf *m*	time wasted	—	tempo morto *m*	tiempo en vacío *m*

	D	E	F	I	Es
tenant's contribution to the construction costs (E)	Baukostenzuschuß *m*	—	participation financière à la construction *f*	contributo alla costruzione *m*	contribución a los costes de construcción *f*
tenant's credit (E)	Pächterkredit *m*	—	crédit agricole aux fermiers *m*	credito ai fittavoli *m*	crédito agrícola a favor de los arrendatarios *m*
tendance à la hausse (F)	Reprise *f*	reprise	—	ripresa *f*	recuperación *f*
tendance de base (F)	Basistrend *m*	basic trend	—	trend di base *m*	tendencia de base *f*
tendance de la bourse (F)	Börsentendenz *f*	stock market trend	—	tendenza borsistica *f*	tendencia bursátil *f*
tendance extraordinaire (F)	Sonderbewegung *f*	extraordinary trend	—	movimento divergente *m*	oscilación extraordinaria *f*
tendencia bursátil (Es)	Börsentendenz *f*	stock market trend	tendance de la bourse *f*	tendenza borsistica *f*	—
tendencia de base (Es)	Basistrend *m*	basic trend	tendance de base *f*	trend di base *m*	—
tendenza borsistica (I)	Börsentendenz *f*	stock market trend	tendance de la bourse *f*	—	tendencia bursátil *f*
tender procedure (E)	Tenderverfahren *n*	—	offre d'emprunts pour la régulation monétaire *f*	asta marginale *f*	sistema de ofertas *m*
Tenderverfahren (D)	—	tender procedure	offre d'emprunts pour la régulation monétaire *f*	asta marginale *f*	sistema de ofertas *m*
tenencia de dinero (Es)	Geldhaltung *f*	money management	tenue d'argent *f*	tenuta di denaro *f*	—
teneur en or (F)	Goldgehalt *m*	gold content	—	contenuto aureo *m*	contenido de oro *m*
tensiones sobre los gastos (Es)	Kostendruck *m*	cost pressure	poids des coûts *m*	pressione dei costi *f*	—
tenue d'argent (F)	Geldhaltung *f*	money management	—	tenuta di denaro *f*	tenencia de dinero *f*
tenue de la caisse (F)	Kassenhaltung *f*	cash accountancy	—	tenuta di cassa *f*	contabilidad de caja *f*
tenuta di cassa (I)	Kassenhaltung *f*	cash accountancy	tenue de la caisse *f*	—	contabilidad de caja *f*
tenuta di denaro (I)	Geldhaltung *f*	money management	tenue d'argent *f*	—	tenencia de dinero *f*
teoría cuantitativa (Es)	Quantitätstheorie *f*	quantity theory	théorie quantitative *f*	teoria quantitativa *f*	—
teoría de financiación (Es)	Finanzierungstheorie *f*	financing theory	théorie de financement *f*	teoria dei finanziamenti *f*	—
teoría degli interessi (I)	Zinstheorie *f*	theory of interest	théorie des intérêts *f*	—	teoría del interés *f*
teoría dei finanziamenti (I)	Finanzierungstheorie *f*	financing theory	théorie de financement *f*	—	teoría de financiación *f*
teoría de imprevisibilidad (Es)	Random-Walk-Theorie *f*	random-walk theory	théorie d'imprévisibilité *f*	teoria Random-Walk *f*	—
teoría de la determinación de la renta (Es)	Einkommenstheorie *f*	theory of income determination	théorie de la détermination du revenu *f*	teoria del reddito *f*	—
teoría de la empresa (Es)	Betriebswirtschaftslehre *f*	business economics	gestion industrielle et commerciale *f*	scienza dell'economia aziendale *f*	—
teoría del interés (Es)	Zinstheorie *f*	theory of interest	théorie des intérêts *f*	teoria degli interessi *f*	—
teoría de liquidez (Es)	Liquiditätstheorie *f*	liquidity theory	théorie de la liquidité *f*	teoria della liquidità *f*	—
teoria della liquidità (I)	Liquiditätstheorie *f*	liquidity theory	théorie de la liquidité *f*	—	teoría de liquidez *f*
teoria del reddito (I)	Einkommenstheorie *f*	theory of income determination	théorie de la détermination du revenu *f*	—	teoría de la determinación de la renta *f*
teoria di Keynes (I)	Keynes'sche Theorie *f*	Keynes Theory	théorie Keynésienne *f*	—	teoría keynesiana *f*
teoría financiera (Es)	Finanztheorie *f*	financial theory	théorie financière *f*	teoria finanziaria *f*	—
teoria finanziaria (I)	Finanztheorie *f*	financial theory	théorie financière *f*	—	teoría financiera *f*
teoria keynesiana (Es)	Keynes'sche Theorie *f*	Keynes Theory	théorie Keynésienne *f*	teoria di Keynes *f*	—
teoria quantitativa (I)	Quantitätstheorie *f*	quantity theory	théorie quantitative *f*	—	teoría cuantitativa *f*
teoria Random-Walk (I)	Random-Walk-Theorie *f*	random-walk theory	théorie d'imprévisibilité *f*	—	teoría de imprevisibilidad *f*
teorie di bilancio (I)	Bilanztheorien *f/pl*	accounting theory	théories de bilan *f/pl*	—	teorías sobre balances *f/pl*
tercer deudor (Es)	Drittschuldner *m*	third-party debtor	tiers débiteur *m*	terzo debitore *m*	—

	D	E	F	I	Es
tercería de dominio (Es)	Aussonderung f	separation of property belonging to a third party from the bankrupt's estate	distraction f	separazione f	—
term funds (E)	Laufzeitfonds m	—	fonds à terme m	fondo a scadenza m	fondos a plazo m/pl
termination (E)	Kündigung f	—	préavis m	preavviso m	preaviso m
Terminbörse (D)	—	futures market	bourse à terme f	mercato a termine m	bolsa de valores a término f
Termindevisen (D)	—	exchange for forward delivery	devises négociées en bourse à terme f/pl	divise a termine f/pl	divisas a plazo f/pl
termine di preavviso (I)	Kündigungsgrundschuld f	land charge not repayable until called	dette foncière remboursable avec préavis f	—	deuda inmobiliaria con preaviso f
termine di preavviso (I)	Kündigungssperrfrist f	non-calling period	délai de blocage de dénonciation m	—	plazo de suspensión de preaviso m
termine di presentazione (I)	Präsentationsfrist f	presentation period	délai de présentation m	—	tiempo útil para la presentación m
termine d'opzione (I)	Bezugsfrist f	subscription period	délai de souscription m	—	plazo de suscripción m
Termineinlagen (D)	—	time deposit	dépôt à échéance convenue m	deposito a scadenza m	depósitos a plazo m/pl
termine presentazione di protesto (I)	Protestzeit f	period of protest	heures de présentation du protêt f/pl	—	período de protesta m
Termingeschäft (D)	—	time bargain	opération à terme f	contratto a termine m	operación a plazo f
termini borsistici (I)	Kurszusätze m/pl	notes appended to quotation	indications supplémentaires de cotation f/pl	—	indicaciones explicativas de las cotizaciones f/pl
Terminkontraktmarkt (D)	—	futures market	marché à terme m	mercato dei contratti a termine m	mercado de contratos de entrega futura m
término de tipo de interés (Es)	Interest Rate Future m	interest rate future	interest rate future m	interest rate future m	—
Terminpapiere (D)	—	forward securities	valeurs à terme f/pl	titoli ammessi a contratti futuri m/pl	títulos a plazo m/pl
terms and conditions of business (E)	Geschäftsbedingungen f/pl	—	conditions commerciales f/pl	condizioni contrattuali f/pl	condiciones comerciales f/pl
terms and conditions of issue (E)	Emissionsbedingungen f/pl	—	conditions de l'émission f/pl	condizioni d'emissione f/pl	condiciones de emisión f/pl
terms of payment (E)	Zahlungsbedingung f	—	condition de payement f	condizione di pagamento f	condición de pago f
terzo debitore (I)	Drittschuldner m	third-party debtor	tiers débiteur m	—	tercer deudor m
tesaurizzazione (I)	Thesaurierung f	accumulation of capital	thésauration f	—	atesoramiento m
tesaurizzazione degli utili (I)	Gewinnthesaurierung f	earnings retention	retention de bénéfices f	—	retención de beneficios f
tetto interessi (I)	Zinskappe f	cap rate of interest	plafond de l'intérêt m	—	plafón de interés m
théorie de financement (F)	Finanzierungstheorie f	financing theory	—	teoria dei finanziamenti f	teoría de financiación f
théorie de la détermination du revenu (F)	Einkommenstheorie f	theory of income determination	—	teoria del reddito f	teoría de la determinación de la renta f
théorie de la liquidité (F)	Liquiditätstheorie f	liquidity theory	—	teoria della liquidità f	teoría de liquidez f
théorie des intérêts (F)	Zinstheorie f	theory of interest	—	teoria degli interessi f	teoría del interés f
théorie d'imprévisibilité (F)	Random-Walk-Theorie f	random-walk theory	—	teoria Random-Walk f	teoría de imprevisibilidad f
théorie financière (F)	Finanztheorie f	financial theory	—	teoria finanziaria f	teoría financiera f
théorie Keynésienne (F)	Keynes'sche Theorie f	Keynes Theory	—	teoria di Keynes f	teoría keynesiana f
théorie quantitative (F)	Quantitätstheorie f	quantity theory	—	teoria quantitativa f	teoría cuantitativa f
theory of income determination (E)	Einkommenstheorie f	—	théorie de la détermination du revenu f	teoria del reddito f	teoría de la determinación de la renta f
theory of interest (E)	Zinstheorie f	—	théorie des intérêts f	teoria degli interessi f	teoría del interés f
thésauration (F)	Thesaurierung f	accumulation of capital	—	tesaurizzazione f	atesoramiento m
Thesaurierung (D)	—	accumulation of capital	thésauration f	tesaurizzazione f	atesoramiento m

	D	E	F	I	Es
Thesaurierungs-fonds (D)	—	accumulative investment fund	fonds de thésauration *m*	fondo di accumulazione *m*	fondo de atesoramiento *m*
third-party debtor (E)	Drittschuldner *m*	—	tiers débiteur *m*	terzo debitore *m*	tercer deudor *m*
third-party mortgage (E)	Fremdhypothek *f*	—	hypothèque constituée au profit d'un tiers *f*	ipoteca a favore di terzi *f*	hipoteca ajena *f*
three months' money (E)	Dreimonatsgeld *n*	—	dépôts à trois mois *m/pl*	prestito a tre mesi *m*	imposición a un plazo de 3 meses *f*
Ticker (D)	—	teleprinter	téléscripteur *m*	ticker *m*	teleimprenta *f*
ticker (I)	Ticker *m*	teleprinter	téléscripteur *m*	—	teleimprenta *f*
tiempo de utilización (Es)	Nutzungsdauer *f*	service life	durée normale d'utilisation *f*	durata di godimento *f*	—
tiempo en vacío (Es)	Leerlauf *m*	time wasted	temps creux *m*	tempo morto *m*	—
tiempo útil para la presentación (Es)	Präsentationsfrist *f*	presentation period	délai de présentation *m*	termine di presentazione *m*	—
tiers débiteur (F)	Drittschuldner *m*	third-party debtor	—	terzo debitore *m*	tercer deudor *m*
Tilgung (D)	—	redemption	amortissement *m*	rimborso *m*	amortización *f*
Tilgungsanleihe (D)	—	redemption loan	emprunt d'amortissement *m*	prestito ammortizzabile *m*	empréstito amortizable *m*
Tilgungsaussetzung (D)	—	subspension of redemption payments	suspension d'amortissement *f*	differimento di rimborso *m*	suspensión de la amortización *f*
Tilgungsfonds (D)	—	redemption fund	fonds d'amortissement *m*	fondo d'ammortamento *m*	fondo de amortización *m*
Tilgungsgewinn (D)	—	gain of redemption	bénéfice d'amortissement *m*	utile di rimborso *m*	beneficio de amortización *m*
Tilgungshypothek (D)	—	amortizable mortgage loan	hypothèque garantissant une créance remboursable à termes périodiques *f*	ipoteca ammortizzabile *f*	hipoteca amortizable *f*
Tilgungsrate (D)	—	amortization instalment	annuité *f*	rata di rimborso *f*	tasa de amortización *f*
Tilgungsrückstände (D)	—	redemption in arrears	arriérés d'amortissement *m/pl*	rate di rimborso arretrate *f/pl*	amortizaciones pendientes *f/pl*
Tilgungsstreckung (D)	—	repayment extension	prolongation du délai de remboursement *f*	proroga di rimborso *f*	extensión del plazo de reintegración *f*
timbratura di banconote (I)	Notenabstempelung *f*	stamping of bank notes	estampillage des billets de banque *m*	—	estampillado de billetes *m*
timbre d'épargne (F)	Sparmarke *f*	savings stamp	—	marca di risparmio *f*	cuota de ahorro *f*
time bargain (E)	Termingeschäft *n*	—	opération à terme *f*	contratto a termine *m*	operación a plazo *f*
time deposit (E)	Termineinlagen *f/pl*	—	dépôt à échéance convenue *m*	deposito a scadenza *m*	depósitos a plazo *m/pl*
time limit (E)	Befristung *f*	—	fixation d'un délai *f*	fissazione di un termine *f*	condición de plazo *f*
time of expiration (E)	Verfallzeit *f*	—	époque de l'échéance *f*	scadenza *f*	plazo de vencimiento *m*
time wasted (E)	Leerlauf *m*	—	temps creux *m*	tempo morto *m*	tiempo en vacío *m*
tipi di deposito (I)	Depotarten *f/pl*	types of deposit	sortes de dépôts *f/pl*	—	tipos de depósito *m/pl*
tipi di emissione (I)	Emissionsarten *f/pl*	types of issuing	sortes d'émission *f/pl*	—	tipos de emisión *m/pl*
tipi di investimento di capitale (I)	Kapitalanlegearten *f/pl*	types of capital investment	sortes d'investissement *f/pl*	—	tipos de inversión *m/pl*
tipi di patrimonio (I)	Vermögensarten *f/pl*	types of property	catégories de patrimoine *f/pl*	—	clases de patrimonio *f/pl*
tipo base (Es)	Eckzins *m*	basic rate of interest	taux d'intérêt de base *m*	interesse di riferimento *m*	—
tipo de cambio (Es)	Wechselkurs *m*	exchange rate	cours du change *m*	cambio *m*	—
tipo de cambio al contado (Es)	Devisenkassakurs *m*	foreign exchange spot operations	taux de change au comptant *m*	corso dei cambi a pronti *m*	—
tipo de cambio de billetes y monedas extranjeras (Es)	Sortenkurs *m*	rate for foreign notes and coins	cours des monnaies étrangères *m*	corso dei cambi *m*	—
tipo de cambio del mercado monetario (Es)	Geldmarktsatz *m*	money market rate	taux d'intérêt sur le marché monétaire *m*	tasso del mercato monetario *m*	—

	D	E	F	I	Es
tipo de cambio fijo (Es)	starrer Wechselkurs *m*	fixed exchange rate	taux de change fixe *m*	cambio fisso *m*	—
tipo de cambio libre (Es)	freier Wechselkurs *m*	freely fluctuating exchange rate	taux de change libre *m*	cambio libero *m*	—
tipo de cambio múltiple (Es)	gespaltener Devisenmarkt *m*	two-tier foreign exchange market	marché des changes où existent deux taux de change pour une même monnaie *m*	mercato dei cambi multipli *m*	—
tipo de cambio múltiple (Es)	gespaltener Wechselkurs *m*	multiple exchange rates	cours du change multiple *m*	cambio multiplo *m*	—
tipo de coste (Es)	Kostenfaktor *m*	cost factor	facteur de coûts *m*	fattore di costo *m*	—
tipo de descuento (Es)	Diskontsatz *m*	discount rate	taux d'escompte *m*	saggio di sconto *m*	—
tipo de descuento variable (Es)	flexibler Diskontsatz *m*	flexible discount rate	taux d'escompte variable *m*	tasso di sconto flessibile *m*	—
tipo de emisión (Es)	Emissionskurs *m*	issue price	cours d'émission *m*	corso d'emissione *m*	—
tipo de interés (Es)	Zinssatz *m*	interest rate	taux d'intérêt *m*	tasso d'interesse *m*	—
tipo de interés (Es)	Geldsatz *m*	money rate	taux de l'argent *m*	tasso monetario *m*	—
tipo de interés calculado (Es)	Kalkulationszinssatz *m*	calculation interest rate	taux d'intérêt de calcul *m*	tasso d'interesse desiderato minimo *m*	—
tipo de interés del mercado (Es)	Marktzins *m*	market rate of interest	taux du marché *m*	tasso d'interesse corrente *m*	—
tipo de interés de un empréstito (Es)	Leihzins *m*	interest rate on a loan	intérêt du capital prêté *m*	interesse *m*	—
tipo de interés interno (Es)	interner Zinsfuß *m*	internal interest rate	taux d'intérêt interne *m*	saggio di rendimento interno *m*	—
tipo de interés para créditos pignoraticios (Es)	Lombardzinsfuß *m*	lending rate	taux d'intérêt de l'argent prêté et garanti par un gage *m*	tasso anticipazioni *m*	—
tipo de pignoración (Es)	Lombardsatz *m*	bankrate for advances against collateral	taux lombard *m*	tasso lombard *m*	—
tipo de pivote (Es)	Leitkurs *m*	central rate	taux central *m*	parità centrale *f*	—
tipo de prolongación (Es)	Prolongationssatz *m*	renewal rate	taux de report *m*	saggio di riporto *m*	—
tipo de referencia (Es)	Spareckzins *m*	basic savings rate	taux-clé d'intérêt bancaire sur les dépôts d'épargne *m*	interesse di riferimento per il risparmio *m*	—
tipo di costo (I)	Kostenart *f*	cost type	coût par nature *m*	—	clase de costes *f*
tipo neto de intereses (Es)	Nettozinssatz *m*	net interest rate	taux d'intérêt net *m*	tasso d'interesse netto *m*	—
tipos de depósito (Es)	Depotarten *f/pl*	types of deposit	sortes de dépôts *f/pl*	tipi di deposito *m/pl*	—
tipos de emisión (Es)	Emissionsarten *f/pl*	types of issuing	sortes d'émission *f/pl*	tipi di emissione *m/pl*	—
tipos de inversión (Es)	Kapitalanlegearten *f/pl*	types of capital investment	sortes d'investissement *f/pl*	tipi di investimento di capitale *m/pl*	—
tipo swap (Es)	Swapsatz *m*	swap rate	taux de swap *m*	tasso swap *m*	—
tirage (F)	Ziehung *f*	drawing	—	estrazione *f*	giro *m*
tirage (F)	Trassierung *f*	drawing	—	traenza *f*	giro *m*
tiré (F)	Bezogener *m*	drawee	—	trattario *m*	librado *m*
tiré (F)	Trassat *n*	drawee	—	trattario *m*	girado *m*
tirelire (F)	Sparbüchse *f*	piggy bank	—	salvadanaio *m*	alcancía *f*
tireur (F)	Trassant *m*	drawer	—	traente *m*	girador *m*
tireur d'une traite (F)	Wechselaussteller *m*	drawer of a bill	—	traente di una cambiale *m*	librador *m*
title-evidencing instrument (E)	Legitimationspapiere *n/pl*		titre nominatif *m*	documenti di legittimazione *m/pl*	títulos de legitimación *m/pl*
titoli (I)	Effekten *pl*	securities	valeurs mobilières *f/pl*	—	efectos *m/pl*
titoli (I)	Stücke *n/pl*	securities	titres *m/pl*	—	títulos *m/pl*
titoli all'ordine non per legge (I)	gewillkürte Orderpapiere *n/pl*	instruments to order by option	titres à ordre par destination *m/pl*	—	valores a la orden por elección *m/pl*
titoli all'ordine per legge (I)	geborene Orderpapiere *n/pl*	instruments to order by law	titres à ordre par nature *m/pl*	—	valores a la orden por naturaleza *m/pl*

	D	E	F	I	Es
titoli al portatore qualificati (I)	qualifizierte Legitimations- papiere *n/pl*	eligible title-evidencing instrument	titre établi à personne dénommée ou à tout autre porteur *m*	—	títulos de legitimación calificados *m/pl*
titoli ammessi a contratti future (I)	Terminpapiere *n/pl*	forward securities	valeurs à terme *f/pl*	—	títulos a plazo *m/pl*
titoli ammessi in borsa (I)	börsengängige Wertpapiere *n/pl*	quoted securities	valeurs négociées en bourse *f/pl*	—	títulos cotizados en bolsa *m/pl*
titoli annullati (I)	vernichtete Wertpapiere *n/pl*	destroyed securities	titres détruits *m/pl*	—	títulos destruidos *m/pl*
titoli a premio (I)	Agiopapiere *n/pl*	securities redeemable at a premium	obligations rembour sables avec prime *f/pl*	—	valores de renta fija reembolsados con una prima *m/pl*
titoli a prezzo d'affezione (I)	historische Wertpapiere *n/pl*	historical securities	titres historiques *m/pl*	—	títulos históricos *m/pl*
titoli a tariffa d'imposizione (I)	tarifbesteuerte Wertpapiere *n/pl*	securities taxed at the standard rate	titres soumis aux impôts en vigueur *m/pl*	—	títulos sometidos a los impuestos en vigor *m/pl*
titoli colpiti da ammortamento (I)	aufgerufene Wert- papiere *n/pl*	securities publicly notified as lost	titres appelés au remboursement *m/pl*	—	títulos retirados de la circulación con aviso *m/pl*
titoli colpiti da fermo (I)	gesperrte Stücke *n/pl*	blocked shares	titres bloqués *m/pl*	—	títulos congelados *m/pl*
titoli con privilegi fiscali (I)	steuerbegünstigte Wertpapiere *n/pl*	tax-privileged securities	titres assortis d'avan- tages fiscaux *m/pl*	—	títulos favorecidos por ventajas fiscales *m/pl*
titoli dati a riporto (I)	Reporteffekten *pl*	contango securities	titres reportés *m/pl*	—	efectos de reporte *m/pl*
titoli di credito (I)	Forderungspapiere *n/pl*	instruments conferring title	titres de créance *m/pl*	—	títulos de crédito *m/pl*
titoli di deposito cauzionale (I)	Kautionseffekten *pl*	guarantee securities	papiers de sûreté *m/pl*	—	valores de fianza *m/pl*
titoli di diritto reale (I)	sachenrechtliche Wertpapiere *n/pl*	property law securities	titres sur un droit réel *m/pl*	—	títulos jurídico-reales *m/pl*
titoli di importo modesto (I)	Kleinstücke *n/pl*	fractional amount	petits titres *m/pl*	—	títulos pequeños *m/pl*
titoli d'investimento (I)	Anlagepapiere *n/pl*	investment securities	valeurs de placement *f/pl*	—	valores de inversión *m/pl*
titoli di prima classe (I)	goldgeränderte Pa- piere *n/pl*	gilt-edged securities	titres à marges dorées *m/pl*	—	seguridades pupilares *f/pl*
titoli di smobilizzo (I)	Mobilisierungspapiere *n/pl*	mobilization papers	titres de mobilisation *m/pl*	—	títulos de mobilización *m/pl*
titoli di Stato (I)	Staatspapiere *n/pl*	public securities	effets publics *m/pl*	—	papeles del Estado *m/pl*
titoli di Stato (I)	Staatsanleihen *f/pl*	public bonds	emprunts d'Etat *m/pl*	—	bonos del Estado *m/pl*
titoli fungibili (I)	vertretbare Wertpapiere *n/pl*	fungible securities	titres fongibles *m/pl*	—	títulos fungibles *m/pl*
titoli girabili (I)	indossable Wertpapiere *n/pl*	endorsable securities	valeurs endossables *f/pl*	—	títulos endosables *m/pl*
titoli leggeri (I)	leichte Papiere *n/pl*	low-priced securities	titres de basse cotation *m/pl*	—	títulos de baja cotización *m/pl*
titoli lombard (I)	Lombardeffekten *pl*	securities serving as collateral	titres remis en nantissement *m/pl*	—	títulos pignoraticios *m/pl*
titoli molto richiesti (I)	Favoriten *m/pl*	seasoned securities	favoris *m/pl*	—	favoritos *m/pl*
titolo morto (I)	totes Papier *n*	inactive security	titre inactif *m*	—	título muerto *m*
titoli non vincolati (I)	freie Stücke *n/pl*	negotiable securities	titres négociables *m/pl*	—	títulos libres *m/pl*
titoli nostri (I)	Nostroeffekten *pl*	securities held by a bank at another bank	effets dans une autre banque *m/pl*	—	efectos a nuestro cargo *m/pl*
titoli pesanti (I)	schwere Papiere *n/pl*	heavy-priced securities	titres chers *m/pl*	—	valores de alta cotización *m/pl*
titoli propri (I)	eigene Effekten *f*	own security holdings	titres propres *m/pl*	—	valores propios *m/pl*
titoli provenienti da paesi esotici (I)	Exoten *m/pl*	highly speculative securities	valeurs extrêmement spéculatives *f/pl*	—	valores especulativos *m/pl*
titoli rimanenti di un'emissione (I)	nasse Stücke *n/pl*	unissued mortgage bonds still in trustee's hands	titres d'une émission pas encore placés *m/pl*	—	títulos todavía no emitidos *m/pl*

	D	E	F	I	Es
titoli rimanenti di un'emissione (I)	Emissionsreste *m/pl*	residual securities of an issue	titres restant d'une émission *m/pl*	—	títulos restantes de una emisión *m/pl*
titoli riscontabili (I)	deckungsfähige Wertpapiere *n/pl*	securities eligible as cover	titres susceptibles d'être déposés en couverture *m/pl*	—	títulos cubiertos por el banco emisor *m/pl*
titoli riscontabili presso la banca centrale (I)	bundesbankfähige Wertpapiere *n/pl*	bills rediscountable at the Federal Bank	titres escomptables au près de la Banque fédérale *m/pl*	—	títulos redescontables en el Banco Federal *m/pl*
titoli venduti allo sportello (I)	Schalterstücke *n/pl*	counter stock	titres de guichet *m/pl*	—	títulos al contado *m/pl*
titolo (I)	Feingewicht *n*	standard	poids de métal fin *m*	—	peso fino *m*
titolo (I)	Feingehalt *n*	standard	titre *m*	—	ley *f*
titolo (I)	Papier *n*	security	titre *m*	—	título *m*
titolo all'ordine (I)	Orderpapier *n*	instrument made out to order	papier à ordre *m*	—	título a la orden *m*
titolo al portatore (I)	Inhaberpapier *n*	bearer securities	titre souscrit au porteur *m*	—	título al portador *m*
titolo arbitrale (I)	Arbitragewert *m*	arbitrage value	valeur d'arbitrage *f*	—	valor de arbitraje *m*
titolo a reddito fisso (I)	Rentenwert *m*	fixed-interest security	valeur à revenu fixe *f*	—	título de renta fija *m*
titolo a reddito fisso (I)	Rente *f*	annuity	rente *f*	—	renta *f*
titoli a reddito fisso in valuta estera (I)	zertifizierte Bonds *m/pl*	certified bonds	bons certifiés *m/pl*	—	bonos certificados *m/pl*
titolo aureo (I)	Goldfeingehalt *m*	fine gold content	poids d'or fin *m*	—	peso fino del oro *m*
titolo del mercato ristretto (I)	Kulissenwert *m*	quotation on the unofficial market	valeur négociée sur le marché libre *f*	—	valor de la bolsa extraoficial *m*
titolo di credito (I)	Wertpapier *n*	security	valeur *f*	—	valor *m*
titolo di credito (I)	Gläubigerpapier *n*	creditor paper	titre créditeur *m*	—	título acreedor *m*
titolo di credito (I)	Kreditaktie *f*	credit share	titre de crédit *m*	—	título de crédito *m*
titolo di credito fondiario (I)	Hypothekenpfandbrief *m*	mortgage debenture	obligation foncière *f*	—	obligación hipotecaria *f*
titolo di credito in valuta estera (I)	Valutaschuldschein *m*	foreign currency certificate of indebtedness	titre de créance en monnaie étrangère *m*	—	pagaré en moneda extranjera *m*
titolo di credito trasferibile (I)	Traditionspapier *n*	negotiable document of title	titre du type classique *m*	—	título de tradición *m*
titolo di credito turistico (I)	Reisekreditbrief *m*	traveller's letter of credit	lettre de crédit circulaire *f*	—	carta de crédito viajero *f*
titolo di debito (I)	Schuldbrief *m*	certificate of indebtedness	titre d'obligation *m*	—	título de deuda *m*
titolo di finanziamento (I)	Finanzierungspapier *n*	funding paper	titres de financement *m/pl*	—	título de financiación *m*
titolo di libera contrattazione (I)	variabler Wert *m*	variable value	valeur variable *f*	—	valor variable *m*
titolo di rendita (I)	Rentenbrief *m*	annuity certificate	titre de rente foncière *m*	—	título de renta *m*
titoli di riflusso (I)	Rückflußstücke *n/pl*	securities repurchased	titres rachetés *m/pl*	—	títulos de reflujo *m/pl*
titolo di sconto (I)	Diskontpapier *n*	discountable paper	titre escomptable *m*	—	título de descuento *m*
titolo di Stato (I)	Bundesanleihe *f*	Federal loan	titre de dette publique *m*	—	empréstito de la Federación *m*
titolo estero (I)	ausländisches Wertpapier *n*	foreign security	valeurs étrangères *f/pl*	—	título extranjero *m*
titolo in deposito collettivo (I)	Girosammelstück *n*	security held on giro-transferable deposit	titre en dépôt collectif *m*	—	título en depósito colectivo *m*
titolo in deposito collettivo (I)	Girosammeldepotstück *n*	security held on giro-transferable deposit	titre en dépôt collectif *m*	—	título en un depósito central de valores *m*
titolo industria di pubblica utilità (I)	Tarifwert *m*	tariff value	valeur au tarif *f*	—	valor arancelario *m*
titolo insider (I)	Insiderpapier *n*	insider security	titre insider *m*	—	título insider *m*
titolo ipotecario (I)	Hypothekenbrief *m*	mortgage deed	cédule hypothécaire *f*	—	carta hipotecaria *f*
titolo liquido (I)	Liquiditätspapier *n*	liquidity papers	titre de liquidité *m*	—	título de liquidez *m*
titolo locale (I)	Lokalpapier *n*	security only traded on a regional stock exchange	valeur régionale *f*	—	título local *m*

	D	E	F	I	Es
titolo negoziabile (I)	lieferbares Wertpapier n	deliverable security	valeur négociable f	—	título de buena entrega m
titolo nominativo (I)	Namenspapier n	registered securities	titre nominatif m	—	título nominal m
titolo obbligazionario (I)	Schuldverschreibung f	debenture stock	obligation f	—	obligación f
titolo obbligazionario di liquidazione (I)	Liquidationsschuldverschreibung f	liquidation bond	obligation de liquidation f	—	bono de liquidación f
titolo primario (I)	Interessenwert m	vested interest stock	action qui fait l'objet d'un achat par un groupe intéressé f	—	valor de interés m
titolo rappresentativo di merci (I)	Warenpapier n	document of title	effet de commerce m	—	valor comercial m
titolo speculativo (I)	Spekulationspapier n	speculative security	valeur spéculative f	—	título especulativo m
titolo unitario (I)	Einheitswert m	standard value	valeur globale intrinsèque f	—	valor unitario m
titre (F)	Feingehalt n	standard	—	titolo m	ley f
titre (F)	Mantel m	share certificate	—	mantello m	título m
titre (F)	Papier n	security	—	titolo m	título m
titre créditeur (F)	Gläubigerpapier n	creditor paper	—	titolo di credito m	título acreedor m
titre de créance en monnaie étrangère (F)	Valutaschuldschein m	foreign currency certificate of indebtedness	—	titolo di credito in valuta estera m	pagaré en moneda extranjera m
titre de crédit (F)	Kreditaktie f	credit share	—	titolo di credito m	título de crédito m
titre de dette publique (F)	Bundesanleihe f	Federal loan	—	titolo di Stato m	empréstito de la Federación m
titre de gage (F)	Warrants m/pl	warrants	—	warrants m/pl	certificados de depósito m/pl
titre d'emprunt convertible (F)	Optionsanleihe f	option bond	—	prestito convertibile m	bono opcional m
titre de rente foncière (F)	Rentenbrief m	annuity certificate	—	titolo di rendita m	título de renta m
titre d'obligation (F)	Schuldbrief m	certificate of indebtedness	—	titolo di debito m	título de deuda m
titre du type classique (F)	Traditionspapier n	negotiable document of title	—	titolo di credito trasferibile m	título de tradición m
titre en dépôt collectif (F)	Girosammeldepotstück n	security held on giro-transferable deposit	—	titolo in deposito collettivo m	título en un depósito central de valores m
titre en dépôt collectif (F)	Girosammelstück n	security held on giro-transferable deposit	—	titolo in deposito collettivo m	título en depósito colectivo m
titre escomptable (F)	Diskontpapier n	discountable paper	—	titolo di sconto m	título de descuento m
titre établi à personne dénommée ou à tout autre porteur (F)	qualifizierte Legitimationspapiere n/pl	eligible title-evidencing instrument	—	titoli al portatore qualificati m/pl	títulos de legitimación calificados m/pl
titre inactif (F)	totes Papier n	inactive security	—	titolo morto m	título muerto m
titre insider (F)	Insiderpapier n	insider security	—	titolo insider m	título insider m
titre le liquidité (F)	Liquiditätspapier n	liquidity papers	—	titolo liquido m	título de liquidez m
titre nominatif (F)	Namenspapier n	registered security	—	titolo nominativo m	título nominal m
titre nominatif (F)	Legitimationspapiere n/pl	title-evidencing instrument	—	documenti di legittimazione m/pl	títulos de legitimación m/pl
titre représentant globalement un paquet d'actions (F)	Sammelaktie f	global share	—	azione globale f	acción global f
titre représentant globalement un paquet d'emprunts (F)	Global-Anleihe f	all-share certificate	—	credito globale m	empréstito global m
titres (F)	Stücke n/pl	securities	—	titoli m/pl	títulos m/pl
titres à marges dorées (F)	goldgeränderte Papiere n/pl	gilt-edged securities	—	titoli di prima classe m/pl	seguridades pupilares f/pl
titres à ordre par destination (F)	gewillkürte Orderpapiere n/pl	instruments to order by option	—	titoli all'ordine non per legge m/pl	valores a la orden por elección m/pl
titres à ordre par nature (F)	geborene Orderpapiere n/pl	instruments to order by law	—	titoli all'ordine per legge m/pl	valores a la orden por naturaleza m/pl
titres appelés au remboursement (F)	aufgerufene Wertpapiere n/pl	securities publicly notified as lost	—	titoli colpiti da ammortamento m/pl	títulos retirados de la circulación con aviso m/pl

	D	E	F	I	Es
titres assortis d' avantages fiscaux (F)	steuerbegünstigte Wertpapiere *n/pl*	tax-privileged securities	—	titoli con privilegi fiscali *m/pl*	títulos favorecidos por ventajas fiscales *m/pl*
titres bloqués (F)	gesperrte Stücke *n/pl*	blocked shares	—	titoli colpiti da fermo *m/pl*	títulos congelados *m/pl*
titres chers (F)	schwere Papiere *n/pl*	heavy-priced securities	—	titoli pesanti *m/pl*	valores de alta cotización *m/pl*
titres de basse cotation (F)	leichte Papiere *n/pl*	low-priced securities	—	titoli leggeri *m/pl*	títulos de baja cotización *m/pl*
titres de créance (F)	Forderungspapiere *n/pl*	instruments conferring title	—	titoli di credito *m/pl*	títulos de crédito *m/pl*
titres de financement (F)	Finanzierungspapier *n*	funding paper	—	titolo di finanziamento *m*	título de financiación *m*
titres de guichet (F)	Schalterstücke *n/pl*	counter stock	—	titoli venduti allo sportello *m/pl*	títulos al contado *m/pl*
titres de mobilisation (F)	Mobilisierungspapiere *n/pl*	mobilization papers	—	titoli di smobilizzo *m/pl*	títulos de mobilización *m/pl*
titres d'emprunt émis en monnaie étrangère (F)	Auslandsbonds *m*	foreign currency bonds	—	obbligazioni in valuta estera *f/pl*	bonos en moneda extranjera *m/pl*
titres de participation (F)	Anteilspapiere *n/pl*	equity securities	—	cedole azionarie *f/pl*	títulos de participación *m/pl*
titres détruits (F)	vernichtete Wertpapiere *n/pl*	destroyed securities	—	titoli annullati *m/pl*	títulos destruidos *m/pl*
titres du marché monétaire (F)	Geldmarktpapier *n*	money market security	—	portafoglio sconto *m*	título del mercado monetario *m*
titres d'une émission pas encore placés (F)	nasse Stücke *n/pl*	unissued mortgage bonds still in trustee's hands	—	titoli rimanenti di un' emissione *m/pl*	títulos todavía no emitidos *m/pl*
titres escomptables auprès de la Banque fédérale (F)	bundesbankfähige Wertpapiere *n/pl*	bills rediscountable at the Federal Bank	—	titoli riscontabili presso la banca centrale *m/pl*	títulos redescontables en el Banco Federal *m/pl*
titres fongibles (F)	vertretbare Wertpapiere *n/pl*	fungible securities	—	titoli fungibili *m/pl*	títulos fungibles *m/pl*
titres historiques (F)	historische Wertpapiere *n/pl*	historical securities	—	titoli a prezzo d'affezione *m/pl*	títulos históricos *m/pl*
titres lancés sur le marché (F)	herauskommendes Material *n*	securities coming on to the market	—	offerta di titoli *f*	material saliente *m*
titres négociables (F)	freie Stücke *n/pl*	negotiable securities	—	titoli non vincolati *m/pl*	títulos libres *m/pl*
titres non cotés officiellement (F)	amtlich nicht notierte Werte *m/pl*	unquoted securities	—	valori non quotati *m/pl*	valores no cotizados oficialmente *m/pl*
titres non déclarés (F)	Bodensatz *m*	undeclared securities	—	giacenza media di depositi a vista *f*	títulos no declarados *m/pl*
titre souscrit au porteur (F)	Inhaberpapier *n*	bearer security	—	titolo al portatore *m*	título al portador *m*
titres propres (F)	eigene Effekten *f*	own security holdings	—	titoli propri *m/pl*	valores propios *m/pl*
titres rachetés (F)	Rückflußstücke *n/pl*	securities repurchased	—	titoli di riflusso *m/pl*	títulos de reflujo *m/pl*
titres remis en nantissement (F)	Lombardeffekten *pl*	securities serving as collateral	—	titoli lombard *m/pl*	títulos pignoraticios *m/pl*
titres reportés (F)	Reporteffekten *pl*	contango securities	—	titoli dati a riporto *m/pl*	efectos de reporte *m/pl*
titres restant d'une émission (F)	Emissionsreste *m/pl*	residual securities of an issue	—	titoli rimanenti di un' emissione *m/pl*	títulos restantes de una emisión *m/pl*
titres soumis aux impôts en vigueur (F)	tarifbesteuerte Wertpapiere *n/pl*	securities taxed at the standard rate	—	titoli a tariffa d'imposizione *m/pl*	títulos sometidos a los impuestos en vigor *m/pl*
titres spéciaux (F)	Spezialwerte *m/pl*	specialties	—	premi omaggio *m/pl*	títulos especiales *m/pl*
titre spéculatif (F)	Hoffnungswert *m*	speculative security	—	valore promettente reddito futuro *m*	título especulativo *m*
titres sur un droit réel (F)	sachenrechtliche Wertpapiere *n/pl*	property law securities	—	titoli di diritto reale *m/pl*	títulos jurídico-reales *m/pl*
titres susceptibles d'être déposé en couverture (F)	deckungsfähige Wertpapiere *n/pl*	securities eligible as cover	—	titoli riscontabili *m/pl*	títulos cubiertos por el banco emisor *m/pl*
titular de acciones (Es)	Anteilseigner *m*	shareholder	porteur de parts *m*	azionista *m*	—

	D	E	F	I	Es
titular de acciones extranjero (Es)	ausländischer Anteilseigner *m*	foreign shareholder	actionnaire étranger *m*	azionista estero *m*	—
título (Es)	Papier *n*	security	titre *m*	titolo *m*	—
título (Es)	Mantel *m*	share certificate	titre *m*	mantello *m*	—
título acreedor (Es)	Gläubigerpapier *n*	creditor paper	titre créditeur *m*	titolo di credito *m*	—
título a la orden (Es)	Orderpapier *n*	instrument made out to order	papier à ordre *m*	titolo all'ordine *m*	—
título al portador (Es)	Inhaberpapier *n*	bearer security	titre souscrit au porteur *m*	titolo al portatore *m*	—
título de buena entrega (Es)	lieferbares Wertpapier *n*	deliverable security	valeur négociable *f*	titolo negoziabile *m*	—
título de crédito (Es)	Kreditaktie *f*	credit share	titre de crédit *m*	titolo di credito *m*	—
título de descuento (Es)	Diskontpapier *n*	discountable paper	titre escomptable *m*	titolo di sconto *m*	—
título de deuda (Es)	Schuldbrief *m*	certificate of indebtedness	titre d'obligation *m*	titolo di debito *m*	—
título de financiación (Es)	Finanzierungspapier *n*	funding paper	titres de financement *m/pl*	titolo di finanziamento *m*	—
títulos de legitimación calificados (Es)	qualifizierte Legitimationspapiere *n/pl*	eligible title-evidencing instrument	titre établi à personne dénommée ou à tout autre porteur *m*	titoli al portatore qualificati *m/pl*	—
título de liquidez (Es)	Liquiditätspapier *n*	liquidity papers	titre de liquidité *m*	titolo liquido *m*	—
título del mercado monetario (Es)	Geldmarktpapier *n*	money market security	titres du marché monétaire *m/pl*	portafoglio sconto *m*	—
título de renta (Es)	Rentenbrief *m*	annuity certificate	titre de rente foncière *m*	titolo di rendita *m*	—
título de renta fija (Es)	Rentenwert *m*	fixed-interest security	valeur à revenu fixe *f*	titolo a reddito fisso *m*	—
título de tradición (Es)	Traditionspapier *n*	negotiable document of title	titre du type classique *m*	titolo di credito trasferibile *m*	—
título en depósito colectivo (Es)	Girosammelstück *n*	security held on giro-transferable deposit	titre en dépôt collectif *m*	titolo in deposito collettivo *m*	—
título en un depósito central de valores (Es)	Girosammeldepotstück *n*	security held on giro-transferable deposit	titre en dépôt collectif *m*	titolo in deposito collettivo *m*	—
título especulativo (Es)	Spekulationspapier *n*	speculative security	valeur spéculative *f*	titolo speculativo *m*	—
título especulativo (Es)	Hoffnungswert *m*	speculative security	titre spéculatif *m*	valore promettente reddito futuro *m*	—
título insider (Es)	Insiderpapier *n*	insider security	titre insider *m*	titolo insider *m*	—
título local (Es)	Lokalpapier *n*	security only traded on a regional stock exchange	valeur régionale *f*	titolo locale *m*	—
título muerto (Es)	totes Papier *n*	inactive security	titre inactif *m*	titolo morto *m*	—
título nominal (Es)	Namenspapier *n*	registered security	titre nominatif *m*	titolo nominativo *m*	—
título oficialmente cotizado (Es)	Schrankenwert *m*	officially quoted security	valeur négociée au marché officiel *f*	valori amnesi alla quotazione afficiale *m/pl*	—
títulos (Es)	Stücke *n/pl*	securities	titres *m/pl*	titoli *m/pl*	—
títulos al contado (Es)	Schalterstücke *n/pl*	counter stock	titres de guichet *m/pl*	titoli venduti allo sportello *m/pl*	—
títulos a plazo (Es)	Terminpapiere *n/pl*	forward securities	valeurs à terme *f/pl*	titoli ammessi a contratti future *m/pl*	—
títulos comerciales a la orden (Es)	kaufmännische Orderpapiere *n/pl*	commercial instruments to order	effets de commerce	effetti commerciali all'ordine *m/pl*	—
títulos congelados (Es)	gesperrte Stücke *n/pl*	blocked shares	titres bloqués *m/pl*	titoli colpiti da fermo *m/pl*	—
títulos cotizados en bolsa (Es)	börsengängige Wertpapiere *n/pl*	quoted securities	valeurs négociées en bourse *f/pl*	titoli ammessi in borsa *m/pl*	—
títulos cubiertos por el banco emisor (Es)	deckungsfähige Wertpapiere *n/pl*	securities eligible as cover	titres susceptibles d' être déposés en couverture *m/pl*	titoli riscontabili *m/pl*	—
títulos de baja cotización (Es)	leichte Papiere *n/pl*	low-priced securities	titres de basse cotation *m/pl*	titoli leggeri *m/pl*	—
títulos de crédito (Es)	Forderungspapiere *n/pl*	instruments conferring title	titres de créance *m/pl*	titoli di credito *m/pl*	—

	D	E	F	I	Es
títulos de legitimación (Es)	Legitimationspapiere *n/pl*	title-evidencing instrument	titre nominatif *m*	documenti di legittimazione *m/pl*	—
títulos de mobilización (Es)	Mobilisierungspapiere *n/pl*	mobilization papers	titres de mobilisation *m/pl*	titoli di smobilizzo *m/pl*	—
títulos de participación (Es)	Anteilspapiere *n/pl*	equity securities	titres de participation *m/pl*	cedole azionarie *f/pl*	—
títulos de reflujo (Es)	Rückflußstücke *n/pl*	securites repurchased	titres rachetés *m/pl*	titoli di riflusso *m/pl*	—
títulos destruidos (Es)	vernichtete Wertpapiere *n/pl*	destroyed securities	titres détruits *m/pl*	titoli annullati *m/pl*	—
títulos endosables (Es)	indossable Wertpapiere *n/pl*	endorsable securities	valeurs endossables *f/pl*	titoli girabili *m/pl*	—
títulos especiales (Es)	Spezialwerte *m/pl*	specialties	titres spéciaux *m/pl*	premi omaggio *m/pl*	—
título extranjero (Es)	ausländisches Wertpapier *n*	foreign security	valeurs étrangères *f/pl*	titolo estero *m*	—
títulos favorecidos por ventajas fiscales (Es)	steuerbegünstigte Wertpapiere *n/pl*	tax-privileged securities	titres assortis d'avantages fiscaux *m/pl*	titoli con privilegi fiscali *m/pl*	—
títulos fungibles (Es)	vertretbare Wertpapiere *n/pl*	fungible securities	titres fongibles *m/pl*	titoli fungibili *m/pl*	—
títulos históricos (Es)	historische Wertpapiere *n/pl*	historical securities	titres historiques *m/pl*	titoli a prezzo d'affezione *m/pl*	—
títulos jurídico-reales (Es)	sachenrechtliche Wertpapiere *n/pl*	property law securities	titres sur un droit réel *m/pl*	titoli di diritto reale *m/pl*	—
títulos libres (Es)	freie Stücke *n/pl*	negotiable securities	titres négociables *m/pl*	titoli non vincolati *m/pl*	—
títulos no declarados (Es)	Bodensatz *m*	undeclared securities	titres non déclarés *m/pl*	giacenza media di depositi a vista *f*	—
títulos pequeños (Es)	Kleinstücke *n/pl*	fractional amount	petits titres *m/pl*	titoli di importo modesto *m/pl*	—
títulos pignoraticios (Es)	Lombardeffekten *pl*	securities serving as collateral	titres remis en nantissement *m/pl*	titoli lombard *m/pl*	—
títulos pupilares (Es)	mündelsichere Papiere *n/pl*	trustee securities	valeur de tout repos *f*	valori di tutto riposo *m/pl*	—
títulos redescontables en el Banco Federal (Es)	bundesbankfähige Wertpapiere *n/pl*	bills rediscountable at the Federal Bank	titres escomptables auprès de la Banque fédérale *m/pl*	titoli riscontabili presso la banca centrale *m/pl*	—
títulos restantes de una emisión (Es)	Emissionsreste *m/pl*	residual securities of an issue	titres restant d'une émission *m/pl*	titoli rimanenti di un' emissione *m/pl*	—
títulos retirados de la circulación con aviso (Es)	aufgerufene Wertpapiere *n/pl*	securities publicly notified as lost	titres appelés au remboursement *m/pl*	titoli colpiti da ammortamento *m/pl*	—
títulos sometidos a los impuestos en vigor (Es)	tarifbesteuerte Wertpapiere *n/pl*	securities taxed at the standard rate	titres soumis aux - impôts en vigueur *m/pl*	titoli a tariffa d'imposizione *m/pl*	—
títulos todavía no emitidos (Es)	nasse Stücke *n/pl*	unissued mortgage bonds still in trustee's hands	titres d'une émission pas encore placés *m/pl*	titoli rimanenti di un' emissione *m/pl*	—
tobacco exchange (E)	Tabakbörse *f*	—	bourse de tabacs *f*	borsa tabacchi *f*	bolsa de tabaco *f*
toma de crédito neta (Es)	Nettokreditaufnahme *f*	net borrowing	emprunt net *m*	indebitamento netto *m*	—
tope de la base de cotización (Es)	Beitragsbemessungsgrenze *f*	income limit for the assessment of contributions	plafond d'assujettissement servant au calcul de la cotisation à l'assurance invalidité-vieillesse *m*	massimale di contributo *m*	—
total capital profitability (E)	Gesamtkapitalrentabilität *f*	—	rentabilité totale du capital *f*	redditività del capitale complessivo *f*	rédito del capital total *m*
total claim (E)	Gesamtforderung *f*	—	créance totale *f*	credito complessivo *m*	crédito total *m*
total credit outstanding (E)	Kreditvolumen *n*	—	volume des crédits *m*	volume creditizio *m*	volumen de créditos *m*
total debt (E)	Gesamtschuld *f*	—	dette solidaire *f*	debito solidale *m*	obligación solidaria *f*
total du bilan (F)	Bilanzsumme *f*	balance sheet total	—	totale del bilancio *m*	suma del balance *f*
totale del bilancio (I)	Bilanzsumme *f*	balance sheet total	total du bilan *m*	—	suma del balance *f*
totalidad del patrimonio (Es)	Gesamtvermögen *n*	aggregate property	avoir total *m*	patrimonio complessivo *m*	—

	D	E	F	I	Es
total market value (E)	Gesamtkurs *m*	—	cours total *m*	quotazione accordata *f*	cotización colectiva *f*
total proceeds (E)	Gesamtertrag *m*	—	produit global *m*	reddito totale *m*	renta total *f*
totes Depot (D)	—	dormant deposit	compte de choses *m*	deposito inattivo *m*	depósito muerto *m*
totes Konto (D)	—	inoperative account	compte sans mouvement *m*	conto inattivo *m*	cuenta muerta *f*
totes Papier (D)	—	inactive security	titre inactif *m*	titolo morto *m*	título muerto *m*
tracer note (E)	Kontrollmitteilung *f*	—	bulletin de contrôle *m*	comunicazione di revisione *f*	control cruzado *m*
tracollo dei prezzi di borsa (I)	Deroute *f*	collapse	déroute *f*	—	fuga desbaratada *f*
trade (E)	Handel *m*	—	commerce *m*	commercio *m*	comercio *m*
trade credit (E)	Warenkredit *m*	—	avance sur marchandises *f*	credito su merci *m*	crédito sobre mercancías *m*
trade practice (E)	Handelsbrauch *m*	—	usage commercial *m*	usanza commerciale *f*	uso comercial *m*
trade tax (E)	Gewerbesteuer *f*	—	impôt sur les bénéfices des professions industrielles et commerciales *m*	tassa d'esercizio *f*	impuesto industrial *m*
trade union bank (E)	Gewerkschaftsbank *f*	—	banque de syndicat *f*	banca del lavoro *f*	banco sindical *m*
trading account (E)	Verkaufskonto *n*	—	compte de ventes *m*	conto vendite *m*	cuenta de ventas *f*
trading in foreign exchange (E)	Usancenhandel *m*	—	commerce de change *m*	commercio delle valute *m*	comercio de cambio *m*
trading in futures on a stock exchange (E)	Börsentermingeschäfte *n/pl*	—	opérations boursières à terme *f/pl*	contratti di borsa a termine *m/pl*	operaciones bursátiles a término *f/pl*
trading in security futures (E)	Wertpapier-Terminhandel *m*	—	marché des valeurs à terme *m*	operazioni a termine in titoli *f/pl*	operaciones de valores a plazo *f/pl*
trading in subscription rights (E)	Bezugsrechthandel *m*	—	marché des droits de souscription *m*	trattazione di diritti d'opzione *f*	comercio de derechos de suscripción *m*
trading on own account (E)	Eigenhandel *m*	—	commerce à propre compte *m*	commercio in proprio *m*	comercio por cuenta propia *m*
Traditionspapier (D)	—	negotiable document of title	titre du type classique *m*	titolo di credito trasferibile *m*	título de tradición *m*
traente (I)	Trassant *m*	drawer	tireur *m*	—	girador *m*
traente di una cambiale (I)	Wechselaussteller *m*	drawer of a bill	tireur d'une traite *m*	—	librador *m*
traenza (I)	Trassierung *f*	drawing	tirage *m*	—	giro *m*
traite (F)	Tratte *f*	draft	—	tratta *f*	letra girada *f*
traite à jour fixe (F)	Tageswechsel *m*	day bill	—	cambiale a scadenza fissa *f*	letra al día fijo *f*
traite à un certain délai de vue (F)	Nachsichtwechsel *m*	after-sight bill	—	cambiale a certo tempo vista *f*	letra a tantos días vista *f*
traite à vue (F)	Sichtwechsel *m*	demand bill	—	cambiale a vista *f*	letra a la vista *f*
traite commerciale (F)	Warenwechsel *m*	commercial bill	—	cambiale commerciale *f*	letra comercial *f*
traite de cavalerie (F)	Reitwechsel *m*	windbill	—	cambiale incrociata *f*	letra cruzada *f*
traite de mobilisation (F)	Mobilisierungstratte *f*	mobilization draft	—	effetto di smobilizzo *m*	letra de mobilización *f*
traite documentaire (F)	Dokumententratte *f*	acceptance bill	—	tratta documentaria *f*	letra documentaria *f*
traite donnée au recouvrement (F)	Inkassowechsel *m*	bill for collection	—	cambiale all'incasso *f*	letra al cobro *f*
traite en blanc (F)	Blanko-Wechsel *m*	blank bill	—	cambiale in bianco *f*	letra en blanco *f*
traite endossée par une banque (F)	bankgirierter Warenwechsel *pl*	bank endorsed bill	—	effetto commerciale girato da banche *m*	letra comercial con endoso bancario *f*
traite fictive (F)	Kellerwechsel *m*	fictitious bill	—	cambiale fittizia *f*	letra de cambio ficticia *f*
traite financière (F)	Leerwechsel *m*	finance bill	—	cambiale vuota *f*	letra al descubierto *f*
traite financière (F)	Finanzwechsel *m*	finance bill	—	cambiale finanziaria *f*	letra bancaria *f*
traite financière acceptée (F)	Finanzakzept *n*	accepted finance bill	—	accettazione bancaria *f*	letra de cambio bancaria *f*
traite globale (F)	Sammeltratte *f*	collective bill	—	tratta collettiva *f*	libranza colectiva *f*

	D	E	F	I	Es
traite libellée en monnaie étrangère (F)	Valuta-Akzept *n*	foreign currency accept	—	accettazione in valuta estera *f*	aceptación en moneda extranjera *f*
traite non à ordre (F)	Rektawechsel *m*	non-negotiable bill of exchange	—	cambiale non all'ordine *f*	letra nominativa *f*
traite pour compte d'autrui (F)	Kommissionstratte *f*	bill of exchange drawn for third-party account	—	tratta per conto terzi *f*	giro por cuenta *m*
traite protestée (F)	Protestwechsel *m*	protested bill	—	cambiale protestata *f*	letra protestada *f*
traite protestée hors des délais (F)	präjudizierter Wechsel *m*	void bill	—	cambiale pregiudicata *f*	letra prejudicada *f*
traite retournée (F)	Rückwechsel *m*	unpaid bill of exchange	—	cambiale di ritorno *f*	letra de recambio *f*
traite tirée (F)	gezogener Wechsel *m*	drawn bill	—	cambiale tratta *f*	letra girada *f*
traite tirée en garantie d'un crédit (F)	Kreditakzept *n*	financial acceptance	—	accettazione bancaria *f*	aceptación de crédito *f*
traite tirée sur débiteur (F)	Debitorenziehung *f*	bills drawn on debtors	—	cambiale tratta sul debitore *f*	letra librada *f*
traite tirée sur l'étranger (F)	Auslandswechsel *m*	foreign bill of exchange	—	cambiale sull'estero *f*	letra sobre el exterior *f*
traite tirée sur l'étranger (F)	Auslandsakzept *n*	bill in foreign currency	—	accettazione estera *f*	letra sobre el extranjero *f*
traite tirée sur soimême (F)	trassiert-eigener Wechsel *m*	bill drawn by the drawer himself	—	cambiale tratta su se stesso *f*	letra girada a su propio cargo *f*
Tranche (D)	—	tranche	tranche *f*	tranche *f*	fracción *f*
tranche (E)	Tranche *f*	—	tranche *f*	tranche *f*	fracción *f*
tranche (F)	Tranche *f*	tranche	—	tranche *f*	fracción *f*
tranche (I)	Tranche *f*	tranche	tranche *f*	—	fracción *f*
tranche de crédit (F)	Kredittranche *f*	credit tranche	—	quota di credito *f*	fracción de crédito *f*
transacción (Es)	Transaktion *f*	transaction	transaction *f*	transazione *f*	—
transacción a término en divisas (Es)	Devisentermingeschäft *n*	forward exchange dealings	opération à terme sur les changes *f*	operazione di cambio a termine *f*	—
transacción de mediación (Es)	Vermittlungsgeschäft *n*	brokerage business	affaire de médiation *f*	operazione di intermediazione *f*	—
transacción de oro (Es)	Goldgeschäft *n*	gold transactions	transaction d'or *f*	operazione in oro *f*	—
transacción en contra (Es)	Gegengeschäft *n*	countertrade	affaire en contrepartie *f*	operazione di compensazione *f*	—
transacciones de cuotas (Es)	Quotenhandel *m*	quota transactions	transactions sur les quotas *f/pl*	mercato di quote di capitale *m*	—
transacciones de paquetes mayores de acciones (Es)	Pakethandel *m*	dealing in large lots	négociation de lots importants *f*	negoziazione di pacchetti azionari *f*	—
transacciones de trueque (Es)	Bartergeschäft *n*	barter transactions	troc *m*	operazione switch *f*	—
transacciones por cuenta ajena (Es)	Kundengeschäft *n*	transactions for third account	opération pour compte de client *f*	operazioni per la clientela *f/pl*	—
transacciones realizadas utilizando información privilegiada (Es)	Insiderhandel *m*	insider trading	opérations d'insider *f/pl*	insider trading *m*	—
transacción financiera (Es)	Finanztransaktion *f*	financial transaction	transaction financière *f*	operazione finanziaria *f*	—
transaction (E)	Transaktion *f*	—	transaction *f*	transazione *f*	transacción *f*
transaction (F)	Transaktion *f*	transaction	—	transazione *f*	transacción *f*
transaction balance (E)	Transaktionskasse *f*	—	solde des transactions *m*	domanda di moneta per transazioni *f*	caja de transacción *f*
transaction d'or (F)	Goldgeschäft *n*	gold transactions	—	operazione in oro *f*	transacción de oro *f*
transaction financière (F)	Finanztransaktion *f*	financial transaction	—	operazione finanziaria *f*	transacción financiera *f*
transaction for delivery by a fixed date (E)	Fixgeschäft *n*		opération à terme fixe *f*	contrattazione a fermo	negocio fijo *m*
transactions for third account (E)	Kundengeschäft *n*		opération pour compte de client *f*	operazioni per la clientela *f/pl*	transacciones por cuenta ajena *f/pl*
transactions on own account (E)	Eigengeschäft *n*		opération en nom personnel et à propre compte *f*	affare in proprio *m*	operación por cuenta propia *f*

	D	E	F	I	Es
transactions par téléphone (F)	Telefonverkehr *m*	telephone dealings	—	negoziazione di titoli per telefono *f*	mercado de valores extrabursátil *m*
transactions sur les quotas (F)	Quotenhandel *m*	quota transactions	—	mercato di quote di capitale *m*	transacciones de cuotas *f/pl*
Transaktion (D)	—	transaction	transaction *f*	transazione *f*	transacción *f*
Transaktionskasse (D)	—	transaction balance	solde des transactions *m*	domanda di moneta per transazioni *f*	caja de transacción *f*
Transaktionskosten (D)	—	conversion charge	frais de transaction *m/pl*	costi di transazione *m/pl*	gastos de transacción *m/pl*
transazione (I)	Transaktion *f*	transaction	transaction *f*	—	transacción *f*
transazione tra privati (I)	Privatgeschäft *n*	private transaction	affaire privée *f*	—	operación privada *f*
Transfer (D)	—	transfer	transfert *m*	trasferimento *m*	transferencia *f*
transfer (E)	Transfer *m*	—	transfert *m*	trasferimento *m*	transferencia *f*
transférabilité illimitée (F)	Devinkulierung *f*	unrestricted transferability	—	svincolamento *m*	devinculación *f*
transfer cheque (E)	Überweisungsscheck *m*	—	chèque postal de virement *m*	bancogiro della banca centrale *m*	cheque de transferencia *m*
transferencia (Es)	Transfer *m*	transfer	transfert *m*	trasferimento *m*	—
transferencia (Es)	Überweisung *f*	remittance	virement *m*	trasferimento *m*	—
transferencia colectiva (Es)	Sammelüberweisung *f*	combined bank transfer	virement global *m*	trasferimento cumulativo *m*	—
transferencia de beneficios (Es)	Gewinnabführung *f*	transfer of profits	transfert du bénéfice *m*	trasferimento degli utili *m*	—
transferencia de recursos (Es)	Ressourcentransfer *m*	transfer of resources	transfert de ressources *m*	trasferimento di risorse *m*	—
transferencia de una plaza a otra (Es)	Ferngiro *m*	long distance giro	virement entre deux places bancaires *m*	bonifico da una piazza all'altra *m*	—
transferencia local (Es)	Platzübertragung *f*	local transfer	virement de place *m*	trasferimento su piazza *m*	—
transferencias (Es)	Überweisungsverkehr *m*	money transfer transactions	virements *m/pl*	bancogiro *m*	—
transferencia sustitutiva (Es)	Ersatzüberweisung *f*	substitute transfer	virement de substitution *m*	trasferimento sostitutivo *m*	—
Transfergarantie (D)	—	guarantee of foreign exchange transfer	garantie des transferts *f*	garanzia di trasferimento *f*	garantía de transferencia *f*
transfer in blank (E)	Blankozession *f*	—	cession en blanc *f*	cessione allo scoperto *f*	cesión en blanco *f*
transfer of an entry (E)	Umbuchung *f*	—	jeu d'écritures *m*	giro di partite *m*	asiento en otra cuenta *m*
transfer of money by means of a clearing system (E)	Giroverkehr *m*	—	opérations de virement *f/pl*	bancogiro *m*	giro de valores *m*
transfer of ownership by way of security (E)	Sicherungsübereignung *f*	—	transfert à titre de sûreté *m*	cessione fiduciaria *f*	transmisión en garantía *f*
transfer of profits (E)	Gewinnabführung *f*	—	transfert du bénéfice *m*	trasferimento degli utili *m*	transferencia de beneficios *f*
transfer of resources (E)	Ressourcentransfer *m*	—	transfert de ressources *m*	trasferimento di risorse *m*	transferencia de recursos *f*
transfert (F)	Transfer *m*	transfer	—	trasferimento *m*	transferencia *f*
transfert à titre de sûreté (F)	Sicherungsübereignung *f*	transfer of ownership by way of security	—	cessione fiduciaria *f*	transmisión en garantía *f*
transfert de ressources (F)	Ressourcentransfer *m*	transfer of resources	—	trasferimento di risorse *m*	transferencia de recursos *f*
transfert du bénéfice (F)	Gewinnabführung *f*	transfer of profits	—	trasferimento degli utili *m*	transferencia de beneficios *f*
transformación de plazos (Es)	Fristentransformation *f*	maturity transformation	transformation d'échéances *f*	trasformazione termini di scadenza *f*	—
transformation d'échéances (F)	Fristentransformation *f*	maturity transformation	—	trasformazione termini di scadenza *f*	transformación de plazos *f*
transmisión en garantía (Es)	Sicherungsübereignung *f*	transfer of ownership by way of security	transfert à titre de sûreté *m*	cessione fiduciaria *f*	—

	D	E	F	I	Es
transmitted accounts (E)	durchlaufende Gelder n/pl	—	fonds en consignation m/pl	denaro d'ordine m	dinero en tránsito m
transmitted loans (E)	durchlaufende Kredite m/pl	—	crédits en consignation m/pl	crediti indiretti m/pl	crédito transitorio m
transparencia del balance (Es)	Bilanzklarheit f	accounting transparency	clarté du bilan f	chiarezza del bilancio f	—
trasferimenti collettivi di giro (I)	Girosammelverkehr m	collective securities deposit operations	opérations de virements collectives f/pl	—	giro central de valores m
trasferimento (I)	Transfer m	transfer	transfert m	—	transferencia f
trasferimento (I)	Überweisung f	remittance	virement m	—	transferencia f
trasferimento bancario (I)	Banküberweisung f	bank transfer	virement bancaire m	—	giro bancario m
trasferimento cumulativo (I)	Sammelüberweisung f	combined bank transfer	virement global m	—	transferencia colectiva f
trasferimento degli utili (I)	Gewinnabführung f	transfer of profits	transfert du bénéfice m	—	transferencia de beneficios f
trasferimento di giro (I)	Girogeschäft n	bank's transaction dealing with cashless transactions	opération de virement f	—	operación de giro f
trasferimento di risorse (I)	Ressourcentransfer m	transfer of resources	transfert de ressources m	—	transferencia de recursos f
trasferimento sostitutivo (I)	Ersatzüberweisung f	substitute transfer	virement de substitution m	—	transferencia sustitutiva f
trasferimento su piazza (I)	Platzübertragung f	local transfer	virement de place m	—	transferencia local f
trasferimento telegrafico (I)	telegrafische Auszahlung f	telegraphic transfer	payement télégraphique m	—	desembolso telegráfico m
trasformazione (I)	Umgründung f	reorganization	réorganisation d'une société f	—	reorganización f
trasformazione termini di scadenza (I)	Fristentransformation f	maturity transformation	transformation d'échéances f	—	transformación de plazos f
traslación de pérdidas (Es)	Verlustvortrag m	carry-forward of the losses	report des pertes m	riporto delle perdite m	—
Trassant (D)	—	drawer	tireur m	traente m	girador m
Trassat (D)	—	drawee	tiré m	trattario m	girado m
trassiert-eigener Scheck (D)	—	cheque drawn by the drawer himself	chèque tiré sur soimême m	assegno tratto su se stesso m	cheque girado a su propio cargo m
trassiert-eigener Wechsel (D)	—	bill drawn by the drawer himself	traite tirée sur soimême m	cambiale tratta su se stesso m	letra girada a su propio cargo f
Trassierung (D)	—	drawing	tirage m	traenza f	giro m
Trassierungskredit (D)	—	acceptance credit	crédit bancaire sur documents m	credito di traenza m	crédito de reembolso m
tratta (I)	Tratte f	draft	traite f	—	letra girada f
tratta collettiva (I)	Sammeltratte f	collective bill	traite globale f	—	libranza colectiva f
tratta documentaria (I)	Dokumententratte f	acceptance bill	traite documentaire f	—	letra documentaria f
trattamento della nazione più favorita (I)	Meistbegünstigung f	most-favoured nation treatment	régime de la nation la plus favorisée m	—	régimen de la nación más favorecida m
tratta per conto terzi (I)	Kommissionstratte f	bill of exchange drawn for third-party account	traite pour compte d'autrui f	—	giro por cuenta m
trattario (I)	Bezogener m	drawee	tiré m	—	librado m
trattario (I)	Trassat n	drawee	tiré m	—	girado m
trattazione di diritti d'opzione (I)	Bezugsrechthandel m	trading in subscription rights	marché des droits de souscription m	—	comercio de derechos de suscripción m
Tratte (D)	—	draft	traite f	tratta f	letra girada f
traveller's cheque (E)	Reisescheck m	—	chèque de voyage m	assegno turistico m	cheque de viaje m
traveller's letter of credit (E)	Reisekreditbrief m	—	lettre de crédit circulaire f	titolo di credito turistico m	carta de crédito viajero f
treasury (E)	Fiskus m	—	fisc m	fisco m	fisco m
Treasury bill (E)	Schatzwechsel m	—	effet du Trésor m	buono del tesoro m	letra de tesorería f
treasury bond (E)	Schatzanweisung f	—	bon du Trésor m	buono del tesoro m	bono del tesoro m

	D	E	F	I	Es
treasury bonds (E)	Schätze *m/pl*	—	obligations du Trésor *f/pl*	buoni del tesoro *m/pl*	bonos del tesoro *m/pl*
treasury stock (E)	Verwaltungsaktien *f/pl*	—	actions de Trésor *f/pl*	azioni amministrate *f/pl*	acciones de tesorería *f/pl*
Trendanalyse (D)	—	trend analysis	analyse de la tendance générale *f*	analisi di tendenza *f*	análisis de la tendencia *m*
trend analysis (E)	Trendanalyse *f*	—	analyse de la tendance générale *f*	analisi di tendenza *f*	análisis de la tendencia *m*
trend di base (I)	Basistrend *m*	basic trend	tendance de base *f*	—	tendencia de base *f*
trend in prices (E)	Preisentwicklung *f*	—	évolution des prix *f*	andamento dei prezzi *m*	evolución de los precios *f*
Trennbanksystem (D)	—	system of specialized banking	système des banques spécialisées *m*	sistema delle banche specializzate *m*	sistema de bancos especializados *m*
Tresor (D)	—	safe	coffre-fort *m*	cassaforte *f*	caja fuerte *f*
Treuhand (D)	—	trust	substitution fidéicommissaire *f*	amministrazione fiduciaria *f*	administración fiduciaria *f*
Treuhandanstalt (D)	—	institutional trustee	fiduciaire institué *m*	istituto fiduciario *m*	instituto fiduciario *m*
Treuhandbanken (D)	—	trust banks	banques dépositaires *f/pl*	banche fiduciarie *f/pl*	bancos fiduciarios *m/pl*
Treuhanddepots (D)	—	trust deposits	dépôts de consignation *m/pl*	depositi per conto altrui *m/pl*	depósitos fiduciarios *m/pl*
Treuhänder (D)	—	trustee	fiduciaire *m*	fiduciario *m*	fiduciario *m*
Treuhandfonds (D)	—	trust funds	fonds fiduciaire *m*	fondo immobiliare fiduciario *m*	fondos fiduciarios *m/pl*
Treuhand-gesellschaft (D)	—	trust company	société fiduciaire *f*	società fiduciaria *f*	sociedad fiduciaria *f*
Treuhandkredit (D)	—	loan on a trust basis	crédit fiduciaire *m*	credito indiretto *m*	crédito fiduciario *m*
triangular arbitrage (E)	Dreiecksarbitrage *f*	—	arbitrage triangulaire *m*	arbitraggio triangolare *m*	arbitraje triangular *m*
tributo sobre beneficios del crédito (Es)	Kreditgewinnabgabe *f*	debts profit levy	taxe sur les bénéfices de crédit *f*	ritenuta sugli utili dei crediti *f*	—
trieuse d'argent (F)	Geldsortiermaschine *f*	money sorting machine	—	macchina per la cernita delle monete *f*	máquina clasificadora de dinero *f*
troc (F)	Bartergeschäft *n*	barter transactions	—	operazione switch *f*	transacciones de trueque *f/pl*
troc (F)	Tausch *m*	barter	—	cambio *m*	trueque *m*
trockener Wechsel (D)	—	negotiable promissory note	billet à ordre *m*	pagherò *m*	pagaré *m*
troy ounce (E)	Feinunze *f*	—	once fine *f*	oncia *f*	onza fina *f*
troy weights (E)	Goldgewichte *n/pl*	—	poids de l'or *m/pl*	unità di misura per l'oro *f/pl*	pesos de oro *m/pl*
trueque (Es)	Tausch *m*	barter	troc *m*	cambio *m*	—
truffa (I)	Betrug *m*	fraud	fraude *f*	—	fraude *m*
trust (E)	Treuhand *f*	—	substitution fidéicommissaire *f*	amministrazione fiduciaria *f*	administración fiduciaria *f*
trust banks (E)	Treuhandbanken *f/pl*	—	banques dépositaires *f/pl*	banche fiduciarie *f/pl*	bancos fiduciarios *m/pl*
trust company (E)	Treuhandgesellschaft *f*	—	société fiduciaire *f*	società fiduciaria *f*	sociedad fiduciaria *f*
trust deposits (E)	Treuhanddepots *n/pl*	—	dépôts de consignation *m/pl*	depositi per conto altrui *m/pl*	depósitos fiduciarios *m/pl*
trustee (E)	Treuhänder *m*	—	fiduciaire *m*	fiduciario *m*	fiduciario *m*
trustee securities (E)	mündelsichere Papiere *n/pl*	—	valeur de tout repos *f*	valori di tutto riposo *m/pl*	títulos pupilares *m/pl*
trust funds (E)	Treuhandfonds *m*	—	fonds fiduciaire *m*	fondo immobiliare fiduciario *m*	fondos fiduciarios *m/pl*
trust investment (E)	Fondsanlagen *f/pl*	—	placements en fonds *m/pl*	investimenti di fondo d'investimento *m/pl*	inversión de fondos *f*
turnover (E)	Umsatz *m*	—	chiffre d'affaires *m*	fatturato *m*	cifra de facturación *f*
turnover balance (E)	Summenbilanz *f*	—	relevé des comptes généraux *m*	bilancio generale *m*	balance de sumas *f*
turnover of money (E)	Geldumsatz *m*	—	roulement de l'argent *m*	circolazione monetaria *f*	giro monetario *m*

	D	E	F	I	Es
tutela degli investimenti (I)	Investitionsschutz *m*	protection of investment	protection de l'investisseur *f*	—	protección del inversor *f*
tutela degli investitori (I)	Anlegerschutz *m*	protection for the investor	protection de l'investisseur *f*	—	protección del inversor *f*
tutela dei capitali (I)	Kapitalschutz *m*	capital protection	protection de capital *f*	—	protección del capital *f*
tutela del credito (I)	Kreditschutz *m*	protection of credit	protection du crédit *f*	—	protección del crédito *f*
two-tier foreign exchange market (E)	gespaltener Devisenmarkt *m*	—	marché des changes où existent deux taux de change pour une même monnaie *m*	mercato dei cambi multipli *m*	tipo de cambio múltiple *m*
types of capital investment (E)	Kapitalanlegearten *f/pl*	—	sortes d'investissement *f/pl*	tipi di investimento di capitale *m/pl*	tipos de inversión *m/pl*
types of deposit (E)	Depotarten *f/pl*	—	sortes de dépôts *f/pl*	tipi di deposito *m/pl*	tipos de depósito *m/pl*
types of issuing (E)	Emissionsarten *f/pl*	—	sortes d'émission *f/pl*	tipi di emissione *m/pl*	tipos de emisión *m/pl*
types of property (E)	Vermögensarten *f/pl*	—	catégories de patrimoine *f/pl*	tipi di patrimonio *m/pl*	clases de patrimonio *f/pl*
Überbringerscheck (D)	—	bearer cheque	chèque au porteur *m*	assegno al portatore *m*	cheque al portador *m*
Überbrückungskredit (D)	—	bridging loan	crédit transitoire *m*	credito per necessità di cassa *m*	crédito transitorio *m*
Überdividende (D)	—	super-dividend	superdividende *m*	dividendo addizionale *m*	dividendo adicional *m*
Überfinanzierung (D)	—	overfinancing	financement exagéré *m*	sovraccapitalizzazione *f*	financiación excesiva *f*
Überfremdung (D)	—	control by foreign capital	envahissement de capitaux étrangers *m*	inforestieramento *m*	extranjerización *f*
Überkapitalisierung (D)	—	overcapitalization	surcapitalisation *f*	sovraccapitalizzazione *f*	sobrecapitalización *f*
Übernahme (D)	—	accept	acceptation *f*	accettazione *f*	aceptación *f*
Übernahmegründung (D)	—	foundation in which founders take all shares	fondation simultanée *f*	costituzione simulatanea *f*	fundación de adquisición *f*
Übernahmekonsortium (D)	—	security-taking syndicate	syndicat bancaire de garantie *m*	consorzio di collocamento *m*	consorcio de suscripción *m*
Übernahmekurs (D)	—	underwriting price	cours payé par le souscripteur au syndicat des banquiers *m*	corso d'acquisto per il consorzio *m*	cambio de adquisición por el banco emisor *m*
Überschuldung (D)	—	excessive indebtedness	surendettement *m*	indebitamento eccessivo *m*	exceso de deudas *m*
Überschuldungsbilanz (D)	—	statement of overindebtedness	bilan de l'endettement *m*	stato di disavanzo patrimoniale *m*	balance de débitos *m*
Überschußreserve (D)	—	surplus reserve	réserve excédentaire *f*	riserva liquida *f*	reserva en exceso *f*
Überschuß-Sparen (D)	—	surplus saving	épargne d'excédents *f*	risparmio con ordine permanente *m*	ahorro de los importes excesivos *m*
Überweisung (D)	—	remittance	virement *m*	trasferimento *m*	transferencia *f*
Überweisungsscheck (D)	—	transfer cheque	chèque postal de virement *m*	bancogiro della banca centrale *m*	cheque de transferencia *m*
Überweisungsträger (D)	—	remittance slip	formulaire de virement *m*	nota d'accredito *f*	formulario de transferencia *m*
Überweisungsverkehr (D)	—	money transfer transactions	virements *m/pl*	bancogiro *m*	transferencias *f/pl*
Überzeichnung (D)	—	over-subscription	souscription surpassée *f*	sottoscrizione eccedente *f*	suscripción en exceso *f*
Überziehen eines Kontos (D)	—	overdraft	découvert de compte *m*	mandare un conto allo scoperto *m*	descubierto *m*
Überziehungskredit (D)	—	credit by way of overdraft	avance sur compte courant *f*	credito su base scoperta *m*	crédito en descubierto *m*
Überziehungsprovision (D)	—	overdraft commission	commission de découvert *f*	provvigione di scoperta *f*	comisión de giro en descubierto *f*
ufficio assegni (I)	Scheckabteilung *f*	cheque department	service des chèques *m*	—	sección de cheques *f*
ufficio borsa (I)	Börsenabteilung *f*	exchange department	service des valeurs en bourse *m*	—	sección de bolsa *f*

	D	E	F	I	Es
ufficio cambi (I)	Devisenabteilung f	foreign exchange department	service des devises m	—	sección de divisas f
ufficio cambi (I)	Wechselstube f	exchange office	bureau de change m	—	casa cambiaria f
ufficio commercio estero (I)	Außenhandels-abteilung f	export department	service étranger m	—	sección de comercio exterior f
ufficio consorzi (I)	Konsortialabteilung f	syndicate department	service de syndicats m	—	sección de consorcios f
ufficio conto correnti postali (I)	Postscheckamt n	postal giro centre	bureau de chèques postaux m	—	oficina de cheques postales f
ufficio crediti (I)	Kreditabteilung f	credit department	service du crédit et des prêts m	—	sección de crédito f
ufficio d'ammissione (I)	Zulassungsstelle f	admission board	commission pour l'admission des valeurs à la cote f	—	oficina de matrícula f
ufficio delle finanze (I)	Finanzamt n	inland revenue office	service de contributions m	—	hacienda f
ufficio di contabilità generale (I)	Hauptbuchhaltung f	chief accountancy	comptabilité générale f	—	contabilidad principal f
ufficio emissioni (I)	Emissionsabteilung f	issue department	service d'émission m	—	sección de emisión f
ufficio federale dei cartelli (I)	Bundeskartellamt n	Federal Cartel Authority	administration fédérale pour la réglementation des cartels f	—	Oficina Federal de Cártel f
ufficio incassi (I)	Inkasso-Abteilung f	collection department	service des encaissements m	—	sección de cobranza f
ufficio organizzazione (I)	Organisations-abteilung f	organization and methods department	service d'organisation m	—	sección de organización f
ufficio per titoli a reddito fisso (I)	Rentenabteilung f	annuity department	service des titres à revenu fixe m	—	sección de títulos de renta fija f
ufficio prelievi speciali (I)	Sonderziehungs-abteilung f	Special Drawing Rights Department	service de tirage spécial m	—	sección de giro especial f
ufficio revisioni (I)	Revisionsabteilung f	audit department	service de vérification m	—	sección de revisión f
ufficio risparmi (I)	Sparabteilung f	savings department	service d'épargne m	—	sección de ahorro f
ufficio titoli (I)	Effektenabteilung f	securities department	service des titres m	—	sección de efectos f
ufficio titoli (I)	Wertpapierabteilung f	securities department	service des valeurs m	—	sección de valores f
Ultimo (D)	—	end of the month	fin de mois f	fine mese m	fin de mes m
Ultimogeld (D)	—	last-day money	fonds remboursables à fin de mois m/pl	prestito per fine mese m	dinero a fin de mes m
Ultimogeschäft (D)	—	last-day business	opération à liquider en fin de mois f	contratto a fine ultimo m	operación a término con vencimiento a fin de mes f
umbral de la rentabilidad (Es)	Gewinnschwelle f	break-even point	seuil de rentabilité m	soglia dell'utile f	—
Umbuchung (D)	—	transfer of an entry	jeu d'écritures m	giro di partite m	asiento en otra cuenta m
Umgründung (D)	—	reorganization	réorganisation d'une société f	trasformazione f	reorganización f
Umlaufmarkt (D)	—	secondary market	marché secondaire m	mercato secondario m	mercado de circulación m
Umlaufvermögen (D)	—	current assets	capital de roulement m	circolante m	capital circulante m
Umsatz (D)	—	turnover	chiffre d'affaires m	fatturato m	cifra de facturación f
Umsatzprovision (D)	—	commission on turnover	commission sur le chiffre d'affaires f	provvigione sul fatturato f	comisión sobre la cifra de facturación f
Umsatzrentabilität (D)	—	net profit ratio	rendement du chiffre d'affaires m	rendimento del fatturato m	rentabilidad del volumen de negocios f
Umschuldung (D)	—	debt rescheduling	conversion de dette f	conversione del debito f	conversión de la deuda f
unanimity rule (E)	Einstimmigkeitsregel f	—	règle d'unanimité f	regola dell'unanimità f	regla de la unanimidad f
uncertainty (E)	Unsicherheit f	—	insécurité f	incertezza f	inseguridad f
uncertificated land charge (E)	Buchgrundschuld f	—	dette foncière inscrite au bureau foncier f	debito iscritto nel libro fondiario m	deuda inmobiliaria registrada f

	D	E	F	I	Es
uncertificated mortgage (E)	Buchhypothek f	—	hypothèque inscrite au livre foncier f	ipoteca iscritta f	hipoteca de registro f
uncollectible (E)	uneinbringliche Forderung f	—	créances irrécupérables f/pl	credito irrecuperabile m	crédito incobrable m
uncovered cheque (E)	ungedeckter Scheck m	—	chèque sans provision m	assegno senza copertura m	cheque descubierto m
uncovered credit (E)	ungedeckter Kredit m	—	crédit sur notoriété m	credito allo scoperto m	crédito descubierto m
undeclared securities (E)	Bodensatz m	—	titres non déclarés m	giacenza media di depositi a vista f	títulos no declarados m/pl
underemployment (E)	Unterbeschäftigung f	—	sous-emploi m	sottoccupazione f	subempleo m
underfinancing (E)	Unterfinanzierung f	—	financement insuffisant m	sottocapitalizzazione f	financiación insuficiente f
undertaking to deal exclusively with one bank or firm (E)	Ausschließlichkeits-erklärung f	—	déclaration d'exclusivité f	dichiarazione d'esclusività f	contrato de exclusividad m
under upward pressure (E)	im Aufwind	—	en progrès	con tendenza ascendente	con tendencia alcesta
undervaluation (E)	Unterbewertung f	—	sous-estimation f	sottovalutazione f	subvaloración f
underwriting business (E)	Emissionsgeschäft n	—	opération de place-ment de parts f	operazione d'emissione f	operación de emisión f
underwriting costs (E)	Emissionskosten pl	—	frais de l'émission m/pl	spese d'emissione f/pl	gastos de emisión m/pl
underwriting price (E)	Übernahmekurs m	—	cours payé par le souscripteur au syndicat des banquiers m	corso d'acquisto per il consorzio m	cambio de adquisición por el banco emisor m
underwriting prospectus (E)	Prospekt bei Emissionen m	—	prospectus d'émission m	prospetto d'emissione m	manifiesto de emisión m
underwriting syndicate (E)	Emissionssyndikat n	—	syndicat bancaire de garantie m	sindacato d'emissione m	sindicato de emisión m
underwriting syndicate (E)	Garantiekonsortium n	—	syndicat bancaire de garantie m	consorzio di garanzia m	consorcio de garantía m
underwriting syndicate (E)	Emissions-konsortium n	—	syndicat bancaire appuyant une émission m	consorzio d'emissione m	consorcio emisor m
undisclosed assignment (E)	stille Zession f	—	cession occulte f	cessione tacita f	cesión tácita f
Und-Konto (D)	—	joint account where all signatories must sign	compte joint m	conto comune m	cuenta colectiva f
unechtes Factoring (D)	—	false factoring	factoring non authentique m	factoring pro solvendo m	factoring falso m
uneinbringliche Forderung (D)	—	uncollectible	créances irrécupérables f/pl	credito irrecuperabile m	crédito incobrable m
unemployment benefit (E)	Arbeitslosengeld n	—	indemnité de chômage f	indennità di disoccupazione f	subsidio de desempleo m
uneven order (E)	krummer Auftrag m	—	ordre de lots irréguliers m	ordine irregolare m	orden de lotes irregulares f
unfair competition (E)	unlauterer Wettbewerb m	—	concurrence déloyale f	concorrenza sleale f	competencia desleal f
ungedeckter Kredit (D)	—	uncovered credit	crédit sur notoriété m	credito allo scoperto m	crédito descubierto m
ungedeckter Scheck (D)	—	uncovered cheque	chèque sans provision m	assegno senza copertura m	cheque descubierto m
unidad de compensación (Es)	Verrechnungseinheit f	clearing unit	unité de compte f	unità di conto f	—
unidad de cuenta (Es)	Rechnungseinheit f	unit of account	unité de compte f	unità di conto f	—
Unidad Monetaria Europea (Es)	Europäische Wäh-rungseinheit f	European Currency Unit [ECU]	Unité monétaire européenne f	Unità Monetaria Europea f	—
unificazione (I)	Unifizierung f	consolidation	consolidation f	—	consolidación f
unified balance sheet (E)	Einheitsbilanz f	—	bilan unique m	bilancio unico m	balance unitario m
unified company (E)	Einheitsgesellschaft f	—	société unitaire f	società unitaria f	sociedad unitaria f
Unifizierung (D)	—	consolidation	consolidation f	unificazione f	consolidación f

	D	E	F	I	Es
union (E)	Verbund m	—	union f	unione f	interconexión f
union (F)	Verbund m	union	—	unione f	interconexión f
unión aduanera (Es)	Zollunion f	customs union	union douanière f	unione doganale f	—
unione doganale (I)	Zollunion f	customs union	union douanière f	—	unión aduanera f
union douanière (F)	Zollunion f	customs union	—	unione doganale f	unión aduanera f
unione (I)	Verbund m	union	union f	—	interconexión f
unione monetaria (I)	Währungsunion f	monetary union	union monétaire f	—	unión monetaria f
Unión Europea (Es)	Europäische Union f	European Union	Union Européenne f	Unione Europea f	—
Unione Europea (I)	Europäische Union f	European Union	Union Européenne f	—	Unión Europea f
Union Européenne (F)	Europäische Union f	European Union	—	Unione Europea f	Unión Europea f
union monétaire (F)	Währungsunion f	monetary union	—	unione monetaria f	unión monetaria f
unión monetaria (Es)	Währungsunion f	monetary union	union monétaire f	unione monetaria f	—
unissued mortgage bonds still in trustee's hands (E)	nasse Stücke n/pl	—	titres d'une émission pas encore placés m/pl	titoli rimanenti di un'emissione m/pl	títulos todavía no emitidos m/pl
unità di conto (I)	Rechnungseinheit f	unit of account	unité de compte f	—	unidad de cuenta f
unità di conto (I)	Verrechnungseinheit f	clearing unit	unité de compte f	—	unidad de compensación f
unità di misura per l'oro (I)	Goldgewichte n/pl	troy weights	poids de l'or m/pl	—	pesos de oro m/pl
Unità Monetaria Europea (I)	Europäische Währungseinheit [ECU] f	European Currency Unit [ECU]	Unité monétaire européene f	—	Unidad Monetaria Europea [UME] f
unité de compte (F)	Rechnungseinheit f	unit of account	—	unità di conto f	unidad de cuenta f
unité de compte (F)	Verrechnungseinheit f	clearing unit	—	unità di conto f	unidad de compensación f
Unité monétaire européene (F)	Europäische Währungseinheit [ECU] f	European Currency Unit [ECU]	—	Unità Monetaria Europea f	Unidad Monetaria Europea [UME] f
unit of account (E)	Rechnungseinheit f	—	unité de compte f	unità di conto f	unidad de cuenta f
Universalbank (D)	—	all-round bank	banque universelle f	banca universale f	banco mixto m
unkompensierte Bilanz (D)	—	unoffset balance sheet	bilan non compensé m	bilancio senza compensazioni m	balance no compensado m
unlauterer Wettbewerb (D)	—	unfair competition	concurrence déloyale f	concorrenza sleale f	competencia desleal f
unlimited power (E)	Generalvollmacht f	—	pouvoir général m	procura generale f	poder general m
unofficial dealings (E)	Freiverkehr m	—	marché libre m	contrattazioni fuori borsa f/pl	mercado libre m
unofficial dealings committee (E)	Freiverkehrsausschuß m	—	comité du marché libre m	commissione operazioni fuori borsa f	comité de mercado libre m
unofficial market (E)	geregelter Freiverkehr m	—	marché libre m	mercato libero disciplinato m	mercado de valores extrabursátil m
unofficial stock market (E)	Kulisse f	—	coulisse f	operatori di borsa m/pl	bolsa extraoficial f
unoffset balance sheet (E)	unkompensierte Bilanz f	—	bilan non compensé m	bilancio senza compensazioni m	balance no compensado m
unpaid bill of exchange (E)	Rückwechsel m	—	traite retournée f	cambiale di ritorno f	letra de recambio f
urquoted securities (E)	amtlich nicht notierte Werte m/pl	—	titres non cotés officiellement m/pl	valori non quotati m/pl	valores no cotizados oficialmente m/pl
unquoted share (E)	nichtnotierte Aktie f	—	action non cotée f	azione non quotata ufficialmente f	acción no cotizada f
unrestricted retained earnings (E)	freie Rücklage f	—	réserve libre f	riserva eventuale f	reservas libres f/pl
unrestricted transferability (E)	Devinkulierung f	—	transférabilité illimitée f	svincolamento m	devinculación f
unsettled account (E)	offene Rechnung f	—	facture pas encore payée f	conto aperto m	factura pendiente f
Unsicherheit (D)	—	uncertainty	insécurité f	incertezza f	inseguridad f
Unterbeschäftigung (D)	—	underemployment	sous-emploi m	sottoccupazione f	subempleo m
Unterbewertung (D)	—	undervaluation	sous-estimation f	sottovalutazione f	subvaloración f
Unterbilanz (D)	—	deficit balance	bilan déficitaire m	bilancio in deficit m/pl	balance deficitario m

	D	E	F	I	Es
unter dem Strich (D)	—	in total	au total	fuori bilancio	en total
Unterfinanzierung (D)	—	underfinancing	financement insuffisant *m*	sottoccapitalizzazione *f*	financiación insuficiente *f*
Unterliquidität (D)	—	lack of liquidity	insufficance de liquidité *f*	liquidità insufficiente *f*	insuficiencia de liquidez *f*
Untermakler (D)	—	intermediate broker	sous-agent *m*	commissionario *m*	subagente *m*
Unternehmen (D)	—	enterprise	entreprise *f*	impresa *f*	empresa *f*
Unternehmens-konzentration (D)	—	business concentration	concentration d'entreprises *f*	concentrazione industriale *f*	concentración empresarial *f*
Unternehmungs-wert (D)	—	corporate value	valeur de l'entreprise *f*	valutazione del capitale *f*	valor de la empresa *m*
Unter-Pari-Emission (D)	—	issue below par	émission au-dessous du pair *f*	emissione sotto la pari *f*	emisión por debajo de la par *f*
Unterschlagung (D)	—	embezzlement	détournement *m*	appropriazione indebita *f*	defraudación *f*
Unterstützunglinie (D)	—	support level	ligne de soutien *f*	linea di sostegno *f*	línea de sostenimiento *f*
Untervollmacht (D)	—	delegated authority	sous-délégation *f*	procura rilasciata dal procuratore *f*	subpoder *m*
Untreue (D)	—	disloyalty	abus de confiance *m*	infedeltà *f*	infidelidad *f*
usage (E)	Usancen *f/pl*	—	usages *m/pl*	usanze *f/pl*	usanzas *f/pl*
usage commercial (F)	Handelsbrauch *m*	trade practice	—	usanza commerciale *f*	uso comercial *m*
usages (F)	Usancen *f/pl*	usage	—	usanze *f/pl*	usanzas *f/pl*
usages commerciaux (F)	Handelsusancen *f/pl*	custom of trade	—	usanze commerciali *f/pl*	uso comercial *m*
usages de la bourse (F)	Börsenusancen *f/pl*	stock exchange customs	—	usanze borsistiche *f/pl*	usos bursátiles *m/pl*
Usancen (D)	—	usage	usages *m/pl*	usanze *f/pl*	usanzas *f/pl*
Usancenhandel (D)	—	trading in foreign exchange	commerce de change *m*	commercio delle valute *m*	comercio de cambio *m*
usanza commerciale (I)	Handelsbrauch *m*	trade practice	usage commercial *m*	—	uso comercial *m*
usanza di pagamento (I)	Zahlungssitte *f*	payment habit	habitude de payement *f*	—	costumbre de pago *f*
usanzas (Es)	Usancen *f/pl*	usage	usages *m/pl*	usanze *f/pl*	—
usanze (I)	Usancen *f/pl*	usage	usages *m/pl*	—	usanzas *f/pl*
usanze borsistiche (I)	Börsenusancen *f/pl*	stock exchange customs	usages de la bourse *m/pl*	—	usos bursátiles *m/pl*
usanze commerciali (I)	Handelsusancen *f/pl*	custom of trade	usages commerciaux *m/pl*	—	uso comercial *m*
U-Schätze (D)	—	non-interest bearing Treasury bond	obligations du Trésor ne produisant pas d'intérêts *f/pl*	buoni del tesoro infruttiferi *m/pl*	letras del Tesoro sin interés *f/pl*
uso comercial (Es)	Handelsusancen *f/pl*	custom of trade	usages commerciaux *m/pl*	usanze commerciali *f/pl*	—
uso comercial (Es)	Handelsbrauch *m*	trade practice	usage commercial *m*	usanza commerciale *f*	—
usos bursátiles (Es)	Börsenusancen *f/pl*	stock exchange customs	usages de la bourse *m/pl*	usanze borsistiche *f/pl*	
usuary (E)	Wucher *m*	—	usure *f*	usura *f*	usura *f*
usufruct (E)	Nießbrauch *m*	—	usufruit *m*	usufrutto *m*	usufructo *m*
usufructo (Es)	Nießbrauch *m*	usufruct	usufruit *m*	usufrutto *m*	—
usufructury right (E)	Nutzungsrecht *n*	—	droit de jouissance *m*	diritto di godimento *m*	derecho de uso *m*
usufruit (F)	Nießbrauch *m*	usufruct	—	usufrutto *m*	usufructo *m*
usufrutto (I)	Nießbrauch *m*	usufruct	usufruit *m*	—	usufructo *m*
usura (Es)	Wucher *m*	usury	usure *f*	usura *f*	—
usura (I)	Wucher *m*	usury	usure *f*	—	usura *f*
usure (F)	Wucher *m*	usury	—	usura *f*	usura *f*
usure en matière de prêt à intérêt (F)	Zinswucher *m*	usury	—	interesse usurario *m*	interés usurario *m*

	D	E	F	I	Es
usury (E)	Zinswucher *m*	—	usure en matière de prêt à intérêt *f*	interesse usurario *m*	interés usurario *m*
utile (I)	Gewinn *m*	profit	bénéfice *m*	—	beneficio *m*
utile contabile (I)	Buchgewinn *m*	book profit	bénéfice comptable *m*	—	beneficio contable *m*
utile di borsa (I)	Kursgewinn *m*	price gain	plus-value sur les cours *f*	—	plusvalía de cotización *m*
utile di coniatura (I)	Münzgewinn *m*	seignorage	monnayage *m*	—	monedaje *m*
utile di rimborso (I)	Tilgungsgewinn *m*	gain of redemption	bénéfice d'amortissement *m*	—	beneficio de amortización *m*
utile di speculazione (I)	Spekulationsgewinn *m*	speculative profit	gain spéculatif *m*	—	beneficio especulativo *m*
utile fittizio (I)	Scheingewinn *m*	fictitious profit	gain fictif *m*	—	beneficio simulado *m*
utile lordo (I)	Bruttogewinn *m*	gross profit	bénéfice brut *m*	—	beneficio bruto *m*
utile rettificato (I)	bereinigter Gewinn *m*	actual profit	produit net d'exploitation *m*	—	beneficio real *m*
utilidad marginal (Es)	Grenznutzen *m*	marginal utility	utilité marginale *f*	rendita marginale *f*	—
utilidad monetaria (Es)	Geldnutzen *m*	utility of funds	utilité monétaire *f*	utilità del denaro *f*	—
utilità del denaro (I)	Geldnutzen *m*	utility of funds	utilité monétaire *f*	—	utilidad monetaria *f*
utilité marginale (F)	Grenznutzen *m*	marginal utility	—	rendita marginale *f*	utilidad marginal *f*
utilité monétaire (F)	Geldnutzen *m*	utility of funds	—	utilità del denaro *f*	utilidad monetaria *f*
utility of funds (E)	Geldnutzen *m*	—	utilité monétaire *f*	utilità del denaro *f*	utilidad monetaria *f*
vacant (E)	vakant	—	vacant	vacante	vacante
vacant (F)	vakant	vacant	—	vacante	vacante
vacante (Es)	vakant	vacant	vacant	vacante	—
vacante (I)	vakant	vacant	vacant	—	vacante
vaglia bancario (I)	Bankanweisung *f*	bank money order	mandat de payement bancaire *m*	—	pago bancario *m*
vaglia espresso (I)	Eilüberweisung *f*	rapid money transfer	virement accéléré *m*	—	giro urgente *m*
vaglia postale (I)	Postanweisung *f*	postal money order	mandat-poste *m*	—	giro postal *m*
vakant (D)	—	vacant	vacant	vacante	vacante
valable aujourd'hui (F)	heute gültig	valid today	—	valido un giorno	válido hoy
vale de ahorro (Es)	Spargeschenk-gutschein *m*	savings gift credit voucher	bon d'épargne *m*	buono regalo di risparmio *m*	—
valeur (F)	Wert *m*	value	—	valore *m*	valor *m*
valeur (F)	Wertpapier *n*	security	—	titolo di credito *m*	valor *m*
valeur actuelle (F)	Barwert *m*	value in cash	—	valore di cassa *m*	valor efectivo *m*
valeur actuelle (F)	Gegenwartswert *m*	present value	—	valore attuale *m*	valor actual *m*
valeur à revenu fixe (F)	Rentenwert *m*	fixed-interest security	—	titolo a reddito fisso *m*	título de renta fija *m*
valeur au tarif (F)	Tarifwert *m*	tariff value	—	titolo industria di pubblica utilità *m*	valor arancelario *m*
valeur commerciale (F)	Geschäftswert *m*	value of the subject matter at issue	—	avviamento *m*	valor comercial *m*
valeur compensée (F)	kompensierte Valuta *f*	value compensated	—	valuta compensata *f*	valuta compensada *f*
valeur compensée (F)	Valuta kompensiert	value compensated	—	valuta compensata *f*	valuta compensada *f*
valeur comptable (F)	Buchwert *m*	accounting value	—	valore di libro *m*	valor contable *m*
valeur comptable (F)	Bilanzkurs *m*	book value	—	prezzo di bilancio *m*	valor contable *m*
valeur d'acquisition (F)	Anschaffungswert *m*	acquisition value	—	valore d'acquisto *m*	valor de adquisición *m*
valeur d'arbitrage (F)	Arbitragewert *m*	arbitrage value	—	titolo arbitrale *m*	valor de arbitraje *m*
valeur de l'argent (F)	Geldwert *m*	value of money	—	valore monetario *m*	valor monetario *m*
valeur de l'entreprise (F)	Unternehmungs-wert *m*	corporate value	—	valutazione del capitale *f*	valor de la empresa *m*
valeur de l'inventaire (F)	Inventarwert *m*	inventory value	—	valore d'inventario *m*	valor del inventario *m*
valeur de remplacement (F)	Reproduktionswert *m*	reproduction value	—	valore reale *m*	valor de reproducción *m*
valeur des éléments incorporels (F)	immaterielle Werte *m/pl*	intangible assets	—	valori immateriali *m/pl*	valores inmateriales *m/pl*

	D	E	F	I	Es
valeur des fonds en dépôt (F)	Verwahrungsbetrag *m*	value of custody	—	importo di deposito *m*	valor de los fondos en depósito *m*
valeur de tout repos (F)	mündelsichere Papiere *n/pl*	trustee securities	—	valori di tutto riposo *m/pl*	títulos pupilares *m/pl*
valeur du gage (F)	Besicherungswert *m*	collateral value	—	valore di garanzia di credito *m*	valor colateral *m*
valeur d'une chose mesurée à son rendement (F)	Ertragswert *m*	capitalized value	—	valore del reddito *m*	valor de la renta *m*
valeur d'usage (F)	Gebrauchswert *m*	value in use	—	valore d'uso *m*	valor de uso *m*
valeur en capital (F)	Kapitalwert *m*	net present value	—	valore del capitale *m*	valor capitalizado *m*
valeur escomptée (F)	Erwartungswert *m*	anticipation term	—	valore stimato *m*	valor esperado *m*
valeur externe de la monnaie (F)	Außenwert der Währung *m*	external value of the currency	—	valore esterno della valuta *m*	valor de la moneda en el exterior *m*
valeur fixe (F)	Festwert *m*	fixed value	—	valore costante *m*	precio fijo *m*
valeur globale intrinsèque (F)	Einheitswert *m*	standard value	—	titolo unitario *m*	valor unitario *m*
valeur habituelle (F)	gemeiner Wert *m*	market value	—	prezzo teorico *m*	valor común *m*
valeur informative (F)	Informationswert *m*	information value	—	valore dell'informazione *m*	valor informativo *m*
valeur intrinsèque (F)	innerer Wert *m*	intrinsic value	—	valore intrinseco *m*	valor intrínseco *m*
valeur moyenne (F)	Mittelwert *m*	average value	—	valore medio *m*	valor medio *m*
valeur négociable (F)	lieferbares Wertpapier *n*	deliverable security	—	titolo negoziabile *m*	título de buena entrega *m*
valeur négociée au marché officiel (F)	Schrankenwert *m*	officially quoted security	—	valori ammessi alla quotazione officiale *m/pl*	título oficialmente cotizado *m*
valeur négociée sur le marché libre (F)	Kulissenwert *m*	quotation on the unofficial market	—	titolo del mercato ristretto *m*	valor de la bolsa extraoficial *m*
valeur nominale (F)	Nominalwert *m*	face value	—	valore nominale *m*	valor nominal *m*
valeur nominale (F)	Nennwert *m*	nominal value	—	valore nominale *m*	valor nominal *m*
valeur portée au bilan (F)	Bilanzwert *m*	balance sheet value	—	valore di bilancio *m*	valor de balance *m*
valeur régionale (F)	Lokalpapier *n*	security only traded on a regional stock exchange	—	titolo locale *m*	título local *m*
valeurs (F)	Valoren *pl*	securities	—	valori *m/pl*	valores *m/pl*
valeurs à terme (F)	Terminpapiere *n/pl*	forward securities	—	titoli ammessi a contratti futuri *m/pl*	títulos a plazo *m/pl*
valeurs de placement (F)	Anlagepapiere *n/pl*	investment securities	—	titoli d'investimento *m/pl*	valores de inversión *m/pl*
valeurs endossables (F)	indossable Wertpapiere *n/pl*	endorsable securities	—	titoli girabili *m/pl*	títulos endosables *m/pl*
valeurs étrangères (F)	ausländisches Wertpapier *n*	foreign security	—	titolo estero *m*	título extranjero *m*
valeurs extrêmement spéculatives (F)	Exoten *m/pl*	highly speculative securities	—	titoli provenienti da paesi esotici *m/pl*	valores especulativos *m/pl*
valeurs immobilisées (F)	Anlagevermögen *n*	fixed assets	—	attivo fisso *m*	activo fijo *m*
valeurs immobilisées financières (F)	Finanzanlagevermögen *n*	financial assets	—	investimenti finanziari *m/pl*	inversiones financieras *f/pl*
valeurs mobilières (F)	Effekten *pl*	securities	—	titoli *m/pl*	efectos *m/pl*
valeurs négociées en bourse (F)	börsengängige Wertpapiere *n/pl*	quoted securities	—	titoli ammessi in borsa *m/pl*	títulos cotizados en bolsa *m/pl*
valeur spéculative (F)	Spekulationspapier *n*	speculative security	—	titolo speculativo *m*	título especulativo *m*
valeurs réalisables à court terme ou disponibles (F)	Barvermögen *n*	cash assets	—	capitale liquido *m*	activo efectivo *m*
valeur sur le marché (F)	Marktwert *m*	fair market value	—	valore di mercato *m*	valor de mercado *m*
valeur variable (F)	variabler Wert *m*	variable value	—	titolo di libera contrattazione *m*	valor variable *m*
valeur vénale (F)	Verkaufswert *m*	selling value	—	valore di realizzo *m*	valor de venta *m*

	D	E	F	I	Es
validation des titres d'emprunt émis en monnaie étrangère (F)	Auslandsbonds-bereinigung *f*	external bonds validation	—	correzione bonds in valuta estera *f*	convalidación de obligaciones en el exterior *f*
válido hoy (Es)	heute gültig	valid today	valable aujourd'hui	valido un giorno	—
valido un giorno (I)	heute gültig	valid today	valable aujourd'hui	—	válido hoy
valid today (E)	heute gültig	—	valable aujourd'hui	valido un giorno	válido hoy
valor (Es)	Wert *m*	value	valeur *f*	valore *m*	—
valor (Es)	Wertpapier *n*	security	valeur *f*	titolo di credito *m*	—
valor actual (Es)	Gegenwartswert *m*	present value	valeur actuelle *f*	valore attuale *m*	—
valor arancelario (Es)	Tarifwert *m*	tariff value	valeur au tarif *f*	titolo industria di pubblica utilità *m*	—
valor capitalizado (Es)	Kapitalwert *m*	net present value	valeur en capital *f*	valore del capitale *m*	—
valor colateral (Es)	Besicherungswert *m*	collateral value	valeur du gage *f*	valore di garanzia di credito *m*	—
valor comercial (Es)	Warenpapier *n*	document of title	effet de commerce *m*	titolo rappresentativo di merci *m*	—
valor comercial (Es)	Geschäftswert *m*	value of the subject matter at issue	valeur commerciale *f*	avviamento *m*	—
valor común (Es)	gemeiner Wert *m*	market value	valeur habituelle *f*	prezzo teorico *m*	—
valor contable (Es)	Buchwert *m*	accounting value	valeur comptable *f*	valore di libro *m*	—
valor contable (Es)	Bilanzkurs *m*	book value	valeur comptable *f*	prezzo di bilancio *m*	—
valor de adquisición (Es)	Anschaffungswert *m*	acquisition value	valeur d'acquisition *f*	valore d'acquisto *m*	—
valor de arbitraje (Es)	Arbitragewert *m*	arbitrage value	valeur d'arbitrage *f*	titolo arbitrale *m*	—
valor de balance (Es)	Bilanzwert *m*	balance sheet value	valeur portée au bilan *f*	valore di bilancio *m*	—
valor de emisión (Es)	Ausgabewert *m*	nominal value	cours d'émission *m*	valore d'emissione *m*	—
valor de interés (Es)	Interessenwert *m*	vested interest stock	action qui fait l'objet d'un achat par un groupe intéressé *f*	titolo primario *m*	—
valor de la bolsa extraoficial (Es)	Kulissenwert *m*	quotation on the unofficial market	valeur négociée sur le marché libre *f*	titolo del mercato ristretto *m*	—
valor de la empresa (Es)	Unternehmungs-wert *m*	corporate value	valeur de l'entreprise *f*	valutazione del capitale *f*	—
valor de la moneda en el exterior (Es)	Außenwert der Währung *m*	external value of the currency	valeur externe de la monnaie *f*	valore esterno della valuta *f*	—
valor de la renta (Es)	Ertragswert *m*	capitalized value	valeur d'une chose mesurée à son rendement *m*	valore del reddito *m*	—
valor del inventario (Es)	Inventarwert *m*	inventory value	valeur de l'inventaire *f*	valore d'inventario *m*	—
valor de los fondos en depósito (Es)	Verwahrungsbetrag *m*	value of custody	valeur des fonds en dépôt *f*	importo di deposito *m*	—
valor de mercado (Es)	Marktwert *m*	fair market value	valeur sur le marché *f*	valore di mercato *m*	—
valores de primera clase (Es)	Primapapiere *n/pl*	prime papers	effets de tout premier ordre *m/pl*	carte commerciali di prim'ordine *f/pl*	—
valor de reproducción (Es)	Reproduktionswert *m*	reproduction value	valeur de remplacement *f*	valore reale *m*	—
valor de uso (Es)	Gebrauchswert *m*	value in use	valeur d'usage *f*	valore d'uso *m*	—
valor de venta (Es)	Verkaufswert *m*	selling value	valeur vénale *f*	valore di realizzo *m*	—
valore (I)	Wert *m*	value	valeur *f*	—	valor *m*
valore aritmetico diritto d'opzione (I)	Bezugsrechtsparität *f*	subscription rights parity	parité des droits de souscription *f*	—	paridad de derecho de suscripción *f*
valore attuale (I)	Gegenwartswert *m*	present value	valeur actuelle *f*	—	valor actual *m*
valore costante (I)	Festwert *m*	fixed value	valeur fixe *f*	—	precio fijo *m*
valore d'acquisto (I)	Anschaffungswert *m*	acquisition value	valeur d'acquisition *f*	—	valor de adquisición *m*
valore del capitale (I)	Kapitalwert *m*	net present value	valeur en capital *f*	—	valor capitalizado *m*
valore dell'informazione (I)	Informationswert *m*	information value	valeur informative *f*	—	valor informativo *m*
valore del reddito (I)	Ertragswert *m*	capitalized value	valeur d'une chose mesurée à son rendement *m*	—	valor de la renta *m*

	D	E	F	I	Es
valore d'emissione (I)	Ausgabewert *m*	nominal value	cours d'émission *m*	—	valor de emisión *m*
valore di bilancio (I)	Bilanzwert *m*	balance sheet value	valeur portée au bilan *f*	—	valor de balance *m*
valore di cassa (I)	Barwert *m*	value in cash	valeur actuelle *f*	—	valor efectivo *m*
valore di garanzia di credito (I)	Besicherungswert *m*	collateral value	valeur du gage *f*	—	valor colateral *m*
valore di libro (I)	Buchwert *m*	accounting value	valeur comptable *f*	—	valor contable *m*
valore di mercato (I)	Marktwert *m*	fair market value	valeur sur le marché *f*	—	valor de mercado *m*
valore d'inventario (I)	Inventarwert *m*	inventory value	valeur de l'inventaire *f*	—	valor del inventario *m*
valore di realizzo (I)	Verkaufswert *m*	selling value	valeur vénale *f*	—	valor de venta *m*
valore d'uso (I)	Gebrauchswert *m*	value in use	valeur d'usage *f*	—	valor de uso *m*
valore esterno della valuta (I)	Außenwert der Währung *m*	external value of the currency	valeur externe de la monnaie *f*	—	valor de la moneda en el exterior *m*
valor efectivo (Es)	Barwert *m*	value in cash	valeur actuelle *f*	valore di cassa *m*	—
valore intrinseco (I)	innerer Wert *m*	intrinsic value	valeur intrinsèque *f*	—	valor intrínseco *m*
valore massimo di voto (I)	Höchststimmrecht *n*	maximum voting right	droit de vote maximum *m*	—	límite máximo de votos *m*
valore medio (I)	Mittelwert *m*	average value	valeur moyenne *f*	—	valor medio *m*
valore monetario (I)	Geldwert *m*	value of money	valeur de l'argent *f*	—	valor monetario *m*
Valoren (D)	—	securities	valeurs *f/pl*	valori *m/pl*	valores *m/pl*
valore nominale (I)	Nennwert *m*	nominal value	valeur nominale *f*	—	valor nominal *m*
valore nominale (I)	Nominalwert *m*	face value	valeur nominale *f*	—	valor nominal *m*
valore promettente reddito futuro (I)	Hoffnungswert *m*	speculative security	titre spéculatif *m*	—	título especulativo *m*
valore reale (I)	Reproduktionswert *m*	reproduction value	valeur de remplacement *f*	—	valor de reproducción *m*
valores (Es)	Valoren *pl*	securities	valeurs *f/pl*	valori *m/pl*	—
valores a la orden por elección (Es)	gewillkürte Orderpapiere *n/pl*	instruments to order by option	titres à ordre par destination *m/pl*	titoli all'ordine non per legge *m/pl*	—
valores a la orden por naturaleza (Es)	geborene Orderpapiere *n/pl*	instruments to order by law	titres à ordre par nature *m/pl*	titoli all'ordine per legge *m/pl*	—
valores de alta cotización (Es)	schwere Papiere *n/pl*	heavy-priced securities	titres chers *m/pl*	titoli pesanti *m/pl*	—
valores de fianza (Es)	Kautionseffekten *pl*	guarantee securities	papiers de sûreté *m/pl*	titoli di deposito cauzionale *m/pl*	—
valores de inversión (Es)	Anlagepapiere *n/pl*	investment securities	valeurs de placement *f/pl*	titoli d'investimento *m/pl*	—
valores de renta fija reembolsados con una prima (Es)	Agiopapiere *n/pl*	securities redeemable at a premium	obligations remboursables avec prime *f/pl*	titoli a premio *m/pl*	—
valores especulativos (Es)	Exoten *m/pl*	highly speculative securities	valeurs extrêmement spéculatives *f/pl*	titoli provenienti da paesi esotici *m/pl*	—
valor esperado (Es)	Erwartungswert *m*	anticipation term	valeur escomptée *f*	valore stimato *m*	—
valores inmateriales (Es)	immaterielle Werte *m/pl*	intangible assets	valeur des éléments incorporels *f*	valori immateriali *m/pl*	—
valores no cotizados oficialmente (Es)	amtlich nicht notierte Werte *m/pl*	unquoted securities	titres non cotés officiellement *m/pl*	valori non quotati *m/pl*	—
valores pendientes de pago (Es)	Float *m*	float	float *m*	float *m*	—
valores propios (Es)	eigene Effekten *pl*	own security holdings	titres propres *m/pl*	titoli propri *m/pl*	—
valores punteros (Es)	Blue Chips *m/pl*	blue chips	blue chips *m/pl*	blue chips *m/pl*	—
valore stimato (I)	Erwartungswert *m*	anticipation term	valeur escomptée *f*	—	valor esperado *m*
valori (I)	Valoren *pl*	securities	valeurs *f/pl*	—	valores *m/pl*
valori ammessi alla quotazione ufficiale (I)	Schrankenwert *m*	officially quoted security	valeur négociée au marché officiel *f*	—	título oficialmente cotizado *m*
valori di tutto riposo (I)	mündelsichere Papiere *n/pl*	trustee securities	valeur de tout repos *f*	—	títulos pupilares *m/pl*
valori immateriali (I)	immaterielle Werte *m/pl*	intangible assets	valeur des éléments incorporels *f*	—	valores inmateriales *m/pl*

valor informativo

428

	D	E	F	I	Es
valor informativo (Es)	Informationswert *m*	information value	valeur informative *f*	valore dell'informazione *m*	—
valori non quotati (I)	amtlich nicht notierte Werte *m/pl*	unquoted securities	titres non cotés officiellement *m/pl*	—	valores no cotizados oficialmente *m/pl*
valor intrínseco (Es)	innerer Wert *m*	intrinsic value	valeur intrinsèque *f*	valore intrinseco *m*	—
valorisation (F)	Bewertung *f*	valuation	—	valutazione *f*	evaluación *f*
valor medio (Es)	Mittelwert *m*	average value	valeur moyenne *f*	valore medio *m*	—
valor monetario (Es)	Geldwert *m*	value of money	valeur de l'argent *f*	valore monetario *m*	—
valor nominal (Es)	Nominalwert *m*	face value	valeur nominale *f*	valore nominale *m*	—
valor nominal (Es)	Nennwert *m*	nominal value	valeur nominale *f*	valore nominale *m*	—
valor unitario (Es)	Einheitswert *m*	standard value	valeur globale intrinsèque *f*	titolo unitario *m*	—
valor variable (Es)	variabler Wert *m*	variable value	valeur variable *f*	titolo di libera contrattazione *m*	—
valuation (E)	Bewertung *f*	—	valorisation *f*	valutazione *f*	evaluación *f*
value (E)	Wert *m*	—	valeur *f*	valore *m*	valor *m*
value-added tax (E)	Mehrwertsteuer *f*	—	taxe à la valeur ajoutée *f*	imposta sul valore aggiunto *f*	impuesto sobre el valor añadido *m*
value compensated (E)	kompensierte Valuta *f*	—	valeur compensée *f*	valuta compensata *f*	valuta compensada *f*
value compensated (E)	Valuta kompensiert	—	valeur compensée *f*	valuta compensata *f*	valuta compensada *f*
value guarantee (E)	Wertsicherung *f*	—	garantie de valeur *f*	garanzia del valore *f*	garantía de valor *f*
value in cash (E)	Barwert *m*	—	valeur actuelle *f*	valore di cassa *m*	valor efectivo *m*
value in use (E)	Gebrauchswert *m*	—	valeur d'usage *f*	valore d'uso *m*	valor de uso *m*
value of custody (E)	Verwahrungsbetrag *m*	—	valeur des fonds en dépôt *f*	importo di deposito *m*	valor de los fondos en depósito *m*
value of money (E)	Geldwert *m*	—	valeur de l'argent *f*	valore monetario *m*	valor monetario *m*
value of the subject matter at issue (E)	Geschäftswert *m*	—	valeur commerciale *f*	avviamento *m*	valor comercial *m*
Valuta (D)	—	foreign exchange	monnaie étrangère *f*	valuta *f*	moneda extranjera *f*
valuta (Es)	Wertstellung *f*	availability date	datation de la valeur en compte *f*	valuta *f*	—
valuta (I)	Wertstellung *f*	availability date	datation de la valeur	en compte *f*	— valuta *f*
valuta (I)	Valutierung *f*	fixing of exchange rate	fixation des cours de change *f*	—	fijación del tipo de cambio *f*
valuta (I)	Valuta *f*	foreign exchange	monnaie étrangère *f*	—	moneda extranjera *f*
Valuta-Akzept (D)	—	foreign currency accept	traite libellée en monnaie étrangère *f*	accettazione in valuta estera *f*	aceptación en moneda extranjera *f*
Valuta-Anleihen (D)	—	loan in foreign currency	emprunt émis en monnaie étrangère *m*	prestiti in valuta estera *m/pl*	empréstitos en moneda extranjera *m/pl*
valuta a regime di controllo (I)	gebundene Währung *f*	linked currency	monnaie liée *f*	—	moneda vinculada *f*
valuta aurea (I)	Goldwährung *f*	gold currency	monnaie à couverture or *f*	—	moneda oro *f*
valuta compensada (Es)	kompensierte Valuta *f*	value compensated	valeur compensée *f*	valuta compensata *f*	—
valuta compensada (Es)	Valuta kompensiert	value compensated	valeur compensée *f*	valuta compensata *f*	—
valuta compensata (I)	Valuta kompensiert	value compensated	valeur compensée *f*	—	valuta compensada *f*
valuta compensata (I)	kompensierte Valuta *f*	value compensated	valeur compensée *f*	—	valuta compensada *f*
valuta d'argento (I)	Silberwährung *f*	silver standard	monnaie en argent *f*	—	patrón plata *m*
valuta d'investimento (I)	Anlagewährung *f*	currency of investment	monnaie d'investissement *f*	—	moneda de inversión *f*
valuta estera (I)	Devisen *f/pl*	currency	devises *f/pl*	—	divisas *f/pl*
valuta estera (I)	Sorte *f*	foreign notes and coins	devise *f*	—	moneda extranjera *f*
valuta estera da esportazioni (I)	Exportdevisen *f/pl*	export exchange	devises obtenues par l'exportation *f/pl*	—	divisas obtenidas mediante la exportación *f/pl*
valuta forte (I)	harte Währung *f*	hard currency	monnaie forte *f*	—	moneda dura *f*

	D	E	F	I	Es
Valutageschäft (D)	—	currency transactions	opération de change *f*	operazione di cambio *f*	operación de divisas *f*
Valutaklausel (D)	—	foreign currency clause	mention de la valeur fournie *f*	clausola valutaria *f*	cláusula de valuta *f*
Valuta kompensiert (D)	—	value compensated	valeur compensée *f*	valuta compensata *f*	valuta compensada *f*
Valutakonto (D)	—	foreign currency account	compte en monnaie étrangère *m*	conto valutario *m*	cuenta de moneda extranjera *f*
Valutakredit (D)	—	foreign currency loan	crédit en monnaie étrangère *m*	credito in valuta estera *m*	crédito en divisas *m*
Valutakupon (D)	—	foreign currency coupon	coupon payable en monnaie étrangère *m*	cedola di un titolo estero *f*	cupón de divisas *m*
valuta libera (I)	freie Währung *f*	freely convertible currency	monnaie librement convertible *f*	—	moneda libre *f*
valuta media (I)	Durchschnittsvaluta *f*	average value date	datation moyenne de la valeur en compte *f*	—	cambio medio *m*
valuta metallica (I)	Metallwährung *f*	metallic currency	monnaie métallique *f*	—	patrón metálico *m*
valuta paniere (I)	Korbwährung *f*	basket currency	monnaie de panier *f*	—	moneda de cesta *f*
Valutapolitik (D)	—	currency policy	politique monétaire *f*	politica valutaria *f*	política de divisas *f*
Valutarisiko (D)	—	exchange risk	risque de perte au change *m*	rischio di cambio *m*	riesgo en el cambio *m*
Valutaschuld-schein (D)	—	foreign currency certificate of indebtedness	titre de créance en monnaie étrangère *m*	titolo di credito in valuta estera *m*	pagaré en moneda extranjera *m*
valutazione (I)	Wertermittlung *f*	determination of the value	évaluation *f*	—	evaluación del valor *f*
valutazione (I)	Bewertung *f*	valuation	valorisation *f*	—	evaluación *f*
valutazione del capitale (I)	Unternehmungswert *m*	corporate value	valeur de l'entreprise *f*	—	valor de la empresa *m*
valutazione del diritto d'opzione (I)	Bezugsrechts-bewertung *f*	subscription rights evaluation	évaluation des droits de souscription *f*	—	evaluación del derecho de suscripción *f*
Valuten (D)	—	foreign exchange	coupons de titres étrangers *m/pl*	cedole di titoli esteri *f/pl*	moneda extranjera *f*
valute pregiate (I)	deckungsfähige Devisen *f/pl*	foreign currencies eligible as cover	devises aptes à servir de couverture *f/pl*	—	divisas cubiertas por el banco emisor *f/pl*
Valutierung (D)	—	fixing of exchange rate	fixation des cours de change *f*	valuta *f*	fijación del tipo de cambio *f*
variabile di flusso (I)	Stromgröße *f*	rate of flow	volume du flux *m*	—	tasa de flujo *f*
variabile endogena (I)	endogene Variable *f*	endogenous variable	variable endogène *f*	—	variable endógena *f*
variable endógena (Es)	endogene Variable *f*	endogenous variable	variable endogène *f*	variabile endogena *f*	—
variable endogène (F)	endogene Variable *f*	endogenous variable	—	variabile endogena *f*	variable endógena *f*
variable market (E)	variabler Markt *m*	—	marché à cours variables *m*	mercato delle libere contrattazioni *m*	mercado variable *m*
variable price (E)	variabler Kurs *m*	—	cours variable *m*	corso variabile *m*	cotización variable *f*
variable price quoting (E)	fortlaufende Notierung *f*	—	cotation variable *f*	libere contrattazioni *f/pl*	cotización variable *f*
variable rate of interest (E)	variabler Zins *m*	—	intérêt variable *m*	interesse variabile *m*	interés variable *m*
variabler Kurs (D)	—	variable price	cours variable *m*	corso variabile *m*	cotización variable *f*
variabler Markt (D)	—	variable market	marché à cours variables *m*	mercato delle libere contrattazioni *m*	mercado variable *m*
variabler Wert (D)	—	variable value	valeur variable *f*	titolo di libera contrattazione *m*	valor variable *m*
variabler Zins (D)	—	variable rate of interest	intérêt variable *m*	interesse variabile *m*	interés variable *m*
variable value (E)	variabler Wert *m*	—	valeur variable *f*	titolo di libera contrattazione *m*	valor variable *m*
variaciones de las partidas (Es)	Bestands-veränderung *f*	inventory change	variation des existences *f*	movimento di scorte *m*	—
variance (E)	Varianz *f*	—	variance *f*	varianza *f*	varianza *f*
variance (F)	Varianz *f*	variance	—	varianza *f*	varianza *f*
Varianz (D)	—	variance	variance *f*	varianza *f*	varianza *f*

	D	E	F	I	Es
varianza (Es)	Varianz f	variance	variance f	varianza f	—
varianza (I)	Varianz f	variance	variance f	—	varianza f
variation des existences (F)	Bestands-veränderung f	inventory change	—	movimento di scorte m	variaciones de las partidas f/pl
veil of money (E)	Geldschleier m	—	voile d'argent m	moneta-velo f	velo monetario m
velocità della circolazione monetaria (I)	Geldumlaufs-geschwindigkeit f	velocity of circulation of money	vitesse de la circulation de la monnaie f	—	ritmo de la circulación del dinero m
velocity of circulation of money (E)	Geldumlaufs-geschwindigkeit f	—	vitesse de la circulation de la monnaie f	velocità della circolazione monetaria f	ritmo de la circulación del dinero m
velo monetario (Es)	Geldschleier m	veil of money	voile d'argent m	moneta-velo f	—
vencimiento (Es)	Fälligkeit f	maturity	échéance f	scadenza f	—
vencimiento a medio plazo (Es)	mittlere Verfallszeit f	mean due date	échéance à moyen terme f	scadenza media f	—
vencimiento de intereses (Es)	Zinstermin m	interest payment date	délai de payement de l'intérêt m	data di godimento f	—
vendedor al descubierto (Es)	Fixer m	bear seller	vendeur à découvert m	scopertista m	—
vendedor de opción (Es)	Stillhalter m	option seller	vendeur d'option m	venditore di un'opzione m	—
vender al descubierto (Es)	fixen	to speculate for a fall	vendre à découvert	vendere allo scoperto	—
vendeur à découvert (F)	Fixer m	bear seller	—	scopertista m	vendedor al descubierto m
vendere allo scoperto (I)	fixen	to speculate for a fall	vendre à découvert	—	vender al descubierto
vendeur d'option (F)	Stillhalter m	option seller	—	venditore di un'opzione m	vendedor de opción m
vendibilità (I)	Vermarktung f	marketing	commercialisation f	—	comercialización f
vendita (I)	Verkauf m	sale	vente f	—	venta f
vendita a contanti (I)	Barverkauf m	cash sale	vente au comptant f	—	venta al contado f
vendita allo scoperto (I)	Leerverkauf m	bear selling	vente à découvert f	—	venta al descubierto f
vendita allo scoperto (I)	Blanko-Verkauf m	short sale	vente à découvert f	—	venta al descubierto f
vendita di pacchetti azionari (I)	Blockverkauf m	block sale	vente en bloc f	—	venta en bloque f
vendita diretta (I)	Direktverkauf m	direct selling	vente directe au consommateur f	—	venta directa f
vendita di titoli (I)	Effektenverkauf m	over-the-counter trading	vente de titres f	—	venta de valores f
venditore di un'opzione (I)	Stillhalter m	option seller	vendeur d'option m	—	vendedor de opción m
vendre à découvert (F)	fixen	to speculate for a fall	—	vendere allo scoperto	vender al descubierto
vendredi noir (F)	Schwarzer Freitag m	Black Friday	—	venerdì nero m	viernes negro m
vendre une option (F)	stillhalten	to sell an option	—	concedere una moratoria	prorrogar
venerdì nero (I)	Schwarzer Freitag m	Black Friday	vendredi noir m	—	viernes negro m
venta (Es)	Verkauf m	sale	vente f	vendita f	—
venta al contado (Es)	Barverkauf m	cash sale	vente au comptant f	vendita a contanti f	—
venta al descubierto (Es)	Leerverkauf m	bear selling	vente à découvert f	vendita allo scoperto f	—
venta al descubierto (Es)	Blanko-Verkauf m	short sale	vente à découvert f	vendita allo scoperto f	—
venta de liquidación (Es)	Ausverkauf m	clearance sale	soldes m/pl	liquidazione f	—
venta de valores (Es)	Effektenverkauf m	over-the-counter trading	vente de titres f	vendita di titoli f	—
venta directa (Es)	Direktverkauf m	direct selling	vente directe au consommateur f	vendita diretta f	—
venta en bloque (Es)	Blockverkauf m	block sale	vente en bloc f	vendita di pacchetti azionari f	—
vente (F)	Verkauf m	sale	—	vendita f	venta f

	D	E	F	I	Es
vente à découvert (F)	Leerverkauf *m*	bear selling	—	vendita allo scoperto *f*	venta al descubierto *f*
vente à découvert (F)	Blanko-Verkauf *m*	short sale	—	vendita allo scoperto *f*	venta al descubierto *f*
vente à l'enchère d'or (F)	Goldauktion *f*	gold auction	—	asta dell'oro *f*	subasta de oro *f*
vente a tempérament (F)	Abzahlungsgeschäft *n*	instalment sale transaction	—	operazione con pagamento rateale *f*	operación a plazos *f*
vente au comptant (F)	Barverkauf *m*	cash sale	—	vendita a contanti *f*	venta al contado *f*
vente de titres (F)	Effektenverkauf *m*	over-the-counter trading	—	vendita di titoli *f*	venta de valores *f*
vente directe au consommateur (F)	Direktverkauf *m*	direct selling	—	vendita diretta *f*	venta directa *f*
vente d'une créance (F)	Forderungskauf *m*	purchase of accounts receivable	—	acquisizione di crediti *f*	compra de créditos *f*
vente en bloc (F)	Blockverkauf *m*	block sale	—	vendita di pacchetti azionari *f*	venta en bloque *f*
venture (E)	Wagnis *n*	—	risque *m*	rischio *m*	riesgo *m*
venture capital (E)	Venture Kapital *n*	—	capital de risque *m*	capitale di rischio *m*	capital de riesgo *m*
Venture Kapital (D)	—	venture capital	capital de risque *m*	capitale di rischio *m*	capital de riesgo *m*
Veräußerungsgewinn (D)	—	gain on disposal	bénéfice d'aliénation *m*	plusvalenza *f*	beneficio de la venta *m*
Verband (D)	—	association	association *f*	federazione *f*	asociación *f*
Verbindlichkeit (D)	—	liability	obligation *f*	debito *m*	obligación *f*
Verbot (D)	—	prohibition	prohibition *f*	divieto *m*	prohibición *f*
verbotene Aktienausgabe (D)	—	prohibited share issue	émission d'actions interdite *f*	emissione vietata d'azioni *f*	emisión de acciones prohibida *f*
Verbraucherkreditgesetz (D)	—	consumer credit act	loi sur les crédits à la consommation *f*	legge sul credito al consumo *f*	ley sobre créditos al consumidor *f*
Verbuchung (D)	—	entry	inscription en compte *f*	registrazione *f*	contabilización *f*
Verbund (D)	—	union	union *f*	unione *f*	interconexión *f*
verdeckte Gewinnausschüttung (D)	—	hidden profit distribution	distribution occulte de bénéfices *f*	partecipazione agli utili velata *f*	distribución oculta *f*
verdecktes Stammkapital (D)	—	quasi-equity capital	capital social occulte *m*	conferimento di un socio *m*	capital social oculto *m*
vereinfachte Kapitalherabsetzung (D)	—	simplified capital reduction	diminution de capital simplifiée *f*	riduzione di capitale semplice *f*	reducción de capital simplificada *f*
Verfalltag (D)	—	day of expiry	jour de l'échéance *m*	giorno di scadenza *m*	día de vencimiento *m*
Verfallzeit (D)	—	time of expiration	époque de l'échéance *f*	scadenza *f*	plazo de vencimiento *m*
verfügbares Einkommen (D)	—	disposable income	revenu disponible *m*	reddito disponibile *f*	renta disponible *f*
Verfügung (D)	—	disposition	disposition *f*	disposizione *f*	disposición *f*
Verfügungsrecht (D)	—	right of disposal	droit de disposition *m*	diritto di disporre *m*	capacidad dispositiva *f*
Vergleichsbilanz (D)	—	comparative balance sheet	bilan au moment de l'ouverture du règlement judiciare *m*	situazione patrimoniale di concordato *m*	balance de comparación *m*
Vergleichsverfahren (D)	—	composition proceedings	procédure de conciliation *f*	procedura di concordato *f*	procedimiento conciliatorio *m*
Vergütung (D)	—	remuneration	rémunération *f*	remunerazione *f*	remuneración *f*
vérification (F)	Prüfung *f*	examination	—	controllo *m*	revisión *f*
vérification (F)	Revision *f*	audit	—	revisione *f*	revisión *f*
vérification de la solvabilité (F)	Bonitätsprüfung *f*	credit check	—	esame di solvibilità *m*	inspección de solvencia *f*
vérification des livres (F)	Buchprüfung *f*	auditing	—	ispezione contabile *f*	revisión contable *f*
vérification des livres de l'entreprise (F)	Betriebsprüfung *f*	investigation by the tax authorities	—	revisione aziendale *f*	revisión *f*
vérification du bilan bancaire (F)	Bankprüfung *f*	audit of the bank balance sheet	—	esame del bilancio *m*	revisión de cuentas del banco *f*

	D	E	F	I	Es
vérification du prospectus (F)	Prospektprüfung	audit of prospectus	—	controllo del prospetto m	examinación del prospecto f
Verjährung (D)	—	limitation of actions	prescription f	prescrizione f	prescripción f
Verkauf (D)	—	sale	vente f	vendita f	venta f
Verkaufskonto (D)	—	trading account	compte de ventes m	conto vendite m	cuenta de ventas f
Verkaufsoption (D)	—	option to sell	option de vente f	opzione di vendita f	opción de venta f
Verkaufswert (D)	—	selling value	valeur vénale f	valore di realizzo m	valor de venta m
Verlust (D)	—	loss	perte f	perdita f	pérdida f
Verlustanteil (D)	—	share in the loss	participation aux pertes f	quota alle perdite f	cuota de pérdidas f
Verlustausgleich (D)	—	loss-compensation	compensation des pertes f	conguaglio dei passivi m	compensación de pérdidas f
Verlustvortrag (D)	—	carry-forward of the losses	report des pertes m	riporto delle perdite m	traslación de pérdidas f
Verlustzuweisung (D)	—	loss allocation	assignation des pertes f	società d'ammortamento f	asignación de pérdidas f
Vermarktung (D)	—	marketing	commercialisation f	vendibilità f	comercialización f
Vermittlungs-geschäft (D)	—	brokerage business	affaire de médiation f	operazione di intermediazione f	transacción de mediación f
Vermögen (D)	—	property	patrimoine m	patrimonio m	patrimonio m
Vermögensanlage (D)	—	investment	investissement de capital m	investimento patrimoniale m	inversión de capital f
Vermögensarten (D)	—	types of property	catégories de patrimoine f/pl	tipi di patrimonio m/pl	clases de patrimonio f/pl
Vermögensberater (D)	—	investment advisor	conseiller en investissement m	consulente patrimoniale m	asesor en materia de inversiones m
Vermögensbilanz (D)	—	asset and liability statement	état du patrimoine m	bilancio patrimoniale m	balance patrimonial m
Vermögensbildung (D)	—	capital formation	formation de capital f	formazione del patrimonio f	formación de capital f
Vermögenseffekten (D)	—	real balance effect	effets patrimoniaux m/pl	effetti patrimoniali m/pl	efectos patrimoniales m/pl
Vermögens-einkommen (D)	—	real balance effect	revenu du capital m	reddito di capitale m	ingresos por capital m/pl
Vermögenspolitik (D)	—	policy relating to capital formation	politique financière f	politica patrimoniale f	política de patrimonios f
Vermögens-rechnung (D)	—	capital account	compte de capital m	situazione patrimoniale f	cálculo del valor neto m
Vermögenssteuer (D)	—	wealth tax	impôt sur la fortune m	imposta sul patrimonio f	impuesto patrimonial m
vermögenswirksame Leistungen (D)	—	capital forming payment	prestations primées f/pl	prestazioni con effetti patrimoniali f/pl	prestaciones que fomentan la formación de capital f/pl
vernichtete Wertpapiere (D)	—	destroyed securities	titres détruits m/pl	titoli annullati m/pl	títulos destruidos m/pl
Veröffentlichung (D)	—	publication	publication f	pubblicazione f	publicación f
Veröffentlichungs-pflicht (D)	—	statutory public disclosure	obligation de publier f	obbligo di pubblicazione m	publicación obligatoria f
Verpfändung (D)	—	pledge	mise en gage f	pignoramento m	pignoración f
Verrechnung (D)	—	compensation	compensation f	compensazione f	compensación f
Verrechnungs-einheit (D)	—	clearing unit	unité de compte f	unità di conto f	unidad de compensación f
Verrechnungs-scheck (D)	—	crossed cheque	chèque à porter en compte m	assegno da accreditare m	cheque cruzado m
versamento (I)	Einzahlung f	payment	payement m	—	aportación f
versamento in contanti (I)	Bareinschuß m	cash loss payment	payement en espèces m	—	reserva en efectivo m
Versandscheck (D)	—	out-of-town cheque	chèque déplacé m	assegno fuori piazza m	cheque sobre otra plaza m
Verschachtelung (D)	—	interlocking	interdépendance f	partecipazione di società al capitale di altre società f	participación de una sociedad en el capital de otra f

	D	E	F	I	Es
verschlossenes Depot (D)	—	safe deposit	dépôt fermé *m*	deposito chiuso *m*	depósito cerrado *m*
Verschuldung (D)	—	indebtedness	endettement *m*	indebitamento *m*	endeudamiento *m*
versement complémentaire (F)	Nachschuß *m*	subsequent payment	—	apporto supplemetare *m*	aportación suplementaria *f*
Versicherung (D)	—	insurance	assurance *f*	assicurazione *f*	seguro *m*
Versicherungsaktie (D)	—	insurance company share	action d'une société d'assurance *f*	azione assicurativa *f*	acción de compañías de seguros *f*
versteckte Arbeitslosigkeit (D)	—	hidden unemployment	chômage caché *m*	disoccupazione camuffata *f*	desempleo disfrazado *m*
versteckte Inflation (D)	—	hidden inflation	inflation larvée *f*	inflazione mascherata *f*	inflación encubierta *f*
vertice internazionale di economia (I)	Weltwirtschafts- gipfel *m*	world economic summit	sommet économique international *m*	—	Cumbre Económica Occidental *f*
Vertrag (D)	—	contract	contrat *m*	contratto *m*	contrato *m*
Vertragsbindung (D)	—	contractual obligation	obligation de respecter le contrat *f*	vincolo di contratto *m*	vínculo contractual *m*
Vertragsstrafe (D)	—	contractual penalty	pénalité *f*	convenzionale *f*	pena contractual *f*
vertretbare Wertpapiere (D)	—	fungible securities	titres fongibles *m/pl*	titoli fungibili *m/pl*	títulos fungibles *m/pl*
Verursacherprinzip (D)	—	polluter pays principle	principe du pollueur payeur *m*	principio di causalità *m*	principio contamina- dor-pagador *m*
Verwahrung (D)	—	custody	dépôt *m*	custodia *f*	custodia *f*
Verwahrungsbetrag (D)	—	value of custody	valeur des fonds en dépôt *f*	importo di deposito *m*	valor de los fondos en depósito *m*
Verwahrungsbuch (D)	—	custody ledger	registre des dépôts *m*	libretto di deposito *m*	libro de custodia *f*
Verwahrungskosten (D)	—	custody fee	coût de garde *m*	spese di custodia *f/pl*	gastos de depósito *m/pl*
Verwaltung (D)	—	administration	administration *f*	amministrazione *f*	administración *f*
Verwaltungsaktien (D)	—	treasury stock	actions de Trésor *f/pl*	azioni amministrate *f/pl*	acciones de tesorería *f/pl*
Verwaltungsgebühr (D)	—	official fees	taxe administrative *f*	tassa amministrativa *f*	derechos administrativos *m/pl*
Verwertungs- konsortien (D)	—	marketing syndicates	consortium de commercialisation *f*	consorzi di utilizzazione *m/pl*	consorcios de comercialización *m/pl*
Verzinsung (D)	—	payment of interest	payement des intérêts *m*	tasso d'interesse *m*	interés *m*
Verzug (D)	—	delay	demeure *f*	mora *f*	demora *f*
Verzugszinsen (D)	—	default interest	intérêts moratoires *m/pl*	interessi moratori *m/pl*	intereses de demora *m/pl*
vested interest stock (E)	Interessenwert *m*	—	action qui fait l'objet d'un achat par un groupe intéressé *f*	titolo primario *m*	valor de interés *m*
videotext account (E)	Tele-Konto *n*	—	compte vidéotex *m*	conto videotel *m*	cuenta videotexto *f*
viernes negro (Es)	Schwarzer Freitag *m*	Black Friday	vendredi noir *m*	venerdì nero *m*	—
vincolamento di capitale (I)	Kapitalbindung *f*	capital tie-up	immobilisation de capitaux *f*	—	vinculación de capital *f*
vincolare (I)	Vinkulieren	restriction of transferability	obliger *f*	—	vinculación *f*
vincolo del capitale (I)	Kapitalbindungs- dauer *f*	duration of capital tie-up	durée de l'immobili- sation de capitaux *f*	—	plazo de vinculación de capital *m*
vincolo di contratto (I)	Vertragsbindung *f*	contractual obligation	obligation de re- specter le contrat *f*	—	vínculo contractual *m*
vinculación (Es)	Vinkulieren	restriction of transferability	obliger *f*	vincolare *m*	—
vinculación al índice (Es)	Indexbindung *f*	index-linking	indexation *f*	indicizzazione *f*	—
vinculación al tipo de interés pactado (Es)	Zinsbindung *f*	interest rate control	engagement sur le taux d'intérêt accordé *m*	prescrizione sui tassi *f*	—
vinculación a reglas (Es)	Regelbindung *f*	rule-bound policy	affectation à des règles *f*	attività vincolata *f*	—

	D	E	F	I	Es
vinculación de capital (Es)	Kapitalbindung f	capital tie-up	immobilisation de capitaux f	vincolamento di capitale m	—
vinculación de precios a nivel internacional (Es)	internationaler Preiszusammenhang m	international price system	interrelation internationale en matière des prix f	interdipendenza internazionale dei prezzi f	—
vinculaciones financieras (Es)	Finanzverflechtung f	financial interlocking	interdépendance financière f	interferenza finanziaria f	—
vínculo contractual (Es)	Vertragsbindung f	contractual obligation	obligation de respecter le contrat f	vincolo di contratto m	—
Vinkulieren (D)	—	restriction of transferability	obliger f	vincolare m	vinculación f
vinkulierte Aktie (D)	—	restricted share	action négociable sous réserve f	azione vincolata f	acción vinculada f
virement (F)	Giro n	credit transfer	—	girata f	giro m
virement (F)	Überweisung f	remittance	—	trasferimento m	transferencia f
virement accéléré (F)	Eilüberweisung f	rapid money transfer	—	vaglia espresso m	giro urgente m
virement bancaire (F)	Banküberweisung f	bank transfer	—	trasferimento bancario m	giro bancario m
virement de place (F)	Platzübertragung f	local transfer	—	trasferimento su piazza m	transferencia local f
virement de substitution (F)	Ersatzüberweisung f	substitute transfer	—	trasferimento sostitutivo m	transferencia sustitutiva f
virement entre deux places bancaires (F)	Ferngiro m	long distance giro	—	bonifico da una piazza all'altra m	transferencia de una plaza a otra f
virement global (F)	Sammelüberweisung f	combined bank transfer	—	trasferimento cumulativo m	transferencia colectiva f
virements (F)	Überweisungsverkehr m	money transfer transactions	—	bancogiro m	transferencias f/pl
virement transmis par le système de virements de télex direct (F)	Blitzgiro m	direct telex transfer system	—	bonifico telegrafico m	giro transmitido por el sistema de transferencia de télex directo m
vitesse de la circulation de la monnaie (F)	Geldumlaufsgeschwindigkeit f	velocity of circulation of money	—	velocità della circolazione monetaria f	ritmo de la circulación del dinero m
voce per memoria (I)	Merkposten m	memorandum item	poste pour mémoire m	—	cifra nominal f
void bill (E)	präjudizierter Wechsel m	—	traite protestée hors des délais f	cambiale pregiudicata f	letra prejudicada f
voile d'argent (F)	Geldschleier m	veil of money	—	moneta-velo f	velo monetario m
volatilidad (Es)	Volatilität f	volatility	volatilité f	volatilità f	—
volatilità (I)	Volatilität f	volatility	volatilité f	—	volatilidad f
Volatilität (D)	—	volatility	volatilité f	volatilità f	volatilidad f
volatilité (F)	Volatilität f	volatility	—	volatilità f	volatilidad f
volatility (E)	Volatilität f	—	volatilité f	volatilità f	volatilidad f
Volksaktie (D)	—	low-denomination share for small savers	action populaire f	azione popolare f	acción popular f
Volkseinkommen (D)	—	national income	revenu national m	reddito nazionale m	renta nacional f
Volksvermögen (D)	—	national wealth	patrimoine national m	ricchezza nazionale f	patrimonio nacional m
Volkswirt (D)	—	economist	économiste m	esperto di economia politica m	economista m
Volkswirtschaft (D)	—	national economy	économie nationale f	economia politica f	economía nacional f
Volkswirtschaftliche Gesamtrechnung (D)	—	national accounting	comptabilité nationale f	contabilità nazionale f	contabilidad nacional f
Volkswirtschaftslehre (D)	—	economics	économie politique f	economia politica f	ciencias económicas f/pl
Vollkaufmann (D)	—	registered trader	commerçant de plein droit m	imprenditore a pieno titolo m	comerciante pleno m
Vollmacht (D)	—	power of attorney	plein pouvoir m	procura f	poder m
Vollstreckung (D)	—	enforcement	exécution f	esecuzione f	ejecución f
volume creditizio (I)	Kreditvolumen n	total credit outstanding	volume des crédits m	—	volumen de créditos m

	D	E	F	I	Es
volume d'affaires (F)	Geschäftsvolumen *n*	volume of business	—	volume d'affari *m*	volumen de negocios *m*
volume d'affari (I)	Geschäftsvolumen *n*	volume of business	volume d'affaires *m*	—	volumen de negocios *m*
volume de la production (F)	Ausbringung *f*	output	—	gettito *m*	volumen de la producción *m*
volume des crédits (F)	Kreditvolumen *n*	total credit outstanding	—	volume creditizio *m*	volumen de créditos *m*
volume di mercato (I)	Marktvolumen *n*	market volume	volume du marché *m*	—	volumen del mercado *m*
volume d'opérations boursières (F)	Börsenumsätze *m/pl*	stock exchange turnover	—	scambi borsistici *m/pl*	volumen de operaciones bursátiles *m*
volume du flux (F)	Stromgröße *f*	rate of flow	—	variabile di flusso *f*	tasa de flujo *f*
volume du marché (F)	Marktvolumen *n*	market volume	—	volume di mercato *m*	volumen del mercado *m*
volumen de créditos (Es)	Kreditvolumen *n*	total credit outstanding	volume des crédits *m*	volume creditizio *m*	—
volumen de la producción (Es)	Ausbringung *f*	output	volume de la production *m*	gettito *m*	—
volumen del mercado (Es)	Marktvolumen *n*	market volume	volume du marché *m*	volume di mercato *m*	—
volumen de negocios (Es)	Geschäftsvolumen *n*	volume of business	volume d'affaires *m*	volume d'affari *m*	—
volumen de operaciones bursátiles (Es)	Börsenumsätze *m/pl*	stock exchange turnover	volume d'opérations boursières *m*	scambi borsistici *m/pl*	—
volumen de pedido (Es)	Auftragsgröße *f*	size of an order	importance de la commande *f*	ampiezza d'ordinazione *f*	—
volumen máximo de crédito disponible (Es)	Kreditplafondierung *f*	credit limitation	fixation d'une limite de crédit *f*	fissazione del fido *f*	—
volumen monetario (Es)	Geldvolumen *n*	volume of money	masse monétaire *f*	massa monetaria *f*	—
volume of business (E)	Geschäftsvolumen *n*	—	volume d'affaires *m*	volume d'affari *m*	volumen de negocios *m*
volume of money (E)	Geldvolumen *n*	—	masse monétaire *f*	massa monetaria *f*	volumen monetario *m*
Vorausklage (D)	—	preliminary injunction	bénéfice de discussion *m*	citazione preventiva *f*	excusión *f*
Vorbörse (D)	—	before hours dealing	marché avant le marché officiel *m*	avant bourse *m*	operaciones antes de la apertura *f/pl*
Vorfinanzierung (D)	—	prefinancing	préfinancement *m*	prefinanziamento *m*	financiación anticipada *f*
Vorkaufsrecht (D)	—	preemption right	droit de préemption *m*	diritto di prelazione *m*	derecho de preferencia *m*
Vorleistung (D)	—	advance performance	prestation exécutée avant l'échéance *f*	prestazione anticipata *f*	anticipo *m*
Vorratsaktie (D)	—	disposable share	action en réserve *f*	azione di riserva *f*	acción de provisión *f*
Vorschaltkonditionen (D)	—	preliminary conditions	conditions préliminaires *f/pl*	condizioni preliminari *f/pl*	condiciones preliminares *f/pl*
Vorschuß (D)	—	advance	avance *f*	anticipo *m*	anticipo *m*
Vorschußzinsen (D)	—	negative advance interest	intérêts payés par anticipation *m/pl*	penalità interessi *f*	interés negativo anticipado *m*
Vorsichtskasse (D)	—	precautionary holding	fonds de réserve *m/pl*	domanda precauzionale di moneta *f*	existencias de precaución *f/pl*
Vorstand (D)	—	board	comité directeur *m*	consiglio d'amministrazione *m*	junta directiva *f*
Vorsteuer (D)	—	input tax	impôt perçu en amont *m*	imposta sul fatturato d'acquisto *f*	impuesto sobre el valor añadido deducible *m*
Vorzugsaktie (D)	—	preference share	action privilégiée *f*	azione privilegiata *f*	acción preferente *f*
Vorzugsdividende (D)	—	preferential dividend	dividende prioritaire *m*	dividendo privilegiato *m*	dividendo preferente *m*
Vorzugskurs (D)	—	preferential price	cours de faveur *m*	corso preferenziale *m*	curso preferencial *m*
Vorzugsobligation (D)	—	preference bond	obligation assortie de droits réservés *f*	obbligazione privilegiata *f*	obligación preferente *f*

	D	E	F	I	Es
vostro account (E)	Vostrokonto *n*	—	votre compte en notre établissement *m*	conto vostro *m*	su cuenta *f*
Vostrokonto (D)	—	vostro account	votre compte en notre établissement *m*	conto vostro *m*	su cuenta *f*
vote de titres en dépôt (F)	Depotabstimmung *f*	securities deposit reconciliation	—	coordinamento dei depositi *m*	voto de título en depósito *m*
voting rights of nominee shareholders (E)	Depotstimmrecht *n*	—	droit de vote d'une banque dépositaire d'actions en compte courant *m*	diritto di voto azioni in deposito *m*	derecho de voto de título en depósito *m*
voting share (E)	Stimmrechtsaktie *f*	—	action à droit de vote simple *f*	azione con diritto di voto *f*	acción con derecho a voto *f*
voto de título en depósito (Es)	Depotabstimmung *f*	securities deposit reconciliation	vote de titres en dépôt *m*	coordinamento dei depositi *m*	—
votre compte en notre établissement (F)	Vostrokonto *n*	vostro account	—	conto vostro *m*	su cuenta *f*
Wachstumsfonds (D)	—	growth fund	fonds d'expansion *m*	fondo di accumulazione *m*	fondo de crecimiento *m*
Wachstumsziel (D)	—	growth target	objectif de croissance *m*	obiettivo di crescita *m*	objetivo de crecimiento *m*
wage in cash (E)	Barlohn *m*	—	salaire en espèces *m*	paga in contanti *f*	salario en efectivo *m*
wage-price spiral (E)	Preis-Lohn-Spirale *f*	—	course des prix et des salaires *f*	spirale dei prezzi e dei salari *f*	espiral precio-salario *f*
Wagnis (D)	—	venture	risque *m*	rischio *m*	riesgo *m*
Währung (D)	—	currency	monnaie *f*	moneta *f*	moneda *f*
Währungsabsicherung (D)	—	safeguarding of the currency	garantie de change *f*	sostegno di una moneta *m*	garantía de cambio *f*
Währungsausgleich (D)	—	currency conversion compensation	alignement des monnaies *m*	conguaglio dei cambi *m*	compensación de cambios *f*
Währungsblock (D)	—	monetary block	bloc monétaire *m*	blocco monetario *m*	bloque monetario *m*
Währungsdumping (D)	—	currency dumping	dumping du change *m*	dumping di valuta *m*	dumping monetario *m*
Währungsfonds (D)	—	monetary fund	fonds monétaire *m*	fondo monetario *m*	fondo monetario *m*
Währungsgebiet (D)	—	currency area	zone monétaire *f*	area monetaria *f*	área monetaria *f*
Währungskonto (D)	—	currency account	compte en monnaies étrangères *m*	conto valutario *m*	cuenta de moneda extranjera *f*
Währungskorb (D)	—	currency basket	panier des monnaies *m*	paniere monetario *m*	cesta de monedas *f*
Währungskrise (D)	—	monetary crisis	crise monétaire *f*	crisi monetaria *f*	crisis monetaria *f*
Währungsordnung (D)	—	monetary system	ordre monétaire *m*	ordinamento valutario *m*	ordenación monetaria *f*
Währungsparität (D)	—	monetary parity	parité des monnaies *f*	parità monetaria *f*	paridad monetaria *f*
Währungspolitik (D)	—	monetary policy	politique monétaire *f*	politica monetaria *f*	política monetaria *f*
Währungspool (D)	—	currency pool	pool monétaire *m*	pool monetario *m*	pool monetario *m*
Währungsreform (D)	—	monetary reform	réforme monétaire *f*	riforma monetaria *f*	reforma monetaria *f*
Währungsreserven (D)	—	monetary reserves	réserves monétaires *f/pl*	riserve valutarie *f/pl*	reservas monetarias *f/pl*
Währungsschuld (D)	—	foreign currency debt	dette d'argent exprimée en unité monétaire étrangère *f*	debito in valuta estera *m*	deuda en moneda extranjera *f*
Währungssubstitution (D)	—	currency substitution	substitution monétaire *f*	sostituzione monetaria *f*	substitución monetaria *f*
Währungsswap (D)	—	currency swap	swap de devises *m*	currency swap *m*	swap en moneda extranjera *m*
Währungssystem (D)	—	monetary system	système monétaire *m*	sistema monetario *m*	sistema monetario *m*
Währungsumstellung (D)	—	currency conversion	adaptation d'une monnaie *f*	riforma monetaria *f*	reforma monetaria *f*
Währungsunion (D)	—	monetary union	union monétaire *f*	unione monetaria *f*	unión monetaria *f*
wait-and-see attitude (E)	Attentismus *m*	—	attentisme *m*	attentismo *m*	atentismo *m*
Wandelanleihen (D)	—	convertible bonds	obligation convertible *f*	prestiti convertibili *m/pl*	empréstitos convertibles *m/pl*

	D	E	F	I	Es
Wandelgeschäft (D)	—	callable forward transaction	marché à option *m*	contratto a termine con opzione di adempimento anticipato *m*	operación de opción *f*
Ware (D)	—	goods	marchandise *f*	merce *f*	mercancía *f*
Warenbeleihung (D)	—	lending on goods	emprunt sur marchandises *m*	prestito su merci *m*	préstamo sobre mercancías *m*
Warenbörse (D)	—	commodity exchange	bourse de marchandises *f*	borsa merci *f*	bolsa de mercancías *f*
Warenkredit (D)	—	trade credit	avance sur marchandises *f*	credito su merci *m*	crédito sobre mercancías *m*
Warenpapier (D)	—	document of title	effet de commerce *m*	titolo rappresentativo di merci *m*	valor comercial *m*
Warentermingeschäft (D)	—	commodity futures trading	opération à livrer *f*	operazione a termine su merci *f*	operación a plazo *f*
Warenwechsel (D)	—	commercial bill	traite commerciale *f* commerciale *f*	cambiale	letra comercial *f*
war loan (E)	Kriegsanleihe *f*	—	emprunt de guerre *m*	prestito di guerra *m*	empréstito de guerra *m*
warrant (I)	Optionsschein *m*	share purchase warrant	coupon d'option *m*	—	documento de opción *m*
Warrants (D)	—	warrants	titre de gage *m*	warrants *m/pl*	certificados de depósito *m/pl*
warrants (E)	Warrants *m/pl*	—	titre de gage *m*	warrants *m/pl*	certificados de depósito *m/pl*
warrants (E)	Anrechtscheine *m/pl*	—	certificats provisoires *m/pl*	certificati provvisori *m/pl*	certificados provisionales *m/pl*
warrants (I)	Warrants *m/pl*	warrants	titre de gage *m*	—	certificados de depósito *m/pl*
watering of capital stock (E)	Kapitalverwässerung *f*	—	augmentation du capital par émission d'actions gratuites ou par incorporation des réserves au fonds social *f*	annacquamento di capitali *m*	depreciación del capital *f*
wealth tax (E)	Vermögenssteuer *f*	—	impôt sur la fortune *m*	imposta sul patrimonio *f*	impuesto patrimonial *m*
Wechsel (D)	—	bill of exchange	lettre de change *f*	cambiale *f*	letra *f*
Wechselakzept (D)	—	acceptance of a bill	acceptation d'un effet *f*	accettazione cambiaria *f*	aceptación cambiaria *f*
Wechselaussteller (D)	—	drawer of a bill	tireur d'une traite *m*	traente di una cambiale *m*	librador *m*
Wechseldiskont (D)	—	discount of bills	escompte d'un effet *m*	sconto cambiario *m*	descuento de letras *m*
Wechseldiskontkredit (D)	—	credit by way of discount of bills	crédit sur effets escomptés *m*	credito per sconto effetti *m*	crédito de descuento cambial *m*
Wechselinkasso (D)	—	collection of bills of exchange	encaissement d'un effet *m*	incasso di cambiale *m*	cobro de letras *m*
Wechselkopie (D)	—	copy of a bill	copie de traite *f*	copiacambiale *f*	copia de una letra *f*
Wechselkurs (D)	—	exchange rate	cours du change *m*	cambio *m*	tipo de cambio *m*
Wechselkursmechanismus (D)	—	exchange rate mechanism	mécanisme du cours du change *m*	meccanismo di cambio *m*	mecanismo de cambio *m*
Wechselkursrisiko (D)	—	foreign exchange risk	risque de change *m*	rischio di cambio *m*	riesgo de cambio *m*
Wechselkurssystem (D)	—	system of exchange rates	système de change *m*	regime dei cambi *m*	sistema de cambios *m*
Wechsellombard (D)	—	collateral loan based on a bill of exchange	avance sur effet nanti *f*	anticipazione su cambiali *f*	letra de cambio tomada en prenda *f*
Wechselnehmer (D)	—	payee of a bill of exchange	preneur d'un effet *m*	beneficiario di una cambiale *m*	endosado *m*
Wechselobligo (D)	—	customer's liability on bills	engagement par lettre de change *m*	cambiale passiva *f*	obligación en letras de cambio *f*
Wechselpensionsgeschäft (D)	—	pledging of bills of exchange against grant of a loan	opération de mise en pension d'effets *f*	pensione di effetti *f*	operación de reporte de letras *f*
Wechselprolongation (D)	—	renewal of a bill of exchange	prolongation de la traite *f*	proroga di cambiale *f*	renovación de la letra *f*

	D	E	F	I	Es
Wechselprotest (D)	—	protest	protêt de traite *m*	protesto cambiario *m*	protesto de una letra *m*
Wechselregreß (D)	—	legal recourse for non-payment of a bill	recours en matière de traite *m*	regresso cambiario *m*	recurso cambiario *m*
Wechselstube (D)	—	exchange office	bureau de change *m*	ufficio cambi *m*	casa cambiaria *f*
weekly return (E)	Wochenausweis *m*	—	bilan hebdomadaire *m*	situazione settimanale *f*	balance semanal *m*
Weichwährung (D)	—	soft currency	monnaie faible *f*	moneta debole *f*	moneda débil *f*
welfare (E)	Wohlfahrt *f*	—	bienfaisance *f*	benessere *m*	beneficencia *f*
Weltbank (D)	—	World Bank	banque mondiale *f*	Banca mondiale *f*	Banco Mundial *m*
Weltbilanz (D)	—	worldwide financial statements	bilan mondial *m*	bilancio internazionale *m*	balance mundial *m*
Weltmarkt (D)	—	world market	marché mondial *m*	mercato internazionale *m*	mercado mundial *m*
Weltwirtschafts-gipfel (D)	—	world economic summit	sommet économique international *m*	vertice internazionale di economia *m*	Cumbre Económica Occidental *f*
Weltwirtschafts-krise (D)	—	worldwide economic crisis	crise économique mondiale *f*	crisi economica internazionale *f*	crisis económica mundial *f*
Werbungskosten (D)	—	publicity expenses	coût de publicité *m*	spese professionali *f/pl*	gastos de publicidad *m/pl*
Wert (D)	—	value	valeur *f*	valore *m*	valor *m*
Wertermittlung (D)	—	determination of the value	évaluation *f*	valutazione *f*	evaluación del valor *f*
Wertpapier (D)	—	security	valeur *f*	titolo di credito *m*	valor *m*
Wertpapier-abteilung (D)	—	securities department	service des valeurs *m*	ufficio titoli *m*	sección de valores *f*
Wertpapieranalyse (D)	—	securities research	analyse des valeurs mobilières *f*	analisi di titoli *f*	análisis de inversiones *m*
Wertpapieranlage (D)	—	investment in securities	placement en valeurs mobilières *m*	investimento in titoli *m*	inversión en valores *f*
Wertpapier-arbitrage (D)	—	arbitrage in securities	arbitrage sur les cours des valeurs mobilières *m*	arbitraggio su titoli *m*	arbitraje de valores *m*
Wertpapierbörse (D)	—	securities market	bourse des titres et valeurs *f*	borsa valori *f*	bolsa de valores *f*
Wertpapier-emission (D)	—	issue of securities	émission de titres *f*	emissione di titoli *f*	emisión de valores *f*
Wertpapierleihe (D)	—	lending on securities	prêt sur valeurs *m*	prestito per l'acquisto di titoli *m*	préstamo sobre títulos *m*
Wertpapiermarkt (D)	—	securities market	marché des valeurs mobilières *m*	mercato mobiliare *m*	mercado de valores *m*
Wertpapierpensions-geschäft (D)	—	credit transaction under repurchase agreement of securities	prise en pension de valeurs mobilières *f*	operazione pronti contro termine *f*	operación de reporte de valores *f*
Wertpapier-sammelbank (D)	—	central depository for securities	banque de dépôts et de virements de titres *f*	banca di deposito di titoli *f*	banco de depósito de valores mobiliarios *m*
Wertpapierspar-vertrag (D)	—	securities-linked savings scheme	contrat d'épargne mobilière *m*	contratto di risparmio in titoli *m*	contrato de ahorro en forma de valores *m*
Wertpapier-Terminhandel (D)	—	trading in security futures	marché des valeurs à terme *m*	operazioni a termine in titoli *f/pl*	operaciones de valores a plazo *f/pl*
Wertpapier-verwahrung (D)	—	safe custody and administration of securities	garde de titres *f*	custodia di titoli *f*	custodia de valores *f*
Wertrechtanleihe (D)	—	government-inscribed debt	emprunt de l'Etat inscrit dans le livre de la dette *m*	obbligazione contabile *f*	empréstito del Estado inscrito en el libro de la deuda *m*
Wertsicherung (D)	—	value guarantee	garantie de valeur *f*	garanzia del valore *f*	garantía de valor *f*
Wertstellung (D)	—	availability date	datation de la valeur en compte *f*	valuta *f*	valuta *f*
Wettbewerbs-beschränkung (D)	—	restraint of competition	restriction apportée à la concurrence *f*	limitazione della concorrenza *f*	restricción a la competencia *f*

	D	E	F	I	Es
whole-bank interest margin calculation (E)	Gesamtzins-spannenrechnung f	—	calcul du total de la marge entre les taux d'intérêt créditeur et débiteur m	calcolo margine d'interesse m	cálculo del margen de beneficio por intereses total m
Widerspruch (D)	—	objection	objection f	obiezione f	objeción f
Widerstandslinie (D)	—	line of resistance	ligne de résistance f	linea di resistenza f	línea de resistencia f
Wiederanlage (D)	—	reinvestment	réinvestissement m	reinvestimento m	reinversión f
windbill (E)	Reitwechsel m	—	traite de cavalerie f	cambiale incrociata f	letra cruzada f
Windhund-verfahren (D)	—	first come-first served principle	principe du premier arrivé et le premier servi m	principio del primo offerente m	principio del primer venido, primer servido m
Winkelbörse (D)	—	bucket shop	bourse du marché en banque f	borsa clandestina f	bolsín m
Wirtschaftskreislauf (D)	—	economic circulation	circuit économique m	circuito economico m	circuito económico m
Wirtschaftskrise (D)	—	economic crisis	crise économique f	crisi economica f	crisis económica f
Wirtschaftsordnung (D)	—	economic order	ordre économique m	ordinamento economico m	orden económico m
Wirtschaftsplan (D)	—	economic plan	plan économique m	piano economico m	plan económico m
Wirtschaftspolitik (D)	—	economic policy	politique économique f	politica economica f	política económica f
Wirtschaftswunder (D)	—	economic miracle	miracle économique m	miracolo economico m	milagro económico m
with a fixed rate of interest (E)	festverzinslich	—	à revenu fixe	a reddito fisso	de renta fija
withdrawal (E)	Entnahme f	—	prélèvement m	prelevamento m	retirada de dinero f
withdrawal of shares (E)	Aktieneinziehung f	—	retrait d'actions m	ritiro di azioni m	redención de acciones f
Wochenausweis (D)	—	weekly return	bilan hebdomadaire m	situazione settimanale f	balance semanal m
Wohlfahrt (D)	—	welfare	bienfaisance f	benessere m	beneficencia f
Wohnungsbau-förderung (D)	—	promotion of housing construction	promotion de la construction de logements f	promozione edilizia residenziale f	fomento de la construcción de viviendas m
working expenses (E)	Betriebskosten pl	—	charges d'exploitation f/pl	costi d'esercizio m/pl	gastos de explotación m/pl
working funds (E)	Betriebsmittel n	—	équipement d'exploitation m	fondi d'esercizio m/pl	fondos de explotación m/pl
World Bank (E)	Weltbank f	—	banque mondiale f	Banca mondiale f	Banco Mundial m
world economic summit (E)	Weltwirtschafts-gipfel m	—	sommet économique international m	vertice internazionale di economia m	Cumbre Económica Occidental f
world market (E)	Weltmarkt m	—	marché mondial m	mercato internazionale m	mercado mundial m
worldwide economic crisis (E)	Weltwirtschaftskrise f	—	crise économique mondiale f	crisi economica internazionale f	crisis económica mundial f
worldwide fincancial statements (E)	Weltbilanz f	—	bilan mondial m	bilancio internazionale m	balance mundial m
writing off (E)	Abschreibung f	—	amortissement m	ammortamento m	amortización f
Wucher (D)	—	usury	usure f	usura f	usura f
Wucherverbot (D)	—	prohibition of usurious money-lending	défense d'usure f	proibizione di usura f	prohibición de usura f
Wuchsaktie (D)	—	growth share	action avec possibilité d'acroissement f	azione con possibilità di sviluppo f	acción con posibilidad de incremento f
yield (E)	Rendite f	—	rendement m	rendimento m	rédito m
yield on shares (E)	Aktienrendite f	—	produit de l' action m	reddito effettivo di azioni m	rédito de las acciones m
Zahl (D)	—	figure	chiffre m	cifra f	número m
Zahlschein (D)	—	payment slip	mandat-carte m	modulo di versamento m	impreso para giro postal m
Zahlstelle (D)	—	payments office	bureau payeur m	cassa di pagamento f	pagaduría f
Zahltag (D)	—	payday	jour de paye m	giorno di pagamento m	día de pago m
Zahlung (D)	—	payment	payement m	pagamento m	pago m

	D	E	F	I	Es
Zahlungsanweisung (D)	—	order to pay	mandat de payement *m*	mandato di pagamento *m*	orden de pago *f*
Zahlungsaufschub (D)	—	extension of time for payment	sursis de payement *m*	dilazione di pagamento *f*	pago aplazado *m*
Zahlungsauftrag (D)	—	order for payment	ordre de payement *m*	ordine di pagamento *m*	delegación de pago *f*
Zahlungsbedingung (D)	—	terms of payment	condition de payement *f*	condizione di pagamento *f*	condición de pago *f*
Zahlungsbilanz (D)	—	balance of payments	balance des payements *f*	bilancia dei pagamenti *f*	balanza de pagos *f*
Zahlungseinstellung (D)	—	cessation of payments	suspension de payement *f*	cessazione di pagamento *f*	suspensión de pagos *f*
Zahlungsmittel (D)	—	means of payment	moyen de payement *m*	mezzo di pagamento *m*	medio de pago *m*
Zahlungsmittel-umlauf (D)	—	notes and coins in circulation	circulation monétaire *f*	circolazione di mezzi di pagamento *f*	medios de pago en circulación *m/pl*
Zahlungssitte (D)	—	payment habit	habitude de payement *f*	usanza di pagamento *f*	costumbre de pago *f*
Zahlungs-unfähigkeit (D)	—	insolvency	insolvabilité *f*	insolvenza *f*	insolvencia *f*
Zahlungsverkehr (D)	—	payment transaction	règlements *m/pl*	pagamenti *m/pl*	movimiento de pagos *m*
Zahlungsverzug (D)	—	failure to pay on due date	demeure du débiteur *f*	mora nel pagamento *f*	retraso en el pago *m*
Zahlungsziel (D)	—	period for payment	délai de payement *m*	dilazione di pagamento *f*	plazo de pago *m*
Zeichnungsschein (D)	—	subscription form	certificat de souscription *m*	bollettino di sottoscrizione *m*	boletín de suscripción *m*
Zentralbank (D)	—	central bank	banque centrale *f*	banca centrale *f*	banco central *m*
Zentralbankgeld (D)	—	central bank money	monnaie banque centrale *f*	moneta creata dalla banca centrale *f*	dinero legal *m*
Zentralbankrat (D)	—	Central Bank Council	Conseil de la banque centrale *m*	consiglio centrale banca centrale *m*	Consejo del Banco Central *m*
Zentrale (D)	—	head office	centrale *f*	centrale *f*	central *f*
Zentralkasse (D)	—	central credit institution	caisse centrale *f*	cassa centrale *f*	caja central *f*
Zerobond (D)	—	zero bond	obligation à coupon zéro *f*	zero coupon bond *m*	bono cero *m*
zero bond (E)	Zerobond *m*	—	obligation à coupon zéro *f*	zero coupon bond *m*	bono cero *m*
zero coupon bond (I)	Zerobond *m*	zero bond	obligation à coupon zéro *f*	—	bono cero *m*
Zertifikat (D)	—	certificate	certificat *m*	certificato *m*	certificado *m*
zertifizierte Bonds (D)	—	certified bonds	bons certifiés *m/pl*	titoli a reddito fisso in valuta estera *m/pl*	bonos certificados *m/pl*
Ziehung (D)	—	drawing	tirage *m*	estrazione *f*	giro *m*
Ziehungsrechte (D)	—	drawing rights	droits de tirage *m/pl*	diritti di prelievo *m/pl*	derechos de giro *m/pl*
Zins (D)	—	interest	intérêt *m*	interesse *m*	interés *m*
Zinsänderungs-risiko (D)	—	risk of change in interest rates	risque de fluctuations d'intérêts *m*	rischio variazione tassi d'interesse *m*	riesgo del cambio del tipo de interés *m*
Zinsanleihe (D)	—	loan repayable in full at a due date	emprunt produisant des intérêts *m*	prestito non ammortizzabile *m*	empréstito produciendo interés *m*
Zinsarbitrage (D)	—	interest rate arbitrage	arbitrage sur les taux de l'intérêt *m*	arbitraggio sui tassi d'interesse *m*	arbitraje en materia de tipos de interés *m*
Zinsbindung (D)	—	interest rate control	engagement sur le taux d'intérêt accordé *m*	prescrizione sui tassi *f*	vinculación al tipo de interés pactado *f*
Zinselastizität (D)	—	interest elasticity	élasticité des intérêts *f*	elasticità degli interessi *f*	elasticidad de los intereses *f*
Zinsendienst (D)	—	interest service	service de l'intérêt *m*	servizio degli interessi *m*	servicio del interés *m*
Zinsertrag (D)	—	income from interests	intérêts perçus *m/pl*	provento d'interessi *m*	rédito *m*
Zinseszins (D)	—	compound interest	intérêt composé *m*	anatocismo *m*	interés compuesto *m*

	D	E	F	I	Es
Zinseszins-rechnung (D)	—	calculation of compound interest	calcul des intérêts composés m	calcolo capitalizza-zione composta m	cálculo de interés compuesto m
Zinsgarantie (D)	—	guaranteed interest	garantie de l'intérêt f	garanzia d'interesse f	garantía de intereses f
Zinsgefälle (D)	—	margin between interest rates	disparité des niveaux d'intérêts f	differenza di interessi f	diferencial de intereses m
Zinskappe (D)	—	cap rate of interest	plafond de l'intérêt m	tetto interessi m	plafón de interés m
Zinskappen-vereinbahrung (D)	—	cap rate of interest agreement	accord d'un plafond d'intérêt m	accordo sul tetto interessi m	acuerdo de un plafón de interés m
Zinsmarge (D)	—	interest margin	marge entre les taux d'intérêt créditeur et débiteur f	margine d'interesse m	margen de interés m
Zinsniveau (D)	—	interest rate level	niveau du taux d'intérêt m	livello degli interessi m	nivel de los tipos de interés m
Zinsparität (D)	—	interest parity	parité des intérêts f	parità dei tassi d'interesse f	paridad del interés f
Zinspolitik (D)	—	interest rate policy	politique en matière d'intérêts f	politica degli interessi f	política de intereses f
Zinsrückstand (D)	—	arrear on interests	intérêt arriéré m	interessi arretrati m/pl	interés retrasado m
Zinssatz (D)	—	interest rate	taux d'intérêt m	tasso d'interesse m	tipo de interés m
Zinsschein (D)	—	coupon	coupon d'intérêts m	cedola d'interessi f	cupón de intereses m
Zinssenkung (D)	—	reduction of the interest rate	réduction des intérêts f	abbassamento del tasso d'interesse m	reducción del tipo de interés f
Zinsspanne (D)	—	interest margin	marge entre les taux d'intérêt créditeur et débiteur f	margine d'interesse m	margen de beneficio por intereses m
Zinsstaffel (D)	—	interest rate table	barème des intérêts m	scaletta f	escala de intereses f
Zinsstruktur (D)	—	interest rate structure	structure des intérêts f	struttura degli interessi f	estructura de los intereses f
Zinsswap (D)	—	interest rate swap	swap d'intérêts m	interest swap m	swap de intereses m
Zinstage (D)	—	quarter days	nombre de jours portant intérêt m	giorni per il calcolo interessi m	número de días de-vengado intereses m
Zinstermin (D)	—	interest payment date	délai de payement de l'intérêt m	data di godimento f	vencimiento de intereses m
Zinstheorie (D)	—	theory of interest	théorie des intérêts f	teoria degli interessi f	teoría del interés f
Zinsüberschuß (D)	—	interest surplus	excédent d'intérêts m	eccedenza degli interessi f	excedente de interés m
zinsvariable Anleihe (D)	—	loan at variable rates	emprunt d'un taux d'intérêt variable m	prestito a tasso d'interesse variabile m	empréstito con un tipo de interés variable m
Zinswucher (D)	—	usury	usure en matière de prêt à intérêt f	interesse usurario m	interés usurario m
Zoll (D)	—	customs duty	droit de douane m	dazio m	aduana f
Zollunion (D)	—	customs union	union douanière f	unione doganale f	unión aduanera f
zona del dólar (Es)	Dollarblock m	dollar area	bloc dollar m	area del dollaro f	—
zona de librecambio (Es)	Freihandelszone f	free trade area	zone de libre-échange f	zona di libero scambio f	—
zona di libero scambio (I)	Freihandelszone f	free trade area	zone de libre-échange f	—	zona de librecambio f
zone de libre-échange (F)	Freihandelszone f	free trade area	—	zona di libero scambio f	zona de librecambio f
zone monétaire (F)	Währungsgebiet n	currency area	—	area monetaria f	área monetaria f
zone monétaire libre (F)	freier Währungsraum m	free currency area	—	area delle valute libere f	área monetaria libre f
Zulassung (D)	—	admission	admission f	ammissione f	admisión f
Zulassungsstelle (D)	—	admission board	commission pour l'admission des valeurs à la cote f	ufficio d'ammissione m	oficina de matrícula f
zurückgestaute Inflation (D)	—	pent-up inflation	inflation refoulée f	inflazione arginata f	inflación detenida f
Zusatzaktie (D)	—	bonus share	action supplémentaire f	azione gratuita f	acción suplementaria f
Zusatzkapital (D)	—	additional capital	capital supplémentaire m	capitale addizionale m	capital suplementario m

	D	E	F	I	Es
Zuschuß (D)	—	allowance	allocation *f*	aggiunta *f*	suplemento *m*
Zustimmung (D)	—	consent	accord *m*	approvazione *f*	consentimiento *m*
Zuteilung (D)	—	allocation	répartition *f*	ripartizione *f*	asignación *f*
Zuteilungsrechte (D)	—	allotment right	droits de répartition *m/pl*	diritti d'assegnazione *m/pl*	derechos de acceso *m/pl*
Zuweisung (D)	—	assignment	assignation *f*	conferimento *m*	atribución *f*
Zuzahlung (D)	—	additional contribution	payement supplémentaire *m*	pagamento supplementare *m*	pago suplementario *m*
Zwangsanleihe (D)	—	compulsory loan	emprunt forcé *m*	prestito forzato *m*	empréstito forzoso *m*
Zwangssparen (D)	—	compulsory saving	épargne forcée *f*	risparmio forzato *m*	ahorro forzoso *m*
Zwecksparen (D)	—	target saving	épargne à un but déterminée *f*	risparmio ad investimento vincolato *m*	ahorro con un fin determinado *m*
Zweigstelle (D)	—	branch	agence *f*	filiale *f*	sucursal *f*
Zwischenaktionär (D)	—	interim shareholder	actionnaire intermédiaire *m*	azionista non permanente *m*	accionista intermedio *m*
Zwischenbilanz (D)	—	interim balance sheet	bilan intermédiaire *m*	bilancio intermedio *m*	balance intermedio *m*
Zwischenfinanzierung (D)	—	interim financing	financement intermédiaire *m*	finanziamento transitorio *m*	financiación interina *f*
Zwischenkredit (D)	—	interim loan	crédit intermédiare *m*	credito transitorio *m*	crédito interino *m*
Zwischenschein (D)	—	provisional receipt	certificat provisoire *m*	certificato provvisorio *m*	certificado de acción *m*
Zwischenzinsen (D)	—	interim interest	intérêts intermédiaires *m/pl*	interessi intercalari *m/pl*	intereses provisionales *m/pl*

	D	E	F	I	Es
1	eins	one	un	uno	uno
2	zwei	two	deux	due	dos
3	drei	three	trois	tre	tres
4	vier	four	quatre	quattro	cuatro
5	fünf	five	cinq	cinque	cinco
6	sechs	six	six	sei	seis
7	sieben	seven	sept	sette	siete
8	acht	eight	huit	otto	ocho
9	neun	nine	neuf	nove	nueve
10	zehn	ten	dix	dieci	diez
11	elf	eleven	onze	undici	once
12	zwölf	twelve	douze	dodici	doce
13	dreizehn	thirteen	treize	tredici	trece
14	vierzehn	fourteen	quatorze	quattordici	catorce
15	fünfzehn	fifteen	quinze	quindici	quince
16	sechzehn	sixteen	seize	sedici	dieciséis
17	siebzehn	seventeen	dix-sept	diciassette	diecisiete
18	achtzehn	eighteen	dix-huit	diciotto	dieciocho
19	neunzehn	nineteen	dix-neuf	diciannove	diecinueve
20	zwanzig	twenty	vingt	venti	veinte
21	einundzwanzig	twenty-one	vingt et un	ventuno	veintiuno
30	dreißig	thirty	trente	trenta	treinta
40	vierzig	forty	quarante	quaranta	cuarenta
50	fünfzig	fifty	cinquante	cinquanta	cincuenta
60	sechzig	sixty	soixante	sessanta	sesenta
70	siebzig	seventy	soixante-dix	settanta	setenta
80	achtzig	eighty	quatre-vingts	ottanta	ochenta
90	neunzig	ninety	quatre-vingt-dix	novanta	noventa
100	einhundert	one hundred	cent	cento	cien
101	einhundertundeins	one hundred and one	cent un	cento uno	ciento uno
200	zweihundert	two hundred	deux cents	duecento	doscientos
1.000	eintausend	one thousand	mille	mille	mil
5.000	fünftausend	five thousand	cinq mille	cinquemila	cinco mil
1.000.000	eine Million	one million	un million	un milione	un millón
1.000.000.000	eine Milliarde	one billion (US) / 1,000 millions (UK)	un milliard	un miliardo	mil millones

D	E	F	I	Es
Wochentage	**days of the week**	**jours de la semaine**	**giorni della settimana**	**días de semana**
Montag	Monday	lundi	lunedì	lunes
Dienstag	Tuesday	mardi	martedì	martes
Mittwoch	Wednesday	mercredi	mercoledì	miércoles
Donnerstag	Thursday	jeudi	giovedì	jueves
Freitag	Friday	vendredi	venerdì	viernes
Samstag	Saturday	samedi	sabato	sábado
Sonntag	Sunday	dimanche	domenica	domingo
Monate	**months**	**mois**	**mesi**	**meses**
Januar	January	janvier	gennaio	enero
Februar	February	février	febbraio	febrero
März	March	mars	marzo	marzo
April	April	avril	aprile	abril
Mai	May	mai	maggio	mayo
Juni	June	juin	giugno	junio
Juli	July	juillet	luglio	julio
August	August	août	agosto	agosto
September	September	septembre	settembre	septiembre
Oktober	October	octobre	ottobre	octubre
November	November	novembre	novembre	noviembre
Dezember	December	décembre	dicembre	diciembre

	D	E	F	I	Es
km	Kilometer *m*	kilometre	kilomètre *m*	chilometro *m*	kilómetro *m*
m	Meter *m*	metre	mètre *m*	metro *m*	metro *m*
dm	Dezimeter *m*	decimetre	décimètre *m*	decimetro *m*	decímetro *m*
cm	Zentimeter *m*	centimetre	centimètre *m*	centimetro *m*	centímetro *m*
mm	Millimeter *m*	millimetre	millimètre *m*	millimetro *m*	milímetro *m*
km²	Quadratkilometer *m*	square kilometre	kilomètre carré *m*	chilometro quadrato *m*	kilómetro cuadrado *m*
m²	Quadratmeter *m*	square metre	mètre carré *m*	metro quadrato *m*	metro cuadrado *m*
cm²	Quadratzentimeter *m*	square centimetre	centimètre carré *m*	centimetro quadrato *m*	centímetro cuadrado *m*
mm²	Quadratmillimeter *m*	square millimetre	millimètre carré *m*	millimetro quadrato *m*	milímetro cuadrado *m*
km³	Kubikkilometer *m*	cubic kilometre	kilomètre cube *m*	chilometro cubico *m*	kilómetro cúbico *m*
m³	Kubikmeter *m*	cubic metre	mètre cube *m*	metro cubico *m*	metro cúbico *m*
cm³	Kubikzentimeter *m*	cubic centimetre	centimètre cube *m*	centimetro cubico *m*	centímetro cúbico *m*
mm³	Kubikmillimeter *m*	cubic millimetre	millimètre cube *m*	millimetro cubico *m*	milímetro cúbico *m*
l	Liter *m*	litre	litre *m*	litro *m*	litro *m*
t	Tonne *f*	ton	tonne *f*	tonnellata *f*	tonelada *f*
kg	Kilogramm *n*	kilogramme	kilogramme *m*	chilogrammo *m*	kilogramo *m*
g	Gramm *n*	gramme	gramme *m*	grammo *m*	gramo *m*
mg	Milligramm *n*	milligramme	milligramme *m*	milligrammo *m*	miligramo *m*